ear NFT User,

ɔs Angeles has one true love: the car. Sure, we love our surfing, Hollywood and avocados, but nothing will ever top ·uising along the open road. We spend so much time in our cars that they define us. We bathe and wax them regu- rly to keep them shining and sparkly, and we feed them premium gas. But this love affair is only so effective if you now where to take your car. And that's why the 2008 NFT guide to Los Angeles is the latest and greatest accessory) this relationship.

ut this book isn't limited to those who love their cars. It's also for those who just need to navigate their way around ıe asphalt-and-concrete country that is Los Angeles. These are people who need to find an alternate route from the affic because some under-aged Hollywood starlet has crashed her car while driving intoxicated, or because UCLA ıns are swarming the streets after finally beating USC in football, or because another wildfire has burnt their normal ɔmmute to a crisp.

nd at NFT, we know it's important to distinguish what's seen on TV to what L.A. is really about. It's not just the eaches and blond hair and lettuce lunches, which can get tiresome after a short while. It's a unique, hip, urban chic ɔwn so diverse that you need a different language dictionary to read the store signs every few miles. So we sent our eighborhood Editors into the streets to explore their favorite places to dine, drink, dance, listen, learn, browse, play, elax, exercise, shop and visit.

ɔr LA locals, written by LA locals, our latest edition continues to uncover the hidden nooks, flavors and materials ıat create the diverse foundation of this city. We'll show you where all the coffee places are along your morning ɔmmute, the location of the nearest gym, the best place for an after-work drink and dinner by your office, and of ɔurse, where to wash your car, among other things.

very special thanks goes out to all the Neighborhood Editors for their contributions, which without there wouldn't e much of a book. And we'd like to give a sunny two-thumbs-up to the NFT staff back in New York for all their late ours, hard work and scrutiny to make this the most comprehensive edition ever.

appy navigating,

in-rin, Jane, and Rob

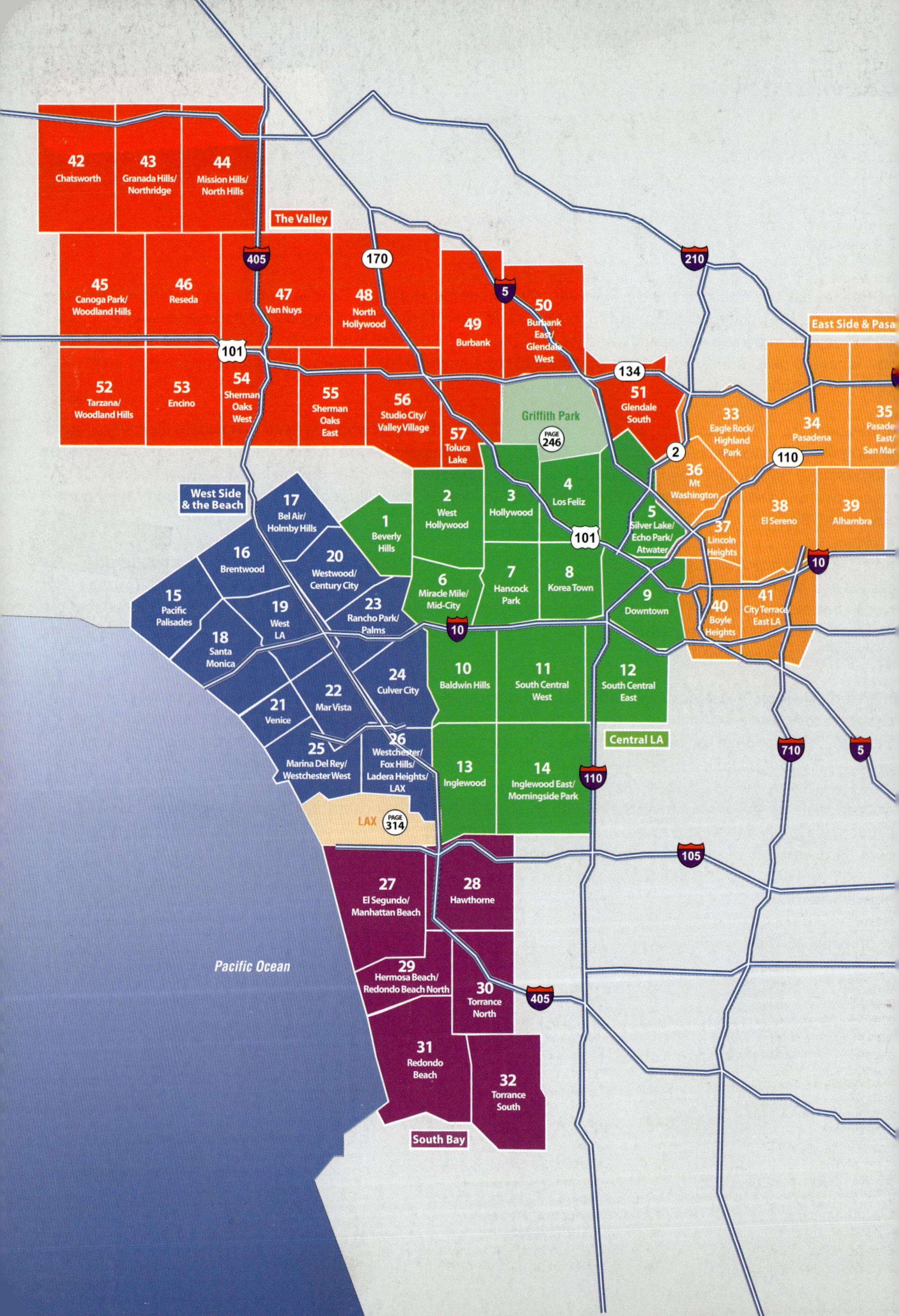

42
Chatsworth
43
Granada Hills/
Northridge
44
Mission Hills/
North Hills
The Valley
45
Canoga Park/
Woodland Hills
46
Reseda
47
Van Nuys
48
North
Hollywood
49
Burbank
50
Burbank
East/
Glendale
West
52
Tarzana/
Woodland Hills
53
Encino
54
Sherman
Oaks
West
55
Sherman
Oaks
East
56
Studio City/
Valley Village
57
Toluca
Lake
51
Glendale
South
Griffith Park
PAGE
246
East Side & Pasa
33
Eagle Rock/
Highland
Park
34
Pasadena
35
Pasade
East/
San Mar
36
Mt
Washington
37
Lincoln
Heights
38
El Sereno
39
Alhambra
40
Boyle
Heights
41
City Terrace/
East LA
West Side
& the Beach
17
Bel Air/
Holmby Hills
16
Brentwood
20
Westwood/
Century City
15
Pacific
Palisades
19
West
LA
23
Rancho Park/
Palms
18
Santa
Monica
24
Culver City
22
Mar Vista
21
Venice
25
Marina Del Rey/
Westchester West
26
Westchester/
Fox Hills/
Ladera Heights/
LAX
LAX
PAGE
314
1
Beverly
Hills
2
West
Hollywood
3
Hollywood
4
Los Feliz
5
Silver Lake/
Echo Park/
Atwater
6
Miracle Mile/
Mid-City
7
Hancock
Park
8
Korea Town
9
Downtown
10
Baldwin Hills
11
South Central
West
12
South Central
East
Central LA
13
Inglewood
14
Inglewood East/
Morningside Park
27
El Segundo/
Manhattan Beach
28
Hawthorne
29
Hermosa Beach/
Redondo Beach North
30
Torrance
North
31
Redondo
Beach
32
Torrance
South
South Bay
Pacific Ocean
405
170
5
210
101
134
2
110
10
710
105

Table of Contents

Central LA

West Side & the Beach

South Bay

East Side & Pasadena

The Valley

Parks & Places

Beaches & Marinas

Sports

Malls

Transit

General Information

Arts & Entertainment

Street Index

Franklin Canyon Reservoir
Greystone Park
Greystone Mansion
BEVERLY HILLS
Beverly Hills Hotel
Will Rogers Memorial Park
Beverly Gardens Park
Beverly Hills Civic Center
Museum of Television and Radio
Prada Store
The Witch's House
Regent Beverly Wilshire Hotel
Academy of Motion Pictures Arts & Sciences
The Los Angeles Country Club
Roxbury Park
West Hollywood Park
Sunset Blvd
W Sunset Blvd
Santa Monica Blvd
Wilshire Blvd
Olympic Blvd
W Pico Blvd
Burton Wy
Coldwater Canyon Dr
N Beverly Dr
S Beverly Dr
Melrose Ave
N Beverly Blvd
Charleville Blvd
Gregory Wy

1/2 mile
.5 km

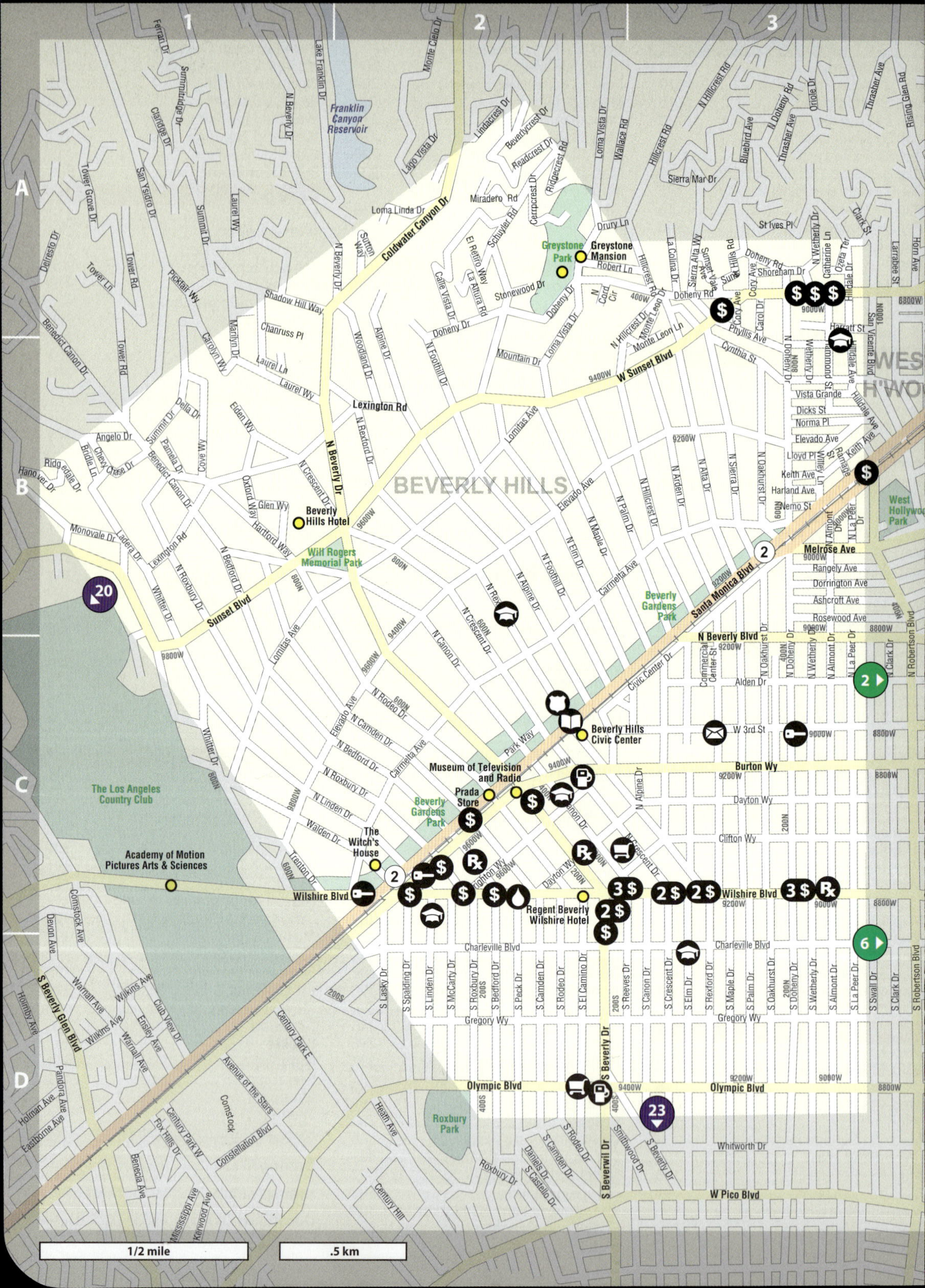

When the rest of the world thinks of Los Angeles, they picture Beverly Hills: palm-lined, broad avenues bursting with beautiful people, homes, and cars. Shopping Rodeo Drive is spendy fun, but locals tend to avoid its garish prices and attitude. For quintessential BH, visit during the holidays, when decorations high above Wilshire Boulevard impart a glitzy charm. The rest of the year, take Little Santa Monica Boulevard if you're just passing through, or stay and enjoy the only freebie in town—two hours free parking in public lots.

Banks

- **Bank of America** • 460 N Beverly Dr
- **Bank of America** • 9461 Wilshire Blvd
- **Bank of the West** • 9401 Wilshire Blvd
- **California National** • 9100 Wilshire Blvd
- **Citibank** • 9059 W Sunset Blvd
- **Citibank** • 9401 Wilshire Blvd
- **City National** • 400 N Roxbury Dr
- **City National** • 9229 W Sunset Blvd
- **Comerica** • 9757 Wilshire Blvd
- **East West** • 450 N Roxbury Dr
- **First Bank & Trust** • 175 S Beverly Dr
- **First Bank & Trust** • 9145 Wilshire Blvd
- **First Republic** • 9593 Wilshire Blvd
- **Fremont Investment & Loan** • 9301 Wilshire Blvd
- **Manufacturers** • 9777 Wilshire Blvd
- **Pacific Western** • 9454 Wilshire Blvd
- **Union** • 9460 Wilshire Blvd
- **US** • 9595 Wilshire Blvd
- **Wachovia** • 9107 Wilshire Blvd
- **Washington Mutual** • 9245 Wilshire Blvd
- **Wells Fargo** • 9000 W Sunset Blvd
- **Wells Fargo** • 9354 Wilshire Blvd
- **Wells Fargo** • 9600 Santa Monica Blvd

Car Rental

- **Beverly Hills Rent A Car** • 9732 S Santa Monica Blvd
- **Budget** • 9815 Wilshire Blvd
- **Midway Car Rental** • 300 S Doheny Dr

Car Washes

- **Aqua Carwash** • 9601 Wilshire Blvd

Gas Stations

- **76** • 427 N Crescent Dr
- **76** • 9460 W Olympic Blvd

Landmarks

- **Academy of Motion Pictures Arts & Sciences** • 8949 Wilshire Blvd
- **Beverly Hills Civic Center** • Rexford Dr & Santa Monica Blvd
- **Beverly Hills Hotel** • 9641 Sunset Blvd
- **Four Seasons Beverly Wilshire** • 9500 Wilshire Blvd
- **Greystone Mansion** • 905 Loma Vista Dr
- **Greystone Park** • 905 Loma Vista Dr
- **Museum of Television & Radio** • 465 N Beverly Dr
- **Prada Store** • 469 N Rodeo Dr
- **The Witch's House** • 516 Walden Dr

Libraries

- **Beverly Hills Public Library** • 444 N Rexford Dr • 310-288-2220

Pharmacies

- **CVS** • 9045 Wilshire Blvd • 310-273-5252
- **CVS** • 9045 Wilshire Blvd • 310-273-5252
- **Rite-Aid** • 300 N Canon Dr • 310-273-3561
- **Rite-Aid** • 463 N Bedford Dr • 310-247-0843

Police

- **Beverly Hills Police** • 464 N Rexford Dr • 310-550-4951

Post Offices

- **US Post Office** • 312 S Beverly Dr • 800-275-8777
- **US Post Office** • 323 N Crescent Dr • 800-275-8777
- **US Post Office** • 325 N Maple Dr • 800-275-8777

Schools

- **Beverly Hills Lingual Institute** • 439 N Canon Dr
- **Beverly Vista Elementary** • 200 S Elm Dr
- **Good Shepherd Catholic** • 148 S Linden Dr
- **Hawthorne Elementary** • 624 N Rexford Dr
- **West Hollywood Elementary** • 970 N Hammond St

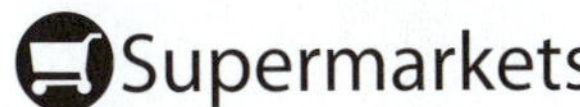

Supermarkets

- **Pavilions** • 9467 W Olympic Blvd
- **Whole Foods Market** • 239 N Crescent Dr

Map 1 • Beverly Hills

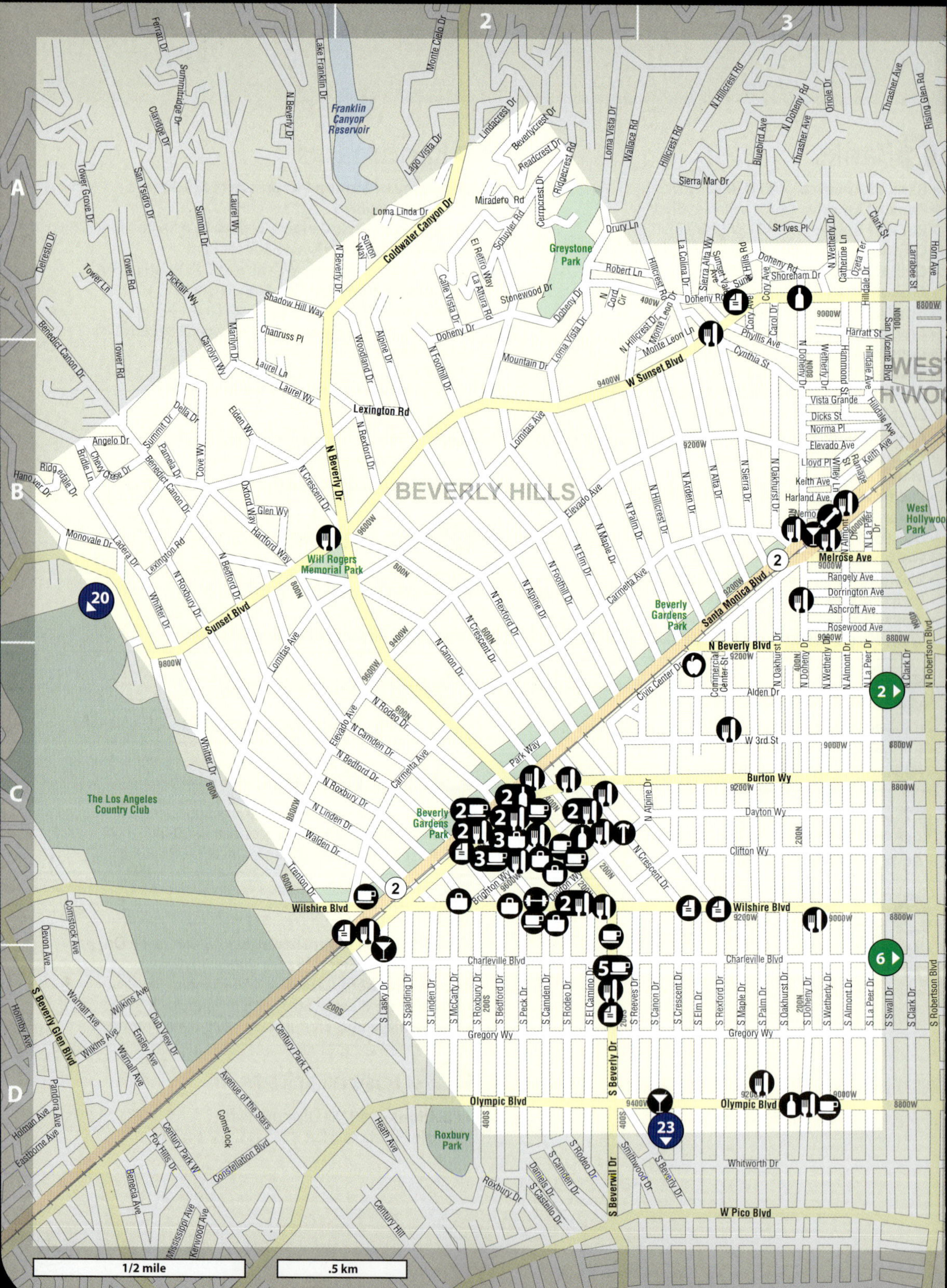

BEVERLY HILLS

Franklin Canyon Reservoir

Greystone Park

Will Rogers Memorial Park

Beverly Gardens Park

West Hollywood Park

The Los Angeles Country Club

Roxbury Park

WEST H'WOOD

Coldwater Canyon Dr

N Beverly Dr

Lexington Rd

W Sunset Blvd

Sunset Blvd

Santa Monica Blvd

Melrose Ave

N Beverly Blvd

W 3rd St

Burton Wy

Dayton Wy

Clifton Wy

Wilshire Blvd

Charleville Blvd

Gregory Wy

Olympic Blvd

Whitworth Dr

W Pico Blvd

S Beverly Dr

S Beverwil Dr

S Beverly Glen Blvd

Century Park E

Avenue of the Stars

Constellation Blvd

Doheny Rd

N Doheny Dr

N Robertson Blvd

S Robertson Blvd

San Vicente Blvd

Civic Center Dr

N Rodeo Dr

N Canon Dr

N Crescent Dr

N Rexford Dr

N Alpine Dr

N Foothill Rd

Lomitas Ave

Elevado Ave

Carmelita Ave

Park Way

A

B

C

D

1

2

3

1/2 mile

.5 km

Sundries / Entertainment

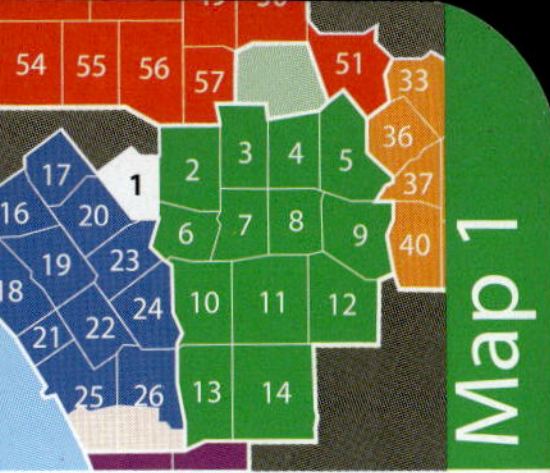

Rodeo Drive is a theme park— complete with high prices, throngs of tourists, and long lines (for the valet). It is not a reliable place to see the beau monde (unless you cruise N Bedford Drive, the plastic surgery capital of the world). Head to Beverly Drive south of Wilshire Boulevard for a more down-to-earth experience: a supermarket, small shops, nail salons, bakeries, cafés, an inspiring newsstand, places to grab lunch or an afternoon yoga class, and a friendly post office.

Coffee

- **Aloha Island Coffee Company** • 153 S Beverly Dr
- **Brighton Coffee Shop** • 9600 Brighton Wy
- **Coffee Bean & Tea Leaf** • 233 S Beverly Dr
- **Coffee Bean & Tea Leaf** • 445 N Beverly Dr
- **Euro Caffé** • 9559 Santa Monica Blvd
- **Graffeo Coffee Roasting** • 315 N Beverly Dr
- **It's Coffee Lovers Time** • 468 N Camden Dr
- **Peet's** • 258 S Beverly Dr
- **Seletoo** • 434 N Camden Dr
- **Splurge** • 9595 Wilshire Blvd
- **Starbucks** • 202 S Beverly Dr
- **Starbucks** • 428 N Beverly Dr
- **Starbucks** • 9844 Wilshire Blvd
- **Urth Caffé** • 267 S Beverly Dr

Copy Shops

- **Beverly Hills Postal Place** • 269 S Beverly Dr • 310-274-7721
- **FedEx Kinko's** • 8950 W Olympic Blvd • 310-285-9591
- **FedEx Kinko's** • 9201 W Sunset Blvd • 310-274-0714
- **FedEx Kinko's** • 9334 Wilshire Blvd • 310-271-1258
- **FedEx Kinko's** • 9680 Santa Monica Blvd • 310-859-2381
- **Mail Boxes Etc** • 9663 Santa Monica Blvd • 310-858-7122
- **Printcraft Printing** • 9301 Wilshire Blvd • 310-247-0234

Farmers Markets

- **Beverly Hills (Sun, 9 am-1 pm)** • 9300 Civic Center Dr

Gyms

- **Sports Club LA** • 9601 Wilshire Blvd • 310-888-8100

Hardware Stores

- **Pioneer & Lucerne Hardware** • 315 N Crescent Dr • 310-276-1167

Liquor Stores

- **Cheese Store of Beverly Hills (Wine only)** • 419 N Beverly Dr
- **Wine Merchant** • 9467 Santa Monica Blvd
- **Wine Shop** • 350 N Canon Dr

Nightlife

- **Bar Noir** • Maison 140 • 140 S Lasky Dr • 310-281-4000
- **The Belvedere** • Peninsula Hotel • 9882 S Santa Monica Blvd • 310-551-2888
- **Blue on Blue** • Avalon Hotel • 9400 W Olympic Blvd • 310-407-7791
- **The Blvd** • Regent Beverly Wilshire • 9500 Wilshire Blvd • 310-275-5200
- **Trader Vic's** • The Beverly Hilton • 9876 Wilshire Blvd • 310-276-6345
- **Writer's Bar at L'Ermitage Hotel** • 9291 Burton Wy • 310-278-3344

Pet Shops

- **Petco** • 508 N Doheny Dr • 310-275-6012

Restaurants

- **Baja Fresh** • 475 N Beverly Dr • 310-858-6690
- **Barney Greengrass** • 9570 Wilshire Blvd • 310-777-5877
- **Basic Bites** • 443 N Beverly Blvd • 310-247-9673
- **The Belvedere** • Peninsula Hotel • 9882 Little Santa Monica Blvd • 310-788-2306
- **Blowfish Sushi** • 9229 Sunset Blvd • 310-887-3848
- **Blue on Blue** • Avalon Hotel • 9400 W Olympic Blvd • 310-407-7791
- **The Blvd** • Regent Beverly Wilshire • 9500 Wilshire Blvd • 310-275-5200
- **Boe on the Crescent** • Beverly Crescent Hotel • 403 N Crescent Dr • 310-247-0505
- **Brighton Coffee Shop** • 9600 Brighton Wy • 310-276-7732
- **Café Talesai** • 9198 W Olympic Blvd • 310-271-9345
- **Crustacean** • 9646 Little Santa Monica Blvd • 310-205-8990
- **Da Pasquale** • 9749 Little Santa Monica Blvd • 310-859-3884
- **Dan Tana's** • 9071 Santa Monica Blvd • 310-275-9444
- **El Torito Grill** • 9595 Wilshire Blvd • 310-550-1599
- **Farm of Beverly Hills** • 439 N Beverly Dr • 310-273-5578
- **Flavor of India** • 9045 Santa Monica Blvd • 310-274-1715
- **The Grill on the Alley** • 9560 Dayton Wy • 310-276-0615
- **Il Cono Gelateria** • 9461 Little Santa Monica Blvd • 310-285-2045
- **Kate Mantilini** • 9101 Wilshire Blvd • 310-278-3699
- **La Conversation** • 638 N Doheny Dr • 310-858-0950
- **La Scala** • 434 N Canon Dr • 310-275-0579
- **Le Pain Quotidien** • 9630 Little Santa Monica Blvd • 310-859-1100
- **Mastro's Steakhouse** • 246 N Canon Dr • 310-888-8782
- **Mulberry Street Pizzeria** • 240 S Beverly Dr • 310-247-8100
- **Mulberry Street Pizzeria** • 347 N Canon Dr • 310-247-8998
- **Nate 'n Al's** • 414 N Beverly Dr • 310-274-0101
- **Nic's** • 453 N Canon Dr • 310-550-5707
- **Polo Lounge** • The Beverly Hills Hotel • 9641 Sunset Blvd • 310-276-2251
- **Sprinkles Cupcakes** • 9635 Little Santa Monica Blvd • 310-274-8765
- **Trader Vic's** • The Beverly Hilton • 9876 Wilshire Blvd • 310-276-6345
- **Xi'an** • 362 N Canon Dr • 310-275-3345

Shopping

- **Anthropologie** • 320 N Beverly Dr • 310-385-7390
- **Barney's New York** • 9570 Wilshire Blvd • 310-276-4400
- **Chanel Boutique** • 400 N Rodeo Dr • 310-278-5500
- **Cheese Store of Beverly Hills (Wine only)** • 419 N Beverly Dr • 310-278-2855
- **Fritelli Donuts** • 350 N Canon Dr • 310-276-1408
- **Geary's of Beverly Hills** • 351 N Beverly Dr • 310-273-4741
- **Giorgio Armani Boutique** • 436 N Rodeo Dr • 310-271-5555
- **Gucci** • 347 N Rodeo Dr • 310-278-3451
- **Mrs Beasley's/Miss Grace Lemon Cake Co** • 255 1/2 S Beverly Dr • 310-276-6516
- **Neiman Marcus** • 9700 Wilshire Blvd • 310-550-5900
- **Prada Epicenter** • 343 N Rodeo Dr • 310-278-8661
- **Ron Herman** • 325 N Beverly Dr • 310-550-0910
- **Saks Fifth Avenue** • 9600 Wilshire Blvd • 310-275-4211
- **Sprinkles Cupcakes** • 9635 Little Santa Monica Blvd • 310-274-8765
- **The Taschen Store** • 354 N Beverly Dr • 310-274-4300

Map 2 • West Hollywood

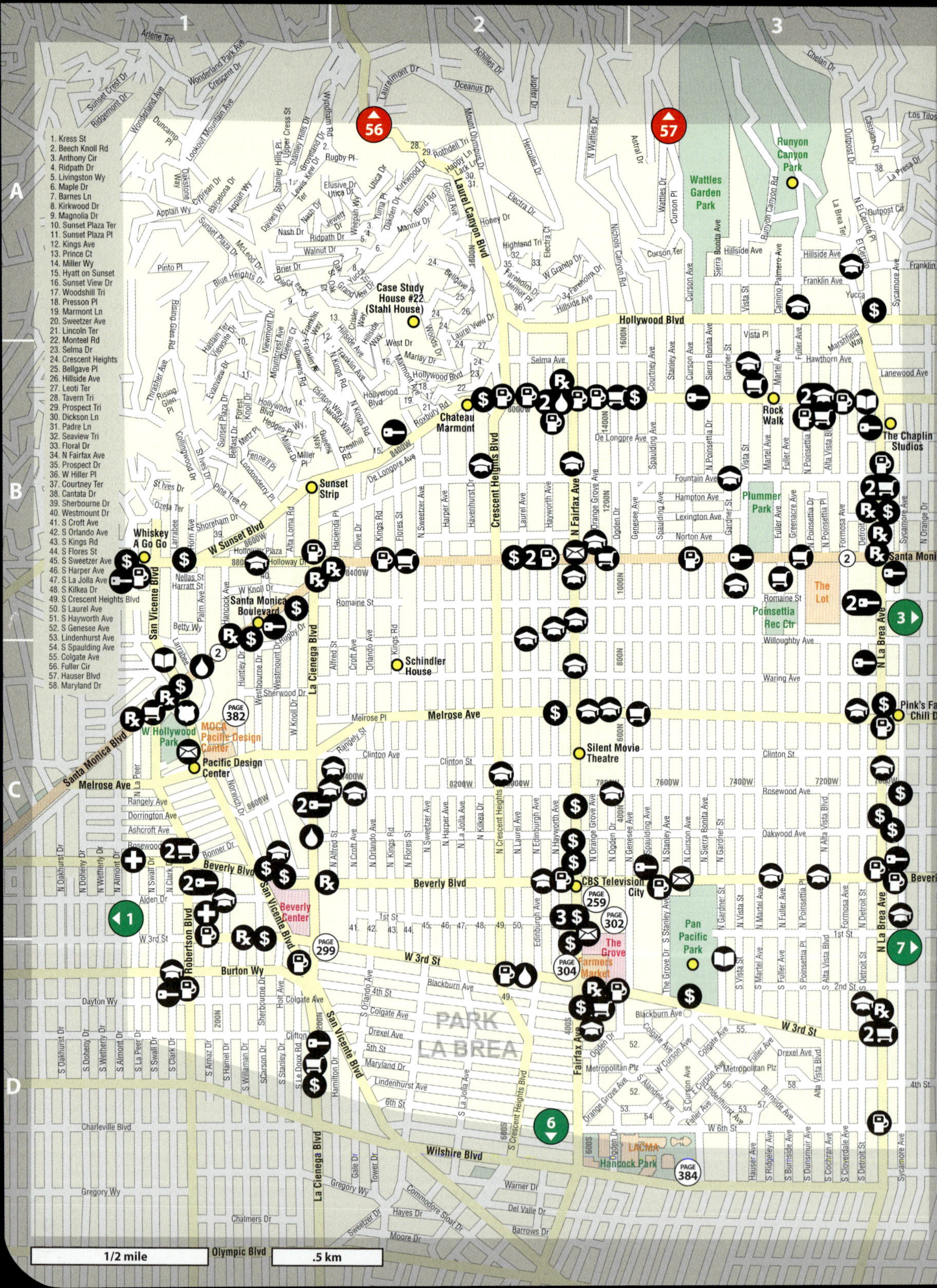

1. Kress St
2. Beech Knoll Rd
3. Anthony Cir
4. Ridpath Dr
5. Livingston Wy
6. Maple Dr
7. Barnes Ln
8. Kirkwood Dr
9. Magnolia Dr
10. Sunset Plaza Ter
11. Sunset Plaza Pl
12. Kings Ave
13. Prince Ct
14. Miller Wy
15. Hyatt on Sunset
16. Sunset View Dr
17. Woodshill Trl
18. Presson Pl
19. Marmont Ln
20. Sweetzer Ave
21. Lincoln Ter
22. Monteel Rd
23. Selma Dr
24. Crescent Heights
25. Bellgave Pl
26. Hillside Ave
27. Leoti Ter
28. Tavern Trl
29. Prospect Trl
30. Dickson Ln
31. Padre Ln
32. Seaview Trl
33. Floral Dr
34. N Fairfax Ave
35. Prospect Dr
36. W Hiller Pl
37. Courtney Ter
38. Cantata Dr
39. Sherbourne Dr
40. Westmount Dr
41. S Croft Ave
42. S Orlando Ave
43. S Kings Rd
44. S Flores St
45. S Sweetzer Ave
46. S Harper Ave
47. S La Jolla Ave
48. S Kilkea Dr
49. S Crescent Heights Blvd
50. S Laurel Ave
51. S Hayworth Ave
52. S Genesee Ave
53. Lindenhurst Ave
54. S Spaulding Ave
55. Colgate Ave
56. Fuller Cir
57. Hauser Blvd
58. Maryland Dr

1/2 mile | .5 km

Visitors trying to make sense of Los Angeles sprawl often encounter locals who cheerfully insist that most attractions are just "20 minutes away." Realistically, these locals must live in WeHo. With the beach, the Valley and downtown all roughly 1,200 seconds from your doorstep, West Hollywood is quite literally the center of the LA universe. Which is great news for the gays, actors, and yuppies that proliferate the neighborhood—even though they'd never be caught dead in the Valley.

Banks

- **Bank of America** • 466 N La Brea Ave
- **Bank of America** • 7800 W Sunset Blvd
- **Bank of America** • 7900 Melrose Ave
- **Bank of America** • 8025 Santa Monica Blvd
- **Bank of America** • 8655 Beverly Blvd
- **Bank of America** • 8921 Santa Monica Blvd
- **Bank of America** • 9021 W Sunset Blvd
- **California National** • 145 S Fairfax Ave
- **California National** • 736 N La Brea Ave
- **California National** • 8601 Santa Monica Blvd
- **Citibank** • 300 S Fairfax Ave
- **Citibank** • 8900 Santa Monica Blvd
- **First Federal** • 400 N La Brea Ave
- **First Federal** • 464 N Fairfax Ave
- **First Federal** • 8653 Beverly Blvd
- **First Regional** • 7083 Hollywood Blvd
- **Gilmore** • 110 S Fairfax Ave
- **National Bank of California** • 145 S Fairfax Ave
- **US** • 8901 Santa Monica Blvd
- **Washington Mutual** • 310 N Fairfax Ave
- **Washington Mutual** • 449 N La Brea Ave
- **Washington Mutual** • 6120 W 3rd St
- **Washington Mutual** • 8150 W Sunset Blvd
- **Wells Fargo** • 1233 N La Brea Ave
- **Wells Fargo** • 137 N Fairfax Ave
- **Wells Fargo** • 8571 Santa Monica Blvd
- **Wells Fargo** • 8625 W 3rd St

Car Rental

- **699 Rent A Car** • 1415 N La Brea Ave
- **Affordable Car Rental** • 1040 N La Brea Ave
- **Annex Enterprises** • 200 N La Cienega Blvd
- **Avon Rent-A-Car** • 7080 Santa Monica Blvd
- **Beverly Hills Rent A Car** • 8929 W Sunset Blvd
- **Beverly Hills Rent-A-Car** • 800 N La Brea Ave
- **Black & White Rent-a-Car** • 8800 Burton Wy
- **Enterprise** • 265 N Robertson Blvd
- **Enterprise** • 463 N La Cienega Blvd
- **Enterprise** • 7100 Beverly Blvd
- **Enterprise** • 8367 W Sunset Blvd
- **Enterprise** • 8583 Santa Monica Blvd
- **Enterprise** • 943 N La Brea Ave
- **Hertz** • 361 N La Brea Ave
- **Hertz** • 450 N La Cienega Blvd
- **Priceless Car Rental** • 7415 Santa Monica Blvd
- **West Hollywood Rent-a-Car** • 7610 W Sunset Blvd

Car Washes

- **Chevron** • 7955 W Sunset Blvd
- **Chevron** • 8017 W 3rd St
- **Medison Car Wash** • 7617 Santa Monica Blvd
- **Royal Car Wash** • 431 N La Cienega Blvd
- **Santa Palm Car Wash** • 8787 Santa Monica Blvd
- **Sunset Car Wash** • 7955 W Sunset Blvd

Gas Stations

- **76** • 5436 W 6th St
- **76** • 7751 Beverly Blvd
- **76** • 7960 Santa Monica Blvd
- **76** • 7979 W Sunset Blvd
- **76** • 8755 W 3rd St
- **Arco** • 7564 Santa Monica Blvd
- **Arco** • 7901 W Sunset Blvd
- **Chevron** • 1107 N La Cienega Blvd
- **Chevron** • 7020 Beverly Blvd
- **Chevron** • 7100 Melrose Ave
- **Chevron** • 7955 W Sunset Blvd
- **Chevron** • 8017 W 3rd St
- **Chevron** • 8101 W Sunset Blvd
- **Exxon** • 391 S Robertson Blvd
- **Exxon** • 7900 Beverly Blvd
- **Exxon** • 8020 Santa Monica Blvd
- **Independent** • 8906 W Sunset Blvd
- **Mobil** • 7100 W Sunset Blvd
- **Mobil** • 7865 W Sunset Blvd
- **Mobil** • 8380 Santa Monica Blvd
- **Mobil** • 8489 Beverly Blvd
- **Shell** • 1309 N La Brea Ave
- **Valero** • 307 N La Brea Ave

Emergency Rooms

- **Cedars-Sinai Medical Center** • 8700 Beverly Blvd

Landmarks

- **Case Study House #22 (Stahl House)** • 1636 Woods Dr
- **CBS Television City** • Beverly Blvd & N Fairfax Ave
- **The Chaplin Studios** • 1416 N La Brea Ave
- **Chateau Marmont** • 8221 W Sunset Blvd
- **Pacific Design Center** • Melrose Ave & San Vicente Blvd
- **Pan Pacific Park** • 7600 Beverly Blvd
- **Pink's Famous Chili Dogs** • 709 N La Brea Ave
- **Rock Walk** • 7435 Sunset Blvd
- **Runyon Canyon Park** • Franklin Ave & Fuller Dr
- **Santa Monica Blvd** • Santa Monica Blvd b/w La Cienega Blvd & Robertson Blvd
- **Schindler House** • 833 N Kings Rd
- **Silent Movie Theatre** • 611 N Fairfax Ave
- **Sunset Strip** • Sunset Blvd b/w N Doheny Dr & N Fairfax Ave
- **Whisky A Go Go** • 8901 Sunset Blvd

Libraries

- **Fairfax Branch Library** • 161 S Gardner St • 323-936-6191
- **West Hollywood** • 715 N San Vicente Blvd • 310-652-5340
- **Will & Ariel Durant Branch** • 7140 W Sunset Blvd • 323-876-2741

Pharmacies

- **CVS** • 6360 W 3rd St • 323-937-3019
- **CVS** • 8491 Santa Monica Blvd • 310-360-7303
- **CVS** • 8491 W Santa Monica Blvd • 310-360-7303
- **CVS/ProCare** • 8635 W 3rd St • 310-652-1080
- **Longs Drugs** • 8490 Beverly Blvd • 323-653-4616
- **Pavilions** • 8969 Santa Monica Blvd • 310-273-5126
- **PharmaCare** • 8607 Santa Monica Blvd • 310-659-9810
- **Ralphs** • 1233 N La Brea Ave • 323-876-5651
- **Ralphs** • 260 S La Brea Ave • 323-937-9383
- **Rite-Aid** • 1130 N La Brea Ave • 323-463-8539
- **Rite-Aid** • 7900 W Sunset Blvd • 323-876-4466
- **Target** • 7100 Santa Monica Blvd • 323-603-0005
- **Vons/Pavillions** • 8969 Santa Monica Blvd • 310-273-5126

Police

- **Los Angeles County Sheriff's Dept-West Hollywood Station** • 780 N San Vicente Blvd • 310-855-8850

Post Offices

- **US Post Office** • 1125 N Fairfax Ave • 800-275-8777
- **US Post Office** • 7610 Beverly Blvd • 800-275-8777
- **US Post Office** • 820 N San Vicente Blvd • 800-275-8777

Schools

- **ABC Little School** • 927 N Fairfax Ave
- **Aviva High** • 7120 Franklin Ave
- **Bais Tzivia for Girls** • 7269 Beverly Blvd
- **Bais Yaakov School for Girls** • 7353 Beverly Blvd
- **Bnos Esther** • 116 N La Brea Ave
- **Bnos Esther** • 7659 Beverly Blvd
- **Center for Early Education** • 563 N Alfred St
- **Cheerful Helpers Therapeutic** • 8730 Alden Dr
- **Daniel Murphy Catholic High** • 241 S Detroit St
- **Dvorskaya Alternative** • 1317 N Cresent Heights Blvd
- **Emanuel Academy** • 8844 Burton Wy
- **Fairfax Senior High** • 7850 Melrose Ave
- **Fountain Day** • 1128 N Orange Grove Ave
- **Gardner St Elementary** • 7450 Hawthorn Ave
- **Hancock Park Elementary** • 408 S Fairfax Ave
- **Just Like Moms Pre-School - Kindergarten** • 1535 N Poinsettia Pl
- **Laurel EEC** • 8023 Willoughby Ave
- **Laurel Elementary** • 925 N Hayworth Ave
- **Los Feliz Charter School For The Arts** • 1265 N Fairfax Ave
- **Maimonides Academy** • 310 Huntley Dr
- **Melrose Ave Elementary** • 731 N Detroit St
- **Ofman Learning Center** • 812 N Fairfax Ave
- **Pacific Hills** • 8628 Holloway Dr
- **Perutz Jacob Hebrew Academy** • 7951 Beverly Blvd
- **Rosewood Ave Elementary** • 503 N Croft Ave
- **Rosewood EEC** • 510 N Alfred St
- **Temple Israel Day** • 7300 Hollywood Blvd
- **West Hollywood Children's Academy** • 1031 N Vista St
- **West Hollywood Community Day** • 1049 N Fairfax Ave
- **Westside Community Adult** • 7850 Melrose Ave
- **Whitman Continuation** • 7795 Rosewood Ave
- **Yeshiva Ohr Elchonon Chabad** • 7215 Waring Ave
- **Yeshiva Rav Isaacsohn** • 540 N La Brea Ave

Supermarkets

- **Bristol Farms** • 7880 W Sunset Blvd
- **Bristol Farms** • 9039 Beverly Blvd
- **Gelson's Markets** • 8330 Santa Monica Blvd
- **Jon's Marketplace** • 1234 N La Brea Ave
- **Pavilions** • 8969 Santa Monica Blvd
- **Ralphs** • 1233 N La Brea Ave
- **Ralphs** • 260 S La Brea Ave
- **Ralphs** • 7257 Sunset Blvd
- **Ralphs** • 9040 Beverly Blvd
- **Smart & Final** • 1041 N Fuller Ave
- **Smart & Final** • 7720 Melrose Ave
- **Trader Joe's** • 263 S La Brea Ave
- **Trader Joe's** • 7304 Santa Monica Blvd
- **Trader Joe's** • 8611 Santa Monica Blvd
- **Whole Foods Market** • 6350 W 3rd St
- **Whole Foods Market** • 7871 Santa Monica Blvd

Map 2 • West Hollywood

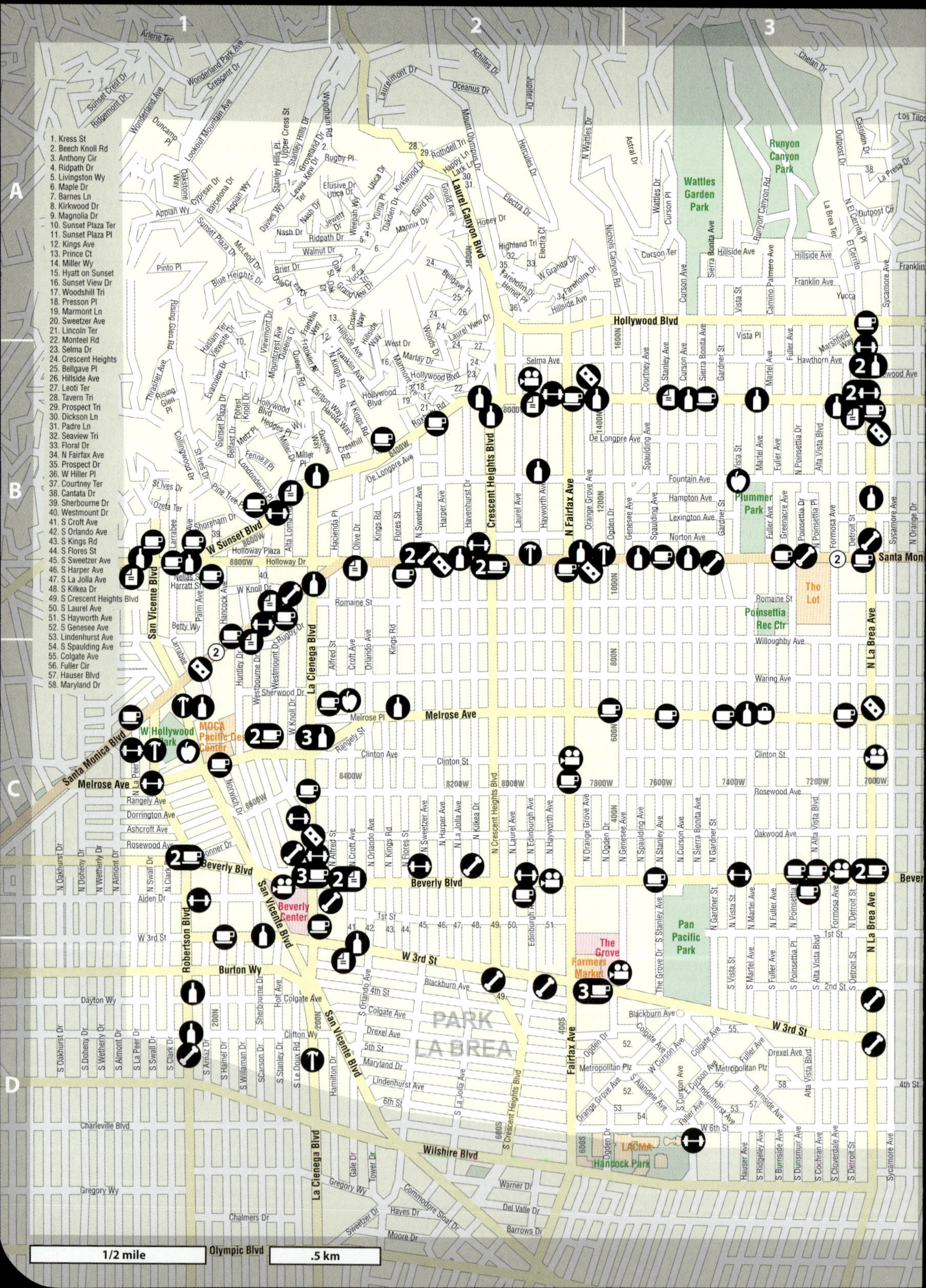

1. Kress St
2. Beech Knoll Rd
3. Anthony Cir
4. Ridpath Dr
5. Livingston Wy
6. Maple Dr
7. Barnes Ln
8. Kirkwood Dr
9. Magnolia Dr
10. Sunset Plaza Ter
11. Sunset Plaza Pl
12. Kings Ave
13. Prince Ct
14. Miller Wy
15. Hyatt on Sunset
16. Sunset View Dr
17. Woodshill Trl
18. Presson Pl
19. Marmont Ln
20. Sweetzer Ave
21. Lincoln Ter
22. Monteel Rd
23. Selma Dr
24. Crescent Heights
25. Bellgave Pl
26. Hillside Ave
27. Leoti Ter
28. Tavern Trl
29. Prospect Trl
30. Dickson Ln
31. Padre Ln
32. Seaview Trl
33. Floral Dr
34. N Fairfax Ave
35. Prospect Dr
36. W Hiller Pl
37. Courtney Ter
38. Cantata Dr
39. Sherbourne Dr
40. Westmount Dr
41. S Croft Ave
42. S Orlando Ave
43. S Kings Rd
44. S Flores St
45. S Sweetzer Ave
46. S Harper Ave
47. S La Jolla Ave
48. S Kilkea Dr
49. S Crescent Heights Blvd
50. S Laurel Ave
51. S Hayworth Ave
52. S Genesee Ave
53. Lindenhurst Ave
54. S Spaulding Ave
55. Colgate Ave
56. Fuller Cir
57. Hauser Blvd
58. Maryland Dr
Runyon Canyon Park
Wattles Garden Park
Hollywood Blvd
Laurel Canyon Blvd
W Sunset Blvd
Santa Monica Blvd
Plummer Park
The Lot
Poinsettia Rec Ctr
Melrose Ave
W Hollywood Park
MOCA Pacific Design Center
Beverly Blvd
Beverly Center
Pan Pacific Park
The Grove Farmers Market
W 3rd St
PARK LA BREA
LACMA
Hancock Park
Wilshire Blvd
Olympic Blvd
La Cienega Blvd
San Vicente Blvd
Robertson Blvd
Crescent Heights Blvd
N Fairfax Ave
N La Brea Ave
1/2 mile
.5 km

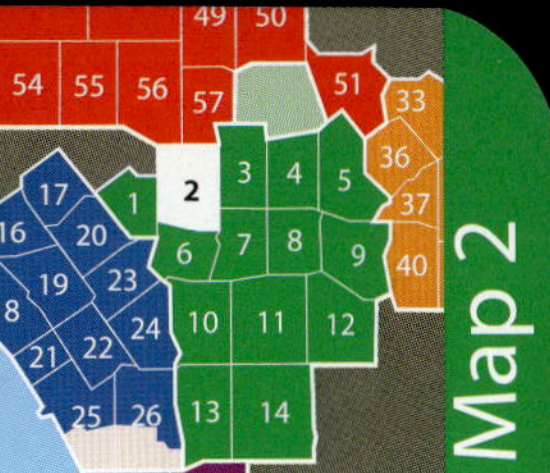

The area boasts some of the most cohesive and walkable micro-neighborhoods in town (try Third Street west of Fairfax Avenue, the changes in demographic along Melrose Avenue from Doheny Drive east to La Brea Avenue, or Fairfax Avenue north of Beverly Boulevard). This does make the installation of The Grove shopping mall, with its faux-village atmosphere, a little ironic. Though in fairness, the dancing fountains are delightful, and the Farmer's Market food and tchotchke stalls have been left just as perfect as they ever were.

Coffee

- **Abbot's Habit Hollywood** • 7554 W Sunset Blvd
- **African Red Tea** • 533 N Fairfax Ave
- **At Coffee Shop** • 7200 Melrose Ave
- **Basix Café** • 8333 Santa Monica Blvd
- **Bob's Coffee & Donuts** • 6333 W 3rd St
- **Buzz Coffee** • 7623 Beverly Blvd
- **Café Et Lait** • 7115 Beverly Blvd
- **Café Europe** • 7701 Santa Monica Blvd
- **Café Marco** • 8200 Santa Monica Blvd
- **Coffee Bean & Tea Leaf** • 300 S La Cienega Blvd
- **Coffee Bean & Tea Leaf** • 5979 W 3rd St
- **Coffee Bean & Tea Leaf** • 6333 W 3rd St
- **Coffee Bean & Tea Leaf** • 7235 Beverly Blvd
- **Coffee Bean & Tea Leaf** • 7502 Melrose Ave
- **Coffee Bean & Tea Leaf** • 7915 W Sunset Blvd
- **Coffee Bean & Tea Leaf** • 8500 Beverly Blvd
- **Coffee Bean & Tea Leaf** • 8735 Santa Monica Blvd
- **Coffee Bean & Tea Leaf** • 8789 W Sunset Blvd
- **Coffee Bean & Tea Leaf** • 8793 Beverly Blvd
- **Coffee Corner** • 6333 W 3rd St
- **Coffee Station** • 7801 Melrose Ave
- **Creative City Café** • 7310 Santa Monica Blvd
- **Cyber Java Internet Store** • 7080 Hollywood Blvd
- **The Design Café** • 8687 Melrose Ave
- **Destini Café** • 349 N La Cienega Blvd
- **Dialog Coffee & Bakery** • 8766 Holloway Dr
- **Dukes Tropicana Coffee Shop** • 8909 W Sunset Blvd
- **Elixir** • 8612 Melrose Ave
- **Insomnia** • 7286 Beverly Blvd
- **Milk** • 7290 Beverly Blvd
- **Peet's** • 8833 W Sunset Blvd
- **Ramma Geni Café** • 8500 Melrose Ave
- **Starbucks** • 100 N La Cienega Blvd
- **Starbucks** • 164 N Robertson Blvd
- **Starbucks** • 6333 W 3rd St
- **Starbucks** • 7055 Sunset Blvd
- **Starbucks** • 7100 Santa Monica Blvd
- **Starbucks** • 7122 Beverly Blvd
- **Starbucks** • 7624 Melrose Ave
- **Starbucks** • 7901 Santa Monica Blvd
- **Starbucks** • 8363 NE Sunset Blvd
- **Starbucks** • 8500 Beverly Blvd
- **Starbucks** • 8500 Beverly Pl
- **Starbucks** • 8595 Santa Monica Blvd
- **Starbucks** • 8949 Santa Monica Blvd
- **Swingers** • 8020 Beverly Blvd
- **Tully's Coffee** • 8631 W 3rd St
- **Urth Caffé** • 8565 Melrose Ave

Copy Shops

- **A Plus Printing & Copy** • 8404 Santa Monica Blvd • 323-656-8061
- **Alpha Print & Copy** • 9030 W Sunset Blvd • 310-273-9460
- **FedEx Kinko's** • 7630 W Sunset Blvd • 323-845-4501
- **FedEx Kinko's** • 8471 Beverly Blvd • 323-782-6905
- **Mail Boxes Etc** • 8391 Beverly Blvd • 323-655-9980
- **New Image Printing** • 7109 W Sunset Blvd • 323-876-1102
- **Printop Copy Center** • 8539 W Sunset Blvd • 310-854-0403
- **Sharp-Print** • 8426 W 3rd St • 310-300-9228
- **Sir Speedy** • 8730 Santa Monica Blvd • 310-657-7210
- **UPS Store** • 8033 W Sunset Blvd • 323-848-8300
- **UPS Store** • 8581 Santa Monica Blvd • 310-289-5952

Farmers Markets

- **Melrose Place (Sun, 9 am-2 pm)** • Melrose Pl & N Croft Ave
- **West Hollywood (Mon, 9 am-2 pm)** • N Vista St & Fountain Ave
- **West Hollywood (Thurs, 2 pm-7 pm)** • 647 N San Vicente Blvd

Gyms

- **24 Hour Fitness** • 8612 Santa Monica Blvd • 310-652-7440
- **Beverly Hills Health & Fitness** • 8301 Beverly Blvd • 323-658-6999
- **Boulevard Health** • 120 N Robertson Blvd • 310-659-5002
- **Crunch** • 8000 W Sunset Blvd • 323-654-4550
- **Curves** • 415 Westmount Dr • 310-854-4428
- **Curves** • 7125 1/2 W Sunset Blvd • 323-851-2878
- **Easton Gym** • 8053 Beverly Blvd • 323-651-3636
- **Emerson Health & Fitness** • 8816 Melrose Ave • 310-858-6812
- **Equinox** • 8590 W Sunset Blvd • 310-289-1900
- **Fitness Factory** • 650 N La Peer Dr • 310-358-1838
- **Groove Fitness** • 1626 N La Brea Ave • 323-960-0660
- **Hollywood Gym** • 1551 N La Brea Ave • 323-845-1420
- **Train West Hollywood** • 624 N La Cienega Blvd • 310-657-4140
- **Vista Fitness (Women only)** • 7421 Beverly Blvd • 323-939-1212

Hardware Stores

- **Anawalt Lumber** • 641 N Robertson Blvd • 310-652-6202
- **Koontz Hardware** • 8914 Santa Monica Blvd • 310-652-0123
- **Laurel Hardware** • 7984 Santa Monica Blvd • 323-656-9605
- **Liz's Antique Hardware** • 453 S La Brea Ave • 323-939-4403
- **Tashman Screens & Hardware** • 7769 Santa Monica Blvd • 323-656-7028

Liquor Stores

- **Almor Liquors** • 7855 W Sunset Blvd
- **Beverages & More** • 7100 Santa Monica Blvd
- **Carmel Liquor** • 8204 Santa Monica Blvd
- **Consumers Liquor** • 7151 W Sunset Blvd
- **Crown Liquor** • 130 N Robertson Blvd
- **Du Vin Wine & Spirits** • 540 N San Vicente Blvd
- **Fountain Liquor** • 7952 Fountain Ave
- **Gil Turner's Fine Wine & Spirits** • 9101 W Sunset Blvd
- **Golden Rule Liquor** • 7753 Santa Monica Blvd
- **Greenblatts Delicatessen & Fine Wines** • 8017 W Sunset Blvd
- **John & Pete's Fine Wine And Spirits** • 621 N La Cienega Blvd
- **John & Pete's Liquor** • 621 N La Cienega Blvd
- **Jon's Market** • 1234 N La Brea Ave
- **Lee's Liquor** • 8572 W 3rd St
- **Limelite Liquors** • 1649 N La Brea Ave
- **Liquor Locker** • 8161 W Sunset Blvd
- **Liquor Mart** • 7580 W Sunset Blvd
- **Liquor Time** • 7873 Santa Monica Blvd
- **Mel & Rose Liquor & Cigars** • 8344 Melrose Ave
- **Melrose Liquors** • 7435 Melrose Ave
- **Monaco Liquor** • 8513 Santa Monica Blvd
- **Pink Dot Market Deli/Grocery** • 8495 W Sunset Blvd
- **Robert Burns Liquor** • 157 N Robertson Blvd
- **Roman's Liquor** • 1529 N La Brea Ave
- **S&S Liquor** • 7600 Santa Monica Blvd
- **St Regis Liquors** • 8401 W 3rd St
- **Sun Bee Food & Liquor** • 8860 W Sunset Blvd
- **Sunset Plaza Liquor** • 7365 W Sunset Blvd
- **Terner's Liquor** • 8850 W Sunset Blvd

Movie Theaters

- **Laemmle Sunset 5** • 8000 W Sunset Blvd • 323-848-3505
- **Loews Beverly Center 13** • 8522 Beverly Blvd • 310-652-7760
- **New Beverly Cinema** • 7165 Beverly Blvd • 323-938-4038
- **Pacific's The Grove Stadium 14** • 189 The Grove Dr • 323-692-0164
- **Regency Fairfax** • 7907 Beverly Blvd • 323-655-4010
- **Regency Fairfax 3** • 7907 Beverly Blvd • 323-655-4012
- **Regent Showcase Theatre** • 614 N La Brea Ave • 323-934-1770
- **Silent Movie Theatre** • 611 N Fairfax Ave • 323-655-2520

Pet Shops

- **Amazon Rainforest Pet Shop** • 7505 Santa Monica Blvd • 323-969-8382
- **Animal Crackers** • 8023 Beverly Blvd • 310-659-1919
- **Animal Farm Pet Shop** • 8270 Santa Monica Blvd • 323-650-7772
- **Centinela Feed & Pet Supplies** • 331 N Robertson Blvd • 310-246-0367
- **Chateau Marmutt** • 8128 W 3rd St • 323-653-2062
- **Collar & Leash Pet Food & Supllies** • 8555 Santa Monica Blvd • 310-657-6638
- **D-O-G Pet Boutique** • 346 N La Cienega Blvd • 310-424-5807
- **For Birds Only** • 7990 Santa Monica Blvd • 323-848-8361
- **For Pets Only** • 310 S La Brea Ave • 323-664-4211
- **Heavy Petting** • 8229 Santa Monica Blvd • 323-656-2626
- **Le Pet Boutique** • 189 The Grove Dr • 323-935-9195
- **Oranda Aquarium** • 7320 Santa Monica Blvd • 323-876-5059
- **Pet Love** • 131 N La Cienega Blvd • 310-659-8490
- **Petco** • 200 S La Brea Ave • 323-934-8444
- **Three Dog Bakery** • 6333 W 3rd St • 323-935-7512

Video Rental

- **20-20 Video** • 7064 W Sunset Blvd • 323-957-2020
- **20-20 Video** • 8208 Santa Monica Blvd • 323-656-2300
- **Blockbuster** • 1508 N Orange Grove Ave • 323-851-2688
- **Blockbuster** • 330 N La Cienega Blvd • 310-659-8366
- **Blockbuster Video** • 1508 N Orange Grove Ave • 323-851-2688
- **Rocket Video** • 726 N La Brea Ave • 323-965-1100
- **Top One Video** • 901 N Fairfax Ave • 323-654-0434
- **Video West** • 805 Larrabee St • 310-659-5762

Map 2 • West Hollywood

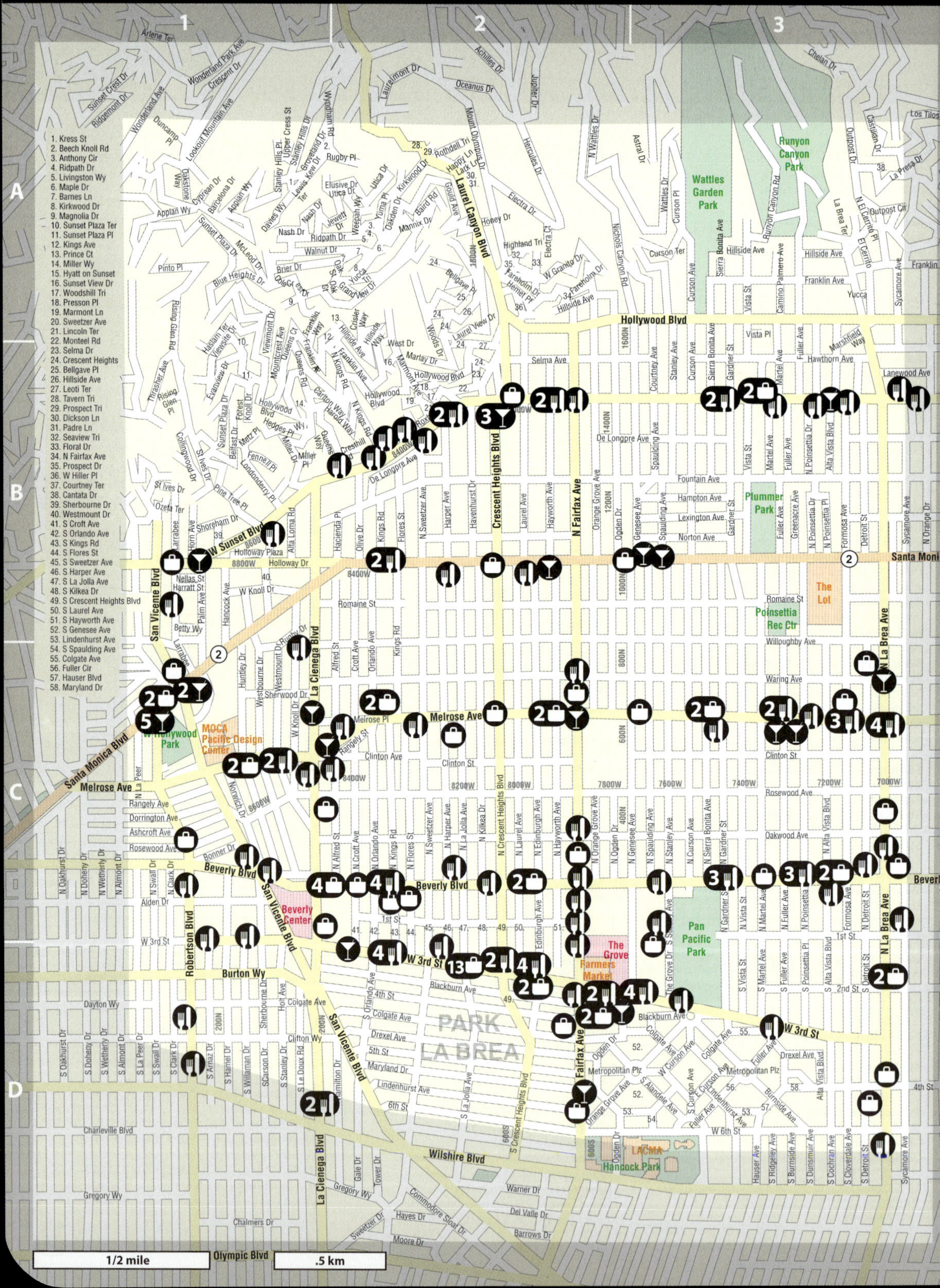

N
1
2
3
A
B
C
D
1. Kress St
2. Beech Knoll Rd
3. Anthony Cir
4. Ridpath Dr
5. Livingston Wy
6. Maple Dr
7. Barnes Ln
8. Kirkwood Dr
9. Magnolia Dr
10. Sunset Plaza Ter
11. Sunset Plaza Pl
12. Kings Ave
13. Prince Ct
14. Miller Wy
15. Hyatt on Sunset
16. Sunset View Dr
17. Woodshill Trl
18. Presson Pl
19. Marmont Ln
20. Sweetzer Ave
21. Lincoln Ter
22. Monteel Rd
23. Selma Dr
24. Crescent Heights
25. Bellgave Pl
26. Hillside Ave
27. Leoti Ter
28. Tavern Trl
29. Prospect Trl
30. Dickson Ln
31. Padre Ln
32. Seaview Trl
33. Floral Dr
34. N Fairfax Ave
35. Prospect Dr
36. W Hiller Pl
37. Courtney Ter
38. Cantata Dr
39. Sherbourne Dr
40. Westmount Dr
41. S Croft Ave
42. S Orlando Ave
43. S Kings Rd
44. S Flores St
45. S Sweetzer Ave
46. S Harper Ave
47. S La Jolla Ave
48. S Kilkea Dr
49. S Crescent Heights Blvd
50. S Laurel Ave
51. S Hayworth Ave
52. S Genesee Ave
53. Lindenhurst Ave
54. S Spaulding Ave
55. Colgate Ave
56. Fuller Cir
57. Hauser Blvd
58. Maryland Dr
Wattles Garden Park
Runyon Canyon Park
Laurel Canyon Blvd
Hollywood Blvd
Crescent Heights Blvd
N Fairfax Ave
W Sunset Blvd
Santa Monica Blvd
Plummer Park
The Lot
Poinsettia Rec Ctr
N La Brea Ave
San Vicente Blvd
La Cienega Blvd
Melrose Ave
W Hollywood Park
MOCA Pacific Design Center
Beverly Blvd
Beverly Center
Robertson Blvd
Burton Wy
W 3rd St
The Grove
Farmers Market
Pan Pacific Park
PARK LA BREA
Fairfax Ave
LACMA
Hancock Park
Wilshire Blvd
Olympic Blvd
1/2 mile
.5 km

If Los Angeles were a high school, this area would be straight-up the most popular kid on campus, beloved by jocks, geeks, brains, stoners, preppies, and the entire pep squad. That it is so much to so many makes it both good and bad. Meantime, the available inventory is impressive. Velvet rope? Check. Art-house cinemas? Check. Sidewalk café tables? Check. Celebrity gawking? Check. Are you with us? Good. Now go out and make some new friends.

Nightlife

- **The Abbey** • 692 N Robertson Blvd • 310-289-8410
- **Bar 1200** • Sunset Marquis Hotel • 1200 N Alta Loma Rd • 310-657-1333
- **Bar at the Standard** • 8300 W Sunset Blvd • 323-650-9090
- **Bar Lubitsch** • 7702 Santa Monica Blvd • 323-654-1234
- **Barney's Beanery** • 8447 Santa Monica Blvd • 323-654-2287
- **Bel Age Hotel** • 1020 N San Vicente Blvd • 866-282-4560
- **Club 7969** • 7969 Santa Monica Blvd • 323-654-0280
- **The Dime** • 442 N Fairfax Ave • 323-651-4421
- **Dominick's** • 8715 Beverly Blvd • 310-652-2335
- **East West** • 8851 Santa Monica Blvd • 310-360-6186
- **El Carmen Tequila & Taco Bar** • 8138 W 3rd St • 323-852-1552
- **El Coyote** • 7312 Beverly Blvd • 323-939-2255
- **The Factory/Ultra Suede** • 652 N La Peer Dr • 310-659-4551
- **Falcon** • 7213 W Sunset Blvd • 323-850-5350
- **Formosa Café** • 7156 Santa Monica Blvd • 323-850-9050
- **Fubar** • 7994 Santa Monica Blvd • 323-654-0396
- **Garden of Eden** • 7080 Hollywood Blvd • 323-465-3336
- **Genghis Cohen** • 740 N Fairfax Ave • 323-653-0640
- **Guy's Bar** • 8713 Beverly Blvd • 818-766-8311
- **Here** • 696 N Robertson Blvd • 310-360-8455
- **House of Blues** • 8430 Sunset Blvd • 323-848-5100
- **Jones** • 7205 Santa Monica Blvd • 323-850-1727
- **Key Club** • 9039 W Sunset Blvd • 310-274-5800
- **La Plaza** • 739 N La Brea Ave • 323-939-0703
- **Largo** • 432 N Fairfax Ave • 323-852-1073
- **Laugh Factory** • 8001 W Sunset Blvd • 323-656-1336
- **Lola's** • 945 N Fairfax Ave • 213-736-5652
- **Micky's** • 8857 Santa Monica Blvd • 310-657-1176
- **Molly Malone's** • 575 S Fairfax Ave • 323-935-1577
- **Monsieur Marcel** • 6333 W 3rd St • 323-932-6855
- **O-bar** • 8279 Santa Monica Blvd • 323-822-3300
- **Pearl** • 665 N Robertson Blvd • 310-358-9191
- **Prey** • 643 N La Cienega Blvd • 310-652-2012
- **Privilege** • 8117 W Sunset Blvd • 323-654-0030
- **Rage** • 8911 Santa Monica Blvd • 310-652-7055
- **Rainbow Bar and Grill** • 9015 Sunset Blvd • 310-278-4232
- **Red Rock** • 8782 Sunset Blvd • 310-854-0710
- **Roxy** • 9009 W Sunset Blvd • 310-276-2222
- **The Ruby** • 7070 Hollywood Blvd • 323-467-7070
- **Saddle Ranch Chop House** • 8371 W Sunset Blvd • 323-656-2007
- **Silent Movie Theatre** • 611 N Fairfax Ave • 323-655-2520
- **The Skybar** • 8440 W Sunset Blvd • 323-650-8999
- **Snake Pit Ale House** • 7529 Melrose Ave • 323-653-2011
- **St Nicks** • 8450 W Third St • 323-655-6917
- **Tower Bar** • Sunset Tower Hotel • 8358 Sunset Blvd • 323-654-7100
- **The Troubadour** • 9081 Santa Monica Blvd • 310-276-6168
- **The Village Idiot** • 7383 Melrose Ave • 323-655-3331
- **Viper Room** • 8852 Sunset Blvd • 310-358-1880
- **Whisky A Go Go** • 8901 Sunset Blvd • 310-652-4202
- **Windows Lounge** • Four Seasons Hotel • 300 S Doheny Dr • 310-273-2222
- **Winston's** • 7746 Santa Monica Blvd • 323-654-0105

Restaurants

- **Ago** • 8478 Melrose Ave • 323-655-6333
- **Albano's Brooklyn Pizza** • 7261 Melrose Ave • 323-934-2494
- **Amalfi** • 143 N La Brea Ave • 323-938-2504
- **Andre's Italian Restaurant** • 6332 W Third St • 323-935-1246
- **Angeli Caffe** • 7274 Melrose Ave • 323-936-9086
- **Angelini Osteria** • 7313 Beverly Blvd • 323-297-0070
- **AOC** • 8022 W 3rd St • 323-653-6359
- **Azami Sushi Café** • 7160 Melrose Ave • 323-939-3816
- **Balboa** • The Grafton Hotel • 8462 W Sunset Blvd • 323-650-8383
- **Barefoot Bar & Grill** • 8722 W 3rd St • 310-276-6223
- **Basix Café** • 8333 Santa Monica Blvd • 323-848-2460
- **Benito's Taco Shop** • 7912 Beverly Blvd • 323-938-7427
- **Beverly Hills Juice Club** • 8382 Beverly Blvd • 323-655-8300
- **BLD** • 7450 Beverly Blvd • 323-930-9744
- **Bossa Nova** • 685 N Robertson Blvd • 310-657-5070
- **Bossa Nova** • 7181 W Sunset Blvd • 323-436-7999
- **Boule** • 420 N La Cienega Blvd • 310-289-9977
- **Buddha's Belly** • 7475 Beverly Blvd • 323-931-8588
- **Bungalow Club** • 7174 Melrose Ave • 323-936-5270
- **Café Angelino** • 8735 W 3rd St • 310-246-1177
- **Café Med** • 8615 Sunset Blvd • 310-652-0445
- **Café Vegan** • 7669 Beverley Blvd • 323-937-3100
- **Campanile** • 624 S La Brea Ave • 323-938-1447
- **Canter's Deli** • 419 N Fairfax Ave • 323-651-2030
- **Chameau** • 339 N Fairfax Ave • 323-951-0039
- **Chateau Marmont** • 8221 W Sunset Blvd • 323-656-1010
- **Chaya Brasserie** • 8741 Alden Dr • 310-859-8833
- **Cheebo** • 7533 W Sunset Blvd • 323-850-7070
- **Chipotle** • 121 N La Cienega Blvd • 310-855-0371
- **Cobras & Matadors** • 7615 Beverly Blvd • 323-932-6178
- **The Courtyard** • 8543 Santa Monica Blvd • 310-358-0301
- **Cynthia's** • 8370 W 3rd St • 323-658-7851
- **Dolce Enoteca** • 8284 Melrose Ave • 323-852-7174
- **Doughboys** • 8136 W 3rd St • 323-651-4202
- **East India Grill** • 345 N La Brea Ave • 323-936-8844
- **Eat Well** • 8252 Santa Monica Blvd • 323-656-1383
- **Ed's Coffee Shop** • 460 N Robertson Blvd • 310-659-8625
- **El Compadre** • 7408 Sunset Blvd • 323-874-7924
- **Falcon** • 7213 W Sunset Blvd • 323-850-5350
- **Farm of Beverly Hills** • 189 The Grove Dr • 323-525-1699
- **Fish Grill** • 7226 Beverly Blvd • 323-937-7162
- **Fogo de Chao** • 133 N La Cienega Blvd • 310-289-7755
- **The French Crêpe Co** • 6333 W 3rd St • 323-934-3113
- **French Quarter Market Place** • 7985 Santa Monica Blvd • 323-654-0898
- **Genghis Cohen** • 740 N Fairfax Ave • 323-653-0640
- **Grace** • 7360 Beverly Blvd • 323-934-4400
- **Greenblatts Delicatessen & Fine Wines** • 8017 W Sunset Blvd • 323-656-0606
- **Griddle Café** • 7916 W Sunset Blvd • 323-874-0377
- **Gumbo Pot** • 6333 W 3rd St • 323-933-0358
- **Hirozen** • 8385 Beverly Blvd • 323-653-0470
- **House of Blues** • 8430 Sunset Blvd • 323-848-5100
- **Hugo's** • 8401 Santa Monica Blvd • 323-654-3993
- **In-N-Out Burger** • 7009 W Sunset Blvd • 800-786-1000
- **The Ivy** • 113 N Robertson Blvd • 310-274-8303
- **JAR** • 8225 Beverly Blvd • 323-655-6566
- **Joan's on Third** • 8350 W 3rd St • 323-655-2285
- **Jones** • 7205 Santa Monica Blvd • 323-850-1727
- **King's Road Café** • 8361 Beverly Blvd • 323-655-9044
- **Kokomo** • Farmer's Market • 6333 W 3rd St • 323-933-0773
- **La Paella** • 476 S San Vicente Blvd • 323-951-0745
- **Lala's** • 7229 Melrose Ave • 323-934-6838
- **Le Pain Quotidien** • 8607 Melrose Ave • 310-854-3700
- **The Little Door** • 8164 W 3rd St • 323-951-1210
- **Los Tacos** • 7954 Santa Monica Blvd • 323-848-9141
- **Loteria Grill** • 6333 W 3rd St • 323-930-2211
- **Lucques** • 8474 Melrose Ave • 323-655-6277
- **M Cafe de Chaya** • 7119 Melrose Ave • 323-525-0588
- **Mandarette** • 8386 Beverly Blvd • 323-655-6115
- **Miyagi's** • 8225 W Sunset Blvd • 323-650-3524
- **Newsroom Café** • 120 N Robertson Blvd • 310-652-4444
- **Numbers Restaurant** • 8741 Santa Monica Blvd • 310-652-7700
- **Opaque** • 8401 W Sunset Blvd • 800-710-1270
- **The Pig** • 612 N La Brea Ave • 323-935-1116
- **Pink's Famous Chili Dogs** • 709 N La Brea Ave • 323-931-4223
- **Quality Food & Beverage** • 8030 W 3rd St • 323-658-5959
- **Real Food Daily** • 414 N La Cienega Blvd • 310-289-9910
- **Saddle Ranch Chop House** • 8371 W Sunset Blvd • 323-656-2007
- **Singapore's Banana Leaf** • 6333 W 3rd St • 323-933-4627
- **The Standard** • 8300 W Sunset Blvd • 323-650-9090
- **Surya India** • 8048 W 3rd St • 323-653-5151
- **Susina Bakery** • 7122 Beverly Blvd • 323-934-7900
- **Sweet Lady Jane** • 8360 Melrose Ave • 323-653-7145
- **Swingers** • 8020 Beverly Blvd • 323-653-5858
- **Tagine** • 132 N Robertson Blvd • 310-360-7535
- **TART** • 115 S Fairfax Ave • 323-556-2608
- **Taste** • 8454 Melrose Ave • 323-852-6888
- **The TEN20 Café** • Wyndham Bel Age Hotel • 1020 N San Vicente Blvd • 310-854-1111
- **Toast** • 8221 W Third St • 323-655-5018
- **Toi** • 7505 1/2 W Sunset Blvd • 323-874-8062
- **Tops** • 8593 Santa Monica Blvd • 310-659-8843
- **Trattoria Amici** • 469 N Doheny Dr • 310-858-0271
- **Ulysses Voyage** • 6333 W Third St • 323-939-9728
- **Urth Caffé** • 8565 Melrose Ave • 310-659-0628
- **Uzbekistan Restaurant** • 7077 W Sunset Blvd • 323-464-3663
- **Vienna Café** • 7356 Melrose Ave • 323-651-3822
- **The Village Idiot** • 7383 Melrose Ave • 323-655-3331
- **Wokcano Café** • 8408 W 3rd St • 323-653-1998
- **Wood Ranch BBQ & Grill** • 189 The Grove Dr • 323-937-6800
- **Yabu** • 521 N La Cienega Blvd • 310-854-0400

Shopping

- **Aardvark's Odd Ark** • 7579 Melrose Ave • 323-655-6769
- **Aero & Co** • 8403 W 3rd St • 323-653-4651
- **Agent Provocateur** • 7961 Melrose Ave • 323-653-0229
- **American Apparel** • 104 N Robertson Blvd • 310-274-6292
- **American Apparel** • 802 N San Vicente Blvd • 310-659-0373
- **American Rag** • 150 S La Brea Ave • 323-935-3154
- **Apple Store** • 189 The Grove Dr • 323-965-8400
- **Beige** • 7274 Beverly Blvd • 323-549-0064
- **Ben Sherman** • 8500 Beverly Blvd • 310-657-3400
- **Betsey Johnson** • 8050 Melrose Ave • 323-852-1534
- **Blick Art Materials** • 7301 Beverly Blvd • 323-933-9284
- **Blueprint** • 8366 Beverly Blvd • 323-653-2439
- **The Bodhi Tree** • 8585 Melrose Ave • 310-659-1733
- **Book Soup** • 8818 W Sunset Blvd • 310-659-3110
- **Button Store** • 8344 W 3rd St • 323-658-5473
- **Centerfold Newsstand** • 716 N Fairfax Ave • 323-651-4822
- **Chado Tea Room** • 8422 1/2 W 3rd St • 323-655-2056
- **Chateau Marmutt** • 8128 W 3rd St • 323-653-2062
- **The Cook's Library** • 8373 W 3rd St • 323-655-3141
- **Cost Plus World Market** • 6333 W 3rd St • 323-935-5530
- **Crate & Barrel** • 189 The Grove Dr • 323-297-0370
- **Decades** • 8214 1/2 Melrose Ave • 323-655-0223
- **Decades Two** • 8214 Melrose Ave • 323-655-1960
- **Denim Doctors** • 8044 W 3rd St • 323-852-0171
- **Diesel** • 8500 Beverly Blvd • 310-652-5504
- **Eduardo Lucero** • 7378 Beverly Blvd • 323-933-2778
- **Ethel** • 8235 1/2 W 3rd St • 323-658-8602
- **Flight 001** • 8235 3rd St • 323-966-0001
- **Fornarina** • 8000 Melrose Ave • 323-782-7901
- **Fred Segal** • 8100 Melrose Ave • 323-651-4129
- **Futurama** • 446 N La Brea Ave • 323-937-4522
- **Golden Apple Comics** • 7018 Melrose Ave • 323-658-6047
- **Guitar Center** • 7425 Sunset Blvd • 323-874-1060
- **Hilary Rush** • 8222 W Third St • 323-852-0088
- **I Martin** • 8330 Beverly Blvd • 323-653-6900
- **Iconology** • 353 S La Brea Ave • 323-965-9666
- **Jet Rag** • 825 N La Brea Ave • 323-939-0528
- **Joan's on Third** • 8350 W 3rd St • 323-655-2285
- **Knit Café** • 8441 Melrose Ave • 323-658-5648
- **Koontz Hardware** • 8914 Santa Monica Blvd • 310-652-0123
- **Kowboyz** • 8050 Beverly Blvd • 323-653-6444
- **Lisa Kline** • 136 S Robertson Blvd • 310-246-0907
- **Liz's Antique Hardware** • 453 S La Brea Ave • 323-939-4403
- **M Frederic** • 189 The Grove Dr • 323-939-9072
- **Madison** • 113 S Robertson Blvd • 310-275-1930
- **Maison Midi** • 148 S La Brea Ave • 323-935-3157
- **Mani's Bakery** • 519 S Fairfax Ave • 323-938-8800
- **Marc Jacobs** • 8400 Melrose Pl • 323-653-5100
- **Marc Jacobs Accessories** • 8401 Melrose Pl • 323-653-0100
- **Me & Ro** • 8405 Melrose Pl • 323-782-1071
- **Milk** • 8209 W Third St • 323-951-0330
- **Miss Sixty** • 8070 Melrose Ave • 323-655-7220
- **Mr Marcel's** • 6333 W 3rd St (Farmers Market) • 323-935-9451
- **Necromance** • 7220 Melrose Ave • 323-934-8684
- **Nordstrom** • 189 The Grove Dr • 323-930-2230
- **Paul Smith** • 8221 Melrose Ave • 323-951-4800
- **Plastica** • 8405 W 3rd St • 323-655-1051
- **Pleasure Chest** • 7733 Santa Monica Blvd • 323-650-1022
- **Politix** • 8552 Beverly Blvd • 310-659-1964
- **Pulp** • 452 S La Brea Ave • 323-937-3505
- **Restoration Hardware** • 131 N La Cienega Blvd • 310-360-9651
- **Ron Herman** • 8100 Melrose Ave • 323-651-4129
- **Sam Ash Music** • 7360 Sunset Blvd • 323-850-1050
- **Samy's Camera** • 431 S Fairfax Ave • 323-938-4400
- **Satine** • 8117 W 3rd St • 323-655-2142
- **SEE Selective Eyewear Elements** • 131 N La Cienega Blvd • 310-360-6998
- **Solomon's** • 447 N Fairfax Ave • 323-653-9045
- **Sonrisa** • 7609 Beverly Blvd • 323-935-8438
- **Soolip** • 8646 Melrose Ave • 310-360-0545
- **Susina Bakery** • 7122 Beverly Blvd • 323-934-7900
- **Sweet 9** • 7361 1/2 Melrose Ave • 323-868-1658
- **Target** • 7100 Santa Monica Blvd • 323-603-0004
- **Tarina Tarantino** • 7957 Melrose Ave • 323-651-5155
- **Trashy Lingerie** • 402 N La Cienega Blvd • 310-652-4543
- **Traveler's Bookcase** • 8375 W 3rd St • 323-655-0575
- **Trina Turk** • 8008 W 3rd St • 323-651-1382
- **Twentieth** • 8057 Beverly Blvd • 323-904-1200
- **Urban Outfitters** • 7650 Melrose Ave • 323-653-3231
- **Virgin Megastore** • 8000 W Sunset Blvd • 323-650-8666
- **Zipper** • 8316 W 3rd St • 323-951-0620

Map 3 • Hollywood

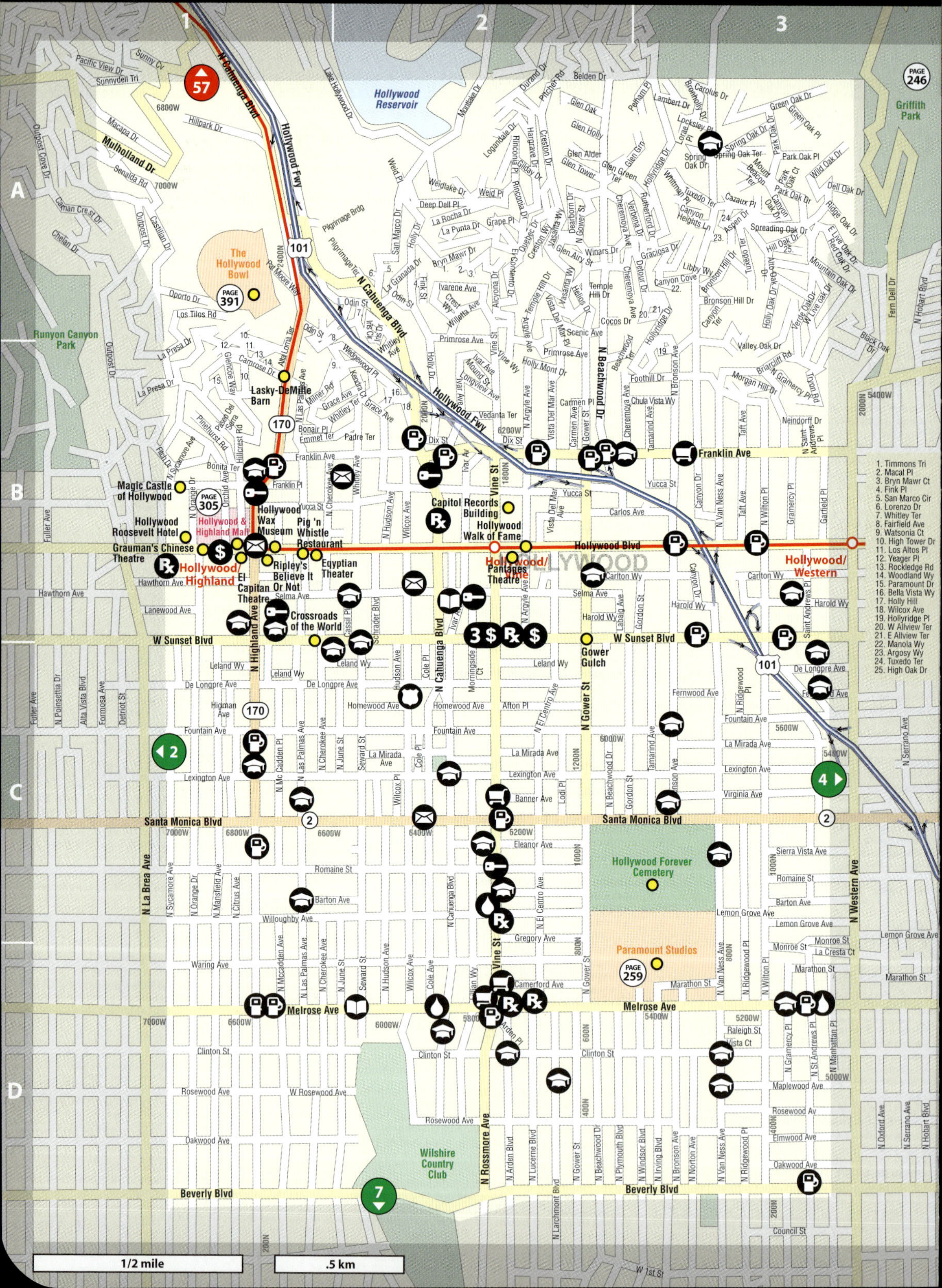

The Hollywood Bowl

Hollywood Reservoir

Runyon Canyon Park

Griffith Park

Lasky-DeMille Barn

Magic Castle of Hollywood

Hollywood Roosevelt Hotel

Hollywood & Highland Mall

Grauman's Chinese Theatre

Hollywood/Highland

El Capitan Theatre

Hollywood Wax Museum

Ripley's Believe It Or Not

Pig 'n Whistle Restaurant

Egyptian Theater

Crossroads of the World

Capitol Records Building

Hollywood Walk of Fame

Pantages Theatre

Hollywood/Vine

Hollywood/Western

Gower Gulch

Hollywood Forever Cemetery

Paramount Studios

Wilshire Country Club

1. Timmons Trl
2. Macal Pl
3. Bryn Mawr Ct
4. Fink Pl
5. San Marco Cir
6. Lorenzo Dr
7. Whitley Ter
8. Fairfield Ave
9. Watsonia Ct
10. High Tower Dr
11. Los Altos Pl
12. Yeager Pl
13. Rockledge Rd
14. Woodland Wy
15. Paramount Dr
16. Bella Vista Wy
17. Holly Hill
18. Wilcox Ave
19. Hollyridge Pl
20. W Allview Ter
21. E Allview Ter
22. Manola Wy
23. Argosy Wy
24. Tuxedo Ter
25. High Oak Dr

1/2 mile

.5 km

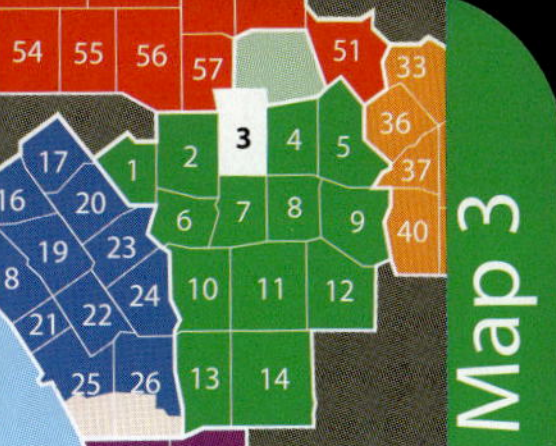

With its population of aspiring actors and middle-America refugees, present-day Hollywood is still much like the city once so described by Lionel Barrymore: "Half the people in Hollywood are dying to be discovered and the other half are afraid they will be." Demographics aside, Hollywood has cleaned up its act of late—at least on the surface. Real estate developments like the W Hotel condo project and the Sunset + Vine residences are yet another step in the ongoing revitalization of Hollywood.

Banks

- **Bank of America** • 6300 Sunset Blvd
- **California National** • 6922 Hollywood Blvd
- **Comerica** • 6255 W Sunset Blvd
- **Washington Mutual** • 1500 Vine St
- **Wells Fargo** • 6320 W Sunset Blvd

Car Rental

- **Basic Car Rental** • 1819 N Cahuenga Blvd
- **Budget** • 6822 Hollywood Blvd
- **Enterprise** • 1770 Ivar Ave
- **Enterprise** • 990 N Vine St
- **Hertz** • 1755 N Highland Ave

Car Washes

- **Celebrity Car Wash** • 901 Vine St
- **Cook's Corner Smog** • 5925 Melrose Ave
- **La Car Wash** • 6061 Santa Monica Blvd
- **Melrose Car Wash** • 5080 Melrose Ave

Gas Stations

- **76** • 4700 Beverly Blvd
- **76** • 5890 Hollywood Blvd
- **76** • 6051 Franklin Ave
- **76** • 6537 Melrose Ave
- **76** • 6678 Santa Monica Blvd
- **Arco** • 5175 Melrose Ave
- **Arco** • 6100 Franklin Ave
- **Chevron** • 1255 N Highland Ave
- **Chevron** • 1787 N Highland Ave
- **Chevron** • 1934 N Cahuenga Blvd
- **Mobil** • 1051 N Highland Ave
- **Mobil** • 5700 Hollywood Blvd
- **Mobil** • 5857 W Sunset Blvd
- **Mobil** • 6228 Franklin Ave
- **Mobil** • 6301 Santa Monica Blvd
- **Mobil** • 6601 Melrose Ave
- **Shell** • 5657 W Sunset Blvd
- **Shell** • 6420 Franklin Ave
- **Valero** • 655 N Rossmore Ave

Landmarks

- **Capitol Records Building** • 1750 N Vine St
- **Crossroads of the World** • 6671 Sunset Blvd
- **El Capitan Theatre** • 6838 Hollywood Blvd
- **Gower Gulch** • W Sunset Blvd & N Gower St
- **Grauman's Chinese Theatre** • 6925 Hollywood Blvd
- **Grauman's Egyptian Theater** • 6712 Hollywood Blvd
- **Hollywood Bowl** • 2301 N Highland Ave
- **Hollywood Forever Cemetery** • 6000 Santa Monica Blvd
- **Hollywood & Highland Mall** • 6801 Hollywood Blvd
- **Hollywood Roosevelt Hotel** • 7000 Hollywood Blvd
- **Hollywood Walk of Fame** • Hollywood Blvd from N Gower St to La Brea Ter
- **Hollywood Wax Museum** • 6767 Hollywood Blvd
- **Lasky-DeMille Barn** • 2100 N Highland Ave
- **Magic Castle of Hollywood** • 7025 Franklin Ave
- **Pantages Theater** • 6233 Hollywood Blvd
- **Paramount Studios** • 5555 Melrose Ave
- **Pig 'n Whistle** • 6714 Hollywood Blvd
- **Ripley's Believe It or Not** • 6780 Hollywood Blvd

Libraries

- **Frances Howard Goldwyn** • 1623 Ivar Ave • 323-856-8260
- **John C Fremont Branch** • 6121 Melrose Ave • 323-962-3521

Pharmacies

- **CVS** • 1747 N Cahuenga Blvd • 323-463-7900
- **CVS** • 861 N Vine St • 323-466-7300
- **Longs Drugs** • 7021 Hollywood Blvd • 323-836-0307
- **Pavilions** • 727 N Vine St • 323-466-7158
- **Rite-Aid** • 6130 W Sunset Blvd • 323-467-4201
- **Vons/Pavillions** • 727 Vine St • 323-466-7158

Police

- **Los Angeles Police Dept** • 1358 Wilcox Ave • 213-972-2971

Post Offices

- **US Post Office** • 1425 N Cherokee Ave • 800-275-8777
- **US Post Office** • 1615 Wilcox Ave • 800-275-8777
- **US Post Office** • 6457 Santa Monica Blvd • 800-275-8777
- **US Post Office** • 6801 Hollywood Blvd • 323-957-2671

Schools

- **ABC Educational Center** • 1129 Cole Ave
- **Assistance League of Southern California** • 1375 N St Andrews Pl
- **Assistance League of Southern California** • 5620 De Longpre Ave
- **Beverly Hills RC** • 6550 Fountain Ave
- **Blessed Sacrament** • 6641 W Sunset Blvd
- **Cheder Menachem** • 5120 Melrose Ave
- **Cheremoya Avenue Elementary** • 6017 Franklin Ave
- **Christ the King Elementary** • 617 N Arden Blvd
- **Frances Blend Special Education** • 5210 Clinton St
- **Grant EEC** • 1559 N St Andrews Pl
- **Grant Elementary** • 1530 N Wilton Pl
- **Hollywood Community Adult** • 1521 N Highland Ave
- **Hollywood Little Red School House** • 1248 N Highland Ave
- **Hollywood Primary Center** • 1115 Tamarind Ave
- **Hollywood Senior High** • 1521 N Highland Ave
- **Hubert Howe Bancroft Middle** • 929 N Las Palmas Ave
- **Joseph le Conte Middle** • 1316 N Bronson Ave
- **Larchmont Charter** • 815 N El Centro Ave
- **Montessori Shir-Hashirim** • 6047 Carlton Wy
- **Neilson Academy** • 2528 Canyon Dr
- **Oaks** • 6817 Franklin Ave
- **Page Private** • 565 N Larchmont Blvd
- **Santa Monica Blvd Community Charter** • 1022 N Van Ness Ave
- **Selma Ave Elementary** • 6611 Selma Ave
- **TCA Arshag Dickranian** • 1200 N Cahuenga Blvd
- **Van Ness Elementary** • 501 N Van Ness Ave
- **Vine EEC** • 6312 Eleanor Ave
- **Vine St Elementary** • 955 Vine St
- **Wagon Wheel** • 653 N Cahuenga Blvd
- **Young Hollywood** • 1547 N McCadden Pl

Supermarkets

- **Gelson's Markets** • 5877 Franklin Ave
- **Pavilions** • 727 Vine St
- **Stop N Shop** • 1123 Vine St

Map 3 • Hollywood

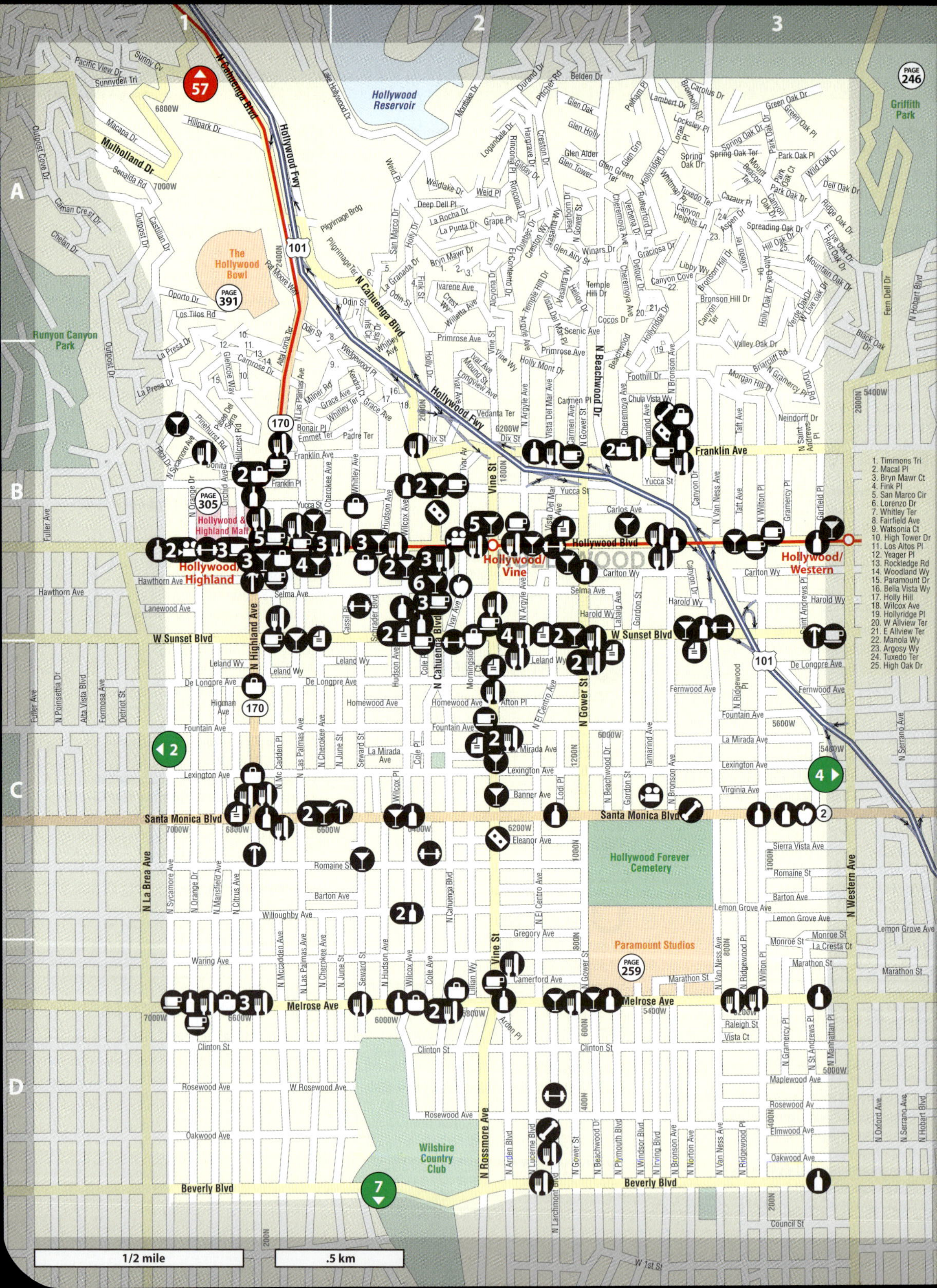

Hollywood Reservoir

The Hollywood Bowl

Runyon Canyon Park

Griffith Park

Hollywood & Highland Mall

Hollywood/Highland

Hollywood/Vine

Hollywood/Western

Hollywood Forever Cemetery

Paramount Studios

Wilshire Country Club

Hollywood Blvd

Franklin Ave

W Sunset Blvd

Santa Monica Blvd

Melrose Ave

Beverly Blvd

1. Timmons Trl
2. Macal Pl
3. Bryn Mawr Ct
4. Fink Pl
5. San Marco Cir
6. Lorenzo Dr
7. Whitley Ter
8. Fairfield Ave
9. Watsonia Ct
10. High Tower Dr
11. Los Altos Pl
12. Rockledge Rd
13. Woodland Wy
14. Paramount Dr
15. Bella Vista Wy
16. Holly Hill
17. Yeager Pl
18. Wilcox Ave
19. Hollyridge Pl
20. W Allview Ter
21. E Allview Ter
22. Manola Wy
23. Argosy Wy
24. Tuxedo Ter
25. High Oak Dr

1/2 mile

.5 km

Sundries / Entertainment

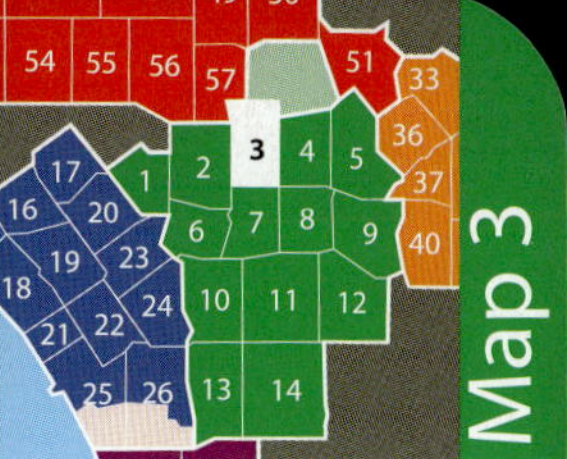

The prostitute-laden, drug-riddled Hollywood Boulevard portrayed in Pretty Woman is long gone. In its place is a bustling thoroughfare, flanked by the ostentatious Hollywood and Highland complex (Live Large!) at one end, and the unwavering Pantages Theatre at the other. In between are a plethora of tacky souvenir shops, mediocre restaurants, nightclubs dripping with underage celebs, and more American Apparel stores than realistically necessary. The omnipresent sidewalk stars and landmarks like Musso & Frank remind us that, despite the changes, this is still Hollywood—land of dreams.

Coffee

- **101 Coffee Shop** • 6145 Franklin Ave
- **Belwood Café** • 6243 Hollywood Blvd
- **Bliss Art House Café** • 1249 Vine St
- **Bourgeois Pig** • 5931 Franklin Ave
- **Café Audrey** • 6701 Hollywood Blvd
- **Caffe Etc** • 6371 Selma Ave
- **Coffee Bean & Tea Leaf** • 6255 W Sunset Blvd
- **Coffee Bean & Tea Leaf** • 6922 Hollywood Blvd
- **Goldberg's Famous Coffee Bar** • 6767 W Sunset Blvd
- **The Green Room** • 6752 Hollywood Blvd
- **Groundwork Coffee** • 1501 N Cahuenga Blvd
- **Hollywood Internet Café** • 1770 N Highland Ave
- **Karma Coffeehouse** • 1544 N Cahuenga Blvd
- **Kelly's Coffee & Fudge** • 6801 Hollywood Blvd
- **Nestle Toll House Café** • 6801 Hollywood Blvd
- **Sabor y Cultura** • 5625 Hollywood Blvd
- **Starbucks** • 1900 N Highland Ave
- **Starbucks** • 6102 W Sunset Blvd
- **Starbucks** • 6745 Hollywood Blvd
- **Starbucks** • 6801 Hollywood Blvd
- **Stir Crazy Coffee Shop** • 6903 Melrose Ave
- **Stir Crazy Coffee Shop** • 6917 Melrose Ave
- **Sunshine Sweet Café** • 6771 Hollywood Blvd

Copy Shops

- **Copy Central** • 6464 W Sunset Blvd • 323-461-1222
- **Davco Printing** • 5825 W Sunset Blvd • 323-466-9591
- **FedEx Kinko's** • 1440 Vine St • 323-871-1300
- **FedEx Kinko's** • 6255 W Sunset Blvd • 323-465-3305
- **Nonstop Printing** • 6140 Hollywood Blvd • 323-464-1640
- **Office Depot** • 1240 Vine St • 323-957-1274
- **Rush Copy** • 6095 W Sunset Blvd • 323-462-7874
- **Sir Speedy** • 6660 W Sunset Blvd • 323-469-0327
- **Staples** • 6450 W Sunset Blvd • 323-467-2155

Farmers Markets

- **Hollywood (Sun, 8 am-1 pm)** • Ivar Ave & Selma Ave
- **Sears Parking Lot (Wed, 12:30-5:30)** • 5601 Santa Monica Blvd

Gyms

- **24 Hour Fitness** • 6380 W Sunset Blvd • 323461-2024
- **Bally Total Fitness** • 1628 N El Centro Ave • 323-461-0227
- **Curves** • 527 N Larchmont Blvd • 323-465-4652
- **Curves** • 5825 W Sunset Blvd • 323-467-8101
- **Gold's Gym** • 1016 Cole Ave • 323-462-7012
- **Hollywood YMCA** • 1553 N Schrader Blvd • 323-467-4161
- **LA Fitness Sports Clubs** • 7021 Hollywood Blvd • 323-462-5199

Hardware Stores

- **Anawalt Lumber** • 1001 N Highland Ave • 323-464-1600
- **Brookstone** • 6801 Hollywood Blvd • 310-553-2248
- **Home Depot** • 5600 W Sunset Blvd • 323-461-3303
- **Stock Building Supply** • 6641 Santa Monica Blvd • 323-469-1951

Liquor Stores

- **Al's Liquor Store** • 5550 Melrose Ave
- **Bogie's Liquor** • 5753 Melrose Ave
- **Colbee Liquor** • 6205 Willoughby Ave
- **Gary's Liquor** • 5067 Melrose Ave
- **Highland Liquor** • 1770 N Highland Ave
- **Hollywood Liquors** • 7040 Hollywood Blvd
- **Howie's Liquor** • 5645 Santa Monica Blvd
- **Hudson Liquor & Deli** • 6023 Melrose Ave
- **Jeffrey K An** • 1515 Wilcox Ave
- **Liquor & Food Mart** • 4657 Beverly Blvd
- **Liquor to Go Go** • 5901 Hollywood Blvd
- **P&J Liquor** • 6170 Santa Monica Blvd
- **P&J Liquor & Deli** • 6480 Santa Monica Blvd
- **Pla-Boy Liquor** • 6435 Yucca St
- **Quaker State Liquor** • 6901 Melrose Ave
- **Quik Stop Liquor** • 6223 Franklin Ave
- **Spirit Shop & Deli** • 6443 W Sunset Blvd
- **St Andrew's Liquor** • 5566 Hollywood Blvd
- **Studio Liquor** • 6759 Santa Monica Blvd
- **Sunset Market & Liquor** • 5825 W Sunset Blvd
- **Tony's Liquor** • 5707 Santa Monica Blvd
- **Victor's Liquor & Delicatessen** • 1915 N Bronson Ave

Movie Theaters

- **ArcLight Hollywood/Cinerama Dome** • 6360 W Sunset Blvd • 323-464-1465
- **Cinespace** • 6356 Hollywood Blvd • 323-817-3456
- **Grauman's Chinese Theatre** • 6925 Hollywood Blvd • 323-464-8111
- **Grauman's Egyptian Theater** • 6712 Hollywood Blvd • 323-466-3456
- **Hollywood Forever Cemetery** • 6000 Santa Monica Blvd • 323-469-1181
- **Mann Chinese 6** • 6801 Hollywood Blvd • 323-464-8111
- **Pacific El Capitan** • 6838 Hollywood Blvd • 323-467-7674
- **Vine Theatre** • 6321 Hollywood Blvd • 323-463-6819

Nightlife

- **Amagi** • 6114 W Sunset Blvd • 323-464-7497
- **ArcLight Café Bar & Balcony** • 6360 W Sunset Blvd • 323-464-1478
- **Arena Nightclub** • 6655 Santa Monica Blvd • 323-462-0714
- **Avalon** • 1735 Vine St • 323-462-8900
- **The Bar** • 5851 Sunset Blvd • 323-468-9154
- **Beauty Bar** • 1638 N Cahuenga Blvd • 323-464-7676
- **Big Wang's** • 1562 N Cahuenga Blvd • 323-469-2449
- **Birds** • 5925 Franklin Ave • 323-465-0175
- **Blu Monkey** • 5521 Hollywood Blvd • 323-957-9000
- **Boardner's** • 1642 N Cherokee Ave • 323-462-9621
- **Burgundy Room** • 1621 N Cahuenga Blvd • 323-465-7530
- **The Cat & Fiddle** • 6530 Sunset Blvd • 323-468-3800
- **Catalina Bar & Grill** • 6725 W Sunset Blvd • 323-466-2210
- **Cinespace** • 6356 Hollywood Blvd • 323-817-3456
- **Circus Disco** • 6655 Santa Monica Blvd • 323-462-1291
- **Dragonfly** • 6510 Santa Monica Blvd • 323-466-6111
- **El Floridita** • 1253 N Vine St • 323-871-8612
- **Element** • 1642 N Las Palmas Ave • 323-460-4632
- **Forty Deuce** • 5574 Melrose Ave • 323-465-4242
- **Frolic Room** • 6245 Hollywood Blvd • 323-462-5890
- **Henry Fonda Music Box** • 6126 Hollywood Blvd • 323-464-0808
- **The Highlands** • 6801 Hollywood Blvd • 323-461-9800
- **Holly's** • 1651 Wilcox Ave • 323-461-1400
- **Hollywood Billiards** • 5750 Hollywood Blvd • 323-465-0115
- **Hollywood Canteen** • 1006 N Seward St • 323-465-0961
- **Hollywood Palladium (Temporarily Closed)** • 6215 W Sunset Blvd • 323-962-7600
- **The Hotel Café** • 1623 1/2 N Cahuenga Blvd • 323-461-2040
- **Ivar** • 6356 Hollywood Blvd • 323-465-4827
- **Joseph's** • 1775 Ivar Ave • 323-462-8697
- **King King** • 6555 Hollywood Blvd • 323-960-5765
- **Knitting Factory** • 7021 Hollywood Blvd • 323-463-0204
- **La Velvet Margarita Cantina** • 1612 N Cahuenga Blvd • 323-469-2000
- **The Larchmont** • 5657 Melrose Ave • 323-467-4068
- **LAX** • 1714 Las Palmas Ave • 323-464-0171
- **Les Deux** • 1638 N Las Palmas Ave • 323-462-7674
- **M-Bar** • 1253 Vine St • 323-856-0036
- **Montmartre Lounge** • 6757 Hollywood Blvd • 323-465-5369
- **Mood** • 6623 Hollywood Blvd • 323-464-6663
- **Musso & Frank Grill Bar** • 6667 Hollywood Blvd • 323-467-5123
- **Nacional** • 1645 Wilcox Ave • 323-962-7712
- **Parc** • 6683 Hollywood Blvd • 323-465-6200
- **Power House** • 1714 N Highland Ave • 323-463-9438
- **Ritual Nightclub** • 1743 N Cahuenga Blvd • 323-463-0060
- **Rokbar** • 1710 N Las Palmas Ave • 323-461-5600
- **The Room** • 1626 N Cahuenga Blvd • 323-462-7196
- **Spider Club at the Avalon** • 1735 Vine St • 323-462-1307
- **Star Shoes** • 6364 Hollywood Blvd • 323-462-7827
- **Three of Clubs** • 1123 N Vine St • 323-462-6441
- **Tokio** • 1640 Cahuenga Blvd • 323-464-2065
- **The Vanguard** • 6021 Hollywood Blvd • 323-463-3331
- **The Well** • 6255 W Sunset Blvd • 323-467-9355
- **White Horse** • 1532 N Western Ave • 323-462-8088
- **Xes** • 1716 N Cahuenga Blvd • 323-461-8190
- **Yamashiro** • 1999 N Sycamore Ave • 323-466-5125

Pet Shops

- **Barking Lot** • 336 N Larchmont Blvd • 323-464-3031
- **Tailwaggers** • 1929 N Bronson Ave • 323-464-9600
- **Yo's Aquarium** • 5846 Santa Monica Blvd • 323-871-2730

Restaurants

- **101 Coffee Shop** • 6145 Franklin Ave • 323-467-1175
- **Ammo** • 1155 N Highland Ave • 323-871-2666
- **Astro Burger** • 5601 Melrose Ave • 323-469-1924
- **Benito's Taco Shop** • 6751 Santa Monica Blvd • 323-466-9333
- **Big Wang's** • 1562 N Cahuenga Blvd • 323-469-2449
- **Birds** • 5925 Franklin Ave • 323-465-0175
- **California Chicken Café** • 6805 Melrose Ave • 323-935-5877
- **California Vegan** • 7300 Sunset Blvd, Unit #A • 323-874-9079
- **Chan Dara** • 310 N Larchmont Blvd • 323-467-1052
- **Cinespace** • 6356 Hollywood Blvd • 323-817-3456
- **Citizen Smith** • 1602 N Cahuenga Blvd • 323-461-5001
- **Crispy Crust** • 1253 Vine St • 323-467-2000
- **Doughboys** • 1156 N Highland Ave • 323-467-9117
- **eat. on sunset** • 1448 N Gower St • 323-461-8800
- **Fabiolus Café** • 5255 Melrose Ave • 323-464-5857
- **Fabiolus Café** • 6270 W Sunset Blvd • 323-467-2882
- **Geisha House** • 6633 Hollywood Blvd • 323-460-6300
- **Hola Fresh Mexican Grill** • 1807 N Cahuenga Blvd • 323-466-0000
- **Hollywood and Vine** • 6263 Hollywood Blvd • 323-464-2345
- **Hungry Cat** • 1535 Vine St • 323-462-2155
- **Kung Pao Kitty** • 6445 Hollywood Blvd • 323-465-0110
- **La Buca** • 5210 Melrose Ave • 323-462-1900
- **La Poubelle** • 5907 Franklin Ave • 323-465-0807
- **Larchmont Deli** • 5210 Beverly Blvd • 323-466-1193
- **Le Oriental Bistro** • 1710 N Highland Ave • 323-462-3388
- **Los Balcones del Peru** • 1360 Vine St • 323-871-9600
- **Magnolia** • 6266 W Sunset Blvd • 323-467-0660
- **Memphis** • 6541 Hollywood Blvd • 323-465-8600
- **Miceli's** • 1646 N Las Palmas Ave • 323-466-3438
- **Musso & Frank Grill** • 6667 Hollywood Blvd • 323-467-7788
- **Off Vine** • 6263 Leland Wy • 323-962-1900
- **Palms Thai** • 5900 Hollywood Blvd • 323-462-5073
- **Pig 'n Whistle** • 6714 Hollywood Blvd • 323-463-0000
- **Pizza Bella** • Whitley Heights Liquor Market • 1900 N Highland Ave • 323-876-5961
- **Red Pearl Kitchen** • 6703 Melrose Ave • 323-525-1415
- **Roscoe's House of Chicken 'n Waffles** • 1514 N Gower St • 323-466-7453
- **Skooby's Hot Dogs** • 6654 Hollywood Blvd • 323-HOT-DOGS
- **Sushi Hiroba** • 776 Vine St • 323-962-7237
- **Truly a Vegan Restaurant** • 5907 Hollywood Blvd • 323-466-7533
- **Xiomara** • 6101 Melrose Ave • 323-461-0601
- **Yamashiro** • 1999 N Sycamore Ave • 323-466-5125

Shopping

- **Amoeba Music** • 6400 Sunset Blvd • 310-245-6400
- **Conservatory Florist** • 1900 N Highland Ave • 323-851-6290
- **Cottage Antiques** • 5870 Melrose Ave • 323-469-6444
- **Counterpoint Records and Books** • 5911 Franklin Ave • 323-957-7965
- **Daily Planet Book Store** • 5931 Franklin Ave • 323-957-0061
- **Edmund's Bookshop** • 6644 Hollywood Blvd • 323-463-3273
- **Frederick's of Hollywood** • 6751 Hollywood Blvd • 323-957-5953
- **Half-Off Clothing** • 660 N Larchmont Blvd • 323-463-6613
- **Hollywood Hills Beauty Center and Spa** • 1915 N Highland Ave • 323-874-5159
- **Hollywood Toy & Costume Shop** • 6600 Hollywood Blvd • 323-464-4444
- **Native** • 5915 Franklin Ave • 323-962-7710
- **Pom Pom** • 6819 Melrose Ave • 323-938-6286
- **Ray the Retoucher** • 1330 N Highland Ave • 323-463-0555
- **Victor's Liquor & Delicatessen** • 1915 N Bronson Ave • 323-464-0275
- **Vine American Party Store** • 5969 Melrose Ave • 323-467-7124

Video Rental

- **Video Hut** • 1931 N Bronson Ave • 323-461-4190
- **Video Hut** • 5810 Santa Monica Blvd • 323-464-4777
- **Yucca Video** • 1817 N Cahuenga Blvd • 323-465-2376

Map 4 • Los Feliz

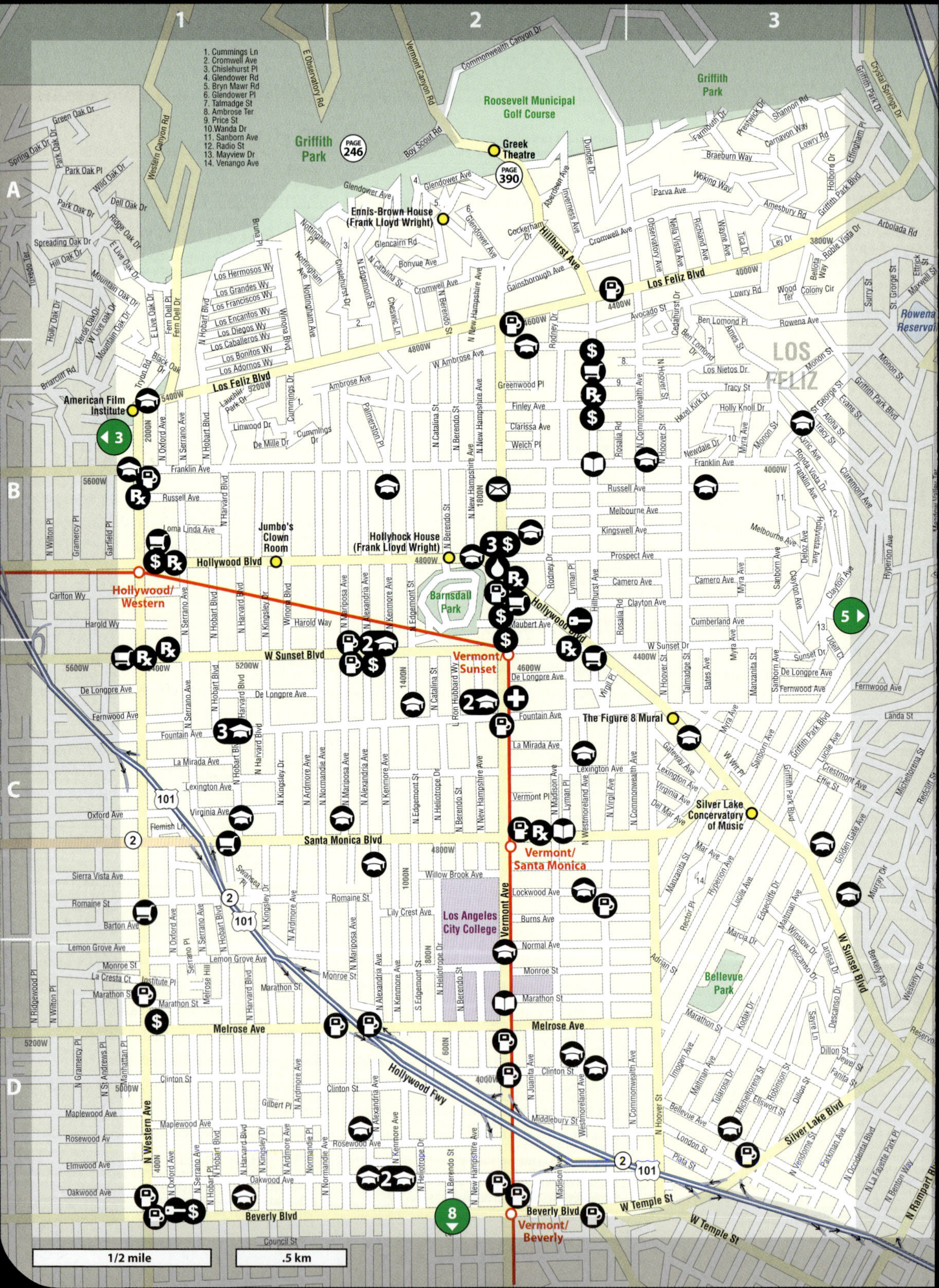

1. Cummings Ln
2. Cromwell Ave
3. Chislehurst Pl
4. Glendower Rd
5. Bryn Mawr Rd
6. Glendower Pl
7. Talmadge St
8. Ambrose Ter
9. Price St
10. Wanda Dr
11. Sanborn Ave
12. Radio St
13. Mayview Dr
14. Venango Ave

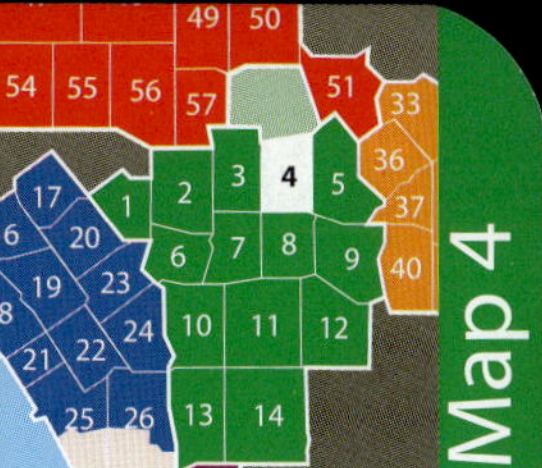

Los Feliz perseveres despite the burden of being America's most hyped neighborhood. It continues to have ample room for everyone—from grannies wearing old cardigans to hipsters wearing...old cardigans. You'll find multimillion-dollar playpens on the hill, as well as crowded studio apartment buildings lining Vermont and Hillhurst Avenues. Los Feliz is home to some of LA's most beloved and relevant attractions—Griffith Park, the Los Angeles Zoo, and the Greek Theater—proving that, even in Los Angeles, sometimes you really can believe the hype.

Banks

- **Bank of America** • 1715 N Vermont Ave
- **Bank of America** • 2035 Hillhurst Ave
- **Bank of America** • 4975 Melrose Ave
- **California National** • 1702 N Vermont Ave
- **California National** • 4500 W Beverly Blvd
- **Citibank** • 1965 N Hillhurst Ave
- **Citibank** • 5000 Sunset Blvd
- **US** • 5454 Hollywood Blvd
- **Washington Mutual** • 1600 N Vermont Ave
- **Wells Fargo** • 1534 N Vermont Ave

Car Rental

- **Enterprise** • 1608 Hillhurst Ave
- **Enterprise** • 4550 Beverly Blvd

Car Washes

- **Vermont Handwash** • 1666 N Vermont Ave

Gas Stations

- **76** • 1270 N Vermont Ave
- **76** • 1300 N Western Ave
- **76** • 304 N Vermont Ave
- **76** • 4456 Los Feliz Blvd
- **76** • 4600 Melrose Ave
- **Arco** • 5025 W Sunset Blvd
- **Chevron** • 1868 N Western Ave
- **Chevron** • 4590 Melrose Ave
- **Chevron** • 4666 Santa Monica Blvd
- **Chevron** • 591 N Vermont Ave
- **Independent** • 4501 Melrose Ave
- **Independent** • 5007 W Sunset Blvd
- **Independent** • 655 N Western Ave
- **Independent** • 924 N Virgil Ave
- **Mobil** • 4605 Beverly Blvd
- **Mobil** • 515 Silver Lake Blvd
- **Mobil** • 657 N Vermont Ave
- **Shell** • 1630 N Vermont Ave
- **Shell** • 341 N Vermont Ave
- **Valero** • 2134 N Vermont Ave

Emergency Rooms

- **Hollywood Presbyterian** • 1300 N Vermont Ave

Landmarks

- **American Film Institute** • 2021 N Western Ave
- **Ennis-Brown House** • 2607 Glendower Ave
- **The Figure 8 Mural** • 4334 W Sunset Blvd
- **Greek Theatre** • 2700 N Vermont Ave
- **Hollyhock House** • 4800 Hollywood Blvd
- **Jumbo's Clown Room** • 5153 Hollywood Blvd
- **Silverlake Conservatory of Music** • 3920 Sunset Blvd

Libraries

- **Cahuenga Branch** • 4591 Santa Monica Blvd • 323-664-6418
- **Los Angeles Main Branch-Braille Institute Library** • 741 N Vermont Ave • 800-808-2555
- **Los Feliz Branch** • 1874 Hillhurst Ave • 323-913-4710

Pharmacies

- **CVS** • 5510 W Sunset Blvd • 323-464-2169
- **Ralphs** • 5429 Hollywood Blvd • 323-957-6830
- **Rite-Aid** • 1637 N Vermont Ave • 323-664-9854
- **Rite-Aid** • 1841 N Western Ave • 323-461-6136
- **Rite-Aid** • 4633 Santa Monica Blvd • 323-666-6125
- **Sav-On** • Albertsons • 2035 Hillhurst Ave • 323-662-5105
- **Vons** • 4520 W Sunset Blvd • 323-662-2121
- **Walgreens** • 5451 W Sunset Blvd • 323-860-7970

Post Offices

- **US Post Office** • 1825 N Vermont Ave • 800-275-8777

Schools

- **Alexandria EEC** • 4304 Rosewood Ave
- **Alexandria Elementary** • 4211 Oakwood Ave
- **Bellevue Primary** • 610 N Micheltorena St
- **Canyon Oakes Ranch** • 1308 L Ron Hubbard Wy
- **Dayton EEC** • 3917 Clinton St
- **Dayton Heights Elementary** • 607 N Westmoreland Ave
- **Dennison Academy** • 4655 Kingswell Ave No 201
- **Franklin Ave Elementary** • 1910 N Commonwealth Ave
- **French Nursery** • 5262 Fountain Ave
- **Funtime Nursery and Day Care** • 400 N Kenmore Ave
- **Harvard Elementary** • 330 N Harvard Blvd
- **Harvard Preschool and Kindergarten** • 1311 N Harvard Blvd
- **Hollywood Los Feliz Corners** • 1839 N Kenmore Ave
- **Hollywood Preschool and Kindergarden** • 1313 N Edgemont St
- **Immaculate Heart** • 5515 Franklin Ave
- **Immaculate Heart Mary** • 1055 N Alexandria Ave
- **John Marshall Senior High** • 3939 Tracy St
- **Kingsley Elementary** • 5200 Virginia Ave
- **Lexington Avenue Primary Center** • 4564 Lexington Ave
- **Lockwood Ave Elementary** • 4345 Lockwood Ave
- **Los Angeles City College** • 855 N Vermont Ave
- **Los Feliz Academy** • 4627 Russell Ave
- **Los Feliz Elementary** • 1740 N New Hampshire Ave
- **Lycee International de Los Angeles** • 4155 Russell Ave
- **Mary's Schoolhouse** • 1334 L Ron Hubbard Wy
- **Micheltorena St Elementary** • 1511 Micheltorena St
- **Our Mother of Good Counsel** • 4622 Ambrose Ave
- **Pacific Southwest Lutheran Learning Center** • 1518 N Alexandria Ave
- **Ramona Elementary** • 1133 N Mariposa Ave
- **Rose Alex Pilibos Arm** • 1615 N Alexandria Ave
- **Silverlake Los Feliz Jewish County** • 1110 Bates Ave
- **St Casimir** • 2714 St George St
- **St Francis of Assisi** • 1550 Maltman Ave
- **Thomas Starr King Junior High** • 4201 Fountain Ave

Supermarkets

- **Albertsons** • 2035 Hillhurst Ave
- **Food 4 Less** • 5420 W Sunset Blvd
- **Jon's Marketplace** • 1601 N Vermont Ave
- **Jon's Marketplace** • 5311 Santa Monica Blvd
- **Ralphs** • 5429 Hollywood Blvd
- **Smart & Final** • 939 N Western Ave
- **Vons** • 4520 W Sunset Blvd

Map 4 • Los Feliz

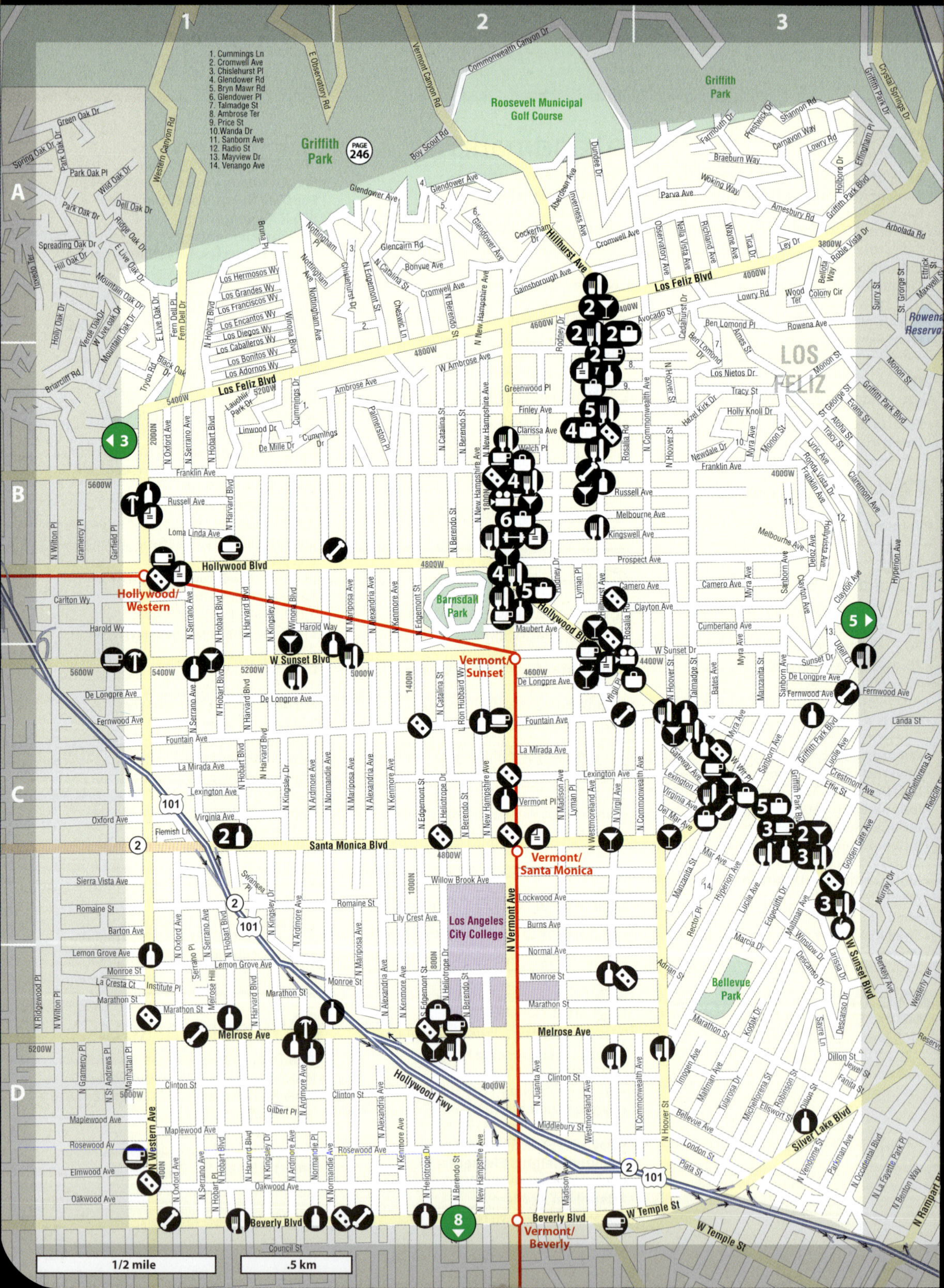

1. Cummings Ln
2. Cromwell Ave
3. Chislehurst Pl
4. Glendower Rd
5. Bryn Mawr Rd
6. Glendower Pl
7. Talmadge St
8. Ambrose Ter
9. Price St
10. Wanda Dr
11. Sanborn Ave
12. Radio St
13. Mayview Dr
14. Venango Ave

Griffith Park

PAGE 246

Roosevelt Municipal Golf Course

Griffith Park

LOS FELIZ

Barnsdall Park

Los Angeles City College

Bellevue Park

Hollywood/Western

Vermont/Sunset

Vermont/Santa Monica

Vermont/Beverly

Los Feliz Blvd

Hollywood Blvd

W Sunset Blvd

Santa Monica Blvd

Melrose Ave

Beverly Blvd

W Temple St

Hollywood Fwy

Hillhurst Ave

N Vermont Ave

N Western Ave

Silver Lake Blvd

1/2 mile

.5 km

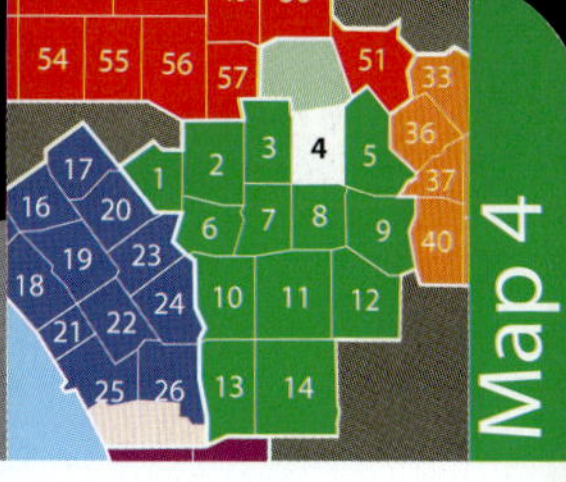

With the newly renovated Griffith Observatory twinkling down on the neighborhood, Los Feliz reminds us that the stars are among us, even where you least expect it. There's a democratic quality to hedonistic pursuits here, and it's not uncommon to see your favorite celebrity catching a film at the Vista or grabbing a bite on Hillhurst. Whether you're enjoying a Bloody Mary at Ye Rustic Inn, or catching Marty & Elayne at the Dresden, in Los Feliz, it's all about brunch, booze, and the pursuit of happiness.

Coffee

- **Café Los Feliz** • 2081 N Hillhurst Ave
- **Café Rosewood** • 429 N Western Ave
- **Café Stella** • 3932 W Sunset Blvd
- **Casbah Café** • 3900 W Sunset Blvd
- **Coffee Bean & Tea Leaf** • 2081 Hillhurst Ave
- **It's a Grind** • 1528 N Vermont Ave
- **Lollicup** • 5259 Hollywood Blvd
- **Lollicup Los Angeles** • 4718 Fountain Ave
- **Night in Tunisia** • 710 N Heliotrope Dr
- **Psychobabble** • 1866 N Vermont Ave
- **Starbucks** • 1700 N Vermont Ave
- **Starbucks** • 5453 Hollywood Blvd
- **Starbucks** • 5545 W Sunset Blvd
- **Tang's Donuts** • 4341 W Sunset Blvd
- **Tsunami Coffee House** • 4019 W Sunset Blvd

Copy Shops

- **Copies Unlimited** • 1823 N Western Ave • 323-462-5532
- **Copy Cat** • 2046 Hillhurst Ave • 323-913-0360
- **Staples** • 4641 Santa Monica Blvd • 323-669-7583
- **UPS Store** • 4470 W Sunset Blvd • 323-644-2621
- **UPS Store** • 5419 Hollywood Blvd • 323-460-6323

Farmers Markets

- **Silver Lake Farmer's Market (Sat, 8 am-1 pm)** • 3700 W Sunset Blvd

Gyms

- **Curves** • 1761 N Vermont Ave • 323-644-9898

Hardware Stores

- **Orchard Supply Hardware** • 5525 W Sunset Blvd • 323-871-1707
- **True Value** • 1801 N Western Ave • 323-467-2129
- **True Value** • 4583 Melrose Ave • 323-663-7232

Liquor Stores

- **Beverly Mart Liquors** • 4003 Beverly Blvd
- **Big Mac's Liquor** • 3735 W Sunset Blvd
- **Bill's Liquor** • 5334 W Sunset Blvd
- **Dexter's Liquor** • 4323 W Sunset Blvd
- **Express Liquor Mart** • 4323 W Sunset Blvd
- **Fountain Liquor** • 4711 Fountain Ave
- **Grand Liquor** • 4669 Melrose Ave
- **Hillhurst Liquor** • 2060 Hillhurst Ave
- **I&A Liquor** • 701 N Normandie Ave
- **JB Liquor** • 1185 N Vermont Ave
- **John & Pat's Fountain Liquor** • 5203 Fountain Ave
- **Jon's Marketplace** • 1601 N Vermont Ave
- **Jon's Marketplace** • 5311 Santa Monica Blvd
- **Jons Market Place** • 5311 Santa Monica Blvd
- **Lees Liquor Mart** • 3907 Fountain Ave
- **Liquor Center** • 861 N Western Ave
- **Liquor Mart of Los Feliz** • 1859 Hillhurst Ave
- **Melrose Market** • 4803 Melrose Ave
- **Mikron Liquor** • 631 Silver Lake Blvd
- **Pacific Liquors** • 4228 Beverly Blvd
- **Pink Elephant Liquors** • 1836 N Western Ave
- **Short Stop** • 5102 Hollywood Blvd
- **T & J Mini Mart** • 5063 W Sunset Blvd
- **Virgil Liquors** • 780 N Virgil Ave

Movie Theaters

- **Five Star Theaters Los Feliz 3** • 1822 N Vermont Ave • 323-664-2169
- **Vista Theatre** • 4473 Sunset Blvd • 323-660-6639

Nightlife

- **4100 Club** • 4100 W Sunset Blvd • 323-666-4460
- **Akbar** • 4356 W Sunset Blvd • 323-665-6810
- **The Derby** • 4500 Los Feliz Blvd • 323-663-8979
- **Drawing Room** • 1800 Hillhurst Ave • 323-665-0135
- **The Dresden Room** • 1760 N Vermont Ave • 323-665-4294
- **Figaro Café** • 1802 N Vermont Ave • 323-662-1587
- **Gauntlet II** • 4219 Santa Monica Blvd • 323-669-9472
- **Good Luck Bar** • 1514 Hillhurst Ave • 323-666-3524
- **Good Microbrew & Grill** • 3725 W Sunset Blvd • 323-660-3645
- **il corral** • 662 N Heliotrope Dr •
- **Jumbo's Clown Room** • 5153 Hollywood Blvd • 323-666-1187
- **Little Temple** • 4519 Santa Monica Blvd • 323-660-4540
- **Malo** • 4326 W Sunset Blvd • 323-664-1011
- **Smog Cutter** • 864 N Virgil Ave • 23-660-4626
- **Tangier Lounge** • 2138 Hillhurst Ave • 323-666-8666
- **Tantra** • 3705 W Sunset Blvd • 323-663-8268
- **Tiki Ti** • 4427 W Sunset Blvd • 323-669-9381
- **Vermont** • 1714 N Vermont Ave • 323-661-6163
- **Ye Rustic Inn** • 1831 Hillhurst Ave • 323-662-5757

Pet Shops

- **Beverly & Normandie Pets** • 4152 Beverly Blvd • 213-382-9314
- **Collar & Leash** • 1836 Hyperion Ave • 323-665-2215
- **Fish Tale** • 4364 Fountain Ave • 323-665-0350
- **For Pets Only** • 1903 Hillhurst Ave • 323-664-4211
- **Four Paws & A Tail** • 3726 W Sunset Blvd • 323-644-7649
- **J's Dog & Cat Grooming** • 5065 Hollywood Blvd • 323-667-1255
- **Kim's Pets & Fish** • 1187 N Vermont Ave • 323-664-3338
- **Pet's Life** • 4562 Beverly Blvd • 323-467-2395
- **Young's Tropical Fish** • 1953 1/2 Hillhurst Ave • 323-663-5665

Restaurants

- **Alcove Bakery & Café** • 1929 Hillhurst Ave • 323-644-0100
- **Alegria on Sunset** • 3510 W Sunset Blvd • 323-913-1422
- **Café Los Feliz** • 2081 N Hillhurst Ave • 323-664-7111
- **Café Stella** • 3932 W Sunset Blvd • 323-666-0265
- **Casbah Café** • 3900 W Sunset Blvd • 323-664-7000
- **Casita Del Campo** • 1920 Hyperion Ave • 323-662-4255
- **Cha Cha Cha** • 656 N Virgil Ave • 323-664-7723
- **Cliff's Edge** • 3626 W Sunset Blvd • 323-666-6116
- **Cobras and Matadors** • 4655 Hollywood Blvd • 323-669-3922
- **Eat Well** • 3916 E Sunset Blvd • 323-664-1624
- **El Conquistador** • 3701 W Sunset Blvd • 323-666-5136
- **Electric Lotus** • 4656 Franklin Ave • 323-953-0040
- **Farfalla Trattoria** • 1978 Hillhurst Ave • 323-661-7365
- **Fred 62** • 1850 N Vermont Ave • 323-667-0062 24
- **Good Microbrew & Grill** • 3725 W Sunset Blvd • 323-660-3645
- **Hollywood Gelato Company** • 1936 Hillhurst Ave • 323-644-3311
- **Home** • 1760 Hillhurst Ave • 323-669-0211
- **House of Pies** • 1869 N Vermont Ave • 323-666-9961
- **The Kitchen** • 4348 Fountain Ave • 323-664-3663
- **Las Ranas Café Restaurant** • 654 N Hoover St • 323-664-1588
- **Maco's Restaurant** • 1820 N Vermont Ave • 323-660-1211
- **Madame Matisse** • 3536 W Sunset Blvd • 323-662-4862
- **Malo** • 4326 W Sunset Blvd • 323-664-1011
- **Mexico City** • 2121 Hillhurst Ave • 323-661-7227
- **Millie's** • 3524 Sunset Blvd • 323-664-0404
- **Mustard Seed Café** • 1948 Hillhurst Ave • 323-660-0670
- **Palermo** • 1858 N Vermont Ave • 323-663-1178
- **Paru's** • 5140 W Sunset Blvd • 323-661-7600
- **Pinkberry** • 1726 N Vermont Ave • 323-661-0411
- **Scoops** • 712 N Heliotrope Dr • 323-906-2649
- **Shin** • 1972 Hillhurst Ave • 323-664-1891
- **Tantra** • 3705 W Sunset Blvd • 323-663-8268
- **Toad House** • 4503 Beverly Blvd • 323-460-7037
- **Vermont** • 1714 N Vermont Ave • 323-661-6163
- **Yai on Vermont** • 1627 N Vermont • 323-644-1076
- **Yuca's** • 2056 Hillhurst Ave • 323-662-1214
- **Zankou Chicken** • 5065 W Sunset Blvd • 323-665-7845

Shopping

- **American Apparel** • 4665 Hollywood Blvd • 323-661-1407
- **Atmosphere** • 1728 N Vermont Ave • 323-666-8420
- **Bicycle Kitchen** • 706 N Heliotrope Dr • 323-NO-CARRO
- **Blue Rooster Art Supplies** • 1718 N Vermont Ave • 323-661-9471
- **Camille Hudson** • 4685 Hollywood Blvd • 323-953-0377
- **Casbah Café** • 3900 W Sunset Blvd • 323-664-7000
- **Cheese Store of Silver Lake** • 3926 W Sunset Blvd • 323-644-7511
- **Glory** • 4659 Hollywood Blvd • 323-644-5679
- **Golden Needle Tailoring** • 2044 Hillhurst Ave • 323-666-3365
- **Gypsy** • 3915 W Sunset Blvd • 323-660-2556
- **Half-Off Clothing** • 1748 N Vermont Ave • 323-665-1526
- **Lovecraft Bio-Fuels** • 4000 W Sunset Blvd • 213-291-8587
- **LS** • 2120 Hillhurst Ave • 323-913-1444
- **Naturemart & Bulk Bin** • 2080 Hillhurst Ave • 323-667-1677
- **Oou** • 1764 N Vermont Ave • 323-665-6263
- **Ozzie Dots** • 4637 Hollywood Blvd • 323-663-2867
- **Reform School** • 4014 Santa Monica Blvd • 323-906-8660
- **Rosetta Stone** • 1958 Hillhurst Ave • 323-913-0369
- **Secret Headquarters** • 3817 W Sunset Blvd • 323-666-2228
- **Serifos** • 3814 W Sunset Blvd • 323-660-7467
- **Skylight Books** • 1818 N Vermont Ave • 323-660-1175
- **Squaresville** • 1800 N Vermont Ave • 323-669-8464
- **Steinberg & Sons** • 4712 Franklin Ave • 323-660-0294
- **Una Mae's** • 4651 Kingswell Ave • 323-662-6137
- **Uncle Jer's** • 4459 W Sunset Blvd • 323-662-6710
- **Village Gourmet** • 1927 Hillhurst Ave • 323-660-3803
- **Wacko** • 4633 Hollywood Blvd • 323-663-0122
- **White Trash Charms** • 1951 Hillhurst Ave • 323-666-9585
- **Y Que Trading Post** • 1770 Vermont Ave • 323-664-0021
- **Zoe & Sage** • 2134 Hillhurst Ave • 323-906-1874

Video Rental

- **Blockbuster** • 4470 Sunset Blvd • 323-661-0791
- **Blockbuster** • 5445 Hollywood Blvd • 323-467-0481
- **Deme A-1 Video** • 1100 N Vermont Ave • 323-669-1230
- **Hollywood Video** • 1075 N Western Ave • 323-464-0294
- **Jerry's Video Room** • 1904 N Hillhurst Ave • 323-666-7471
- **LA Video** • 720 N Western Ave • 323-465-0705
- **LA Video & Music** • 788 N Virgil Ave • 323-906-1282
- **Mondo Video A-Go-Go** • 4328 Melrose Ave • 323-953-8896
- **Sanahin Video** • 5230 W Sunset Blvd • 323-906-8557
- **Super Videoland** • 1189 N Vermont Ave • 323-661-2583
- **Video Hot** • 4207 Beverly Blvd • 323-668-1616
- **Video Hut** • 1864 N Vermont Ave • 323-661-4680
- **Video Market** • 3605 W Sunset Blvd • 323-663-6000
- **Video Universal Rental** • 1306 N Edgemont St • 323-660-2169
- **Winn Video** • 4855 Santa Monica Blvd • 323-953-9732

Map 5 • Silver Lake / Echo Park / Atwater

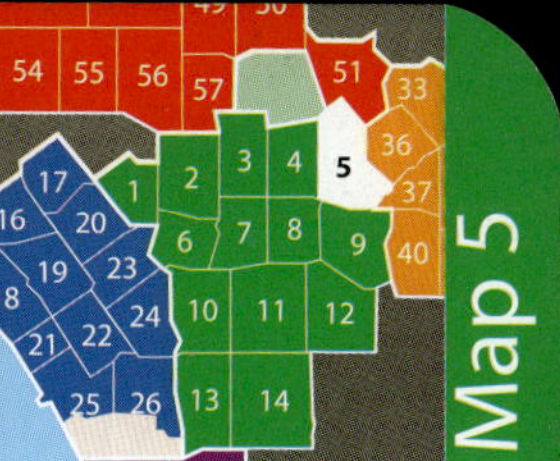

Silver Lake has established itself as a muse of West Coast indie culture for artists and writers like Beck, Jonathan Lethem, and (alas) Elliot Smith, to name a few. Young, hip, up-and-comers who can afford the skyrocketing housing costs continue their migration toward points east, while the neighborhood remains home to Latino families whose culture is still an integral part of the local scene. Late summer's Sunset Junction street fair brings them all together for a day of food, fun, art, and—of course—music.

Banks

- **Bank of America** • 1572 W Sunset Blvd
- **Bank of America** • 2420 Glendale Blvd
- **Citibank** • 1900 Sunset Blvd
- **Citibank** • 2450 Glendale Blvd
- **East West** • 2496 Glendale Blvd
- **Union** • 3355 Glendale Blvd
- **Wells Fargo** • 2933 Los Feliz Blvd
- **Wells Fargo** • 3250 Glendale Blvd

Car Rental

- **Alpha Rent a Car** • 1750 Glendale Blvd

Car Washes

- **Best Way Hand Car Wash** • 1185 W Sunset Blvd
- **Carwash On Sunset** • 2028 W Sunset Blvd
- **Los Feliz Car Wash** • 3013 Los Feliz Blvd

Gas Stations

- **76** • 1000 Elysian Park Ave
- **76** • 2035 W Sunset Blvd
- **76** • 2580 Glendale Blvd
- **76** • 2635 Hyperion Ave
- **76** • 3053 Los Feliz Blvd
- **76** • 3070 Glendale Blvd
- **Arco** • 1605 Glendale Blvd
- **Arco** • 2466 Riverside Dr
- **Arco** • 3073 Los Feliz Blvd
- **Chevron** • 2427 Fletcher Dr
- **Chevron** • 3050 Los Feliz Blvd
- **Independent** • 1467 W Sunset Blvd
- **Independent** • 3047 Glendale Blvd
- **Valero** • 2918 Riverside Dr

Landmarks

- **Angelus Temple** • 1100 Glendale Blvd
- **Dodger Stadium** • 1000 Elysian Park Ave
- **Echo Park** • Glendale Blvd & Park Ave
- **Richard Neutra Houses** • 2200 Silver Lake Blvd
- **Rowena Reservoir** • Corner of Hyperion Ave & Rowena Ave
- **Silver Lake Reservoir** • Silverlake Blvd & Duane St

Libraries

- **Atwater Branch** • 3379 Glendale Blvd • 323-664-1353
- **Edendale Branch** • 2011 W Sunset Blvd • 213-207-3000

Pharmacies

- **CVS** • 2530 Glendale Blvd • 323-666-1285
- **Pharmacare** • 3224 Glendale Blvd • 323-663-6231
- **Rite-Aid** • 1433 Glendale Blvd • 213-483-3468
- **Walgreens** • 1625 W Sunset Blvd • 213-482-9286

Post Offices

- **US Post Office** • 1525 N Alvarado St • 800-275-8777
- **US Post Office** • 3370 Glendale Blvd • 800-275-8777

Schools

- **Allesandro Elementary** • 2210 Riverside Dr
- **Atwater Avenue Elementary** • 3271 Silver Lake Blvd
- **Baxter Montessori** • 2101 Echo Park Ave
- **Clifford St Elementary** • 2150 Duane St
- **Dream Center Academy** • 2301 Bellevue Ave
- **Elysian Heights Elementary** • 1562 Baxter St
- **Glenfeliz Blvd Elementary** • 3955 Glenfeliz Blvd
- **Glenfeliz EEC** • 3745 Dover Pl
- **Golden West Christian** • 1310 Liberty St
- **Holy Trinity** • 3716 Boyce Ave
- **Ivanhoe Elementary** • 2828 Herkimer St
- **Kids' World** • 2442 Hyperion Ave
- **Learning Kingdom** • 2772 Rowena Ave
- **Logan EEC** • 1712 Montana St
- **Logan St Elementary** • 1711 Montana St
- **Lyric Preschool & Kindergarten** • 2328 Hyperion Ave
- **Mayberry St Elementary** • 2414 Mayberry St
- **Solano Ave Elementary** • 615 Solano Ave
- **St Teresa of Avila** • 2215 Fargo St

Supermarkets

- **Gelson's Markets** • 2725 Hyperion Ave
- **Ralphs** • 2520 Glendale Blvd
- **Trader Joe's** • 2738 Hyperion Ave
- **Vons** • 1342 N Alvarado St

Map 5 • Silver Lake / Echo Park / Atwater

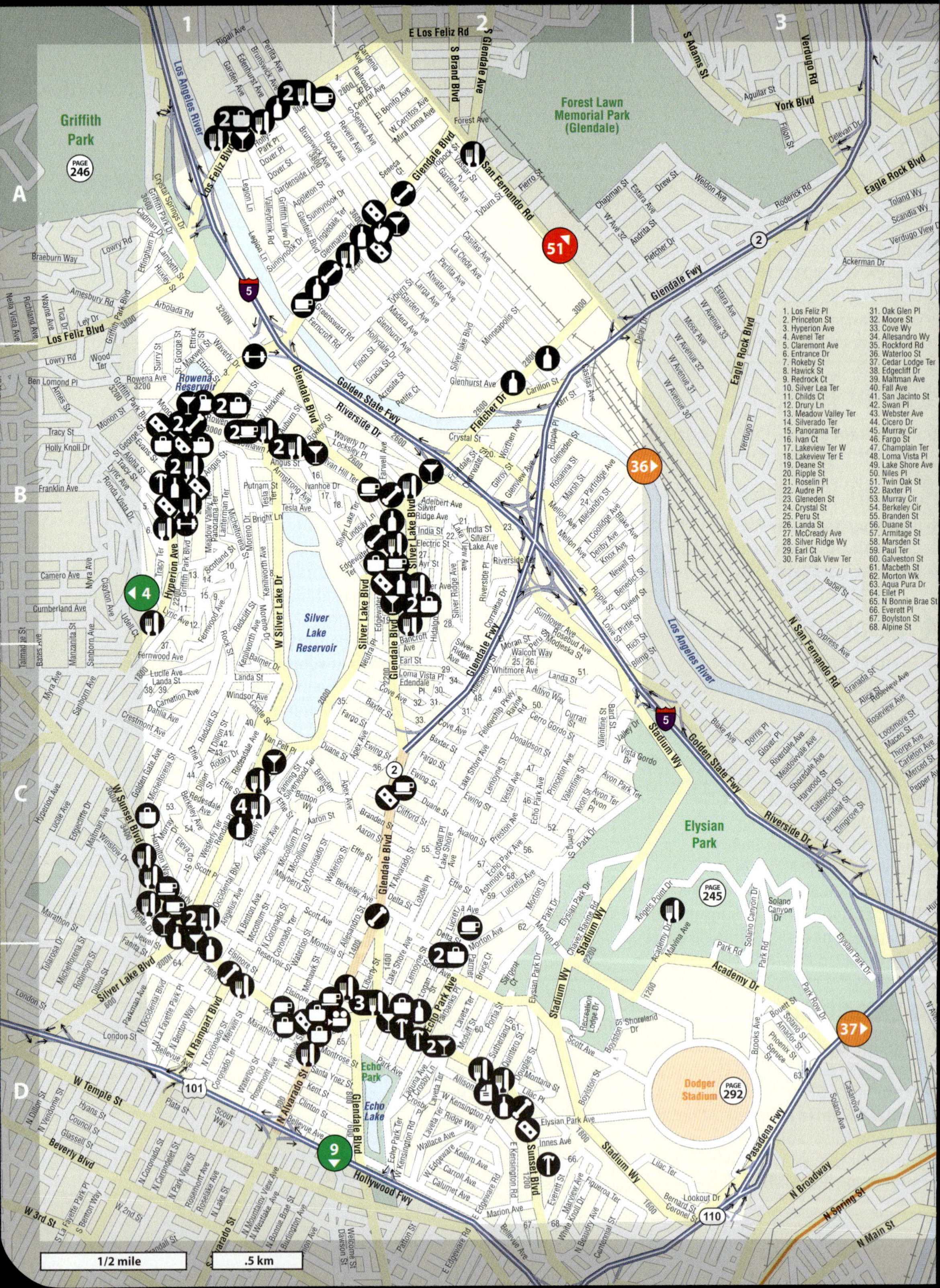

N
1
2
3
A
B
C
D
Griffith Park
PAGE 246
Forest Lawn Memorial Park (Glendale)
Silver Lake Reservoir
Rowena Reservoir
Elysian Park
PAGE 245
Dodger Stadium
PAGE 292
Echo Park
Echo Lake
Los Angeles River
Golden State Fwy
Glendale Fwy
Hollywood Fwy
Pasadena Fwy
E Los Feliz Rd
Los Feliz Blvd
Glendale Blvd
San Fernando Rd
N San Fernando Rd
Riverside Dr
Hyperion Ave
Silver Lake Blvd
W Silver Lake Dr
Sunset Blvd
W Sunset Blvd
Alvarado St
N Alvarado St
Echo Park Ave
Stadium Wy
Academy Dr
Fletcher Dr
Eagle Rock Blvd
York Blvd
Verdugo Rd
W Temple St
Beverly Blvd
W 3rd St
N Broadway
N Spring St
N Main St
1. Los Feliz Pl
2. Princeton St
3. Hyperion Ave
4. Avenel Ter
5. Claremont Ave
6. Entrance Dr
7. Rokeby St
8. Hawick St
9. Redrock Ct
10. Silver Lea Ter
11. Childs Ct
12. Drury Ln
13. Meadow Valley Ter
14. Silverado Ter
15. Panorama Ter
16. Ivan Ct
17. Lakeview Ter W
18. Lakeview Ter E
19. Deane St
20. Ripple St
21. Roselin Pl
22. Audre Pl
23. Gleneden St
24. Crystal St
25. Peru St
26. Landa St
27. McCready Ave
28. Silver Ridge Wy
29. Earl Ct
30. Fair Oak View Ter
31. Oak Glen Pl
32. Moore St
33. Cove Wy
34. Allesandro Wy
35. Rockford Rd
36. Waterloo St
37. Cedar Lodge Ter
38. Edgecliff Dr
39. Maltman Ave
40. Fall Ave
41. San Jacinto St
42. Swan Pl
43. Webster Ave
44. Cicero Dr
45. Murray Cir
46. Fargo St
47. Champlain Ter
48. Loma Vista Pl
49. Lake Shore Ave
50. Niles Pl
51. Twin Oak St
52. Baxter Pl
53. Murray Cir
54. Berkeley Cir
55. Branden St
56. Duane St
57. Armitage St
58. Marsden St
59. Paul Ter
60. Galveston St
61. Macbeth St
62. Morton Wk
63. Aqua Pura Dr
64. Ellet Pl
65. N Bonnie Brae St
66. Everett Pl
67. Boylston St
68. Alpine St
1/2 mile
.5 km

Sundries / Entertainment

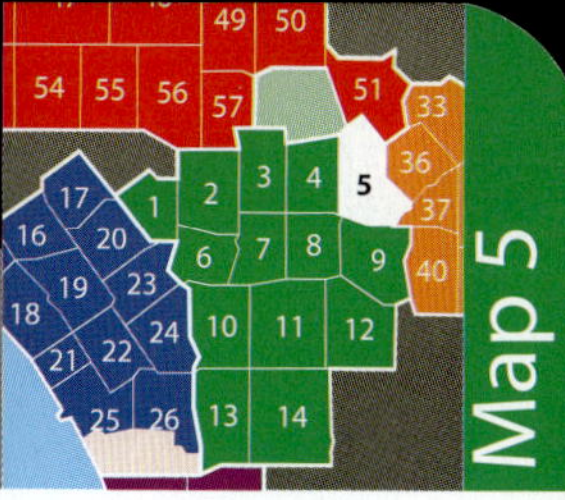

Take a drive along Silver Lake, Hyperion, or Rowena on any day, and you'll see sidewalk cafés packed with shaggy-haired cool kids. After you're done thinking "Don't these people work?" you'll realize that the neighborhood is at once esoteric and eclectic. Want authentic Mexican grub? Got it. Looking for the best undiscovered restaurants and boutiques? Check. Rocking clubs? Definitely. And a fancy cheese store? Yup—that, too. It's enough to make you quit your day job, stop washing your hair, and join a band.

Coffee

- **Café Tropical** • 2900 W Sunset Blvd
- **Chango** • 1559 Echo Park Ave
- **Coffee Table** • 2930 Rowena Ave
- **The Downbeat Café** • 1202 N Alvarado St
- **Kaldi Coffee & Tea** • 3147 Glendale Blvd
- **Silverlake Coffee** • 2388 Glendale Blvd
- **Starbucks** • 2134 Sunset Blvd
- **Starbucks** • 2556 Glendale Blvd
- **Starbucks** • 2560 Glendale Blvd
- **Starbucks** • 2919 Los Feliz Blvd

Copy Shops

- **ER Copies** • 1439 W Sunset Blvd • 213-482-3804

Farmers Markets

- **Atwater Village (Sun, 10 am-2 pm)** • 3250 Glendale Blvd

Gyms

- **Body Builders Gym** • 2516 Hyperion Ave • 323-668-0802
- **Curves** • 2724 Griffith Park Blvd • 323-912-9205

Hardware Stores

- **Baller Hardware Lumber & Paint** • 2505 Hyperion Ave • 323-668-7420
- **Reliable Do It Center** • 1229 W Sunset Blvd • 213-250-3970
- **True Value** • 2505 Hyperion Ave • 323-665-4149

Liquor Stores

- **Bill's Liquor** • 3150 Glendale Blvd
- **Bogie's Liquor** • 2560 Hyperion Ave
- **House of Spirits** • 1314 Echo Park Ave
- **Kopper Keg Liquors** • 3237 Glendale Blvd
- **Los Feliz Liquor** • 3006 Los Feliz Blvd
- **M&W Liquor** • 2801 Fletcher Dr
- **Plaza Liquors** • 2829 W Sunset Blvd
- **Ray's Liquor** • 2730 Fletcher Dr
- **Silver Glen Liquor** • 2474 Glendale Blvd
- **Silver Lake Liquor Store** • 1620 Silver Lake Blvd
- **Silverlake Wine (Wine only)** • 2395 Glendale Blvd
- **Silversun Liquor** • 2901 W Sunset Blvd

Movie Theaters

- **Echo Park Film Center** • 1200 N Alvarado St • 213-484-8846

Nightlife

- **Bigfoot Lodge** • 3172 Los Feliz Blvd • 323-662-9227
- **Club Tee Gee** • 3210 Glendale Blvd • 323-669-9631
- **The Echo** • 1822 W Sunset Blvd • 213-413-8200
- **Gold Room** • 1558 W Sunset Blvd • 213-482-5259
- **Johnny's Bar** • 2939 W Sunset Blvd • 323-660-2276
- **Mixville Bar** • 2838 Rowena Ave • 323-666-2000
- **MJ's** • 2810 Hyperion Ave • 323-660-1503
- **Red Lion Tavern** • 2366 Glendale Blvd • 323-662-5337
- **The Roost** • 3100 Los Feliz Blvd • 323-664-7272
- **Rudolpho's** • 2500 Riverside Dr • 323-669-1226
- **Short Stop** • 1455 W Sunset Blvd • 213-482-4942
- **Silverlake Lounge** • 2906 Sunset Blvd • 323-666-2407
- **Spaceland** • 1717 Silver Lake Blvd • 323-661-4380
- **Tam O'Shanter** • 2980 Los Feliz Blvd • 323-664-0228

Pet Shops

- **Catts & Doggs Pet Boutique** • 2833 Hyperion Ave • 323-953-8383
- **Fish on the Wall** • 2334 Fletcher Dr • 323-468-0103
- **Jimmy's Pet Store** • 1548 Glendale Blvd • 213-413-8013
- **LA Tropical Fish Pet & Supplies** • 1371 W Sunset Blvd • 213-482-9131
- **Pampered Birds** • 3183 Glendale Blvd • 323-662-7807
- **Pet Express** • 2472 Glendale Blvd • 323-668-2255
- **Pets Lover** • 3400 Glendale Blvd • 323-913-3368
- **Tiffany's Pet Food** • 2854 W Sunset Blvd • 323-662-7173

Restaurants

- **Astro Family Restaurant** • 2300 Fletcher Dr • 323-663-9241
- **Baracoa Cuban Café** • 3175 Glendale Blvd • 323-665-9590
- **Blair's** • 2903 Rowena Ave • 323-660-1882
- **Brite Spot Family Restaurant** • 1918 W Sunset Blvd • 213-484-9800
- **Café Tropical** • 2900 W Sunset Blvd • 323-661-8391
- **The Downbeat Café** • 1202 N Alvarado St • 213-483-3955
- **Dusty's** • 3200 W Sunset Blvd • 323-906-1018
- **Edendale Grill** • 2838 Rowena Ave • 323-666-2000
- **Gingergrass** • 2396 Glendale Blvd • 323-644-1600
- **Hard Times Pizza Co** • 2664 Griffith Park Blvd • 323-661-5656
- **India Sweets and Spices** • 3126 Los Feliz Blvd • 323-345-0360
- **La Parrilla** • 3129 W Sunset Blvd • 323-661-8055
- **Leela Thai** • 1737 Silver Lake Blvd • 323-660-6100
- **Mae Ploy** • 2606 W Sunset Blvd • 213-353-9635
- **Masa of Echo Park** • 1800 W Sunset Blvd • 213-989-1558
- **Michelangelo Pizzeria** • 1637 Silver Lake Blvd • 323-660-4843
- **Mimi's Café** • 2925 Los Feliz Blvd • 323-668-1715
- **Nicky D's Wood-Fired Pizza** • 2764 Rowena Ave • 323-664-3333
- **Pho' Café** • 2841 W Sunset Blvd • 213-413-0888
- **Police Academy Café** • 1880 Academy Dr • 323-221-5222
- **Rambutan Thai** • 2835 W Sunset Blvd • 213-273-8424
- **Red Lion Tavern** • 2366 Glendale Blvd • 323-662-5337
- **Soycafe** • 1997 Hyperion Ave • 323-663-7888
- **Spain** • 1866 Glendale Blvd • 323-667-9045
- **Taix** • 1911 W Sunset Blvd • 213-484-1265
- **Tam O'Shanter** • 2980 Los Feliz Blvd • 323-664-0228

Shopping

- **American Apparel** • 2111 W Sunset Blvd • 213-484-6464
- **Bittersweet Butterfly** • 1406 Micheltorena St • 323-660-4303
- **Edna Harte & Fay** • 2941 Rowena Ave • 323-661-4070
- **Grometville** • 2876 Rowena Ave • 323-665-5524
- **Island LS** • 3038 Rowena Blvd • 323-665-7454
- **The Kids Are Alright** • 2201 W Sunset Blvd • 213-413-4014
- **Le Pink** • 1545 Echo Park Ave • 323-661-7465
- **Mini-Melt** • 3151 Los Feliz Blvd • 323-668-1212
- **Panty Raid** • 2378 Glendale Blvd • 323-668-1888
- **Pot-ted** • 3158 Los Feliz Blvd • 323-665-3801
- **Rockaway Records** • 2395 Glendale Blvd • 323-664-3232
- **Say Cheese** • 2800 Hyperion Ave • 323-665-0545
- **Sea Level Records** • 1716 W Sunset Blvd • 213-989-0146
- **Show Pony** • 1543 Echo Park Ave • 213-482-7676
- **Silverlake Wine** • 2395 Glendale Blvd • 323-662-9024
- **Sirens and Sailors** • 1104 Mohawk St • 213-483-5423
- **Video Journeys** • 2730 Griffith Park Blvd • 323-663-5857

Video Rental

- **20-20 Video** • 2522 Glendale Blvd • 323-665-2020
- **50 50 Video** • 1717 W Sunset Blvd • 213-353-0406
- **Asian Star Video (Chinese & Thai)** • 1498 W Sunset Blvd • 213-481-2896
- **Blockbuster** • 2656 Griffith Park Blvd • 323-665-6764
- **Go Video** • 2147 W Sunset Blvd • 213-413-0860
- **Silverlake Video** • 3206 Glendale Blvd • 323-666-5570
- **Video Active** • 2522 Hyperion Ave • 323-669-8544
- **Video House** • 1864 Glendale Blvd • 323-663-9175
- **Video Hut** • 2732 Hyperion Ave • 323-660-1166
- **Video Journeys** • 2730 Griffith Park Blvd • 323-663-5857
- **VideoCzar** • 3332 Glendale Blvd • 323-661-2978

Map 6 • Miracle Mile / Mid-City

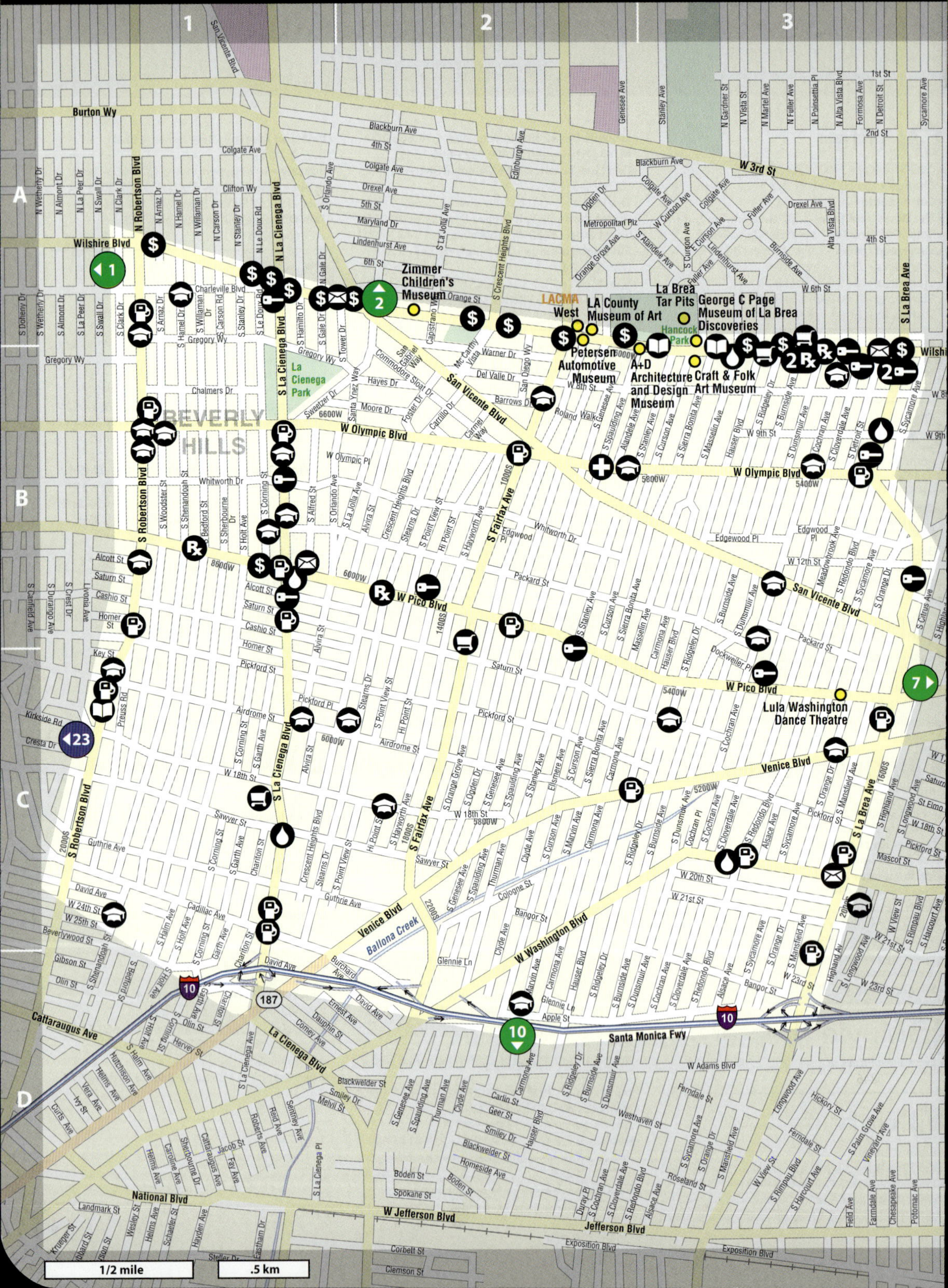

1 2 3

A B C D

BEVERLY HILLS

Zimmer Children's Museum

LACMA West

LA County Museum of Art

La Brea Tar Pits

George C Page Museum of La Brea Discoveries

Hancock Park

Petersen Automotive Museum

A+D Architecture and Design Museum

Craft & Folk Art Museum

La Cienega Park

Lula Washington Dance Theatre

Ballona Creek

Santa Monica Fwy

1/2 mile

.5 km

Essentials

"Miracle Mile" is the stretch of real estate on Wilshire Boulevard between La Brea and Fairfax Avenues. Once a snappy, Art Deco-influenced shopping destination, this area has become a bit scruffy with age. You can still see the Art Deco, but now Miracle Mile draws traffic for its Museum Row, including the La Brea Tar Pits, the Peterson Automotive Museum, and the Los Angeles Craft and Folk Art Museum. Check out the LA County Museum of Art during construction for its much-anticipated Renzo Piano transformation.

Banks

- **Bank Leumi USA** • 8383 Wilshire Blvd
- **Bank of America** • 5304 Wilshire Blvd
- **Bank of America** • 8381 Wilshire Blvd
- **Bank of America** • 8501 W Pico Blvd
- **Bank of America** • 8760 Wilshire Blvd
- **California Bank & Trust** • 6500 Wilshire Blvd
- **Citibank** • 5660 Wilshire Blvd
- **Citibank** • 8485 Wilshire Blvd
- **City National** • 6100 Wilshire Blvd
- **Comerica** • 6301 Wilshire Blvd
- **Washington Mutual** • 8500 Wilshire Blvd
- **Wells Fargo** • 5601 Wilshire Blvd
- **Wells Fargo** • 6245 Wilshire Blvd
- **Wells Fargo** • 8501 Wilshire Blvd

Car Rental

- **Aviv Rent a Car** • 8946 W Pico Blvd
- **Dollar** • 732 S La Brea Ave
- **Dream Boats Rent A Car** • 8500 Wilshire Blvd
- **Edson Luxury Car Rental** • 5455 Wilshire Blvd
- **Enterprise** • 1234 S La Brea Ave
- **Enterprise** • 1435 S La Cienega Blvd
- **Enterprise** • 5406 Wilshire Blvd
- **Enterprise** • 800 S La Brea Ave
- **Hertz** • 1103 S La Cienega Blvd
- **Horizon** • 5226 W Pico Blvd
- **Premier Car Rental** • 5651 W Pico Blvd

Car Washes

- **Expert Car Wash** • 900 S La Brea Ave
- **La Cienega Car Wash** • 1907 S La Cienega Blvd
- **Oasis Hand Wash & Detail** • 5700 Wilshire Blvd
- **Shell** • 5164 W Washington Blvd
- **Shell** • 8500 W Pico Blvd

Gas Stations

- **76** • 1004 S La Cienega Blvd
- **76** • 1515 S La Brea Ave
- **76** • 1701 S Robertson Blvd
- **Arco** • 5301 W Olympic Blvd
- **Arco** • 5420 Venice Blvd
- **BP** • 8770 W Olympic Blvd
- **Chevron** • 1865 S La Brea Ave
- **Chevron** • 2065 S La Cienega Blvd
- **Exxon** • 1460 S La Cienega Blvd
- **Independent** • 5801 W Pico Blvd
- **Mobil** • 2305 S La Cienega Blvd
- **Shell** • 1502 S Robertson Blvd
- **Shell** • 2339 S La Brea Ave
- **Shell** • 5164 W Washington Blvd
- **Shell** • 6101 W Olympic Blvd
- **Shell** • 8500 W Pico Blvd

Emergency Rooms

- **Olympic Medical Center** • 5900 W Olympic Blvd

Landmarks

- **A+D Museum** • 5900 Wilshire Blvd
- **Craft & Folk Art Museum** • 5800 Wilshire Blvd
- **George C Page Museum of La Brea Discoveries** • 5801 Wilshire Blvd
- **La Brea Tar Pits** • Wilshire Blvd & S Curson Ave
- **LACMA West (former May Co Building)** • 6067 Wilshire Blvd
- **Los Angeles County Museum of Art** • 5905 Wilshire Blvd
- **Lula Washington Dance Theatre** • 5041 W Pico Blvd
- **Petersen Automotive Museum** • 6060 Wilshire Blvd
- **Zimmer Children's Museum** • 6505 Wilshire Blvd

Libraries

- **Balch Art Research Library** • 5905 Wilshire Blvd • 323-857-6116
- **Goethe Institute-Los Angeles** • 5750 Wilshire Blvd • 323-525-3388
- **Robertson Branch** • 1719 S Robertson Blvd • 310-840-2147

Pharmacies

- **CVS** • 5985 W Pico Blvd • 323-965-9161
- **Longs Drugs** • 1843 S La Cienega Blvd • 310-558-0373
- **Ralphs** • 5601 Wilshire Blvd • 323-936-0050
- **Rite-Aid** • 5575 Wilshire Blvd • 323-954-7193
- **Walgreens** • 5467 Wilshire Blvd • 323-525-0646
- **Walgreens** • 8770 W Pico Blvd • 310-275-2117

Post Offices

- **US Post Office** • 1270 S Alfred St • 800-275-8777
- **US Post Office** • 4960 W Washington Blvd • 800-275-8777
- **US Post Office** • 5350 Wilshire Blvd • 800-275-8777
- **US Post Office** • 8383 Wilshire Blvd • 800-275-8777

Schools

- **Aloha** • 5042 Venice Blvd
- **Bais Chana** • 9041 W Pico Blvd
- **Bais Chaya Mushka** • 9051 W Pico Blvd
- **Carthay Center Elementary** • 6351 W Olympic Blvd
- **Cathedral Chapel** • 755 S Cochran Ave
- **Crescent Heights Blvd Elementary** • 1661 S Crescent Heights Blvd
- **Crescent Heights EEC** • 1700 Alvira St
- **Donna Ro** • 4946 W 20th St
- **Hillel Hebrew Academy** • 9120 W Olympic Blvd
- **Holy Spirit Elementary** • 1418 S Burnside Ave
- **Horace Mann Elementary** • 8701 Charleville Blvd
- **Joannes Taylor** • 1372 S Cochran Ave
- **Kabbalah Center** • 1046 S Robertson Blvd
- **Los Angeles Center for Enriched Studies** • 5931 W 18th St
- **Marvin Ave Children's Center** • 2341 S Curson Ave
- **Marvin Elementary** • 2411 Marvin Ave
- **Netan Eli High** • 1445 S Robertson Blvd
- **Ohr Haemet Institute for Girls** • 1030 S Robertson Blvd
- **Page Private** • 419 S Robertson Blvd
- **Rabbi Jacob Pressman Academy** • 1055 S La Cienega Blvd
- **Rejoice in Jesus Christian** • 1304 S Cochran Ave
- **Saturn St Elementary** • 5360 Saturn St
- **Shalhevet High** • 910 S Fairfax Ave
- **Shenandoah St Elementary** • 2450 S Shenandoah St
- **St Mary Magdalen** • 1223 S Corning St
- **Torat Hayim Hebrew Academy** • 1210 S La Cienega Blvd
- **Westside Jewish Comm Pre-School** • 5870 W Olympic Blvd
- **Yeshiva Gedolah of Los Angeles** • 5444 W Olympic Blvd
- **Yeshiva University High of Los Angeles** • 1619 S Robertson Blvd

Supermarkets

- **Ralphs** • 5601 Wilshire Blvd
- **Smart & Final** • 1835 S La Cienega Blvd
- **Smart & Final** • 5555 Wilshire Blvd
- **Vons** • 1430 S Fairfax Ave

Map 6 • **Miracle Mile / Mid-City**

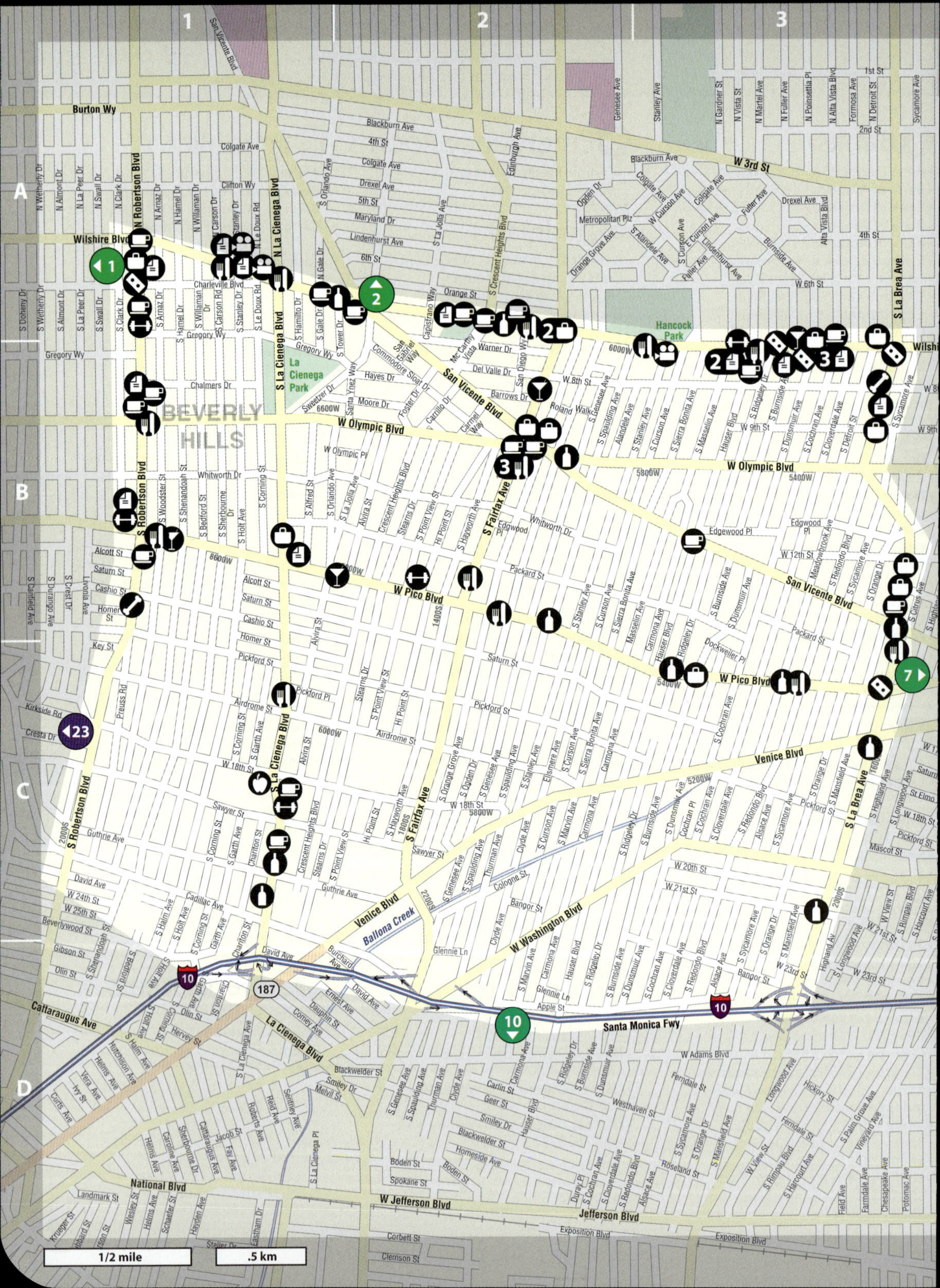

N

1
2
3
A
B
C
D

Burton Wy
Wilshire Blvd
W 3rd St
W 6th St
W 8th St
W 9th St
W Olympic Blvd
W Pico Blvd
Venice Blvd
W Washington Blvd
Santa Monica Fwy
W Adams Blvd
W Jefferson Blvd
Jefferson Blvd
National Blvd
Exposition Blvd
San Vicente Blvd
La Cienega Blvd
N Robertson Blvd
S Robertson Blvd
N La Cienega Blvd
S La Cienega Blvd
S Fairfax Ave
S La Brea Ave
Cattaraugus Ave
Hancock Park
La Cienega Park
BEVERLY HILLS
Ballona Creek
Metropolitan Plz
6000W
5800W
5400W
6600W
8600W
5200W
10
187

1/2 mile
.5 km

For those who like to be in the middle of it all, what's not to like about the Miracle Mile? You have easy access to museums like LACMA, shops with chic gear like Kitson, and tasty garlic chicken at restaurants like Versailles. You just have to contend with nightmarish parking, congested traffic, homes priced well over a million dollars, and condominiums costing nearly as much.

Coffee

- **Anny's** • 265 S Robertson Blvd
- **Backdoor Boba** • 5484 Wilshire Blvd
- **Black Dog Coffee** • 5657 Wilshire Blvd, Ste 150
- **Café Latte** • 6254 Wilshire Blvd
- **Coffee Bean And Tea Leaf** • 1945 S La Cienega Blvd
- **Coffee Bean & Tea Leaf** • 1845 S La Cienega Blvd
- **Coffee Bean & Tea Leaf** • 8328 Wilshire Blvd
- **E&M Café** • 1032 S Fairfax Ave
- **Kelly's Coffee & Fudge Factory** • 6361 Wilshire Blvd
- **La Peer Coffee Shop** • 8920 Wilshire Blvd
- **Paddington's Tea Room** • 355 S Robertson Blvd
- **Pasquale's Grand Brew Café** • 5616 San Vicente Blvd
- **Starbucks** • 1258 S La Brea Ave
- **Starbucks** • 257 S La Cienega Blvd
- **Starbucks** • 6066 W Olympic Blvd
- **Starbucks** • 8783 W Pico Blvd
- **Starbucks** • 9049 W Olympic Blvd
- **Taistee Coffee Shop** • 6200 Wilshire Blvd

Copy Shops

- **City Print** • 5328 Wilshire Blvd • 323-456-7966
- **Copy Copy** • 8621 Wilshire Blvd • 310-659-8171
- **Copy USA** • 850 S La Brea Ave • 213-384-8184
- **Easy Copy** • 8582 Wilshire Blvd • 310-657-7777
- **FedEx Kinko's** • 5500 Wilshire Blvd • 323-937-0126
- **Ford Graphics** • 900 S Robertson Blvd • 310-657-0040
- **Moonlight Printing** • 137 S Robertson Blvd • 310-657-7528
- **Office Depot** • 5665 Wilshire Blvd • 323-965-0673
- **Printing and More** • 5657 Wilshire Blvd • 323-935-8080
- **Staples** • 1833 La Cienega Blvd • 310-202-5343
- **Staples** • 5407 Wilshire Blvd • 323-965-5240
- **UPS Store** • 1171 S Robertson Blvd • 310-860-0856
- **UPS Store** • 5482 Wilshire Blvd • 323-939-6001
- **Wilcopy** • 6380 Wilshire Blvd, Ste 100 • 323-651-1677

Farmers Markets

- **La Cienega Farmer's Market (Thurs, 3 pm-7 pm)** • 1801 La Cienega Blvd

Gyms

- **Bolder Fitness** • 8810 W Pico Blvd • 310-276-5505
- **Curves** • 5945 W Pico Blvd • 323-931-5940
- **LA Fitness Sports Club** • 1833 La Cienega Blvd • 310-202-6823
- **LA Fitness Sports Club** • 5950 Wilshire Blvd • 323-934-6150
- **Quick's Fitness Center** • 473 S Robertson Blvd • 310-271-7933

Liquor Stores

- **Beverly Hills Beverage** • 8318 Wilshire Blvd
- **Century Liquor** • 5431 W Pico Blvd
- **L&E Liquors** • 1298 S La Brea Ave
- **La Brea Liquor** • 1617 S La Brea Ave
- **Le Chateau Wines & Spirits** • 6252 Wilshire Blvd
- **Midtown Liquor** • 5956 W Olympic Blvd
- **Pinchers** • 5121 W Pico Blvd
- **PM Liquor** • 1976 S La Cienega Blvd
- **Sunshine Liquor** • 5677 W Pico Blvd
- **Teddy's Liquor** • 2112 S La Brea Ave
- **Thriftown Liquor** • 2043 S La Cienega Blvd
- **Vendome Wines & Spirits** • 9153 W Olympic Blvd

Movie Theaters

- **Bing Theater at LACMA** • 5905 Wilshire Blvd • 323-857-6000
- **The Fine Arts Theatre** • 8556 Wilshire Blvd • 310-360-0455
- **Laemmle Music Hall 3** • 9036 Wilshire Blvd • 310-274-6860

Nightlife

- **El Rey** • 5515 Wilshire Blvd • 323-936-6400
- **The Joint** • 8771 W Pico Blvd • 310-275-2619
- **The Mint** • 6010 Pico Blvd • 323-954-9400
- **Tom Bergin's** • 840 S Fairfax Ave • 323-936-7151

Pet Shops

- **Pet Club** • 778 S La Brea Ave • 323-933-8811
- **Petco** • 1475 S Robertson Blvd • 310-282-8166

Restaurants

- **Baja Guadalajara Grill** • 1663 S La Cienega Blvd • 310-860-1165
- **Black Dog Coffee** • 5657 Wilshire Blvd • 323-933-1976
- **Café Latte** • 6254 Wilshire Blvd • 323-936-5213
- **Crazy Fish** • 9105 W Olympic Blvd • 310-550-8547
- **Fu's Palace** • 8751 W Pico Blvd • 310-271-7887
- **Lucy's** • 1373 S La Brea Ave • 323-938-4337
- **Luna Park** • 672 S La Brea Ave • 323-934-2110
- **Merkato** • 1036 S Fairfax Ave • 323-935-1775
- **Natalee Thai** • 998 S Robertson Blvd • 310-855-9380
- **Nyala Ethiopian Cuisine** • 1076 S Fairfax Ave • 323-936-5918
- **Rosalind's** • 1044 S Fairfax Ave • 323-936-2486
- **Roscoe's House of Chicken 'n Waffles** • 5006 W Pico Blvd • 323-934-4405
- **Versailles** • 1415 S La Cienega Blvd • 310-289-0392
- **Wi Jammin** • 5103 Pico Blvd • 323-965-9809

Shopping

- **99 Cent Store** • 6121 Wilshire Blvd • 323-939-9991
- **Ace Gallery** • 5514 Wilshire Blvd • 323-935-4411
- **Albertson Wedding Chapel** • 5318 Wilshire Blvd • 323-937-4919
- **Bang a Drum** • 1255 S La Brea Ave • 800-495-1109
- **City Spa** • 5325 Pico Blvd • 323-938-4800
- **Feldmar Watch** • 9000 W Pico Blvd • 310-274-8016
- **Hansen's Cakes** • 1072 S Fairfax Ave • 323-936-4332
- **Kitson** • 115 S Robertson Blvd • 310-859-2652
- **Marinello Beauty School** • 6111 Wilshire Blvd • 323-938-2005
- **Miauhaus** • 1201 S La Brea Ave • 323-933-6150
- **Oh My Nappy Hair!** • 805 S La Brea Ave • 323-939-3999
- **Pearl Art and Craft Supplies** • 1250 S La Cienega Blvd • 310-854-4900
- **Tom Bergin's** • 840 S Fairfax Ave • 323-936-7151
- **Up Health Merchants** • 6051 San Vicente Blvd • 323-935-3020

Video Rental

- **20-20 Video** • 6161 W Pico Blvd • 310-551-2020
- **Blockbuster** • 270 S Robertson Blvd • 310-854-0991
- **Blockbuster Video** • 677 S La Brea Ave • 323-936-7122
- **Hollywood Video** • 3939 Crenshaw Blvd • 323-293-5762
- **Hollywood Video** • 5522 Wilshire Blvd • 323-937-5647
- **Top Video** • 4972 W Pico Blvd • 323-935-6960

N

Hancock Park
Country Club Park
Mid-City
Wilshire Country Club
Los Angeles High Memorial Park
Harold A Henry Park
Queen Anne Rec Center
Getty House
Los Altos Apartments
Wilshire Ebell Theatre & Club
Wiltern LG
Beverly Blvd
W 3rd St
Wilshire Blvd
W Olympic Blvd
San Vicente Blvd
W Pico Blvd
Venice Blvd
W Washington Blvd
Crenshaw Blvd
N La Brea Ave
S La Brea Ave
S Western Ave
Santa Monica Fwy
1. Abbey Pl
2. 11th Pl
3. W 11th St
4. W 12th St
5. S Ridgewood Pl
PAGE 397
1/2 mile
.5 km

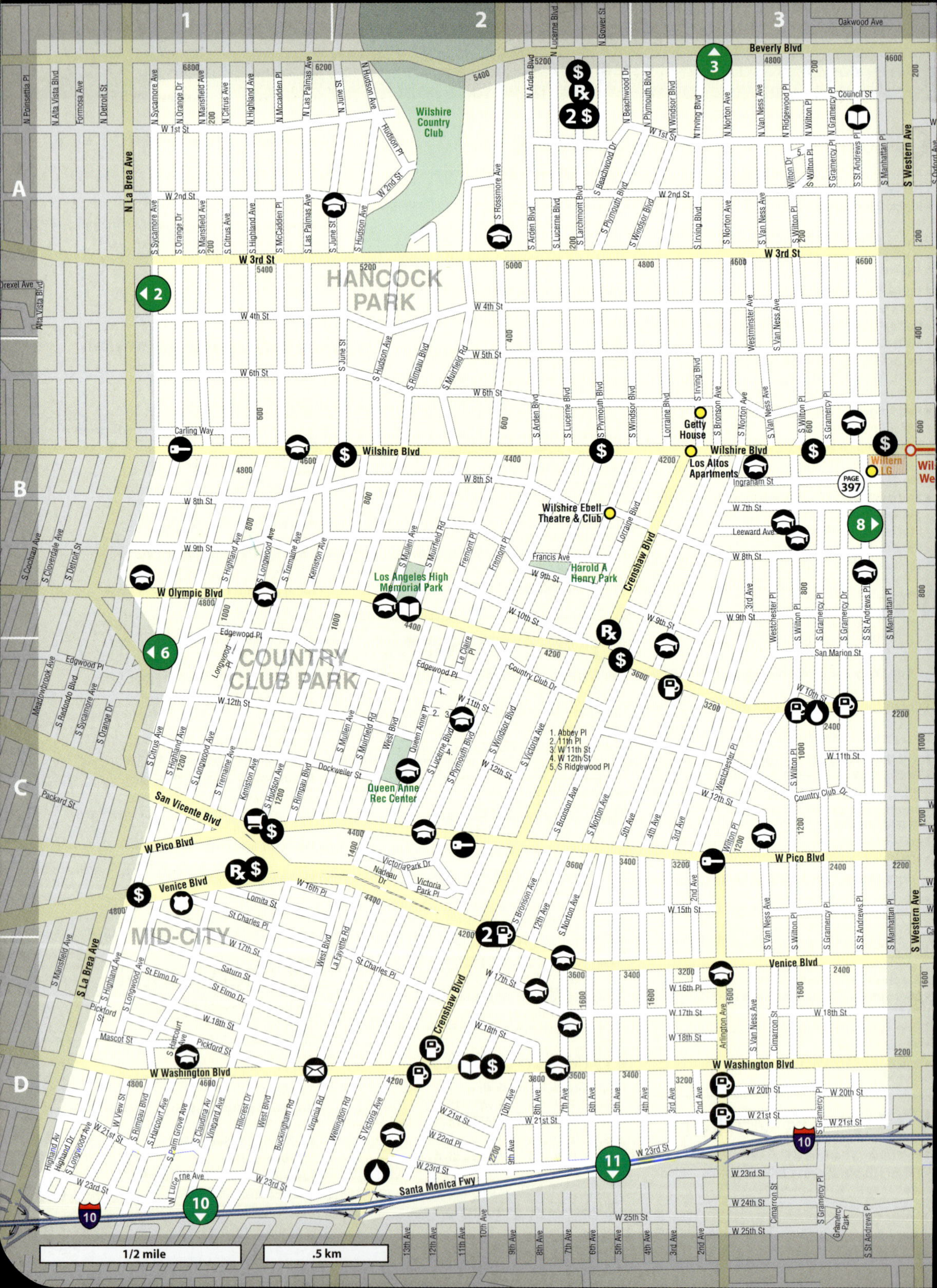

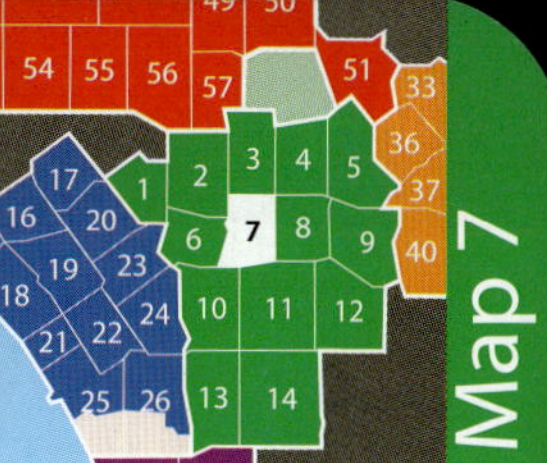

Before there was a such thing as the 'westside,' Hancock Park was home to the Hollywood elite—and it still packs a serious celebrity punch. Bordering Hollywood and K-town, this exclusive neighborhood hosts some of the most impressive mansions in LA and its sprawling green lawns and quiet streets make for the perfect lazy Sunday drive.

Banks

- **Bank of America** • 100 N Larchmont Blvd
- **Bank of America** • 4077 W Washington Blvd
- **Bank of America** • 4649 Venice Blvd
- **Broadway Federal** • 4800 Wilshire Blvd
- **Broadway Federal** • 4835 Venice Blvd
- **California National** • 157 N Larchmont Blvd
- **Hanmi** • 3737 W Olympic Blvd
- **Washington Mutual** • 101 N Larchmont Blvd
- **Washington Mutual** • 4333 Wilshire Blvd
- **Wells Fargo** • 245 N Larchmont Blvd
- **Wells Fargo** • 4700 W Pico Blvd
- **Wilshire State** • 3832 Wilshire Blvd

Car Rental

- **Enterprise** • 3412 W Pico Blvd
- **Enterprise** • 5151 Wilshire Blvd
- **Hertz** • 4334 W Pico Blvd

Car Washes

- **Car Wash** • 2345 Crenshaw Blvd
- **Olympic Car Wash** • 3554 W Olympic Blvd

Gas Stations

- **76** • 2121 Arlington Ave
- **76** • 3477 W Olympic Blvd
- **76** • 3481 W Olympic Blvd
- **76** • 4176 Venice Blvd
- **Chevron** • 1009 Crenshaw Blvd
- **Chevron** • 1907 Arlington Ave
- **Independent** • 4169 Venice Blvd
- **Mobil** • 1925 Crenshaw Blvd
- **Mobil** • 3950 W Olympic Blvd

Landmarks

- **Getty House (Mayor's official residence)** • 605 S Irving Blvd
- **Los Altos Apartments** • 4121 Wilshire Blvd
- **Wilshire Ebell Theatre & Club** • 4401 W 8th St
- **Wiltern Theater** • 3780 Wilshire Blvd

Libraries

- **Memorial Branch** • 4625 W Olympic Blvd • 323-938-2732
- **Washington Irving Branch** • 4117 W Washington Blvd • 323-734-6303
- **Wilshire Library** • 149 N St Andrews Pl • 323-957-4550

Pharmacies

- **CVS** • 4707 W Venice Blvd • 323-938-2523
- **Rite-Aid** • 226 N Larchmont Blvd • 323-467-1366
- **Rite-Aid** • 959 Crenshaw Blvd • 323-939-7911

Police

- **Los Angeles Police Dept** • 4861 W Venice Blvd • 213-473-0476

Post Offices

- **US Post Office** • 4040 W Washington Blvd • 800-275-8777

Schools

- **3rd St Elementary** • 201 S June St
- **Alta Loma Elementary** • 1745 Vineyard Ave
- **Arlington Heights Elementary** • 1717 7th Ave
- **John Burroughs Middle** • 600 S McCadden Pl
- **Johnnie L Cochran Jr Middle** • 4066 W 17th St
- **King Learning Academy** • 2250 Crenshaw Blvd
- **Los Angeles Community Adult** • 4650 W Olympic Blvd
- **Los Angeles Senior High** • 4650 W Olympic Blvd
- **Los Angeles Tech Center** • 3721 W Washington Blvd
- **Marlborough** • 250 S Rossmore Ave
- **Pico** • 4436 W Pico Blvd
- **Pio Pico Elementary** • 1512 S Arlington Ave
- **Queen Anne EEC** • 1191 S Lucerne Blvd
- **Queen Anne Pl Elementary** • 1212 Queen Anne Pl
- **Roennes** • 4701 W Washington Blvd
- **Sound of Music Preschool** • 1256 S Van Ness Ave
- **St Andrews Preschool & Kindergarten** • 845 S St Andrews Pl
- **St Gregory Nazianzen** • 911 S Norton Ave
- **St James** • 625 S St Andrews Pl
- **St Jeanne De Lestonnac** • 4001 Venice Blvd
- **St Paul Elementary** • 1908 S Bronson Ave
- **Wilshire Crest Elementary** • 5241 W Olympic Blvd
- **Wilshire Elementary** • 4900 Wilshire Blvd
- **Wilshire Park Elementary** • 4063 Ingraham St
- **Wilton Pl Elementary** • 745 S Wilton Pl
- **Wilton Place EEC** • 4030 Leeward Ave
- **Yavneh Hebrew Academy** • 5353 W 3rd St

Supermarkets

- **Ralphs** • 4760 W Pico Blvd

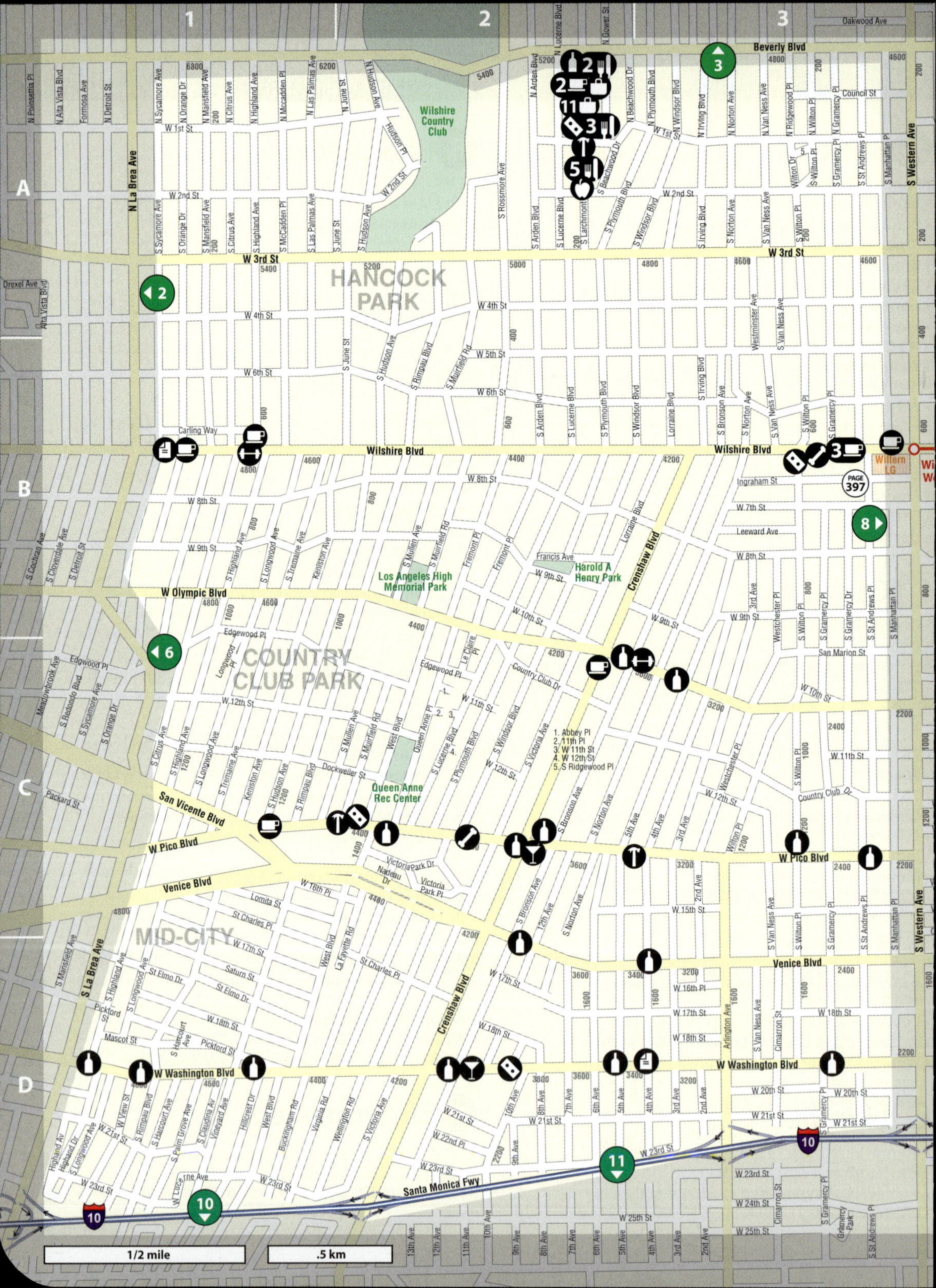

Map 7 • Hancock Park

Sundries / Entertainment

Stroll Larchmont Village for a glimpse of the bucolic: mothers pushing strollers and uniformed teens grabbing cappuccinos after school. The Sunday Farmer's Market is colorful and convivial, and the oenophile staff at Larchmont Village Wine & Cheese will recommend the perfect vintage if you let them know what's for dinner—their deli sandwiches are a local secret you shouldn't miss! If you fancy a bit more fuss, try Le Petit Greek or give Girasole a go for mouthwatering Italian fare.

Coffee

- **Café Americano** • 4001 Wilshire Blvd
- **Café Sicily** • 5001 Wilshire Blvd
- **Coffee Bean & Tea Leaf** • 135 N Larchmont Blvd
- **Coffeecana** • 3959 Wilshire Blvd
- **Noah's New York Bagels** • 250 N Larchmont Blvd
- **Peet's** • 124 N Larchmont Blvd
- **Romeo & Juliet** • 1032 Crenshaw Blvd
- **Sam's Bagels** • 150 N Larchmont Blvd
- **Starbucks** • 206 N Larchmont Blvd
- **Starbucks** • 4700 W Pico Blvd
- **Starbucks** • 5020 Wilshire Blvd
- **Tea Room** • 3839 Wilshire Blvd

Copy Shops

- **Color & Copy** • 5162 Wilshire Blvd • 323-634-9010
- **Copy Service Express** • 3408 W Washington Blvd • 323-737-3036

Farmers Markets

- **Larchmont Farmer's Market (Sun, 10 am-2 pm)** • N Larchmont Blvd & Beverly Blvd

Gyms

- **Century Sports Club** • 4120 W Olympic Blvd • 323-954-1020
- **Curves** • 5001 Wilshire Blvd • 323-937-8767

Hardware Stores

- **Oaxaca** • 3711 W Pico Blvd • 323-731-7971
- **Orchard Supply Hardware** • 4801 Venice Blvd • 323-930-6060
- **True Value** • 152 N Larchmont Blvd • 213-463-5783

Liquor Stores

- **Bacchus** • 4159 W Pico Blvd
- **Dallas Liquor Market** • 4111 Venice Blvd
- **Grand Prize Liquor & Deli** • 4555 W Washington Blvd
- **Jack's Cigars** • 3720 W Olympic Blvd
- **LA Liquor** • 4816 W Washington Blvd
- **Larchmont Village Wine, Spirits, & Cheese** • 223 N Larchmont Blvd
- **Midway Liquor** • 3186 W Pico Blvd
- **Olympic Liquors** • 3533 W Olympic Blvd
- **Reggie's Liquor** • 4161 W Washington Blvd
- **Showplace Liquors** • 3401 Venice Blvd
- **Sixth Avenue Liquor** • 3526 W Washington Blvd
- **T&G Liquor Store** • 4879 W Washington Blvd
- **Three Jays Liquor** • 2333 W Washington Blvd
- **Tony's Liquor** • 4485 W Pico Blvd
- **Victoria Plaza Liquors** • 4226 W Pico Blvd
- **Wilton Market & Liquor** • 3271 W Pico Blvd

Nightlife

- **Jewel's Catch One** • 4067 W Pico Blvd • 323-737-1159
- **Mixed Nuts Comedy Club** • 4000 W Washington Blvd • 323-735-6622

Pet Shops

- **Fumi's Tropical Fish** • 4158 W Pico Blvd • 323-731-5255
- **Kyoto Aquarium** • 3952 Wilshire Blvd • 213-487-7302

Restaurants

- **Café du Village** • 139 N Larchmont Blvd • 323-466-3996
- **Girasole** • 225 1/2 N Larchmont Blvd • 323-464-6978
- **Kiku Sushi** • 246 N Larchmont Blvd • 323-464-1200
- **La Bottega Marino** • 203 N Larchmont Blvd • 323-962-1325
- **La Luna** • 113 N Larchmont Blvd • 323-962-2130
- **Le Petit Greek** • 127 N Larchmont Blvd • 323-464-5160
- **Noah's New York Bagels** • 250 N Larchmont Blvd • 323-466-2924
- **Prado** • 244 N Larchmont Blvd • 323-467-3871
- **Village Pizzeria** • 131 N Larchmont Blvd • 323-465-5566
- **Z Pizza** • 123 N Larchmont Blvd • 323-466-6969

Shopping

- **Absolute Tickets** • 144 N Larchmont Blvd • 323-957-6699
- **Center for Yoga** • 230 1/2 N Larchmont Blvd • 323-464-1276
- **Chevalier Bookshop** • 126 N Larchmont Blvd • 323-465-1334
- **Hans Custom Optik** • 212 N Larchmont Blvd • 323-462-5195
- **Kicks Sole Provider** • 143 N Larchmont Blvd • 323-468-9794
- **Landis Department Store** • 140 N Larchmont Blvd • 323-465-7998
- **Larchmont Beauty Center** • 208 N Larchmont Blvd • 323-461-0162
- **Larchmont News Stand** • 230 N Larchmont Blvd •
- **Larchmont Village Wine, Spirits, & Cheese** • 223 N Larchmont Blvd • 323-856-8699
- **Leonidas Belgian Chocolates** • 201 N Larchmont Blvd • 323-860-7966
- **Picket Fences** • 214 N Larchmont • 323-467-2140

Video Rental

- **Blockbuster** • 147 N Larchmont Blvd • 323-461-3341
- **No 1 Video** • 4409 W Pico Blvd • 323-932-6299
- **Oscar Video (Korean)** • 4001 Wilshire Blvd • 213-384-7770
- **Video 21** • 4020 W Washington Blvd • 323-730-8927

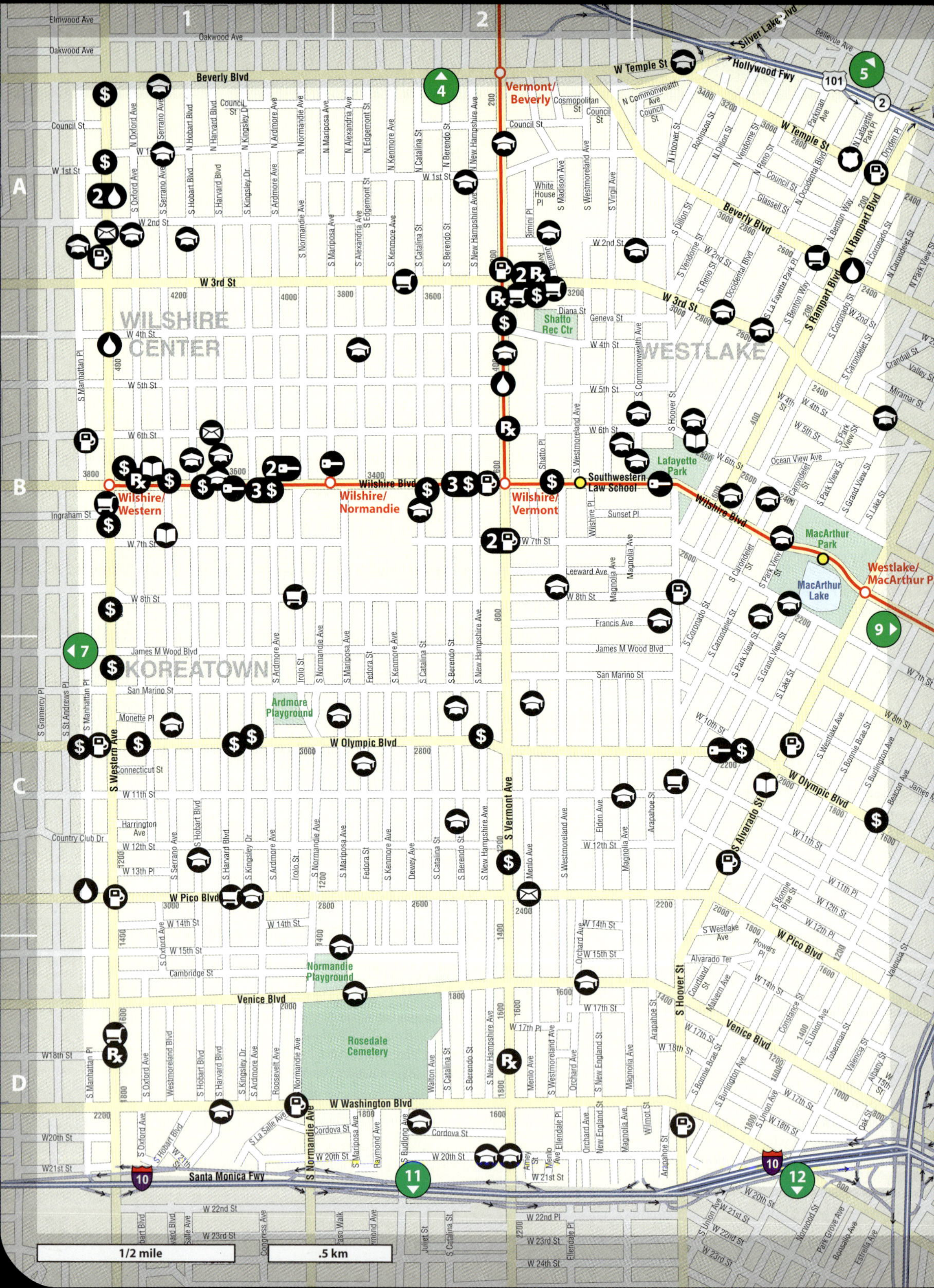

Map 8 • Korea Town

1
2
3
A
B
C
D

WILSHIRE CENTER
WESTLAKE
KOREATOWN

Wilshire/ Western
Wilshire/ Normandie
Wilshire/ Vermont
Vermont/ Beverly
Westlake/ MacArthur Park
Southwestern Law School

Shatto Rec Ctr
Lafayette Park
MacArthur Park
MacArthur Lake
Ardmore Playground
Normandie Playground
Rosedale Cemetery

Beverly Blvd
W Temple St
Hollywood Fwy
Silver Lake Blvd
W 3rd St
Wilshire Blvd
W Olympic Blvd
W Pico Blvd
Venice Blvd
W Washington Blvd
Santa Monica Fwy
S Western Ave
S Vermont Ave
S Normandie Ave
S Hoover St
S Alvarado St
N Rampart Blvd
S Rampart Blvd

1/2 mile
.5 km

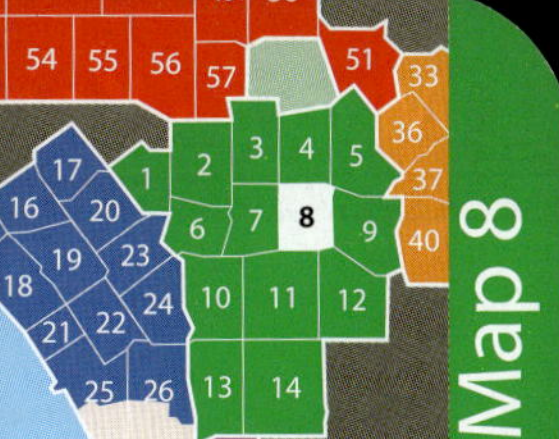

Korea Town is a bustling epicenter of nightlife and restaurants nestled against Wilshire Boulevard's business district. Mention K-Town to most non-Korean Los Angeles residents, and you'll immediately bring three things to mind: reasonable rents, karaoke, and barbecue. And although the Korean population has given way to a rising Hispanic majority in recent years, many of the storefronts and signs remain in Korean and the culture is imprinted on every corner.

Banks

- **Banco Popular** • 3360 W Olympic Blvd
- **Bank of America** • 1232 S Vermont Ave
- **Bank of America** • 3045 Wilshire Blvd
- **Bank of America** • 3320 W Olympic Blvd
- **Bank of America** • 3442 Wilshire Blvd
- **Bank of the West** • 3347 Wilshire Blvd
- **California Bank & Trust** • 3250 Wilshire Blvd
- **California Center** • 2222 W Olympic Blvd
- **California Center** • 253 N Western Ave
- **California Center** • 3435 Wilshire Blvd
- **California Center** • 3525 W 8th St
- **Citibank** • 270 N Vermont Ave
- **Citibank** • 3530 Wilshire Blvd
- **City National** • 1730 W Olympic Blvd
- **First Federal** • 351 S Vermont Ave
- **Hanmi** • 120 S Western Ave
- **Hanmi** • 3099 W Olympic Blvd
- **Hanmi** • 3250 W Olympic Blvd
- **Hanmi** • 3660 Wilshire Blvd
- **Hanmi** • 928 S Western Ave
- **Hanmi** • 933 S Vermont Ave
- **Nara** • 2727 W Olympic Blvd
- **Nara** • 3680 Wilshire Blvd
- **Nara** • 3701 Wilshire Blvd
- **US** • 3461 W 3rd St
- **Washington Mutual** • 3731 Wilshire Blvd
- **Wells Fargo** • 3550 Wilshire Blvd
- **Wells Fargo** • 670 S Western Ave
- **Wilshire State** • 3200 Wilshire Blvd
- **Wilshire State** • 841 S Western Ave

Car Rental

- **Allied Rent-a-Car** • 3540 Wilshire Blvd
- **Budget** • 3600 Wilshire Blvd
- **Dollar** • 2320 W Olympic Blvd
- **Dollar** • 3515 Wilshire Blvd
- **Enterprise** • 3435 Wilshire Blvd
- **Midway Car Rental** • 2926 Wilshire Blvd

Car Washes

- **4th & Western Car Wash** • 401 S Western Ave
- **Narys Car Wash** • 2570 Beverly Blvd
- **Pico Car Wash** • 3131 W Pico Blvd
- **Silverlake Car Wash** • 3595 Beverly Blvd
- **Sun Hand Car Wash** • 128 S Western Ave
- **Wilshire Car Wash** • 505 S Vermont Ave

Gas Stations

- **76** • 1000 S Vermont Ave
- **76** • 3501 W 3rd St
- **76** • 4000 W 6th St
- **76** • 801 S Hoover St
- **76** • 801 S Western Ave
- **Arco** • 1205 S Alvarado St
- **Chevron** • 2503 W Pico Blvd
- **Chevron** • 3325 W 6th St
- **Chevron** • 3625 Beverly Blvd
- **Chevron** • 3817 W 3rd St
- **Mobil** • 1904 W Washington Blvd
- **Mobil** • 1940 S Hoover St
- **Mobil** • 2608 W Temple St
- **Mobil** • 3309 W Olympic Blvd
- **Mobil** • 958 S Alvarado St
- **Shell** • 1303 S Western Ave
- **Shell** • 270 S Western Ave
- **Shell** • 3201 Wilshire Blvd
- **Shell** • 700 S Vermont Ave

Landmarks

- **MacArthur Park** • Wilshire Blvd & S Alvarado St
- **Southwestern Law School** • 3050 Wilshire Blvd

Libraries

- **Felipe De Neve Branch** • 2820 W 6th St • 213-384-7676
- **Pico Union Branch** • 1030 S Alvarado St • 213-368-7545
- **Pio Pico Koreatown Branch** • 694 S Oxford Ave • 213-368-7647

Pharmacies

- **CVS** • 1701 S Western Ave • 323-731-9247
- **CVS** • 3751 Wilshire Blvd • 213-385-5030
- **Ralphs** • 3410 W 3rd St • 213-480-3112
- **Rite-Aid** • 1815 S Vermont Ave • 323-735-0774
- **Rite-Aid** • 334 S Vermont Ave • 213-381-5257
- **Vons** • 3461 W 3rd St • 213-382-5971
- **Walgreens** • 3201 W 6th St • 213-251-0179

Police

- **Los Angeles Police Dept** • 2710 W Temple St • 213-485-4061

Post Offices

- **US Post Office** • 2390 W Pico Blvd • 800-275-8777
- **US Post Office** • 265 S Western Ave • 800-275-8777
- **US Post Office** • 3751 W 6th St • 800-275-8777

Schools

- **Berendo Middle** • 1157 S Berendo St
- **Berkeley Hall** • 16000 Mulholland Dr
- **The Beverly Academy** • 224 N Serrano Ave
- **Bishop Conaty-Our Lady of Love** • 2900 W Pico Blvd
- **Cahuenga Elementary** • 220 S Hobart Blvd
- **Camino Nuevo Charter Academy** • 635 S Harvard Blvd
- **Camino Nuevo High** • 2990 W 6th St
- **Camino Nuevo High School Charter** • 3500 W Temple St
- **Charles H Kim Elementary** • 225 S Oxford Ave
- **Commonwealth Elementary** • 215 S Commonwealth Ave
- **Frank Del Olmo Elementary** • 100 N New Hampshire Ave
- **Gabriella Charter** • 631 S Commonwealth Ave
- **Giraffe Charter** • 436 S Alexandria Ave
- **Green Pastures Academy** • 760 S Westmoreland Ave
- **Hobart Blvd Elementary** • 980 S Hobart Blvd
- **Hobart EEC** • 982 S Serrano Ave
- **Hoover St Elementary** • 2726 Francis Ave
- **Kingsley Montessori** • 347 S Kingsley Dr
- **Korean Baptist Church** • 975 S Berendo St
- **La Fayette Park Primary Center** • 310 S La Fayette Park Pl
- **La First Preschool** • 2029 W Washington Blvd
- **LA Leadership Academy** • 668 S Catalina St
- **La Western** • 743 S Grand View St
- **Leo Politi Elementary** • 2481 W 11th St
- **Linden Center West** • 2706 Wilshire Blvd
- **Los Angeles Academy of Arts & Enterprise Charter** • 3119 W 6th St
- **Los Angeles Christian** • 1620 W 20th St
- **Los Angeles Christian** • 2001 S Vermont Ave
- **Los Angeles Elementary** • 1211 S Hobart Blvd
- **Loyola High** • 1901 Venice Blvd
- **MacArthur Park PC** • 2300 W 7th St
- **Magnolia Ave Elementary** • 1626 Orchard Ave
- **Mariposa-Nabi Primary Center** • 987 S Mariposa Ave
- **McAlister High** • 611 S Carondelet St
- **Metropolitan Adult Skill Center** • 2801 W 6th St
- **Mid-Wilshire Christian** • 221 S Juanita Ave
- **New Horizon** • 434 S Vermont Ave
- **Newton Preschool** • 1035 Fedora St
- **Pilgrim** • 540 S Commonwealth Ave
- **Precious Blood** • 307 S Occidental Blvd
- **Rainbow Child Development Center** • 938 Menlo Ave
- **Salvin Special Ed Center** • 1925 S Budlong Ave
- **Serrano Lily Academy** • 103 N Serrano Ave
- **St Brendan** • 238 S Manhattan Pl
- **St Thomas Apostle Elementary** • 2632 W 15th St
- **Virgil Middle** • 152 N Vermont Ave
- **White Elementary** • 2401 Wilshire Blvd
- **White House Place Primary Center** • 108 S Bimini Pl
- **Wilshire Smiling Tree Preschool-K** • 611 S Hobart Blvd

Supermarkets

- **Food 4 Less** • 1091 S Hoover St
- **Food 4 Less** • 1717 S Western Ave
- **Jon's Supermarket** • 3334 W 8th St
- **Jon's Supermarket** • 3667 W 3rd St
- **Ralphs** • 3410 W 3rd St
- **Ralphs** • 670 S Western Ave
- **Smart & Final** • 2720 Beverly Blvd
- **Smart & Final** • 2949 W Pico Blvd
- **Vons** • 3461 W 3rd St

Map 8 • Korea Town

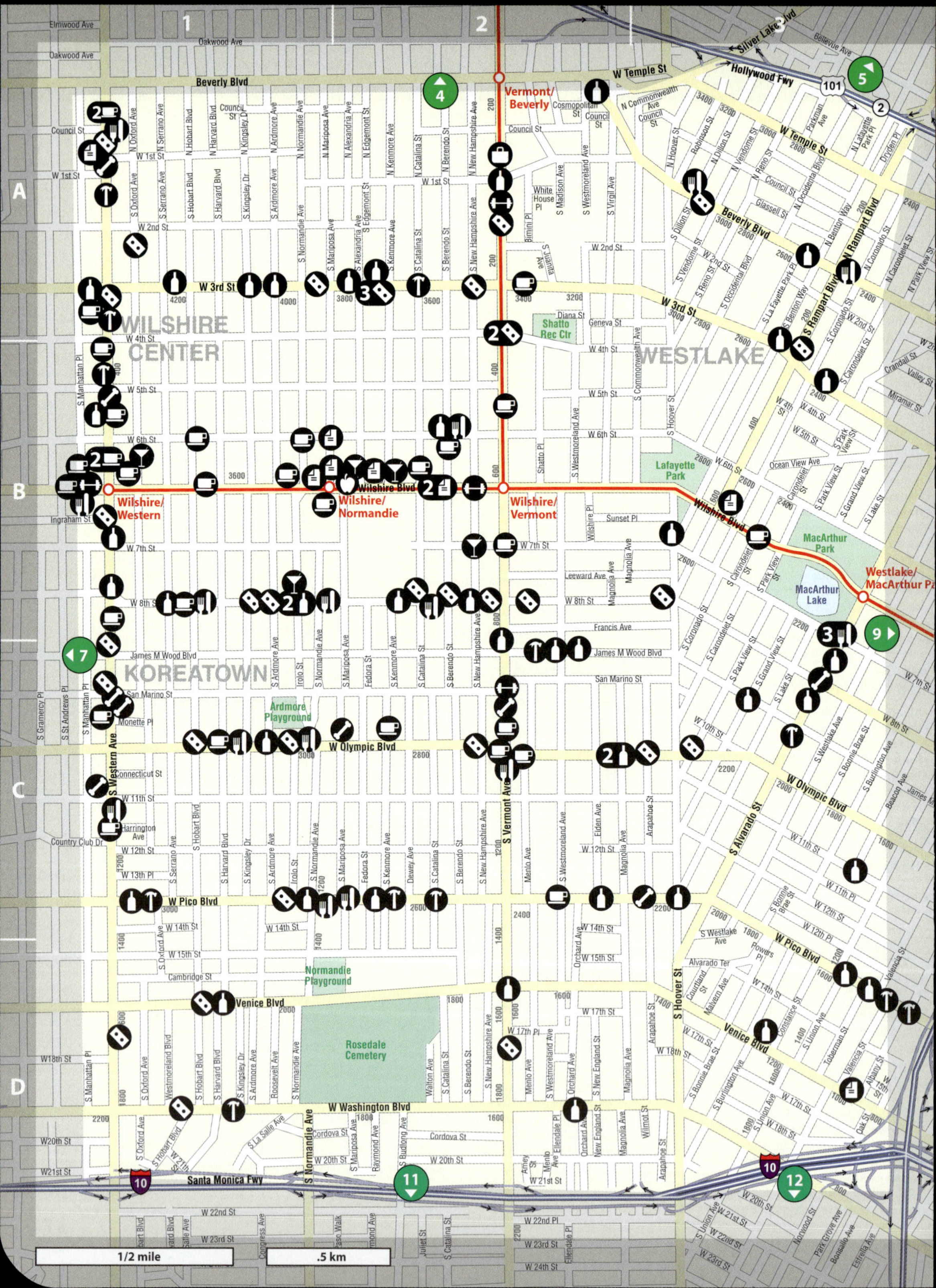

1
2
3
A
B
C
D
Beverly Blvd
W Temple St
Hollywood Fwy
Silver Lake Blvd
Vermont/ Beverly
Wilshire/ Western
Wilshire/ Normandie
Wilshire/ Vermont
Westlake/ MacArthur Park
WILSHIRE CENTER
WESTLAKE
KOREATOWN
W 3rd St
W 4th St
W 5th St
W 6th St
Wilshire Blvd
W 7th St
W 8th St
James M Wood Blvd
San Marino St
W Olympic Blvd
W 11th St
W 12th St
W Pico Blvd
Venice Blvd
W Washington Blvd
Santa Monica Fwy
Shatto Rec Ctr
Lafayette Park
MacArthur Park
MacArthur Lake
Ardmore Playground
Normandie Playground
Rosedale Cemetery
S Western Ave
S Vermont Ave
S Hoover St
S Alvarado St
S Normandie Ave
1/2 mile
.5 km

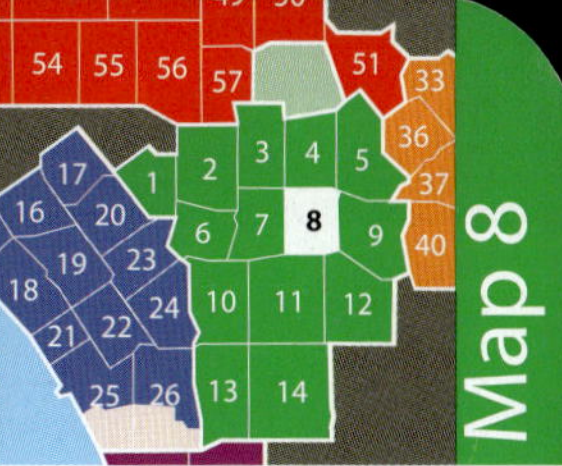

Going out for a night on the K-town? Three words: Korean barbecue + karaoke . Try Soot Bull Jeep for a no-frills dining experience with a handful of friends. Follow up a feast of kimchi and short ribs with generous amounts of sake and bad 80s tunes at Orchid Karaoke. Orchid offers private rooms and dining service, so you don't have to leave your seat for a fresh drink or snacks. Add a few soju cocktails, and your night is complete.

Coffee

- **Baristar** • 698 S Vermont Ave
- **Café Aristo** • 664 S Catalina St
- **Café de Flora** • 210 N Western Ave
- **Café Latte** • 3130 W Olympic Blvd, Ste 100
- **Café Moet** • 3832 Wilshire Blvd
- **Café Patio** • 3324 W 6th St
- **Café Village** • 3464 W 8th St
- **Coffee Break** • 363 S Western Ave
- **Coffee House Cona** • 425 S Western Ave
- **Coffee Tree** • 2881 W Olympic Blvd
- **Coffee Zone** • 3240 Wilshire Blvd
- **Coffeetime** • 851 S Western Ave
- **Donuts & Coffee Shop** • 207 N Western Ave
- **Essence Coffee** • 3458 Wilshire Blvd
- **Faru** • 975 S Vermont Ave
- **I Love Boba** • 1144 S Western Ave
- **I Love BOBA** • 534 S Western Ave
- **Ice Kiss** • 3407 W 6th St
- **K-Town Café** • 974 S Western Ave
- **Koffea** • 610 S Berendo St
- **Lollicup** • 3805 W 6th St
- **New Seoul Hotel Coffee House** • 2666 W Olympic Blvd
- **Olive Snackshop** • 3325 Wilshire Blvd
- **Pronto Caffe & Tea** • 3530 Wilshire Blvd, Ste 102
- **Starbucks** • Vons • 3461 W 3rd St
- **Starbucks** • 3680 Wilshire Blvd
- **Sunshine Café** • 2500 Wilshire Blvd
- **Vienna Coffee** • 2716 W Olympic Blvd

Copy Shops

- **Color & Copy** • 3460 Wilshire Blvd • 213-381-0077
- **Copy Express LA** • 3321 Wilshire Blvd • 213-380-0062
- **Copy USA** • 3377 Wilshire Blvd • 213-384-8184
- **FedEx Kinko's** • 3345 Wilshire Blvd • 213-381-4129
- **Ford Graphics** • 934 Venice Blvd • 213-745-2134
- **Just Fill** • 3435 Wilshire Blvd • 213-738-8116
- **Pip Printing** • 3550 W 6th St • 213-386-4200
- **Saver Office Supplies** • 143 N Western Ave • 323-469-8401
- **Universal Reprographics** • 2706 Wilshire Blvd • 213-365-7750

Farmers Markets

- **Wilshire Center (Fri, 11:30 am-3 pm)** • S Mariposa Ave & Wilshire Blvd

Gyms

- **24 Hour Fitness** • 3699 Wilshire Blvd • 213-388-2700
- **Natura Sports Health Club** • 3240 Wilshire Blvd • 213-637-9640

Hardware Stores

- **A&B Ace Hardware** • 513 S Western Ave • 213-389-6529
- **Alvarado Paint & Hardware** • 915 S Alvarado St • 213-382-1305
- **Callahan True Value** • 139 S Western Ave • 213-387-3336
- **Catalina Hardware & Paint** • 3615 W 3rd St • 213-384-3059
- **D&D Hardware** • 2831 James M Wood Blvd • 213-386-6220
- **J&C Hardware** • 1426 W Pico Blvd • 213-748-1530
- **Orlando's Key Shop & Hardware** • 2024 W Washington Blvd • 323-737-5017
- **Pico Building Supply** • 2595 W Pico Blvd • 213-388-5102
- **Tool Max Hardware** • 2656 W Pico Blvd • 213-386-5284
- **Villanueva's Hardware** • 3030 W Pico Blvd • 323-737-1099
- **West Coast Maintenance Materials** • 337 S Western Ave • 213-387-2245

Liquor Stores

- **3rd St Liquors** • 4023 W 3rd St
- **8 OK Liquors** • 749 S Western Ave
- **A&A Liquors** • 111 S Vermont Ave
- **Albert's Liquors** • 3088 W Pico Blvd
- **Amigos Liquor** • 2601 W 7th St
- **Ant Liquor** • 2701 W 8th St
- **Ardmore Liquor** • 4056 W 3rd St
- **Ashibi Liquor** • 4376 W 3rd St
- **Catalina Liquor** • 3130 W 8th St
- **Cheyenne Liquor Store** • 1611 S Vermont Ave
- **Crest Liquors** • 2543 W 3rd St
- **Dick's Beverage House** • 3315 W 6th St
- **Garden Liquor** • 1479 W Washington Blvd
- **Gary's Liquors** • 2171 Venice Blvd
- **Gourmet Liquors** • 826 S Alvarado St
- **Hiro's Liquor & Groceries** • 2340 W Pico Blvd
- **Hope Liquor** • 687 S Hoover St
- **Imperial Liquor** • 1602 W Pico Blvd
- **J&F Liquor** • 1512 W Pico Blvd
- **J&H Liquors** • 1154 Venice Blvd
- **Jeff's Liquor** • 1683 W 11th St
- **Jon's Supermarket** • 3334 W 8th St
- **Jon's Supermarket** • 3667 W 3rd St
- **Kumano Liquor** • 2801 W Pico Blvd
- **LA Pit Stop** • 2571 W Olympic Blvd
- **Ladd Liquor** • 4217 W 3rd St
- **Lawrence Liquor** • 2301 W James M Wood Blvd
- **Lucky Liquor** • 2201 W Pico Blvd
- **Nadee's Liquor** • 863 S Vermont Ave
- **Occidental Liquor** • 2755 Beverly Blvd
- **Ocean Liquor** • 760 S Alvarado St
- **Olympic Liquors** • 3060 W Olympic Blvd
- **Oxford Mini Mart** • 3502 W 8th St
- **Park Liquor** • 3554 Beverly Blvd
- **Service Liquor House** • 3803 W 3rd St
- **Silver Liquor & Deli** • 2717 W 3rd St
- **Superior Liquor** • 2700 W Pico Blvd
- **Topper Liquor** • 3061 W 8th St
- **West Seven Liquor Store** • 707 S Western Ave
- **Western Liquor** • 553 S Western Ave
- **Westmoreland Market** • 2800 James M Wood Blvd

Nightlife

- **Brass Monkey** • 659 Mariposa Ave • 213-381-7047
- **HMS Bounty** • 3357 Wilshire Blvd • 213-385-7275
- **La Fonda De Los Camperos** • 2501 Wilshire Blvd • 213-380-5055
- **Orchid Karaoke Club** • 607 S Oxford Ave, 2nd Fl • 213-251-8886
- **The Prince** • 3198 7th St • 213-389-1586
- **R Bar** • 3331 W 8th St • 213-387-7227

Pet Shops

- **Blanquis Pet and Supplies** • 2251 W Pico Blvd • 213-487-1290
- **Hanmi Pet Shop** • 1048 S Western Ave • 323-731-8882
- **Hobby Life Center** • 533 S Western Ave • 323-262-9999
- **JC Pet Shop and Supplies** • 1233 S Western Ave • 323-252-3173
- **Puppy in Style** • 974 S Western Ave • 323-732-1130
- **Puppy Land** • 2921 W Olympic Blvd • 213-385-0050
- **Sunny Pet Shop** • 955 S Vermont Ave, Ste B • 213-487-7778
- **Western Pet Center (Birds)** • 533 S Western Ave • 213-381-3435
- **World Pet Shop & Bonsai** • 151 N Western Ave • 323-469-9977

Restaurants

- **Cassell's Hamburgers** • 3266 W 6th St • 213-480-5000
- **Dong Il Jang** • 3455 W 8th St • 213-383-5757
- **El Cholo** • 1121 S Western Ave • 323-734-2773
- **El Farolito** • 2737 W Pico Blvd • 323-731-4329
- **Guelaguetza** • 3014 W Olympic Blvd • 213-427-0608
- **Hodori** • 1001 S Vermont Ave, Ste 102 • 213-383-3554
- **Langers** • 704 S Alvarado St • 213-483-8050
- **Lowenbrau Keller** • 3211 Beverly Blvd • 213-382-5723
- **M Grill** • 3832 Wilshire Blvd • 213-389-2770
- **Mama's Hot Tamales** • 2122 W Seventh St • 213-487-4300
- **Papa Cristo's** • 2771 W Pico Blvd • 323-737-2970
- **Parao** • 3680 Wilshire Blvd • 213-383-8686
- **Pipers** • 222 N Western Ave • 323-465-7701
- **Soot Bull Jeep** • 3136 W 8th St • 213-387-3865
- **Taylor's Steak House** • 3361 W 8th St • 213-382-8449
- **Tommy's** • 2575 Beverly Blvd • 213-389-9060

Shopping

- **Seafood Market** • 110 N Vermont Ave • 323-953-2689

Video Rental

- **20-20 Video** • 142 S Vermont Ave • 213-380-0202
- **20-20 Video** • 1720 S Vermont Ave • 323-734-2020
- **50 50 Video** • 2411 W Olympic Blvd • 213-384-4585
- **A&T Video Center** • 272 S Rampart Blvd • 213-387-6161
- **CALA Video** • 3810 W 3rd St • 213-388-3744
- **Central Video (Korean)** • 3072 W 8th St • 213-389-2111
- **Chung's Video (Korean)** • 244 S Oxford Ave • 213-384-9900
- **Cinema Story** • 401 S Vermont Ave • 213-383-6211
- **Corner Video (Korean)** • 2528 W Olympic Blvd • 213-388-2255
- **El Chasis Video** • 2980 W 8th St • 213-385-4702
- **Excalibur Video** • 1724 S Western Ave • 323-731-1801
- **Han Nam Video (Korean)** • 2716 W Olympic Blvd • 213-487-1225
- **Hollywood Video** • 650 S Western Ave • 213-385-7233
- **Korea Town Plaza Video (Korean)** • 928 S Western Ave • 213-480-8080
- **Korean Video Store (Korean)** • 401 S Vermont Ave • 213-386-7116
- **LA Korean Video (Korean)** • 326 S Western Ave • 213-389-4989
- **Lucky Video (Korean)** • 124 N Western Ave • 323-460-4398
- **Mickey Video (Korean)** • 3134 W Olympic Blvd • 323-732-8399
- **Super Video (Korean)** • 3338 W 8th St • 213-380-0550
- **Video Target** • 3128 W 8th St • 213-487-6035
- **Video Tek (Korean)** • 849 S Western Ave • 213-382-0714
- **Virgil Video** • 2161 Venice Blvd • 323-734-6007
- **World Video** • 3362 W 8th St • 213-487-0068

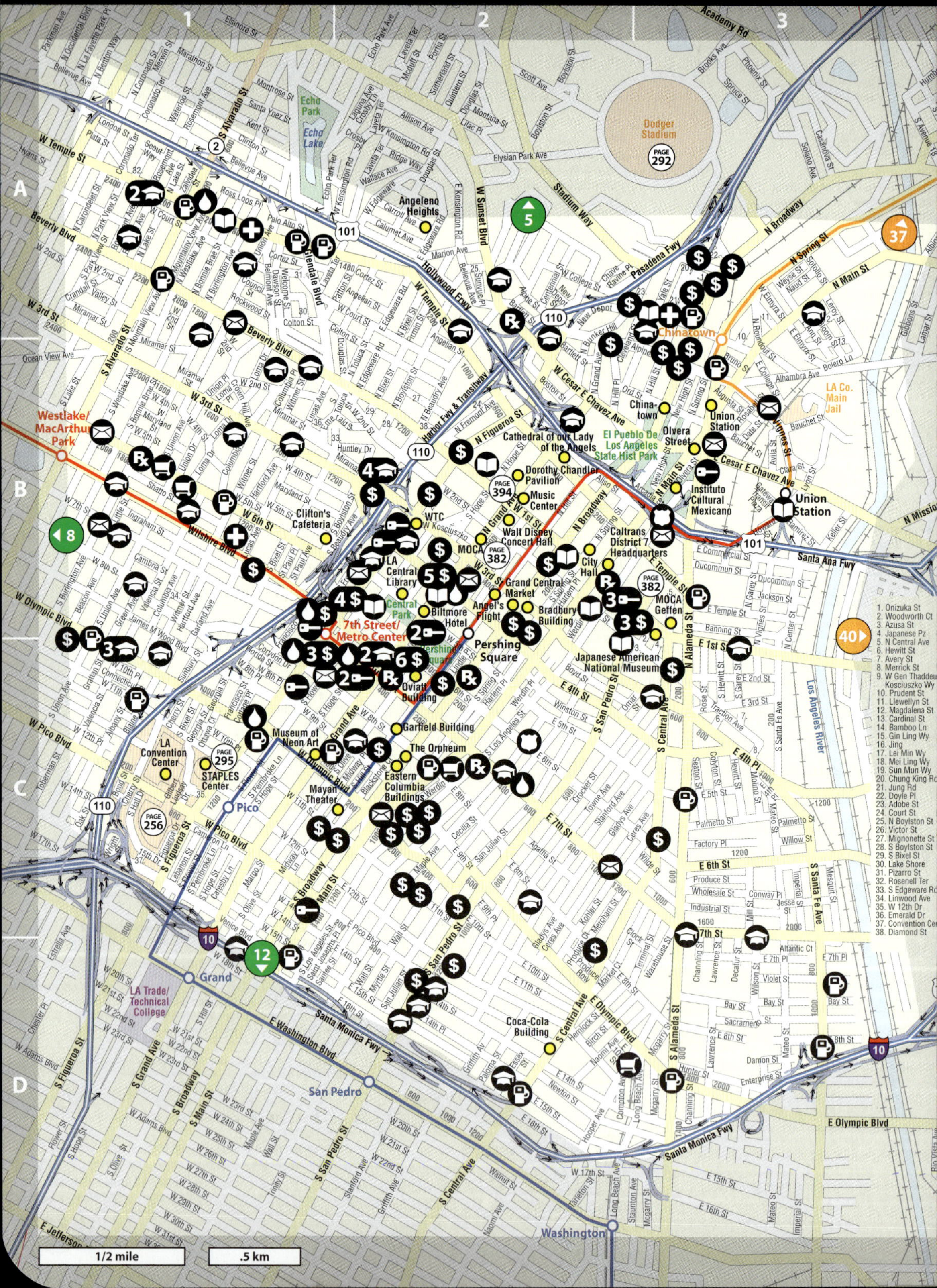

Map 9 • Downtown

N

1
2
3
A
B
C
D

Echo Park
Echo Lake
Dodger Stadium
PAGE 292
Angeleno Heights
Chinatown
China-town
Union Station
Olvera Street
El Pueblo De Los Angeles State Hist Park
Instituto Cultural Mexicano
LA Co. Main Jail
Cathedral of our Lady of the Angels
Dorothy Chandler Pavilion
Music Center
PAGE 394
Walt Disney Concert Hall
MOCA
PAGE 382
City Hall
Caltrans District 7 Headquarters
MOCA Geffen
PAGE 382
Japanese American National Museum
WTC
Clifton's Cafeteria
LA Central Library
Central Park
Biltmore Hotel
Angel's Flight
Grand Central Market
Bradbury Building
Pershing Square
7th Street/ Metro Center
Westlake/ MacArthur Park
Oviatt Building
Garfield Building
Museum of Neon Art
The Orpheum
Eastern Columbia Buildings
Mayan Theater
LA Convention Center
STAPLES Center
PAGE 295
PAGE 256
Pico
Grand
San Pedro
Washington
LA Trade/ Technical College
Coca-Cola Building
Los Angeles River

Pasadena Fwy
Hollywood Fwy
Harbor Fwy & Transitway
Santa Monica Fwy
Santa Ana Fwy
W Temple St
Beverly Blvd
W 3rd St
W 6th St
Wilshire Blvd
W Olympic Blvd
W Pico Blvd
W Cesar E Chavez Ave
N Broadway
N Spring St
N Main St
N Figueroa St
S Figueroa St
S Grand Ave
S Broadway
S Main St
S San Pedro St
S Central Ave
S Alameda St
E Olympic Blvd
E Washington Blvd
E 7th St
E 6th St
E 1st St
S Alvarado St
Glendale Blvd
Sunset Blvd
Stadium Way

101
110
10
2
5
8
12
37
40

1. Onizuka St
2. Woodworth Ct
3. Azusa St
4. Japanese Pz
5. N Central Ave
6. Hewitt St
7. Avery St
8. Merrick St
9. W Gen Thaddeu Kosciuszko Wy
10. Prudent St
11. Llewellyn St
12. Magdalena St
13. Cardinal St
14. Bamboo Ln
15. Gin Ling Wy
16. Jing
17. Lei Min Wy
18. Mei Ling Wy
19. Sun Mun Wy
20. Chung King Rc
21. Jung Rd
22. Doyle Pl
23. Adobe St
24. Court St
25. N Boylston St
26. Victor St
27. Mignonette St
28. S Boylston St
29. S Bixel St
30. Lake Shore
31. Pizarro St
32. Rosenell Ter
33. S Edgeware Rc
34. Linwood Ave
35. W 12th Dr
36. Emerald Dr
37. Convention Cer
38. Diamond St

1/2 mile
.5 km

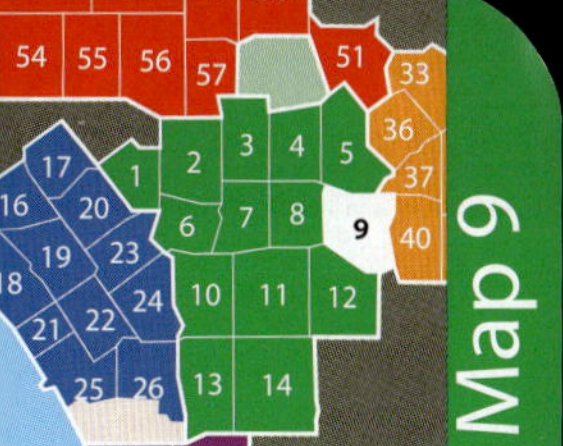

Downtown's revitalization has placed Skid Row residents on the doorsteps of yuppie loft dwellers—a juxtaposition that is (amazingly) working. Head south to find portfolio-toting FIDM students and the Fashion District, or explore Little Tokyo and Chinatown's galleries and restaurants to the north. From Downtown's epicenter, visit Gehry's Walt Disney concert hall and the MOCA; stroll the Jewelry District for wholesale goodies; stock up on veggies at Grand Central Market and (for you early-birds) don't miss the vibrant Flower District.

Banks

- **Banco Popular** • 354 S Spring St
- **Bank Leumi USA** • 600 Wilshire Blvd
- **Bank of America** • 100 S Broadway
- **Bank of America** • 110 E 9th St
- **Bank of America** • 1127 S Hill St
- **Bank of America** • 1625 W Olympic Blvd
- **Bank of America** • 2101 W 6th St
- **Bank of America** • 333 S Hope St
- **Bank of America** • 550 S Hill St
- **Bank of America** • 590 S Central Ave
- **Bank of America** • 600 Wilshire Blvd
- **Bank of America** • 850 N Broadway
- **Bank of America** • 888 W 7th St
- **Bank of the West** • 300 S Grand Ave
- **Bank of the West** • 333 S Alameda St
- **Bank of the West** • 915 Wilshire Blvd
- **California Bank & Trust** • 101 S San Pedro St
- **California Bank & Trust** • 550 S Hope St
- **California Center** • 1059 S San Pedro St
- **California Center** • 1205 S Broadway
- **California Credit Union** • 333 S Beaudry Ave
- **California Credit Union** • 420 N Rosenell Ter
- **California National** • 221 S Figueroa St
- **Cathay** • 777 N Broadway
- **Cathay** • 800 W 6th St
- **Citibank** • 110 E 9th St
- **Citibank** • 324 E 1st St
- **Citibank** • 787 W 5th St
- **Citibank** • 800 N Hill St
- **City National** • 355 S Grand Ave
- **City National** • 525 S Flower St
- **City National** • 606 S Olive St
- **Comerica** • 110 E 9th St
- **Comerica** • 201 N Figueroa St
- **East West** • 624 S Grand Ave
- **East West** • 942 N Broadway
- **Far East National** • 350 S Grand Ave
- **Far East National** • 350 S Grand Ave
- **Far East National** • 977 N Broadway
- **Far East National** • 977 N Broadway
- **First Bank & Trust** • 711 W College St
- **First Republic** • 901 W 7th St
- **Hanmi** • 726 E 12th St
- **Hanmi** • 950 S Los Angeles St
- **Manufacturers** • 200 S San Pedro St
- **Manufacturers** • 515 S Figueroa St
- **Nara** • 1122 S Wall St
- **Pacific Western** • 444 S Flower St
- **Preferred** • 601 S Figueroa St
- **Union** • 120 S San Pedro St
- **Union** • 445 S Figueroa St
- **Union** • 900 S Main St
- **United Commercial** • 767 N Hill St
- **US** • 633 W 5th St
- **Washington Mutual** • 400 S Hope St
- **Washington Mutual** • 725 S Figueroa St
- **Washington Mutual** • 855 S Hill St
- **Wells Fargo** • 1200 Wilshire Blvd
- **Wells Fargo** • 1244 E 8th St
- **Wells Fargo** • 333 S Grand Ave
- **Wells Fargo** • 333 S Spring St
- **Wells Fargo** • 707 Wilshire Blvd
- **Wells Fargo** • 988 N Hill St
- **Wilshire State** • 1122 Maple Ave
- **Wilshire State** • 1300 S San Pedro St

Car Rental

- **Allied Rent A Car** • 1333 S Main St
- **Avis** • 888 S Figueroa St
- **Budget** • 800 N Alameda St
- **Enterprise** • 404 S Figueroa St
- **Enterprise** • 506 S Grand Ave
- **Enterprise** • 530 S Olive St
- **Enterprise** • 718 Wilshire Blvd
- **Enterprise** • 930 Wilshire Blvd
- **Hertz** • 333 S Figueroa St
- **Hertz** • 711 S Hope St
- **Hertz** • 800 N Alameda St
- **Sakura Rent-a-Car** • 120 S Los Angeles St
- **Sakura Rent-a-Car** • 248 E 1st St

Car Washes

- **Aztec Auto Detailing** • 948 W 8th St
- **Chevron** • 811 W Olympic Blvd
- **Joe's Car Wash** • 400 E 7th St
- **Leo's Car Wash** • 700 S Flower St
- **Mario's Hand Wash & Auto Detailing** • 1000 Wilshire Blvd
- **Shell** • 400 N Alvarado St
- **Valet Car Wash** • 355 S Grand Ave

Gas Stations

- **76** • 1307 W 6th St
- **76** • 1800 E Olympic Blvd
- **Arco** • 1045 Blaine St
- **Arco** • 2106 W Temple St
- **Chevron** • 1516 S Main St
- **Chevron** • 1600 W Olympic Blvd
- **Chevron** • 501 Glendale Blvd
- **Chevron** • 811 W Olympic Blvd
- **Chevron** • 901 N Alameda St
- **Independent** • 812 S Main St
- **Independent** • 900 N Hill St
- **Independent** • 930 S Santa Fe Ave
- **Shell** • 1520 Santa Fe Ave
- **Shell** • 1541 S Central Ave
- **Shell** • 400 N Alvarado St
- **Shell** • 504 W Olympic Blvd
- **Texaco** • 500 S Alameda St
- **Valero** • 2041 Beverly Blvd

Emergency Rooms

- **City of Angels** • 1711 W Temple St
- **Good Samaritan** • 1225 Wilshire Blvd
- **Pacific Alliance** • 531 W College St

Landmarks

- **Angel's Flight** • W 4th St & Hill St
- **Angeleno Heights** • Carroll/Kellam/W Kensington Aves
- **Biltmore Hotel** • 506 S Grand Ave
- **Bradbury Building** • 304 S Broadway
- **Caltrans District 7 Headquarters** • 100 S Main St
- **Cathedral of Our Lady of the Angels** • 555 W Temple St
- **Chinatown** • 700-1000 N Broadway
- **City Hall** • 200 N Spring St
- **Clifton's Cafeteria** • 648 S Broadway
- **Coca-Cola Building** • 1334 S Central Ave
- **Dorothy Chandler Pavilion** • 135 N Grand Ave
- **Eastern Columbia Buildings** • 849 S Broadway
- **El Pueblo de Los Angeles Historical Monument** • Main St & Cesar E Chavez Ave
- **Garfield Building** • 403 W 8th St
- **The Geffen Contemporary at MOCA** • 152 N Central Ave
- **Grand Central Market** • 317 S Broadway
- **Instituto Cultural Mexicano** • 125 Paseo de la Plz
- **Japanese American National Museum** • 369 E 1st St
- **LA Convention Center** • 1201 S Figueroa St
- **Los Angeles Central Library** • 630 W 5th St
- **Mayan Theater** • 1038 S Hill St
- **MOCA** • 250 S Grand Ave
- **Music Center** • 135 N Grand Ave
- **Olvera Street** • Olvera St
- **The Orpheum** • 842 S Broadway
- **Oviatt Building** • 617 S Olive St
- **STAPLES Center** • 1111 S Figueroa St
- **Union Station** • 800 N Alameda St
- **Walt Disney Concert Hall** • 141 S Grand Ave
- **World Trade Center** • 350 S Figueroa St

Libraries

- **Chinatown Branch** • 639 N Hill St • 213-620-0925
- **Echo Park Library** • 1410 W Temple St • 213-250-7808
- **Franklin D Murphy Library (temporarily closed)** • 244 S San Pedro St • 213-628-2725
- **LA County Law Library** • 301 W 1st St • 213-629-3531
- **Little Tokyo Branch** • 203 S Los Angeles St • 213-612-0525
- **Los Angeles Central Library** • 630 W 5th St • 213-228-7000
- **MTA Library** • 1 Gateway Plz • 213-922-4859
- **Water & Power Library** • 111 N Hope St • 213-367-1995

Pharmacies

- **CVS** • 1050 Sunset Blvd • 213-975-1165
- **CVS** • 201 N Los Angeles St • 213-620-1494
- **Rite-Aid** • 1744 W 6th St • 213-413-2458
- **Rite-Aid** • 501 S Broadway • 213-623-5820
- **Rite-Aid** • 600 W 7th St • 213-896-0083
- **Rite-Aid** • 700 S Los Angeles St • 213-614-9574

Police

- **Los Angeles Police Dept** • 251 E 6th St • 213-485-3294
- **Los Angeles Police Dept - Administrative Office** • 150 N Los Angeles St • 213-485-2121

Post Offices

- **US Post Office** • 100 W Olympic Blvd • 800-275-8777
- **US Post Office** • 1055 N Vignes St • 800-275-8777
- **US Post Office** • 1122 E 7th St • 800-275-8777
- **US Post Office** • 1660 Beverly Blvd • 800-275-8777
- **US Post Office** • 1808 W 7th St • 800-275-8777
- **US Post Office** • 2005 W 6th St • 213-483-4098
- **US Post Office** • 300 N Los Angeles St • 800-275-8777
- **US Post Office** • 350 S Grand Ave • 800-275-8777
- **US Post Office** • 505 S Flower St • 800-275-8777
- **US Post Office** • Macy's • 750 W 7th St • 800-275-8777
- **US Post Office** • 900 N Alameda St • 213-617-4404

Schools

- **10th St Elementary** • 1000 Grattan St
- **9th St Elementary** • 820 Towne Ave
- **Ann St Elementary** • 126 E Bloom St
- **Belmont Senior High** • 1575 W 2nd St
- **Betty Plasencia Elementary** • 1321 Cortez St
- **CA Academy for Liberal Studies Early College High** • 700 Wilshire Blvd
- **Camino Nuevo Charter Middle** • 653 S Burlington Ave
- **Castelar EEC** • 840 Yale St
- **Castelar Elementary** • 840 Yale St
- **CDS Elementary** • 450 N Grand Ave
- **CDS Secondary** • 333 S Beaudry Ave
- **Center For Advanced Transition Skills** • 333 S Beaudry Ave
- **Central Continuation** • 716 E 14th St
- **City of Angels Independent Study** • 1449 S San Pedro St
- **Citylife Downtown Charter** • 1501 Wilshire Blvd
- **Citylife Downtown Charter** • 700 Wilshire Blvd
- **Cruz EEC** • 1020 Valencia St
- **DBM/Electronic Information Magnet** • 1081 W Temple St
- **De La Hoya Animo Senior High** • 350 S Figueroa St
- **Elementary Community Day** • 333 S Beaudry Ave
- **Esperanza Elementary** • 680 Little St
- **Evans Community Adult** • 717 N Figueroa St
- **Evelyn Thurman Gratts Elementary** • 309 Lucas Ave
- **Friedman OCC Center** • 1646 S Olive St
- **Harris Newmark Continuation High** • 134 Witmer St
- **Immaculate Conception** • 830 Green Ave
- **Jardin D La Infancia** • 307 E 7th St
- **LA Trade/Technical College** • 400 W Washington Blvd
- **Lake Street Primary** • 135 N Lake St
- **Los Angelitos EEC** • 400 W 9th St
- **Lumbini Child Development Center** • 505 E 3rd St
- **Metropolitan Continuation** • 727 Wilson St
- **New Academy for Science & Arts** • 379 Loma Dr
- **New Covenant Academy** • 1111 W Sunset Blvd
- **Nishi Hongwanji Child Development Center** • 815 E 1st St
- **Olympic PC** • 950 S Albany St
- **Our Lady of Loretto** • 258 N Union Ave
- **Para Los Ninos Charter** • 1617 E 7th St
- **Personal Coaching Systems** • 1725 Beverly Blvd
- **ROP Center** • 333 S Beaudry Ave
- **Rosemont Ave Elementary** • 421 Rosemont Ave
- **Rosemont EEC** • 430 Rosemont Ave
- **St Nicholas Primary** • 2300 W 3rd St
- **St Turibius Elementary** • 1524 Essex St
- **Tri-C Community Day** • 716 E 14th St
- **Union Ave Elementary** • 150 S Burlington Ave

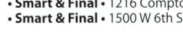

Supermarkets

- **Food 4 Less** • 1700 W 6th St
- **Rons** • 805 S Main St
- **Smart & Final** • 1216 Compton Ave
- **Smart & Final** • 1500 W 6th St

Map 9 • Downtown

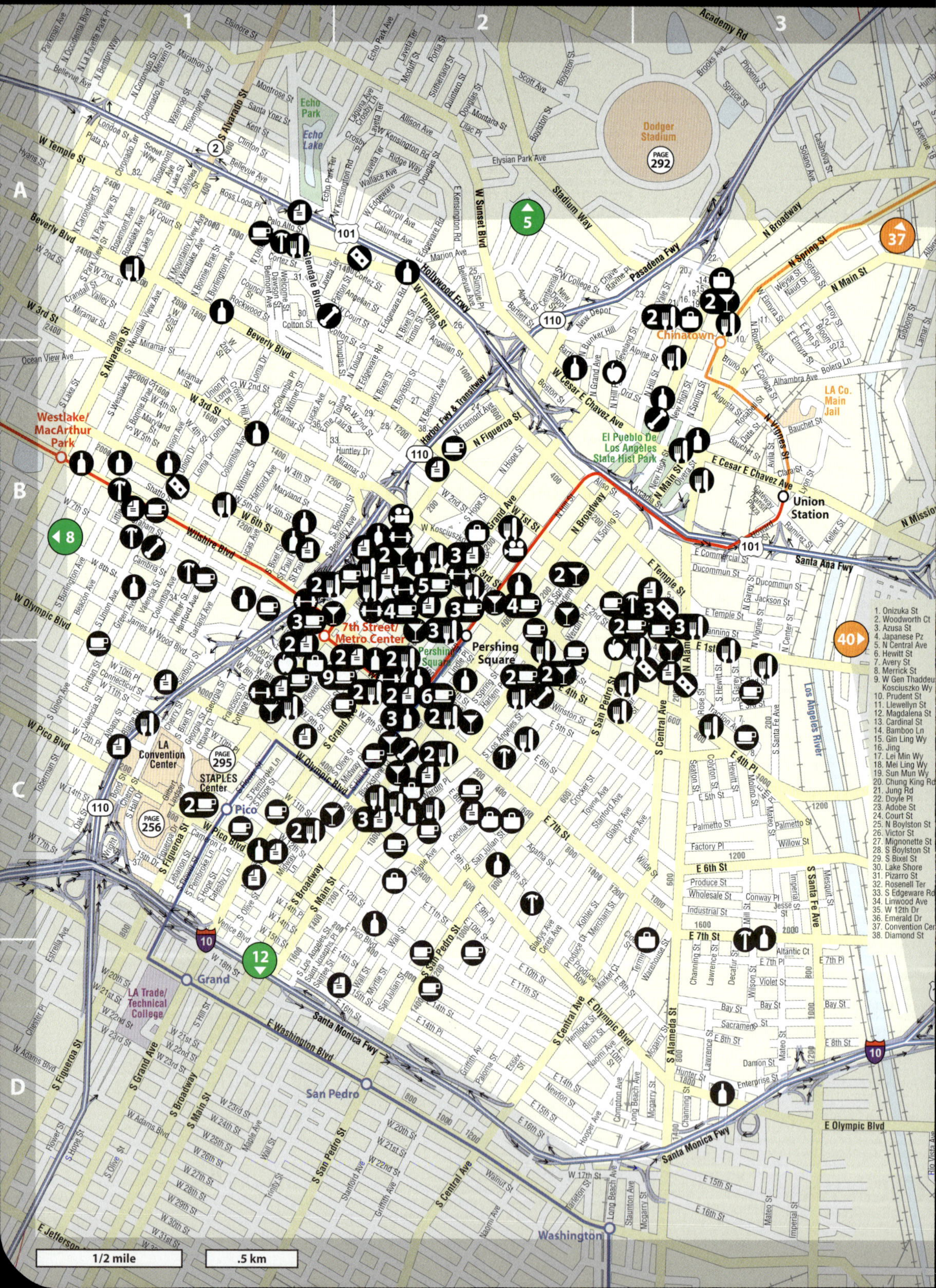

Echo Park
Echo Lake
Dodger Stadium
PAGE 292
Chinatown
LA Co. Main Jail
El Pueblo De Los Angeles State Hist Park
Union Station
Westlake/MacArthur Park
7th Street/Metro Center
Pershing Square
LA Convention Center
STAPLES Center
PAGE 295
PAGE 256
Pico
Grand
LA Trade/Technical College
San Pedro
Washington
Los Angeles River

1. Onizuka St
2. Woodworth Ct
3. Azusa St
4. Japanese Pz
5. N Central Ave
6. Hewitt St
7. Avery St
8. Merrick St
9. W Gen Thaddeu Kosciuszko Wy
10. Prudent St
11. Llewellyn St
12. Magdalena St
13. Cardinal St
14. Bamboo Ln
15. Gin Ling Wy
16. Jing
17. Lei Min Wy
18. Mei Ling Wy
19. Sun Mun Wy
20. Chung King Rd
21. Jung Rd
22. Doyle Pl
23. Adobe St
24. Court St
25. N Boylston St
26. Victor St
27. Mignonette St
28. S Boylston St
29. S Bixel St
30. Lake Shore
31. Pizarro St
32. Rosenell Ter
33. S Edgeware Rd
34. Linwood Ave
35. W 12th Dr
36. Emerald Dr
37. Convention Cen
38. Diamond St

1/2 mile
.5 km

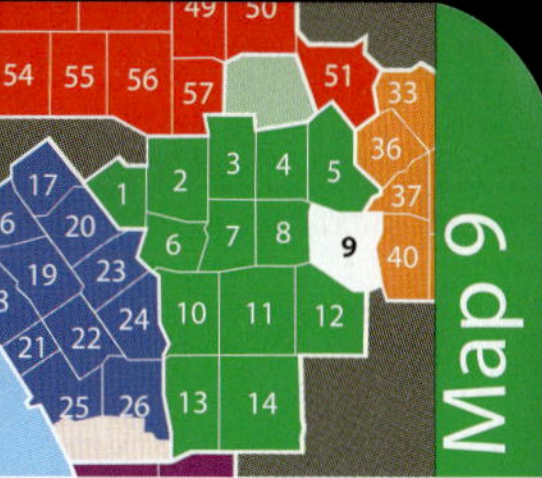

Downtown is (slowly) reclaiming its former throne as LA's premier dining district. The Water Grill boasts superb seafood and spectacular views; while Philippe's famous French-dip sandwiches draw crowds from miles away. Local professionals lounge at Ciudad and the Standard for happy hour. The Edison oozes Great Gatsby glam with dancing flappers and hi-brow drinks. Concert-goers enjoy the old-world charm of the Orpheum and the neighboring Broadway Bar, while local hipsters flock to the Golden Gopher, Downtown's resident dive bar.

Coffee

- **Banquette Café** • 400 S Main St
- **The Bishop Coffee & Gourmet** • 816 S Grand Ave
- **Blue Diamond** • 631 S Hill St
- **Boba Loca** • 623 E 12th St
- **Bruno Coffee** • 502 W 6th St
- **Café Sprout** • 1300 S San Pedro St
- **Café Take 5** • 328 E 1st St
- **City Bean** • 700 S Flower St
- **Coffee Bean & Tea Leaf** • 210 E Olympic Blvd
- **Coffee Bean & Tea Leaf** • 601 W 5th St
- **Coffee Bean & Tea Leaf** • 801 W 7th St
- **Coffee Shop** • 915 Wilshire Blvd
- **Corner Bakery Café** • 801 S Figueroa St
- **Emerson's Café** • 606 S Olive St
- **Gourmet Coffee & Nuts** • 505 S Flower St
- **Gourmet Coffee Wherhouse Downtown** • 811 Traction Ave
- **Green Spot** • 1015 Crocker St
- **Groundwork** • 108 W 2nd St
- **Happy Time Snack** • 819 Santee St
- **Harlls Café** • 317 S Broadway
- **Jolt-Bar Café** • 1055 W 7th St
- **LA Boulangeries Café** • 238 E 6th St
- **Larry's Cookie** • 221 N Figueroa St
- **Le Café Bonjour** • 640 S Hill St
- **Lollicup** • 988 N Hill St
- **Lost Souls Café** • 124 W 4th St
- **Marie Café** • 733 W 7th St
- **Metropol** • 923 E 3rd St
- **Moose's Juices** • 444 S Flower St
- **Moxie** • 1433 W 7th St
- **Park Central Coffee Shop** • 412 W 6th St
- **Poirier & Co** • 550 S Hope St
- **Primo's Expresso Americana** • 333 S Spring St
- **Quality Coffee Shop** • 1238 W 7th St
- **Ric's Café** • 350 S Grand Ave
- **Seven Star Coffee 2** • 701 S Broadway
- **Starbucks**
  - 10925 Atlantic Ave
  - 1111 S Grand Ave
  - 120 S Los Angeles St
  - 1201 S Figueroa St (South Hall)
  - 1201 S Figueroa St (West Hall)
  - 138 S Central Ave
  - 1601 Wilshire Blvd
  - 217 N Hill St
  - 300 E 9th St
  - 330 S Hope St
  - 333 S Hope St
  - 350 S Grand Ave
  - 400 S Hope St
  - 400 S Hope St
  - 444 S Flower St, Ste 170
  - 445 S Figueroa St
  - 505 S Flower St
  - 523 W 6th St
  - 555 W 5th St
  - 633 W 5th St
  - 695 S Figueroa St
  - 735 S Figueroa St
- **Time Snack** • 1541 W Olympic Blvd
- **Tokyo Café** • 116 Judge John Aiso St
- **Tribal Café** • 1651 W Temple St
- **Trimana Restaurant** • 611 W 6th St
- **Vieta Coffee** • 800 W 6th St

Copy Shops

- **101 Printing** • 820 S Main St • 213-489-5050
- **Ace Copy Center** • 1001 S Hill St • 213-746-0222
- **Capitol Reprographics** • 350 S Figueroa St • 310-593-8100
- **Color & Copy** • 100 S San Pedro St • 213-625-8808
- **Color & Copy** • 1300 W Olympic Blvd • 213-736-5550
- **Concord Document Services** • 1321 W 12th St • 213-680-1114
- **Copy LA** • 1001 S Broadway • 213-746-3391
- **Copy Star** • 1515 Maple Ave • 213-744-1738
- **Copy Vision** • 123 S Figueroa St • 213-687-9994
- **Copy World** • 1338 S Grand Ave • 323-467-1222
- **Copypage** • 350 S Grand Ave • 213-412-1449
- **Copypage** • 865 S Figueroa St • 213-439-9656
- **Digital Color Copy** • 1622 S Hill St • 213-749-1292
- **Downtown Reprographics** • 640 S Olive St • 213-488-3332
- **FedEx Kinko's** • 110 E 9th St • 213-623-3614
- **FedEx Kinko's** • 330 S Hope St • 213-620-8615
- **FedEx Kinko's** • 554 S Grand Ave • 213-623-8129
- **FedEx Kinko's** • 735 S Figueroa St • 213-624-9409
- **FedEx Kinko's** • 835 Wilshire Blvd • 213-892-1700
- **Graphic Copy** • 811 Wilshire Blvd • 213-627-3083
- **LA Best Copies** • 621 W 6th St • 213-622-1622
- **LA Reprographics** • 601 W 5th St • 213-673-4460
- **Minuteman Press** • 600 W 9th St • 213-627-2604
- **Office Depot** • 401 E 2nd St • 213-628-5000
- **Pip Printing** • 1644 Wilshire Blvd • 213-483-4646
- **Pip Printing** • 700 Wilshire Blvd • 213-489-2333
- **Precision Copy** • 333 S Hope St, Ste C400 • 213-617-2332
- **Quality Digital Solutions** • 1625 Palo Alto St • 213-989-7800
- **Ready Reproductions** • 1212 S Olive St • 213-749-2041
- **Unlimited Copy** • 1111 W 6th St • 213-250-8951
- **Unlimited Reprographics** • 444 S Flower St • 213-892-9000

Farmers Markets

- **Little Tokyo (Tues, 10 am-2 pm)** • E 2nd St & S San Pedro St
- **Los Angeles-7th & Figueroa (Thurs, Fri, Sat, 10 am-4 pm)** • 735 S Figueroa St
- **Los Angeles-Chinatown (Thurs, 4 pm-8 pm)** • 727 N Hill St

Gyms

- **24 Hour Fitness** • 505 S Flower St • 213-683-1400
- **Bally Total Fitness** • 700 S Flower St • 213-624-3933
- **Curves** • 350 S Grand Ave • 213-628-4444
- **Gold's Gym** • 735 S Figueroa St • 213-688-1441
- **Los Angeles Athletic Club** • 431 W 7th St • 213-625-2211

Hardware Stores

- **7th & Union Hardware** • 1622 W 7th St • 213-483-5138
- **Anzen Hardware** • 309 E 1st St • 213-628-7600
- **Cooper Ace Hardware** • 1645 W Temple St • 213-483-3353
- **Douglas Hardware** • 1811 E 7th St • 213-622-4666
- **Gumbi** • 656 S Los Angeles St • 213-629-1518
- **Home Depot** • 1675 Wilshire Blvd • 213-273-8464
- **Terminal Hardware** • 824 E 8th St • 213-624-4078

Liquor Stores

- **Annex Liquors** • 1607 W 6th St
- **Best Liquor Store** • 722 S Hill St
- **Bixel Liquor** • 467 S Bixel St
- **Duke's Liquor** • 818 S San Pedro St
- **Esquire Liquor & Deli** • 619 S Olive St
- **French Kitchen** • 404 S Figueroa St
- **Friendly Liquor** • 1553 W 8th St
- **George's Liquor** • 1300 W Temple St
- **George's Liquor** • 700 N Broadway
- **Gourmet Liquors** • 1476 W 3rd St
- **Gourmet Wines & Spirits** • 626 Wilshire Blvd
- **Grand Central Liquor** • 317 S Broadway
- **Hope Liquor** • 1216 W 7th St
- **Jason's Wine & Spirits** • 110 E 9th St
- **Jo's Liquor** • 333 W Pico Blvd
- **Lees Liquor** • 1800 W 6th St
- **Macy Liquor** • 111 W Cesar E Chavez Ave
- **Mark's Liquor** • 1259 W 6th St
- **OT Liquor** • 1920 E Olympic Blvd
- **Pete's Liquor** • 1234 Maple Ave
- **Sam's Liquor** • 2001 W 6th St
- **Sorrento Liquor** • 801 W Cesar E Chavez Ave
- **TD Beer & Wine** • 1948 E 7th St
- **Union Liquor Store** • 1703 Beverly Blvd

Movie Theaters

- **Laemmle Grande 4** • 345 S Figueroa St • 213-617-0268
- **REDCAT** • 631 W 2nd St • 213-237-2800

Nightlife

- **Bar 107** • 107 W 4th St • 213-625-7382
- **Bonavista Lounge** • Bonaventure Hotel • 404 S Figueroa St • 213-236-0802
- **Broadway Bar** • 830 S Broadway • 213-614-9909
- **Ciudad** • Union Bank Plaza • 445 S Figueroa St • 213-486-5171
- **The Edison** • 108 W 2nd St • 213-613-0000
- **Gallery Bar** • Millennium Biltmore Hotel • 506 S Grand Ave • 213-624-1011
- **The Golden Gopher** • 417 W 8th St • 213-614-8001
- **Hop Louie** • 950 Mei Ling Wy • 213-628-4244
- **La Cita** • 336 S Hill St • 213-687-7111
- **Mayan Theater** • 1038 S Hill St • 213-746-4287
- **Mountain Bar** • 473 Gin Ling Wy • 213-625-7500
- **Oiwake** • 122 Japanese Village Plz Mall • 213-628-2678
- **Pete's Café & Bar** • 400 S Main St • 213-617-1000
- **Point Moorea Lounge** • Wilshire Grand Hotel • 930 Wilshire Blvd • 213-833-5100
- **Redwood Bar & Grill** • 316 W 2nd St • 213-680-2600
- **Roof Bar at the Standard Downtown** • 550 S Flower St • 213-892-8080
- **The Smell** • 247 S Main St •
- **Stock Exchange** • 618 S Spring St • 213-489-3877
- **Veranda Bar** • Figueroa Hotel • 939 S Figueroa St • 213-627-8971

Pet Shops

- **Al's Pet Supplies** • 430 S Los Angeles St • 213-622-1215
- **Canary Pet Shop** • 222 Glendale Blvd • 213-482-9622
- **Liberty Fish & Pet Shop** • 665 N Broadway • 213-628-9664

Restaurants

- **410 Boyd** • 410 Boyd St • 213-617-2491
- **626 Reserve** • 626B S Spring St • 213-627-9800
- **Angelique Café** • 840 S Spring St • 213-623-8698
- **Angelique Café** • 840 S Spring St • 213-623-8698
- **Blossom** • 426 S Main St • 213-623-1973
- **Brooklyn Bagel** • 2217 Beverly Blvd • 213-413-4114
- **Café Pinot** • 700 W 5th St • 213-239-6500
- **Casa La Golondrina** • W 17 Olvera St • 213-628-4349
- **Checkers** • Hilton • 535 S Grand Ave • 213-624-0000
- **Cicada** • 617 S Olive St • 213-488-9488
- **Ciudad** • Union Bank Plaza • 445 S Figueroa St • 213-486-5171
- **Clifton's Cafeteria** • 648 S Broadway • 213-627-1673
- **Dakokuya** • 327 E 1st St • 213-626-1680
- **Emerson's** • 862 S Los Angeles St • 213-623-8807
- **Emerson's Café** • 606 S Olive St • 213-623-3006
- **Empress Pavilion** • 988 N Hill St • 213-617-9898
- **Engine Co No 28** • 644 S Figueroa St • 213-624-6996
- **Lamonica's NY Pizza** • 518 W 6th St • 213-614-1100
- **Mikado Sushi Roll & Teriyaki** • 1001 S Broadway • 213-746-1481
- **Mrs Beasley's** • 735 S Figueroa St • 213-228-0227
- **Nick & Stef's Steakhouse** • Wells Fargo Ctr • 330 S Hope St • 213-680-0330
- **Noe** • Omni Hotel • 251 S Olive St • 213-356-4100
- **Oomasa** • 100 Japanese Village Plz Mall • 213-623-9048
- **Original Pantry Café** • 877 S Figueroa St • 213-972-9279
- **Pacific Dining Car** • 1310 W 6th St • 213-483-6000
- **Patina** • Walt Disney Concert Hall • 141 S Grand Ave • 213-972-3331
- **Pete's Café & Bar** • 400 S Main St • 213-617-1000
- **Philippe the Original** • 1001 N Alameda St • 213-628-3781
- **Plum Tree Inn** • 913 N Broadway • 213-613-1819
- **R-23** • 923 E 2nd St • 213-687-7178
- **Rustic Canyon Wine Bar** • 1119 Wilshire Blvd • 310-393-7050
- **Señor Fish** • 422 E 1st St • 213-625-0566
- **Seoul Jung Korean** • 930 Wilshire Blvd • 213-688-7880
- **The Standard** • 550 S Flower St • 213-892-8080
- **Suehiro Café** • 337 E 1st St • 213-626-9132
- **Sushi Gen** • 422 E 2nd St • 213-617-0552
- **Tiara Café** • 127 E 9th St • 213-623-3663
- **TOT** • 345 E 2nd St • 213-680-0344
- **Traxx at Union Station** • 800 N Alameda St • 213-625-1999
- **Tribal Café** • 1651 W Temple St • 213-483-4458
- **Via Café** • 451 Gin Ling Wy • 213-617-1481
- **Water Grill** • 544 S Grand Ave • 213-891-0900
- **Windows Steaks and Martinis** • SBC Tower • 1150 S Olive St • 213-746-1554
- **Yang Chow** • 819 N Broadway • 213-625-0811
- **Zip** • 744 E 3rd St • 213-680-3770

Shopping

- **7 + Fig at Ernst & Young Plaza** • 735 S Figueroa St • 213-955-7150
- **American Apparel** • 374 E 2nd St • 213-687-0467
- **American Apparel Factory Store** • 747 Warehouse St • 213-488-0226
- **California Market Center** • 110 E 9th St • 213-630-3600
- **Grand Central Market** • 317 S Broadway • 213-625-5006
- **LA Flower Market** • 766 Wall St • 213-622-1966
- **The MOCA Store** • 250 S Grand Ave • 213-621-1710
- **Moskatel's** • 733 San Julian St • 213-689-4590
- **Munky King** • 441 Gin Ling Wy • 213-620-8787
- **Ooga Booga** • 943 N Broadway, #203 • 213-617-1105
- **Santee Alley** • Maple Ave & E 12th St • 213-488-1153

Video Rental

- **B&C Video Rental** • 1416 W 6th St • 213-484-5383
- **J Wave (Japanese)** • 319 E 2nd St • 213-687-9920
- **Sun Video** • 450 E 2nd St • 213-625-0700
- **Tokyo Market (Japanese)** • 339 E 1st St • 213-620-0033
- **Video Z** • 1460 W Temple St • 213-481-0996

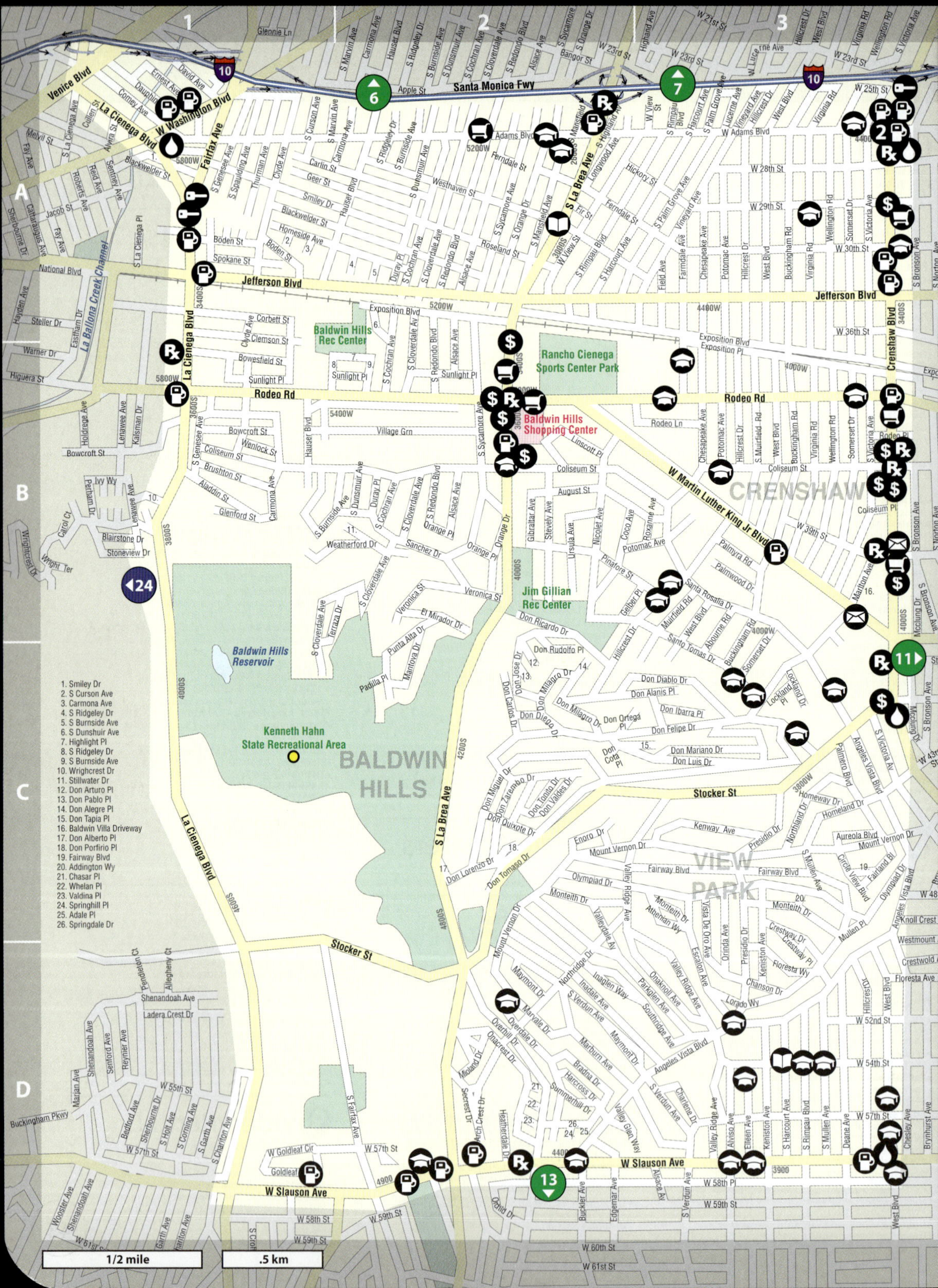

Map 10 • Baldwin Hills

1. Smiley Dr
2. S Curson Ave
3. Carmona Ave
4. S Ridgeley Dr
5. S Burnside Ave
6. S Dunshuir Ave
7. Highlight Pl
8. S Ridgeley Dr
9. S Burnside Ave
10. Wrighcrest Dr
11. Stillwater Dr
12. Don Arturo Pl
13. Don Pablo Pl
14. Don Alegre Pl
15. Don Tapia Pl
16. Baldwin Villa Driveway
17. Don Alberto Pl
18. Don Porfirio Pl
19. Fairway Blvd
20. Addington Wy
21. Chasar Pl
22. Whelan Pl
23. Valdina Pl
24. Springhill Pl
25. Adale Pl
26. Springdale Dr

1/2 mile

.5 km

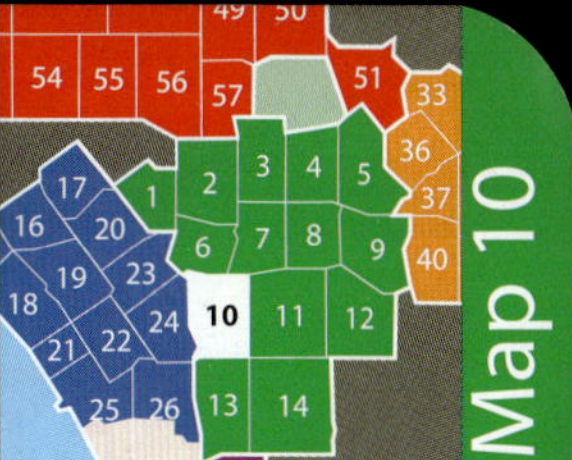

Baldwin Hills is a well-to-do African-American community whose first claim to fame was hosting the world's first Olympic Village in 1932. Post-Olympics, this mid-city swath of rolling hills became the gilded, exclusive enclave of the rich and famous—called the "Black Beverly Hills." Today's roster of homeowners now includes more doctors, dentists, lawyers, and other professionals than top entertainment and sports stars.

Banks

- **Bank of America** • 2907 Crenshaw Blvd
- **Bank of America** • 3615 S La Brea Ave
- **Bank of America** • 3945 Crenshaw Blvd
- **California Bank & Trust** • 3810 Crenshaw Blvd
- **Comerica** • 3825 Crenshaw Blvd
- **US** • 3605 S La Brea Ave
- **Washington Mutual** • 3738 Crenshaw Blvd
- **Washington Mutual** • 3747 S La Brea Ave
- **Wells Fargo** • 3480 S La Brea Ave
- **Wells Fargo** • 3649 Stocker St

Car Rental

- **Enterprise** • 3318 S La Cienega Blvd
- **Galpin Rent-A-Car** • 3200 La Cienega Blvd

Car Washes

- **Crenshaw Car Wash** • 4220 Crenshaw Blvd
- **Mr Polish** • 2605 S La Cienega Blvd
- **Shell** • 3645 Crenshaw Blvd
- **Slauson Hand Car Wash** • 3615 W Slauson Ave

Gas Stations

- **76** • 4856 W Slauson Ave
- **76** • 5100 W Jefferson Blvd
- **Arco** • 3412 Crenshaw Blvd
- **Arco** • 5884 Washington Blvd
- **Chevron** • 2538 Crenshaw Blvd
- **Chevron** • 2546 S La Brea Ave
- **Chevron** • 3063 Crenshaw Blvd
- **Chevron** • 3742 S La Brea Ave
- **Chevron** • 4701 W Slauson Ave
- **Independent** • 3708 W Slauson Ave
- **Mobil** • 4380 W Adams Blvd
- **Mobil** • 5776 Washington Blvd
- **Shell** • 2545 S Crenshaw Blvd
- **Shell** • 3645 Crenshaw Blvd
- **Shell** • 4660 W Slauson Ave
- **Thrifty** • 4406 Adams Blvd
- **Valero** • 3300 S La Cienega Blvd
- **Valero** • 3950 W Martin Luther King Jr Blvd

Landmarks

- **Kenneth Hahn State Recreation Area** • 4100 S La Cienega Blvd

Libraries

- **Baldwin Hills Branch** • 2906 S La Brea Ave • 323-733-1196
- **View Park** • 3854 W 54th St • 323-293-5371

Pharmacies

- **CVS** • 3741 Crenshaw Blvd • 323-298-5595
- **CVS** • Albertsons • 3901 Crenshaw Blvd • 323-295-3330
- **CVS** • 4501 W Slauson Ave • 323-292-4114
- **CVS** • 5101 W Rodeo Dr • 323-936-0279
- **Rite-Aid** • 3550 S La Brea Ave • 323-293-9397
- **Rite-Aid** • 3566 Rodeo Pl • 323-295-3323
- **Target** • 3535 S La Cienega Blvd • 310-895-1132
- **Walgreens** • 3724 Crenshaw Blvd • 323-292-7261
- **Walmart** • 4101 Crenshaw Blvd • 323-299-8246

Post Offices

- **US Post Office** • 3650 W Martin Luther King Jr Blvd • 800-275-8777
- **US Post Office** • 3894 Crenshaw Blvd • 800-275-8777

Schools

- **54th St Elementary** • 5501 Eileen Ave
- **Ascension Lutheran** • 5820 West Blvd
- **Baldwin Hills Elementary** • 5421 Rodeo Rd
- **CCDC of Little Angels** • 3808 W 54th St
- **Cienega Elementary** • 2611 S Orange Dr
- **Cleophas Oliver Learning Center** • 4449 W Adams Blvd
- **Coliseum St Elementary** • 4400 Coliseum St
- **Communion Christian Academy (second location)** • 4729 W Slauson Ave
- **Del Carousel Elementary** • 3944 W Slauson Ave
- **Hillcrest Center for Enriched Studies Music Magnet** • 4041 Hillcrest Dr
- **Hillcrest Dr Elementary** • 4041 Hillcrest Dr
- **Ivie League Christian** • 4416 W Slauson Ave
- **Junior Blind of America** • 5300 Angeles Vista Blvd
- **Kids Preparatory Academy** • 3770 Santa Rosalia Dr
- **Little Lamb-Lamb of God Christ** • 3717 S La Brea Ave
- **Marlton** • 4000 Santo Tomas Dr
- **New Designs (MS)** • 3770 Santa Rosalia Dr
- **Slausen Learning Center** • 4000 W Slauson Ave
- **St Bernadette Elementary** • 4196 Marlton Ave
- **Stella Middle Charter** • 2636 Mansfield Ave
- **Susan Miller Dorsey Senior High** • 3537 Farmdale Ave
- **View Park Continuation** • 4701 Rodeo Rd
- **View Park Preparatory Accelerated Charter** • 3751 W 54th St
- **View Park Preparatory Accelerated High** • 5749 Crenshaw Blvd
- **View Park Preparatory Accelerated Middle** • 5701 Crenshaw Blvd
- **Virginia Rd Elementary** • 2925 Virginia Rd
- **West Angeles Christian Academy** • 3010 S Crenshaw Blvd
- **Windsor Hills Math & Science Elementary** • 5215 Overdale Dr

Supermarkets

- **Albertsons** • 3480 S La Brea Ave
- **Albertsons** • 3901 Crenshaw Blvd
- **Ralphs** • 3670 Crenshaw Blvd
- **Ralphs** • 5080 Rodeo Rd
- **Ranch Market** • 5212 W Adams Blvd
- **Smart & Final** • 2929 Crenshaw Blvd

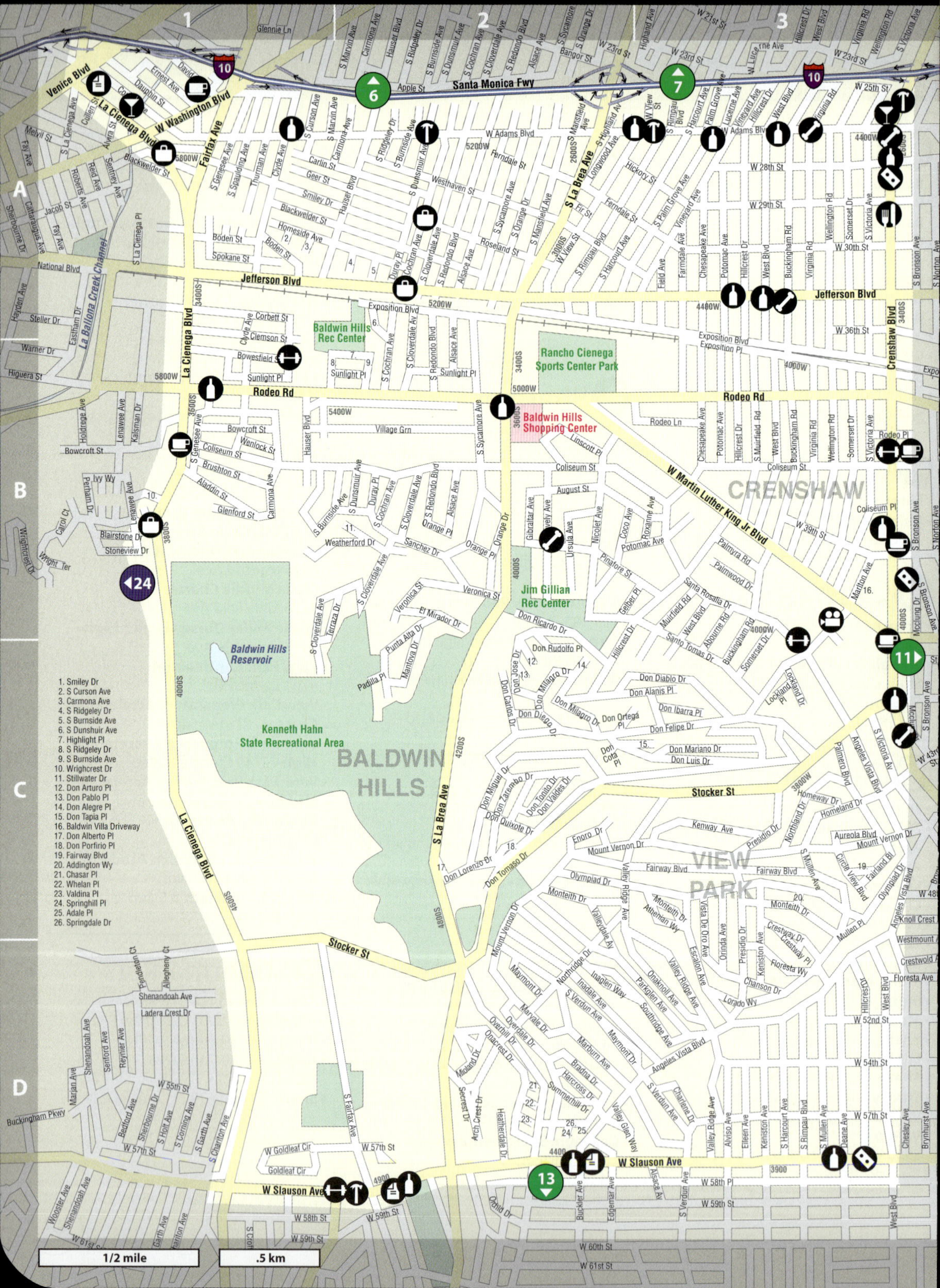

Map 10 • Baldwin Hills

1. Smiley Dr
2. S Curson Ave
3. Carmona Ave
4. S Ridgeley Dr
5. S Burnside Ave
6. S Dunshuir Ave
7. Highlight Pl
8. S Ridgeley Dr
9. S Burnside Ave
10. Wrighcrest Dr
11. Stillwater Dr
12. Don Arturo Pl
13. Don Pablo Pl
14. Don Alegre Pl
15. Don Tapia Pl
16. Baldwin Villa Driveway
17. Don Alberto Pl
18. Don Porfirio Pl
19. Fairway Blvd
20. Addington Wy
21. Chasar Pl
22. Whelan Pl
23. Valdina Pl
24. Springhill Pl
25. Adale Pl
26. Springdale Dr

1/2 mile

.5 km

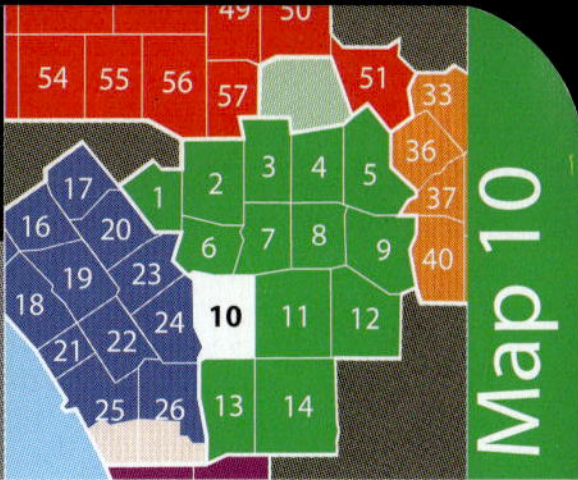

Perched atop Baldwin Hills, Kenneth Hahn State Recreation Area hovers under the radar of even long-time Angelenos, but its five miles of hiking trails, many playgrounds, and stocked fishing pond are heavily trafficked on the weekends. Of course, commuters from Hollywood, Mid-City, and elsewhere will have seen the recreation center's signage as they take the unofficial freeway alternative route to LAX: La Brea Avenue south to Century Boulevard, then west into the sunset.

Coffee

- **City Bean** • 5801 Washington Blvd
- **Coffee Beanery** • 3745 S La Brea Ave
- **Krispy Kreme Doughnuts** • 4034 Crenshaw Blvd
- **Starbucks** • 3722 Crenshaw Blvd
- **Tak's Coffee Shop** • 3870 Crenshaw Blvd

Copy Shops

- **Copies Plus** • 4401 W Slauson Ave • 323-296-1470
- **Efiximage** • 2632 S La Cienega Blvd • 310-559-2200
- **UPS Store** • 4859 W Slauson Ave • 323-291-4800

Gyms

- **24 Hour Fitness** • 5045 W Slauson Ave • 323-293-2481
- **Curves** • 3737 S Crenshaw Blvd • 323-295-3737
- **YMCA** • 3820 Santa Rosalia Dr • 323-292-9195

Hardware Stores

- **Ace** • 2620 Crenshaw Blvd • 323-733-9157
- **Home Depot** • 4925 W Slauson Ave • 323-298-4610
- **Slater Hardware** • 5365 W Adams Blvd • 323-931-0989
- **Sonora Hardware** • 4860 W Adams Blvd • 323-766-1396

Liquor Stores

- **Adam's Liquor** • 4620 W Adams Blvd
- **Arcade Liquor** • 4431 W Slauson Ave
- **Baldwin Hills Liquor** • 3629 S La Brea Ave
- **Bottle Bar Liquors** • 2642 Crenshaw Blvd
- **Cabin Liquor Store** • 5633 W Adams Blvd
- **Gubby's Liquor** • 4800 W Adams Blvd
- **Holiday Liquor** • 4966 W Adams Blvd
- **Janet's Liquor** • 4028 W Jefferson Blvd
- **Ladera Liquor** • 4834 W Slauson Ave
- **Liquor, Bank & Deli** • 3600 Stocker St
- **PG's Liquor** • 4407 W Jefferson Blvd
- **T&D Liquor** • 3860 W Slauson Ave
- **Tag's Liquor** • 3866 Crenshaw Blvd
- **Wine Cellar** • 5747 Rodeo Rd

Movie Theaters

- **AMC Magic Johnson Theatre 15** • 4020 Marlton Ave • 323-290-5900

Nightlife

- **Café Club Fais Do-Do** • 5253 W Adams Blvd • 323-954-8080
- **The Living Room** • 2636 Crenshaw Blvd • 323-735-8748
- **Mandrake** • 2692 S La Cienega Blvd • 310-837-3297

Pet Shops

- **James' Tropical Fish** • 4273 Crenshaw Blvd • 323-294-6490
- **Pet Center** • 4105 W Jefferson Blvd • 323-734-1445
- **Pets Planet** • 3651 S La Brea Ave • 323-293-1212
- **Tokyo Aquarium** • 4600 W Adams Blvd • 323-735-7553

Restaurants

- **Tasty Q** • 2959 Crenshaw Blvd • 323-735-8325

Shopping

- **Berbere Imports** • 3049 S La Cienega Blvd • 310-842-3842
- **Graphaids** • 3030 La Cienega Blvd • 310-204-1212
- **Normandie Pate** • 3022 S Cochran Ave • 323-939-5528

Video Rental

- **Home Video Club** • 2803 Crenshaw Blvd • 323-730-1322
- **Rick's Video** • 3608 W Slauson Ave • 323-299-2950
- **Video Club** • 4130 Crenshaw Blvd • 323-294-8997

1. W Prescott Ct
2. Humphrey Wk
3. Norumbega Ct
4. Rochester Cir
5. Santa Barbara Ct
6. Kansas Ave

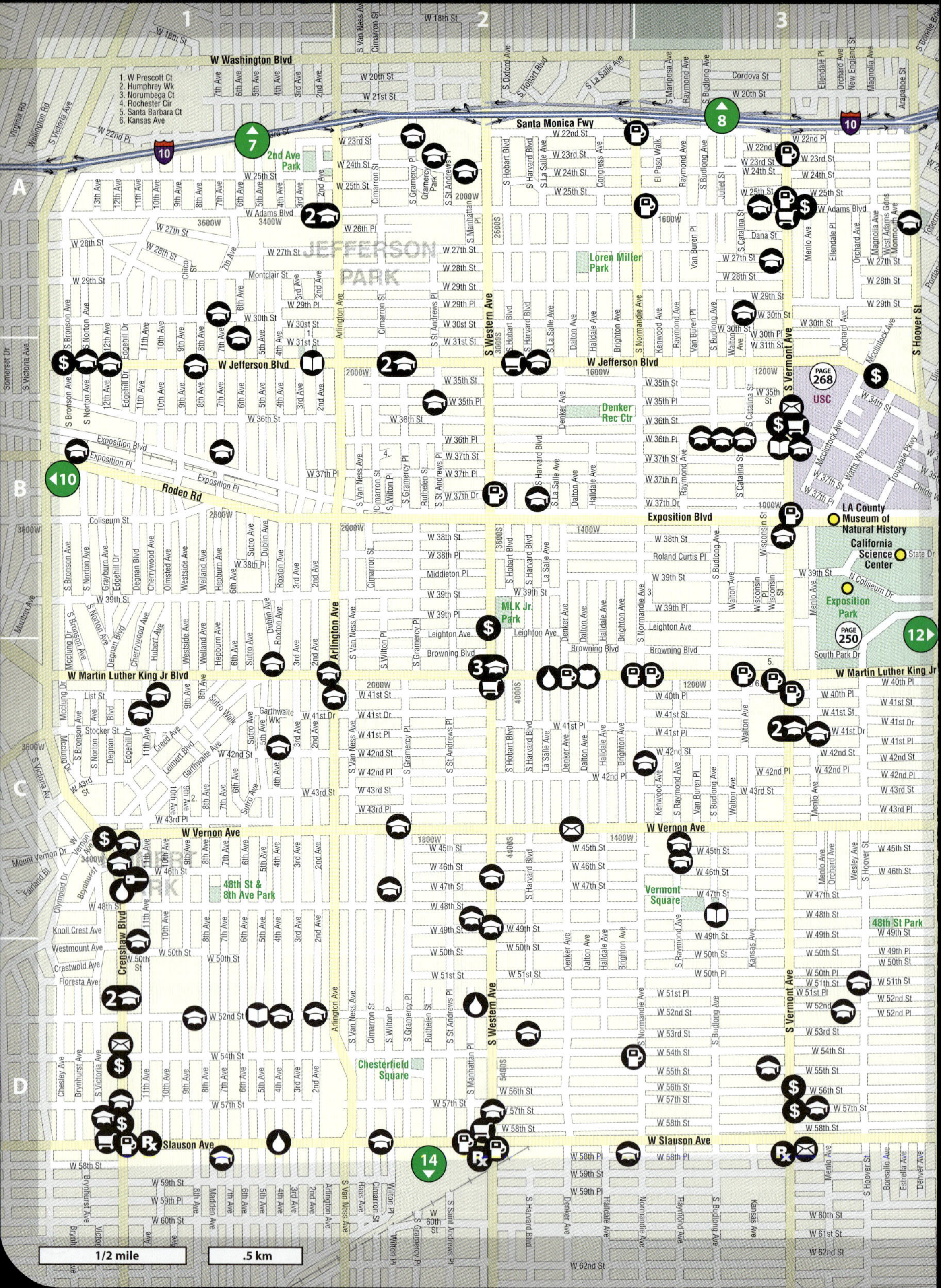

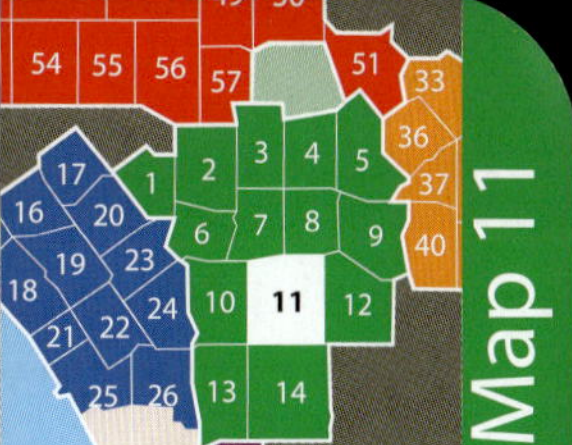

This area sees pretty heavy traffic during the college football season, when intoxicated, cardinal-and-gold clad students and alumni go to cheer on the USC Trojans. The USC campus itself is a hotbed of activity, with free concerts, lectures, and cheap movies—and local residents are encouraged to bring the family. On the southwest side is Leimert Park Village, a shopping and arts district with an emphasis on African-American culture.

Banks

- **Bank of America** • 4103 S Western Ave
- **Bank of America** • 5471 Crenshaw Blvd
- **Bank of America** • 5700 S Vermont Ave
- **Bank of America** • 985 W Jefferson Blvd
- **Citibank** • 3615 S Vermont Ave
- **Downey Savings & Loan** • 2600 S Vermont Ave
- **Union** • 3501 W Jefferson Blvd
- **US** • 5760 Crenshaw Blvd
- **Washington Mutual** • 4401 Crenshaw Blvd
- **Washington Mutual** • 5717 S Vermont Ave

Car Rental

- **Enterprise** • 4610 Crenshaw Blvd

Car Washes

- **A Moment's Notice Hand Carwash** • 4727 Crenshaw Blvd
- **Flores Hand Car Wash** • 5201 S Western Ave
- **Red Carpet Carwash** • 1620 W Martin Luther King Jr Blvd
- **Walter's Car Wash** • 2601 W Slauson Ave

Gas Stations

- **76** • 1403 W Adams Blvd
- **76** • 3774 S Western Ave
- **76** • 5816 S Western Ave
- **All Star Gas** • 1100 W Martin Luther King Jr Blvd
- **Arco** • 1355 W Martin Luther King Jr Blvd
- **Arco** • 3775 S Vermont St
- **Arco** • 5407 S Normandie Ave
- **Arco** • 5804 Crenshaw Blvd
- **Chevron** • 1691 W Adams Blvd
- **Chevron** • 2202 S Vermont Ave
- **Independent** • 1010 W Martin Luther King Jr Blvd
- **Independent** • 1404 W Martin Luther King Jr Blvd
- **Independent** • 1515 W Martin Luther King Jr Blvd
- **Valero** • 2217 S Normandie Ave

Landmarks

- **California Science Center** • 700 State Dr
- **Exposition Park** • Menlo Ave & S Park Dr
- **LA County Museum of Natural History** • 900 Exposition Blvd

Libraries

- **Angeles Mesa** • 2700 W 52nd St • 323-292-4328
- **Exposition Park Branch** • 3665 S Vermont Ave • 323-732-0169
- **Jefferson Branch** • 2211 W Jefferson Blvd • 323-734-8573
- **Vermont Square Branch** • 1201 W 48th St • 323-290-7405

Pharmacies

- **CVS** • 5822 S Vermont Ave • 323-750-5222
- **Rite-Aid** • 3230 W Slauson Ave • 323-295-9661
- **Walgreens** • 1800 W Slauson Ave • 323-292-1941

Police

- **Los Angeles Police Dept** • 1546 W Martin Luther King Jr Blvd • 213-485-2582

Post Offices

- **US Post Office** • 1515 W Vernon Ave • 800-275-8777
- **US Post Office** • 3585 S Vermont Ave • 800-275-8777
- **US Post Office** • 5472 Crenshaw Blvd • 800-275-8777
- **US Post Office** • 5832 S Vermont Ave • 323-778-5015

Schools

- **24th St EEC** • 2101 W 24th St
- **24th St Elementary** • 2055 W 24th St
- **36th St EEC** • 3556 S St Andrews Pl
- **37th St EEC** • 1204 W 36th Pl
- **42nd St Elementary** • 4231 4th Ave
- **52nd St EEC** • 901 W 52nd St
- **52nd St Elementary** • 816 W 51st St
- **6th Ave EEC** • 3124 7th Ave
- **Al Madinah** • 3510 Exposition Pl
- **Angeles Mesa Elementary** • 2611 W 52nd St
- **Audubon Middle** • 4120 11th Ave
- **Bright Elementary** • 1771 W 36th St
- **Burton Green** • 3787 S Vermont Ave
- **Celerity Nascent Charter** • 3417 W Jefferson Blvd
- **College-Ready Academy High** • 1729 W Martin Luther King Jr Blvd
- **College-Ready Middle Academy** • 2023 S Union Ave
- **Community Harvest Charter** • 3202 W Adams Blvd
- **Concord** • 2828 W Jefferson Blvd
- **Creative Learning Center** • 2320 W Martin Luther King Jr Blvd
- **Crenshaw Arts-Technology High** • 5125 Crenshaw Blvd
- **Crenshaw Montessori Academy** • 4914 Crenshaw Blvd
- **Crenshaw Senior High** • 5010 11th Ave
- **Crenshaw Tot Academy** • 5148 Crenshaw Blvd
- **Crescendo Charter** • 4900 S Western Ave
- **Divine Providence Kindergarten** • 2620 Monmouth Ave
- **Dorothy Brown** • 3502 S Normandie Ave
- **Foshay Learning Center** • 3751 S Harvard Blvd
- **Golden Day** • 4476 Crenshaw Blvd
- **Holy Name of Jesus Elementary** • 1955 W Jefferson Blvd
- **John W Mack Elementary** • 3020 S Catalina St
- **Joseph Pomeroy Widney High** • 2302 S Gramercy Pl
- **Just Beginning** • 1712 W Jefferson Blvd
- **Leon Garr Learning Institute** • 5101 S Western Ave
- **Little Citizens Elementary** • 3672 Seventh Ave
- **Little Citizens Westside Academy** • 4256 S Western Ave
- **Manual Arts Community Adult** • 4131 S Vermont Ave
- **Manual Arts Senior High** • 4131 S Vermont Ave
- **Marcus Garvey** • 2916 W Slauson Ave
- **Marie Fegan** • 2069 W Slauson Ave
- **Martin Luther King Jr Elementary** • 3989 S Hobart Blvd
- **Menlo Ave Elementary** • 4156 Menlo Ave
- **Mid-City Magnet** • 3150 W Adams Blvd
- **Missionette Christian Academy** • 1915 W Vernon Ave
- **Mount Calvary Christian** • 1033 W 55th St
- **Nativity** • 943 W 57th St
- **New Heights Charter** • 4126 Arlington Ave
- **Normandie Ave Elementary** • 4505 S Raymond Ave
- **Normandie EEC** • 4407 S Raymond Ave
- **Owens Community Day** • 2400 W 54th St
- **Parks/Huerta Primary** • 1020 W 58th Pl
- **Perry-Meadows Learning Center** • 1986 W Jefferson Blvd
- **Sixth Ave Elementary** • 3109 6th Ave
- **Spirit Child Development Center** • 3651 S Vermont Ave
- **St Agnes Parish** • 1478 W Adams Blvd
- **St Cecilia Elementary** • 4224 S Normandie Ave
- **Testimonial Christian** • 5701 S Western Ave
- **Today's Fresh Start Charter** • 4514 Crenshaw Blvd
- **Transfiguration** • 4020 Roxton Ave
- **University of Southern California** • Exposition Blvd & S Vermont Ave
- **Vermont Ave Elementary** • 1435 W 27th St
- **Vernon R Byrd Child Development** • 4724 S Wilton Pl
- **View Park Preparatory Accelerated Charter High** • 5701 Crenshaw Blvd
- **View Park Preparatory Accelerated Charter Middle** • 5749 Crenshaw Blvd
- **WDM Islamic Learning Center/SCM** • 1758 W 49th St
- **Weemes Elementary** • 1260 W 36th Pl
- **Western Ave Elementary** • 1724 W 53rd St
- **Westside Academy / Little Citizens** • 3411 12th Ave
- **Whitney Young Continuation** • 3051 W 52nd St

Supermarkets

- **Food 4 Less** • 1748 S Jefferson Blvd
- **Food 4 Less** • 1820 W Slauson Ave
- **Ralphs** • 2600 S Vermont Ave
- **Ralphs** • 3300 W Slauson Ave
- **Ralphs** • 4030 S Western Ave
- **Smart & Final** • 3607 S Vermont Ave

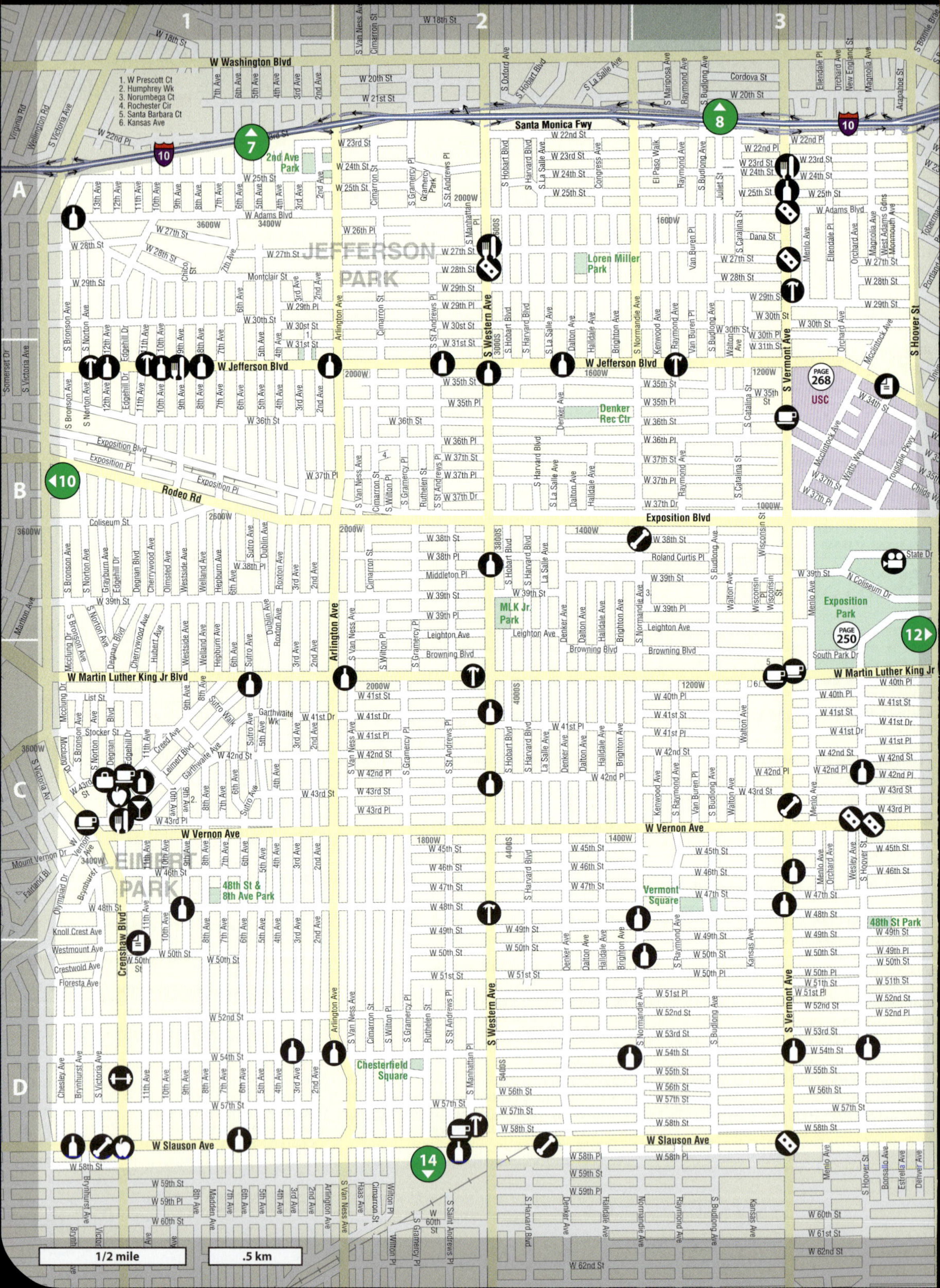

1. W Prescott Ct
2. Humphrey Wk
3. Norumbega Ct
4. Rochester Cir
5. Santa Barbara Ct
6. Kansas Ave
W Washington Blvd
Santa Monica Fwy
W Jefferson Blvd
Exposition Blvd
W Martin Luther King Jr Blvd
W Vernon Ave
W Slauson Ave
Crenshaw Blvd
Arlington Ave
S Western Ave
S Vermont Ave
S Hoover St
Rodeo Rd
JEFFERSON PARK
LEIMERT PARK
USC
2nd Ave Park
Loren Miller Park
Denker Rec Ctr
MLK Jr. Park
Exposition Park
48th St & 8th Ave Park
Vermont Square
48th St Park
Chesterfield Square
PAGE 268
PAGE 250
1/2 mile
.5 km

Sundries / Entertainment

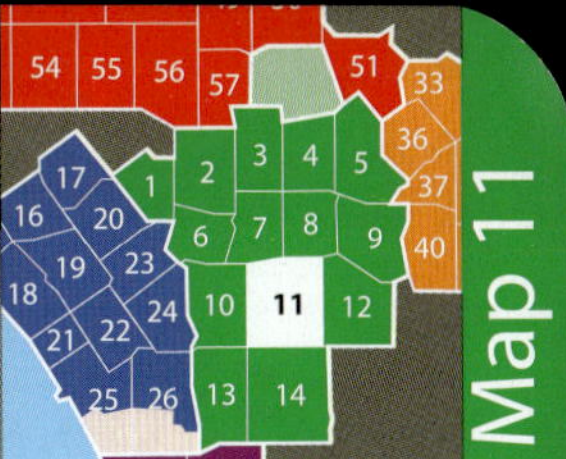

Harold & Belle's Restaurant may have the best Cajun and Creole cooking this side of the Mississippi: Go for the gumbo. However, it's only one of many culinary choices in the Leimert Park Village area, the heart of this community. This area includes a farmers' market and African-American specialty shops such as Zambezi Bazaar. Adjacent to USC, Exposition Park features an admirable rose garden.

Coffee

- **Boba Loca** • 3617 S Vermont Ave
- **Lucy Florence Coffeehouse** • 3351 W 43rd St
- **Starbucks** • 1005 W Martin Luther King Jr Blvd
- **Starbucks** • 1850 W Slauson Ave
- **Starbucks** • 4371 Crenshaw Blvd
- **Swiss Valley Ice Cream Coffee Shop** • 1023 W Martin Luther King Jr Blvd

Copy Shops

- **Awesome Print Copy & Graphic Design** • 4936 Crenshaw Blvd • 323-292-0352
- **Copies Ink** • 907 W Jefferson Blvd • 213-744-1511

Farmers Markets

- **Leimert Park Village (Sat, 9 am–2 pm)** • W 43rd St & Degnan Blvd
- **Los Angeles - Harambee (Sat, 10 am–4 pm)** • Crenshaw Blvd & W Slauson Ave
- **St Agnes Catholic Church (Wed; Jun–Aug, 1 pm–6 pm; Sept-May, 2 pm–5 pm)** • 1432 W Adams Blvd

Gyms

- **Black Diamond Fitness** • 5436 Crenshaw Blvd • 323-291-0294

Hardware Stores

- **Bravo's Hardware** • 1439 W Jefferson Blvd • 323-735-3777
- **Home Depot** • 1830 W Slauson Ave • 323-292-1397
- **J&J Hardware** • 1755 W Martin Luther King Jr Blvd • 323-290-0909
- **Peterson's True Value** • 4823 S Western Ave • 323-292-5310
- **RPM Hardware & Lumber** • 3001 W Jefferson Blvd • 323-737-6282
- **Tak's Hardware** • 3318 W Jefferson Blvd • 323-732-6966
- **True Value** • 2929 S Vermont Ave • 323-734-4488

Liquor Stores

- **7 Kings Liquor** • 4051 Leimert Blvd
- **ABIC Liquor** • 3115 S Western Ave
- **Borigol Liquor** • 2833 W Jefferson Blvd
- **Century Liquor** • 2115 W Jefferson Blvd
- **Century Liquor** • 2301 W 54th St
- **Century Liquor** • 3894 S Western Ave
- **G&I Liquor** • 3504 W Slauson Ave
- **Gee-Gee Liquors** • 5028 S Normandie Ave
- **Hubert's Liquor** • 4307 Leimert Blvd
- **Jesse's Liquor** • 2527 W 54th St
- **John's Liquor** • 2428 S Vermont Ave
- **Kenny's Liquor** • 3104 W 48th St
- **LA Liquor** • 1403 W 54th St
- **Lucky Liquor** • 2109 W Martin Luther King Jr Blvd
- **Marvin's Liquor & Deli** • 1650 W Jefferson Blvd
- **Print Liquor** • 5400 S Hoover St
- **Rogo Liquors** • 4626 S Vermont Ave
- **Saki Liquor** • 3300 W Jefferson Blvd
- **Slauson Liquor** • 2825 W Slauson Ave
- **St Andrew's Liquor** • 1894 W Jefferson Blvd
- **T's Liquor** • 3019 W Jefferson Blvd
- **Two & One Liquor Store** • 4829 S Normandie Ave
- **West-Vern Liquor** • 4381 S Western Ave
- **Wine Barrel Liquors** • 4250 S Hoover St

Movie Theaters

- **California Science Center IMAX** • 700 State Dr • 213-744-7400

Nightlife

- **Babe's Ricky Inn** • 4339 Leimert Blvd • 323-295-9112

Pet Shops

- **34 Pet Shop** • 3434 W Slauson Ave • 323-291-6115
- **Exotic Fish & Birds** • 1279 W 38th St • 323-742-6454
- **Pet Slauson** • 1680 W Slauson Ave • 323-751-7924
- **Tong's Tropical Fish & Pets** • 4327 S Vermont Ave • 323-235-4370

Restaurants

- **Aunt Rosa Lee's Mississippi Soul Food** • 2781 S Western Ave • 323-733-8586
- **Harold & Belle's** • 2920 W Jefferson Blvd • 323-735-3376
- **La Barca** • 2414 S Vermont Ave • 323-735-6567
- **Phillip's Barbecue** • 4307 Leimert Blvd • 323-292-7613

Shopping

- **Zambezi Bazaar** • 4334 Degnan Blvd • 323-299-6383

Video Rental

- **Alpha Video** • 807 W Vernon Ave • 323-233-8930
- **Blockbuster** • 728 Vernon Ave • 323-238-0146
- **Echo Video & Mini Mart** • 2701 S Western Ave • 323-735-7411
- **Johnny's Video** • 2709 S Vermont Ave • 323-733-0862
- **Omni Video** • 5862 S Vermont Ave • 323-759-7100
- **Video World** • 2604 S Vermont Ave • 323-733-1877

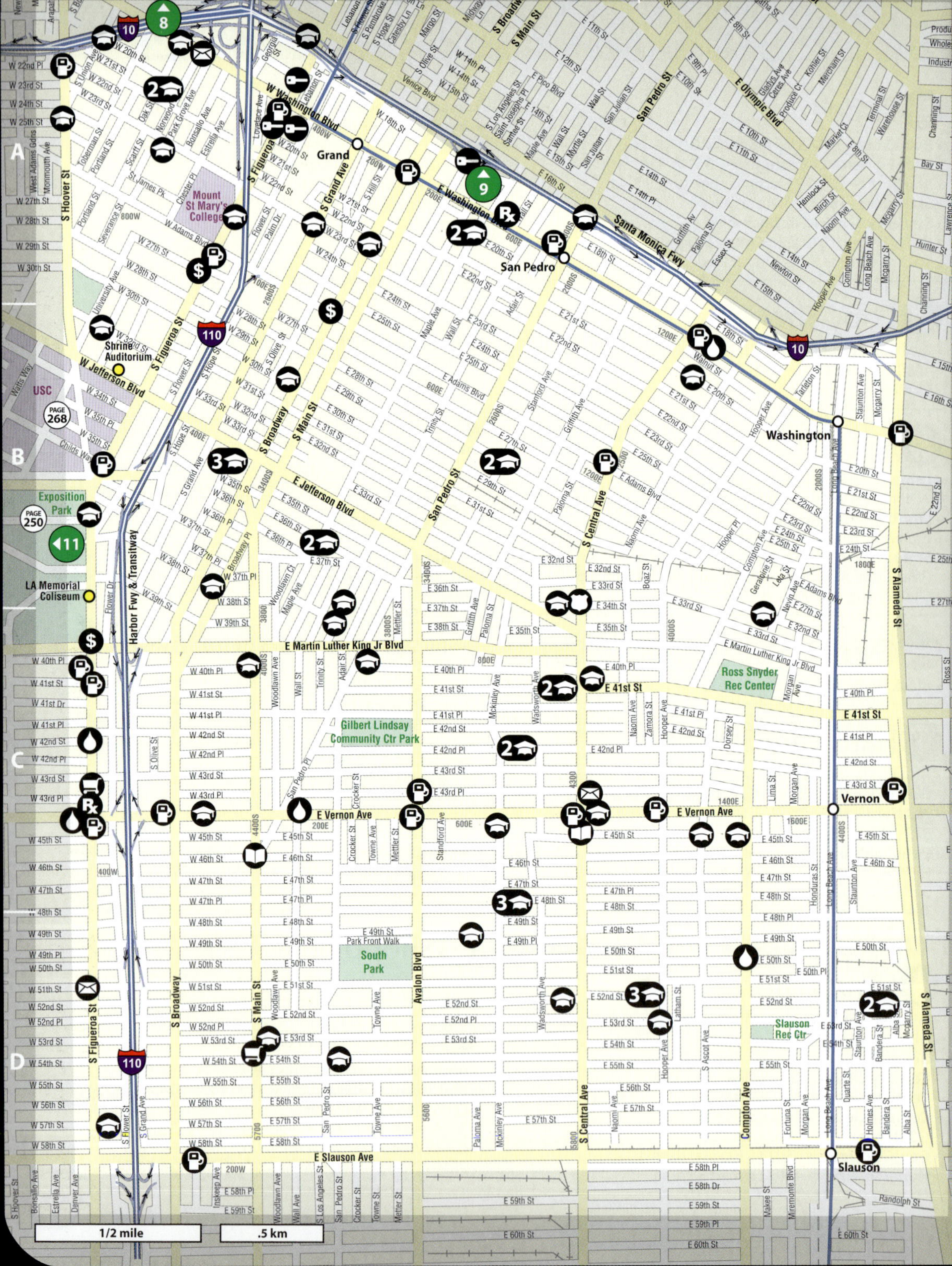
Pico
Grand
San Pedro
Washington
Vernon
Slauson
USC
Shrine Auditorium
Exposition Park
LA Memorial Coliseum
Mount St Mary's College
Gilbert Lindsay Community Ctr Park
South Park
Ross Snyder Rec Center
Slauson Rec Ctr
Santa Monica Fwy
Harbor Fwy & Transitway
PAGE 268
PAGE 250
1/2 mile
.5 km

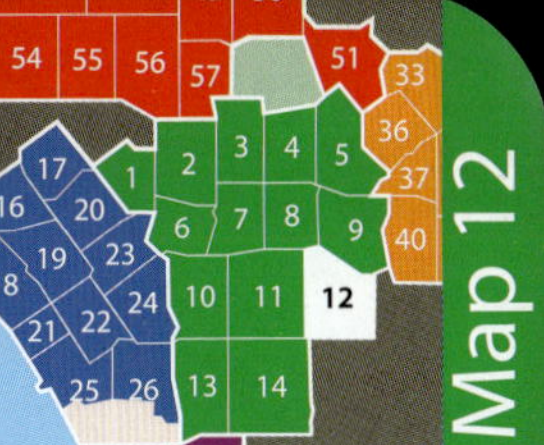

This is one of those edgy areas where an aging urban neighborhood rubs up against the well-manicured lawns and sprawling edifices of a university campus. Downtown's new developments are also slowly encroaching on the neighborhood, home to a large Latino and African-American population. The area's reputation for crime is still accurate, but programs through USC and non-profits are working to make it a safer place for families and kids.

Banks

- **Bank of America** • 2703 S Figueroa St
- **Broadway Federal** • 4001 S Figueroa St
- **Wells Fargo** • 141 W Adams Blvd

Car Rental

- **Downtown Rent-a-Car** • 1740 S Los Angeles St
- **Enterprise** • 1801 S Figueroa St
- **Enterprise** • 1944 S Figueroa St
- **Midway Car Rental** • 2001 S Figueroa St

Car Washes

- **Figueroa Car Wash** • 4200 S Figueroa St
- **La Hand Car Wash** • 181 E Vernon Ave
- **Martinez Hand Car Wash** • 5000 Compton Ave
- **Shell** • 1317 E Washington Blvd
- **Shell** • 4403 S Figueroa St

Gas Stations

- **76** • 1900 S Broadway
- **76** • 505 W Vernon Ave
- **Arco** • 1800 E Slauson Ave
- **Arco** • 2211 S Hoover St
- **Arco** • 4321 S Alameda St
- **Arco** • 4424 S Central Ave
- **Arco** • 4442 S Avalon Blvd
- **Chevron** • 3584 S Figueroa St
- **Chevron** • 4000 S Figueroa St
- **Chevron** • 525 W Washington Blvd
- **Chevron** • 650 E Washington Blvd
- **Exxon** • 4368 Avalon Blvd
- **Mobil** • 1690 S Alameda St
- **Mobil** • 254 W Slauson Ave
- **Mobil** • 2620 S Figueroa St
- **Mobil** • 315 W Vernon Ave
- **Shell** • 1317 E Washington Blvd
- **Shell** • 4403 S Figueroa St
- **Valero** • 1285 E Vernon Ave
- **Valero** • 2603 S Central Ave

Landmarks

- **LA Memorial Coliseum** • 3911 S Figueroa St
- **Shrine Auditorium** • 665 W Jefferson Blvd

Libraries

- **Junipero Serra Branch** • 4607 S Main St • 323-234-1685
- **Vernon Branch** • 4504 S Central Ave • 323-234-9106

Pharmacies

- **Rite-Aid** • 4322 S Figueroa St • 323-235-3535
- **Rite-Aid** • 446 E Washington Blvd • 213-747-9581

Police

- **Los Angeles Police Dept** • 3400 S Central Ave • 310-846-6547

Post Offices

- **US Post Office** • 4352 S Central Ave • 800-275-8777
- **US Post Office** • 5115 S Figueroa St • 800-275-8777
- **US Post Office** • 819 W Washington Blvd • 800-275-8777

Schools

- **20th St Elementary** • 1353 E 20th St
- **28th St EEC** • 747 E 28th St
- **28th St Elementary** • 2807 Stanford Ave
- **49th St Elementary** • 750 E 49th St
- **Accelerated Elementary** • 119 E 37th St
- **Animo Film & Theater Arts Charter** • 2501 S Hoover St
- **Animo Jackie Robinson** • 3500 S Hill St
- **Animo Justice Charter High** • 3500 S Hill St
- **Animo Pat Brown Charter** • 3801 Broadway Pl
- **Animo Ralph Bunche Charter** • 892 E 48th St
- **Annenberg (Wallis) High** • 4000 S Main St
- **Arco Iris Primary Center** • 4504 Ascot Ave
- **Ascot Elementary** • 1447 E 45th St
- **Aurora Elementary** • 1050 E 52nd Pl
- **Central LA Area New Middle** • 3500 S Hill St
- **College Ready Academy Senior High #4** • 644 W 17th St
- **Downtown Value** • 950 W Washington Blvd
- **Dr Theodore T Alexander Jr Science Center** • 3737 S Figueroa St
- **Figueroa Christian Day Care** • 455 W 57th St
- **George Washington Carver Middle** • 4410 McKinley Ave
- **Harmony Elementary** • 899 E 42nd St
- **Harmony Elementary State Preschool** • 898 E 42nd St
- **Holmes Avenue Elementary** • 5108 Holmes Ave
- **Holmes EEC** • 1810 E 52nd St
- **Hooper EEC** • 1224 E 52nd St
- **Hooper Elementary** • 1225 E 52nd St
- **Hooper New Primary Center** • 1280 E 52nd St
- **Jefferson New Continuation High** • 1921 Maple Ave
- **John Adams Middle** • 151 W 30th St
- **Johnson Community Day** • 333 E 54th St
- **La Senda Antigua Charter** • 631 E Adams Blvd
- **Lanterman High** • 2328 St James Pl
- **Lizarraga Elementary** • 401 E 40th Pl
- **Los Angeles Academy Middle** • 644 E 56th St
- **Main St Elementary** • 129 E 53rd St
- **Maple Primary Center** • 3601 Maple Ave
- **Mount St Mary's College—Doheny Campus** • 10 Chester Pl
- **Nevin Elementary** • 1569 E 32nd St
- **Norwood EEC** • 855 W 21st St
- **Norwood Elementary** • 2020 Oak St
- **Orthopaedic Hospital Medical Magnet High** • 300 W 23rd St
- **Page Multicultural Learning Academy** • 216 W Vernon Ave
- **Richard Merkin Middle Academy** • 2023 S Union Ave
- **Roberti EEC** • 1156 E Vernon Ave
- **San Pedro St Elementary** • 1635 S San Pedro St
- **Santee Education Complex** • 1921 Maple Ave
- **St Odilia** • 5300 Hooper Ave
- **St Vincent Elementary** • 2333 S Figueroa St
- **Star Christian** • 2120 Estella Ave
- **Synergy Charter** • 1010 E 34th St
- **Thomas Jefferson Community Adult** • 1319 E 41st St
- **Thomas Jefferson Senior High** • 1319 E 41st St
- **Trinity EEC** • 3816 Trinity St
- **Trinity St Elementary** • 3736 Trinity St
- **USC Performing Arts** • 822 W 32nd St
- **Victory Baptist Day** • 4802 McKinley Ave
- **Victory Baptist Day Elementary** • 892 E 48th St
- **Wadsworth EEC** • 1047 E 41st St
- **Wadsworth Elementary** • 981 E 41st St
- **West Vernon Ave Elementary** • 4312 S Grand Ave

Supermarkets

- **Food 4 Less** • 5318 S Main St
- **Ralphs** • 4360 S Figueroa St

Map 12 • South Central East

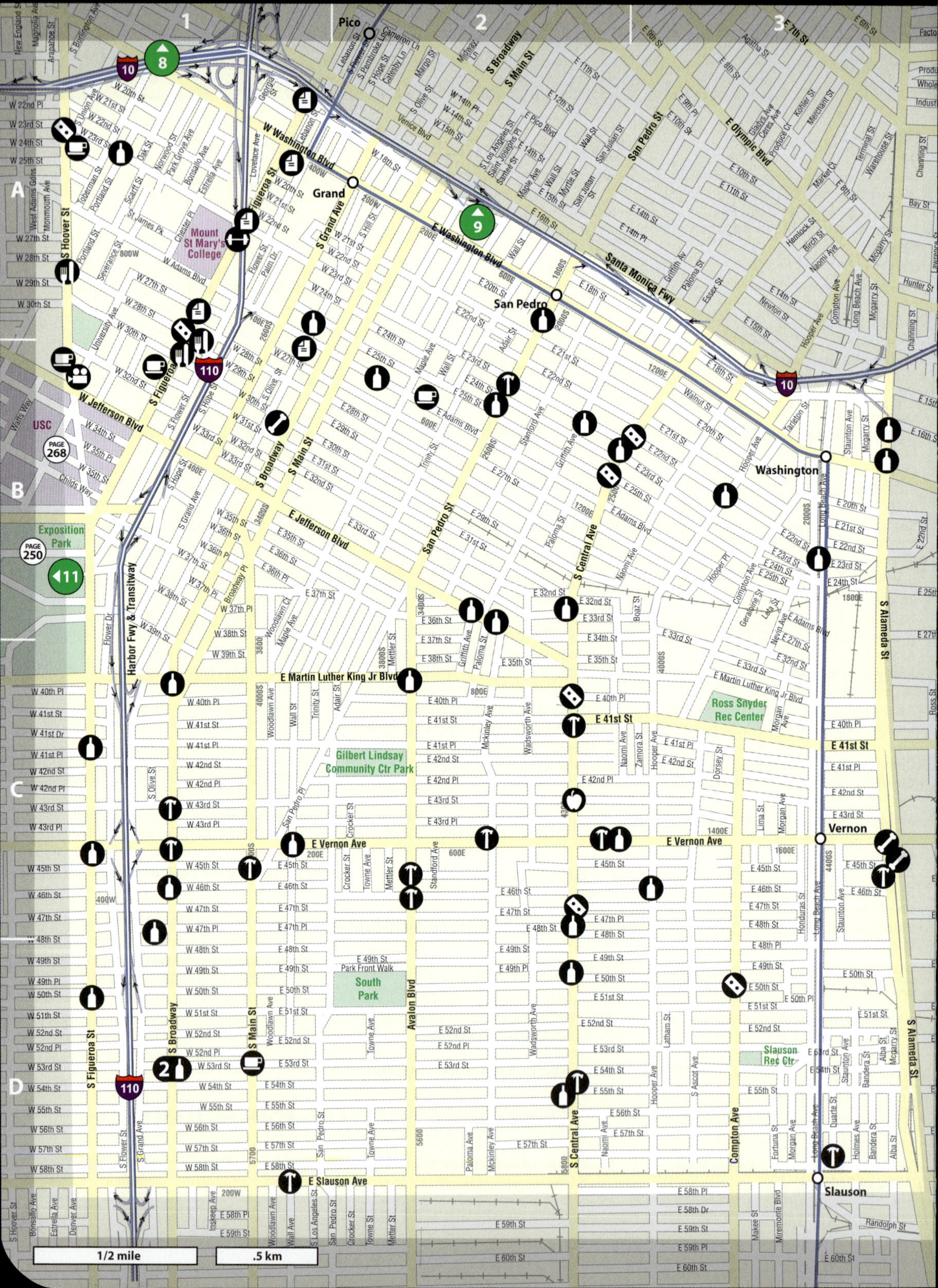

Pico
Grand
San Pedro
Washington
Vernon
Slauson
Mount St Mary's College
USC
PAGE 268
Exposition Park
PAGE 250
Gilbert Lindsay Community Ctr Park
South Park
Ross Snyder Rec Center
Slauson Rec Ctr
Santa Monica Fwy
Harbor Fwy & Transitway
W Washington Blvd
E Washington Blvd
W Jefferson Blvd
E Jefferson Blvd
E Martin Luther King Jr Blvd
E Vernon Ave
E Slauson Ave
E 41st St
S Figueroa St
S Broadway
S Main St
S Grand Ave
San Pedro St
Avalon Blvd
S Central Ave
Compton Ave
Long Beach Ave
S Alameda St
S Hoover St
E Olympic Blvd
1/2 mile
.5 km

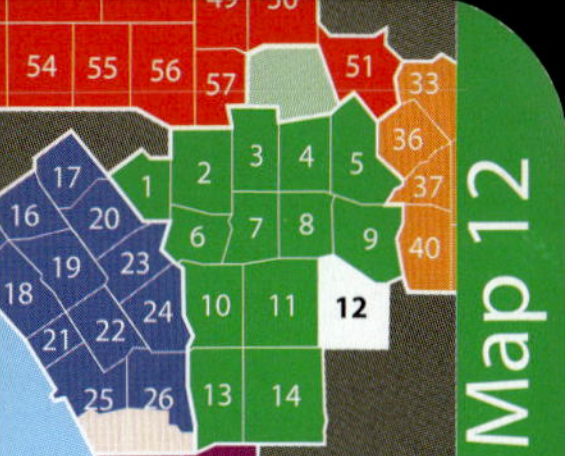

The 29th Street Café is an adorable and slightly vanilla nod to the neighborhood's history, housed in the Davis House which was built in 1896. Kids and grown-ups can test their skateboarding skills at the Gilbert Lindsay Skate Park on 42nd Place. The Shrine Auditorium sees it fair share of awards events, concerts, and celebrities. And during the off-season, the Coliseum and Sports Arena act as venues for some of the city's biggest concerts and sports events. Check www.lacoliseum.com for the events calendar.

Coffee

- **Coffee Factory** • 3014 S Figueroa St
- **Coffee Times Donuts** • 5333 S Main St
- **Lady Effie's Tea Parlor** • 453 E Adams Blvd
- **Ragazzi Room** • 2316 S Union Ave
- **Starbucks** • 3303 S Hoover St

Copy Shops

- **FedEx Kinko's** • 2723 S Figueroa St • 213-747-8341
- **Office Depot** • 2020 Figueroa St • 213-741-0576
- **Pip Printing** • 2600 S Hill St • 213-749-5321
- **Staples** • 1701 S Figueroa St • 213-746-6330
- **UPS Store** • 2202 S Figueroa St • 213-749-1249

Farmers Markets

- **Los Angeles Central Ave (Sat, 9 am–1 pm)** • 43rd St & Central Ave

Gyms

- **Curves** • 2268 Figueroa St • 213-746-3488

Hardware Stores

- **Alameda Hardware** • 4501 S Alameda St • 323-235-5940
- **Avalon Tools & Supplies** • 4514 Avalon Blvd • 323-232-6516
- **Barbara's Hardware** • 4609 Avalon Blvd • 323-232-4514
- **E&J Tools** • 1717 E Slauson Ave • 323-585-6004
- **Flores Hardware** • 4121 S Central Ave • 323-234-3623
- **Garcia Hardware** • 2414 S San Pedro St • 213-749-0992
- **Hardware Express** • 823 E Vernon Ave • 323-235-1722
- **Jalisco Hardware** • 5423 S Central Ave • 323-231-3340
- **Los Perritos Tools** • 4752 S Broadway • 323-232-1602
- **Main Building Materials** • 4308 S Broadway • 323-235-6253
- **Marce's** • 4500 S Main St • 323-233-9320
- **Villanueva's Hardware** • 1177 E Vernon Ave • 323-234-6340
- **Workman Industries** • 200 E Slauson Ave • 323-234-6421

Liquor Stores

- **A&J Liquors** • 200 E Vernon Ave
- **A&J Liquors** • 2527 S Hill St
- **Ace Liquors** • 2525 Griffith Ave
- **Arby's Liquor** • 5501 S Central Ave
- **Bestway Liquors** • 4157 S Figueroa St
- **Buddy's Liqour** • 3231 S Central Ave
- **C&C Liquor** • 4606 S Broadway
- **Central Liquor Market** • 5000 S Central Ave
- **Elisa's Liquor Store** • 2312 Long Beach Ave
- **Empire Liquor Store** • 1100 E 22nd St
- **Express Liquor** • 1601 S Alameda St
- **Gordon's Liquors & Wines** • 842 E Jefferson Blvd
- **Harry's Corner** • 2315 S Central Ave
- **JKO Liquor** • 255 E Adams Blvd
- **Johnny's Liquor** • 4000 S Broadway
- **Koko's Liquor** • 5029 S Figueroa St
- **Lee's Liquor** • 934 W 23rd St
- **Los Altos Liquor** • 4625 Hooper Ave
- **Louie's Liquor** • 908 E Jefferson Blvd
- **Maple Liquor** • 2401 S San Pedro St
- **Peewee Liquor** • 5323 S Broadway
- **Prince Liquor** • 1161 E Vernon Ave
- **Reggie's Liquor & Junior Market** • 4426 S Figueroa St
- **SH Liquor Market** • 4006 Avalon Blvd
- **Steve's Liquor** • 1501 E 22nd St
- **Toni's Liquor & Deli** • 5955 West Blvd
- **Wally's Liquor** • 1955 S San Pedro St
- **Webb's Liquor Store & Sundries** • 4762 S Central Ave

Movie Theaters

- **Flagship University Village 3** • 3323 S Hoover St • 213-748-6321

Pet Shops

- **Bark Avenue** • 3016 S Hill St • 213-748-7485
- **Giron's Pet Store** • 4501 S Alameda St • 323-231-4360
- **Ramirez Pet Shop** • 4433 S Alameda St • 323-846-6805

Restaurants

- **29th Street Café** • 2827 S Hoover St • 213-746-2929
- **Chano's Drive-In** • 3000 S Figueroa St • 213-747-3944
- **Pasta Roma** • 2827 S Figueroa St • 213-742-0303

Video Rental

- **Central Video** • 2204 S Central Ave • 213-749-7716
- **Compton Video** • 5035 Compton Ave • 323-233-2822
- **Danny Boy Video** • 2506 S Central Ave • 323-234-4412
- **Eve's Video** • 4068 S Central Ave • 323-234-0473
- **Hernandez Video** • 4754 S Central Ave • 323-231-0213
- **Little Hollywood Video** • 1105 W 23rd St • 213-741-1303
- **Video Hits** • 2813 S Figueroa St • 213-748-2928

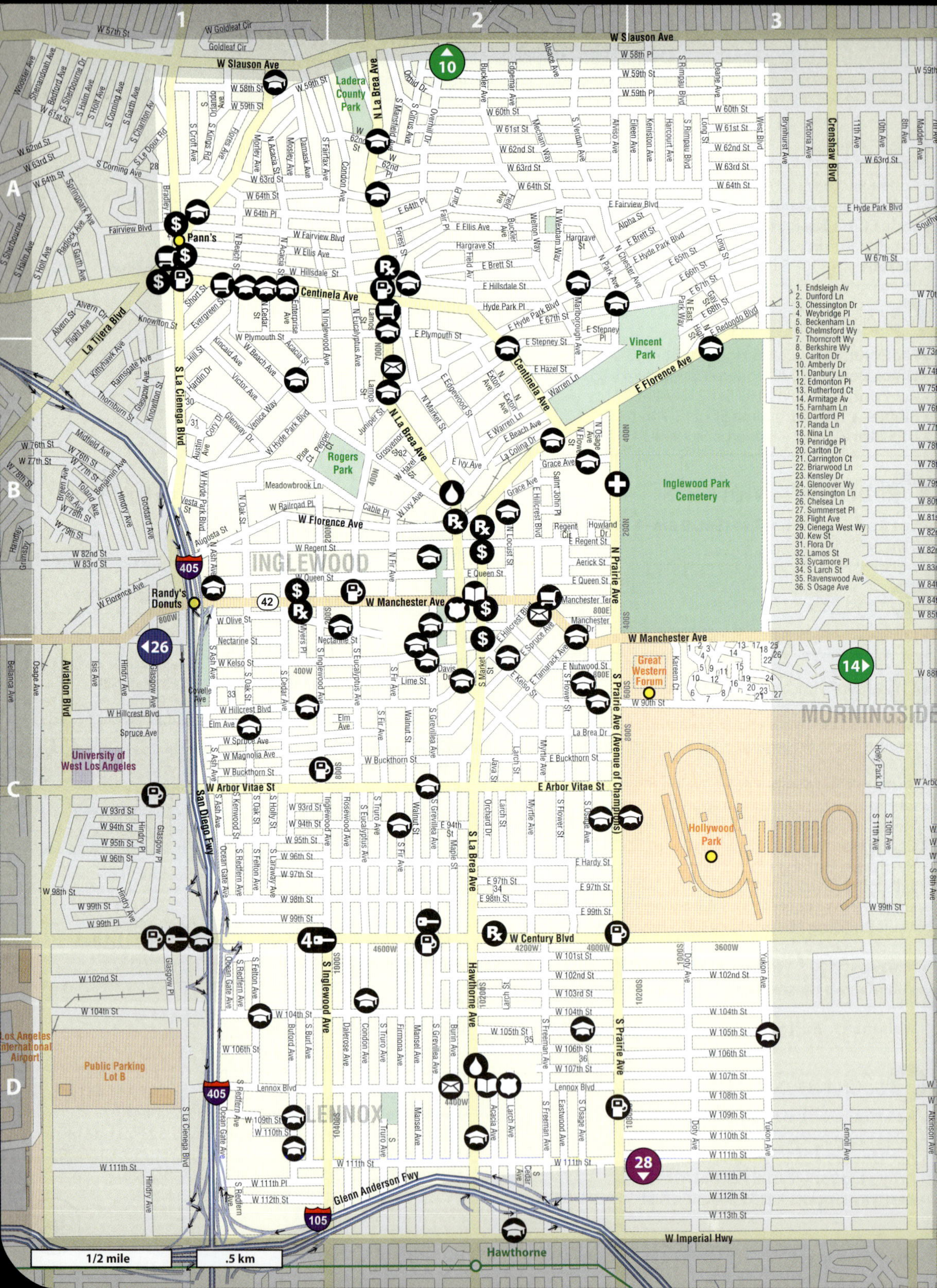

Map 13 • Inglewood

INGLEWOOD

LENNOX

MORNINGSIDE

Ladera County Park

Rogers Park

Vincent Park

Inglewood Park Cemetery

Great Western Forum

Hollywood Park

University of West Los Angeles

Los Angeles International Airport

Public Parking Lot B

Pann's

Randy's Donuts

Hawthorne

San Diego Fwy

Glenn Anderson Fwy

1. Endsleigh Av
2. Dunford Ln
3. Chessington Dr
4. Weybridge Pl
5. Beckenham Ln
6. Chelmsford Wy
7. Thorncroft Wy
8. Berkshire Wy
9. Carlton Dr
10. Amberly Dr
11. Danbury Ln
12. Edmonton Pl
13. Rutherford Ct
14. Armitage Av
15. Farnham Ln
16. Dartford Pl
17. Randa Ln
18. Nina Ln
19. Penridge Pl
20. Carlton Dr
21. Carrington Ct
22. Briarwood Ln
23. Kensley Dr
24. Glenoover Wy
25. Kensington Ln
26. Chelsea Ln
27. Summerset Pl
28. Flight Ave
29. Cienega West Wy
30. Kew St
31. Flora Dr
32. Lamos St
33. Sycamore Pl
34. S Larch St
35. Ravenswood Ave
36. S Osage Ave

1/2 mile

.5 km

Essentials

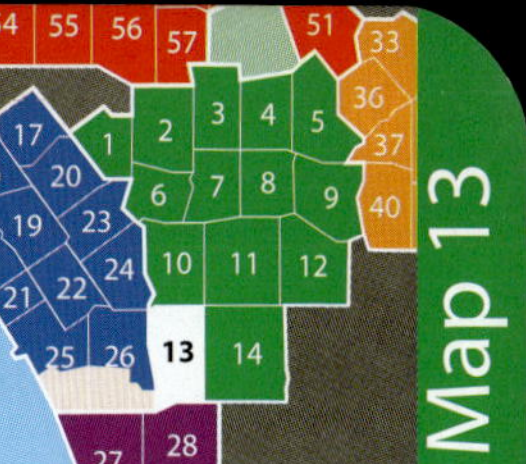

While North Inglewood's charming, sylvan avenues played stunt double for the Yourtown, Midwest backdrop of Wayne's World, much of the city's residual grittiness reflects the loss of its adored Lakers to the Staples Center (Map 9). But if former Laker Magic Johnson has his way, Inglewood will be just fine. Johnson gets the assist for bringing Starbucks, TGI Friday's, and a burst of commercial energy to the area.

Banks

- **Bank of America** • 330 E Manchester Blvd
- **Bank of America** • 6611 La Cienega Westway St
- **Broadway Federal** • 170 N Market St
- **Downey Savings & Loan** • 5245 Centinela Ave
- **Union** • 6719 La Tijera Blvd
- **US** • 500 E Manchester Blvd
- **Wells Fargo** • 400 S Market St

Car Rental

- **Arrow Rent A Car** • 4505 W Century Blvd
- **GA Car Rental** • 4840 W Century Blvd
- **Priceless Car Rental** • 4831 W Century Blvd

Car Washes

- **Inglewood Car Wash** • 320 N La Brea Ave
- **Lennox Car Wash** • 10709 Hawthorne Blvd

Gas Stations

- **76** • 400 W Arbor Vitae
- **76** • 4520 W Century Blvd
- **76** • 633 W Manchester Blvd
- **Chevron** • 4015 W Century Blvd
- **Independent** • 1244 S Inglewood Ave
- **Independent** • 145 E Manchester Blvd
- **Mobil** • 1079 N La Brea Ave
- **Mobil** • 5215 W Centinela Ave
- **Thrifty** • 4130 W Century Blvd
- **Valero** • 10800 S Prairie Blvd

Emergency Rooms

- **Daniel Freeman Memorial** • 333 N Prairie Ave

Landmarks

- **Great Western Forum** • Manchester Ave & Prairie Ave
- **Hollywood Park** • 1050 S Prairie Ave
- **Pann's Diner** • 6710 La Tijera Blvd
- **Randy's Donuts** • 805 W Manchester Blvd

Libraries

- **Inglewood Public Library** • 101 W Manchester Blvd • 310-412-5380
- **Lennox** • 4359 Lennox Blvd • 310-674-0385

Pharmacies

- **CVS** • 4345 W Century Blvd • 310-672-6078
- **The Medicine Shoppe** • 1101 N La Brea Ave • 310-412-6088
- **Sav-On** • 222 N Market St • 310-671-0441
- **Vons** • 500 E Manchester Blvd • 310-677-0501
- **Walgreens** • 230 N La Brea Ave • 310-671-2471

Police

- **Inglewood Police Dept** • 1 W Manchester Blvd • 310-412-5111

Post Offices

- **US Post Office** • 300 E Hillcrest Blvd • 800-275-8777
- **US Post Office** • 4443 Lennox Blvd • 800-275-8777
- **US Post Office** • 811 N La Brea Ave • 800-275-8777

Schools

- **A Bright Beginning** • 712 E Manchester Blvd
- **Academy for Early Learning** • 1020 N Park Ave
- **AF Williams Christian Academy** • 1437 W Centinela Ave
- **Buelah Payne Elementary** • 215 W 94th St
- **Buford Elementary** • 4919 W 109th St
- **Centinela Elementary** • 1123 Marlborough Ave
- **Century Community Charter** • 901 S Maple St
- **City Honors High** • 155 W Kelso St
- **Claude Hudnall Elementary** • 331 W Olive St
- **Communion Christian Academy** • 6201 S La Brea Ave
- **Cornerstone Learning Academy** • 1009 N Market St
- **Crusaders Christian Preschool** • 601 Centinela Ave
- **Culture and Language Academy of Success** • 434 S Grevillea Ave
- **Culture & Language Academy of Success** • 100 E Nutwood St
- **Debbie's Child Care Development** • 521 S Osage Ave
- **Dolores Huerta Elementary** • 11036 Hawthorne Blvd
- **Felton Elementary** • 10417 Felton Ave
- **First Lutheran Preschool** • 600 W Queen St
- **Frank D Parent Elementary** • 5354 W 64th St
- **George W Crozier Junior High** • 151 N Grevillea Ave
- **Highland Elementary** • 430 Venice Wy
- **Hillcrest High** • 441 W Hillcrest Blvd
- **Inglewood Christian** • 215 E Hillcrest Blvd
- **Inglewood High** • 231 S Grevillea Ave
- **Jefferson Elementary** • 10322 Condon Ave
- **K Anthony** • 1003 S Prairie Ave
- **Kids' Castle Child Care Center** • 745 N La Brea Ave
- **La Tijera Elementary** • 1415 S La Tijera Blvd
- **The Learning Zone** • 901 E Redondo Blvd
- **Lennox Mathematics, Science, and Technology Academy** • 4125 W 105th St
- **Lennox Middle** • 11033 Buford Ave
- **Moffett Elementary** • 11050 Larch Ave
- **Morningside High** • 10500 Yukon Ave
- **Oak St Elementary** • 633 S Oak St
- **Saluson Learning Center** • 260 N Locust St
- **St John Chrysotom Elementary** • 530 E Florence Ave
- **St Mary's Academy** • 701 Grace Ave
- **Tender Care Kindergarten** • 335 E Spruce Ave
- **United World International Learning Center** • 5020 W 58th Pl
- **University of Children** • 1518 Centinela Ave
- **Wilder's Preparatory Academy Charter** • 830 N La Brea Ave
- **WIlliam H Kelso Elementary** • 809 E Kelso St
- **Wiz** • 121 W Arbor Vitae
- **Worthington Elementary** • 11101 Yukon Ave

Supermarkets

- **Ralphs** • 5245 W Centinela Ave
- **Ralphs** • 950 N La Brea Ave
- **Smart & Final** • 1575 Centinela Ave
- **Vons** • 500 E Manchester Blvd

Map 13 • Inglewood

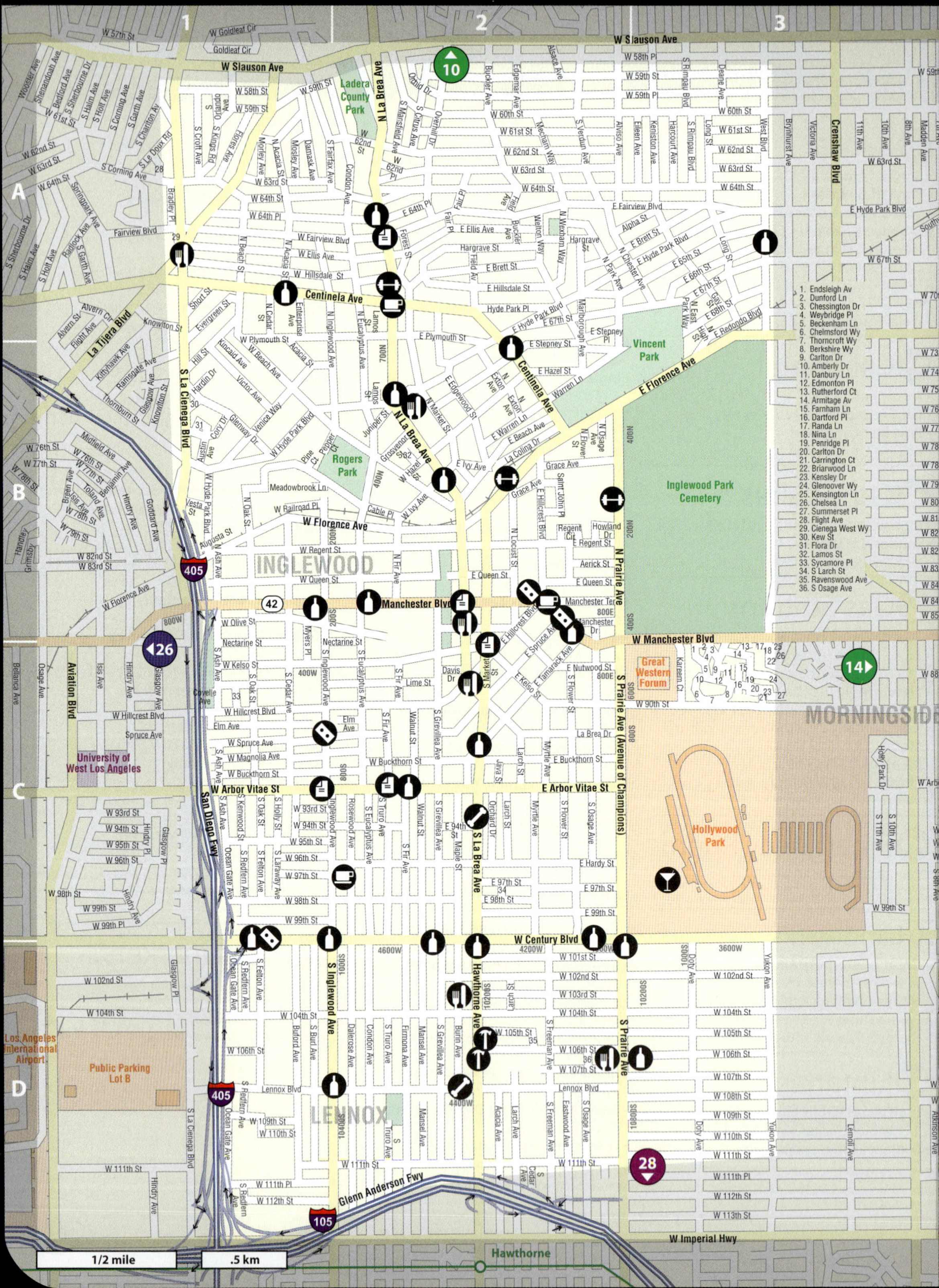

1. Endsleigh Av
2. Dunford Ln
3. Chessington Dr
4. Weybridge Pl
5. Beckenham Ln
6. Chelmsford Wy
7. Thorncroft Wy
8. Berkshire Wy
9. Carlton Dr
10. Amberly Dr
11. Danbury Ln
12. Edmonton Pl
13. Rutherford Ct
14. Armitage Av
15. Farnham Ln
16. Dartford Pl
17. Randa Ln
18. Nina Ln
19. Penridge Pl
20. Carlton Dr
21. Carrington Ct
22. Briarwood Ln
23. Kensley Dr
24. Glenoover Wy
25. Kensington Ln
26. Chelsea Ln
27. Summerset Pl
28. Flight Ave
29. Cienega West Wy
30. Kew St
31. Flora Dr
32. Lamos St
33. Sycamore Pl
34. S Larch St
35. Ravenswood Ave
36. S Osage Ave

1/2 mile

.5 km

Sundries / Entertainment

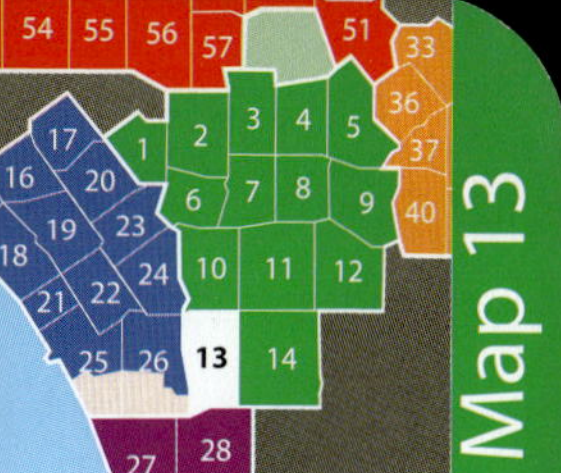

Downtown Inglewood's pedestrian-friendly Market Street is a veritable wormhole back in time, with mom-and-pop establishments you won't find in the malls elsewhere in the city. This area is an odd counterbalance to the acres of condominiums covering the areas adjacent to LAX and nearby industrial centers.

Coffee

- **Howling Monk** • 1134 S Eucalyptus Ave
- **Starbucks** • Vons • 500 E Manchester Blvd
- **Starbucks** • 941 N La Brea Ave

Copy Shops

- **AG&R Instant Printing Copy Center** • 226 W Arbor Vitae St • 310-412-0423
- **Copies Plus** • 240 S La Brea • 310-674-6970
- **D'Menace Copies & Communications** • 1323 N La Brea Ave • 310-677-1683
- **Mina Printing** • 428 W Arbor Vitae St • 310-677-5501
- **Postal Plus Business Copy** • 309 E Hillcrest Blvd • 310-672-9097

Gyms

- **Curves** • 979 N La Brea Ave • 310-673-9043
- **Huff N Puff Gym** • 400 E Florence Ave • 310-672-5055
- **YMCA** • 333 N Prairie Ave • 310-671-7615

Hardware Stores

- **Inglewood True Value** • 10600 Hawthorne Blvd • 323-678-6261

Liquor Stores

- **Airport Liquors & Groceries** • 420 N La Brea Ave
- **Airport Westerner Liquor** • 4500 W Century Blvd
- **Andy's Liquors** • 440 W Manchester Blvd
- **Banks of Scotland Liquor** • 5014 W Century Blvd
- **Big G Liquor** • 400 W Manchester Blvd
- **Century Discount Liquor** • 4082 W Century Blvd
- **Happy Time Liquors** • 730 N La Brea Ave
- **Hyde Park Liquor** • 622 Centinela Ave
- **Inglewood Liquor** • 10805 S Inglewood Ave
- **JR's Liquor** • 10025 S Inglewood Ave
- **Liquorette** • 1400 Centinela Ave
- **Martino's Liquor** • 706 E Manchester Blvd
- **Mr B's Liquor** • 10025 S Prairie Ave
- **Nelson's Liquor Store** • 1435 N La Brea Ave
- **Star Liquor** • 201 W Arbor Vitae St
- **Teds Liquor** • 10625 S Prairie Ave
- **Tran's Liquor** • 10021 Hawthorne Blvd

Nightlife

- **Hollywood Park** • 1050 S Prairie Ave • 310-419-1500

Pet Shops

- **Distributors Feed** • 4435 Lennox Blvd • 310-677-0200
- **Inglewood Pet Shop** • 979 S La Brea Ave • 310-677-2225

Restaurants

- **Ibex Ethiopian Restaurant** • 630 N La Brea Ave • 310-673-3392
- **La Costa Mariscos Restaurant** • 597 S La Brea Ave • 310-672-2083
- **La Perla Restaurant** • 10623 S Prairie Ave • 310-677-5277
- **Little Belize Restaurant** • 217 E Nutwood St • 323-574-4003
- **Pann's Diner** • 6710 La Tijera Blvd • 323-776-3770
- **Thai Plate Restaurant** • 10311 Hawthorne Blvd • 310-412-0111

Video Rental

- **Blockbuster Video** • 500 E Manchester Blvd • 310-680-9860
- **Carrousel Video** • 913 S Inglewood Ave • 310-677-1888
- **Hollywood Video** • 425 E Manchester Blvd • 310-677-6510
- **Video Vision** • 5008 W Century Blvd • 310-674-0004

Map 14 • Inglewood East / Morningside Park

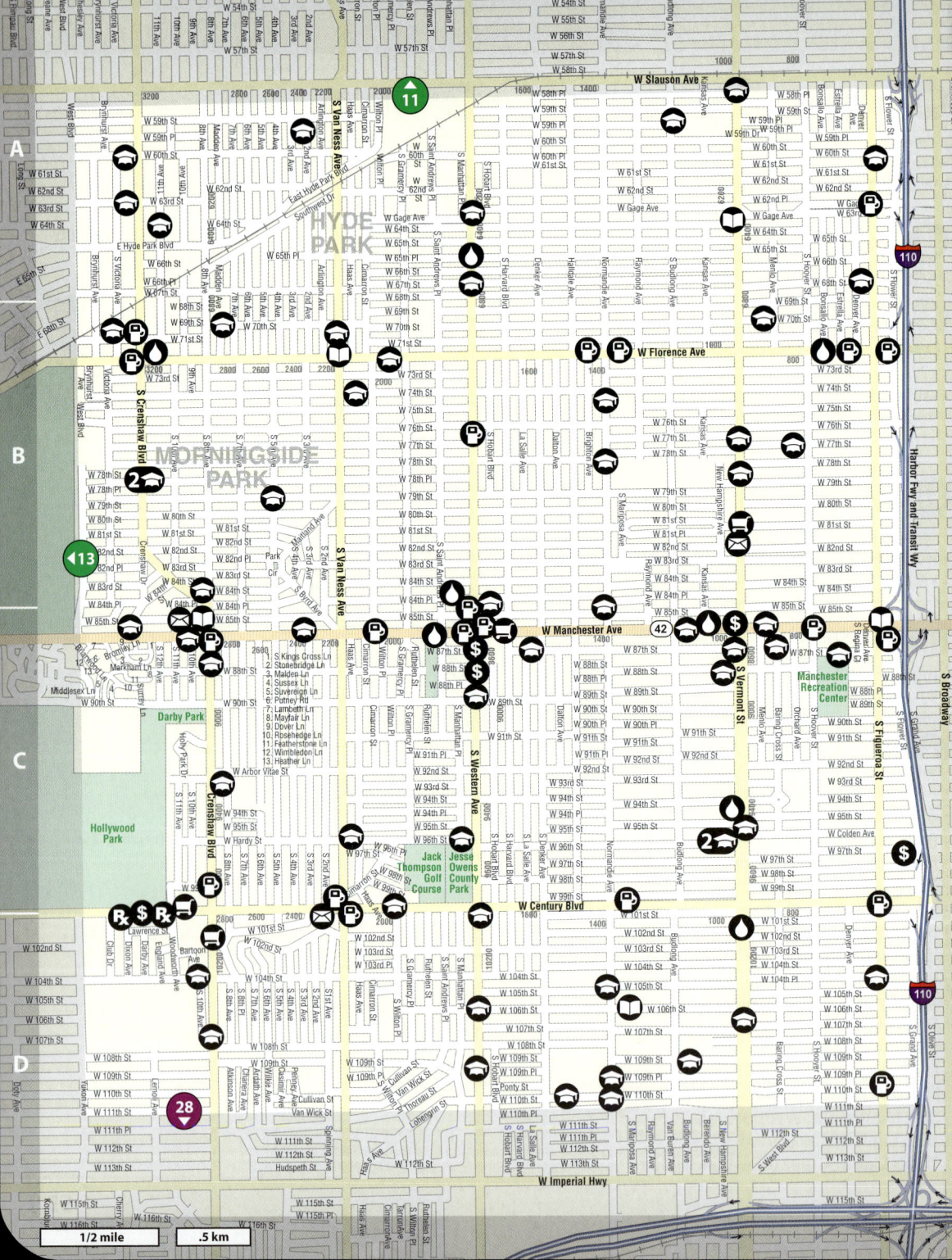

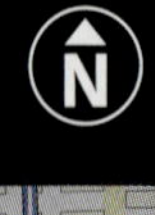

Shedding its inner-city vibe, Morningside Park is becoming more like its neighboring communities in the South Bay. Residential areas here are bisected by commercial throughways filled with shopping centers anchored by big-box retailers like Costco. These mini-malls, however, still make room for the local mom-and-pop businesses.

Banks

- **Bank of America** • 8701 S Western Ave
- **Union** • 8811 S Western Ave
- **US** • 3366 W Century Blvd
- **Washington Mutual** • 1027 W Manchester Ave
- **Washington Mutual** • 3520 W Century Blvd

Car Rental

- **LAX Rent-a-Car** • 4900 W Century Blvd

Car Washes

- **EJ Hand Car Wash** • 2320 W Manchester Ave
- **Magic Car Wash** • 1923 W Manchester Ave
- **Manchester Car Wash** • 1111 W Manchester Ave
- **Mike's Hand Car Wash** • 10135 S Vermont Ave
- **Royal Oasis Hand Car Wash** • 9421 S Vermont Ave
- **Simms Car Wash** • 3312 W Florence Ave
- **Spot Car Wash** • 701 W Florence Ave
- **The Spot Hand Car Wash** • 6522 S Western Ave

Gas Stations

- **76** • 10000 S Figueroa St
- **76** • 1350 W Florence Ave
- **76** • 8600 S Figueroa St
- **76** • 9830 Crenshaw Blvd
- **Arco** • 1403 Century Blvd
- **Arco** • 2050 W Manchester Ave
- **Arco** • 3411 W Florence Ave
- **Arco** • 615 W Florence Ave
- **Arco** • 7600 S Western Ave
- **Arco** • 800 W Manchester Ave
- **Chevron** • 428 W Florence Ave
- **Chevron** • 9920 S Hoover St
- **Independent** • 11025 S Figueroa St
- **Independent** • 2138 W Century Blvd
- **Mobil** • 1803 W Manchester Ave
- **Mobil** • 7130 Crenshaw Blvd
- **Shell** • 1400 W Florence Ave
- **Shell** • 3100 W Manchester Blvd
- **Shell** • 8611 S Western Ave
- **Valero** • 1359 W Century Blvd
- **Valero** • 6303 S Figueroa St

Libraries

- **Hyde Park-Miriam Matthews Branch** • 2205 W Florence Ave • 323-750-7241
- **John Muir Branch** • 1005 W 64th St • 323-789-4800
- **Mark Twain Branch** • 9621 S Figueroa St • 323-755-4088
- **Morningside Park Branch** • 3202 W 85th St • 310-412-5400
- **Woodcrest** • 1340 W 106th St • 323-757-9373

Pharmacies

- **Target** • 3471 W Century Blvd • 310-677-5937
- **Walgreens** • 3331 W Century Blvd • 310-671-1523

Post Offices

- **US Post Office** • 2200 W Century Blvd • 800-275-8777
- **US Post Office** • 3212 W 85th St • 800-275-8777
- **US Post Office** • 8200 S Vermont Ave • 800-275-8777

Schools

- **59th St Elementary** • 5939 2nd Ave
- **68th St Elementary** • 612 W 68th St
- **74th St Elementary** • 2112 W 74th St
- **95th St EEC** • 1027 W 96th St
- **95th St Elementary** • 1109 W 96th St
- **Academy of Basic Learning** • 10457-A S Figueroa St
- **Albert F Monroe Junior High** • 10711 S 10th Ave
- **Ambassadors for Christ Christian** • 1400 W 105th St
- **Amino Inglewood Charter High** • 3425 W Manchester Blvd
- **Barrett Elementary** • 419 W 98th St
- **Bret Harte Middle** • 9301 S Hoover St
- **Budlong Ave Elementary** • 5940 S Budlong Ave
- **Bundle of Joy Christian Academy** • 10963 S Western Ave
- **Cavalry Christian** • 2400 W 85th St
- **Century Park Elementary** • 10935 Spinning Ave
- **Charter Academy Middle and High** • 2941 W 70th St
- **Children's Enrichment Center** • 3209 W Manchester Blvd
- **Citizen Learning Academy** • 6715 S Western Ave
- **Cleophas Oliver Learning Academy** • 1902 W Florence Ave
- **Clyde Woodworth Elementary** • 3200 W 104th St
- **Cope Academy of Learning** • 3320 W 85th St
- **Daniel Freeman Elementary** • 2602 W 79th St
- **Danny J Bakewell Sr Primary Center** • 8621 Baring Cross St
- **Duke Ellington High** • 1541 W 110th St
- **Faith Children's Center** • 2057 W Century Blvd
- **Famli Circle Schools** • 8505 S Western Ave
- **Frederick KC Price** • 7901 S Vermont Ave
- **Fresh Starts Child Enrichment** • 7867 Crenshaw Blvd
- **George Washington Preparatory High** • 10860 S Denker Ave
- **Horace Mann Middle** • 7001 S St Andrews Pl
- **Hyde Park Blvd Elementary** • 3140 Hyde Park Blvd
- **Hyde Park EEC** • 6428 11th Ave
- **Imani Enrichment Academy of Learning** • 1408 W 110th St
- **John Muir Middle** • 5929 S Vermont Ave
- **Junior Technologies** • 9537 S Vermont Ave
- **K Anthony** • 8420 Crenshaw Blvd
- **KIPP Academy of Opportunity** • 7019 S Van Ness Ave
- **La Salle Ave Elementary** • 8715 La Salle Ave
- **Little Rainbow Childrens' Center** • 7419 S Normandie Ave
- **Manchester Ave Elementary** • 661 W 87th St
- **Manhattan Pl Elementary** • 1850 W 96th St
- **Marie Fegan** • 8477 S Normandie Ave
- **Mikes EEC** • 7720 S Vermont Ave
- **Miller Elementary** • 830 W 77th St
- **Nelson Christian** • 10531 S Western Ave
- **New Creations Christian Faith** • 8862 S Western Ave
- **New W Technical Academy** • 10531 S Vermont Ave
- **Nikka Tiffany** • 7112 S Victoria Ave
- **Normandie Christian** • 6306 S Normandie Ave
- **Opportunities Unlimited Charter High** • 8825 S Vermont Ave
- **Puente Charter** • 10000 S Western Ave
- **Raymond Ave Elementary** • 7511 Raymond Ave
- **San Pedro Academy** • 1145 W Manchester Ave
- **Sixty-First Street Elementary** • 6020 S Figueroa St
- **Southern California Academy Of Arts and Sciences** • 10513 S Vermont Ave
- **St Eugene** • 9521 Haas Ave
- **St John the Evangelist** • 6028 S Victoria Ave
- **St Michael's Elementary** • 1027 W 87th St
- **St Raphael's Elementary** • 924 W 70th St
- **Tijay Renee Academy** • 8722 Crenshaw Blvd
- **Toddler Technical University** • 7861 S Normandie Ave
- **Warren Lane Elementary** • 9330 S 8th Ave
- **Woodcrest Elementary** • 1151 W 109th St
- **Woodcrest Nazarene** • 10936 S Normandie Ave
- **Youth Opportunities Unlimited** • 915 W Manchester Ave

Supermarkets

- **Food 4 Less** • 3200 W Century Blvd
- **Ralphs** • 1730 W Manchester Ave
- **Smart & Final** • 10100 Crenshaw Blvd
- **Smart & Final** • 8137 S Vermont Ave

Map 14 • Inglewood East / Morningside Park

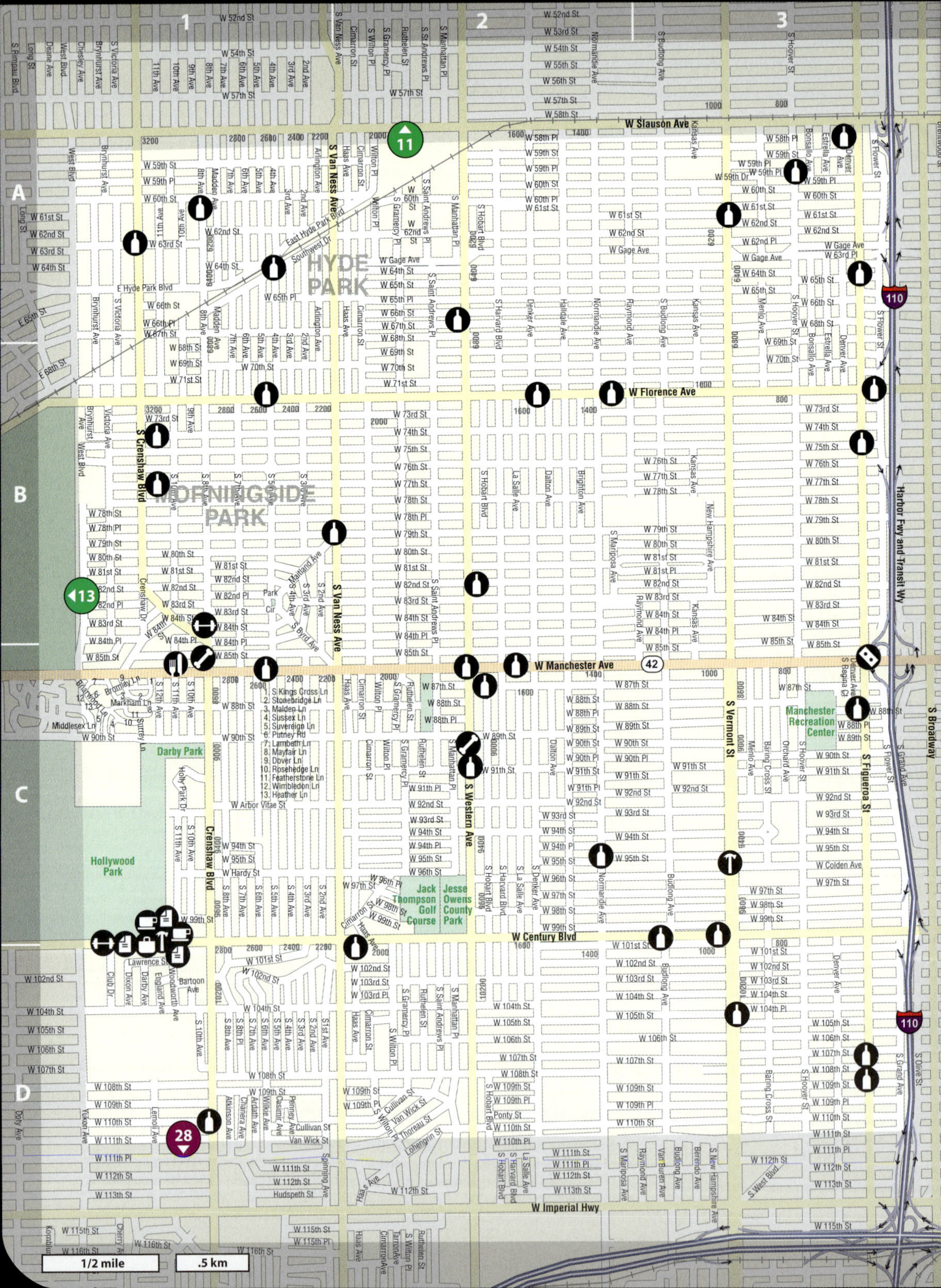

HYDE PARK

MORNINGSIDE PARK

W Slauson Ave

W Florence Ave

W Manchester Ave

W Century Blvd

W Imperial Hwy

S Crenshaw Blvd

S Van Ness Ave

S Western Ave

S Vermont St

S Figueroa St

Harbor Fwy and Transit Way

S Broadway

Darby Park

Hollywood Park

Manchester Recreation Center

Jack Thompson Golf Course

Jesse Owens County Park

1. S Kings Cross Ln
2. Stonebridge Ln
3. Malden Ln
4. Sussex Ln
5. Sovereign Ln
6. Putney Rd
7. Lambeth Ln
8. Mayfair Ln
9. Dover Ln
10. Rosehedge Ln
11. Featherstone Ln
12. Wimbledon Ln
13. Heather Ln

1/2 mile

.5 km

The area south of the 10 and bordered by Imperial Highway on the south features blocks of vintage homes with manicured gardens and, despite some of the area's rough edges, it is primarily residential. The neon exception to the urban landscape is the Hollywood Park Race Track and Casino with its thoroughbred racing season and year-round nightclubs and card rooms.

Coffee

- **Coffee Bean & Tea Leaf** • 3396 W Century Blvd
- **Starbucks** • 3351 W Century Blvd

Copy Shops

- **Office Depot** • 3330 W Century Blvd • 310-419-9274
- **Staples** • 3451 W Century Blvd • 310-673-6800
- **UPS Store** • 3550 W Century Blvd • 310-677-3030

Gyms

- **Bally Total Fitness** • 3531 W Century Blvd • 310-672-6002
- **Curves** • 8409 8th Ave • 323-971-1382

Hardware Stores

- **Ferreteria Lemus Supply** • 9510 S Vermont Ave • 323-418-8041
- **Home Depot** • 3363 Century Blvd • 310-677-1944

Liquor Stores

- **8th Liquor Mart** • 6007 8th Ave
- **Al's Liquor** • 10751 S Figueroa St
- **All Star Liquor & Market** • 6300 Crenshaw Blvd
- **B&B Liquors** • 8207 S Western Ave
- **Bookers Liquor & Jr Market** • 5879 S Figueroa St
- **Bottoms Up Liquor** • 6424 S Vermont Ave
- **E&O Liquor** • 10466 S Vermont Ave
- **Florence Liquor** • 1534 W Florence Ave
- **Franks Liquor** • 8720 S Western Ave
- **Giant Store** • 455 W Florence Ave
- **Gil's Liquor** • 10815 S Figueroa St
- **Gin's Liquor Store** • 11001 Crenshaw Blvd
- **Holiday Liquor** • 9150 S Western Ave
- **Irene's Liquor Store** • 8825 S Figueroa St
- **M&J Liquor** • 7405 Crenshaw Blvd
- **Mr Spirit's Liquor** • 6818 S Western Ave
- **Porche Liquor** • 7528 S Figueroa St
- **Ralph's Drive-In Liquor** • 2130 W Century Blvd
- **Red's Liquor** • 1201 W Century Blvd
- **Red's Liquor** • 2600 Southwest Dr
- **San's Liquor** • 7911 S Van Ness Ave
- **Shyrea's Liquor** • 1753 W Century Blvd
- **Silver Dollar Liquor** • 1650 W Manchester Ave
- **SMB's Liquors** • 9467 S Normandie Ave
- **Sunshine Liquor** • 2619 W Florence Ave
- **Susie's Liquor** • 5953 S Hoover St
- **Vee's Liquor** • 7707 Crenshaw Blvd
- **Vermont Liquor** • 6107 S Vermont Ave

Pet Shops

- **James' Tropical Fish** • 8519 Crenshaw Blvd • 323-758-4406
- **R T Pet & Food General Warehouse** • 8902 S Western Ave • 323-778-1400

Restaurants

- **M&M Soul Food Restaurant** • 3300 W Manchester Blvd • 310-673-5031

Shopping

- **Costco** • 3560 W Century Blvd • 310-242-2774

Video Rental

- **A&N Video** • 519 W Manchester Ave • 323-971-6249

Map 15 • Pacific Palisades

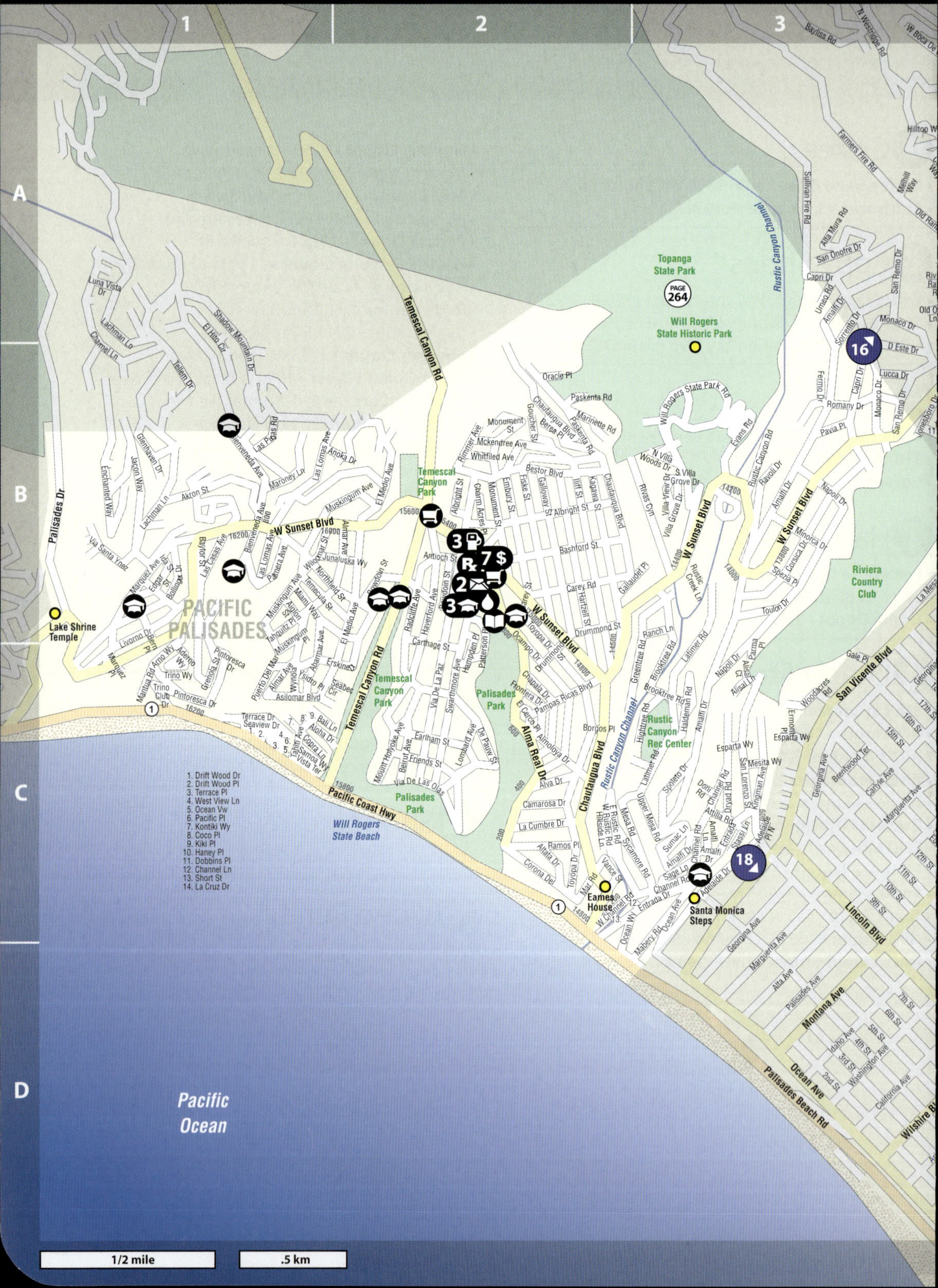

PACIFIC PALISADES

Topanga State Park

PAGE 264

Will Rogers State Historic Park

Temescal Canyon Park

Temescal Canyon Park

Palisades Park

Rustic Canyon Rec Center

Riviera Country Club

Lake Shrine Temple

Eames House

Santa Monica Steps

Will Rogers State Beach

Pacific Ocean

1. Drift Wood Dr
2. Drift Wood Pl
3. Terrace Pl
4. West View Ln
5. Ocean Vw
6. Pacific Pl
7. Kontiki Wy
8. Coco Pl
9. Kiki Pl
10. Haney Pl
11. Dobbins Pl
12. Channel Ln
13. Short St
14. La Cruz Dr

1/2 mile

.5 km

Made up of streets winding continuously through the hills, out to endless ocean views and down into surprisingly lush canyons, the Pacific Palisades are one of LA's most beautiful areas, home to many celebs and movie moguls—as the lavish homes might suggest. This remote-yet-close Los Angeles neighborhood is nestled between the Pacific Ocean and Topanga State Park, so awe-inspiring hikes and romantic beach strolls are literally right outside your door. Or the movie mogul's over-sized door, anyway.

Banks

- **Bank of America** • 15314 W Sunset Blvd
- **California National** • 15305 W Sunset Blvd
- **Citibank** • 15215 Sunset Blvd
- **First Federal** • 15135 W Sunset Blvd
- **US** • 15245 W Sunset Blvd
- **Washington Mutual** • 15200 W Sunset Blvd
- **Wells Fargo** • 1012 Swarthmore Ave

Car Washes

- **Palisades Car Wash** • 890 Alma Real Dr

Gas Stations

- **76** • 15400 W Sunset Blvd
- **Mobil** • 15281 W Sunset Blvd
- **Shell** • 15401 W Sunset Blvd

Landmarks

- **Eames House** • 203 Chautauqua Blvd
- **Santa Monica Steps** • 4th St & Adelaide Dr
- **Self Realization Fellowship Lake Shrine Temple** • 17190 W Sunset Blvd
- **Will Rogers State Historic Park** • Sunset Blvd

Libraries

- **Pacific Palisades Branch** • 861 Alma Real Dr • 310-459-2754

Pharmacies

- **CVS** • 864 Swarthmore Ave • 310-459-8449

Post Offices

- **US Post Office** • 15209 W Sunset Blvd • 800-275-8778
- **US Post Office** • 15243 La Cruz Dr • 800-275-8779

Schools

- **Canyon Elementary** • 421 Entrada Dr
- **Corpus Christi** • 890 Toyopa Dr
- **Marquez Elementary** • 16821 Marquez Ave
- **Pacific Palisades Elementary** • 800 Via De La Paz
- **Palisades Charter High** • 15777 Bowdoin St
- **St Matthew's Episcopal** • 1031 Bienveneda Ave
- **Temescal Canyon High** • 777 Temescal Cyn Rd
- **Village** • 780 Swarthmore Ave

Supermarkets

- **Gelson's Market** • 15424 W Sunset Blvd
- **Ralphs** • 15120 W Sunset Blvd

Map 15 • Pacific Palisades

1 2 3

A B C D

PACIFIC PALISADES

Topanga State Park

PAGE 264

Will Rogers State Historic Park

Temescal Canyon Park

Palisades Park

Rustic Canyon Rec Center

Riviera Country Club

Will Rogers State Beach

Pacific Ocean

16

18

1. Drift Wood Dr
2. Drift Wood Pl
3. Terrace Pl
4. West View Ln
5. Ocean Vw
6. Pacific Pl
7. Kontiki Wy
8. Coco Pl
9. Kiki Pl
10. Haney Pl
11. Dobbins Pl
12. Channel Ln
13. Short St
14. La Cruz Dr

W Sunset Blvd · Pacific Coast Hwy · Temescal Canyon Rd · Chautauqua Blvd · Alma Real Dr · Palisades Dr · San Vicente Blvd · Montana Ave · Ocean Ave · Palisades Beach Rd · Lincoln Blvd · Rustic Canyon Channel · Wilshire Blvd

1/2 mile

.5 km

Sundries / Entertainment

Amenities in the Palisades are generally limited to the village, just off Sunset Boulevard along Swarthmore Avenue. But Santa Monica is just a short hop down the PCH, a longer drive across the more serpentine Sunset Boulevard, or perhaps a meandering slow-cut through Santa Monica canyon.

Coffee

- **Coffee Bean & Tea Leaf** • 15278 Antioch St
- **Starbucks** • 15300 Sunset Blvd

Farmers Markets

- **Pacific Palisades (Sun, 8 am-1:30 pm)** • Swarthmore Ave & W Sunset Blvd

Gyms

- **Canyon Athletic** • 139 Entrada Dr • 310-459-2409
- **Curves** • 881 Alma Real Dr • 310-459-1003
- **Palisades-Malibu YMCA** • 821 Via De La Paz • 310-454-5591
- **Spectrum Club** • 17383 Sunset Blvd • 310-459-2582

Hardware Stores

- **Norris Hardware** • 15140 W Sunset Blvd • 310-454-4116

Liquor Stores

- **State Beach Liquor** • 14801 Pacific Coast Hwy

Nightlife

- **The Hideout** • 112 W Channel Rd • 310-429-1851
- **Pearl Dragon** • 15229 Sunset Blvd • 310-459-9790

Restaurants

- **A La Tarte Bistrot** • 1037 Swarthmore Ave • 310-459-6635
- **Dante Palisades Restaurant** • 1032 Swarthmore Ave • 310-459-7561
- **Giorgio Baldi** • 114 W Channel Rd • 310-573-1660
- **Kay 'n Dave's** • 15246 W Sunset Blvd • 310-459-8118
- **Marix Tex Mex Café** • 118 Entrada Dr • 310-459-8596
- **Modo Mio Cucina Rustica** • 15200 W Sunset Blvd • 310-459-0979
- **Patrick's Roadhouse** • 106 Entrada Dr • 310-459-4544
- **Pure Energy Café** • 17383 W Sunset Blvd • 310-573-4105
- **Robek's Juice** • 15280 Antioch St • 310-230-3991
- **Terry's** • 1028 Swarthmore Ave • 310-454-6467

Shopping

- **Benton's Sporting Goods** • 1038 Swarthmore Ave • 310-459-8451
- **Gelson's Market** • 15424 W Sunset Blvd • 310-459-4483
- **Gift Garden Antiques** • 15266 Antioch St • 310-459-4114
- **Ivy Greene for Kids** • 1020 Swarthmore Ave • 310-230-0301
- **Palisades Playthings** • 1041 Swarthmore Ave • 310-454-8648
- **The Prince's Table** • 1051 Swarthmore Ave • 310-573-3667
- **Village Books** • 1049 Swarthmore Ave • 310-454-4063
- **Vivian's Boutique** • 970 Monument St • 310-573-1326
- **Whispers** • 1013 Swarthmore Ave • 310-454-5582

Video Rental

- **Blockbuster** • 970 Monument St • 310-230-3002
- **Palisades Video Plus** • 542 Palisades Dr • 310-230-1688

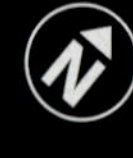

Map 16 • Brentwood

1
2
3
A
B
C
D
BRENTWOOD
Topanga State Park
Rustic Canyon
Crestwood Hills Park
Getty Center
Barrington Recreation Center
Brentwood Country Club
Veterans Administration
Wadsworth Veterans Administration Medical Center
Sunset Blvd
San Vicente Blvd
Montana Ave
Wilshire Blvd
San Diego Fwy
N Sepulveda Blvd
S Sepulveda Blvd
405
PAGE 264
PAGE 386
15
17
18
19
20
1. Lindenwood Ln
2. Bluestone Ter
3. Bluegrass Ln
4. Bluegrass Way
5. Glenmere Way
6. Pontoon Pl
7. Castlegate Dr
8. Brentridge Ln
9. Brentridge Dr
10. Norway Ln
11. Kiel St
12. Ocean Pl
13. Stonehaven Way
14. Little Park Ln
15. Mandeville Ln
16. Haney Pl
17. Dobbins Pl
1/2 mile
.5 km

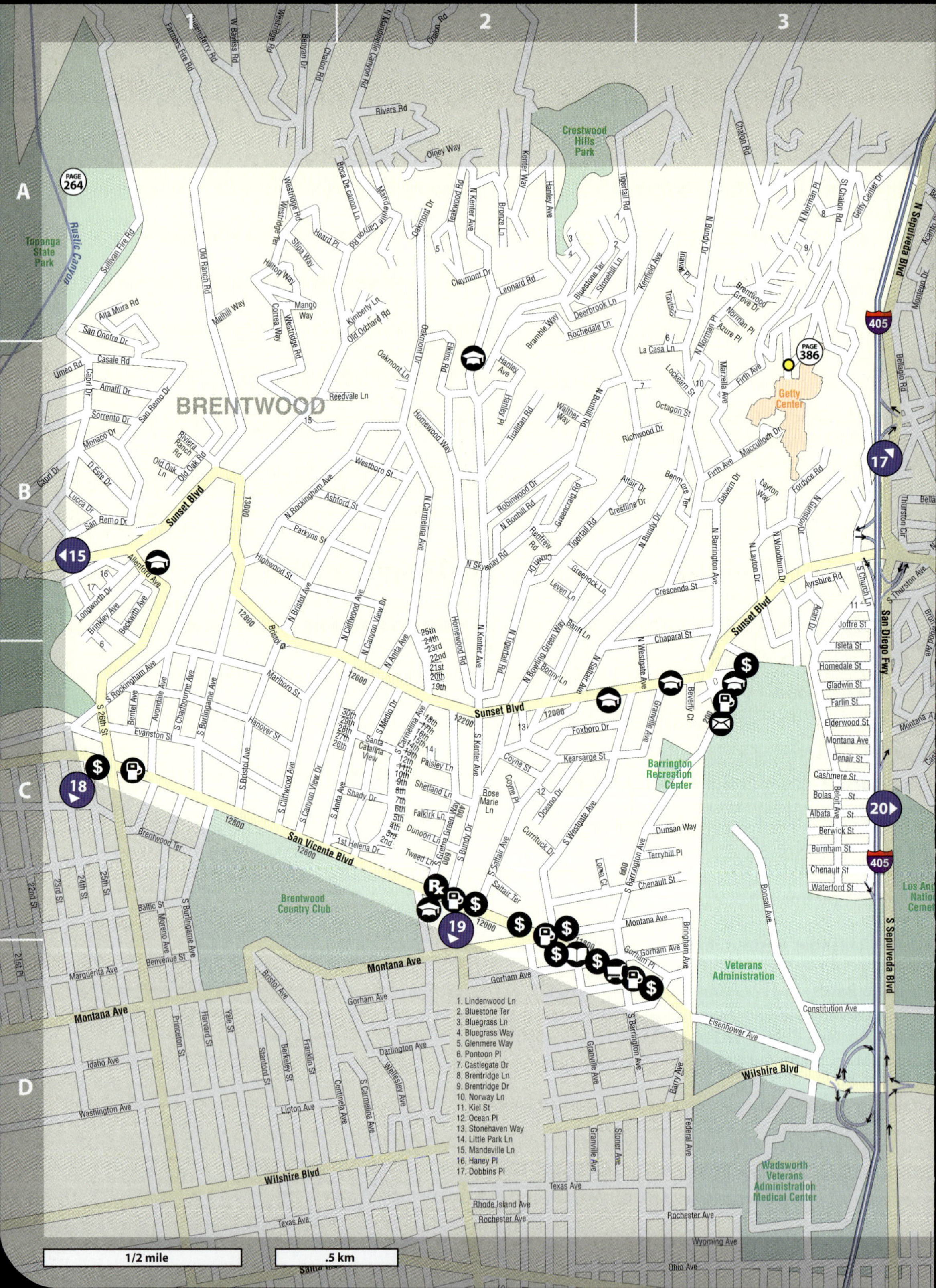

O. J. Simpson put Brentwood on most Americans' radar, but this neighborhood is back to being the quietly affluent place it once was. San Vicente Boulevard serves as a shady and pleasant place for a jog or bike ride (complete with a bicycle lane) and is the scene of the annual Kickin' Cancer 5K run (www.kickincancer.com). Many young professionals prefer the rent over here compared to neighboring Santa Monica, but parking can be a nightmare. Carry cash, valet often.

Banks

- **Bank of America** • 11911 San Vicente Blvd
- **California National** • 11777 San Vicente Blvd
- **Citibank** • 11726 San Vicente Blvd
- **Comerica** • 12001 San Vicente Blvd
- **Union** • 11661 San Vicente Blvd
- **Washington Mutual** • 226 26th St
- **Wells Fargo** • 11836 San Vicente Blvd
- **Wells Fargo** • 143 S Barrington Pl

Gas Stations

- **76** • 12037 San Vicente Blvd
- **76** • 13060 San Vicente Blvd
- **Chevron** • 110 S Barrington Ave
- **Chevron** • 11852 San Vincente Blvd
- **Independent** • 11811 San Vicente Blvd

Landmarks

- **Getty Center** • 1200 Getty Center Dr

Libraries

- **Donald Bruce Kaufman** • 11820 San Vicente Blvd • 310-575-8273

Pharmacies

- **Longs Drugs** • 11941 San Vicente Blvd • 310-440-4162

Post Offices

- **US Post Office** • 200 S Barrington Ave • 800-275-8777

Schools

- **Archer School for Girls** • 11725 W Sunset Blvd
- **Brentwood** • 100 S Barrington Pl
- **Brentwood Science** • 740 Gretna Green Wy
- **Kenter Canyon Elementary** • 645 N Kenter Ave
- **Paul Revere Middle** • 1450 Allenford Ave
- **St Martin of Tours Elementary** • 11955 W Sunset Blvd

Supermarkets

- **Whole Foods Market** • 11737 San Vicente Blvd

1. Lindenwood Ln
2. Bluestone Ter
3. Bluegrass Ln
4. Bluegrass Way
5. Glenmere Way
6. Pontoon Pl
7. Castlegate Dr
8. Brentridge Ln
9. Brentridge Dr
10. Norway Ln
11. Kiel St
12. Ocean Pl
13. Stonehaven Way
14. Little Park Ln
15. Mandeville Ln
16. Haney Pl
17. Dobbins Pl

1/2 mile

.5 km

You'll see an outpost of every quirky but popular chain restaurant here, including Chin Chin and Ben & Jerry's. There are a few independents that are worth noting, however. We love the pastas at Pizzicotto, and Coral Tree Café offers a perfect first-date atmosphere. Brentwood is home to one of LA's best independent booksellers, Dutton's—it has an impressive selection and an atmosphere geared toward serious readers. Book signings and other events here keep bibliophiles coming back for more.

Coffee

- **Brew-N-Beans** • 11911 San Vicente Blvd
- **Coffee Bean & Tea Leaf** • 11698 San Vicente Blvd
- **The Coral Tree Café** • 11645 San Vicente Blvd
- **Mart Coffee & Juice Bar** • 225 26th St
- **Peet's** • 11750 San Vicente Blvd
- **Starbucks** • 11700 Barrington Ct
- **Starbucks** • 11707 San Vicente Blvd
- **Starbucks** • 13050 San Vicente Blvd

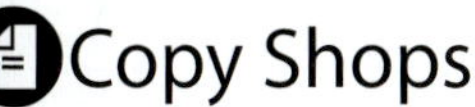

Copy Shops

- **Brentwood Printing** • 11726 San Vicente Blvd • 310-826-1011
- **Mail Boxes Etc** • 149 S Barrington Ave • 310-472-8850

Farmers Markets

- **Brentwood (Sun, 9 am-1 pm)** • S Gretna Green Wy & San Vicente Blvd

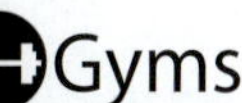

Gyms

- **Curves** • 11777 San Vicente Blvd • 310-571-2422
- **Pro Gym** • 11943 Montana Ave • 310-826-6624

Liquor Stores

- **Briggs Wines & Spirits** • 13038 San Vicente Blvd

Pet Shops

- **Petspot** • 11720 Barrington Ct • 310-471-8169

Restaurants

- **A Votre Sante** • 13016 San Vicente Blvd • 310-451-1813
- **The Brentwood** • 148 S Barrington Ave • 310-476-3511
- **Cheesecake Factory** • 11647 San Vicente Blvd • 310-826-7111
- **Chin Chin** • 11740 San Vicente Blvd • 310-826-2525
- **City Bakery** • 225 26th St • 310-656-3040
- **The Coral Tree Café** • 11645 San Vicente Blvd • 310-979-8733
- **Daily Grill** • Brentwood Gardens • 11677 San Vicente Blvd • 310-442-0044
- **Gaucho Grill** • 11754 San Vicente Blvd • 310-447-7898
- **La Scala Presto** • 11740 San Vicente Blvd • 310-826-6100
- **Le Pain Quotidien** • 11702 Barrington Ct • 310-476-0969
- **Pizzicotto** • 11758 San Vicente Blvd • 310-442-7188
- **Reddi Chick BBQ** • 225 26th St • 310-393-5238
- **Toscana** • 11633 San Vicente Blvd • 310-820-2448
- **Vincenti** • 11930 San Vicente Blvd • 310-207-0127

Shopping

- **Dutton's Brentwood** • 11975 San Vicente Blvd • 310-476-6263
- **Falconhead** • 11911 San Vicente Blvd • 310-471-7075
- **PJ London** • 11661 San Vicente Blvd • 310-826-4649
- **Porta Bella** • 11715 San Vicente Blvd • 310-820-2550
- **Ron Herman** • 11677 San Vicente Blvd • 310-207-0927
- **Sugar Paper** • 225 26th St #27 • 310-451-7870
- **SusieCakes** • 11708 San Vicente Blvd • 310-442-2253
- **Terra Cotta** • 11922 San Vicente Blvd • 310-826-7878
- **Whole Foods Market** • 11737 San Vicente Blvd • 310-826-4433

Video Rental

- **Blockbuster** • 11770 San Vicente Blvd • 310-207-3837

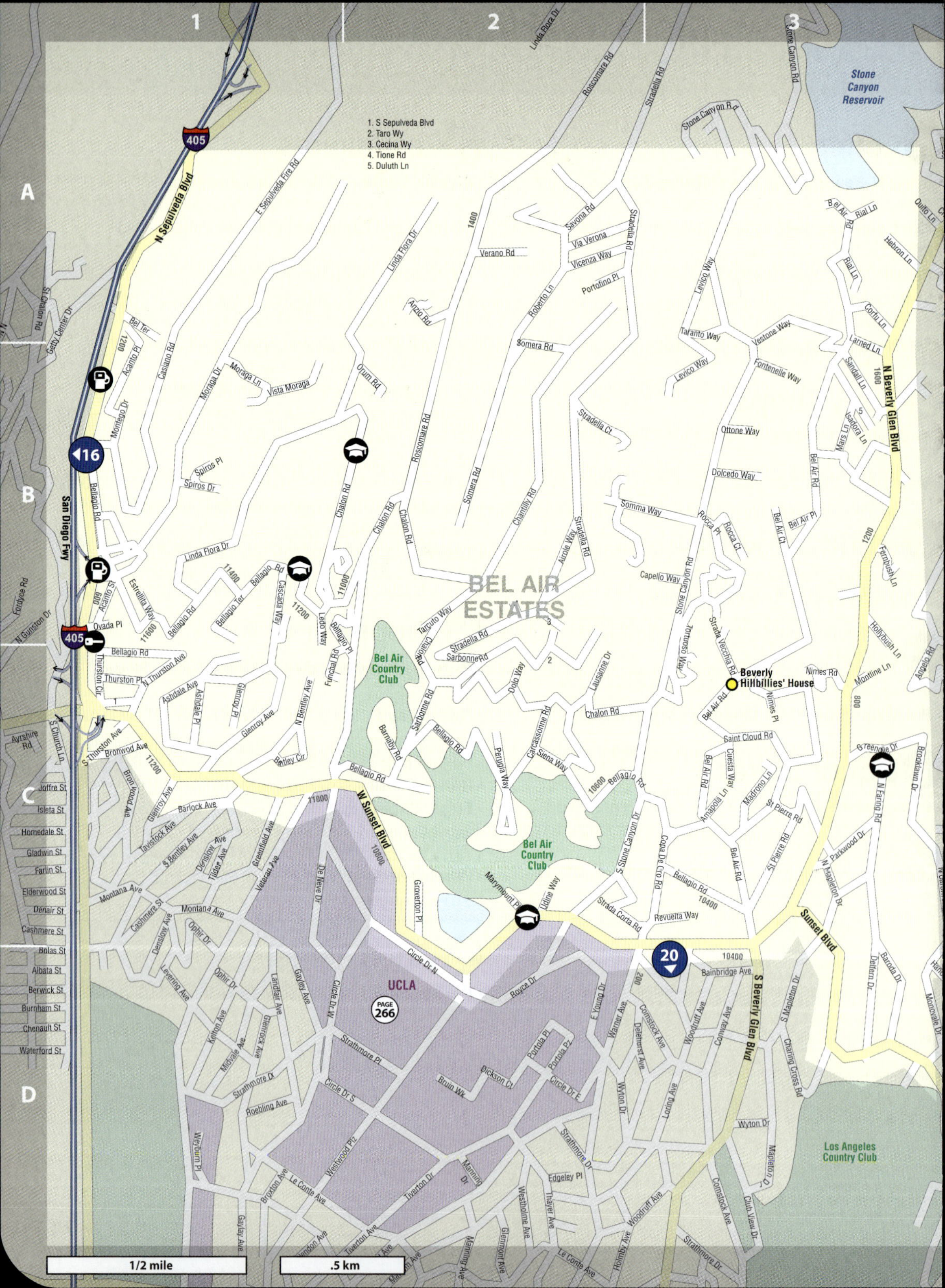

1 2 3

A B C D

1. S Sepulveda Blvd
2. Taro Wy
3. Cecina Wy
4. Tione Rd
5. Duluth Ln

Stone Canyon Reservoir

BEL AIR ESTATES

Bel Air Country Club

Bel Air Country Club

Beverly Hillbillies' House

UCLA

PAGE 266

Los Angeles Country Club

San Diego Fwy

405

16

20

N Sepulveda Blvd

W Sunset Blvd

Sunset Blvd

N Beverly Glen Blvd

S Beverly Glen Blvd

Stone Canyon Rd

Stradella Rd

Roscomare Rd

Linda Flora Dr

Chalon Rd

Bellagio Rd

Bel Air Rd

Moraga Dr

Casiano Rd

E Sepulveda Fire Rd

Getty Center Dr

Church Ln

Thurston Ave

Bronwood Ave

Hilgard Ave

Westwood Plz

Le Conte Ave

Strathmore Dr

Tiverton Ave

Gayley Ave

Levering Ave

Veteran Ave

Wilshire Blvd

Mapleton Dr

Comstock Ave

Woodruff Ave

Conway Ave

Loring Ave

Holmby Ave

Warner Ave

Wyton Dr

Circle Dr N

Circle Dr S

Royce Dr

Strada Corta Rd

St Pierre Rd

Copa De Oro Rd

Bel Air Pl

Montana Ave

Joffre St

Isleta St

Homedale St

Gladwin St

Farlin St

Elderwood St

Denair St

Cashmere St

Bolas St

Albata St

Berwick St

Burnham St

Chenault St

Waterford St

1/2 mile

.5 km

Both of these neighborhoods are almost completely residential. Celebrity devotees can purchase star maps that chart some of the celebrity homes, or rather, their 15-foot tree barrier fencing. The roads are confusing and it's easy to get lost in Bel Air, but the homes you can see are so stunning to look at that you may not mind.

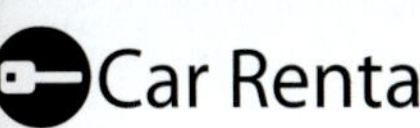

Car Rental

- **Rocket Rent a Car** • 525 N Sepulveda Blvd

Gas Stations

- **76** • 800 N Sepulveda Blvd
- **Chevron** • 670 N Sepulveda Blvd

Landmarks

- **Beverly Hillbillies' House** • 700 Bel Air Rd

Schools

- **Community Magnet Center** • 11301 Bellagio Rd
- **Harvard-Westlake (second location)** • 700 N Faring Rd
- **John Thomas Dye** • 11414 Chalon Rd
- **Marymount High** • 10643 W Sunset Blvd

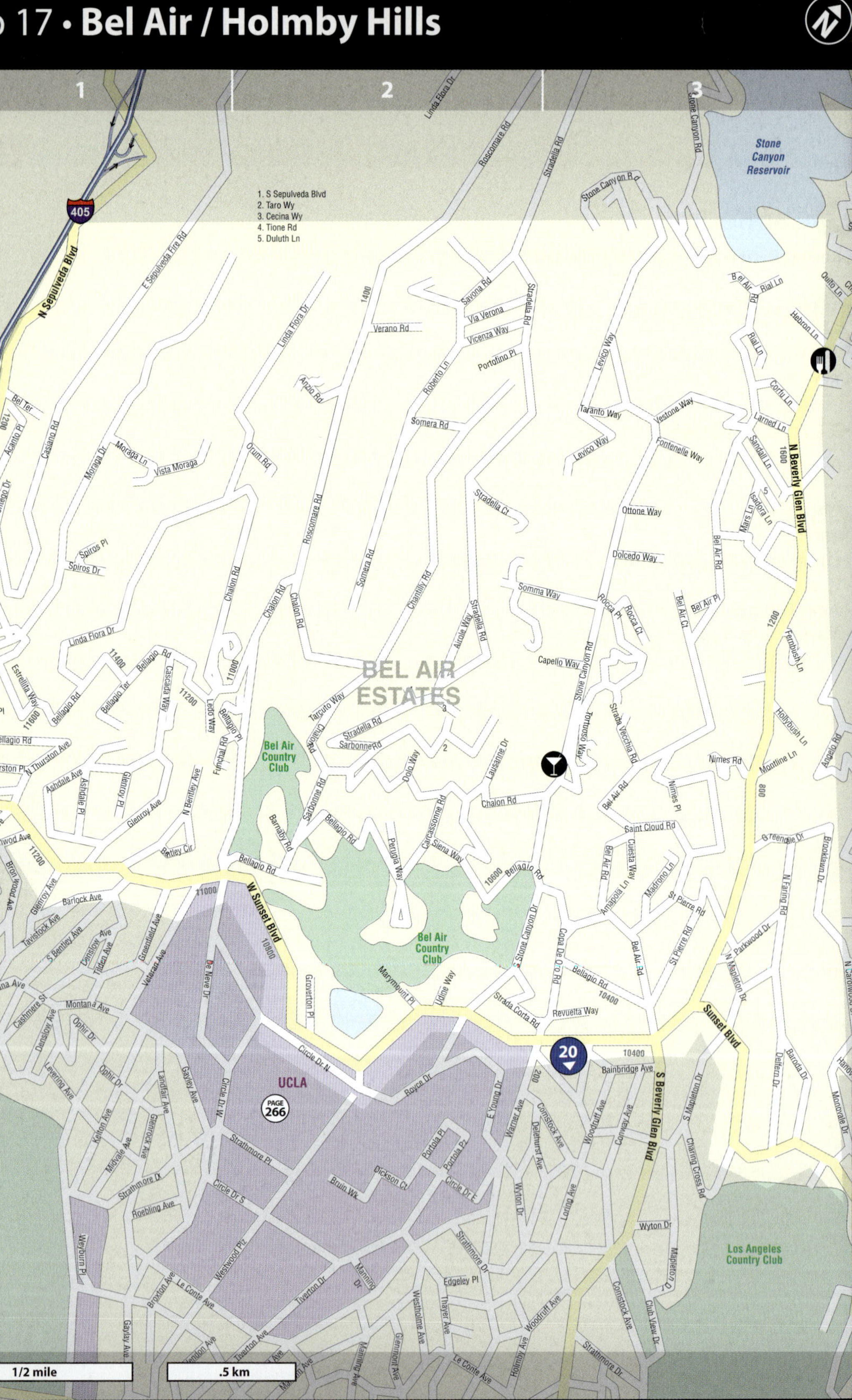

1. S Sepulveda Blvd
2. Taro Wy
3. Cecina Wy
4. Tione Rd
5. Duluth Ln
BEL AIR ESTATES
Bel Air Country Club
UCLA
Stone Canyon Reservoir
Los Angeles Country Club
1/2 mile
.5 km

Sundries / Entertainment

The Hotel Bel Air might be Los Angeles County's most beautiful hotel. The grounds are exquisitely maintained; it's easy to understand why so many couples wed here, and why Oscar nominees take up temporary residence here for a little calm and serenity before the awards.

Nightlife

- **Hotel Bel Air Lounge** • 701 Stone Cyn Rd • 310-472-1211

Restaurants

- **Bel Air Bar & Grill** • 662 N Sepulveda Blvd • 310-440-5544
- **Hotel Bel Air Dining Room** • 701 Stone Cyn Rd • 310-472-1211

1. Esparta Way
2. Foxtail Dr
3. Larkin Pl
4. Winnett Pl
5. Arroyo Vista Dr
6. Seaside Ter
7. Seaview Ter
8. Pacific Ter
9. Vicente Ter
10. Arcadia Ter
11. Pacific Ter
12. Marine Ter
13. Moss Ave
14. Goldsmith St
15. Ruskin St
16. Bentley Ct
17. Marine Pl N
18. Lincoln Ct
19. Longfellow St

1/2 mile

.5 km

Santa Monica's beachy artist community has already given way to families, young professionals, tourists, and now condominiums. While residents do their best to avoid 3rd Street Promenade unless they need a last-minute clothing item, book, or gift, they do shop along the boutique and café-lined Main Street. Montana Avenue also offers a wealth of cafés, restaurants, baby clothing stores, and jewelry shops for the well-heeled. Santa Monicans also play outside, thanks to the ocean bike path, the bluffs above, and the famous Santa Monica stairs.

Banks

- **Bank of America** • 1301 4th St
- **Bank of America** • 1430 Wilshire Blvd
- **Bank of the West** • 407 Colorado Ave
- **California Bank & Trust** • 100 Wilshire Blvd
- **California National** • 201 Santa Monica Blvd
- **Citibank** • 1505 Montana Ave
- **Citibank** • 501 Santa Monica Blvd
- **First Entertainment Credit Union** • 2425 Colorado Ave
- **First Federal** • 1630 Montana Ave
- **First Federal** • 1750 Ocean Park Blvd
- **First Federal** • 2827 Main St
- **First Federal** • 401 Wilshire Blvd
- **First Regional** • 501 Santa Monica Blvd
- **Pacific Western** • 120 Wilshire Blvd
- **Preferred** • 524 Wilshire Blvd
- **Union** • 1101 Montana Ave
- **Union** • 2001 Wilshire Blvd
- **Union** • 429 Santa Monica Blvd
- **US** • 1401 Wilshire Blvd
- **US** • 2221 Santa Monica Blvd
- **US** • 400 Wilshire Blvd
- **Washington Mutual** • 1333 4th St
- **Wells Fargo** • 1300 4th St
- **Wells Fargo** • 2444 Wilshire Blvd
- **World Savings & Loan** • 729 Montana Ave

Car Rental

- **Ava's** • 842 11th St
- **Avis** • 1027 Broadway
- **Avon Rent-A-Car** • 2411 Lincoln Blvd
- **Beverly Hills Rent A Car** • 1719 Wilshire Blvd
- **Budget** • 1723 Wilshire Blvd
- **Enterprise** • 1100 Colorado Ave
- **Enterprise** • 1702 Santa Monica Blvd
- **Enterprise** • 2487 Lincoln Blvd
- **Enterprise** • 2700 Lincoln Blvd
- **Hertz** • 101 Wilshire Blvd
- **Hertz** • 1426 Santa Monica Blvd
- **Hertz** • 1700 Ocean Ave
- **Midway Car Rental** • 1901 Ocean Ave
- **Rent 4 Less** • 3202 Lincoln Blvd

Car Washes

- **Bonus Car Wash & Auto Detail** • 2800 Lincoln Blvd
- **Lincoln Blvd Car Wash** • 1624 Lincoln Blvd
- **Wilshire West Detail & Car Wash** • 2320 Wilshire Blvd

Gas Stations

- **76** • 1402 Santa Monica Blvd
- **76** • 1944 Pico Blvd
- **76** • 2120 Lincoln Blvd
- **Arco** • 2555 Lincoln Blvd
- **Arco** • 332 Pico Blvd
- **Chevron** • 1330 Santa Monica Blvd
- **Chevron** • 1732 Lincoln Blvd
- **Chevron** • 432 Wilshire Blvd
- **Exxon** • 1801 Lincoln Blvd
- **Mobil** • 731 Santa Monica Blvd
- **Shell** • 1866 Lincoln Blvd

Landmarks

- **3rd Street Promenade** • 3rd St b/w Broadway & Wilshire
- **Heritage Square** • Main St & Ocean Park Blvd
- **Santa Monica Civic Auditorium/ Civic Center** • 1855 Main St
- **Santa Monica Pier** • Ocean Ave & Colorado Ave

Libraries

- **LA County Law Library-Santa Monica** • 1725 Main St • 310-260-3644
- **Santa Monica Fairview Branch** • 2101 Ocean Park Blvd • 310-450-0443
- **Santa Monica Montana Avenue Branch** • 1704 Montana Ave • 310-829-7081
- **Santa Monica Ocean Park Branch** • 2601 Main St • 310-392-3804
- **Santa Monica Public Library** • 601 Santa Monica Blvd • 315-458-8600
- **Santa Monica Public Library (temporarily closed)** • 1343 6th St • 310-458-8600

Pharmacies

- **CVS** • 1411 Lincoln Blvd • 310-319-1318
- **Ralphs** • 1644 Cloverfield Blvd • 310-582-3915
- **Rite-Aid** • 1331 Wilshire Blvd • 310-458-0731
- **Rite-Aid** • 1808 Wilshire Blvd • 310-829-3951
- **Vons** • 710 Broadway • 310-260-0263
- **Walgreens** • 1932 Wilshire Blvd • 310-829-9264

Police

- **Santa Monica Police Headquarters** • 333 Olympic Dr • 310-458-8411

Post Offices

- **US Post Office** • 1025 Colorado Ave • 800-275-8777
- **US Post Office** • 1217 Wilshire Blvd • 800-275-8777
- **US Post Office** • 1248 5th St • 800-275-8777
- **US Post Office** • 2720 Neilson Wy • 800-275-8777

Schools

- **Carlthorp** • 438 San Vicente Blvd
- **Concord High** • 1831 Wilshire Blvd
- **Crossroads Elementary** • 1714 21st St
- **Delphi Academy** • 1229 4th St
- **Franklin Elementary** • 2400 Montana Ave
- **FSG Lighthouse** • 1220 20th St
- **Garden of Angels** • 1009 18th St
- **John Adams Middle** • 2425 16th St
- **John Muir Elementary** • 2526 6th St
- **Lincoln Middle** • 1501 California Ave
- **McKinley Elementary** • 2401 Santa Monica Blvd
- **New Path Montessori** • 1962 20th St
- **New Roads Elementary** • 1512 Pearl St
- **Olympic High** • 721 Ocean Park Blvd
- **Pacific Center for Creative Learning** • 1008 11th St
- **Pacifica Christian High** • 1730 Wilshire Blvd
- **PS #1 Elementary** • 1454 Euclid St
- **Roosevelt Elementary** • 801 Montana Ave
- **Santa Monica Alternative** • 2525 5th St
- **Santa Monica College** • 1900 Pico Blvd
- **Santa Monica High** • 601 Pico Blvd
- **Santa Monica Montessori** • 1909 Colorado Ave
- **SMMUSD Community Day** • 1401 Olympic Blvd
- **Soledad Enrichment Action** • 141 S Fetterly Ave
- **St Anne** • 2015 Colorado Ave
- **St John** • 1339 20th St
- **St Monica Elementary** • 1039 7th St
- **St Monica's High** • 1030 Lincoln Blvd
- **Westside Waldorf** • 1229 4th St
- **Will Rogers Elementary** • 2401 14th St

Supermarkets

- **Albertsons** • 2627 Lincoln Blvd
- **Pavilions** • 820 Montana Ave
- **Ralphs** • 1644 Cloverfield Blvd
- **Vons** • 1311 Wilshire Blvd
- **Vons** • 710 Broadway
- **Whole Foods Market** • 2201 Wilshire Blvd
- **Wild Oats** • 1425 Montana Ave
- **Wild Oats** • 500 Wilshire Blvd

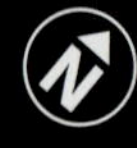

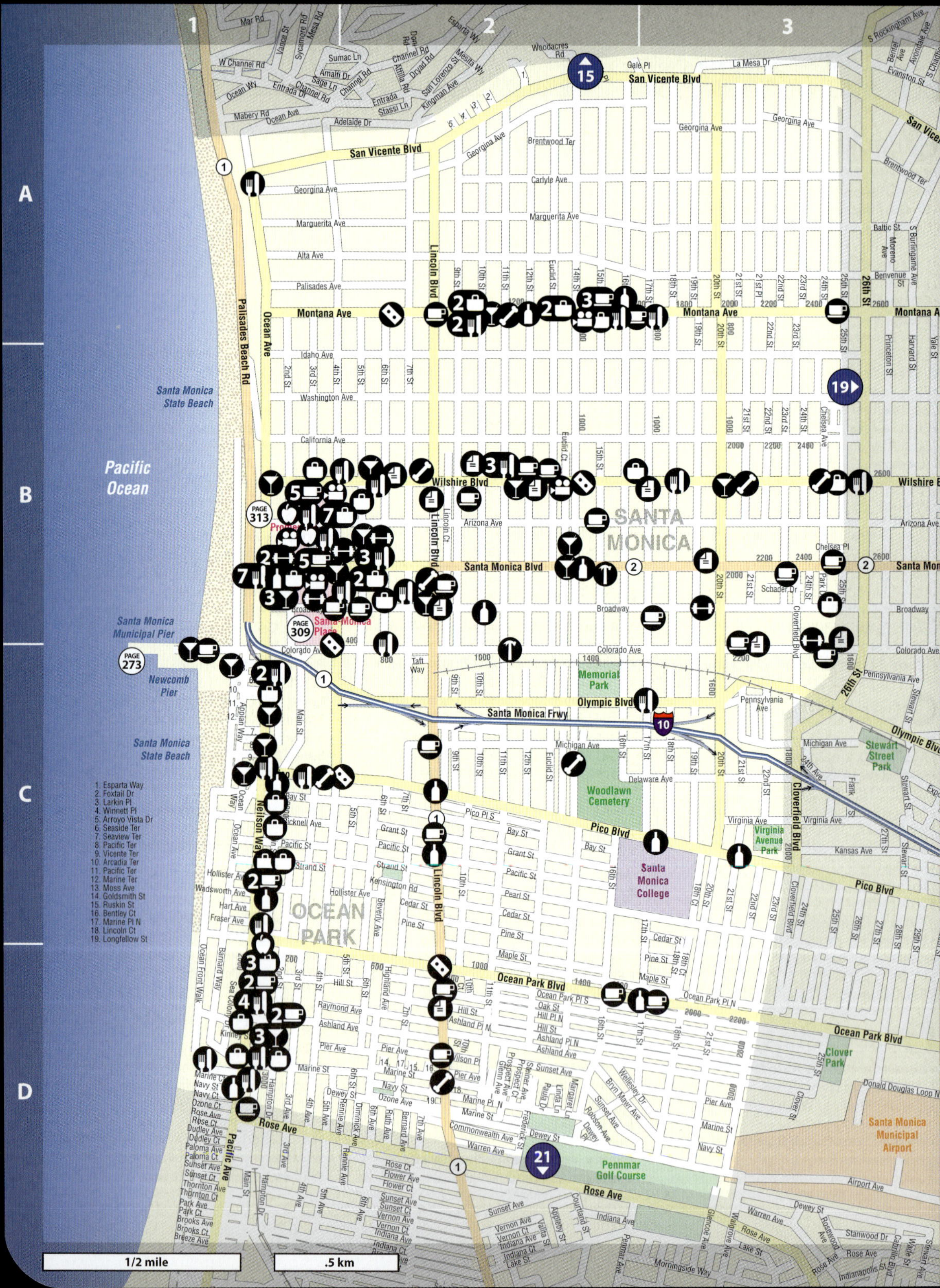

Pacific Ocean
Santa Monica State Beach
Santa Monica Municipal Pier
Newcomb Pier
SANTA MONICA
OCEAN PARK
Memorial Park
Woodlawn Cemetery
Santa Monica College
Virginia Avenue Park
Stewart Street Park
Clover Park
Pennmar Golf Course
Santa Monica Municipal Airport
Santa Monica Place
Santa Monica Frwy
San Vicente Blvd
Montana Ave
Wilshire Blvd
Santa Monica Blvd
Broadway
Colorado Ave
Olympic Blvd
Pico Blvd
Ocean Park Blvd
Rose Ave
Lincoln Blvd
Ocean Ave
Palisades Beach Rd
Main St
Cloverfield Blvd
26th St
PAGE 313
PAGE 309
PAGE 273
1. Esparta Way
2. Foxtail Dr
3. Larkin Pl
4. Winnett Pl
5. Arroyo Vista Dr
6. Seaside Ter
7. Seaview Ter
8. Pacific Ter
9. Vicente Ter
10. Arcadia Ter
11. Pacific Ter
12. Marine Ter
13. Moss Ave
14. Goldsmith St
15. Ruskin St
16. Bentley Ct
17. Marine Pl N
18. Lincoln Ct
19. Longfellow St
1/2 mile
.5 km

A weekend in Santa Monica should begin at the Farmers' Market (on Arizona on Saturdays, Main St. on Sundays). Then take a walk along the bluffs or bike ride on the beach path followed by lunch and shopping on Main St. Next, try the Library Ale House for its personal brews and neighboring Rick's Tavern for its burgers. Finally, check out REI: Outdoorsy Santa Monicans were pretty excited when it opened its doors on 4th street, transforming the once seedy Promenade neighbor into the next up-and-coming place to shop.

Coffee

- **18th Street Coffee House** • 1725 Broadway
- **Amelia's** • 2645 Main St
- **Angelato Café** • 301 Arizona Ave
- **Café Bolivar** • 1741 Ocean Park Blvd
- **Caffé Divine** • 500 Broadway
- **Coffee Bean and Tea Leaf** • 321 Santa Monica Blvd
- **Coffee Bean & Tea Leaf** • 1312 3rd St Prom
- **Coffee Bean & Tea Leaf** • 1426 Montana Ave
- **Coffee Bean & Tea Leaf** • 1804 Lincoln Blvd
- **Coffee Bean & Tea Leaf** • 200 Santa Monica Blvd
- **Coffee Bean & Tea Leaf** • 2901 Main St
- **Coffee Bean & Tea Leaf** • 380 Santa Monica Pier
- **Coffee Bean & Tea Leaf** • 829 Wilshire Blvd
- **Cutting Board** • 1260 15th St
- **Groundwork Coffee** • 2908 Main St
- **Infuzion Café** • 1149 3rd St
- **It's A Grind Coffee House** • 602 Santa Monica Blvd
- **Krispy Kreme Doughnuts** • 1231 Wilshire Blvd
- **Pane Dolce** • 1627 Montana Ave
- **Peet's** • 1401 Montana Ave
- **Peet's** • 2439 Main St
- **Starbucks** • 1201 3rd St Promenade
- **Starbucks** • 1311 Wilshire Blvd
- **Starbucks** • 1356 3rd St Prom
- **Starbucks** • 1426 Montana Ave
- **Starbucks** • 2200 Colorado Ave
- **Starbucks** • 2461 Santa Monica Blvd
- **Starbucks** • Albertsons • 2627 Lincoln Blvd
- **Starbucks** • 2671 Main St
- **Starbucks** • 3020 Lincoln Blvd
- **Starbucks** • 308 Wilshire Blvd
- **Starbucks** • 3110 Main St
- **Starbucks** • 701 Montana Ave
- **Starbucks** • 710 Broadway
- **Starbucks Coffee and Hear Music** • 1429 3rd St Prom
- **Swingers** • 802 Broadway
- **Talking Stick** • 1630 Ocean Park Blvd
- **Tully's Coffee** • 2425 Colorado Ave
- **Urth Caffé** • 2327 Main St
- **Velocity Café** • 2127 Lincoln Blvd

Copy Shops

- **Copypage** • 2450 Colorado Ave • 310-453-3600
- **FedEx Kinko's** • 601 Wilshire Blvd • 310-576-7710
- **FedEx Kinko's** • 925 Wilshire Blvd • 310-394-2914
- **Printing Palace** • 2300 Lincoln Blvd • 310-451-5151
- **Santa Monica Copy Printing** • 924 Wilshire Blvd • 310-319-1341
- **Sir Speedy** • 1909 Santa Monica Blvd • 310-829-3022
- **Staples** • 1501 Lincoln Blvd • 310-577-6740
- **Staples** • 1610 Wilshire Blvd • 310-828-7779
- **UPS Store** • 1223 Wilshire Blvd • 310-458-6878
- **UPS Store** • 2633 Lincoln Blvd • 310-396-5707

Farmers Markets

- **Farmers' Market (Wed, 9 am-2 pm; Sat, 8:30 am-1 pm)** • Arizona Ave & 2nd St
- **Santa Monica Saturday Organic (Sat, 8:30-1 pm)** • Arizona Ave & 3rd St Prom
- **Santa Monica (Sun, 9:30 am- 1 pm)** • Ocean Park Blvd & Main St

Gyms

- **24 Hour Fitness** • 1417 2nd St • 310-255-0008
- **Curves** • 1335 4th St • 310-917-1371
- **Curves** • 1919 Broadway • 310-582-9181
- **Easton Gym** • 1233 3rd St Prom • 310-395-4441
- **Equinox** • 201 Santa Monica Blvd • 310-593-8888
- **Santa Monica Family YMCA** • 1332 6th St • 310-393-2721
- **Tri Fit** • 2425 Colorado Ave • 310-829-2227

Hardware Stores

- **Busy Bee Hardware,** • 1521 Santa Monica Blvd • 310-395-1158
- **Fisher Lumber** • 1600 Lincoln Blvd • 310-395-0956
- **True Value** • 1636 11th St • 310-450-6556

Liquor Stores

- **A&E Liquor Mart** • 2116 Pico Blvd
- **Bill's Liquor** • 2202 Lincoln Blvd
- **Davey Jones Liquor Locker** • 63 Navy St
- **Davey Jones Liquor Locker** • 63 Navy St
- **Duck Blind** • 1102 Montana Ave
- **Ed's Liquor** • 825 Pico Blvd
- **Fireside Liquors** • 1421 Montana Ave
- **Frank's Liquor** • 115 Broadway
- **Hank's Liquor** • 1436 Santa Monica Blvd
- **Ladd Liquor** • 1011 Broadway
- **Marty's Liquor** • 1736 Ocean Park Blvd
- **Moore's Liquors** • 1713 Pico Blvd
- **Santa Monica Liquor** • 1001 Wilshire Blvd
- **Star Liquor** • 1929 Main St
- **Surf Liquor** • 2522 Main St

Movie Theaters

- **Aero Theater** • 1328 Montana Ave • 310-260-1528
- **AMC Broadway Cinemas 4** • 1441 3rd St Prom • 310-458-1506
- **AMC Santa Monica 7 Plex** • 1310 3rd St Prom • 310-289-4262
- **Laemmle Monica 4** • 1332 2nd St • 310-394-9744
- **Landmark NuWilshire Theatre** • 1314 Wilshire Blvd • 310-281-8223
- **Mann Criterion 6** • 1313 3rd St Prom • 310-395-1599

Nightlife

- **14 Below** • 1348 14th St • 310-451-5040
- **Bar Copa** • 2810 Main St • 310-452-2445
- **Big Dean's Café** • 1615 Ocean Front Wk • 310-393-2666
- **Cameo Bar** • Viceroy Hotel • 1819 Ocean Ave • 310-260-7500
- **Casa del Mar** • 1910 Ocean Wy • 310-581-5533
- **Circle Bar** • 2926 Main St • 310-450-0508
- **Cock N' Bull Pub** • 2947 Lincoln Blvd • 310-399-9696
- **Father's Office** • 1018 Montana Ave • 310-393-2337
- **The Gaslite** • 2030 Wilshire Blvd • 310-829-2382
- **Grill Restaurant** • Fairmont Miramar Hotel • 101 Wilshire Blvd • 310-319-3111
- **Harvelle's** • 1432 4th St • 310-395-1676
- **Library Alehouse** • 2911 Main St • 310-314-4855
- **Loews Santa Monica Beach Hotel** • 1700 Ocean Ave • 310-458-6700
- **Lounge 217** • 217 Broadway • 310-394-6336
- **Ma'Kai** • 101 Broadway Ave • 310-434-1511
- **O'Brien's** • 2941 Main St • 310-396-4725
- **Renee's Courtyard** • 522 Wilshire Blvd • 310-451-9341
- **The Room SM** • 1323 Santa Monica Blvd • 310-458-0707
- **Rusty's Surf Ranch** • 256 Santa Monica Pier • 310-393-7437
- **Shutters** • 1 Pico Blvd • 310-458-0030
- **Temple Bar** • 1026 Wilshire Blvd • 310-393-6611
- **Voda** • 1449 2nd St • 310-394-9774
- **Ye Olde King's Head** • 116 Santa Monica Blvd • 310-451-1402
- **Zanzibar** • 1301 5th St • 310-451-2221

Pet Shops

- **Animal Kingdom** • 300 Pico Blvd • 310-392-4074
- **Aquarium & Pet Center** • 826 Wilshire Blvd • 310-395-1009
- **Centinela Feed & Pet Supplies** • 1448 Lincoln Blvd • 310-451-7140
- **Consolidated Pet Supplies** • 1840 14th St • 310-393-9393
- **Nature's Grooming & Boutique** • 3110 Main St, Ste 104 • 310-392-8758
- **Pets of Wilshire** • 2102 Wilshire Blvd • 310-453-7676
- **Wagging Tail** • 1123 Montana Ave • 310-656-9663

Restaurants

- **17th Street Café** • 1610 Montana Ave • 310-453-2771
- **Akbar Cuisine of India** • 2627 Wilshire Blvd • 310-586-7469
- **Angelato Café** • 301 Arizona Ave • 310-656-9999
- **Babalu** • 1002 Montana Ave • 310-395-2500
- **Bagel Nosh** • 1629 Wilshire Blvd • 310-451-8771
- **Bay Cities Italian Deli** • 1517 Lincoln Blvd • 310-395-8279
- **Border Grill** • 1445 4th St • 310-451-1655
- **Broadway Deli** • 1457 3rd St Prom • 310-451-0616
- **Buffalo Club** • 1520 Olympic Blvd • 310-450-8600
- **Café Montana** • 1534 Montana Ave • 310-829-3990
- **California Chicken Café** • 2401 Wilshire Blvd • 310-453-0477
- **Cha Cha Chicken** • 1906 Ocean Ave • 310-581-1684
- **Chaya Venice** • 110 Navy St • 310-396-1179
- **Chez Jay** • 1657 Ocean Ave • 310-395-1741
- **Chinois on Main** • 2709 Main St • 310-392-9025
- **Dhaba** • 2104 Main St • 310-399-9452
- **El Cholo** • 1025 Wilshire Blvd • 310-899-1106
- **Falafel King** • 1315 3rd St Prom • 310-587-2551
- **Finn McCool's** • 2702 Main St • 310-452-1734
- **Fritto Misto** • 601 Colorado Ave • 310-458-2829
- **Fromin's Delicatessen** • 1832 Wilshire Blvd • 310-829-5443
- **The Galley** • 2442 Main St • 310-452-1934
- **Houston's** • 202 Wilshire Blvd • 310-576-7558
- **Jack 'n Jill's** • 510 Santa Monica Blvd • 310-656-1501
- **Library Alehouse** • 2911 Main St • 310-314-4855
- **The Lobster** • 1602 Ocean Ave • 310-458-9294
- **Lula** • 2720 Main St • 310-392-5711
- **Ma'Kai** • 101 Broadway Ave • 310-434-1511
- **Mani's** • 2507 Main St • 310-396-7700
- **Michael D's Café & Catering** • 234 Pico Blvd • 310-452-8737
- **Musha** • 424 Wilshire Blvd • 310-576-6330
- **Newsroom Café** • 530 Wilshire Blvd • 310-319-9100
- **Ocean Ave Seafood** • 1401 Ocean Ave • 310-394-5669
- **Omelette Parlor** • 2732 Main St • 310-399-7892
- **On the Waterfront Café** • 205 Ocean Front Wk • 310-392-0322
- **Sushi Roku** • 1401 Ocean Ave • 310-458-4771
- **Toi on Wilshire** • 1120 Wilshire Blvd • 310-394-7804
- **Trastevere** • 1360 3rd St Prom • 310-319-1985
- **Tudor House** • 1403 2nd St • 310-451-4107
- **World Café** • 2820 Main St • 310-392-1661
- **Ye Olde King's Head** • 116 Santa Monica Blvd • 310-451-1402

Shopping

- **Acorn Store** • 1220 5th St • 310-451-5845
- **Apple Store** • 1248 3rd St Prom • 310-576-1011
- **Continental Shop** • 1619 Wilshire Blvd • 310-453-8655
- **Eames Office** • 850 Pico Blvd • 310-396-5991
- **Fred Segal** • 500 Broadway • 310-394-9814
- **Helen's Cycles** • 2501 Broadway • 310-829-1836
- **Herb King** • 2305 Main St • 310-399-4470
- **Holy Guacamole, Neighborhood Taco Stand and Hot Sauce Emporium** • 2906 Main St • 310-314-4850
- **Horizons West** • 2011 Main St • 310-392-1122
- **Kiehl's** • 1516 Montana Ave • 310-255-0055
- **Le Sanctuaire** • 2710 Main St • 310-581-8999
- **London Sole** • 1331 Montana Ave • 310-255-0937
- **Number One Beauty Supply** • 1426 Montana Ave • 310-394-6968
- **One Life Natural Foods** • 3001 Main St • 310-392-4501
- **Palmetto** • 1034 Montana Ave • 310-395-6687
- **Pump Station** • 2415 Wilshire Blvd • 310-998-1981
- **Puzzle Zoo** • 1413 3rd St Prom • 310-393-9201
- **REI** • 402 Santa Monica Blvd • 310-458-4370
- **Santa Monica Farms** • 2015 Main St • 310-396-4069
- **Segway Los Angeles** • 1660 Ocean Ave • 310-395-1395
- **Starbucks Coffee and Hear Music** • 1429 3rd St Prom • 310-319-9527
- **Step!** • 1004 Montana Ave • 310-899-4409
- **Tao Healing Arts Center** • 2309 Main St • 310-396-4877
- **This Little Piggy Wears Cotton** • 309 Wilshire Blvd • 310-260-2727
- **Tiffany & Jax** • 1244 3rd St Prom • 310-260-8656
- **Tudor House** • 1403 2nd St • 310-451-4107
- **West Elm** • 1433 4th St • 310-576-7270
- **Wildfiber** • 1453 14th St • 310-458-2748
- **ZJ Boarding House** • 2619 Main St • 310-392-5646

Video Rental

- **Blockbuster** • 1402 Wilshire Blvd • 310-394-7792
- **Blockbuster** • 2602 Lincoln Blvd • 310-392-3228
- **Blockbuster** • 625 Montana Ave • 310-393-5131
- **Vidiots** • 302 Pico Blvd • 310-392-8508

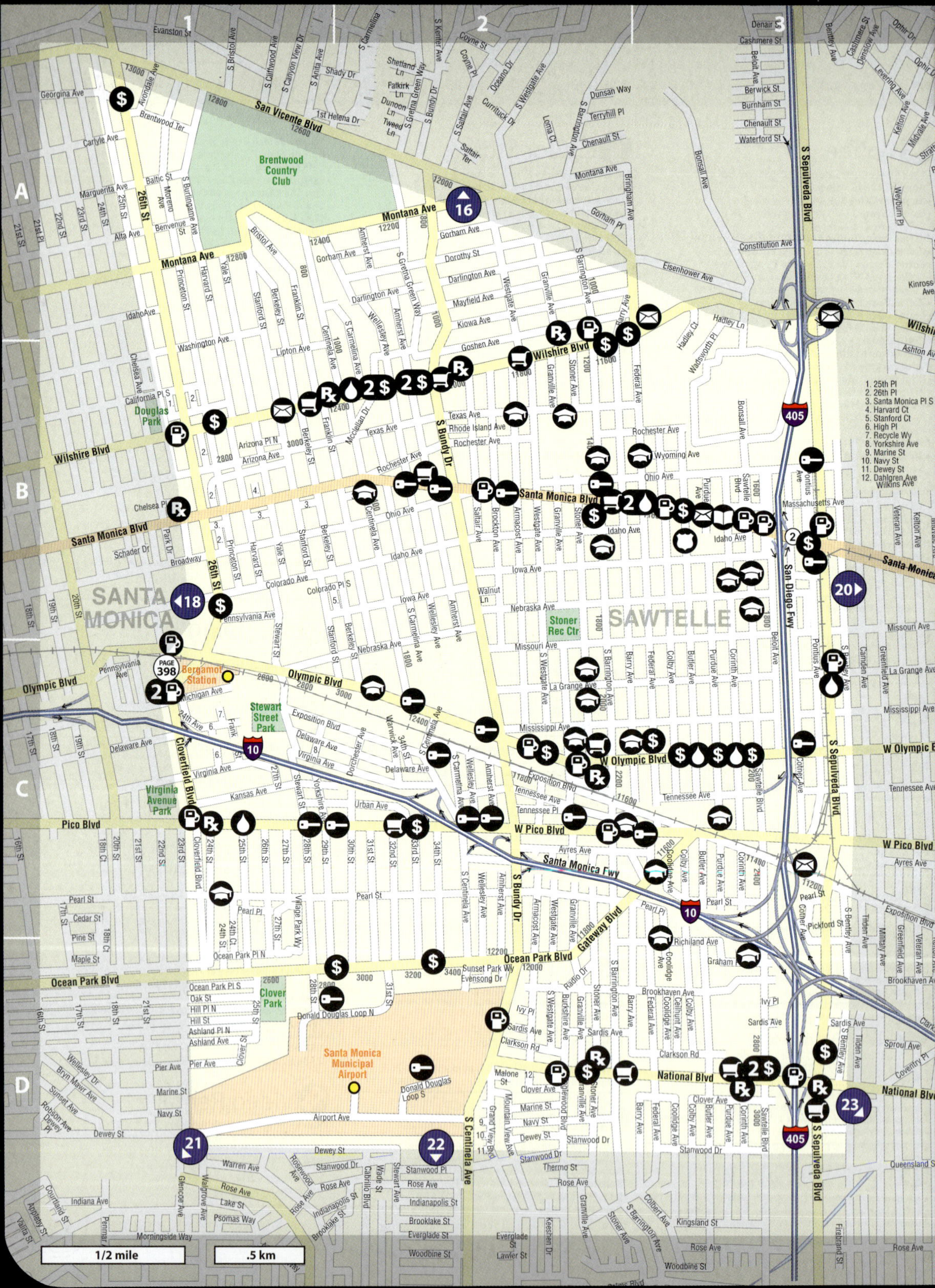

1. 25th Pl
2. 26th Pl
3. Santa Monica Pl S
4. Harvard Ct
5. Stanford Ct
6. High Pl
7. Recycle Wy
8. Yorkshire Ave
9. Marine St
10. Navy St
11. Dewey St
12. Dahlgren Ave

Often referred to as "The Westside," West LA/Santa Monica East is a part of town with its own hidden diamonds in the rough. Most residents of the area will agree that the proximity to the beach, wealth of shopping and dining options, cheaper rents, and easy access to the 10 and 405 freeways make it a great place to live.

Banks

- **Bank of America** • 11501 Santa Monica Blvd
- **Bank of America** • 287 26th St
- **Bank of America** • 2930 S Sepulveda Blvd
- **Bank of America** • 3320 Ocean Park Blvd
- **California Bank & Trust** • 11345 W Olympic Blvd
- **City National** • 11500 W Olympic Blvd
- **City National** • 1620 26th St
- **First Bank & Trust** • 11835 W Olympic Blvd
- **First Federal** • 11310 National Blvd
- **First Federal** • 12401 Wilshire Blvd
- **Fremont Investment & Loan** • 12424 Wilshire Blvd
- **Guaranty Bank of California** • 12301 Wilshire Blvd
- **Pacific Western** • 11150 W Olympic Blvd
- **US** • 12100 Wilshire Blvd
- **US** • 3302 Pico Blvd
- **Washington Mutual** • 11285 National Blvd
- **Washington Mutual** • 11766 Wilshire Blvd
- **Washington Mutual** • 2701 Wilshire Blvd
- **Wells Fargo** • 11377 W Olympic Blvd
- **Wells Fargo** • 11727 W Olympic Blvd
- **Wells Fargo** • 2940 Ocean Park Blvd
- **World Savings & Loan** • 11601 Wilshire Blvd

Car Rental

- **A Bundy Rent A Car** • 12333 W Pico Blvd
- **Absolutely Ugly Rent-A-Car** • 2270 Centinela Ave
- **Avis** • 11901 Santa Monica Blvd
- **California Rent-a-Car** • 11725 Santa Monica Blvd
- **Dreamboats Rent-a-Car** • 2929 Pico Blvd
- **Enterprise** • 11151 W Olympic Blvd
- **Enterprise** • 11779 W Pico Blvd
- **Enterprise** • 12101 Olympic Blvd
- **Enterprise** • 12207 Santa Monica Blvd
- **Enterprise** • 3300 Olympic Blvd
- **Hertz** • 3223 Donald Douglas Loop S
- **Midway Car Rental** • 1800 S Sepulveda Blvd
- **Midway Car Rental** • 2828 Donald Douglas Loop N
- **OK Rent a Car** • 12301 Santa Monica Blvd
- **Rapid Rent-a-Car** • 11590 W Pico Blvd
- **Rent-a-Wreck** • 12333 W Pico Blvd
- **Rodeo Automotive** • 2802 Pico Blvd

Car Washes

- **76** • 2001 S Sepulveda Blvd
- **Blue Wave Car Wash** • 11602 Santa Monica Blvd
- **Mr Detail Auto Waxing** • 11500 W Olympic Blvd
- **Santa Monica Car Wash & Detail** • 2510 Pico Blvd
- **Shell** • 11574 Santa Monica Blvd
- **Shine for Show** • 11755 Wilshire Blvd
- **West LA Car Wash** • 11350 W Olympic Blvd

Gas Stations

- **76** • 11280 National Blvd
- **76** • 11305 Santa Monica Blvd
- **76** • 11675 W Pico Blvd
- **76** • 11954 Santa Monica Blvd
- **76** • 2001 S Sepulveda Blvd
- **76** • 2601 Wilshire Blvd
- **76** • 2876 S Bundy Dr
- **Arco** • 11748 W Olympic Blvd
- **Arco** • 1819 Cloverfield Blvd
- **Chevron** • 11261 Santa Monica Blvd
- **Chevron** • 11951 W Olympic Blvd
- **Exxon** • 1770 Cloverfield Blvd
- **Mobil** • 11666 Wilshire Blvd
- **Mobil** • 1660 S Sepulveda Blvd
- **Shell** • 11574 Santa Monica Blvd
- **Shell** • 11944 W Olympic Blvd
- **Shell** • 1802 Cloverfield Blvd

Landmarks

- **Bergamot Station** • 2525 Michigan Ave
- **Santa Monica Municipal Airport** • 3223 Donald Douglas Loop S

Libraries

- **West Los Angeles Regional** • 11360 Santa Monica Blvd • 310-575-8323

Pharmacies

- **CVS** • 12015 W Wilshire Blvd • 310-479-6500
- **CVS** • 2505 Santa Monica Blvd • 310-828-6456
- **CVS** • 3010 S Sepulveda Blvd • 310-478-9821
- **Longs Drugs** • 3202 Wilshire Blvd • 310-829-5523
- **Pavilions** • 11750 Wilshire Blvd • 310-473-6138
- **Ralphs** • 11727 W Olympic Blvd • 310-444-0603
- **Rite-Aid** • 11321 National Blvd • 310-479-5729
- **Rite-Aid** • 2412 Pico Blvd • 310-450-7624

Police

- **Los Angeles Police Dept** • 1663 Butler Ave • 310-444-0701

Post Offices

- **US Post Office** • 11270 Exposition Blvd • 800-275-8777
- **US Post Office** • 11301 Wilshire Blvd • 800-275-8777
- **US Post Office** • 11420 Santa Monica Blvd • 800-275-8777
- **US Post Office** • 3010 WIlshire Blvd • 213-738-9714

Schools

- **Brawerman Elementary** • 11661 W Olympic Blvd
- **Brockton Ave Elementary** • 1309 Armacost Ave
- **Daniel Webster Middle** • 11330 W Graham Pl
- **Edison Language Academy Charter** • 2425 Kansas Ave
- **Grant Elementary** • 2368 Pearl St
- **Indian Springs Continuation** • 1441 S Barrington Ave
- **New Horizon** • 1819 Sawtelle Blvd
- **New Roads** • 3131 Olympic Blvd
- **New West Charter Middle** • 11625 W Pico Blvd
- **Nora Sterry Elementary** • 1730 Corinth Ave
- **Park Century** • 2040 Stoner Ave
- **Poseidon** • 11811 W Pico Blvd
- **Richland Ave Elementary** • 11562 Richland Ave
- **Richland EEC** • 2623 Coolidge Ave
- **Southern California Montessori** • 1430 Centinela Ave
- **St Joan of Arc Elementary** • 11561 Gateway Blvd
- **St Sebastian** • 1430 Federal Ave
- **Sterry EEC** • 1747 Sawtelle Blvd
- **University Senior High** • 11800 Texas Ave
- **West LA Baptist** • 1609 S Barrington Ave
- **Westview** • 2000 Stoner Ave
- **Wildwood** • 11811 W Olympic Blvd

Supermarkets

- **Albertsons** • 3105 Wilshire Blvd
- **Pavilions** • 11750 Wilshire Blvd
- **Ralphs** • 11361 National Blvd
- **Ralphs** • 11727 W Olympic Blvd
- **Ralphs** • 12057 Wilshire Blvd
- **Smart & Final** • 11221 W Pico Blvd
- **Smart & Final** • 12210 Santa Monica Blvd
- **Trader Joe's** • 3212 Pico Blvd
- **Vons** • 11674 Santa Monica Blvd
- **Vons** • 3118 S Sepulveda Blvd
- **Whole Foods Market** • 11666 National Blvd

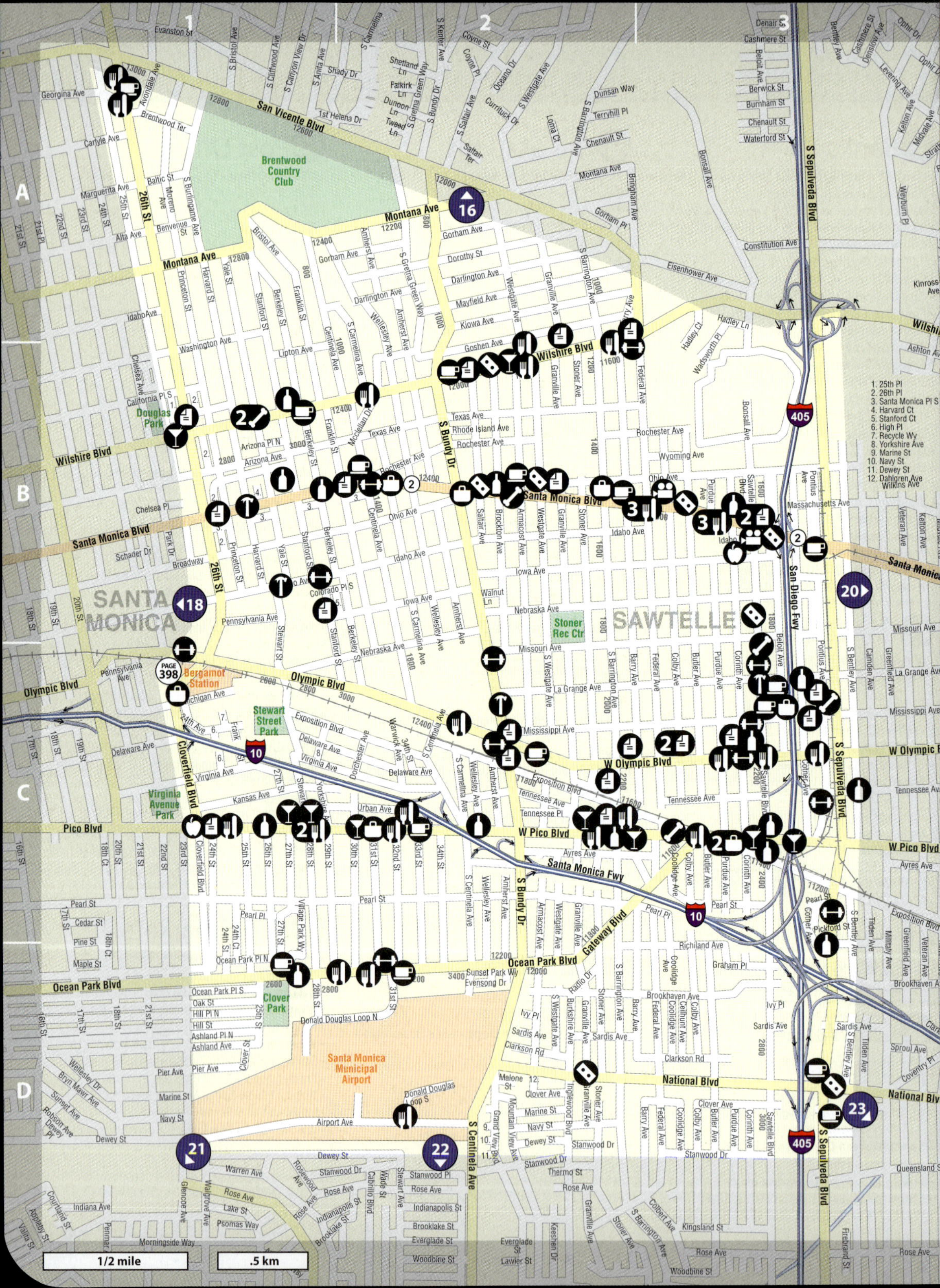

1. 25th Pl
2. 26th Pl
3. Santa Monica Pl S
4. Harvard Ct
5. Stanford Ct
6. High Pl
7. Recycle Wy
8. Yorkshire Ave
9. Marine St
10. Navy St
11. Dewey St
12. Dahlgren Ave

Brentwood Country Club

Douglas Park

SANTA MONICA

SAWTELLE

Stoner Rec Ctr

Bergamot Station

Stewart Street Park

Virginia Avenue Park

Clover Park

Santa Monica Municipal Airport

San Vicente Blvd

Montana Ave

Wilshire Blvd

Santa Monica Blvd

Olympic Blvd

W Olympic Blvd

Pico Blvd

W Pico Blvd

Ocean Park Blvd

National Blvd

Santa Monica Fwy

San Diego Fwy

S Sepulveda Blvd

S Bundy Dr

26th St

Cloverfield Blvd

S Centinela Ave

PAGE 398

16 18 20 21 22 23

1/2 mile

.5 km

A variety of restaurants illustrate the neighborhood's diversity. A mini-Japantown lies along Sawtelle north of Olympic, with an array of Japanese BBQ, sushi, noodle houses, and cutesy trendy shops. Yashima provides comfort food in the form of udon and scallion rice. Along Pico and Centinela is a bit of hip nightlife. The Arsenal serves up tunes and cocktails, while wine bar Air Conditioned pours wine tastings every Tuesday. For a quiet night at the movies, independent theater reigns in this neighborhood with the NuArt and Royal theaters.

Coffee

- **Balcony** • 12431 Rochester Ave
- **Brew N Beans** • 11150 Santa Monica Blvd
- **Calle Vista Coffee** • 11207 National Blvd
- **Coffee Bean & Tea Leaf** • 11913 W Olympic Blvd
- **Coffee Bean & Tea Leaf** • 3150 Ocean Park Blvd
- **Literati Café** • 12081 Wilshire Blvd
- **Lollicup** • 2012 Sawtelle Blvd
- **The Office** • 256 26th St
- **Starbucks** • 11155 Santa Monica Blvd
- **Starbucks** • 11280 W Olympic Blvd
- **Starbucks** • 11705 National Blvd
- **Starbucks** • 12100 Santa Monica Blvd
- **Starbucks** • 2525 Wilshire Blvd
- **Starbucks** • 2901 Ocean Park Blvd
- **Starbucks** • Albertsons • 3105 Wilshire Blvd
- **Starbucks** • 3118 S Sepulveda Blvd
- **Tanner's Coffee Company** • 11901 Santa Monica Blvd
- **Unurban** • 3301 Pico Blvd
- **Volcano Tea** • 2111 Sawtelle Blvd
- **Watta Express** • 2716 Ocean Park Blvd

Copy Shops

- **Advance Graphics & Printing** • 2233 Barry Ave • 310-473-7002
- **Blair Graphics** • 1740 Stanford St • 310-829-4621
- **Copy Depot & Printing** • 1635 Sawtelle Blvd • 310-473-5152
- **Copyco Printing** • 11555 W Olympic Blvd • 310-478-1776
- **Copyland** • 11717 W Pico Blvd • 310-479-3957
- **FedEx Kinko's** • 11819 Wilshire Blvd • 310-477-7756
- **FedEx Kinko's** • 2139 S Bundy Dr • 310-826-8122
- **Image Square** • 1627 Stanford St • 310-586-2333
- **Mail Boxes Etc** • 1158 26th St • 310-453-4111
- **Office Depot** • 2231 S Barrington Ave • 310-478-7103
- **Phantom Lithography** • 11279 Santa Monica Blvd • 310-478-4667
- **Pip Printing** • 2612 Santa Monica Blvd • 310-315-9625
- **Printers Company** • 11601 Wilshire Blvd • 310-477-8818
- **Quality Digital Solutions** • 11159 Mississippi Ave • 310-914-7606
- **Reliable Graphics** • 3212 Santa Monica Blvd • 310-453-7991
- **Sir Speedy** • 11660 W Olympic Blvd • 310-473-9256
- **Staples** • 2052 Bundy Dr • 310-826-0442
- **Super Fast Copying & Binding Systems** • 2358 Pico Blvd • 310-452-3352
- **Universal Reprographics** • 2043 Pontius Ave • 310-458-3523
- **UPS Store** • 11301 W Olympic Blvd • 310-445-4014
- **UPS Store** • 11870 Santa Monica Blvd • 310-207-1530
- **West LA Print & Copy** • 11577 Olympic Blvd • 310-473-5620

Farmers Markets

- **Santa Monica Pico (Sat, 8 am-1 pm)** • Pico Blvd & Cloverfield Blvd
- **West LA Civic (Sun, 9 am-2 pm)** • 1645 Corinth Ave

Gyms

- **24 Hour Fitness** • 2929 31st St • 310-450-4464
- **Bally Total Fitness** • 1914 S Bundy Dr • 310-820-7571
- **Bodies In Motion** • 12100 Olympic Blvd • 310-836-8000
- **Curves** • 2130 Sawtelle Blvd • 310-836-3050
- **Joe's Gym** • 11601 Wilshire Blvd • 310-966-1999
- **Powerhouse Gym** • 11400 W Olympic Blvd • 310-914-5120
- **Spectrum Club** • 2425 Olympic Blvd • 310-829-4995
- **Sports Club LA** • 1835 S Sepulveda Blvd • 310-473-1447
- **WestsideFamily YMCA** • 11311 La Grange Ave • 310-477-1511

Hardware Stores

- **George's Hardware & Garden Supply** • 2060 Sawtelle Blvd • 310-479-1280
- **Hardware Express** • 2834 Colorado Ave • 310-829-1184
- **Orchard Supply Hardware** • 2020 S Bundy Dr • 310-571-3838
- **Tool Power** • 2828 Santa Monica Blvd • 310-453-2012

Liquor Stores

- **2020 (wine only)** • 2020 Cotner Ave
- **Brockton Liquor** • 11932 Santa Monica Blvd
- **Hai's Liquor** • 11701 W Pico Blvd
- **In & Out Liquor** • 2130 Sawtelle Blvd
- **J & M Liquor** • 11306 Santa Monica Blvd
- **Jan's Liquors** • 12300 W Pico Blvd
- **Jerry's Liquor** • 2923 Wilshire Blvd
- **King Liquor** • 3102 Santa Monica Blvd
- **Signature Wines & Spirits** • 2717 Ocean Park Blvd
- **Sunset Plaza Liquor** • 2602 Pico Blvd
- **Wine Expo** • 2933 Santa Monica Blvd
- **Wine House (wine only)** • 2311 Cotner Ave

Movie Theaters

- **Laemmle Royal** • 11523 Santa Monica Blvd • 310-477-5581
- **Landmark NuArt Theatre** • 11272 Santa Monica Blvd • 310-281-8223

Nightlife

- **Air Conditioned** • 2819 Pico Blvd • 310-829-3700
- **The Arsenal** • 12012 W Pico Blvd • 310-575-5511
- **The Joker** • 2827 Pico Blvd • 310-828-9235
- **Liquid Kitty** • 11780 W Pico Blvd • 310-473-3707
- **McCabe's Guitar Shop** • 3101 Pico Blvd • 310-828-4497
- **Plan B** • 11637 W Pico Blvd • 310-312-3633
- **Q's Billiards** • 11835 Wilshire Blvd • 310-477-7550
- **The Shack** • 2518 Wilshire Blvd • 310-449-1171
- **Sonny McLean's Irish Pub & Restaurant** • 2615 Wilshire Blvd • 310-449-1811

Pet Shops

- **4 Paws and More** • 11544 W Pico Blvd • 310-312-6774
- **Elaine's Pet Depot** • 2919 Wilshire Blvd • 310-828-4545
- **Petco** • 2910 Wilshire Blvd • 310-586-1963
- **Pets Salon** • 12243 Santa Monica Blvd • 310-207-0838
- **The Reef Hotspot** • 2037 Pontius Ave • 310-478-4707

Restaurants

- **Asakuma** • 11701 Wilshire Blvd • 310-826-0013
- **Bandera** • 11700 Wilshire Blvd • 310-477-3524
- **Benito's Taco Shop** • 11614 Santa Monica Blvd • 310-442-9924
- **Bombay Café** • 12021 W Pico Blvd • 310-473-3388
- **Chez Mimi** • 246 26th St • 310-393-0558
- **Don Antonio's** • 11755 W Pico Blvd • 310-312-2090
- **Hide Sushi** • 2040 Sawtelle Blvd • 310-477-7242
- **Il Forno** • 2901 Ocean Park Blvd • 310-450-1241
- **Il Grano** • 11359 Santa Monica Blvd • 310-477-7886
- **Il Moro** • 11400 W Olympic Blvd • 310-575-3530
- **Javan** • 11500 Santa Monica Blvd • 310-207-5555
- **Josie Restaurant** • 2424 Pico Blvd • 310-581-9888
- **Kay 'n Dave's** • 262 26th St • 310-260-1355
- **La Bottega Marino** • 11363 Santa Monica Blvd • 310-477-7777
- **Lares** • 2909 Pico Blvd • 310-829-4559
- **Lazy Daisy** • 11913 Wilshire Blvd • 310-477-8580
- **Le Saigon** • 11611 Santa Monica Blvd • 310-312-2929
- **Nook Neighborhood Bistro** • 11628 Santa Monica Blvd • 310-207-5160
- **Rae's Restaurant** • 2901 Pico Blvd • 310-828-7937
- **Sushi Sasabune** • 12400 Wilshire Blvd • 310-268-8380
- **Tlapazola Grill** • 11676 Gateway Blvd • 310-477-1577
- **Typhoon** • Santa Monica Airport • 3221 Donald Douglas Loop S • 310-390-6565
- **Valentino** • 3115 Pico Blvd • 310-829-4313
- **Violet** • 3221 Pico Blvd • 310-453-9113
- **Vito** • 2807 Ocean Park Blvd • 310-450-4999
- **Yabu** • 11820 W Pico Blvd • 310-473-9757
- **Yashima** • 11301 W Olympic Blvd, Ste 210 • 310-473-5297
- **Zabie's** • 3003 Ocean Park Blvd • 310-392-9036

Shopping

- **Any Occasion Balloons** • 12009 W Pico Blvd • 310-473-9963
- **Giant Robot Store** • 2015 Sawtelle Blvd • 310-478-1819
- **Graphaids** • 12400 Santa Monica Blvd • 310-820-0445
- **Hiromi Paper International** • Bergamot Station • 2525 Michigan Ave • 310-998-0098
- **McCabe's Guitar Shop** • 3101 Pico Blvd • 310-828-4497
- **Musicians' Supply Shop** • 12010 Ohio Ave • 310-478-7836
- **Record Surplus** • 11609 W Pico Blvd • 310-478-4217
- **Utrecht Arts Supplies** • 11677 Santa Monica Blvd • 310-478-5775

Video Rental

- **20-20 Video** • 11550 Santa Monica Blvd • 310-478-2020
- **20-20 Video** • 3000 S Sepulveda Blvd • 310-836-2020
- **Blockbuster** • 11700 National Blvd • 310-391-8233
- **Blockbuster** • 12112 Santa Monica Blvd • 310-447-2481
- **Cinefile Video** • 11280 Santa Monica Blvd • 310-312-8836
- **Hollywood Video** • 11870 Santa Monica Blvd • 310-207-1485
- **Odyssey Video** • 11910 Wilshire Blvd • 310-477-2523
- **Video Addict (Asian)** • 1818 Sawtelle Blvd • 310-312-5083

Map 20 • Westwood / Century City

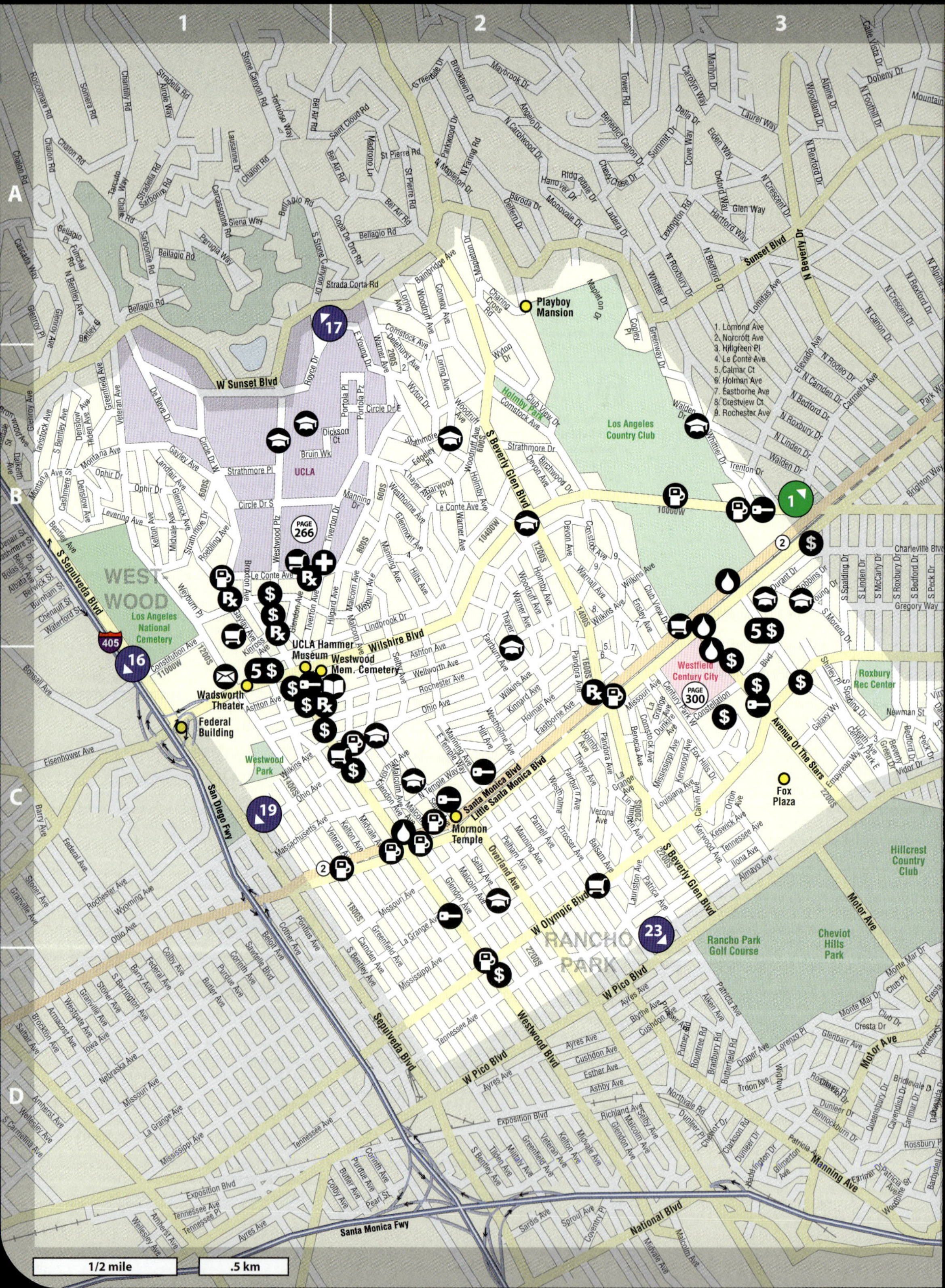
N
1
2
3
A
B
C
D
UCLA
PAGE 266
WEST WOOD
Los Angeles National Cemetery
405
16
17
19
23
1
Playboy Mansion
Los Angeles Country Club
Holmby Park
1. Lomond Ave
2. Norcroft Ave
3. Hillgreen Pl
4. Le Conte Ave
5. Calmar Ct
6. Holman Ave
7. Eastborne Ave
8. Crestview Ct
9. Rochester Ave
Westfield Century City
PAGE 300
Roxbury Rec Center
Fox Plaza
Hillcrest Country Club
Rancho Park Golf Course
Cheviot Hills Park
RANCHO PARK
UCLA Hammer Museum
Westwood Mem. Cemetery
Wadsworth Theater
Federal Building
Westwood Park
Mormon Temple
W Sunset Blvd
Sunset Blvd
Wilshire Blvd
Santa Monica Blvd
Little Santa Monica Blvd
W Olympic Blvd
W Pico Blvd
National Blvd
S Sepulveda Blvd
Sepulveda Blvd
San Diego Fwy
Santa Monica Fwy
Westwood Blvd
S Beverly Glen Blvd
Avenue Of The Stars
Motor Ave
Manning Ave
N Beverly Dr
1/2 mile
.5 km

By day, people come and go through Century City's office buildings. By night, it becomes a ghost town, unless you're at the recently renovated Century City Mall and AMC Movie Theatres. Nearby Westwood is always heavily populated—UCLA students, moviegoers, and sports fans. Consequently, street parking will test your patience and parallel parking abilities. For book enthusiasts, come to the LA Times Festival of Books at UCLA during April. Movie fans can try catching star sightings at a Mann Theatre movie premiere.

Banks

- **Bank of America** • 10960 Wilshire Blvd
- **Bank of America** • 2049 Century Park E
- **Bank of America** • 930 Westwood Blvd
- **Bank of the West** • 10929 Wilshire Blvd
- **California Bank & Trust** • 1940 Century Park E
- **California Credit Union** • 2215 Westwood Blvd
- **California National** • 1460 Westwood Blvd
- **California National** • 1800 Ave of the Stars
- **Citibank** • 1072 Westwood Blvd
- **Citibank** • 1801 Ave of the Stars
- **Citibank (Banamex USA)** • 2029 Century Park E
- **City National** • 10889 Wilshire Blvd
- **City National** • 1800 Century Park E
- **City National** • 2029 Century Park E
- **Comerica** • 10900 Wilshire Blvd
- **East West** • 1900 Ave of the Stars
- **First Regional** • 1801 Century Park E
- **First Republic** • 1888 Century Park E
- **Pacific Western** • 10250 Constellation Blvd
- **Preferred** • 1801 Century Park E
- **Union** • 10900 Wilshire Blvd
- **Union** • 1901 Ave of the Stars
- **US** • 10866 Wilshire Blvd
- **Washington Mutual** • 10901 Wilshire Blvd
- **Washington Mutual** • 1550 Westwood Blvd
- **Washington Mutual** • 1925 Century Park E
- **Wells Fargo** • 10920 Wilshire Blvd
- **Wells Fargo** • 1801 Ave of the Stars

Car Rental

- **Avis** • 1234 Westwood Blvd
- **Basic Car Rental** • 10687 Santa Monica Blvd
- **Enterprise** • 10799 Santa Monica Blvd
- **Hertz** • 2021 Westwood Blvd
- **Hertz** • 2025 Ave of the Stars

Car Washes

- **Blue Wave Car Wash** • 10854 Santa Monica Blvd
- **Century City** • 1800 Ave of the Stars
- **Mario's Hand Wash & Auto Detailing** • 10100 Santa Monica Blvd
- **Mr Polish** • 1901 Ave of the Stars

Gas Stations

- **76** • 10389 Santa Monica Blvd
- **76** • 9988 Wilshire Blvd
- **Chevron** • 10867 Santa Monica Blvd
- **Chevron** • 10984 Le Conte Ave
- **Chevron** • 1465 Glendale Blvd
- **Exxon** • 10991 Santa Monica Blvd
- **Mobil** • 10857 Santa Monica Blvd
- **Mobil** • 10863 W Olympic Blvd
- **Thrifty** • 10801 Santa Monica Blvd

Emergency Rooms

- **UCLA Medical Center** • 10833 Le Conte Ave

Landmarks

- **Federal Building** • Wilshire Blvd & Sepulveda Blvd
- **Fox Plaza (a.k.a "the Die Hard building")** • 2121 Ave of the Stars
- **Mormon Temple** • 10777 Santa Monica Blvd
- **Playboy Mansion** • 10236 Charing Cross Rd
- **UCLA Hammer Museum** • 10889 Wilshire Blvd
- **Wadsworth Theater** • 11000 Wilshire Blvd
- **Westwood Memorial Cemetery** • 1218 Glendon Ave

Libraries

- **Westwood Branch** • 1246 Glendon Ave • 310-474-1739

Pharmacies

- **CVS** • 1001 Westwood Blvd • 310-209-9141
- **CVS** • 10889 Wellworth Ave • 310-474-2152
- **Ralphs** • 10861 Le Conte Ave • 310-824-5994
- **Rite-Aid** • 1101 Westwood Blvd • 310-209-0708
- **Walgreens** • 10407 Santa Monica Blvd • 310-481-7123

Post Offices

- **US Post Office** • 11000 Wilshire Blvd • 800-275-8777

Schools

- **Beverly Hills High** • 241 S Moreno Dr
- **Beverly Hills Montessori** • 1105 N Laurel Ave
- **El Rodeo Elementary** • 605 N Whittier Dr
- **Fairburn Ave Elementary** • 1403 Fairburn Ave
- **Moreno High** • 214 Moreno Dr
- **Ralph Waldo Emerson Middle** • 1650 Selby Ave
- **Sinai Akiba Academy** • 10400 Wilshire Blvd
- **St Paul the Apostle** • 1536 Selby Ave
- **UCLA** • 405 Hilgard Ave
- **UCLA Neuropsychiatric Institute** • 760 Westwood Plz
- **Warner Ave Elementary** • 615 Holmby Ave
- **Westwood Elementary** • 2050 Selby Ave

Supermarkets

- **Bristol Farms** • 1515 Westwood Blvd
- **Gelson's Markets** • 10250 Santa Monica Blvd
- **Ralphs** • 10309 W Olympic Blvd
- **Ralphs** • 10861 Le Conte Ave
- **Whole Foods Market** • 1050 S Gayley Ave

1. Lomond Ave
2. Norcroft Ave
3. Hillgreen Pl
4. Le Conte Ave
5. Calmar Ct
6. Holman Ave
7. Eastborne Ave
8. Crestview Ct
9. Rochester Ave

UCLA

PAGE 266

Westwood

Los Angeles National Cemetery

Los Angeles Country Club

Holmby Park

Westfield Century City

PAGE 300

Roxbury Rec Center

Westwood Park

Rancho Park

Rancho Park Golf Course

Cheviot Hills Park

Hillcrest Country Club

1/2 mile

.5 km

The symbiotic relationship Westwood has with UCLA gives rise to so many unhealthy but delectable and inexpensive places to eat: In N' Out Burger (with a drive thru window!), Diddy Reece Cookies (just thirty-five cents a cookie—best when they're still warm), and Falafel King (extra baba ganoush, please).For the true Westwood experience, see a movie here on opening night. With some of the best and oldest remaining one-screen movie houses around, and enthusiastic and loyal crowds, it's a tradition you can't miss.

Coffee

- **Boba Loca** • 10946 Weyburn Ave
- **Bolee's Gourmet** • 10100 Santa Monica Blvd
- **City Bean** • 2121 Ave of The Stars
- **City Bean Coffee** • 10911 Lindbrook Dr
- **Coffee Bean & Tea Leaf** • 1001 Gayley Ave
- **Coffee Bean & Tea Leaf** • 10401 Santa Monica Blvd
- **Coffee Bean & Tea Leaf** • 11049 Santa Monica Blvd
- **Coffee Bean & Tea Leaf** • 1500 Westwood Blvd
- **Coffee Bean & Tea Leaf** • 1940 Century Park E
- **Coffee Bean & Tea Leaf** • 950 Westwood Blvd
- **Coffee Zinio** • 1731 Westwood Blvd
- **Cup-O-Coffee** • 2347 Kerwood Ave
- **Green Tea Terrace** • 1037 Westwood Blvd
- **Habibi Café** • 923 Broxton Ave
- **Kelly's Coffee & Fudge** • 10250 Santa Monica Blvd
- **Peet's** • 1154 Westwood Blvd
- **Peet's** • 1854 Westwood Blvd
- **Starbucks** • 10955 W Weyburn Ave
- **Starbucks** • 1161 Westwood Blvd
- **Starbucks** • 1875 Century Park E
- **Starbucks** • 1898 Westwood Blvd
- **Starbucks** • 1999 Ave of the Stars
- **Starbucks** • 2049 Century Park E
- **Starbucks** • 2215 Westwood Blvd

Copy Shops

- **ABC Copy & Print** • 1557 Westwood Blvd • 310-473-2813
- **Budget Printing & Copy** • 1718 Westwood Blvd • 310-444-1478
- **Copy Central** • 925 Westwood Blvd • 310-207-5952
- **Copy to Go Printing** • 1311 Westwood Blvd • 310-478-5455
- **Copypage** • 10250 Constellation Blvd • 310-203-0404
- **Copypage** • 1999 Ave of the Stars • 310-788-8601
- **Copypage** • 2029 Century Park E • 310-226-8640
- **Copytron & Printing** • 1377 Westwood Blvd • 310-473-0773
- **Doggie Logic** • 10100 Santa Monica Blvd • 310-556-7751
- **FedEx Kinko's** • 10924 Weyburn Ave • 310-443-5501
- **FedEx Kinko's** • 1520 Westwood Blvd • 310-475-0789
- **FedEx Kinko's** • 1925 Century Park E • 310-203-9928
- **Mail Boxes Etc** • 1875 Century Park E • 310-286-1875
- **Mail Boxes Etc** • 914 Westwood Blvd • 310-208-5022
- **Next Print** • 1632 Westwood Blvd • 310-441-5999
- **Print Run Services** • 952 Gayley Ave • 310-824-5150
- **Repro Solutions** • 10780 Santa Monica Blvd • 310-441-4333
- **Staples** • 10830 Santa Monica Blvd • 310-441-1734
- **Summitt Reprographics** • 1801 Ave of The Stars • 310-788-3481
- **Sunshine Instant Printing** • 10900 Wellworth Ave • 310-479-5939
- **Unlimited Reprographics** • 1880 Century Park E • 310-282-0202
- **Westwood Copies** • 1001 Gayley Ave • 310-208-3233

Farmers Markets

- **Farmers' Market-Century City (Thurs, 11:30 am-3 pm)** • Constellation Blvd & Ave of the Stars
- **Westwood Village (Thurs, 1 pm-7 pm)** • Weyburn Ave & Westwood Blvd

Gyms

- **Curves** • 10966 Le Conte Ave • 310-443-9044
- **Equinox Fitness** • 10220 Constellation Blvd • 310-552-8026
- **Equinox Fitness Club** • 10960 Wilshire Blvd • 310-954-8950
- **LA Fitness Sports Clubs** • 10921 Wilshire Blvd • 310-209-5002

Hardware Stores

- **Boulevard Hardware** • 1456 Westwood Blvd • 310-475-0795

Liquor Stores

- **Frank's Liquor** • 10559 Santa Monica Blvd
- **Wally's Wines & Liquors** • 2107 Westwood Blvd

Movie Theaters

- **AMC Avco Center Cinemas** • 10840 Wilshire Blvd • 310-475-0714
- **AMC Century 15** • 10250 Santa Monica Blvd • 310-289-4262
- **Billy Wilder Theater at the Hammer Museum** • 10899 Wilshire Blvd • 310-206-3456
- **Landmark Regent Theatre** • 1045 Broxton Ave • 310-281-8223
- **Majestic Crest Theatre** • 1262 Westwood Blvd • 310-474-7866
- **Mann Bruin** • 948 Broxton Ave • 310-208-8998
- **Mann Festival Westwood 1** • 10887 Lindbrook Dr • 310-248-6266
- **Mann Village Theatre Westwood** • 961 Broxton Ave • 310-208-5576

Nightlife

- **The Century Club** • 10131 Constellation Blvd • 310-553-6000
- **Westwood Brewing Company** • 1097 Glendon Ave • 310-209-2739
- **Whiskey Blue** • W Hotel • 930 Hilgard Ave • 310-443-8232

Pet Shops

- **Judy's Pet Depot** • 1278 Westwood Blvd • 310-470-4210
- **Petco** • 1873 Westwood Blvd • 310-441-2073

Restaurants

- **Big Chill** • 10850 Olympic Blvd • 310-441-0643
- **Carvel Ice Cream** • 11037 Santa Monica Blvd • 310-444-0011
- **Clementine** • 1751 Ensley Ave • 310-552-1080
- **Diddy Riese Cookies** • 926 Broxton Ave • 310-208-0448
- **Earth, Wind & Flour** • 1776 Westwood Blvd • 310-470-2499
- **Falafel King** • 1059 Broxton Ave • 310-208-4444
- **Gardens on Glendon** • 1139 Glendon Ave • 310-824-1818
- **Houston's** • 10250 Santa Monica Blvd • 310-557-1285
- **In-N-Out Burger** • 922 Gayley Ave • 800-786-1000
- **Johnnie's NY Pizzeria** • Fox Apartments • 10251 Santa Monica Blvd • 310-553-1188
- **La Bruschetta** • 1621 Westwood Blvd • 310-477-1052
- **La Cachette** • 10506 Santa Monica Blvd • 310-470-4992
- **Matteo's Hoboken** • 2323 Westwood Blvd • 310-474-1109
- **Napa Valley Grille** • 1100 Glendon Ave • 310-824-3322
- **Stan's Donuts** • 10948 Weyburn Ave • 310-208-8660
- **Tengu** • 10853 Lindbrook Dr • 310-209-0071

Shopping

- **Bristol Farms** • 1515 Westwood Blvd • 310-481-0100
- **Cost Plus World Market** • 10860 Santa Monica Blvd • 310-441-5115
- **Restoration Hardware** • 10250 Santa Monica Blvd • 310-551-4995
- **Sugar Paper** • 1749 Ensley Ave • 310-277-7804
- **The Writer's Store** • 2040 Westwood Blvd • 310-441-5151

Video Rental

- **Hollywood Video** • 10250 S Santa Monica Blvd • 310-201-4712
- **Hollywood Video** • 10951 Wilshire Blvd • 310-443-5644
- **Hollywood Video** • 2201 Westwood Blvd • 310-475-0636

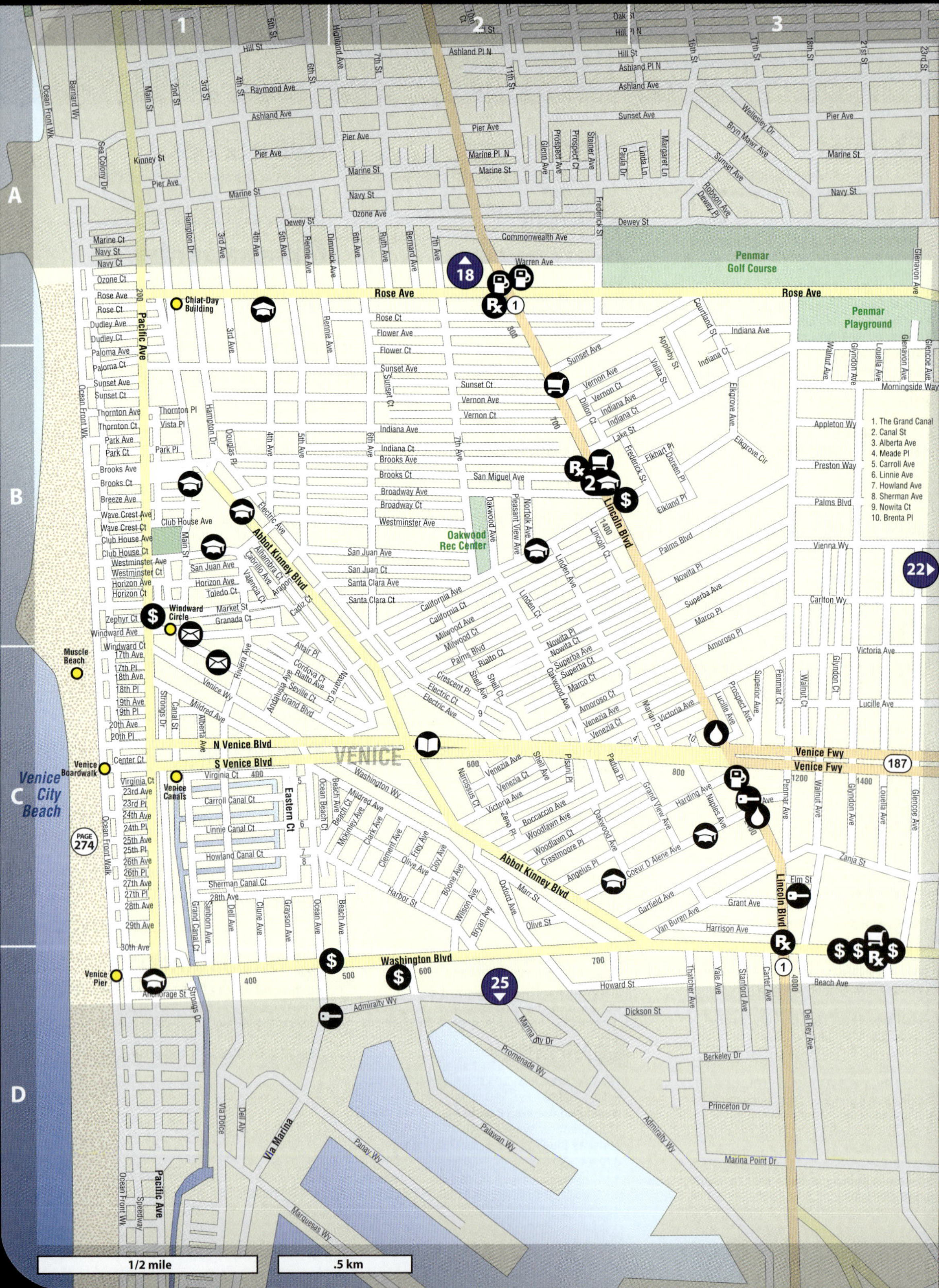

1. The Grand Canal
2. Canal St
3. Alberta Ave
4. Meade Pl
5. Carroll Ave
6. Linnie Ave
7. Howland Ave
8. Sherman Ave
9. Nowita Ct
10. Brenta Pl

1/2 mile

.5 km

Essentials

Venice is where LA comes to check out the waves, the sun, and each other in bikinis. The beachfront boardwalk grooves to a smooth carnival beat Abbott Kinney leans back local and sells upscale design, and the canals showcase mini, domestic architectural wonders. Meanwhile, Lincoln Blvd offers up a multitude of places to get a new tire and a smog check.

Banks

- **Bank of America** • 121 Windward Ave
- **Downey Savings & Loan** • 13401 Washington Blvd
- **Downey Savings & Loan** • 8824 S Sepulveda Blvd
- **First Coastal** • 590 Washington Blvd
- **First Federal** • 13405 Washington Blvd
- **Washington Mutual** • 1415 Lincoln Blvd
- **Wells Fargo** • 13400 Washington Blvd
- **Wells Fargo** • 514 Washington Blvd

Car Rental

- **California Rent-A-Car** • 2423 Lincoln Blvd
- **Enterprise** • 4111 Via Marina
- **Hertz** • 2519 Lincoln Blvd

Car Washes

- **Lincoln Millennium Car Wash** • 2454 Lincoln Blvd
- **Marina Car Wash** • 2305 Lincoln Blvd

Gas Stations

- **76** • 300 Lincoln Blvd
- **Arco** • 251 Lincoln Blvd
- **Chevron** • 2400 Lincoln Blvd

Landmarks

- **Chiat-Day Building** • 340 Main St
- **Muscle Beach** • 1817 Ocean Front Wk
- **Venice Boardwalk** • Ocean Front Wk
- **Venice Canals** • Venice Blvd & Pacific Ave
- **Venice Pier** • Far west end of Washington Blvd
- **Windward Circle** • Main St & Windward Ave

Libraries

- **Venice Branch** • 501 S Venice Blvd • 310-821-1769

Pharmacies

- **CVS** • 219 Lincoln Blvd • 310-392-3983
- **Rite-Aid** • 888 Lincoln Blvd • 310-396-2838
- **Sav-On** • Albertsons • 13401 Washington Blvd • 310-821-0904
- **Walgreens** • 4009 Lincoln Blvd • 310-823-7152

Post Offices

- **US Post Office** • 1601 Main St • 800-275-8777
- **US Post Office** • 313 Grand Blvd • 800-275-8777

Schools

- **Animo Venice Charter High** • 1015 Lincoln Blvd
- **Animo Venice Charter High** • 841 California Ave
- **Broadway Elementary** • 1015 Lincoln Blvd
- **Coeur D'Alene Ave Elementary** • 810 Coeur D'Alene Ave
- **Ecole Clairefontaine** • 226 Westminster Ave
- **First Lutheran** • 815 Venice Blvd
- **St Mark's Elementary** • 912 Coeur D'Alene Ave
- **Venice Skills Center** • 611 5th Ave
- **Westminster Ave Elementary** • 1010 Abbot Kinney Blvd
- **Westminster EEC** • 1010 Main St
- **Westside Leadership Magnet** • 104 Anchorage St

Supermarkets

- **Albertsons** • 13401 Washington Blvd
- **Ralphs** • 910 Lincoln Blvd
- **Smart & Final** • 604 Lincoln Blvd

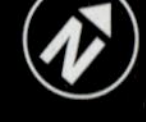

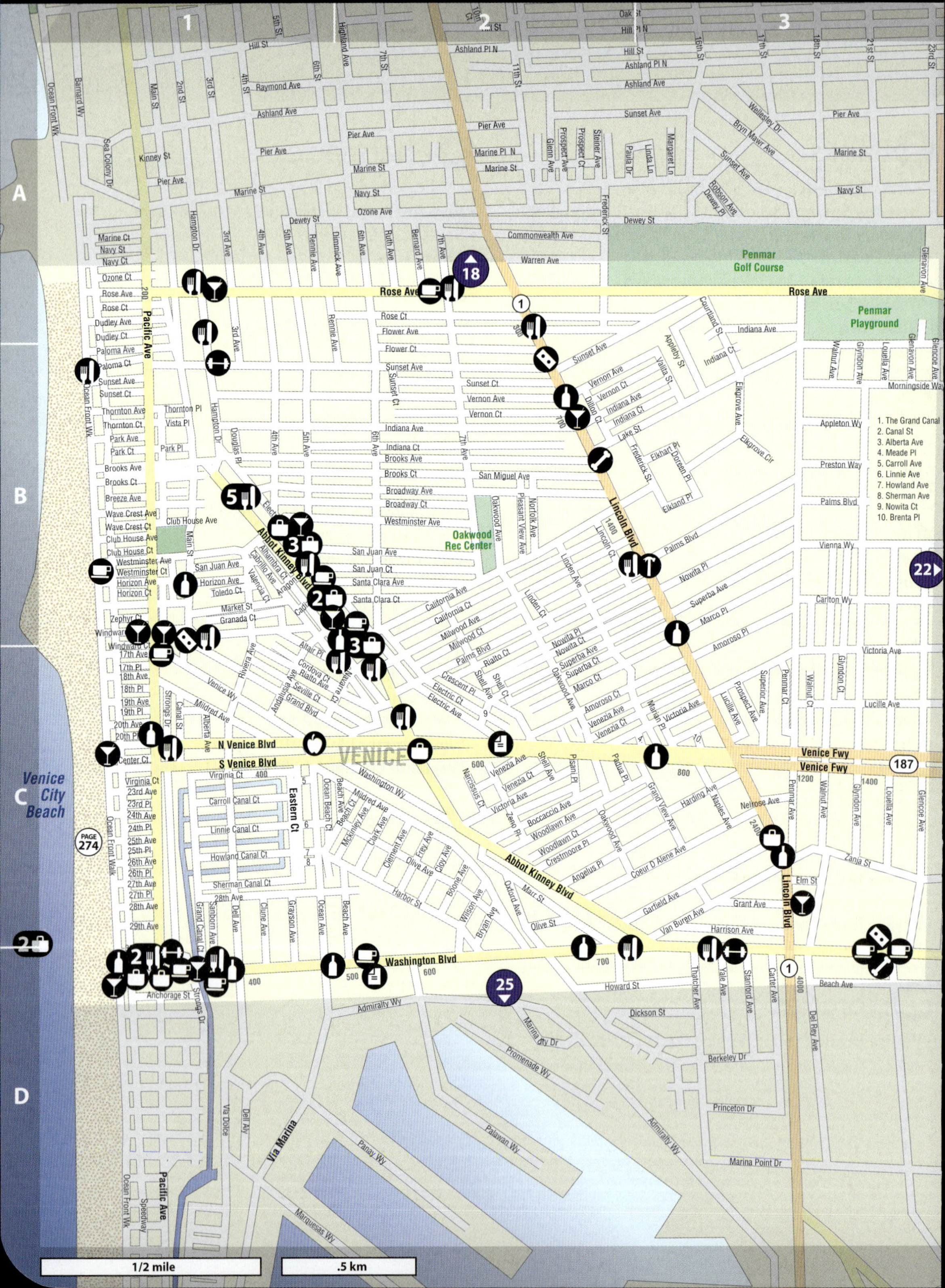

1
2
3
A
B
C
D
Penmar Golf Course
Penmar Playground
Oakwood Rec Center
Venice City Beach
VENICE
18
22
25
PAGE 274
1. The Grand Canal
2. Canal St
3. Alberta Ave
4. Meade Pl
5. Carroll Ave
6. Linnie Ave
7. Howland Ave
8. Sherman Ave
9. Nowita Ct
10. Brenta Pl
Rose Ave
Lincoln Blvd
Abbot Kinney Blvd
Pacific Ave
N Venice Blvd
S Venice Blvd
Venice Fwy
Washington Blvd
Ocean Front Wk
Main St
Hampton Dr
Rennie Ave
Oakwood Ave
Walnut Ave
Glyndon Ave
Louella Ave
Glencoe Ave
Glenavon Ave
Ashland Ave
Hill St
Pier Ave
Marine St
Navy St
Ozone Ave
Dewey St
Commonwealth Ave
Warren Ave
Sunset Ave
Vernon Ave
Indiana Ave
Brooks Ave
Broadway Ave
Westminster Ave
San Juan Ave
Santa Clara Ave
California Ave
Milwood Ave
Palms Blvd
Superba Ave
Victoria Ave
Harding Ave
Zanja St
Grant Ave
Harrison Ave
Beach Ave
Howard St
Admiralty Wy
Via Marina
Via Dolce
Marquesas Wy
Panay Wy
Palawan Wy
Promenade Wy
Dickson St
Berkeley Dr
Princeton Dr
Marina Point Dr
Speedway
Eastern Ct
Grand Canal Ct
Carroll Canal Ct
Linnie Canal Ct
Howland Canal Ct
Sherman Canal Ct
Anchorage St
Strongs Dr
Dell Ave
Ocean Ave
Mildred Ave
Andalusia Ave
Riviera Ave
Zeno Pl
Woodlawn Ave
Crestmoore Pl
Angelus Pl
Coeur D Alene Ave
Garfield Ave
Van Buren Ave
Elm St
Del Rey Ave
187
1
1/2 mile
.5 km

Venice is an artist colony striving to survive amid the juxtaposition of million-dollar homes and drug houses, walk streets and canals. For those with some disposable income, head to shabby chic Abbott Kinney for great shops and restaurants. Joe's French-California cuisine is one of the best fusion spots in LA, while wine and tunes go hand-in-hand at The Other Room's exposed-brick wine bar. Venice Beach is great for surfing, but skip Venice walk - head to Washington Blvd. instead for more weird-people watching.

Coffee

- **Abbot's Habit** • 1401 Abbot Kinney Blvd
- **Coffee Bean & Tea Leaf** • 80 Windward Ave
- **The Cow's End** • 34 Washington Blvd
- **Groundwork Coffee Company** • 3 Westminster Ave
- **Groundwork Coffee Company** • 671 Rose Ave
- **Jin Patisserie** • 1202 Abbot Kinney Blvd
- **Joni's Coffee Roaster Café** • 552 Washington Blvd
- **Starbucks** • 100 Washington Blvd
- **Starbucks** • Albertsons • 13401 Washington Blvd
- **Starbucks** • 13431 Washington Blvd

Copy Shops

- **Graphic Details** • 660 Venice Blvd • 310-823-2679
- **UPS Store** • 578 Washington Blvd • 310-827-4657

Farmers Markets

- **Venice (Fri, 7 am-11 am)** • Venice Blvd & Venice Wy

Gyms

- **Boditron Fitness Academy** • 134 Washington Blvd • 310-574-8785
- **Gold's Gym** • 360 Hampton Dr • 310-392-6004
- **World Gym** • 3205 Washington Blvd • 310-827-8019

Hardware Stores

- **True Value** • 1609 Lincoln Blvd • 310-821-1027

Liquor Stores

- **Alan's Market** • 339 Washington Blvd
- **Bob's Liquor** • 727 Lincoln Blvd
- **Day & Night Liquor & Market** • 1002 Venice Blvd
- **Joe's Liquor** • 1901 Lincoln Blvd
- **Lincoln Liquor Locker** • 2498 Lincoln Blvd
- **Lucky Stop** • 1360 Abbot Kinney Blvd
- **Marina Del Rey Liquormart** • 753 Washington Blvd
- **Munis Liquor** • 2022 Pacific Ave
- **Nick's Liquor** • 11 Washington Blvd
- **Trading Post Liquor** • 1313 Main St
- **Wolf's Liquor** • 536 Washington Blvd

Nightlife

- **Baja Cantina** • 311 Washington Blvd • 310-821-2252
- **The Brig** • 1515 Abbot Kinney Blvd • 310-399-7537
- **Firehouse** • 213 Rose Ave • 310-396-6810
- **James' Beach** • 60 N Venice Blvd • 310-823-5396
- **The Other Room** • 1201 Abbot Kinney Blvd • 312-226-6300
- **Red Garter** • 2536 Lincoln Blvd • 310-306-8300
- **Roosterfish** • 1302 Abbot Kinney Blvd • 310-392-2123
- **The Town House** • 52 Windward Ave • 310-392-4040
- **Venice Whaler Bar & Grill** • 2 Washington Blvd • 310-821-8737

Pet Shops

- **Allan's Aquarium & Pet Center** • 845 Lincoln Blvd • 310-399-5464
- **Pet Stuff** • 13400 Washington Blvd • 310-306-5175

Restaurants

- **Abbot's Pizza** • 1407 Abbot Kinney Blvd • 310-396-7334
- **Axe** • 1009 Abot Kinney Blvd • 310-664-9787
- **Baja Cantina** • 311 Washington Blvd • 310-821-2252
- **Bay Cities Italian Deli** • 1517 Lincoln Blvd • 310-395-8279
- **Beechwood** • 822 Washington Blvd • 310-448-8884
- **The Brick House** • 826 Hampton Dr • 310-581-1639
- **C&O Trattoria** • 31 Washington Blvd • 310-823-9491
- **Café 50's** • 838 Lincoln Blvd • 310-399-1955
- **Café Buna** • 3105 Washington Blvd • 310-823-2430
- **Canal Club** • 2025 Pacific Ave • 310-823-3878
- **Casablanca** • 220 Lincoln Blvd • 310-392-5751
- **Hal's Bar & Grill** • 1349 Abbot Kinney Blvd • 310-396-3105
- **Hama Sushi** • 213 Windward Ave • 310-396-8783
- **Jin Patisserie** • 1202 Abbot Kinney Blvd • 310-399-8801
- **Joe's** • 1023 Abbot Kinney Blvd • 310-399-5811
- **Killer Shrimp** • 523 Washington Blvd • 310-578-2293
- **La Cabana Restaurant and Bar** • 738 Rose Ave • 310-392-7973
- **Lilly's French Café** • 1031 Abbot Kinney Blvd • 310-314-0004
- **Primitivo Wine Bistro** • 1025 Abbot Kinney Blvd • 310-396-5353
- **Rose Café** • 220 Rose Ave • 310-399-0711
- **The Terrace Café** • 7 Washington Blvd • 310-578-1530
- **Wabi-Sabi** • 1635 Abbot Kinney Blvd • 310-314-2229

Shopping

- **Ananda** • 1354 Abbot Kinney Blvd • 310-399-4186
- **Brick Lane** • 1132 Abbot Kinney Blvd • 310-392-2525
- **Daisy Arts** • 1312 Abbot Kinney Blvd • 310-396-8463
- **DNA** • 411 Rose Ave • 310-399-0341
- **Equator Books** • 1103 Abbot Kinney Blvd • 310-399-5544
- **Firefly** • 1413 Abbot Kinney Blvd • 310-450-6288
- **Green House Smoke Shop** • 1428 Abbot Kinney Blvd • 310-450-6420
- **Heist** • 1104 Abot Kinney Blvd • 310-450-6531
- **Helen's Cycles** • 2472 Lincoln Blvd • 310-306-7843
- **Hydro Lab** • 1140 Abbot Kinney Blvd • 310-450-7221
- **Samy's Camera** • 585 Venice Blvd • 310-450-4551
- **The Starting Line** • 114 Washington Blvd • 310-827-3035
- **Venice Bike & Skate** • 21 Washington Blvd • 310-301-4011
- **Waraku** • 1225 Abbot Kinney Blvd • 310-452-5300

Video Rental

- **Hollywood Video** • 13411 Washington Blvd • 310-821-7884
- **Jungle Video** • 423 Lincoln Blvd • 310-314-7777
- **Main St Video** • 1600 Main St • 310-821-7838

1. Coolidge Pl
2. Craigview Av
3. Corinth Ave
4. Rurdue Ave
5. S Barrington
6. Butler Ave
7. Vienna Way
8. Marco Pl
9. Francis Pl
10. Regent St
11. Westminste
12. Bradson Pl
13. Patrae St
14. Verdi St

Mar Vista Tract

Mar Vista Rec Center

Culver West Park

Mar Vista Gardens

Venice Blvd

Washington Blvd

Washington Pl

Culver Blvd

S Centinela Ave

San Diego Fwy

Marina Fwy

Marina Expy

Ballona Creek

Centinela Creek

Sepulveda Channel

1/2 mile | .5 km

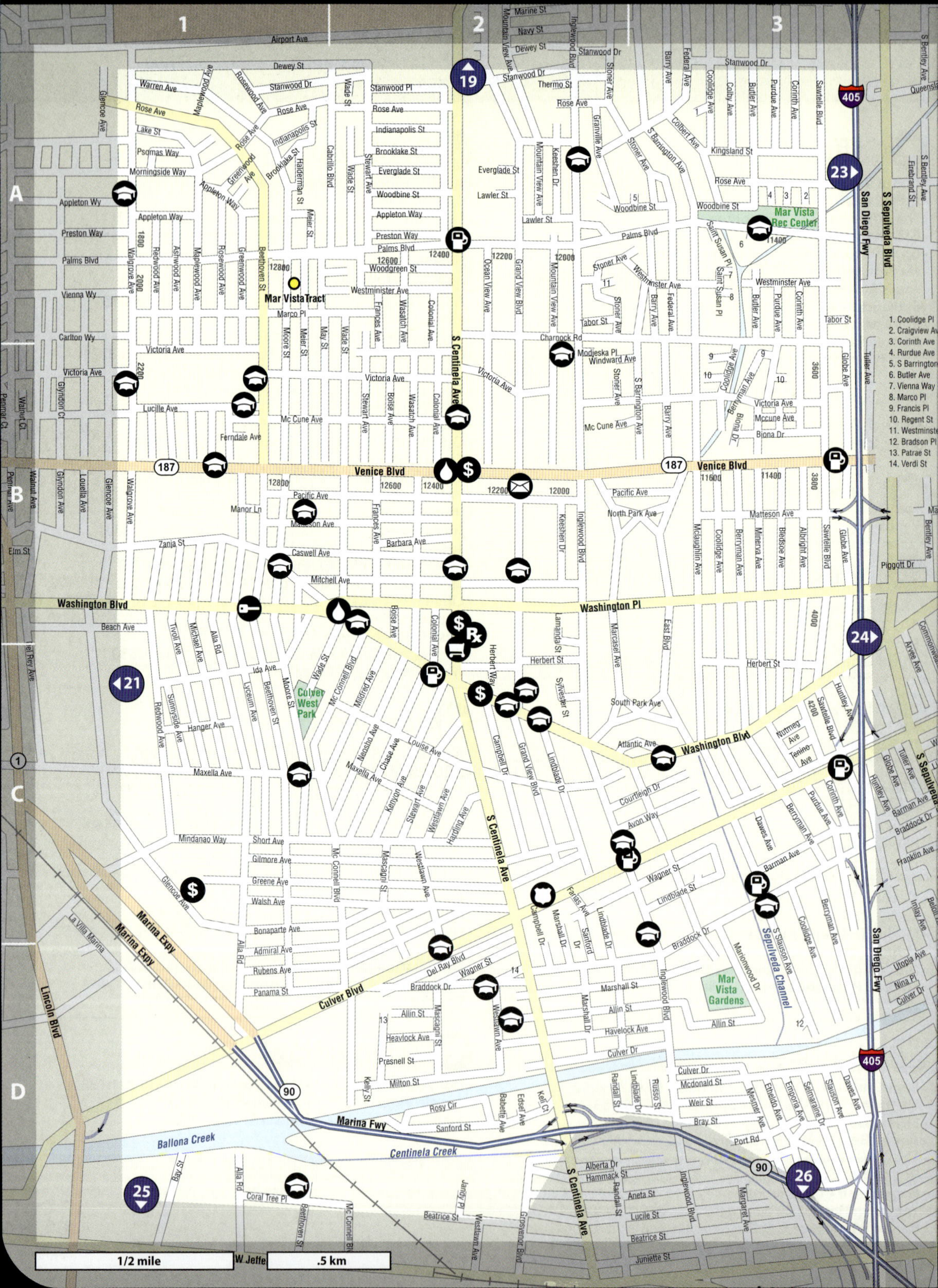

Ah, the Westside. Where you can be a yuppie without getting grief. Mar Vista is the'burbs with a twist. Quiet little neighborhood of pricey homes between Old Money Marina Del Rey and newly hip Culver City. Far enough west to still get ocean breezes. This easy-on-the-attitude community has enough local businesses and neighborhood joints that you won't have to fight traffic to grab a bite, raise a glass, or grocery shop.

Banks

- **Bank of America** • 12316 W Washington Blvd
- **Citibank** • 4375 Glencoe Ave
- **Union** • 4032 S Centinela Ave
- **Washington Mutual** • 12335 Venice Blvd

Car Rental

- **Marathon Rent-A-Car** • 12903 W Washington Blvd

Car Washes

- **Car Wash Coin Op** • 12415 Venice Blvd
- **Handy J Car Wash** • 12681 W Washington Blvd

Gas Stations

- **76** • 11305 Culver Blvd
- **Arco** • 12000 Culver Blvd
- **Arco** • 12332 W Washington Blvd
- **Arco** • 4661 S Slauson Ave
- **Chevron** • 3500 S Centinela Ave
- **Independent** • 11284 Venice Blvd

Landmarks

- **Mar Vista Tract** • 3500 Block of Beethoven St , Moore St, & Meier St, just south of Palms Blvd

Libraries

- **Mar Vista Branch** • 12006 Venice Blvd • 310-390-3454

Pharmacies

- **Rite-Aid** • 4046 S Centinela Ave • 310-391-0255

Police

- **Los Angeles Police Dept** • 12312 Culver Blvd • 310-482-6334

Post Offices

- **US Post Office** • 3826 Grand View Blvd • 800-275-8777

Schools

- **Beethoven EEC** • 12939 Lucille Ave
- **Beethoven St Elementary** • 3711 Beethoven St
- **Braddock Dr Elementary** • 4711 Inglewood Blvd
- **Culver Christian** • 11312 W Washington Blvd
- **Culver City Adventist** • 11828 W Washington Blvd
- **Grand View Blvd Elementary** • 3951 Grand View Blvd
- **Mar Vista Elementary** • 3330 Granville Ave
- **Marina del Rey Middle** • 12500 Braddock Dr
- **Marina EEC** • 4908 Westlawn Ave
- **Mark Twain Middle** • 2224 Walgrove Ave
- **McBride Special Education Center** • 3960 Centinela Ave
- **Montessori Preschool** • 12676 W Washington Blvd
- **Ocean Charter** • 12606 Culver Blvd
- **Pacifica Montessori** • 3734 Centinela Ave
- **Phoenix Continuation** • 12971 Zanja St
- **Shining Path Montessori** • 11500 Culver Blvd
- **Short Ave Elementary** • 12814 Maxella Ave
- **St Gerard Majella Elementary** • 4471 Inglewood Blvd
- **Stoner Ave Elementary** • 11735 Braddock Dr
- **Summit View West** • 12101 W Washington Blvd
- **Thomas Bradley Environmental Science & Humanities Charter Magnet** • 3875 Dublin Ave
- **Venice Senior High** • 13000 Venice Blvd
- **Village Glen** • 4160 Grand View Blvd
- **Walgrove Ave Elementary** • 1630 Walgrove Ave
- **Westside Christian Academy** • 12767 Pacific Ave
- **Westside Neighborhood** • 5401 Beethoven St
- **Wildwood** • 12201 Washington Pl
- **Windward** • 11350 Palms Blvd

Supermarkets

- **Vons** • 4030 S Centinela Ave

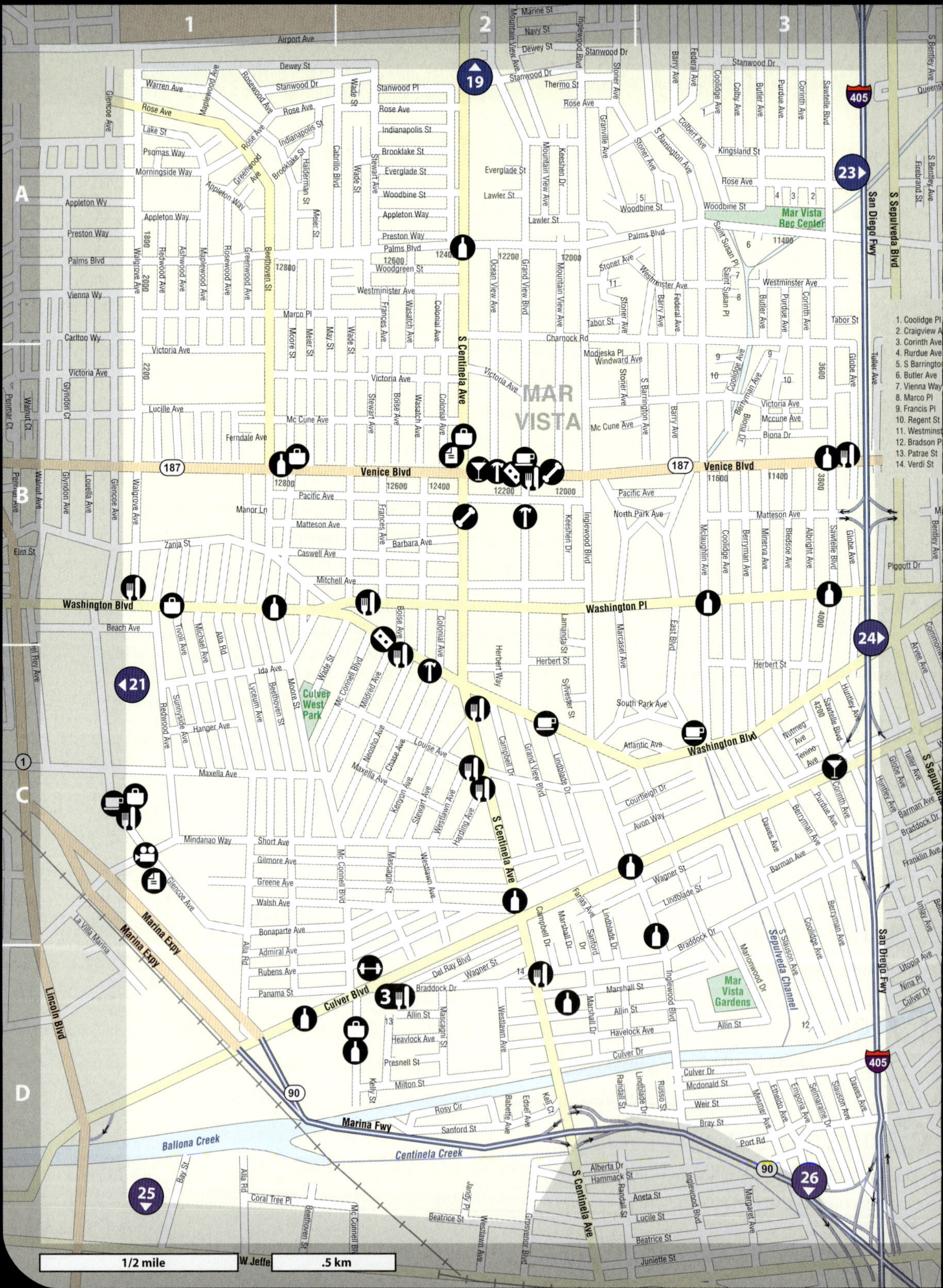

1. Coolidge Pl
2. Craigview A
3. Corinth Ave
4. Rurdue Ave
5. S Barringto
6. Butler Ave
7. Vienna Way
8. Marco Pl
9. Francis Pl
10. Regent St
11. Westminst
12. Bradson P
13. Patrae St
14. Verdi St

1/2 mile

.5 km

Is Mar Vista flashy? Not so much. But that's its appeal. Good neighborhood eateries, wide, tree-lined streets made for walking, and it's a straight shot to Venice. Little League on Saturday. For excitement, get a dog, or peruse the local bowling alley. For live music and libations served from vinyl-clad nurses, head down to Good Hurt.

Coffee

- **Panini Coffee & Café** • 4325 Glencoe Ave
- **Rumor Mill** • 11739 W Washington Blvd
- **Rutts Hawaiian Café** • 12114 W Washington Blvd
- **Venice Grind** • 12224 Venice Blvd

Copy Shops

- **FedEx Kinko's** • 4325 Glencoe Ave • 310-827-2297
- **UPS Store** • 12405 Venice Blvd • 310-915-6580

Gyms

- **Curves** • 12740 Culver Blvd • 310-301-6733

Hardware Stores

- **B & B Hardware Sales** • 12450 W Washington Blvd • 310-390-9413
- **Dick's True Value** • 12216 Venice Blvd • 310-397-3220
- **Stock Building Supply** • 3860 Grand View Blvd • 310-881-2000

Liquor Stores

- **A&M Liquors** • 11700 Washington Pl
- **Beverage Warehouse** • 4935 McConnell Ave
- **Bill's Liquor** • 11700 Culver Blvd
- **Dicoteca Licorerea La Mexicana** • 4513 Inglewood Blvd
- **Happy Corner Liquors** • 4584 S Centinela Ave
- **Hillcrest Liquors** • 11300 Venice Blvd
- **Jay's Liquor** • 11305 Washington Pl
- **The Los Angeles Wine Company** • 4935 McConnell Ave
- **Rajmohan's Liquors** • 12815 Venice Blvd
- **Sun Liquor Shop** • 12827 W Washington Blvd
- **Super Liquor & Deli** • 4704 Inglewood Blvd
- **Westside Liquor** • 3501 S Centinela Ave

Movie Theaters

- **United Artists Marina del Rey 6** • 4335 Glencoe Ave • 310-823-3959

Nightlife

- **Dear John's** • 11208 Culver Blvd • 310-397-0276
- **Good Hurt** • 12249 Venice Blvd • 310-390-1076

Pet Shops

- **Centinela Feed & Pet Supplies** • 3860 S Centinela Ave • 310-398-2134
- **Kirby's Pet Depot** • 12112 Venice Blvd • 310-313-1801

Restaurants

- **Asaya Restaurant** • 12740 Culver Blvd, #A • 310-823-8944
- **Aunt Kizzy's Back Porch** • 4325 Glencoe Ave • 310-578-1005
- **Centinela Café** • 4800 S Centinela Ave • 310-391-2585
- **Cora's Mexican Food** • 12565 W Washington Blvd • 310-390-2007
- **Empanada's Place** • 3811 Sawtelle Blvd • 310-391-0888
- **Fioretto Trattoria** • 12740 Culver Blvd • 310-448-8000
- **Maxwell's Café** • 13329 W Washington Blvd • 310-306-7829
- **Outdoor Grill** • 12630 Washington Pl • 310-636-4745
- **Paco's Tacos** • 4141 S Centinela Ave • 310-391-9616
- **Pepy's Galley** • 12125 Venice Blvd • 310-390-0577
- **Ronnie's Diner** • 12740 Culver Blvd, # J • 310-578-9399
- **Sakura Japanese Restaurant** • 4345 S Centinela Ave • 310-822-7790
- **Taqueria Sanchez** • 4341 S Centinela Ave • 310-822-8880

Shopping

- **A Mano Yarn Center** • 12808 Venice Blvd • 310-397-7170
- **The Los Angeles Wine Company** • 4935 McConnell Ave • 310-306-9463
- **Mitsuwa Marketplace** • 3760 S Centinela Ave • 310-398-2113
- **Prebica Coffee** • 4325 Glencoe Ave • 310-823-4446
- **Vanity Room** • 13217 W Washington Blvd • 310-306-3336

Video Rental

- **La Mexicana Video Rental (Spanish)** • 12612 W Washington Blvd • 310-390-9691
- **Video Exhibition** • 12200 Venice Blvd • 310-737-0053

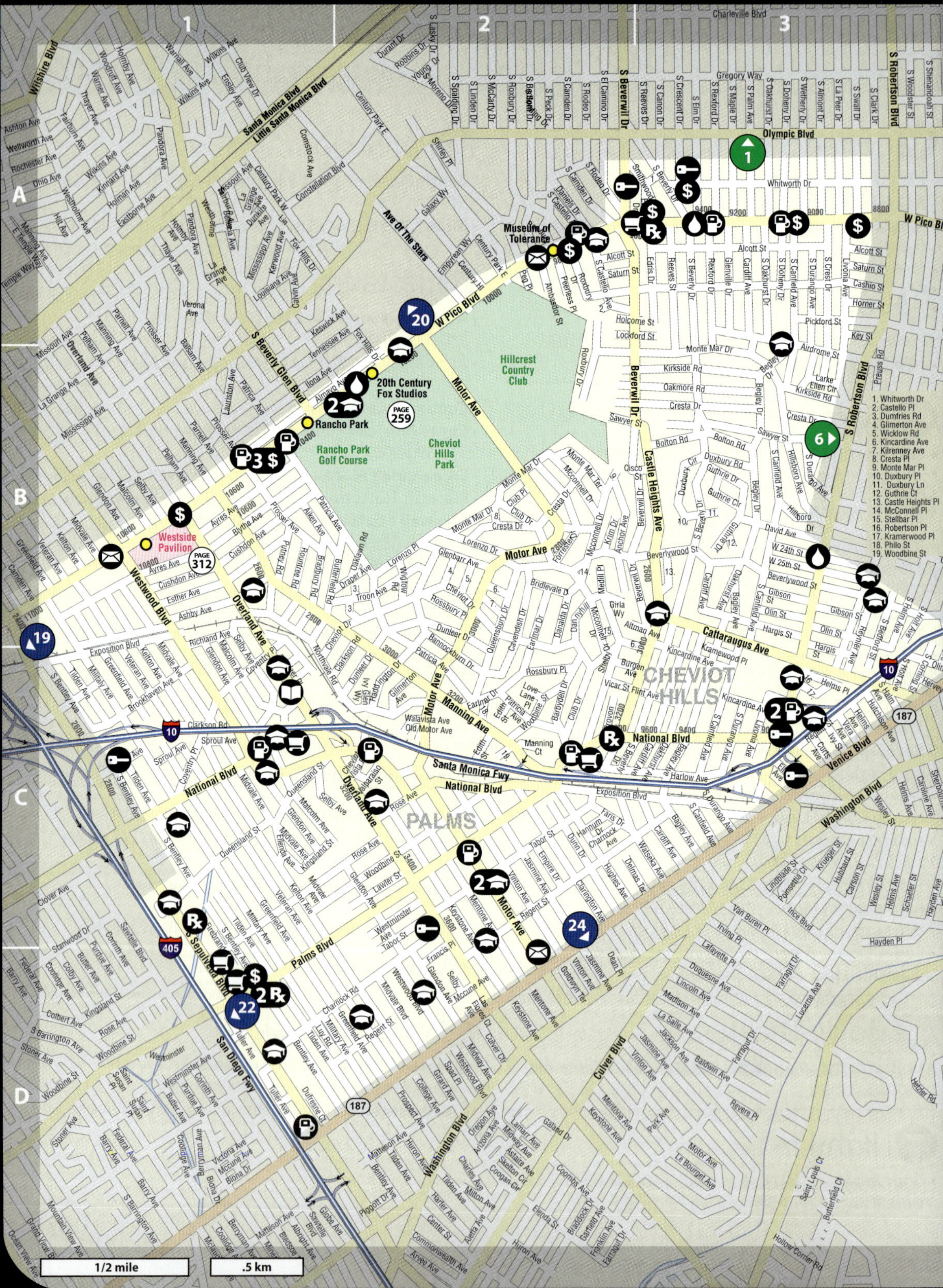

Map 23 • Rancho Park / Palms

Museum of Tolerance

20th Century Fox Studios

PAGE 259

Rancho Park

Rancho Park Golf Course

Cheviot Hills Park

Hillcrest Country Club

Westside Pavilion

PAGE 312

CHEVIOT HILLS

PALMS

1. Whitworth Dr
2. Castello Pl
3. Dumfries Rd
4. Glimerton Ave
5. Wicklow Rd
6. Kincardine Ave
7. Kilrenney Ave
8. Cresta Pl
9. Monte Mar Pl
10. Duxbury Pl
11. Duxbury Ln
12. Guthrie Ct
13. Castle Heights Pl
14. McConnell Pl
15. Stellbar Pl
16. Robertson Pl
17. Kramerwood Pl
18. Philo St
19. Woodbine St

1/2 mile

.5 km

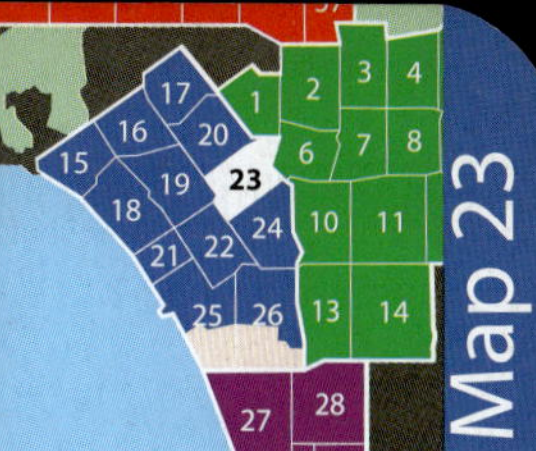

Rancho Park is like Beverly Hills with better taste. This suburban-flavored neighborhood has all the best trappings of small-town America—lovely houses with nice lawns, a walkable downtown area, and plenty of outdoor space for summer evening activity. Plus, it's nestled between Westwood and Culver City, so if you need a little more action, it's not hard to find.

Banks

- **Bank of America** • 10731 W Pico Blvd
- **California National** • 2566 Overland Ave
- **Citibank** • 10680 W Pico Blvd
- **Citibank** • 1180 S Beverly Dr
- **First Federal** • 9618 W Pico Blvd
- **Washington Mutual** • 10701 W Pico Blvd
- **Washington Mutual** • 9080 W Pico Blvd
- **Washington Mutual** • 9800 W Pico Blvd
- **Wells Fargo** • 10789 W Pico Blvd
- **Wells Fargo** • 11116 Palms Blvd
- **Wells Fargo** • 8901 W Pico Blvd

Car Rental

- **Avon Rent-A-Car** • 1100 S Beverly Dr
- **Downtown Car & Truck Rental** • 8919 Ellis Ave
- **Hertz** • 1150 S Beverly Dr
- **Rent 4 Less** • 3638 Overland Ave
- **Westside Car Rental** • 3071 S Robertson Blvd

Car Washes

- **Century West Car Wash** • 9500 W Pico Blvd
- **Crown Car Wash** • 10399 W Pico Blvd
- **Robertson Car Wash** • 2460 S Robertson Blvd

Gas Stations

- **76** • 9081 W Pico Blvd
- **76** • 9779 W Pico Blvd
- **76** • 9930 National Blvd
- **Arco** • 3479 Motor Ave
- **Chevron** • 10815 National Blvd
- **Chevron** • 3029 S Robertson Blvd
- **Chevron** • 3775 S Sepulveda Blvd
- **Exxon** • 10691 W Pico Blvd
- **Mobil** • 10611 National Blvd
- **Mobil** • 9448 W Pico Blvd
- **Shell** • 10564 W Pico Blvd
- **Valero** • 3071 S Robertson Blvd

Landmarks

- **20th Century Fox Studios** • 10201 Pico Blvd
- **Museum of Tolerance** • 9786 W Pico Blvd
- **Rancho Park** • 10460 W Pico Blvd
- **Westside Pavilion Cinemas** • 10800 W Pico Blvd

Libraries

- **Palms-Rancho Park Branch** • 2920 Overland Ave • 310-840-2142

Pharmacies

- **Longs Drugs** • 3458 S Sepulveda Blvd • 310-839-9055
- **Longs Drugs** • 9618 W Pico Blvd • 310-858-1855
- **The Medicine Shoppe** • 11126 Palms Blvd • 310-837-1030
- **Rite-Aid** • 9864 National Blvd • 310-836-0623
- **Sav-On** • Albertsons • 3443 S Sepulveda Blvd • 310-915-9251

Post Offices

- **US Post Office** • 10850 W Pico Blvd • 800-275-8777
- **US Post Office** • 3751 Motor Ave • 800-275-8777
- **US Post Office** • 9911 W Pico Blvd • 800-275-8777

Schools

- **Adat Shalom Preschool/Kindergarten** • 3030 Westwood Blvd
- **Alexander Hamilton Senior High** • 2955 S Robertson Blvd
- **Canfield Ave Elementary** • 9233 Airdrome St
- **Castle Heights Elementary** • 9755 Cattaraugus Ave
- **Charnock Rd Elementary** • 11133 Charnock Rd
- **Cheviot Hills Continuation** • 9200 Cattaraugus Ave
- **Clover Ave Elementary** • 11020 Clover Ave
- **Le Lycee Francais de LA** • 10361 W Pico Blvd
- **Le Lycee Francais de LA** • 3261 Overland Ave
- **Mel-O-Dee Montessori Center** • 3659 Motor Ave
- **New World Montessori** • 10520 Regent St
- **Notre Dame Academy Elementary** • 2911 Overland Ave
- **Notre Dame Academy Girls High** • 2851 Overland Ave
- **Overland Ave Elementary** • 10650 Ashby Ave
- **Pacifica Community Charter** • 3754 Dunn Dr
- **Palms Elementary** • 3520 Motor Ave
- **Palms Middle** • 10860 Woodbine St
- **Redeemer Baptist Elementary** • 10792 National Blvd
- **Shenandoah EEC** • 8861 Beverlywood St
- **St Timothy** • 10479 W Pico Blvd
- **Sunshine Learning Center** • 3704 Westwood Blvd
- **Temple Isaiah Preschool and Kindergarten** • 10345 W Pico Blvd
- **UCLA Early Care & Education** • 3233 S Sepulveda Blvd
- **Vista** • 3200 Motor Ave
- **Yeshiva University High** • 9760 W Pico Blvd

Supermarkets

- **Albertsons** • 3443 S Sepulveda Blvd
- **Ralphs** • 9616 W Pico Blvd
- **Trader Joe's** • 10850 National Blvd
- **Trader Joe's** • 3456 S Sepulveda Blvd
- **Vons** • 9860 National Blvd

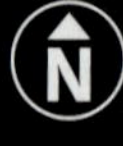

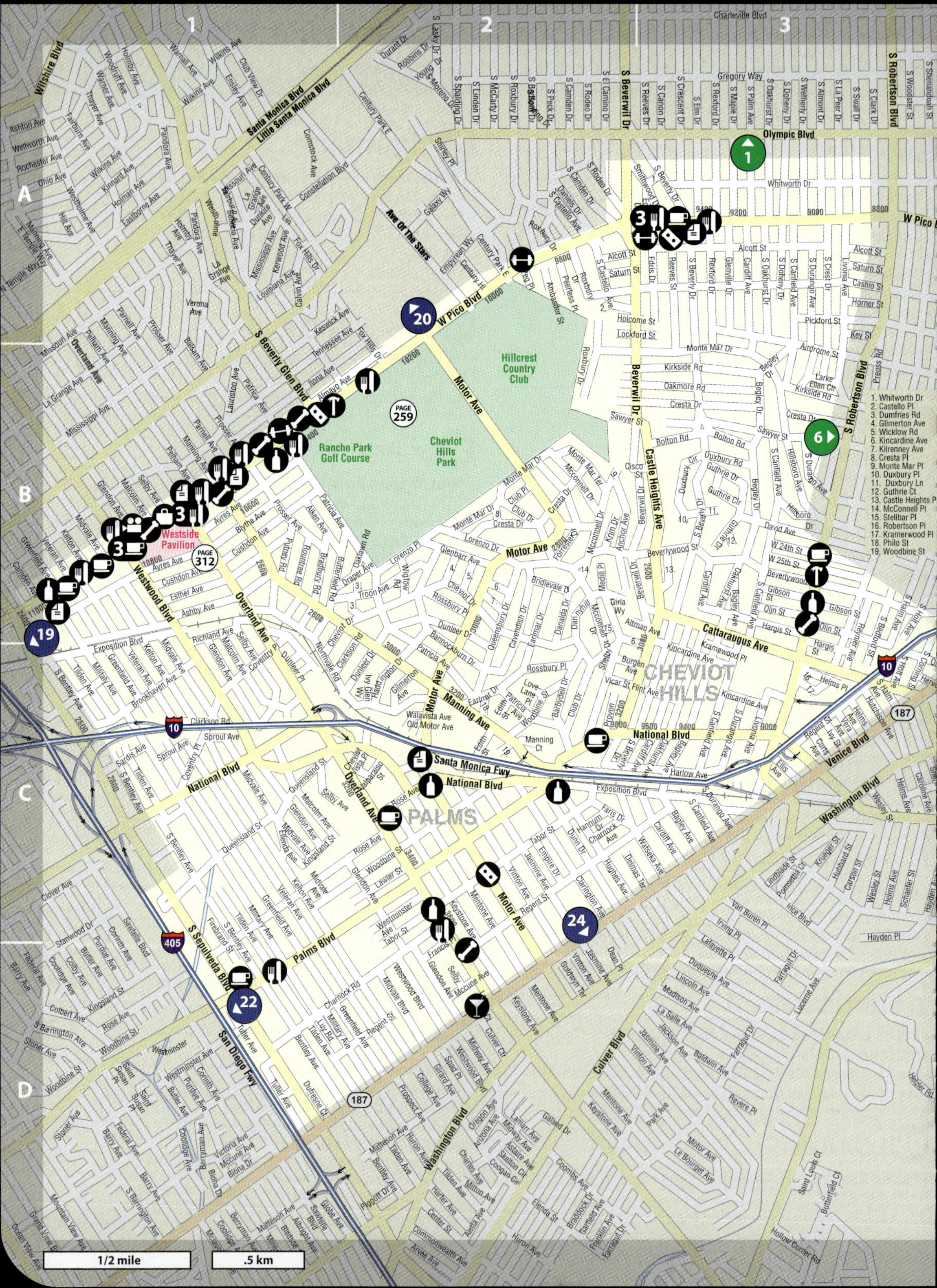

Westside Pavilion
Rancho Park Golf Course
Cheviot Hills Park
Hillcrest Country Club
CHEVIOT HILLS
PALMS
PAGE 259
PAGE 312
Olympic Blvd
W Pico Blvd
Santa Monica Blvd
Little Santa Monica Blvd
Wilshire Blvd
Santa Monica Fwy
San Diego Fwy
National Blvd
Venice Blvd
Washington Blvd
Culver Blvd
Motor Ave
Overland Ave
Westwood Blvd
S Beverly Glen Blvd
S Sepulveda Blvd
Palms Blvd
Manning Ave
Castle Heights Ave
Beverwil Dr
S Robertson Blvd
Cattaraugus Ave
1. Whitworth Dr
2. Castello Pl
3. Dumfries Rd
4. Glimerton Ave
5. Wicklow Rd
6. Kincardine Ave
7. Kilrenney Ave
8. Cresta Pl
9. Monte Mar Pl
10. Duxbury Pl
11. Duxbury Ln
12. Guthrie Ct
13. Castle Heights Pl
14. McConnell Pl
15. Stellbar Pl
16. Robertson Pl
17. Kramerwood Pl
18. Philo St
19. Woodbine St
1/2 mile
.5 km

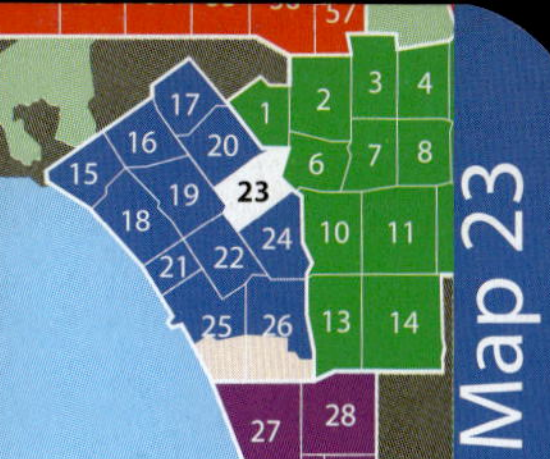

Start off your day on the links at Rancho Park Golf Course. Be sure to make a tee-time reservation, however, as it's reportedly the busiest in the world. It's located at the Cheviot Hills Recreation Center, which also contains tennis courts, basketball hoops, baseball diamonds, and more. Afterwards, get some actual exercise fighting for a seat at the legendary Apple Pan. Do some shopping across the street at the Westside Pavilion, then end your day with dinner and dancing Brazilian style at Zabumba.

Coffee

- **Café Toros** • 3300 Overland Ave
- **Coffee Bean & Tea Leaf** • 10800 W Pico Blvd
- **Coffee Bean & Tea Leaf** • 10897 W Pico Blvd
- **Coffee Bean & Tea Leaf** • 3470 S Sepulveda Blvd
- **Coffee Bean & Tea Leaf** • 9541 W Pico Blvd
- **Miss Donuts** • 2520 S Robertson Blvd
- **Starbucks** • 10911 Pico Blvd
- **Starbucks** • 9824 National Blvd
- **Ugo an Italian Café** • 10915 W Pico Blvd

Copy Shops

- **Ford Graphics** • 2435 Military Ave • 310-477-6501
- **Office Depot** • 9527 W Pico Blvd • 910-551-3006
- **OSG Printing & Copy** • 10665 W Pico Blvd • 310-475-9740
- **Printex** • 3272 Motor Ave • 310-278-0008
- **UPS Store** • 10573 W Pico Blvd • 310-474-7383

Gyms

- **24 Hour Fitness** • 9911 W Pico Blvd • 310-553-7600
- **Curves** • 10522 W Pico Blvd • 310-836-3050
- **Curves** • 9618 W Pico Blvd • 310-858-7546

Hardware Stores

- **Anawalt Lumber** • 11060 W Pico Blvd • 310-478-0324
- **Emil's Hardware** • 2525 S Robertson Blvd • 310-839-8571

Liquor Stores

- **Bob's Food Mart & Liquors** • 10000 National Blvd
- **Dave's Liquors** • 2704 S Robertson Blvd
- **Hillis Liquors** • 3308 Motor Ave
- **Joseph Liquor** • 11304 W Pico Blvd
- **Overland Liquor** • 3585 Overland Ave
- **Rancho Park Liquors** • 10526 W Pico Blvd

Movie Theaters

- **Westside Pavilion Cinemas** • 10800 W Pico Blvd • 310-281-8223

Nightlife

- **Zabumba** • 10717 Venice Blvd • 310-841-6225

Pet Shops

- **Centinela Feed & Pet Supplies** • 11055 W Pico Blvd • 310-473-5099
- **Helen's Pet Depot** • 10531 W Pico Blvd • 310-470-2922
- **Many Paws** • 2730 S Robertson Blvd • 310-837-1710
- **Westside Pet Stop** • 10588 W Pico Blvd • 310-202-1076

Restaurants

- **Apple Pan** • 10801 W Pico Blvd • 310-475-3585
- **Bourbon Street Shrimp** • 10928 W Pico Blvd • 310-474-0007
- **Carvel Ice Cream** • 9618 W Pico Blvd • 310-278-5411
- **Delmonico's Seafood Grille** • 9320 W Pico Blvd • 310-550-7737
- **Factor's Famous Deli** • 9420 W Pico Blvd • 310-278-9175
- **Guelaguetza** • 11127 Palms Blvd • 310-837-1153
- **Gyu-kaku** • 10925 W Pico Blvd • 310-234-8641
- **Hop Li** • 10974 W Pico Blvd • 310-441-3708
- **Jack Sprat's** • 10668 W Pico Blvd • 310-837-6662
- **John O'Groat's** • 10516 W Pico Blvd • 310-204-0692
- **Junior's** • 2379 Westwood Blvd • 310-475-5771
- **La Serenata Gourmet** • 10924 W Pico Blvd • 310-441-9667
- **Lot 1224** • Loews Beverly Hills Hotel • 1224 S Beverlywil Dr • 310-277-2800
- **Milky Way** • 9108 W Pico Blvd • 310-859-0004
- **Overland Café** • 3601 Overland Ave • 310-559-9999
- **Zen Bakery** • 10988 Pico Blvd • 310-475-6727

Shopping

- **Adventure 16** • 11161 Pico Blvd • 310-473-4574

Video Rental

- **Blockbuster** • 9618 W Pico Blvd • 310-858-3822
- **Laser Blazer** • 10587 W Pico Blvd • 310-475-4788
- **Pro Video** • 10401 Tabor St • 310-202-1508

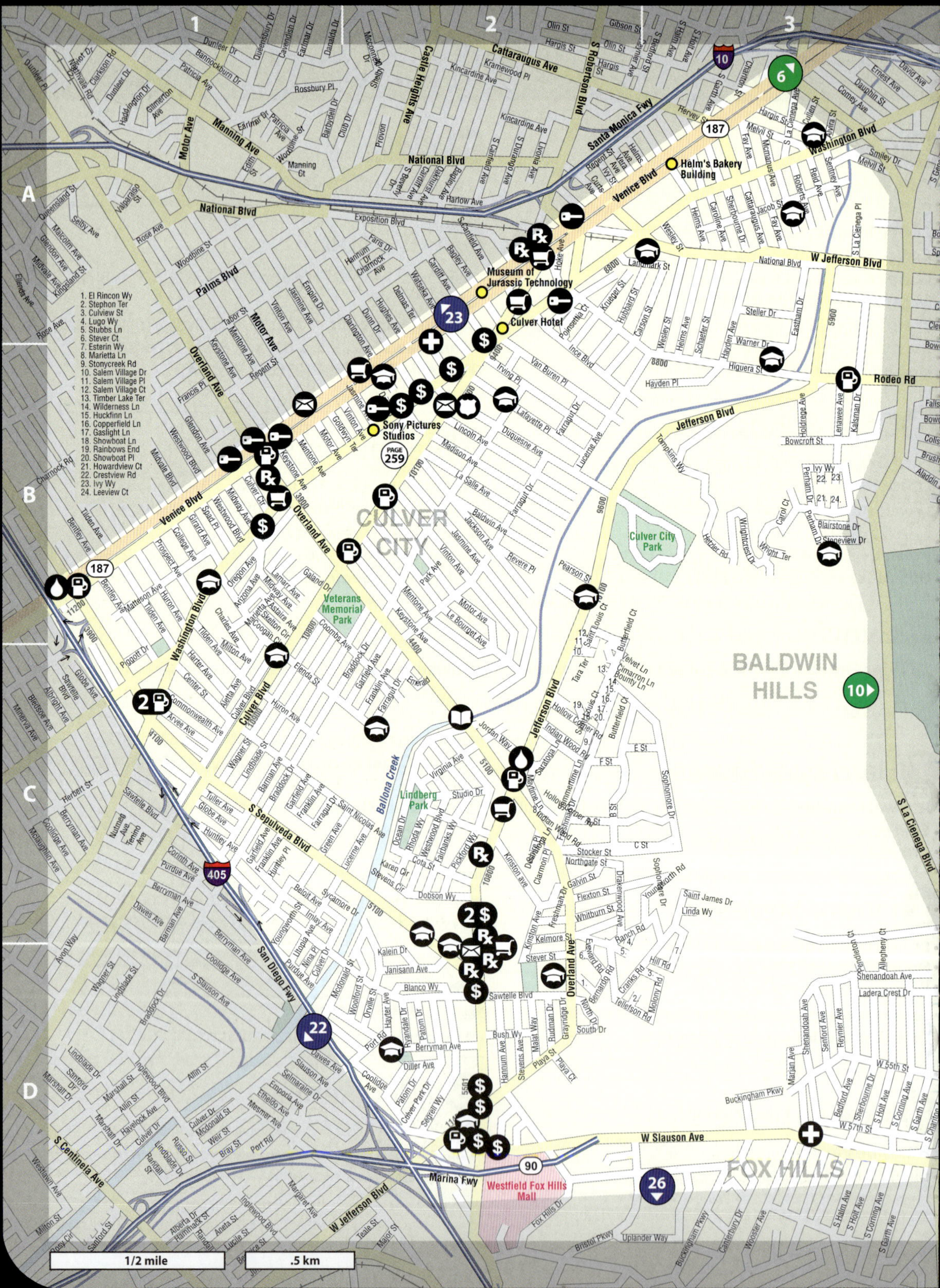

Map 24 • Culver City

1. El Rincon Wy
2. Stephon Ter
3. Culview St
4. Lugo Wy
5. Stubbs Ln
6. Stever Ct
7. Esterin Wy
8. Marietta Ln
9. Stonycreek Rd
10. Salem Village Dr
11. Salem Village Pl
12. Salem Village Ct
13. Timber Lake Ter
14. Wilderness Ln
15. Huckfinn Ln
16. Copperfield Ln
17. Gaslight Ln
18. Showboat Ln
19. Rainbows End
20. Showboat Pl
21. Howardview Ct
22. Crestview Rd
23. Ivy Wy
24. Leeview Ct

Helm's Bakery Building

Museum of Jurassic Technology

Culver Hotel

Sony Pictures Studios

PAGE 259

CULVER CITY

Culver City Park

Veterans Memorial Park

Lindberg Park

BALDWIN HILLS

FOX HILLS

Westfield Fox Hills Mall

1/2 mile

.5 km

Culver City used to be the New Jersey of Los Angeles, but call it the armpit no more. Not only are people realizing the charm behind the once-undignified real estate, but they are now turning the entire area into a gentrified bohemia. Today there are tons of great places to eat and hang out along Washington Blvd. The addition of the Kirk Douglas Theatre has even added (gasp!) a touch of class to the joint, and the Helms Bakery Building is the new swank furniture mecca.

Banks

- **Bank of America** • 3809 Culver Ctr
- **Bank of America** • 5541 S Sepulveda Blvd
- **Bank of America** • 9453 Culver Blvd
- **Bank of the West** • 9735 Washington Blvd
- **Citibank** • 5700 S Sepulveda Blvd
- **First Entertainment Credit Union** • 10000 W Washington Blvd
- **First Federal** • 10784 Jefferson Blvd
- **First Federal** • 5573 Sepulveda Blvd
- **US** • 5399 S Sepulveda Blvd
- **Washington Mutual** • 10970 Jefferson Blvd
- **Washington Mutual** • 5670 Sepulveda Blvd
- **Washington Mutual** • 9801 Washington Blvd
- **Wells Fargo** • 10011 Washington Blvd
- **Wells Fargo** • 11030 Jefferson Blvd

Car Rental

- **Enterprise** • 10757 Venice Blvd
- **Enterprise** • 8949 Venice Blvd
- **G&R Car rental** • 10620 Venice Blvd
- **G&R Car Rental** • 10620 Venice Blvd
- **Hertz** • 11201 Washington Blvd
- **Hertz** • 9055 Washington Blvd

Car Washes

- **Chevron** • 10649 Jefferson Blvd
- **Shine & Brite Hand Car Wash** • 11166 Venice Blvd

Gas Stations

- **76** • 10638 Culver Blvd
- **Arco** • 11181 W Washington Blvd
- **Arco** • 5851 Rodeo Rd
- **Arco** • 6300 W Slauson Ave
- **Chevron** • 10649 Jefferson Blvd
- **Chevron** • 11197 Washington Pl
- **Shell** • 10646 Venice Blvd
- **Shell** • 3801 Sepulveda Blvd
- **Valero** • 10332 Culver Blvd

Emergency Rooms

- **Brotman** • 3828 Delmas Ter

Landmarks

- **Culver Hotel** • 9400 Culver Blvd
- **Helm's Bakery Building** • 3233 Helms Ave
- **Museum of Jurassic Technology** • 9341 Venice Blvd
- **Sony Pictures Studios** • 10202 W Washington Blvd

Libraries

- **Culver City Julian Dixon** • 4975 Overland Ave • 310-559-1676

Pharmacies

- **Albertsons** • 8985 Venice Blvd • 310-202-6167
- **CVS** • 8985 Venice Blvd • 310-838-1049
- **Pavilions** • 11030 Jefferson Blvd • 310-398-8044
- **Rite-Aid** • 11096 Jefferson Blvd • 310-397-3931
- **Rite-Aid** • 3802 Culver Center St • 310-837-2122
- **Target** • 10820 Jefferson Blvd • 310-836-7087
- **Vons** • 11030 Jefferson Blvd • 310-398-8044

Police

- **Culver City Police Dept** • 4040 Duquesne Ave • 310-837-1221

Post Offices

- **US Post Office** • 11111 Jefferson Blvd • 800-275-8777
- **US Post Office** • 9942 Culver Blvd • 800-275-8777

Schools

- **Culver City Middle** • 4601 Elenda St
- **Culver City Senior High** • 4401 Elenda St
- **Culver Park Continuation** • 5303 Berryman Ave
- **Echo Horizon** • 3430 McManus Ave
- **El Marino Elementary** • 11450 Port Rd
- **El Rincon Elementary** • 11177 Overland Ave
- **Eras Center** • 5350 Machado Rd
- **Farragut Elementary** • 10820 Farragut Dr
- **La Ballona Elementary** • 10915 Washington Blvd
- **Linwood E Howe Elementary** • 4100 Irving Pl
- **Ohr Eliahu Academy** • 5950 Stoneview Dr
- **Play Mountain Place** • 6063 Hargis St
- **St Augustine Elementary** • 3819 Clarington Ave
- **STAR Academy** • 10101 Jefferson Blvd
- **Temple Akiba** • 5249 S Sepulveda Blvd
- **Turningpoint** • 8780 National Blvd
- **Venture** • 11477 Jefferson Blvd
- **West Los Angeles College** • 9000 Overland Ave
- **Willows Community** • 8509 Higuera St

Supermarkets

- **Albertsons** • 8985 Venice Blvd
- **Pavilions** • 11030 Jefferson Blvd
- **Ralphs** • 10772 Jefferson Blvd
- **Ralphs** • 3827 Culver Ctr
- **Smart & Final** • 10113 Venice Blvd
- **Trader Joe's** • 9290 Culver Blvd

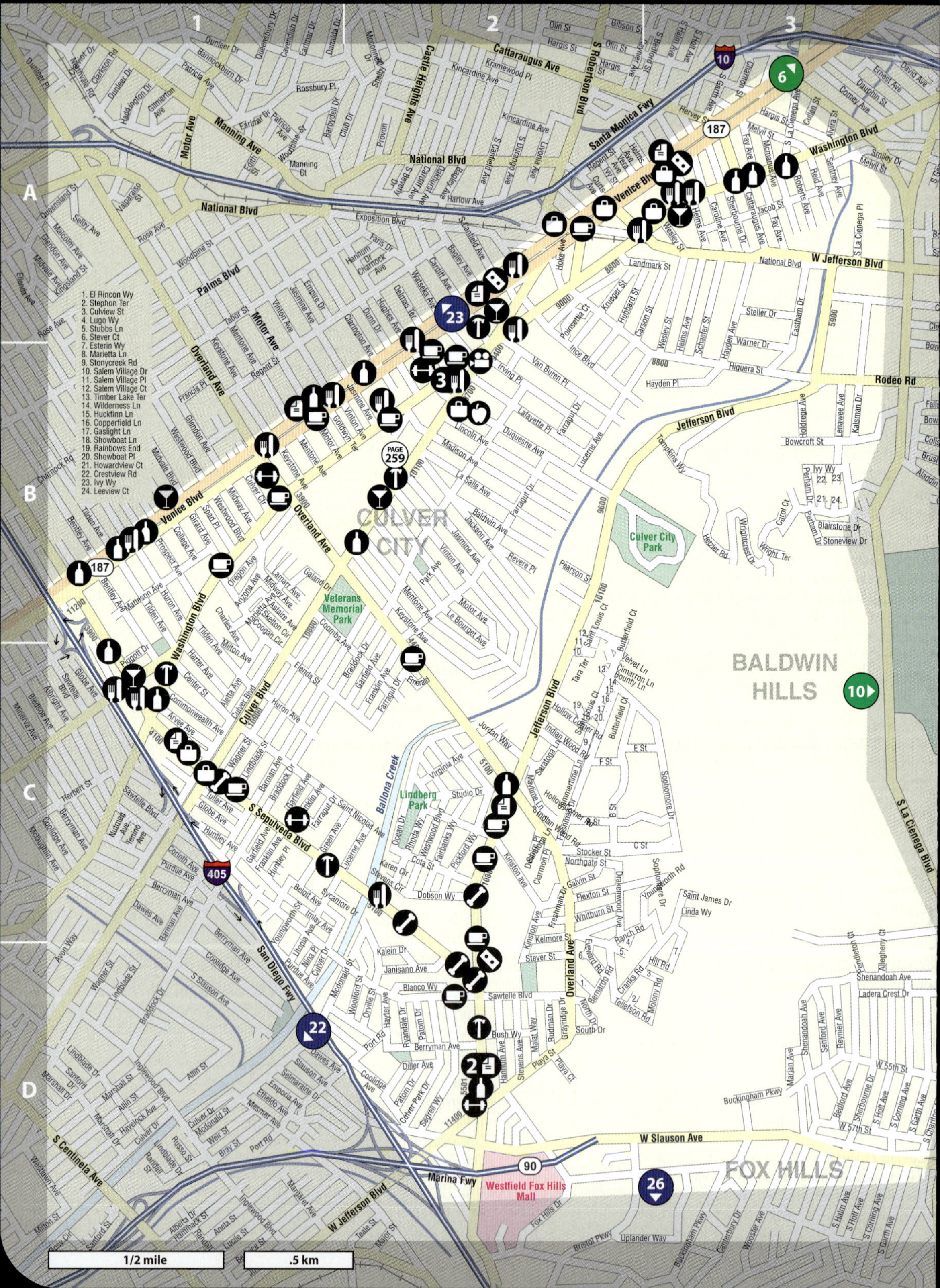

N
1
2
3
A
B
C
D
1. El Rincon Wy
2. Stephon Ter
3. Culview St
4. Lugo Wy
5. Stubbs Ln
6. Stever Ct
7. Esterin Wy
8. Marietta Ln
9. Stonycreek Rd
10. Salem Village Dr
11. Salem Village Pl
12. Salem Village Ct
13. Timber Lake Ter
14. Wilderness Ln
15. Huckfinn Ln
16. Copperfield Ln
17. Gaslight Ln
18. Showboat Ln
19. Rainbows End
20. Showboat Pl
21. Howardview Ct
22. Crestview Rd
23. Ivy Wy
24. Leeview Ct
CULVER CITY
BALDWIN HILLS
FOX HILLS
Culver City Park
Veterans Memorial Park
Lindberg Park
Westfield Fox Hills Mall
Ballona Creek
Santa Monica Fwy
San Diego Fwy
Marina Fwy
Venice Blvd
Washington Blvd
W Jefferson Blvd
Jefferson Blvd
National Blvd
Overland Ave
Culver Blvd
S Sepulveda Blvd
Sawtelle Blvd
W Slauson Ave
Rodeo Rd
S La Cienega Blvd
S Robertson Blvd
Motor Ave
Palms Blvd
Manning Ave
Castle Heights Ave
Cattaraugus Ave
Exposition Blvd
PAGE 259
23
22
26
6
10
10
405
187
90
1/2 mile
.5 km

Suddenly, formerly boring Culver City lays claim to some of the best old-school and new eateries in LA. There's always a line at the family-owned Tito's Tacos. Johnnie's Pastrami still serves up legendary sandwiches. And we'll always have the Jazz Bakery for good tunes. But suddenly the rise of new, even trendy, places have popped up – like wine bar BottleRock, and La Dijonaise, the French restaurant without the hefty cost and attitude. Even the Helms Bakery furniture stores come with wine tasting events.

Coffee

- **Apothecary Café** • 3831 Hughes Ave
- **Coffee Bean & Tea Leaf** • 10401 Venice Blvd
- **Conservatory for Coffee** • 10117 Washington Blvd
- **Essential Chocolate Collection** • 10868 Washington Blvd
- **Kings Café** • 5508 Sawtelle Blvd
- **Starbucks** • 10705 W Washington Blvd
- **Starbucks** • 10820 Jefferson Blvd
- **Starbucks** • Safeway • 11030 Jefferson Blvd
- **Starbucks** • 8985 Venice Blvd
- **Starbucks** • 9718 Washington Blvd
- **Synergy Café** • 4455 Overland Ave
- **Tanner's Coffee** • 4342 Sepulveda Blvd
- **Wanna Bagel** • 10780 Jefferson Blvd

Copy Shops

- **Copymax** • 8985 Venice Blvd • 310-836-5244
- **FedEx Kinko's** • 5575 Sepulveda Blvd • 310-313-2578
- **Office Depot** • 5640 Sepulveda Blvd • 310-390-4023
- **Pip Printing** • 9401 Venice Blvd • 310-837-6151
- **Reprographics** • 4215 Sepulveda Blvd • 310-391-0416
- **UPS Store** • 10401 Venice Blvd • 310-287-2269
- **UPS Store** • 10736 Jefferson Blvd • 310-558-4778

Farmers Markets

- **Culver City (Tues, 2 pm-7 pm)** • Culver Blvd & Main St

Gyms

- **Bally Total Fitness** • 3827 Overland Ave • 310-204-2030
- **Culver-Palms Family YMCA** • 4500 Sepulveda Blvd •
- **Curves** • 3861 Hughes Ave • 310-202-8653
- **Liberty Fitness** • 11409 Jefferson Blvd • 310-572-9356

Hardware Stores

- **A-1 Hardware** • 11119 Washington Blvd • 310-559-9594
- **Culver City Industrial Hardware** • 5429 Sepulveda Blvd • 310-398-1251
- **Stellar True Value** • 3833 Main St • 310-839-2321
- **Tools to Go** • 10248 Culver Blvd • 310-815-8555
- **Westwood Power Tools** • 4824 Sepulveda Blvd • 323-870-8088

Liquor Stores

- **3J** • 11156 Washington Blvd
- **Al's Liquor Store** • 6142 Washington Blvd
- **Albert's Liquors** • 5565 Sepulveda Blvd
- **Big Seven Liquors** • 10217 Venice Blvd
- **Crest Jr Market & Liquor** • 11127 Venice Blvd
- **Culver Liquor** • 10548 Culver Blvd
- **Liquor Barrel** • 3923 Sepulveda Blvd
- **Nick Anthony's Wine And Spirits** • 10725 Jefferson Blvd
- **Palm Tree Liquor** • 10425 Venice Blvd
- **Palm Tree Liquor** • 10425 Venice Blvd
- **R&Z Liquor** • 8582 Washington Blvd

Movie Theaters

- **Pacific Culver Stadium 12** • 9500 Culver Blvd • 310-360-9565

Nightlife

- **Backstage** • 10400 Culver Blvd • 310-839-3892
- **BottleRock** • 3847 Main St • 310-836-9463
- **Cinema Bar** • 3967 Sepulveda Blvd • 310-390-1328
- **Jazz Bakery** • 3223 Helms Ave • 310-271-9039
- **Saints & Sinners** • 10899 Venice Blvd • 310-842-8066

Pet Shops

- **Apex Aquariums** • 4338 Sepulveda Blvd • 310-391-0305
- **The Aquarium** • 5403 Sepulveda Blvd • 310-390-1240
- **Centinela Feed & Pet Supplies** • 5299 Sepulveda Blvd • 310-572-6107
- **Petco** • 5347 S Sepulveda Blvd • 310-390-7255
- **Petsmart** • 10900 W Jefferson Blvd • 310-390-5120

Restaurants

- **Bamboo** • 10835 Venice Blvd • 310-287-0668
- **Beacon** • 3280 Helms Ave • 310-838-7500
- **Café Brasil** • 10831 Venice Blvd • 310-837-8957
- **Café Surfas** • 8777 Washington Blvd • 310-558-1458
- **Conservatory for Coffee** • 10117 Washington Blvd • 310-558-0436
- **Ford's Filling Station** • 9531 Culver Blvd • 310-202-1470
- **Honey's Kettle Fried Chicken** • 9537 Culver Blvd • 310-202-5453
- **In-N-Out Burger** • 9245 W Venice Blvd • 800-786-1000
- **Johnnie's Pastrami** • 4017 Sepulveda Blvd • 310-397-6654
- **La Dijonaise Café et Boulangerie** • Helms Bldg • 8703 Washington Blvd • 310-287-2770
- **Natalee Thai** • 10101 Venice Blvd • 310-202-7003
- **Petrelli's Steakhouse** • 5615 S Sepulveda Blvd • 310-397-1438
- **S&W Country Diner** • 9748 W Washington Blvd • 310-204-5136
- **Santa Maria Barbecue Company** • 9552 Washington Blvd • 310-842-8169
- **Tito's Tacos** • 11222 Washington Pl • 310-391-5780
- **Versailles** • 10319 Venice Blvd • 310-558-3168

Shopping

- **Allied Model Trains** • 4411 Sepulveda Blvd • 310-313-9353
- **Civilization** • 8884 Venice Blvd • 310-202-8883
- **Culver City Home Brewing Supply** • 4358 1/2 Sepulveda Blvd • 310-397-3453
- **Dovetail** • 8918 Venice Blvd • 310-559-9431
- **HD Buttercup** • 3225 Helms Ave • 310-558-8900
- **Last Chance** • 8712 Washington Blvd • 310-287-2333
- **Surfas** • 8777 W Washington Blvd • 310-559-4770

Video Rental

- **Blockbuster** • 11010 Jefferson Blvd • 310-915-1192
- **Blockbuster** • 9201 Venice Blvd • 310-837-1286
- **Hollywood Video** • 8985 Venice Blvd • 310-559-4942

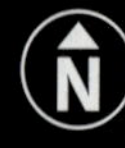

Map 25 • Marina del Rey / Westchester West

N
1
2
3
A
B
C
D
Electric Ave
Abbot Kinney Blvd
Washington Blvd
Washington Wy
N Venice Blvd
S Venice Blvd
Pacific Ave
Via Marina
Admiralty Wy
Admiralty Park
Marina City Towers
Marina City Dr
Promenade Wy
Palawan Wy
Panay Wy
Marquesas Wy
Tahiti Wy
Bora Bora Wy
NW Passage
Marina del Rey
Burton Chase Park
Mindanao Wy
Bali Wy
Fiji Wy
Fisherman's Village
Ballona Wetlands
MARINA DEL REY
PLAYA DEL REY
Bolona Creek
Culver Blvd
Lincoln Blvd
Marina Expy
90
Glencoe Ave
Maxella Ave
Del Rey Ave
1. Burrell Pl
2. Burrell St
3. Viola Pl
4. Schooner Ave
5. Fowling St
6. Campdell St
S Centinela Ave
W Jefferson Blvd
Runway Rd
Discovery Creek
Loyola Marymount University
W 80th St
W Manchester Ave
42
Westchester Rec Center
Otis College
1
La Tijera Blvd
Loyola Blvd
Del Rey Lagoon Park
Vista Del Mar
Pershing Drive
Northside Pkwy
Airport Service Rd
Sandpiper St
World Way West
Los Angeles International Airport
PAGE 314
PAGE 276
Venice County Beach
Dockweiler State Beach
Pacific Ocean
21
22
26
27
West Imperial Hwy
W Imperial Ave
Hillcrest St
Virginia St
Cedar St
Pepper St
Eucalyptus Dr
Cypress St
1/2 mile
.5 km

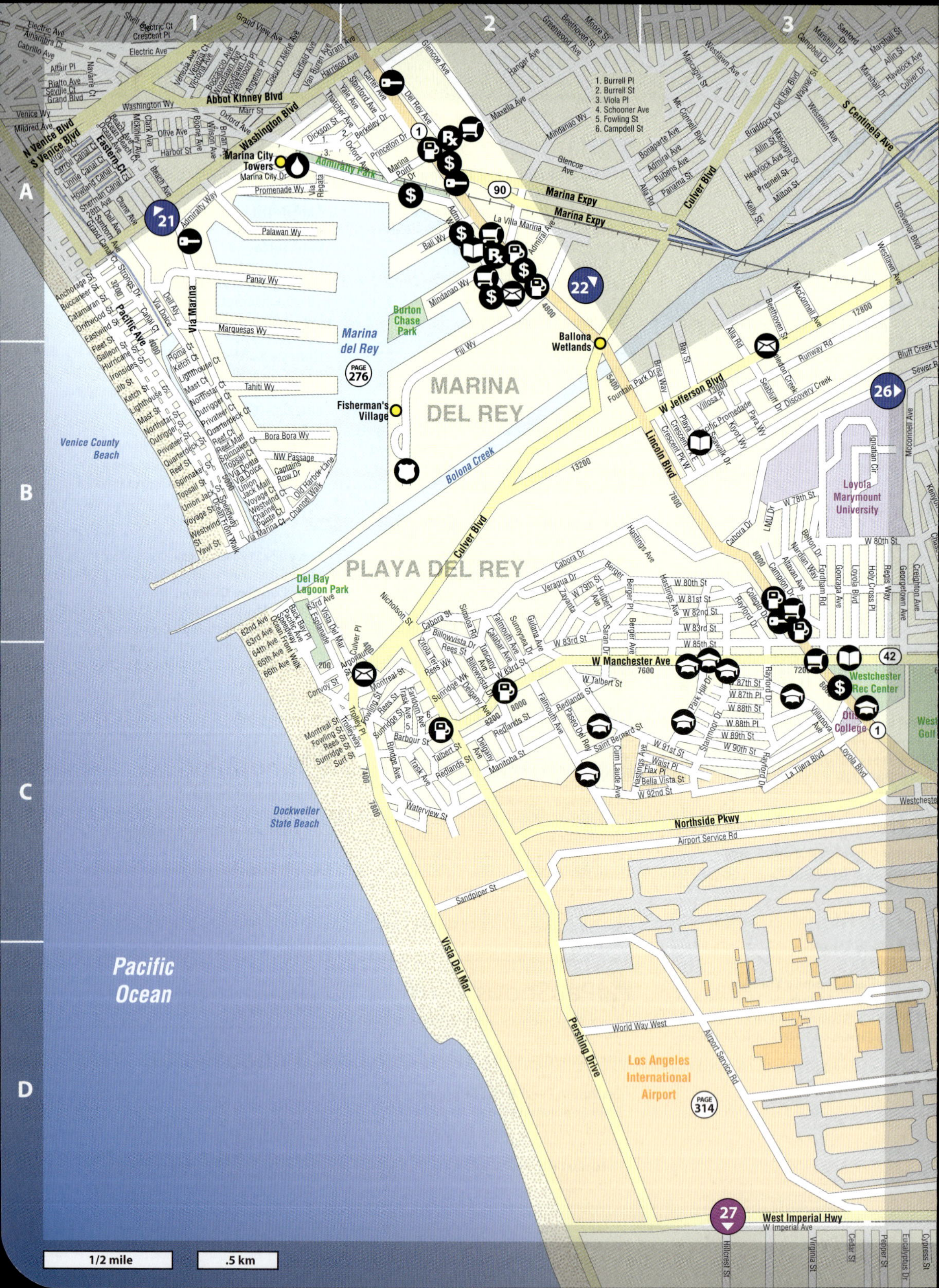

As the world's largest manmade harbor, Marina del Rey can boast over 5,000 boats and yachts in residence. With the number of upscale condominium buildings that have gone up in recent years, this town at the end of the 90 Freeway can rival most places in the number of luxury condo units, too. At any rate, with the marina views, dinner cruises, and picnics by the shore, it almost sounds romantic.

Banks

- **Bank of America** • 4754 Admiralty Wy
- **Bank of America** • 9001 Lincoln Blvd
- **Downey Savings & Loan** • 4311 Lincoln Blvd
- **First Bank & Trust** • 4519 Admiralty Wy
- **US** • 4700 Lincoln Blvd
- **Washington Mutual** • 4676 Admiralty Wy

Car Rental

- **Beverly Hills Rent-a-Car** • 4363 Lincoln Blvd
- **Eagle Rider Motorcycle Rental** • 4110 Lincoln Blvd
- **Hertz** • 4100 Admiralty Wy

Car Washes

- **Mr Polish** • 4333 Admiralty Wy

Gas Stations

- **76** • 4300 Lincoln Blvd
- **76** • 8300 Lincoln Blvd
- **Arco** • 8007 W Manchester Ave
- **Chevron** • 4680 Lincoln Blvd
- **Mobil** • 449 W Manchester
- **Shell** • 4770 Lincoln Blvd
- **Shell** • 8126 Lincoln Blvd

Landmarks

- **Ballona Wetlands** • Around Ballona Creek
- **Fisherman's Village** • 13755 Fiji Wy
- **Marina City Towers** • 4333 Admiralty Wy

Libraries

- **Lloyd Taber** • 4533 Admiralty Wy • 310-821-3415
- **Playa Vista Branch** • 6400 Playa Vista Dr • 310-437-6680
- **Westchester Branch** • 7114 W Manchester Ave • 310-348-1096

Pharmacies

- **CVS** • 13171 Mindanao Wy • 310-821-8908
- **Ralphs** • 4311 Lincoln Blvd • 310-574-0909

Police

- **Los Angeles County Sheriff's Dept- Marina del Rey Station** • 13851 Fiji Wy • 310-823-7762

Post Offices

- **US Post Office** • 13031 W Jefferson Blvd • 800-275-8777
- **US Post Office** • 215 Culver Blvd • 800-275-8777
- **US Post Office** • 4766 Admiralty Wy • 800-275-8777

Schools

- **Del Rey Continuation** • 8701 Park Hill Dr
- **Loyola Marymount Univeristy** • 1 LMU Dr
- **Loyola Village Elementary** • 8821 Villanova St
- **Otis College of Art & Design** • 9045 Lincoln Blvd
- **Paseo del Rey Elementary** • 7751 Paseo Del Rey
- **St Anastansia Elementary** • 8631 S Stanmoor Dr
- **St Bernard High** • 9100 Falmouth Ave
- **Westchester Senior High** • 7400 W Manchester Ave
- **Westchester-Emerson Community Adult** • 7400 W Manchester Ave

Supermarkets

- **Bristol Farms** • 8448 Lincoln Blvd
- **Gelson's Markets** • 13455 Maxella Ave
- **Ralphs** • 4311 Lincoln Blvd
- **Ralphs** • 4700 Admiralty Wy
- **Ralphs** • 8701 Lincoln Blvd

Map 25 • Marina del Rey / Westchester West

1. Burrell Pl
2. Burrell St
3. Viola Pl
4. Schooner Ave
5. Fowling St
6. Campdell St

PAGE 276

PAGE 314

21 22 26 27

Right next door to LAX, you'll never have a shortage of airplanes overhead in this part of town. Westchester is a neighborhood undergoing transition, and with construction continuing at nearby Playa Vista, new luxury homes going up on the bluffs, and the replacement of the old Furama Hotel, the bulldozer is becoming a fixture in the area. At least you can still count on finding great sushi at Kanpai and designer duds at the Jennifer Jeanne Boutique on Lincoln Boulevard.

Coffee

- **Coffee Bean & Tea Leaf** • 13020 Pacific Prom
- **Coffee Bean & Tea Leaf** • 13420 Maxella Ave
- **Johnnie's Coffee** • 13455 Maxella Ave
- **KC's Café** • 8320 Lincoln Blvd
- **Starbucks** • 4264 Lincoln Blvd
- **Starbucks** • 4724 Admiralty Wy
- **Tanner's Coffee** • 200 Culver Blvd

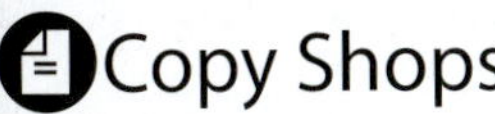

Copy Shops

- **Copypage** • 5418 McConnell Ave • 310-822-1620
- **UPS Store** • 13428 Maxella Ave • 310-827-4000
- **UPS Store** • 322 Culver Ave • 310-448-1218
- **UPS Store** • 4712 Admiralty Wy • 310-827-9002

Gyms

- **Curves** • 8327 Lincoln Blvd • 310-670-2517
- **LA Fitness Sports Clubs** • 13455 Maxella Ave • 310-827-0904
- **Marina City Club** • 4333 Admiralty Wy • 310-822-0611
- **Marina Fitness Center** • 14045 Panay Wy • 310-821-1662

Hardware Stores

- **Home Depot** • 12975 W Jefferson Blvd • 310-822-3330

Liquor Stores

- **Century Marina Liquors** • 8526 Lincoln Blvd
- **Dales Jr** • 8105 W Manchester Ave
- **Del Rey Liquors** • 8367 W Manchester Ave
- **Marina Liquor** • 4148 Via Marina
- **Sandune Liquor** • 317 Culver Blvd

Movie Theaters

- **Cineplex Marina Marketplace** • 13455 Maxella Ave • 310-827-9588

Nightlife

- **Brennan's** • 4089 Lincoln Blvd • 310-821-6622

Restaurants

- **Alejo's** • 4002 Lincoln Blvd • 310-822-0095
- **Alejo's** • 8343 Lincoln Blvd • 310-670-6677
- **Antica Pizzeria** • 13455 Maxella Ave • 310-577-8182
- **Ballona** • 13455 Maxella Ave • 310-822-8979
- **Café Del Rey** • 4451 Admiralty Wy • 310-823-6395
- **Caffe Pinguini** • 6935 Pacific Ave • 310-306-0117
- **Casa Escobar** • 14160 Palawan Wy • 310-822-2199
- **Hacienda Del Rey** • 8347 Lincoln Blvd • 310-670-8588
- **Jer-ne** • Ritz Carlton • 4375 Admiralty Wy • 323-574-4333
- **Kanpai Japanese Sushi Bar and Grill** • 8325 Lincoln Blvd • 310-338-7223
- **The Shack** • 185 Culver Blvd • 310-823-6222
- **Shanghai Red's** • 13813 Fiji Wy • 310-823-4522
- **Tandoor-A-India** • 8406 Pershing Dr • 310-822-1435
- **Tony P's Dockside Grill** • 4445 Admiralty Wy • 310-823-4534
- **The Warehouse** • 4499 Admiralty Wy • 310-823-5451

Shopping

- **Jennifer Jeanne Boutique** • 8328 Lincoln Blvd • 310-338-9300

Video Rental

- **Blockbuster** • 8101 Manchester Ave • 310-578-2243
- **Odyssey Video** • 4240 Lincoln Blvd • 310-823-2780

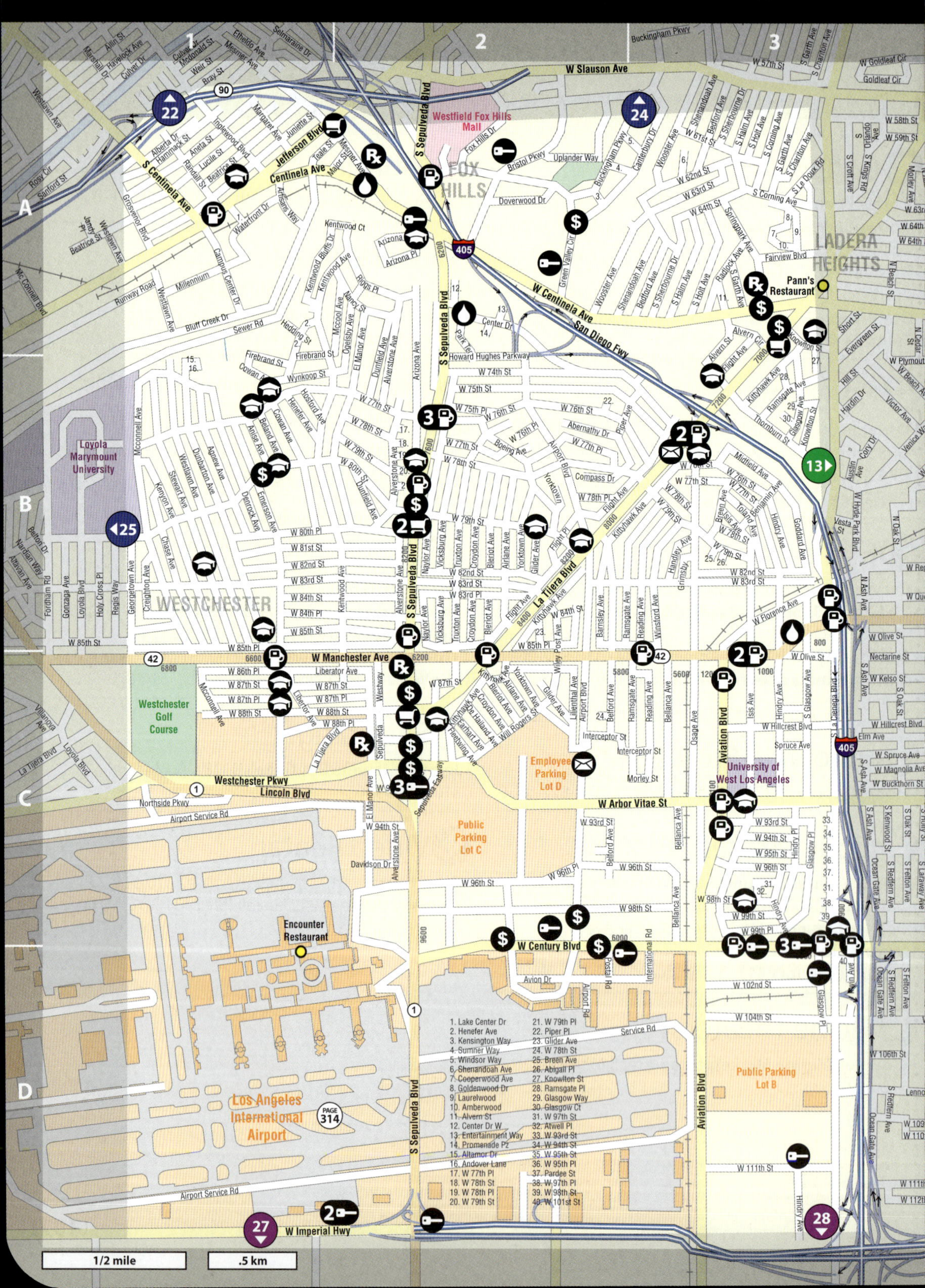
Westfield Fox Hills Mall
FOX HILLS
LADERA HEIGHTS
Pann's Restaurant
Loyola Marymount University
WESTCHESTER
Westchester Golf Course
Employee Parking Lot D
Public Parking Lot C
University of West Los Angeles
Encounter Restaurant
Los Angeles International Airport
PAGE 314
Public Parking Lot B
W Slauson Ave
W Centinela Ave
San Diego Fwy
Jefferson Blvd
Centinela Ave
S Centinela Ave
S Sepulveda Blvd
La Tijera Blvd
W Manchester Ave
Westchester Pkwy
Lincoln Blvd
W Arbor Vitae St
W Century Blvd
Aviation Blvd
W Imperial Hwy
Airport Service Rd
Howard Hughes Parkway
1. Lake Center Dr
2. Henefer Ave
3. Kensington Way
4. Sumner Way
5. Windsor Way
6. Shenandoah Ave
7. Cooperwood Ave
8. Goldenwood Dr
9. Laurelwood
10. Amberwood
11. Alvern St
12. Center Dr W
13. Entertainment Way
14. Promenade Pz
15. Altamor Dr
16. Andover Lane
17. W 77th Pl
18. W 78th St
19. W 78th Pl
20. W 79th St
21. W 79th Pl
22. Piper Pl
23. Glider Ave
24. W 78th St
25. Breen Ave
26. Abigail Pl
27. Knowlton St
28. Ramsgate Pl
29. Glasgow Way
30. Glasgow Ct
31. W 97th St
32. Atwell Pl
33. W 93rd St
34. W 94th St
35. W 95th St
36. W 95th Pl
37. Pardee St
38. W 97th Pl
39. W 98th St
40. W 101st St
1/2 mile
.5 km

If you're coming through Fox Hills or Ladera Heights, you probably either live in the neighborhood or you're making your way out to LAX. For those of you with golf clubs and a day off, or a long flight delay, come out to the putting green at the Westchester Golf Course. Or if you need new sneakers, the selection at Westfield Fox Hills Mall is more than enough to keep you busy for a while.

Banks

- **Bank of America** • 8946 S Sepulveda Blvd
- **Citibank** • 8800 S Sepulveda Blvd
- **Citibank** • 9841 Airport Blvd
- **City National** • 6033 W Century Blvd
- **First Federal** • 6053 W Century Blvd
- **First Federal** • 8750 S Sepulveda Blvd
- **Washington Mutual** • 8915 S Sepulveda Blvd
- **Wells Fargo** • 5377 W Centinela Ave
- **Wells Fargo** • 5899 Green Valley Cir
- **Wells Fargo** • 8814 S Sepulveda Blvd

Car Rental

- **A C Rent-A-Car** • 9142 S Sepulveda Blvd
- **A-One Rent a Car** • 6502 Arizona Ave
- **Aa'a Rent A Car** • 5959 W Century Blvd
- **Advantage Rent-a-Car** • 1030 W Manchester Blvd
- **Alamo** • 9020 Aviation Blvd
- **All States Car Rental** • 8705 La Tijera Blvd
- **Allied Rent-a-Car** • 5280 W Century Blvd
- **Ariana Rent-a-Car** • 6201 W 87th St
- **Atwest Rent a Car** • 5777 W Century Blvd
- **Avis** • 9217 Airport Blvd
- **Beverly Hills Rent-a-Car** • 9220 S Sepulveda Blvd
- **Budget** • 9775 Airport Blvd
- **Deluxe Rent A Car** • 11101 Hindry Ave
- **Discount Rent a Car** • 941 W Manchester Blvd
- **Discovery Car Rental** • 6333 Bristol Pkwy
- **Dollar** • 5630 W Arbor Vitae St
- **Easy Rent-a-Car** • 9142 S Sepulveda Blvd
- **Enterprise** • 5400 W Century Blvd
- **Enterprise** • 6160 Bristol Pkwy
- **Enterprise** • 8734 Bellanca Ave
- **Fox Rent a Car** • 5500 W Century Blvd
- **Global Rent a Car** • 5249 W Century Blvd
- **Hertz** • 5711 W Century Blvd
- **Hertz** • 5855 W Century Blvd
- **Hertz** • 9000 Airport Blvd
- **Hertz** • 6411 W Imperial Hwy
- **Los Angeles Rent-a-Car** • 8911 Bellanca Ave
- **Lucky Rent-a-Car** • 8620 Airport Blvd
- **Midway Car Rental** • 6201 W Imperial Hwy
- **Midway Car Rental** • 6411 W Imperial Hwy
- **Midway Car Rental** • 6225 W Century Blvd
- **National** • 9020 Aviation Blvd
- **Payless Car Rental** • 10121 Glasgow Pl
- **Rent 4 Less** • 5250 W Century Blvd
- **Rex Rent A Car** • 9200 S Sepulveda Blvd
- **Ritz Rent-A-Car** • 9100 S Sepulveda Blvd
- **Sakura Rent-a-Car** • 5250 W Century Blvd
- **Sunrise Rent-a-Car** • 9204 Airport Blvd
- **Super Cheap Car Rental** • 10212 S La Cienega Blvd
- **Thrifty** • 5440 W Century Blvd
- **United Rent-a-Car** • 5250 W Century Blvd

Car Washes

- **Howard Hughes Handwash** • 6080 Center Dr
- **Jet Car Wash** • 941 W Manchester Blvd
- **Playa Vista Car Care** • 6900 S Centinela Ave

Gas Stations

- **76** • 12401 W Jefferson Blvd
- **76** • 5552 W Century Blvd
- **76** • 7400 La Tijera Blvd
- **76** • 8525 S Sepulveda Blvd
- **Arco** • 1110 W Manchester Blvd
- **Arco** • 5201 Century Blvd
- **Arco** • 7370 La Tijera Blvd
- **Arco** • 9200 Aviation Blvd
- **Chevron** • 5156 W Century Blvd
- **Chevron** • 6101 W Manchester Ave
- **Chevron** • 6900 S Centinela Ave
- **Chevron** • 7360 La Tijera Blvd
- **Chevron** • 7550 S Sepulveda Blvd
- **Exxon** • 9131 Aviation Blvd
- **Mobil** • 6100 Sepulveda Blvd
- **Mobil** • 6600 W Manchester Ave
- **Mobil** • 7601 S Sepulveda Blvd
- **Mobil** • 8307 S La Cienega Blvd
- **Shell** • 5551 W Century Blvd
- **Shell** • 804 W Manchester Blvd
- **Valero** • 5800 W Manchester Ave

Landmarks

- **Encounter Restaurant** • 209 World Wy N
- **Pann's Restaurant** • 6710 La Tijera Blvd

Pharmacies

- **CVS** • 5399 W Centinela Ave • 310-670-3335
- **CVS** • 5748 Messmer Ave • 310-915-0981
- **CVS** • 6299 S Bristol Pkwy • 310-641-4426
- **CVS** • 8601 S Sepulveda Blvd • 310-645-8258
- **Longs Drugs** • 8900 Sepulveda Westway • 310-258-0265

Post Offices

- **US Post Office** • 7381 La Tijera Blvd • 800-275-8777
- **US Post Office** • 9029 Airport Blvd • 800-275-8777

Schools

- **Animo Leadership High** • 1155 W Arbor Vitae St
- **Animo Leadership High** • 1155 W Arbor Vitae St
- **B'Nai Tikvah Nursery & Kindergarten** • 8820 Sepulveda Eastway
- **Ballona Creek Academy** • 8228 Stewart Ave
- **Carousel** • 7899 La Tijera Blvd
- **Cowan Ave Elementary** • 7615 Cowan Ave
- **Kentwood EEC** • 8376 Dunbarton Ave
- **Kentwood Elementary** • 8401 Emerson Ave
- **La Tijera United Methodist** • 7400 Osage Ave
- **Ladera Heights Prep** • 6901 Knowlton Pl
- **Living Word Christian Academy** • 6520 Arizona Ave
- **Los Angeles Open Charter** • 5540 W 77th St
- **Middle College High** • 5431 W 98th St
- **Orville Wright Middle** • 6550 W 80th St
- **Playa del Rey Elementary** • 12221 Juniette St
- **St Jerome** • 5580 Thornburn St
- **University of West Los Angeles School of Law** • 9920 S La Cienega Blvd
- **Visitation Elementary** • 8740 Emerson Ave
- **Westchester Lutheran Middle** • 7831 S Sepulveda Blvd
- **Westport Heights Elementary** • 6011 W 79th St

Supermarkets

- **Albertsons** • 5750 Mesmer Ave
- **Ralphs** • 8824 S Sepulveda Blvd
- **Trader Joe's** • 8645 S Sepulveda Blvd
- **Vons** • 6571 W 80th St
- **Vons** • 6921 La Tijera Blvd

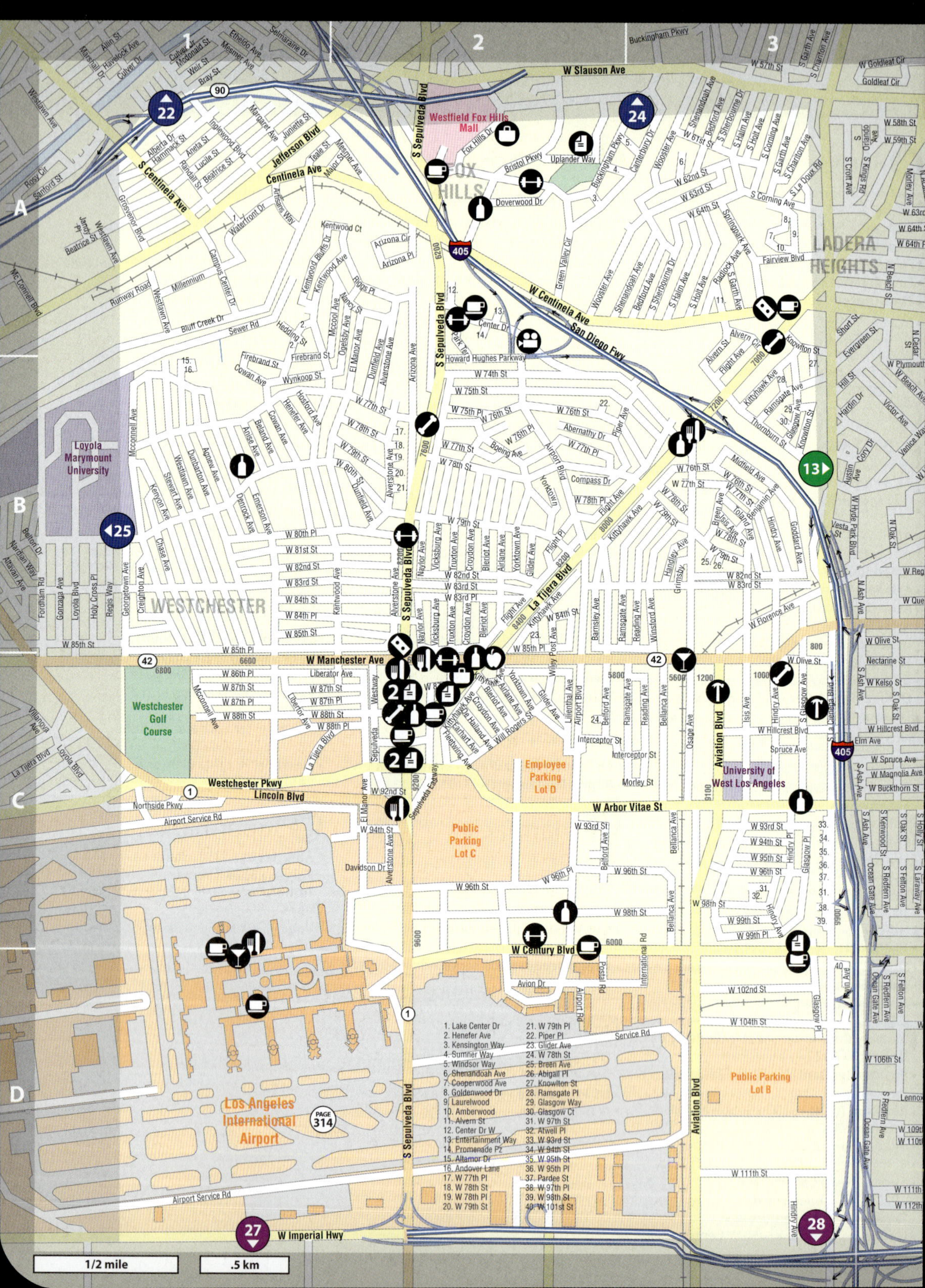
1
2
3
A
B
C
D
Westfield Fox Hills Mall
FOX HILLS
LADERA HEIGHTS
WESTCHESTER
Loyola Marymount University
Westchester Golf Course
University of West Los Angeles
Employee Parking Lot D
Public Parking Lot C
Public Parking Lot B
Los Angeles International Airport
PAGE 314
W Slauson Ave
S Sepulveda Blvd
Jefferson Blvd
Centinela Ave
S Centinela Ave
W Centinela Ave
San Diego Fwy
Howard Hughes Parkway
La Tijera Blvd
W Manchester Ave
Westchester Pkwy
Lincoln Blvd
W Arbor Vitae St
W Century Blvd
Aviation Blvd
W Imperial Hwy
Airport Service Rd
W Florence Ave
22
24
25
13
27
28
405
90
42
1
1. Lake Center Dr
2. Henefer Ave
3. Kensington Way
4. Sumner Way
5. Windsor Way
6. Shenandoah Ave
7. Cooperwood Ave
8. Goldenwood Dr
9. Laurelwood
10. Amberwood
11. Alvern St
12. Center Dr W
13. Entertainment Way
14. Promenade Pz
15. Altamor Dr
16. Andover Lane
17. W 77th Pl
18. W 78th St
19. W 78th Pl
20. W 79th St
21. W 79th Pl
22. Piper Pl
23. Glider Ave
24. W 78th St
25. Breen Ave
26. Abigail Pl
27. Knowlton St
28. Ramsgate Pl
29. Glasgow Way
30. Glasgow Ct
31. W 97th St
32. Atwell Pl
33. W 93rd St
34. W 94th St
35. W 95th St
36. W 95th Pl
37. Pardee St
38. W 97th Pl
39. W 98th St
40. W 101st St
1/2 mile
.5 km

LAX ranks as the fifth-busiest airport in the world based on passenger traffic, second in the country. With all the long lines at security checkpoints, cops cracking down on idling passengers, and growing flight delays, the airport can only stand to improve – but it hasn't. And after the closing of the Encouter Restaurant in the middle of LAX, there's not much else to the neighborhood, though it's still an area many people call home.

Coffee

- **Coffee Co** • 8751 La Tijera Blvd
- **Eurotal** • 380 World Wy
- **Eurotal** • 500 World Wy
- **Java Java** • 300 World Wy
- **LAX Café** • 5250 W Century Blvd
- **Starbucks** • LAX • 201 World Wy
- **Starbucks** • 294 Fox Hills Mall
- **Starbucks** • 5301 Centinela Ave
- **Starbucks** • 5855 W Century Blvd
- **Starbucks** • 6081 Center Dr
- **Starbucks** • 8817 S Sepulveda Blvd

Copy Shops

- **FedEx Kinko's** • 5855 W Century Blvd • 310-665-5955
- **Fox Hills Printing Center** • 5815 Uplander Wy • 310-649-2867
- **M&M Printing** • 8626 S Sepulveda Blvd • 310-417-3875
- **Office Depot** • 8900 S Sepulveda Blvd • 310-568-0600
- **The Printing Spot** • 8711 La Tijera Blvd • 310-670-7075
- **Staples** • 8704 S Sepulveda Blvd • 310-342-5113
- **UPS Store** • 8939 S Sepulveda Blvd • 310-216-1324

Farmers Markets

- **Westchester (Wed, 8:30 am-1 pm)** • W 87th St & Truxton Ave

Gyms

- **24 Hour Fitness** • 5959 W Century Blvd • 310-410-9909
- **Curves** • 5839 Green Valley Cir • 310-348-8727
- **Curves** • 6204 W Manchester Ave • 310-337-0810
- **Spectrum Club** • 6833 Park Ter • 310-216-3060
- **Westchester Family YMCA** • 8015 S Sepulveda Blvd • 310-670-4316

Hardware Stores

- **Home Depot** • 8801 S La Cienega Blvd • 310-417-9051
- **Southland Lumber & Supply** • 8710 Aviation Blvd • 310-641-8150

Liquor Stores

- **A&A Liquors** • 6200 W Manchester Ave
- **Kentwood Mini Market** • 7923 Emerson Ave
- **Purdy Liquor** • 5919 W 98th St
- **Regal Liquor** • 6295 Bristol Pkwy
- **Sear's Liquor** • 5206 Arbor Vitae St
- **Stan's Liquor** • 842 W Manchester Blvd
- **Stewart's Liquor** • 7411 La Tijera Blvd

Movie Theaters

- **The Bridge: Cinema de Lux** • 6081 Center Dr • 310-568-3375

Nightlife

- **Sky Bar Lounge at Encounter Restaurant** • 209 World Wy • 310-215-5151
- **Westchester Sports Grill** • 5630 W Manchester Ave • 310-670-2366

Pet Shops

- **Aquatic Outlet** • 427 Hindry Ave • 310-641-4664
- **Centinela Feed & Pet Supplies** • 7600 S Sepulveda Blvd • 310-216-9261
- **Eco-Pet** • 6955 La Tijera Blvd • 310-645-8892
- **Petco** • 8801 S Sepulveda Blvd • 310-645-7198

Restaurants

- **Buggy Whip** • 7420 La Tijera Blvd • 310-645-7131
- **Encounter Restaurant** • 209 World Wy N • 310-215-5151
- **In-N-Out Burger** • 9149 S Sepulveda Blvd • 800-786-1000
- **Paco's Tacos** • 6212 W Manchester Ave • 310-645-8692
- **Panera Bread** • 8647 S Sepulveda Blvd • 310-641-9200

Shopping

- **D3 International** • 8705 Truxton Ave • 310-568-9118
- **Westfield Fox Hills Mall** • 294 Fox Hills Mall • 310-390-5073

Video Rental

- **Blockbuster** • 5325 W Centinela Ave • 310-645-8211
- **Blockbuster** • 8813 S Sepulveda Blvd • 310-649-3699

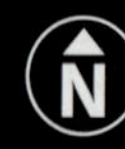

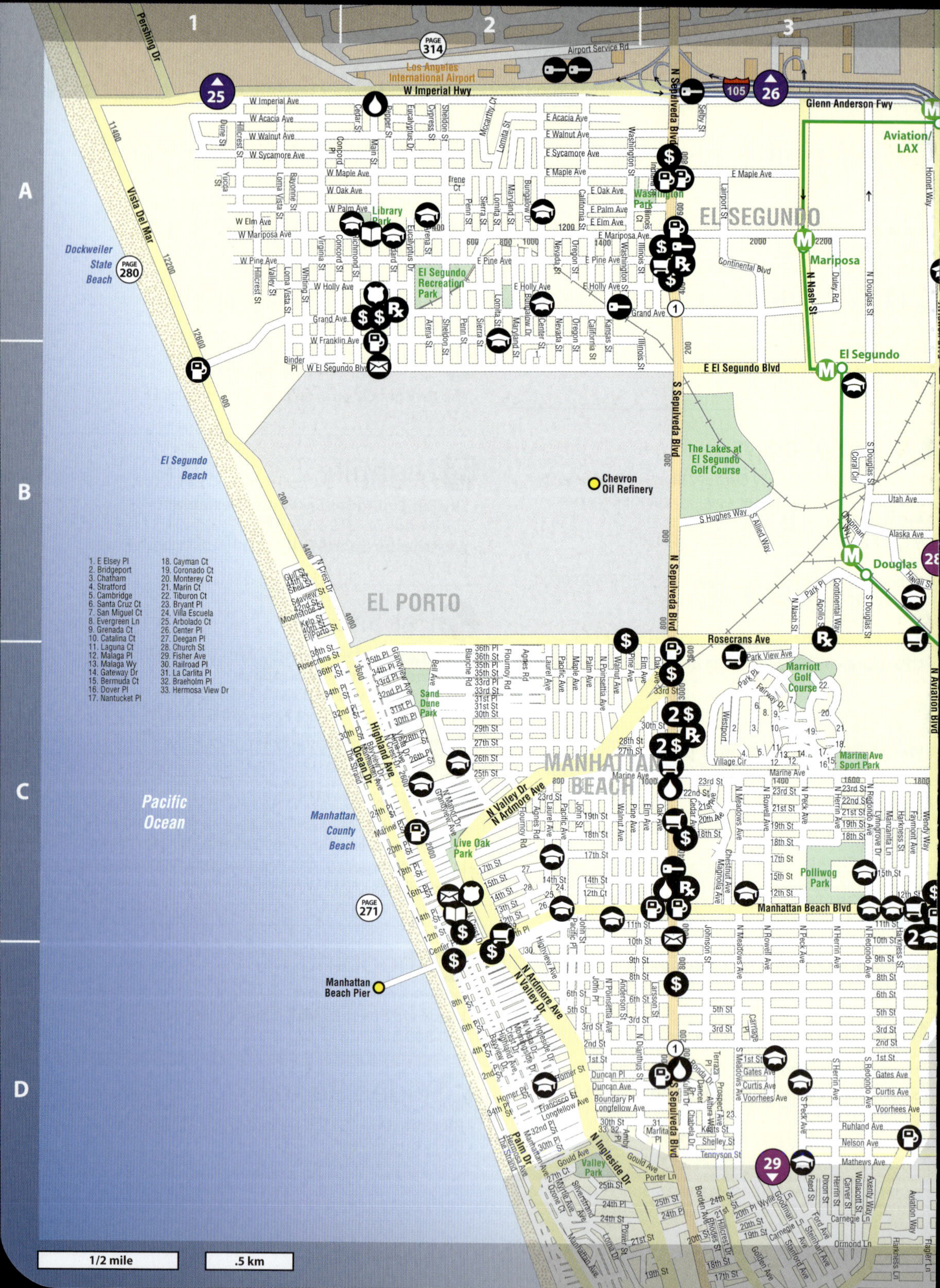

1
2
3
PAGE 314
Los Angeles International Airport
Airport Service Rd
W Imperial Hwy
25
105
26
Glenn Anderson Fwy
Aviation/LAX
Mariposa
El Segundo
Douglas
28
EL SEGUNDO
Library Park
Washington Park
El Segundo Recreation Park
Dockweiler State Beach
PAGE 280
Vista Del Mar
Pershing Dr
E El Segundo Blvd
N Sepulveda Blvd
S Sepulveda Blvd
Rosecrans Ave
The Lakes at El Segundo Golf Course
Chevron Oil Refinery
El Segundo Beach
EL PORTO
Marriott Golf Course
Marine Ave Sport Park
Sand Dune Park
MANHATTAN BEACH
Live Oak Park
Polliwog Park
Manhattan Beach Blvd
Manhattan County Beach
PAGE 271
Manhattan Beach Pier
Pacific Ocean
Highland Ave
N Ardmore Ave
N Valley Dr
Valley Park
29
A
B
C
D
1. E Elsey Pl
2. Bridgeport
3. Chatham
4. Stratford
5. Cambridge
6. Santa Cruz Ct
7. San Miguel Ct
8. Evergreen Ln
9. Grenada Ct
10. Catalina Ct
11. Laguna Ct
12. Malaga Pl
13. Malaga Wy
14. Gateway Dr
15. Bermuda Ct
16. Dover Pl
17. Nantucket Pl
18. Cayman Ct
19. Coronado Ct
20. Monterey Ct
21. Marin Ct
22. Tiburon Ct
23. Bryant Pl
24. Villa Escuela
25. Arbolado Ct
26. Center Pl
27. Deegan Pl
28. Church St
29. Fisher Ave
30. Railroad Pl
31. La Carlita Pl
32. Braeholm Pl
33. Hermosa View Dr
1/2 mile
.5 km

This area continues to grow, and has hit the big time with the opening of Raleigh Studios Manhattan Beach, where shows like *CSI: Miami* now film. Traffic on the 405 used to lighten up just past LAX, but the new businesses that have opened along El Segundo Boulevard and Rosecrans Avenue have, unfortunately, extended the congestion farther south.

Banks

- **Bank of America** • 1200 Highland Ave
- **Bank of America** • 3016 Sepulveda Blvd
- **Bank of America** • 835 N Sepulveda Blvd
- **Bank of the West** • 3500 Aviation Blvd
- **Bay Cities National** • 3005 N Sepulveda Blvd
- **Citibank** • 2710 Sepulveda Blvd
- **Comerica** • 2321 Rosecrans Ave
- **First Coastal** • 1800 N Sepulveda Blvd
- **First Coastal** • 275 Main St
- **Union** • 2910 N Sepulveda Blvd
- **Union** • 400 Manhattan Beach Blvd
- **US** • 3300 N Sepulveda Blvd
- **Washington Mutual** • 130 E Grand Ave
- **Washington Mutual** • 201 Manhattan Beach Blvd
- **Washington Mutual** • 550 N Sepulveda Blvd
- **Washington Mutual** • 700 S Sepulveda Blvd
- **Wells Fargo** • 3110 N Sepulveda Blvd
- **Wells Fargo** • 500 N Sepulveda Blvd

Car Rental

- **Discovery Rent a Car** • 525 N Sepulveda Blvd
- **Enterprise** • 1605 E Grand Ave
- **Hertz** • 6201 W Imperial Hwy
- **Manhattan Beach Toyota Rent a Car** • 1500 N Sepulveda Blvd

Car Washes

- **El Segundo Auto Spa Self Service Car Wash** • 118 E Imperial Ave
- **Manhattan Car Wash** • 300 S Sepulveda Blvd
- **Manhattan Spray Kleen** • 1307 N Sepulveda Blvd
- **Red Carpet Hand Wash** • 2414 N Sepulveda Blvd

Gas Stations

- **76** • 2121 Highland Ave
- **76** • 603 N Sepulveda Blvd
- **76** • 770 N Sepulveda Blvd
- **Arco** • 1002 Manhattan Beach Blvd
- **Chevron** • 101 S Sepulveda Blvd
- **Chevron** • 2301 N Aviation Blvd
- **Chevron** • 232 Main St
- **Chevron** • 3633 N Sepulveda Blvd
- **Chevron** • 601 Vista Del Mar
- **Independent** • 1100 Manhattan Beach Blvd
- **Mobil** • 1865 Manhattan Beach Blvd
- **Mobil** • 765 N Sepulveda Blvd

Landmarks

- **Chevron Oil Refinery** • East of Sepulveda Blvd, north of Rosecrans Ave
- **Manhattan Beach Pier** • West of Manhattan Beach Blvd

Libraries

- **El Segundo Public Library** • 111 W Mariposa Ave • 310-524-2722
- **Manhattan Beach** • 1320 Highland Ave • 310-545-8595

Pharmacies

- **CVS** • 2900 N Sepulveda Blvd • 310-546-3481
- **Longs Drugs** • 1570 S Rosecrans Ave • 310-536-9255
- **Ralphs** • 500 N Sepulveda Blvd • 310-615-3025
- **Rite-Aid** • 220 E Grand Ave • 310-640-2715
- **Target** • 1200 N Sepulveda Blvd • 310-546-1731

Police

- **El Segundo City Police Dept** • 348 Main St • 310-524-2200
- **Manhattan Beach Police Dept** • 420 15th St • 310-802-5100

Post Offices

- **US Post Office** • 1007 N Sepulveda Blvd • 800-275-8777
- **US Post Office** • 425 15th St • 800-275-8777

Schools

- **American Martyrs** • 1701 Laurel Ave
- **Arena High** • 630 Arena St
- **Aurelia Pennekamp Elementary** • 110 S Rowell Ave
- **Center St Elementary** • 700 Center St
- **Del Sol** • 1700 Manhattan Beach Blvd
- **Der Kinder Garden** • 1843 10th St
- **El Segundo High** • 640 Main St
- **El Segundo Middle** • 332 Center St
- **First Lutheran Circle of Love** • 1100 N Poinsettia Ave
- **Grand View Elementary** • 455 24th St
- **Magic Rainbow Pre School** • 1159 N Aviation Blvd
- **Manhattan Academy** • 1740 Manhattan Beach Blvd
- **Manhattan Beach Middle** • 1501 Redondo Ave
- **Meadows Avenue Elementary** • 1200 N Meadows Ave
- **Mira Costa High** • 701 S Peck Ave
- **Montessori** • 315 S Peck Ave
- **Montessori School of Manhattan Beach #2** • 2617 Bell Ave
- **Opal Robinson Elementary** • 80 Morningside Dr
- **Pacific Elementary** • 1200 Pacific Ave
- **Richard Henry Dana Intermediate** • 13500 Aviation Blvd
- **Richmond St Elementary** • 615 Richmond St
- **S Bay Children's Center** • 2270 E El Segundo Blvd
- **St Anthony** • 233 Lomita St
- **Vistamar** • 737 Hawaii St

Supermarkets

- **Bristol Farms** • 1570 Rosecrans Ave
- **Ralphs** • 2700 N Sepulveda Blvd
- **Ralphs** • 500 N Sepulveda Blvd
- **Trader Joe's** • 1800 Rosecrans Ave
- **Trader Joe's** • 1821 Manhattan Beach Blvd
- **Vons** • 410 Manhattan Beach Blvd

1. E Elsey Pl
2. Bridgeport
3. Chatham
4. Stratford
5. Cambridge
6. Santa Cruz Ct
7. San Miguel Ct
8. Evergreen Ln
9. Grenada Ct
10. Catalina Ct
11. Laguna Ct
12. Malaga Pl
13. Malaga Wy
14. Gateway Dr
15. Bermuda Ct
16. Dover Pl
17. Nantucket Pl
18. Cayman Ct
19. Coronado Ct
20. Monterey Ct
21. Marin Ct
22. Tiburon Ct
23. Bryant Pl
24. Villa Escuela
25. Arbolado Ct
26. Center Pl
27. Deegan Pl
28. Church St
29. Fisher Ave
30. Railroad Pl
31. La Carlita Pl
32. Braeholm Pl
33. Hermosa View Dr

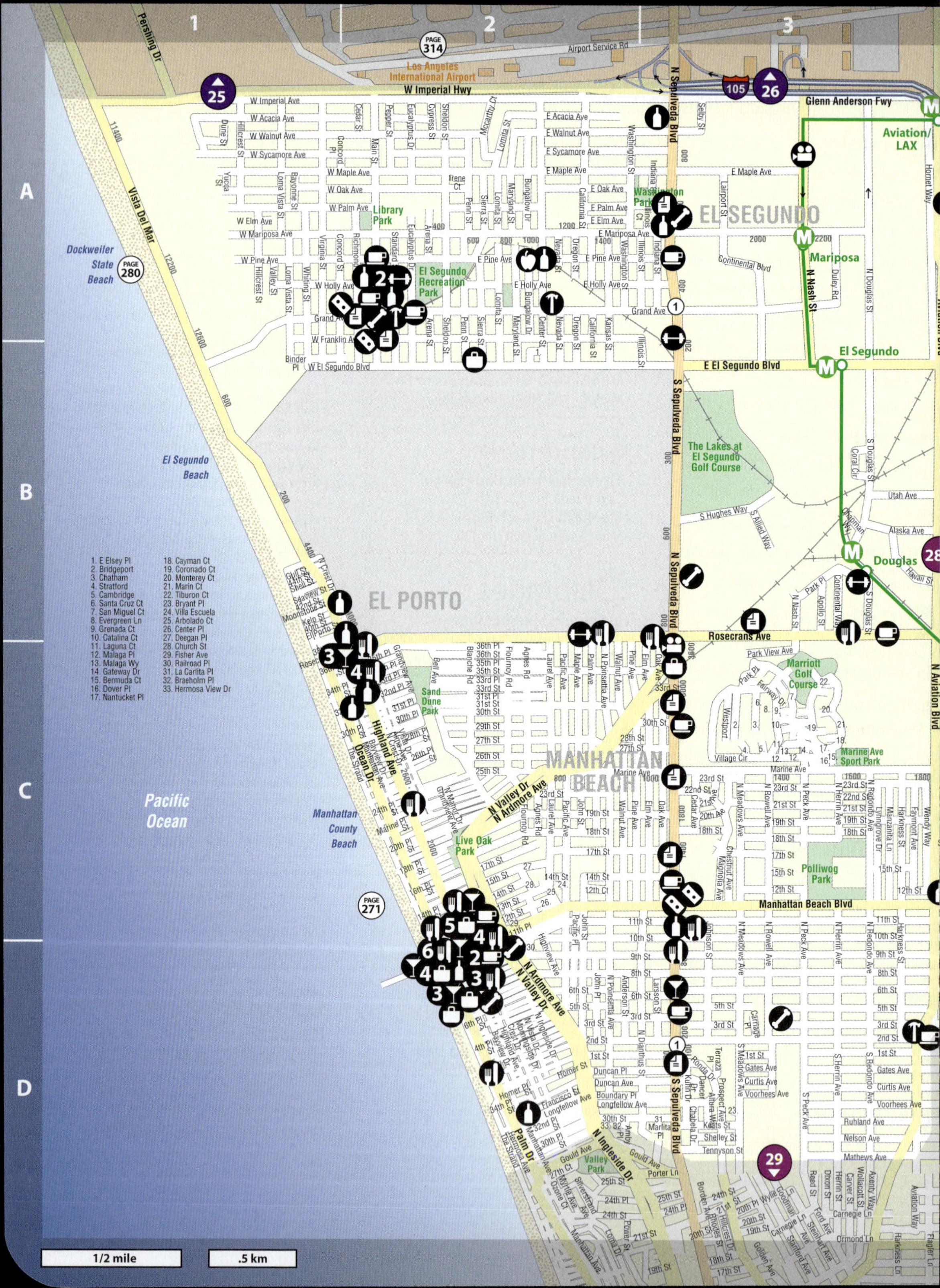

A mostly residential community, this area has a more mature nightlife scene compared to its rowdy neighbor, Hermosa Beach. You'll find an abundance of eccentric shops and inexpensive cafés and bistros like Café Pierre, a French restaurant that has been in town since 1977. The shops and restaurant near the main pier of Manhattan County Beach draw the biggest crowds. Local residents love the nearby El Porto Beach for its quiet(er) shores and great waves .

Coffee

- **Blue Butterfly Coffee** • 351 Main St
- **Coffee Bean & Tea Leaf** • 3008 N Sepulveda Blvd
- **Coffee Bean & Tea Leaf** • 321 Manhattan Beach Blvd
- **Manhattan Coffee** • 350 N Sepulveda Blvd
- **Our Daily Grind** • 503 Main St
- **Peet's** • 328 Manhattan Beach Blvd
- **Saxbys Coffee** • 210 N Aviation Blvd
- **Starbucks** • Target • 1200 N Sepulveda Blvd
- **Starbucks** • 2231 Rosecrans Ave
- **Starbucks** • 233 Manhattan Beach Blvd
- **Starbucks** • 310 E Grand Ave
- **Starbucks** • 530 N Sepulveda Blvd

Copy Shops

- **Copy Shop** • 309 S Sepulveda Blvd • 310-374-3666
- **Dial Instant Printers** • 2313 N Sepulveda Blvd • 310-546-4679
- **FedEx Kinko's** • 630 N Sepulveda Blvd • 310-322-9141
- **Office Depot** • 1700 Rosencrans Ave • 310-536-9969
- **Pip Printing** • 116 W Grand Ave • 310-322-7441
- **Pip Printing** • 3201 N Sepulveda Blvd • 310-545-5617
- **UPS Store** • 1601 N Sepulveda Blvd • 310-545-1260
- **UPS Store** • 214 Main St • 310-640-8589

Farmers Markets

- **Farmers' Market-El Segundo (Thurs, 3pm-7pm)** • Main St & E Pine Ave

Gyms

- **24 Hour Fitness** • 1500 Rosecrans Ave • 310-536-9300 ㉔
- **Bodysmart on Main** • 505 Main St • 310-414-1400
- **Club at Pacific Corporate Towers** • 200 N Sepulveda Blvd • 310-563-1442
- **Curves** • 433 Main St • 310-414-0004
- **Spectrum Club** • 2250 Park Pl • 310-643-6878

Hardware Stores

- **Ace** • 203 E Grand Ave • 310-322-4545
- **Manhattan True Value** • 1005 N Aviation Blvd • 310-372-2402
- **S&S Hardware** • 1111 E Grand Ave • 310-322-9404

Liquor Stores

- **Bacchus (wine only)** • 1000 Manhattan Ave
- **Dan's Liquor** • 3232 Manhattan Ave
- **El Porto Market & Deli** • 4103 Highland Ave
- **Hollymain Liquor** • 404 Main St
- **Jon's Liquor** • 3508 Aviation Blvd
- **Leonard's Liquor** • 630 N Sepulveda Blvd
- **Lindy's Liquor & Deli** • 11720 Aviation Blvd
- **Moon's Market** • 3307 Highland Ave
- **Mr D's Liquor** • 1100 N Sepulveda Blvd
- **Players Liquor** • 3804 Highland Ave
- **Sepulveda Wine** • 917 N Sepulveda Blvd
- **Village Liquor** • 506 Center St

Movie Theaters

- **Old Town Music Hall** • 140 Richmond St • 310-322-2592
- **Pacific Beach Cities 16** • 831 N Nash St • 310-607-9630
- **Pacific Manhattan Village** • 3560 N Sepulveda Blvd • 310-640-1258

Nightlife

- **Baja Sharkeez** • 3801 Highland Ave • 310-545-6563
- **Beaches** • 117 Manhattan Beach Blvd • 310-545-2523
- **Ercole's** • 1101 Manhattan Ave • 310-372-1997
- **Hennessey's** • 313 Manhattan Beach Blvd • 310-546-4813
- **Mr Pockets** • 516 N Sepulveda Blvd• 310-372-4343
- **OB's** • 3610 Highland Ave • 310-546-1542
- **Panchos** • 3615 Highland Ave • 310-545-6670
- **Shark's Cove** • 309 Manhattan Beach Blvd • 310-545-2683
- **Shellback Tavern** • 116 Manhattan Beach Blvd • 310-376-7857
- **Side Door** • 900 Manhattan Ave • 310-372-1684

Pet Shops

- **Buster & Sullivan** • 451 Manhattan Beach Blvd • 310-802-1410
- **Critter Corral Pet Shop** • 118 W Grand Ave • 310-322-3077
- **Jim's Exotic Fish** • 630 N Sepulveda Blvd • 310-322-3474
- **PetSmart** • 730 S Sepulveda Blvd • 310-333-0602
- **We Love Pets** • 815 Manhattan Ave • 310-372-1212

Restaurants

- **Avenue** • 1141 Manhattan Ave • 310-802-1973
- **Back Home in Lahaina** • 916 N Sepulveda Blvd • 310-374-0111
- **Bora Bora** • 3505 Highland Ave • 310-545-6464
- **Café Pierre** • 317 Manhattan Beach Blvd • 310-545-5252
- **Corkscrew Café** • 2201 Highland Ave • 310-546-7160
- **Cozymel's** • 2171 Rosecrans Ave • 310-606-5464
- **El Tarasco** • 316 Rosecrans Ave • 310-545-4241
- **Fonzs** • 1017 Manhattan Ave • 310-376-1536
- **Houston's** • 1550 Rosecrans Ave • 310-643-7211
- **Il Fornaio** • 1800 Rosecrans Ave • 310-725-9555
- **The Kettle** • 1138 Highland Ave • 310-545-8511
- **Le Pain Quotidien** • 451 Manhattan Beach Blvd • 310-546-6411
- **Local Yolk** • 3414 Highland Ave • 310-546-4407
- **Mama D's** • 1125 Manhattan Ave • 310-546-1492
- **Mangiamos** • 128 Manhattan Beach Blvd • 310-318-3434
- **Manhattan Beach Brewing Company** • 124 Manhattan Beach Blvd • 310-798-2744
- **North End Café** • 3421 Highland Ave • 310-546-4782
- **Petros** • 451 Manhattan Beach Blvd • 310-545-4100
- **Rock'n Fish** • 120 Manhattan Beach Blvd • 310-379-9900
- **Sloopy's** • 3416 Highland Ave • 310-545-1373
- **Talias** • 1148 Manhattan Ave • 310-545-6884
- **Towne** • 1142 Manhattan Ave • 310-545-5405
- **Uncle Bill's Pancake House** • 1305 Highland Ave • 310-545-5177
- **Versailles** • 1000 N Sepulveda Blvd • 310-937-6829

Shopping

- **Bombshell** • 320 Manhattan Beach Blvd • 310-372-0777
- **Diane's** • 125 Manhattan Beach Blvd • 310-546-5868
- **Dollyrocker** • 212 Manhattan Beach Blvd • 310-374-3396
- **Fry's Electronics** • 3600 Sepulveda Blvd • 310-364-3797
- **GeoDecor** • 130 Penn St • 310-322-4043
- **Growing Wild** • 1201 Highland Ave • 310-545-4432
- **Katwalk** • 312 Manhattan Beach Blvd • 310-798-7399
- **Lucky Brand Dungarees** • 1113 Manhattan Ave • 310-798-8000
- **Magpie** • 1141 Highland Ave • 310-546-5132
- **Manhattan Surf & Sports** • 300 Manhattan Beach Blvd • 310-318-7055
- **Michael Stars** • 1114 Manhattan Ave • 310-376-8700
- **Sequins** • 912 Manhattan Ave • 310-798-1788
- **Skechers USA** • 1121 Manhattan Ave • 310-318-3116
- **Tabula Rasa Essentials** • 919 Manhattan Ave • 310-318-3385

Video Rental

- **Blockbuster** • 1130 Sepulveda Blvd • 310-545-8659
- **Blockbuster** • 131 W Grand Ave • 310-414-9194
- **Blockbuster Video** • 1200 N Sepulveda Blvd • 310-545-3579
- **Main Street Video** • 239 Main St • 310-322-8700

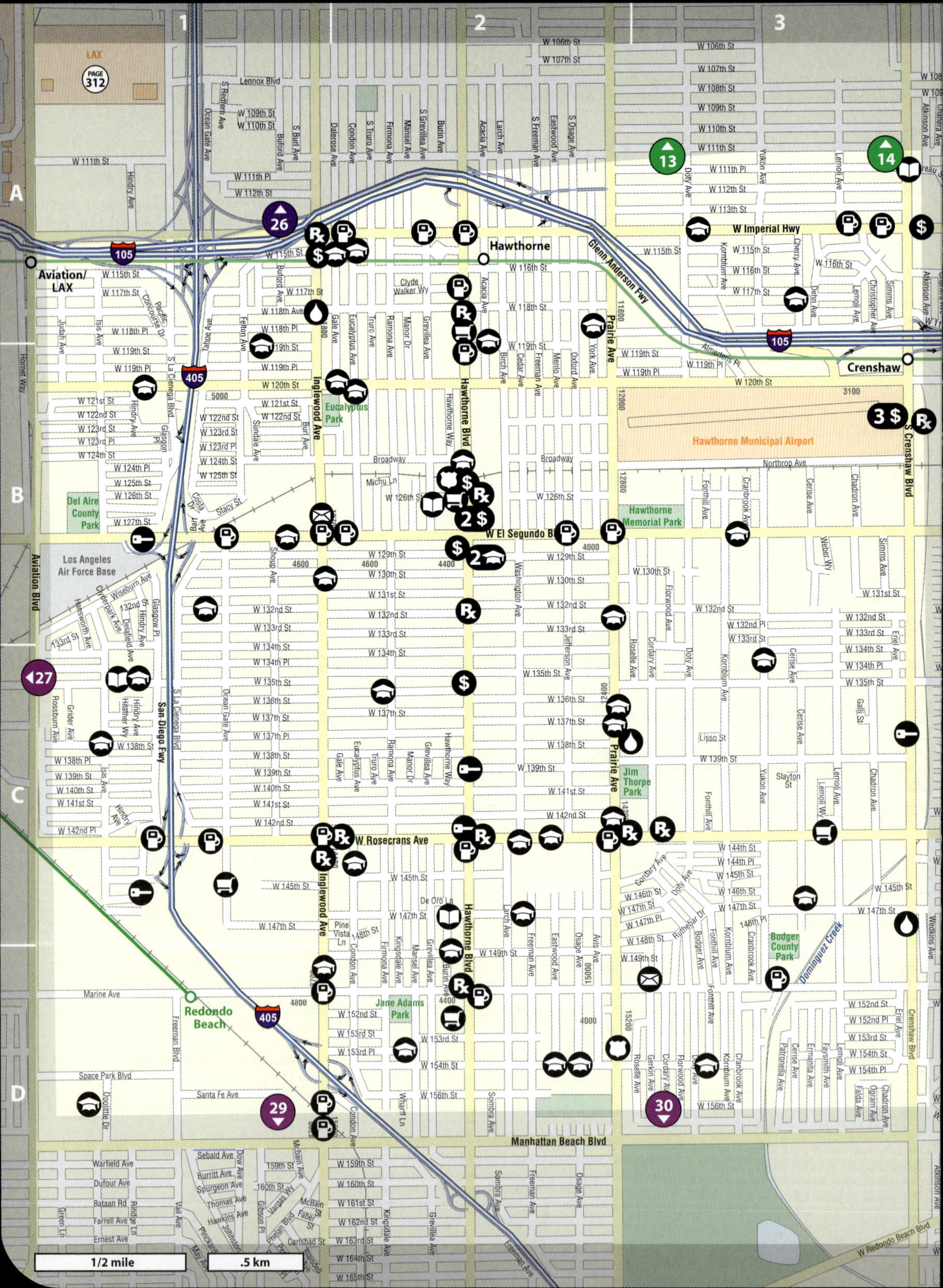

Map 28 • Hawthorne

1
2
3
A
B
C
D

LAX
PAGE 312
Lennox Blvd
W 106th St
W 107th St
W 108th St
W 109th St
W 110th St
W 111th St
W 111th Pl
W 112th St
W 113th St
W Imperial Hwy
Hawthorne
Aviation/ LAX
W 115th St
W 116th St
W 117th St
W 118th Ave
W 118th St
W 118th Pl
W 119th St
W 119th Pl
W 120th St
Glenn Anderson Fwy
Crenshaw
Prairie Ave
Inglewood Ave
Hawthorne Blvd
Eucalyptus Park
Hawthorne Municipal Airport
Northrop Ave
Broadway
Michu Ln
W 126th St
Del Aire County Park
W El Segundo Blvd
Hawthorne Memorial Park
Los Angeles Air Force Base
Aviation Blvd
San Diego Fwy
W 129th St
W 130th St
W 131st St
W 132nd St
W 133rd St
W 134th St
W 135th St
W 136th St
W 137th St
W 138th St
W 139th St
W 140th St
W 141st St
W 142nd St
W Rosecrans Ave
Jim Thorpe Park
W 144th St
W 145th St
W 146th St
W 147th St
W 148th St
W 149th St
Bodger County Park
Dominguez Creek
Jane Adams Park
Marine Ave
Redondo Beach
W 152nd St
W 153rd St
W 154th St
W 156th St
Space Park Blvd
Santa Fe Ave
Manhattan Beach Blvd
W 159th St
W 160th St
W 161st St
W 162nd St
W 163rd St
W 164th St
W 165th St
W Redondo Beach Blvd
Crenshaw Blvd
1/2 mile
.5 km

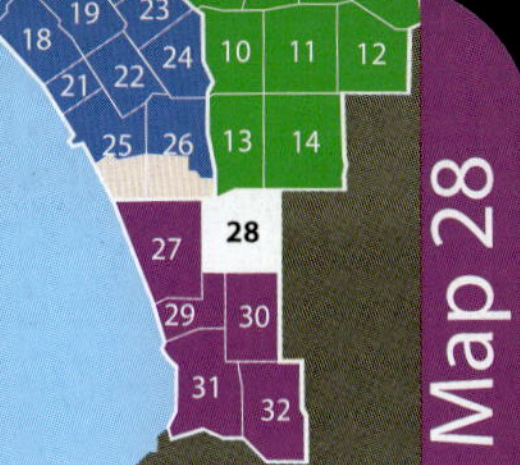

Encompassing six square miles, ensconced by three major freeways—the 405, 105, and 110—Hawthorne calls itself the "hub of the South Bay." With LAX on its border and Northrop Grumman, one of Hawthorne's largest businesses, the city is driven by the aerospace and air transport industries, making it known as the "cradle of aviation." Hawthorne's own municipal airport is appropriately known as Jack Northrop Field.

Banks

- **Bank of America** • 11525 Crenshaw Blvd
- **Bank of America** • 12547 Hawthorne Blvd
- **Citibank** • 12710 Hawthorne Blvd
- **Citibank** • 2940 W Imperial Hwy
- **Union** • 12801 Hawthorne Blvd
- **Washington Mutual** • 12645 Hawthorne Blvd
- **Wells Fargo** • 11305 S Crenshaw Blvd
- **Wells Fargo** • 13545 Hawthorne Blvd
- **Wells Fargo** • 4001 Inglewood Ave

Car Rental

- **Atlas Rent A Car** • 5250 W El Segundo Blvd
- **Enterprise** • 13901 Hawthorne Blvd
- **Enterprise** • 14800 Hindry Ave
- **Rent 4 Less** • 15312 Hawthorne Blvd
- **Town Rent A Car** • 13815 Crenshaw Blvd

Car Washes

- **Camino Car Wash** • 14701 Crenshaw Blvd
- **E-Z Self Service Car Wash** • 11817 Inglewood Ave
- **Excellent Car Wash And Detailing** • 13762 Prairie Ave

Gas Stations

- **76** • 12806 S Prairie Ave
- **76** • 3101 W Imperial Hwy
- **76** • 4008 W Rosecrans Ave
- **76** • 5105 W Rosecrans Ave
- **Arco** • 2730 Marine Ave
- **Arco** • 4009 W Rosecrans Ave
- **Arco** • 4015 W El Segundo Blvd
- **Chevron** • 12801 Inglewood Ave
- **Chevron** • 14305 Hawthorne Blvd
- **Independent** • 11741 Hawthorne Blvd
- **Independent** • 3760 W Imperial Hwy
- **Shell** • 15106 Hawthorne Blvd
- **Shell** • 15606 Inglewood Ave
- **Shell** • 4750 W Rosecrans Ave
- **Shell** • 4755 W Imperial Hwy
- **Thrifty** • 11890 S Hawthorne Blvd
- **Thrifty** • 5038 W El Segundo Blvd
- **Thrifty** • 5230 Rosecrans Ave
- **Valero** • 11402 Hawthorne Blvd

Libraries

- **Crenshaw-Imperial Branch** • 11141 Crenshaw Blvd • 310-412-5403
- **Hawthorne** • 12700 Grevillea Ave • 310-679-8193
- **Lawndale Library** • 14615 Burin Ave • 310-676-0177
- **Wiseburn** • 5335 W 135th St • 310-643-8880

Pharmacies

- **CVS** • 11831 Hawthorne Blvd • 310-973-6723
- **CVS** • 15103 Hawthorne Blvd • 310-679-7619
- **CVS** • 15103 S Hawthorne Blvd • 310-679-7619
- **CVS** • 3880 W Rosecrans Blvd • 310-675-0359
- **CVS** • 4775 W Rosecrans Ave • 310-263-7330 (24)
- **Rite-Aid** • 11340 Crenshaw Blvd • 323-757-2811
- **Rite-Aid** • 13141 Hawthorne Blvd • 310-675-9322
- **Sav-On** • Albertsons • 12630 S Hawthorne Blvd • 310-675-3636
- **Sav-On** • 4775 W Rosecrans Ave • 310-973-7356
- **Vons** • 4001 Inglewood Ave • 310-349-0860
- **Walgreens** • 14250 Prairie Ave • 310-978-9167 (24)

Police

- **Hawthorne Police Dept** • 12501 S Hawthorne Blvd • 310-675-4443
- **Lawndale Sheriff Service Center** • 15331 Prairie Ave • 310-219-2750

Post Offices

- **US Post Office** • 12700 Inglewood Ave • 800-275-8777
- **US Post Office** • 4320 Marine Ave • 800-275-8777

Schools

- **Academic Academy Center** • 4321 W Rosecrans Ave
- **Academy of the Two Hearts** • 5150 W 132nd St
- **Al-Huda Islamic** • 12227 Hawthorne Wy
- **Bennett-Kew Elementary** • 11710 Cherry Ave
- **Billy Mitchell Elementary** • 14429 Condon Ave
- **Bud Carlson Middle** • 13838 Yukon Ave
- **Del Aire Day Care** • 4955 W 119th St
- **Environmental Charter** • 4234 W 147th St
- **Eucalyptus Elementary** • 12044 Eucalyptus Ave
- **Explorers In Learning Academy** • 4754 W 120th St
- **Hawthorne Academy** • 12500 Ramona Ave
- **Hawthorne High** • 4859 W El Segundo Blvd
- **Hawthorne Mathematics & Science Academy** • 4467 W Broadway
- **Hawthorne Middle** • 4366 W 129th St
- **Jane Addams Elementary** • 4535 W 153rd Pl
- **Jefferson Elementary** • 4091 W 139th St
- **Juan Cabrillo Elementary** • 5309 W 135th St
- **Juan de Anza Elementary** • 5234 W 120th St
- **Kornblum Elementary** • 3630 W El Segundo Blvd
- **The Launching Pad** • 3707 Doolittle Dr
- **Lawndale High** • 14901 Inglewood Ave
- **Leuzinger High** • 4118 W Rosecrans Ave
- **Mark Twain Elementary** • 3728 W 154th St
- **Nellies Educational Center** • 4720 W Imperial Hwy
- **New Journey Christian** • 14204 Prairie Ave
- **Peter Burnett Elementary** • 5403 W 138th St
- **Prairie Elementary** • 13703 Prairie Ave
- **Prairie Vista Middle** • 13600 Prairie Ave
- **Ramona Elementary** • 4617 W 136th St
- **RK Lloyde High** • 14901 Inglewood Ave
- **South Bay Lutheran High** • 3600 W Imperial Hwy
- **St Joseph's Elementary** • 11886 Acacia Ave
- **SW Day** • 14600 Cerise Ave
- **Trinity Lutheran** • 4783 W 130th St
- **Vine Christian Academy** • 3210 W 155th St
- **Washington Elementary** • 4339 W 129th St
- **Will Rogers Middle** • 4110 W 154th St
- **William Anderson Elementary** • 4110 W 154th St
- **York Elementary** • 11838 York Ave
- **Zela Davis Elementary** • 13435 S Yukon Ave

Supermarkets

- **Albertsons** • 12630 Hawthorne Blvd
- **Food 4 Less** • 14500 Ocean Gate Ave
- **Ralphs** • 11873 Hawthorne Blvd
- **Smart & Final** • 15205 Hawthorne Blvd
- **Vons** • 4001 Inglewood Ave

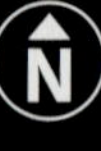

N
1
2
3
A
B
C
D
LAX
PAGE 312
13
14
26
27
29
30
105
405
Aviation/ LAX
Hawthorne
Crenshaw
Redondo Beach
W Imperial Hwy
Glenn Anderson Fwy
San Diego Fwy
Aviation Blvd
Inglewood Ave
Hawthorne Blvd
Prairie Ave
S Crenshaw Blvd
W El Segundo Blvd
W Rosecrans Ave
Manhattan Beach Blvd
Marine Ave
Space Park Blvd
Santa Fe Ave
W Redondo Beach Blvd
Lennox Blvd
W 111th St
W 115th St
W 120th St
Broadway
Northrop Ave
Hawthorne Municipal Airport
Eucalyptus Park
Del Aire County Park
Los Angeles Air Force Base
Hawthorne Memorial Park
Jim Thorpe Park
Jane Adams Park
Bodger County Park
Dominguez Creek
1/2 mile
.5 km

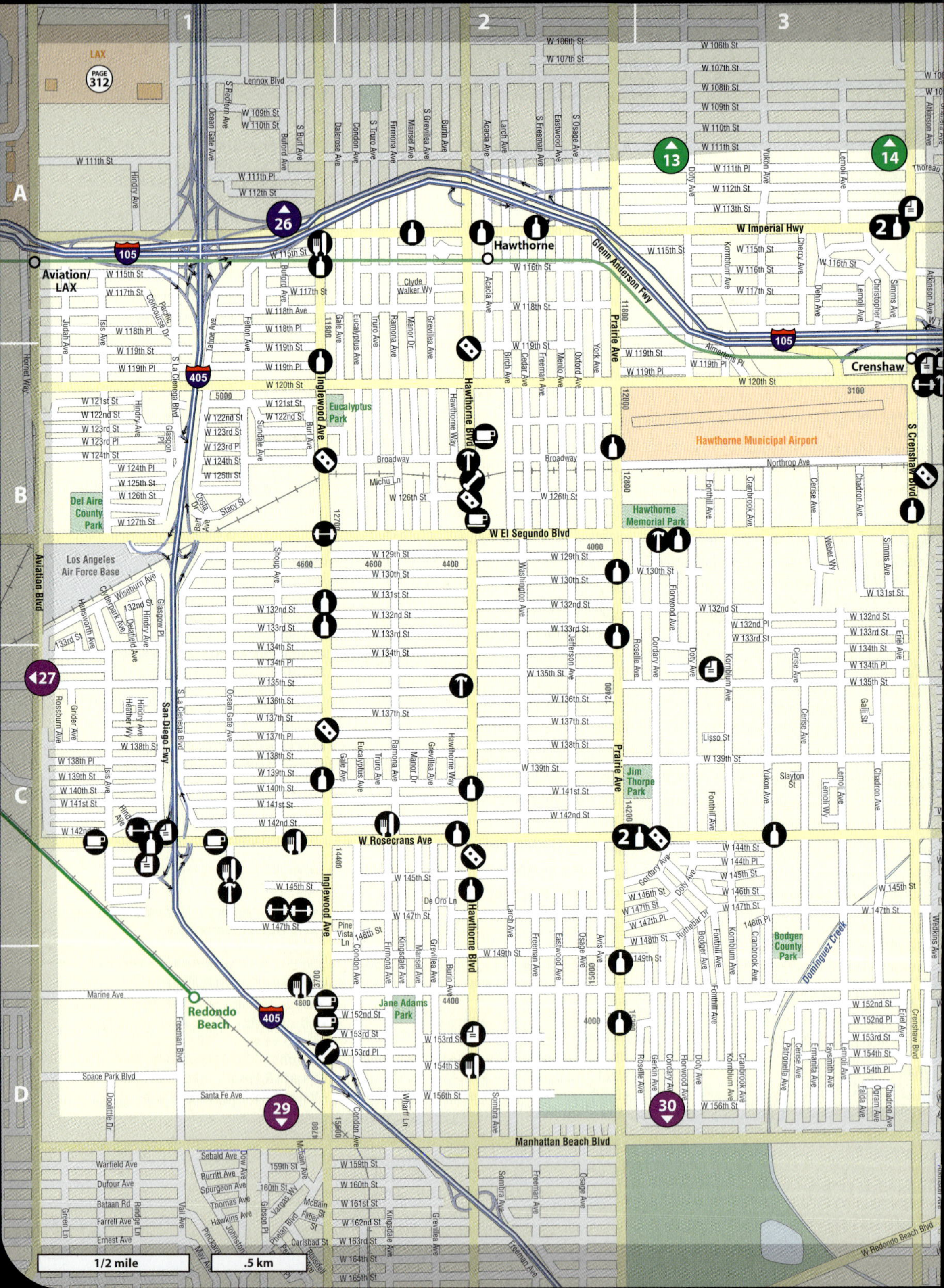

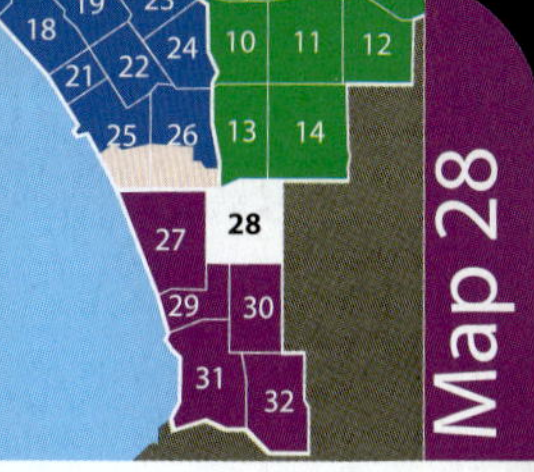

Rising South Bay real estate prices and an active city council have pushed this older, blue collar-flavored municipality to spruce up. Families and young professionals once eyeing a house in Manhattan Beach have skittered into Hawthorne, creating new and revamped recreational facilities and the Larry Guidi Skateboard Park. Hawthorne is home to Blue Bird Liquor, the luckiest place in LA to buy a lottery ticket. There's a line around the block when the jackpot gets big!

Coffee

- **Coffee Attic** • 3901 Inglewood Ave
- **Starbucks** • 12770 Hawthorne Blvd
- **Starbucks** • 2909 W 120th St
- **Starbucks** • 4001 Inglewood Ave
- **Starbucks** • 5030 W Rosecrans Ave
- **Starbucks** • 5378 W Rosecrans Ave
- **White's Bakery** • 12215 Hawthorne Blvd

Copy Shops

- **A&H Printing Services** • 14027 Hawthorne Blvd • 310-644-4975
- **Expresso Courier & Printing** • 11344 Crenshaw Blvd • 323-755-0222
- **FedEx Kinko's** • 5201 W Rosecrans Ave • 310-297-6850
- **Office Depot** • 14501 Ocean Gate Ave • 310-970-0226
- **Staples** • 14401 Hindry Ave • 310-297-0815
- **UPS Store** • 15228 Hawthorne Blvd • 310-973-7500
- **UPS Store** • 2851 W 120th St • 323-777-8388

Gyms

- **24 Hour Fitness** • 2831 W 120th St • 323-756-2466
- **Bally Total Fitness** • 5001 El Segundo Blvd • 310-263-7520
- **Curves** • 5261 W Rosecrans Ave • 310-727-9958
- **Gold's Gym** • 4917 W 147th St • 310-263-2900
- **Gold's Gym** • 4949 W 147th St • 310-263-2900

Hardware Stores

- **CWH Hardware** • 12329 Hawthorne Blvd • 310-263-0222
- **Hawthorne True Value** • 13532 Hawthorne Blvd • 310-676-2253
- **Home Depot** • 14603 Ocean Gate Ave • 310-644-9600
- **Lowe's** • 2800 120th St • 323-327-4000
- **True Value** • 3856 W El Segundo Blvd • 310-676-5497

Liquor Stores

- **Art's Rite Liquor** • 14000 Inglewood Ave
- **Avenue Liquor** • 13305 Inglewood Ave
- **Blue Bird Liquor** • 13746 Hawthorne Blvd
- **BMW Liquor** • 4533 W Imperial Hwy
- **Coast Liquor Store** • 11935 Inglewood Ave
- **Frank's Liquor** • 12329 Prairie Ave
- **G&G Liquors** • 14989 Prairie Ave
- **Jacks Liquor** • 4700 W Imperial Hwy
- **M&C Liquor** • 13201 Inglewood Ave
- **Mel & Leo's Liquor** • 14245 Hawthorne Blvd
- **Mr B's Mini Mart** • 3500 W Rosecrans Ave
- **Northgate Liquor** • 3930 W Rosecrans Ave
- **Plaza Liquor** • 11601 Inglewood Ave
- **Pound Penny Liquor & Market** • 13353 Prairie Ave
- **Ramp West Market & Liquor** • 5241 W Rosecrans Ave
- **S&D Liquor** • 3910 W Rosecrans Ave
- **S&P Liquor Store** • 13007 Prairie Ave
- **SK Liquor** • 15202 Prairie Ave
- **Snappy Food Mart** • 4172 W Imperial Hwy
- **South Bay Market Liquor** • 12726 Crenshaw Blvd
- **Ted's Liquor** • 14609 Hawthorne Blvd
- **Variety Liquor** • 4669 W Imperial Hwy
- **Young's Liquor** • 3800 W El Segundo Blvd

Pet Shops

- **Petco** • 3901 Inglewood Ave • 310-355-1370
- **Su Aquarium** • 12625 Hawthorne Blvd • 310-675-8652

Restaurants

- **Daphne's Greek Café** • 2700 Marine Ave • 310-676-9165
- **El Pollo Inka** • Lawndale Plaza • 15400 Hawthorne Blvd • 310-676-6665
- **Guru Palace** • 4850 W Rosecrans Ave • 310-675-5533
- **In-N-Out Burger** • 3801 Inglewood Ave • 800-786-1000
- **Piggies** • 4601 W Rosecrans Ave • 310-679-6326

Video Rental

- **Blockbuster** • 3909 W Rosecrans Blvd • 310-644-1970
- **Cali Games** • 14401 Hawthorne Blvd • 310-978-0880
- **Hollywood Video** • 11344 Crenshaw Blvd • 323-756-1750
- **Hollywood Video** • 12750 Hawthorne Blvd • 310-679-5797
- **Movie Time** • 13731 Inglewood Ave • 310-973-0750
- **Video Town** • 12404 Inglewood Ave • 310-675-5747
- **Videomax** • 11911 Hawthorne Blvd • 310-644-7345

Map 29 • Hermosa Beach / Redondo Beach North

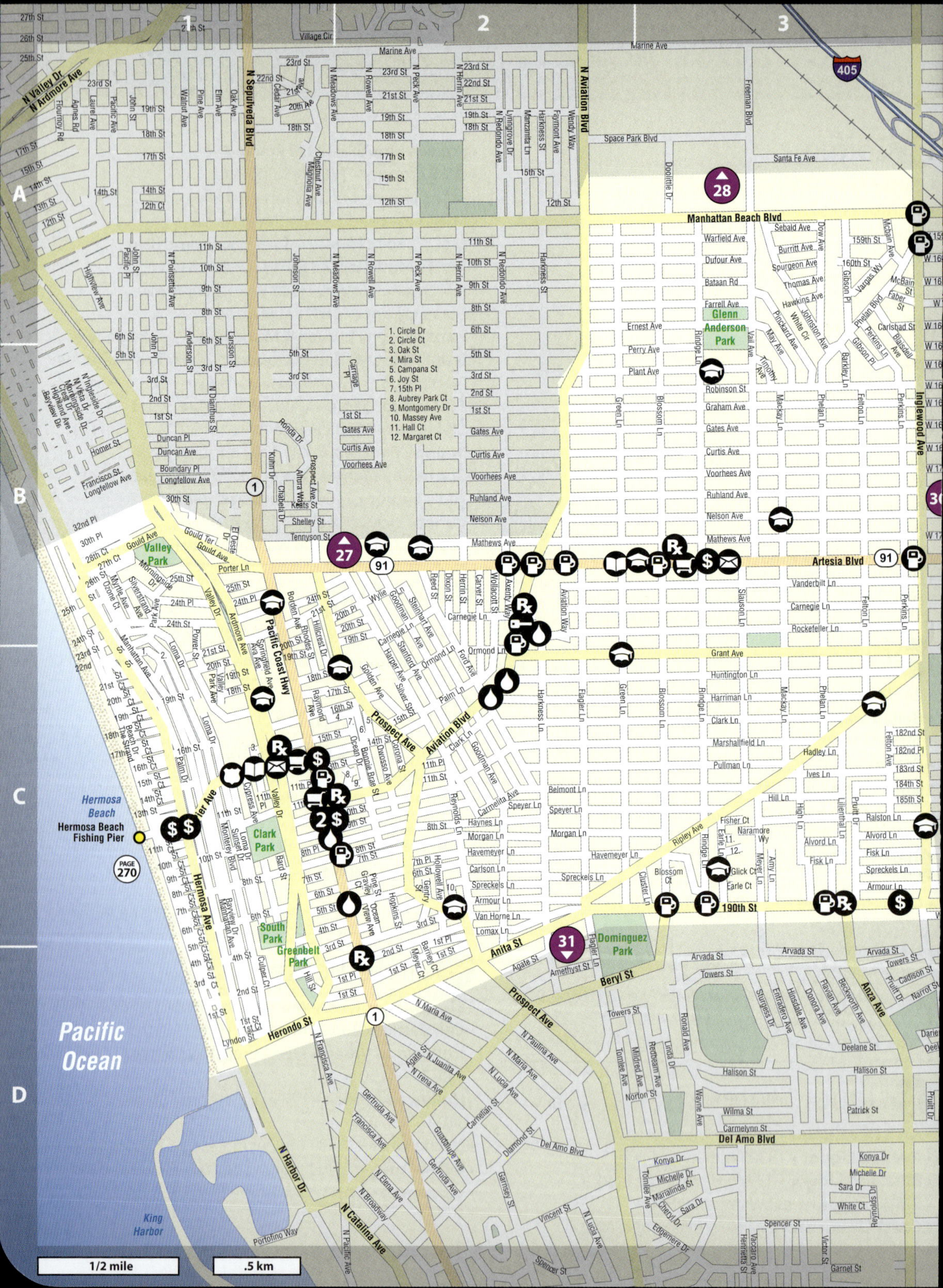
N
1
2
3
A
B
C
D
405
28
27
31
30
91
1
2
PAGE 270
Manhattan Beach Blvd
Artesia Blvd
Marine Ave
N Sepulveda Blvd
N Aviation Blvd
Pacific Coast Hwy
Aviation Blvd
Prospect Ave
Hermosa Ave
Pier Ave
Valley Dr
Herondo St
Inglewood Ave
Grant Ave
190th St
Anita St
Beryl St
Del Amo Blvd
N Harbor Dr
N Catalina Ave
Space Park Blvd
Santa Fe Ave
Ripley Ave
Anza Ave
Valley Park
Glenn Anderson Park
Clark Park
South Park
Greenbelt Park
Dominguez Park
Hermosa Beach
Hermosa Beach Fishing Pier
Pacific Ocean
King Harbor
1. Circle Dr
2. Circle Ct
3. Oak St
4. Mira St
5. Campana St
6. Joy St
7. 15th Pl
8. Aubrey Park Ct
9. Montgomery Dr
10. Massey Ave
11. Hall Ct
12. Margaret Ct
1/2 mile
.5 km

Essentials

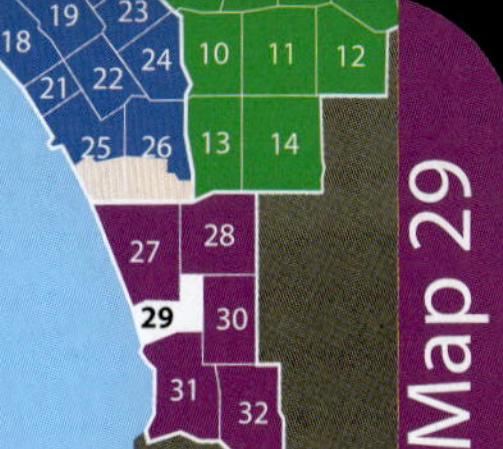

Part quaint beach town, part post-college town, Hermosa Beach is an unusual combination of homey and hoppin'. You'll know you're there when you begin to notice the street signs, which are brown with an almost antique typeface. Hermosa is anything but outdated, however. Whether you want to stroll through an art gallery with a latte, blade on the Strand, or catch the sunset during happy hour, you'll find somewhere to do it near the cross streets of Pier and Hermosa avenues.

Banks

- **Bank of America** • 90 Pier Ave
- **Citibank** • 81 Pier Ave
- **First Federal** • 1100 Pacific Coast Hwy
- **First Federal** • 2233 Artesia Blvd
- **Wells Fargo** • 1501 Pacific Coast Hwy

Car Rental

- **Hertz** • 1740 Aviation Blvd

Car Washes

- **Auto Spa Self Service Car Wash** • 1616 Aviation Blvd
- **Auto Spa Self Service Car Wash** • 620 Pacific Coast Hwy
- **Aviation Auto Spa** • 1616 Aviation Blvd
- **Hermosa Beach Car Wash** • 1000 Pacific Coast Hwy
- **Pacific Auto Cleaning** • 1449 Aviation Blvd

Gas Stations

- **76** • 3601 Inglewood
- **76** • 5404 W 190th St
- **Arco** • 1131 Pacific Coast Hwy
- **Arco** • 15922 Inglewood Ave
- **Arco** • 1800 W Artesia Blvd
- **Chevron** • 1633 Aviation Blvd
- **Chevron** • 2118 Artesia Blvd
- **Mobil** • 2714 Artesia Blvd
- **Mobil** • 931 Pacific Coast Hwy
- **Shell** • 1700 Artesia Blvd

Landmarks

- **Hermosa Beach Fishing Pier** • End of Pier Ave

Libraries

- **Hermosa Beach Public Library** • 550 Pier Ave • 310-379-8475
- **Redondo Beach North Branch** • 2000 Artesia Blvd • 310-318-0677

Pharmacies

- **CVS** • 155 Pacific Coast Hwy • 310-372-4345
- **CVS** • 5020 W 190th St • 310-370-5607
- **CVS** • 711 Pier Ave • 310-374-6266
- **Ralphs** • 1100 Pacific Coast Hwy • 310-374-2435
- **Rite-Aid** • 1720 Aviation Blvd • 310-376-4460
- **Sav-On** • 2115 Artesia Blvd • 310-370-1513

Police

- **Hermosa Beach Police Dept** • 540 Pier Ave • 310-318-0360

Post Offices

- **US Post Office** • 2215 Artesia Blvd •
- **US Post Office** • 565 Pier Ave • 800-275-8777

Schools

- **Adams Middle** • 2600 Ripley Ave
- **Beach Cities Child Development Center** • 850 Inglewood Ave
- **Birney Elementary** • 1600 Green Ln
- **Coast Christian** • 525 Earle Ln
- **Hermosa Valley Elementary** • 1645 Valley Dr
- **Hermosa View Elementary** • 1800 Prospect Ave
- **Hope Chapel Academy** • 2420 Pacific Coast Hwy
- **Jefferson Elementary** • 600 Harkness Ln
- **Journey of Faith Christian** • 1243 Artesia Blvd
- **Lincoln Elementary** • 2223 Plant Ave
- **Madison Elementary** • 2200 Mackay Ln
- **Our Lady of Guadalupe** • 340 Massey Ave
- **St Lawerence Martyr Elementary** • 1950 S Prospect Ave
- **Washington Elementary** • 1100 Lilienthal Ln

Supermarkets

- **Albertsons** • 2115 Artesia Blvd
- **Albertsons** • 2510 Pacific Coast Hwy
- **Ralphs** • 1100 Pacific Coast Hwy
- **Vons** • 715 Pier Ave

Map 29 • Hermosa Beach / Redondo Beach North

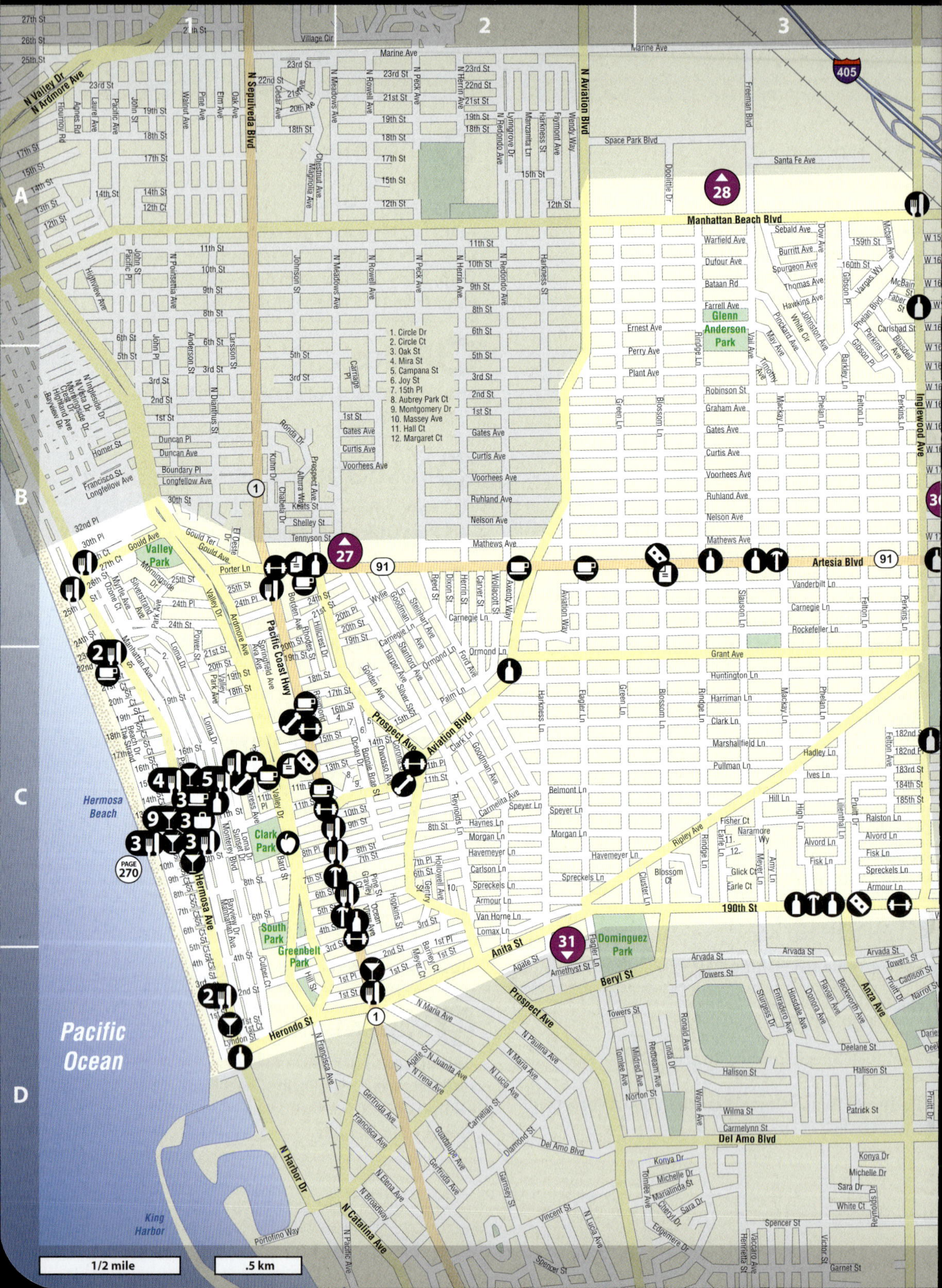

1. Circle Dr
2. Circle Ct
3. Oak St
4. Mira St
5. Campana St
6. Joy St
7. 15th Pl
8. Aubrey Park Ct
9. Montgomery Dr
10. Massey Ave
11. Hall Ct
12. Margaret Ct

Hermosa Beach

Pacific Ocean

King Harbor

Valley Park

Clark Park

South Park

Greenbelt Park

Glenn Anderson Park

Dominguez Park

Manhattan Beach Blvd

Artesia Blvd

Pacific Coast Hwy

N Sepulveda Blvd

N Aviation Blvd

Aviation Blvd

Prospect Ave

Hermosa Ave

Herondo St

Anita St

190th St

Del Amo Blvd

N Harbor Dr

N Catalina Ave

Inglewood Ave

Marine Ave

Space Park Blvd

Santa Fe Ave

Grant Ave

Ripley Ave

Beryl St

PAGE 270

1/2 mile

.5 km

Sundries / Entertainment

If you're under 25 or over 30 and experiencing a midlife crisis, Pier Avenue is the place to go for a night out. Go early or spend the evening standing in queue on the pier. Bleached blond hair and flip-flops is the dress code. Patrick Molloys represents your typical Hermosa scene (practice saying "dude" like you mean it), while Mermaid has no lines, stiff drinks and a great view of the Strand. Paisano's dishes up New York style pizza late, and pick-up volleyball is always available on the beach.

Coffee

- **Coffee Bean & Tea Leaf** • 1133 Artesia Blvd
- **Coffee Bean & Tea Leaf** • 1227 Hermosa Ave
- **Coffee Bean & Tea Leaf** • 1617 Pacific Coast Hwy
- **Fox Hollow Café** • 1700 Artesia Blvd
- **Java Man** • 157 Pier Ave
- **Planet Earth Eco Café** • 509 Pier Ave
- **Starbucks** • 1100 Pacific Coast Hwy
- **Starbucks** • 1303 Hermosa Ave
- **Starbucks** • 1904 Artesia Blvd
- **Starbucks** • 5050 190th St

Copy Shops

- **FedEx Kinko's** • 1139 Artesia Blvd • 310-379-7433
- **UPS Store** • 2110 Artesia Blvd • 310-318-3000
- **UPS Store** • 703 Pier Ave • 310-374-4420

Farmers Markets

- **Hermosa Beach (Fri, 12 pm-4 pm)** • Valley Dr b/w 10th St & 8th St

Gyms

- **24 Hour Fitness** • 1601 Pacific Coast Hwy • 310-374-4524
- **Bally Total Fitness** • 1133 Artesia Blvd • 310-372-0068
- **Curves** • 1147 Aviation Blvd • 310-372-2440
- **Gorgeous! Women's Fitness Center** • 4850 190th St • 310-542-7741
- **The Gym** • 339 Pacific Coast Hwy • 310-379-7141

Hardware Stores

- **Anza True Value** • 2441 190th St • 310-376-0852
- **Kurt True Value** • 2404 Artesia Blvd • 310-376-3494
- **Learned Lumber** • 635 Pacific Coast Hwy • 310-374-3406
- **Triangle Hardware** • 403 Pacific Coast Hwy • 310-372-2414

Liquor Stores

- **Abe's Liquor** • 240 Pier Ave
- **B&K Liquor** • 16210 Inglewood Ave
- **Coast Liquor** • 400 Pacific Coast Hwy
- **Dawn To Dust Liquor** • 2 Hermosa Ave
- **Manhattan Liquors** • 1157 Artesia Blvd
- **McNamara's Liquor** • 4703 Artesia Blvd
- **Mr B's Liquor** • 2433 190th St
- **Number One Liquor** • 1520 Aviation Blvd
- **Paul's Liquor** • 2218 Artesia Blvd
- **Quick Stop** • 2301 Artesia Blvd
- **Robert's Liquor** • 74 Pier Ave
- **Three Kings Liquor** • 5126 190th St

Nightlife

- **Aloha Sharkeez (temporarily closed)** • 52 Pier Ave • 310-374-7823
- **Café Boogaloo** • 1238 Hermosa Ave • 310-318-2324
- **Comedy & Magic Club** • 1018 Hermosa Ave • 310-372-1193
- **Dragon** • 22 Pier Ave • 310-372-4462
- **Fat Face Fenner's Fishack** • 53 Pier Ave, 2nd Floor • 310-379-5550
- **Hennessey's** • 8 Pier Ave • 310-372-5759
- **Hermosa Beach Yacht Club** • 66 Hermosa Ave • 310-376-6767
- **The Lighthouse Café** • 30 Pier Ave • 310-376-9833
- **Mermaid** • 11 Pier Ave • 310-374-9344
- **Patrick Molloy's** • 50-A Pier Ave • 310-798-9762
- **The Pitcher House** • 142 Pacific Coast Hwy • 310-374-0626
- **Sangria** • 68 Pier Ave • 310-376-4412
- **Shark's Cove** • 1220 Hermosa Ave • 310-798-3932
- **The Underground** • 1334 Hermosa Ave • 310-318-3818

Pet Shops

- **Bow Wow Boutique** • 433 Pier Ave • 310-372-7722
- **Pet Mart** • 1054 Aviation Blvd • 310-376-4724
- **The Petcare Company-Store** • 1630 Pacific Coast Hwy • 310-372-1980

Restaurants

- **Back on the Beach** • 445 Pacific Coast Hwy • 310-393-8282
- **Big Mike's Philly Steaks & Subs** • 1314 Hermosa Ave • 310-798-1499
- **Bobo's Chinese Deli** • 934 Hermosa Ave • 310-372-8559
- **Bottle Inn** • 26 22nd St • 310-376-9595
- **Buona Vita** • 439 Pier Ave • 310-379-7626
- **Club Sushi** • 1200 Hermosa Ave • 310-372-5939
- **Créme de la Crepe** • 424 Pier Ave • 310-937-2822
- **El Burrito Jr** • 919 Pacific Coast Hwy • 310-316-5058
- **El Gringo** • 2620 Hermosa Ave • 310-376-1381
- **Fritto Misto** • 316 Pier Ave • 310-318-6098
- **Good Stuff on the Strand** • 1286 The Strand • 310-374-2334
- **Havana Mania** • 3615 Inglewood Ave • 310-725-9075
- **Hennessey's Tavern** • 8 Pier Ave • 310-372-5759
- **Il Boccaccio** • 39 Pier Ave • 310-376-0211
- **Jackson's Village Bistro** • 517 Pier Ave • 310-376-6714
- **La Sosta Enoteca** • 2700 Manhattan Ave • 310-318-1556
- **Le Petit Café** • 190 Hermosa Ave • 310-379-1400
- **Martha's 22nd Street Grill** • 25 22nd St • 301-376-7786
- **Mediterraneo** • 73 Pier Ave • 310-318-2666
- **Paisano's** • 1132 Hermosa Ave • 310-376-9883
- **Pedone's Pizza** • 1332 Hermosa Ave • 310-376-0949
- **Phuket Thai** • 901 N Pacific Coast Hwy • 310-374-9598
- **Ragin' Cajun Café** • 422 Pier Ave • 310-376-7878
- **The Spot** • 110 2nd St • 310-376-2355
- **Sushi Duke** • 201 Hermosa Ave • 310-406-8986
- **Sushi Sei** • 1040 Hermosa Ave • 310-379-6900
- **Union Cattle** • 1301 Manhattan Ave • 310-798-8227

Shopping

- **Re:Style** • 138 Pier Ave • 310-379-1706
- **Splash Bath & Body** • 132 Pier Ave • 310-376-7270
- **Star's Antique Market** • 526 Pier Ave • 310-318-2800
- **Yak & Yeti** • 116 Pier Ave • 310-406-2890

Video Rental

- **Blockbuster** • 5050 190th St • 310-793-9802
- **Blockbuster** • 709 Pier Ave • 310-379-1834
- **Hollywood Video** • 2101 Artesia Blvd • 310-921-3102

N

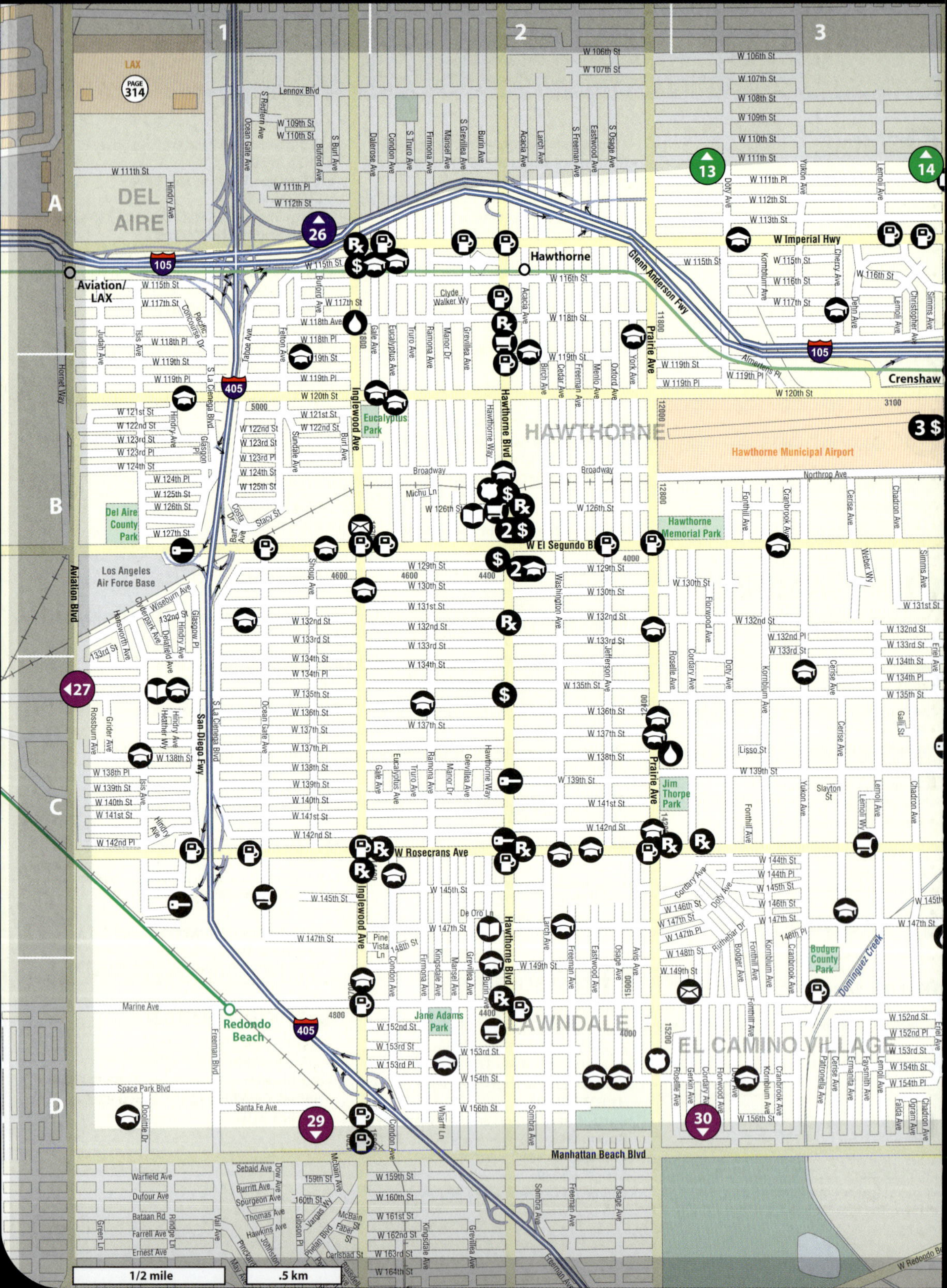

LAX
DEL AIRE
Aviation/ LAX
Hawthorne
HAWTHORNE
Hawthorne Municipal Airport
Crenshaw
Del Aire County Park
Los Angeles Air Force Base
Eucalyptus Park
Hawthorne Memorial Park
Jim Thorpe Park
Jane Adams Park
LAWNDALE
EL CAMINO VILLAGE
Redondo Beach
Budger County Park
W Imperial Hwy
Glenn Anderson Fwy
Inglewood Ave
Hawthorne Blvd
Prairie Ave
W El Segundo Blvd
W Rosecrans Ave
Manhattan Beach Blvd
Aviation Blvd
San Diego Fwy
Marine Ave
Space Park Blvd
Santa Fe Ave
Dominguez Creek

1/2 mile
.5 km

This is primarily a suburban area characterized by tract homes and large chain stores, though it too is making way for the residential push coming from Redondo. The main social hub of the area is the South Bay Galleria, which is decidedly more upscale than neighboring Del Amo Mall (Map 32). The local community college, El Camino, is also worth a gander for recent North High grads or those wishing to rejoin the educational world.

Banks

- **Bank of America** • 1603 Hawthorne Blvd
- **Bank of America** • 17512 Crenshaw Blvd
- **First Bank & Trust** • 20016 Hawthorne Blvd
- **Union** • 1413 Hawthorne Blvd
- **Washington Mutual** • 17200 Hawthorne Blvd
- **Washington Mutual** • 4840 190th St
- **Wells Fargo** • 4340 Artesia Blvd

Car Rental

- **Budget** • 20522 Hawthorne Blvd
- **Enterprise** • 18800 Hawthorne Blvd
- **Enterprise** • 20340 Hawthorne Blvd
- **Enterprise** • 20625 Hawthorne Blvd
- **Hertz** • 18409 Hawthorne Blvd
- **Midway Rent-A-Car** • 20125 Hawthorne Blvd
- **Rent 4 Less** • 4111 W Redondo Beach Blvd

Car Washes

- **AAA Galleria Hand Car Wash** • 4641 Artesia Blvd
- **Artesian Car Wash** • 17500 Prairie Ave
- **Bay Cities Carwash** • 4457 Manhattan Beach Blvd
- **Del Amo Car Wash** • 20505 Hawthorne Blvd
- **Lawndale Car Wash** • 17111 Hawthorne Blvd

Gas Stations

- **76** • 4373 W 182nd St
- **Arco** • 16518 Hawthorne Blvd
- **Arco** • 18180 Prairie Ave
- **Arco** • 3015 W 182nd St
- **Chevron** • 16926 Hawthorne Blvd
- **Chevron** • 17405 Crenshaw Blvd
- **Chevron** • 3962 Artesia Blvd
- **Independent** • 4000 Redondo Beach Blvd
- **Mobil** • 19009 Crenshaw Blvd
- **Shell** • 18910 Crenshaw Blvd
- **Shell** • 3101 Artesia Blvd
- **Shell** • 3975 W 190th St

Libraries

- **LA County Law Library** • 825 Maple Ave • 310-222-8816
- **North Torrance Branch** • 3604 Artesia Blvd • 310-323-7200

Pharmacies

- **CVS** • 15718 Hawthorne Blvd • 313-970-7440
- **CVS** • 4320 Redondo Beach Blvd • 310-542-7327
- **Ralphs** • 1413 Hawthorne Blvd • 310-370-8784
- **Ralphs** • 17500 Crenshaw Blvd • 310-327-0675
- **Target** • 1601 Kingsdale Ave • 310-750-0004

Police

- **Torrance Police Dept** • 3300 Civic Center Dr • 310-320-2611

Post Offices

- **US Post Office** • 18080 Crenshaw Blvd • 800-275-8777
- **US Post Office** • 1815 Hawthorne Blvd • 800-275-8777

Schools

- **ABC Playhouse** • 18213 Prairie St
- **Ascension Luthern Elementary** • 17910 S Prairie Ave
- **Bayside Learning Center** • 18119 Prairie Ave
- **Crenshaw Children's Center** • 18909 Crenshaw Blvd
- **Edison Elementary** • 3800 W 182nd St
- **El Camino College** • 16007 Crenshaw Blvd
- **Evelyn Carr Elementary** • 3404 W 168th St
- **Jubilee Torrance Academy** • 18015 Prairie Ave
- **North High** • 3620 W 182nd St
- **Philip Magruder Middle** • 4100 W 185th St
- **School of Life** • 18090 Prairie Ave
- **South Bay Junior Academy** • 4400 Del Amo Blvd
- **St Catherine's Laboure** • 3846 Redondo Beach Blvd
- **Switzer Center** • 2201 Amapola Ct
- **TJ's Learning Center** • 4422 W 172nd St
- **William Green Elementary** • 4520 W 168th St
- **Yukon Elementary** • 17815 Yukon Ave

Supermarkets

- **Ralphs** • 1413 Hawthorne Blvd
- **Ralphs** • 17500 Crenshaw Blvd
- **Trader Joe's** • 19720 Hawthorne Blvd

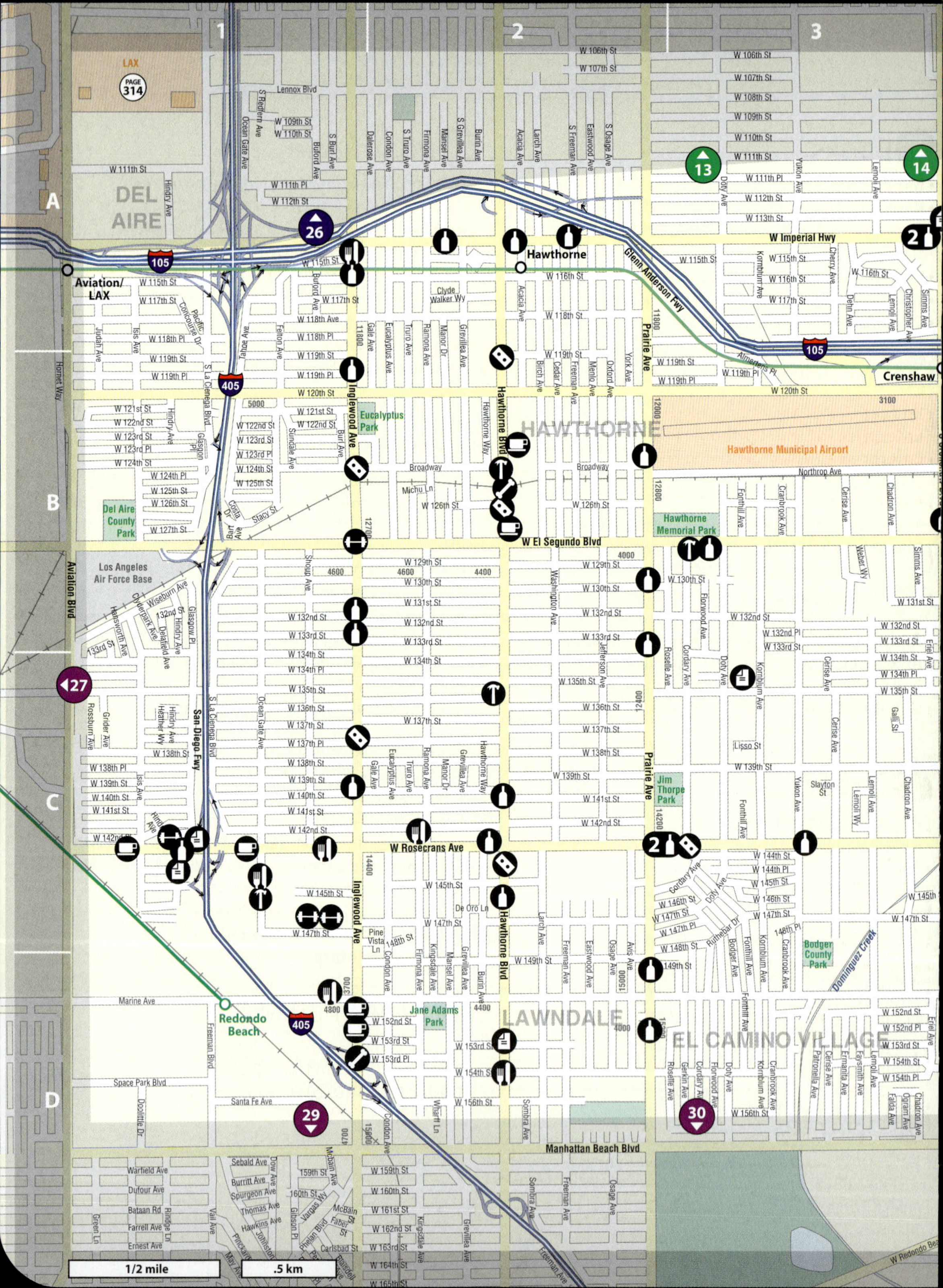

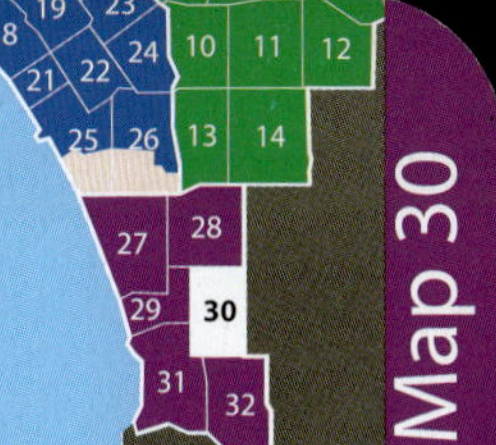

Those passing through will recognize Torrance High School, where the gang from Beverly Hills *90210* actually went to school. It was the same setting for *Buffy the Vampire Slayer*. Columbia Regional Park, just around the corner, hosts youth and soccer tournaments throughout the year. And for local golfers, the Alondra County Golf Course is your standard 18-hole, 3-par course, but without the long wait.

Coffee

- **Boba Time** • 1815 Hawthorne Blvd
- **Coffee Bean & Tea Leaf** • 20301 Hawthorne Blvd
- **Fox Hollow Drive Thru Coffee** • 19150 Hawthorne Blvd
- **Starbucks** • 1450 190th St
- **Starbucks** • 1601 Kingsdale Ave
- **Starbucks** • 17400 Hawthorne Blvd
- **Starbucks** • 1815 Hawthorne Blvd
- **Starbucks** • 3931 W Artesia Blvd

Copy Shops

- **Copier Fax Land** • 16402 Hawthorne Blvd • 310-214-4636
- **Office Depot** • 19800 Hawthorne Blvd • 310-214-9179

Gyms

- **Bally Total Fitness** • 20040 Hawthorne Blvd • 310-542-3511
- **Curves** • 4230 Redondo Beach Blvd • 310-371-1122
- **Ladies Workout Express** • 4447 Redondo Beach Blvd • 310-921-6332
- **West End Racquet & Health Club** • 4343 Spencer St • 310-542-7373

Hardware Stores

- **Rockler Woodworking and Hardware** • 20725 Hawthorne Blvd • 310-542-1466

Liquor Stores

- **ABC Liquors** • 3709 W 190th St
- **Epicure** • 3943 Artesia Blvd
- **Gourmet Cheese & Wine Market** • 1815 Hawthorne Blvd
- **J's Liquor** • 3133 Artesia Blvd
- **Jug's Liquor Mart** • 15814 Hawthorne Blvd
- **M&M Liquor** • 4015 W 182nd St
- **Mr J's Liquor** • 15734 Hawthorne Blvd
- **Pennysavers Liquor Mart** • 4507 Artesia Blvd

Movie Theaters

- **AMC Galleria - South Bay Cinema 16** • 1815 Hawthorne Blvd • 310-289-4262
- **Redondo Beach Cinema 3** • 1509 Hawthorne Blvd • 310-371-4567

Pet Shops

- **Centinela Feed & Pet Supplies** • 22840 Hawthorne Blvd • 310-373-4437
- **Centinela Feed & Pet Supplies (Mega Store)** • 2727 Maricopa St • 310-212-1030
- **Pet City** • 18305 Hawthorne Blvd • 310-542-6442
- **Pet Club** • 16919 Hawthorne Blvd • 310-542-6674
- **Pets Plus** • 17440 Crenshaw Blvd • 310-719-7088

Restaurants

- **Flossie's Restaurant** • 3566 Redondo Beach Blvd • 310-352-4037

Video Rental

- **Blockbuster** • 17124 Hawthorne Blvd • 310-371-5498

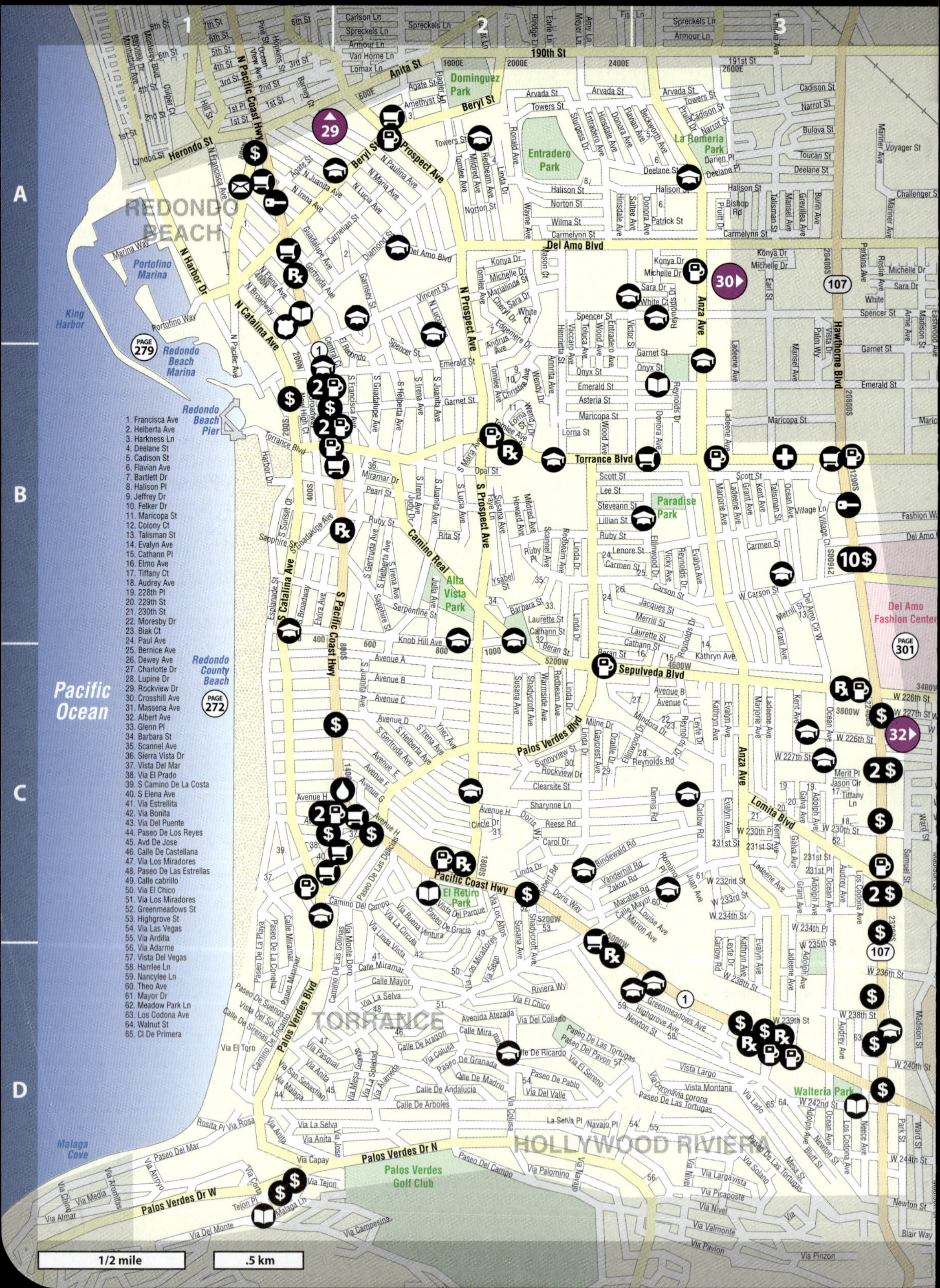

N
1
2
3
A
B
C
D
REDONDO BEACH
TORRANCE
HOLLYWOOD RIVIERA
Pacific Ocean
King Harbor
Portofino Marina
Redondo Beach Marina
Redondo Beach Pier
Redondo County Beach
Malaga Cove
Dominguez Park
Entradero Park
La Romeria Park
Paradise Park
Alta Vista Park
El Retiro Park
Walteria Park
Palos Verdes Golf Club
Del Amo Fashion Center
PAGE 279
PAGE 272
PAGE 301
29
30
32
1. Francisca Ave
2. Helberta Ave
3. Harkness Ln
4. Deelane St
5. Cadison St
6. Flavian Ave
7. Bartlett Dr
8. Halison Pl
9. Jeffrey Dr
10. Felker Dr
11. Maricopa St
12. Colony Ct
13. Talisman St
14. Evalyn Ave
15. Cathann Pl
16. Elmo Ave
17. Tiffany Ct
18. Audrey Ave
19. 228th Pl
20. 229th St
21. 230th St
22. Moresby Dr
23. Biak Ct
24. Paul Ave
25. Bernice Ave
26. Dewey Ave
27. Charlotte Dr
28. Lupine Dr
29. Rockview Dr
30. Crosshill Ave
31. Massena Ave
32. Albert Ave
33. Glenn Pl
34. Barbara St
35. Scannel Ave
36. Sierra Vista Dr
37. Vista Del Mar
38. Via El Prado
39. S Camino De La Costa
40. S Elena Ave
41. Via Estrellita
42. Via Bonita
43. Via Del Puente
44. Paseo De Los Reyes
45. Avd De Jose
46. Calle De Castellana
47. Via Los Miradores
48. Paseo De Las Estrellas
49. Calle cabrillo
50. Via El Chico
51. Via Los Miradores
52. Greenmeadows St
53. Highgrove St
54. Via Las Vegas
55. Via Ardilla
56. Via Adarme
57. Vista Del Vegas
58. Harrlee Ln
59. Nancylee Ln
60. Theo Ave
61. Mayor Dr
62. Meadow Park Ln
63. Los Codona Ave
64. Walnut St
65. Cl De Primera
190th St
Del Amo Blvd
Torrance Blvd
Sepulveda Blvd
Pacific Coast Hwy
N Pacific Coast Hwy
S Pacific Coast Hwy
Palos Verdes Blvd
Palos Verdes Dr N
Palos Verdes Dr W
Hawthorne Blvd
Anza Ave
Lomita Blvd
Camino Real
N Prospect Ave
S Prospect Ave
N Catalina Ave
S Catalina Ave
N Harbor Dr
Beryl St
Anita St
Herondo St
1/2 mile
.5 km

Essentials

It's hard to beat living, working, or playing by the beach. A solid school district, many parks, and areas such as the Redondo Beach Pier/King Harbor (a typical, touristy, crowded beach boardwalk) and the Hollywood Riviera, with its cool boutiques and hip restaurants, ensure that there is something for everyone.

Banks

- **Bank of America** • 1601 S Pacific Coast Hwy
- **Bank of America** • 21700 Hawthorne Blvd
- **Bank of America** • 22 Malaga Cove Plz
- **Bank of America** • 222 N Catalina Ave
- **Bank of America** • 4206 Pacific Coast Hwy
- **Bank of the West** • 23865 Hawthorne Blvd
- **Bay Cities National** • 1333 S Pacific Coast Hwy
- **Bay Cities National** • 23550 Hawthorne Blvd
- **California Bank & Trust** • 21515 Hawthorne Blvd
- **California Credit Union** • 22733 Hawthorne Blvd
- **California National** • 22150 Hawthorne Blvd
- **Cathay** • 23226 Hawthorne Blvd
- **Chinatrust** • 22939 Hawthorne Blvd
- **Comerica** • 21535 Hawthorne Blvd
- **Downey Savings & Loan** • 4350 W Pacific Coast Hwy
- **East West** • 23737 Hawthorne Blvd
- **Farmers & Merchants** • 22400 Hawthorne Blvd
- **Hanmi** • 21838 Hawthorne Blvd
- **Malaga** • 2514 Via Tejon
- **Preferred** • 21615 Hawthorne Blvd
- **Union** • 1401 Pacific Coast Hwy
- **Union** • 21201 Hawthorne Blvd
- **Union** • 24030 Hawthorne Blvd
- **United Commercial** • 23211 Hawthorne Blvd
- **US** • 1217 N Catalina Ave
- **Wachovia** • 21705 Hawthorne Blvd
- **Washington Mutual** • 1600 S Pacific Coast Hwy
- **Washington Mutual** • 21660 Hawthorne Blvd
- **Wells Fargo** • 1701 S Elena Ave
- **Wells Fargo** • 21323 Hawthorne Blvd
- **Wells Fargo** • 301 S Pacific Coast Hwy

Car Rental

- **Dollar** • 21333 Hawthorne Blvd
- **Enterprise** • 816 N Irena

Car Washes

- **Chevron** • 1500 S Pacific Coast Hwy

Gas Stations

- **76** • 21190 Hawthorne Blvd
- **76** • 247 S Pacific Coast Hwy
- **Arco** • 1890 S Pacific Coast Hwy
- **Arco** • 3900 Sepulveda Blvd
- **Arco** • 4205 Pacific Coast Hwy
- **Chevron** • 1500 S Pacific Coast Hwy
- **Chevron** • 1630 S Elena Ave
- **Chevron** • 5230 Sepulveda Blvd
- **Mobil** • 20306 Anza Ave
- **Mobil** • 246 S Pacific Coast Hwy
- **Mobil** • 4202 Pacific Coast Hwy
- **Shell** • 1200 Beryl St
- **Shell** • 23140 Hawthorne Blvd
- **Shell** • 4530 Torrance Blvd
- **Thrifty** • 4925 Torrance Blvd

Emergency Rooms

- **Little Company of Mary** • 4101 Torrance Blvd

Libraries

- **El Retiro Branch** • 126 Vista Del Parque • 310-375-0922
- **Henderson Branch** • 4805 Emerald St • 310-371-2075
- **Malaga Cove Library** • 2400 Via Campesina • 310-377-9584
- **Redondo Beach Public Library** • 303 N Pacific Coast Hwy • 310-318-0675
- **Walteria Branch** • 3815 W 242nd St • 310-375-8418

Pharmacies

- **CVS** • 4235 Pacific Coast Hwy • 310-373-6847
- **CVS** • 4625 Torrance Blvd • 310-370-7919
- **Longs Drugs** • 1880 S Pacific Coast Hwy • 310-316-6492
- **Ralphs** • 5035 Pacific Coast Hwy • 310-378-5214
- **Rite-Aid** • 3860 Sepulveda Blvd • 310-373-5884
- **Rite-Aid** • 401 N Pacific Coast Hwy • 310-372-9029
- **Sav-On** • Albertsons • 21035 Hawthorne Blvd • 310-540-6807
- **Walgreens** • 4142 Pacific Coast Hwy • 310-375-9019
- **Walgreens** • 535 S Pacific Coast Hwy • 310-540-2228

Police

- **Redondo Beach Police Dept Main Station** • 401 Diamond St • 310-379-2477

Post Offices

- **US Post Office** • 1201 N Catalina Ave • 800-275-8777

Schools

- **Alta Vista Elementary** • 815 Knob Hill Ave
- **Anza Elementary** • 21400 Ellenwood Dr
- **Bert M Lynn Middle** • 5038 Halison St
- **Beryl Heights** • 920 Beryl St
- **Bishop Montgomery High** • 5430 Torrance Blvd
- **Bishop Mora Salesian High** • 960 S Soto St
- **Calle Mayor Middle** • 4800 Calle Mayor
- **Carden Dominion** • 320 Knob Hill Ave
- **Goldensun Academy** • 5265 Bindewald Rd
- **Jefferson Middle** • 21717 Talisman St
- **Joseph Arnold Elementary** • 4100 W 227th St
- **Los Angeles International** • 23800 Hawthorne Blvd
- **Menorah Community Day** • 1101 Camino Real
- **Nick G Parras Middle** • 200 N Lucia
- **Redondo Shores High** • 1000 Del Amo St
- **Redondo Union High** • 631 Vincent Park
- **Richardson Middle** • 23751 Nancy Lee Ln
- **Riveria Hall Lutheran** • 330 Palos Verdes Blvd
- **Riviera Elementary** • 365 Paseo De Arena
- **Seaside Elementary** • 4651 Sharynne Ln
- **South Bay Faith Academy** • 101 S Pacific Coast Hwy
- **South Bay High** • 4025 W 226th St
- **South High** • 4801 Pacific Coast Hwy
- **St James Elementary** • 4625 Garnet St
- **Towers Elementary** • 5600 Towers St
- **Tulita Elementary** • 1520 S Prospect Ave
- **Victor Elementary** • 4820 Spencer St
- **West High** • 20401 Victor St

Supermarkets

- **Albertsons** • 1516 S Pacific Coast Hwy
- **Albertsons** • 21035 Hawthorne Blvd
- **Albertsons** • 615 N Pacific Coast Hwy
- **Bristol Farms** • 1700 Pacific Coast Hwy
- **Pavilions** • 4705 Torrance Blvd
- **Ralphs** • 5035 Pacific Coast Hwy
- **Smart & Final** • 332 S Pacific Coast Hwy
- **Trader Joe's** • 1761 S Elena Ave
- **Vons** • 1212 Beryl St
- **Vons** • 245 Palos Verdes Blvd
- **Whole Foods Market** • 405 N Pacific Coast Hwy

Map 31 • Redondo Beach

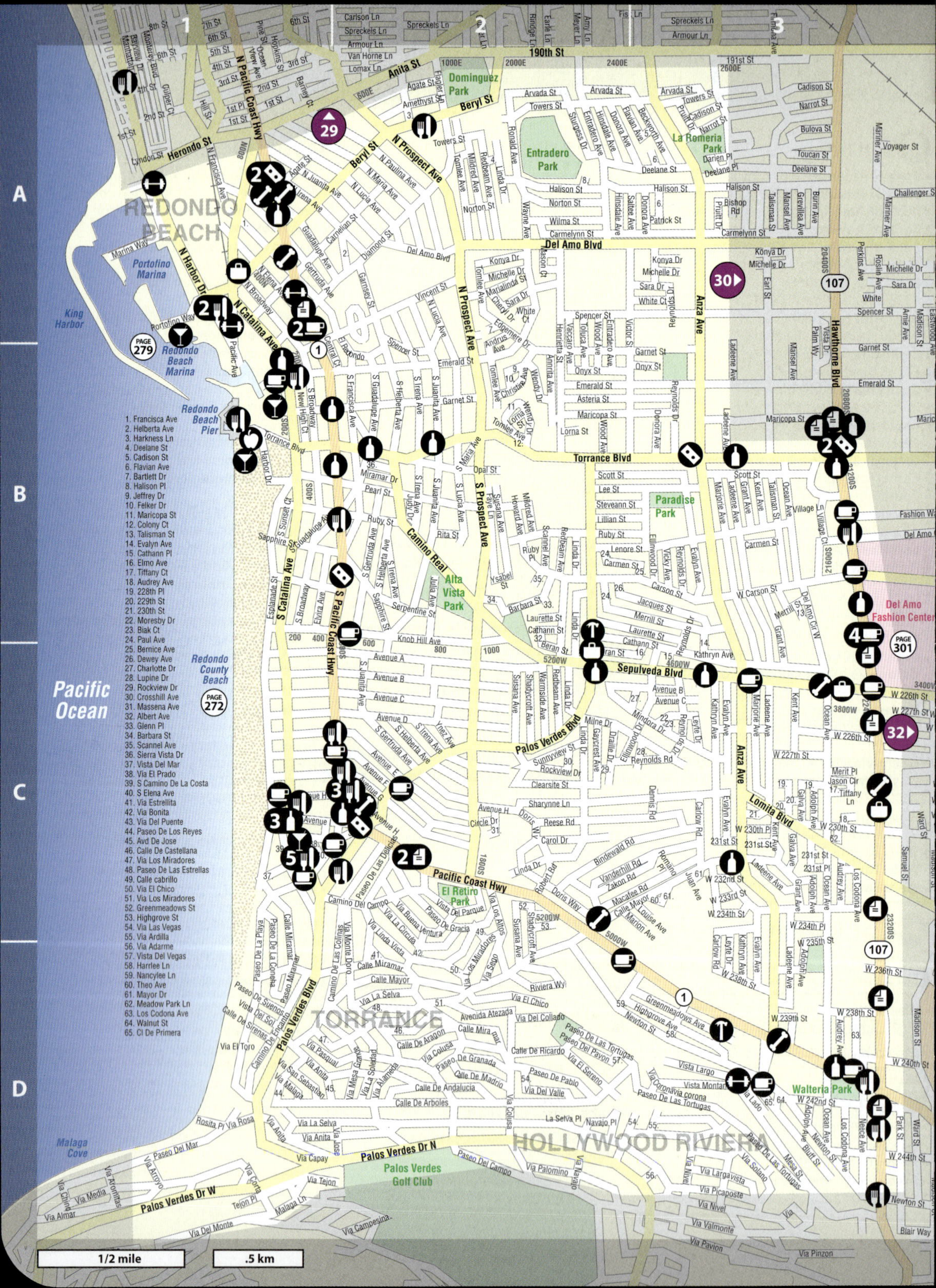

1. Francisca Ave
2. Helberta Ave
3. Harkness Ln
4. Deelane St
5. Cadison St
6. Flavian Ave
7. Bartlett Dr
8. Halison Pl
9. Jeffrey Dr
10. Felker Dr
11. Maricopa St
12. Colony Ct
13. Talisman St
14. Evalyn Ave
15. Cathann Pl
16. Elmo Ave
17. Tiffany Ct
18. Audrey Ave
19. 228th Pl
20. 229th St
21. 230th St
22. Moresby Dr
23. Biak Ct
24. Paul Ave
25. Bernice Ave
26. Dewey Ave
27. Charlotte Dr
28. Lupine Dr
29. Rockview Dr
30. Crosshill Ave
31. Massena Ave
32. Albert Ave
33. Glenn Pl
34. Barbara St
35. Scannel Ave
36. Sierra Vista Dr
37. Vista Del Mar
38. Via El Prado
39. S Camino De La Costa
40. S Elena Ave
41. Via Estrellita
42. Via Bonita
43. Via Del Puente
44. Paseo De Los Reyes
45. Avd De Jose
46. Calle De Castellana
47. Via Los Miradores
48. Paseo De Las Estrellas
49. Calle cabrillo
50. Via El Chico
51. Via Los Miradores
52. Greenmeadows St
53. Highgrove St
54. Via Las Vegas
55. Via Ardilla
56. Via Adarme
57. Via Del Vegas
58. Harrlee Ln
59. Nancylee Ln
60. Theo Ave
61. Mayor Dr
62. Meadow Park Ln
63. Los Codona Ave
64. Walnut St
65. Cl De Primera

At last count, Redondo Beach features fourteen parks, some of which are designed for camping. The Seaside Lagoon is a great place for a family picnic and swim in its shallow 70-degree saltwater. Redondo attracts the post-post-collegiate crowd, but it has a tame and lackluster nightlife.

Coffee

- **Carissimo Bakery** • 1611 S Catalina Ave
- **Catalina Coffee Company** • 126 N Catalina Ave
- **Coffee Bean & Tea Leaf** • 21300 Hawthorne Blvd
- **Coffee Cartel** • 1820 S Catalina Ave
- **Gloria Jean's Gourmet Coffees** • 275 Del Amo Fashion Ctr
- **Green Patio Café** • 24002 Vista Montana
- **Kelly's Coffee & Fudge** • 223 Del Amo Fashion Sq
- **La Caffita** • 420 N Pacific Coast Hwy
- **Peet's** • 1418 S Pacific Coast Hwy
- **Starbucks** • 1516 S Pacific Coast Hwy
- **Starbucks** • 1749 S Elena Ave
- **Starbucks** • Albertsons • 21035 Hawthorne Blvd
- **Starbucks** • 21209A Hawthorne Blvd
- **Starbucks** • 300 N Pacific Coast Hwy
- **Starbucks** • 3737 Pacific Coast Hwy
- **Starbucks** • 5005 Pacific Coast Hwy
- **Starbucks** • 6 Del Amo Fashion Ctr

Copy Shops

- **Acro Printing** • 23780 Hawthorne Blvd • 310-791-2651
- **FedEx Kinko's** • 1770 S Pacific Coast Hwy • 310-792-8635
- **FedEx Kinko's** • 21023 Hawthorne Blvd • 310-316-8455
- **FedEx Kinko's** • 23325 Hawthorne Blvd • 310-373-2530 
- **Mail Boxes Etc** • 21143 Hawthorne Blvd • 310-540-1370
- **Pro Print** • 24205 Hawthorne Blvd • 310-378-8518
- **Sir Speedy** • 21213 Hawthorne Blvd • 310-543-5114
- **Staples** • 22025 Hawthorne Blvd • 310-540-3093
- **UPS Store** • 1874 S Pacific Coast Hwy • 310-792-1747
- **UPS Store** • 409 N Pacific Coast Hwy • 310-798-3013
- **UPS Store** • 800 S Pacific Coast Hwy • 310-540-6323

Farmers Markets

- **Redondo Beach-Harbor Dr (Thurs, 8 am-1 pm)** • N Harbor Dr & W Torrance Blvd

Gyms

- **Curves** • 409 N Pacific Coast Hwy • 310-379-6588
- **Gold's Gym** • 200 N Harbor Dr • 310-374-5522
- **Spectrum Club** • 819 N Harbor Dr • 310-376-9443

Hardware Stores

- **Orchard Supply Hardware** • 4340 Pacific Coast Hwy • 310-375-3077
- **Woods Ace Hardware** • 22217 Palos Verdes Blvd • 310-540-5355

Liquor Stores

- **Beverages & More!** • 21301 Hawthorne Blvd
- **Catalina Liquor & Deli** • 144 N Catalina Ave
- **Chateau Liquor Store** • 4545 Sepulveda Blvd
- **Friends Of The Vine (Wine only)** • 221 Avenida Del Norte
- **House of Cigars & Liquor** • 400 S Pacific Coast Hwy
- **King's Liquor & Gourmet** • 4435 Torrance Blvd
- **Liquor Depot** • 801 Torrance Blvd
- **Mr S Liquor** • 3885 Pacific Coast Hwy
- **Nick's Liquor Store** • 510 N Pacific Coast Hwy
- **Okay Liquor** • 22216 Palos Verdes Blvd
- **Party House Liquor** • 1817 S Catalina Ave
- **Pierside Liquors** • 310 Torrance Blvd
- **Pony Square Liquors** • 1882 S Pacific Coast Hwy
- **Prince Liquor** • 4425 Calle Mayor
- **Red Eye Liquor Store** • 21186 Hawthorne Blvd
- **Ruby's Liquor** • 443 S Pacific Coast Hwy
- **Village Spirit Liquors** • 1711 S Catalina Ave
- **VIP Liquor & Market** • 604 Torrance Blvd
- **Walteria Country Liquor** • 24212 Hawthorne Blvd

Nightlife

- **Mickie Finz Fish House and Bar** • 1710 S Catalina Ave • 310-316-6658
- **Naja's Place** • 154 Internatl Boardwalk • 310-376-9951
- **The Portofino Hotel & Yacht Club** • 260 Portofino Wy • 310-379-8481
- **Tony's on the Pier** • 210 Fishermans Wharf • 310-374-1442

Pet Shops

- **Animal Lovers Pet Shop** • 5141 Calle Mayor • 310-378-3052
- **Aquatic Fantasy** • 531 N Pacific Coast Hwy • 310-798-7333
- **Centinela Feed & Pet** • 413 N Pacific Coast Hwy • 310-318-2653
- **KOOL Dog KAFE** • 1666 S Pacific Coast Hwy • 310-944-3232
- **Paws Pet Supplies & Grooming** • 4172 Pacific Coast Hwy • 310-375-1559
- **Petco** • 537 N Pacific Coast Hwy • 310-374-7969
- **Petsmart** • 3855 Sepulveda Blvd • 310-316-9047

Restaurants

- **Bluewater Grill** • 665 N Harbor Dr • 310-318-3474
- **The Bull Pen** • 314 Ave I • 310-375-7797
- **Captain Kidd's** • 209 N Harbor Dr • 310-372-7703
- **Catalina Coffee Company** • 126 N Catalina Ave • 310-318-2499
- **Chez Melange** • 1716 S Pacific Coast Hwy • 310-540-1222
- **Christine** • 24530 Hawthorne Blvd • 310-373-1952
- **Cialuzzis** • 601 N Pacific Coast Hwy • 310-374-8581
- **El Torito Grill** • 21321 Hawthorne Blvd • 310-543-1896
- **Gina Lee's Bistro** • 211 Palos Verdes Blvd • 310-375-4462
- **The Green Temple Vegetarian Restaurant** • 1700 S Catalina Ave • 310-944-4525
- **Hennessey's Tavern** • 1712 S Catalina Ave • 310-540-8443
- **HT Grill** • 1701 S Catalina Ave • 310-791-4849
- **Japonica** • 1304 S Pacific Coast Hwy • 310-316-9477
- **Kincaids** • 500 Fishermans Wharf • 310-318-6080
- **The Original Pancake House** • 1756 S Pacific Coast Hwy • 310-543-9875
- **Pedone Pizza** • 1821 S Catalina Ave • 310-373-6397
- **Redondo Beach Brewing Company** • 1814 S Catalina Ave • 310-316-8477
- **Riviera Mexican Grill** • 1615 S Pacific Coast Hwy • 310-540-2501
- **Splash** • Crowne Plaza • 300 N Harbor Dr • 310-798-5348
- **W's China Bistro** • 1410 S Pacific Coast Hwy • 310-792-1600
- **Zazou** • 1810 S Catalina Ave • 310-540-4884

Shopping

- **Cookin Stuff** • 22217 Palos Verdes Blvd • 310-371-2220
- **Cost Plus World Market** • 22929 Hawthorne Blvd • 310-378-8331
- **Dive N Surf** • 504 N Broadway • 310-372-8423
- **Lindbergh Nutrition** • 3804 Sepulveda Blvd • 310-378-9490

Video Rental

- **20-20 Video** • 705 N Pacific Coast Hwy • 310-376-2020
- **Blockbuster** • 1900 S Pacific Coast Hwy • 310-316-8957
- **Blockbuster** • 21841 Hawthorne Blvd • 310-540-6373
- **Hollywood Video** • 21149 Hawthorne Blvd • 310-316-9306
- **Movies N You** • 4641 Torrance Blvd • 310-370-8280
- **Premieres Video** • 725 S Pacific Coast Hwy • 310-316-9336

Map 32 • Torrance South

N
1
2
3
A
B
C
D
TORRANCE
LOMITA
Del Amo Fashion Center
PAGE 301
Madrona Marsh Nature Preserve
Charles Wilson Community Park
Torrance Park
Hickory Park
Sur La Brea Park
Lomita Park
Zamperini Field (Torrance Municipal Airport)
30
31
107
213
Torrance Blvd
W Carson St
Sepulveda Blvd
Lomita Blvd
Pacific Coast Hwy
Crenshaw Blvd
Hawthorne Blvd
Madrona Ave
Maple Ave
S Western Ave
Del Amo Ctr
Plaza Del Amo
Skypark Dr
1/2 mile
.5 km
1. Eastwood Ct
2. Osage Ct
3. Benner Ave
4. Primm Wy
5. Pitcairn Wy
6. Glencoe Wy
7. Clarellen St
8. Normallin St
9. Faircross St
10. Forrester Dr
11. Veronica Ln
12. Aubrey Ln
13. Bani Ave
14. Noelle Ct
15. Becknel Ave
16. Stratford Dr
17. Forrester Dr
18. 254th St
19. Plum Ave
20. Park Del Amo
21. Date Ave
22. Elm Ave
23. Shelbourne Wy
24. Atwood Wy
25. Cambridge Wy
26. Santa Cruz Ct
27. Border Ave
28. Modesto Ave
29. Andreo Ave
30. Eshelman Wy
31. Padron Pl
32. Milan Ln
33. Laura Lee Ln
34. Eshelman Wy
35. Leola St

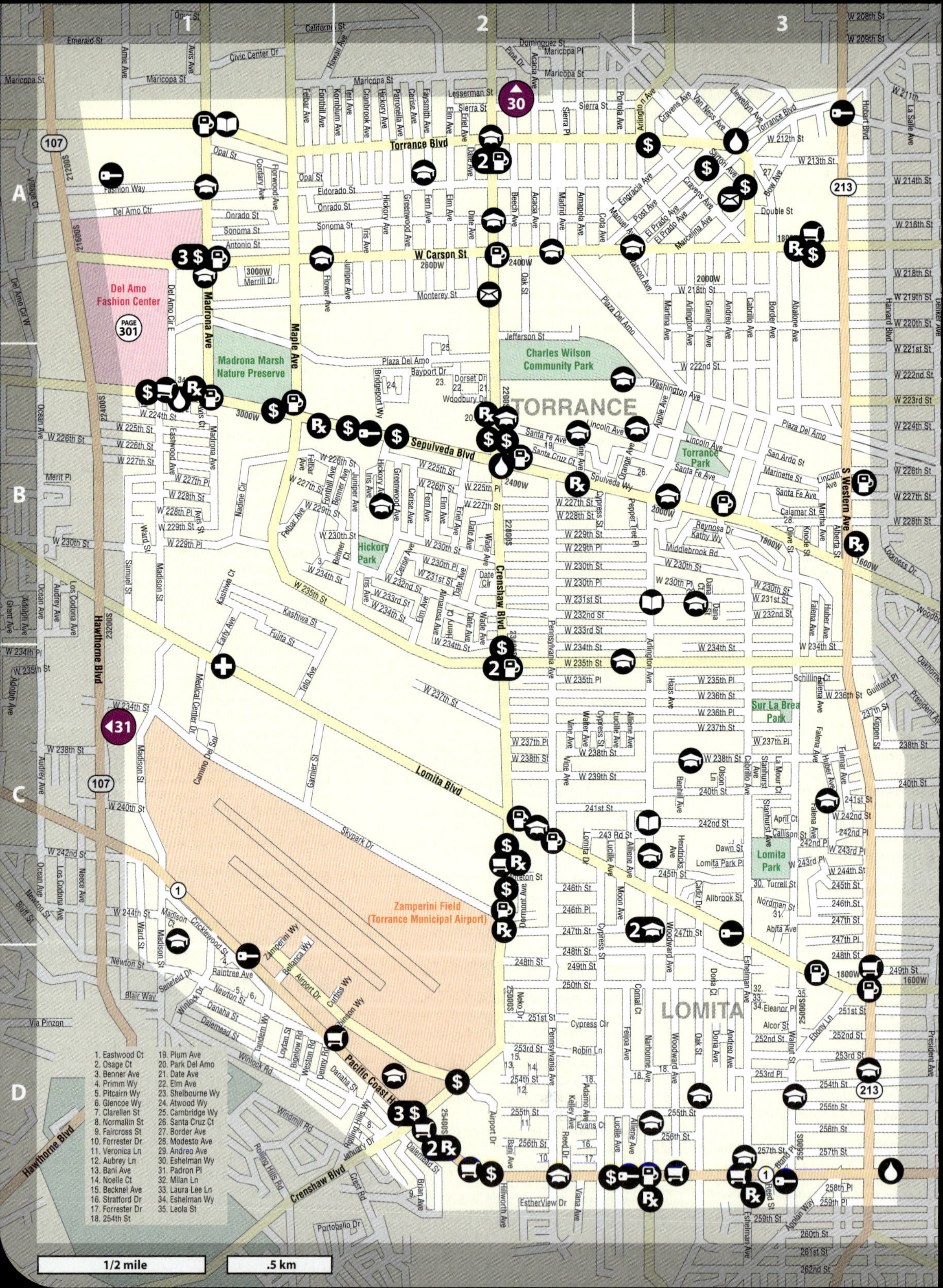

Del Amo Fashion Center is the highlight of this area, considered one of the largest malls in the country. Down the street is the Madrona Marsh Nature Preserve, one of the few remaining wetlands in an urban setting, well-preserved by the local nature society. And the family-owned Torrance Bakery makes both a mean sandwich and a beautiful wedding cake, as well as a gamut of pastries.

Banks

- **Bank of America** • 1255 Sartori Ave
- **Bank of America** • 25435 Crenshaw Blvd
- **California Center** • 2742 W Sepulveda Blvd
- **Citibank** • 2700 Pacific Coast Hwy
- **City National** • 3424 W Carson St
- **Downey Savings & Loan** • 1770 Carson St
- **First Federal** • 2177 Pacific Coast Hwy
- **First Federal** • 23415 Crenshaw Blvd
- **First Federal** • 3422 W Carson St
- **Fremont Investment & Loan** • 3440 W Carson St
- **Hanmi** • 2370 Crenshaw Blvd
- **Nara** • 3030 Sepulveda Blvd
- **Preferred** • 3501 Sepulveda Blvd
- **Union** • 25345 Crenshaw Blvd
- **US** • 2270 Pacific Coast Hwy
- **US** • 2860 Sepulveda Blvd
- **Washington Mutual** • 2121 Torrance Blvd
- **Washington Mutual** • 2750 Pacific Coast Hwy
- **Wells Fargo** • 1403 Sartori Ave
- **Wells Fargo** • 24325 Crenshaw Blvd
- **Wells Fargo** • 24439 Crenshaw Blvd
- **Wilshire State** • 2390 Crenshaw Blvd

Car Rental

- **Avis** • 2814 Sepulveda Blvd
- **Enterprise** • 21176 S Western Ave
- **Enterprise** • 2230 Pacific Coast Hwy
- **Enterprise** • 3311 Pacific Coast Hwy
- **Exclusive Car Rentals** • 2020 Lomita Blvd # 6
- **Hertz** • 3635 Fashion Wy
- **Hertz Local Edition** • 1939 Pacific Coast Hwy

Car Washes

- **76** • 2476 Sepulveda Blvd
- **Bubble Bath Hand Wash** • 1831 Torrance Blvd
- **Chevron** • 3405 Sepulveda Blvd
- **Harbor Car Wash** • 1662 Pacific Coast Hwy
- **Torrance Auto Spa** • 1751 Crenshaw Blvd

Gas Stations

- **76** • 2476 Sepulveda Blvd
- **Arco** • 1210 Crenshaw Blvd
- **Arco** • 22620 Western Ave
- **Arco** • 23510 Crenshaw Blvd
- **Arco** • 2380 Lomita Blvd
- **Chevron** • 1700 Crenshaw Blvd
- **Chevron** • 23420 Crenshaw Blvd
- **Chevron** • 2761 Cabrillo Ave
- **Chevron** • 3405 Sepulveda Blvd
- **Exxon** • 1886 Lomita Blvd
- **Exxon** • 3401 Torrance Blvd
- **Independent** • 25001 Western Ave
- **Mobil** • 1640 Crenshaw Blvd
- **Mobil** • 25808 Narbonne Ave
- **Mobil** • 3006 Sepulveda Blvd
- **Mobil** • 3328 W Carson St
- **Shell** • 2477 Lomita Blvd
- **Shell** • 2504 Torrance Blvd
- **Valero** • 24650 Crenshaw Blvd

Emergency Rooms

- **Torrance Memorial** • 3330 Lomita Blvd

Libraries

- **Katy Geissert Civic Center Library** • 3301 Torrance Blvd • 310-618-5959
- **Lomita** • 24200 Narbonne Ave • 310-539-4515
- **Southeast Branch** • 23115 Arlington Ave • 310-530-5044

Pharmacies

- **CVS** • 2001 Pacific Coast Hwy • 310-517-9535
- **CVS** • 25829 Narbonne Ave • 310-517-8520
- **CVS** • 3020 Sepulveda Blvd • 310-534-1264
- **Longs Drugs** • 24663 Crenshaw Blvd • 310-784-0395
- **Ralphs** • 1770 Carson St • 310-787-8861
- **Rite-Aid** • 2240 W Sepulveda Blvd • 310-325-0868
- **Rite-Aid** • 2545 Pacific Coast Hwy • 310-325-8420
- **Target** • 3433 Sepulveda Blvd • 310-370-1021
- **Vons** • 24325 Crenshaw Blvd • 310-784-1025
- **Walgreens** • 22930 S Western Ave • 310-517-1851
- **Walgreens** • 2690 Pacific Coast Hwy • 310-517-0351
- **Walgreens** • 2976 Sepulveda Blvd • 310-534-0078

Post Offices

- **US Post Office** • 1433 Marcelina Ave • 800-275-8777
- **US Post Office** • 2510 Monterey St • 800-275-8777
- **US Post Office** • 25131 Narbonne Ave • 800-275-8777
- **US Post Office** • 291 Del Amo Fashion Sq • 800-275-8777

Schools

- **Branch of Hope** • 2370 W Carson St
- **Chabad of South Bay** • 24412 Narbonne Ave
- **The Childrens Place** • 1215 Crenshaw Blvd
- **The Childrens Place** • 1625 Crenshaw Blvd
- **Coastal Academy** • 25501 Oak St
- **Discovery World Academy** • 25533 Narbonne Ave
- **Fern Elementary** • 1314 Fern Ave
- **First Lutheran** • 2900 W Carson St
- **Fleming Middle** • 25425 Walnut St
- **Francisco Bravo Medical Magnet High** • 1200 N Cornwell St
- **Harbour Church** • 1716 W 254th St
- **Hickory Elementary** • 2800 W 227th St
- **Hickory Tree** • 21720 Madrona Ave
- **Howard Wood Elementary** • 2250 W 235th St
- **Hull Middle** • 2080 W 231st St
- **John Adams Elementary** • 2121 W 238th St
- **Kindercare** • 2785 Pacific Coast Hwy
- **Kurt T Shery High** • 2600 Vine St
- **Lomita Elementary** • 2211 247th St
- **Madrona Middle** • 21364 Madrona Ave
- **Nativity** • 2371 W Carson St
- **Nishiyamato Academy** • 2458 Lomita Blvd
- **Pacific Coast Montessori** • 2342 Pacific Coast Hwy
- **Pacific Lutheran High** • 2150 Sepulveda Blvd
- **Southern California Regional Occupation Center** • 2300 Crenshaw Blvd
- **St Margaret Mary** • 25515 Eshelman Ave
- **Sunnyside** • 24002 Huber Ave
- **Torrance Community Day** • 2291 Washington Ave
- **Torrance Elementary** • 2125 Lincoln Ave
- **Torrance High** • 2200 Carson St
- **Walteria Elementary** • 24456 Madison St

Supermarkets

- **Albertsons** • 2130 Pacific Coast Hwy
- **Ralphs** • 1770 Carson St
- **Ralphs** • 24911 Western Ave
- **Ralphs** • 3455 Sepulveda Blvd
- **Smart & Final** • 2775 Pacific Coast Hwy
- **Trader Joe's** • 2545 Pacific Coast Hwy
- **Vons** • 24325 Crenshaw Blvd
- **Whole Foods Market** • 2655 Pacific Coast Hwy

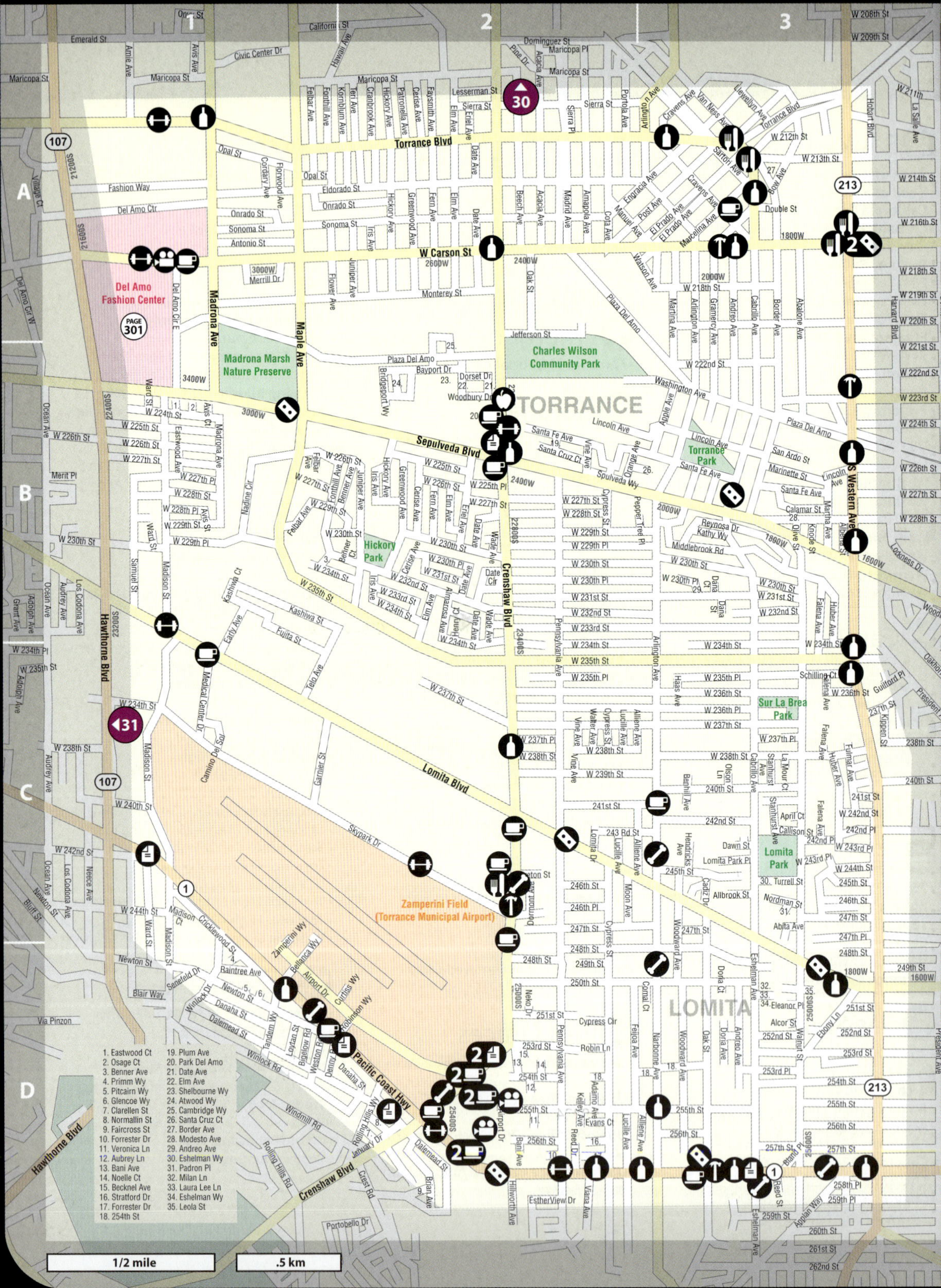

Del Amo Fashion Center

PAGE 301

Madrona Marsh Nature Preserve

Charles Wilson Community Park

TORRANCE

Torrance Park

Hickory Park

Sur La Brea Park

Lomita Park

Zamperini Field (Torrance Municipal Airport)

LOMITA

1. Eastwood Ct
2. Osage Ct
3. Benner Ave
4. Primm Wy
5. Pitcairn Wy
6. Glencoe Wy
7. Clarellen St
8. Normallin St
9. Faircross St
10. Forrester Dr
11. Veronica Ln
12. Aubrey Ln
13. Bani Ave
14. Noelle Ct
15. Becknel Ave
16. Stratford Dr
17. Forrester Dr
18. 254th St
19. Plum Ave
20. Park Del Amo
21. Date Ave
22. Elm Ave
23. Shelbourne Wy
24. Atwood Wy
25. Cambridge Wy
26. Santa Cruz Ct
27. Border Ave
28. Modesto Ave
29. Andreo Ave
30. Eshelman Wy
31. Padron Pl
32. Milan Ln
33. Laura Lee Ln
34. Eshelman Wy
35. Leola St

1/2 mile

.5 km

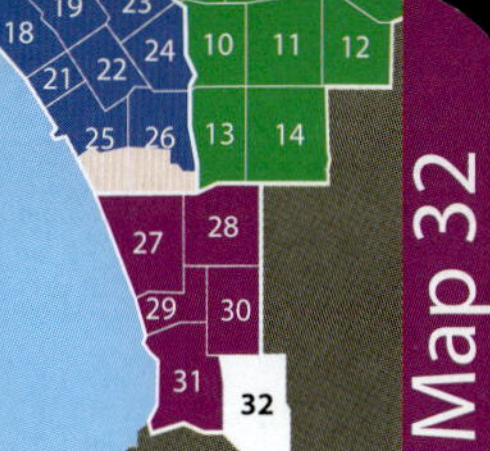

Torrance is home to an annual Oktoberfest, held at the Alpine Village on Torrance Boulevard every autumn. There you can enjoy Bavarian pretzels, sausage and, after some really good German beer, a chorus or two of the Chicken Dance. Enjoy!

Coffee

- **Awakings Coffee House** • 24100 Narbonne Ave
- **Boba Loca** • 22501 Crenshaw Blvd
- **Boba Paradise** • 25412 Crenshaw Blvd
- **Boston Cream Bagel's and Donuts** • 24200 Crenshaw Blvd
- **Coffee Bean & Tea Leaf** • 25345 Crenshaw Blvd
- **Kelly's Coffee & Fudge** • 2595 Airport Dr
- **Krispy Kreme Doughnuts** • 2795 Pacific Coast Hwy
- **Starbucks** • 2104 Pacific Coast Hwy
- **Starbucks** • Albertsons • 2130 Pacific Coast Hwy
- **Starbucks** • 2370 Crenshaw Blvd
- **Starbucks** • Vons • 24325 Crenshaw Blvd
- **Starbucks** • 24427 Crenshaw Blvd
- **Starbucks** • 25348 Crenshaw Blvd
- **Starbucks** • 3525 W Carson St
- **Tormed Bistro** • 3400 Lomita Blvd
- **Torrance Bakery** • 1341 El Prado Ave

Copy Shops

- **Copy Rite** • 1962 Pacific Coast Hwy • 310-530-7282
- **Copymax** • 3665 Pacific Coast Hwy • 310-791-0097
- **Office Depot** • 24313 Crenshaw Blvd • 310-326-3291
- **Postal Annex** • 24325 Crenshaw Blvd • 310-326-3498
- **Staples** • 2748 Pacific Coast Hwy • 310-784-2410
- **UPS Store** • 2390 Crenshaw Blvd • 310-787-9564
- **UPS Store** • 2785 Pacific Coast Hwy • 310-530-8411

Farmers Markets

- **Torrance (Tues, 8 am-12 pm; Sat, 8 am-1 pm)** • 2200 Crenshaw Blvd

Gyms

- **24 Hour Fitness** • 2685 Pacific Coast Hwy • 310-534-5100
- **Curves** • 2366 Pacific Coast Hwy • 310-326-6777
- **Curves** • 3535 Torrance Blvd • 310-540-0083
- **LA Fitness Sports Club** • 3550 W Carson St • 310-921-9890
- **Ladies Workout Express** • 2370 Crenshaw Blvd • 310-328-9348
- **Rolling Hills Athletic Club** • 3601 Lomita Blvd • 310-791-2700
- **South End Racquet & Health Club** • 2800 Skypark Dr • 310-530-0630

Hardware Stores

- **Brookstone** • 252 Del Amo Fashion Sq • 310-542-9424
- **Harbor Freight Tools** • 2040 Pacific Coast Hwy, Ste B • 310-326-7942
- **Home Depot** • 24451 Crenshaw Blvd • 310-325-9600
- **Lovelady Hardware** • 1967 W Carson St • 310-328-4274
- **Lowe's** • 22255 S Western Ave • 310-787-1469

Liquor Stores

- **Ace Hi Liquors** • 25511 Narbonne Ave
- **Bottle Shop** • 2087 Torrance Blvd
- **Brite Spot Liquor** • 1725 Pacific Coast Hwy
- **Cory's Liquor** • 1954 W Carson St
- **El Dorado Liquor** • 23421 S Western Ave
- **Frank's Liquor** • 1601 Cabrillo Ave
- **International Liquor Store** • 2515 W Carson St
- **J&S Liquor** • 23804 Crenshaw Blvd
- **Lomita Liquor & Deli** • 2022 Pacific Coast Hwy
- **McCowan Liquor** • 22802 S Western Ave
- **Moran's Liquor** • 2354 Pacific Coast Hwy
- **Mr K's Liquor** • 3405 Torrance Blvd
- **One Stop Liquor & Market** • 22540 S Western Ave
- **Royal Liquor** • 3114 Pacific Coast Hwy
- **Sam's Liquor** • 1810 Lomita Blvd
- **Town Pump Wine & Spirits** • 22505 Crenshaw Blvd

Movie Theaters

- **AMC Del Amo 18** • 3525 W Carson St, Space 73 •
- **AMC Rolling Hills 20** • 2591 Airport Dr • 310-289-4262

Pet Shops

- **John's Tropical Fish (Fish only)** • 1937 Pacific Coast Hwy • 310-539-7755
- **Lomita Feed Store** • 24403 Narbonne Ave • 310-326-4738
- **Neptune's Reef** • 2851 Pacific Coast Hwy • 310-534-2323
- **Petco** • 24413 Crenshaw Blvd • 310-530-5945
- **Reptile Finders** • 1856 Pacific Coast Hwy • 310-325-3366
- **Steers N Stripes** • 24831 Narbonne Ave • 310-534-0678
- **Wild Birds Unlimited** • 25416 Crenshaw Blvd • 310-326-2473

Restaurants

- **Aioli** • 1261 Cabrillo Ave • 310-320-9200
- **Depot** • 1250 Cabrillo Ave • 310-787-7501
- **In-N-Out Burger** • 24445 Crenshaw Blvd • 800-786-1000
- **Koji BBQ Buffet** • 1725 W Carson St • 310-787-1820
- **Mishima** • 21605 S Western Ave • 310-320-2089

Video Rental

- **Hollywood Video** • 2549 Pacific Coast Hwy • 310-539-5508
- **K Video** • 3030 Sepulveda Blvd • 310-539-1112
- **Sakura Video (Japanese)** • 2383 Lomita Blvd • 310-325-0306
- **Super Movies N You** • 2113 Pacific Coast Hwy • 310-539-9088
- **Tri-Video** • 1658 W Carson St • 310-212-5358
- **Video Access** • 1820 Lomita Blvd • 310-325-4418
- **Video Japan Number 2 (Japanese)** • 1735 W Carson St • 310-787-1131

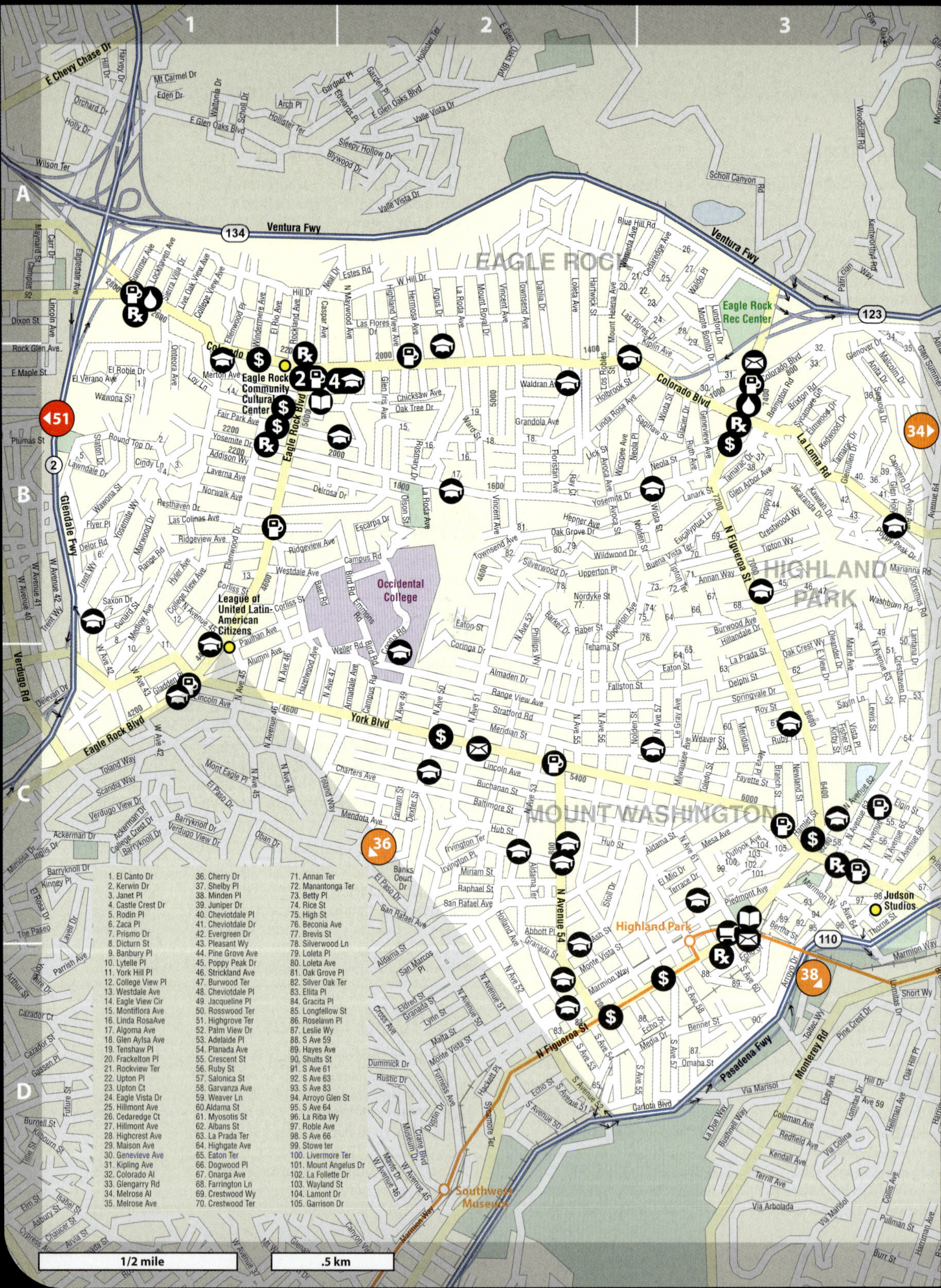

Map 33 • Eagle Rock / Highland Park

1. El Canto Dr
2. Kerwin Dr
3. Janet Pl
4. Castle Crest Dr
5. Rodin Pl
6. Zaca Pl
7. Prismo Dr
8. Dicturn St
9. Banbury Pl
10. Lytelle Pl
11. York Hill Pl
12. College View Pl
13. Westdale Ave
14. Eagle View Cir
15. Montiflora Ave
16. Linda RosaAve
17. Algoma Ave
18. Glen Aylsa Ave
19. Tenshaw Pl
20. Frackelton Pl
21. Rockview Ter
22. Upton Pl
23. Upton Ct
24. Eagle Vista Dr
25. Hillmont Ave
26. Cedaredge Ct
27. Hillmont Ave
28. Highcrest Ave
29. Maison Ave
30. Genevieve Ave
31. Kipling Ave
32. Colorado Al
33. Glengarry Rd
34. Melrose Al
35. Melrose Ave
36. Cherry Dr
37. Shelby Pl
38. Minden Pl
39. Juniper Dr
40. Cheviotdale Pl
41. Cheviotdale Dr
42. Evergreen Dr
43. Pleasant Wy
44. Pine Grove Ave
45. Poppy Peak Dr
46. Strickland Ave
47. Burwood Ter
48. Cheviotdale Pl
49. Jacqueline Pl
50. Rosswood Ter
51. Highgrove Ter
52. Palm View Dr
53. Adelaide Pl
54. Planada Ave
55. Crescent St
56. Ruby St
57. Salonica St
58. Garvanza Ave
59. Weaver Ln
60. Aldama St
61. Myosotis St
62. Albans St
63. La Prada Ter
64. Highgate Ave
65. Eaton Ter
66. Dogwood Pl
67. Onarga Ave
68. Farrington Ln
69. Crestwood Wy
70. Crestwood Ter
71. Annan Ter
72. Manantonga Ter
73. Betty Pl
74. Rice St
75. High St
76. Beconia Ave
77. Brevis St
78. Silverwood Ln
79. Loleta Pl
80. Loleta Ave
81. Oak Grove Pl
82. Silver Oak Ter
83. Ellita Pl
84. Gracita Pl
85. Longfellow St
86. Roselawn Pl
87. Leslie Wy
88. S Ave 59
89. Hayes Ave
90. Shults St
91. S Ave 61
92. S Ave 63
93. S Ave 83
94. Arroyo Glen St
95. S Ave 64
96. La Riba Wy
97. Roble Ave
98. S Ave 66
99. Stowe ter
100. Livermore Ter
101. Mount Angelus Dr
102. La Follette Dr
103. Wayland St
104. Lamont Dr
105. Garrison Dr

1/2 mile | .5 km

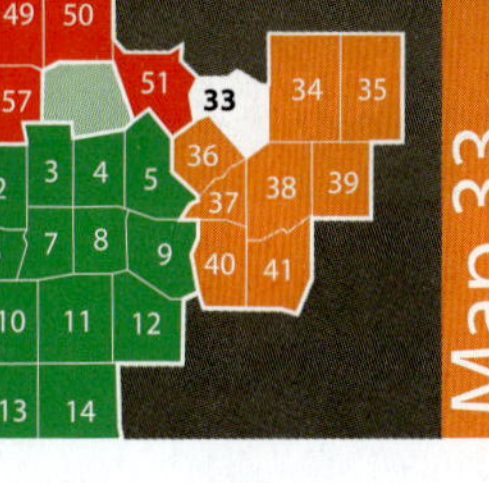

There are essentially two Eagle Rocks: One is north of Colorado Blvd, packed with wide, tree-lined streets and gigantic Craftsman homes. The south side features more humble housing, but a lot of new neighbors are fixing up their places and giving the Northsiders a run for their money. Beyond that, the south side is getting more and more great shops, cafés, and restaurants every day, making its tag as "the next Silver Lake" all that much more believable.

Banks

- **Bank of America** • 2263 Colorado Blvd
- **Bank of America** • 5515 N Figueroa St
- **Citibank** • 5015 Eagle Rock Blvd
- **Citibank** • 5053 York Blvd
- **Union** • 6301 N Figueroa St
- **Washington Mutual** • 4945 Eagle Rock Blvd
- **Washington Mutual** • 5700 N Figueroa St
- **Wells Fargo** • 7311 N Figueroa St

Car Washes

- **76** • 2711 Colorado Blvd
- **JJ's Hand Car Wash** • 7320 N Figueroa St

Gas Stations

- **76** • 2711 Colorado Blvd
- **76** • 4755 Eagle Rock Blvd
- **Alliance** • 405 N Ave 64
- **Chevron** • 6405 York Blvd
- **Chevron** • 7368 N Figueroa St
- **Independent** • 5404 York Blvd
- **Mobil** • 2207 Colorado Blvd
- **Mobil** • 6174 York Blvd
- **Shell** • 2200 Colorado Blvd
- **Valero** • 1871 Colorado Blvd

Landmarks

- **Eagle Rock Community Cultural Center** • 2225 Colorado Blvd
- **Judson Studios** • 200 S Ave 66
- **League of United Latin-American Citizens** • 4512 Eagle Rock Blvd

Libraries

- **Arroyo Seco Regional** • 6145 N Figueroa St • 323-255-0537
- **Eagle Rock** • 5027 Caspar Ave • 323-258-8078

Pharmacies

- **CVS** • 2240 Fair Park Ave • 323-254-7346
- **CVS** • 5944 N Figueroa Ave • 323-478-8310
- **Rite-Aid** • 6305 York Blvd • 323-550-1317
- **Target** • 2626 Colorado Blvd • 323-258-5101
- **Vons** • 7311 N Figueroa St • 323-254-7241
- **Walgreens** • 2222 Colorado Blvd • 323-254-4593

Post Offices

- **US Post Office** • 5132 York Blvd • 800-275-8777
- **US Post Office** • 5930 N Figueroa St • 800-275-8777
- **US Post Office** • 7435 N Figueroa St • 800-275-8777

Schools

- **ABC Child Development** • 5443 Ash St
- **Academia Avance** • 115 N Ave 53
- **American Montessori** • 4475 Eagle Rock Blvd
- **Annandale Elementary** • 6125 Poppy Peak Dr
- **Benjamin Franklin Senior High** • 820 N Ave 54
- **Buchanan St Elementary** • 5024 Buchanan St
- **Dahlia Heights Elementary** • 5063 Floristan Ave
- **Delevan Dr Elementary** • 4168 W Ave 42
- **Eagle Rock Elementary** • 2057 Fair Park Ave
- **Eagle Rock Junior-Senior High** • 1750 Yosemite Dr
- **Eagle Rock Montessori** • 1439 Colorado Blvd
- **Franklin Community Adult** • 820 N Ave 54
- **Garvanza Elementary** • 317 N Ave 62
- **Good Shepherd Lutheran** • 6338 N Figueroa St
- **Harvest Christian Academy** • 5066 Ellenwood Dr
- **Highland Park Continuation** • 928 N Ave 53
- **Luther Burbank Middle** • 6460 N Figueroa St
- **Meridian Early Education Center** • 6124 Ruby Pl
- **Monte Vista EEC** • 5509 Ash St
- **Monte Vista St Elementary** • 5423 Monte Vista St
- **Montessori Children's World** • 4371 Eagle Rock Blvd
- **Occidental College** • 1600 Campus Rd
- **Optimist High** • 6957 N Figueroa St
- **Renaissance Arts Academy** • 1800 Colorado Blvd
- **Renaissance Arts Academy** • 2109 Merton Ave
- **Riordan PC** • 5531 Monte Vista St
- **Rockdale Elementary** • 1303 Yosemite Dr
- **St Dominic Elementary** • 2005 Merton Ave
- **St Ignatius Elementary** • 6025 Monte Vista St
- **Westminster Academy** • 1495 Colorado Blvd
- **Yorkdale Elementary** • 5657 Meridian St

Supermarkets

- **Albertsons** • 4211 Eagle Rock Blvd
- **Smart & Final** • 6060 N Figueroa St
- **Super A Foods** • 2245 Yosemite Dr
- **Super A Foods** • 5250 York Blvd
- **Trader Joe's** • 1566 Colorado Blvd
- **Vons** • 7311 N Figueroa St

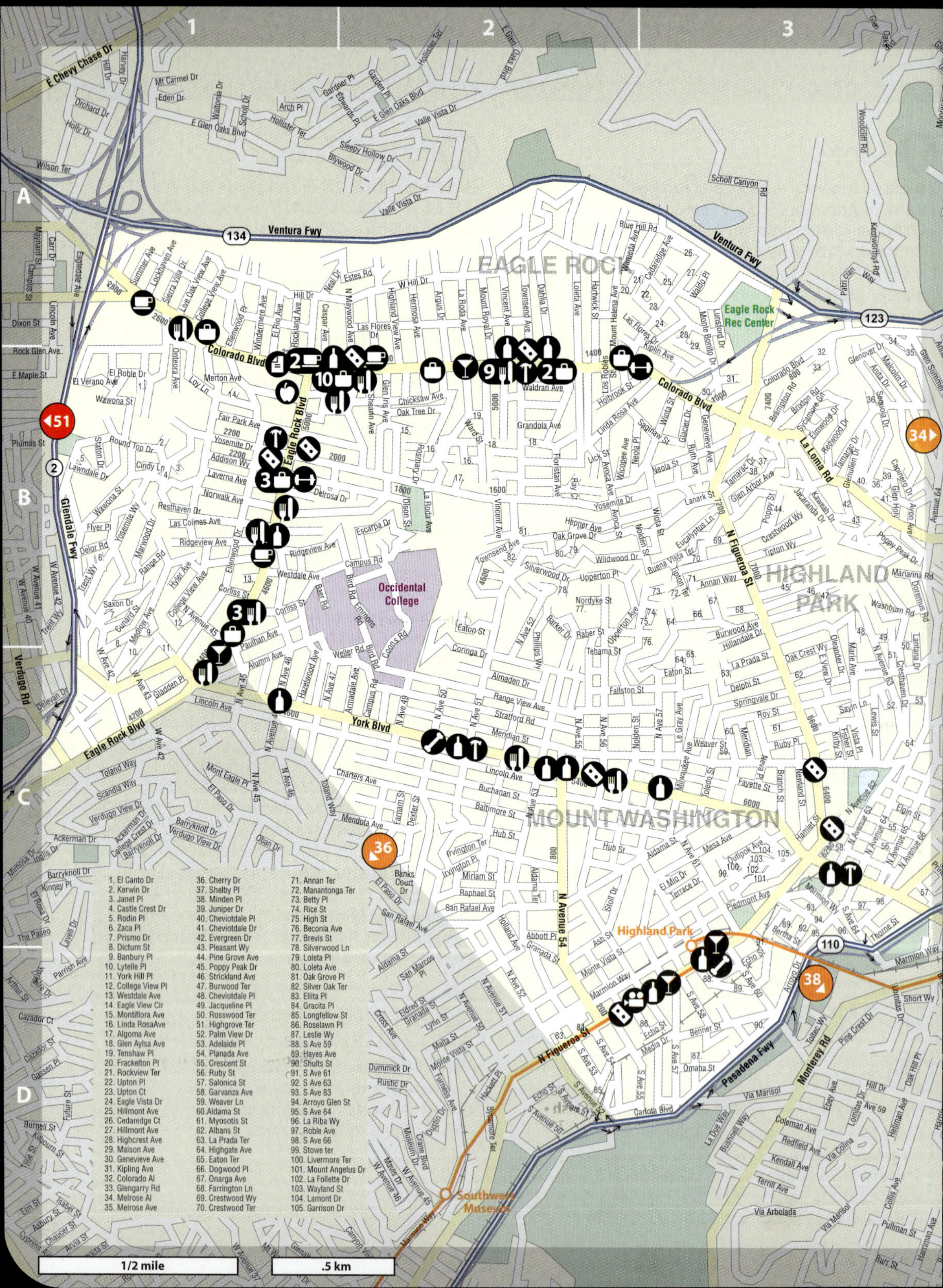

N
1
2
3
A
B
C
D
EAGLE ROCK
HIGHLAND PARK
MOUNT WASHINGTON
Eagle Rock Rec Center
Occidental College
Highland Park
Southwest Museum
Ventura Fwy
Colorado Blvd
Eagle Rock Blvd
York Blvd
N Figueroa St
N Avenue 54
Glendale Fwy
Pasadena Fwy
Verdugo Rd
134
123
110
2
51
34
36
38
1. El Canto Dr
2. Kerwin Dr
3. Janet Pl
4. Castle Crest Dr
5. Rodin Pl
6. Zaca Pl
7. Prismo Dr
8. Dicturn St
9. Banbury Pl
10. Lytelle Pl
11. York Hill Pl
12. College View Pl
13. Westdale Ave
14. Eagle View Cir
15. Montiflora Ave
16. Linda RosaAve
17. Algoma Ave
18. Glen Aylsa Ave
19. Tenshaw Pl
20. Frackelton Pl
21. Rockview Ter
22. Upton Pl
23. Upton Ct
24. Eagle Vista Dr
25. Hillmont Ave
26. Cedaredge Ct
27. Hillmont Ave
28. Highcrest Ave
29. Maison Ave
30. Genevieve Ave
31. Kipling Ave
32. Colorado Al
33. Glengarry Rd
34. Melrose Al
35. Melrose Ave
36. Cherry Dr
37. Shelby Pl
38. Minden Pl
39. Juniper Dr
40. Cheviotdale Pl
41. Cheviotdale Dr
42. Evergreen Dr
43. Pleasant Wy
44. Pine Grove Ave
45. Poppy Peak Dr
46. Strickland Ave
47. Burwood Ter
48. Cheviotdale Pl
49. Jacqueline Pl
50. Rosswood Ter
51. Highgrove Ter
52. Palm View Dr
53. Adelaide Pl
54. Planada Ave
55. Crescent St
56. Ruby St
57. Salonica St
58. Garvanza Ave
59. Weaver Ln
60.Aldama St
61. Myosotis St
62. Albans St
63. La Prada Ter
64. Highgate Ave
65. Eaton Ter
66. Dogwood Pl
67. Onarga Ave
68. Farrington Ln
69. Crestwood Wy
70. Crestwood Ter
71. Annan Ter
72. Manantonga Ter
73. Betty Pl
74. Rice St
75. High St
76. Beconia Ave
77. Brevis St
78. Silverwood Ln
79. Loleta Pl
80. Loleta Ave
81. Oak Grove Pl
82. Silver Oak Ter
83. Ellita Pl
84. Gracita Pl
85. Longfellow St
86. Roselawn Pl
87. Leslie Wy
88. S Ave 59
89. Hayes Ave
90. Shults St
91. S Ave 61
92. S Ave 63
93. S Ave 83
94. Arroyo Glen St
95. S Ave 64
96. La Riba Wy
97. Roble Ave
98. S Ave 66
99. Stowe ter
100. Livermore Ter
101. Mount Angelus Dr
102. La Follette Dr
103. Wayland St
104. Lamont Dr
105. Garrison Dr
1/2 mile
.5 km

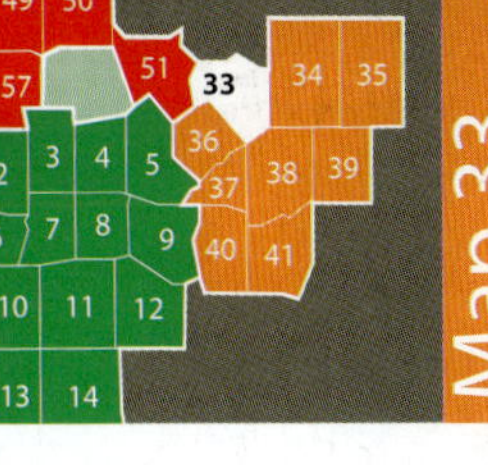

Over the past few years, Eagle Rock has seen shady liquor stores shut down and fancy wine stores open up. There are more and more cute boutiques lining Eagle Rock Blvd. The east side has arrived, as demonstrated by the gourmet cupcake shop, Auntie Em's. But its old-school roots remain: Some of the best burgers around are served at The Bucket and low-key but yummy Vietnamese can be found at Blue Hen.

Coffee

- **The Coffee Table** • 1958 Colorado Blvd
- **Mocha Express** • 2700 Colorado Blvd
- **Pat and Lorraine's Coffee Shop** • 4720 Eagle Rock Blvd
- **Starbucks** • 2218 Colorado Blvd
- **Swork Coffee** • 2160 Colorado Blvd

Copy Shops

- **Super Copy** • 2256 Colorado Blvd • 323-255-5800

Farmers Markets

- **Eagle Rock Farmer's Market (Fri 5 am-8:30 pm)** • 2100 Merton Ave

Gyms

- **Curves** • 1414 W Colorado Blvd • 626-796-1667
- **Curves** • 4870 Eagle Rock Blvd • 323-259-5800

Hardware Stores

- **Do It Best Hardware** • 5040 York Blvd • 323-254-6843
- **Eagle Rock Lumber & Hardware** • 2223 Fair Park Ave • 323-255-1451
- **Garvanza Hardware** • 6324 York Blvd • 323-256-3211
- **Tritch True Value** • 1620 Colorado Blvd • 323-255-8222

Liquor Stores

- **Amigos Liquor** • 5611 N Figueroa St
- **Bert's Liquor** • 4604 York Blvd
- **Beverage Liquor Shop** • 1605 Colorado Blvd
- **Cal's Liquor** • 5326 York Blvd
- **Colorado Wine Company (Wine only)** • 2114 Colorado Blvd
- **Dan's Liquors** • 5711 York Blvd
- **Eagle Rock Market** • 4729 Eagle Rock Blvd
- **Highland Park Liquors** • 5900 N Figueroa St
- **Liquor Azteca de Oro** • 5049 York Blvd
- **Marios Liquor** • 5421 York Blvd
- **One's Liquor** • 1664 Colorado Blvd
- **York Square Liquors** • 6312 York Blvd

Movie Theaters

- **Highland Theater** • 5604 N Figueroa St • 323-256-6383

Nightlife

- **All Star Lanes** • 4459 Eagle Rock Blvd • 323-254-2579
- **The Chalet** • 1630 Colorado Blvd • 323-258-8800
- **Little Cave** • 5922 N Figueroa St • 323-255-6871
- **Mr T's Bowl** • 5621 1/2 N Figueroa St • 323-256-7561

Pet Shops

- **Birdman Pet Shop** • 5926 N Figueroa St • 323-344-0696
- **Verdugo Pet Shop** • 5022 York Blvd • 323-255-2327

Restaurants

- **Auntie Em's Kitchen** • 4616 Eagle Rock Blvd • 323-255-0800
- **Blue Hen Vietnamese Kitchen** • 1743 Colorado Blvd • 323-982-9900
- **The Bucket** • 4541 Eagle Rock Blvd • 323-257-5654
- **Café Beaujolais** • 1712 Colorado Blvd • 323-255-5111
- **Capri Restaurant** • 4604 Eagle Rock Blvd • 323-257-3225
- **Casa Bianca** • 1650 Colorado Blvd • 323-256-9617
- **Classic Thai Restaurant** • 1708 Colorado Blvd • 323-478-0530
- **The Coffee Table** • 1958 Colorado Blvd • 323-255-2200
- **Colombo's** • 1833 Colorado Blvd • 323-254-9138
- **Dave's Chillin-n-Grillin** • 2152 Colorado Blvd • 323-490-0988
- **Eagle Rock Italian Bakery & Deli** • 1726 Colorado Blvd • 323-255-8224
- **El Arco Iris** • 5684 York Blvd • 323-254-3401
- **El Huarache Azteca** • 5225 York Blvd • 323-478-9572
- **Fatty's & Co** • 1627 Colorado Blvd • 323-254-8804
- **Mia Sushi** • 4741 Eagle Rock Blvd • 323-256-2562
- **Original Tommy's** • 1717 Colorado Blvd • 323-982-1746
- **Pete's Blue Chip** • 1701 Colorado Blvd • 323-478-9022
- **Señor Fish** • 4803 Eagle Rock Blvd • 323-257-7167
- **Sicha Siam** • 4403 Eagle Rock Blvd • 323-344-8285
- **Spitz** • 2506 Colorado Blvd • 323-257-5600
- **Villa Sombrero** • 6101 York Blvd • 323-256-9784

Shopping

- **The Blissful Soul** • 4870 Eagle Rock Blvd • 323-258-6900
- **Blue Healer Imports** • 5058 Eagle Rock Blvd • 323-982-9111
- **Cactus** • 4534 Eagle Rock Blvd • 323-256-6117
- **Colorado Wine Company** • 2114 Colorado Blvd • 323-478-1985
- **Don's Music** • 4873 Eagle Rock Blvd • 323-255-3551
- **Dr Music** • 1812 Colorado Blvd • 323-258-9010
- **F*Art** • 2120 Colorado Blvd • 323-254-3278
- **Galco's Soda Pop Stop** • 5702 York Blvd • 323-255-7115
- **Imix Books** • 5052 Eagle Rock Blvd • 323-257-2512
- **Lily Simone** • 5022 Eagle Rock Blvd • 323-254-0530
- **Lucy Finch** • 5054 Eagle Rock Blvd • 323-255-2565
- **Mini-Melt Too** • 1613 Colorado Blvd • 323-258-2300
- **Owl Talk** • 5060-B Eagle Rock Blvd • 323-258-2465
- **Rockin' Baby Shop** • 5048 Eagle Rock Blvd • 888-645-2227
- **Stained Glass Supplies** • 2104 Colorado Blvd • 323-254-4361
- **SW Hill Country** • 1412 Colorado Blvd • 323-256-2500
- **Swanky Blanky** • 4807 Eagle Rock Blvd • 323-478-9306
- **That Yarn Store** • 1578 #4 W Colorado Blvd • 323-256-9276
- **Twerps** • 5060 Eagle Rock Blvd • 323-256-7608

Video Rental

- **Best Video** • 6473 N Figueroa St • 323-257-8586
- **Blockbuster** • 2175 Colorado Blvd • 323-255-2445
- **Blockbuster** • 6312 N Figueroa St • 323-259-5980
- **Planet Video** • 5445 N Figueroa St • 323-982-9064
- **Video 808** • 1608 Colorado Blvd • 323-259-8282
- **Video Hut** • 4927 Eagle Rock Blvd • 323-257-2222
- **Video Street 56** • 5544 York Blvd • 323-349-0622

Map 34 • Pasadena

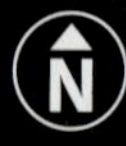

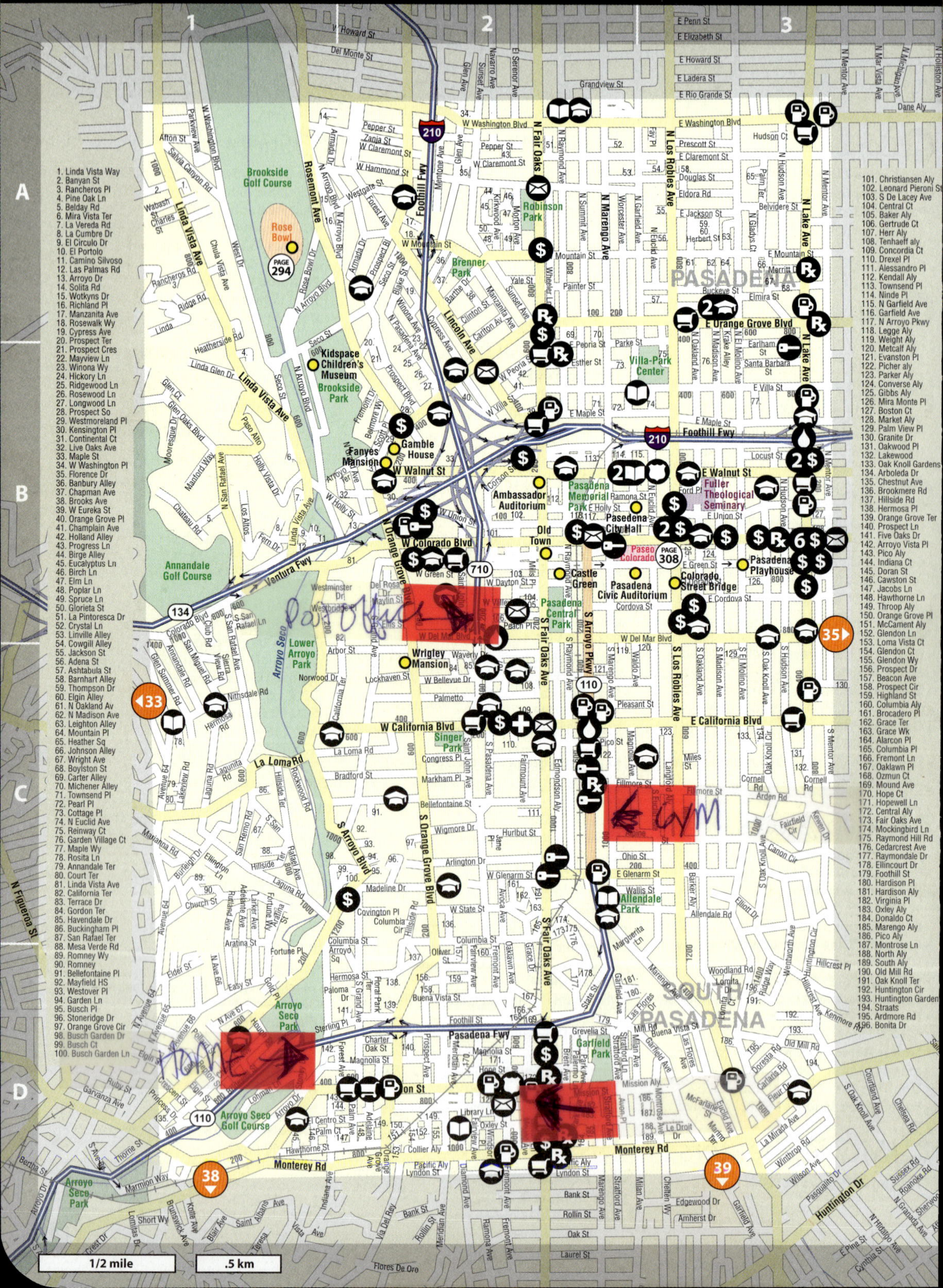

1. Linda Vista Way
2. Banyan St
3. Rancheros Pl
4. Pine Oak Ln
5. Belday Rd
6. Mira Vista Ter
7. La Vereda Rd
8. La Cumbre Dr
9. El Circulo Dr
10. El Portolo
11. Camino Silvoso
12. Las Palmas Rd
13. Arroyo Dr
14. Solita Rd
15. Wotkyns Dr
16. Richland Pl
17. Manzanita Ave
18. Rosewalk Wy
19. Cypress Ave
20. Prospect Ter
21. Prospect Cres
22. Mayview Ln
23. Winona Wy
24. Hickory Ln
25. Ridgewood Ln
26. Rosewood Ln
27. Longwood Ln
28. Prospect So
29. Westmoreland Pl
30. Kensington Pl
31. Continental Ct
32. Live Oaks Ave
33. Maple St
34. W Washington Pl
35. Florence Dr
36. Banbury Alley
37. Chapman Ave
38. Brooks Ave
39. W Eureka St
40. Orange Grove Pl
41. Champlain Ave
42. Holland Alley
43. Progress Ln
44. Birge Alley
45. Eucalyptus Ln
46. Birch Ln
47. Elm Ln
48. Poplar Ln
49. Spruce Ln
50. Glorieta St
51. La Pintoresca Dr
52. Crystal Ln
53. Linville Alley
54. Cowgill Alley
55. Jackson St
56. Adena St
57. Ashtabula St
58. Barnhart Alley
59. Thompson Dr
60. Elgin Alley
61. N Oakland Av
62. N Madison Ave
63. Leighton Alley
64. Mountain Pl
65. Heather Sq
66. Johnson Alley
67. Wright Ave
68. Boylston St
69. Carter Alley
70. Michener Alley
71. Townsend Pl
72. Pearl Pl
73. Cottage Pl
74. N Euclid Ave
75. Reinway Ct
76. Garden Village Ct
77. Maple Wy
78. Rosita Ln
79. Annandale Ter
80. Court Ter
81. Linda Vista Ave
82. California Ter
83. Terrace Dr
84. Gordon Ter
85. Havendale Dr
86. Buckingham Pl
87. San Rafael Ter
88. Mesa Verde Rd
89. Romney Wy
90. Romney
91. Bellefontaine Pl
92. Mayfield HS
93. Westover Pl
94. Garden Ln
95. Busch Pl
96. Stoneridge Dr
97. Orange Grove Cir
98. Busch Garden Dr
99. Busch Ct
100. Busch Garden Ln
101. Christiansen Aly
102. Leonard Pieroni St
103. S De Lacey Ave
104. Central Ct
105. Baker Aly
106. Gertrude Ct
107. Herr Aly
108. Tenhaeff aly
109. Concordia Ct
110. Drexel Pl
111. Alessandro Pl
112. Kendall Aly
113. Townsend Pl
114. Ninde Pl
115. N Garfield Ave
116. Garfield Ave
117. N Arroyo Pkwy
118. Legge Aly
119. Weight Aly
120. Metcalf Aly
121. Evanston Pl
122. Picher aly
123. Parker Aly
124. Converse Aly
125. Gibbs Aly
126. Mira Monte Pl
127. Boston Ct
128. Market Aly
129. Palm View Pl
130. Granite Dr
131. Oakwood Pl
132. Lakewood
133. Oak Knoll Gardens
134. Arboleda Dr
135. Chestnut Ave
136. Brookmere Rd
137. Hillside Rd
138. Hermosa Pl
139. Orange Grove Ter
140. Prospect Ln
141. Five Oaks Dr
142. Arroyo Vista Pl
143. Pico Aly
144. Indiana Ct
145. Doran St
146. Cawston St
147. Jacobs Ln
148. Hawthorne Ln
149. Throop Aly
150. Orange Grove Pl
151. McCament Aly
152. Glendon Ln
153. Loma Vista Ct
154. Glendon Ct
155. Glendon Wy
156. Prospect Dr
157. Beacon Ave
158. Prospect Cir
159. Highland St
160. Columbia Aly
161. Brocadero Pl
162. Grace Ter
163. Grace Wk
164. Alarcon Pl
165. Columbia Pl
166. Fremont Ln
167. Oaklawn Pl
168. Ozmun Ct
169. Mound Ave
170. Hope Ct
171. Hopewell Ln
172. Central Aly
173. Fair Oaks Ave
174. Mockingbird Ln
175. Raymond Hill Rd
176. Cedarcrest Ave
177. Raymondale Dr
178. Ellincourt Dr
179. Foothill St
180. Hardison Pl
181. Hardison Aly
182. Virginia Pl
183. Oxley Aly
184. Donaldo Ct
185. Marengo Aly
186. Pico Aly
187. Montrose Ln
188. North Aly
189. South Aly
190. Old Mill Rd
191. Oak Knoll Ter
192. Huntington Cir
193. Huntington Garden
194. Straats
195. Ardmore Rd
196. Bonita Dr
PASADENA
SOUTH PASADENA
Brookside Golf Course
Rose Bowl
PAGE 294
Kidspace Children's Museum
Brookside Park
Robinson Park
Brenner Park
Villa-Park Center
Gamble House
Fenyes Mansion
Ambassador Auditorium
Pasadena Memorial Park
Fuller Theological Seminary
Pasadena City Hall
Old Town
Paseo Colorado
PAGE 308
Castle Green
Pasadena Civic Auditorium
Colorado Street Bridge
Pasadena Playhouse
Pasadena Central Park
Wrigley Mansion
Lower Arroyo Park
Annandale Golf Course
Singer Park
Allendale Park
Arroyo Seco Park
Arroyo Seco Golf Course
Garfield Park
Foothill Fwy
Ventura Fwy
Pasadena Fwy
1/2 mile
.5 km

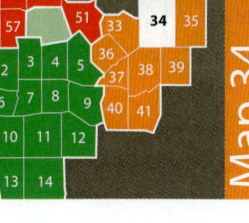

More culture than couture, Pasadena has long been LA's artsy fartsy half brother and the most happenin' habitude on the eastside. Pasadena may be synonymous with "Old Town," but there's more than just Colorado Blvd going on. The Jet Propulsion Lab smarty-pants are doing their science thing. Golfers can go posh at Brookside Country Club or on the cheap at Arroyo Seco. And if Colorado's restaurant row is totally booked, Fair Oaks is fast becoming a gastronomical haven.

Banks

- **Bank of America** • 145 W California Blvd
- **Bank of America** • 399 E Colorado Blvd
- **Bank of America** • 880 E Colorado Blvd
- **Bank of America** • 929 Fair Oaks Ave
- **Bank of the West** • 587 E Colorado Blvd
- **California Credit Union** • 95 S Lake Ave
- **California National** • 102 S Lake Ave
- **California National** • 1153 Fair Oaks Ave
- **Citibank** • 161 W California Blvd
- **Citibank** • 201 N Garfield Ave
- **Citibank** • 285 S Lake Ave
- **Citibank** • 315 E Colorado Blvd
- **Citizens Business** • 225 E Colorado Blvd
- **Citizens Business** • 901 Fair Oaks Ave
- **City National** • 89 S Lake Ave
- **Comerica** • 35 N Lake Ave
- **Community** • 505 E Colorado Blvd
- **Community** • 790 E Colorado Blvd
- **East West** • 1001 Fair Oaks Ave
- **East West** • 135 N Los Robles Ave
- **Far East National** • 301 N Lake Ave
- **First Entertainment Credit Union** • 55 N St John Ave
- **Fremont Investment & Loan** • 300 N Lake Ave
- **Pacific Western** • 200 S Los Robles Ave
- **Pacific Western** • 625 Fair Oaks Ave
- **Union** • 70 S Lake Ave
- **United Commercial** • 199 S Los Robles Ave
- **US** • 720 E Colorado Blvd
- **Washington Mutual** • 860 E Colorado Blvd
- **Wells Fargo** • 1000 Fair Oaks Ave
- **Wells Fargo** • 350 W Colorado Blvd
- **Wells Fargo** • 655 N Fair Oaks Ave
- **Wells Fargo** • 82 S Lake Ave

Car Rental

- **Avis** • 570 N Lake Ave
- **Budget** • 750 S Arroyo Pkwy
- **Enterprise** • 1060 S Fair Oaks Ave
- **Enterprise** • 267 W Colorado Blvd
- **Rent 4 Less** • 665 S Arroyo Pkwy

Car Washes

- **Arroyo-California Car Wash** • 605 S Arroyo Pkwy
- **Pasadena Auto Wash** • 164 W Del Mar Blvd
- **Royal Hand Wash** • 850 S Arroyo Pkwy

Gas Stations

- **76** • 122 N Lake Ave
- **76** • 155 E Glenarm St
- **76** • 475 W Colorado Blvd
- **76** • 675 N Lake Ave
- **76** • 911 E Washington Blvd
- **Arco** • 445 E Walnut St
- **Arco** • 736 Mission St
- **Chevron** • 1200 Fair Oaks Ave
- **Chevron** • 1400 Mission St
- **Chevron** • 160 E California Blvd
- **Independent** • 2601 Mission St
- **Independent** • 960 E Washington Blvd
- **Mobil** • 290 S Arroyo Pkwy
- **Mobil** • 392 N Lake Ave
- **Mobil** • 400 N Fair Oaks Ave
- **Mobil** • 474 S Lake Ave
- **Shell** • 200 N Fair Oaks Ave
- **Shell** • 632 N Garfield Ave

Emergency Rooms

- **Huntington Memorial** • 100 W California Blvd

Landmarks

- **Ambassador Auditorium** • 131 S St John Ave
- **Castle Green** • 99 S Raymond Ave
- **Colorado Street Bridge** • 171 S Los Robles Ave
- **Fenyes Mansion** • 470 W Walnut St
- **Gamble House** • 4 Westmoreland Pl
- **Kidspace—An Interactive Museum** • 480 N Arroyo Blvd
- **Old Town** • Fair Oaks Ave & Colorado Blvd
- **Pasadena City Hall** • 100 N Garfield Ave
- **Pasadena Civic Auditorium** • 300 E Green St
- **Pasadena Playhouse State Theater** • 39 S El Molino Ave
- **Rose Bowl** • 991 Rosemont Ave
- **Wrigley Mansion** • 391 S Orange Grove Blvd

Libraries

- **Allendale Branch** • 1130 S Marengo Ave • 626-744-7260
- **LA County Law Library-Pasadena** • 300 E Walnut St • 626-356-5253
- **La Pintoresca Branch** • 1355 N Raymond Ave • 626-744-7268
- **Pasadena Central** • 285 E Walnut St • 626-744-4066
- **San Rafael Branch** • 1240 Nithsdale Rd • 626-744-7270
- **South Pasadena Library** • 1100 Oxley St • 626-403-7340
- **Villa Parke Community Center Branch** • 363 E Villa St • 626-744-6510

Pharmacies

- **CVS** • 20 E Orange Grove Blvd • 626-795-6609
- **CVS** • 727 S Arroyo Pkwy • 626-795-3810
- **CVS** • 900 N Lake Ave • 626-794-4418
- **Pavilions** • 1213 Fair Oaks Ave • 626-799-4156
- **Rite-Aid** • 914 Fair Oaks Ave • 626-441-3702
- **Target** • 777 E Colorado Blvd • 626-795-5472
- **Vons** • 1213 Fair Oaks Ave • 626-799-4156
- **Vons** • 155 W California Blvd • 626-577-2594
- **Vons** • 655 N Fair Oaks Ave • 626-578-1336
- **Walgreens** • 670 N Lake Ave • 626-585-8926

Police

- **Pasadena Police Dept** • 207 N Garfield Ave • 626-744-4501
- **South Pasadena Police Dept** • 1422 Mission St • 626-403-7270

Post Offices

- **US Post Office** • 1001 Fremont Ave • 800-275-8777
- **US Post Office** • 1100 N Fair Oaks Ave • 800-275-8777
- **US Post Office** • 1355 N Mentor Ave • 626-794-8053
- **US Post Office** • 281 E Colorado Blvd • 800-275-8777
- **US Post Office** • 600 Lincoln Ave • 800-275-8777
- **US Post Office** • 870 S Raymond Ave • 800-275-8777
- **US Post Office** • 99 W California Blvd • 800-275-8777

Schools

- **Aria Montessori** • 693 S Euclid Ave
- **Arroyo Vista Elementary** • 335 El Centro St
- **Blair High** • 1201 S Marengo Ave
- **Chandler** • 1005 Armada Dr
- **Elworth Christian Preschool** • 500 E Colorado Blvd
- **Friends Western** • 524 E Orange Grove Blvd
- **Fuller Theological Seminary** • 135 N Oakland Ave
- **Hillsides Education Center** • 940 Ave 64
- **Institute for Redesign of Learning** • 625 S Fair Oaks Ave
- **International Montessori Academy** • 355 W Green St
- **Lake Ave Christian** • 393 N Lake Ave
- **Madison Elementary** • 515 E Ashtabula St
- **Maranatha High** • 169 S Saint John Ave
- **Mayfield Junior** • 405 S Euclid Ave
- **Mayfield Senior** • 500 Bellefontaine St
- **New Horizon** • 651 N Orange Grove Blvd
- **Oak Knoll Kinderhaus** • 1200 N Lake Ave
- **Pacific Oaks** • 714 W California Blvd
- **Pasadena Montessori** • 280 S Los Robles Ave
- **Roosevelt Elementary** • 315 N Pasadena Ave
- **Rose City High** • 325 S Oak Knoll Ave
- **San Pascual Ave Elementary** • 815 San Pascual Ave
- **San Rafael Elementary** • 1090 Nithsdale Rd
- **Sequoyah** • 535 S Pasadena Ave
- **Southwestern Academy** • 2800 Monterey Rd
- **St Andrew's Elementary** • 42 Chestnut St
- **St James Parish Day** • 1325 Monterey Rd
- **St Monica Academy** • 301 N Orange Grove Blvd
- **Waverly (second location)** • 67 W Bellevue Dr
- **Westridge School for Girls** • 324 Madeline Dr

Supermarkets

- **Bristol Farms** • 606 Fair Oaks Ave
- **Farm Fresh Ranch Market** • 475 E Orange Grove Blvd
- **Food 4 Less** • 1329 N Lake Ave
- **Gelson's Markets** • 245 E Green St
- **Pavilions** • 1213 Fair Oaks Ave
- **Pavilions** • 845 E California Blvd
- **Ralphs** • 160 N Lake Ave
- **Ralphs** • 320 W Colorado Blvd
- **Smart & Final** • 401 N Fair Oaks Ave
- **Trader Joe's** • 610 S Arroyo Pkwy
- **Trader Joe's** • 613 Mission St
- **Vons** • 1129 Fair Oaks Ave
- **Vons** • 155 W California Blvd
- **Vons** • 655 N Fair Oaks Ave
- **Wild Oats** • 603 S Lake Ave

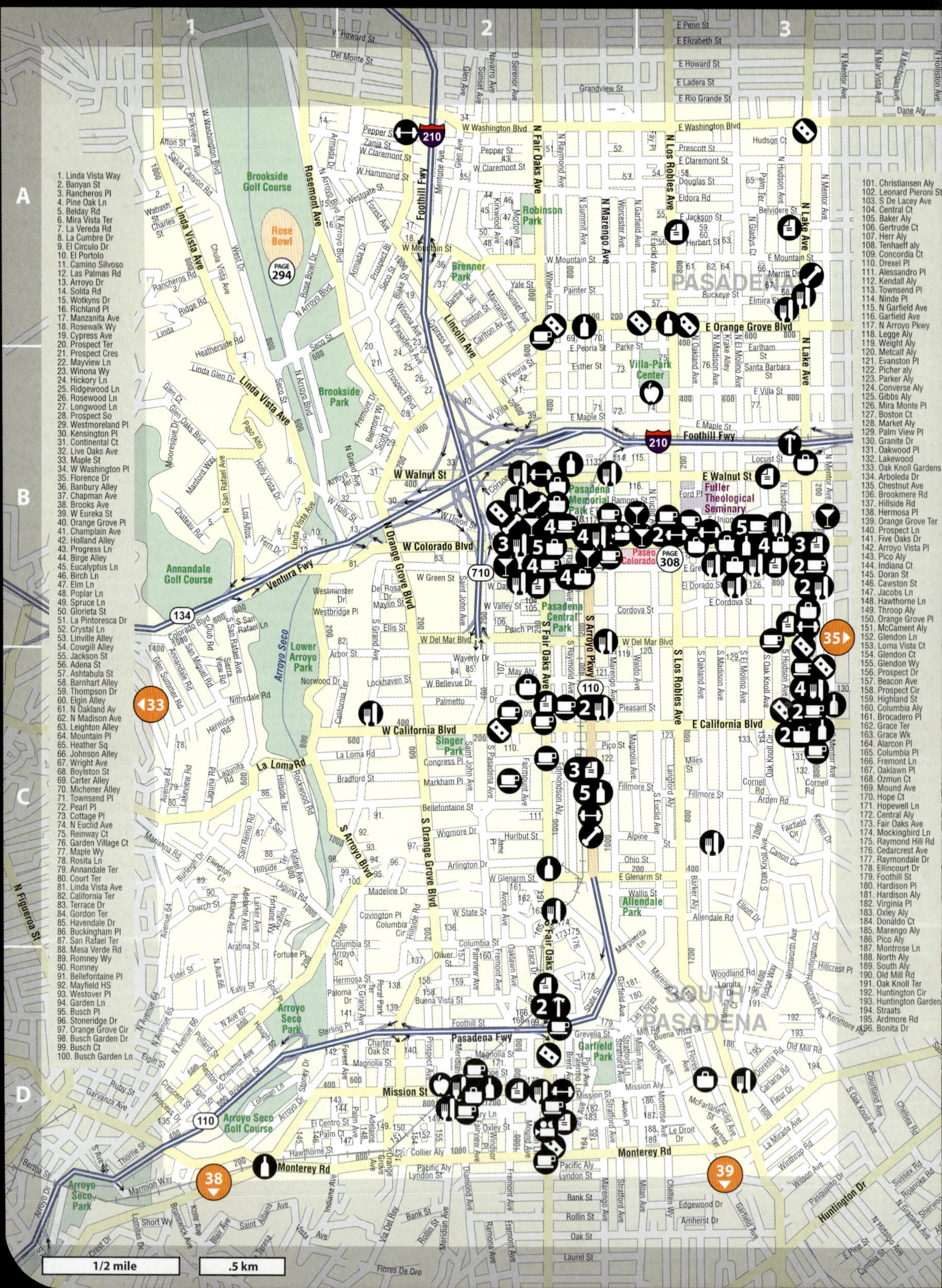

1. Linda Vista Way
2. Banyan St
3. Rancheros Pl
4. Pine Oak Ln
5. Belday Rd
6. Mira Vista Ter
7. La Vereda Rd
8. La Cumbre Dr
9. El Circulo Dr
10. El Portolo
11. Camino Silvoso
12. Las Palmas Rd
13. Arroyo Dr
14. Solita Rd
15. Wotkyns Dr
16. Richland Pl
17. Manzanita Ave
18. Rosewalk Wy
19. Cypress Ave
20. Prospect Ter
21. Prospect Cres
22. Mayview Ln
23. Winona Wy
24. Hickory Ln
25. Ridgewood Ln
26. Rosewood Ln
27. Longwood Ln
28. Prospect So
29. Westmoreland Pl
30. Kensington Pl
31. Continental Ct
32. Live Oaks Ave
33. Maple St
34. W Washington Pl
35. Florence Dr
36. Banbury Alley
37. Chapman Ave
38. Brooks Ave
39. W Eureka St
40. Orange Grove Pl
41. Champlain Ave
42. Holland Alley
43. Progress Ln
44. Birge Alley
45. Eucalyptus Ln
46. Birch Ln
47. Elm Ln
48. Poplar Ln
49. Spruce Ln
50. Glorieta St
51. La Pintoresca Dr
52. Crystal Ln
53. Linville Alley
54. Cowgill Alley
55. Jackson St
56. Adena St
57. Ashtabula St
58. Barnhart Alley
59. Thompson Dr
60. Elgin Alley
61. N Oakland Av
62. N Madison Ave
63. Leighton Alley
64. Mountain Pl
65. Heather Sq
66. Johnson Alley
67. Wright Ave
68. Boylston St
69. Carter Alley
70. Michener Alley
71. Townsend Pl
72. Pearl Pl
73. Cottage Pl
74. N Euclid Ave
75. Reinway Ct
76. Garden Village Ct
77. Maple Wy
78. Rosita Ln
79. Annandale Ter
80. Court Ter
81. Linda Vista Ave
82. California Ter
83. Terrace Dr
84. Gordon Ter
85. Havendale Dr
86. Buckingham Pl
87. San Rafael Ter
88. Mesa Verde Rd
89. Romney Wy
90. Romney
91. Bellefontaine Pl
92. Mayfield HS
93. Westover Pl
94. Garden Ln
95. Busch Pl
96. Stoneridge Dr
97. Orange Grove Cir
98. Busch Garden Dr
99. Busch Ct
100. Busch Garden Ln
101. Christiansen Aly
102. Leonard Pieroni St
103. S De Lacey Ave
104. Central Ct
105. Baker Aly
106. Gertrude Ct
107. Herr Aly
108. Tenhaeff aly
109. Concordia Ct
110. Drexel Pl
111. Alessandro Pl
112. Kendall Aly
113. Townsend Pl
114. Ninde Pl
115. N Garfield Ave
116. Garfield Ave
117. N Arroyo Pkwy
118. Legge Aly
119. Weight Aly
120. Metcalf Aly
121. Evanston Pl
122. Picher aly
123. Parker Aly
124. Converse Aly
125. Gibbs Aly
126. Mira Monte Pl
127. Boston Ct
128. Market Aly
129. Palm View Pl
130. Granite Dr
131. Oakwood Pl
132. Lakewood
133. Oak Knoll Gardens
134. Arboleda Dr
135. Chestnut Ave
136. Brookmere Rd
137. Hillside Rd
138. Hermosa Pl
139. Orange Grove Ter
140. Prospect Ln
141. Five Oaks Dr
142. Arroyo Vista Pl
143. Pico Aly
144. Indiana Ct
145. Doran St
146. Cawston St
147. Jacobs Ln
148. Hawthorne Ln
149. Throop Aly
150. Orange Grove Pl
151. McCament Aly
152. Glendon Ln
153. Loma Vista Ct
154. Glendon Ct
155. Glendon Wy
156. Prospect Dr
157. Beacon Ave
158. Prospect Cir
159. Highland St
160. Columbia Aly
161. Brocadero Pl
162. Grace Ter
163. Grace Wk
164. Alarcon Pl
165. Columbia Pl
166. Fremont Ln
167. Oaklawn Pl
168. Ozmun Ct
169. Mound Ave
170. Hope Ct
171. Hopewell Ln
172. Central Aly
173. Fair Oaks Ave
174. Mockingbird Ln
175. Raymond Hill Rd
176. Cedarcrest Ave
177. Raymondale Dr
178. Ellincourt Dr
179. Foothill St
180. Hardison Pl
181. Hardison Aly
182. Virginia Pl
183. Oxley Aly
184. Donaldo Ct
185. Marengo Aly
186. Pico Aly
187. Montrose Ln
188. North Aly
189. South Aly
190. Old Mill Rd
191. Oak Knoll Ter
192. Huntington Cir
193. Huntington Garden
194. Straats
195. Ardmore Rd
196. Bonita Dr

1/2 mile
.5 km

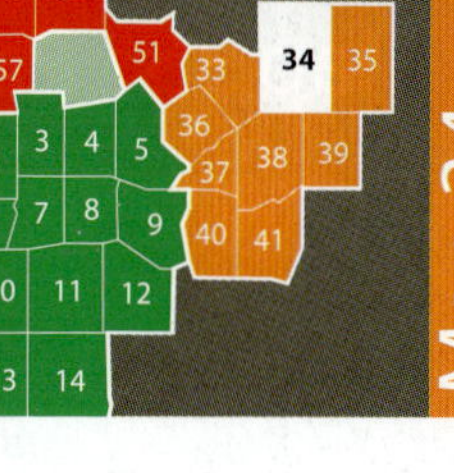

Whether you've a taste for experimental art, independent theater, or outstanding cuisine, the Pasadena palette is always colorful and eclectic, making it the best reason to never venture into LA proper again. Old Town is chock-a-block with great restaurants, bars, and non-stop shopping action. Stock up on rare CDs at Canterbury Records, dine lavishly at the enduringly popular Mi Piace, or enter bargain shopping nirvana every second Sunday of the month at the famous Rose Bowl Flea Market.

Coffee

- **Bamboo Tea House** • 700 E Colorado Blvd
- **Buster's Ice Cream & Coffee Shop** • 1006 Mission St
- **Café Alibi** • 84 S Fair Oaks Ave
- **Café Atlantic** • 69 N Raymond Ave
- **Café Latte** • 55 S Lake Ave
- **Coffee Bean & Tea Leaf** • 18 S Fair Oaks Ave
- **Coffee Bean & Tea Leaf** • 415 S Lake Ave
- **Coffee Bean & Tea Leaf** • 700 S Fair Oaks Ave
- **Coffee Tree** • 696 E Colorado Blvd
- **Equator Coffee House** • 22 Mills Pl
- **Hey That's Amore** • 27 E Holly St
- **Java Filling Station** • 222 E Colorado Blvd
- **Jones Coffee Roasters** • 537 S Raymond Ave
- **Kaldi Coffee & Tea** • 1019 El Centro St
- **Kitty's Café** • 109 E Union St
- **Muddy Joes** • 146 S Lake Ave
- **Peet's** • 605 S Lake Ave
- **Plaza Café** • 802 Fairmount Ave
- **Rose Tree Cottage** • 828 E California Blvd
- **Shubert's Café** • 451 E Colorado Blvd
- **Starbucks** • 1000 Fair Oaks Ave
- **Starbucks** • 117 W Colorado Blvd
- **Starbucks** • Vons • 1213 Fair Oaks Ave
- **Starbucks** • 155 W California Blvd
- **Starbucks** • 408 E Colorado Blvd
- **Starbucks** • 454 N Fair Oaks Ave
- **Starbucks** • 556 S Fair Oaks Ave
- **Starbucks** • 575 S Lake Ave
- **Starbucks** • 671 N Fair Oaks Ave
- **Starbucks** • Target • 777 E Colorado Blvd
- **Starbucks** • 82 S Lake Ave
- **Tiffany's Coffee** • 263 E Colorado Blvd
- **ZELI Coffee Bar** • 695 E Colorado Blvd
- **Zona Rosa** • 15 S El Molino Ave

Copy Shops

- **Cantu Graphics** • 1421 Mission St • 626-441-5631
- **Copy Rite** • 908 E Colorado Blvd • 626-405-9800
- **Copymax** • 721 E Colorado Blvd • 626-449-5676
- **FedEx Kinko's** • 135 N Los Robles Ave • 626-356-0483
- **FedEx Kinko's** • 460 Fair Oaks Ave • 626-403-6690
- **FedEx Kinko's** • 855 E Colorado Blvd • 626-793-6336
- **Ford Graphics** • 681 S Raymond Ave • 626-583-1122
- **Image Quest Plus** • 275 S Lake Ave • 626-744-1333
- **PMX Print N Copy Center** • 739 E Walnut St, Ste 100 • 626-584-6962
- **Print X-Press & Copy Center** • 718 E Green St • 626-440-9472
- **Quick & Easy Copy Service** • 1015 N Lake Ave • 626-794-9187
- **Reliable Graphics** • 61 Valley St • 626-449-6555
- **Staples** • 875 S Arroyo Pwy • 626-578-3490
- **UPS Store** • 1107 Fair Oaks Ave • 626-799-4589
- **UPS Store** • 556 S Fair Oaks Ave • 626-564-0690

Farmers Markets

- **Pasadena Villa Park (Tues, 9 am-1 pm)** • 363 E Villa St
- **South Pasadena (Thurs 4 pm- 8 pm)** • Meridian Ave & Mission St

Gyms

- **24 Hour Fitness** • 525 E Colorado Blvd • 626-795-7121 24
- **Bally Total Fitness** • 45 S Arroyo Pkwy • 626-577-8588
- **Bodies In Motion** • 900 S Arroyo Pkwy • 626-577-2211
- **Curves** • 1270 Lincoln Ave • 626-797-5890
- **Curves** • 906 Fair Oaks Ave • 626-403-9615
- **Equinox** • 260 E Colorado Blvd • 626-685-4800
- **LA Fitness Sports Club** • 201 S Lake Ave • 626-568-3598
- **Pasadena Athletic Club** • 25 W Walnut St • 323-681-6943

Hardware Stores

- **Orchard Supply Hardware** • 452 Fair Oaks Ave • 626-403-8115
- **True Value** • 409 N Fair Oaks Ave • 626-792-2196

Liquor Stores

- **Andy's Liquors** • 124 E Orange Grove Blvd
- **Beverages & More** • 885 S Arroyo Pkwy
- **Bow Tie Wines & Spirits** • 753 S Arroyo Pkwy
- **Chronicle Wine Cellar (wine only)** • 913 E California Blvd
- **Foremost Liquor** • 301 Monterey Rd
- **Gerlach's Drive in Liquors** • 1075 S Fair Oaks Ave
- **Heritage Wine Co** • 155 N Raymond Ave
- **Milt's Liquor** • 400 E Orange Grove Blvd
- **Mission Wines (wine only)** • 1114 Mission St
- **Nose Wine Cellar (Wine only)** • 696 E Colorado Blvd
- **Vendome Wine & Spirits (wine only)** • 906 Granite Dr

Movie Theaters

- **Laemmle One Colorado Cinemas** • 42 Miller Aly • 626-744-1224
- **Laemmle Playhouse 7** • 673 E Colorado Blvd • 626-844-6444
- **Landmark Rialto Theatre** • 1023 Fair Oaks Ave • 626-388-2122
- **Pacific Paseo Stadium 14** • 336 E Colorado Blvd • 626-568-9690

Nightlife

- **Bodega Wine Bar** • 260 E Colorado Blvd • 626-793-4300
- **Club 41** • 41 S De Lacey Ave • 626-795-4141
- **Freddie's 35er Bar** • 12 E Colorado Blvd • 626-356-9315
- **Ice House Comedy Club** • 24 N Mentor Ave • 626-577-1894
- **Jake's Café and Billiards** • 38 W Colorado Blvd • 626-568-1602
- **Lucky Baldwin's** • 17 S Raymond Ave • 626-795-0652
- **McMurphy's** • 72 Fair Oaks Ave • 626-666-1445
- **The Muse** • 54 E Colorado Blvd • 626-793-0608
- **Yard House** • 330 E Colorado Blvd • 626-577-9273

Pet Shops

- **Angel's Tropical Fish** • 847 N Lake Ave • 626-798-3473
- **Pet's Delight** • 725 Fair Oaks Ave • 626-799-2935
- **Petco** • 845 S Arroyo Pkwy • 626-577-2600
- **Three Dog Bakery** • 24 Smith Aly • 626-440-0443

Restaurants

- **750ml** • 966 Mission St • 626-799-0711
- **Akbar Cuisine of India** • 44 N Fair Oaks Ave • 626-577-9916
- **Arroyo Chop House** • 536 S Arroyo Pkwy • 626-577-7463
- **Bar Celona** • 46 E Colorado Blvd • 626-405-1000
- **Beckham Grill** • 77 W Walnut St • 626-796-3399
- **BrenArt Café and Gallery** • 53 E Union St • 626-796-7460
- **Burger Continental** • 535 S Lake Ave • 626-792-6634
- **Café Atlantic** • 69 N Raymond Ave • 626-796-7350
- **Café Bizou** • 91 N Raymond Ave • 626-792-9923
- **Café Santorini** • 64 W Union St • 626-564-4200
- **Celestino** • 141 S Lake Ave • 626-795-4006
- **Club 41** • 41 S De Lacey Ave • 626-795-4141
- **CrepeVine Bistro & Wine Bar** • 36 W Colorado Blvd, Ste 1 • 626-796-7250
- **Firefly Bistro** • 1009 El Centro St • 626-441-2443
- **Five Sixty-One** • 561 E Green St • 626-405-1561
- **Gordon Biersch** • 41 Hugus Aly • 626-449-0052
- **Hop Li** • 526 Alpine St • 213-680-3939
- **Houston's** • 320 S Arroyo Pkwy • 626-577-6001
- **Julienne** • 2649 Mission St • 626-441-2299
- **Kansai** • 36 S Fair Oaks Ave • 626-564-1560
- **La Luna Negra** • 44 W Green St • 626-844-4331
- **La Maschera Ristorante** • 82 N Fair Oaks Ave • 626-304-0004
- **Magnolia Restaurant** • 492 S Lake Ave • 626-584-1126
- **Maison Akira** • 713 E Green St • 626-796-9501
- **Marston's** • 151 E Walnut St • 626-796-2459
- **Mi Piace** • 25 E Colorado Blvd • 626-795-3131
- **Parkway Grill** • 510 S Arroyo Pkwy • 626-795-1001
- **Pie 'N Burger** • 913 E California Blvd • 626-795-1123
- **Radhika's** • 140 Shoppers Ln • 626-744-0994
- **The Raymond** • 1250 S Fair Oaks Ave • 626-441-3136
- **Roscoe's House of Chicken n' Waffles** • 830 N Lake Ave • 626-791-4890
- **The School Café** • 561 E Green St • 626-683-7319
- **Shiro** • 1505 Mission St • 626-799-4774
- **Tonny's** • 843 E Orange Grove Blvd • 626-797-0866
- **Twin Palms** • 101 W Green St • 626-577-2567
- **Xiomara** • 69 N Raymond Ave • 626-796-2520
- **Yahaira's Café** • 698 E Colorado Blvd • 626-844-3254
- **Yujean Kang's** • 67 N Raymond Ave • 626-585-0855

Shopping

- **Angels School Supply** • 600 E Colorado Blvd • 626-584-0855
- **The Art Store** • 44 S Raymond Ave • 626-795-4985
- **Assistance League of Pasadena** • 820 E California Blvd • 626-449-6590
- **Bungalow News** • 746 E Colorado Blvd • 626-795-9456
- **Canterbury Record Shop** • 805 E Colorado Blvd • 626-792-7184
- **Canyon Beachwear** • 34 Hugus Aly • 626-564-0752
- **Carroll & Co** • 146 S Lake Ave • 626-396-7060
- **Dreams of Tibet** • 20 E Holly St • 626-585-8100
- **Elisa B** • 12 Douglas Aly • 626-792-4746
- **Fine Kicks** • 88 E Colorado Blvd • 626-744-0656
- **Heritage Wine Co** • 155 N Raymond Ave • 800-630-WINE
- **Jacob Maarse Florists** • 655 E Green St • 626-449-0246
- **Lather** • 106 W Colorado Blvd • 626-396-9636
- **Lush** • 24 E Colorado Blvd • 626-792-0901
- **Messarian Oriental Rugs** • 493 E Colorado Blvd • 626-792-9858
- **Nicole's Gourmet Imports** • 921 Meridian Ave • 626-441-9600
- **Paperwhites** • 2491 Mission St • 626-441-2196
- **Pasadena Antique Mall** • 444 S Fair Oaks • 626-449-7606
- **Penny Lane Records & Tapes** • 12 W Colorado Blvd • 626-564-0161
- **Rose Tree Cottage** • 828 E California Blvd • 626-793-3337
- **Run with Us** • 235 N Lake Ave • 626-568-3331
- **Stats** • 120 S Raymond Ave • 626-795-9308
- **Target** • 777 E Colorado Blvd • 626-795-5472
- **Three Dog Bakery** • 24 Smith Aly • 626-440-0443
- **Vroman's Bookstore** • 695 E Colorado Blvd • 626-449-5320
- **Z Gallerie** • 42 W Colorado Blvd • 626-578-1538

Video Rental

- **Blockbuster** • 1100 Fair Oaks Ave • 626-441-8112
- **Blockbuster** • 151 W California Blvd • 626-440-7074
- **Blockbuster** • 320 S Lake Ave • 626-568-9874
- **Hollywood Video** • 25 E California Blvd • 626-304-9340
- **Ito Video** • 41 E Orange Grove Blvd • 626-683-9503
- **Pasadena Video** • 453 E Orange Grove Blvd • 626-744-9698
- **Penny Lane Music & Video** • 569 S Lake Ave • 626-568-9999
- **Pepe's Video Store** • 313 E Orange Grove Blvd • 626-792-7127
- **Q Video** • 1279 N Lake Ave • 626-398-8686

Map 35 • Pasadena East / San Marino

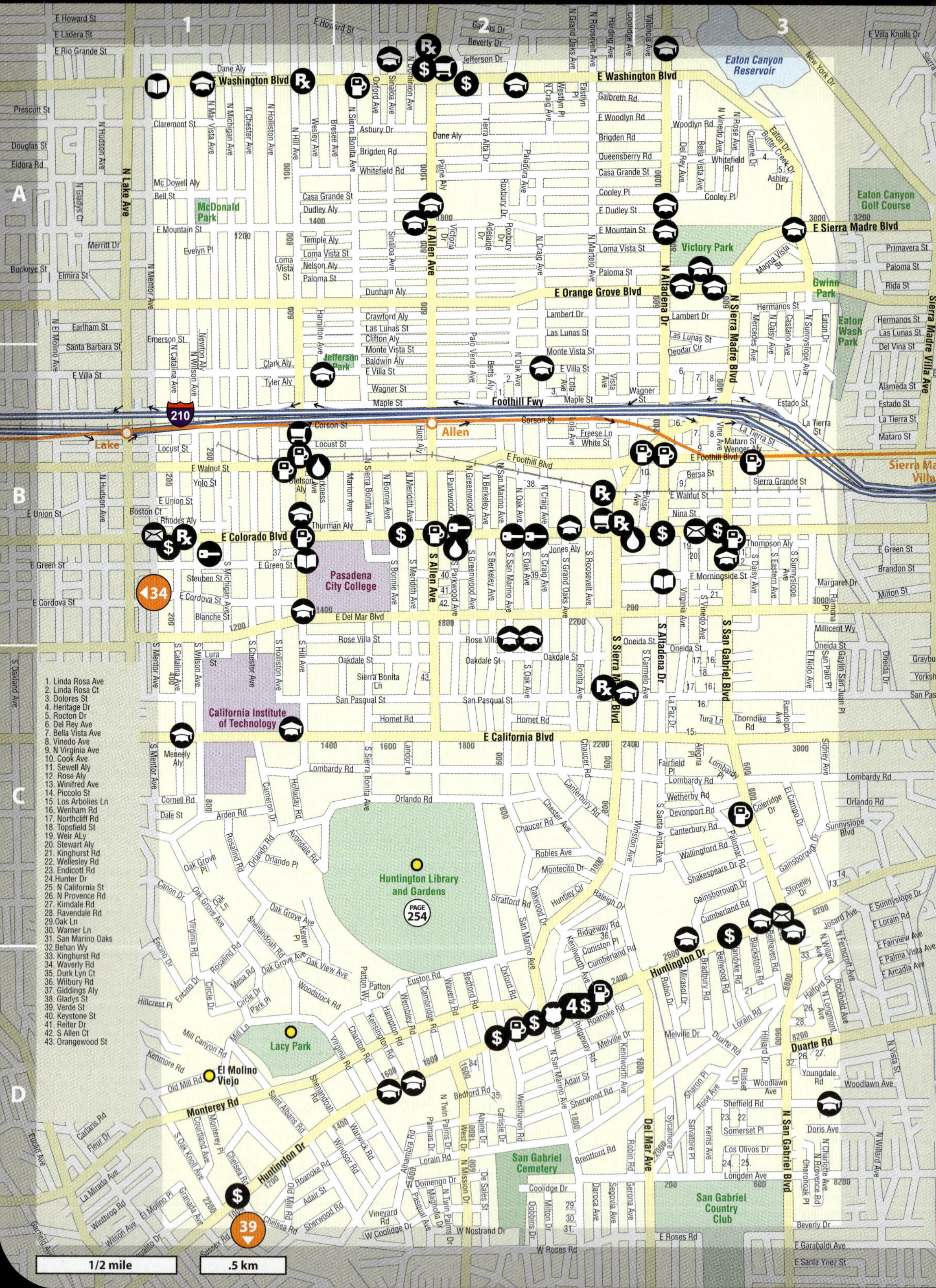

Washington Blvd
E Washington Blvd
E Orange Grove Blvd
Foothill Fwy
E Colorado Blvd
E Del Mar Blvd
E California Blvd
Huntington Dr
Monterey Rd
Duarte Rd
E Sierra Madre Blvd
N Lake Ave
N Allen Ave
S Allen Ave
N Altadena Dr
S Altadena Dr
N Sierra Madre Blvd
S Sierra Madre Blvd
S San Gabriel Blvd
N San Gabriel Blvd
Del Mar Ave
Eaton Canyon Reservoir
Eaton Canyon Golf Course
McDonald Park
Jefferson Park
Victory Park
Gwinn Park
Eaton Wash Park
Pasadena City College
California Institute of Technology
Huntington Library and Gardens
Lacy Park
El Molino Viejo
San Gabriel Cemetery
San Gabriel Country Club
Lake
Allen
Sierra Madre Villa

1. Linda Rosa Ave
2. Linda Rosa Ct
3. Dolores St
4. Heritage Dr
5. Rocton Dr
6. Del Rey Ave
7. Bella Vista Ave
8. Vinedo Ave
9. N Virginia Ave
10. Cook Ave
11. Sewell Aly
12. Rose Aly
13. Winifred Ave
14. Piccolo St
15. Los Arbolies Ln
16. Wenham Rd
17. Northcliff Rd
18. Topsfield St
19. Weir ALy
20. Stewart Aly
21. Kinghurst Rd
22. Wellesley Rd
23. Endicott Rd
24. Hunter Dr
25. N California St
26. N Provence Rd
27. Kimdale Rd
28. Ravendale Rd
29. Oak Ln
30. Warner Ln
31. San Marino Oaks
32. Behan Wy
33. Kinghurst Rd
34. Waverly Rd
35. Durk Lyn Ct
36. Wilbury Rd
37. Giddings Aly
38. Gladys St
39. Verde St
40. Keystone St
41. Reiter Dr
42. S Allen Ct
43. Orangewood St

34
39
PAGE 254

1/2 mile
.5 km

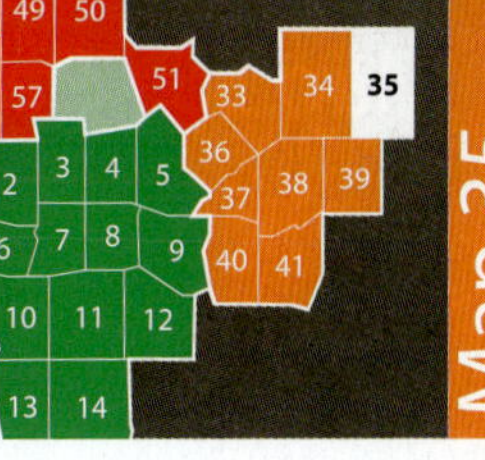

When you venture east past Lake Avenue along Colorado, the cute shops and restaurants become drab auto repair shops, dingy motels, and whatnot. But head south and you'll see not only some of the smartest people at Cal Tech (whose seismic expertise is needed for all of our earthquakes), but some of the richest. The homes around Pasadena City College and the resplendent Huntington Library and Gardens are worth the drive just to see how the other half lives.

Banks

- **Bank of America** • 1687 E Colorado Blvd
- **Bank of America** • 2180 Huntington Dr
- **Bank of the West** • 2395 Huntington Dr
- **Bank of the West** • 2500 E Colorado Blvd
- **Chinatrust** • 2956 Huntington Dr
- **Citizens Business** • 1010 E Colorado Blvd
- **Citizens Business** • 980 Huntington Dr
- **East West** • 2090 Huntington Dr
- **East West** • 2295 Huntington Dr
- **Washington Mutual** • 1845 E Washington Blvd
- **Washington Mutual** • 2270 Huntington Dr
- **Washington Mutual** • 2670 E Colorado Blvd
- **Wells Fargo** • 1390 N Allen Ave
- **Wells Fargo** • 2355 Huntington Dr

Car Rental

- **All-Rite Rent-a-Car** • 1150 E Colorado Blvd
- **Enterprise** • 1890 E Colorado Blvd
- **Hertz** • 2070 E Colorado Blvd
- **Value Rent-a-Car** • 2106 E Colorado Blvd

Car Washes

- **Chevron** • 1400 E Colorado Blvd
- **Sparkle Car Wash** • 2400 E Colorado Blvd
- **Walnut-Hill Hand Car Wash** • 1465 E Walnut St

Gas Stations

- **76** • 200 N Hill Ave
- **76** • 2390 Huntington Dr
- **76** • 911 S San Gabriel Blvd
- **Arco** • 2800 E Foothill Blvd
- **Chevron** • 1400 E Colorado Blvd
- **Chevron** • 233 N Altadena Dr
- **Independent** • 1600 E Washington Blvd
- **Mobil** • 1813 E Colorado Blvd
- **Mobil** • 210 N Sierra Madre Blvd
- **Shell** • 2716 E Colorado Blvd
- **Valero** • 2155 Huntington Dr

Landmarks

- **El Molino Viejo** • 1120 Old Mill Rd
- **Huntington** • 1151 Oxford Rd
- **Lacy Park** • 1500 Virginia Rd

Libraries

- **Hill Avenue Branch** • 55 S Hill Ave • 626-744-7264
- **Lamanda Park Branch** • 140 S Altadena Dr • 626-744-7266
- **Santa Catalina Branch** • 999 E Washington Blvd • 626-744-7272

Pharmacies

- **CVS** • 451 S Sierra Madre Blvd • 626-564-8681
- **Rite-Aid** • 1038 E Colorado Blvd • 626-796-5539
- **Rite-Aid** • 1421 E Washington Blvd • 626-296-0245
- **Rite-Aid** • 2330 E Walnut St • 626-304-2725
- **Vons** • 1390 N Allen Ave • 626-798-0764
- **Vons** • 2355 E Colorado Blvd • 626-449-4110

Police

- **San Marino Police Dept** • 2200 Huntington Dr • 626-300-0720

Post Offices

- **US Post Office** • 2609 E Colorado Blvd • 800-275-8777
- **US Post Office** • 2960 Huntington Dr • 800-275-8777
- **US Post Office** • 967 E Colorado Blvd • 800-275-8777

Schools

- **Assumption Elementary** • 2660 E Orange Grove Blvd
- **California Academy for Liberal Studies** • 3838 Eagle Rock Blvd
- **California Institute of Technology** • 1200 E California Blvd
- **Carver Elementary** • 3100 Huntington Dr
- **Chaim Weizmann Community Day** • 1434 N Altadena Dr
- **Frostig** • 971 N Altadena Dr
- **Grace Christian Academy** • 73 N Hill Ave
- **Hamilton Elementary** • 2089 Rose Villa St
- **Huntington Middle** • 1700 Huntington Dr
- **Jefferson Elementary** • 1500 E Villa St
- **LH Tavlian Pre School** • 1317 Sinaloa Ave
- **Living Way Christian Academy** • 2495 E Mountain St
- **Longfellow Elementary** • 1065 E Washington Blvd
- **Marshall Fundamental** • 990 N Allen Ave
- **Norma Coombs Elementary** • 2600 Paloma St
- **Oddessy Charter** • 725 N Altadena Dr
- **Our School** • 1800 E Mountain St
- **Pasadena City College** • 1570 E Colorado Blvd
- **Pasadena High** • 2925 E Sierra Madre Blvd
- **Pasadena Progressive Monessori** • 615 S Catalina Ave
- **Polytechnic** • 1030 E California Blvd
- **San Marino High** • 2701 Huntington Dr
- **San Marino Montessori** • 444 S Sierra Madre Blvd
- **St Gregory** • 2215 E Colorado Blvd
- **St Philip the Apostle** • 161 S Hill Ave
- **Sts Felicita & Perpetua** • 2955 Huntington Dr
- **Valentine Elementary** • 1650 Huntington Dr
- **Villa Esperanza** • 2116 E Villa St
- **Walden** • 74 S San Gabriel Blvd
- **Washington Elementary** • 300 N San Marino Ave
- **Webster Elementary** • 2101 E Washington Blvd
- **Woodrow Wilson Elementary** • 8317 Sheffield Rd

Supermarkets

- **Smart & Final** • 1382 Locust St
- **Vons** • 1390 N Allen Ave
- **Vons** • 2355 E Colorado Blvd

Map 35 • Pasadena East / San Marino

1. Linda Rosa Ave
2. Linda Rosa Ct
3. Dolores St
4. Heritage Dr
5. Rocton Dr
6. Del Rey Ave
7. Bella Vista Ave
8. Vinedo Ave
9. N Virginia Ave
10. Cook Ave
11. Sewell Aly
12. Rose Aly
13. Winifred Ave
14. Piccolo St
15. Los Arbolies Ln
16. Wenham Rd
17. Northcliff Rd
18. Topsfield St
19. Weir ALy
20. Stewart Aly
21. Kinghurst Rd
22. Wellesley Rd
23. Endicott Rd
24. Hunter Dr
25. N California St
26. N Provence Rd
27. Kimdale Rd
28. Ravendale Rd
29. Oak Ln
30. Warner Ln
31. San Marino Oaks
32. Behan Wy
33. Kinghurst Rd
34. Waverly Rd
35. Durk Lyn Ct
36. Wilbury Rd
37. Giddings Aly
38. Gladys St
39. Verde St
40. Keystone St
41. Reiter Dr
42. S Allen Ct
43. Orangewood St

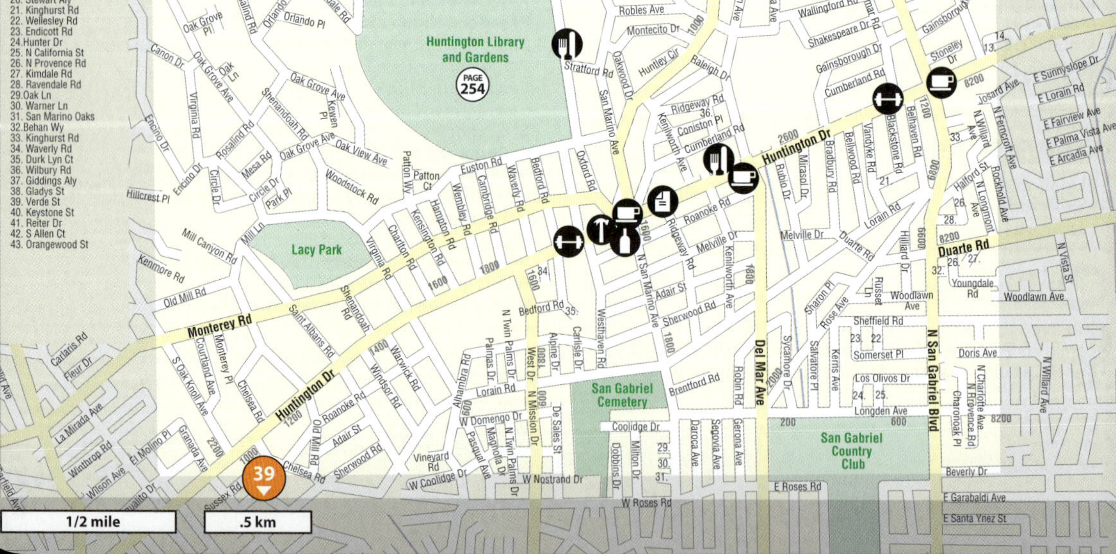

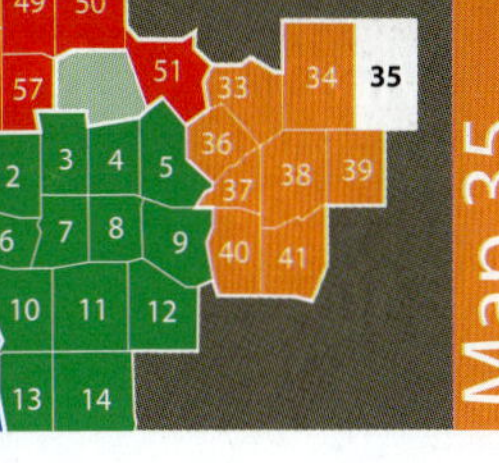

If you're looking to get back to nature, strangely enough, the east side of Pasadena is probably the place. The 150-acre Huntington Library and Gardens will take you away from it all with wide-open spaces for lounging, gawking, and relaxing. Lacy Park, Pasadena City College, and the Cal Tech campuses are also welcome retreats for nature lovers. Hungry? Go French provincial at Madeleine's or English proper at the Rose Garden Tea Room. Posh nosh ain't your thing? There's always Zankou Chicken.

Coffee

- **Café Culture** • 1359 N Altadena Dr
- **Coffee Beanery** • 1225 E Washington Blvd
- **Coffee Club** • 12 Harkness Ave
- **Lollicup** • 1491 E Colorado Blvd
- **Lollicup** • 2506 Huntington Dr
- **Starbucks** • Vons • 1390 N Allen Ave
- **Starbucks** • 161 N Hill Ave
- **Starbucks** • 1687 E Colorado Blvd
- **Starbucks** • 1830 E Washington Blvd
- **Starbucks** • 2265 Huntington Dr
- **Starbucks** • Vons • 2355 E Colorado Blvd
- **Starbucks** • 3007 Huntington Dr

Copy Shops

- **Baughman Printing Company** • 1842 E Walnut St • 626-793-0753
- **Book Mart & Copy Center** • 1535 E Colorado Blvd • 626-683-3391
- **Econoprint Printing & Graphics Center** • 1765 E Colorado Blvd • 626-795-1000
- **Office Depot** • 1130 E Colorado Blvd • 626-666-6900
- **Office Depot** • 325 N Altadena Dr • 626-792-5800
- **Print Stop** • 300 N Allen Ave • 626-577-0510
- **Printcraft Copy Center** • 985 E Colorado Blvd • 626-584-6971
- **UPS Store** • 1443 E Washington Blvd • 626-529-0325
- **UPS Store** • 2275 Huntington Dr • 626-795-1999

Farmers Markets

- **Pasadena Victory Park (Sat, 8:30 am-1 pm)** • Paloma St & E Sierra Madre Blvd

Gyms

- **Curves** • 1250 E Green St • 626-793-9711
- **Curves** • 1311 N Altadena Dr • 626-794-5294
- **Curves** • 2920 Huntington Dr • 626-287-1513
- **Evolution Fitness** • 2370 E Colorado Blvd • 626-793-5353
- **Gold's Gym** • 36 S Altadena Dr • 626-304-1133
- **Women's World Fitness Center** • 2000 Huntington Dr • 626-284-7741

Hardware Stores

- **Berg Hardware** • 495 N Altadena Dr • 626-793-6161
- **Crown City Hardware** • 1047 N Allen Ave • 626-794-1188
- **Davis Lumber** • 1787 E Walnut St • 626-792-7104
- **San Marino Hardware** • 2134 Huntington Dr • 626-282-6536

Liquor Stores

- **Allen Villa Beverage** • 490 N Allen Ave
- **Foothill Liquor** • 2547 E Foothill Blvd
- **Golden Liquor** • 2895 E Colorado Blvd
- **Liquor Mart** • 2044 E Colorado Blvd
- **Mission Liquor** • 1801 E Washington Blvd
- **Pat's Liquors** • 1072 E Colorado Blvd
- **Wine Connections (wine only)** • 2154 Huntington Dr

Movie Theaters

- **Academy 6** • 1003 E Colorado Blvd • 626-229-9400

Pet Shops

- **Lucky & Mimi Pet Shop & Salon** • 2439 E Colorado Blvd • 626-227-4399
- **Pasadena Tropical Fish** • 2982 E Colorado Blvd • 626-449-4987

Restaurants

- **Bistro 45** • 45 S Mentor Ave • 626-795-2478
- **Café Verde** • 961 E Green St • 626-356-9811
- **Europane** • 950 E Colorado Blvd • 626-577-1828
- **In-N-Out Burger** • 2114 E Foothill Blvd • 800-786-1000
- **Madeleine's Restaurant** • 1030 E Green St • 626-440-7087
- **Rose Garden Tea Room** • 1151 Oxford Rd • 626-405-2100
- **Sushi Bar Yoshida** • 2026 Huntington Dr • 626-281-9292
- **The Vault Bar & Grill** • 2675 E Colorado Blvd • 626-683-3344
- **Zankou Chicken** • 1415 E Colorado Blvd • 818-244-1937

Shopping

- **Aardvark's** • 1253 E Colorado Blvd • 626-583-9109

Video Rental

- **Plaza Video** • 1832 E Colorado Blvd • 626-793-2451
- **Star Video** • 1878 E Washington Blvd • 626-791-9708
- **Video Grand** • 376 N Allen Ave • 626-578-1640

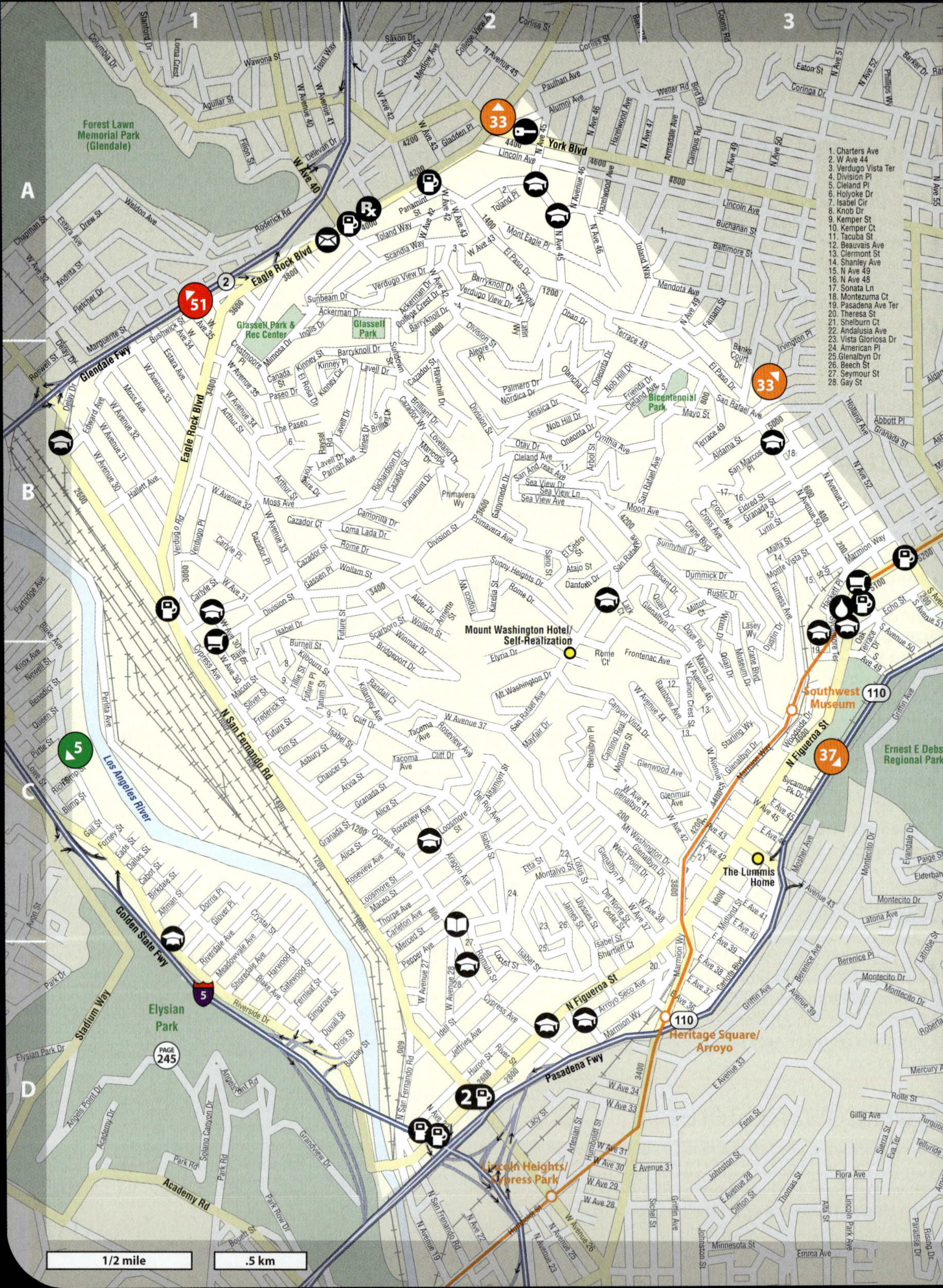

Map 36 • Mt Washington

1. Charters Ave
2. W Ave 44
3. Verdugo Vista Ter
4. Division Pl
5. Cleland Pl
6. Holyoke Dr
7. Isabel Cir
8. Knob Dr
9. Kemper St
10. Kemper Ct
11. Tacuba St
12. Beauvais Ave
13. Clermont St
14. Shanley Ave
15. N Ave 49
16. N Ave 48
17. Sonata Ln
18. Montezuma Ct
19. Pasadena Ave Ter
20. Theresa St
21. Shelburn Ct
22. Andalusia Ave
23. Vista Gloriosa Dr
24. American Pl
25. Glenalbyn Dr
26. Beech St
27. Seymour St
28. Gay St

Forest Lawn Memorial Park (Glendale)

Glassell Park & Rec Center

Glassell Park

Bicentennial Park

Mount Washington Hotel/ Self-Realization

Southwest Museum

The Lummis Home

Ernest E Debs Regional Park

Elysian Park

Heritage Square/ Arroyo

Lincoln Heights/ Cypress Park

Los Angeles River

Glendale Fwy

Golden State Fwy

Pasadena Fwy

PAGE 245

1/2 mile

.5 km

Mt. Washington is feeling the energy from the new, young money that's moving into one of the few affordable areas left in Los Angeles. Once-shady neighborhoods are perking up, and new businesses are coming along every day. That's not to say this place isn't without its gangs, graffiti, and crime problems (but really, which part of LA isn't?). It's just shaping up nicely, especially in the hilly parts, which offer great views of downtown and the surrounding area.

Car Rental

- **Enterprise** • 4442 York Blvd

Car Washes

- **Highland Car Wash** • 5128 N Figueroa St

Gas Stations

- **76** • 105 N Ave 52
- **76** • 2250 N Figueroa St
- **Arco** • 2135 San Fernando Rd
- **Arco** • 4380 Eagle Rock Blvd
- **Chevron** • 2601 N Figueroa St
- **Chevron** • 4005 Eagle Rock Blvd
- **Independent** • 2600 N Figueroa St
- **Independent** • 4236 Eagle Rock Blvd
- **Shell** • 5137 N Figueroa St
- **Thrifty** • 2251 N Figueroa St

Landmarks

- **The Lummis Home** • 200 E Ave 43
- **Mount Washington Hotel/Self-Realization** • 3880 San Rafael Ave

Libraries

- **Cypress Park Branch** • 1150 Cypress Ave • 323-224-0039

Pharmacies

- **Rite-Aid** • 4044 Eagle Rock Blvd • 323-254-8642

Post Offices

- **US Post Office** • 3950 Eagle Rock Blvd • 800-275-8777

Schools

- **Aldama Elementary** • 632 N Ave 50
- **Aragon Ave Elementary** • 1118 Aragon Ave
- **Arroyo Seco** • 4805 Sycamore Ter
- **Divine Saviour** • 624 Cypress Ave
- **Dorris Pl Elementary** • 2225 Dorris Pl
- **Florence Nightingale Middle** • 3311 N Figueroa St
- **Glassell Park Elementary** • 2211 W Ave 30
- **Loreto St Elementary** • 3408 Arroyo Seco Ave
- **Mount Washington Elementary** • 3981 San Rafael Ave
- **Ribet Academy** • 2911 San Fernando Rd
- **St Bernard Elementary** • 3254 Verdugo Rd
- **Sycamore Grove** • 4900 N Figueroa St
- **Toland Way EEC** • 4505 Toland Wy
- **Toland Way Elementary** • 4545 Toland Wy

Supermarkets

- **Food 4 Less** • 5100 N Figueroa St
- **Super A Foods** • 2925 Division St

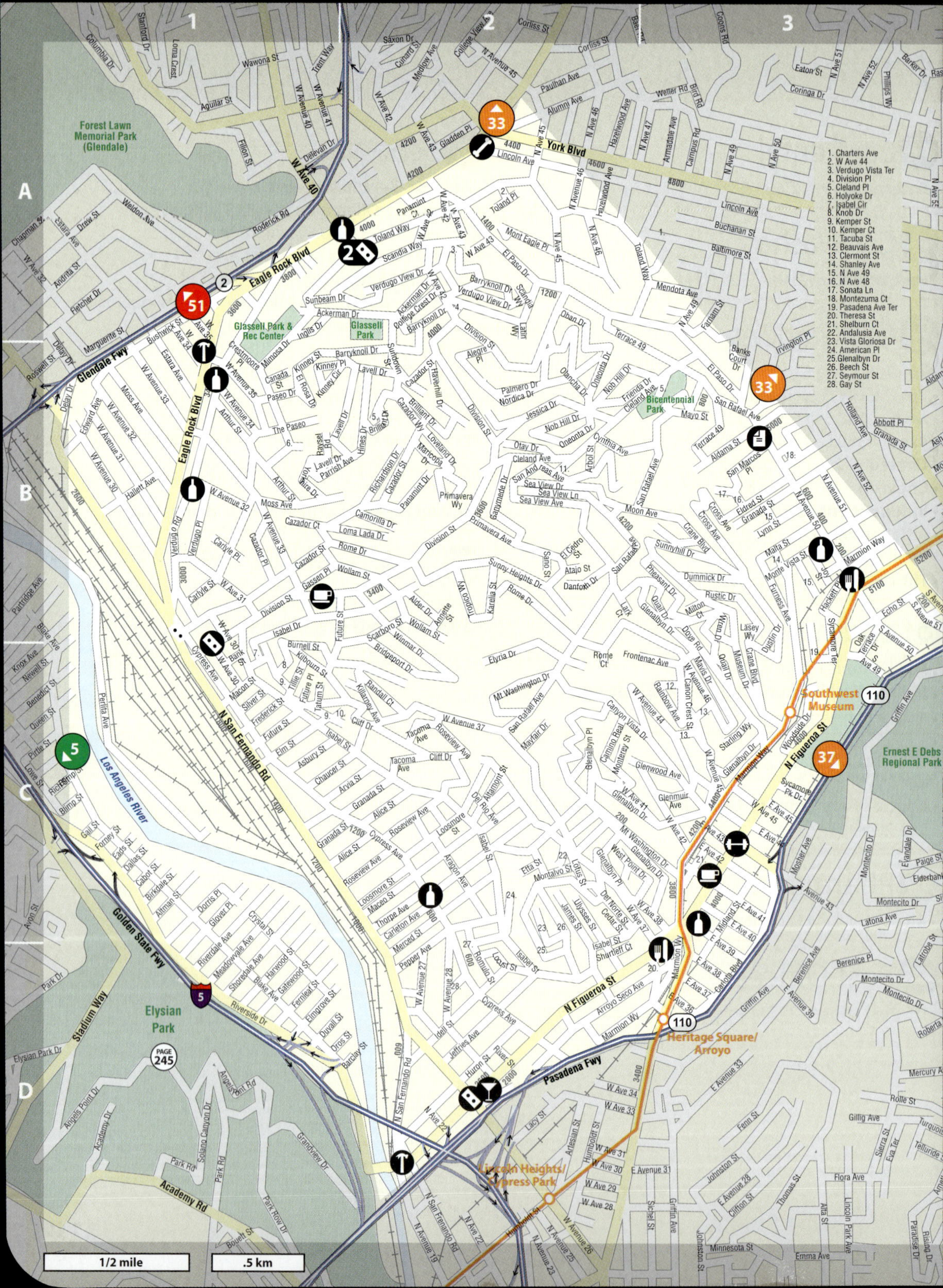

Map 36 • Mt Washington

1. Charters Ave
2. W Ave 44
3. Verdugo Vista Ter
4. Division Pl
5. Cleland Pl
6. Holyoke Dr
7. Isabel Cir
8. Knob Dr
9. Kemper St
10. Kemper Ct
11. Tacuba St
12. Beauvais Ave
13. Clermont St
14. Shanley Ave
15. N Ave 49
16. N Ave 48
17. Sonata Ln
18. Montezuma Ct
19. Pasadena Ave Ter
20. Theresa St
21. Shelburn Ct
22. Andalusia Ave
23. Vista Gloriosa Dr
24. American Pl
25. Glenalbyn Dr
26. Beech St
27. Seymour St
28. Gay St

1/2 mile | .5 km

Local businesses still rule Mt. Washington. That just means it's a great place to get authentic Mexican food (like the terrific brunches at La Abeja) and you can find a dive bar that hasn't been completely overrun by the cool elite (or you could just go to hipster hang Footsie's). If you're looking for a retail chain, you need to drive to Glendale or Pasadena.

Coffee

- **Julie's Gourmet Café** • 3329 Division St
- **Rock Rose Café** • 4108 N Figueroa St

Copy Shops

- **The Copierman** • 720 N Ave 50 • 323-255-8606

Gyms

- **Curves** • 4319 N Figueroa St • 323-224-0044

Hardware Stores

- **Home Depot** • 2055 N Figueroa St • 323-342-9495
- **Verdugo True Value** • 3516 Eagle Rock Blvd • 323-255-5191

Liquor Stores

- **Barney's Liquors** • 5001 Monte Vista St
- **Cypress Liquor** • 1207 Cypress Ave
- **Golden Liquor** • 3924 N Figueroa St
- **L&M Liquor** • 4010 Eagle Rock Blvd
- **Mike's Liquor** • 3192 Verdugo Rd
- **S&J Liquor** • 925 Cypress Ave

Nightlife

- **Footsie's** • 2640 N Figueroa St • 323-221-6900

Pet Shops

- **Hal's Eagle Rock Pet Shop** • 4374 Eagle Rock Blvd • 323-255-5714

Restaurants

- **Chico's** • 100 N Ave 50 • 323-254-2445
- **La Abeja** • 3700 N Figueroa St • 323-221-0474

Video Rental

- **21 Video** • 2211 N San Fernando Rd • 323-221-1793
- **J Video** • 2933 Division St • 323-223-5525
- **Landmark Video (Filipino)** • 3756 W Ave 40 • 323-256-0969
- **Penny Lane Music & Video** • 1661 E Colorado Blvd • 626-535-0949
- **Video Club of LA** • 3756 W Ave 40 • 323-255-9883

Map 37 • Lincoln Heights

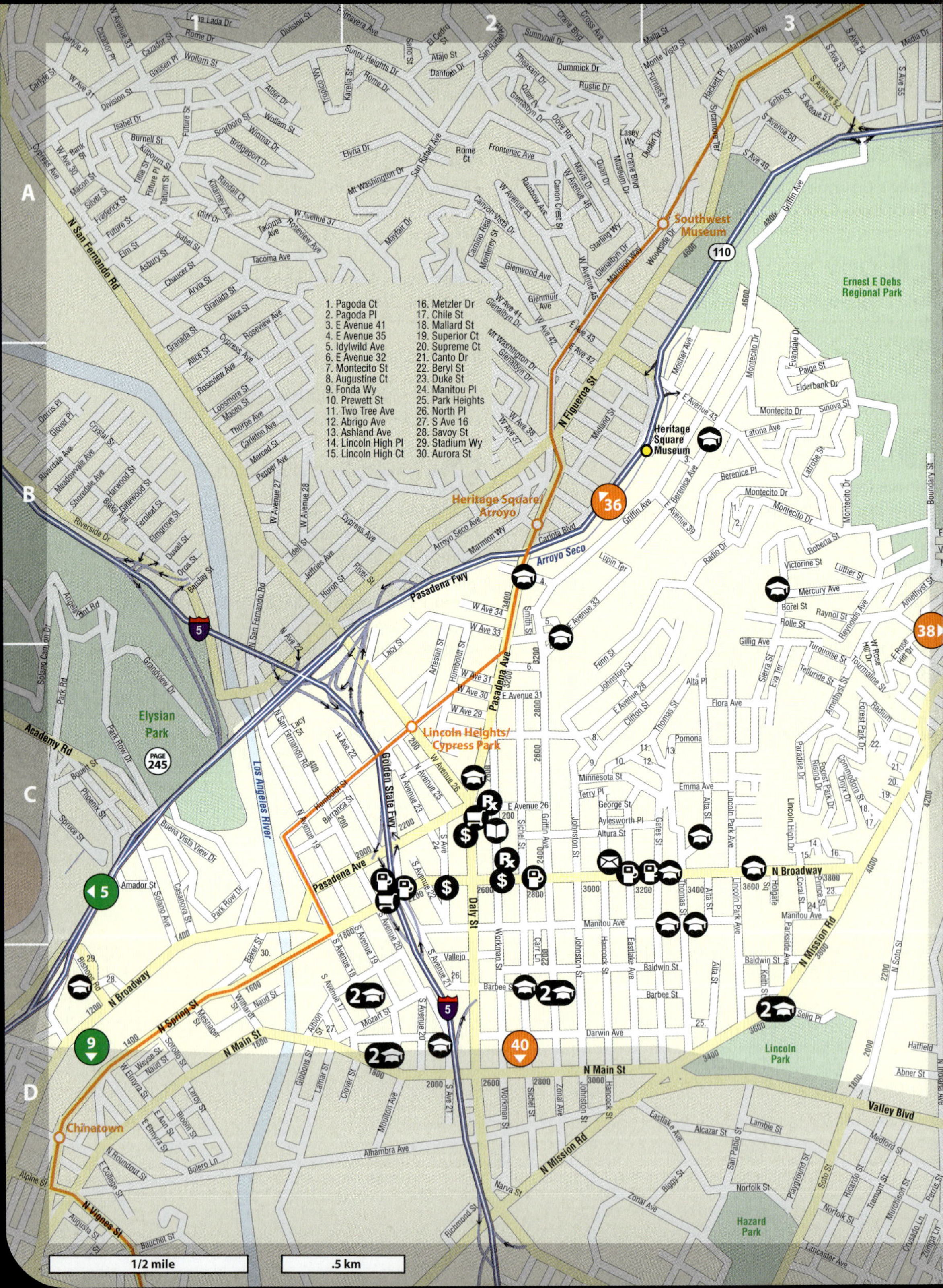

1. Pagoda Ct
2. Pagoda Pl
3. E Avenue 41
4. E Avenue 35
5. Idylwild Ave
6. E Avenue 32
7. Montecito St
8. Augustine Ct
9. Fonda Wy
10. Prewett St
11. Two Tree Ave
12. Abrigo Ave
13. Ashland Ave
14. Lincoln High Pl
15. Lincoln High Ct
16. Metzler Dr
17. Chile St
18. Mallard St
19. Superior Ct
20. Supreme Ct
21. Canto Dr
22. Beryl St
23. Duke St
24. Manitou Pl
25. Park Heights
26. North Pl
27. S Ave 16
28. Savoy St
29. Stadium Wy
30. Aurora St

1/2 mile

.5 km

Lincoln Heights is one of LA's oldest neighborhoods, and in its 125 years it has housed a mélange of immigrant enclaves and tourist curios (Ostrich farm, anyone?). While most of the ethnic population has become uniformly Mexican and many of the recreation sites have closed, Lincoln Heights maintains its identity. There are delightful restaurants and walkable areas throughout the sea of concrete.

Banks

- **Bank of America** • 2400 N Broadway
- **East West** • 2601 N Broadway
- **Wells Fargo** • 2511 Daly St

Gas Stations

- **76** • 2001 N Broadway
- **Arco** • 2829 N Broadway
- **Independent** • 3130 N Broadway
- **Shell** • 3200 N Broadway
- **Thrifty** • 2214 N Broadway

Landmarks

- **Heritage Square Museum** • 3800 N Homer St

Libraries

- **Lincoln Heights Branch** • 2530 Workman St • 323-226-1692

Pharmacies

- **CVS** • 2419 Workman St • 323-223-9059
- **Rite-Aid** • 111 E Ave 26 • 323-222-8876

Post Offices

- **US Post Office** • 3001 N Broadway • 800-275-8777

Schools

- **Abraham Lincoln Senior High** • 3501 N Broadway
- **Albion EEC** • 348 S Ave 18
- **Albion Street Elementary** • 322 S Ave 18
- **Boyle Heights Continuation** • 544 S Mathews St
- **Cathedral High** • 1253 Bishop Rd
- **Crittenton High** • 234 E Ave 33
- **East Los Angeles Adult Skill Center** • 3921 Selig Pl
- **Gates EEC** • 2306 Thomas St
- **Gates St Elementary** • 3333 Manitou Ave
- **Glen Alta Elementary** • 3410 Sierra St
- **Griffin Elementary** • 2025 Griffin Ave
- **Hillside Elementary** • 120 E Ave 35
- **Jardin De Ninos EEC** • 3921 Selig Pl
- **Kipp LA College Prep** • 1855 N Main St
- **Latona Ave Elementary** • 4312 Berenice Ave
- **Little Flower Missionary House** • 2434 Gates St
- **Milagro Charter Elementary** • 1855 N Main St
- **Milagro Charter Elementary** • 2635 Pasadena Ave
- **Our Lady Help of Christians** • 2024 Darwin Ave
- **Pubelo de Los Angeles Continuation** • 2506 Alta St
- **Sacred Heart Elementary** • 2109 Sichel St
- **Sacred Heart High** • 2111 Griffin Ave

Supermarkets

- **Smart & Final** • 2019 Pasadena Ave
- **Vons** • 2511 Daly St

Map 37 • Lincoln Heights

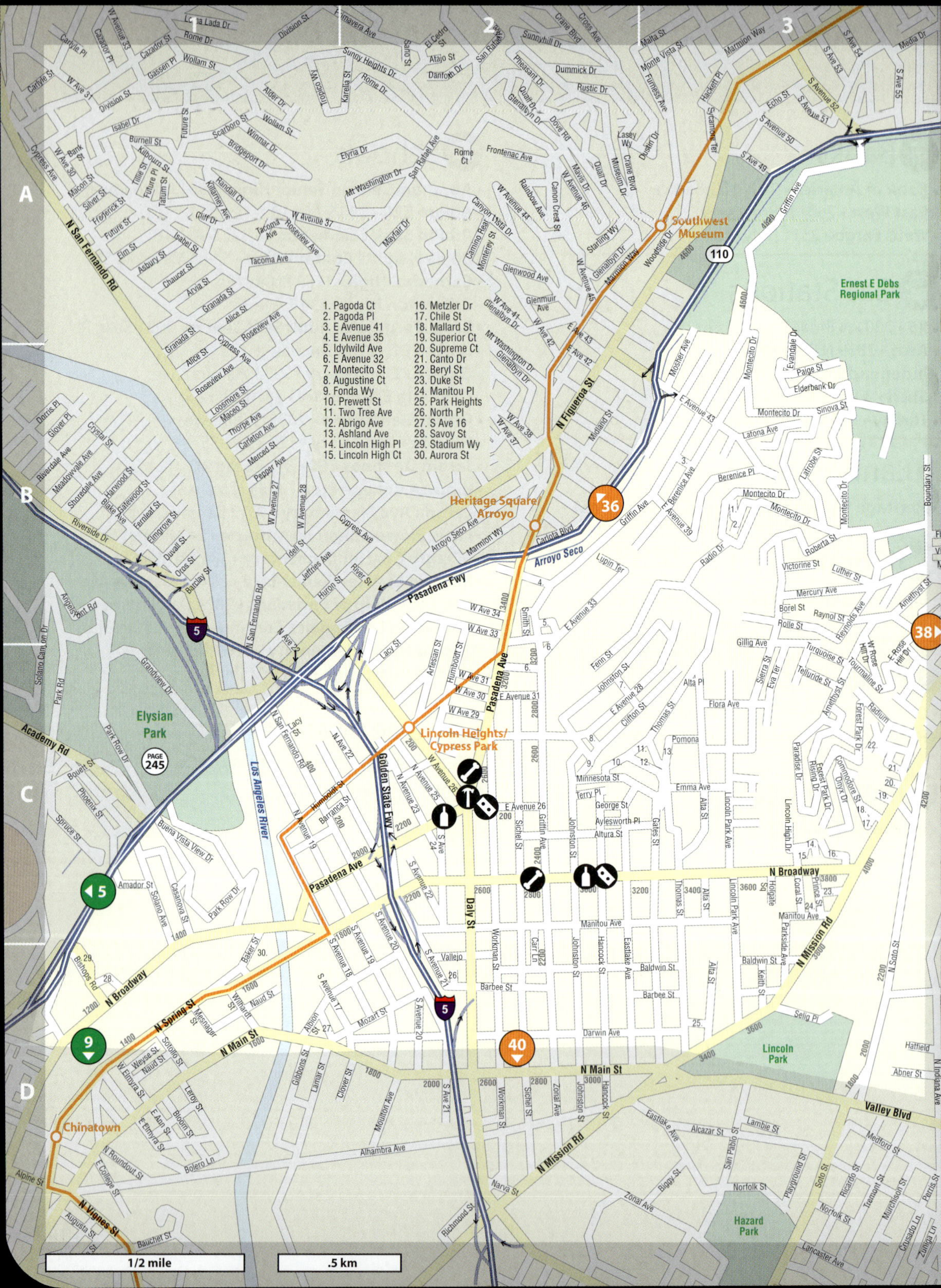

1. Pagoda Ct
2. Pagoda Pl
3. E Avenue 41
4. E Avenue 35
5. Idylwild Ave
6. E Avenue 32
7. Montecito St
8. Augustine Ct
9. Fonda Wy
10. Prewett St
11. Two Tree Ave
12. Abrigo Ave
13. Ashland Ave
14. Lincoln High Pl
15. Lincoln High Ct
16. Metzler Dr
17. Chile St
18. Mallard St
19. Superior Ct
20. Supreme Ct
21. Canto Dr
22. Beryl St
23. Duke St
24. Manitou Pl
25. Park Heights
26. North Pl
27. S Ave 16
28. Savoy St
29. Stadium Wy
30. Aurora St

PAGE 245
36
38
40
5
9

Lincoln Heights is home to the San Antonio Winery (Map 40), the only LA winery to survive Prohibition. Tours are available, along with dinner and live music on the weekends. Also in the area is The Brewery (Map 40), the world's largest artist community, where over 500 artists live and work in a converted Pabst Blue Ribbon brewery. Find inspiration at one of the Brewery's semi-annual ArtWalks, when the studio doors are open to the public.

Hardware Stores

- **5 Points Hardware** • 2615 Pasadena Ave • 323-225-6423

Liquor Stores

- **Mandala Liquor** • 2920 N Broadway
- **Royal Liquor** • 2501 Pasadena Ave

Pet Shops

- **Jack's Pet Shop** • 2634 Pasadena Ave • 323-225-6315
- **Pete's Pet Supply** • 2828 N Broadway • 323-227-6060

Video Rental

- **Hollywood Video** • 3030 N Broadway • 323-221-3201
- **Star Video** • 112 E Ave 26 • 323-222-9046

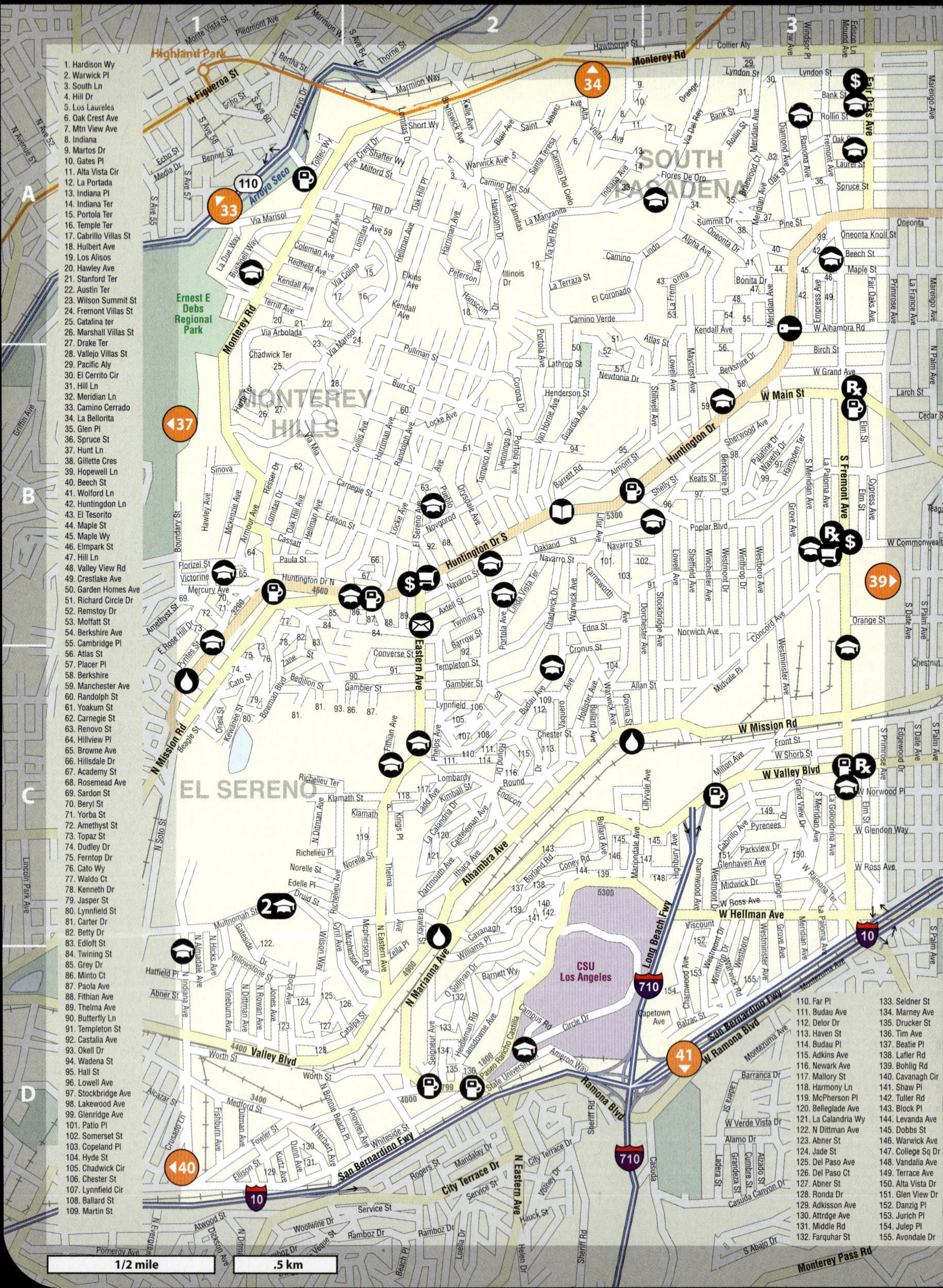

1. Hardison Wy
2. Warwick Pl
3. South Ln
4. Hill Dr
5. Los Laureles
6. Oak Crest Ave
7. Mtn View Ave
8. Indiana
9. Martos Dr
10. Gates Pl
11. Alta Vista Cir
12. La Portada
13. Indiana Pl
14. Indiana Ter
15. Portola Ter
16. Temple Ter
17. Cabrillo Villas St
18. Hulbert Ave
19. Los Alisos
20. Hawley Ave
21. Stanford Ter
22. Austin Ter
23. Wilson Summit St
24. Fremont Villas St
25. Catalina ter
26. Marshall Villas St
27. Drake Ter
28. Vallejo Villas St
29. Pacific Aly
30. El Cerrito Cir
31. Hill Ln
32. Meridian Ln
33. Camino Cerrado
34. La Bellorita
35. Glen Pl
36. Spruce St
37. Hunt Ln
38. Gillette Cres
39. Hopewell Ln
40. Beech St
41. Wolford Ln
42. Huntingdon Ln
43. El Tesorito
44. Maple St
45. Maple Wy
46. Elmpark St
47. Hill Ln
48. Valley View Rd
49. Crestlake Ave
50. Garden Homes Ave
51. Richard Circle Dr
52. Remstoy Dr
53. Moffatt St
54. Berkshire Ave
55. Cambridge Pl
56. Atlas St
57. Placer Pl
58. Berkshire
59. Manchester Ave
60. Randolph St
61. Yoakum St
62. Carnegie St
63. Renovo St
64. Hillview Pl
65. Browne Ave
66. Hilsdale Dr
67. Academy St
68. Rosemead Ave
69. Sardon St
70. Beryl St
71. Yorba St
72. Amethyst St
73. Topaz St
74. Dudley Dr
75. Ferntop Dr
76. Cato Wy
77. Waldo Ct
78. Kenneth Dr
79. Jasper St
80. Lynnfield St
81. Carter Dr
82. Betty Dr
83. Edloft St
84. Twining St
85. Grey Dr
86. Minto Ct
87. Paola Ave
88. Fithian Ave
89. Thelma Ave
90. Butterfly Ln
91. Templeton St
92. Castalia Ave
93. Okell Dr
94. Wadena St
95. Hall St
96. Lowell Ave
97. Stockbridge Ave
98. Lakewood Ave
99. Glenridge Ave
100. Garfield Ave
101. Patio Pl
102. Somerset St
103. Copeland Pl
104. Hyde St
105. Chadwick Cir
106. Chester St
107. Lynnfield Cir
108. Ballard St
109. Martin St
110. Far Pl
111. Budau Ave
112. Delor Dr
113. Haven St
114. Budau Pl
115. Adkins Ave
116. Newark Ave
117. Mallory St
118. Harmony Ln
119. McPherson Pl
120. Belleglade Ave
121. La Calandria Wy
122. N Dittman Ave
123. Abner St
124. Jade St
125. Del Paso Ave
126. Del Paso Ct
127. Abner St
128. Ronda Dr
129. Adkisson Ave
130. Attrdge Ave
131. Middle Rd
132. Farquhar St
133. Seldner St
134. Marney Ave
135. Drucker St
136. Tim Ave
137. Beatie Pl
138. Lafler Rd
139. Bohlig Rd
140. Cavanagh Cir
141. Shaw Pl
142. Tuller Rd
143. Block Pl
144. Levanda Ave
145. Dobbs St
146. Warwick Ave
147. College Sq Dr
148. Vandalia Ave
149. Terrace Ave
150. Alta Vista Dr
151. Glen View Dr
152. Danzig Pl
153. Jurich Pl
154. Julep Pl
155. Avondale Dr

1/2 mile | .5 km

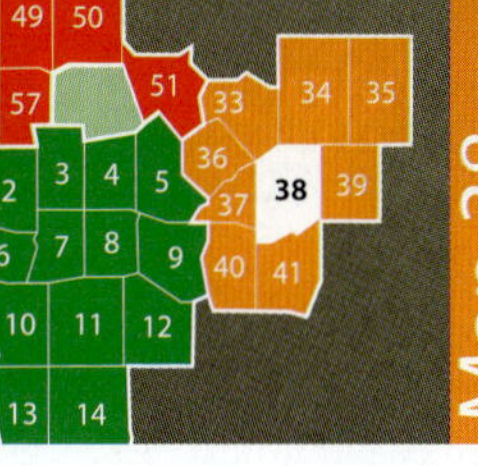

You'll never mistake El Sereno for Beverly Hills, but it has *corazón* (heart, to non-Spanish speakers) and a deep sense of community. Ringed by snow-capped mountains and minutes from downtown and Pasadena, El Sereno is a quiet little gem of a neighborhood. The eclectic mix of small unassuming businesses and family-owned Hispanic restaurants make it a great place to get your car worked on, grab a couple of tamales, and watch the freight trains lumbering through this working-class town.

Banks

- **Bank of America** • 2400 W Commonwealth Ave
- **Washington Mutual** • 1305 Fair Oaks Ave
- **Washington Mutual** • 4887 Huntington Dr N

Car Rental

- **Enterprise** • 1106 Huntington Dr

Car Washes

- **Fast Carwash** • 5509 Alhambra Ave
- **Valley Hand Car Wash** • 4941 Valley Blvd

Gas Stations

- **76** • 475 S Ave 60
- **76** • 5376 S Huntington Dr
- **Arco** • 3201 W Valley Blvd
- **Arco** • 4860 S Huntington Dr
- **Chevron** • 1535 N Eastern Ave
- **Chevron** • 2600 W Valley Blvd
- **Mobil** • 1600 N Eastern Ave
- **Mobil** • 2601 W Main St
- **Shell** • 4590 Huntington Dr

Libraries

- **El Sereno Branch** • 5226 Huntington Dr S • 323-255-9201

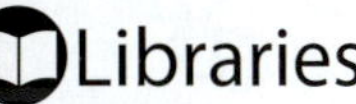

Pharmacies

- **CVS** • 2532 W Valley Blvd • 626-308-1001
- **Sav-On** • Albertsons • 2400 W Commonwealth Ave • 626-576-3900
- **Walgreens** • 2551 W Main St • 626-281-1637

Post Offices

- **US Post Office** • 3316 N Eastern Ave • 800-275-8777
- **US Post Office** • 4875 Huntington Dr • 800-275-8777

Schools

- **Academia Semillas Del Pueblo #2** • 4990 Huntington Dr S
- **Academia Semillas Del Pueblo Charter** • 4736 Huntington Dr S
- **All Saints** • 3420 Portola Ave
- **Almansor Center** • 1955 Fremont Ave
- **Bushnell Way Elementary** • 5507 Bushnell Wy
- **Busy Bees Wonderland** • 1851 W Imperial Hwy
- **California State University-Los Angeles** • 5151 State University Dr
- **Cesar Chavez Elementary** • 5243 Oakland St
- **El Sereno EEC** • 3802 Pueblo Ave
- **El Sereno Elementary** • 3838 Rosemead Ave
- **El Sereno Middle** • 2839 N Eastern Ave
- **Emery Park Elementary** • 2821 W Commonwealth Ave
- **Farmdale Elementary** • 2660 Ruth Swiggett Dr
- **Fremont Elementary** • 2001 S Elm St
- **Holy Family Elementary** • 1301 Rollin St
- **Huntington Dr Elementary** • 4435 Huntington Dr N
- **John C Fremont Elementary** • 3320 Las Palmas Ave
- **Kingston** • 4555 Multnomah St
- **LA County High School for the Arts** • 5151 State University Dr
- **Monterey Hills Elementary** • 1624 Via del Rey
- **Multnomah St Elementary** • 2101 N Indiana St
- **Our Lady of Guadalupe** • 4522 Browne Ave
- **Pacific Christian High** • 625 Coleman Ave
- **Sherman** • 1000 S Fremont Ave
- **Sierra Park Elementary** • 3170 Budau Ave
- **Sierra Vista Elementary** • 4342 Alpha St
- **South Pasadena Middle** • 1600 Oak St
- **South Pasadena Senior High** • 1401 Fremont Ave
- **Woodrow Wilson Senior High** • 4500 Multnomah St

Supermarkets

- **Albertsons** • 2400 W Commonwealth Ave
- **Food 4 Less** • 4910 Huntington Dr S

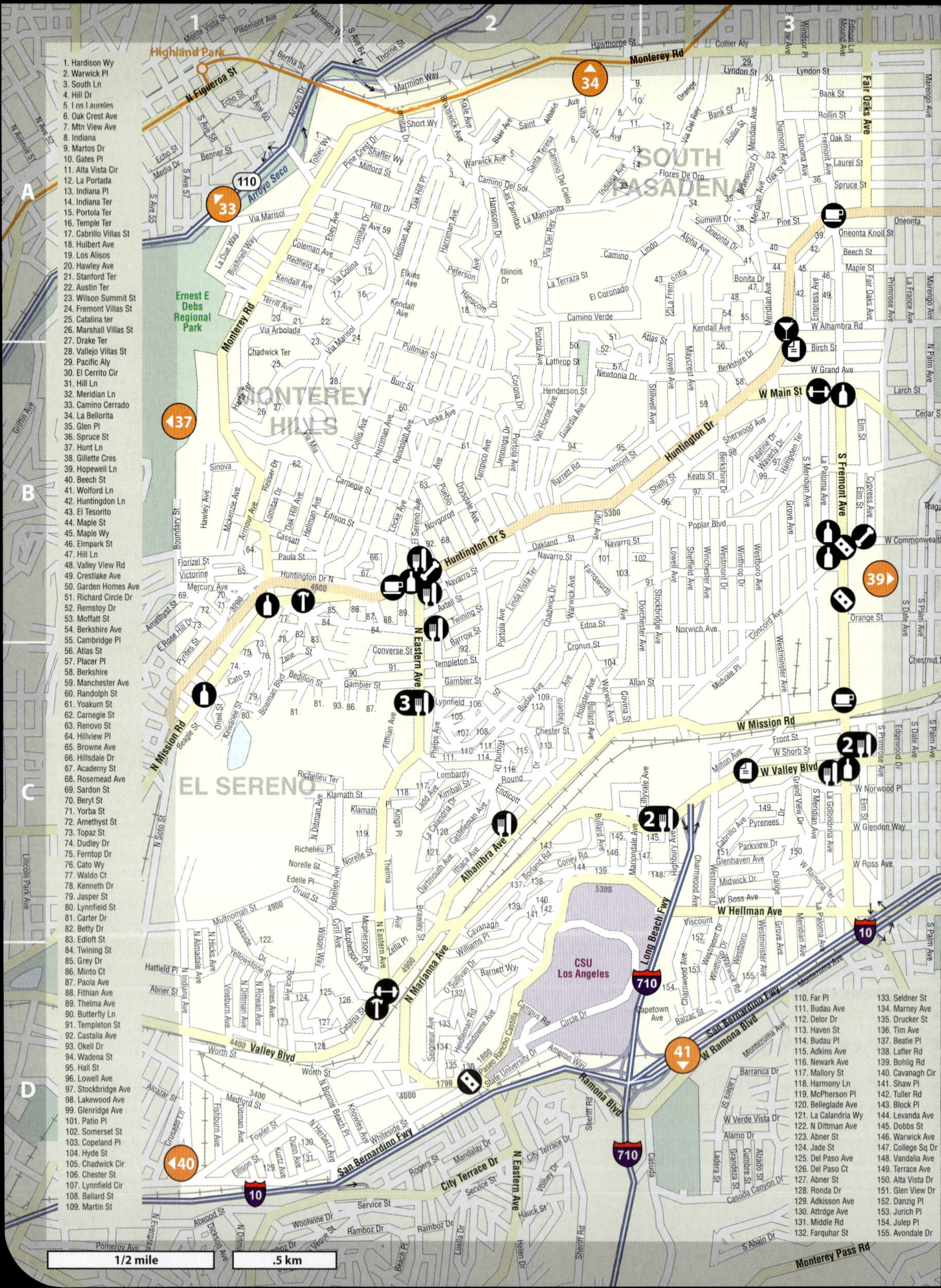

Map 38 • El Sereno

1. Hardison Wy
2. Warwick Pl
3. South Ln
4. Hill Dr
5. Los Laureles
6. Oak Crest Ave
7. Mtn View Ave
8. Indiana
9. Martos Dr
10. Gates Pl
11. Alta Vista Cir
12. La Portada
13. Indiana Pl
14. Indiana Ter
15. Portola Ter
16. Temple Ter
17. Cabrillo Villas St
18. Hulbert Ave
19. Los Alisos
20. Hawley Ave
21. Stanford Ter
22. Austin Ter
23. Wilson Summit St
24. Fremont Villas St
25. Catalina ter
26. Marshall Villas St
27. Drake Ter
28. Vallejo Villas St
29. Pacific Aly
30. El Cerrito Cir
31. Hill Ln
32. Meridian Ln
33. Camino Cerrado
34. La Bellorita
35. Glen Pl
36. Spruce St
37. Hunt Ln
38. Gillette Cres
39. Hopewell Ln
40. Beech St
41. Wolford Ln
42. Huntingdon Ln
43. El Tesorito
44. Maple St
45. Maple Wy
46. Elmpark St
47. Hill Ln
48. Valley View Rd
49. Crestlake Ave
50. Garden Homes Ave
51. Richard Circle Dr
52. Remstoy Dr
53. Moffatt St
54. Berkshire Ave
55. Cambridge Pl
56. Atlas St
57. Placer Pl
58. Berkshire
59. Manchester Ave
60. Randolph St
61. Yoakum St
62. Carnegie St
63. Renovo St
64. Hillview Pl
65. Browne Ave
66. Hillsdale Dr
67. Academy St
68. Rosemead Ave
69. Sardon St
70. Beryl St
71. Yorba St
72. Amethyst St
73. Topaz St
74. Dudley Dr
75. Ferntop Dr
76. Cato Wy
77. Waldo Ct
78. Kenneth Dr
79. Jasper St
80. Lynnfield St
81. Carter Dr
82. Betty Dr
83. Edloft St
84. Twining St
85. Grey Dr
86. Minto Ct
87. Paola Ave
88. Fithian Ave
89. Thelma Ave
90. Butterfly Ln
91. Templeton St
92. Castalia Ave
93. Okell Dr
94. Wadena St
95. Hall St
96. Lowell Ave
97. Stockbridge Ave
98. Lakewood Ave
99. Glenridge Ave
101. Patio Pl
102. Somerset St
103. Copeland Pl
104. Hyde St
105. Chadwick Cir
106. Chester St
107. Lynnfield Cir
108. Ballard St
109. Martin St
110. Far Pl
111. Budau Ave
112. Delor Dr
113. Haven St
114. Budau Pl
115. Adkins Ave
116. Newark Ave
117. Mallory St
118. Harmony Ln
119. McPherson Pl
120. Belleglade Ave
121. La Calandria Wy
122. N Dittman Ave
123. Abner St
124. Jade St
125. Del Paso Ave
126. Del Paso Ct
127. Abner St
128. Ronda Dr
129. Adkisson Ave
130. Attridge Ave
131. Middle Rd
132. Farquhar St
133. Seldner St
134. Marney Ave
135. Drucker St
136. Tim Ave
137. Beatie Pl
138. Lafler Rd
139. Bohlig Rd
140. Cavanagh Cir
141. Shaw Pl
142. Tuller Rd
143. Block Pl
144. Levanda Ave
145. Dobbs St
146. Warwick Ave
147. College Sq Dr
148. Vandalia Ave
149. Terrace Ave
150. Alta Vista Dr
151. Glen View Dr
152. Danzig Pl
153. Jurich Pl
154. Julep Pl
155. Avondale Dr

1/2 mile | .5 km

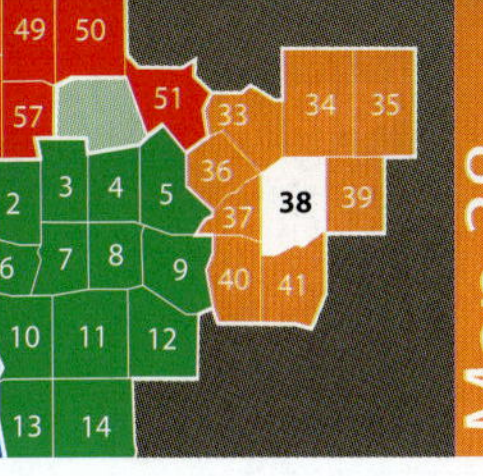

Take a right if you want to eat down-home Chinese; hang a left for authentic Mexican *comidas*. El Sereno is a multicultural grab bag of restaurants, bodegas, and funky hilltop 'hoods with downtown views. Don't miss the El Sereno Christmas and July 4th parades down Huntington Drive and, of course, Cinco de Mayo in the Park.

Coffee

- **Antigua Cultural Coffee House** • 4836 Huntington Dr S
- **Starbucks** • 1190 S Fremont Ave
- **Starbucks** • 1318 Huntington Dr

Copy Shops

- **Image One Graphics** • 200 N Huntington Dr • 626-943-8100
- **Sharp Image Copier** • 2960 W Valley Blvd • 626-458-8000

Gyms

- **Curves** • 2718 W Main St • 626-284-2744
- **Curves** • 4815 Valley Blvd • 323-223-4348

Hardware Stores

- **Newland True Value** • 4938 Huntington Dr S • 323-227-1933
- **Valley Hardware** • 4757 Valley Blvd • 323-222-9670

Liquor Stores

- **7-Eleven Food Stores** • 601 S Fremont Ave
- **International Liquor Food Market** • 16 S Fremont Ave
- **Mickey's Liquor** • 4904 Huntington Dr S
- **Nate's Friendly Liquor** • 4412 Huntington Dr S
- **Pete's Liquor** • 2639 W Valley Blvd
- **Tropic Liquor** • 210 N Huntington Dr

Pet Shops

- **David's Pet Shop** • 4913 Huntington Dr N • 323-226-9007
- **Petsmart** • 2568 W Commonwealth Ave • 626-284-3390

Restaurants

- **Baguette du Jour** • 2436 W Valley Blvd • 626-282-0109
- **Bamboo House** • 2718 W Valley Blvd • 626-458-8888
- **Brazusa** • 4880 Huntington Dr • 323-342-9422
- **El Kora De Nayarit** • 4863 Huntington Dr N • 323-223-3322
- **Gaeta's Deli** • 3107 N Eastern Ave • 323-227-5054
- **Garfono's Pizza** • 5468 Valley Blvd • 323-225-5464
- **Lee Kam Kee** • 2505 W Valley Blvd • 626-282-7720
- **Mi Casita Real Mexican Food** • 5189 Alhambra Ave • 323-225-4800
- **The Original Taco Room** • 5472 Valley Blvd • 323-227-0284
- **Tamale Man** • 3320 N Eastern Ave • 323-221-5954
- **Taqueria Guadalupana** • 3100 N Eastern Blvd • 323-441-1036

Shopping

- **Kohl's Department Store** • 1201 S Fremont Ave • 626-289-7250

Video Rental

- **Blockbuster** • 2581 W Commonwealth Ave • 626-576-4550
- **Neighborhood Video of Alhambra** • 2148 S Fremont Ave • 626-282-6146
- **Videostory** • 1689 N Eastern Ave • 323-262-8850

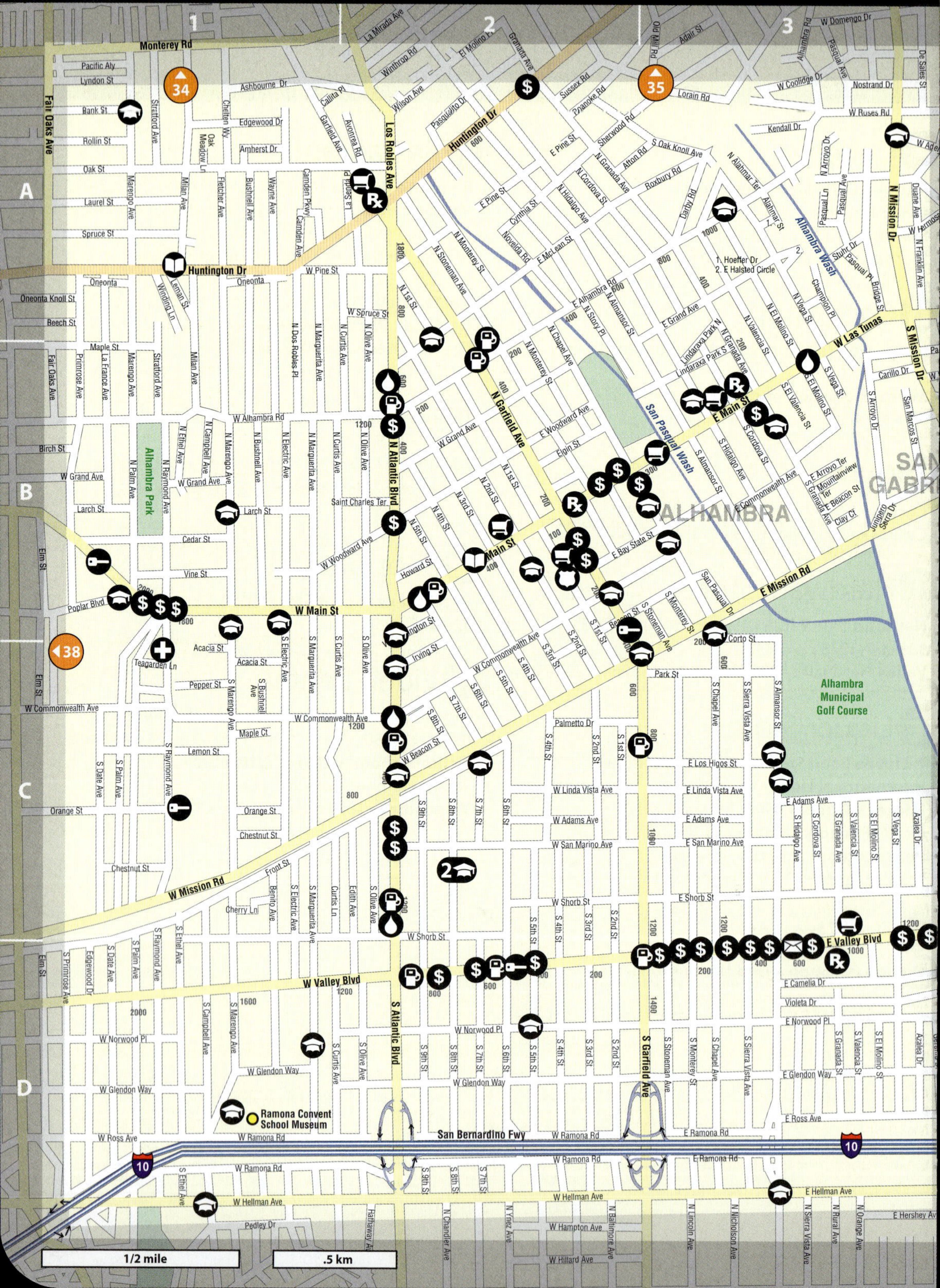

Map 39 • Alhambra

Monterey Rd
Huntington Dr
Los Robles Ave
N Atlantic Blvd
S Atlantic Blvd
N Garfield Ave
S Garfield Ave
W Main St
E Main St
W Las Tunas
W Mission Rd
E Mission Rd
W Valley Blvd
E Valley Blvd
N Mission Dr
S Mission Dr
Fair Oaks Ave
San Bernardino Fwy
10
Alhambra Park
Alhambra Municipal Golf Course
San Pasqual Wash
Alhambra Wash
ALHAMBRA
Ramona Convent School Museum
34
35
38
1. Hoeffer Dr
2. E Halsted Circle
1/2 mile
.5 km

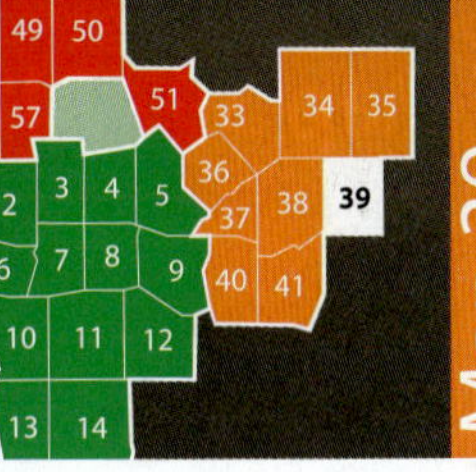

Alhambra bills itself proudly as the "Gateway to the San Gabriel Valley." But this sleepy little town is rapidly coming into its own as a destination of choice, especially for connoisseurs of incredible Chinese food and devotees of traditional Chinese medicine. It's also the new hot real estate market. Its wide, tree-lined streets boast some of the last affordable housing east of downtown. There's easy commuting access to Pasadena, the financial district, and the mountain communities. It's also that rarity in Southern California—a walking town.

Banks

- **Bank of America** • 160 E Main St
- **Bank of America** • 300 N Atlantic Blvd
- **Bank of America** • 444 E Valley Blvd
- **Bank of the West** • 100 S Garfield Ave
- **Bank of the West** • 1833 N Atlantic Blvd
- **Bank of the West** • 331 N Atlantic Blvd
- **Bank of the West** • 855 W Valley Blvd
- **California Bank & Trust** • 230 E Valley Blvd
- **Cathay** • 43 E Valley Blvd
- **Cathay** • 601 N Atlantic Blvd
- **Cathay** • 701 S Atlantic Blvd
- **Citibank** • 1 W Bay State St
- **East West** • 1881 W Main St
- **East West** • 403 W Valley Blvd
- **East West** • 805 Huntington Dr
- **Far East National** • 105 E Valley Blvd
- **Far East National** • 809 S Atlantic Blvd
- **First Bank & Trust** • 711 W Valley Blvd
- **Preferred** • 325 E Valley Blvd
- **United Commercial** • 1211 E Valley Blvd
- **Washington Mutual** • 401 E Valley Blvd
- **Washington Mutual** • 808 E Main St
- **Wells Fargo** • 123 S Chapel Ave
- **Wells Fargo** • 1910 W Main St
- **Wells Fargo** • 345 E Main St
- **Wells Fargo** • 726 E Valley Blvd
- **World Savings & Loan** • 1300 E Valley Blvd

Car Rental

- **Avis** • 330 S Garfield Ave
- **Budget** • 539 W Valley Blvd
- **Enterprise** • 2201 W Main St

Car Washes

- **76** • 707 W Main St
- **Boulevard Hand Car Wash** • 389 S Atlantic Blvd
- **Butch's Beauty Shine** • 1200 E Main St
- **Monterey Park Car Wash** • 521 N Atlantic Blvd

Gas Stations

- **76** • 1201 S Atlantic Blvd
- **76** • 525 N Atlantic Blvd
- **76** • 601 W Valley Blvd
- **76** • 707 W Main St
- **76** • 848 S Garfield Ave
- **Chevron** • 300 S Atlantic Blvd
- **Exxon** • 600 N Garfield Ave
- **Mobil** • 1000 W Valley Blvd
- **Shell** • 1401 S Garfield Ave
- **Valero** • 600 N Garfield Ave

Emergency Rooms

- **Alhambra** • 100 S Raymond Ave

Landmarks

- **Ramona Convent School Museum** • 1701 W Ramona Rd

Libraries

- **Alhambra Library** • 410 W Main St • 626-570-5008
- **San Marino Public Library** • 1890 Huntington Dr • 626-300-0777

Pharmacies

- **CVS** • 816 E Main St • 626-284-0602
- **Ralphs** • 1745 Garfield Ave • 626-799-2926
- **Rite-Aid** • 69 E Main St • 626-300-8049
- **Rite-Aid** • 920 E Valley Blvd • 626-281-8422

Police

- **Alhambra Police Dept** • 211 S 1st St • 626-570-5107

Post Offices

- **US Post Office** • 1603 W Valley Blvd • 800-275-8777

Schools

- **Alhambra Community Day** • 1000 S 8th St
- **Alhambra High** • 101 S 2nd St
- **All Souls** • 29 S Electric Ave
- **Calvin Coolidge Elementary** • 421 N Mission Dr
- **Century High** • 20 S Marengo Ave
- **Children Montessori Center** • 19 N Hidalgo Ave
- **Dr Sun Yatsen Chinese** • 225 S Atlantic Blvd
- **Emmaus Lutheran** • 840 S Almansor St
- **First Baptist Church Alhambra** • 101 S Atlantic Blvd
- **Garfield Elementary** • 110 W McLean St
- **Granada Elementary** • 100 S Granada Ave
- **Granada Park United Methodist** • 1850 W Hellman Ave
- **Independence High** • 1000 S 8th St
- **Kumon Math & Reading Center** • 330 S Garfield Ave
- **Leeway** • 9 N Almansor St
- **Lily S Garden Preschool** • 616 S Chapel Ave
- **Marengo Elementary** • 1400 Marengo Ave
- **Marguerita Elementary** • 1603 S Marguerita Ave
- **Mark Keppel High** • 501 E Hellman Ave
- **Martha Baldwin Elementary** • 900 S Almansor Ave
- **Oneonta Montessori** • 2221 Poplar Blvd
- **Park Elementary** • 301 N Marengo Ave
- **Payke Gymnastics Academy** • 107 S Garfield Ave
- **Ramona Convent Secondary** • 1701 W Ramona Rd
- **Ramona Elementary** • 509 W Norwood Pl
- **St Therese** • 1106 E Alhambra Rd
- **Triumph Education Center** • 29 N Garfield Ave
- **William Northrup Elementary** • 409 S Atlantic Blvd

Supermarkets

- **Max Foods** • 1000 E Valley Blvd
- **Ralphs** • 1745 Garfield Ave
- **Ralphs** • 345 E Main St
- **Smart & Final** • 725 E Main St
- **Super A Foods** • 300 W Main St

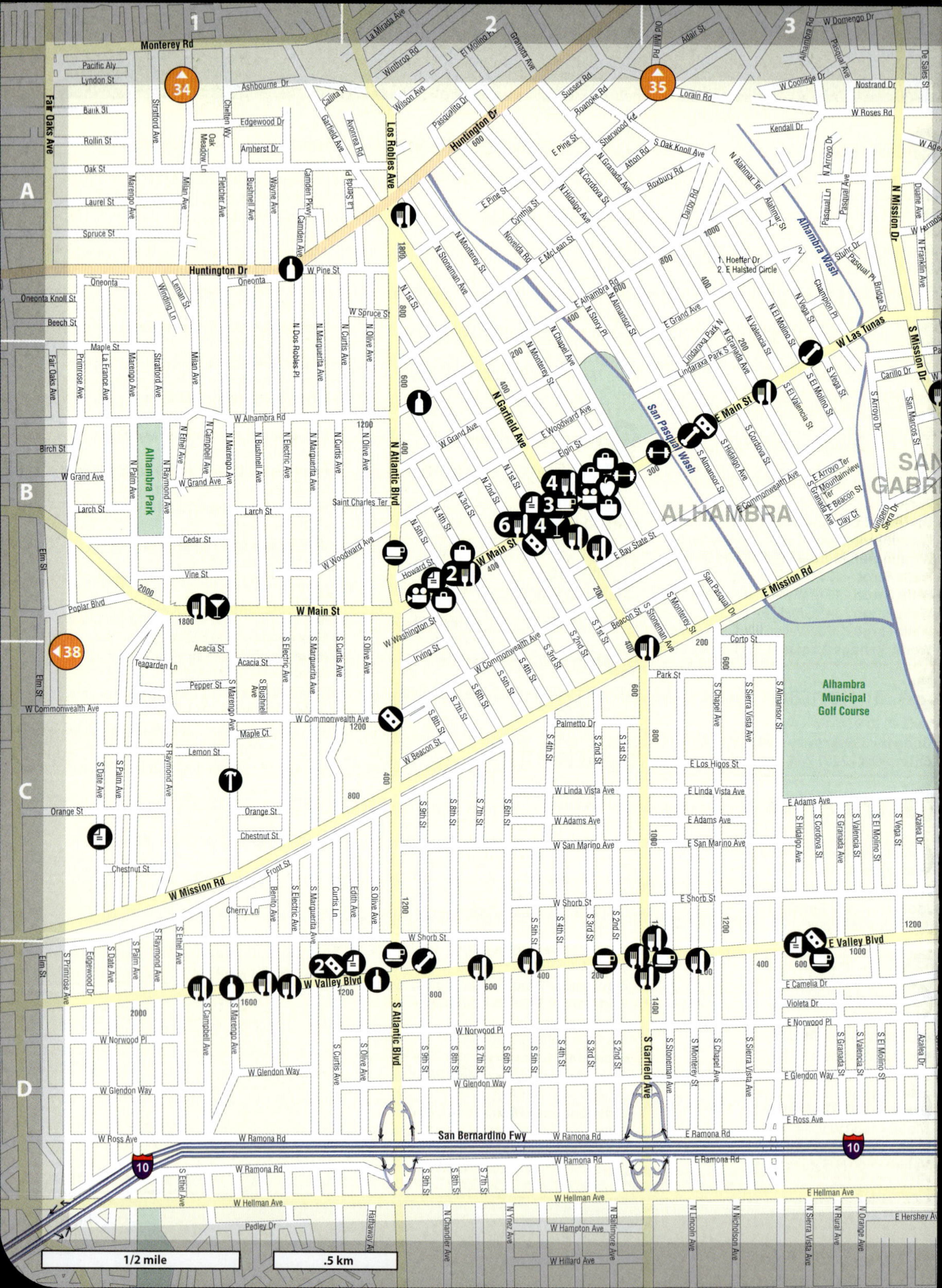

Map 39 • Alhambra

ALHAMBRA

SAN GABR

Alhambra Park

Alhambra Municipal Golf Course

Alhambra Wash

San Pasqual Wash

San Bernardino Fwy

10

34

35

38

1. Hoeffer Dr
2. E Halsted Circle

Monterey Rd · Huntington Dr · Los Robles Ave · N Atlantic Blvd · S Atlantic Blvd · N Garfield Ave · S Garfield Ave · W Main St · E Main St · W Las Tunas · W Mission Rd · E Mission Rd · W Valley Blvd · E Valley Blvd · N Mission Dr · S Mission Dr · Fair Oaks Ave · W Pine St · W Alhambra Rd · E Alhambra Rd · W Grand Ave · E Grand Ave · W Commonwealth Ave · E Commonwealth Ave · W Woodward Ave · E Woodward Ave · W Shorb St · E Shorb St · W Ramona Rd · E Ramona Rd · W Hellman Ave · E Hellman Ave · W Norwood Pl · E Norwood Pl · W Glendon Way · E Glendon Way · W Ross Ave · E Ross Ave · W Adams Ave · E Adams Ave · W Linda Vista Ave · E Linda Vista Ave · W San Marino Ave · E San Marino Ave · E Los Higos St · Palmetto Dr · Park St · Corto St · E Camelia Dr · Violeta Dr · Poplar Blvd · Acacia St · Pepper St · Lemon St · Orange St · Chestnut St · Cedar St · Vine St · Larch St · Birch St · Beech St · Maple St · Oneonta · Spruce St · Laurel St · Oak St · Rollin St · Bank St · Lyndon St · Pacific Aly · Ashbourne Dr · Edgewood Dr · Amherst Dr · Lorain Rd · Nostrand Dr · W Roses Rd · Kendall Dr · W Coolidge Dr · W Domengo Dr · Pedley Dr · W Hampton Ave · W Hillard Ave · E Hershey Av

1/2 mile

.5 km

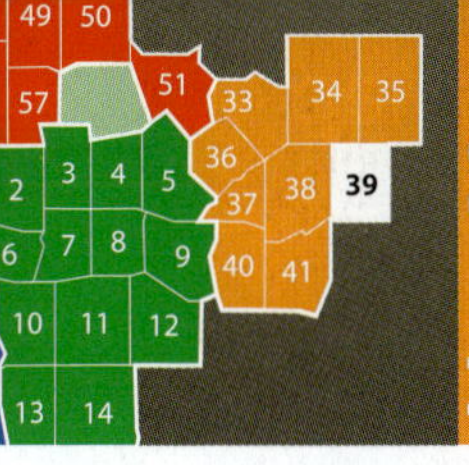

Ozzie and Harriet eat out. Alhambra has plenty to offer: a laid-back, small town Main Street with foot traffic and summertime street music, snow-capped mountains, and great restaurants. Its proximity to predominantly Chinese Monterey Park and Hispanic El Sereno ensures an eclectic smorgasbord of dining options. A must try is Crepe in the Grip – where the French delight becomes portable for your afternoon shopping needs.

Coffee

- **Coffee Bean & Tea Leaf** • 9 E Main St
- **I Browse Coffee** • 11 W Main St
- **Jungle Boba** • 405 W Main St
- **Lollicup** • 228 W Valley Blvd
- **Starbucks** • 1 E Valley Blvd
- **Starbucks** • 101 W Main St
- **Starbucks** • 141 N Atlantic Blvd
- **Starbucks** • 810 E Valley Blvd
- **Tea Station** • 560 W Main St
- **Valley Tea & Coffee** • 1101 W Valley Blvd

Copy Shops

- **Alhambra Blueprint** • 17 N 1st St • 626-289-4455
- **Office Depot** • 1200 W Valley Blvd • 626-943-0900
- **Sal Aguilar Printing** • 718 S Date Ave • 626-570-6746
- **Staples** • 610 E Valley Blvd • 626-281-6900
- **UPS Store** • 560 W Main St • 626-284-8298

Farmers Markets

- **Alhambra (Sun, 8:30 am–1 pm)** • S Monterey St b/w E Main St & E Bay State St

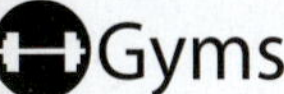

Gyms

- **Curves** • 244 E Main St • 626-282-2999
- **LA Fitness Sports Clubs** • 412 E Main St • 626-299-5980

Hardware Stores

- **Home Depot** • 500 S Marengo Ave • 626-458-9800

Liquor Stores

- **Lee's Liquor** • 1152 W Valley Blvd
- **Marengo Liquor** • 1700 W Valley Blvd
- **Ocean Liquor** • 2005 Huntington Dr
- **Super Store** • 320 W Alhambra Rd

Movie Theaters

- **Edwards Atlantic Cinemas** • 700 W Main St • 626-458-9748
- **Edwards Renaissance Stadium 14** • 1 E Main St • 626-300-8312

Nightlife

- **Azul Bar and Nightclub** • 129 W Main St • 626-282-6320
- **California Brewing Co** • 100 W Main St • 626-943-8430
- **The Granada** • 17 S 1st St • 626-227-2572
- **Havana House** • 133 W Main St • 626-576-0547
- **Jay-dee Café** • 1843 W Main St • 626-281-6887

Pet Shops

- **Atlantic Aquarium** • 1419 S 9th St • 626-576-0028
- **McCormick's Pet Emporium** • 644 E Main St • 626-289-4393
- **Tropical Reef Oasis** • 1117 E Main St, Ste 102 • 626-284-2607

Restaurants

- **Angelo's Italian Restaurant** • 1540 W Valley Blvd • 626-282-0153
- **Charlie's Trio Café** • 47 W Main St • 626-284-4943
- **Crane Sushi** • 17 W Main St • 626-458-0388
- **Crazy Sushi** • 201 E Bay State St • 626-282-3557
- **Crepe in the Grip** • 7 E Valley Blvd • 626-284-1237
- **Cuban Bistro** • 28 W Main St • 626-308-3350
- **The Diner on Main** • 201 W Main St • 626-281-3488
- **El Ranchero Restaurant** • 511 S Garfield Ave • 626-281-3452
- **Fosselman's Ice Cream Parlor** • 1824 W Main St • 626-282-6533
- **Green Papaya Thai** • 1800 W Valley Blvd • 626-282-1291
- **The Hat** • 1 W Valley Blvd • 626-282-0140
- **Hecho en Mexico** • 4976 S Huntington Dr • 323-226-0010
- **Hop Woo** • 1 W Main St • 626-289-7938
- **Indo Kitchen** • 5 N 4th St • 626-282-1676
- **La Parilla Mexicana** • 2938 W Valley Blvd • 626-289-2412
- **Little London Fish & Chips** • 19 S Garfield Ave • 626-282-4477
- **Mahan Indian Restaurant** • 2 S Garfield Ave • 626-458-6299
- **Mission 261** • 261 S Mission Dr • 626-588-1666
- **MPV Seafood** • 1412 S Garfield Ave • 626-289-3018
- **Noodle Planet** • 700 W Valley Blvd • 626-282-8855
- **Perfectly Sweet** • 126 W Main St • 626-282-9400
- **Pho 79** • 29 S Garfield Ave • 626-289-0239
- **Phoenix Food Boutique** • 220 E Valley Blvd • 626-299-1918
- **Rick's Drive In & Out** • 132 W Main St • 626-576-8519
- **Sam Woo Barbeque** • 514 W Valley Blvd • 626-281-0038
- **Señor Fish** • 115 W Main St • 626-299-7550
- **Thai Purple** • 27 N Garfield Ave • 626-300-9083
- **Twohey's** • 1224 N Atlantic Blvd • 626-284-7387
- **Wahib's Middle East** • 910 E Main St • 626-576-1048
- **Yazmin Malaysian Restaurant** • 27 E Main St • 626-308-2036

Shopping

- **Lieberg's Hallmark Shop** • 101 E Main St • 626-282-8454
- **Mervyn's** • 150 E Main St • 626-300-0888
- **Mi Casita Rustica** • 135 W Main St • 626-576-8143
- **Penny Lane** • 110 W Main St • 626-457-5787
- **Ross Dress for Less** • 201 E Main St • 626-281-8453

Video Rental

- **Blockbuster** • 1334 W Valley Blvd • 626-289-3829
- **China Town Video (Chinese)** • 1227 W Valley Blvd • 626-458-6246
- **Hollywood Video** • 701 E Main St • 626-308-3427
- **Penny Lane** • 110 W Main St • 626-457-5787
- **Video 101** • 1100 W Commonwealth Ave • 626-308-3883

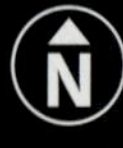

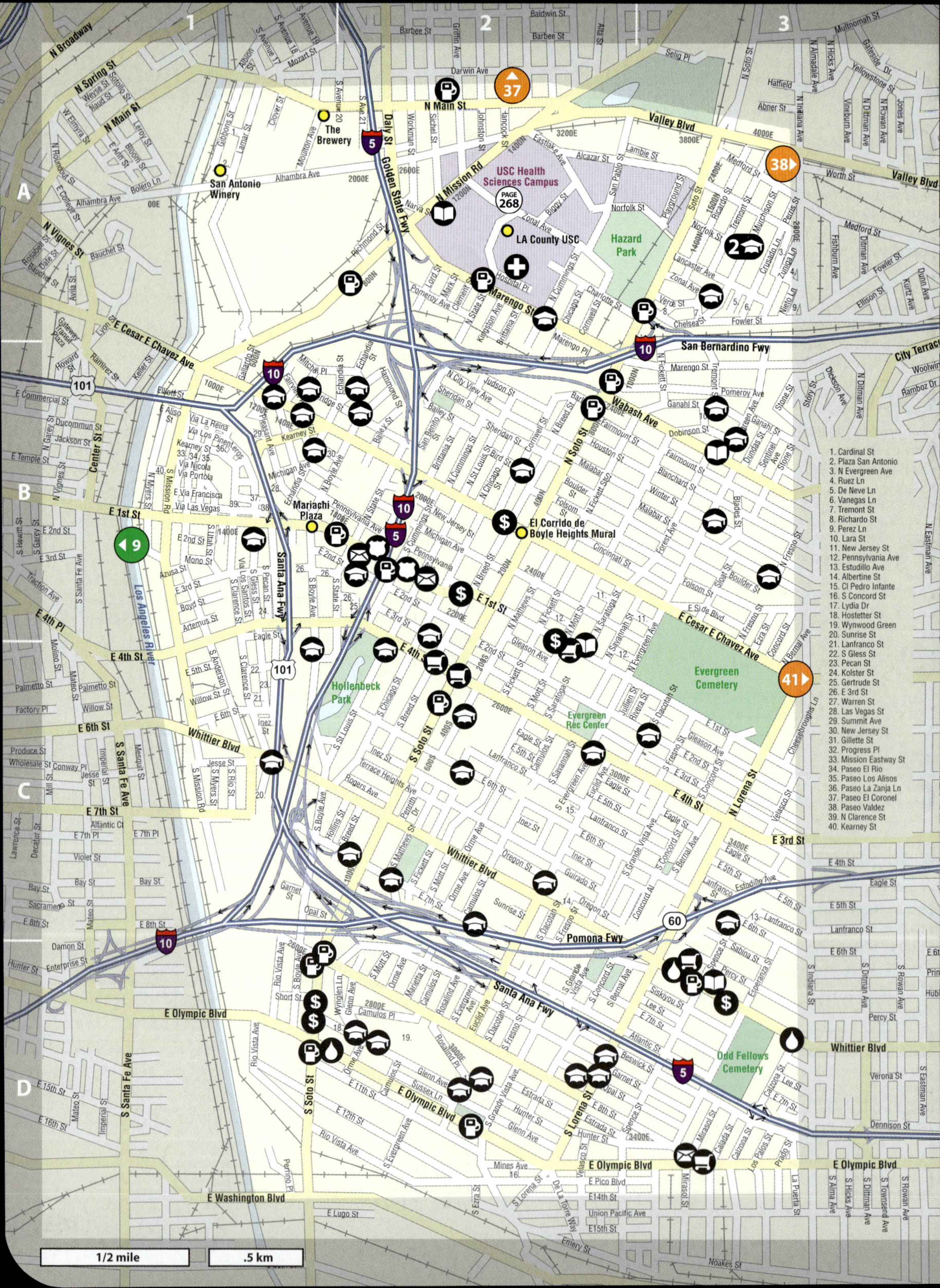

N
1
2
3
A
B
C
D
The Brewery
San Antonio Winery
USC Health Sciences Campus
PAGE 268
LA County USC
Hazard Park
Mariachi Plaza
El Corrido de Boyle Heights Mural
Hollenbeck Park
Evergreen Rec Center
Evergreen Cemetery
Odd Fellows Cemetery
Los Angeles River
Golden State Fwy
San Bernardino Fwy
Santa Ana Fwy
Pomona Fwy
Valley Blvd
E Cesar E Chavez Ave
E 1st St
E 4th St
Whittier Blvd
E Olympic Blvd
E Washington Blvd
N Mission Rd
N Main St
S Soto St
N Soto St
S Lorena St
E 3rd St
Wabash Ave
37
38
41
9
1. Cardinal St
2. Plaza San Antonio
3. N Evergreen Ave
4. Ruez Ln
5. De Neve Ln
6. Vanegas Ln
7. Tremont St
8. Richardo St
9. Perez Ln
10. Lara St
11. New Jersey St
12. Pennsylvania Ave
13. Estudillo Ave
14. Albertine St
15. Cl Pedro Infante
16. S Concord St
17. Lydia Dr
18. Hostetter St
19. Wynwood Green
20. Sunrise St
21. Lanfranco St
22. S Gless St
23. Pecan St
24. Kolster St
25. Gertrude St
26. E 3rd St
27. Warren St
28. Las Vegas St
29. Summit Ave
30. New Jersey St
31. Gillette St
32. Progress Pl
33. Mission Eastway St
34. Paseo El Rio
35. Paseo Los Alisos
36. Paseo La Zanja Ln
37. Paseo El Coronel
38. Paseo Valdez
39. N Clarence St
40. Kearney St
1/2 mile
.5 km

As one of the city's last untapped housing resources, Boyle Heights has recently enjoyed a real estate boom. Situated just east of the LA River, the area is still predominantly Hispanic and home to perhaps the most superb Mexican food in all of Los Angeles. Mariachi Plaza hosts local mariachi bands looking to book their next quinceanera while entertaining the passersby. The area is also known for a number of community grassroots efforts, including some impressive mural commissions near Cesar E Chavez Ave and Soto Street.

Banks

- **Bank of America** • 1308 S Soto St
- **Bank of America** • 2305 E Cesar E Chavez Ave
- **Bank of America** • 3475 Whittier Blvd
- **US** • 2708 E 1st St
- **Washington Mutual** • 1350 S Soto St
- **Washington Mutual** • 2301 E 1st St

Car Washes

- **Bob's Hand Car Wash** • 3629 Whittier Blvd
- **The Sunshine Car Wash** • 2740 E Olympic Blvd
- **Tio Car Wash** • 3442 Whittier Blvd

Gas Stations

- **76** • 1171 S Soto St
- **76** • 1800 E 4th St
- **76** • 1848 Marengo St
- **Arco** • 3401 Whittier Blvd
- **Arco** • 401 S Soto St
- **Chevron** • 1101 N Mission Rd
- **Exxon** • 2740 E Olympic Blvd
- **Independent** • 1203 N Soto St
- **Independent** • 2829 N Main St
- **Independent** • 918 N Soto St
- **Mobil** • 1010 N Soto St
- **Mobil** • 1166 S Soto St
- **Shell** • 1410 S Soto St
- **Shell** • 2005 E 4th St
- **Texaco** • 3154 E Olympic Blvd

Emergency Rooms

- **LA County USC Medical Center** • 1200 N State St

Landmarks

- **The Brewery** • 620 Moulton Ave
- **El Corrido de Boyle Heights Mural** • 2336 E Cesar E Chavez Ave
- **LA County USC Medical Center** • 1200 N State St
- **Mariachi Plaza** • Boyle Ave & 1st St
- **San Antonio Winery** • 737 Lamar St

Libraries

- **Benjamin Franklin Branch** • 2200 E 1st St • 323-263-6901
- **Malabar Branch** • 2801 Wabash Ave • 323-263-1497
- **Nursing Library** • 1237 N Mission Rd • 323-226-6521
- **Robert Louis Stevenson Branch** • 803 Spence St • 323-268-4710

Police

- **Los Angeles Police Dept** • 1936 E 1st St • 323-266-5964

Post Offices

- **US Post Office** • 2016 E 1st St • 800-275-8777
- **US Post Office** • 3641 E 8th St • 800-275-8777

Schools

- **1st St Elementary** • 2820 E 1st St
- **2nd St Elementary** • 1942 E 2nd St
- **Assumption** • 3016 Winter St
- **Breed Elementary** • 2226 E 3rd St
- **Bridge EEC** • 648 Echandia St
- **Bridge Elementary** • 605 N Boyle Ave
- **Carmen Lomas Garza Primary Center** • 2750 Hostetter St
- **Christopher Dena Elementary** • 1314 Dacotah St
- **Dacotah EEC** • 3142 Lydia Dr
- **Dena New Primary Center** • 2705 Hostetter St
- **Dolores Mission Elementary** • 170 S Gless St
- **East Los Angeles College** • 1301 E Cesar E Chavez Ave
- **East Los Angeles Occupational Center** • 2100 Marengo St
- **Euclid Ave Elementary** • 806 Euclid Ave
- **Evergreen EEC** • 1027 N Evergreen Ave
- **Evergreen Elementary** • 2730 Ganahl St
- **Hollenbeck Middle** • 2510 E 6th St
- **Lane Elementary** • 1500 Cesar E Chavez Ave
- **Light and Life** • 207 S Dacotah St
- **Lorena St Elementary** • 1015 S Lorena St
- **Los Angeles City Baptist** • 709 Spence St
- **Malabar St Elementary** • 3200 Malabar St
- **Murchison EEC** • 1537 Murchison St
- **Murchison Elementary** • 1501 Murchison St
- **Oscar Dela Hoya Amino Charter High** • 1114 S Lorena St
- **Our Lady of the Rosary of Talp** • 411 S Evergreen Ave
- **Puente Charter** • 501 S Boyle Ave
- **Resurrection** • 3360 E Opal St
- **Roosevelt Community Adult** • 456 S Mathews St
- **San Antonio de Padua** • 1500 Bridge St
- **Santa Isabel Elementary** • 2424 Whittier Blvd
- **Santa Teresita** • 2646 Zonal Ave
- **Sheridan St Elementary** • 416 Cornwell St
- **Soto St EEC** • 2616 E 7th St
- **Soto St Elementary** • 1020 S Soto St
- **St Mary** • 416 S St Louis St
- **Sunrise Elementary** • 2821 E 7th St
- **Theodore Roosevelt Senior High** • 456 S Mathews St
- **Utah Elementary** • 255 Gabriel Garcia Marquez St
- **White Memorial Adventist** • 1605 New Jersey St

Supermarkets

- **Food 4 Less** • 2750 E 1st St
- **Food 4 Less** • 3654 E Olympic Blvd
- **Smart & Final** • 2308 E 4th St
- **Super A Foods** • 425 S Soto St
- **Vallarta Supermarket** • 3425 Whittier Blvd

Map 40 • Boyle Heights

1. Cardinal St
2. Plaza San Antonio
3. N Evergreen Ave
4. Ruez Ln
5. De Neve Ln
6. Vanegas Ln
7. Tremont St
8. Richardo St
9. Perez Ln
10. Lara St
11. New Jersey St
12. Pennsylvania Ave
13. Estudillo Ave
14. Albertine St
15. Cl Pedro Infante
16. S Concord St
17. Lydia Dr
18. Hostetter St
19. Wynwood Green
20. Sunrise St
21. Lanfranco St
22. S Gless St
23. Pecan St
24. Kolster St
25. Gertrude St
26. E 3rd St
27. Warren St
28. Las Vegas St
29. Summit Ave
30. New Jersey St
31. Gillette St
32. Progress Pl
33. Mission Eastway St
34. Paseo El Rio
35. Paseo Los Alisos
36. Paseo La Zanja Ln
37. Paseo El Coronel
38. Paseo Valdez
39. N Clarence St
40. Kearney St

1/2 mile | .5 km

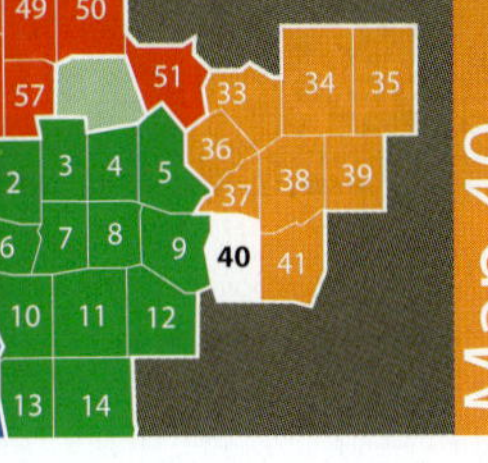

Those on a sojourn for the world's most perfect taco need look no farther than Boyle Heights. With fleet of traveling taco trucks, there's ample opportunity to sample the local specialty even if you're just passing through town. The popular chain King Taco serves arguably some of the best, fast Mexican food in the city. Put the fanfare to the test yourself by sampling the *dulce* and *horchata* at the local bakeries, or make a night of it at La Serenata de Garibaldi across from Mariachi Plaza or La Parilla on Cesar Chavez Ave.

Coffee

- **Bradford Coffee** • 1607 Perrino Pl

Copy Shops

- **Davis Blue Print Co** • 3205 N Main St • 323-225-4703

Gyms

- **Curves** • 2421 Whittier Blvd • 323-263-1311

Hardware Stores

- **Moe's Hardware Store** • 3044 Wabash Ave • 323-268-0824

Liquor Stores

- **Amigos Liquor** • 3124 E 4th St
- **B&G Liquors** • 1529 E 1st St
- **Beverage Center** • 6033 Whittier Blvd
- **Brooklyn Liquor** • 2101 E Cesar E Chavez Ave
- **JT Ramirez Market** • 736 S Soto St
- **Major Liquor** • 2335 E 1st St
- **Marengo Ranch Market & Liquor** • 2901 Marengo St
- **Ole Dad Davis Liquor** • 1462 S Grande Vista Ave
- **Regency Liquor** • 1260 S Soto St
- **S&M Liquor Store** • 3000 N Main St
- **Xochitl** • 3200 E 1st St

Nightlife

- **Barbara's at the Brewery** • Brewery Art Complex • 620 Moulton Ave • 323-221-9204

Pet Shops

- **Elias Pet Shop** • 2500 E Cesar E Chavez Ave • 323-263-3138
- **Happy Pets** • 2011 E 1st St • 323-265-3614
- **VIP Pet Shop** • 305 N Soto St • 323-266-1166

Restaurants

- **Barbara's at the Brewery** • Brewery Art Complex • 620 Moulton Ave • 323-221-9204
- **Ciro's** • 705 N Evergreen St • 323-267-8637
- **El Tepeyac** • 812 N Evergreen Ave • 323-267-8668
- **King Taco** • 2400 E Cesar E Chavez Ave • 323-264-3940
- **La Parrilla** • 2126 E Cesar E Chavez Ave • 323-262-3434
- **La Serenata de Garibaldi** • 1842 E 1st St • 323-265-2887

Shopping

- **Skeletons in the Closet** • 1100 N Mission Rd • 323-343-0760

Video Rental

- **Joyce's Videos** • 2830 Wabash Ave • 323-261-5385
- **S&S Video (Spanish)** • 3358 E Olympic Blvd • 323-780-3981
- **Video Century** • 919 S Soto St • 323-262-5003

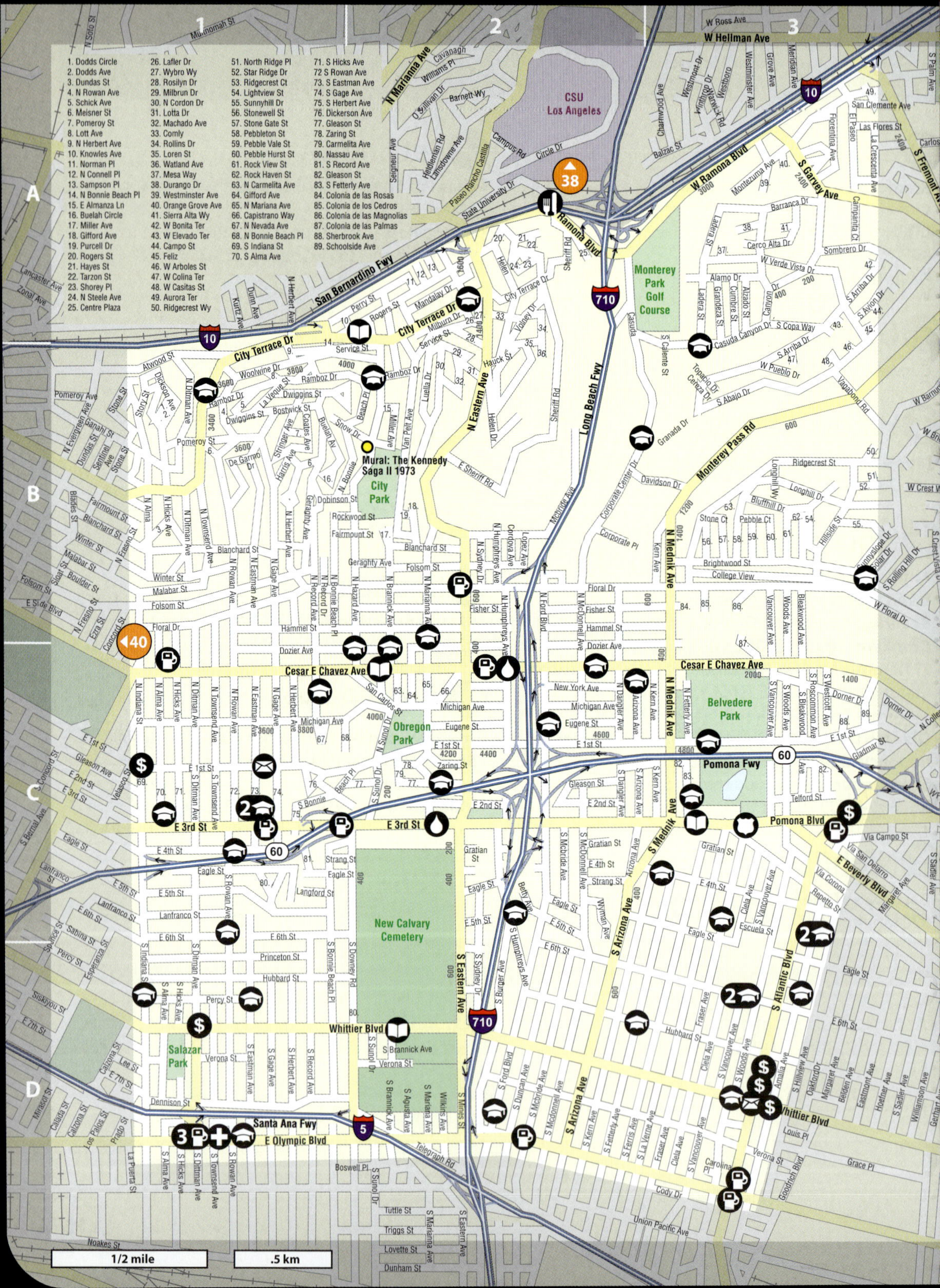

1. Dodds Circle
2. Dodds Ave
3. Dundas St
4. N Rowan Ave
5. Schick Ave
6. Meisner St
7. Pomeroy St
8. Lott Ave
9. N Herbert Ave
10. Knowles Ave
11. Norman Pl
12. N Connell Pl
13. Sampson Pl
14. N Bonnie Beach Pl
15. E Almanza Ln
16. Buelah Circle
17. Miller Ave
18. Gifford Ave
19. Purcell Dr
20. Rogers St
21. Hayes St
22. Tarzon St
23. Shorey Pl
24. N Steele Ave
25. Centre Plaza
26. Lafler Dr
27. Wybro Wy
28. Rosilyn Dr
29. Milbrun Dr
30. N Cordon Dr
31. Lotta Dr
32. Machado Ave
33. Comly
34. Rollins Dr
35. Loren St
36. Watland Ave
37. Mesa Way
38. Durango Dr
39. Westminster Ave
40. Orange Grove Ave
41. Sierra Alta Wy
42. W Bonita Ter
43. W Elevado Ter
44. Campo St
45. Feliz
46. W Arboles St
47. W Colina Ter
48. W Casitas St
49. Aurora Ter
50. Ridgecrest Wy
51. North Ridge Pl
52. Star Ridge Dr
53. Ridgecrest Ct
54. Lightview St
55. Sunnyhill Dr
56. Stonewell St
57. Stone Gate St
58. Pebbleton St
59. Pebble Vale St
60. Pebble Hurst St
61. Rock View St
62. Rock Haven St
63. N Carmelita Ave
64. Gifford Ave
65. N Mariana Ave
66. Capistrano Way
67. N Nevada Ave
68. N Bonnie Beach Pl
69. S Indiana St
70. S Alma Ave
71. S Hicks Ave
72. S Rowan Ave
73. S Eastman Ave
74. S Gage Ave
75. S Herbert Ave
76. Dickerson Ave
77. Gleason St
78. Zaring St
79. Carmelita Ave
80. Nassau Ave
81. S Record Ave
82. Gleason St
83. S Fetterly Ave
84. Colonia de las Rosas
85. Colonia de los Cedros
86. Colonia de las Magnolias
87. Colonia de las Palmas
88. Sherbrook Ave
89. Schoolside Ave

1/2 mile | .5 km

Back when Los Angeles was still called "El Pueblo de Nuestra Senora la Reina de los Angeles de Porciuncula," East LA was the center of Mexican culture. Today is no different, and a tour of the area reveals an homage to the motherland. Home-style restaurants, spectacular murals, and unique shops abound with *el espiritu de la raza*.

Banks

- **Bank of America** • 941 S Atlantic Blvd
- **Cathay** • 250 S Atlantic Blvd
- **Citibank** • 3479 E 1st St
- **East West** • 855 S Atlantic Blvd
- **Washington Mutual** • 5301 Whittier Blvd
- **Wells Fargo** • 3800 Whittier Blvd

Car Washes

- **Ricky's Hand Car Wash** • 4247 E 3rd St
- **Shell** • 4357 E Caesar E Chavez Ave

Gas Stations

- **76** • 3860 E 3rd St
- **76** • 3915 E Olympic Blvd
- **76** • 5200 E Olympic Blvd
- **Arco** • 3541 E Cesar E Chavez Ave
- **Arco** • 3834 E 3rd St
- **Arco** • 3949 E Dennison Ave
- **Arco** • 4625 E Olympic Blvd
- **Arco** • 705 N Eastern Ave
- **Chevron** • 250 S Atlantic Blvd
- **Exxon** • 5050 E Olympic Blvd
- **Mobil** • 301 S Atlantic Blvd
- **Shell** • 4357 E Cesar E Chavez Ave
- **Valero** • 1060 S Ditman Ave

Emergency Rooms

- **Los Angeles Community** • 4081 E Olympic Blvd

Landmarks

- **Mural: The Kennedy Saga II 1973 (City Terrace Park)** • 1126 N Hazard Ave

Libraries

- **Anthony Quinn Public Library** • 3965 E Cesar E Chavez Ave • 323-264-7715
- **City Terrace** • 4025 City Terrace Dr • 323-261-0295
- **East Los Angeles** • 4837 E 3rd St • 323-264-0155
- **El Camino Real** • 4264 Whittier Blvd • 323-269-8102

Police

- **Los Angeles County Sheriff's Dept** • 5019 E 3rd St • 323-264-4151

Post Offices

- **US Post Office** • 3729 E 1st St • 800-275-8777
- **US Post Office** • 975 S Atlantic Blvd • 800-275-8777

Schools

- **4th St Elementary** • 420 Amalia Ave
- **4th St New Primary Center** • 469 Amalia Ave
- **Amanecer Primary Center** • 832 S Eastman Ave
- **Belvedere EEC** • 221 S Eastman Ave
- **Belvedere Elementary** • 3724 E 1st St
- **Belvedere Middle** • 312 N Record Ave
- **Brightwood Elementary** • 1701 Brightwood St
- **Brooklyn Ave Elementary** • 4620 Cesar E Chavez Ave
- **Brooklyn EEC** • 329 N Arizona Ave
- **Central City Value** • 5156 Whittier Blvd
- **City Terrace Elementary** • 4350 City Terrace Dr
- **Cornerstone Learning Academy** • 2421 W Jefferson Blvd
- **David Wark Griffith Middle** • 4765 E 4th St
- **East Los Angeles Day** • 1260 S Monterey Pass Rd
- **Eastman Ave Elementary** • 4112 E Olympic Blvd
- **Ford Blvd Elementary** • 1112 S Ford Blvd
- **Garfield Community Adult** • 5101 E 6th St
- **Hammel EEC** • 452 N Marianna Ave
- **Hammel St Elementary** • 438 N Brannick Ave
- **Harrison St Elementary** • 3529 City Terrace Dr
- **Humphreys Ave Elementary** • 500 S Humphreys Ave
- **James A Garfield High** • 5101 E 6th St
- **Marianna Ave Elementary** • 4215 Gleason St
- **Monterey Continuation High** • 466 Fraser Ave
- **Monterey Highlands Elementary** • 400 Casuda Cyn Dr
- **Morris K Hamasaki Elementary** • 4865 E 1st St
- **Our Lady of Guadalupe** • 436 N Hazard Ave
- **Our Lady of Lourdes** • 315 S Eastman Ave
- **Perez Special Education Center** • 4540 Michigan Ave
- **Perez State Preschool** • 4540 Michigan Ave
- **Ramona High** • 231 S Alma Ave
- **Robert F Kennedy Elementary** • 4010 E Ramboz Dr
- **Robert Louis Stevenson Middle** • 725 S Indiana St
- **Rowan Ave Elementary** • 600 S Rowan Ave
- **Soledad Enrichment Action** • 3763 E 4th St
- **St Alphonsus** • 552 Amalia Ave

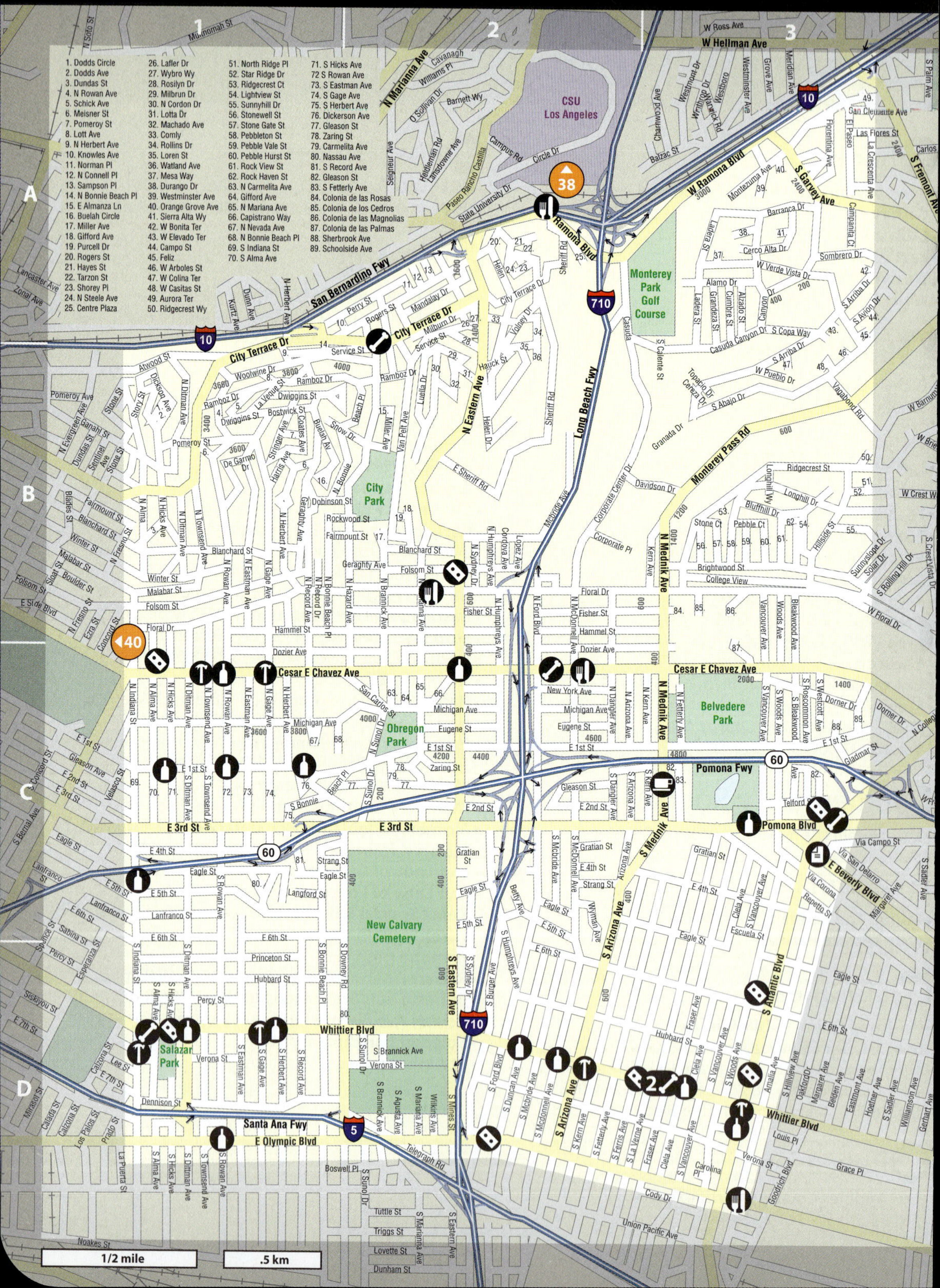

Map 41 • City Terrace / East LA

1. Dodds Circle
2. Dodds Ave
3. Dundas St
4. N Rowan Ave
5. Schick Ave
6. Meisner St
7. Pomeroy St
8. Lott Ave
9. N Herbert Ave
10. Knowles Ave
11. Norman Pl
12. N Connell Pl
13. Sampson Pl
14. N Bonnie Beach Pl
15. E Almanza Ln
16. Buelah Circle
17. Miller Ave
18. Gifford Ave
19. Purcell Dr
20. Rogers St
21. Hayes St
22. Tarzon St
23. Shorey Pl
24. N Steele Ave
25. Centre Plaza
26. Lafler Dr
27. Wybro Wy
28. Rosilyn Dr
29. Milbrun Dr
30. N Cordon Dr
31. Lotta Dr
32. Machado Ave
33. Comly
34. Rollins Dr
35. Loren St
36. Watland Ave
37. Mesa Way
38. Durango Dr
39. Westminster Ave
40. Orange Grove Ave
41. Sierra Alta Wy
42. W Bonita Ter
43. W Elevado Ter
44. Campo St
45. Feliz
46. W Arboles St
47. W Colina Ter
48. W Casitas St
49. Aurora Ter
50. Ridgecrest Wy
51. North Ridge Pl
52. Star Ridge Dr
53. Ridgecrest Ct
54. Lightview St
55. Sunnyhill Dr
56. Stonewell St
57. Stone Gate St
58. Pebbleton St
59. Pebble Vale St
60. Pebble Hurst St
61. Rock View St
62. Rock Haven St
63. N Carmelita Ave
64. Gifford Ave
65. N Mariana Ave
66. Capistrano Way
67. N Nevada Ave
68. N Bonnie Beach Pl
69. S Indiana St
70. S Alma Ave
71. S Hicks Ave
72 S Rowan Ave
73. S Eastman Ave
74. S Gage Ave
75. S Herbert Ave
76. Dickerson Ave
77. Gleason St
78. Zaring St
79. Carmelita Ave
80. Nassau Ave
81. S Record Ave
82. Gleason St
83. S Fetterly Ave
84. Colonia de las Rosas
85. Colonia de los Cedros
86. Colonia de las Magnolias
87. Colonia de las Palmas
88. Sherbrook Ave
89. Schoolside Ave

CSU Los Angeles

Monterey Park Golf Course

City Park

Obregon Park

Belvedere Park

New Calvary Cemetery

Salazar Park

San Bernardino Fwy

Long Beach Fwy

Pomona Fwy

Santa Ana Fwy

City Terrace Dr

Cesar E Chavez Ave

E 3rd St

Whittier Blvd

E Olympic Blvd

W Ramona Blvd

Monterey Pass Rd

Pomona Blvd

N Eastern Ave

S Atlantic Blvd

38

40

1/2 mile

.5 km

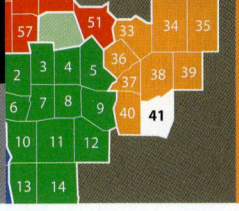

East LA's dynamic culture may finally be getting the credit it deserves. With LA Mayor Antonio Villaraigosa as one of City Terrace's native sons, and artists and authors such as Sesshu Foster emerging on the scene, the flavor of East LA is finding its way to widespread recognition. If you often argue with friends about the best "authentic" Mexican food in LA, play the trump card with two of East LA's best—try the rich mole sauce at Tamayo and savory tamales at Tamales Lilianas.

Coffee

- **Coffee Bean & Tea Leaf** • 209 S Mednik Ave

Copy Shops

- **UPS Store** • 5280 E Beverly Blvd • 323-869-6959

Hardware Stores

- **Brooklyn Hardware** • 3734 E Cesar E Chavez Ave • 323-264-6260
- **Eddie Dillen True Value** • 4615 Whittier Blvd • 626-810-2645
- **Indiana Home Supply** • 944 S Indiana St • 323-265-2008
- **Marce's** • 1012 S Atlantic Blvd • 323-269-8375
- **Santiago Noemi** • 3948 Whittier Blvd • 323-263-1044
- **Villanueva's Hardware** • 3516 E Cesar E Chavez Ave • 323-266-0650

Liquor Stores

- **Andy's Liquors** • 4312 E Cesar E Chavez Ave
- **Atlantic Liquors** • 1010 S Atlantic Blvd
- **Ayutla Liquor** • 3548 E 1st St
- **Eddie's Drive-In Liquor Store** • 5024 Whittier Blvd
- **Green Mill Liquor** • 3812 Whittier Blvd
- **John's Liquor** • 405 S Indiana St
- **Lim Fung Liquor** • 3563 E Cesar E Chavez Ave
- **Paco's Liquor** • 5048 E 3rd St
- **Pueblo Liquor** • 4600 Whittier Blvd
- **Safety Liquor** • 4635 Whittier Blvd
- **Sam's Liquor** • 3984 Whittier Blvd
- **Victoria's Liquor** • 3882 E 1st St
- **Winn's Liquor Store** • 4048 E Olympic Blvd
- **Zozaya Market & Liquor** • 116 N Rowan Ave

Pet Shops

- **Bob's Tropical Fish** • 234 S Atlantic Blvd • 323-261-6675
- **Inez Pet Shop** • 3825 Whittier Blvd • 323-266-2320
- **Jesse's Pet Shop** • 3875 Whittier Blvd • 323-262-7947
- **Lucky Pets** • 4001 1/4 City Terrace Dr • 323-262-3112
- **Pet Shop Casa Galleros** • 4516 E Cesar E Chavez Ave • 323-780-5811

Restaurants

- **Granny's Donuts** • 1681 N Eastern Ave • 323-266-6918
- **Juanito's** • 4214 E Floral Dr • 323-268-2365
- **Tamales Lilianas** • 4629 E Cesar E Chavez Ave • 323-780-7265
- **Tamayo** • 5300 E Olympic Blvd • 323-260-4700

Video Rental

- **20-20 Video** • 4975 Whittier Blvd • 323-266-0202
- **5050 Video Music & Games** • 4528 Whittier Blvd • 323-263-5050
- **Blockbuster** • 3431 E Cesar E Chavez Ave • 323-307-0786
- **JC Video Superstore** • 5161 Pomona Blvd • 323-266-1055
- **Nancy's Video** • 715 1/2 S Atlantic Blvd • 323-268-5849
- **Video Camacho (Spanish)** • 710 N Eastern Ave, Ste C • 323-268-5152
- **Videoland** • 3857 Whittier Blvd • 323-266-2553

N

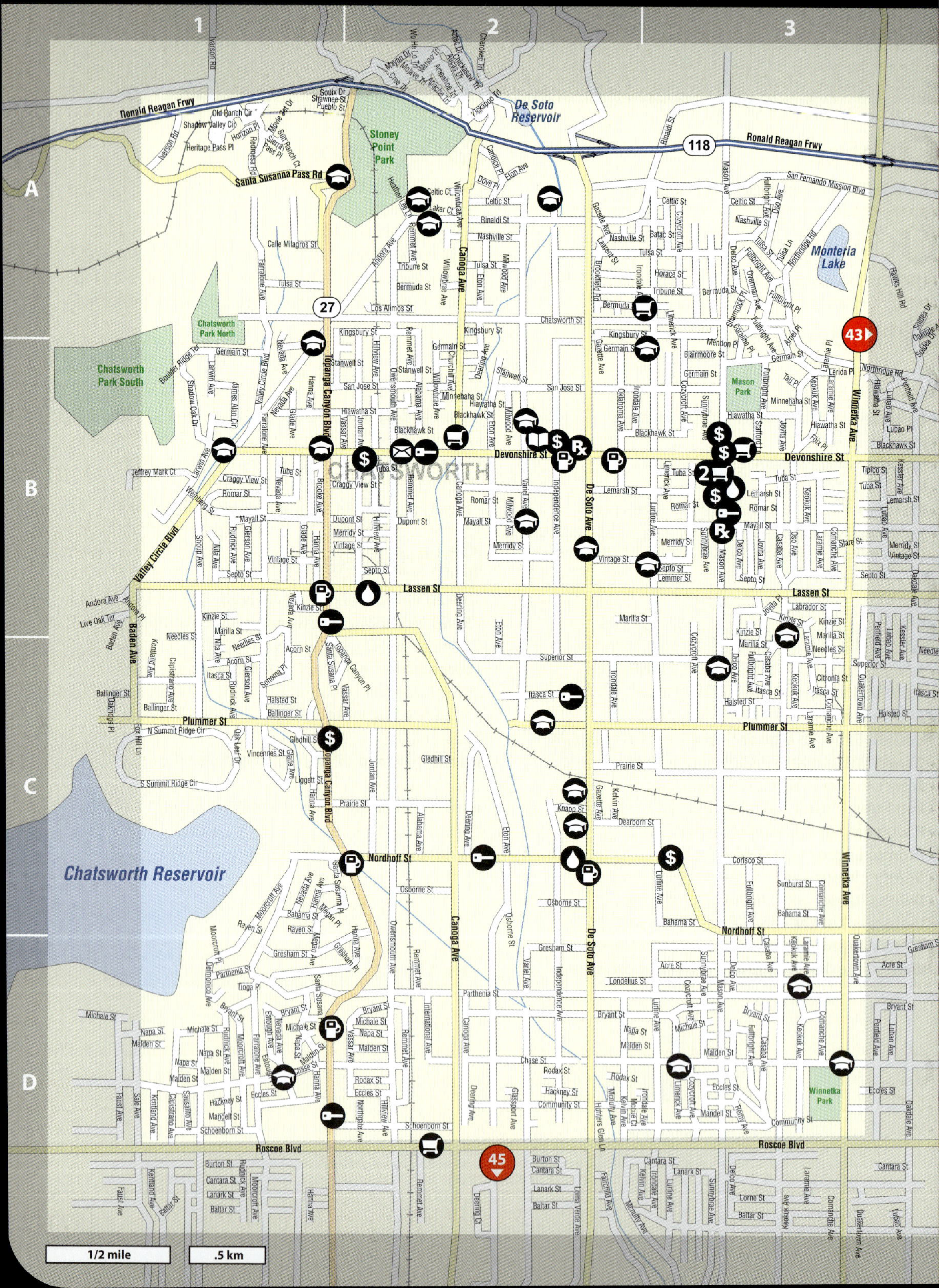

1
2
3
A
B
C
D
Ronald Reagan Frwy
118
27
De Soto Reservoir
Stoney Point Park
Chatsworth Park North
Chatsworth Park South
Monteria Lake
Mason Park
Winnetka Park
Chatsworth Reservoir
CHATSWORTH
Topanga Canyon Blvd
Canoga Ave
De Soto Ave
Winnetka Ave
Devonshire St
Lassen St
Plummer St
Nordhoff St
Roscoe Blvd
Valley Circle Blvd
Santa Susanna Pass Rd
San Fernando Mission Blvd
43
45
1/2 mile
.5 km

Remote Chatsworth is an eclectic community. Horse country, it has been the site of countless TV and movie westerns over the years, and Roy Rogers and Dale Evans are among the folks who have called the place home. More recent residents are a bit different—Charles Manson and his "family" set up camp at the Spahn Ranch and Marilyn Manson (no relation, of course) is rumored to reside there today.

Banks

- **Bank of America** • 20699 Nordhoff St
- **Bank of America** • 21001 Devonshire St
- **Citibank** • 20520 Devonshire St
- **City National** • 9400 Topanga Cyn Blvd
- **Union** • 21821 Devonshire St
- **Washington Mutual** • 10370 Mason Ave
- **Wells Fargo** • 10250 Mason Ave

Car Rental

- **Enterprise** • 21310 Nordhoff St
- **Enterprise** • 8364 Topanga Cyn Blvd
- **Enterprise** • 9800 Topanga Cyn Blvd
- **Hertz** • 10170 Mason Ave
- **Hertz** • 20944 Itasca St
- **Hertz** • 21510 Devonshire St

Car Washes

- **Chatsworth Car Wash** • 10241 Mason Ave
- **M&S Professional Detail** • 20914 Nordhoff St
- **Stoney Point Car Wash** • 21930 Lassen St

Gas Stations

- **76** • 13455 Osborne St
- **76** • 20841 Devonshire St
- **Arco** • 9110 Topanga Cyn Blvd
- **Chevron** • 20904 Devonshire St
- **Mobil** • 9906 Topanga Cyn Blvd
- **Shell** • 20850 Devonshire St
- **Valero** • 9061 De Soto Ave

Libraries

- **Chatsworth Branch** • 21052 Devonshire St • 818-341-4276

Pharmacies

- **Rite-Aid** • 10120 Mason Ave • 818-349-7213
- **Walgreens** • 20901 Devonshire St • 818-341-4339

Post Offices

- **US Post Office** • 21606 Devonshire St • 800-275-8777

Schools

- **Aggeler Opportunity High** • 21050 Plummer St
- **Canyon Vista Children's Learning** • 10616 Andora Ave
- **Chatsworth Hills Academy** • 21523 Rinaldi St
- **Chatsworth Park Elementary** • 22005 Devonshire St
- **Chatsworth Senior High** • 10027 Lurline Ave
- **CHIME Charter Middle** • 22280 Devonshire St
- **East Valley Academy** • 20206 Londelius St
- **Ernest Lawrence Middle** • 10100 Variel Ave
- **Germain St Elementary** • 20730 Germain St
- **Great Beginnings** • 10324 Variel Ave
- **James Jordan Middle** • 20920 Knapp St
- **Leap High** • 20920 Knapp St
- **Limerick Ave Elementary** • 8530 Limerick Ave
- **Meraj Academy** • 11070 Old Santa Susana Pass Rd
- **Nevada Ave Elementary** • 22120 Chase St
- **Our Redeemer Lutheran** • 8520 Winnetka Ave
- **Sierra Canyon** • 11052 Independence Ave
- **St John Eudes Elementary** • 9925 Mason Ave
- **St Paul's Christian Academy** • 21621 Heather Lee Lane
- **Stoney Point Continuation** • 10010 De Soto Ave
- **Superior St Elementary** • 9756 Oso Ave

Supermarkets

- **Ralphs** • 21431 Devonshire St
- **Smart & Final** • 10340 Mason Ave
- **Trader Joe's** • 10330 Mason Ave
- **Vallarta Supermarket** • 21555 Roscoe Blvd
- **Vons** • 20440 Devonshire St

N

1
2
3
A
B
C
D
Ronald Reagan Frwy
118
27
Stoney Point Park
De Soto Reservoir
Chatsworth Park North
Chatsworth Park South
Mason Park
Monteria Lake
Chatsworth Reservoir
Winnetka Park
CHATSWORTH
Santa Susanna Pass Rd
Topanga Canyon Blvd
Canoga Ave
De Soto Ave
Winnetka Ave
Devonshire St
Lassen St
Plummer St
Nordhoff St
Roscoe Blvd
Valley Circle Blvd
San Fernando Mission Blvd
Chatsworth St
43
45
1/2 mile
.5 km

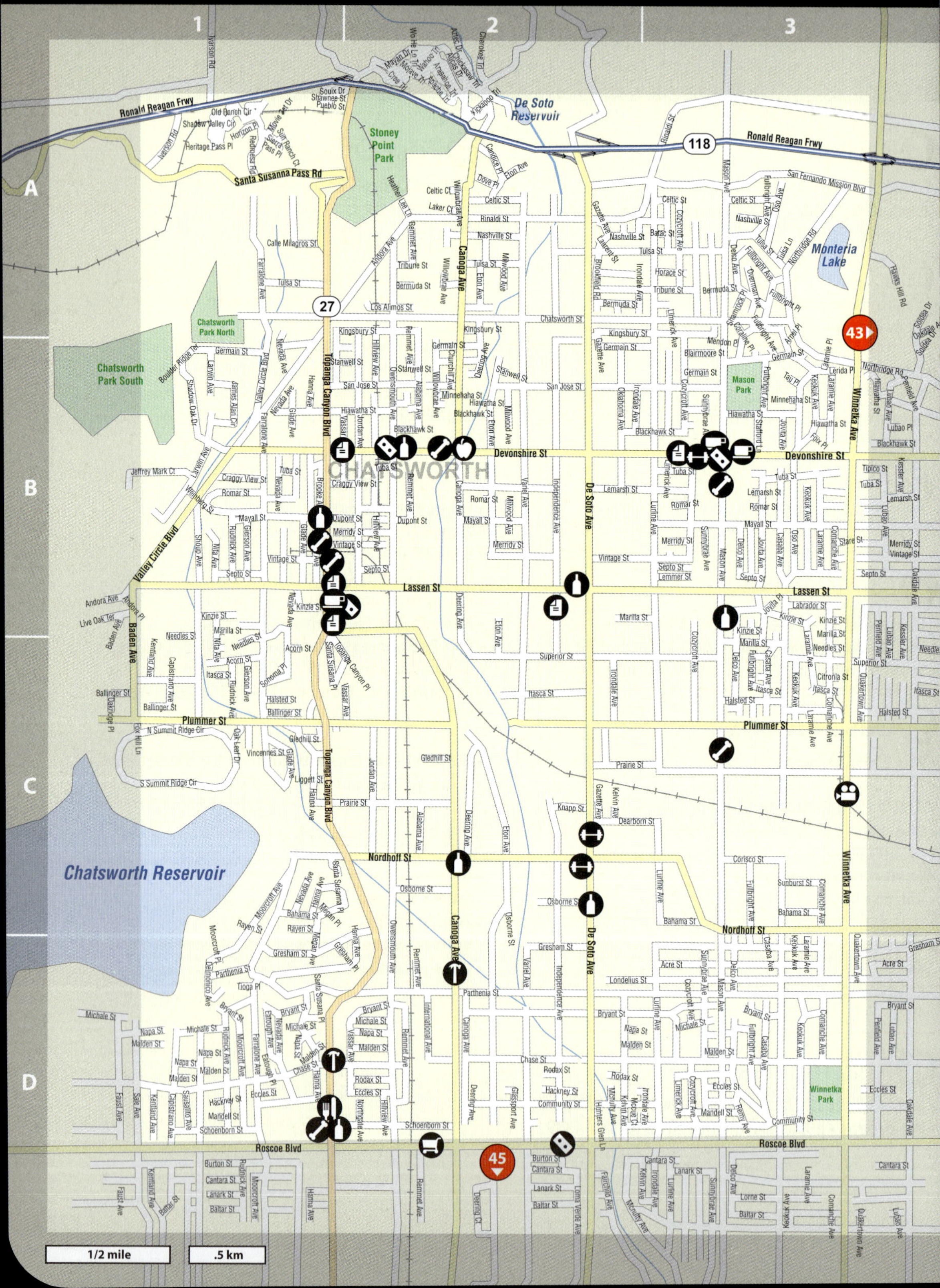

Sundries / Entertainment

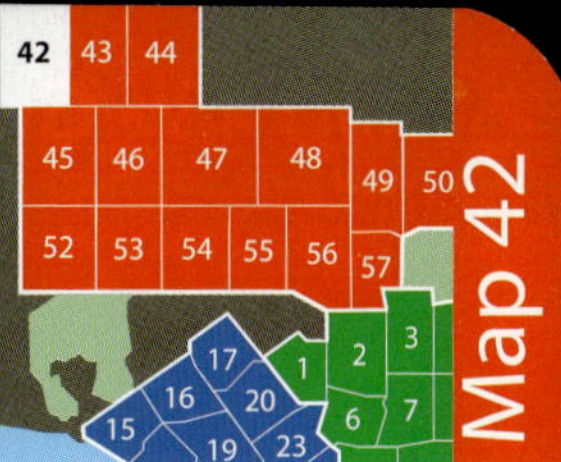

To casual observers, Chatsworth may appear to be interchangeable with any other of LA's Valley suburbs. But sleepy little Chatsworth has one dubious distinction—it's the epicenter of the porn industry, home to countless production companies, video distributors, and the industry bible, *Adult Video News*. Or so we've been told. Aside from adult merchandise, shoppers can choose from an array of stores scattered about, but no central malls to speak of.

Coffee

- **Starbucks** • Vons • 20440 Devonshire St
- **Starbucks** • 20516 Devonshire St
- **Starbucks** • 9935 Topanga Cyn Blvd

Copy Shops

- **All Valley Printing** • 9721 Canoga Ave • 818-709-8734
- **Dot Copy & Print** • 21901 Devonshire St • 818-882-2232
- **Postnet** • 9909 Topanga Cyn Blvd • 818-349-1099
- **Unlimited Printing** • 9829 Independence Ave • 818-882-1212
- **UPS Store** • 20555 Devonshire St • 818-349-2584
- **UPS Store** • 9800 Topanga Cyn Blvd • 818-709-1858

Farmers Markets

- **Chatsworth (Sat, 8 am-1 pm)** • Devonshire St & Canoga Ave

Gyms

- **Bally Total Fitness** • 9143 De Soto Ave • 818-882-5912
- **Curves** • 20521 Devonshire St • 818-341-2643
- **Powerhouse Gym** • 20914 Nordhoff St • 818-775-0300

Hardware Stores

- **Lowe's** • 8383 Topanga Cyn Blvd • 818-610-1960
- **Plumbing City True Value** • 8751 Canoga Ave • 818-341-1622

Liquor Stores

- **AMS Liquor** • 20930 Lassen St
- **Chatsworth Liquor** • 21615 Devonshire St
- **City Market** • 21404 Nordhoff St
- **De Soto Plaza Liquor** • 8935 De Soto Ave
- **Dorose Liquor** • 9857 Mason Ave
- **Liquid Wines & Spirits (wine only)** • 10100 Topanga Cyn Blvd
- **Tally-Ho Liquor** • 8356 Topanga Cyn Blvd

Movie Theaters

- **Pacific Winnetka 21 Theaters** • 9201 Winnetka Ave • 818-501-5121

Pet Shops

- **Exotic Life Fish & Reptiles** • 9919 Topanga Cyn Blvd • 818-341-1007
- **Pacific Aquatic West** • 21413 Devonshire St • 818-886-6083
- **Quality Reptiles (Reptiles only)** • 9410 De Soto Ave • 818-678-0364
- **Red Barn Feed and Saddlery** • 8393 Topanga Cyn Blvd • 818-887-7388
- **Reptile Depot** • 10120 Topanga Cyn Blvd • 818-576-1508
- **Valley Pet** • 10218 Mason Ave • 818-349-5520

Restaurants

- **Los Chilenos** • 8408 Topanga Cyn Blvd • 818-716-4169

Video Rental

- **Blockbuster** • 20516 Devonshire St • 818-727-7166
- **DVD Access** • 21700 Devonshire St • 818-885-7199
- **Video Maxx** • 9820 Topanga Cyn Blvd, Ste A • 818-885-8002

N

1
2
3
A
B
C
D
Porter Ranch Park
Ronald Reagan Frwy
118
Rinaldi St
GRANADA HILLS
Monteria Lake
Winnetka Ave
Tampa Ave
Reseda Blvd
Zelzah Ave
Chatsworth St
Devonshire St
Northridge Park
Plummer St
Northridge Fashion Center
PAGE 307
California State University Northridge
Nordhoff St
Vanalden Park
NORTHRIDGE
Winnetka Park
Roscoe Blvd
42
44
45
46
1/2 mile
.5 km

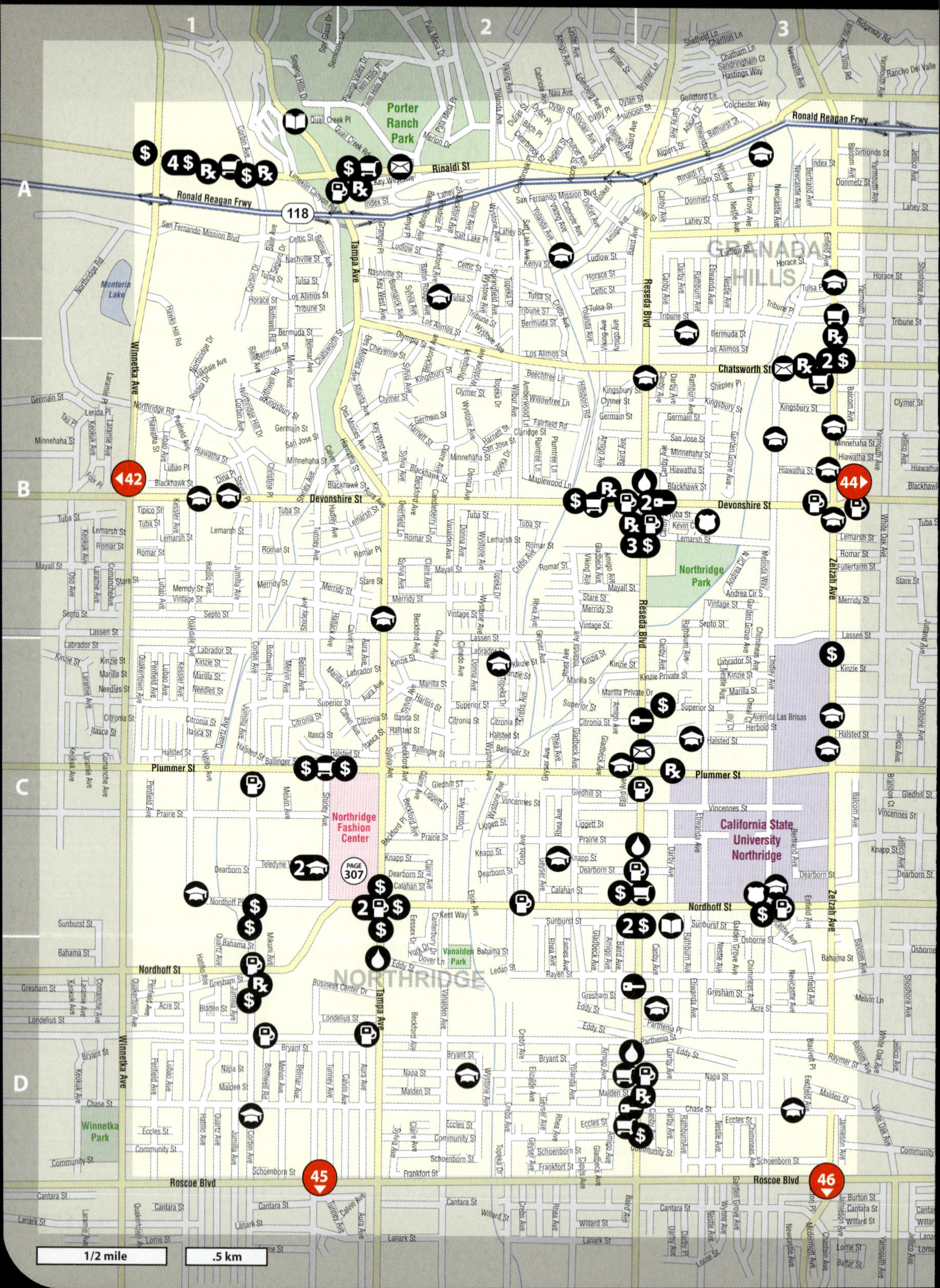

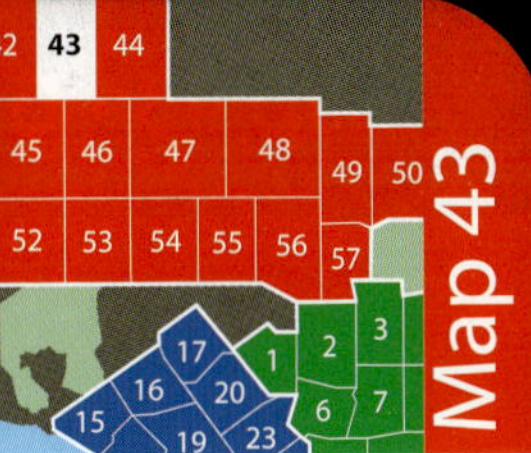

Granada Hills used to be home to wide open spaces and the citrus groves for which Southern California was once known, but it's now in the hands of the developers. Strip malls and chain restaurants are opening up right and left. Northridge is a bustling suburb, thanks to Cal State Northridge's 30,000+ students and the Northridge Fashion Center mall.

Banks

- **Banco Popular** • 19821 Rinaldi St
- **Bank of America** • 10200 Reseda Blvd
- **Bank of America** • 19240 Nordhoff St
- **Bank of America** • 19789 Rinaldi St
- **Bank of the West** • 19953 Rinaldi St
- **California Center** • 10147 Reseda Blvd
- **California National** • 19450 Plummer St
- **Cathay** • 9045 Corbin Ave
- **Citibank** • 19350 Rinaldi Ave
- **Citibank** • 9051 Tampa Ave
- **Fremont Investment & Loan** • 10240 Reseda Blvd
- **Union** • 19781 Rinaldi St
- **Union** • 19921 Rinaldi St
- **Union** • 9110 Tampa Ave
- **Washington Mutual** • 17900 Chatsworth St
- **Washington Mutual** • 18601 Devonshire St
- **Washington Mutual** • 19500 Plummer St
- **Washington Mutual** • 19837 Rinaldi St
- **Washington Mutual** • 9055 Reseda Blvd
- **Washington Mutual** • 9111 Corbin Ave
- **Wells Fargo** • 18010 Chatsworth St
- **Wells Fargo** • 18111 Nordhoff St
- **Wells Fargo** • 8812 Corbin Ave
- **Wells Fargo** • 9119 Reseda Blvd
- **Wells Fargo** • 9851 Zelzah Ave
- **Wilshire State** • 8401 Reseda Blvd
- **World Savings & Loan** • 9036 Reseda Blvd

Car Rental

- **Advantage Rent-a-Car** • 8834 Reseda Blvd
- **Avis** • 9545 Reseda Blvd
- **Dollar** • 18473 Devonshire St
- **Enterprise** • 8438 Reseda Blvd
- **Thrifty** • 18501 Devonshire St

Car Washes

- **Buena Vista Self-Service Car Wash** • 8639 Reseda Blvd
- **Classic Car Wash** • 18470 Devonshire St
- **Cruisers Car Wash** • 8870 Tampa Ave
- **Northridge Car Wash** • 9240 Reseda Blvd

Gas Stations

- **76** • 11240 Tampa Ave
- **76** • 18050 Nordhoff St
- **76** • 19301 Nordhoff St
- **76** • 9455 Reseda Blvd
- **Alliance** • 8900 Corbin Ave
- **Arco** • 18473 Devonshire St
- **Arco** • 18855 Nordhoff St
- **Arco** • 9454 Corbin Ave
- **Chevron** • 19260 Nordhoff St
- **Mobil** • 17836 Devonshire St
- **Mobil** • 18501 Devonshire St
- **Mobil** • 19655 Parthenia St
- **Northridge Car Wash** • 9240 Reseda Blvd
- **Shell** • 17915 Devonshire St
- **Shell** • 19301 Parthenia St
- **Thrifty** • 8606 Reseda Blvd

Libraries

- **Northridge Branch** • 9051 Darby Ave • 818-886-3640
- **Porter Ranch Branch** • 11371 Tampa Ave • 818-360-5706

Pharmacies

- **CVS** • 10181 Reseda Blvd • 818-993-4125
- **CVS** • Albertsons • 8530 Reseda Blvd • 818-341-7104
- **Longs Drugs** • 18020 Chatsworth St • 818-831-4152
- **Longs Drugs** • 19783 Rinaldi St • 818-368-6279
- **Ralphs** • 19781 Rinaldi St • 818-832-3156
- **Rite-Aid** • 10811 Zelzah Ave • 818-360-8411
- **Rite-Aid** • 18444 Plummer St • 818-349-6267
- **Target** • 8840 Corbin Ave • 818-739-0043
- **Walgreens** • 18515 Devonshire St • 818-363-1067
- **Walmart** • 19821 Rinaldi St • 818-832-0643

Police

- **CSU Northridge Police Dept** • 18111 Nordhoff St • 818-677-2111
- **Los Angeles Police Dept** • 10250 Etiwanda Ave • 818-832-0633

Post Offices

- **US Post Office** • 18039 Chatsworth St • 800-275-8777
- **US Post Office** • 19300 Rinaldi St • 800-275-8777
- **US Post Office** • 9534 Reseda Blvd • 800-275-8777

Schools

- **Alfred Bernhard Nobel Middle** • 9950 Tampa Ave
- **Apple Tree Education** • 18510 Plummer St
- **Beckford Ave Elementary** • 19130 Tulsa St
- **Calahan St Elementary** • 18722 Knapp St
- **California State University Northridge** • 18111 Nordhoff St
- **Chaminade College Preparatory Middle** • 19800 Devonshire St
- **Child & Family Studies Center** • 18330 Halsted St
- **Cornerstone Christian Academy** • 11031 Yolanda Ave
- **Darby Ave Elementary** • 10818 Darby Ave
- **Egremont** • 19850 Devonshire St
- **First Lutheran Elementary** • 18355 Roscoe Blvd
- **First Presbyterian** • 10400 Zelzah St
- **Granada Hills Baptist Elementary** • 10949 Zelzah Ave
- **Granada Hills Charter High** • 10535 Zelzah Ave
- **Kidsville USA** • 8464 Corbin Ave
- **Kirk Douglas High** • 10500 Lindley Ave
- **Napa St Elementary** • 19010 Napa St
- **New Heights Preparatory** • 8756 Canby Ave
- **New Life Pre-School Kindergarten** • 10650 Reseda Blvd
- **Northpoint** • 9650 Zelzah Ave
- **Northridge Academy Senior High** • 9601 Zelzah Ave
- **Northridge Middle** • 17960 Chase St
- **Our Lady of Lourdes** • 18437 Superior St
- **Sierra Canyon School** • 19809 Nordhoff Pl
- **Temple Ahavat Shalom Early Chi** • 18200 Rinaldi Pl
- **Topeka Dr Elementary** • 9815 Topeka Dr

Supermarkets

- **Albertsons** • 18555 Devonshire St
- **CVS** • 8530 Reseda Blvd
- **Gelson's Supermarket** • 19500 Plummer St
- **Ralphs** • 10823 Zelzah Ave
- **Ralphs** • 18010 Chatsworth St
- **Ralphs** • 19781 Rinaldi St
- **Vallarta Supermarket** • 8453 Reseda Blvd
- **Vons** • 9119 Reseda Blvd
- **Whole Foods Market** • 19340 Rinaldi St

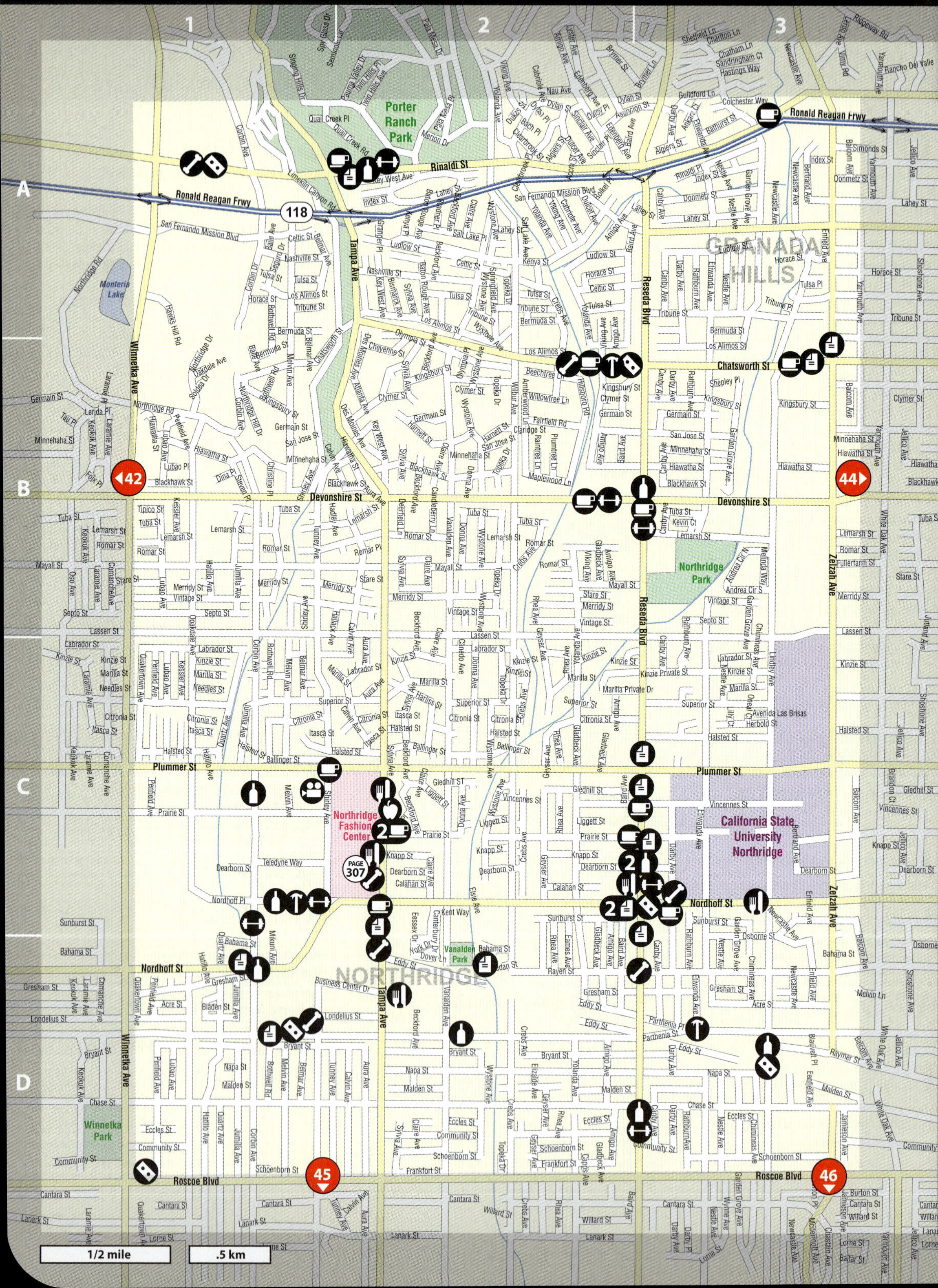

1 2 3

A B C D

Ronald Reagan Frwy

118

Rinaldi St

Porter Ranch Park

Granada Hills

Monteria Lake

Chatsworth St

Devonshire St

Northridge Park

Plummer St

Northridge Fashion Center

PAGE 307

California State University Northridge

Nordhoff St

Vanalden Park

Northridge

Winnetka Park

Roscoe Blvd

Winnetka Ave

Tampa Ave

Reseda Blvd

Zelzah Ave

42 44 45 46

1/2 mile .5 km

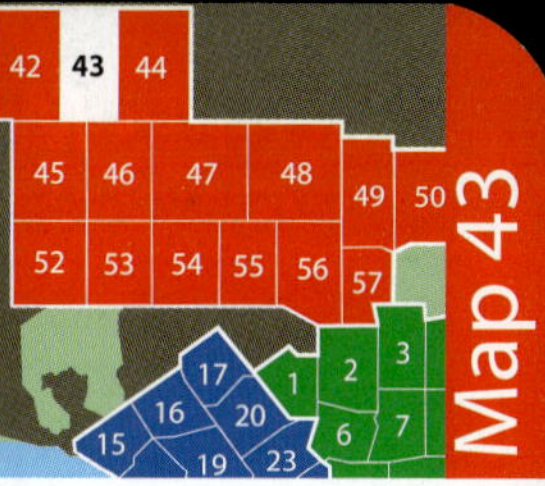

The area's original name was "Zelzah," a biblical name meaning "oasis." This was a reference to a water spring that no longer runs, but which lies buried deep beneath the intersection of Parthenia and Reseda. That spring served as a water cooler for the local Indians—apparently providing both refreshment and a place to discuss the previous night's episode of *Lost*.

Coffee

- **Barclays Coffee & Tea** • 8976 Tampa Ave
- **Café Donut** • 19362 Rinaldi St
- **Coffee Bean & Tea Leaf** • 18705 Devonshire St
- **Daily Grind Coffee House and Café** • 18131 Chatsworth St
- **Gloria Jeans Coffee** • 9301 Tampa Ave
- **Kellys Coffee & Fudge** • 9301 Tampa Ave
- **Lollicup** • 18429 Nordhoff St
- **Muddhouse Coffee** • 9255 Reseda Blvd
- **Starbucks** • 10235 Reseda Blvd
- **Starbucks** • 18100 Chatsworth St
- **Starbucks** • 19500 Plummer St
- **Starbucks** • 19759 Rinaldi St
- **Starbucks** • 9420 Reseda Blvd

Copy Shops

- **ASAP Copy & Print** • 9250 Reseda Blvd • 818-700-7999
- **FedEx Kinko's** • 10725 Zelzah Ave • 818-366-3761
- **FedEx Kinko's** • 9000 Tampa Ave • 818-701-0362
- **Mail Boxes Etc** • 9420 Reseda Blvd • 818-349-2252
- **Minuteman Press** • 19709 Nordhoff St • 818-341-1003
- **Northridge Printing & Copy Center** • 9130 Reseda Blvd • 818-775-0255
- **Office Depot** • 19611 Parthenia St • 818-727-7090
- **Postnet** • 9135 Reseda Blvd •
- **Precision Instant Printing** • 8959 Reseda Blvd • 818-993-6010
- **Sun Star Copy** • 9514 Reseda Blvd • 818-718-6151
- **UPS Store** • 17939 Chatsworth St • 818-360-6144
- **UPS Store** • 19360 Rinaldi St • 818-360-0144

Farmers Markets

- **Northridge (Wed, 5 pm-9 pm)** • 9301 Tampa Ave

Gyms

- **Bally Total Fitness** • 8948 Corbin Ave • 818-885-7417
- **Bodies In Motion** • 10155 Reseda Blvd • 818-700-4900
- **Curves** • 19300 Rinaldi St • 818-368-3811
- **Curves** • 8458 Reseda Blvd • 818-773-7342
- **Gold's Gym** • 9150 B Reseda Blvd • 818-772-1400
- **LA Fitness Sports Clubs** • 18679 Devonshire St • 818-832-5496
- **Total Woman** • 19456 Nordhoff St • 818-772-8900

Hardware Stores

- **Lowe's** • 19601 Nordhoff St • 818-477-9022
- **Orchard Supply Hardware** • 18060 Chatsworth St • 818-363-7557
- **Stock Building Supply** • 18300 Parthenia St • 818-885-6322

Liquor Stores

- **International Liquor & Jr Market** • 9250 Reseda Blvd
- **Jolly Jug Liquor** • 8464 Reseda Blvd
- **King Arthur Liquors** • 9348 Corbin Ave
- **Liquor Stop-N-Go Market** • 20001 Roscoe Blvd
- **Lorenzo's Liquor** • 19061 Parthenia St
- **Napa in the Valley (wine only)** • 8876 Corbin Ave
- **Northridge Liquor** • 9157 Reseda Blvd
- **Porter Plaza Liquor** • 19344 Rinaldi St
- **Village Liquor** • 8642 Lindley Ave
- **Wine Etc** • 19520 Nordhoff St
- **Wines & Spirits of the World** • 10318 Reseda Blvd

Movie Theaters

- **Pacific Fashion Center 10** • 9400 Shirley Ave • 818-501-5121

Pet Shops

- **Ocean Pet Tropical Fish** • 8906 Reseda Blvd • 818-700-4971
- **Pet Terrific (birds only)** • 8745 Shirley Ave • 818-775-9889
- **Petco** • 19869 Rinaldi St • 818-368-3062
- **Petco** • 8800 Tampa Ave • 818-993-1871
- **PetPeople** • 18040 Chatsworth St • 818-832-0771
- **Petworld** • 9301 Tampa Ave, Unit 74 • 818-993-6951
- **Prestige Pet Supply** • 18425 Nordhoff St • 818-772-6611

Restaurants

- **Claim Jumper Restaurant** • 9429 Tampa Ave • 818-718-2882
- **El Torrito Mexican Grill** • 8855 Tampa Ave • 818-349-1607
- **Maria's Italian Kitchen Northridge** • 9161 Reseda Blvd • 818-341-5114
- **On the Border Mexican Café** • 9301 Tampa Ave, # 210 • 818-885-2060
- **University Club at Cal State** • 18111 Nordhoff St • 818-677-2076

Video Rental

- **Blockbuster** • 17945 Chatsworth St • 818-363-7094
- **Blockbuster** • 18497 Nordhoff Blvd • 818-700-9949
- **Blockbuster** • 19767 Rinaldi St • 818-363-9617
- **Filmasia (Indian)** • 8652 Lindley Ave • 818-341-8786
- **Video Hut** • 20021 Roscoe Blvd • 818-775-1222
- **Video Super Shop** • 19643 Parthenia St • 818-701-1133

N

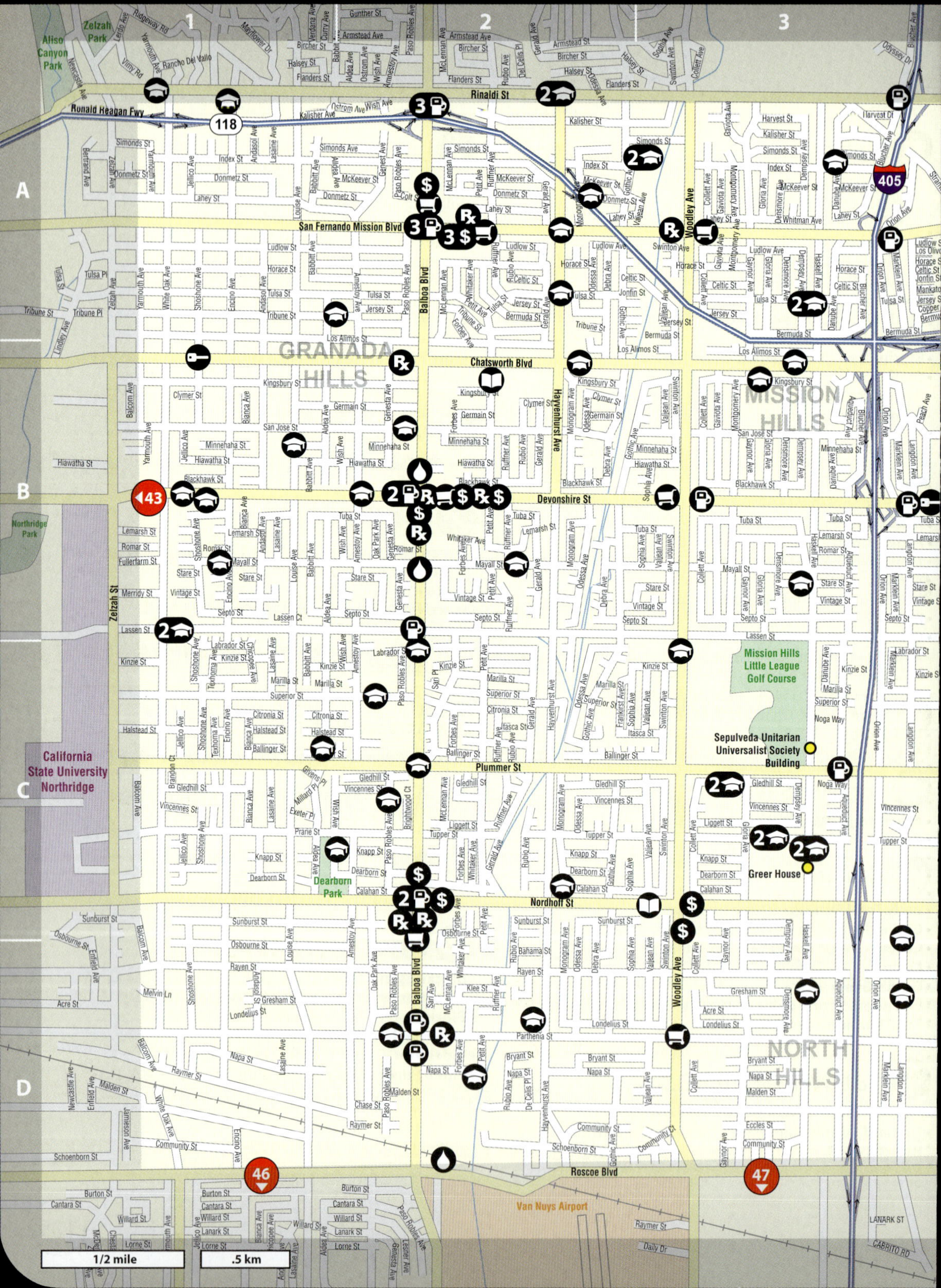

Aliso Canyon Park
Zelzah Park
Ronald Reagan Fwy
118
405
Rinaldi St
San Fernando Mission Blvd
Chatsworth Blvd
Devonshire St
Plummer St
Nordhoff St
Roscoe Blvd
Balboa Blvd
Woodley Ave
Haybenhurst Ave
Zelzah St
GRANADA HILLS
MISSION HILLS
NORTH HILLS
Northridge Park
California State University Northridge
Mission Hills Little League Golf Course
Sepulveda Unitarian Universalist Society Building
Greer House
Dearborn Park
Van Nuys Airport
43
46
47
1/2 mile
.5 km

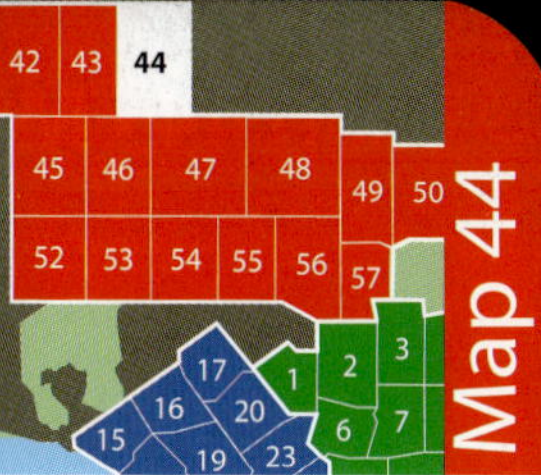

North Hills' Haskell Avenue is home to two of the community's most distinctive buildings: Frank Lloyd Wright Jr.'s Greer House, and the Sepulveda Universalist Society Building, which locals have dubbed "the Onion" for its oddly bulbous shape. Larger, and dearer to the hearts of those more interested in brew than architecture, is the Budweiser Brewery on Roscoe. And for the more spiritually inclined, there is the Mission of San Fernando, for which Mission Hills is named.

Banks

- **Bank of America** • 16944 San Fernando Mission Blvd
- **Bank of America** • 8720 Balboa Blvd
- **Bank of the West** • 16900 Nordhoff St
- **California Credit Union** • 9026 Woodley Ave
- **Citibank** • 16152 Nordhoff St
- **Citibank** • 16800 Devonshire St
- **Downey Savings & Loan** • 16940 Devonshire St
- **Washington Mutual** • 11160 Balboa Blvd
- **Wells Fargo** • 10225 Balboa Blvd
- **Wells Fargo** • 16830 San Fernando Mission Blvd
- **World Savings & Loan** • 16844 San Fernando Mission Blvd

Car Rental

- **Enterprise** • 15439 Devonshire St
- **Enterprise** • 17602 Chatsworth St

Car Washes

- **Balboa Car Wash** • 10125 Balboa Blvd
- **Great American Car Wash** • 16919 Roscoe Blvd
- **North Hills Car Wash** • 10315 Balboa Blvd

Gas Stations

- **76** • 11062 Balboa Blvd
- **76** • 17000 Rinaldi St
- **76** • 8658 Balboa Blvd
- **Arco** • 11454 Balboa Blvd
- **Arco** • 15508 Devonshire St
- **Arco** • 15705 Nordhoff St
- **Arco** • 17000 Devonshire St
- **Arco** • 8700 Balboa Blvd
- **Chevron** • 16156 Devonshire St
- **Chevron** • 17009 Rinaldi St
- **Chevron** • 17011 Devonshire St
- **Chevron** • 9106 Balboa Blvd
- **Mobil** • 16955 San Fernando Mission Blvd
- **Mobil** • 16958 Nordhoff St
- **Mobil** • 17011 Lassen St
- **Shell** • 11105 Balboa Blvd
- **Shell** • 15540 Rinaldi St
- **Shell** • 17000 Roscoe Blvd
- **Valero** • 15544 San Fernando Mission Blvd

Landmarks

- **Greer House** • 9200 Haskell Ave
- **Sepulveda Unitarian Universalist Society Building** • 9550 Haskell Ave

Libraries

- **Granada Hills Branch** • 10640 Petit Ave • 818-368-5687
- **Mid-Valley Regional Branch Library** • 16244 Nordhoff St • 818-895-3650

Pharmacies

- **CVS** • 10208 Balboa Blvd • 818-368-5635
- **CVS** • 9038 Balboa Blvd • 818-891-0956
- **The Medicine Shoppe** • 16915 Devonshire St • 818-366-8857
- **Ralphs** • 16940 Devonshire St • 818-831-4962
- **Rite-Aid** • 16930 Parthenia St • 818-895-2724
- **Sav-On** • 16201 San Fernando Mission Blvd • 818-366-9557
- **Target** • 8999 Balboa Blvd • 818-924-9002
- **Vons** • 16830 San Fernando Mission Blvd • 818-831-5059
- **Walgreens** • 17010 Chatsworth St • 818-360-0871

Schools

- **Abraham Joshua Heschel** • 17701 Devonshire St
- **Agape Preschool and Kindergarten** • 10452 Louise Ave
- **Andasol Ave Elementary** • 10126 Encino Ave
- **Art of Learning Academy** • 9535 Aldea Ave
- **Balboa Gifted / High Ability Magnet Elementary** • 17020 Labrador St
- **Casa Montessori** • 17633 Lassen St
- **Centers of Learning** • 8854 Haskell Ave
- **Danube Ave Elementary** • 11220 Danube Ave
- **De La Salle Elementary** • 16535 Chatsworth St
- **Dearborn St Elementary** • 9240 Wish Ave
- **Einstein High** • 15938 Tupper St
- **Elam EEC** • 15950 Tupper St
- **George K Porter Middle** • 15960 Kingsbury St
- **Gledhill EEC** • 16058 Gledhill St
- **Gledhill Elementary** • 16030 Gledhill St
- **Granada Elementary** • 17170 Tribune St
- **Haskell Elementary** • 15850 Tulsa St
- **Haskell Math/Science Magnet** • 15850 Tulsa St
- **Highland Hall Waldorf** • 17100 Superior St
- **Hillcrest Christian** • 17531 Rinaldi St
- **Holy Martyrs Armenian Elementary** • 16617 Parthenia St
- **Imagine Academy Charter** • 16651 Rinaldi St
- **Jane Addams Continuation** • 16341 Donmetz St
- **John F Kennedy High** • 11254 Gothic Ave
- **Kennedy-San Fernando Community Adult** • 11254 Gothic Ave
- **Kindercare Learning Center** • 17730 Rinaldi St
- **Knollwood Kindergarten** • 17034 Parthenia St
- **Langdon Elementary** • 8817 Langdon Ave
- **Los Angeles Baptist High** • 9825 Woodley Ave
- **Mayall Elementary** • 16701 Mayall St
- **Monroe High** • 9229 Haskell Ave
- **North Valley Charter Academy** • 16551 Rinaldi St
- **Oliver Wendell Holmes Middle** • 9351 Paso Robles Ave
- **Our Lady of Peace Elementary** • 9022 Langdon Ave
- **Our Savior First Lutheran** • 16603 San Fernando Mission Blvd
- **Parthenia Elementary** • 16825 Napa St
- **Patrick Henry Middle** • 17340 San Jose St
- **Pinecrest** • 17081 Devonshire St
- **San Fernando Valley Academy** • 17601 Lassen St
- **St Nicholas** • 9501 Balboa Blvd
- **St Stephen S Lutheran Preschool** • 15950 Chatsworth St
- **Temple Ramat Zion Nursery** • 17655 Devonshire St
- **Tulsa St Elementary** • 10900 Hayvenhurst Ave
- **Valley Community Charter** • 16514 Nordhoff St
- **Valley Presbyterian** • 9240 Haskell Ave
- **Vintage Math/Science Magnet** • 15848 Stare St

Supermarkets

- **Albertsons** • 16201 San Fernando Mission Blvd
- **Albertsons** • 9022 Balboa Blvd
- **Food 4 Less** • 16208 Parthenia St
- **Ralphs** • 16940 Devonshire St
- **Smart & Final** • 16210 Devonshire St
- **Trader Joe's** • 11114 Balboa Blvd
- **Vons** • 16830 San Fernando Mission Blvd

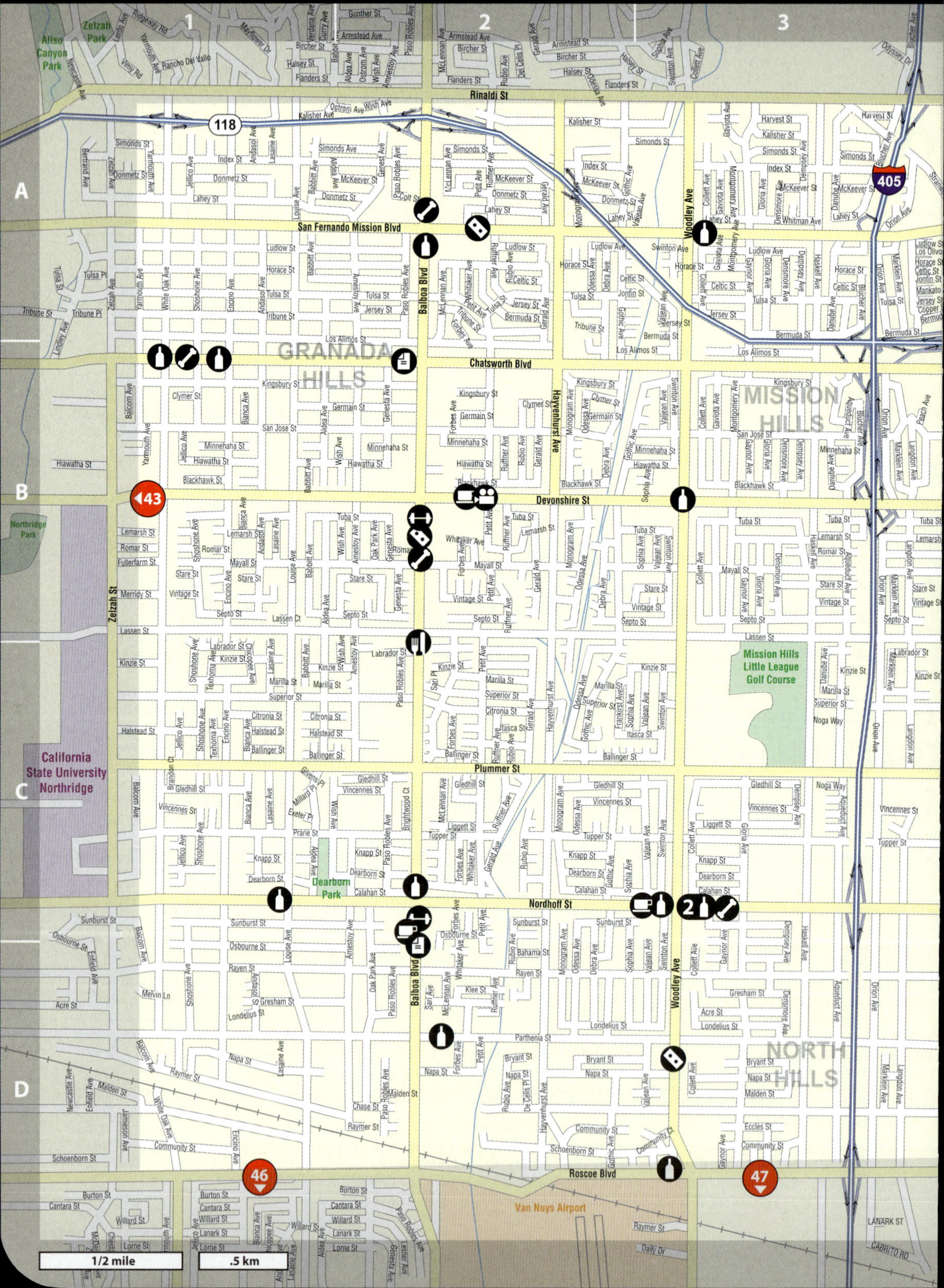

1 2 3

A B C D

Granada Hills

Mission Hills

North Hills

Aliso Canyon Park

Zelzah Park

Northridge Park

California State University Northridge

Mission Hills Little League Golf Course

Dearborn Park

Van Nuys Airport

Rinaldi St

San Fernando Mission Blvd

Chatsworth Blvd

Devonshire St

Plummer St

Nordhoff St

Roscoe Blvd

Balboa Blvd

Woodley Ave

Haynvenhurst Ave

Zelzah St

118

405

43

46

47

1/2 mile

.5 km

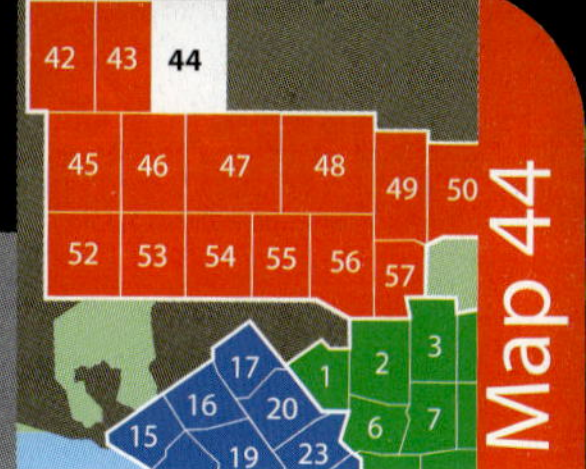

Though most of the homes in Mission Hills and North Hills were built in the fifties, if you look hard you can find a few adobes that have been standing since the early 19th century.

Coffee

- **Perks** • 9028 Balboa Blvd
- **Starbucks** • 16222 Nordhoff St
- **Starbucks** • 16850 Devonshire Blvd

Copy Shops

- **Staples** • 17020 Chatsworth St • 818-831-8095
- **UPS Store** • 9018 Balboa Blvd • 818-894-4993

Gyms

- **Curves** • 9024 Balboa Ave • 818-920-7205
- **Northridge Athletic Club** • 10211 Balboa Blvd • 818-993-3696

Liquor Stores

- **Alda Liquors** • 16151 Roscoe Blvd
- **Balboa Liquor** • 16904 Parthenia St
- **Cheers Liquor** • 16205 Devonshire St
- **Continental Liquor** • 9114 Balboa Blvd
- **Country Club Liquor & Delicatessen** • 11067 Balboa Blvd
- **Frank's Liquor & Deli** • 16210 Nordhoff St
- **Highland Liquor** • 16163 San Fernando Mason Blvd
- **Joe's Liquor** • 16151 Nordhoff St
- **Party Pantry** • 16145 Parthenia St
- **Safeway Liquor** • 17702 Chatsworth St
- **Stardust Liquor** • 17503 Chatsworth St
- **Turner's Liquor** • 8305 Balboa Blvd

Movie Theaters

- **Mann Granada Hills 9** • 16830 Devonshire St • 818-363-3679

Pet Shops

- **All Pet Headquarters** • 11130 Balboa Blvd • 818-368-0269
- **C&C Pet Food for Less** • 16134 Nordhoff St • 818-830-1452
- **Fumi's Tropical Fish** • 17606 Chatsworth St • 818-363-3710
- **Tags Pet Supplies** • 10142 Balboa Blvd • 818-832-0110

Restaurants

- **In-N-Out Burger** • 9858 Balboa Blvd • 800-786-1000

Video Rental

- **Hollywood Video** • 10207 Balboa Blvd • 818-700-8931
- **Hollywood Video** • 8635 Woodley Ave • 818-830-7489
- **Video Allstars** • 16848 San Fernando Mission Blvd • 818-360-6988

N

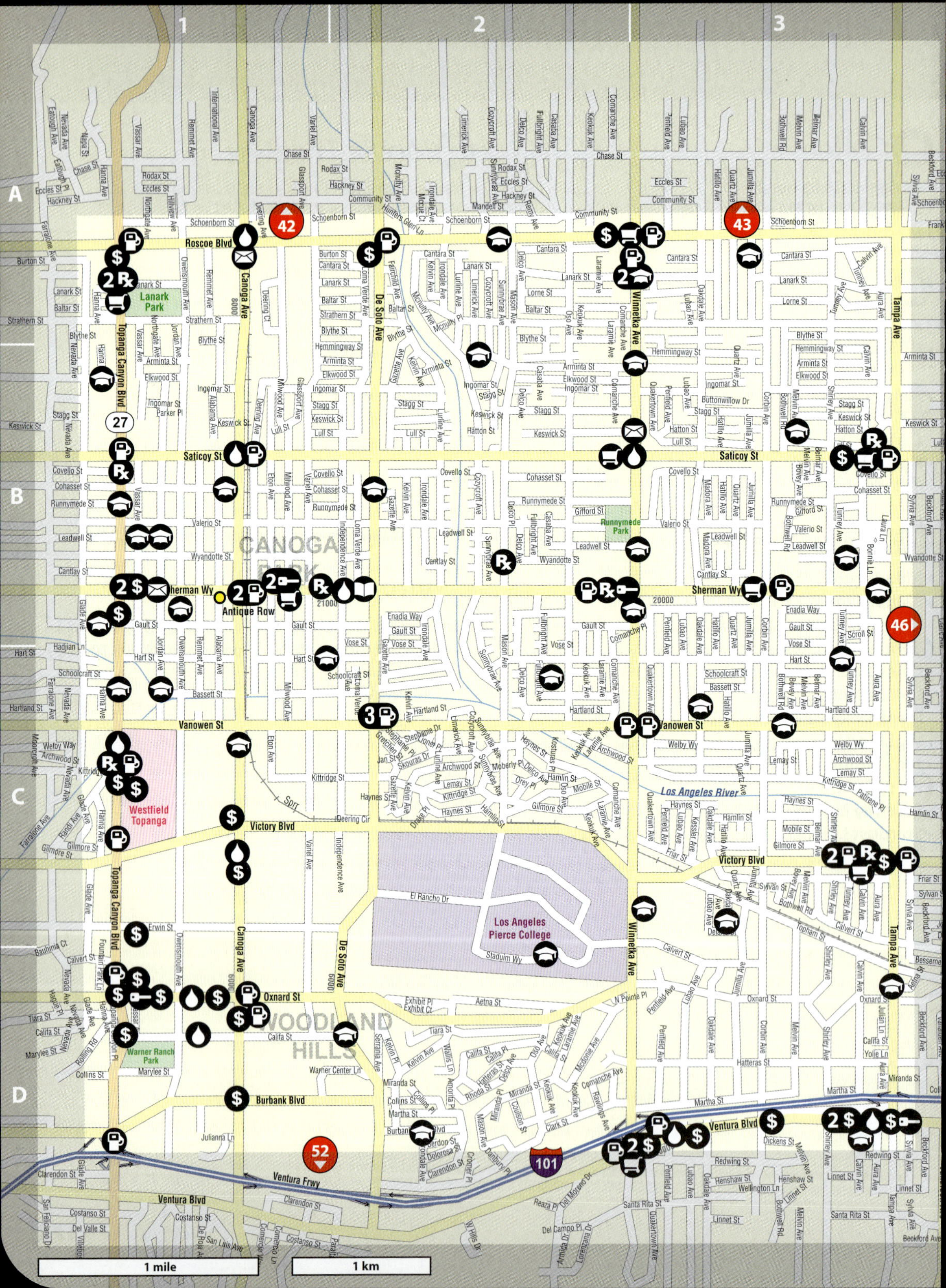

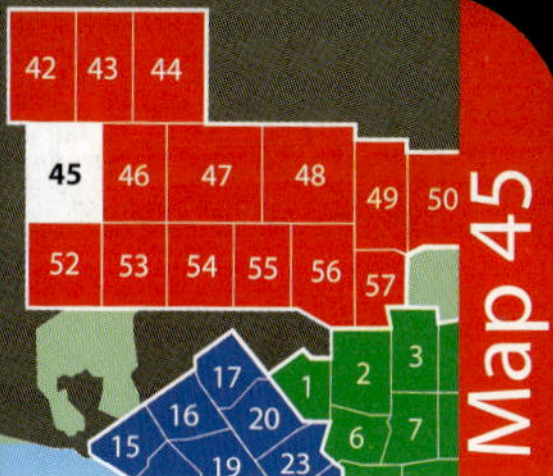

Warner Center, which lies between Topanga Canyon Blvd and Canoga Ave just north of Ventura Blvd, is a small city of office buildings, chain stores and restaurants, and big corporations. But just a stone's throw away sits Pierce College, a two-year community college with an emphasis on agriculture. The college boasts a working farm, a veterinary science program, and a "green" philosophy that includes solar power and drought-resistant plants—adding a rustic charm to what would otherwise be a wasteland of pre-fab business parks.

Banks

- **Bank of America** • 20118 Roscoe Blvd
- **Bank of the West** • 19858 Ventura Blvd
- **California Credit Union** • 6037 Topanga Canyon Blvd
- **California National** • 19500 Ventura Blvd
- **Citibank** • 19255 Ventura Blvd
- **Citibank** • 21945 Erwin St
- **Citibank** • 7119 Topanga Cyn Blvd
- **City National** • 21800 Oxnard St
- **Comerica** • 5700 Canoga Ave
- **Downey Savings & Loan** • 20060 Ventura Blvd
- **First Bank & Trust** • 5939 Canoga Ave
- **First Bank & Trust** • 6300 Canoga Ave
- **Manufacturers** • 21550 Oxnard St
- **Union** • 5855 Topanga Cyn Blvd
- **Washington Mutual** • 19315 Saticoy St
- **Washington Mutual** • 19323 Victory Blvd
- **Washington Mutual** • 19436 Ventura Blvd
- **Washington Mutual** • 20040 Ventura Blvd
- **Washington Mutual** • 21901 Sherman Wy
- **Washington Mutual** • 6633 Topanga Cyn Blvd
- **Wells Fargo** • 19900 Ventura Blvd
- **Wells Fargo** • 21834 Sherman Wy
- **Wells Fargo** • 6001 Topanga Cyn Blvd
- **Wells Fargo** • 6500 Canoga Ave
- **Wells Fargo** • 6600 Topanga Canyon Blvd
- **Wells Fargo** • 8201 Topanga Cyn Blvd
- **Wells Fargo** • 8231 De Soto Ave

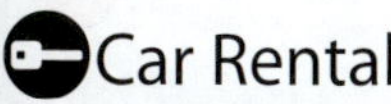

Car Rental

- **Budget** • 21339 Sherman Wy
- **Enterprise** • 19228 Ventura Blvd
- **Enterprise** • 21330 Sherman Wy
- **Hertz** • 21850 Oxnard St
- **Point Car Rental-Sales** • 20112 Sherman Wy

Car Washes

- **76** • 6760 Topanga Cyn Blvd
- **Canoga Park Car Wash** • 21004 Sherman Wy
- **Chevron** • 20021 Ventura Blvd
- **Fiesta Car Wash** • 21403 Saticoy St
- **Marv's Car Wash** • 20238 Saticoy St
- **Steve's Detailing & Hand Car Wash** • 6326 Canoga Ave
- **Steve's Hand Car Wash & Fine Auto Detailing Inc** • 21625 Califa St
- **Tarzana Car Wash** • 19348 Ventura Blvd
- **Topanga Car Wash** • 6829 Topanga Cyn Blvd
- **Warner Center Auto Detail** • 21600 Oxnard St
- **West Hills Car Wash** • 8301 Canoga Ave

Gas Stations

- **76** • 20105 Vanowen St
- **76** • 5601 Topanga Cyn Blvd
- **76** • 6760 Topanga Cyn Blvd
- **76** • 8308 De Soto Ave
- **Alliance** • 7601 Topanga Cyn Blvd
- **Arco** • 20055 Vanowen St
- **Arco** • 20951 Vanowen St
- **Arco** • 8255 Winnetka Ave
- **Canoga Park Alliance** • 20901 Vanowen St
- **Chevron** • 19156 Ventura Blvd
- **Chevron** • 19650 Sherman Wy
- **Chevron** • 20021 Ventura Blvd
- **Chevron** • 21403 Sherman Wy
- **Chevron** • 21935 Roscoe Blvd
- **Chevron** • 5960 Canoga Ave
- **Chevron** • 6061 Topanga Cyn Blvd
- **Independent** • 19304 Saticoy St
- **Mobil** • 19248 Victory Blvd
- **Mobil** • 20101 Roscoe Blvd
- **Mobil** • 20101 Ventura Blvd
- **Mobil** • 20910 Vanowen St
- **Mobil** • 21403 Saticoy St
- **Mobil** • 6423 Topanga Cyn Blvd
- **Shell** • 21404 Sherman Wy
- **Shell** • 22001 Vanowen St
- **Thrifty** • 6000 Canoga Ave
- **Valero** • 20250 Sherman Wy

Landmarks

- **Antique Row** • 21500 block of Sherman Wy

Libraries

- **Canoga Park Branch** • 20939 Sherman Wy • 818-887-0320

Pharmacies

- **CVS** • 19353 Victory Blvd • 818-996-4742
- **CVS** • 21051 Sherman Wy • 818-348-6222
- **CVS** • 8201 Topanga Cyn Blvd • 818-340-2388
- **Rite-Aid** • 20141 Sherman Wy • 818-882-0202
- **Rite-Aid** • 8230 Topanga Cyn Blvd • 818-348-5126
- **Sav-On** • Albertsons • 19307 Saticoy St • 818-885-1525
- **Sav-On** • Albertsons • 7224 Mason Ave • 818-346-5667
- **Target** • 6700 Topanga Canyon Blvd • 818-746-9923
- **Walgreens** • 20505 Sherman Wy • 818-719-6599
- **Walgreens** • 7560 Topanga Cyn Blvd • 818-340-4031

Police

- **Los Angeles Police Dept** • 19020 Vanowen St • 818-374-7611

Post Offices

- **US Post Office** • 21801 Sherman Wy • 800-275-8777
- **US Post Office** • 7655 Winnetka Ave • 800-275-8777
- **US Post Office** • 8201 Canoga Ave • 800-275-8777

Schools

- **Agbu Manoogian-Demirdjian** • 6844 Oakdale Ave
- **Blythe St Elementary** • 18730 Blythe St
- **Buonora Child Development Center** • 19325 Sherman Wy
- **Calvert St Elementary** • 19850 Delano St
- **Canoga Park EEC** • 7355 Vassar Ave
- **Canoga Park Elementary** • 7438 Topanga Cyn Blvd
- **Canoga Park Lutheran** • 7357 Jordan Ave
- **Canoga Park Preschool and Kindergarten** • 7839 Topanga Cyn Blvd
- **Canoga Park Senior High** • 6850 Topanga Cyn Blvd
- **Castle Oaks Children's Center** • 6739 Corbin Ave
- **Coutin** • 7119 Owensmouth Ave
- **Diane S Leichman Special Education Center** • 19034 Gault St
- **Faucher Academy** • 19414 Ventura Blvd
- **Fullbright Ave Elementary** • 6940 Fullbright Ave
- **Green Gables** • 8217 Winnetka Ave
- **Grover Cleaveland High** • 8140 Vanalden Ave
- **Hart St Elementary** • 21040 Hart St
- **John A Sutter Middle** • 7330 Winnetka Ave
- **Kirk of the Valley** • 19620 Vanowen St
- **Little Wonders Montessori** • 20550 Roscoe Blvd
- **Melvin Ave Elementary** • 7700 Melvin Ave
- **Morning Star Christian Academy** • 8232 Jumilla Ave
- **Multicultural Learning Center** • 7510 De Soto Ave
- **New Canoga Park Elementary** • 21425 Cohasset St
- **Our Lady of the Valley** • 22041 Gault St
- **Owensmouth Continuation** • 6921 Jordan Ave
- **Shirley Ave Elementary** • 19452 Hart St
- **St Joseph the Worker** • 19812 Cantlay St
- **St Martin-In-The-Fields Parish** • 7136 Winnetka Ave
- **Sunny Brae Ave Elementary** • 20620 Arminta St
- **Sven Lokrantz Special Education Center** • 19451 Wyandotte St
- **Tutor Time** • 5855 De Soto Ave
- **Vanalden Ave Elementary** • 19019 Delano St
- **West Valley Christian Academy** • 7911 Winnetka Ave
- **West Valley Occupational Center** • 6200 Winnetka Ave
- **Winnetka Ave Elementary** • 8240 Winnetka Ave
- **Woodcrest** • 6043 Tampa Ave
- **Wooden High** • 18741 Elkwood St
- **Woodland Hills Academy** • 20800 Burbank Blvd

Supermarkets

- **Albertsons** • 19307 Saticoy St
- **Albertsons** • 7224 Mason Ave
- **Food 4 Less** • 20155 Saticoy St
- **Jon's Market** • 20151 Roscoe Blvd
- **Ralphs** • 20060 Ventura Blvd
- **Smart & Final** • 19718 Sherman Wy
- **Vallarta Supermarket** • 21208 Sherman Way
- **Vons** • 19333 Victory Blvd
- **Vons** • 8201 Topanga Cyn Blvd

Map 45 • Canoga Park / Woodland Hills

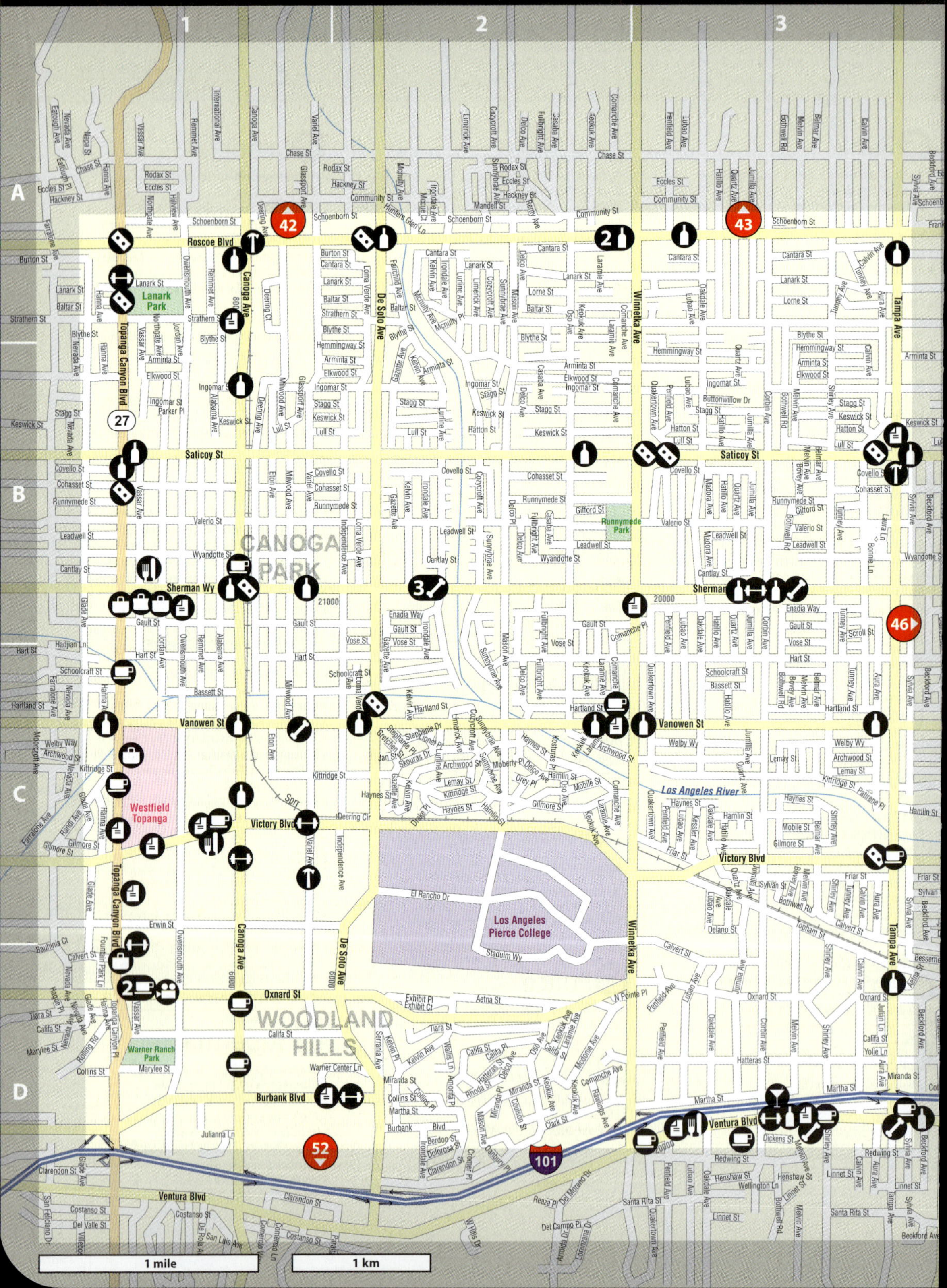
N
1
2
3
A
B
C
D
42
43
46
52
27
101
Roscoe Blvd
Saticoy St
Sherman Wy
Vanowen St
Victory Blvd
Oxnard St
Burbank Blvd
Ventura Blvd
Topanga Canyon Blvd
Canoga Ave
De Soto Ave
Winnetka Ave
Tampa Ave
Schoenborn St
Chase St
Cantara St
Lanark St
Strathern St
Blythe St
Keswick St
Covello St
Cohasset St
Runnymede St
Valerio St
Leadwell St
Cantlay St
Wyandotte St
Gault St
Vose St
Hart St
Schoolcraft St
Bassett St
Hartland St
Kittridge St
Haynes St
Calvert St
Califa St
Marylee St
Erwin St
Collins St
Lanark Park
Runnymede Park
Warner Ranch Park
Westfield Topanga
Los Angeles Pierce College
Los Angeles River
CANOGA PARK
WOODLAND HILLS
El Rancho Dr
Stadium Wy
21000
20000
8000
6000
1 mile
1 km

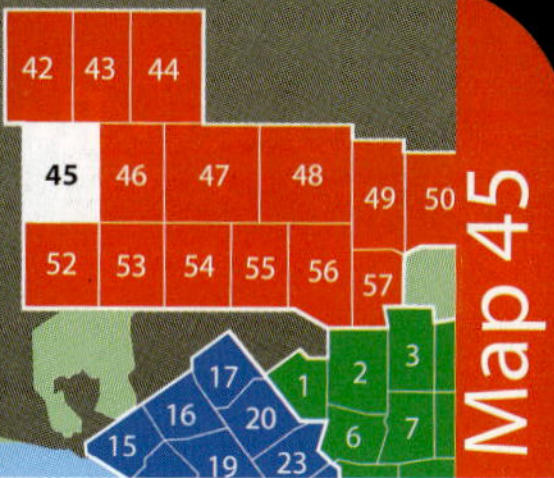

Antique Row, the 21500 block of Sherman Way, might be Canoga Park's most charming thoroughfare. It's home to the Follow Your Heart Market & Café, birthplace of Vegenaise, a "mayonnaise alternative" allowing vegans everywhere to say goodbye to dry Tofurkey club sandwiches. Nearby (and not quite so charming), the behemoth Westfield Topanga seems to add new stores by the hour, already including a Neiman Marcus, a revamped Nordstrom, and a two-story Target. Our advice: skip the Tofurkey, grab some of Target's Choxie chocolates instead.

Coffee

- **Coffee Bean & Tea Leaf** • 19732 Ventura Blvd
- **Coffee Bean & Tea Leaf** • 21801 Oxnard St
- **Coffee Bean & Tea Leaf** • 5780 Canoga Ave
- **Coffee Junction** • 19221 Ventura Blvd
- **Planet Cyber Coffee House & Computer Center** • 6911 Topanga Canyon Blvd
- **Rocky Roaster** • 7239 Canoga Ave
- **Starbucks** • 19313 Victory Blvd
- **Starbucks** • 19522 Ventura Blvd
- **Starbucks** • 20054 Ventura Blvd
- **Starbucks** • 21504 Victory Blvd
- **Starbucks** • Marriott • 21850 Oxnard St
- **Starbucks** • 5960 Canoga Ave
- **Starbucks** • 6600 Topanga Cyn Blvd
- **Village Café** • 20122 Vanowen St

Copy Shops

- **A Woodland Printing & Copy** • 7124 Owensmouth Ave • 818-999-2679
- **Copies Plus Printing** • 19911 Ventura Blvd • 818-346-1919
- **Copy Center** • 20113 Vanowen St • 818-883-6283
- **FedEx Kinko's** • 21816 Victory Blvd • 818-884-4465
- **JNS Copy Service** • 21041 Burbank Blvd • 818-887-8563
- **Mail Boxes Etc** • 19528 Ventura Blvd • 818-343-4377
- **Office Depot** • 6227 Topanga Cyn Blvd • 818-716-7770
- **Sir Speedy** • 21430 Strathern St • 818-346-2280
- **Staples** • 21500 Victory Blvd • 818-999-0091
- **Universal Copy** • 7141 Winnetka Ave • 818-887-2559
- **UPS Store** • 6433 Topanga Cyn Blvd • 818-704-5808
- **VIP Prints** • 7630 Tampa Ave • 818-609-1013

Gyms

- **Curves** • 19710 Ventura Blvd • 818-340-9614
- **Curves** • 19762 Sherman Wy • 818-264-1313
- **Curves** • 21151 Victory Blvd • 818-702-0230
- **Curves** • 8201 Topanga Cyn Blvd • 818-888-4770
- **Gold's Gym** • 20971 Burbank Blvd • 818-226-3890
- **LA Fitness Sports Club** • 6336 Canoga Ave • 818-884-1100
- **Total Woman** • 6100 Topanga Cyn Blvd • 818-710-7606

Hardware Stores

- **Home Depot** • 21218 Roscoe Blvd • 818-348-9400
- **Home Depot** • 6345 Variel Ave • 818-716-9141
- **Tampa Hardware** • 7543 Tampa Ave • 818-709-0354

Liquor Stores

- **Alcon Cut-Rate Liquor** • 21315 Saticoy St
- **Amber Liquor** • 20263 Saticoy St
- **Aria Liquors** • 22015 Vanowen St
- **Beverages & More** • 6520 Canoga Ave
- **Bottle Bin Liquor** • 20915 Vanowen St
- **Corbin Liquor** • 19661 Ventura Blvd
- **Duke of Bourbon** • 20908 Roscoe Blvd
- **Imperial Liquor** • 20152 Roscoe Blvd
- **J&J Liquor** • 6042 Tampa Ave
- **Jon's Market** • 20151 Roscoe Blvd
- **King's Delight** • 21925 Saticoy St
- **Knight Life Liquor** • 19245 Saticoy St
- **Kwik-Stop Liquor** • 19663 Sherman Wy
- **Ladin's Liquor & Deli** • 20857 Sherman Wy
- **Liquor Mart** • 7547 Topanga Cyn Blvd
- **Liquor Works** • 19200 Ventura Blvd
- **Lucky 7 Liquor** • 19322 Vanowen St
- **Mustang Liquor** • 21121 Sherman Wy
- **Papa Mac's Liquor** • 8219 Canoga Ave
- **Portofino Liquor** • 19756 Sherman Wy
- **Rocket Liquor** • 21413 Vanowen St
- **S&K Liquor** • 8240 Tampa Ave
- **Star's Cork 'n' Bottle Shop** • 7801 Canoga Ave
- **Super Store** • 20043 Vanowen St
- **US Liquor** • 20127 Vanowen St
- **West End Liquor** • 21500 Sherman Wy

Movie Theaters

- **AMC Promenade 16** • 21801 Oxnard St • 818-883-2262

Nightlife

- **Corbin Bowl** • 19616 Ventura Blvd • 818-996-2695

Pet Shops

- **Aquarium City** • 21723 Sherman Wy • 818-887-7369
- **C&C Aquatics** • 21724 Sherman Wy • 818-340-9923
- **C&C'S Pet Food for Less** • 21720 Sherman Wy • 818-348-3018
- **Discount Bird & Pet Supplies** • 19640 Sherman Wy • 818-343-1040
- **Parrots Naturally** • 19224 Ventura Blvd • 818-708-7277
- **Shani's Four Your Paws Only** • 19576 Ventura Blvd • 818-881-5155
- **Vivid Aquariums Warehouse** • 21126 Vanowen St • 818-348-3288

Restaurants

- **Follow Your Heart Café** • 21825 Sherman Wy • 818-348-3240
- **In-N-Out Burger** • 19920 Ventura Blvd • 800-786-1000
- **Pasta Pomodoro** • 21600 Victory Blvd • 818-340-2400

Shopping

- **Babyland** • 7134 Topanga Cyn Blvd • 818-704-7848
- **Green Thumb Nursery** • 21812 Sherman Wy • 818-340-6400
- **Kake Kreations** • 21851 Sherman Wy • 818-346-7621
- **Promenade At Woodland Hills** • 6100 Topanga Cyn Blvd • 818-594-8732
- **Westfield Topanga** • 6600 Topanga Cyn Blvd • 818-594-8732

Video Rental

- **20-20 Video** • 19371 Saticoy St • 818-885-0202
- **Blockbuster** • 19339 Victory Blvd • 818-708-2887
- **Blockbuster** • 8201 Topanga Cyn Blvd • 818-348-7196
- **Hollywood Video** • 8301 Topanga Cyn Blvd • 818-713-0591
- **M&K Video** • 20942 Roscoe Blvd • 818-773-9454
- **Mega Value Video** • 20147 Saticoy St • 818-886-1968
- **Mega Value Video** • 6842 De Soto Ave • 818-598-1475
- **Sunshine Groceries (Indian)** • 7518 Topanga Cyn Blvd • 818-887-6917
- **Video 10** • 20030 Saticoy St • 818-341-0771
- **Video Stage** • 21418 Sherman Wy • 818-887-4234

Map 46 • Reseda

1
2
3
A
B
C
D
Roscoe Blvd
Saticoy St
Sherman Wy
Vanowen St
Victory Blvd
Burbank Blvd
Ventura Fwy
Ventura Blvd
Reseda Blvd
White Oak Ave
Balboa Blvd
Tampa Ave
Vanalden Ave
Haynenhurst Ave
Gresham St
Parthenia St
Napa St
Raymer St
Chase St
Community St
Schoenborn St
Bryant St
Maiden St
Eccles St
Frankfort St
Cantara St
Lanark St
Strathern St
Blythe St
Arminta St
Elkwood St
Ingomar St
Keswick St
Lull St
Stagg St
Cohasset St
Runnymede St
Valerio St
Leadwell St
Wyandotte St
Cantlay St
Enadia Way
Gault St
Vose St
Hart St
Schoolcraft St
Bassett St
Hartland St
Welby Way
Archwood St
Lemay Pl
Kittridge St
Haynes St
Hamlin St
Gilmore St
Friar St
Sylvan St
Erwin St
Calvert St
Topham St
Oxnard St
Hatteras St
Miranda St
Collins St
Martha St
Killion St
Clark St
Margate St
Magnolia Blvd
Weddington St
Mccormick St
Santa Rita St
Canasta St
Linnet Dr
Addison St
Morrison St
Moorpark St
Van Nuys Airport
Reseda Park and Recreation Center
Jesse Owens Park
Louise Park
Lake Balboa Park
Lake Balboa
Los Angeles River
Balboa Sports Center
Balboa Golf Course
Encino Golf Course
Woodley Golf Course
Van Nuys Golf Course
43
44
45
47
53
101
1. Cantara St
2. Willard St
3. Lanark St
4. Lorne St
5. Baltar St
6. Arminta St
7. Hemmingway St
8. Elkwood St
9. Driscoll Ave
10. Ostrom Ave
11. Wish Ave
12. Nestle Ave
13. Wynne Ave
14. Garden Grove Ave
15. Chimineas Ave
16. Wyandotte St
17. Canby Ave
18. Bianca Ave
19. Lasaine Ave
20. Jellico Ave
21. Lasaine Ave
22. Delano St
23. Lyptus Ct
24. Newcastle Ave
25. Bertrand Ave
26. Enfield Ave
27. Alonzo Ave
28. Jamieson Ave
29. Balcom Ave
30. Yarmouth Ave
31. Emelita St
32. Hatteras St
33. Bromley St
34. Andasol Ave
35. Mclennan Ave
36. Killion St
37. Albers St
38. Forbes Ave
39. Aldea Ave
40. Ostrom Ave
1 mile
1 km

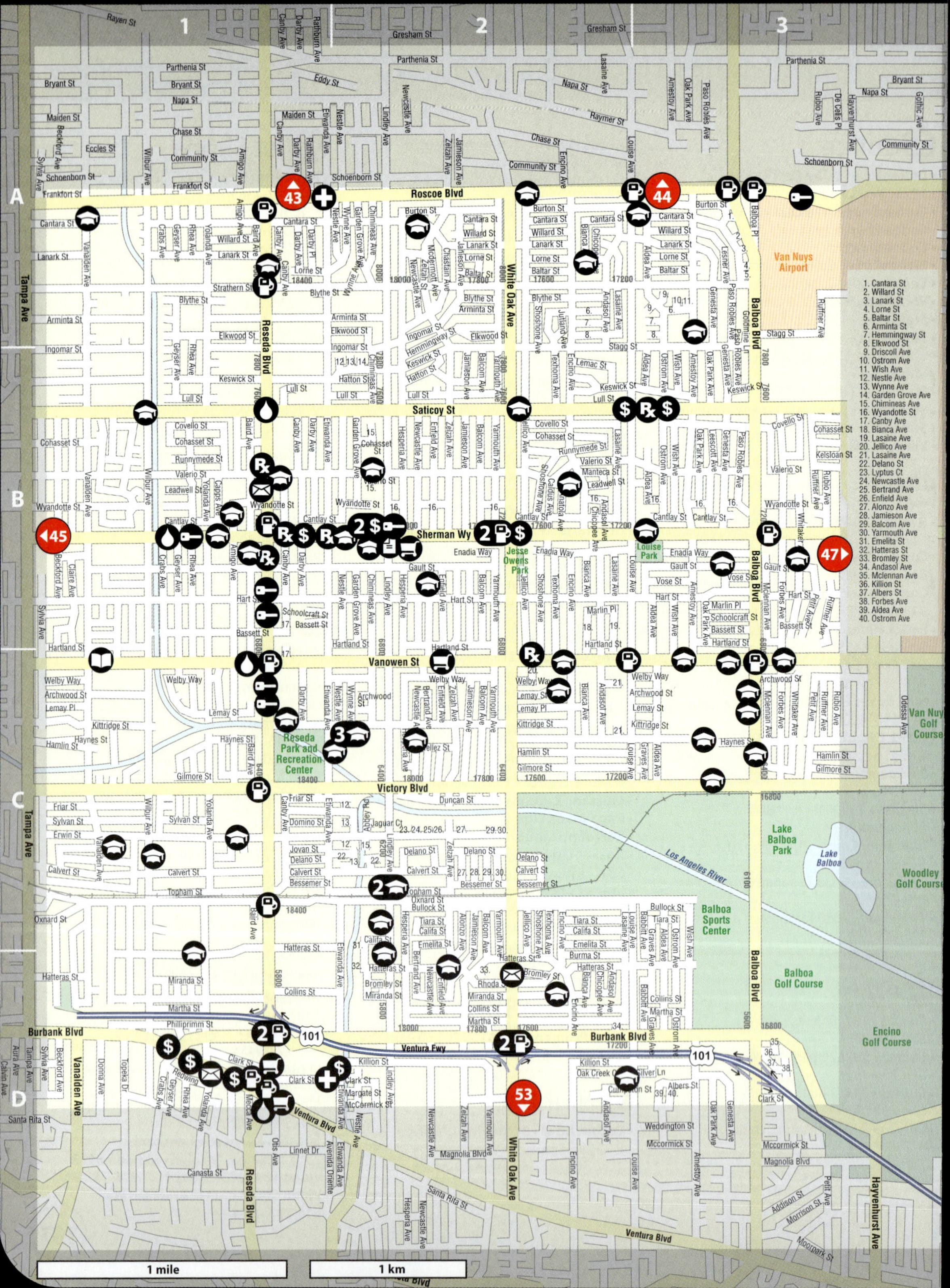

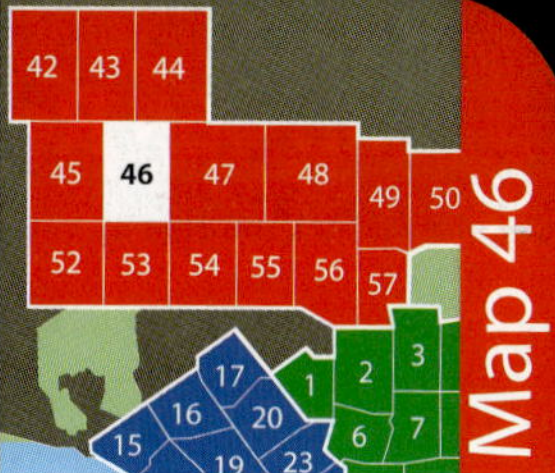

Reseda is more blue collar than upmarket neighbors Encino and Tarzana, but it alone has been immortalized in a Tom Petty song, "Free Fallin'." A mostly-forgotten fact about the 1994 Northridge earthquake is that the epicenter was actually not located in Northridge, but in Reseda, at the intersection of Wilbur Avenue and Saticoy Street. This conclusion wasn't drawn until about a week after the quake, by which time the media had churned out their graphics and packaged their segments—accuracy be damned.

Banks

- **Bank of America** • 18120 Sherman Wy
- **Citibank** • 18260 Sherman Wy
- **Downey Savings & Loan** • 17250 Saticoy St
- **First Federal** • 18585 Ventura Blvd
- **Nara** • 17639 Sherman Wy
- **Washington Mutual** • 17204 Saticoy St
- **Washington Mutual** • 18705 Ventura Blvd
- **Wells Fargo** • 18400 Sherman Wy
- **Wells Fargo** • 18801 Ventura Blvd

Car Rental

- **Discount Rent-a-Car** • 7002 Reseda Blvd
- **Domestic Car Rentals** • 18128 Sherman Wy
- **Enterprise** • 6653 Reseda Blvd
- **Hertz** • 16700 Roscoe Blvd
- **Hertz** • 6728 Reseda Blvd
- **Rent 4 Less** • 6944 Reseda Blvd
- **Rent-a-Wreck** • 18738 Sherman Wy

Car Washes

- **Coast Motor Detailing** • 18500 Ventura Blvd
- **Quality Car Wash** • 7601 Reseda Blvd
- **Sherman Car Wash** • 18815 Sherman Wy
- **Vanowen Car Wash** • 18514 Vanowen St

Gas Stations

- **76** • 17300 Vanowen St
- **76** • 17704 Sherman Wy
- **76** • 18524 Ventura Blvd
- **76** • 8247 Reseda Blvd
- **Arco** • 16851 Sherman Wy
- **Arco** • 6039 Reseda Blvd
- **Chevron** • 17255 Roscoe Blvd
- **Chevron** • 7208 Reseda Blvd
- **Exxon** • 5605 Reseda Blvd
- **Independent** • 6801 Reseda Blvd
- **Mobil** • 18468 Burbank Blvd
- **Mobil** • 18510 Victory Blvd
- **Mobil** • 5553 White Oak Ave
- **Shell** • 17660 Burbank Blvd
- **Shell** • 17707 Sherman Wy
- **Shell** • 18500 Ventura Blvd
- **Shell** • 6801 Balboa Blvd
- **Shell** • 8000 Reseda Blvd
- **Valero** • 16930 Roscoe Blvd

Emergency Rooms

- **Encino-Tarzana Regional Medical Center-Tarzana Campus** • 18321 Clark St
- **Northridge - Roscoe Campus** • 18300 Roscoe Blvd

Libraries

- **West Valley Regional** • 19036 Vanowen St • 818-345-9806

Pharmacies

- **CVS** • 18247 Sherman Wy • 818-345-9640
- **CVS** • 7400 Reseda Blvd • 818-776-2600
- **The Medicine Shoppe** • 17650 Vanowen St • 818-996-2878
- **The Medicine Shoppe** • 7111 Reseda Blvd • 818-345-5397
- **Rite-Aid** • 17266 Saticoy St • 818-345-1543
- **Walgreens** • 18430 Sherman Wy • 818-343-4513

Post Offices

- **US Post Office** • 5609 Yolanda Ave • 800-275-8777
- **US Post Office** • 5805 White Oak Ave • 800-275-8777
- **US Post Office** • 7320 Reseda Blvd • 800-275-8777

Schools

- **American Hebrew Academy** • 6134 Lindley Ave
- **Anatola Ave Elementary** • 7364 Anatola Ave
- **Bertrand Ave Elementary** • 7021 Bertrand Ave
- **Birmingham Senior High** • 17000 Haynes St
- **Cantara St Elementary** • 17950 Cantara St
- **Cleveland EEC** • 19031 Strathern St
- **Community Charter Early College High** • 16945 Sherman Wy
- **Emelita Elementary** • 17931 Hatteras St
- **Encino Academy** • 6100 Lindley Ave
- **Eretz Alliance** • 6170 Wilbur Ave
- **Fred E Lull Special Education** • 17551 Miranda St
- **Garden Grove Elementary** • 18141 Valerio St
- **Gault St Elementary** • 17000 Gault St
- **Grey Continuing High** • 18230 Kittridge St
- **Heart of the Valley Christ** • 18644 Sherman Wy
- **High Tech High** • 17111 Victory Blvd
- **Independence Continuation** • 6501 Balboa Blvd
- **Lemay EEC** • 17553 Lemay St
- **Lemay St Elementary** • 17520 Vanowen St
- **Lewis Carroll Academy** • 19000 Saticoy St
- **Lorne St Elementary** • 17440 Lorne St
- **Lycee International de los Angeles** • 5933 Lindley Ave
- **Magnolia Science Academy** • 18238 Sherman Wy
- **Miller High** • 8218 Vanalden Ave
- **Netan-Eli Hebrew Academy** • 7350 Reseda Blvd
- **New Horizon Christian** • 8055 Reseda Blvd
- **Newcastle Elementary** • 6520 Newcastle Ave
- **The Northridge Community** • 8212 Louise Ave
- **Oak Meadow** • 17645 Saticoy St
- **Pinecrest-Whiteoak** • 17643 Roscoe Blvd
- **Playmates of Reseda** • 7119 Baird Ave
- **Reseda Community Adult** • 18230 Kittridge St
- **Reseda Elementary** • 7265 Amigo Ave
- **Reseda Senior High** • 18230 Kittridge St
- **Sage Academy** • 5901 Lindley Ave
- **Sherman Oaks Center for Enriched Students** • 18605 Erwin St
- **St Bridget of Sweden** • 7120 Whitaker Ave
- **St Catherine of Siena** • 18125 Sherman Wy
- **Stagg St Elementary** • 7839 Amestoy Ave
- **Tierra Montessori** • 18706 Hatteras St
- **Trinity Lutheran High** • 18425 Kittridge St
- **Valley Magnet** • 6701 Balboa Blvd
- **Valley Montessori** • 17249 Sherman Wy
- **Vanalden EEC** • 6212 Vanalden Ave
- **West Valley Special Education** • 6649 Balboa Blvd
- **Westmark** • 5461 Louise Ave
- **William Mulholland Middle** • 17120 Vanowen St
- **Zane Grey Continuation** • 6510 Etiwanda Ave

Supermarkets

- **Gelson's Supermarket** • 5500 Reseda Blvd
- **Jon's Marketplace** • 18135 Sherman Wy
- **Ralphs** • 17250 Saticoy St
- **Ralphs** • 18300 Vanowen St
- **Trader Joe's** • 17640 Burbank Blvd
- **Vons** • 18439 Ventura Blvd

Map 46 • Reseda

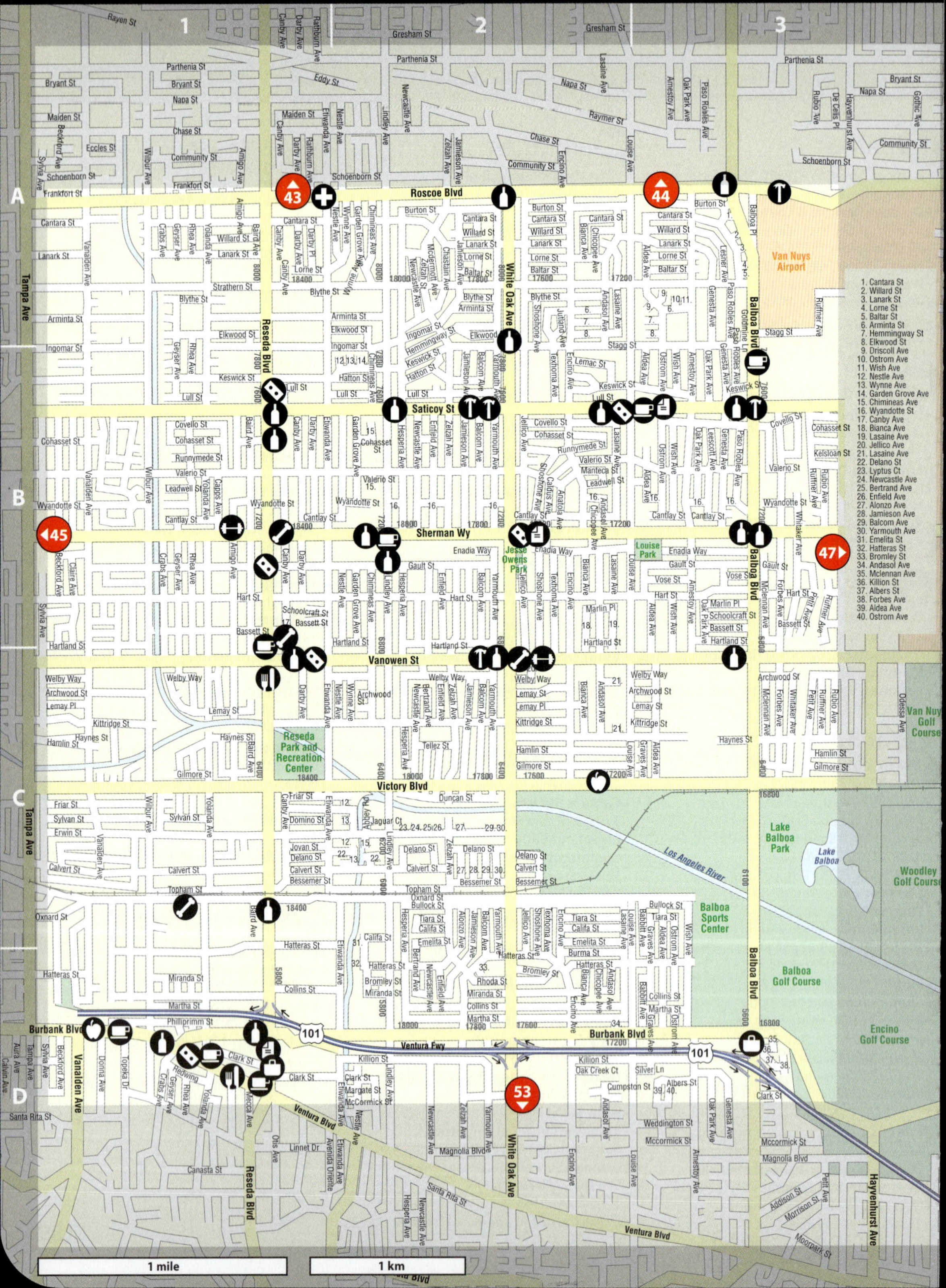

N
1
2
3
A
B
C
D
Roscoe Blvd
Saticoy St
Sherman Wy
Vanowen St
Victory Blvd
Burbank Blvd
Ventura Fwy
Ventura Blvd
Reseda Blvd
White Oak Ave
Balboa Blvd
Tampa Ave
Vanalden Ave
Haynvenhurst Ave
Van Nuys Airport
Jesse Owens Park
Louise Park
Reseda Park and Recreation Center
Lake Balboa Park
Lake Balboa
Los Angeles River
Balboa Sports Center
Balboa Golf Course
Encino Golf Course
Woodley Golf Course
Van Nuys Golf Course
43
44
45
47
53
101
1. Cantara St
2. Willard St
3. Lanark St
4. Lorne St
5. Baltar St
6. Arminta St
7. Hemmingway St
8. Elkwood St
9. Driscoll Ave
10. Ostrom Ave
11. Wish Ave
12. Nestle Ave
13. Wynne Ave
14. Garden Grove Ave
15. Chimineas Ave
16. Wyandotte St
17. Canby Ave
18. Bianca Ave
19. Lasaine Ave
20. Jellico Ave
21. Lasaine Ave
22. Delano St
23. Lyptus Ct
24. Newcastle Ave
25. Bertrand Ave
26. Enfield Ave
27. Alonzo Ave
28. Jamieson Ave
29. Balcom Ave
30. Yarmouth Ave
31. Emelita St
32. Hatteras St
33. Bromley St
34. Andasol Ave
35. Mclennan Ave
36. Killion St
37. Albers St
38. Forbes Ave
39. Aldea Ave
40. Ostrom Ave
1 mile
1 km

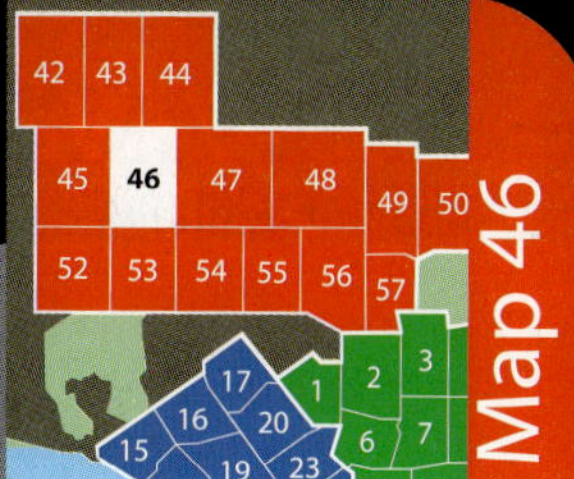

Lake Balboa Park is a lovely place to spend a weekend day. Rent a paddleboat and work your way across the lake, or grab a fishing rod—the lake is stocked regularly by the Department of Fish and Game. The park is also surrounded by three golf courses, and hosts the Valley Jazz Festival.

Coffee

- **Café Donuts** • 7161 Lindley Ave
- **Coffee Bean & Tea Leaf** • 18505 Ventura Blvd
- **Lillo Caffe** • 7716 Balboa Blvd
- **Peet's** • 18973 Ventura Blvd
- **Starbucks** • 17272 Saticoy St
- **Starbucks** • 18668 Ventura Blvd
- **Starbucks** • 6840 Reseda Blvd

Copy Shops

- **Office Depot** • 5530 Reseda Blvd • 818-708-7587
- **UPS Store** • 17216 Saticoy St • 818-774-9095
- **Variety Printing & Graphics** • 17618 Sherman Wy • 818-705-4422

Farmers Markets

- **Encino (Sun, 8 am–1 pm)** • 17400 Victory Blvd
- **Tarzana (Sun, 8 am–12 pm)** • 19130 Ventura Blvd

Gyms

- **Curves** • 17624 Sherman Wy • 818-668-8433
- **The Sport Club** • 18570 Sherman Wy • 818-758-8459

Hardware Stores

- **Home Depot** • 16800 Roscoe Blvd • 818-780-5448
- **M&M Tools** • 7544 Balboa Blvd • 818-989-7514
- **Marcos- Hardware & Garden Supply** • 17734 Saticoy St • 818-705-1804
- **Reseda Hardware** • 17729 Vanowen St • 818-345-6467
- **Tool Depot** • 17746 Saticoy St • 818-881-0146

Liquor Stores

- **A&A Liquor** • 17311 Roscoe Blvd
- **Al's Drive-In Liquor** • 18444 Saticoy St
- **Bob's Liquor** • 17315 Saticoy St
- **Farm Boy's Liquor** • 6026 Reseda Blvd
- **Jon's Market** • 18135 Sherman Wy
- **L&M Liquor** • 18400 Vanowen St
- **Lindley Liquor** • 7137 Lindley Ave
- **Liquor Bank** • 16925 Vanowen St
- **Party House Liquor & Wine** • 18839 Ventura Blvd
- **Pour House Liquor** • 7448 Reseda Blvd
- **Rainbow Liquor** • 18033 Saticoy St
- **Red Dragon** • 17705 Vanowen St
- **Spirits World** • 18523 Burbank Blvd
- **Valli-Ho** • 16925 Sherman Wy
- **Wagon Wheel Liquor** • 17724 Roscoe Blvd
- **Western Liquor** • 7143 Balboa Blvd
- **Wine & Liquor Depot** • 16938 Saticoy St

Pet Shops

- **3 Day Pet Supply** • 6924 Canby Ave • 818-342-1212
- **LA Paloma Pet Shop** • 18411 Sherman Wy • 818-881-5352
- **Red Barn Feed and Saddlery** • 18601 Oxnard St • 818-345-2510
- **Tams Pet Food & Supplies** • 17635 Vanowen St • 818-343-6873

Restaurants

- **Amber's Chicken Kitchen** • 16900 Burbank Blvd • 818-995-3200
- **Madeleine Bistro** • 18621 Ventura Blvd • 818-758-6971
- **Melody's Mexican Kitchen** • 6747 Reseda Blvd • 818-609-9062

Shopping

- **Beauty Collection** • 18517 Ventura Blvd • 818-881-8393
- **Hobby Shack** • 5541 Balboa Blvd • 818-995-1162

Video Rental

- **Blockbuster** • 17288 Saticoy St • 818-342-8835
- **Hollywood Video** • 18346 Vanowen St • 818-344-1890
- **Unique Video** • 7146 Reseda Blvd • 818-757-0058
- **Video All Star** • 7622 Reseda Blvd • 818-344-8129
- **Western Video (Korean)** • 17639 Sherman Wy • 818-708-2496

Map 47 • Van Nuys

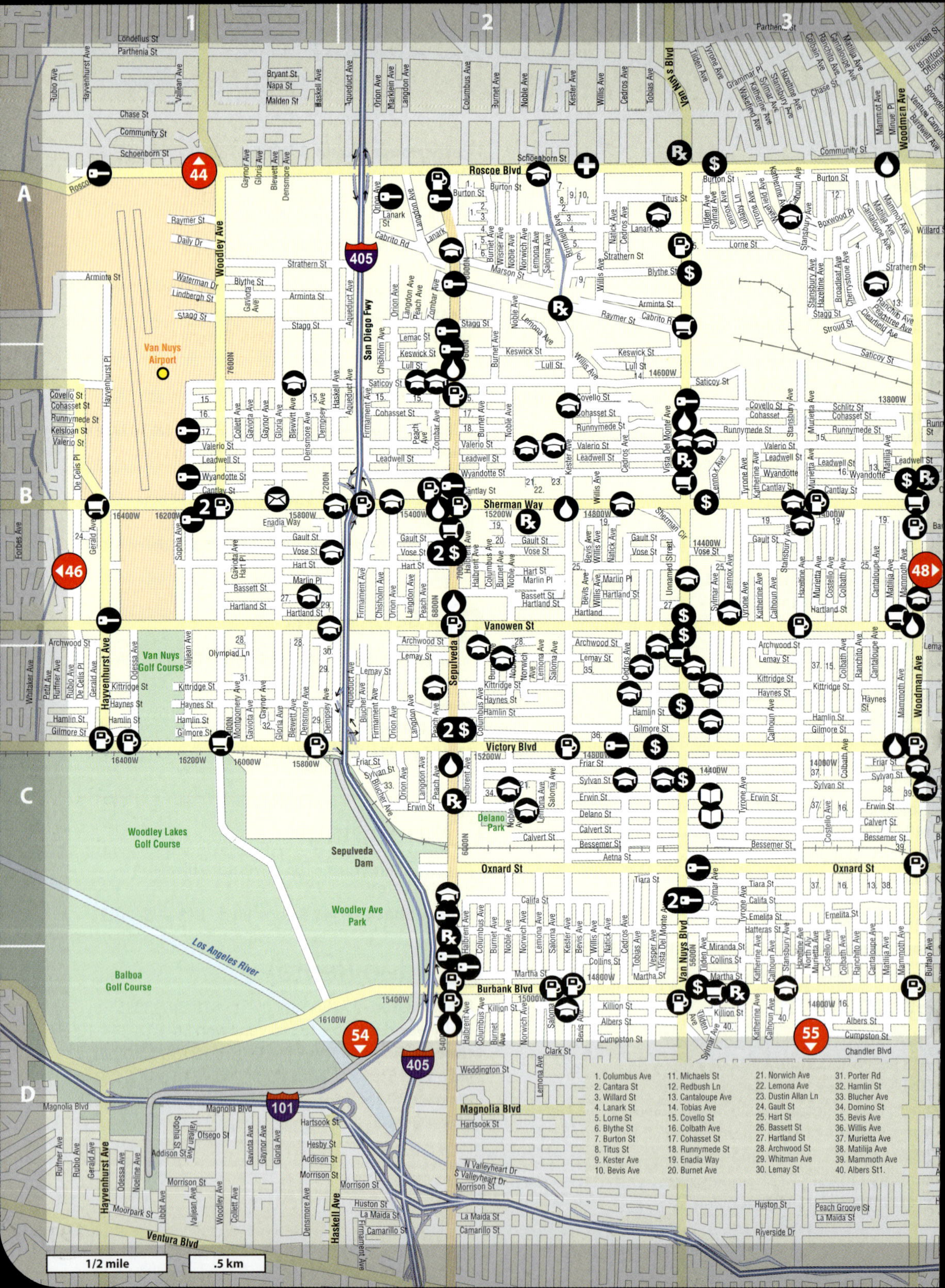

1. Columbus Ave
2. Cantara St
3. Willard St
4. Lanark St
5. Lorne St
6. Blythe St
7. Burton St
8. Titus St
9. Kester Ave
10. Bevis Ave
11. Michaels St
12. Redbush Ln
13. Cantaloupe Ave
14. Tobias Ave
15. Covello St
16. Colbath Ave
17. Cohasset St
18. Runnymede St
19. Enadia Way
20. Burnet Ave
21. Norwich Ave
22. Lemona Ave
23. Dustin Allan Ln
24. Gault St
25. Hart St
26. Bassett St
27. Hartland St
28. Archwood St
29. Whitman Ave
30. Lemay St
31. Porter Rd
32. Hamlin St
33. Blucher Ave
34. Domino St
35. Bevis Ave
36. Willis Ave
37. Murietta Ave
38. Matilija Ave
39. Mammoth Ave
40. Albers St1.

1/2 mile | .5 km

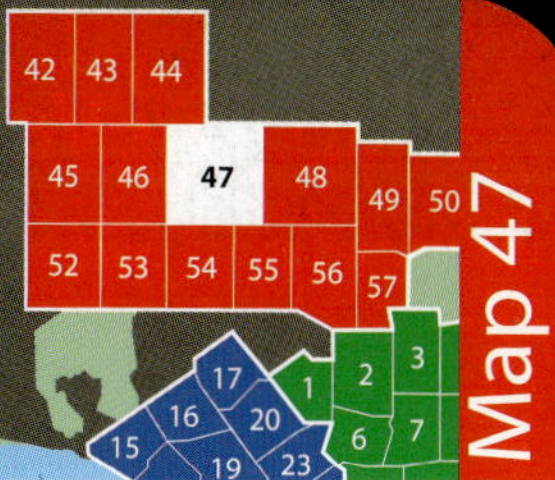

Traffic along Van Nuys' main thoroughfares and freeways is always a hassle during rush hour. Burbank Boulevard is usually a speedy and convenient east/west alternative to the 101 Freeway, and it turns into a mini-freeway between Sepulveda and Balboa Boulevards. When traveling north or south, always opt for Kester over the infinitely more congested Van Nuys or Sepulveda Boulevards.

Banks

- **Bank of America** • 6551 Van Nuys Blvd
- **Bank of America** • 7060 Sepulveda Blvd
- **Bank of America** • 7255 Woodman Ave
- **California National** • 14545 Victory Blvd
- **Citibank** • 6750 Van Nuys Blvd
- **Downey Savings & Loan** • 14440 Burbank Blvd
- **East West** • 6450 Sepulveda Blvd
- **Hanmi** • 14427 Sherman Wy
- **Union** • 14360 Roscoe Blvd
- **United Commercial** • 6440 Sepulveda Blvd
- **Washington Mutual** • 6300 Van Nuys Blvd
- **Washington Mutual** • 7108 Sepulveda Blvd
- **Washington Mutual** • 7950 Van Nuys Blvd
- **Wells Fargo** • 6800 Van Nuys Blvd

Car Rental

- **699 Rent-a-Car** • 14627 Victory Blvd
- **Advantage Rent-a-Car** • 5951 Van Nuys Blvd
- **Budget** • 5651 Sepulveda Blvd
- **Economy Rent-a-Car** • 7256 Sepulveda Blvd
- **Enterprise** • 5845 Sepulveda Blvd
- **Enterprise** • 7277 Valjean Ave
- **Enterprise** • 8230 Sepulveda Blvd
- **Enterprise Rent A Car** • 14436 Oxnard St
- **Excel Rent-a-Car** • 16506 Vanowen St
- **Hertz** • 16644 Roscoe Blvd
- **Hertz** • 5858 Van Nuys Blvd
- **Hertz** • 7155 Valjean Ave
- **Hertz** • 7435 Valjean Ave
- **Hertz** • 7724 Van Nuys Blvd
- **Hertz** • 8244 Orion Ave
- **Midway Car Rental** • 7240 Hayvenhurst Ave

Car Washes

- **Auto Hand Wash** • 13716 Victory Blvd
- **Buena Vista Self-Service Car Wash** • 14900 Sherman Wy
- **Buena Vista Self-Service Car Wash** • 15311 Saticoy St
- **Panorama Car Wash** • 13800 Roscoe Blvd
- **Sherman Oaks Auto Resort** • 5546 Sepulveda Blvd
- **Tri Star Car Wash** • 6344 Sepulveda Blvd
- **Valley Car Wash** • 7530 Van Nuys Blvd
- **Van Nuys Express Wash** • 7157 Sepulveda Blvd
- **Vanowen Coin-Op Carwash** • 13720 Vanowen St
- **Wash World** • 6810 Sepulveda Blvd

Gas Stations

- **76** • 14903 Burbank Blvd
- **76** • 15650 Sherman Wy
- **76** • 16505 Victory Blvd
- **76** • 6003 Woodman Ave
- **Alliance** • 16103 Sherman Wy
- **Arco** • 14114 Vanowen St
- **Arco** • 14903 Victory Blvd
- **Arco** • 15711 Victory Blvd
- **Arco** • 7557 Sepulveda Blvd
- **Chevron** • 14850 Burbank Blvd
- **Chevron** • 15255 Sherman Wy
- **Chevron** • 16455 Victory Blvd
- **Chevron** • 5600 Sepulveda Blvd
- **Chevron** • 7200 Woodman Ave
- **Exxon** • 8250 Sepulveda Blvd
- **Independent** • 14053 Sherman Wy
- **Mobil** • 15303 Sherman Wy
- **Mobil** • 16106 Sherman Wy
- **Mobil** • 5560 Van Nuys Blvd
- **Shell** • 13703 Victory Blvd
- **Shell** • 15805 Roscoe Blvd
- **Shell** • 5556 Sepulveda Blvd
- **Shell** • 5600 Woodman Ave
- **Thrifty** • 6810 Sepulveda Blvd
- **Thrifty** • 8050 Van Nuys Blvd

Emergency Rooms

- **Mission Community** • 14850 Roscoe Blvd

Landmarks

- **Van Nuys Airport** • 16461 Sherman Wy

Libraries

- **LA County Law Library** • 6230 Sylmar Ave • 818-374-2499
- **Van Nuys Branch** • 6250 Sylmar Ave • 818-756-8453

Pharmacies

- **CVS** • 15232 Sherman Wy • 818-374-3480
- **CVS** • 6201 N Sepulveda Blvd • 818-373-5005
- **Ralphs** • 14440 Burbank Blvd • 818-989-5422
- **Rite-Aid** • 7239 Woodman Ave • 818-781-7127
- **Sav-On** • Albertsons • 7227 Van Nuys Blvd • 818-787-8081
- **Target** • 14920 Raymer St • 818-922-1002
- **Target** • 5711 Sepulveda Blvd • 818-779-0321
- **Walmart** • 8333 Van Nuys Blvd • 818-830-0350

Police

- **Los Angeles Police Dept** • 6240 Sylmar Ave • 818-756-8343

Post Offices

- **US Post Office** • 15701 Sherman Wy • 800-275-8777
- **US Post Office** • 6200 Van Nuys Blvd • 800-275-8777

Schools

- **ABC Little** • 14926 Burbank Blvd
- **ABC Little** • 6447 Woodman Ave
- **Bassett St Elementary** • 15756 Bassett St
- **Burton St Elementary** • 8111 Calhoun Ave
- **Charter High School Of Arts-Multimedia & Performing** • 6952 Van Nuys Blvd
- **Children's Community** • 14702 Sylvan St
- **Children's Corner Preschool** • 7023 Haskell Ave
- **Childrens Circle Nursery** • 6328 Woodman Ave
- **Cohassett St Elementary** • 15810 Saticoy St
- **Columbus Ave Academy** • 6700 Columbus Ave
- **Crawford Academy** • 14530 Sylvan St
- **Crossroads** • 6843 Lennox Ave
- **East Valley New Continuation High** • 14630 Lanark St
- **Erikson High** • 6305 Woodman Ave
- **Foundations Community** • 14646 Sherman Wy
- **Grace Christian Academy** • 6510 Peach Ave
- **Happy Preschool Land** • 15727 Vanowen St
- **Hazeltine Ave Elementary** • 7150 Hazeltine Ave
- **The Keystone Van Nuys Campus** • 7533 Van Nuys Blvd
- **Kindergarten Learning Center** • 6555 Sylmar Ave
- **Knowledge Intermediate School Power School of Learning** • 6729 Vesper Ave
- **Los Angeles Hebrew High** • 5900 Sepulveda Blvd
- **Montclair** • 8071 Sepulveda Blvd
- **Montessori House of Children** • 6252 Woodman Ave
- **NW Day** • 7400 Van Nuys Blvd
- **Pacific Ridge** • 15339 Saticoy St
- **Pacific Ridge** • 15339 Saticoy St
- **Panorama Senior High** • 8015 Van Nuys Blvd
- **Pinecrest** • 14111 Sherman Wy
- **Ranchito Ave Elementary** • 7940 Ranchito Ave
- **Robert Fulton College Prep** • 7477 Kester Ave
- **Serendipity Early Care** • 14125 Burbank Blvd
- **St Elisabeth Elementary** • 6635 Tobias Ave
- **Sun Flower Montessori** • 15520 Sherman Wy
- **Sylvan Park EEC** • 15011 Delano St
- **Sylvan Park Elementary** • 6238 Noble Ave
- **Valerio Primary Center** • 14935 Valerio St
- **Valerio St Elementary** • 15035 Valerio St
- **Valley** • 15700 Sherman Wy
- **Valley High** • 6650 Van Nuys Blvd
- **Van Nuys Community Adult** • 6535 Cedros Ave
- **Van Nuys Elementary** • 6464 Sylmar Ave
- **Van Nuys Middle** • 5435 Vesper Ave
- **Van Nuys Senior High** • 6535 Cedros Ave
- **Vista Middle** • 15040 Roscoe Blvd
- **Will Rogers Continuation** • 15141 Lemay St

Supermarkets

- **Albertsons** • 7227 Van Nuys Blvd
- **Food 4 Less** • 16530 Sherman Wy
- **Jon's Market** • 6655 Van Nuys Blvd
- **Jon's Marketplace** • 7134 Sepulveda Blvd
- **Ralphs** • 14440 Burbank Blvd
- **Ralphs** • 7221 Woodman Ave
- **Smart & Final** • 7815 Van Nuys Blvd
- **Vallarta Supermarket** • 13715 Vanowen St
- **Vallarta Supermarket** • 16107 Victory Blvd

Roscoe Blvd
Sherman Way
Vanowen St
Victory Blvd
Oxnard St
Burbank Blvd
Magnolia Blvd
Ventura Blvd
Woodley Ave
Sepulveda Blvd
Van Nuys Blvd
Woodman Ave
San Diego Fwy
Van Nuys Airport
Van Nuys Golf Course
Woodley Lakes Golf Course
Balboa Golf Course
Sepulveda Dam
Woodley Ave Park
Delano Park
Los Angeles River

1. Columbus Ave	11. Michaels St	21. Norwich Ave	31. Porter Rd
2. Cantara St	12. Redbush Ln	22. Lemona Ave	32. Hamlin St
3. Willard St	13. Cantaloupe Ave	23. Dustin Allan Ln	33. Blucher Ave
4. Lanark St	14. Tobias Ave	24. Gault St	34. Domino St
5. Lorne St	15. Covello St	25. Hart St	35. Bevis Ave
6. Blythe St	16. Colbath Ave	26. Bassett St	36. Willis Ave
7. Burton St	17. Cohasset St	27. Hartland St	37. Murietta Ave
8. Titus St	18. Runnymede St	28. Archwood St	38. Matilija Ave
9. Kester Ave	19. Enadia Way	29. Whitman Ave	39. Mammoth Ave
10. Bevis Ave	20. Burnet Ave	30. Lemay St	40. Albers St1.

1/2 mile .5 km

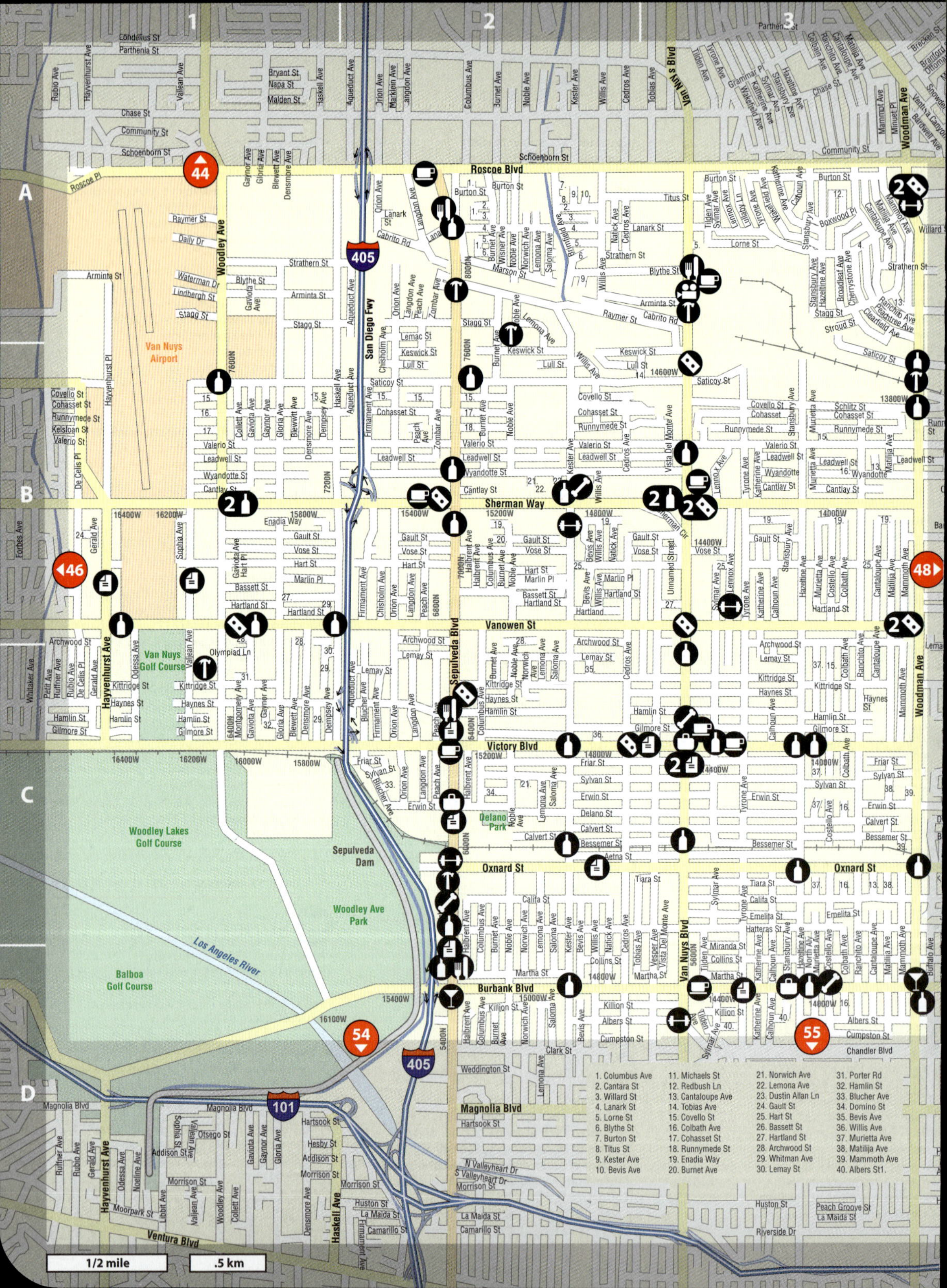

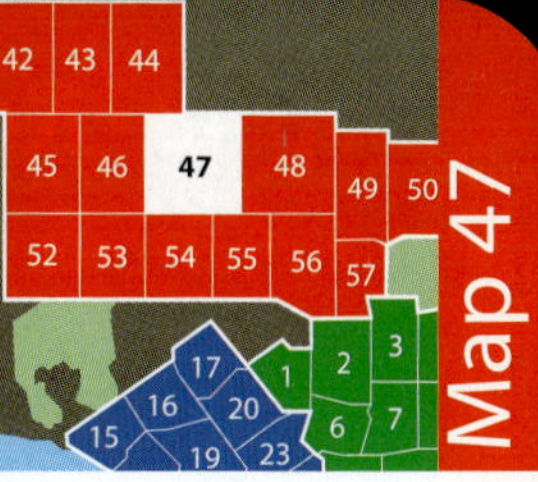

Cars are a big part of Van Nuys' identity. Van Nuys Boulevard was once a drag strip for teenagers out cruising in their hot rods, and it now serves as Automobile Row for consumers looking to trade in their set of wheels for something new. The old General Motors assembly plant is now The Plant (7800 Van Nuys Blvd.), a strip mall that houses a plethora of shopping and dining options and a decent 16-screen movie theater.

Coffee

- **Boba Loca Van Nuys** • 6411 Sepulveda Blvd
- **Java Groove Coffee** • 14310 Victory Blvd
- **Krispy Kreme Doughnuts** • 7249 Van Nuys Blvd
- **Starbucks** • 14431 Burbank Blvd
- **Starbucks** • 15355 Sherman Wy
- **Starbucks** • 15430 Roscoe Blvd
- **Starbucks** • Albertsons • 7227 Van Nuys Blvd
- **Starbucks** • 7902 Van Nuys Blvd
- **Won's Coffee Shop** • 14440 Gilmore St

Copy Shops

- **FedEx Kinko's** • 5810 Sepulveda Blvd • 818-780-2123
- **Ford Graphics** • 6920 Hayvenhurst Ave • 818-781-0513
- **Kopy-Rite** • 6325 Van Nuys Blvd • 818-787-1667
- **Office Depot** • 6440 S Sepulveda Blvd • 818-780-9916
- **Platinum Copy** • 14328 Victory Blvd • 818-779-0779
- **Priorty Graphics** • 6961 Valjean Ave • 818-908-2700
- **Staples** • 6104 Sepulveda Blvd • 818-908-2360
- **UPS Store** • 6311 Van Nuys Blvd • 818-781-9000
- **Valley Instant Press** • 14806 Oxnard St • 818-786-5793
- **VIP Printing** • 14619 Victory Blvd • 818-994-2216

Gyms

- **Curves** • 5512 Van Nuys Blvd • 818-782-8783
- **Curves** • 7135 Kester Ave • 818-902-2100
- **Curves** • 8205 Woodman Ave • 818-781-0101
- **LA Fitness Sports Clubs** • 5990 Sepulveda Blvd • 818-988-7411
- **YMCA** • 6901 Lennox Ave • 818-902-3894

Hardware Stores

- **Callahan Whsle Hardware** • 6666 Valjean Ave • 818-988-4611
- **CWH** • 7910 Sepulveda Blvd • 818-787-0525
- **Handiman Hardware** • 7730 Burnet Ave • 818-988-0700
- **Home Depot** • 7870 E Van Nuys Blvd • 818-373-0046
- **Orchard Supply Hardware** • 5960 Sepulveda Blvd • 818-779-7292
- **Peterson Lumber & Supply** • 7610 Woodman Ave • 818-782-9320

Liquor Stores

- **Adam's Liquor** • 14556 Vanowen St
- **Allan's Liquor** • 16060 Vanowen St
- **Amar Liquor** • 14900 Burbank Blvd
- **AMS Liquor** • 5658 Sepulveda Blvd
- **Beverages & More** • 5820 Sepulveda Blvd
- **Casino Liquors** • 14900 Victory Blvd
- **Confetti Liquors** • 13674 Oxnard St
- **D&K Liquor** • 15245 Saticoy St
- **F&R Liquor** • 14040 Burbank Blvd
- **George's Liquor** • 14102 Oxnard St
- **Gigis Liquor** • 14038 Victory Blvd
- **Harvest Markets** • 14055 Burbank Blvd
- **In & Out Liquor Mart & Deli** • 7650 Woodman Ave
- **Jon's Market** • 6655 Van Nuys Blvd
- **Jon's Market** • 7134 Sepulveda Blvd
- **Jons Market** • 7134 Sepulveda Blvd
- **Liquor Palace 2** • 13649 Burbank Blvd
- **Lloyd's Liquor Market** • 7219 Kester Ave
- **Louie's Liquors** • 16461 Vanowen St
- **Michael's Liquor** • 7510 Woodman Pl
- **One Stop Liquor & Market** • 14521 Sherman Wy
- **Pat's Liquors** • 6020 Kester Ave
- **Sam's Liquor** • 15717 Vanowen St
- **Sherman Liquors & Jr Market** • 16045 Sherman Wy
- **Short Stop 25** • 14411 Victory Blvd
- **Short Stop 28** • 6073 Van Nuys Blvd
- **Tori Liquor & Jr Market** • 7300 Sepulveda Blvd
- **Triangle Liquors** • 8120 Sepulveda Blvd
- **Valley Liquor** • 7357 Van Nuys Blvd
- **Woodley Liquors** • 7550 Woodley Ave

Movie Theaters

- **Mann Plant 16** • 7876 Van Nuys Blvd • 818-779-0323

Nightlife

- **Robin Hood Pub** • 13640 Burbank Blvd • 818-994-6045

Pet Shops

- **Birds Plus** • 14041 Burbank Blvd • 818-901-1187
- **Doggie Pros** • 7244 Kester Ave • 310-227-1752
- **Helen's Bird Shop** • 6455 Van Nuys Blvd • 818-909-6814
- **Petco** • 5850 Sepulveda Blvd • 818-997-4009

Restaurants

- **Dr Hogly Wogly's BBQ** • 8136 Sepulveda Blvd • 818-780-6701
- **In-N-Out Burger** • 7930 Van Nuys Blvd • 800-786-1000
- **Sam Woo Barbeque** • 6450 Sepulveda Blvd • 818-988-6813
- **Zankou Chicken** • 5658 Sepulveda Blvd • 818-781-0615

Shopping

- **Big Kid Collectable Toy Mall** • 14109 Burbank Blvd • 818-785-9208
- **Educative Toys & Supplies** • 6416 Van Nuys Blvd • 818-782-5580
- **Star Restaurant Equipment & Supply** • 6178 Sepulveda Blvd • 818-782-4460

Video Rental

- **20-20 Video** • 6440 Sepulveda Blvd • 818-780-2020
- **Blockbuster** • 13722 Sherman Wy • 818-781-9734
- **Hollywood Video** • 7221 Van Nuys Blvd • 818-997-0706
- **Prael (Thai)** • 8205 Woodman Ave • 818-376-1976
- **Speed Video** • 16065 Vanowen St • 818-785-3051
- **Unique Video** • 7650 Van Nuys Blvd • 818-989-1563
- **Video City** • 8245 Woodman Ave • 818-786-4950
- **Video Japan (Japanese)** • 15355 Sherman Wy • 818-786-0850
- **Video Rose** • 14655 Victory Blvd • 818-989-4050
- **Video Supermart Valley (Korean)** • 7130 Van Nuys Blvd • 818-997-7410
- **Videomen** • 14522 Vanowen St • 818-786-3561

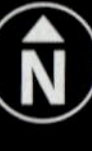

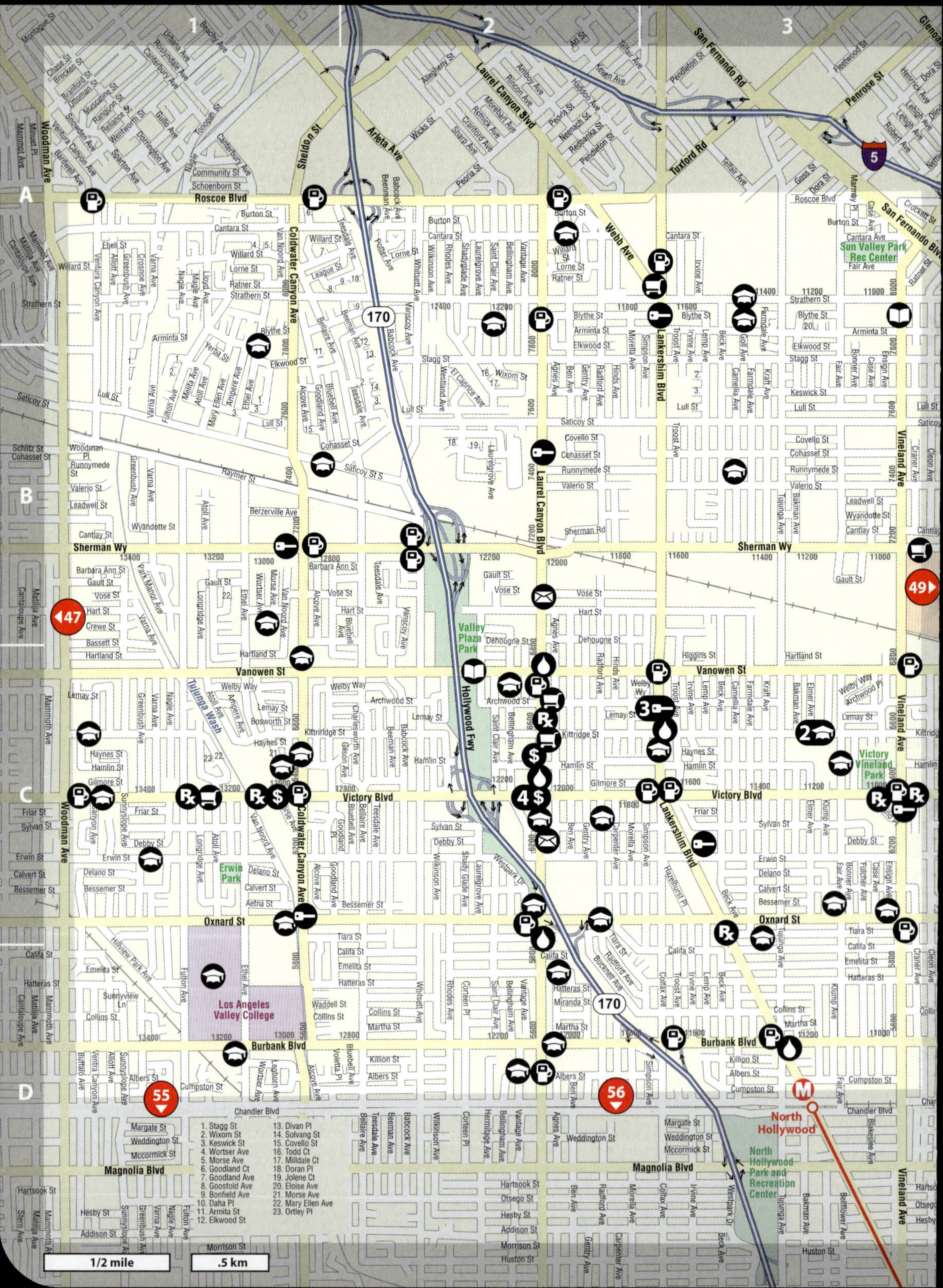

N
1
2
3
A
B
C
D
Roscoe Blvd
Sherman Wy
Vanowen St
Victory Blvd
Oxnard St
Burbank Blvd
Chandler Blvd
Magnolia Blvd
Saticoy St
Woodman Ave
Coldwater Canyon Ave
Laurel Canyon Blvd
Lankershim Blvd
Vineland Ave
San Fernando Rd
Tuxford Rd
Sheldon St
Arleta Ave
Webb Ave
Hollywood Fwy
Tujunga Wash
170
5
47
49
55
56
Valley Plaza Park
Erwin Park
Los Angeles Valley College
Sun Valley Park Rec Center
Victory Vineland Park
North Hollywood
North Hollywood Park and Recreation Center
1. Stagg St
2. Wixom St
3. Keswick St
4. Wortser Ave
5. Morse Ave
6. Goodland Ct
7. Goodland Ave
8. Goosfold Ave
9. Bonfield Ave
10. Daha Pl
11. Armita St
12. Elkwood St
13. Divan Pl
14. Solvang St
15. Covello St
16. Todd Ct
17. Milldale Ct
18. Doran Pl
19. Jolene Ct
20. Eloise Ave
21. Morse Ave
22. Mary Ellen Ave
23. Ortley Pl
1/2 mile
.5 km

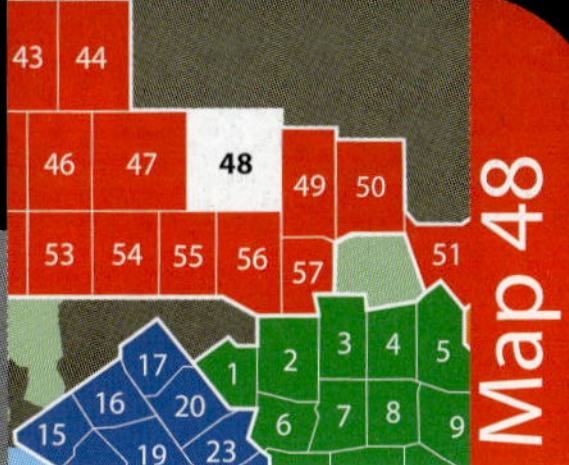

While North Hollywood is often considered the nuts and bolts of Hollywood's entertainment industry, it has actually evolved into an entertaining place in and of itself. With studio tours, an arts festival, live theater, and an art house movie theatre due to open, North Hollywood has come into its own for tourists and locals alike. The NoHo Arts District is teeming with theaters, galleries, shops, cafés, and restaurants. With the Metro Red Line leading directly under the hill, it's easier than ever to enjoy all that North Hollywood has to offer. While

Banks

- **Bank of America** • 6600 Laurel Cyn Blvd
- **California National** • 6350 Laurel Cyn Blvd
- **Citibank** • 13003 Victory Blvd
- **Washington Mutual** • 6400 Laurel Cyn Blvd
- **Wells Fargo** • 12160 Victory Blvd

Car Rental

- **Any Price Rent A Car** • 7441 Laurel Canyon Blvd
- **Enterprise** • 12959 Sherman Wy
- **Enterprise** • 6343 Vineland Ave
- **Hertz** • 6712 Lankershim Blvd
- **Hertz** • 7918 Lankershim Blvd
- **Horizon** • 6644 Lankershim Blvd
- **Horizon Rent A Car** • 6638 Lankershim Blvd
- **Rent 4 Less** • 6051 Vineland Ave
- **Studio Self Storage** • 6200 Lankershim Blvd

Car Washes

- **Buena Vista Self-Service Car Wash** • 6809 Laurel Cyn Blvd
- **Lankershim Car Wash** • 6622 Lankershim Blvd
- **National Car Wash** • 5950 Laurel Cyn Blvd
- **Plaza Car Wash** • 6462 Laurel Cyn Blvd
- **Tujunga Car Wash** • 5553 Tujunga Ave

Gas Stations

- **76** • 11407 Burbank Blvd
- **76** • 11705 Victory Blvd
- **76** • 12856 Sherman Wy
- **76** • 5969 Laurel Cyn Blvd
- **76** • 7955 Laurel Cyn Blvd
- **Arco** • 12050 Roscoe Blvd
- **Arco** • 13605 Roscoe Blvd
- **Arco** • 6757 Laurel Cyn Blvd
- **Arco** • 6804 Vineland Ave
- **Arco** • 8004 Lankershim Blvd
- **BP** • 6800 Lankershim Blvd
- **Chevron** • 11000 Victory Blvd
- **Chevron** • 12950 Victory Blvd
- **Chevron** • 5544 Laurel Cyn Blvd
- **Chevron** • 7214 Whitsett Ave
- **Mobil** • 11680 Burbank Blvd
- **Mobil** • 12500 Sherman Wy
- **Shell** • 11680 Victory Blvd
- **Shell** • 12858 Roscoe Blvd
- **Shell** • 5957 Vineland Ave
- **Valero** • 13666 Victory Blvd
- **Valero** • 7004 Laurel Cyn Blvd

Libraries

- **Sun Valley Branch** • 7935 Vineland Ave • 818-764-1338
- **Valley Plaza Branch** • 12311 Vanowen St • 818-765-9251

Pharmacies

- **CVS** • 10945 Victory Blvd • 818-487-0119
- **CVS** • 13021 Victory Blvd • 818-760-2861
- **CVS** • 5969 Lankershim Blvd • 818-761-4235
- **Rite-Aid** • 6639 Laurel Cyn Blvd • 818-982-0695
- **Target** • 11051 Victory Blvd • 818-487-9351
- **Walgreens** • 13231 Victory Blvd • 818-623-9358

Police

- **Los Angeles Police Dept** • 11640 Burbank Blvd • 818-623-4016

Post Offices

- **US Post Office** • 6242 Vantage Ave • 800-275-8777
- **US Post Office** • 6535 Lankershim Blvd • 800-275-8777
- **US Post Office** • 7035 Laurel Cyn Blvd • 800-275-8777

Schools

- **Adat Ari El** • 12020 Burbank Blvd
- **Arminta EEC** • 7911 Goll Ave
- **Arminta St Elementary** • 11530 Strathern St
- **Bellingham PC** • 6728 Bellingham Ave
- **Burbank Blvd Elementary** • 12215 Albers St
- **Camellia Ave Elementary** • 7451 Camellia Ave
- **Charles Leroy Lowman Special Education Center** • 12827 Saticoy St
- **Coldwater Canyon Ave Elementary** • 6850 Coldwater Cyn Ave
- **Erwin St Elementary** • 13400 Erwin St
- **Fair Ave Elementary** • 6501 Fair Ave
- **Fair EEC** • 11300 Kittridge St
- **Greenwood Preschool and Elementary** • 6003 Fair Ave
- **James Madison Middle** • 13000 Hart St
- **John B Monlux Elementary** • 6051 Bellaire Ave
- **Kiddie Academy** • 6543 Lankershim Blvd
- **Kittridge St Elementary** • 13619 Kittridge St
- **Laurel Hall** • 11919 Oxnard St
- **Laurence** • 13639 Victory Blvd
- **London Continuation** • 12924 Oxnard St
- **Los Angeles Valley College** • 5800 Fulton Ave
- **Maud Booth Family Center** • 11243 Kitteridge St
- **Maurice Sendak Elementary** • 11414 Tiara St
- **Messiah Lutheran** • 12020 Cantara St
- **Montessori Academy of N Hollywood** • 6000 Ensign Ave
- **Or Hachaim Academy** • 6021 Laurel Cyn Blvd
- **Princeton College Preparatory** • 5622 Colfax Ave
- **Red Apple Preschool** • 12052 Emelita St
- **San Fernando Valley Professional** • 6215 Laurel Cyn Blvd
- **Saticoy Elementary** • 7850 Ethel Ave
- **St Jane Frances de Chantal** • 12950 Hamlin St
- **Strathern St Elementary** • 7939 St Clair Ave
- **Summit View** • 6455 Coldwater Cyn Ave
- **Ulysses S Grant Senior High** • 13000 Oxnard St
- **Victory Blvd Elementary** • 6315 Radford Ave
- **Village Glen** • 13130 Burbank Blvd

Supermarkets

- **Food 4 Less** • 8035 Webb Ave
- **Ralphs** • 6657 Laurel Cyn Blvd
- **Smart & Final** • 6601 N Laurel Cyn Blvd
- **Vallarta Supermarket** • 10950 Sherman Way

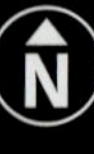

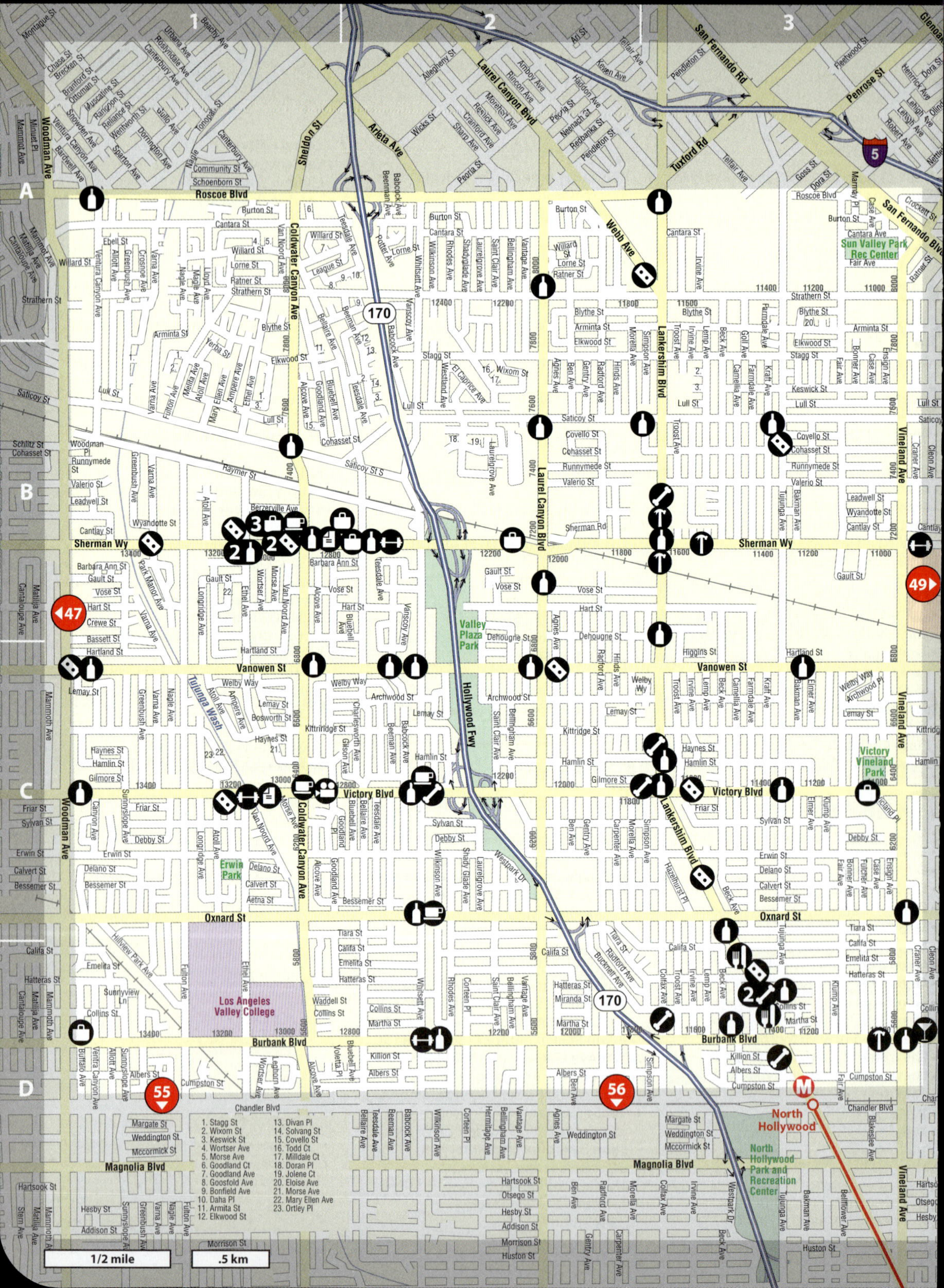

N
1
2
3
A
B
C
D
Roscoe Blvd
Sherman Wy
Vanowen St
Victory Blvd
Oxnard St
Burbank Blvd
Magnolia Blvd
Chandler Blvd
Saticoy St
Woodman Ave
Coldwater Canyon Ave
Laurel Canyon Blvd
Lankershim Blvd
Vineland Ave
Hollywood Fwy
Sheldon St
Arleta Ave
San Fernando Rd
Tuxford Rd
Penrose St
Webb Ave
Tujunga Wash
170
5
47
49
55
56
Valley Plaza Park
Erwin Park
Los Angeles Valley College
Sun Valley Park Rec Center
Victory Vineland Park
North Hollywood
North Hollywood Park and Recreation Center
1. Stagg St
2. Wixom St
3. Keswick St
4. Wortser Ave
5. Morse Ave
6. Goodland Ct
7. Goodland Ave
8. Goosfold Ave
9. Bonfield Ave
10. Daha Pl
11. Armita St
12. Elkwood St
13. Divan Pl
14. Solvang St
15. Covello St
16. Todd Ct
17. Milldale Ct
18. Doran Pl
19. Jolene Ct
20. Eloise Ave
21. Morse Ave
22. Mary Ellen Ave
23. Ortley Pl
1/2 mile
.5 km

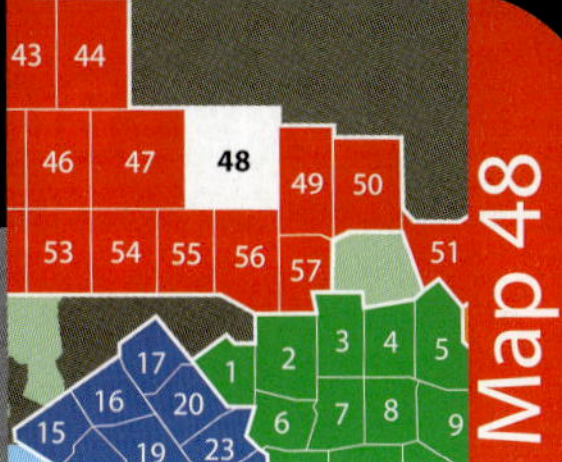

NoHo will never be accused of being posh, it excels in the interesting and the offbeat. Its used-clothing stores are treasure chests offering outfits worn in TV shows and movies. While the area isn't defined by a specific cuisine and doesn't exactly qualify as an LA dining destination, there are plenty of dining options from Chinese to Italian to Indian. With a liquor store seemingly on every street corner, there's sure to be plenty of wino-rific fun.

Coffee

- **Bobo Loca** • 12901 Sherman Wy
- **The Coffee Bar** • 12444 Victory Blvd
- **House of Bonjour** • 12453 Oxnard St
- **Starbucks** • 12848 Victory Blvd

Copy Shops

- **Staples** • 12807 Sherman Wy • 818-503-7960
- **UPS Store** • 13029 Victory Blvd • 818-623-9988

Gyms

- **Bally Total Fitness** • 13069 Victory Blvd • 818-506-4208
- **Curves** • 12501 Burbank Blvd • 818-762-2305
- **Curves** • 12650 Sherman Wy • 818-764-9282
- **Gold's Gym** • 6233 Laurel Cyn Blvd • 818-506-4600
- **Powerhouse Gym** • 10950 Sherman Wy • 818-565-5533

Hardware Stores

- **CWH** • 7303 Lankershim Blvd • 818-982-2121
- **Home Depot** • 11600 Sherman Wy • 818-764-9600
- **Stock Building Supply** • 7151 Lankershim Blvd • 818-982-6046
- **True Value** • 11000 Burbank Blvd • 818-769-4421

Liquor Stores

- **7&7 Liquor Junior Mart** • 13654 Victory Blvd
- **A&S Liquors** • 5745 Tujunga Ave
- **Arrow Liquor** • 12521 Vanowen St
- **Brothers Market** • 7050 Laurel Cyn Blvd
- **Carmel Liquor** • 12516 Vanowen St
- **Circus Liquor** • 5600 Vineland Ave
- **Circus Liquors** • 6417 Lankershim Blvd
- **D&R Liquors** • 6917 Lankershim Blvd
- **Dale's Junior Liquor Store** • 12500 Oxnard St
- **Danny's Liquor & Market** • 7202 Lankershim Blvd
- **Dorose Liquors** • 13560 Roscoe Blvd
- **Fair House Liquor** • 12903 Sherman Wy
- **Gigi's Liquor 2** • 12114 Vanowen St
- **Gip Liquor** • 13100 Sherman Wy
- **Handy Mart Liquors** • 8012 Laurel Cyn Blvd
- **Imperial Liquor** • 13324 Vanowen St
- **Joe's Liquor** • 12521 Victory Blvd
- **K-1 Liquor** • 13056 Sherman Wy
- **Kim's Liquor** • 5940 Lankershim Blvd
- **Ladd Liquor** • 13646 Vanowen St
- **Ladd Liquors** • 11336 Vanowen St
- **Metro Liquor** • 6400 Tujunga Ave
- **Phil's Liquor & Deli** • 11510 Burbank Blvd
- **Roy's Liquors** • 12441 Burbank Blvd
- **Sal's Liquor** • 7552 Laurel Cyn Blvd
- **Saticoy Liquor** • 11415 Saticoy St
- **Short Stop 26** • 12861 Vanowen St
- **Short Stop 30** • 12650 Sherman Wy
- **Sunrise Liquors** • 12931 Saticoy St
- **Urban Liquors** • 8323 Lankershim Blvd
- **USA Liquor** • 6530 Lankershim Blvd
- **Valley Liquor** • 11723 Saticoy St
- **Vineland Wine Cellar** • 6012 Vineland Ave

Movie Theaters

- **Century North Hollywood** • 12827 Victory Blvd • 818-508-6004

Nightlife

- **Rawhide** • 10937 Burbank Blvd • 818-760-9798

Pet Shops

- **Aquarium Village (fish only)** • 11734 Victory Blvd • 818-985-3813
- **Bird House** • 5742 Lankershim Blvd • 818-766-4269
- **Deep Sea Aquarium** • 7355 Lankershim Blvd • 818-764-0875
- **Dog House** • 5742 Lankershim Blvd • 818-753-4325
- **Dragon Aquarium** • 6507 Lankershim Blvd • 818-508-9611
- **Fish Pond** • 12459 Oxnard St • 818-766-8343
- **Pet Stop** • 5505 1/2 Tujunga Ave • 818-760-7387

Restaurants

- **In-N-Out Burger** • 5864 Lankershim Blvd • 800-786-1000
- **Miss Peaches Southern Cuisine** • 5643 Lankershim Blvd • 818-760-4924

Shopping

- **99 Cents Store** • 12711 Sherman Wy • 818-764-9991
- **Baklava Factory** • 12909 Sherman Wy • 818-764-1011
- **Big Lots** • 13005 Sherman Wy • 818-982-1687
- **K-Mart** • 13007 Sherman Wy • 818-764-0250
- **Michael's** • 12809 Sherman Wy • 818-901-8321
- **Plummer's** • 12240 Sherman Way • 818-765-0401
- **Robin Hood** • 13638 Burbank Blvd • 818-994-6045

Video Rental

- **Blockbuster** • 6112 Lankershim Blvd • 818-487-6929
- **Hollywood Video** • 8065 Webb Ave • 818-504-6438
- **Planet Video** • 13041 Victory Blvd • 818-508-9429
- **SK Video (Thai)** • 13124 Sherman Wy • 818-764-1666
- **Video 9 (Thai)** • 12980 Sherman Wy • 818-765-8106
- **Video Center** • 5751 Lankershim Blvd • 818-760-4722
- **Video Citi** • 11650 Victory Blvd • 818-980-1505
- **Video Citi** • 12051 Vanowen St • 818-982-0414
- **Video Hut** • 13648 Vanowen St • 818-994-5878
- **Video Hut** • 7563 Tujunga Ave • 818-982-7020
- **Video Market** • 13434 Sherman Wy • 818-982-8488
- **Video Universe** • 12937 Sherman Wy • 818-764-8842

Map 49 • Burbank

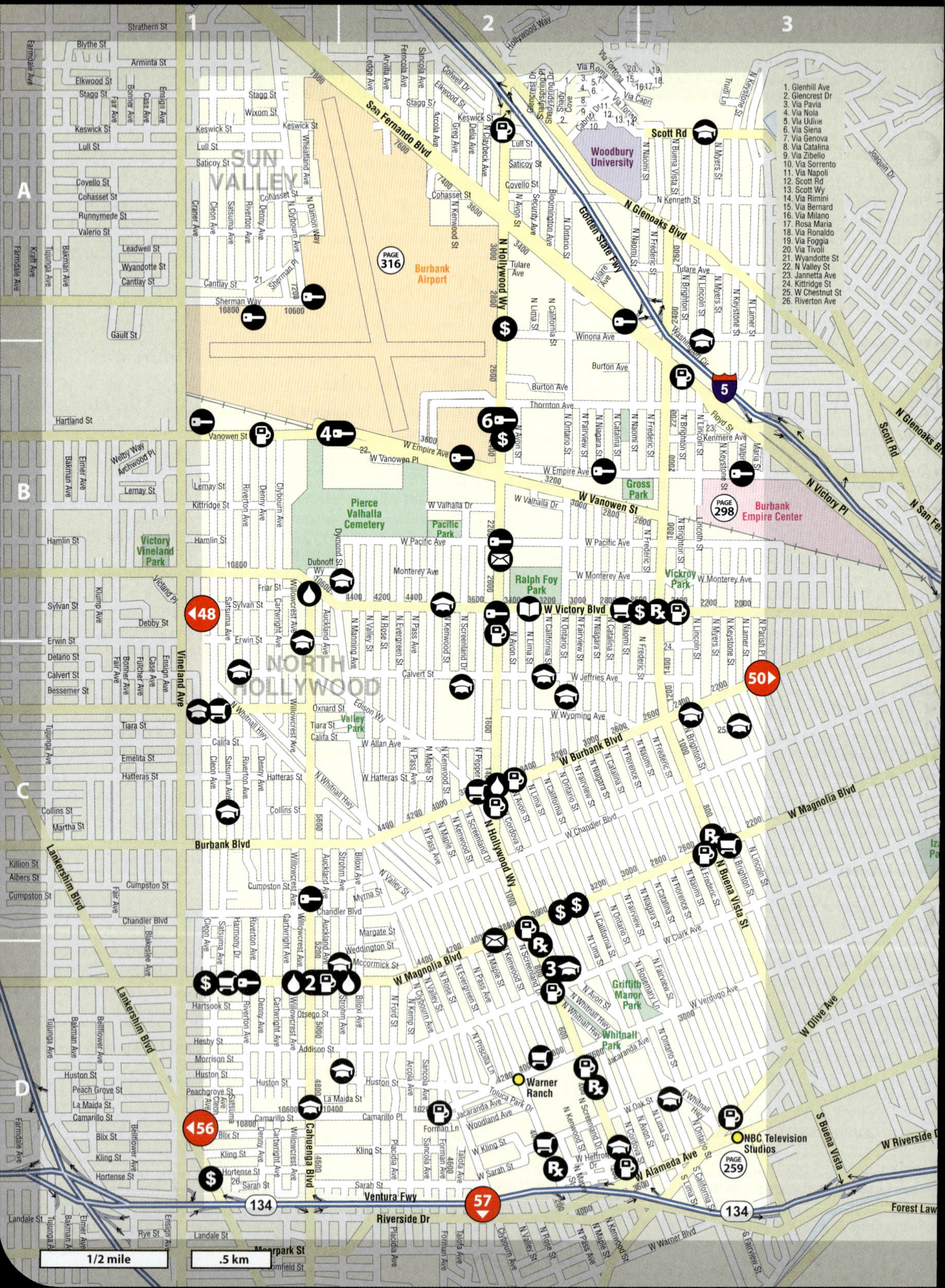

1. Glenhill Ave
2. Glencrest Dr
3. Via Pavia
4. Via Nola
5. Via Udine
6. Via Siena
7. Via Genova
8. Via Sorrento
9. Via Zibello
10. Via Sorrento
11. Via Napoli
12. Scott Rd
13. Scott Wy
14. Via Rimini
15. Via Bernard
16. Via Milano
17. Rosa Maria
18. Via Ronaldo
19. Via Foggia
20. Via Tivoli
21. Wyandotte St
22. N Valley St
23. Jannetta Ave
24. Kittridge St
25. W Chestnut St
26. Riverton Ave

1/2 mile

.5 km

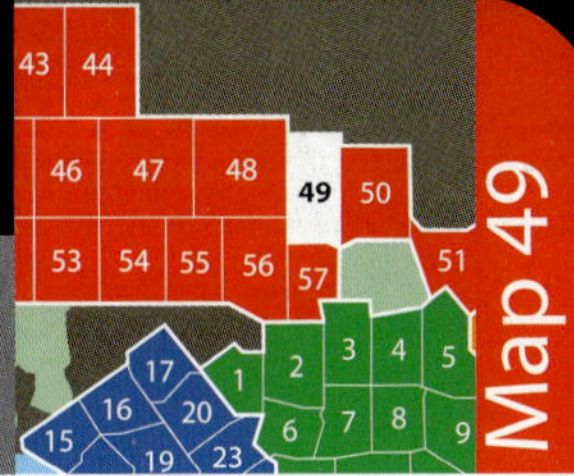

Everyone comes to Burbank, but it's not just for Ikea (Map 50) and studio tours. The Bob Hope Airport can shave hours off your travels. One of the coolest decorating jobs in town is just next door at Fry's Electronics, with its 1950s-era invaders-from-outer-space motif, complete with a flying saucer that seems to have missed the runway and crashed into the store. It's not unusual to see Jay Leno tooling along Hollywood Way between the NBC studios and the facility that houses his collection of cars.

Banks

- **Bank of America** • 3400 W Magnolia Blvd
- **City National** • 4605 Lankershim Blvd
- **Community** • 2800 N Hollywood Wy
- **Downey Savings & Loan** • 2600 W Victory Blvd
- **Lockheed Federal Credit Union** • 2340 Hollywood Wy
- **Washington Mutual** • 3521 W Magnolia Blvd
- **Wells Fargo** • 10900 Magnolia Blvd

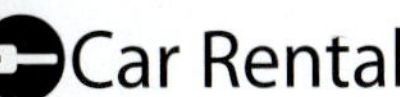

Car Rental

- **Ace Rent-A-Car** • 4320 W Vanowen St
- **Advantage Rent-a-Car** • 2890 W Empire Ave
- **Airport Car Rental Center** • 10929 Vanowen St
- **Alamo** • 2627 N Hollywood Wy
- **Avis** • 2627 N Hollywood Wy
- **Budget** • 2220 N Hollywood Wy
- **Burbank Airport Rent-A-Car** • 5424 Cahuenga Blvd
- **Discovery Rent A Car** • 1976 N Hollywood Wy
- **Enterprise** • 2612 N Hollywood Wy
- **EZ Rent A Car** • 2900 N San Fernando Blvd
- **Hertz** • 10750 Sherman Wy
- **Hertz** • 2100 W Empire Ave
- **Hertz** • 2627 N Hollywood Wy
- **Hertz** • 2800 Clybourn Ave
- **Hertz** • 3750 Empire Ave
- **Hertz** • 4511 W Empire Ave
- **Hertz** • 4531 W Empire Ave
- **Horizon** • 2627 N Hollywood Wy
- **National** • 2627 N Hollywood Wy
- **Rent 4 Less** • 4320 W Vanowen St
- **Rent-a-Wreck** • 10860 Burbank Blvd

Car Washes

- **HWB Car Wash** • 3600 W Burbank Blvd
- **In-N-Out Car Wash** • 10505 Victory Blvd
- **Toluca Lake Car Wash** • 10515 Magnolia Blvd
- **Zeavy Car Wash** • 10605 Burbank Blvd

Gas Stations

- **76** • 1401 N Hollywood Wy
- **76** • 200 N Hollywood Wy
- **76** • 2421 W Victory Blvd
- **Arco** • 10601 Magnolia Blvd
- **Exxon** • 2417 N San Fernando Blvd
- **Independent** • 10740 Vanowen St
- **Independent** • 1951 N Hollywood Wy
- **Independent** • 3600 W Burbank Blvd
- **Mobil** • 3020 W Olive Ave
- **Shell** • 2500 W Magnolia Blvd
- **Shell** • 550 N Hollywood Wy
- **Shell** • 7710 N Hollywood Wy
- **Valero** • 3701 W Magnolia Blvd
- **Valero** • 800 N Hollywood Wy

Landmarks

- **NBC Television Studios** • 3000 W Alameda Ave
- **Warner Ranch** • Verdugo Ave & Pass Ave

Libraries

- **Northwest Branch** • 3323 W Victory Blvd • 818-238-5640

Pharmacies

- **CVS** • 1615 W Verdugo Ave • 818-845-9332
- **CVS** • 2500 W Victory Blvd • 818-955-8200
- **CVS** • 511 Hollywood Wy • 818-841-0710
- **Dana Drug Store & Boutique** • 317 N Pass Ave • 818-562-1177
- **Rite-Aid** • 935 N Hollywood Wy • 818-841-5336
- **Walgreens** • 2501 W Magnolia Blvd • 818-841-1685

Post Offices

- **US Post Office** • 2140 N Hollywood Wy • 800-275-8777
- **US Post Office** • 3810 W Magnolia Blvd • 800-275-8777

Schools

- **Bret Harte Children's Center** • 1421 N Ontario St
- **Bret Harte Elementary** • 3200 W Jeffries Ave
- **Burbank Montessori Academy** • 217 N Hollywood Wy
- **Burlington** • 242 N Burlington Ave
- **Dubnoff Elementary** • 10526 Dubnoff Wy
- **George Washington Elementary** • 2322 N Lincoln St
- **Joyces Toluca Lake Pre-School** • 10512 Magnolia Blvd
- **Kindechicks** • 10837 Collins St
- **Luther Burbank Middle** • 3700 W Jeffries Ave
- **Magnolia Park (Special Education)** • 827 N Avon St
- **Media Center Montessori** • 3711 W Clark Ave
- **Monterey High** • 1915 W Monterey Ave
- **Montessori Children's Academie** • 2400 W Burbank Blvd
- **New Generation** • 3821 W Victory Blvd
- **Oxnard St Elementary** • 10912 Oxnard St
- **Providencia Elementary** • 1919 N Ontario St
- **Robert Louis Stevenson Elementary** • 3333 W Oak St
- **St Francis Xavier** • 3601 Scott Rd
- **St Patrick** • 10626 Erwin St
- **Theodore Roosevelt Elementary** • 850 N Cordova St
- **Thomas Edison Elementary** • 2110 W Chestnut St
- **Toluca Crossroads** • 4814 Cahugena Blvd
- **Toluca Lake EEC** • 4915 Strohm Ave
- **Toluca Lake Elementary** • 4840 Cahuenga Blvd
- **Valley Montessori** • 10816 Calvert St
- **Woodbury University** • 7500 Glenoaks Blvd

Supermarkets

- **Albertsons** • 3830 W Verdugo Ave
- **Handy Market** • 2514 W Magnolia Blvd
- **Ralphs** • 10900 Magnolia Blvd
- **Ralphs** • 2600 W Victory Blvd
- **Smart & Final** • 3708 W Burbank Blvd
- **Vallarta Supermarket** • 10859 Oxnard St
- **Vons** • 301 N Pass Ave

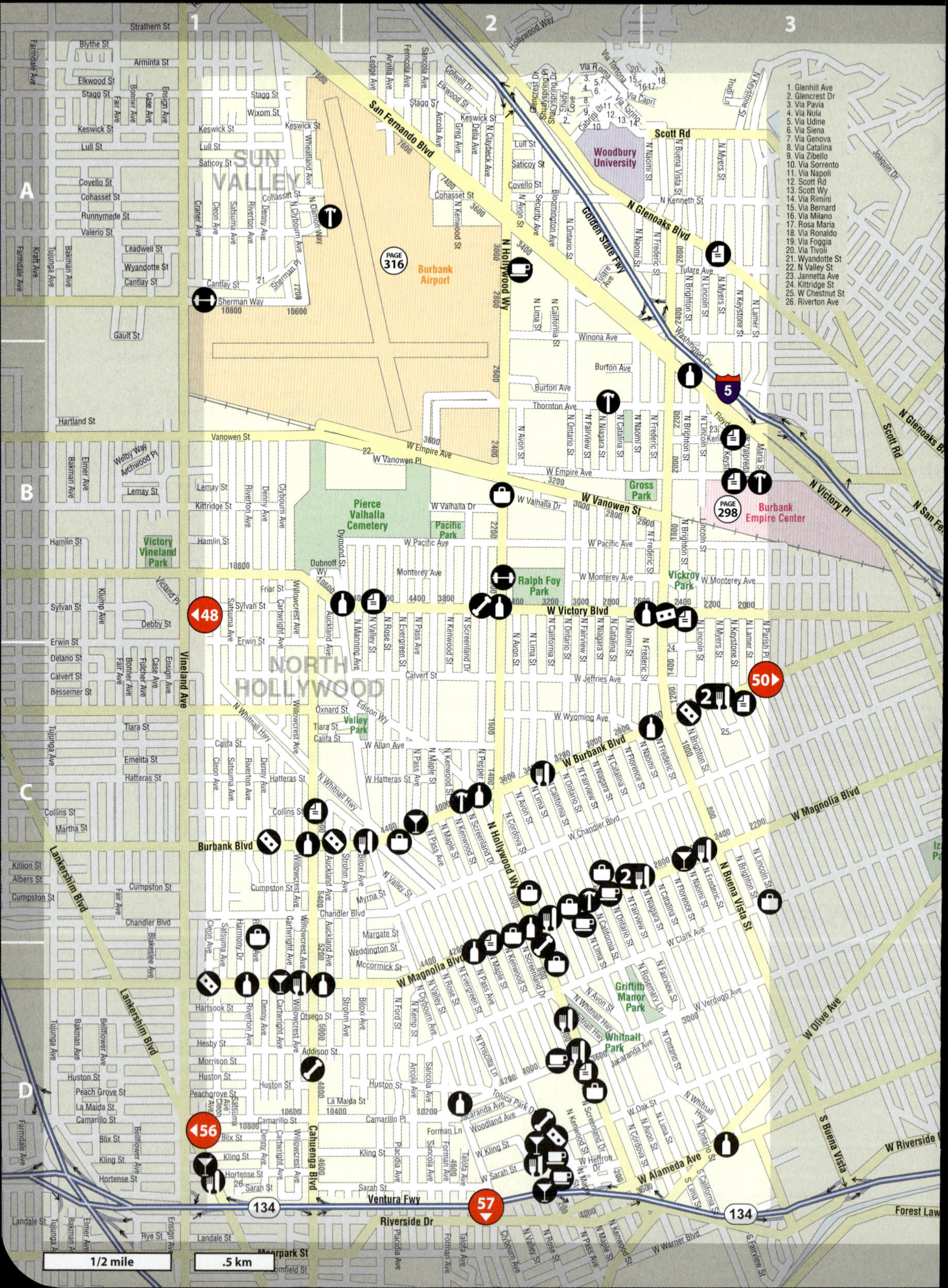

N
1
2
3
A
B
C
D
SUN VALLEY
NORTH HOLLYWOOD
Woodbury University
Burbank Airport
PAGE 316
Burbank Empire Center
PAGE 298
Pierce Valhalla Cemetery
Pacific Park
Victory Vineland Park
Ralph Foy Park
Gross Park
Vickroy Park
Valley Park
Griffith Manor Park
Whitnall Park
48
50
56
57
5
134
San Fernando Blvd
Golden State Fwy
N Glenoaks Blvd
N Hollywood Wy
Scott Rd
W Empire Ave
W Vanowen St
Vanowen St
W Victory Blvd
W Burbank Blvd
Burbank Blvd
W Magnolia Blvd
W Olive Ave
W Alameda Ave
W Riverside Dr
Riverside Dr
Ventura Fwy
Lankershim Blvd
Vineland Ave
Cahuenga Blvd
N Buena Vista St
S Buena Vista
Forest Law
N Victory Pl
N San Fe
Sherman Way
Moorpark St
W Verdugo Ave
W Chandler Blvd
W Monterey Ave
W Pacific Ave
W Valhalla Dr
Winona Ave
Burton Ave
Thornton Ave
Tulare Ave
N Kenneth St
W Jeffries Ave
W Wyoming Ave
W Clark Ave
Toluca Park Dr
W Warner Blvd
1. Glenhill Ave
2. Glencrest Dr
3. Via Pavia
4. Via Nola
5. Via Udine
6. Via Siena
7. Via Genova
8. Via Catalina
9. Via Zibello
10. Via Sorrento
11. Via Napoli
12. Scott Rd
13. Scott Wy
14. Via Rimini
15. Via Bernard
16. Via Milano
17. Rosa Maria
18. Via Ronaldo
19. Via Foggia
20. Via Tivoli
21. Wyandotte St
22. N Valley St
23. Jannetta Ave
24. Kittridge St
25. W Chestnut St
26. Riverton Ave
1/2 mile
.5 km

Burbank may seem all residential, industrial, and corporate, and that's because it is. But don't overlook the nooks and crannies. Magnolia Boulevard is a walkable strip of restaurants, shops, and salons. Nosing around the studios will yield all sorts of great industry-secret restaurants and bars. Joe Mantegna serves up Chicago-style dogs and Eli's cheesecake at Taste Chicago. Harry Potter fans will go mad as a box of frogs over the generous display of props, costumes, and set pieces housed on the Warner Brothers lot.

Coffee

- **Romancing the Bean** • 3208 1/2 W Magnolia Blvd
- **Simply Coffee & Boutique** • 940 N Lima St
- **Starbucks** • 2950 N Hollywood Wy
- **Starbucks** • 301 N Pass Ave
- **Starbucks** • 347 N Pass Ave
- **Starbucks** • Albertsons • 3830 W Verdugo Ave

Copy Shops

- **A Express** • 531 N Hollywood Wy • 818-566-8542
- **Concepts Printing & Copying** • 5668 Cahuenga Blvd • 818-752-8330
- **Copy & Mail** • 2829 N Glenoaks Blvd • 818-843-1010
- **Image Copy** • 1909 W Burbank Blvd • 818-955-9444
- **Nonstop Printing** • 3820 W Magnolia Blvd • 818-846-3864
- **Pip Printing** • 2111 Kenmere Ave • 818-845-2474
- **Staples** • 2080 Empire Ave • 818-238-2928
- **Turbo Graphics** • 4300 W Victory Blvd • 818-563-5278
- **UPS Store** • 2416 W Victory Blvd • 818-559-6335

Gyms

- **Miami Fitness** • 1611 W Verdugo Ave • 818-566-7547
- **Valley Powerhouse Gym & Fitness Center** • 10950 Sherman Wy • 818-565-5533
- **World Gym** • 2010 N Hollywood Wy • 818-563-4203

Hardware Stores

- **Do It Center** • 3221 W Magnolia Blvd • 818-845-8301
- **Estrada Hardware** • 3110 N Damon Wy • 818-840-8029
- **Lowe's** • 2000 Empire Ave • 818-557-2300
- **Lucky's Hardware** • 3814 W Burbank Blvd • 818-845-8338
- **Reno Hardware & Supply** • 2901 Thornton Ave • 818-842-3667

Liquor Stores

- **A&O Liquors** • 3117 W Olive Ave
- **Aero Liquor Store** • 2527 W Burbank Blvd
- **Bamford Liquor & Deli** • 10575 Magnolia Blvd
- **La Paz Liquor** • 4101 W Magnolia Blvd
- **Liquor Palace** • 3801 W Burbank Blvd
- **Magnolia Liquor** • 3801 W Magnolia Blvd
- **Nelson's Liquor** • 4420 W Victory Blvd
- **Prestige Wines & Spirits** • 10101 Camarillo St
- **Riverton Liquors** • 10800 Magnolia Blvd
- **Royal Liquor** • 5600 Cahuenga Blvd
- **Starlite Liquor** • 3510 W Victory Blvd
- **Tip Top Liquor** • 2501 W Victory Blvd
- **Vista** • 2415 N San Fernando Blvd

Nightlife

- **Champs Sports Pub** • 4103 W Burbank Blvd • 818-840-9493
- **Dimples** • 3413 W Olive Ave • 818-842-2336
- **The Library Lounge** • 322 N Pass Ave • 818-842-8887
- **Match** • 4657 Lankershim Blvd • 818-766-0116
- **NoBar** • 10622 Magnolia Blvd • 818-753-0545
- **Sardos** • 259 N Pass Ave • 818-846-8126
- **Tinhorn Flats** • 2623 Magnolia Blvd • 818-567-2470

Pet Shops

- **Peggy Woods Pet Emporium** • 923 N Hollywood Wy • 818-848-0123
- **Pet Mania** • 353 N Pass Ave • 818-848-5512
- **Petco** • 3525 W Victory Blvd • 818-566-8528
- **Pride 'n Joy** • 5670 Cahuenga Blvd • 818-760-4337

Restaurants

- **Buchanan Arms** • 2013 W Burbank Blvd • 818-845-0692
- **Chili John's** • 2108 W Burbank Blvd • 818-846-3611
- **Coral Café** • 3321 W Burbank Blvd • 818-566-9725
- **Full o' Life** • 2515 W Magnolia Blvd • 818-845-8343
- **Le Petit Chateau** • 4615 Lankershim Blvd • 818-769-1812
- **Mucho Mas** • 10405 Burbank Blvd • 818-980-0300
- **Pinocchio's** • 3103 W Magnolia Blvd • 818-845-3517
- **Poquito Mas** • 10651 Magnolia Blvd • 818-994-8226
- **Porto's Bakery & Café** • 3614 W Magnolia Blvd • 818-846-9100
- **Santa Fe Tacos** • 353 N Pass Ave • 818-563-4324
- **Taste Chicago** • 603 N Hollywood Wy • 818-563-2800
- **Tony's Bella Vista** • 3116 W Magnolia Blvd • 818-843-0164

Shopping

- **Arte de Mexico** • 5356 Riverton Ave • 818-769-5090
- **Atomic Records** • 3812 W Magnolia Blvd • 818-848-7090
- **Dark Delicacies** • 4213 W Burbank Blvd • 818-556-6660
- **Fry's Electronics** • 2311 N Hollywood Wy • 818-526-8100
- **It's a Wrap** • 3315 W Magnolia Blvd • 818-567-7366
- **Jelly Bean Factory** • 927 N Hollywood Wy • 818-848-4806
- **Monte Carlo** • 3103 Magnolia Blvd • 818-845-3517
- **Otto's Import Store & Delicatessen** • 2320 W Clark Ave • 818-845-0433
- **Swift** • 3212 W Magnolia Blvd • 818-558-1289
- **The Train Shack** • 1030 N Hollywood Wy • 818-842-3330
- **Western Bagel** • 513 N Hollywood Wy • 818-567-0413

Video Rental

- **Blockbuster** • 2420 W Burbank Blvd • 818-566-1193
- **Hollywood Video** • 10930 Magnolia Blvd • 818-763-4866
- **Hollywood Video** • 2484 W Victory Blvd • 818-559-2560
- **Lakeside Video** • 353 N Pass Ave • 818-848-2001
- **Twisted Video** • 10530 Burbank Blvd • 818-508-0559
- **Video 91** • 10723 Burbank Blvd • 818-766-0684

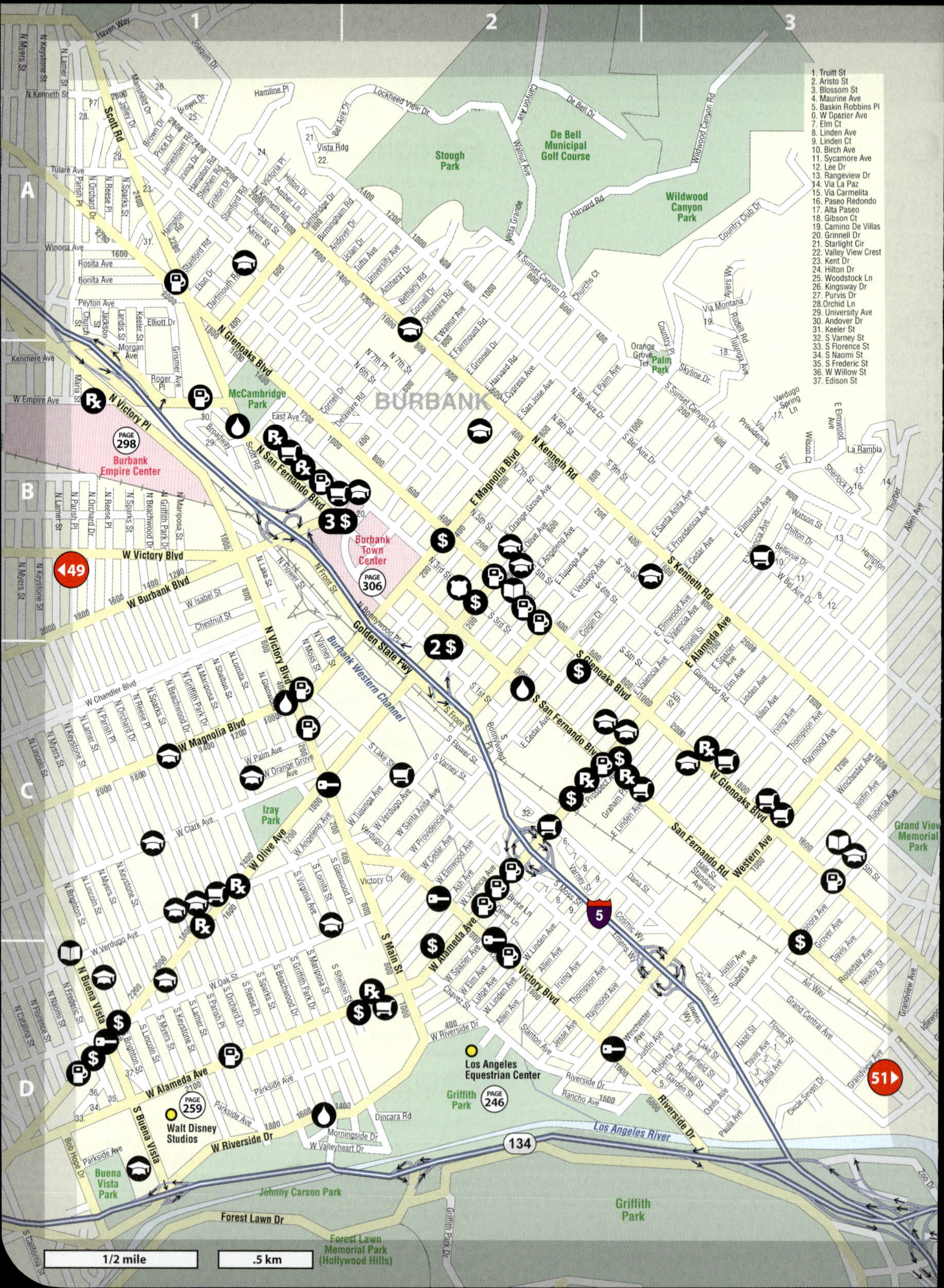

Map 50 • Burbank East / Glendale West

1. Truitt St
2. Aristo St
3. Blossom St
4. Maurine Ave
5. Baskin Robbins Pl
6. W Spazier Ave
7. Elm Ct
8. Linden Ave
9. Linden Ct
10. Birch Ave
11. Sycamore Ave
12. Lee Dr
13. Rangeview Dr
14. Via La Paz
15. Via Carmelita
16. Paseo Redondo
17. Alta Paseo
18. Gibson Ct
19. Camino De Villas
20. Grinnell Dr
21. Starlight Cir
22. Valley View Crest
23. Kent Dr
24. Hilton Dr
25. Woodstock Ln
26. Kingsway Dr
27. Purvis Dr
28. Orchid Ln
29. University Ave
30. Andover Dr
31. Keeler St
32. S Varney St
33. S Florence St
34. S Naomi St
35. S Frederic St
36. W Willow St
37. Edison St

1/2 mile | .5 km

Burbank is an entertainment powerhouse. Not only can you ride horses at the Los Angeles Equestrian Center, but the Pickwick Center on Riverside Drive offers bowling, ice-skating, banquet facilities, and other stuff we probably don't even know about. There are plenty of parks to crash even if you don't live in the area. And even without all of that, the less congested streets make Burbank a nice breather from the regular LA madness.

Banks

- **Bank of America** • 142 E Olive Ave
- **Bank of America** • 6400 San Fernando Rd
- **California National** • 240 N San Fernando Blvd
- **Citibank** • 360 E Magnolia Blvd
- **Comerica** • 801 N San Fernando Blvd
- **Downey Savings & Loan** • 1750 W Olive Ave
- **Downey Savings & Loan** • 25 E Alameda Ave
- **First Entertainment Credit Union** • 2520 W Olive Ave
- **Union** • 601 S Glenoaks Blvd
- **Vista Federal Credit Union** • 2411 W Olive Ave
- **Washington Mutual** • 100 N 1st St
- **Washington Mutual** • 1030 S San Fernando Blvd
- **Washington Mutual** • 1110 W Alameda Ave
- **Washington Mutual** • 840 N San Fernando Blvd
- **Wells Fargo** • 250 E Olive Ave
- **Wells Fargo** • 900 N San Fernando Blvd

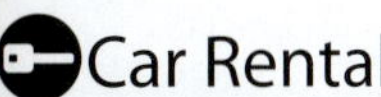

Car Rental

- **Ace Rent-A-Car** • 1633 Victory Blvd
- **All-Rite Rent-a-Car** • 810 S Victory Blvd
- **Avis** • 2509 W Olive Ave
- **Enterprise** • 110 S Victory Blvd

Car Washes

- **Burbank Pitstop** • 1420 N San Fernando Blvd
- **Classic Hand Car Wash** • 506 S San Fernando Blvd
- **Magnolia Car Wash** • 910 W Magnolia Blvd
- **Sonora Car Wash** • 1521 Riverside Dr

Gas Stations

- **76** • 280 W Alameda Ave
- **76** • 901 N San Fernando Blvd
- **Arco** • 201 W Alameda Ave
- **Arco** • 250 S Glenoaks Blvd
- **Chevron** • 100 S Glenoaks Blvd
- **Chevron** • 140 E Alameda Ave
- **Chevron** • 1501 W Glenoaks Blvd
- **Chevron** • 1655 Victory Blvd
- **Chevron** • 2501 W Olive Ave
- **Chevron** • 439 W Alameda Blvd
- **Independent** • 1638 N San Fernando Blvd
- **Independent** • 1919 W Alameda Ave
- **Independent** • 2005 N Glenoaks Blvd
- **Mobil** • 349 S Glenoaks Blvd
- **Shell** • 181 W Alameda Ave
- **Shell** • 400 N Victory Blvd
- **Valero** • 341 N Victory Blvd

Landmarks

- **Los Angeles Equestrian Center** • 480 Riverside Dr
- **Walt Disney Studios** • 500 S Buena Vista

Libraries

- **Buena Vista Branch** • 300 N Buena Vista St • 818-238-5620
- **Burbank Central Library** • 110 N Glenoaks Blvd • 818-238-5600
- **Grandview Library** • 1535 5th St • 818-548-2049

Pharmacies

- **CVS** • 1015 N San Fernando Blvd • 818-841-0810
- **Pavilions** • 1110 W Alameda Ave • 818-567-0086
- **Ralphs** • 1100 N San Fernando Blvd • 818-845-5112
- **Rite-Aid** • 1505 W Olive Ave • 818-846-7843
- **Sav-On** • 101 E Alameda Ave • 818-563-2724
- **Sav-On** • Albertsons • 1855 W Glenoaks Blvd • 818-246-4934
- **Target** • 1800 W Empire Ave • 818-238-0239
- **Walgreens** • 1028 S San Fernando Blvd • 818-729-9283

Police

- **Burbank Police Dept** • 200 N 3rd St • 818-238-3000

Post Offices

- **US Post Office** • 135 E Olive Ave • 800-275-8777
- **US Post Office** • 1634 N San Fernando Blvd • 800-275-8777
- **US Post Office** • 6444 San Fernando Rd • 800-275-8777

Schools

- **Balboa Elementary** • 1844 Bel Aire Dr
- **Bellarmine-Jefferson High** • 465 E Olive Ave
- **Benjamin Franklin Elementary** • 1610 Lake St
- **Burbank High** • 902 N 3rd St
- **Burbank USD Community Day** • 330 N Buena Vista St
- **Burroughs High** • 1920 Clark Ave
- **David Starr Jordan Middle** • 420 S Mariposa St
- **First Lutheran** • 1001 S Glenoaks Blvd
- **Jefferson Elementary** • 1540 5th St
- **Joaquin Miller Elementary** • 720 E Providencia Ave
- **Media Center Montessori** • 1601 W Magnolia Blvd
- **Montessori Academy** • 1920 W Glenoaks Blvd
- **Muir Middle** • 1111 N Kenneth Rd
- **Music Box Preschool and Kindergarten** • 720 S Main St
- **Options for Youth-Burbank Charter** • 1701 W Verdugo Ave
- **Providence High** • 511 S Buena Vista St
- **Ralph Waldo Emerson Elementary** • 720 E Cypress Ave
- **St Finbar** • 2120 W Olive Ave
- **St Robert Bellarmine** • 154 N 5th St
- **Steady Circle** • 310 E Alameda Ave
- **Stepping Stones** • 332 E Valencia Ave
- **Thomas Jefferson Elementary** • 1900 N 6th St
- **Walt Disney Elementary** • 1220 W Orange Grove Ave
- **William McKinley Elementary** • 349 W Valencia Ave

Supermarkets

- **Albertsons** • 1855 W Glenoaks Blvd
- **Jon's Market** • 1717 W Glenoaks Blvd
- **Pavilions** • 1110 W Alameda Ave
- **Ralphs** • 1100 N San Fernando Blvd
- **Ralphs** • 25 E Alameda Ave
- **Smart & Final** • 6850 San Fernando Rd
- **Trader Joe's** • 230 E Alameda Ave
- **Trader Joe's** • 345 S Lake Blvd
- **Vons** • 1011 N San Fernando Blvd
- **Vons** • 1820 W Verdugo Ave

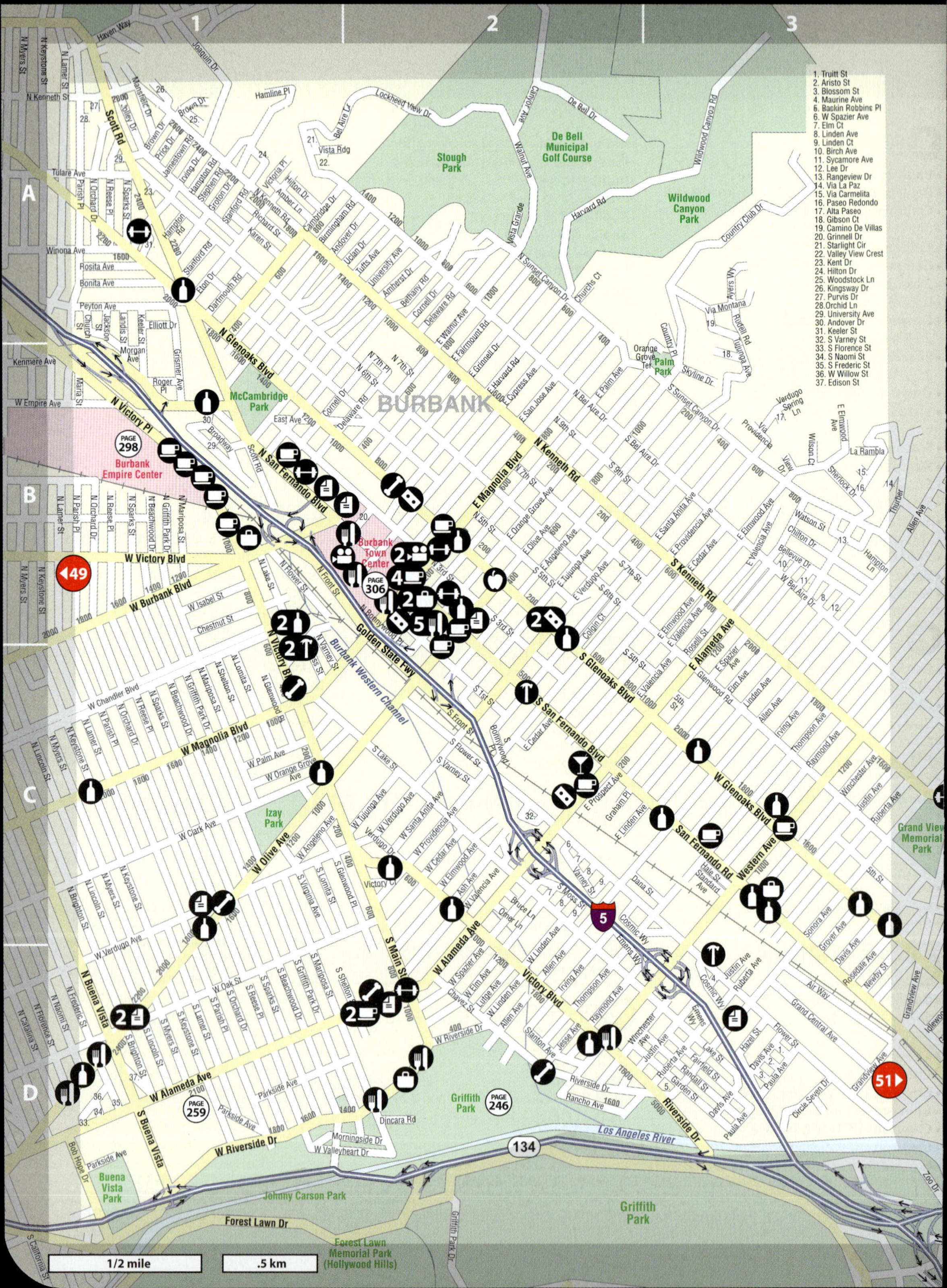

Map 50 • Burbank East / Glendale West

1. Truitt St
2. Aristo St
3. Blossom St
4. Maurine Ave
5. Backin Robbins Pl
6. W Spazier Ave
7. Elm Ct
8. Linden Ave
9. Linden Ct
10. Birch Ave
11. Sycamore Ave
12. Lee Dr
13. Rangeview Dr
14. Via La Paz
15. Via Carmelita
16. Paseo Redondo
17. Alta Paseo
18. Gibson Ct
19. Camino De Villas
20. Grinnell Dr
21. Starlight Cir
22. Valley View Crest
23. Kent Dr
24. Hilton Dr
25. Woodstock Ln
26. Kingsway Dr
27. Purvis Dr
28. Orchid Ln
29. University Ave
30. Andover Dr
31. Keeler St
32. S Varney St
33. S Florence St
34. S Naomi St
35. S Frederic St
36. W Willow St
37. Edison St

BURBANK

Burbank Empire Center PAGE 298

Burbank Town Center PAGE 306

PAGE 259

Griffith Park PAGE 246

49

51

1/2 mile | .5 km

Sundries / Entertainment

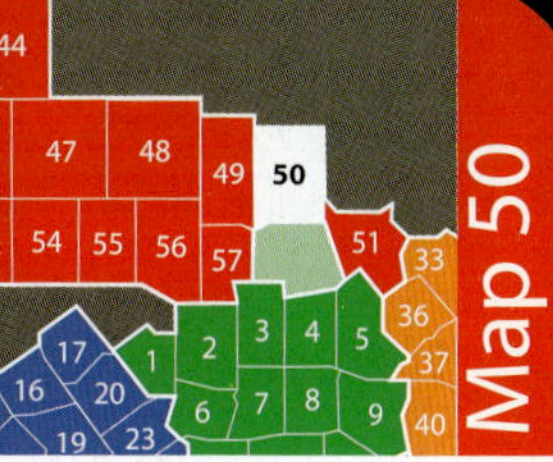

The Burbank Town Center mall is just the start of the town's retail therapy options. The pedestrian-friendly shop-, bar-, and restaurant-lined San Fernando Road (a "scene" in its own right); and the ginormous Empire Center are on hand to fulfill any type of spree. Sure, it's not quite the Grove or Hollywood & Highland, but avoiding that traffic for this more maneuverable area is a deal that's simply priceless.

Coffee

- **Boba Loca** • 148 N San Fernando Blvd
- **Café Chalet** • 150 E Olive Ave
- **Coffee Bean & Tea Leaf** • 1521 N Victory Pl
- **Coffee Bean & Tea Leaf** • 340 N San Fernando Blvd
- **Gloria Jean's Coffee** • 201 E Magnolia Blvd, Ste 242
- **Indoor Café** • 1301 N Victory Pl
- **Kelly's Coffee & Fudge** • 201 E Magnolia Blvd
- **Krispy Kreme Doughnuts** • 1521 N Victory Pl
- **Patrick's Café** • 6320 San Fernando Rd
- **San Marco Coffee Roasting** • 401 N Glenoaks Blvd
- **Starbucks** • 1001 N San Fernando Blvd
- **Starbucks** • Vons • 1110 W Alameda Ave
- **Starbucks** • 113 E Alameda Ave
- **Starbucks** • 1190 Alameda Ave
- **Starbucks** • The Great Indoors • 1301 N Victory Pl
- **Starbucks** • 1703 W Glenoaks Blvd
- **Starbucks** • 1711 N Victory Pl
- **Starbucks** • 300 N San Fernando Blvd

Copy Shops

- **Color Images Copy and Print** • 2320 W Olive Ave • 818-567-2900
- **Command Print + Graphics** • 1807 W Verdugo Ave • 818-260-9678
- **Copy Central** • 2300 W Olive Ave • 818-841-8800
- **FedEx Kinko's** • 250 E Olive Ave • 818-558-3900
- **Ford Graphics** • 608 Sonora Ave • 818-241-4181
- **Office Depot** • 228 E Burbank Blvd • 818-848-2591
- **Staples** • 1060 W Almeda Dr • 818-558-3350
- **UPS Store** • 928 N San Fernando Blvd • 818-842-5200

Farmers Markets

- **Burbank (Sat, 8 am–12:30 pm)** • E Olive Ave & S Glenoaks Blvd

Gyms

- **Burbank YMCA** • 321 E Magnolia Blvd • 818-845-8551
- **Curves** • 1090 N San Fernando Blvd • 818-842-1007
- **Curves** • 1416 Kenneth Rd • 818-551-1600
- **Curves** • 940 W Alameda Ave • 818-558-3591
- **World Gym** • 226 E Palm Ave • 818-954-0021

Hardware Stores

- **Burbank Paint** • 548 S San Fernando Blvd • 818-845-2684
- **Home Depot** • 1200 S Flower St • 818-556-1563
- **Orchard Supply Hardware** • 641 N Victory Blvd • 818-557-2755
- **Stock Building Supply** • 640 N Victory Blvd • 818-842-2177

Liquor Stores

- **ABC Liquor & Deli** • 2112 W Magnolia Blvd
- **Ace Liquors** • 1740 Victory Blvd
- **Alameda Liquor** • 929 S Victory Blvd
- **Burbank Liquor** • 500 S Glenoaks Blvd
- **Castle Liquors** • 6808 San Fernando Rd
- **Favorite Liquor** • 533 S Victory Blvd
- **Favorite Liquor & Deli** • 533 S Victory Blvd
- **Glenmar Liquors** • 2000 N Glenoaks Blvd
- **Jon's Market** • 1717 W Glenoaks Blvd
- **K&K Liquor** • 515 N Victory Blvd
- **Legacy Liquor** • 1800 W Olive Ave
- **M&M Liquors** • 1951 W Glenoaks Blvd
- **Prime Liquor Jr Market** • 101 N Victory Blvd
- **Roy's Liquor** • 1627 N San Fernando Blvd
- **Roy's Liquor Store** • 6520 San Fernando Rd
- **Selene Liquor Market** • 1427 W Glenoaks Blvd
- **Thirst Quencher Liquors** • 440 N Glenoaks Blvd
- **UM Liquor** • 401 N Victory Blvd
- **Village Liquor** • 211 E Olive Ave
- **Village Market** • 2713 W Olive Ave

Movie Theaters

- **AMC Burbank 16** • 125 E Palm Ave • 818-953-9800
- **AMC Media Center 8** • 201 E Magnolia Blvd • 818-953-9800
- **AMC Media Center North 6** • 770 N 1st St • 818-953-9800

Nightlife

- **The Blue Room** • 916 S San Fernando Blvd • 323-849-2779

Pet Shops

- **Burbank Pet Plaza** • 1080 W Alameda Ave • 818-557-0144
- **Millennium Pets** • 409 N Victory Blvd • 818-845-7305
- **Pet Haven Pets & Supplies** • 626 N Glenoaks Blvd • 818-260-0511
- **Pets R Us** • 839 W Glenoaks Blvd • 818-553-8060
- **Scales 'N' Tails** • 1720 W Verdugo Ave • 818-842-6496
- **Stephens Hay & Grain** • 1840 Riverside Dr • 818-242-4540

Restaurants

- **Gordon Biersch** • 145 S San Fernando Blvd • 818-569-5240
- **Gourmet 88** • 230 N San Fernando Blvd • 818-848-8688
- **Harry's Family Restaurant** • 920 N San Fernando Blvd • 818-842-8755
- **In-N-Out Burger** • 761 N 1st St • 800-786-1000
- **Knight Restaurant** • 138 N San Fernando Blvd • 818-845-4516
- **Mambo's Café** • 1701 Victory Blvd • 818-545-8613
- **Market City Caffé** • 164 E Palm Ave • 818-840-7036
- **Picanha Churrascaria** • 269 E Palm Ave • 818-972-2100
- **Poquito Mas** • 2635 W Olive Ave • 818-563-2252
- **Ribs USA** • 2711 W Olive Ave • 818-841-8872
- **Riverside Café** • 1221 W Riverside Dr • 818-563-3567
- **Romano's Macaroni Grill** • 102 E Magnolia Blvd • 818-729-9405
- **Viva Fresh** • 900 W Riverside Dr • 818-845-2425

Shopping

- **EQ3** • 308 N San Fernando Blvd • 818-841-8110
- **Firing Line Indoor Shooting Ranges** • 1060 North Lake St • 818-954-9810
- **Pickwick Center** • 1001 Riverside Dr • 818-845-5300
- **Skyblupink** • 314 N San Fernando Blvd • 818-845-0226
- **Valley Dealer Exchange** • 6530 San Fernando Rd • 818-845-4090

Video Rental

- **20-20 Video** • 600 S Glenoaks Blvd • 818-559-2300
- **Blockbuster** • 324 S Glenoaks Blvd • 818-972-9292
- **Goodtime Video** • 520 N Glenoaks Blvd • 818-558-5618
- **Hollywood Video** • 105 E Alameda Ave • 818-845-0553

Map 51 • Glendale South

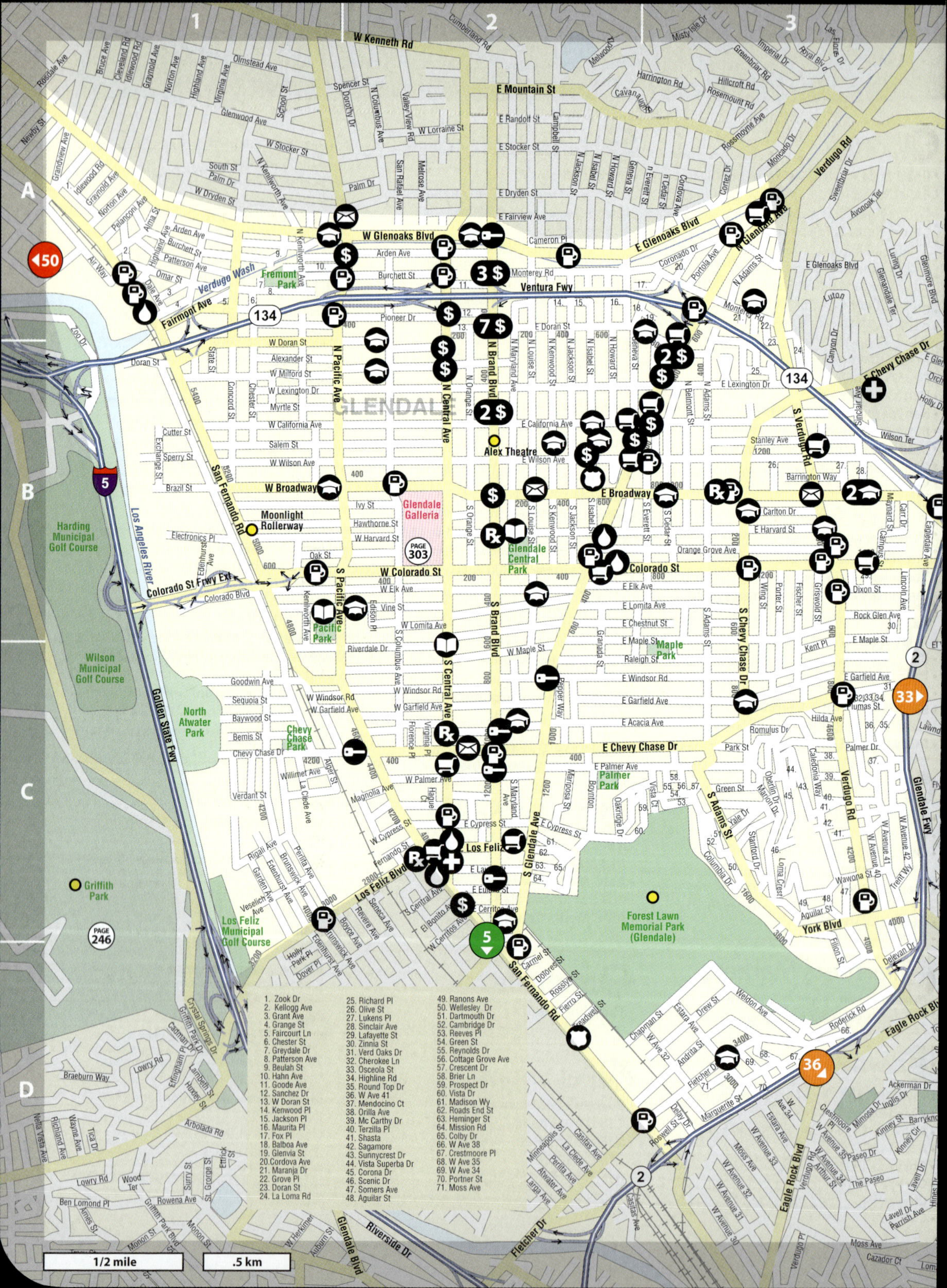

N
1
2
3
A
B
C
D
W Kenneth Rd
E Mountain St
W Glenoaks Blvd
E Glenoaks Blvd
Verdugo Wash
Fremont Park
Ventura Fwy
134
Fairmont Ave
GLENDALE
N Pacific Ave
N Central Ave
N Brand Blvd
Alex Theatre
W Broadway
E Broadway
Glendale Galleria
PAGE 303
Moonlight Rollerway
San Fernando Rd
Harding Municipal Golf Course
Los Angeles River
5
Colorado St Frwy Ext
W Colorado St
E Colorado St
Glendale Central Park
Pacific Park
S Central Ave
S Brand Blvd
S Glendale Ave
S Verdugo Rd
S Chevy Chase Dr
E Chevy Chase Dr
Maple Park
Wilson Municipal Golf Course
North Atwater Park
Chevy Chase Park
Golden State Fwy
Palmer Park
Los Feliz Blvd
Griffith Park
PAGE 246
Los Feliz Municipal Golf Course
Forest Lawn Memorial Park (Glendale)
York Blvd
Verdugo Rd
Glendale Fwy
Eagle Rock Blvd
Riverside Dr
Glendale Blvd
Fletcher Dr
150
33
36
1. Zook Dr
2. Kellogg Ave
3. Grant Ave
4. Grange St
5. Faircourt Ln
6. Chester St
7. Greydale Dr
8. Patterson Ave
9. Beulah St
10. Hahn Ave
11. Goode Ave
12. Sanchez Dr
13. W Doran St
14. Kenwood Pl
15. Jackson Pl
16. Maurita Pl
17. Fox Pl
18. Balboa Ave
19. Glenvia St
20. Cordova Ave
21. Maranja Dr
22. Grove Pl
23. Doran St
24. La Loma Rd
25. Richard Pl
26. Olive St
27. Lukens Pl
28. Sinclair Ave
29. Lafayette St
30. Zinnia St
31. Verd Oaks Dr
32. Cherokee Ln
33. Osceola St
34. Highline Rd
35. Round Top Dr
36. W Ave 41
37. Mendocino Ct
38. Orilla Ave
39. Mc Carthy Dr
40. Terzilla Pl
41. Shasta
42. Sagamore
43. Sunnycrest Dr
44. Vista Superba Dr
45. Corona Dr
46. Scenic Dr
47. Somers Ave
48. Aguilar St
49. Ranons Ave
50. Wellesley Dr
51. Dartmouth Dr
52. Cambridge Dr
53. Reeves Pl
54. Green St
55. Reynolds Dr
56. Cottage Grove Ave
57. Crescent Dr
58. Brier Ln
59. Prospect Dr
60. Vista Dr
61. Madison Wy
62. Roads End St
63. Heminger St
64. Mission Rd
65. Colby Dr
66. W Ave 38
67. Crestmoore Pl
68. W Ave 35
69. W Ave 34
70. Portner St
71. Moss Ave
1/2 mile
.5 km

To those in the know, Glendale is quite the gem. It is regularly listed as one of the safest cities in the state, if not the country. It offers a little bit of the old (check out classic screenings and events at the historic Alex Theatre) with the new (the three-level Glendale Galleria packs 'em in). And thanks to Glendale's prevalent Armenian presence, you can score some of the best baklava around at the bakeries along Colorado Boulevard.

$ Banks

- **Bank of America** • 203 N Glendale Ave
- **Bank of America** • 345 N Brand Blvd
- **Bank of America** • 3812 San Fernando Rd
- **Bank of the West** • 400 N Glendale Ave
- **California Credit Union** • 701 N Brand Blvd
- **California National** • 600 N Brand Blvd
- **Citibank** • 414 N Central Ave
- **Citibank** • 700 N Brand Blvd
- **City National** • 550 N Brand Blvd
- **Community** • 100 N Brand Blvd
- **Downey Savings & Loan** • 211 N Glendale Ave
- **East West** • 520 N Central Ave
- **First Regional** • 655 N Central Ave
- **Nara** • 831 N Pacific Ave
- **National Bank of California** • 520 N Brand Blvd
- **Pacific Western** • 400 N Brand Blvd
- **Union** • 330 N Brand Blvd
- **US** • 311 W Los Feliz Rd
- **US** • 561 N Glendale Ave
- **US** • 701 N Brand Blvd
- **Wachovia** • 611 E Wilson Ave
- **Washington Mutual** • 500 N Glendale Ave
- **Washington Mutual** • 620 N Brand Blvd
- **Wells Fargo** • 535 N Brand Blvd

Car Rental

- **Avis** • 100 W Glenoaks Blvd
- **Budget** • 1124 S Brand Blvd
- **Enterprise** • 1510 S Brand Blvd
- **Enterprise** • 1820 S Brand Blvd
- **Enterprise** • 827 S Glendale Ave
- **Hertz** • 1001 S Brand Blvd
- **Rent 4 Less** • 511 W Chevy Chase Dr

Car Washes

- **Antique Car Wash** • 236 S Glendale Ave
- **California Car Wash** • 3940 San Fernando Rd
- **California Car Wash Detail** • 1411 S Central Ave
- **Cars On Broadway Carwash** • 361 W Broadway
- **Galleria Car Wash** • 5720 San Fernando Rd
- **Glendale Car Wash** • 725 E Colorado St

Gas Stations

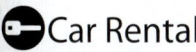

- **76** • 200 N Glendale Ave
- **76** • 901 N Central Ave
- **76** • 901 N Glendale Ave
- **Alliance** • 925 S Verdugo Rd
- **Arco** • 1118 N Glendale Ave
- **Arco** • 144 N Verdugo Rd
- **Arco** • 3680 San Fernando Rd
- **Arco** • 4103 Verdugo Rd
- **Arco** • 5800 San Fernando Rd
- **Chevron** • 1101 E Colorado Blvd
- **Chevron** • 2960 W Broadway
- **Chevron** • 3100 N San Fernando Rd
- **Chevron** • 466 W Broadway
- **Chevron** • 501 E Glenoaks Blvd
- **Chevron** • 825 N Central Ave
- **Independent** • 501 W Colorado St
- **Mobil** • 1028 S Brand Blvd
- **Mobil** • 1324 S Central Ave
- **Mobil** • 250 S Glendale Ave
- **Mobil** • 301 S Verdugo Rd
- **Mobil** • 700 N Glendale Ave
- **Mobil** • 800 N Pacific Ave
- **Shell** • 1401 E Colorado St
- **Shell** • 625 N Pacific Ave

Emergency Rooms

- **Glendale Adventist** • 1509 Chevy Chase Dr
- **Glendale Memorial** • 1420 S Central Ave

Landmarks

- **Alex Theatre** • 216 N Brand Blvd
- **Forest Lawn Memorial Park** • 1712 S Glendale Ave
- **Griffith Park** • 4730 Crystal Springs Dr
- **Moonlight Rollerway** • 5110 San Fernando Rd

Libraries

- **Glendale Central Library** • 222 E Harvard St • 818-548-2030
- **Pacific Park Branch** • 501 S Pacific Ave • 818-548-3760
- **Sons of the Revolution Library** • 600 S Central Ave • 818-240-1775

Pharmacies

- **CVS** • 1122 E Broadway • 818-547-0170
- **Longs Drugs** • 221 N Glendale Ave • 818-247-7218
- **Rite-Aid** • 216 S Brand Blvd • 818-243-1126
- **Rite-Aid** • 531 N Glendale Ave • 818-241-9770
- **Sav-On** • Albertsons • 1000 S Central Ave • 818-246-5679
- **Vons** • 311 W Los Feliz Rd • 818-246-8189

Police

- **Glendale Police Dept** • 131 N Isabel St • 818-548-4840
- **Los Angeles Police Dept** • 3353 N San Fernando Rd • 213-485-2563

Post Offices

- **US Post Office** • 1009 N Pacific Ave • 800-275-8777
- **US Post Office** • 101 N Verdugo Rd • 800-275-8777
- **US Post Office** • 120 E Chevy Chase Dr • 800-275-8777
- **US Post Office** • 313 E Broadway • 800-275-8777

Schools

- **A Adventist Children's Center** • 234 N Isabel St
- **Academy for Arts & Education** • 1479 E Broadway
- **Allan F Daily High** • 220 N Kenwood Pl
- **Bonnie Day Preschool + K** • 534 W Glenoaks Blvd
- **Cerritos Elementary** • 120 E Cerritos Ave
- **Columbus Elementary** • 425 W Milford St
- **First Lutheran** • 1300 E Colorado St
- **Fletcher Dr Elementary** • 3350 Fletcher Dr
- **Glendale Kindergarten** • 225 S Verdugo Rd
- **Glendale Montessori** • 413 W Doran St
- **Glendale Senior High** • 1440 E Broadway
- **Holy Family Elementary** • 400 S Louise St
- **Holy Family High** • 400 E Lomita Ave
- **Horace Mann Elementary** • 501 E Acacia Ave
- **Incarnation Parish** • 123 W Glenoaks Blvd
- **Jewel City Community Day** • 1440 E Broadway
- **John Marshall Elementary** • 1201 E Broadway
- **John Muir Elementary** • 912 S Chevy Chase Dr
- **RD White Elementary** • 744 E Doran St
- **Sonshine Christian Nursery** • 522 W Broadway
- **St Mary's Armenian Tufenkian** • 1200 Carlton Dr
- **Theodore Roosevelt Middle** • 222 E Acacia Ave
- **Thomas Edison Elementary** • 435 S Pacific Ave
- **Tobinworld** • 920 E Broadway
- **Washington Irving Middle** • 3010 Estara Ave
- **Woodrow Wilson Middle** • 1221 Monterey Rd
- **Zion Lutheran** • 301 N Isabel St

Supermarkets

- **Albertsons** • 1000 S Central Ave
- **Jon's Market** • 600 E Colorado St
- **Ralphs** • 1010 N Glendale Ave
- **Ralphs** • 1416 E Colorado St
- **Ralphs** • 211 N Glendale Ave
- **Smart & Final** • 210 N Verdugo Rd
- **Trader Joe's** • 130 N Glendale Ave
- **Vons** • 311 W Los Feliz Rd
- **Vons** • 561 N Glendale Ave
- **Whole Foods Market** • 331 N Glendale Ave

Map 51 • Glendale South

N
1
2
3
A
B
C
D
50
33
36
5
134
2
PAGE 303
PAGE 246
Glendale Galleria
GLENDALE
Harding Municipal Golf Course
Wilson Municipal Golf Course
Griffith Park
North Atwater Park
Chevy Chase Park
Pacific Park
Fremont Park
Glendale Central Park
Maple Park
Palmer Park
Los Feliz Municipal Golf Course
Forest Lawn Memorial Park (Glendale)
Los Angeles River
Golden State Fwy
Glendale Fwy
Ventura Fwy
Colorado St Frwy Ext
W Kenneth Rd
E Mountain St
W Glenoaks Blvd
E Glenoaks Blvd
W Broadway
E Broadway
W Colorado St
E Colorado St
E Chevy Chase Dr
E Los Feliz Rd
Los Feliz Blvd
San Fernando Rd
N Pacific Ave
S Pacific Ave
N Central Ave
S Central Ave
S Brand Blvd
S Glendale Ave
N Glendale Ave
S Chevy Chase Dr
Verdugo Rd
York Blvd
Eagle Rock Blvd
Riverside Dr
Glendale Blvd
Fletcher Dr
1. Zook Dr
2. Kellogg Ave
3. Grant Ave
4. Grange St
5. Faircourt Ln
6. Chester St
7. Greydale Dr
8. Patterson Ave
9. Beulah St
10. Hahn Ave
11. Goode Ave
12. Sanchez Dr
13. W Doran St
14. Kenwood Pl
15. Jackson Pl
16. Maurita Pl
17. Fox Pl
18. Balboa Ave
19. Glenvia St
20.Cordova Ave
21. Maranja Dr
22. Grove Pl
23. Doran St
24. La Loma Rd
25. Richard Pl
26. Olive St
27. Lukens Pl
28. Sinclair Ave
29. Lafayette St
30. Zinnia St
31. Verd Oaks Dr
32. Cherokee Ln
33. Osceola St
34. Highline Rd
35. Round Top Dr
36. W Ave 41
37. Mendocino Ct
38. Orilla Ave
39. Mc Carthy Dr
40. Terzilla Pl
41. Shasta
42. Sagamore
43. Sunnycrest Dr
44. Vista Superba Dr
45. Corona Dr
46. Scenic Dr
47. Somers Ave
48. Aguilar St
49. Ranons Ave
50. Wellesley Dr
51. Dartmouth Dr
52. Cambridge Dr
53. Reeves Pl
54. Green St
55. Reynolds Dr
56. Cottage Grove Ave
57. Crescent Dr
58. Brier Ln
59. Prospect Dr
60. Vista Dr
61. Madison Wy
62. Roads End St
63. Heminger St
64. Mission Rd
65. Colby Dr
66. W Ave 38
67. Crestmoore Pl
68. W Ave 35
69. W Ave 34
70. Portner St
71. Moss Ave
1/2 mile
.5 km

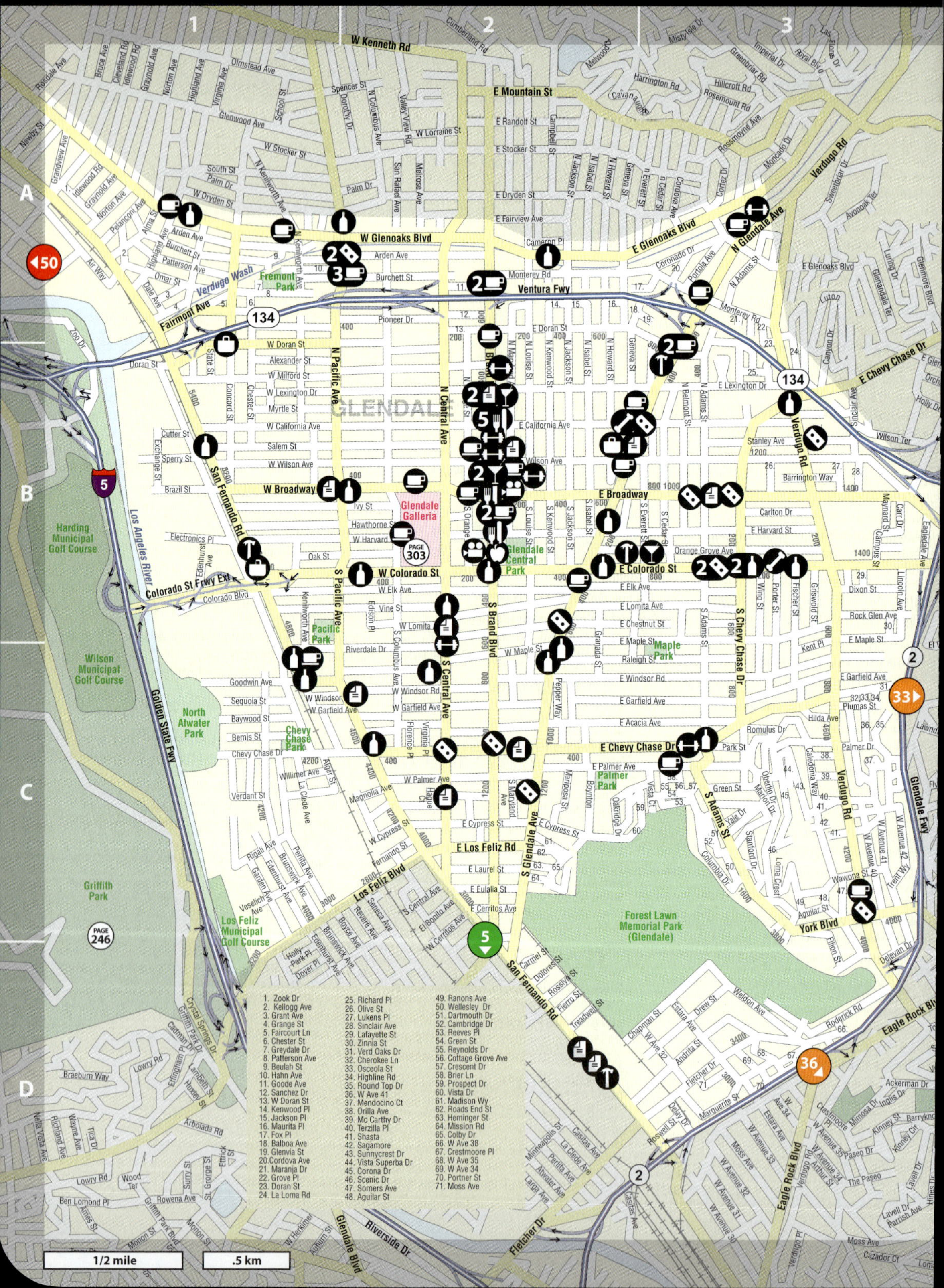

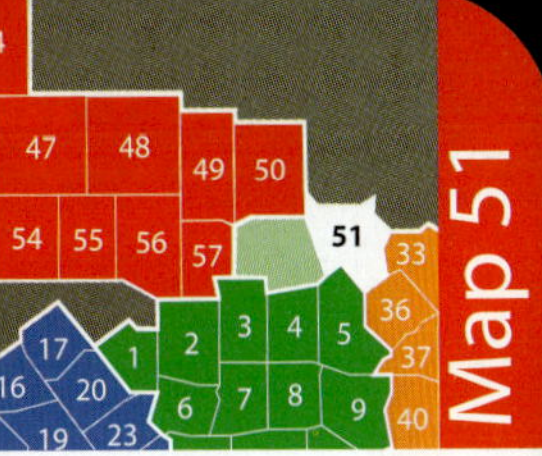

Wanna get a car? Head to the line of dealerships along the "Brand Boulevard of Cars." Then go north along Brand to flaunt your new purchase at one of the many internationally flavored restaurants in this hopping area. How about some rock? The Scene is a legit answer to Silver Lake's Spaceland. And with a new loft/dining/shopping mecca going in across the street from the Glendale Galleria in a few years, there will be more reasons than ever to come to Glendale to dump your cash.

Coffee

- **Boba House** • 818 N Pacific Ave
- **Brand Coffee** • 701 N Brand Blvd
- **Coffee Bean & Tea Leaf** • 300A N Glendale Ave
- **Coffee Cup of Glendale** • 535 N Brand Blvd
- **Coffee Express** • 742 N Glendale Ave
- **Edna's Coffee & Grocery** • 420 S Glendale Ave
- **Favorite Place** • 115 W Wilson Ave
- **Gloria Jean Gourmet Coffee** • 1151 Glendale Galleria
- **Java Time** • 525 N Glendale Ave
- **Just Coffee** • 1010 N Glendale Ave
- **Kelly's Coffee & Fudge** • 2217 Glendale Galleria
- **La Goccia Espresso Bar** • 101 N Brand Blvd
- **Lady Gourmet** • 700 N Brand Blvd
- **Maui Wowi** • 604 W Glenoaks Blvd
- **REVO Coffee & Cigarette Café** • 1022 E Chevy Chase Dr
- **Sidewalk Café** • 901 W Glenoaks Blvd
- **Starbucks** • 114 N Brand Blvd
- **Starbucks** • 130 S Brand Blvd
- **Starbucks** • 203 N Glendale Ave
- **Starbucks** • 469 Burchett St
- **Starbucks** • Vons • 561 N Glendale Ave
- **Tiffany's Coffee** • 900 N Pacific Ave
- **Urartu Coffee** • 119 N Maryland Ave
- **Urban Café** • 100 W Broadway
- **Verdugo Bagels** • 4169 Verdugo Rd
- **Vieta Coffee** • 4720 San Fernando Rd

Copy Shops

- **BJ's Printing Emporium** • 323 N Brand Blvd • 818-551-7840
- **Copy Central** • 330 N Brand Blvd • 818-502-0100
- **FedEx Kinko's** • 225 N Brand Blvd • 818-500-1811
- **K&K Copy** • 1220 S Central Ave • 818-507-7636
- **Mail Boxes Etc** • 1125 E Broadway • 818-242-4270
- **Mail Boxes Etc** • 249 N Brand Blvd • 818-244-4448
- **Minuteman Press** • 446 S Central Ave • 818-500-1620
- **Office Depot** • 515 W Broadway • 818-242-2582
- **Pip Printing** • 4614 San Fernando Rd • 818-956-0912
- **Staples** • 213 N Glendale Ave • 818-240-2133
- **Staples** • 3360 N San Fernando Rd • 818-242-0228
- **VR Printing** • 204 E Chevy Chase Dr, Ste 6 • 818-240-8466

Farmers Markets

- **Farmers Market-Glendale (Thurs, 9:30 am–1 pm)** • 100 N Brand Blvd

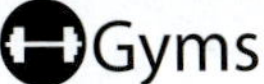

Gyms

- **24 Hour Fitness** • 240 N Brand Blvd • 818-240-5111
- **24 Hour Fitness** • 450 N Brand Blvd • 818-247-4334
- **Bally Total Fitness** • 623 S Central Ave • 818-240-2425
- **Curves** • 1010 Glendale Ave • 818-244-3030
- **Curves** • 1022 E Chevy Chase Dr • 818-242-4553
- **Total Woman** • 601 N Brand Blvd • 818-552-2027
- **World Gym** • 1001 E Colorado Blvd • 818-243-1600
- **YMCA** • 140 N Louise St • 818-240-4130

Hardware Stores

- **Colorado Hardware** • 701 E Colorado St • 818-549-0909
- **Home Depot** • 5040 San Fernando Rd • 818-246-9600
- **Stock Building Supply** • 3250 N San Fernando Rd • 323-478-2200
- **Virgil's Hardware** • 520 N Glendale Ave • 818-846-8750

Liquor Stores

- **8 Eleven Liquor** • 1311 E Colorado St
- **A-1 Liquor** • 1145 E Colorado St
- **Adam's Square Liquor** • 1021 E Chevy Chase Dr
- **B&C Liquor** • 102 W Colorado St
- **Best Liquor Meat & Deli** • 205 S Glendale Ave
- **Broadway Liquors** • 465 W Broadway
- **Cavalier Liquor** • 1307 W Glenoaks Blvd
- **Colorado Liquor** • 468 W Colorado St
- **Esquire Liquor** • 5300 San Fernando Rd
- **Glendale House of Liquor** • 420 S Glendale Ave
- **Gourmet Liquors** • 715 S Central Ave
- **Hammered Liquor Store** • 708 S Glendale Ave
- **House of Liquor** • 1008 E Colorado St
- **Jon's Market** • 600 E Colorado St
- **Liquor Zone** • 424 S Central Ave
- **Mitchall's Liquor** • 333 N Verdugo Rd
- **Old Green Mill Liquor House** • 4520 San Fernando Rd
- **Pacific Food Mart** • 1008 N Pacific Ave
- **Red Carpet Wines & Spirits** • 400 E Glenoaks Blvd
- **Topline Wine & Spirit** • 556 Riverdale Dr
- **Topline Wine & Spirits** • 4718 San Fernando Rd
- **Vens Liquors** • 825 W Glenoaks Blvd
- **Windsor Liquor** • 801 S Glendale Ave

Movie Theaters

- **Mann Glendale Exchange 10** • 128 N Maryland Ave • 818-549-0045
- **Mann Glendale Marketplace 4** • 144 S Brand Blvd • 818-547-3352

Nightlife

- **Far Niente** • 204 N Brand Blvd • 818-242-3835
- **Jax Bar and Grill** • 339 N Brand Blvd • 818-500-1604
- **Maurizio's** • 135 N Maryland Ave • 818-247-5600
- **The Scene** • 806 E Colorado St • 818-241-7029

Pet Shops

- **Petco** • 231 N Glendale Ave • 818-548-0411
- **Tropical Imports (fish only)** • 1134 E Colorado St • 818-240-9356

Restaurants

- **Carousel** • 304 N Brand Blvd • 818-246-7775
- **Damon's Steakhouse** • 317 N Brand Blvd • 818-507-1510
- **Eat Well** • 1013 S Brand Blvd • 818-243-5928
- **Ichiban** • 120 S Brand Blvd • 818-242-9966
- **Max's of Manila** • 313 W Broadway • 818-637-7751
- **Porto's Bakery & Café** • 315 N Brand Blvd • 818-956-5996

Shopping

- **Cost Plus World Market** • 223 N Glendale Ave • 818-241-2112
- **Glendale Costume** • 746 W Doran St • 818-244-1161
- **Luigi's Pottery & Gardenware** • 5630 San Fernando Rd • 818-246-7579

Video Rental

- **20-20 Video** • 1023 S Brand Blvd • 818-240-2020
- **ABC Video (Asian)** • 4108 Verdugo Rd • 323-257-7225
- **Blockbuster** • 1000 E Colorado St • 818-549-0801
- **Blockbuster** • 306 N Glendale Ave • 818-547-1146
- **Blockbuster** • 900 N Pacific Ave • 818-507-4392
- **Chaterian** • 1022 E Broadway • 818-242-6928
- **Glendale Video Shop (Korean)** • 1100 S Central Ave, Ste B • 818-240-9880
- **Glendale Videograph** • 620 S Glendale Ave • 818-240-5463
- **Hyungje Video (Korean)** • 831 N Pacific Ave • 818-551-1077
- **The Movie Place** • 222 N Verdugo Rd • 818-502-0200
- **Mundo Latino (Spanish)** • 1250 S Glendale Ave • 818-241-2263
- **Pop's Video** • 1121 E Colorado St • 818-242-0777
- **Q Video** • 1144 E Broadway • 818-244-8228

Map 52 • Tarzana / Woodland Hills

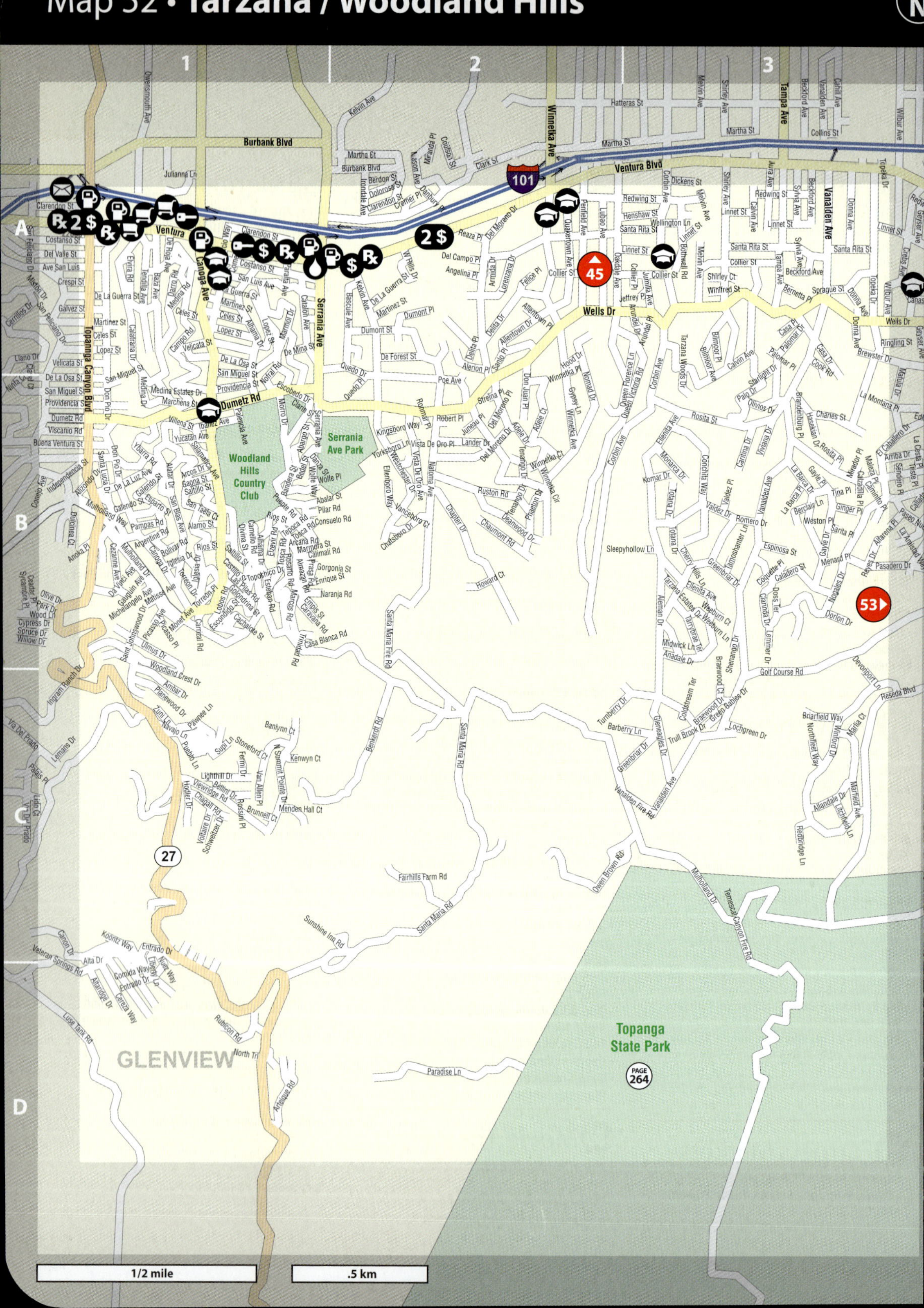

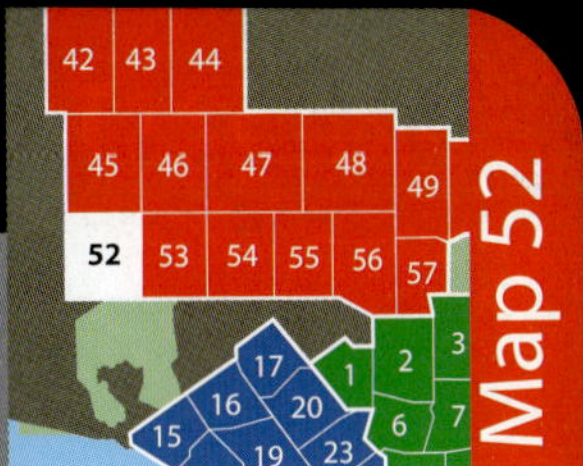

As in most Valley suburbs, Ventura Blvd serves as a dividing line for the "Haves" and the "Have Mores." Homes north of the boulevard are largely condos and rental apartments, while larger, more expensive single-family homes are found to the south. Woodland Hills and Tarzana are home to almost any chain restaurant or store one could ever need, with most found on either Topanga Canyon Blvd or Canoga Ave, north of Ventura.

Banks

- **Bank of America** • 22004 Sherman Wy
- **Bank of America** • 5440 Topanga Cyn Blvd
- **Bank of America** • 5959 Canoga Ave
- **Citibank** • 22000 Ventura Blvd
- **Fremont Investment & Loan** • 20640 Ventura Blvd
- **Washington Mutual** • 22001 Ventura Blvd
- **Wells Fargo** • 20642 Ventura Blvd
- **Wells Fargo** • 21108 Ventura Blvd
- **World Savings & Loan** • 20800 Ventura Blvd

Car Rental

- **Enterprise** • 21118 Ventura Blvd
- **Vista Ford Rent a Car** • 21501 Ventura Blvd

Car Washes

- **Beverly Catalina Car Wash** • 4000 Beverley Blvd

Gas Stations

- **76** • 20905 Ventura Blvd
- **76** • 21940 Ventura Blvd
- **Arco** • 22004 Clarendon St
- **Chevron** • 5356 Canoga Ave
- **Shell** • 20900 Ventura Blvd

Pharmacies

- **CVS** • 22050 Ventura Blvd • 818-346-2207
- **Longs Drugs** • 21055 Ventura Blvd • 818-226-9215
- **Rite-Aid** • 21949 Ventura Blvd • 818-348-5542
- **Target** • 20801 Ventura Blvd • 818-992-3386

Post Offices

- **US Post Office** • 22121 Clarendon St • 800-275-8777

Schools

- **Chime Charter** • 19722 Collier St
- **Halsey** • 21321 Costanso St
- **Henry David Thoreau Continuation** • 5429 Quakertown Ave
- **Kol Tikvah** • 20400 Ventura Blvd
- **Serrania Ave Elementary** • 5014 Serrania Ave
- **St Luke Lutheran** • 5312 Comercio Wy
- **St Mel Elementary** • 20874 Ventura Blvd
- **Topanga Mountain** • 21338 Dumetz Rd
- **Wilbur Ave Elementary** • 5213 Crebs Ave
- **William Howard Taft Senior High** • 5461 Winnetka Ave

Supermarkets

- **Ralphs** • 21909 Ventura Blvd
- **Vons** • 21821 Ventura Blvd
- **Whole Foods Market** • 21347 Ventura Blvd

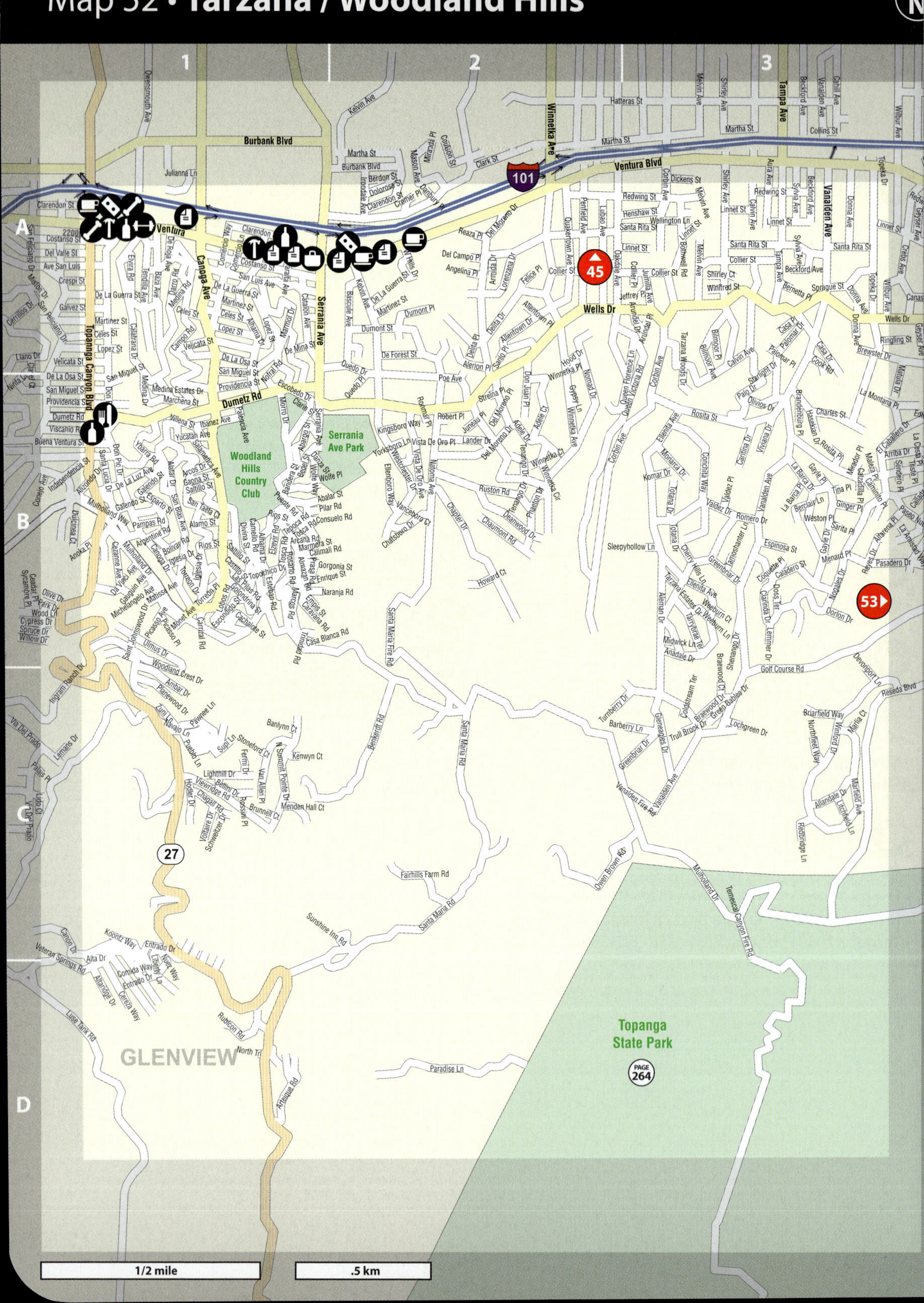

Burbank Blvd
Ventura Blvd
Topanga Canyon Blvd
Canoga Ave
Serrania Ave
Dumetz Rd
Wells Dr
Winnetka Ave
Tampa Ave
Vanalden Ave
Woodland Hills Country Club
Serrania Ave Park
Topanga State Park
GLENVIEW
Mulholland Dr
Santa Maria Rd
Reseda Blvd
1/2 mile
.5 km

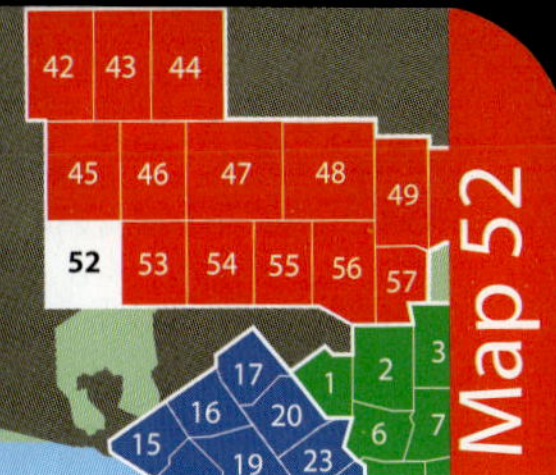

If it's a suburban mecca you seek, look no further. This area is home to quiet communities, mini malls, and some of the easiest parking in the Los Angeles area. However, the most entertainment you're likely to find in these parts is waiting in line at the nearby Wal-Mart. In the summer, when temperatures soar above 100 degrees, hunker down with a group at Corbin Bowl (Map 45). Corbin offers low regular rates and late-night weekend bowling complete with black light, disco lights, and fog.

Coffee

- **Coffee Bean & Tea Leaf** • 21851 Ventura Blvd
- **Mom's Coffee Shop** • 20501 Ventura Blvd
- **Starbucks** • Target • 20801 Ventura Blvd
- **Starbucks** • 5422 Topanga Cyn Blvd

Copy Shops

- **California Copy & Printing Center** • 21416 Ventura Blvd • 818-703-8686
- **Function Junction** • 20841 Ventura Blvd • 818-710-8841
- **UPS Store** • 20929 Ventura Blvd • 818-702-0456
- **Whitmont Copy** • 21031 Ventura Blvd • 818-340-9200
- **Woodland Hills Printing** • 21602 Ventura Blvd • 818-888-6702

Farmers Markets

- **Woodland Hills (Sat, 8 am–4 pm)** • 6200 block of Topanga Cyn Blvd

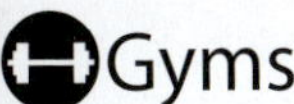

Gyms

- **Curves** • 21800 Ventura Blvd • 818-883-8853

Hardware Stores

- **Ace** • Warner Ctr • 21142 Ventura Blvd • 818-348-4844
- **Franklin's True Value** • 21936 Ventura Blvd • 818-347-6800

Liquor Stores

- **Carlson's Liquor** • 21900 Ventura Blvd
- **Déjà Vu Liquors** • 21056 Ventura Blvd
- **Embassy Liquor** • 4879 Topanga Cyn Blvd

Pet Shops

- **California Pet Center** • 21906 Ventura Blvd • 818-716-5933
- **Petco** • 21943 Ventura Blvd • 818-346-9397

Restaurants

- **Toast** • 20969 Ventura Blvd • 818-992-5500

Shopping

- **Crazy Inkjets** • 4867 Topanga Cyn Blvd • 818-346-5538

Video Rental

- **Blockbuster** • 21937 Ventura Blvd • 818-713-9990
- **Unique Video** • 20812 Ventura Blvd • 818-883-4611

Map 53 • Encino

N
1
2
3
A
B
C
D
46
52
54
101
PAGE 264
Ventura Blvd
Reseda Blvd
White Oak Ave
Balboa Blvd
Valley Vista Blvd
Rancho St
Mulholland Dr
Haskell Ave
Hayvenhurst Ave
Burbank Blvd
Caballero Creek
El Caballero Country Club
Encino Reservoir
Encino Park
Rancho de los Encinos State Historical Park
Topanga State Park
San Vincente Mountain Park
Mandeville Canyon Rd
1. Green Vista Dr
2. Octavia Pl
3. Rochelle Pl
4. Bosque Dr
5. Shileno Pl
6. Huerta Ct
7. Toquet Dr
8. Corinthian Dr
9. Tarzana St
10. Polora St
11. Sugarman St
12. Greenbrier Ln
13. Marblehead Wy
14. Torrey Pines Ln
15. Green Meadow Ct
16. Deer View Ct
17. Anastasia Dr
18. Lake Vista Ct
19. Avd Puerto Vallarta
20. Weddington St
21. Clark St
22. Shoshone Ave
23. Addison St
24. Hartsook St
25. Forbes Ave
26. Whitaker Ave
27. Saville Ave
1/2 mile
.5 km

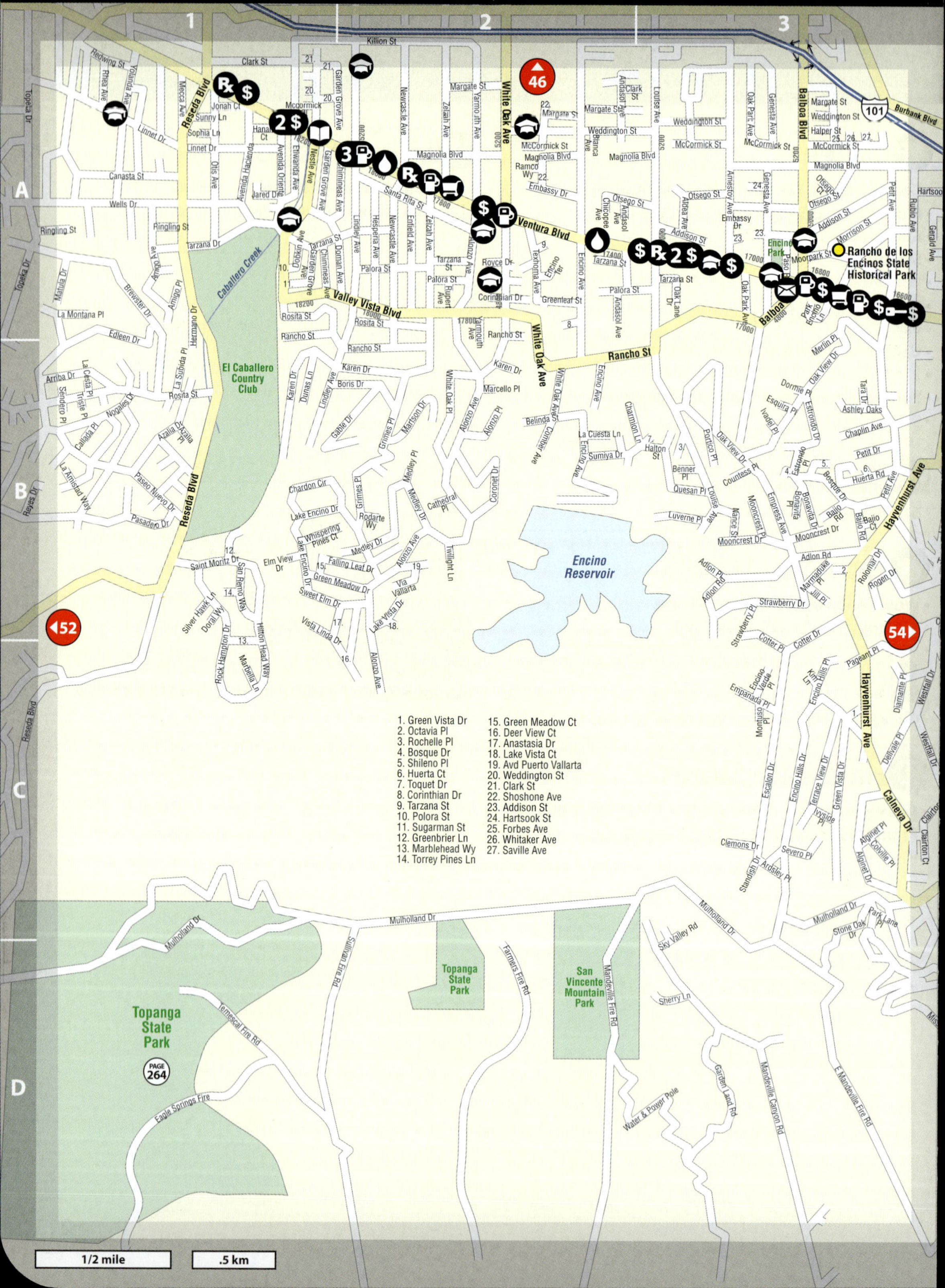

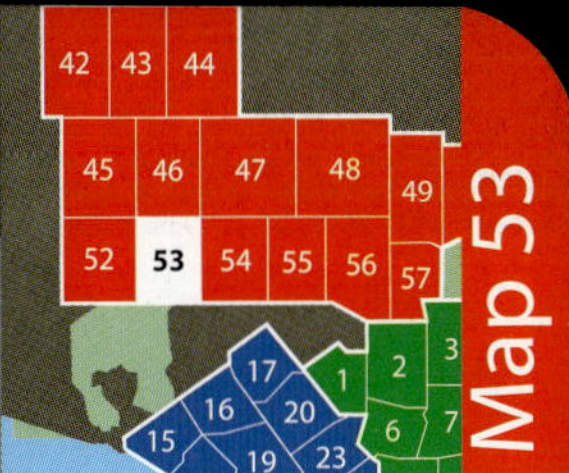

Encino's location, convenient to both the 405 and the 101 freeways, makes it one of LA's most desirable suburbs. It's about as "Valley" as the Valley gets, having been immortalized in Frank Zappa's "Valley Girl," *The Karate Kid*, *Fast Times at Ridgemont High*, and—just as important, culturally—*Match Game* with Gene Rayburn and Brett Somers.

Banks

- **Bank of America** • 16640 Ventura Blvd
- **Bank of America** • 18337 Ventura Blvd
- **California National** • 16830 Ventura Blvd
- **Downey Savings & Loan** • 17250 Ventura Blvd
- **East West** • 18321 Ventura Blvd
- **First Bank & Trust** • 17777 Ventura Blvd
- **First Regional** • 16830 Ventura Blvd
- **Union** • 16633 Ventura Blvd
- **Wachovia** • 17323 Ventura Blvd
- **Washington Mutual** • 17107 Ventura Blvd
- **Wells Fargo** • 17232 Ventura Blvd

Car Rental

- **Enterprise** • 16616 Ventura Blvd

Car Washes

- **76** • 20905 Ventura Blvd
- **Encino Chevron Car Wash** • 18081 Ventura Blvd
- **Premier Car Wash** • 17432 Ventura Blvd

Gas Stations

- **76** • 16900 Ventura Blvd
- **76** • 17849 Ventura Blvd
- **Arco** • 18076 Ventura Blvd
- **Chevron** • 18081 Ventura Blvd
- **Mobil** • 17661 Ventura Blvd
- **Shell** • 16801 Ventura Blvd
- **Shell** • 18101 Ventura Blvd

Landmarks

- **Rancho de los Encinos State Historical Park** • 16756 Moorpark St

Libraries

- **Encino-Tarzana Branch** • 18231 Ventura Blvd • 818-343-1983

Pharmacies

- **CVS** • 17320 Ventura Blvd • 818-995-0071
- **Longs Drugs** • 18441 Ventura Blvd • 818-996-1000
- **Rite-Aid** • 17864 Ventura Blvd • 818-345-5456

Post Offices

- **US Post Office** • 4930 Balboa Blvd • 800-275-8777

Schools

- **Crespi Carmelite High** • 5031 Alonzo Ave
- **Encino Elementary** • 16941 Addison St
- **Encino Presbyterian Childrens Center** • 4963 Balboa Blvd
- **Gaspar de Portola Middle** • 18720 Linnet St
- **Holy Martyrs Elementary & Ferrahian High** • 5300 White Oak Ave
- **Learning Center Foundation** • 16944 Ventura Blvd
- **Los Encinos Elementary** • 17114 Ventura Blvd
- **Nestle Ave Elementary** • 5060 Nestle Ave
- **Our Lady of Grace** • 17720 Ventura Blvd

Supermarkets

- **Ralphs** • 17840 Ventura Blvd
- **Smart & Final** • 16847 Ventura Blvd

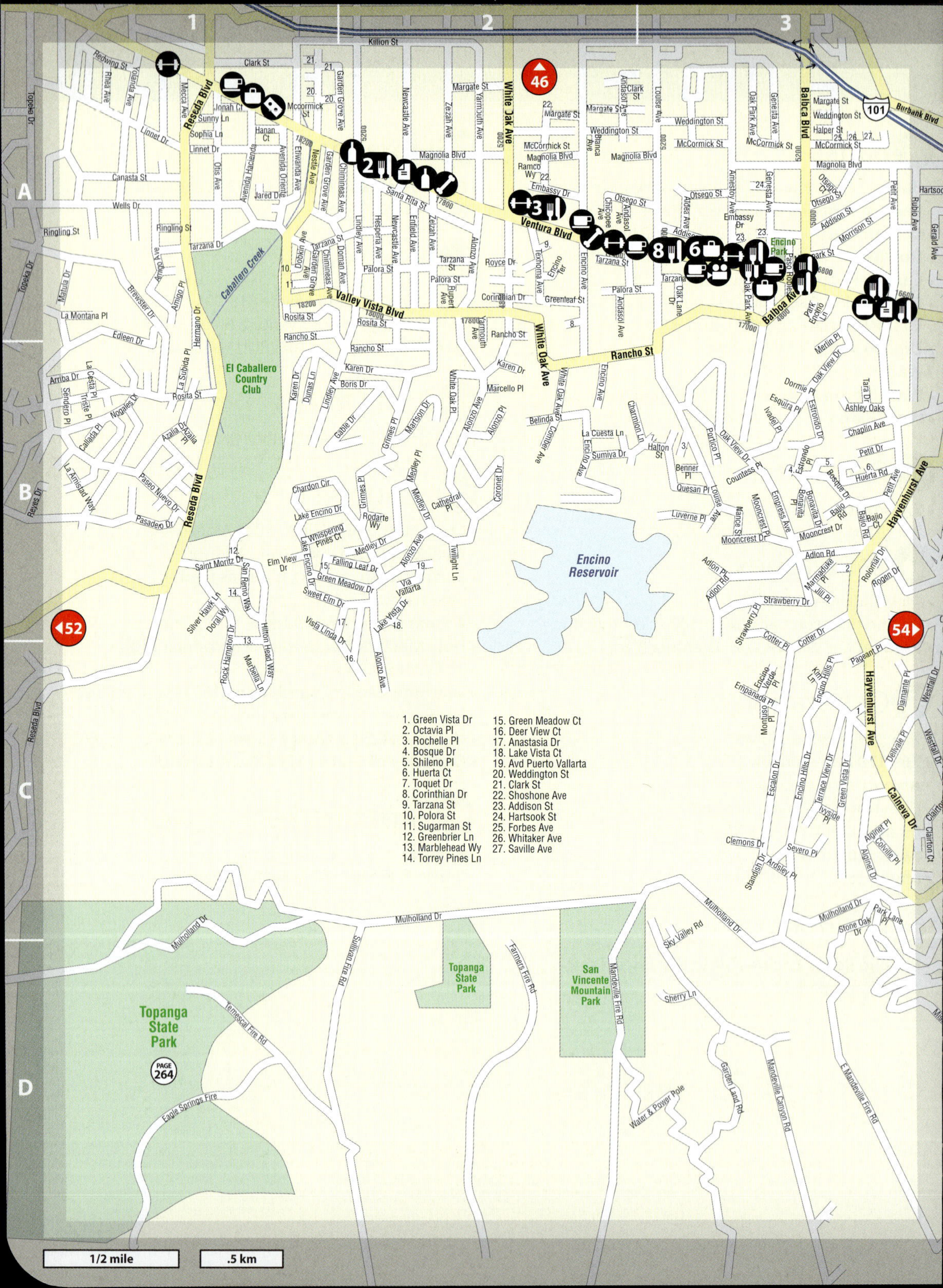

1. Green Vista Dr
2. Octavia Pl
3. Rochelle Pl
4. Bosque Dr
5. Shileno Pl
6. Huerta Ct
7. Toquet Dr
8. Corinthian Dr
9. Tarzana St
10. Polora St
11. Sugarman St
12. Greenbrier Ln
13. Marblehead Wy
14. Torrey Pines Ln
15. Green Meadow Ct
16. Deer View Ct
17. Anastasia Dr
18. Lake Vista Ct
19. Avd Puerto Vallarta
20. Weddington St
21. Clark St
22. Shoshone Ave
23. Addison St
24. Hartsook St
25. Forbes Ave
26. Whitaker Ave
27. Saville Ave

1/2 mile | .5 km

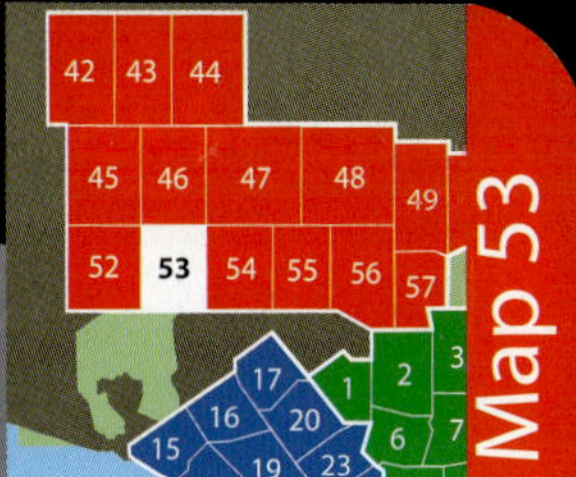

It seems like any halfway decent restaurant is opening up a branch in Encino these days. Mulberry Street Pizza (17040 Ventura Blvd) and Versailles (17410 Ventura Blvd) both started someplace edgier before coming to the 'burbs. In 2007, Encino even exported one of its own—The Stand, hands down the best hot dog restaurant in LA, now feeds hungry agents at the new CAA building in Century City.

Coffee

- **Coffee Bean & Tea Leaf** • 17301 Ventura Blvd
- **Coral Tree Café** • 17499 Ventura Blvd
- **Nuts Landing** • 17028 Ventura Blvd
- **Starbucks** • 17308 Ventura Blvd
- **Starbucks** • Vons • 18439 Ventura Blvd
- **Unique Café** • 18381 Ventura Blvd

Copy Shops

- **FedEx Kinko's** • 16652 Ventura Blvd • 818-788-4243
- **Mail Boxes Etc** • 18034 Ventura Blvd • 818-705-4496

Gyms

- **Bally Total Fitness** • 17401 Ventura Blvd • 818-382-6060
- **Bodies In Motion** • 17031 Ventura Blvd • 818-995-7700
- **Curves** • 17627 Ventura Blvd • 818-986-7212

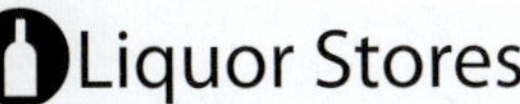

Liquor Stores

- **C&C Liquor** • 18089 Ventura Blvd
- **Encino Park Liquor** • 18001 Ventura Blvd

Movie Theaters

- **Laemmle Town Center 5** • 17200 Ventura Blvd • 818-981-9847

Pet Shops

- **Petco** • 17919 Ventura Blvd • 818-343-1124
- **Pride 'n Joy** • 17324 Ventura Blvd • 818-501-8767

Restaurants

- **Bagel Nosh Deli & Restaurant** • 17271 Ventura Blvd • 818-995-4545
- **Baklava Factory** • 17145 Ventura Blvd • 818-728-1600
- **Buca di Beppo** • 17500 Ventura Blvd • 818-995-3288
- **California Wok** • 16656 Ventura Blvd • 818-386-0561
- **Catch 21** • 17316 Ventura Blvd • 818-789-3474
- **Chili My Soul** • 4928 Balboa Blvd • 818-981-7685
- **Jerry's Famous Deli** • 16650 Ventura Blvd • 818-906-1800
- **Jerusalem Pizza** • 17942 Ventura Blvd • 818-758-9595
- **Johnny Rockets** • 16901 Ventura Blvd • 818-981-5900
- **Kaiten Sushi** • 17302 Ventura Blvd • 818-986-7003
- **More Than Waffles** • 17200 Ventura Blvd • 818-789-5937
- **Mulberry Street Pizzeria** • 17040 Ventura Blvd • 818-906-8881
- **The Stand** • 17000 Ventura Blvd • 818-788-2700
- **Versailles** • 17410 Ventura Blvd • 818-906-0756
- **Vittorio's Italian Cucina** • 17644 Ventura Blvd • 818-986-9074

Shopping

- **Antik Shop** • 4909 Genesta Ave • 818-990-5990
- **Hansen's Cakes** • 18432 Ventura Blvd • 818-708-1208
- **Herbalogics** • 17200 Ventura Blvd • 818-990-9990
- **The Knot Garden** • 17200 Ventura Blvd • 818-986-6642
- **Mitzvahland** • 16733 Ventura Blvd • 818-788-5758
- **Nuts Landing** • 17028 Ventura Blvd • 818-990-3211
- **Rag Tattoo** • 17245 Ventura Blvd • 818-990-7244
- **Sneaker Warehouse** • 16736 Ventura Blvd • 818-995-8999

Video Rental

- **Blockbuster** • 18419 Ventura Blvd • 818-342-7618

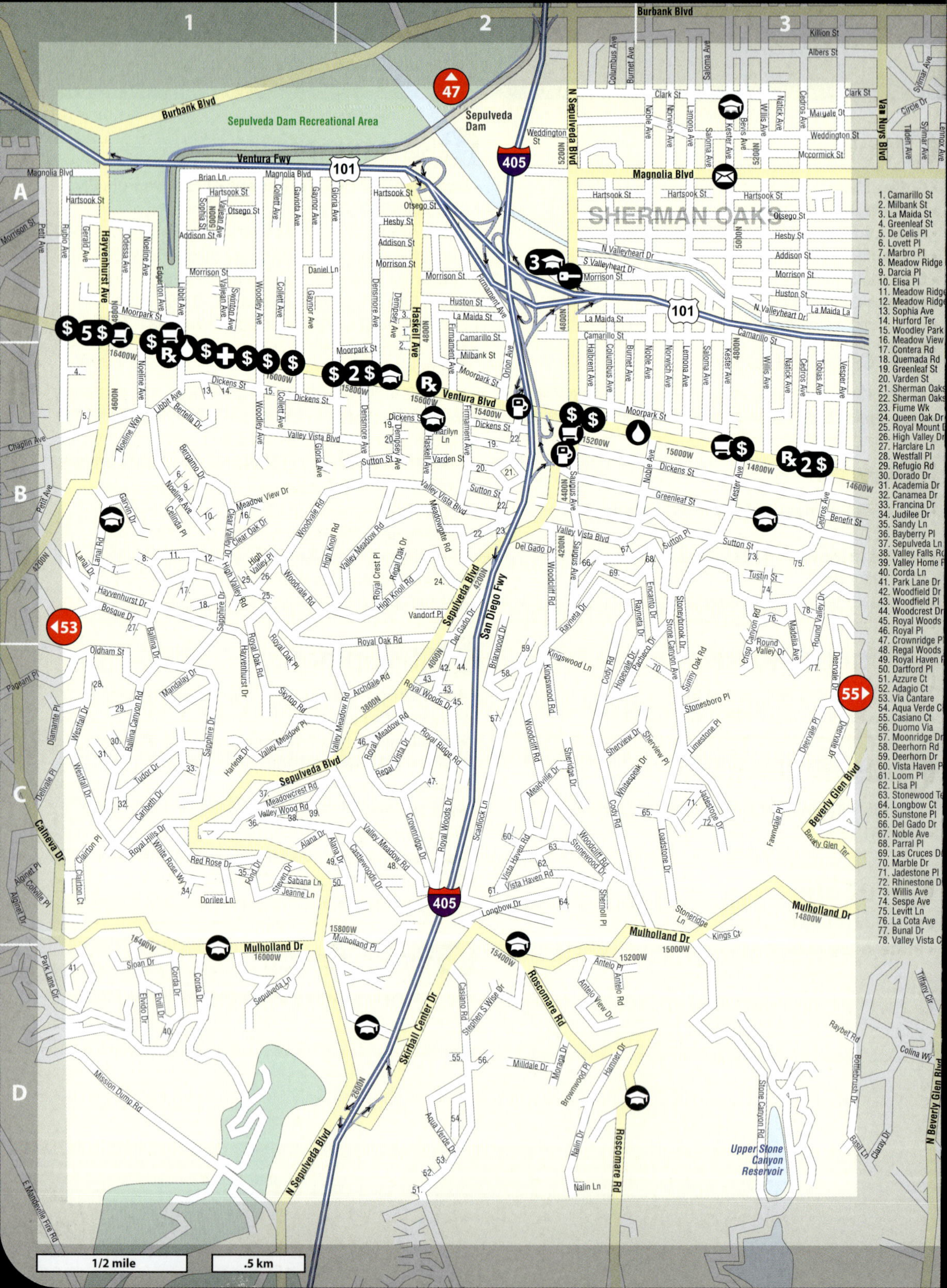

Map 54 • Sherman Oaks West

Sepulveda Dam Recreational Area

Sepulveda Dam

SHERMAN OAKS

Ventura Fwy

San Diego Fwy

Upper Stone Canyon Reservoir

1. Camarillo St
2. Milbank St
3. La Maida St
4. Greenleaf St
5. De Celis Pl
6. Lovett Pl
7. Marbro Pl
8. Meadow Ridge
9. Darcia Pl
10. Elisa Pl
11. Meadow Ridg
12. Meadow Ridg
13. Sophia Ave
14. Hurford Ter
15. Woodley Park
16. Meadow View
17. Contera Rd
18. Quemada Rd
19. Greenleaf St
20. Varden St
21. Sherman Oaks
22. Sherman Oaks
23. Fiume Wk
24. Queen Oak Dr
25. Royal Mount D
26. High Valley Dr
27. Harclare Ln
28. Westfall Pl
29. Refugio Rd
30. Dorado Dr
31. Academia Dr
32. Canamea Dr
33. Francina Dr
34. Judilee Dr
35. Sandy Ln
36. Bayberry Pl
37. Sepulveda Ln
38. Valley Falls Rd
39. Valley Home P
40. Corda Ln
41. Park Lane Dr
42. Woodfield Dr
43. Woodfield Pl
44. Woodcrest Dr
45. Royal Woods
46. Royal Pl
47. Crownridge Pl
48. Regal Woods
49. Royal Haven
50. Dartford Pl
51. Azzure Ct
52. Adagio Ct
53. Via Cantare
54. Aqua Verde C
55. Casiano Ct
56. Duomo Via
57. Moonridge Dr
58. Deerhorn Rd
59. Deerhorn Dr
60. Vista Haven P
61. Loom Pl
62. Lisa Pl
63. Stonewood Te
64. Longbow Ct
65. Sunstone Pl
66. Del Gado Dr
67. Noble Ave
68. Parral Pl
69. Las Cruces D
70. Marble Dr
71. Jadestone Pl
72. Rhinestone D
73. Willis Ave
74. Sespe Ave
75. Levitt Ln
76. La Cota Ave
77. Bunal Dr
78. Valley Vista C

1/2 mile

.5 km

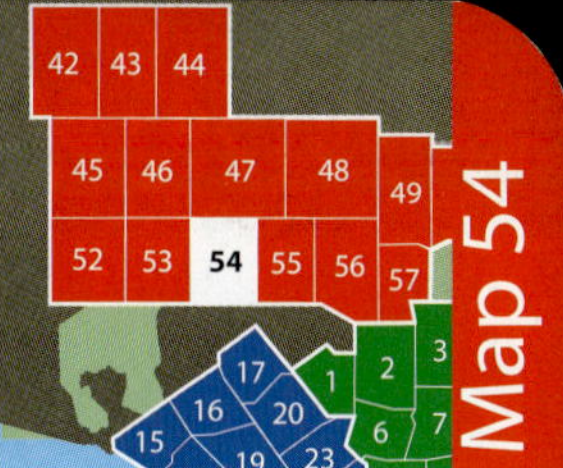

Sherman Oaks is home to the most congested freeway interchange in the nation—the intersection of the 405 and 101 freeways. Local surface streets have been unable to provide relief due to a lengthy Caltrans project intended to improve the connections and on-ramps. We remain dubious. Our advice: Avoid the whole ugly mess. Get on the 405 at either Burbank Blvd or Valley Vista, and avoid the 101 altogether during anything approximating a rush hour.

Banks

- **Bank Leumi USA** • 16530 Ventura Blvd
- **Bank of America** • 14701 Ventura Blvd
- **Bank of the West** • 15165 Ventura Blvd
- **Bank of the West** • 16027 Ventura Blvd
- **California Bank & Trust** • 16130 Ventura Blvd
- **Citibank** • 15233 Ventura Blvd
- **Citibank** • 16601 Ventura Blvd
- **Citibank** • 3812 Sepulveda Blvd
- **City National** • 15260 Ventura Blvd
- **City National** • 16133 Ventura Blvd
- **Comerica** • 15303 Ventura Blvd
- **Downey Savings & Loan** • 16325 Ventura Blvd
- **First Federal** • 16500 Ventura Blvd
- **Manufacturers** • 16255 Ventura Blvd
- **National Bank of California** • 14724 Ventura Blvd
- **US** • 15910 Ventura Blvd
- **Washington Mutual** • 15260 Ventura Blvd
- **Washington Mutual** • 16437 Ventura Blvd
- **Wells Fargo** • 14855 Ventura Blvd
- **Wells Fargo** • 15760 Ventura Blvd

Car Rental

- **Enterprise** • 4940 S Sepulveda Blvd

Car Washes

- **Encino Auto Wash** • 16300 Ventura Blvd
- **Sherman Oaks Car Wash** • 15150 Ventura Blvd

Gas Stations

- **76** • 15410 Ventura Blvd
- **Mobil** • 4528 Sepulveda Blvd

Emergency Rooms

- **Encino-Tarzana Regional Medical Center—Encino Campus** • 16237 Ventura Blvd

Pharmacies

- **CVS** • 14735 Ventura Blvd • 818-788-0208
- **Ralphs** • 16325 Ventura Blvd • 818-728-4515
- **Rite-Aid** • 15630 Ventura Blvd • 818-783-2449

Post Offices

- **US Post Office** • 14900 Magnolia Blvd • 800-275-8777

Schools

- **Charter High School of Arts-Multimedia & Performing** • 15355 Morrison St
- **Curtis** • 15871 Mulholland Dr
- **Emek Hebrew Academy** • 15365 Magnolia Blvd
- **Kester Ave Elementary** • 5353 Kester Ave
- **Lanai Rd Elementary** • 4241 Lanai Rd
- **Los Angeles International** • 15355 Morrison St
- **Milken Community High** • 15800 Zeldins Wy
- **Mirman School for Gifted Children** • 16180 Mulholland Dr
- **Roscomare Rd Elementary** • 2425 Roscomare Rd
- **Sherman Oaks Elementary** • 14755 Greenleaf St
- **St Cyril of Jerusalem** • 4548 Haskell Ave
- **Stephen S Wise Temple Elementary** • 15500 Stephen S Wise Dr
- **Valley Beth Shalom Day** • 15739 Ventura Blvd
- **Westland** • 16200 Mulholland Dr

Supermarkets

- **Gelson's Markets** • 16450 Ventura Blvd
- **Pavilions** • 14845 Ventura Blvd
- **Ralphs** • 16325 Ventura Blvd
- **Whole Foods Market** • 4520 Sepulveda Blvd

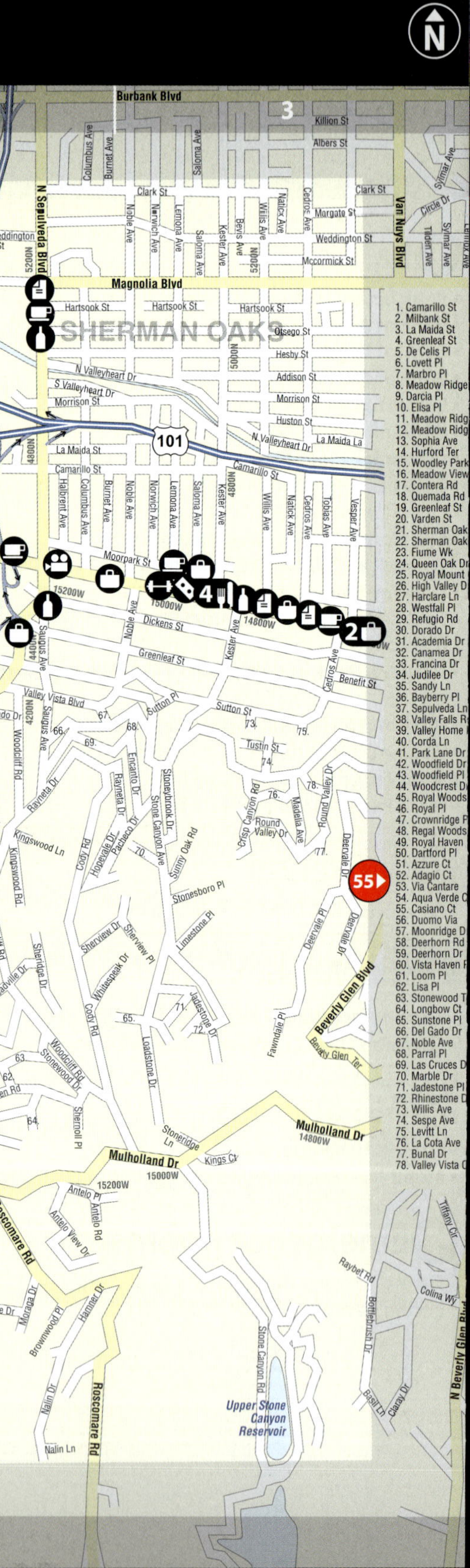
Burbank Blvd
Sepulveda Dam Recreational Area
Sepulveda Dam
Ventura Fwy
101
405
Magnolia Blvd
SHERMAN OAKS
Ventura Blvd
N Sepulveda Blvd
Van Nuys Blvd
Sepulveda Blvd
San Diego Fwy
Mulholland Dr
Skirball Center Dr
Roscomare Rd
Beverly Glen Blvd
N Beverly Glen Blvd
Upper Stone Canyon Reservoir
47
53
55
1/2 mile
.5 km
1. Camarillo St
2. Milbank St
3. La Maida St
4. Greenleaf St
5. De Celis Pl
6. Lovett Pl
7. Marbro Pl
8. Meadow Ridge
9. Darcia Pl
10. Elisa Pl
11. Meadow Ridg
12. Meadow Ridg
13. Sophia Ave
14. Hurford Ter
15. Woodley Park
16. Meadow View
17. Contera Rd
18. Quemada Rd
19. Greenleaf St
20. Varden St
21. Sherman Oak
22. Sherman Oak
23. Fiume Wk
24. Queen Oak Dr
25. Royal Mount
26. High Valley D
27. Harclare Ln
28. Westfall Pl
29. Refugio Rd
30. Dorado Dr
31. Academia Dr
32. Canamea Dr
33. Francina Dr
34. Judilee Dr
35. Sandy Ln
36. Bayberry Pl
37. Sepulveda Ln
38. Valley Falls R
39. Valley Home
40. Corda Ln
41. Park Lane Dr
42. Woodfield Dr
43. Woodfield Pl
44. Woodcrest D
45. Royal Woods
46. Royal Pl
47. Crownridge P
48. Regal Woods
49. Royal Haven
50. Dartford Pl
51. Azzure Ct
52. Adagio Ct
53. Via Cantare
54. Aqua Verde C
55. Casiano Ct
56. Duomo Via
57. Moonridge D
58. Deerhorn Rd
59. Deerhorn Dr
60. Vista Haven R
61. Loom Pl
62. Lisa Pl
63. Stonewood T
64. Longbow Ct
65. Sunstone Pl
66. Del Gado Dr
67. Noble Ave
68. Parral Pl
69. Las Cruces D
70. Marble Dr
71. Jadestone Pl
72. Rhinestone D
73. Willis Ave
74. Sespe Ave
75. Levitt Ln
76. La Cota Ave
77. Bunal Dr
78. Valley Vista

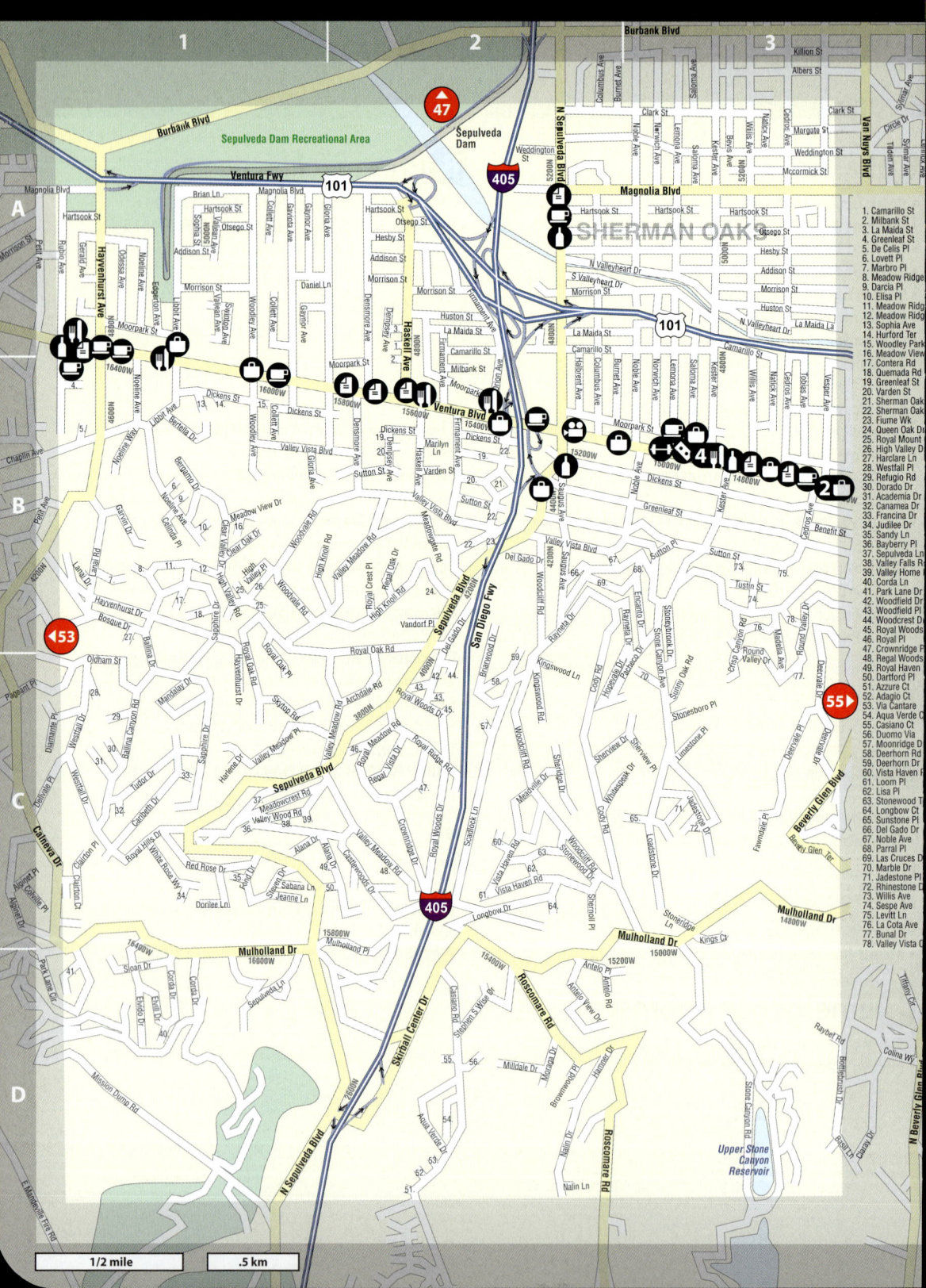

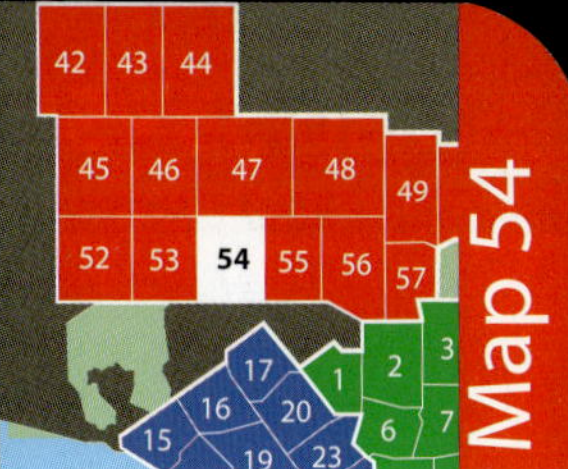

The urbanization of the Sherman Oaks/Studio City communities took a turn for the better when plans were announced to renovate the Galleria's 16-plex movie theatre and reopen it as the ArcLight Sherman Oaks, complete with black box auditoriums, gift shop, and café. One can only hope that this development will allow the grown-ups to take back the Galleria -- or force local teens to eschew dumb comedies for ponderous art house fare.

Coffee

- **Café Bonjour** • 16550 Ventura Blvd
- **Coffee Bean & Tea Leaf** • 16101 Ventura Blvd
- **Miracle Coffee & Pastry** • 5150 Sepulveda Blvd
- **Starbucks** • 14622 Ventura Blvd
- **Starbucks** • 15030 Ventura Blvd
- **Starbucks** • 15303 Ventura Blvd
- **Starbucks** • 16461 Ventura Blvd
- **Suzy's Coffee Shop & Deli** • 16501 Ventura Blvd

Copy Shops

- **All Printing & Graphic Service** • 15616 Ventura Blvd • 818-783-0510
- **FedEx Kinko's** • 15720 Ventura Blvd • 818-783-2680
- **Landmark Print & Copy** • 14762 Ventura Blvd • 818-783-4900
- **Office Depot** • 16571 Ventura Blvd • 818-907-1741
- **Pip Printing** • 15826 Ventura Blvd • 818-986-9245
- **Redi-Quik Printing and Service Center** • 5152 Sepulveda Blvd • 818-986-3424
- **UPS Store** • 14622 Ventura Blvd • 818-990-5930

Gyms

- **24 Hour Fitness** • 15301 Ventura Blvd • 818-728-6777
- **Max Fitness Personal Training Ctr** • 15037 Ventura Blvd • 818-501-4436

Liquor Stores

- **Oak's Liquor** • 5148 Sepulveda Blvd
- **Rubio Liquor & Grocery** • 16573 Ventura Blvd
- **Valley Beverage** • 14901 Ventura Blvd
- **Wines of the World** • 4534 Saugus Ave

Movie Theaters

- **Pacific Galleria Stadium** • 15301 Ventura Blvd • 818-501-5121

Restaurants

- **California Chicken Café** • 15601 Ventura Blvd • 818-789-8056
- **Delmonico's Lobster House** • 16358 Ventura Blvd • 818-986-0777
- **Katsu-Ya Encino** • 16542 Ventura Blvd • 818-788-2396
- **Marmalade Café** • 14910 Ventura Blvd • 818-905-8872
- **Mel's Drive-In** • 14846 Ventura Blvd • 818-990-6357
- **Panzanella** • 14928 Ventura Blvd • 818-784-4400
- **Wiener Factory** • 14917 Ventura Blvd • 818-789-2676

Shopping

- **Buffalo Exchange** • 14621 Ventura Blvd • 818-783-3420
- **Cost Plus World Market** • 15201 Ventura Blvd • 818-205-9620
- **Drum Connection** • 4846 Libbit Ave • 818-788-5550
- **Gregory's Toys** • 16101 Ventura Blvd • 818-906-2212
- **Handmade Galleries** • 14556 Ventura Blvd • 818-382-3444
- **The Laughter Store** • 15140 Ventura Blvd • 866-LAUGH-42
- **Party City** • 14735-A Ventura Blvd • 818-981-0099
- **Rubyjean** • 15000 Ventura Blvd, #101 • 818-990-2200
- **Sherman Oaks Galleria** • Sepulveda Blvd & Ventura Blvd • 818-382-4100

Video Rental

- **Blockbuster** • 14936 Ventura Blvd • 818-788-6162

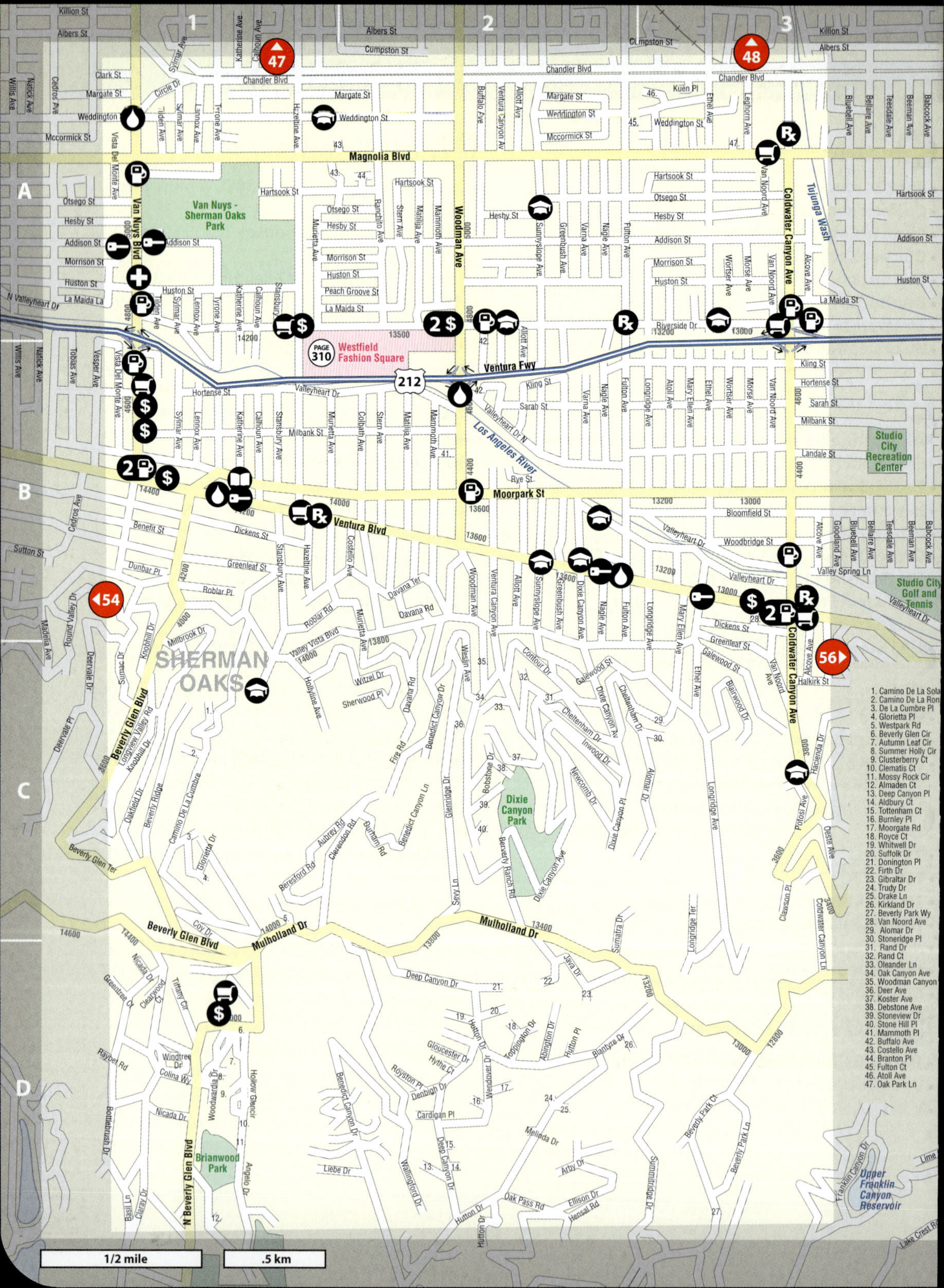

N
1
2
3
A
B
C
D
47
48
54
56
Chandler Blvd
Magnolia Blvd
Van Nuys Blvd
Woodman Ave
Coldwater Canyon Ave
Van Nuys - Sherman Oaks Park
Westfield Fashion Square
PAGE 310
Ventura Fwy
212
Los Angeles River
Tujunga Wash
Moorpark St
Ventura Blvd
Riverside Dr
Valleyheart Dr
Studio City Recreation Center
Studio City Golf and Tennis
SHERMAN OAKS
Beverly Glen Blvd
Mulholland Dr
Dixie Canyon Park
Brianwood Park
N Beverly Glen Blvd
Upper Franklin Canyon Reservoir
1. Camino De La Sola
2. Camino De La Ron
3. De La Cumbre Pl
4. Glorietta Pl
5. Westpark Rd
6. Beverly Glen Cir
7. Autumn Leaf Cir
8. Summer Holly Cir
9. Clusterberry Ct
10. Clematis Ct
11. Mossy Rock Cir
12. Almaden Ct
13. Deep Canyon Pl
14. Aldbury Ct
15. Tottenham Ct
16. Burnley Pl
17. Moorgate Rd
18. Royce Ct
19. Whitwell Dr
20. Suffolk Dr
21. Donington Pl
22. Firth Dr
23. Gibraltar Dr
24. Trudy Dr
25. Drake Ln
26. Kirkland Dr
27. Beverly Park Wy
28. Van Noord Ave
29. Alomar Dr
30. Stoneridge Pl
31. Rand Dr
32. Rand Ct
33. Oleander Ln
34. Oak Canyon Ave
35. Woodman Canyon
36. Deer Ave
37. Koster Ave
38. Debstone Ave
39. Stoneview Dr
40. Stone Hill Pl
41. Mammoth Pl
42. Buffalo Ave
43. Costello Ave
44. Branton Pl
45. Fulton Ct
46. Atoll Ave
47. Oak Park Ln
1/2 mile
.5 km

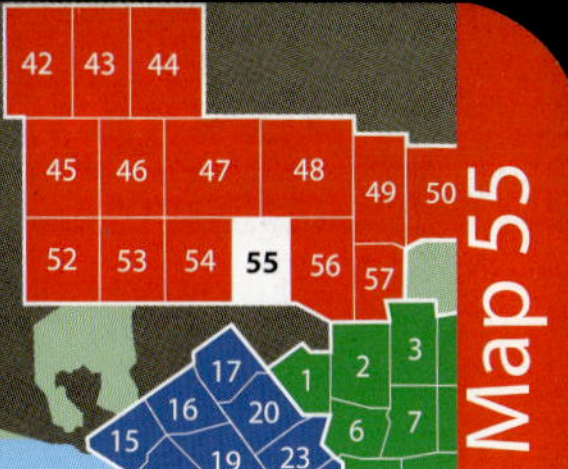

If Studio City is the Valley's answer to West Hollywood, then Sherman Oaks is its Beverly Hills. Mini-mansions are everywhere, while mega-mansions are found south Ventura Boulevard in areas like the Longridge Estates. The area features a high-end mall, good public and private schools, and easy access to the Westside via Coldwater Canyon or Beverly Glen. Rush hour traffic can be a drag, but both roads provide pleasant drives that make you realize things could be a lot worse.

Banks

- **Bank of America** • 13700 Riverside Dr
- **California National** • 14475 Ventura Blvd
- **Citibank** • 4464 Van Nuys Blvd
- **Downey Savings & Loan** • 13701 Riverside Dr
- **Downey Savings & Loan** • 4520 Van Nuys Blvd
- **First Federal** • 2920 N Beverly Glen Cir
- **Washington Mutual** • 13949 Ventura Blvd
- **Washington Mutual** • 14111 Riverside Dr
- **Wells Fargo** • 12930 Ventura Blvd

Car Rental

- **Enterprise** • 14235 Ventura Blvd
- **Enterprise** • 5005 Van Nuys Blvd
- **Hertz** • 13119 Ventura Blvd
- **Midway Car Rental** • 9876 Wilshire Blvd
- **Sherman Oaks Car Rental** • 13336 Ventura Blvd
- **Specialty Auto Rentals and Sales** • 5015 Van Nuys Blvd

Car Washes

- **Fashion Square Car Wash** • 4625 Woodman Ave
- **Handy J Car Wash** • 14311 Ventura Blvd
- **Rob's Car Wash** • 5300 Van Nuys Blvd
- **Ventura Car Wash** • 13320 Ventura Blvd

Gas Stations

- **76** • 12863 Ventura Blvd
- **76** • 13650 Riverside Dr
- **76** • 14478 Ventura Blvd
- **76** • 4822 Van Nuys Blvd
- **Arco** • 4359 Coldwater Cyn Ave
- **Chevron** • 12860 Riverside Dr
- **Chevron** • 14505 Ventura Blvd
- **Mobil** • 12904 Ventura Blvd
- **Shell** • 4441 Van Nuys Blvd
- **Shell** • 5161 Van Nuys Blvd
- **Valero** • 4715 Van Nuys Blvd
- **Valero** • 4804 Coldwater Cyn Ave

Emergency Rooms

- **Sherman Oaks** • 4929 Van Nuys Blvd

Libraries

- **Sherman Oaks Library** • 14245 Moorpark St • 818-205-9716

Pharmacies

- **Ralphs** • 12842 Ventura Blvd • 818-761-7211
- **Ralphs** • 14049 Ventura Blvd • 818-784-3005
- **Rite-Aid** • 13333 Riverside Dr • 818-907-1431
- **Walgreens** • 5224 Coldwater Cyn Ave • 818-487-2715

Schools

- **The Buckley School** • 3900 Stansbury Ave
- **CE Merdinian Armenian Evangelical Elementary** • 13330 Riverside Dr
- **Chandler Elementary** • 14030 Weddington St
- **Dixie Canyon Ave Elementary** • 4220 Dixie Cyn Ave
- **Emerson Academy for Arts and Sciences** • 4182 Sunnyslope Ave
- **Harvard-Westlake** • 3700 Coldwater Cyn Ave
- **Notre Dame High** • 13645 Riverside Dr
- **Riverside Dr Elementary** • 13061 Riverside Dr
- **Robert A Millikan Middle** • 5041 Sunnyslope Ave
- **St Francis De Sales Elementary** • 13368 Valleyheart Dr

Supermarkets

- **Gelson's Markets** • 4520 Van Nuys Blvd
- **Ralphs** • 12842 Ventura Blvd
- **Ralphs** • 12921 Magnolia Blvd
- **Ralphs** • 14049 Ventura Blvd
- **Trader Joe's** • 14119 Riverside Dr
- **Whole Foods Market** • 12905 Riverside Dr

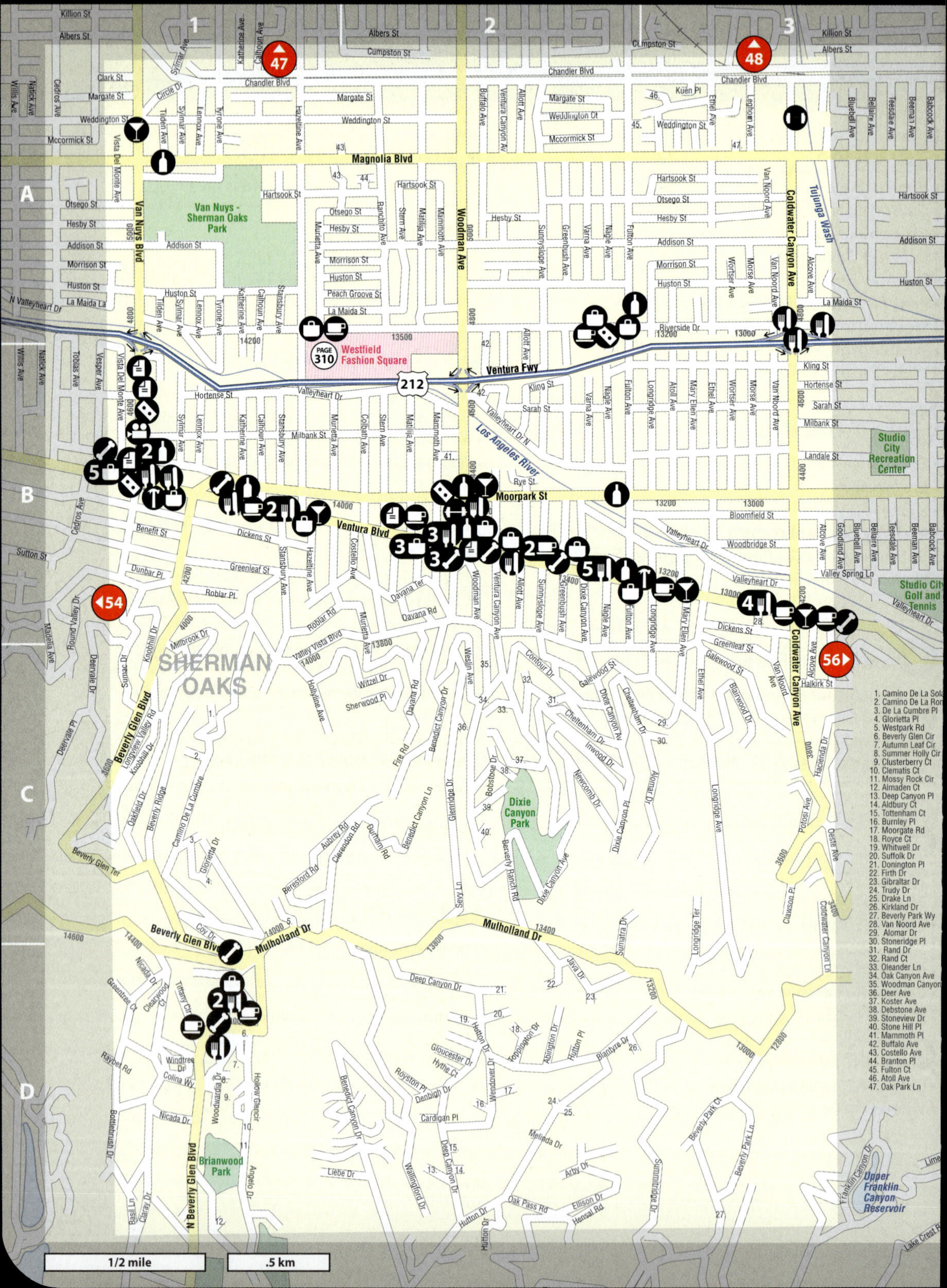

47
48
54
56
PAGE 310

Van Nuys - Sherman Oaks Park
Westfield Fashion Square
Ventura Fwy
212
Los Angeles River
Studio City Recreation Center
Studio City Golf and Tennis
SHERMAN OAKS
Dixie Canyon Park
Brianwood Park
Upper Franklin Canyon Reservoir
Tujunga Wash

Magnolia Blvd
Ventura Blvd
Moorpark St
Mulholland Dr
Van Nuys Blvd
Woodman Ave
Coldwater Canyon Ave
Beverly Glen Blvd
N Beverly Glen Blvd

1. Camino De La Sola
2. Camino De La Ron
3. De La Cumbre Pl
4. Glorietta Pl
5. Westpark Rd
6. Beverly Glen Cir
7. Autumn Leaf Cir
8. Summer Holly Cir
9. Clusterberry Ct
10. Clematis Ct
11. Mossy Rock Cir
12. Almaden Ct
13. Deep Canyon Pl
14. Aldbury Ct
15. Tottenham Ct
16. Burnley Pl
17. Moorgate Rd
18. Royce Ct
19. Whitwell Dr
20. Suffolk Dr
21. Donington Pl
22. Firth Dr
23. Gibraltar Dr
24. Trudy Dr
25. Drake Ln
26. Kirkland Dr
27. Beverly Park Wy
28. Van Noord Ave
29. Alomar Dr
30. Stoneridge Pl
31. Rand Dr
32. Rand Ct
33. Oleander Ln
34. Oak Canyon Ave
35. Woodman Canyon
36. Deer Ave
37. Koster Ave
38. Debstone Ave
39. Stoneview Dr
40. Stone Hill Pl
41. Mammoth Pl
42. Buffalo Ave
43. Costello Ave
44. Branton Pl
45. Fulton Ct
46. Atoll Ave
47. Oak Park Ln

1/2 mile
.5 km

Sundries / Entertainment

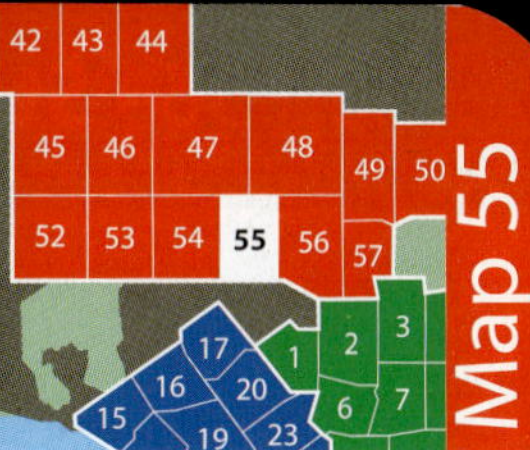

Dining in Sherman Oaks has never been better. Senor Fred has killer margaritas and delicious food to boot. Gyu Kaku is Japan's sublime take on Korean barbecue, while Boneyard Bistro represents an American take on grilling. For dessert, check out Leda's Bakeshop for her mini-cupcakes. They're indulgent but not overkill, and there's a flavor for every mood you're in. We like the Dulce de Leche.

Coffee

- **Ciao Coffee & Tea Company** • 4566 Van Nuys Blvd
- **Coffee Bean & Tea Leaf** • 12930 Ventura Blvd
- **Coffee Bean & Tea Leaf** • 14006 Riverside Dr
- **Coffee Roaster** • 13567 Ventura Blvd
- **Espresso Grounded** • 14241 Ventura Blvd
- **Lulu's Beehive** • 13203 Ventura Blvd
- **Sphinx Café** • 13718 Ventura Blvd
- **Starbucks** • 12824 Ventura Blvd
- **Starbucks** • 13351 Riverside Dr
- **Starbucks** • 13535 Ventura Blvd
- **Starbucks** • 2952 N Beverly Glen Cir

Copy Shops

- **FedEx Kinko's** • 4556 Van Nuys Blvd • 818-906-2679
- **M&M Quality Printing** • 13908 Ventura Blvd • 818-907-0290
- **Tip Top Printing & Copy Center** • 4454 Van Nuys Blvd • 818-783-0949
- **UPS Store** • 13636 Ventura Blvd • 818-906-3544

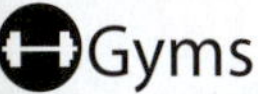

Gyms

- **Curves** • 4348 Woodman Ave • 818-981-7985
- **LA Fitness Sports Clubs** • 5300 Coldwater Cyn Ave • 818-505-0772

Hardware Stores

- **Checker Paint** • 14434 Ventura Blvd • 818-784-0192
- **Studio City Ace Hardware** • 13241 Ventura Blvd • 818-784-6274

Liquor Stores

- **Cheers Liquor & Deli** • 14230 Ventura Blvd
- **Fulton Square Liquors** • 4824 Fulton Ave
- **Metro Liquor** • 14431 Magnolia Blvd
- **Party House Liquors** • 13300 Moorpark St
- **Short Stop 24** • 4344 Woodman Ave
- **Silver Liquor** • 4405 Woodman Ave
- **Tony's Liquor** • 13368 Ventura Blvd
- **Tropicana Liquors** • 4346 Van Nuys Blvd
- **Wine N' Liquor Basket** • 4454 Van Nuys Blvd

Movie Theaters

- **Pacific Sherman Oaks 5** • 14424 Millbank St • 818-501-5121

Nightlife

- **Coda** • 5248 Van Nuys Blvd • 818-783-7518
- **Cozy's** • 14058 Ventura Blvd • 818-986-6000
- **The Green Frog** • 13625 Moorpark St • 818-788-4812
- **Lulu's Beehive** • 13203 Ventura Blvd • 818-986-2233
- **Muddy Moose Bar & Grill** • 12833 Ventura Blvd • 818-755-5000

Pet Shops

- **All Paws** • 13756 Ventura Blvd • 818-788-2797
- **All the Fish U Can Wish** • 13605 Ventura Blvd • 818-783-7199
- **Aquarium Center** • 14255 Ventura Blvd • 818-501-3544
- **Pets Naturally** • 13459 Ventura Blvd • 818-784-1233
- **Pets of Belair** • 2924 Beverly Glen Cir • 310-475-7977
- **Pride 'n Joy** • 13717 Ventura Blvd • 818-784-6243
- **Three Dog Bakery** • 14545 Ventura Blvd • 818-304-0440
- **Underwater Depot** • 13708 Ventura Blvd • 818-789-7323

Restaurants

- **Bistro Garden at Coldwater** • 12950 Ventura Blvd • 818-501-0202
- **Boneyard Bistro** • 13539 Ventura Blvd • 818-906-7427
- **Café Bizou** • 14016 Ventura Blvd • 818-788-3536
- **Carnival Restaurant** • 4356 Woodman Ave • 818-784-3469
- **Casa Vega** • 13301 Ventura Blvd • 818-788-4868
- **The Dip** • 14333 Ventura Blvd • 818-501-1850
- **The Great Greek** • 13362 Ventura Blvd • 818-905-5250
- **Gyu Kaku** • 14457 Ventura Blvd • 818-501-5400
- **Hugo's** • 12851 Riverside Dr • 818-761-8985
- **Hugo's Tacos** • 4749 Coldwater Cyn • 818-762-7771
- **Il Tiramisu** • 13705 Ventura Blvd • 818-986-2640
- **In-N-Out Burger** • 4444 Van Nuys Blvd • 800-786-1000
- **Iroha** • 12953 Ventura Blvd • 818-990-9559
- **Jinky's** • 14120 Ventura Blvd • 818-981-2250
- **Le Chine Wok** • 2958 Beverly Glen Cir • 310-475-1146
- **Le Petit Restaurant** • 13360 Ventura Blvd • 818-501-7999
- **Maria's Italian Kitchen** • 13353 Ventura Blvd • 818-906-0783
- **Marrakesh** • 13003 Ventura Blvd • 818-788-6354
- **Max** • 13355 Ventura Blvd • 818-784-2915
- **Mazzarino's** • 12920 1/2 Riverside Dr • 818-788-5050
- **Mistral Brasserie** • 13422 Ventura Blvd • 818-981-6650
- **Mulholland Grill** • 2932 Beverly Glen Cir • 310-470-6223
- **Pinot Bistro** • 12969 Ventura Blvd • 818-990-0500
- **Rive Gauche** • 14106 Ventura Blvd • 818-990-3573
- **Senor Fred** • 13730 Ventura Blvd • 818-789-3200
- **Stanley's** • 13817 Ventura Blvd • 818-986-4623

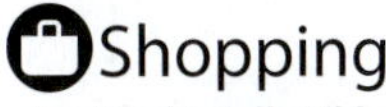

Shopping

- **Aunt Teek's Collectibles** • 14080 Ventura Blvd • 818-784-3341
- **Baxter Northrup Music** • 14534 Ventura Blvd • 818-788-7510
- **Beauty Collection** • 13351 Riverside Dr • 818-789-4999
- **Bel Air Spa** • 2980 N Beverly Glen Cir • 310-470-6362
- **Belle Gray** • 13812 Ventura Blvd • 818-789-4021
- **Bloomingdale's** • 14060 Riverside Dr • 818-325-2200
- **Burgundy Blue Outlet** • 4818 Fulton Ave • 818-981-7446
- **Café Unforgettable Cakes** • 14550 Ventura Blvd • 818-783-5628
- **Doll Shoppe** • 13300 Riverside Dr • 818-784-3655
- **Juvenile Shop** • 13356 Ventura Blvd • 818-986-6214
- **Leda's Bakeshop** • 13722 Ventura Blvd • 818-386-9644
- **Lightbulbs Unlimited** • 14446 Ventura Blvd • 818-501-3492
- **Mark's Garden** • 13838 Ventura Blvd • 818-906-1718
- **Pink Cheeks** • 14562 Ventura Blvd • 818-906-8225
- **Runnergy** • 13541 Ventura Blvd • 818-905-0020
- **Second Spin Records** • 14564 Ventura Blvd • 818-986-6866
- **Sportie LA** • 14510 Ventura Blvd • 818-990-7575
- **Tinker** • 4337 Woodman Ave • 818-784-7991

Video Rental

- **Blockbuster** • 13303 Riverside Dr • 818-501-8335
- **Blockbuster** • 4560 Van Nuys Blvd • 818-990-1695
- **Hollywood Video** • 14525 Ventura Blvd • 818-986-1874
- **Video Hut** • 13713 Moorpark St • 818-385-0067

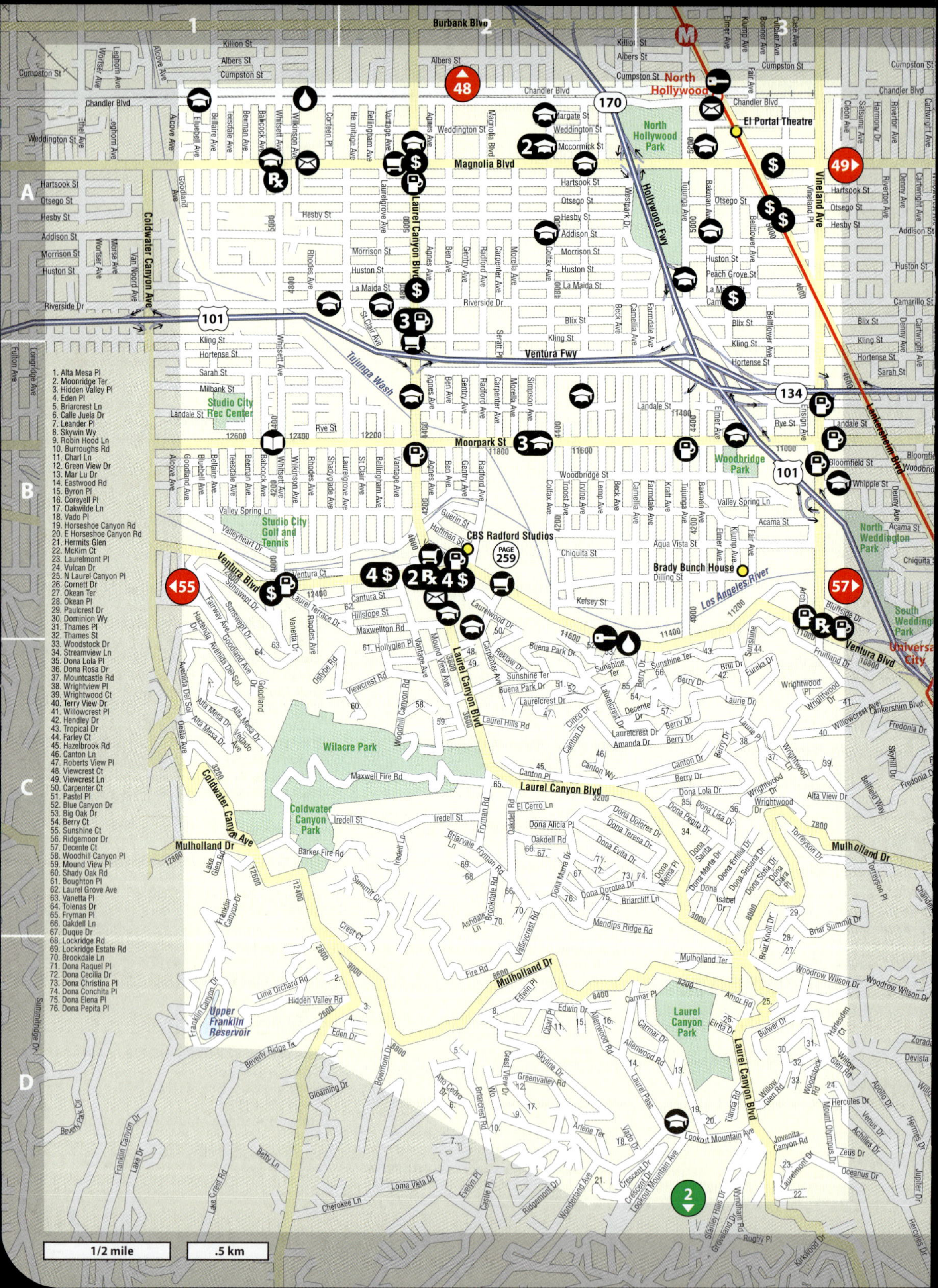

Map 56 • Studio City / Valley Village

1. Alta Mesa Pl
2. Moonridge Ter
3. Hidden Valley Pl
4. Eden Pl
5. Briarcrest Ln
6. Calle Juela Dr
7. Leander Pl
8. Skywin Wy
9. Robin Hood Ln
10. Burroughs Rd
11. Charl Ln
12. Green View Dr
13. Mar Lu Dr
14. Eastwood Rd
15. Byron Pl
16. Coreyell Pl
17. Oakwilde Ln
18. Vado Pl
19. Horseshoe Canyon Rd
20. E Horseshoe Canyon Rd
21. Hermits Glen
22. McKim Ct
23. Laurelmont Pl
24. Vulcan Dr
25. N Laurel Canyon Pl
26. Cornett Dr
27. Okean Ter
28. Okean Pl
29. Paulcrest Dr
30. Dominion Wy
31. Thames Pl
32. Thames St
33. Woodstock Dr
34. Streamview Ln
35. Dona Lola Pl
36. Dona Rosa Dr
37. Mountcastle Rd
38. Wrightview Pl
39. Wrightwood Ct
40. Terry View Dr
41. Willowcrest Pl
42. Hendley Dr
43. Tropical Dr
44. Farley Ct
45. Hazelbrook Rd
46. Canton Ln
47. Roberts View Pl
48. Viewcrest Ct
49. Viewcrest Ln
50. Carpenter Ct
51. Pastel Pl
52. Blue Canyon Dr
53. Big Oak Dr
54. Berry Ct
55. Sunshine Ct
56. Ridgemoor Dr
57. Decente Ct
58. Woodhill Canyon Pl
59. Mound View Pl
60. Shady Oak Rd
61. Boughton Pl
62. Laurel Grove Ave
63. Vanetta Pl
64. Tolenas Dr
65. Fryman Pl
66. Oakdell Ln
67. Duque Dr
68. Lockridge Rd
69. Lockridge Estate Rd
70. Brookdale Ln
71. Dona Raquel Pl
72. Dona Cecilia Dr
73. Dona Christina Pl
74. Dona Conchita Pl
75. Dona Elena Pl
76. Dona Pepita Pl

1/2 mile | .5 km

While families are drawn to cheaper housing in Valley Village and twenty-somethings are ever-insistent on their Studio City zip codes, no one (including cartographers, residents, and the USPS) seems to agree on neighborhood boundaries. But the Studio City Farmers Market is clearly the nexus of its universe. Every Sunday brings together produce-happy locals and tired parents carting their tots in for a carnival of face-painting, petting zoos, and a moon bouncer. What spells unity better than mango-jalapeno jam and pony rides?

Banks

- **Bank of America** • 12223 Ventura Blvd
- **Bank of America** • 5025 Lankershim Blvd
- **Bank of America** • 5201 Laurel Cyn Blvd
- **California Credit Union** • 11221 Camarillo St
- **Citibank** • 12191 Ventura Blvd
- **Citibank** • 4821 Laurel Cyn Blvd
- **Citibank** • 5077 Lankershim Blvd
- **City National** • 12001 Ventura Pl
- **City National** • 12515 Ventura Blvd
- **Comerica** • 12050 Ventura Blvd
- **First Republic** • 12070 Ventura Blvd
- **Union** • 12185 Ventura Blvd
- **Washington Mutual** • 12051 Ventura Blvd
- **Wells Fargo** • 11135 Magnolia Blvd
- **Wells Fargo** • 12251 Ventura Blvd

Car Rental

- **Enterprise** • 11575 Ventura Blvd
- **Enterprise** • 5401 Lankershim Blvd

Car Washes

- **Galaxy Car Wash** • 12444 Chandler Blvd
- **Studio City Car Wash** • 11514 Ventura Blvd

Gas Stations

- **76** • 10974 Ventura Blvd
- **76** • 10984 Riverside Dr
- **76** • 4654 Laurel Cyn Blvd
- **Arco** • 12500 Ventura Blvd
- **Arco** • 5158 Laurel Cyn Blvd
- **Chevron** • 10960 Moorpark St
- **Chevron** • 4757 Laurel Cyn Blvd
- **Independent** • 4388 Tujunga Ave
- **Mobil** • 11001 Ventura Blvd
- **Mobil** • 4359 Laurel Cyn Blvd
- **Mobil** • 4377 Vineland Ave
- **Mobil** • 4801 Laurel Cyn Blvd
- **Shell** • 12007 Ventura Blvd

Landmarks

- **Brady Bunch House** • 11222 Dilling St
- **CBS Radford Studios** • 4024 Radford Ave
- **El Portal Theatre** • 5269 Lankershim Blvd

Libraries

- **North Hollywood Regional** • 5211 Tujunga Ave • 818-766-7185
- **Studio City Branch** • 12511 Moorpark St • 818-755-7873

Pharmacies

- **CVS** • 12143 Ventura Blvd • 818-980-1502
- **Longs Drugs** • 12100 Ventura Blvd • 818-763-5562
- **Rite-Aid** • 10989 Ventura Blvd • 818-980-1797
- **Rite-Aid** • 12511 Magnolia Blvd • 818-506-8795

Post Offices

- **US Post Office** • 11304 Chandler Blvd • 800-275-8777
- **US Post Office** • 12450 Magnolia Blvd • 800-275-8777
- **US Post Office** • 3950 Laurel Cyn Blvd • 800-275-8777

Schools

- **ABC Little School** • 11728 Moorpark St
- **ADC Middle** • 11728 Moorpark St
- **Amelia Earhart Continuation** • 5355 Colfax Ave
- **Beth Hillel Day** • 12326 Riverside Dr
- **Briarwood Pre-School & Kindergarten** • 12150 Riverside Dr
- **Bridges Academy** • 3921 Laurel Cyn Blvd
- **Campbell Hall Episcopal** • 4533 Laurel Cyn Blvd
- **Carlson Hospital Home School 1944** • 10952 Whipple St
- **Carpenter Ave Elementary** • 3909 Carpenter Ave
- **Colfax Ave Elementary** • 11724 Addison St
- **Country** • 5243 Laurel Cyn Blvd
- **Emek Hebrew Academy Nursery** • 12732 Chandler Blvd
- **Hollywood Alternative Schooling** • 11712 Moorpark St
- **Lankershim Elementary** • 5250 Bakman Ave
- **North Hollywood Community Adult** • 5231 Colfax Ave
- **North Hollywood High** • 5231 Colfax Ave
- **Oakwood Elementary** • 11230 Moorpark St
- **Oakwood Secondary** • 11600 Magnolia Blvd
- **St Paul's First Lutheran** • 11330 McCormick St
- **Valley Torah High** • 12517 Chandler Blvd
- **Walter Reed Middle** • 4525 Irvine Ave
- **The Wesley** • 4832 Tujunga Ave
- **Wonderland Ave Elementary** • 8510 Wonderland Ave

Supermarkets

- **Gelson's Markets** • 4738 Laurel Cyn Blvd
- **Jon's Market** • 12122 Magnolia Blvd
- **Trader Joe's** • 11976 Ventura Blvd
- **Vons** • 4033 Laurel Cyn Blvd

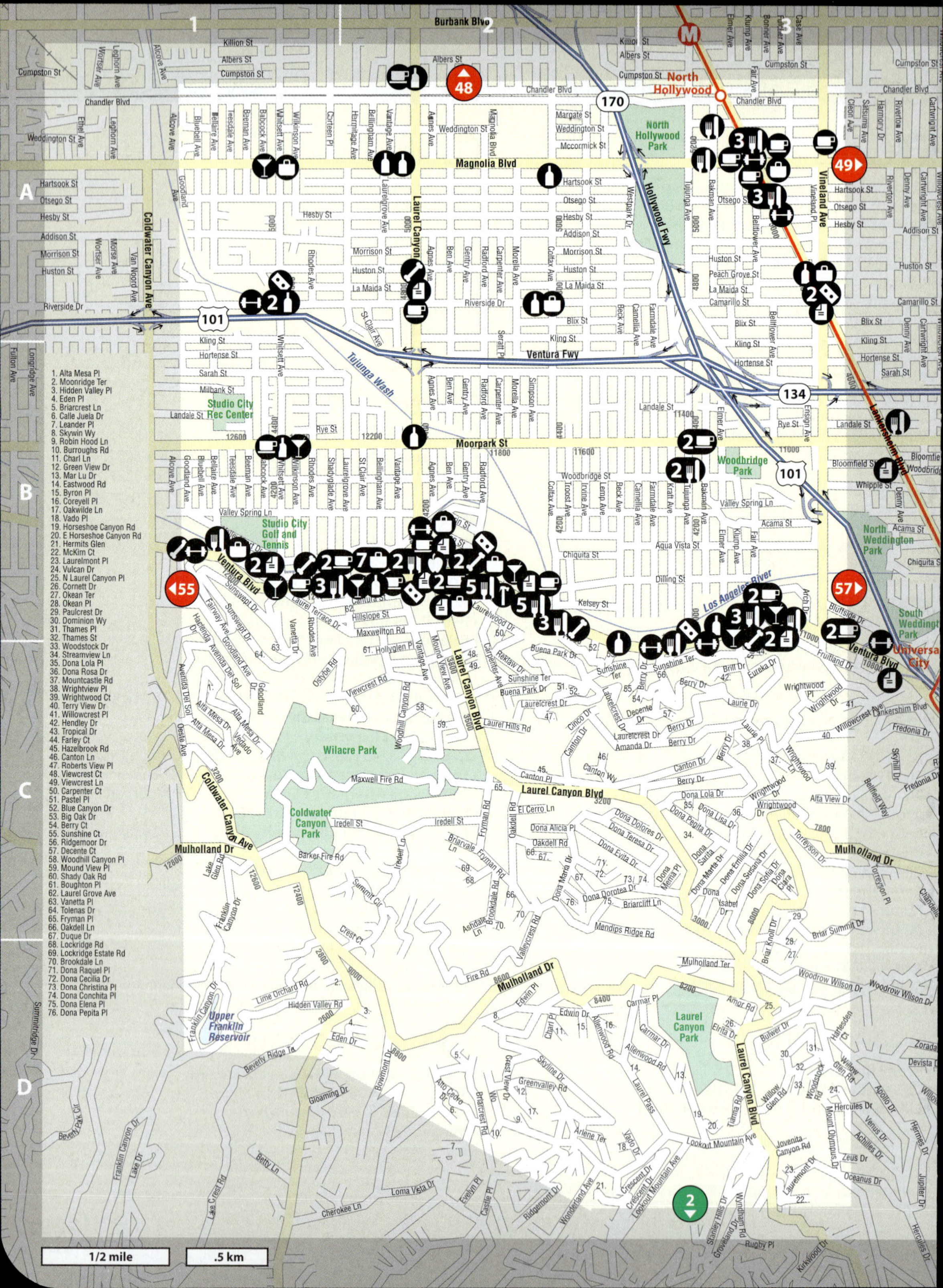

Map 56 • Studio City / Valley Village

1. Alta Mesa Pl
2. Moonridge Ter
3. Hidden Valley Pl
4. Eden Pl
5. Briarcrest Ln
6. Calle Juela Dr
7. Leander Pl
8. Skywin Wy
9. Robin Hood Ln
10. Burroughs Rd
11. Charl Ln
12. Green View Dr
13. Mar Lu Dr
14. Eastwood Rd
15. Byron Pl
16. Coreyell Pl
17. Oakwilde Ln
18. Vado Pl
19. Horseshoe Canyon Rd
20. E Horseshoe Canyon Rd
21. Hermits Glen
22. McKim Ct
23. Laurelmont Pl
24. Vulcan Dr
25. N Laurel Canyon Pl
26. Cornett Dr
27. Okean Ter
28. Okean Pl
29. Paulcrest Dr
30. Dominion Wy
31. Thames Pl
32. Thames St
33. Woodstock Dr
34. Streamview Ln
35. Dona Lola Pl
36. Dona Rosa Dr
37. Mountcastle Rd
38. Wrightview Pl
39. Wrightwood Ct
40. Terry View Dr
41. Willowcrest Pl
42. Hendley Dr
43. Tropical Dr
44. Farley Ct
45. Hazelbrook Rd
46. Canton Ln
47. Roberts View Pl
48. Viewcrest Ct
49. Viewcrest Ln
50. Carpenter Ct
51. Pastel Pl
52. Blue Canyon Dr
53. Big Oak Dr
54. Berry Ct
55. Sunshine Ct
56. Ridgemoor Dr
57. Decente Ct
58. Woodhill Canyon Pl
59. Mound View Pl
60. Shady Oak Rd
61. Boughton Pl
62. Laurel Grove Ave
63. Vanetta Pl
64. Tolenas Dr
65. Fryman Pl
66. Oakdell Ln
67. Duque Dr
68. Lockridge Rd
69. Lockridge Estate Rd
70. Brookdale Ln
71. Dona Raquel Pl
72. Dona Cecilia Dr
73. Dona Christina Pl
74. Dona Conchita Pl
75. Dona Elena Pl
76. Dona Pepita Pl

1/2 mile | .5 km

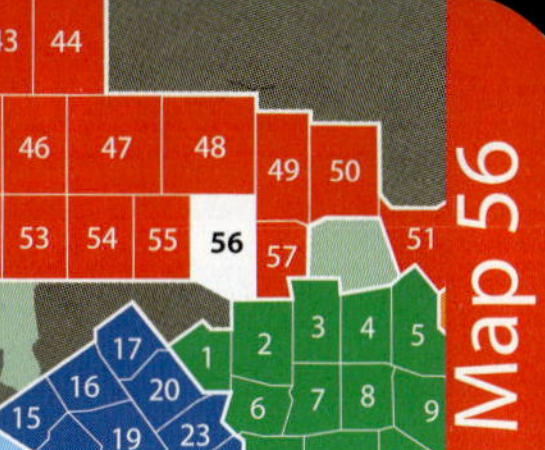

While it once seemed that there was LA proper and there was the Valley and neither the 'twain shall meet, Studio City is hard at work to distinguish itself as a reason to change the direction of traffic over the hill. Branching off of the smorgasbord of Ventura Blvd, there is a spread of trendy bars and restaurants (Firefly, Spark's, Sapphire, Wine Bistro, Lala's, Aura, and Clear), shopping, and sushi joints as far as the eye can see.

Coffee

- **Amsterdam Café** • 10905 Magnolia Blvd
- **Aroma Café** • 4360 Tujunga Ave
- **Caffe Neo** • 11239 Ventura Blvd
- **Coffee Bean & Tea Leaf** • 12050 Ventura Blvd
- **Coffee Bean & Tea Leaf** • 12501 Ventura Blvd
- **Coffee Fix** • 12508 Moorpark St
- **Coffee Time** • 5424 Laurel Canyon Blvd
- **Du-par's** • 12036 Ventura Blvd
- **Great India Café** • 12321 Ventura Blvd
- **Indie Coffee and Tea** • 5211 Lankershim Blvd
- **Jennifer's Coffee Connection** • 4397 Tujunga Ave
- **Jumpin-Java** • 11919 Ventura Blvd
- **Peet's** • 12215 Ventura Blvd
- **Starbucks** • 10965 Ventura Blvd
- **Starbucks** • 12170 Ventura Blvd
- **Starbucks** • Vons • 4033 Laurel Cyn Blvd
- **Starbucks** • 4800 Laurel Cyn Blvd
- **Starbucks** • 5166 A Lankershim Blvd
- **Vivian's Millennium Café** • 10968 Ventura Blvd

Copy Shops

- **Copies Unlimited** • 12548 Ventura Blvd • 818-985-5235
- **FedEx Kinko's** • 12101 Ventura Blvd • 818-980-2679
- **Minuteman Press** • 10807 Fruitland Dr • 818-762-7501
- **NOHO Copy and Printing** • 4795 Vineland Ave • 818-755-4542
- **Nuprint & Graphics** • 3962 Laurel Cyn Blvd • 818-509-0003
- **Office Depot** • 11211 Ventura Blvd • 818-760-4414
- **Pink Copy Center** • 12080 Ventura Pl • 818-762-8100
- **Staples** • 12605 Ventura Blvd • 818-753-6390
- **Studio Copy Center** • 11839 Ventura Blvd • 818-766-6161
- **UPS Store** • 11271 Ventura Blvd • 818-509-2988
- **UPS Store** • 4804 Laurel Cyn Blvd • 818-509-0802

Farmers Markets

- **Studio City Farmers Market (8 am–1 pm)** • Ventura Pl b/w Laurel Cyn Blvd & Ventura Blvd

Gyms

- **Bally Total Fitness** • 11315 Ventura Blvd • 818-760-7800
- **Body Image** • 5077 Lankershim Blvd • 818-761-8840
- **Cardio Barre** • 12530 Riverside Dr • 818-761-4525
- **Curves** • 1135 Magnolia Blvd • 818-332-1369
- **Curves** • 11440 Ventura Blvd • 818-762-0022
- **North Hollywood Gym** • 5126 Lankershim Blvd • 818-766-8888
- **Studio City Fitness** • 12733 Ventura Blvd • 818-506-1436

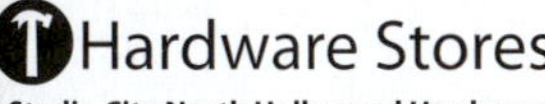

Hardware Stores

- **Studio City North Hollywood Hardware** • 11847 Ventura Blvd • 818-980-2453

Liquor Stores

- **Colfax Liquors** • 11710 Riverside Dr
- **Flask Liquor & Wine** • 12194 Ventura Blvd
- **Gourmet Wine** • 4803 Whitsett Ave
- **Hughie's Liquor** • 12121 Magnolia Blvd
- **J&J Wines & Spirits** • 11312 Ventura Blvd
- **Jon's Market** • 12122 Magnolia Blvd
- **Laurel Park Liquors** • 4407 Laurel Cyn Blvd
- **Liquor Center** • 5424 Laurel Cyn Blvd
- **Nelson's Liquor 2** • 5144 Colfax Ave
- **Oasis Liquor** • 4800 Whitsett Ave
- **Ringside Liquors** • 12500 Moorpark St
- **Sam's Liquor Store** • 4832 Lankershim Blvd
- **Valley Liquor** • 11418 Moorpark St
- **Vendome Liquor & Wine** • 11555 Ventura Blvd

Nightlife

- **Aura** • 12215 Ventura Blvd • 818-487-1488
- **Clear** • 11916 Ventura Blvd • 818-980-4811
- **Firefly** • 11720 Ventura Blvd • 818-762-1833
- **Fox & Hounds** • 11100 Ventura Blvd • 818-763-7976
- **Foxfire Room** • 12516 Magnolia Blvd • 818-766-1344
- **La Ve Lee** • 12514 Ventura Blvd • 818-980-8158
- **Maeve's Residuals** • 11042 Ventura Blvd • 818-761-8301
- **Oyster House Saloon** • 12446 Moorpark St • 818-761-8686
- **Platinum Live** • 11345 Ventura Blvd • 818-753-1771
- **The Sapphire** • 11938 Ventura Blvd • 818-506-0777

Pet Shops

- **Mark's Pet Supplies** • 12077 Ventura Pl • 818-760-4300
- **Mark's Tropical Fish** • 12063 Ventura Pl • 818-762-7700
- **Maxwell Dog** • 12336 Ventura Blvd • 818-505-8411
- **Omar's Exotic Birds** • 11222 Ventura Blvd • 818-985-9003
- **Pam's Pet Palace** • 4841 Laurel Cyn Blvd • 818-762-9035
- **Petco** • 12800 Ventura Blvd • 818-506-6416
- **Rusty's Discount Pet Center** • 11672 Ventura Blvd • 818-769-9085

Restaurants

- **Art's Deli** • 12224 Ventura Blvd • 818-762-1221
- **Asanebo** • 11941 Ventura Blvd • 818-760-3348
- **Caioti Pizza Café** • 4346 Tujunga Ave • 818-761-3588
- **Camille's Sidewalk Café** • 12265 Ventura Blvd • 818-623-9009
- **Carney's Express** • 12601 Ventura Blvd • 818-761-8300
- **Daichan** • 11288 Ventura Blvd • 818-980-8450
- **Dragon X** • 11400 Ventura Blvd • 818-487-7000
- **Du-par's** • 12036 Ventura Blvd • 818-766-4437
- **Eclectic Café** • 5156 Lankershim Blvd • 818-760-2233
- **Ernie's Taco House** • 4410 Lankershim Blvd • 818-985-4654
- **Firefly** • 11720 Ventura Blvd • 818-762-1833
- **Good Earth Restaurant & Bakery** • 12345 Ventura Blvd • 818-506-7400
- **Katsu-ya** • 11680 Ventura Blvd • 818-985-6976
- **Killer Shrimp** • 4000 Colfax Ave • 818-508-1570
- **La Loggia** • 11814 Ventura Blvd • 818-985-9222
- **Lala's Argentine Grill** • 11935 Ventura Blvd • 818-623-4477
- **Matsuda** • 11837 Ventura Blvd • 818-760-3917
- **Maximilians** • 11330 Weddington St • 818-980-6294
- **Mexicali** • 12161 Ventura Blvd • 818-985-1744
- **My Little Cupcake** • 11925 Ventura Blvd • 818-985-2253
- **Next Door at La Loggia** • 11814 Ventura Blvd • 818-985-9222
- **Noosh Deli** • 5118 Lankershim Blvd • 818-769-1844
- **Panera Bread** • 12131 Ventura Blvd • 818-762-2226
- **Pit Fire Pizza** • 5211 Lankershim Blvd • 818-980-2949
- **Salomi** • 5225 Lankershim Blvd • 818-506-0130
- **Sitton's North Hollywood Diner** • 11329 Magnolia Blvd • 818-761-3341
- **Sparks Woodfire Grill** • 11801 Ventura Blvd • 818-623-8883
- **Sushi Dan Rockin' Sushi** • 11056 Ventura Blvd • 818-985-2254
- **Sushi Nozawa** • 11288 Ventura Blvd • 818-508-7017
- **Suzanne's Country Deli** • 11273 Ventura Blvd • 818-762-9494
- **Teru Sushi** • 11940 Ventura Blvd • 818-763-6201
- **Todai** • 11239 Ventura Blvd #2 • 818-762-8311
- **Tokyo Delve's Sushi Bar** • 5239 Lankershim Blvd • 818-766-3868
- **Vegan Plate** • 11943 Ventura Blvd • 818-506-9015
- **Vitello's** • 4349 Tujunga Ave • 818-769-0905
- **Wine Bistro** • 11915 Ventura Blvd • 818-766-6233

Shopping

- **The Artisan Cheese Gallery** • 12023 Ventura Blvd • 818-505-0207
- **Bedfellows** • 12250 Ventura Blvd • 818-985-0500
- **Crossroads Trading Co** • 12300 Ventura Blvd • 818-761-6200
- **Dari** • 12184 Ventura Blvd • 818-762-3274
- **The Flask** • 12194 Ventura Blvd • 818-761-5373
- **Hoity Toity** • 4381 Tujunga Ave • 818-766-2503
- **The Ivy** • 12318 Ventura Blvd • 818-762-9844
- **King's Western Wear** • 11450 Ventura Blvd • 818-761-1162
- **Kit Kraft Hobby Shop** • 12109 Ventura Place • 818-509-9739
- **La Knitterie Parisienne** • 12642 Ventura Blvd • 818-766-1515
- **Laura's Designer Resale Boutique** • 12426 Ventura Blvd • 818-752-2835
- **Marie et Cie** • 11704 Riverside Dr • 818-508-5049
- **Maxwell Dog** • 12336 Ventura Blvd • 818-505-8411
- **Portrait of a Bookstore** • 4360 Tujunga Ave • 818-769-3853
- **Samuel French's Theatre & Film Bookshop** • 11963 Ventura Blvd • 818-752-0535
- **Storyopolis** • 12348 Ventura Blvd • 818-509-5600
- **Tennis Ace** • 12544 Ventura Blvd • 818-762-8751
- **Tuesday Morning** • 11239 Ventura Blvd • 818-508-5334
- **Verona** • 4350 Tujunga Ave • 818-508-6377
- **Village Gourmet** • 4357 Tujunga Ave • 818-487-3807
- **Village Market** • 11653 Moorpark St • 818-761-4848
- **Voila Boutique** • 12500 Magnolia Blvd • 818-766-9449

Video Rental

- **20-20 Video** • 12113 Ventura Blvd • 818-762-2020
- **Blockbuster** • 11978 Ventura Blvd • 818-505-9753
- **Blockbuster** • 4821 Lankershim Blvd • 818-505-1800
- **Odyssey Video** • 4810 Vineland Ave • 818-769-2001
- **Video Club** • 4811 Whitsett Ave • 818-766-2388
- **Video West** • 11376 Ventura Blvd • 818-760-0096

Map 57 • Universal City / Toluca Lake

TOLUCA LAKE

Warner Bros Studios

Lakeside Country Club

Los Angeles River

Universal Studios

Universal City

Campo de Cahuenga

CityWalk

Weddington Park North

Weddington Park South

Falcon Theatre

Bob's Big Boy

MOUNT OLYMPUS

Hollywood Reservoir

Runyon Canyon Park

1. Toluca Lake Ln
2. Velma Dr
3. De Witt Dr
4. Charleston Wy
5. Blair Cres
6. Winnie Dr
7. La Sombra Dr
8. La Falda Pl
9. Wonder View Pl
10. Hollycrest Pl
11. Benda Pl
12. Primera Pl
13. Wonder View Pz
14. Kentucky Dr
15. Terry View Dr
16. Oakley Dr
17. Carse Dr
18. Hild Tr
19. Springlet Tr
20. Sycamore Tr
21. Goodview Tr
22. Oak Point Dr
23. Pyramid Dr
24. Las Alturas St
25. Vista Crest Dr
26. Cahuenga Park Tr
27. Park Center Dr
28. Palo Vista Dr
29. Soper Dr
30. Nichols Canyon Rd
31. Chandelle Pl
32. Flynn Ranch Rd
33. Firenze Pl
34. Seattle Pl
35. La Castana Dr
36. Bantam Pl

1/2 mile

.5 km

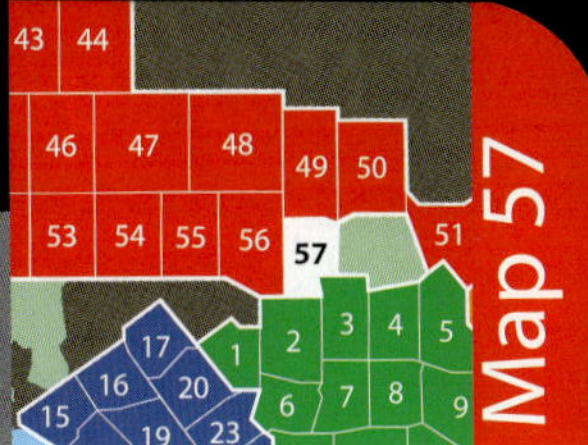

Where's the lake in Toluca Lake? If you don't have a home or a friend there, chances are you'll never see it. The enclave itself has a small-town feel, with a village of neighborhood shops and restaurants on Riverside Drive as well as a collection of beautiful mansions bordering the Lakeside Country Club and the private lake itself. As for its neighbor, Universal City amounts to little more than the studio, the theme park, and the hyper-stimulating, always-crowded CityWalk.

Banks

- **Bank of America** • 110 Universal City Plz
- **Bank of America** • 255 N Pass Ave
- **Bank of America** • 4123 W Olive Ave
- **California National** • 10100 Riverside Dr
- **Citibank** • 4000 W Alameda Ave
- **Citizens Business** • 4100 W Alameda Ave
- **City National** • 3500 W Olive Ave
- **First Entertainment Credit Union** • 6735 Forest Lawn Dr
- **Fremont Investment & Loan** • 10933 Ventura Blvd
- **Union** • 3900 W Alameda Ave
- **Washington Mutual** • 4455 Lankershim Blvd
- **Wells Fargo** • 10225 Riverside Dr
- **World Savings & Loan** • 10064 Riverside Dr

Car Rental

- **Enterprise** • 3500 Cahuenga Blvd W
- **Enterprise** • 3600 Barham Blvd
- **Midway Car Rental** • 4201 Lankershim Blvd

Car Washes

- **Lakeside Car Wash** • 3700 W Riverside Dr

Gas Stations

- **Arco** • 3704 Cahuenga Blvd
- **Arco** • 4506 Lankershim Blvd
- **Chevron** • 3701 W Riverside Dr
- **Chevron** • 3780 Cahuenga Blvd
- **Mobil** • 10570 Riverside Dr
- **Mobil** • 3240 Cahuenga Blvd W

Landmarks

- **Bob's Big Boy** • 4211 Riverside Dr
- **Campo de Cahuenga** • 3912 Lankershim Blvd
- **CityWalk** • Universal Center Dr
- **Falcon Theatre** • 4252 W Riverside Dr
- **Hollywood Reservoir** • East of Hwy 101
- **Universal Studios** • 100 Universal Center Dr
- **Warner Brothers Studios** • 4000 Warner Blvd

Police

- **Los Angeles County Sheriff's Dept-Universal Citywalk** • 1000 Universal Studios Blvd • 818-622-9539

Post Offices

- **US Post Office** • 10063 Riverside Dr • 800-275-8777

Schools

- **Rio Vista Elementary** • 4243 Satsuma Ave
- **St Charles Borromeo** • 10850 Moorpark St
- **Valley View Elementary** • 6921 Woodrow Wilson Dr

Supermarkets

- **Ralphs** • 10901 Ventura Blvd
- **Trader Joe's** • 10130 Riverside Dr

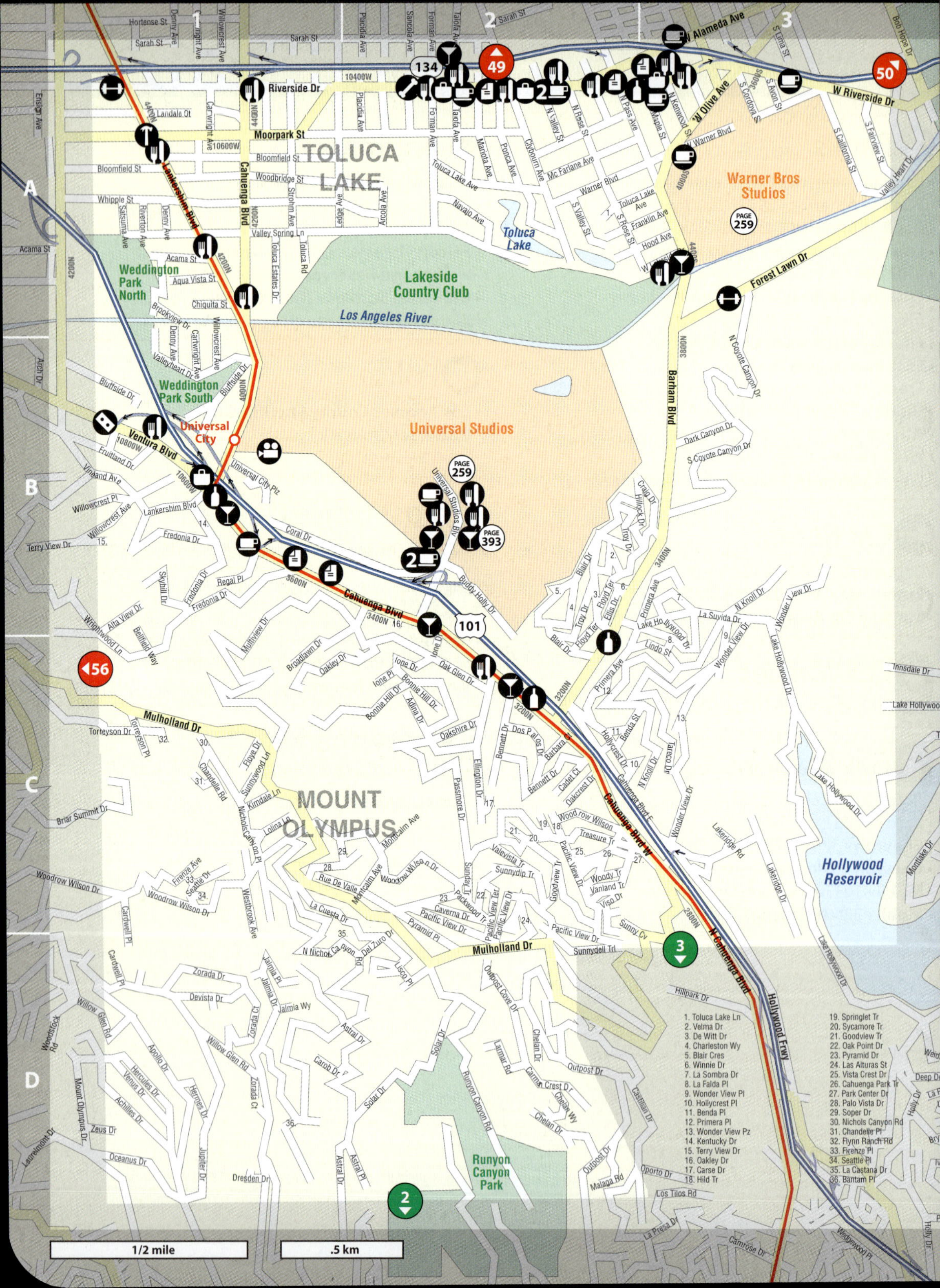

Toluca Lake
Lakeside Country Club
Los Angeles River
Warner Bros Studios
Universal Studios
Universal City
Weddington Park North
Weddington Park South
Mount Olympus
Hollywood Reservoir
Runyon Canyon Park
Riverside Dr
W Riverside Dr
W Alameda Ave
Moorpark St
Lankershim Blvd
Cahuenga Blvd
Ventura Blvd
Barham Blvd
Forest Lawn Dr
Mulholland Dr
Hollywood Frwy
N Cahuenga Blvd
W Olive Ave

1. Toluca Lake Ln
2. Velma Dr
3. De Witt Dr
4. Charleston Wy
5. Blair Cres
6. Winnie Dr
7. La Sombra Dr
8. La Falda Pl
9. Wonder View Pl
10. Hollycrest Pl
11. Benda Pl
12. Primera Pl
13. Wonder View Pz
14. Kentucky Dr
15. Terry View Dr
16. Oakley Dr
17. Carse Dr
18. Hild Tr
19. Springlet Tr
20. Sycamore Tr
21. Goodview Tr
22. Oak Point Dr
23. Pyramid Dr
24. Las Alturas St
25. Vista Crest Dr
26. Cahuenga Park Tr
27. Park Center Dr
28. Palo Vista Dr
29. Soper Dr
30. Nichols Canyon Rd
31. Chandelle Pl
32. Flynn Ranch Rd
33. Firenze Pl
34. Seattle Pl
35. La Castana Dr
36. Bantam Pl

1/2 mile
.5 km

Sundries / Entertainment

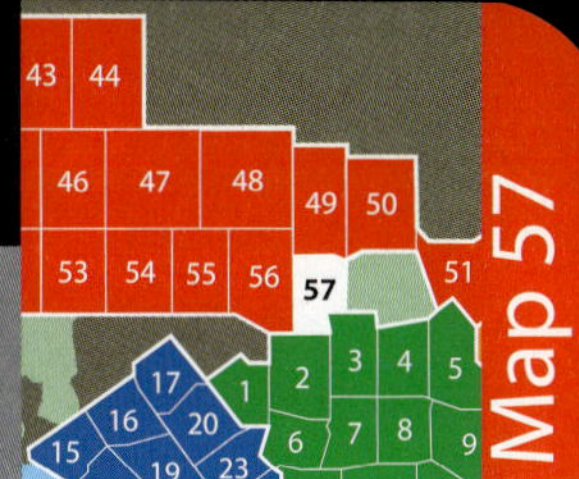

At Universal CityWalk, parking fees ($10 for regular parking, a whopping $17 for preferred parking) turn simply seeing a movie into a major investment. But this year's promotion refunds that fee as "Universal Dollars," which can be redeemed at any food purveyor in the complex, making dinner-and-a-movie seem like a good deal. And strolling CityWalk is entertainment in its own right, whether you crave the sensory overload of wall-to-wall neon, flashing lights and torrents of music flowing from every door, or you're simply into people-watching.

Coffee

- **Coffee Bean & Tea Leaf** • 1000 Universal Studios Blvd
- **Coffee Bean & Tea Leaf** • 10121 Riverside Dr
- **Igloo Café** • 171 N Maple St
- **Priscilla's Coffee** • 4150 W Riverside Dr
- **Starbucks** • 100 Universal City Plz
- **Starbucks** • 3400 W Riverside Dr
- **Starbucks** • 3800 W Alameda Ave
- **Starbucks** • 4000 Warner Blvd
- **Starbucks** • 4207 Riverside Dr
- **Starbucks / Café Puccino** • 1000 Universal Studios Blvd

Copy Shops

- **FedEx Kinko's** • 3575 Cahuenga Blvd W • 323-876-3481
- **FedEx Kinko's** • 3817 W Riverside Dr • 818-569-4914
- **FedEx Kinko's** • 4100 W Riverside Dr • 818-567-1044
- **Universal Print & Copy** • 3535 Cahuenga Blvd • 323-876-3500
- **UPS Store** • 10061 Riverside Dr • 818-506-4388

Gyms

- **Sports Center** • 6711 Forest Lawn Dr • 323-851-6000

Hardware Stores

- **Rick's Hardware** • 4382 Lankershim Blvd • 818-508-7948

Liquor Stores

- **House of Ambrose** • 3331 Barham Blvd
- **Maple Liquor** • 4001 W Riverside Dr
- **Spirit Cellar** • 3278 Cahuenga Blvd W
- **Universal Liquors** • 3797 Cahuenga Blvd
- **Vendome Liquor & Wine** • 10600 Riverside Dr

Movie Theaters

- **Citywalk Stadium 19 with IMAX** • 100 Universal City Plz • 818-508-0588

Nightlife

- **The Baked Potato** • 3787 Cahuenga Blvd • 818-980-1615
- **BB King's Blues Club** • 100 Universal Center Dr • 818-622-5464
- **The Casting Office** • 3256 Cahuenga Blvd W • 323-851-4300
- **Minibar** • 3413 Cahuenga Blvd W • 323-882-6965
- **Rumba Room** • 1000 Universal Studios Blvd • 818-622-1226
- **The Smoke House** • 4420 W Lakeside Dr • 818-845-3731
- **Timmy Nolan's** • 10111 Riverside Dr • 818-985-3359

Pet Shops

- **Four Paws Only of Toluca Lake** • 10214 Riverside Dr • 818-760-3366

Restaurants

- **Bacco Trattoria** • 3821 W Riverside Dr • 818-845-8036
- **Barsac Brasserie** • 4212 Lankershim Blvd • 818-760-7081
- **Buca di Beppo** • 1000 Universal Studios Blvd • 818-509-9463
- **Ca' del Sole** • 4100 Cahuenga Blvd • 818-985-4669
- **California Canteen** • 3311 Cahuenga Blvd • 323-876-1702
- **Chez Nous** • 10550 Riverside Dr • 818-760-0288
- **Don Cuco** • 3911 W Riverside Dr • 818-842-1123
- **Miceli's** • 3655 Cahuenga Blvd W • 323-851-3345
- **Mo's** • 4301 Riverside Dr • 818-845-3009
- **Paty's** • 10001 Riverside Dr • 818-761-0041
- **Priscilla's Coffee** • 4150 W Riverside Dr • 818-843-5707
- **Prosecco Restaurant** • 10144 Riverside Dr • 818-505-0930
- **The Smoke House** • 4420 W Lakeside Dr • 818-845-3731
- **Steak Joynt** • 4354 Lankershim Blvd • 818-761-9899
- **Versailles** • 1000 Universal Studios Blvd • 818-505-0093
- **Wolfgang Puck Café** • 1000 Universal Studios Blvd • 818-985-9653
- **Yamakawa** • 10118 Riverside Dr • 818-763-8355
- **Zach's Italian Café** • 10820 Ventura Blvd • 818-762-4225

Shopping

- **Cinema Secrets Beauty Supply** • 4400 W Riverside Dr • 818-846-0579
- **Geographia Map & Travel** • 4000 W Riverside Dr • 818-848-1414
- **Iliad Bookshop** • 5400 Cahuenga Blvd • 818-509-2665
- **Pergolina** • 10139 Riverside Dr • 818-508-7708
- **Simply Nature Day Spa** • 10067 Riverside Dr • 818-506-8927
- **Steel Casey** • 10624 Ventura Blvd • 818-763-5667
- **Weekendz Only** • 10139 1/2 Riverside Dr • 818-752-3695

Video Rental

- **Blockbuster** • 10911 Ventura Blvd • 818-762-9257

Peck Park
Leland Park
110
47
N Front St
W Summerland Ave
N Western Ave
S Weymouth Ave
Miraleste Dr
N Gaffey St
S Gaffey St
N Pacific Ave
S Pacific Ave
N Harbor Blvd
W 9th St
W 19th St
W 22nd St
W 25th St
S Western Ave
W Paseo Del Mar
S Crescent Ave
Shepard St
San Pedro Peninsula Hospital
ART Walk
San Pedro Farmer's Market
Los Angeles Harbor
Friendship Park
Averill Park
San Pedro High School
Ports O' Call
Palos Verdes Shores
Fort MacArthur Lower Reservation
PAGE 278
Cabrillo Marina
Angels Gate Cultural Center
Angels Gate Park
Point Fermin Park
Cabrillo Beach
Cabrillo Beach Bathhouse
Cabrillo Beach Fishing Pier
Point Fermin Lighthouse
Pacific Ocean

General Information

City of San Pedro Website: www.sanpedro.com
Chamber of Commerce: 310-832-7272; www.sanpedrochamber.com

Overview

On the southern side of the Palos Verdes Peninsula you will find that this fiercely proud community has undergone major renovation in recent years—a revitalization that is ongoing. This port city relies heavily on its boating traffic, giving it a slight industrial feel as ships and barges float in and out from all parts of the world. However, San Pedro also takes great pride in the community's historical look that, despite the palm trees, resembles a New England fishing town. Hidden delights await San Pedro visitors, from the Mediterranean-style Cabrillo Beach Bathhouse (3800 Stephen M White Dr, 310-548-7554) built in 1932, to the charming seaside village of Ports O' Call, to the always enlightening Angels Gate Cultural Center (3601 S Gaffey St, 310-519-0936; www.angelsgateart.org) and the Victorian-era Point Fermin Lighthouse and Park (807 Paseo Del Mar). You can also visit the Korean Friendship Bell (and visit the sick seals while you are in the park: www.marinemammalcare.org), see the grunion run at night at Cabrillo Beach (check the internet for days and times), or find amazing tide pools below the cliffs. A must-experience is the Sunken City, a neighborhood that fell over the cliffs because of seismic shifting (walk south from Point Fermin Lighthouse and hop the wall).

As befits a seafaring town, some of the country's foremost tattoo parlors can be found in San Pedro. It also boasts the Warner Grand Theatre (478 W 6th St, 310-548-7672; www.warnergrand.org), an opulent Art Deco venue built in 1931 that is rich in both history and culture. Visit Green Hills Memorial Park to visit the graves of Charles Bukowski and The Minutemen's D Boon. But what defines and distinguishes San Pedro most is the weekly ART Walk. On the first Thursday of every month, art galleries, retail shops, restaurants, and street vendors celebrate creativity by staying open late and offering discounts and specials. Live entertainment accompanies the action throughout the historic downtown Arts District, located between 4th and 8th Streets and Pacific Avenue and Centre Street, a neighborhood with terrific vintage shops selling cool and unusual wares. Visit www.1stthursday.com for an extensive list of participating establishments.

San Pedro is also a bridge away from Long Beach via Terminal Island (St. Vincent Thomas Bridge), and has ferries to Catalina Island for fantastic day trips.

How to Get There

From downtown LA, take the Harbor Freeway south (110 S) to Gaffey Street, then head south to San Pedro.

Banks

- **Bank of America** • 800 N Western Ave
- **US** • 1000 N Western Ave
- **US** • 1221 S Gaffey St
- **Washington Mutual** • 1001 S Pacific Ave
- **Washington Mutual** • 980 N Western Ave

Landmarks

- **Angel's Gate Cultural Center** • 3601 S Gaffey St
- **Art Walk** • W 4th St & S Pacific Ave
- **Cabrillo Beach Bathhouse** • 3800 Stephen M White Dr
- **Catalina Express Terminal** • Swinford St & N Harbor Blvd
- **Point Fermin Lighthouse** • 807 W Paseo Del Mar
- **Ports O' Call** • 1100 Nagoy Wy
- **San Pedro Farmer's Market** • Mesa St, b/w 6th & 7th Sts

Movie Theaters

- **Warner Grand Theatre** • 478 W 6th St

Nightlife

- **Godmother's** • 302 W 7th St
- **June's Bar** • 1100 S Pacific Ave

Restaurants

- **6th Street Bistro** • 354 W 6th St
- **Ante's Restaurant** • 729 Ante Perkov Wy
- **Beach City Grill** • 376 W 6th St
- **Marcello Tuscany Room** • 470 W 7th St
- **Nam's Red Door** • 2253 S Pacific Ave
- **Pacific Diner** • 3821 S Pacific Ave
- **Papadakis Taverna** • 301 W 6th St
- **Ports O' Call Restaurant** • Berth 76
- **Rex's Café** • 2136 S Pacific Ave
- **Think Bistro** • 1420 W 25th St
- **Think Café** • 302 W 5th St
- **The Whale and Ale** • 327 W 7th St

Shopping

- **Coyote Antiques** • 387 W 6th St
- **Office Depot** • 810 N Western Ave
- **Ramona Bakery** • 1101 S Pacific Ave
- **Sav-On** • 950 N Western Ave

General Information

City of Malibu Phone: 310-456-2489
City of Malibu Website: www.ci.malibu.ca.us
Weather/Surf Reports: http://beaches.co.la.ca.us/BandH/Beaches/main.htm

Overview

When outsiders fantasize about Southern California, it's not the smog-filled sky of downtown LA that runs through their minds. It's the sandy beaches and sunny skies of Malibu and its 21-mile coastline—the city that inspired a coconutty rum and perhaps the most famous Barbie doll ever. It's the place where Baywatch lifeguards roam and the rich and famous come to play.

The area's first settlers were the Chumash Indians. The names of some of their villages are still a part of local culture—Ojai, Mugu, and Zuma, to name just a few. But Malibu's current residents are a very different tribe indeed. For instance, The Colony, a gated community, is home to a wide array of celebrities, business-folk, and anyone else that can spare the $7 million-plus that it takes to buy a parcel of beachfront land.

Depending upon weather and other acts of God (like the fires and mudslides that frequently strike this beautiful stretch of coastline), Malibu is about a 45-minute trip from downtown LA, or approximately 35 miles. The best thing about Malibu is definitely its isolation. You feel as though you've left LA and gone somewhere else. The worst thing about Malibu is...its isolation. You feel as though you've left LA and gone somewhere else. Somewhere very far away.

The Beaches

Beaches are the main attraction in Malibu, and you have a number from which to choose. Keep in mind that dogs are not allowed on any public beach, and parking is a big challenge. There are three options: 1) Pay whatever the day's going rate is at parking lots conveniently located at each Malibu beach. 2) Find street parking in Malibu's residential areas—which then requires hiking down to the beach, often with the added challenge of crossing the PCH (Malibu's answer to the video game *Frogger*). 3) Get all of the planets to align just so, allowing you to score that perfect parking spot on the beach side of the PCH, right outside the entrance to your chosen beach. We grudgingly admit that option #1 may be your best bet.

Many of Malibu's private beaches are accessible to the public via causeways or public gates. Some of Malibu's more popular public beaches are:

- **Topanga State Beach** • Located along the PCH at Topanga Canyon Boulevard. Popular for surfing. Call 310-457-9701 for the northern surf report. Good luck finding parking.
- **Malibu Lagoon State Beach** • Located just west of the Malibu Pier. Features a bird sanctuary as well as the Malibu Lagoon Museum.
- **Malibu Surfrider Beach** • Home of the Malibu Pier, located along the 23000 block of the PCH. This is one of the most famous surfing beaches in the world.
- **Dan Blocker Beach** • Named for the actor who played "Hoss" on the TV series *Bonanza*. He was one of the original owners of this stretch of beach, along with his co-stars, Lorne Greene and Michael Landon, who donated it to the state after Blocker's death. This beach is on the PCH between Puerco Canyon and Corral Canyon.
- **Point Dume State Beach** • This state-owned beach is accessed from Westward Beach Road. One of the area's most beautiful beaches, it features nearby hiking trails, reefs for scuba diving, and tide pools.
- **Zuma Beach** • This very popular beach is located on the PCH, just west of Heathercliff Drive. It's expansive, is home to a number of volleyball courts, and tends to be very crowded in the summer.
- **Robert H. Meyer Memorial State Beach** • This is actually a grouping of three small beaches—El Pescador, La Piedra, and El Matador. They are located about 10 miles west of Malibu proper. Lots of rocky cliffs, sand dunes, and picturesque sunsets.
- **Nicholas Canyon Beach** • Located at 33850 Pacific Coast Highway. Lots of room for lying out in the sun or tossing a Frisbee.

The Adamson House

Located at Malibu Lagoon State Beach, the Adamson House was the home of Merritt Huntley Adamson and his wife Rhoda Rindge Adamson, whose family, the Rindges, once owned the Malibu Spanish Land Grant (as the area was originally known). The house features liberal use of the ceramic tile manufactured by the then-famous Malibu Potteries. The Adamson House and the adjacent Malibu Lagoon Museum are open Wednesday through Saturday from 11 am to 3 pm, while the grounds are open daily from 8 am until sunset. Admission to the adjoining Malibu Lagoon Museum is free while

tours of the Adamson House cost $5 for adults, $2 for children aged 6–16 years, and nothing for children 5 years and under. The property is also available for weddings and other special events, though weekend wedding season requires a year-and-a-half wait, so be prepared for a long engagement. 310-456-8432; www.adamsonhouse.org.

Malibu Creek State Park

What is now a 7,000-acre state park once belonged to motion picture studio Twentieth Century Fox, which used the park as a double for Korea in the TV series *M*A*S*H*. The park is home to some 30 miles of hiking and riding trails, as well as a campground featuring sixty campsites, with barbecues, showers, and bathroom facilities. The park's entrance is located along Las Virgenes/Malibu Canyon Road, just south of Mulholland Highway. 818-880-0367; www.parks.ca.gov/.

Pepperdine University

It's hard to imagine getting any studying done on a campus just a few hundred yards from the ocean, but Pepperdine students manage to pull it off (well…sometimes; we guess the curfew helps). Visible from PCH with its enormous thin cross stretching toward the heavens that created Malibu, Pepperdine sprawls across some of the greenest acreage in the land. The campus may be best known as the location for the 1970s TV spectacular *The Battle of the Network Stars*, but Pepperdine is represented by 15 NCAA Division I athletic teams in sports ranging from men's water polo to women's golf. The university's Center for the Arts typically hosts an eclectic lineup of events including piano recitals, modern dance, and children's theater. 24255 Pacific Coast Hwy, 310-506-4000; www.pepperdine.edu.

Where to Eat

Malibu relies upon the PCH as its Main Street and most of the town's dining establishments are located along either side. Dining experiences in Malibu tend to be one extreme or the other—either ultra-casual or ultra-pricey. Here are some restaurants that we recommend at both ends of the spectrum:

- **Coogies**, Malibu Colony Plaza, 23750 PCH, 310-317-1444. Upscale diner fare. This unpretentious restaurant is healthier than the typical diner and is a great bet for breakfast by the beach.
- **Neptune's Net**, 42505 PCH, 310-457-3095. Seafood. Though it's almost at the Ventura county line, this place is worth the drive. Very "beachy," Neptune's Net serves up a variety of seafood either steamed or fried.
- **Duke's Malibu**, 21150 PCH, 310-317-0777. California-Hawaiian. Lots of seafood dishes served amidst a fun, surfer theme dedicated to famed surfer Duke Paoa Kahanamoku. Avoid the Sunday brunch—the bar menu is always better—and try to snag a table at the barefoot bar.
- **Marmalade Café**, 3894 Cross Creek Rd, 310-317-4242. California-style sandwiches and salads. If you want a nice lunch in a nice setting, this is the place to go. Their food also travels well as take-out, and they have a great catering business too.
- **Taverna Tony**, Malibu Country Mart, 23410 Civic Center Wy, 310-317-9667. Greek. Delicious food in a fun, festive setting with live music.
- **Geoffrey's**, 27400 PCH, 310-457-1519. California-eclectic. Pronounced "Joffrey's," this restaurant serves delicious food that merits the snooty attitude you may occasionally encounter here. This is one of the most beautiful and romantic restaurants in LA.
- **Reel Inn**, 18661 PCH, 310- 456-8221. An old Malibu holdover, the Reel Inn has been a reliable and casual seafood outpost for decades. Fresh snapper, shrimp, and calamari are on the picnic table menu, with requisite cold beer in abundance.
- **Moonshadows**, 20356 PCH, 310-456-3010. The fancy-ish restaurant's food hardly compares to its ocean views, but it's not terrible. The highlight is the outdoor patio with cabanas and futons. A giant spotlight shines on the ocean like moonlight, hence the establishment's name.

How to Get There

With few exceptions, it's difficult to go anywhere in Malibu without encountering the Pacific Coast Highway for at least some of the trip. From the southern half of LA, the easiest option is to take the 10 Freeway to the PCH and head north. On summer weekends, the PCH becomes a virtual parking lot, but at least you can enjoy the smell and view of the ocean.

From the Valley and points north, your best bet is to hop on the 101 Freeway and head north toward Ventura. Exit at Las Virgenes and follow the signs for Las Virgenes Road/Malibu Canyon; then take Malibu Canyon Road to the PCH. If you're planning on going even further north into Malibu, you can also exit the 101 at Kanan Road, which becomes Kanan Dume Road and terminates at the PCH.

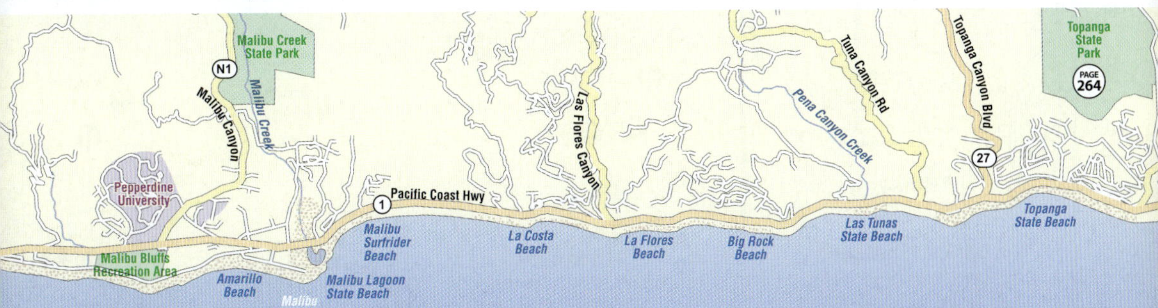

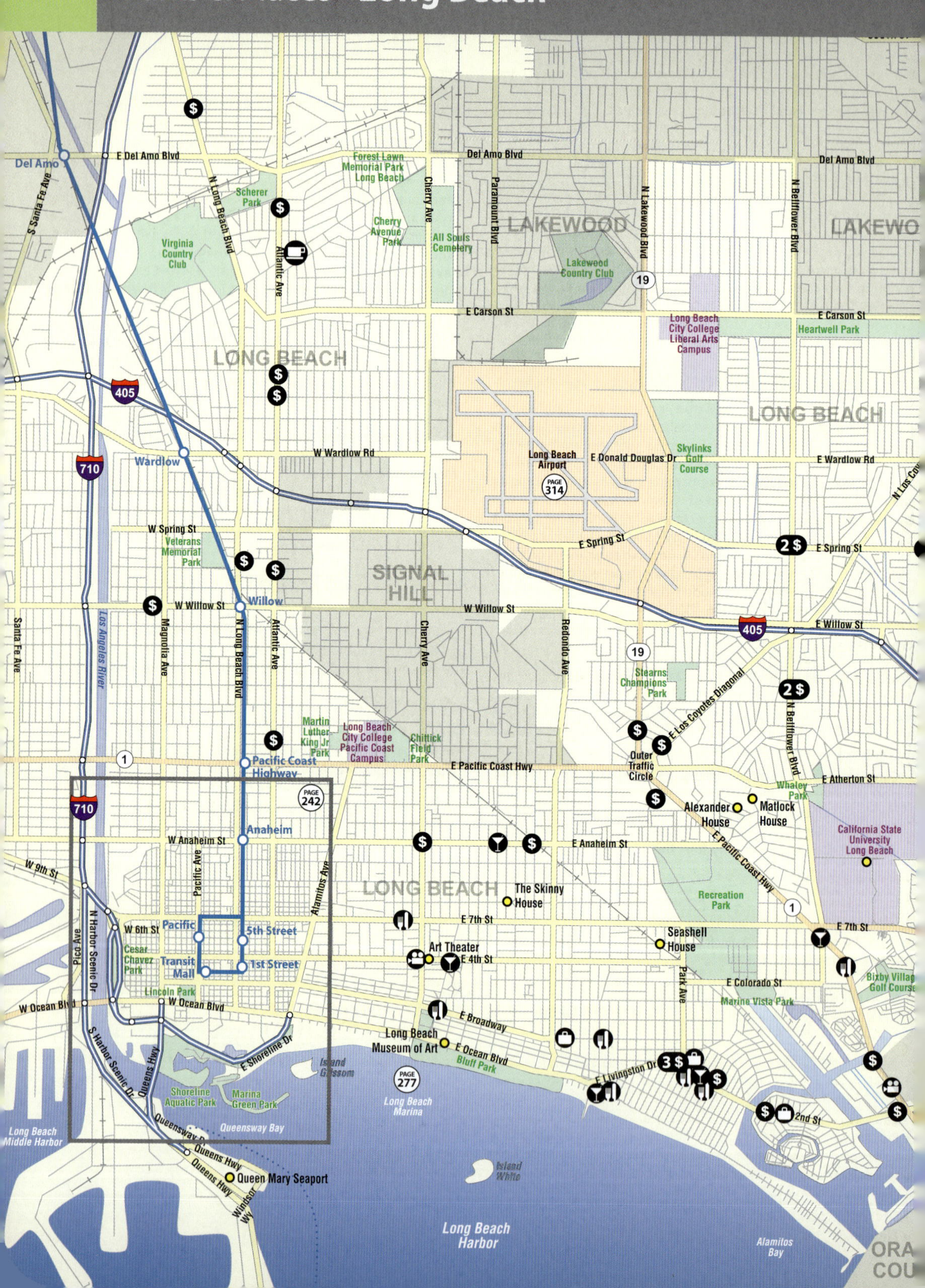

Del Amo
E Del Amo Blvd
Forest Lawn Memorial Park Long Beach
Del Amo Blvd
Scherer Park
Cherry Avenue Park
All Souls Cemetery
LAKEWOOD
Lakewood Country Club
Virginia Country Club
S Santa Fe Ave
N Long Beach Blvd
Atlantic Ave
Cherry Ave
Paramount Blvd
N Lakewood Blvd
N Bellflower Blvd
19
E Carson St
Long Beach City College Liberal Arts Campus
Heartwell Park
LONG BEACH
405
710
Wardlow
W Wardlow Rd
Long Beach Airport
E Donald Douglas Dr
PAGE 314
Skylinks Golf Course
E Wardlow Rd
W Spring St
Veterans Memorial Park
E Spring St
E Spring St
SIGNAL HILL
W Willow St
Willow
W Willow St
E Willow St
Los Angeles River
Magnolia Ave
Santa Fe Ave
Redondo Ave
Stearns Champions Park
E Los Coyotes Diagonal
Martin Luther King Jr Park
Long Beach City College Pacific Coast Campus
Chittick Field Park
Pacific Coast Highway
E Pacific Coast Hwy
1
Outer Traffic Circle
E Atherton St
Whaley Park
Alexander House
Matlock House
California State University Long Beach
PAGE 242
Anaheim
W Anaheim St
E Anaheim St
W 9th St
Pacific Ave
Alamitos Ave
The Skinny House
E Pacific Coast Hwy
Recreation Park
W 6th St
Pacific
5th Street
E 7th St
E 7th St
Seashell House
Cesar Chavez Park
Transit Mall
1st Street
Art Theater
E 4th St
N Harbor Scenic Dr
Pico Ave
Park Ave
E Colorado St
Bixby Village Golf Course
Lincoln Park
W Ocean Blvd
Marina Vista Park
E Broadway
Long Beach Museum of Art
E Ocean Blvd
Bluff Park
E Shoreline Dr
Island Grissom
PAGE 277
Long Beach Marina
E Livingston Dr
2nd St
S Harbor Scenic Dr
Queens Hwy
Shoreline Aquatic Park
Marina Green Park
Queensway Bay
Long Beach Middle Harbor
Queensway Dr
Queens Hwy
Queen Mary Seaport
Windsor Wy
Island White
Long Beach Harbor
Alamitos Bay

Overview

The birthplace of both the silent film industry and Snoop Dogg, Long Beach holds the distinction of being the most ethnically diverse metropolis in the United States. The first silent movie studio—Balboa Studios—was located here, and today numerous television shows and feature films continue to be shot in the area. Perhaps its biggest claim to fame is the Port of Long Beach, the second busiest port in the United States and one of the largest in the world. Despite the great earthquake of 1933, Long Beach has managed to successfully retain much of its charm, as evidenced in the Art Deco architecture along Ocean Boulevard. A massive downtown revitalization aimed at attracting a young, artsy crowd with new lofts, cafés, and theaters has also helped to develop the city.

Long Beach is home to approximately 500,000 people who love living in this city with all their hearts. The city is divided into pocket neighborhoods, each as different as the next. Belmont Shore is the quintessential beach community, with narrow streets and open-minded residents. Belmont Heights and Bluff Park are where the former residents of Belmont Shore go once they have kids and want a yard. North Long Beach is a residential working-class neighborhood near the 405 Freeway. Bixby Knolls is suburbia near the beach, with the usual lineup of ranch homes and minivans. Shoreline Village is a tourist's paradise, with shops and restaurants on the north end of the 11-mile beach.

How to Get There

Although it sits only 21 miles from downtown Los Angeles, the roads to Long Beach are often congested and fraught with delays. Find your way to the 405 or the 5 and head south, taking either freeway to the 710 S. The 10 also intersects with the 710 east of downtown LA, so that's a viable option as well.

Banks

- **Bank of America** • 101 E Willow St
- **Bank of America** • 150 Long Beach Blvd
- **Bank of America** • 2240 N Bellflower Blvd
- **Bank of America** • 5101 E 2nd St
- **Bank of America** • 600 W Willow St
- **Bank of America** • 6351 E Spring St
- **City National** • 6265 E 2nd St
- **Comerica** • 1650 Ximeno Ave
- **Farmers & Merchants** • 2302 N Bellflower Blvd
- **Farmers & Merchants** • 2801 Atlantic Ave
- **Farmers & Merchants** • 3140 E Anaheim St
- **Farmers & Merchants** • 4827 E 2nd St
- **First Bank & Trust** • 3850 Atlantic Ave
- **Union** • 1900 Atlantic Ave
- **Union** • 5430 E 2nd St
- **Washington Mutual** • 3901 Atlantic Ave
- **Washington Mutual** • 4571 E Los Coyotes Diagonal
- **Washington Mutual** • 5200 E 2nd St
- **Washington Mutual** • 6300 E Spring St
- **Wells Fargo** • 1930 N Lakewood Blvd
- **Wells Fargo** • 2096 N Bellflower Blvd
- **Wells Fargo** • 4540 Atlantic Ave
- **Wells Fargo** • 4601 E 2nd St
- **Wells Fargo** • 6290 E Pacific Coast Hwy

Landmarks

- **Alexander House** • 5281 El Roble St
- **Art Theater** • 2025 E 4th St
- **California State University at Long Beach** • 1250 N Bellflower Blvd
- **Long Beach Museum of Art** • 2300 E Ocean Blvd
- **Matlock House** • 1560 Ramillo Ave
- **Queen Mary Seaport** • 1126 Queens Hwy
- **Seashell House** • 4325 E 6th St
- **The Skinny House** • 798 Gladys Ave

Movie Theaters

- **AMC Theatres Marina Pacifica 12** • 6346 E Pacific Coast Hwy
- **Art Theater** • 2025 E 4th St
- **United Artists Long Beach Marketplace 6** • 6601 E Pacific Coast Hwy

Nightlife

- **49ers Tavern** • 5660 E Pacific Coast Hwy
- **The Belmont Brewing Company** • 25 39th Pl
- **Joe Jost's** • 2803 E Anaheim St
- **Murphy's Pub** • 4918 E 2nd St
- **Portfolio Coffee House** • 2300 E 4th St

Restaurants

- **Bono's** • 4901 E 2nd St
- **Christy's** • 3937 E Broadway
- **Chuck's Coffee Shop** • 4120 E Ocean Blvd
- **Enrique's** • 6210 E Pacific Coast Hwy
- **La Rizza's** • 1837 E 7th St
- **Open Sesame** • 5215 E 2nd St
- **Park Pantry** • 2104 E Broadway

Shopping

- **5001** • 5001 E 2nd St
- **Buffalo Exchange** • 4608 E 2nd St
- **Kitchen Outfitters** • 5666 E 2nd St
- **Olives Gourmet Grocer** • 3510 E Broadway

W 5th St
W Cowles St
W 14th Ct
W 14th St
E 14th St
E 15th St
E New York St
Magnolia Ave
Pacific Ave
Long Beach Blvd
Atlantic Ave
W Anaheim St
Anaheim
E Anaheim St
W 12th St
Moro Pl
Regal Wy
E 12th St
E Lily Wy
E Atlas Wy
E 11th St
W 11th St
St Mary's Medical Center
Drake Park
W 10th St
E 10th St
Emerald Pl
W Nardo Wy
E Nardo Wy
W 9th St
E 9th St
W Cypress Wy
E Cypress Wy
York Rite Masonic Temple
W 8th St
E 8th St
Ruby Pl
W La Reina Wy
E La Reina Wy
N Harbor Scenic Dr
710
Pico Ave
W 7th St
E 7th St
Cobre Wy
W 6th St
5th Street
Museum of Latin-American Art
Cereza Wy
W 5th St
E 5th St
Pacific
Cesar E Chavez Park
W Melrose Wy
Long Beach Plaza
W 4th St
E 4th St
Roble Wy
W 3rd St
E 3rd St
Maple Wy
Edison Theatre
W Broadway
E Broadway
Alamitos Ave
E Alta Wy
World Trade Center Long Beach Convention & Visitors Bureau
Lincoln Park
1st Street
E 1st St
Transit Mall
W Ocean Blvd
E Ocean Blvd
W Windsor Pl
Villa Riviera
Adelaide A Tichenor House
W Seaside Wy
W Shoreline Dr
E Seaside Wy
S Pine Ave
Ocean Shore St
Catalina Landing
Long Beach Convention & Entertainment Center
Bay St
The Pike at Rainbow Harbor
Aquarium of the Pacific
E Shoreline Dr
Rainbow Lagoon Park
Marina Green Park
Shoreline Park
Shoreline Village
Shoreline Village Dr
Queensway Bridge
PAGE 277
Island Grissom
Long Beach Marina
Queensway Bay
Queensway Dr

You can also take the Metro Blue Line to downtown Long Beach from either the 7th Street/Metro Center stop or the Pico Boulevard stop (near the Los Angeles Convention Center) for a round-trip fare of $2.50. The train makes several stops in Long Beach, including one at the Transit Mall on 1st Street, between Pine and Pacific. 800-COMMUTE; www.mta.net.

Once you've arrived, Long Beach Transit (562-591-2301) offers several services, such as the Pine Avenue Link and the Passport, that shuttle visitors all over town from the Queen Mary to Pine Avenue and Belmont Shore. Fares are reasonable at $0.90, with discounted rates for seniors, disabled riders, and children. Another transportation alternative is the AquaBus. This 40-foot-long water taxi costs just $1 and will ferry you to a number of Long Beach's coastal attractions. There are stops at the Aquarium, the Queen Mary, Catalina Landing, Shoreline Village, Pine Avenue Circle at Dock 7, and the Coast Hotel. The AquaLink water taxi is another option for nautical travel, but while it's faster and bigger than the AquaBus, this boat costs $3 to ride and only makes stops at Alamitos Bay Landing, the Queen Mary, and the Aquarium. 800-481-3470; www.lbtransit.com/Services/Aqualink.aspx.

Attractions

Catalina

The Catalina Express ferry service currently monopolizes the seaways in the 22 mile stretch between mainland California and Catalina Island. The boats leave Long Beach for Catalina from two ports—Catalina Landing (7 times daily with an eighth departure option on Fridays and Saturdays) and Queen Mary (3 times on weekends only, depending on the season)—and the journey is approximately one hour long. Take sunscreen, a beach towel, and Dramamine—the ride is often a rough one. A round-trip adult ticket costs $59 and reservations are recommended. 800-481-3470; www.catalinaexpress.com.

You can also opt for a quicker route (15 minutes) via the Island Express Helicopter Service for $156 round trip per person. For just a little bit more, Island Express offers daily packages at $210 per person that include flight, taxi, and two Santa Catalina Island Company Discovery tours. 800-2-AVALON; www.islandexpress.com.

Whether by air or by sea, once you land you can take advantage of all the leisure activities the island has to offer,

Banks

- **Bank of America** • 5253 N Long Beach Blvd
- **California Bank & Trust** • 444 W Ocean Blvd
- **Citibank** • 1 World Trade Ctr
- **City National** • 11 Golden Shore St
- **Comerica** • 301 E Ocean Blvd
- **Farmers & Merchants** • 302 Pine Ave
- **First Bank & Trust** • 100 Oceangate
- **International City** • 249 E Ocean Blvd
- **Union** • 400 Oceangate
- **Washington Mutual** • 401 E Ocean Blvd
- **Wells Fargo** • 111 W Ocean Blvd

Landmarks

- **Adelaide A Tichenor House** • 852 E Ocean Blvd
- **Aquarium of the Pacific** • 100 Aquarium Wy
- **Catalina Landing** • 330 Golden Shore St
- **Edison Theater** • 213 E Broadway
- **Long Beach Convention & Visitor's Bureau** • 1 World Trade Ctr
- **Museum of Latin-American Art** • 628 Alamitos Ave
- **The Pike at Rainbow Harbor** • S Pine Ave & W Shoreline Dr
- **Shoreline Village** • 419 Shoreline Village Dr
- **The Villa Riviera Hotel** • 800 E Ocean Blvd

Movie Theaters

- **AMC Theatres Pine Square 16** • 245 Pine Ave
- **Cinemark at the Pike** • 99 S Pine Ave

Nightlife

- **Blue Café** • 210 The Promenade N
- **Mariposa** • 135 Pine Ave
- **Rock Bottom Brewery** • 1 Pine Ave
- **The Sky Room** • 40 S Locust Ave
- **V20** • 81 Aquarium Wy

Restaurants

- **555 East** • 555 E Ocean Blvd
- **Alegria** • 115 Pine Ave
- **Cha Cha** • 762 Pacific Ave
- **Gladstone's** • 330 S Pine Ave
- **King's Fish House** • 100 W Broadway
- **L'Opera** • 101 Pine Ave
- **La Traviata** • 301 Cedar Ave
- **Long Beach Café** • 615 E Ocean Blvd
- **The Madison** • 102 Pine Ave
- **Parker's Lighthouse** • 435 Shoreline Village Dr
- **Uncle Al's Seafood** • 400 E 1st St
- **Utopia** • 445 E 1st St
- **Wasabi Japanese Restaurant** • 200 Pine Ave
- **Yard House** • Shoreline Village• 401 Shoreline Village Dr

Shopping

- **Acres of Books** • 240 Long Beach Blvd
- **City Place** • 275 E 4th St
- **Mood Swings** • 455 E Ocean Blvd
- **Nordstrom Rack** • 300 The Promenade N
- **The Pike at Rainbow Harbor** • Pine Ave & Shoreline Dr
- **Z Gallerie** • 230 Pine Ave

Catalina Cont'd
from renting a golf cart to snorkeling and parasailing—all with that kitschy ski resort town feel…minus the skiing. There's camping available on both sides of the island: Avalon has restaurants within walking distance or a trolley shuttle ride away, while sites at Two Harbors come with fewer tourists, but also less running, water for the more rugged camper. www.catalina.com.

Queen Mary
Once a vessel that ferried WWII troops, movie stars, and heads of state across the Atlantic Ocean, the *Queen Mary* has since retired and is now a floating hotel and museum available for weddings, bar mitzvahs, and rubber stamp conventions – for real. In all seriousness, the ship is awesome in scope and historical significance. The *Queen Mary* offers something for the tourist in you—from brunch and hotel stays to ghost tours and comedy shows. A popular filming location, the liner boasts recent cameos in *Arrested Development* and *Pearl Harbor*, reminding us that Hollywood is just a hop, skip, and a freeway away. 562-435-3511; www.queenmary.com.

Admission: A "First Class Passage" that includes admission to all of the boat's attractions costs $29.95 for each adult, $26.95 for seniors and members of the military, and $18.95 for kids 5–11. Smaller packages are also available.

Directions: The *Queen Mary* is located at 1126 Queens Highway, at the south end of the 710 Freeway.

Aquarium of the Pacific
The Aquarium of the Pacific opened with much fanfare—and a massive PR campaign—in 1998. Don't expect to see Atlantic salmon or Maine lobsters here—this aquarium lives up to its name by focusing solely on the Pacific Ocean's three regions: Southern California/Baja, the Tropical Pacific, and the Northern Pacific. While San Diego's Sea World relies heavily upon flashy acts like Shamu to draw visitors, the Aquarium of the Pacific emphasizes interactive education over entertainment. 562-590-3100; www.aquariumofpacific.org.

Admission: Packages start at $20.95 for adults, $11.95 for children ages 3–11, and $17.95 for seniors. Additional options include a Behind-the-Scenes tour and an Ocean Experience tour for a few extra bucks. The aquarium is open every day from 9 am until 6 pm. It's closed on Christmas and for the entire weekend of the Toyota Grand Prix, which is usually in April. If you want to avoid lines, online ticketing is available for an additional $1.50 fee per ticket.

Directions: Take the 405 S to the 710 S, and follow the signs to Downtown Long Beach and the Aquarium. The Aquarium is located at 100 Aquarium Way, off Shoreline Drive. Parking is available at a municipal lot located just a few feet from the Aquarium. The cost is $6 with an Aquarium ticket stub, $7 without.

Long Beach Convention & Entertainment Center
Located at 300 East Ocean Boulevard, this complex is home to an eclectic assortment of events. Long Beach's professional hockey team, the Ice Dogs, plays its home games at the Long Beach Arena; the Terrace Theater hosts a variety of plays and musical performances; and the Convention Center includes a large ballroom that serves as the site for many a senior prom. 562-436-3636; www.longbeachcc.com.

The Ice Dogs, who play from October until early April, are part of the ECHL. Check their schedule at www.icedogs.com. Game tickets are available through Ticketmaster at 213-480-3232 or online at www.ticketmaster.com.

Directions: Take the 405 S to the 710 S and head for the Downtown exits. The 710 turns into Shoreline Drive. Follow this to Linden and turn into the parking lot.

Shoreline Village
Designed to look like an old-fashioned fishing village, Shoreline Village is a collection of shops, restaurants, and amusements that might best be described as "quaint." Don't get us wrong—Skee-ball has its time and place, and sometimes Shoreline Village might prove to be that place. The area also caters to more athletic pursuits such as rollerblading, bike riding, and sailing, as well as offering a number of great restaurants and tasty snack shops. 562-435-2668; www.shorelinevillage.com.

Directions: Take the 710 S and follow signs for the Aquarium. Continue past the Aquarium and Pine Avenue, and turn right onto Shoreline Village Drive. Two hours of parking is free with any purchase.

Hours: Shoreline Village is open seven days a week from 10 am until 9 pm, closing an hour later during the summer months.

The Pike at Rainbow Harbor
Today's Pike at Rainbow Harbor is in many ways reminiscent of the celebrated Pike of yore. Over 100 years ago, the Pike was one of the most famous beachside amusement parks on the West Coast with rides, a pier, movie houses, shops, and cafés. The *new* Pike at Rainbow Harbor includes modern-day incarnations of commercialized fun, including dining options such as Bubba Gump Shrimp Co. and Smoothie King, a 14-screen multiplex, and an antique carousel. The Pike, covering 18 acres of downtown waterfront, is located smack-dab between the Convention Center and the Aquarium. www.shopthepike.com.

Directions: Take the 405 S to the 710 S and head for the Downtown exits. The 710 turns into Shoreline Drive. Park anywhere between Pine and Chestnut Avenues, or in Shoreline Village, and then walk a few steps north. There's limited free parking with validation, but beware of the $24 lost-ticket fee.

Toyota Grand Prix
For one weekend every April, Long Beach turns into Daytona Beach and the sound of revving car engines echoes throughout the usually subdued downtown area. The real draw of the Grand Prix is the Pro/Celebrity Race, where the likes of Patrick Dempsey, William Shatner, Martina Navratilova, and Frankie Muniz get fast and furious with the best of the pros. Tickets are available online at www.longbeachgp.com, or by calling 888-82-SPEED.

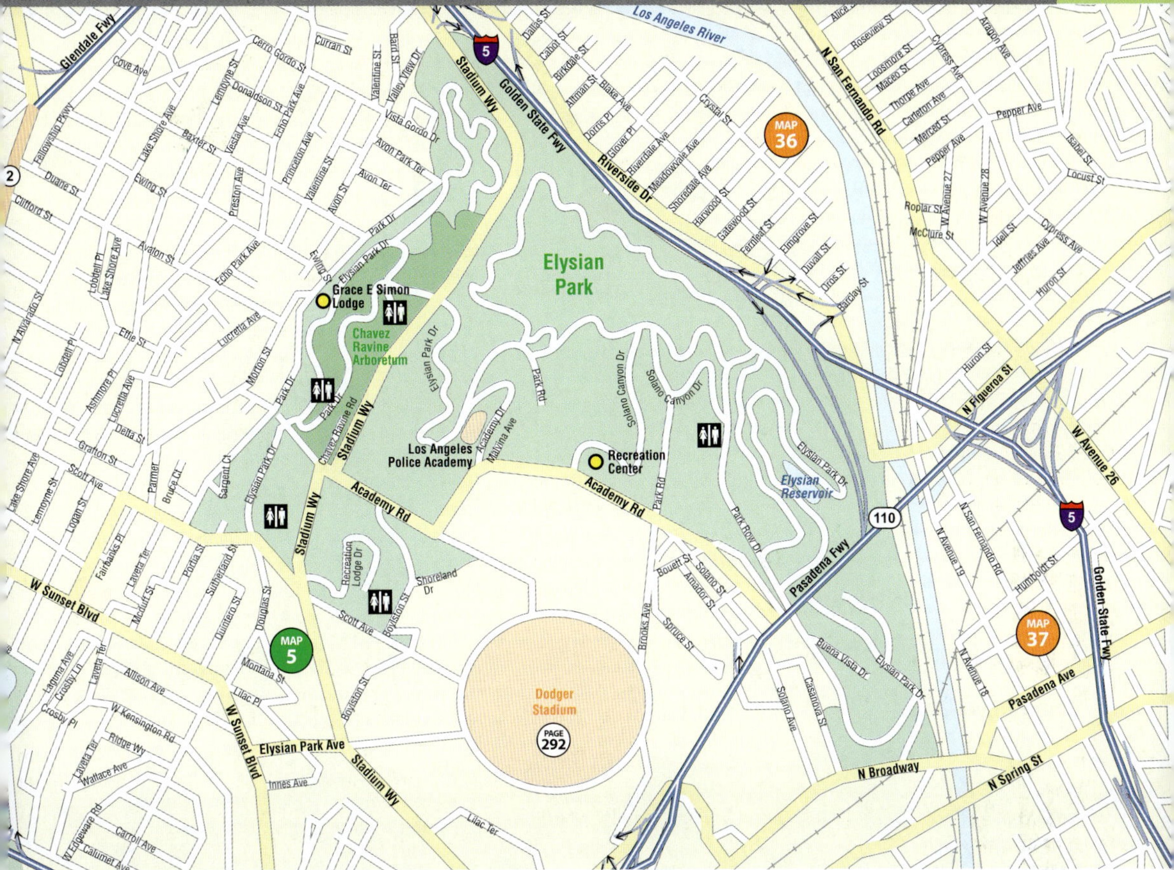

General Information

NFT Maps: 5, 36 & 37
Address: 835 Academy Rd
Los Angeles, CA 90012
Phone: 213-485-5054
Website: www.laparks.org/dos/parks/facility/elysianPk.htm

Overview

When Los Angeles was founded in 1781, more than 600 acres of parkland was set aside for public use. That allotted land, today known as Elysian Park, is the oldest and second-largest park in the LA area. The majority of the park, crisscrossed with hiking trails, has been maintained in its original state since it opened. In 1965, the "Citizens Committee to Save Elysian Park" formed to organize public support to preserve the parkland as public open space. Over 40 years later, the park has seen no redevelopment, but the committee continues to "arouse public and official awareness of the value of saving the last of these Pueblo lands set aside two centuries ago." (The park actually includes the last large piece of Pueblo land granted to the city by Carlos III, King of Spain, in 1781.) Despite the presence of the Police Academy (and their shooting range), one can still get away from it all and enjoy a relaxing respite from the city. But don't wander too far while alone. Even with the high occupancy of officers-in-training, the more isolated sections of the park are just that—and not always the safest, especially when it gets dark. Use the buddy system—in daylight—and aside from the fault line running underneath the park, you should be fine.

Practicalities

The central picnic area on Stadium Way has several barbecue pits, a small human-made lake, and a children's play area. The Recreation Center has basketball courts and volleyball. A café at the Police Academy is open to the public on weekdays from 6 am until 3 pm. The annual Chinatown Firecracker 10K Run passes through the park every February.

Admission to the park and arboretum is free. Elysian Park is located next to Dodger Stadium and the Police Academy and can be reached from the 5 or 110 Freeways (exit Stadium Way). The Chavez Ravine Arboretum is on the west side of Stadium Way near the Grace E. Simon Lodge.

FYI: If you're headed to a game at Dodger Stadium, park near Elysian Park (on Douglas Street or Stadium Way), then cut along the park and up to the stadium. Nature and a parking alternative—you gotta love it.

Chavez Ravine Arboretum

In 1893, the Los Angeles Horticultural Society established the arboretum and extensive botanical gardens in Elysian Park. The Chavez Ravine Arboretum was declared "City Historical-Cultural Monument Number 48" in 1967, and today Los Angeles Beautiful sponsors the arboretum. Many of the trees are the oldest and largest of their kind in California—some even in the United States—and there are over 1,000 tree species from around the world that can be grown in the arboretum's moderate climate. The Los Angeles Beautiful Arbor Day is held annually at the Chavez Ravine Arboretum. 213-485-5054; www.laparks.com/dos/horticulture/chavez.htm.

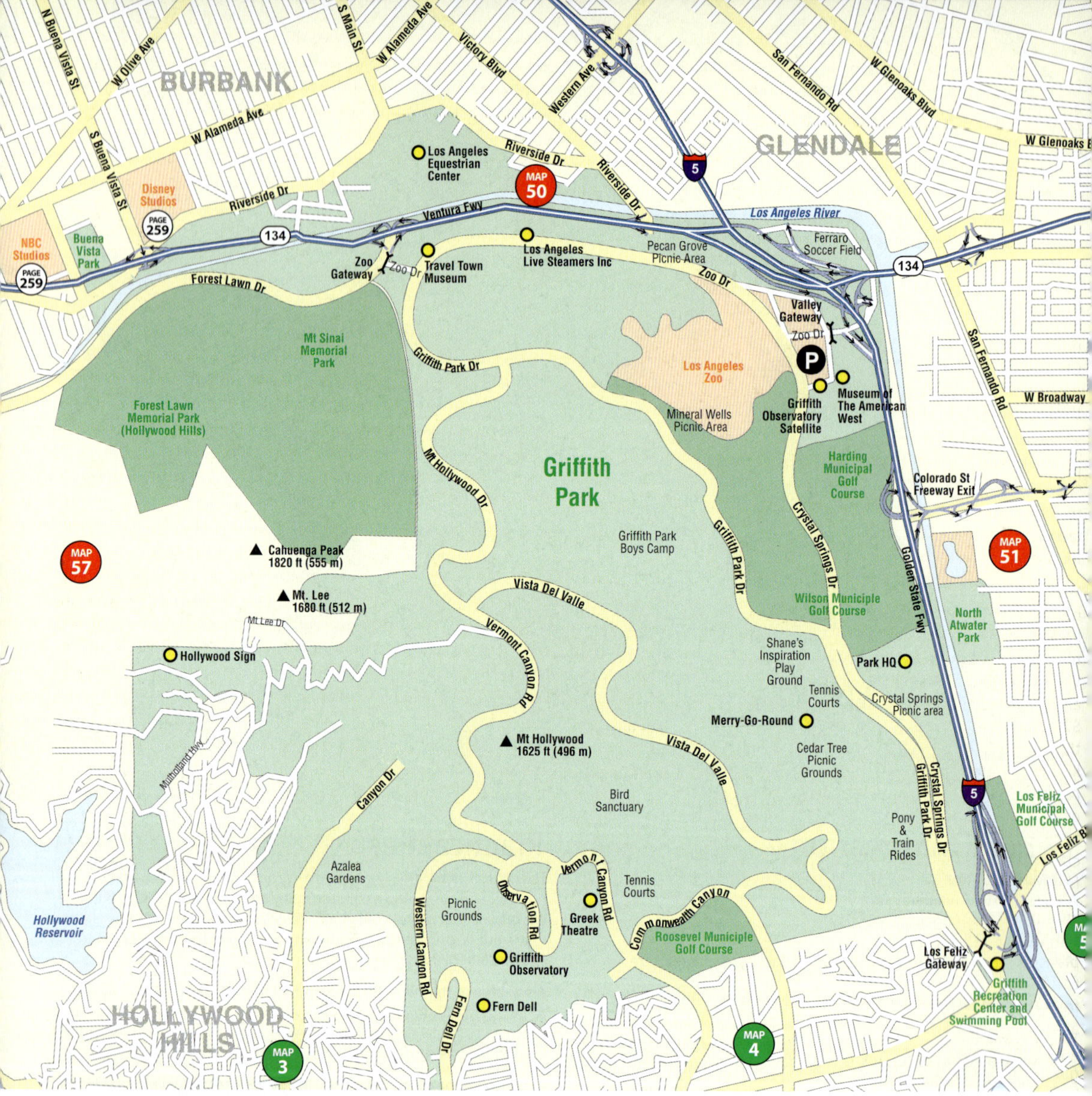

General Information

NFT Maps:	3, 4, 5, 50, 51 & 57
Address:	4730 Crystal Springs Dr Los Angeles, CA 90027
Phone:	323-913-4688
Website:	www.laparks.org/dos/parks/griffithPK/index.htm
Hours:	5 am–10:30 pm, daily (bridle trails, hiking paths, and mountain roads close at sunset)

Overview

It's one of LA's great tragedies that we Angelenos do not make better or more frequent use of Griffith Park. It's the largest municipal park in the United States, far larger than New York's Central Park, yet not nearly as convenient. Sure, it's easily accessible from both the 5 and the 134 freeways, but Griffith Park is still a hike (pun intended) from the Westside, a slow crawl from the West Valley, and might as well be a world away from the South Bay. Most park-goers come to Griffith Park for its museums and attractions (the Zoo, the Greek Theatre, etc.), but these are just the beginning of the wide variety of activities the park has to offer.

Unfortunately, brush fires hit Griffith Park hard in 2007. Dante's View and Captain's Roost, both scenic respites for weary hikers, were both destroyed, and the bird sanctuary suffered heavy damage as well. The burn areas remain closed until further notice, and barbecues and fires of any kind are now prohibited as well. For updated information about repair status, openings, and closings, check http://lagriffithpark.blogspot.com/ before making your trip to the park.

Practicalities

Located northwest of downtown LA, Griffith Park is easily reached from either I-5 or the 134. From I-5, get off at Los Feliz Boulevard, Griffith Park (direct entry), or Zoo Drive. From 134 eastbound, take either the Forest Lawn Drive or Victory Boulevard exits. From 134 westbound, take Zoo Drive or Forest Lawn Drive. Speed at your own risk: the 25 mph speed limit on all park roads is strictly enforced.

Activities

Located within the park are facilities for golf (Harding, Los Feliz, Roosevelt, and Wilson Municipal golf courses); swimming (the Plunge Pool is open in summer months); hiking; jogging; horseback riding; tennis (Griffith-Riverside Pay, Vermont Pay, and the free Griffith Park Drive Courts); soccer (John Ferraro Athletic Fields at the northeast corner of the park); and camping and picnicking at one of the five main picnic areas.

Several playgrounds are located throughout the park, usually near picnic areas. The newest among them, Shane's Inspiration, is a "boundless playground" designed to allow children with disabilities to play alongside their able-bodied peers. Bicycles, including tandems, can be rented from Crystal Springs Bike and Skate Rental, located in a shack behind the Crystal Springs Ranger Station.

Young park-goers also enjoy the pony and train rides located near the Los Feliz Boulevard entrance to the park. The Griffith Park Southern Railroad takes riders on a one-mile-plus ride over a meadow, through an old Western town, and past a Native American village. The hours of operation are 10 am to 4:30 pm on weekdays, and the train runs until 5 pm on Saturdays and Sundays. Tickets cost $2 for adults and $1.50 for kids ages 1–13. The pony rides come in three speeds—slow, slower, and barely breathing—but neither the kids nor the horses ever seem to mind. There is also a surprisingly peppy merry-go-round located between the Zoo and the Los Feliz entrance to the park that's always worth a spin. The Fern Dell "hike" is an easy walk for a parent with a stroller or even a more mobile small child. This nature walk is located at the Fern Dell Drive entrance and features waterfalls, tunnels, and a picnic area for snacking.

From Thanksgiving until New Year's, Griffith Park hosts the annual LADWP Holiday Light Festival from 5 pm until 10 pm nightly. Music plays over twinkling light displays intended both to dazzle and to celebrate the history of LA. However, because the program is free, you might argue that there are finer light shows to be seen at some of the nearby mansions of Toluca Lake and Los Feliz. But a wiser, more polite person would argue that this is the LADWP's gift to the City of Los Angeles and we should appreciate it for the kind, holiday gesture that it is. And, of course, for its considerable kitsch value. The light show really does draw the crowds, so you might consider parking at the zoo and going through the mile-long display on foot.

Griffith Park Museums

Griffith Observatory

2800 E Observatory Rd, 323-664-1181; www.griffithobservatory.org

After closing its doors and shutting down its telescopes in January 2002 for a much-needed renovation, the observatory reopened in 2007, just in time for its 71st anniversary. At first glance, you might not even notice many of the multi-million- dollar improvements, since so much care went into retaining the observatory's Art Deco style, and because a majority of the expansion is hidden beneath the front lawn. But the Hall of Science is bigger, there's a 200-seat presentation theater (called the Leonard Nimoy Event Horizon Theater, for all the Trekkies in the house), classrooms, conference rooms, an expanded book store, and just about anything else a stargazer could hope to find. Admission is free if you're a pedestrian or cyclist, but the Observatory now follows a Getty-like system that forces visitors to reserve parking and shuttle services in advance. Parking is available at Hollywood & Highland or the Observatory Satellite (near the zoo), and a shuttle reservation is $8 for adults, $4 for children. Visit the above website to reserve your spot.

Museum of the American West

4700 Western Heritage Wy, 323-667-2000; www.autry-museum.org

Part museum of history, part art gallery, the Museum of the American West is devoted to the stories, the people, the cultures, and the events that have shaped the legacy of the region. Learn about Spanish explorers, discover how the genre of the western evolved through radio, movies, and television, and see paintings by Remington and Russell. Grab a bite at the museum's Golden Spur Café (open for breakfast and lunch). Hours: Tues–Sun, 10 am–5 pm. Admission costs $9 for adults, $5 for students and seniors, $3 for children ages 2–12, and is free for all on the second Tuesday of every month.

Greek Theatre

2700 N Vermont Canyon Rd, 323-665-5857; www.greektheatrela.com

Built with funds left to the city by Griffith J. Griffith, LA's outdoor theater has been hosting live music under the stars since 1930. In recent years, the 6,100-seat venue has hosted Sir Paul McCartney, The White Stripes, Tina Turner, Elton John, and the Russian National Ballet, just to name a few. At the ripe old age of 75, the theater recently underwent a multi-million-dollar facelift that has improved the acoustics and comfort of the outdoor arena. Tickets to performances can be purchased in person at the box office, or through Ticketmaster.

Los Angeles Zoo

5333 Zoo Dr, 323-644-4200; www.lazoo.org

The Los Angeles Zoo is located in Griffith Park at the junction of the Ventura (134) and Golden State (5) Freeways. The most popular attractions are the Red Ape Rain Forest, the Treetops Terrace, and the newly renovated Sea Lion Cliffs, though we're still eagerly awaiting the end to the seemingly eternal construction of the new gorilla and elephant habitats. The zoo is open daily from 10 am until 5 pm (except on Christmas Day). Note that the zoo puts animals in for the night an hour before closing time. Admission costs $10 for adults, $7 for seniors, and $5 for children ages 2 to 12. Children under two and parking are both free. Annual memberships are a smart move for families with children. Packages start at $45.

Travel Town Museum

5200 Zoo Dr, 323-662-5874; www.traveltown.org

Travel Town Museum is an outdoor museum that spotlights the railroad heritage of the western US. The collection includes locomotives, freight cars, passenger cars, and a couple of cabooses, as well as a miniature train ride for kids (one of three in the park). Hours: Mon-Fri: 10 am–5 pm; Sat–Sun: 10 am–6 pm. Admission and parking are free, and a ride on the miniature train costs just $2.

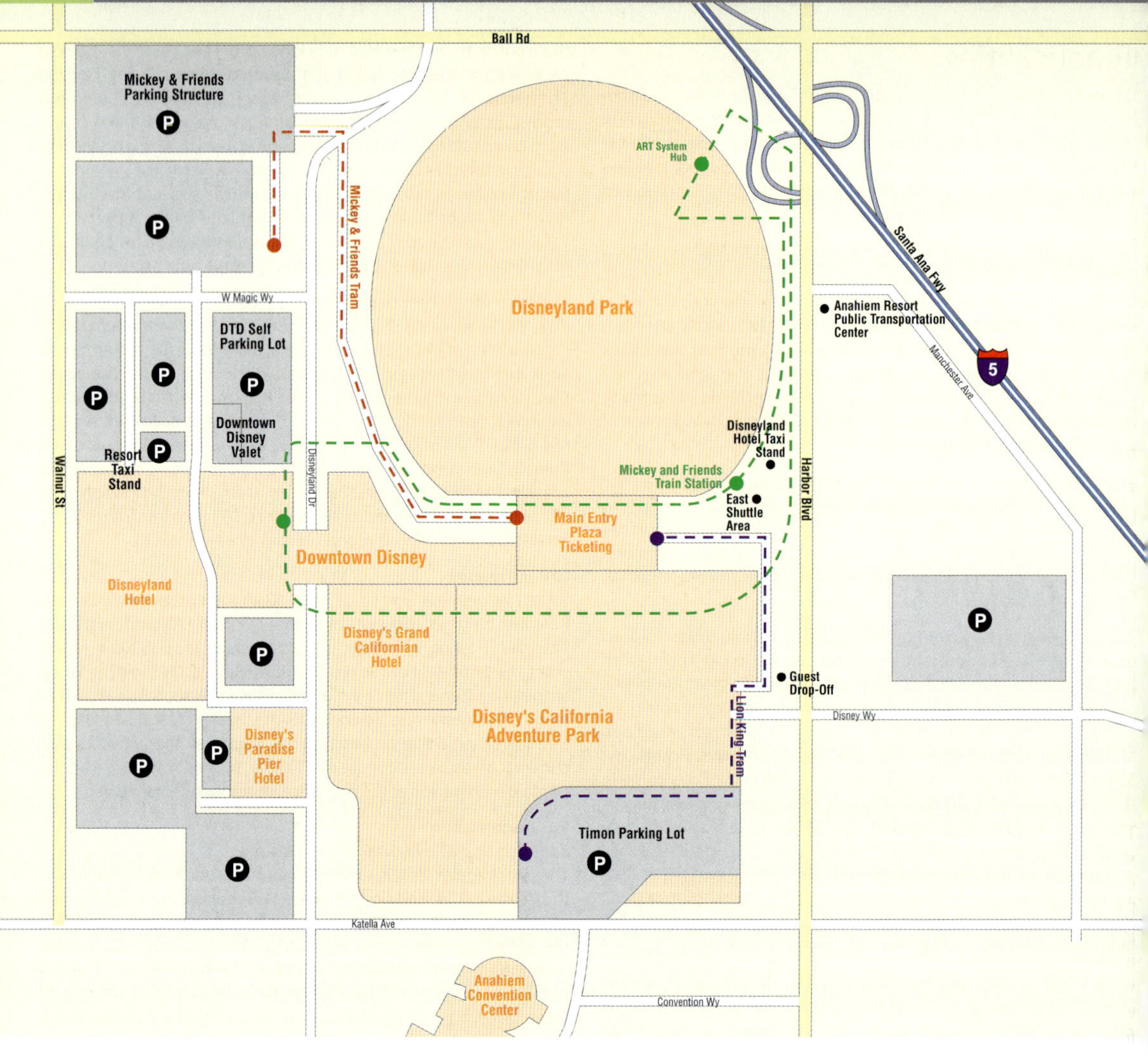

General Information

Address:	1313 S Harbor Blvd Anaheim, CA 92803-3232
Disneyland Info (recorded):	714-781-4565
Disneyland Info (operator):	714-781-7290
Disneyland Travel Packages:	714-520-5060
Disneyland Resort Hotels:	714-956-6425
Disneyland Ticketing:	714-781-4400
Website:	www.disneyland.com

Overview

Sure, you can walk around all day with a chip on your shoulder blaming "The Happiest Place on Earth" for sucking your pocketbook dry at every turn. And, yes, the crowds can be a total pain. But there's something so pleasantly surreal about a visit to the Magic Kingdom. The staff is almost militant about being kind; there's usually some childhood memory running through your head, whether you like it or not; and the second there's a chill in the air—*whammo*!—the hot chocolate carts arrive at your service. It's like…magic!

Though Disneyland kicked off 2007 with an uncharacteristically edgy promotion—Red Hot Chili Peppers' music accompanying both the Space Mountain ride and California Adventure's California Screamin' roller coaster — things have calmed down at the House of Mouse. The new attraction for 2007 and 2008 is actually an old one: the ancient, snooze-inducing Submarine Voyage has been retooled to tie in to "Finding Nemo." And if there's even a little bit of the Force within you, take your inner Jedi to Tomorrowland Terrace to check out the Jedi Training Academy, where young boys' heads implode as they defend their galaxy against a living and breathing Darth Vader.

If you're heading to Disneyland with a group of adults, cruise in during the evening (at least during the summer, when the park is open late) or ditch work for shorter lines and more breathing room. For popular rides, always look for the Fastpass kiosks near the ride entrances. These allow you to take a ticket and return at an appointed time to join the less congested Fastpass queue

The Downtown Disney district, just outside the park's gates, is a loose collection of shops and restaurants, most of which appeal to kids ranging from youngster (Build-A-Bear, Lego) to tween (Club Libby Lu) to Jeff Spicoli (Quiksilver). The restaurants generally offer wider menus and better food than you'll find inside the park, though with few exceptions (Jamba Juice, Wetzel's Pretzels), they won't necessarily save you any money. The World of Disney store is conveniently located next to the parking-lot trams, guaranteeing that you give Disney the last dollar in your wallet before returning to your car at the end of the day.

The California Adventure Park has never quite lived up to the Disney standard. Annual passport holders may park-hop, and can thus experience rides like the Twilight Zone Tower of Terror (which is really quite frightening) and the Soarin' Over California motion ride. Take a little girl to the Princess Celebration (lunch or dinner) at Ariel's Grotto and you will be a rock star, at least until you tell them it's time to leave the park and go home. But if you only have one day at Disneyland, forgo the Park Hopper ticket and save the $20 difference for food and souvenirs. Did we say "and"? We meant food *or* souvenirs. It is Disneyland, after all.

Hours of Operation

The park's hours change depending on the season. During the summer months, school vacations, and holidays, Disneyland is usually open from 9 am until 9 pm, and California Adventure Park is open from 10 am until 7 pm. In the off-season, Disneyland is open from 10 am until 8 pm, and California Adventure Park is open from 10 am until 6 pm. Call the park, or check their website, for more accurate times before heading down. The website is also useful for finding out what rides may be closed for maintenance on any given day. (After all, there's nothing more disappointing than having your Pirates of the Caribbean dreams squashed due to renovations.) The website also lists daily, weekly, and monthly special entertainment events.

Entrance Fees

There are not many places you'll visit where the child admission fee cuts off at 9 years of age—but Disneyland is one of them. One-day general admission tickets to Disneyland or California Adventure Park cost $63 for regular admission and $53 for children (3–9) (children three and under enter for free). The two-day Park Hopper ticket costs $122 for regular admission and $102 for children and gains you entry to both parks. Disney sometimes posts special deals on their website, so make sure you check it before you buy tickets—it also saves time waiting in the entrance line. Disneyland typically offers reduced rates to Southern California residents for Park Hopper tickets and annual passports, so if you plan on visiting the park twice or more during the year, this may be a wise investment.

Lockers

For tourists on the move, or for visitors who inexplicably brought along valuables to the park, there are lockers located outside the main entrances to Disneyland and California Adventure. Locker rentals cost between $7 and $15 per day.

Package Check

If you purchase more mouse ears than you can carry while inside the park, you may leave your packages at the Newsstand (Main Entrance), Star Trader (Tomorrowland), or Pioneer Mercantile (Frontierland) and pick them up on your way out.

Kennels

Traveling with your pooch can create problems, and orchestrating a trip to Disneyland is no exception to this rule. Hotels in the Disneyland Resort do not allow pets, but if you're passing through and plan on staying elsewhere overnight, indoor day kennel facilities, located to the right of the Main Entrance of Disneyland, are available for $15 a day.

How to Get There—Driving

Traveling southbound on I-5 (Golden State/Santa Ana Freeway), exit at Disneyland Drive and turn left (south). Follow the signs to the Mickey & Friends Parking Structure. If you're traveling northbound on I-5 (Santa Ana Freeway), exit on Katella Avenue and turn left (west). Proceed across Katella Avenue and merge onto Disney Way (on the left). Follow the signs to the most convenient parking area. The same goes for if you're traveling eastbound or westbound on the 22 (Garden Grove Freeway).

Parking

Once in the Mickey & Friends parking lot, head to the escalators, which take you directly to the Mickey & Friends Loading Zone. Trams collect visitors and drop them off at the Mickey & Friends Tram Station, located within walking distance of both theme parks. Parking costs $11 a day for cars, $13 for oversized vehicles, and $18 for buses.

How to Get There—Mass Transit

All of the LA area airports provide shuttle services to the Disneyland Resort. Bus 460 goes somewhere near the park, but we recommend driving a car or taking a shuttle if you can.

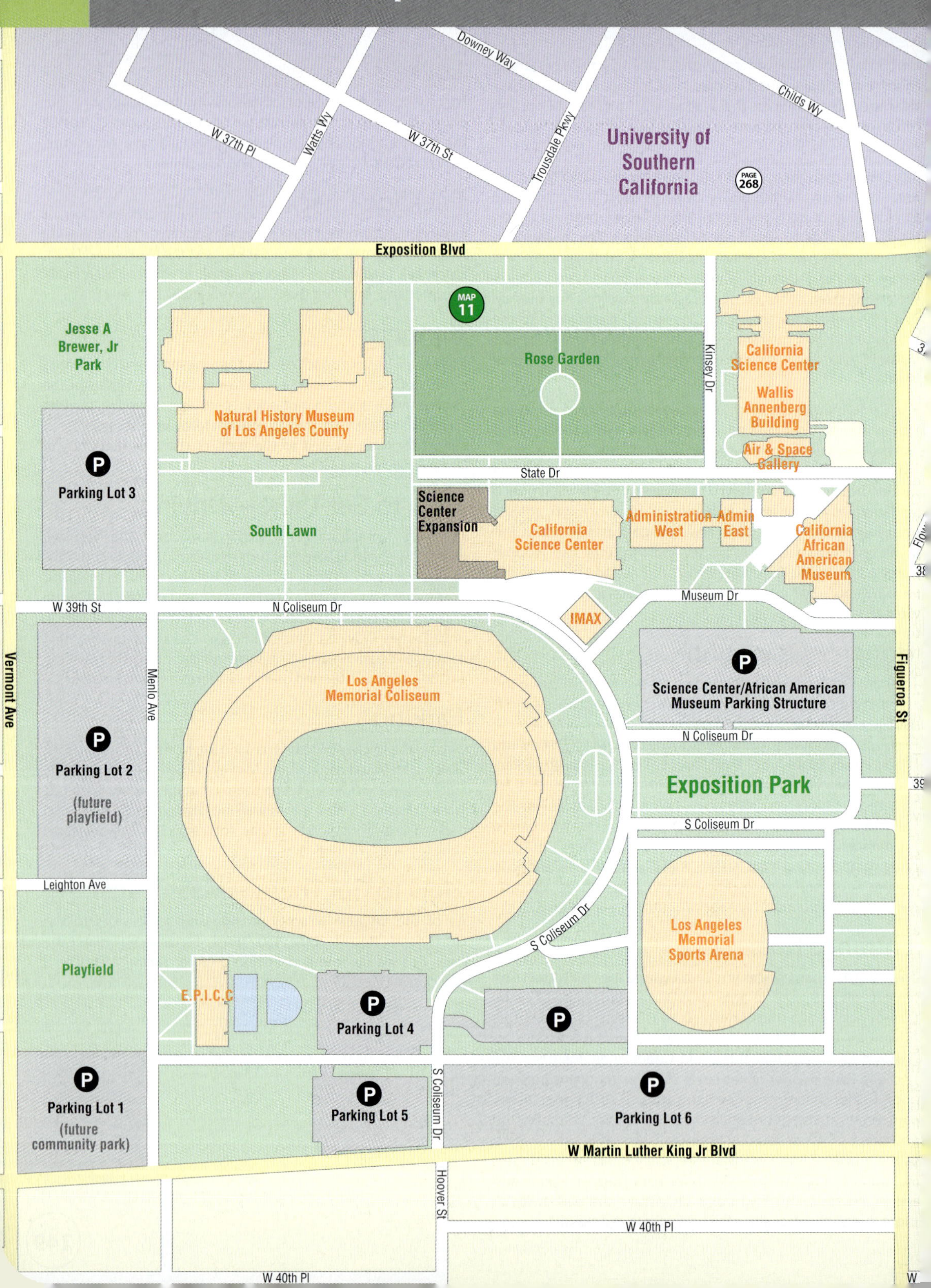

Downey Way
Childs Wy
W 37th Pl
Watts Wy
W 37th St
Trousdale Pkwy
University of Southern California
PAGE 268
Exposition Blvd
MAP 11
Jesse A Brewer, Jr Park
Rose Garden
Kinsey Dr
California Science Center
Wallis Annenberg Building
Air & Space Gallery
Natural History Museum of Los Angeles County
P
Parking Lot 3
State Dr
Science Center Expansion
South Lawn
California Science Center
Administration West
Admin East
California African American Museum
W 39th St
N Coliseum Dr
Museum Dr
IMAX
P
Science Center/African American Museum Parking Structure
Vermont Ave
Menlo Ave
Los Angeles Memorial Coliseum
Figueroa St
N Coliseum Dr
P
Parking Lot 2
(future playfield)
Exposition Park
S Coliseum Dr
Leighton Ave
Los Angeles Memorial Sports Arena
S Coliseum Dr
Playfield
E.P.I.C.C
P
Parking Lot 4
P
P
Parking Lot 1
(future community park)
P
Parking Lot 5
S Coliseum Dr
P
Parking Lot 6
W Martin Luther King Jr Blvd
Hoover St
W 40th Pl
W 40th Pl

Overview

NFT Map: 11

Exposition Park is bounded by Figueroa Street to the east, Martin Luther King Jr. Boulevard to the south, Menlo Avenue to the west, and Exposition Boulevard to the north. The grounds face the University of Southern California's (USC) campus, tying the two into a blend of extensive education and learning. Originally called Agricultural Park, the area was developed in 1876 as a showground for agricultural and horticultural fairs. In June 1923, the Los Angeles Memorial Coliseum, named in honor of those who died in World War I, was completed. The stadium was enlarged for the 1932 Olympics and also hosted the 1984 Olympics. Today Exposition Park houses the Natural History Museum, IMAX Theater, Rose Garden, California Science Center, California African American Museum, LA Memorial Coliseum, and the indoor Los Angeles Memorial Sports Arena.

Los Angeles Memorial Coliseum & Los Angeles Memorial Sports Arena

The history of the Coliseum/Sports Arena complex spans eight decades. It is the only arena in the world to play host to two Olympiads (10th and 23rd), two Super Bowls (1st and 7th), and one World Series (1959). In the past, the complex has played host to the Rams, the Dodgers, and the Lakers, and was the expansion home of the San Diego Chargers and the Kings. Today, the Coliseum is home to USC's juggernaut Trojan football team (call 213-740-GOSC for tickets) and various other special events. Autumn is particularly vibrant during home games – if you're trying to visit the park then, traffic and parking will be double nightmares. Check the website (www.lacoliseum.com) for event details. The main box office switchboard is open from 10 am to 6 pm and can be reached at 213-747-7111.

Rose Garden

The 7.5-acre Rose Garden was completed in 1928, and there were 15,793 roses in full bloom for the opening. Today the sunken garden contains more than 20,000 rose bushes representing 190-plus varieties. It's the perfect place for an afternoon stroll and a nearby retreat when the screaming at the Coliseum during USC football season starts to become a headache. In Southern California, roses bloom from March to November. The garden is open daily, free to the public, and located within Exposition Park at 701 State Drive (213-765-0114). While beautiful during the day, it's awfully sketchy at night—like much of its neighborhood.

Natural History Museum of LA County

The Natural History Museum houses many California-specific exhibits not found at other natural museums. Its Marine Hall highlights Californian ocean life, and its California history section shows a chronological progression since the 1500s. The museum is located at 900 Exposition Boulevard in Exposition Park, across from USC between Vermont Avenue and Figueroa Street. Parking is available off Menlo Avenue. The fee for parking will run between $6 and $10, depending on events in the Exposition Park area. The museum's opening hours are 9:30 am until 5 pm Monday to Friday and 10 am until 5 pm Saturday and Sunday. Adults can expect to pay $9 for entry, seniors and students are $6.50, and children 5–12 are $2. If you schedule your visit on the first Tuesday of the month, it won't cost you a cent! Although the museum is open during USC football games, we highly recommend that you avoid the Exposition Park area at all costs on those days unless you're attending the game. 213-763-DINO; www.nhm.org.

California Science Center & IMAX

You can't miss the giant jet airplane sitting out front. The Science Center is open daily from 10 am until 5 pm, and admission to Science Center exhibition halls is free. The IMAX is open daily and admission is $8 adults, $5.75 seniors and students, and $4.75 children. Check the website (www.californiasciencecenter.org) or call 213-744-7400 for show information. Parking is $6 per car, $10 for buses or oversized vehicles, and the entrance to the visitor parking lot is on Figueroa at 39th Street.

California African American Museum

The California African American Museum researches, collects, preserves, and interprets the art, history, and culture of African Americans, with emphasis on California and the western United States. The museum is open Wednesdays through Saturdays, from 10 am until 4 pm. Admission is free. 213-744-7432; www.caamuseum.org.

How to Get There—Driving

From the north, take 101 S to 110 S, exit at Martin Luther King Jr. Boulevard W, and enter on Hoover Street. From the south, take 405 N to 110 N, exit at Martin Luther King Jr. Boulevard W, and enter on Hoover Street. From the west, take 10 E to the 110 S and follow the above directions. From the east, take 10 W to 110 S and follow the above directions.

Parking

There are parking spaces located at various places within the park. Parking rates and availability will vary for special events. Four-hour and two-hour metered parking is available on Figueroa Street and Jefferson Boulevard. There are a number of lots on the streets surrounding the park, and the usual week-day rate is $3. Rates vary when special events are in progress, and the average cost of parking in a lot is $10. You can also park at any of the USC lots for $7 a day, except on game days and special events where parking may not be available to non-Trojans, in which case the price of a parking spot escalates and locals rent out their driveways and yards for a considerable bargain.

How to Get There—Mass Transit

If you're taking public transport, take the Metro Rail Red Line or Blue Line to the 7th Street/Metro Center Station then catch the Dash F bus at the corner of Seventh and Flower. The bus will stop in front of the University of Southern California across the street from the Natural History Museum on Exposition Boulevard.

A10 A11 A12 A14 A15 A16 A17

Farmers Market Pl

E10 E11 E12 E14 E15 E16 E17 E20

Earl's Service Historic Gilmore Gas Station

Clock Tower

Gate 1 Gate 2 Gate 3 Gate 4 Gate 6 Gate 7 Gate 9 Gate 10 Gate 11 Gate 12 Gate 15

706 708 710 816 818 712 718 720 612 614 616 618 622 623 624 738 740 742 744 750 020 010

508 510 412 514 518 522 524 528 530 540 542 548

West Patio

East Patio

408 416 310 418 424 426 428 430 434 432 436 450 448 P11 P20 P10

312 316 318 322 210 211 212 216 218 220 222 226 228 230 234 236 326 328 330 334 336 350

112 116 120 122 126 130 134 138 144 148 150

Fairfax Ave

W 3rd St

Gilmore Ln

Rosewood

Oakwood A

Beverly B

N Hayworth Ave

S Hayworth Ave

1st St

2nd St

The Grove

PAGE 304

Farmers Market

Genesee Ave

Stanley Ave

Pan Pacific Park

N Gardner St

N Vista St

N Martel Ave

N Fuller Ave

N Poinsettia Pl

N Alta Vista Blvd

Formosa Ave

N Detroit St

N La Brea Ave

MAP 2

Blackburn Ave

Colgate Ave

Ogden Dr

W Curson Ave

Fuller Ave

Drexel Ave

General Information

NFT Map: 2
Address: 6333 W 3rd St
Los Angeles, CA 90036
Phone: 323-933-9211
Website: www.farmersmarketla.com
Hours: Mon–Fri: 9 am–9 pm; Sat: 9 am–8 pm; Sun: 10 am–7 pm

Overview

The Farmers Market opened in the 1930s as a humble dirt lot where farmers parked their trucks and sold their produce right off their tailgates. Over the years, it's slowly morphed into an occasional motley crew of souvenir shops and food stalls. And even though it was scaled back a few years ago to make way for the fancy, schmancy Grove shopping mall, it's still one of the best melting-pot LA experiences around. Old timers are eating the same Sunday brunch they've been looking forward to for years; there's always a young, semi-recognizable Hollywood type from TV's latest teen drama or cash-cow horror to point and gawk at; and hipsters are drawn to it for the kitsch, good grub, seasonal festivals, and, during the right time of year, live music. Plus, when you're with a group of friends that can't decide on what to eat, this place is a godsend.

Where to Shop

There are two kinds of shops at the Farmers Market—the kinds that sell food and the kinds that don't. It's hard to go wrong with any of the food-sellers. Mr. Marcel Gourmet Market has an extensive selection of imported cheese, and you can watch the whole candy-making process at Littlejohn's English Toffee House. Magee's House of Nuts has been in operation at the Farmers Market since it began and will open your eyes to a world of nut butters that goes far beyond peanuts. The Fruit Company always offers a wide variety of fruits that are consistently fresher and more reasonably priced than any local supermarket.

The Farmers Market's other businesses are a bit more eclectic and can be somewhat hit-or-miss. By Candlelight has an impressive selection of candles and Light My Fire sells bottled hot sauce that ranges from mild to downright combustible. There are also many shops that cater to the tourist crowd and sell cheap, Hollywood-themed souvenirs. If you're hoping to do some serious shopping of the mainstream variety, hop on the trolley (or take a short walk) and head over to The Grove.

Where to Eat

There may be no better place for breakfast in all of LA than Kokomo Café, one of the Farmers Market's few sit-down dining establishments. This casual café serves up an eclectic breakfast and lunch menu and, best of all, their egg dishes come with coffeecake. Even with its new fancy remodel, Du-par's has an old-school feel that tourists and locals can't resist. Then, there's always the food court. If you can handle the wait, the French Crepe Company serves 'em up sweet and savory. The Gumbo Pot dishes the tastiest Gumbo YaYa this side of the Mississippi and is tucked away in a courtyard corner with a bar to help wash down the spicy stuff. And no matter how much you've gorged, you must try at least one of Bob's Coffee and Doughnuts' doughy delights—they're considered by many to have the best donuts in town. Some of the finest Mexican dishes west of Alvarado are found at ¡Lotería! Grill. For a more elegant Farmers Market experience, check out the wine bar at Mr. Marcel Pain Vin et Fromage. In other words, it's pretty much impossible to go wrong here.

How to Get There—Driving

To drive to the Farmers Market from almost anywhere south of the Valley or north of LAX, your best bet is to take surface streets. The Grove's opening has made 3rd Street slower going than it used to be, and Beverly Boulevard isn't much better. Take whichever east-west thoroughfare you choose until you hit Fairfax Avenue, and head north. You can't miss the Farmers Market at the corner of 3rd and Fairfax. If you're coming from the Westside or South Bay, you might hop on the 10 Freeway, exit at Fairfax, and head north. Valley residents can hop on the 101 and exit at Highland. Take Highland to 3rd Street and turn right. Continue on 3rd until you reach Fairfax, and the Farmers Market will be on your right.

Parking

Before the opening of The Grove, parking at the Farmers Market was a challenge, but at least it was free. To discourage mall patrons from hogging the smallish parking lot, however, the Farmers Market now charges for parking. With validation, you get two hours of free parking and the third hour is just $1.

A10. Gilmore Bank, 549-2100*
A11. Farmers Market Postal Center, 933-2322
A12. Chipotle, 857-0608
A14. Unique Tan, 933-2826
A15. Elements Spa & Salon, 933-0212
A16. Beauty Collection Apothecary, 930-0300
A17. The Children's Place, 939-1813
CT1. Tashen, 933-9211
E10. Cost Plus World Market, 935-5530
E11. Coffee Bean and Tea Leaf, 857-0461
E12. Francesca's Collection, 935-2474
E14. Jack Gallery, 933-4833
E16. Duck Soup, 549-9101
E17. Marmalade Café, 954-0088
E20. Party America, 965-0700
P10. Sur La Table, 954-9190
P11. Designer Details, 931-9632
P20. Kado, 933-0055
010. Bath & Body Works, 965-1724
020. Kado, 933-0055
112. Starbucks, 965-9594
116. Sheltam's News on Third, 934-1875
120. Kokomo Café, 933-0773
122. Singapore's Banana Leaf, 933-4627
126,130. Pinkberry, 933-9211
138. Tusquellas Seafoods, 938-1919
150. Mr. Marcel Gourmet Market, 935-9451
210. Du-par's Restaurant, 933-8446
211. Du-par's Pie Shop, 933-8446
212. T, 930-0076
216. Farmers Market Poultry, 936-8158
218. Magee's House of Nuts, 938-4127
220. Sticker Planet, 939-6933
222. Tbilisi & Yerevan Bakery, 930-2355
226. Puritan Poultry, 938-0312
230. Light My Fire, 930-2484
236, 144. Mr. Marcel Pain Vin et Fromage, 939-7792
310. Deano's Gourmet Pizza, 935-6373
312. The Gumbo Pot, 933-0358
316. Thee's Continental Pastries, 937-1968
318. The French Crepe Company, 934-3113
322. ¡Lotería! Grill, 930-2211
326. 326 Beer & Wine, 549-2156
328. Treasures of the Pacific, 936-9208
330. J&T Bread Bin Bakery, 936-0785
334. The Village, 936-9340
336. Moishe's Restaurant, 936-4998
350. Huntington Meats & Sausages, 938-5383
408. E.B.'s Beer & Wine, 549-2157
412. Charlie's Coffee Shop, 933-0616
416. Gill's Old Fashioned Ice Cream, 936-7986
424. The Salad Bar, 933-3204
426, 428. By Candlelight, 549-0458
430. Gift & Gadget Nook, 933-1898
432. Littlejohn's English Toffee House, 936-5379
434. Sushi a Go Go, 930-7874
436. Tusquellas Fish & Oyster Bar, 939-2078
448. Patsy D'Amore's Pizza, 938-4938
450. Bob's Coffee and Doughnuts, 933-8929
508. Peking Kitchen, 936-1949
510. La Korea, 936-3930
514. Marconda's Meats, 938-5131
522, 418. Ultimate Nut & Candy Company, 938-1555
524. Essence of Nature, 931-9593
528. Gadget Nook, 933-1898
530. Country Bakery, 937-1968
540. Phil's Deli & Grill, 936-3704
542. Coffee Corner, 938-0278
548. Bennett's Ice Cream, 939-6786
518. The Fruit Company, 936-6363
614. Lustre, 933-6449
616. Farmers Market Variety Store, 933-1086
618. Pampas Grill, 931-1928
622. The Refresher, 939-6786
624. Magee's Kitchen, 938-4127
706. Johnny Rockets, 937-2093
708. Market Optometrix, 936-5140
710. Three Dog Bakery, 935-7512
712. Farmers Market Shoe Repair/Shine, 939-5622
718. Sporte Fashion, 932-6454
720. Kip's Toyland, 939-8334
738. Weiss Jewelry, 934-1623
740. Bryan's Pit Barbecue, 931-2869
742. Market Grill, 934-0424
744. China Depot, 937-6868
750. Ulysses Voyage Greek Restaurant, 939-9728
816. Farm Fresh Produce, 931-3773
818. Farmers Market Newsstand, 934-0318
818, 116. Lottery Booth, 934-0318

**All area codes 323 unless noted*

Directors Dr
Orlando Rd
North Rd
N Perimeter
Main Gate
Mausoleum N Dr
Orange Grove
Median Rd
Mausoleum
E Mausoleum Dr
MAP 35
W Perimeter
E Perimeter
Visitor Parking
Palm Dr
Teaching Greenhouse
Bing Children's Garden
Botanical Center
Staff Parking
Chinese Garden (Phase I)
Head House
Conservatory
Deodar Rd
Garage Rd
Dorothy Collins Brown Garden
Boone Gallery
North Vista/ Camellias
Vista Dr
Munger Research Center
Arabella Gallery
Ikebana Rd
Ginza Dr
Erburu Gallery
Scott Gallery (American Art)
Library Exhibition Hall
Gift Shop
Visitor Center
Friends' Hall
Oxford Gate
Shakespeare Garden
Huntington Circle
Herb Garden
Tea Room & Café
Library Rd
Desert Conservatory
Rose Garden
Huntington Gallery (British & Continental Art)
Japanese House
Jungle Garden
Palm Garden
Oxford Rd
Subtropical Garden
Zen Garden
Japanese Garden
Ombu Ln
Ombu Circle
Bonsai Court
Lily Ponds
Desert Garden Rd
Desert Garden
Australian Garden
S Garden Dr
Euston Gate
Euston Rd

General Information

NFT Map: 35
Address: 1151 Oxford Rd
San Marino, CA 91108
Phone: 626-405-2100
Website: www.huntington.org
Hours: Tues–Fri: 12 pm–4:30 pm;
Sat–Sun: 10:30 am–4:30 pm
Admission: adults $15, seniors $12, students $10, youth (ages 5–11) $6;
Free first Thursday of each month, and always free for members and children under five.

Overview

Part library, part research center, part art gallery, part botanical garden, the Huntington's diverse collection of art and flora is a retreat for researchers or families simply looking to get away from it all. The 150 acres of gardens, covered with 14,000 varieties of plants, has the look of a picturesque college campus on steroids, with plenty of room to stretch out, run around with the kids, or simply doze off in the sun. The best way to see the gardens is by joining up with a free group tour—otherwise you risk missing out on the Desert Garden's menacing cacti or the lush canopy of the Jungle Garden. Kids go crazy over the Children's Garden, where you'll see groups of them running through and squealing over the fog grotto and the prism tunnel, while tired parents rest their weary feet. For a Zen experience, stroll the winding path in the Japanese Garden past the bonsai trees and rock garden and through the bamboo grove. Well-informed docents are permanently stationed in the herb and rose gardens to answer any horticulture questions. And what's all of that construction? Oh, just the largest classical Chinese garden ever constructed outside of China, which, when completed, will stand as 12-acres of total tranquility.

Art Collections

The majestic Huntington is best-known for its collection of British and French art from the 18th and 19th centuries. Highlights include Thomas Gainsborough's celebrated *The Blue Boy* and Sir Thomas Lawrence's *Pinkie*. The Virginia Steele Scott Gallery showcases the works of American painters from the 1730s to the 1930s. This intimate gallery is the perfect place to contemplate masterworks by Sargent, Bellows, and Hopper. In the Library building, the Arabella Huntington Memorial Collection contains 18th-century French furniture, sculpture, and Renaissance paintings.

The Library

The library includes some of the world's most famous rare books—including a Gutenberg Bible and a world-class edition of Shakespeare's complete works. These pieces are on display for the general public, but only professional researchers can gain access to the library's entire collection, which specializes in 15th-century European books, maritime and scientific history, and Renaissance cartography, among other things. Yeah…we knew we'd scare you back out into the gardens.

Dining & Shopping

Treat your favorite aunt to afternoon tea in the Rose Garden Tea Room for an all-you-can-eat buffet of scones, tea sandwiches, and petit fours. Reservations are required (626-683-8131). For a more casual snack or sandwich, try the adjoining café (although it'll cost you about as much as lunch at the Tea Room). If you're harboring romantic (or thrifty) fantasies of picnicking in the gardens, we will crush them for you right now: the Huntington has a strict "no picnics" policy.

The Huntington's spacious gift shop stocks coffee-table books and scholarly titles relating to its varied collections—it's the perfect place to score Mother's Day presents.

How to Get There—Driving

The Huntington is adjacent to Pasadena in the city of San Marino, about 12 miles northeast of downtown Los Angeles. The Huntington has two entrance gates: one on Oxford Road and one at Allen Avenue, just south of California Boulevard.

From the Harbor or Pasadena Freeways (110): Take the 110 N towards Pasadena where it turns into Arroyo Parkway. Turn right on California Boulevard and continue for about three miles. At Allen Avenue, turn right and proceed two blocks to the Huntington's gates.

Foothill Freeway (210): Traveling westbound on the 210, exit at the Allen Avenue off-ramp in Pasadena. Turn left and drive south for two miles to the Huntington's gates. Traveling eastbound on the 210, exit at Hill Avenue and drive alongside the freeway for about three blocks. Turn right at Allen Avenue and head south for two miles to the Huntington's gates.

Santa Monica Monica Freeway (10): Take the 10 E to the 110 N and follow the above directions for the 110.

From San Bernardino Freeway (10): Exit at San Gabriel Boulevard and go north for three miles. Turn left on Huntington Drive and continue for one mile, then make a right on Monterey Road. Bear right onto Oxford Road and continue to the Huntington's gates.

How to Get There—Mass Transit

The Metro Gold Line (Allen Avenue stop) and a few MTA bus routes (the 79 and the 379) stop between one to 1.5 miles from the Huntington. For the most updated routes visit www.mta.net or www.foothilltransit.org.

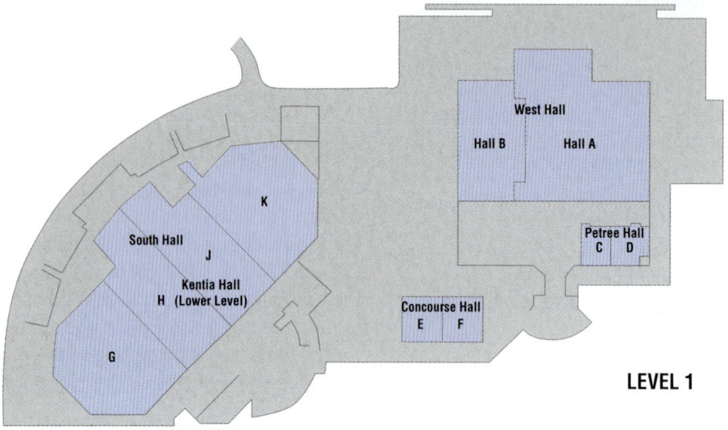

West Hall
Hall B
Hall A
K
South Hall
J
Kentia Hall
H (Lower Level)
Petree Hall
C D
Concourse Hall
E F
G

LEVEL 1

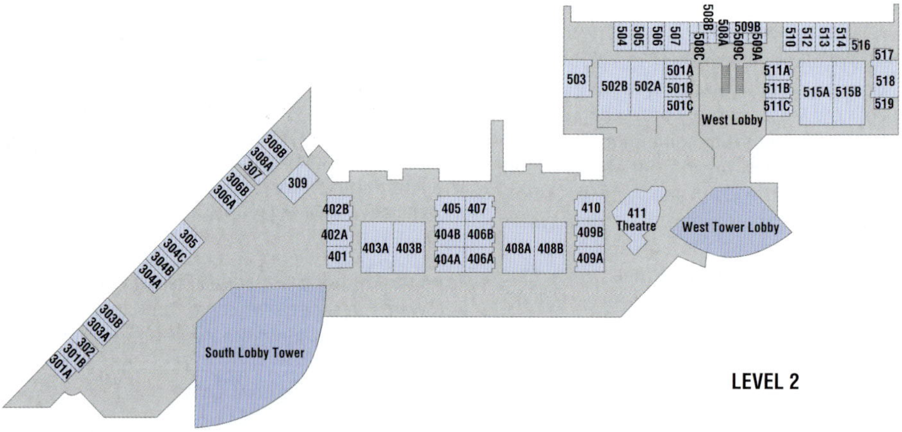

508B 508A 509B
504 505 506 507 508C 509C 509A 510 512 513 514 516
517
503 502B 502A 501A 501B 501C 511A 511B 511C 515A 515B 518 519
West Lobby
308B 308A 307 306B 306A
309
402B 402A 401 403A 403B
405 407 404B 406B 404A 406A
408A 408B
410 409B 409A
411 Theatre
West Tower Lobby
305 304C 304B 304A
303B 303A 302 301B 301A
South Lobby Tower

LEVEL 2

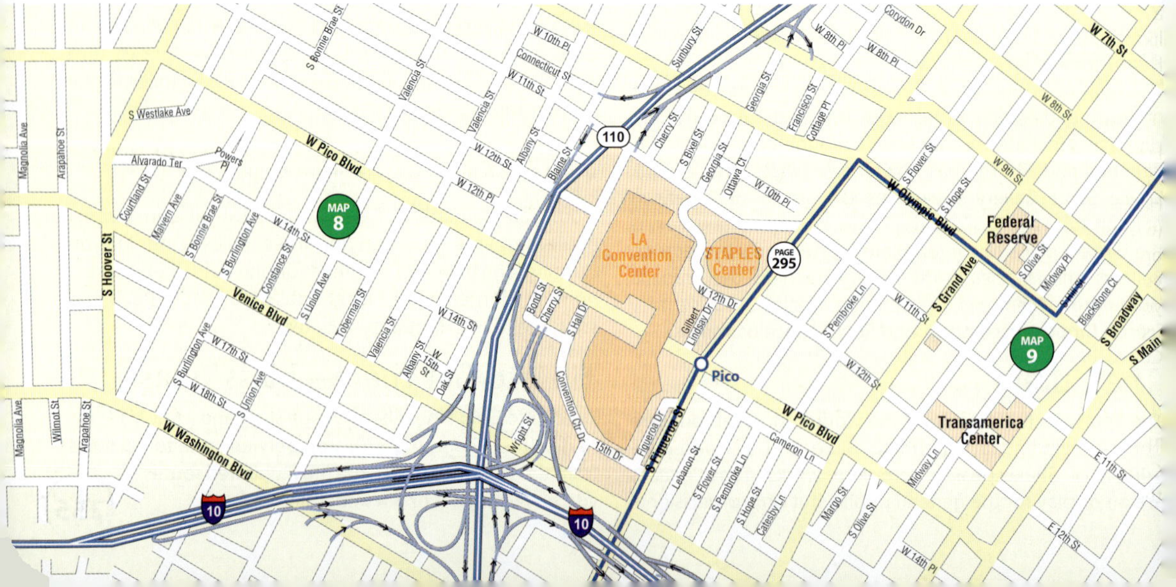

W 7th St
W 8th Pl
W 8th Pl
Corydon Dr
W 8th St
W 10th Pl
Connecticut St
W 11th St
S Bonnie Brae St
Valencia St
Valencia St
Sunbury St
Georgia St
Francisco St
Cottage Pl
S Westlake Ave
110
W Pico Blvd
W 12th St
Albany St
Blaine St
Cherry St
S Bixel St
Georgia St
Ottawa Ct
W 10th Pl
W 9th St
Magnolia Ave
Arapahoe St
Alvarado Ter
Powers Pl
W 12th Pl
S Flower St
S Hope St
W Olympic Blvd
Federal Reserve
Courtland St
Malvern Ave
S Bonnie Brae St
S Burlington Ave
W 14th St
MAP 8
LA Convention Center
STAPLES Center
PAGE 295
S Grand Ave
S Olive St
Midway Pl
S Hill St
Blackstone Ct
S Broadway
S Main
S Hoover St
Constance St
Venice Blvd
S Union Ave
Toberman St
W 12th Dr
Gilbert Lindsay Dr
Bond St
Cherry St
S Hall Dr
W 14th St
S Pembroke Ln
W 11th St
MAP 9
S Burlington Ave
W 17th St
Valencia St
Albany St
W 15th St
Oak St
Pico
W 12th St
S Burlington Ave
W 18th St
S Union Ave
Convention Ctr Dr
Magnolia Ave
Wilmot St
Arapahoe St
W Washington Blvd
Wright St
Figueroa Dr
S Figueroa St
W Pico Blvd
Transamerica Center
15th Dr
Cameron Ln
E 11th St
Lebanon St
S Flower St
S Pembroke Ln
S Hope St
Catesby Ln
Margo St
S Olive St
Midway Ln
10
10
E 12th St
W 14th Pl

General Information

NFT Maps: 8 & 9
Address: 1201 S Figueroa St
Los Angeles, CA 90015
Phone: 213-741-1151
Website: www.lacclink.com

Overview

Yes, it's ugly and, yes, the parking is outrageously overpriced, but sooner or later you'll probably find yourself wandering through the large, airy halls with a glazed look in your eyes. And you'll probably drop a bundle on some home improvement gewgaw, car, cruise, or brand-new personality. (They sometimes rent out their meeting rooms for EST-like marathon weekends.) Recent shows have included the 50th Annual LA Boat Show, Wizard World, and Erotica LA. For years the LACC was home to the E3 Electronic Entertainment Expo, but E3 has since undergone restructuring that will diffuse the rabidly popular annual trade show. Not to worry—the calendar of events never goes slack: cue Baby Celebration LA, Star Wars Celebration IV, and the Women of Destiny and Purpose Conference!

The Convention Center is impossible to miss from the street, and its glass-and-girder exterior is clearly visible from both the 10 and 110 Freeways. That doesn't mean you can actually get to it, but it will appear comfortingly close as you pass a pleasant hour cruising through the downtown one-way street system. The building's design allows for a maximum amount of natural light to flood the lobbies and concourses, in stark contrast to the windowless exhibit halls and meeting rooms, where it's easy to lose track of time—especially if you keep your eyes on the floor; thanks to an art installation in the '90s, a map of the world flanks the floor of the main lobby, while a constellation map blankets the floor of the upstairs lobby. The Convention Center has three major exhibit halls, West Hall, South Hall, and Kentia Hall (located beneath South Hall), as well as fifty-four meeting rooms. It's possible to book anything from a small, intimate gathering for less than twenty people to a large-scale event for over 20,000. The really big exhibitions, like the Auto Show, tend to be held in either the South or West Halls—sometimes even both.

How to Get There—Driving

Located just a stone's throw from STAPLES Center at the intersection of the Santa Monica Freeway (10) and the Harbor Freeway (110), the Los Angeles Convention Center is (theoretically) easily accessible from any part of LA. The simplest option is to exit the 110 at Pico Boulevard and head north. But if you're coming from the West Side or Central Los Angeles area, you may be better off skipping the freeways altogether and using either Olympic or Pico Boulevards to get downtown. The Convention Center's cross street is Figueroa Street.

Parking

There are five parking structures available to patrons of the Convention Center that all charge $12 per day. Parking for the West Hall is located just north of Pico Boulevard. Make a right turn at the intersection of Cherry Street and 12th Street into the parking garage. To park near the South Hall, look for Convention Center Drive just off Venice Boulevard on the center's south side.

How to Get There—Mass Transit

Mass transit. Great concept. The Metro Blue Line stops on Pico Boulevard for both the Convention Center and STAPLES Center. This is a convenient alternative from the Valley, as well as the South Bay.

Buses 30, 31, 81, 381, 439, 442, 444, 445, 446, 447, 460, LX422, LX423, LX448, and LX419 also stop near the Convention Center.

Where to Eat

Pack a lunch. If you must eat-in, the Galaxy Café located in the lobby of the West Building is probably the center's nicest. (Bear in mind this is a relative recommendation. You don't go to the Convention Center to eat. You go to buy cars, Jacuzzis, or all-inclusive package deals. Consider, then, that you're actually dining at your local car dealership or travel agent.) It offers the option of outdoor seating and boasts a full bar (should you be at the Center against your will and need a power hour), though it's only open for breakfast and lunch. Inside the South Building is the more casual Compass Café, which offers a variety of sandwiches, salads, and beverages. Do not, under any circumstances, patronize the concession stands inside both the West and South exhibit halls. We're talking airport prices and sad-looking food.

Better to get some fresh air and take a stroll to some of the local landmarks surrounding the center. Here are some nearby eateries that are worth a visit:

- **Philippe's the Original**,
  1001 N Alameda St, 213-628-3781.
  Fabulous deli. They supposedly invented the French Dip sandwich. Would you even think of ordering anything else?
- **Original Pantry Café**,
  877 S Figueroa St, 213-972-9279.
  American/comfort food. The restaurant never closes. It's an LA landmark, known for heaping helpings of American classics cooked from scratch.
- **Langer's**,
  704 S Alvarado St, 213-483-8050.
  Deli menu. Their pastrami sandwich is legendary.
- **Ciudad**,
  445 S Figueroa St, 213-486-5171.
  Latin food. The chefs/owners of Santa Monica's Border Grill take their act downtown. After a marathon of meetings and exhibits, take a siesta and check out their rum sampler.
- **Pacific Dining Car**,
  1310 W Sixth St, 213-483-6000.
  Steaks and chops. This meat-and-potatoes restaurant is an LA institution that leaves the engine running 24 hours.

General Information

Address: 26101 Magic Mountain Pkwy
Valencia, CA 91355
Phone: 661-255-4100 or 818-367-5965
Website: www.sixflags.com/parks/magicmountain
Hours: Open year-round. Hours are generally 10 am–10 pm, but vary daily. See website for specific hours and dates.
Entry: $59.99 adult fare, $29.99 for kids under 48" free for kids 2 and under for Magic Mountain; $29.99 adult fare, $20.99 for kids under 48", free for kids 2 and under for Hurricane Harbor

Overview

The more viable option for those who prefer thrill rides to the G-rated fairy fare over in Anaheim. Though Six Flags, who acquired Magic Mountain in 1979, toyed with selling the park in 2006, a recent Q1 announcement showed that the Mountain would prevail. With the debut of the flying coaster Tatsu in 2006, Magic Mountain officially set the record (beating out Cedar Point in Ohio) for most roller coasters at a theme park with a whopping 17 rides; however, because one of the Mountain's coasters has been dismantled and another is "standing but not operating" (SBNO), Cedar Point will regain the title when its 17th coaster opens for the 2007 season. So maybe the mighty Mountain has to forfeit its title—for now—but it unequivocally holds the record for the highest concentration of obnoxious preteens in any given place. The motley equation of hormones, sunburn, and skewed centers of gravity combine to effect a navigational free-for-all. Be prepared to swim upstream, and if you're bringing small children, consider leashes.

Tickets

Reduced rates are available for advanced purchase through the website and via promotions throughout the season. You can also look for discounted deals at Ralphs supermarkets, as well as on specially-marked cans of Coke. For those who live within 300 miles of the park, Season Passes are undoubtedly the best deal—a one-time cost of $69.99 will buy you a year's worth of long lines and overpriced, greasy food. Individual tickets and season passes can be purchased online at www.sixflagsticketing.com.

For the Kiddies

Bugs Bunny World offers easy-going rides and games for kids 48 inches and under, while Bugs, Yosemite Sam, et al. amble around for photo ops. Goliath Jr., the choo-choo train version of the popular full-sized Goliath, offers mini-thrills for tykes and tired-but-not-to-be-outdone parents alike.

Thrill Rides

The longstanding rival competition with Cedar Point in Sandusky, Ohio, has upped the ante for Magic Mountain, which now houses 17 coasters and boasts 11 world records. The jewel of the park is X, a "four-dimensional" thrill ride that loops and twists riders strapped to 360-degree rotating chairs—it's the only ride in the park worth the sometimes three-hour wait (what's a wait, really, to those inured to Southern California freeways?). Park-goers can count on the same long lines at Déjà Vu and Tatsu, Magic Mountain's newest "flying" rollercoaster. Goliath and Scream, both solid steel coasters, are always worth checking out if the wait at the other three becomes unbearable.

Hurricane Harbor Water Park

With the exception of a six-story blue-and-yellow funnel slide known as Tornado, Hurricane Harbor typically offers the same water slides and kiddie pools as most water parks. Expect speed slides, wave pools, and a "scenic" inner-tube river.

Insider Tips

To avoid the extremely long lines and young crowds, we suggest you visit on a weekday during the school year. The theme park is also sprawled across a mountain (hence the oh-so-creative name), so expect to give your thighs a solid workout while climbing up and down the park's hills. Comfortable shoes are an absolute necessity, as is sneaking in your own bottled water—unless you don't mind dropping $15 on a day's worth of H_2O.

Make a Night of It

Where to stay in or near Valencia:

- **Country Side Inn,** 14955 Roxford St, Sylmar, 866-427-3219
- **Holiday Inn Express,** 27513 Wayne Mills Pl, Valencia, 661-284-2101
- **Rodeway Inn,** 31558 Castaic Rd, Castaic, 661-295-1100
- **Hilton Garden Inn,** 27710 The Old Road, Valencia, 661-254-8800
- **Best Western Valencia,** 27413 Wayne Mills Pl, Valencia, 661-255-0555

How to Get There

Take I-5 north to the Magic Mountain Parkway exit. Turn left at the signal at the bottom of the exit ramp, then proceed along the parkway to the park's parking entrance. Parking costs $15 per day.

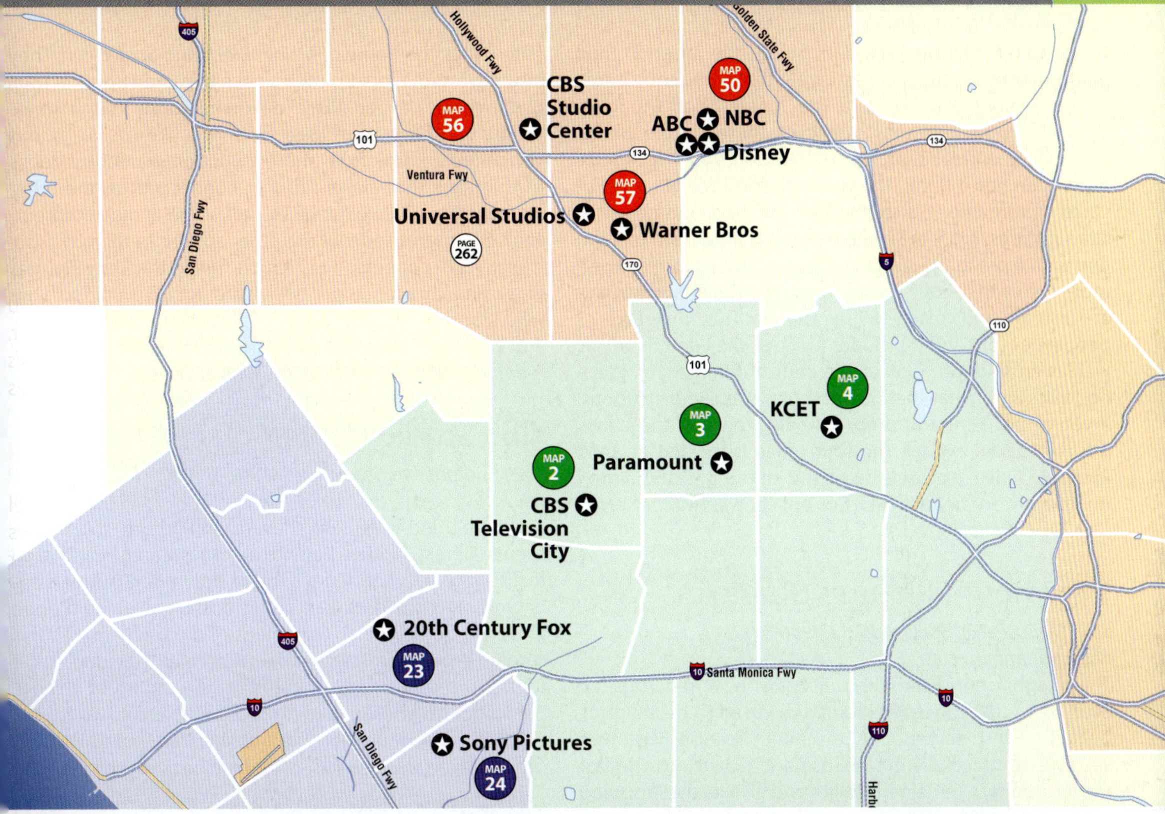

Overview

Depending upon whom you ask, LA is many things: a fashion capital of the US, the modern purveyor of the raw food diet, or the center of the real-estate universe. But with the past century of its history and the most current Census Bureau report at hand, we're pretty sure it's safe to say that LA is the mecca of the film and television industries. In the city that coined the word "tourism," those industries are primed to cart and prod you through the mazes of their studios; but don't be fooled, as all Tinsel Town tours are not created equal.

Be you resident, tourist, or the next Martin Scorsese, knowing what you're in for could save you hours of frustration. The studios aren't what they used to be. The studios are sliding ever more toward operating as giant service providers to production companies. Post- 9/11, the days when Steven Spielberg stole away from his tour at Universal and faked employment there until he was officially hired are long gone. Many tours were cancelled or have changed since then, and security is tighter at some studios than it is at LAX. So expect to bring photo ID to all tours and make reservations. But there is still some good stuff out there and plenty of tourist-y fun to be had. Just keep your ears to the ground: changes are afoot. The WB and UPN have joined forces to form the CW (CBS Warner Bros.) in Burbank (much to the chagrin of UPN employees who were accustomed to staying on the proper side of the hill). CBS is looking to move its operations over to the Valley completely, making it a regular bastion of network television and film production. So take our suggestions below and keep alert. LA's entertainment industry redefines itself more frequently than the Madonna of yesteryear.

Warner Bros. Studio

4000 Warner Blvd, Burbank, 818-977-8687; www2.warnerbros.com/vipstudiotour

The Warner Bros. Studios tour is the créme de la créme of studio tours. The Warner Bros. lots in Burbank are like a miniature Disneyland. The buildings look like decorative castles with towering posters of the popular shows taped at the studio, and its renowned WB emblem looms over the gates of its main building. When the average person pictures a California studio with row upon row of cream-colored square buildings lined with crisscrossing little roads and palm trees, this is it. On their 2 1/4-hour VIP Tour (this is the basic tour, but for $42 per person, you'd better be a VIP), you'll be driven about the 100-acre facility on a small tram to see things like the New York Street, the raised El train platform from *ER*, the Midwest Street that is currently home to the *Gilmore Girls* 'hood, or The Jungle. Scoff though a skeptical know-it-all may, many of these simple things are quite a surreal sight to be had and you'll recognize more than you'd think. The tour also includes glimpses of current productions, a stop at the gift shop, and potential star sightings. Tours are given weekdays from 9 am to 3 pm and until 4 pm in the summer months. There's also an even more involved 5-hour Deluxe Tour that departs weekdays at 10:30 am and costs $150 per person. They only take 12 people per tour and it includes lunch at the commissary as well as an in-depth look at the craft of filmmaking. We're not quite sure what that means, but we're awfully curious. If you've got a mint to drop, they also rent out their back lots for special events. The tour office is located at 3400 Riverside Drive, just outside of the studio gates. Children under eight are not allowed. Current shows: *Two and a Half Men, ER, Cold Case.*

Paramount Pictures Studio

5555 Melrose Ave, Hollywood, 323-956-1777; www.paramount.com

The magnificent Paramount Studios is a reminder of everything that the Hollywood studio used to be: magical, beautiful, and powerful. A romantic Spanish villa that sits ever so gracefully off Melrose and Gower, it's the last movie studio to remain in Hollywood and its eye-popping splendor sprawls over a mass nearly the size of Disneyland. From the main gate immortalized in *Sunset Boulevard*, to the iconic Paramount water tower, the studio is as classic as old Hollywood itself. The Paramount Studio's walking tour has been reinstated after a post-9/11 hiatus and, for the film enthusiast, just the chance to walk in the same steps as Gary Cooper, Claudette Colbert, and Audrey Hepburn is enough in itself, as is the chance to have lunch at the studio's famous Commissary. But sadly, the studio tour is a letdown, owing largely to an uninspired itinerary and guides that seem passively interested at best in the studio's rich history. For the $35 ticket price, the tour should definitely allow you to see more than just soundstage exteriors. Our advice? Save your money (and your feet) and take in a TV show taping where you're guaranteed to see the inside of a soundstage—not to mention a famous face or two. Current shows: *Girlfriends, Dr. Phil, Judge Judy.*

Sony Pictures Studios

10202 W Washington Blvd, Culver City, 323-520-TOUR; www.sonypicturesstudios.com

The design and main gate of Sony Pictures Studios are a little too clean and corporate, and their Main Street really does feel like a facade. It's all very Disney-esque, and not in a good way. Though this is the old MGM studio where *The Wizard of Oz* was shot, Sony seems more interested in billing it as the home of *Men in Black* and *Spiderman*. They also have some lots up their sleeve that aren't on the tour, over where Hayden Place deadends. Sony has a series of lots that have been used for shows like *Las Vegas*, but you'd never know from the distribution-warehouse-looks of the place that make it just as nondescript as the other surrounding office complexes. Still, there is much more to see here than at some of the other options in this city. Also, it's only $25 per person, parking is free in the Sony Pictures Plaza, and children under twelve are not allowed. Tours are held Monday through Friday at 9:30 am, 10:30 am, 1:30 pm, and 2:30 pm. Group tours are also available. Current shows: *Jeopardy!, Wheel of Fortune, The King of Queens.*

CBS Studio Center

4024 Radford Ave, Studio City, 818-655-5000; www.cbssc.com

Tucked behind Ventura Boulevard on Radford, this facility seems almost hidden behind sushi restaurants and strip malls, until you accidentally head down Radford or drive down Colfax to Ventura—then it doesn't seem so hidden at all. That blissful, naive moment of discovery makes this studio center seem pretty sweet. Too bad they don't offer tours. So that just leaves attending the taping of a show. But kudos to you for finding it! Shows: *According to Jim, The Bernie Mac Show*, and the late *That '70s Show* and *Will & Grace*. FYI: *Seinfeld* was also shot here back in the day.

CBS Television City

7800 Beverly Blvd, Los Angeles, 323-575-2458; www.cbs.com

Not to be confused with CBS Studio Center, Television City films such gems as *The Price is Right* and *The Late Late Show*. If you want to see a taping and you don't care which show it is, you can walk up to the studio's ticket office (near the corner of Beverly & Fairfax) and pick up tickets. If you're after tickets for a specific show, you'll need to call 323-575-2458 (live) or 323-575-2449 (*The Price is Right* recorded hotline) in advance.

NBC Studios

3000 W Alameda Ave (at Bob Hope Dr), Burbank, 818-840-3537; www.nbc.com

NBC is the only television studio in LA to offer tours. From the outside it looks like a bland corporate office building, and it's not exactly in a lively section of Burbank. To top that off, it's only a 70-minute walking tour and—sorry to spoil the surprise–it's basically just a visit to *The Tonight Show* set. However, entry can be gained for the bargain price of $7.50 for adults, $6.75 for seniors, $4 for children ages 5–12, and free for kids under 5. They do take you deep into the belly of NBC (even if it's just a lot of viewing-from-afar and standing-behind-the-velvet-rope kind of deal). Maybe empty sets, display cases, and seeing Jay Leno's parking space is your thing—or maybe it will be when Conan takes the reins. If not, you can always just go to see a taping of *The Tonight Show*, and lining up for free tickets to shows with a live studio audience might even be more fun. If you do plan on seeing *The Tonight Show*, tickets are available in person the day of taping or in advance by mail. We suggest you phone ahead for availability if you plan on lining up, otherwise you might just get a good view of the corporate building with no glimpse at Leno's parking space to soften the blow.

ABC TV

2300 Riverside Dr, Burbank, 818-460-7477; www.abc.com

The ABC TV Studios have been recently relocated to the Disney Studio lot in Burbank. The studios still do not offer public tours, but tickets to some shows can be obtained. For more information, visit the network's website to find out which ticket agents provide free tickets to shows such as *America's Funniest Home Videos* and *Dancing with the Stars*.

Disney Studios

500 S Buena Vista St, Burbank, 818-560-1000; www.disney.com

If there's one thing Disney can do better than anyone else, its set up a great photo op. And that's pretty much all you can do at the Walt Disney Studios: take a picture of the elaborate stone and glass building and the 160-foot stone statues of the Seven Dwarfs seemingly holding up the front of its roof. The studio is closed to the public, which really is a pity because it's a Disney fan's dream. You can wander through the hugely impressive prop warehouse where a good deal of the stuff is quite recognizable (like Madonna's *Evita* portrait), you can ogle at an original Multiplane camera on display (the pioneering technology that made *Snow White and the Seven Dwarfs* possible), there are trailers belonging to people like, say, Jennifer Garner, and the studio also hosts a lovely miniature museum with everything from Mary Poppins' iconic blue dress to vintage Mickey memorabilia and an impressive art archive. The back lot's manicured lanes and lawns are typical, formulaic Disney: homogenous and sterile, but it's a formula we're all suckers for, admit it. The studio would make for a killer tour and also make a lot of fans happy—but you'll just have to make do with snapping a picture at the main gate.

KCET Studio

4401 W Sunset Blvd, Hollywood, 323-953-5289; www.kcet.org

KCET, the local public television (PBS) station Channel 28, is a historic studio where classics like *The Jazz Singer* were filmed. Sadly, they have temporarily suspended free walking tours for security reasons.

Universal Studios

100 Universal City Plz, Universal City, 800-UNIVERSAL; www.universalstudios.com

If this studio tour feels like a theme park ride, that's because it is. Universal Studios is really more like 60% theme park, 40% studio, and the theme park features are certainly more famous. The studio itself is part of the Universal City experience, which includes the CityWalk, a mini Las Vegas of restaurants, shops, stores, and a movie theater. As you ride their tram tour, you'll suffer the onslaught of *Jaws* and *King Kong*. There are several rides and shows within the park for favorite spectacle blockbusters like *Back to the Future*, *Jurassic Park*, *Terminator*, and *War of the Worlds*. There are TV shows taped here as well, and film production is always in full swing, but the theme park experience—standing in the extremely long lines after the $61 ticket price—can become somewhat trying. Nevertheless, Universal Studios remains a tour favorite—you just can't get attacked by a shark and a giant ape on the same day anywhere else. If you do decide to take this wild ride, try visiting their website before you go as they often have special reduced rate offers and deals that allow free entry for the rest of the year with the purchase of a full price ticket.

20th Century Fox

10201 W Pico Blvd, Century City; www.fox.com

You can see this studio by heading south down Avenue of the Stars (though this is a misnomer of a street, really), and it'll be on your right just before Pico. Much of what used to be this studio's back lots were sold off to make room for the Century City shopping centers. The facilities that have remained or relocated continue to shoot movies and television. Most of these television shows do not require live audiences, but you can get tickets for the few shows, like *Reba*, by contacting Audiences Unlimited (see below).

Audiences Unlimited

Audiences Unlimited is an agency that distributes free tickets to the tapings of television shows. Call 818-753-3470, visit www.tvtickets.com, or get tickets through the mail (include an SASE) by writing to Audiences Unlimited, 100 Universal City Plz, Bldg 153, Universal City, CA 91608. Be sure to specify the name of the show, date, and number of people in your party. However, we suggest visiting the website or calling the company directly. The tickets are free, so they don't exactly have trouble handing them out.

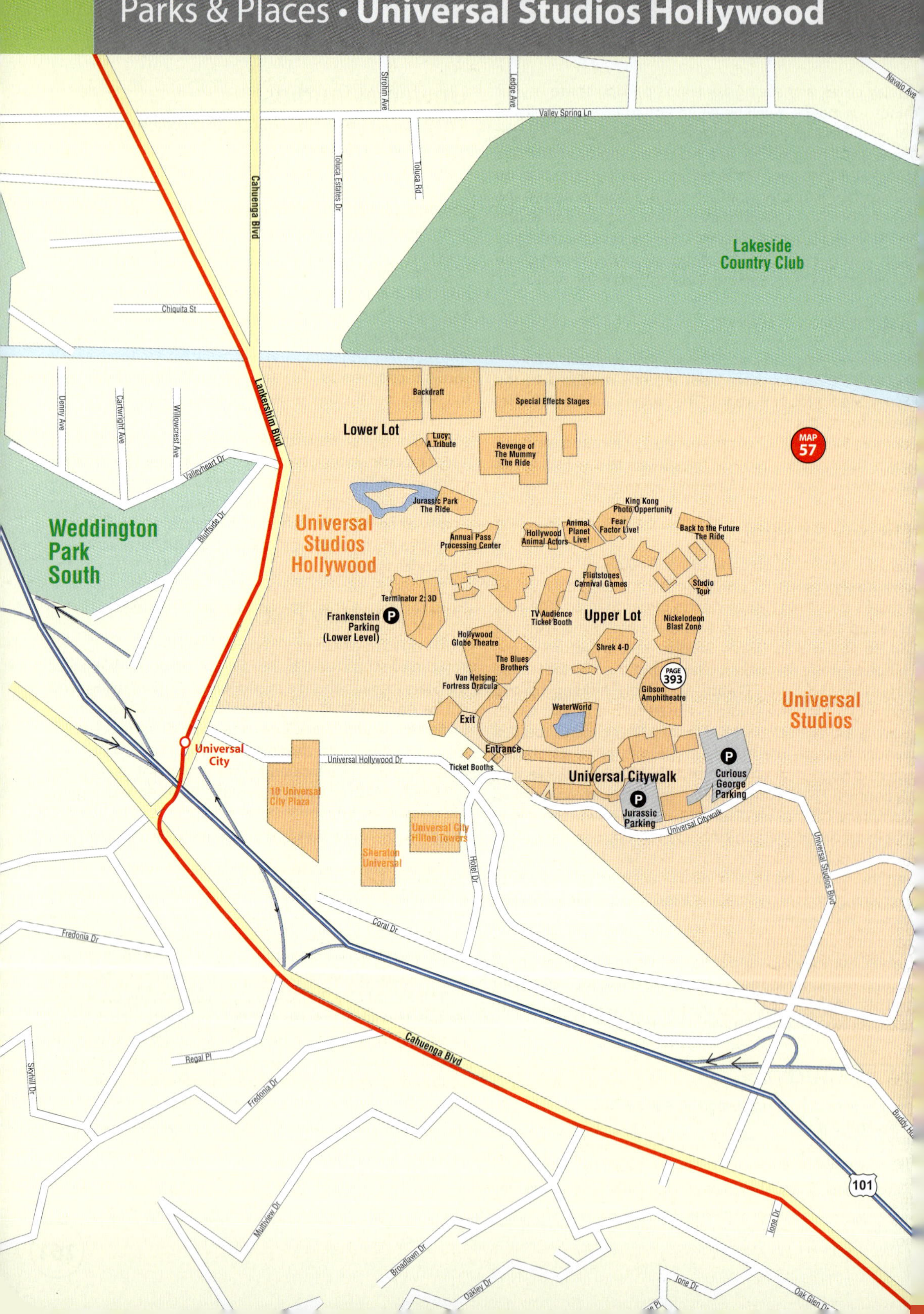
Navajo Ave
Strohm Ave
Ledge Ave
Valley Spring Ln
Cahuenga Blvd
Toluca Estates Dr
Toluca Rd
Lakeside Country Club
Chiquita St
Lankershim Blvd
Denny Ave
Cartwright Ave
Willowcrest Ave
Valleyheart Dr
Bluffside Dr
Weddington Park South
Backdraft
Special Effects Stages
Lower Lot
Lucy: A Tribute
Revenge of The Mummy The Ride
MAP 57
Jurassic Park The Ride
Universal Studios Hollywood
King Kong Photo Oppertunity
Animal Planet Live!
Fear Factor Live!
Hollywood Animal Actors
Annual Pass Processing Center
Back to the Future The Ride
Flintstones Carnival Games
Studio Tour
Terminator 2: 3D
Frankenstein Parking (Lower Level)
TV Audience Ticket Booth
Upper Lot
Nickelodeon Blast Zone
Hollywood Globe Theatre
Shrek 4-D
The Blues Brothers
PAGE 393
Van Helsing: Fortress Dracula
Gibson Amphitheatre
Universal Studios
WaterWorld
Exit
Universal City
Entrance
Universal Hollywood Dr
Ticket Booths
Universal Citywalk
Curious George Parking
Jurassic Parking
10 Universal City Plaza
Universal City Hilton Towers
Sheraton Universal
Hotel Dr
Universal Studios Blvd
Coral Dr
Fredonia Dr
Cahuenga Blvd
Regal Pl
Skyhill Dr
Fredonia Dr
Buddy Ho
101
Multiview Dr
Broadlawn Dr
Ione Dr
Oakley Dr
Oak Glen Dr

General Information

NFT Map: 57
Address: 100 Universal City Plaza
Universal City, CA 91608
Park Information: 800-UNIVERSAL
Special Events: 818-622-3036
Lost & Found: 818-622-3522
Group Sales: 800-959-9688 x2
Website: www.universalstudioshollywood.com

Overview

If you live in Hollywood, you've probably a) seen a movie being filmed during your daily commute, b) been to a show taping, c) worked as an extra, or d) all of the above. Universal Studios, with its hissing animatronic Jaws and silly stunt shows, doesn't offer much of an escape from your daily grind.

However, if you've got out-of-town guests, send them to Universal immediately; it rivals Disneyland with its interactive attractions for both kids (*Shrek 4-D*) and adults (the new *Fear Factor Live*). Aunt Mary will flip when she sees *Desperate Housewives*' Wisteria Lane and Uncle Jerry can channel his inner Tom Cruise while viewing the actual set of *War of the Worlds*. The park is much more manageable than the Happiest Place on Earth, and rides, like *Revenge of the Mummy* are always improving.

Just outside the theme park gates, CityWalk truly embraces the concept of Hollywood hype. Garish storefronts beckon you into knick-knack shops and the restaurant roster reads like a condensed sampling of LA's most popular eateries: Saddle Ranch Chop House, Wolfgang Puck Café, and Daily Grill all have locations here. Even locals come out to appreciate movies at the 19-screen CityWalk Cinemas, (call 818-508-0711 for movie times), music at B.B. King's Blues Club, and seasonal treats like a wintertime outdoor skating rink. The new VIP Party Pass gives you access to all CityWalk clubs with a couple of free drinks and a ride on Saddle Ranch's mechanical bull thrown in. (You'll pay for it the morning after.)

Hours of Operation

Universal Studios is open all year (except Thanksgiving and Christmas), but operating hours are subject to change without notice, so call the park or check the website before you plan your visit. Typically the park is open from 9 am until 9 pm on weekends during peak times, and 9 am until 8 pm during busy weekdays. During the slower months, it's open from 10 am until 6 pm. But again, check before you go.

Entrance Fees

One-day tickets cost $61 for adults and $51 for those under 48 inches tall. Children 2 and under—regardless of height—are free. Book tickets online using Universal's Print@Home option to avoid the lines. If money is no object, consider purchasing the Front of Line Pass for $109.95, which allows you to cut to the front of the line for rides and snag the best seats in the house for any performance.

Check the website for packages and deals like the Southern California CityPass which allows you to visit multiple parks in SoCal at a flat rate. Promotions are abundant during high season and vary wildly, so be sure to check everything from the supermarket to your empty Coke can for special coupons.

Lockers

Cash and credit card–operated rental lockers are located just inside the park at varying costs depending on size. And since they're inside the park, you can keep adding junk as the day goes by.

Package Delivery

If you buy merchandise within the park and you don't feel like schlepping it around, there's a handy delivery service that will have your parcels waiting for you as you leave. The pickup point is located near the exit at Universal Film Co.

Kennels

If you can't bear to leave your pet at home or if you're passing through on a longer journey, Universal provides a complimentary kennel service for park guests. Go to the Guest Services window at the entrance to the park, and your pet will be escorted to the facilities by one of the guest service representatives.

How to Get There—Driving

Universal Studios Hollywood is located between Hollywood and the San Fernando Valley, just off the 101 Hollywood/Ventura Freeway. Exit at Universal Center Drive or Lankershim Boulevard and follow the signs to the parking areas.

Parking

Preferred Parking ($20) is located in the Rocky & Bullwinkle Lot and is one of the closest parking lots to the theme park. If you would prefer to park your car yourself, general parking is located in the Curious George Garage, Jurassic Parking Garage, and the Frankenstein and Woody Woodpecker Lots. All are within walking distance to any Universal destination and cost $10 for the day. If you simply must save your cash for that Jurassic Park t-shirt, park at the bottom of the hill and take the free tram to the park.

How to Get There—Mass Transit

Universal Studios is the only Southern Californian theme park accessible by subway. Take the Metro Red Line to Universal City. MTA Buses 96, 150, 152, 156, 163, 166, 240, and 750 also run to Universal City Station. Shuttles, airport, and charter services are available to and from Universal Studios Hollywood with SuperShuttle. A free tram will take you to the top of the hill upon arrival. 800-258-3826; www.supershuttle.com.

Topanga State Park
Mulholland Dr
Mulholland Dr (unpaved)
Reseda Blvd
Caballero Canyon Trail
Encino Reservoir
Department of Water & Power (No Public Access)
San Vincente Mountain
Bent Arrow Trail
Garapito Canyon Trail
Cheney Fire Rd
Fire Rd 30
Eagle Springs
Hub Junction (2,000 ft)
Eagle Junction
Camping
Musch Meadows
Musch Trail
Topanga Canyon Blvd
Old Topanga Canyon Rd
Dead Horse Trail
Entrada Rd
Eagle Springs Fire Rd
Trippet Ranch
Topanga
Santa Ynez Canyon Trail
Waterfall
Temescal Ridge Trail
Rogers Rd Trail
Sullivan Ridge Fire Rd
Sullivan Canyon Fire Rd
Canyon Fire Rd
Michael Ln
Chastain Pkwy
Lone Oak
Rustic Canyon Trail
Non-Maintained Trail
East Topanga Fire Rd
Santa Ynez Reservior
Palisades Highlands
Skull Rock
Bienveneda Trail
Temescal Canyon Trail
Parker Mesa Overlook (1,525 ft)
Palisades Dr
Bienveneda Ave
Will Rogers State Historical Park
Los Liones Trail
Los Liones Dr
Sunset Blvd
Temescal Canyon Rd
Pacific Coast Hwy
Topanga State Beach
Santa Monica Bay
MAP 52
MAP 53
MAP 16
MAP 15
27
1

General Information

NFT Maps:	15, 16, 52 & 53
Address:	20825 Entrada Rd Topanga, CA 90290
Phone:	310-455-2465
California State Parks Website:	www.parks.ca.gov

Overview

Depending on which translation you accept, *topanga* means "the place above," or "the place where the mountains meet the sea," *or* "the place of green water" (and we just thought it meant "really big"). Located entirely within Los Angeles's city limits (although you wouldn't know it by visiting), Topanga State Park's 11,000 acres make it the largest wilderness located within the boundaries of a major city *in the entire world*. It feels more like New Mexico than Los Angeles. It also has its own community complete with homes, local artists, churches, restaurants, and a historical society—secluded far away from the LA bustle.

Bottom line—it's beautiful. It's *the* place to hit the trails (they've got over 36 miles worth of those) enjoy some nature (take two antihistamines and check out the spring blooms), or bring a book and read trailside. Topanga offers breathtaking views of the ocean and plenty of fresh air—which you'll need once you actually get out of your car and witness just what Mother Nature has in store for you.

Practicalities

The park is open daily from 8 am until dusk. Entry into the park is free, but parking costs $4 per vehicle. Depending on where you hit the trails, street parking is close and free. From Pacific Coast Highway (1), travel north on Topanga Canyon Boulevard, past the post office at the center of the village, then turn right onto Entrada Road. Keep to the left until you reach the park's main parking lot (about one mile). From the Ventura Freeway (101), exit at Topanga Canyon Boulevard, drive south over the crest of the mountains and proceed three miles to Entrada Road and turn left. Follow the above directions from here.

Activities

Topanga is ideal for uninterrupted walking, running, cycling, and horseback riding (although horse rentals are not available at the park). Mountain bikers are supposedly restricted to the fire roads, but they often fly down the pedestrian-only paths anyway. Dogs are not allowed on backcountry trails (but the free-range mountain lions are okay; whatever). There are many marked trails for hikers, most of which can be accessed from Trippet Ranch (off Entrada Road), a former "gentleman's ranch" used as a weekend escape from the city back in the day. In addition to the Park Office, Trippet Ranch provides parking facilities, picnic areas, and a great little Visitor's Center that offers guided walking tours on Sunday mornings. If it's relaxation, not activity, that you're after, you might want to try the self-guided nature trail (the trail map costs a quarter and is available at the parking lot) or join one of the Sunday guided walks with experts well-versed in the flora and fauna of the area. Call the park for more information about walk schedules.

Topanga's restaurants are worth visiting. Writers, poets, and city people looking to escape bring their laptops, books, and blankets to spend a day by the giant fireplace at **Froggy's Fish Market & Restaurant** (1105 N Topanga Canyon Blvd). In tune with its surroundings, Froggy's serves healthier items on its menu as well as burgers and quesadillas. **Inn of the Seventh Ray** (128 Old Topanga Canyon Rd) is a wildly romantic restaurant with vegan and vegetarian options, but the restaurant's mouth-melting rack of lamb would make anyone eat meat again.

Another visual highlight of the park is the blooming flowers that attract thousands of avid gardeners and photographers each year. For information on the different varieties of flowers that grow in the park, call 818-768-3533.

Hiking Trails

Many of the park's trails can be accessed from Trippet Ranch. The Eagle Springs loop begins at the Eagle Junction, just under two miles from Trippet. A climb up the northern section of the loop will afford you a nice panoramic view of the park. At the eastern end of the Eagle Springs loop, you'll come to the Hub Junction, from where you can take the Temescal Ridge Trail south or the fire road north, or simply circle back and complete the Eagle Springs loop to Trippet Ranch.

To reach the unpaved Mullholland Drive, hike north from Hub Junction, and follow the fire road for two miles through chaparral. Heading south on the Temescal Ridge Trail leads you high above the canyons to gorgeous views of sycamore and oak riparian forests below.

Another option from Trippet Ranch is to walk east to the Topanga Fire Road and then north for a short distance to the Santa Ynez Trail. As you descend into the Santa Ynez Canyon, look out for the crumbly sandstone formations with pockets where moisture collects—there are tiny cliff gardens in these areas. Near the bottom of the trail is a short 0.8-mile trail leading to a lovely waterfall (assuming there's been any rainfall, that is) that's definitely worth a look.

Shorter hikes can be taken from other parking lots in Topanga State Park. From the Los Liones Drive parking lot, you can complete a 1.7-mile loop hike on the Los Liones Trail. For a longer hike, take the East Topanga Fire Road to the Parker Mesa Overlook for stunning views of the canyon. The Overlook can also be accessed from Paseo Miramar. From PCH, take Sunset Blvd north and a left onto Paseo Miramar to the top, then park on the street. The nearly 90-degree climb makes for a great workout with incredible ocean views.

If you park in the first lot on Entrada Road (if you hit Trippet Ranch, you've gone too far), you can take the 1.1-mile Dead Horse Trail to Trippet Ranch.

To access the Caballero Canyon Trail or the Bent Arrow Trail, take Reseda Boulevard into the Caballero Canyon Park lot and head out from there.

Camping

Camping facilities are available on a first-come, first-served basis. Your best bet is to follow the Musch Trail to the Musch Trail Campground, but we recommend contacting the park directly for more information before heading out.

Bel Air Country Club
MAP 17
MAP 20
Easton Women's Softball Field
UCLA Guest House
Krieger Child Care Center
De Neve Dr
Marymount Pl
Udine Way
Stone Canyon Dr
Groverton Pl
Sunset Blvd
Bellagio Rd
Veteran Ave
Greenfield Ave
Cashmere St
Ophir Dr
Gayley Ave
Levering Ave
Recreation Center, Sunset Canyon
Sunset Tennis Courts
Hitch Residential Suites
Hedrick Hall
Canyon Point
Courtside
Delta Terrace
Covel Commons
Sproul Hall
Campbell Hall
Orn Hort Area Buildings
Sycamore Tennis Courts
Rieber Hall
Saxon Residential Suites
Southern Regional Library Facility
Dogwood
Cedar
De Neve Plaza
Evergreen
Dykstra Hall
Bradley International Hall
Charles E Young Dr
Drake Track Stadium
Intramural Field
Wooden Center
LA Tennis Center
Pauley Pavillion
Morgan Center
Spaulding Field
Strathmore Dr
Strathmore Building
Campus Services Building I
Facilities Management
Police
Fernald Center
University Residence
Seeds University Elementary School
Rosenfield Library
Anderson School of Management
Collins
Cornell
Charles E Young Research Library
Melnitz Hall (James Bridges Theater)
East Melnitz
Broad Center
Macgowan Hall (Freud Playhouse, Little Theater)
Public Policy Building
UCLA Guest House
Bunche Hall
Rolfe Hall
Campbell Hall
LuValle Commons
Fowler Museum
Royce Hall
Haines Hall
Perloff Hall
Dickson Plaza
Dodd Hall
Law
Kaufman Hall
Fountain
Westwood Plz
Powell Library
Humanities
Murphy Hall
Student Activity Center
Physics
Schoenberg Hall
Kerchkoff Hall
Knudsen Hall
West Alumni Center
Ackerman Union
Moore Hall
Portola Plaza Building
Faculty Center
Engineering I
Mathematical Sciences
Franz Hall
Geology
Slichter Hall
Engineering IV
Boelter Hall
Young Hall
Boyer
Molecular Sciences
Gonda
Neuroscience Research
Lakretz
Life Sciences
Charles E Young Dr S
Hershey Hall
Botany
School of Medicine
Lath House
Plant Growth Center
Clinical Research
Jules Stein Institute
Marion Davis Children's Center
Emergency Center
Morton Med
UCLA Medical Plaza
Doris Stein
Faculty Apartments
Landfair Ave
Strathmore Dr
Roebling Ave
Kelton Ave
Midvale Ave
UCLA Extension
Ueberroth Building
Le Conte Ave
Hilgard Ave
Charing
Comstock
Malcolm Ave
Selby Ave
Cypress Court
Aloe Court
Magnolia Court
Faculty Apartments
Broxton Plaza
Geffen Playhouse
Bank of America Building
Tiverton
Jacaranda Court
Warren Hall
Weyburn Ave
Olive Court
Westwood Center
Weyburn Apartments
Palm Court
Glendon Ave
Westwood Blvd
Broxton Ave
Tiverton Ave
Lindbrook Dr
Los Angeles National Cemetery
Science & Technology Research
Rehab Center
Gayley Center
Weyburn Pl
Capital Programs
Fire Department
Kinross Ave
UCLA/Armand Hammer Museum
Lindbrook Center
Wilshire Blvd
Oppenheimer Tower
Westwood Ashton Memorial Park
Ashton Ave
Wellworth
Kinross Bldg
Wilshire Center
S Sepulveda Blvd
405
Constitution Ave
2. NW Auditorium
3. Office of Residential Life
4. Acosta Training Center
5. North Campus Student Center
6. Graduate School of Education and Information Studies Building
7. MacDonald Medical Research Laboratory
8. West Medical Center

General Information

NFT Maps: 17 & 20
Address: 405 Hilgard Ave
Los Angeles, CA 90095
Phone: 310-825-4321
Website: www.ucla.edu

Overview

Located on a picturesque campus in Westwood, UCLA is a behemoth public research university that offers 127 undergraduate degree programs and 200 graduate degree programs. Its faculty of Nobel prize laureates, MacArthur grant winners, and National Medal of Science winners has earned UCLA an international reputation for academic excellence. The school has also consistently produced champion sports teams and athletes since it was founded in 1919.

UCLA's Extension Program is extremely popular and offers continuing education for adults in topics ranging from architecture to screenwriting to wine tasting. The courses, offered quarterly, are popular among locals debating career changes, as well as those merely interested in bettering themselves.

Tuition

For the 2007-2008 academic year, living expenses for undergraduate students (including books, registration fees, supplies, room and board, transportation, health insurance, and other personal costs) were estimated by the university to cost $16,836-$23.976 for California residents, and $36,456-$43,596 for students from out of state (costs vary depending on living accommodations).

Facilities

The UCLA campus is like a small city - indeed, during the 1984 Olympics, parts of the campus comprised the Olympic Village. UCLA has its own police department and fire marshal, and a range of services including shops, restaurants, post offices, and banks. Eleven parking and information booths located across the campus will aid visitors in their confusion about where to park. UCLA's circular drive loops around the entire campus and is easy to navigate. If you're just popping in, metered parking is available for 25¢ per eight minutes (go heavy on the quarters) or $8 for the entire day. Student parking (granted quarterly through application) is assigned on a need-based point system, which takes into consideration class standing, employment/academic obligations, and commuter distance.

Culture on Campus

UCLA also provides the community with a variety of cultural programs. The university is affiliated with the Geffen Playhouse in Westwood (10886 Le Conte Ave, 310-208-5454), which has been the LA stop for Broadway plays such as *The Weir* and *Wit*. On campus, UCLA LIVE! at Royce Hall (www.uclalive.org, 310-825-2101) has hosted a wide variety of music, literary, and dance programs, from the Los Angeles Philharmonic to jazz legend Alice Coltrane to French actress Isabelle Huppert. The Fowler Museum of Cultural History holds an impressive collection of art from Africa, Asia, and the Pacific (fowler.ucla.edu, 310-825-4361). The Hammer Museum hosts cutting-edge readings, screenings, and music and art celebrations throughout the year (www.hammer.ucla.edu, 310-443-7000). The annual student talent show, *Spring Sing*, doubles as a convocation for recipients of the George and Ira Gershwin Award, which honors music industry magnates (James Taylor and Burt Bacharach are recent awardees). And each April, UCLA is home to the *Los Angeles Times's* Festival of Books—the literary event of the year.

Sports

You don't need to be affiliated with the university to appreciate the talents of UCLA's athletes, though you'll want to curb any lurking support of the cross-town Trojans. UCLA's top-ten nationally ranked teams include men's water polo, women's soccer, women's volleyball, and men's basketball. For up-to-date information, scores, and schedules, check out the official athletics website at uclabruins.cstv.com. Ticket prices for football and men's basketball games depend on the event. All other sporting events cost $4 with a student ID and $6 without. For tickets, call 310-825-2101.

Department Contact Information

College of Letters & Science 310-825-9009
Graduate Admissions 310-825-7290
Undergraduate Admissions 310-825-3101
Anderson School of Management 310-825-7982
Graduate School of Education
and Information Studies 310-825-8326
UCLA Extension (UNEX) 310-826-9971
or 818-784-7006
School of the Arts & Architecture 310-206-6465
The Henry Samueli School of
Engineering & Applied Science 310-825-8162
School of Dentistry 310-825-2337
School of Law 310-207-4736
School of Medicine 310-825-6373
School of Nursing 310-825-7181
School of Public Health 310-825-6381
School of Public Affairs 310-206-7568
School of Theater, Film and TV 310-825-5761

General Information

NFT Maps:	11,12 & 40
Mailing Address:	University Park Campus University of Southern California Los Angeles, CA 90089
Location:	University Park, b/w Figueroa St, Exposition Park, Vermont Ave & Jefferson Blvd
Phone:	213-740-2311
Website:	www.usc.edu

Overview

The University of Southern California opened its doors with 53 students in 1880, when the city of Los Angeles was still in its frontier, beta version. Four years later, three of the original 53—one women, two men—became the first class to graduate from the private school. Enrollment has since jumped to more than 33,000, and the school now straddles two main campuses.

The University Park Campus, home to USC's College of Letters, Arts & Sciences and 15 professional schools, is located three miles south of downtown Los Angeles. Seven miles from the University Park Campus, the 50-acre Health Sciences Campus houses the medical and pharmaceutical schools, as well as programs in occupational therapy, physical therapy, and nursing. A shuttle bus runs between the two campuses approximately every hour throughout the week.

USC's film school boasts an impressive pedigree. Its founding faculty included Douglas Fairbanks and D. W. Griffith, and it has churned out equally famous alumni, including George Lucas and Robert Zemeckis. USC rejected filmmaker Steven Spielberg's application (oops!); he has since sucked up his pride and now sits on the USC Board of Trustees. At least one USC alumnus has been nominated for an Academy Award every year since 1973. Talk about hegemony.

Tuition

For the 2005–2006 academic year, annual undergraduate tuition and fees total about $35,810 (based on 12–18 units for two semesters). Add on the cost of room, board, books, supplies, and transportation, and your education is going to cost you about $49,598 a year.

Parking

Parking on campus costs $7. There are also a smattering of one-hour metered parking spaces available, and a couple of lots inside campus offer two-hour parking for $4. Four-hour and two-hour metered parking is available on Figueroa Street and Jefferson Boulevard. $3- to $5-a-day lots are available Monday through Friday across the street from the campus on Figueroa Street (next to the Sizzler restaurant) and on Jefferson Boulevard (next to the Shrine Auditorium). Parking rates for these lots may vary for special events.

Culture on Campus

USC hosts a plethora of academic and arts events, from concerts and theater performances to exhibits and public lectures. Many events are inexpensive (if not free) and can be found on the USC website at www.usc.edu/calendar. Throughout the academic year, USC's prestigious Thornton School of Music, USC Fisher Gallery, and the KUSC classical radio station are among the many campus cultural institutions that stage full schedules of arts-related events. For a schedule of performances by the Thornton's symphony, chamber orchestra, wind ensemble, and choir, check out www.usc.edu/music. The USC orchestra also performs regularly at Disney Hall, home of the LA Philharmonic. (Frank Gehry, the architect of the famous performance hall, was a USC man himself!)

Sports

USC's top-ten nationally ranked teams include men's water polo, women's water polo, women's swimming, and women's golf. The USC Trojan football team was the back-to-back 2003 and 2004 National Championship winner and played for the 2005 National Championship, but to the cheer of a particular Westwood rival, lost to the Texas Longhorns at the Pasadena Rose Bowl, despite having two Heisman trophy winners—Reggie Bush and Matt Leinert on board. For up-to-date information, scores, and schedules, check out the official athletics website at www.usctrojans.com. For tickets, call 213-740-4672.

Department Contact Information

Admissions 213-740-1111
College of Letters, Arts & Sciences 213-740-2531
Leventhal School of Accounting 213-740-4838
School of Architecture 213-740-2723
Marshall School of Business 213-740-6422
School of Cinematic Arts 213-740-2804
Annenberg School for Communication 213-740-6180
School of Dentistry........ 213-740-2800
Rossier School of Education 213-740-0224
Viterbi School of Engineering........ 213-740-4530
School of Fine Arts 213-740-2787
Leonard Davis School of Gerontology........ 213-740-6060
Occupational Science and Occupational Therapy... 323-442-2850
Department of Biokinesiology and Physical Therapy 332-442-2900
The Law School 213-740-7331
Keck School of Medicine 323-442-1900
Thornton School of Music 213-740-6935
School of Pharmacy........ 323-442-1369
School of Policy, Planning & Development........ 213-740-6842
School of Social Work 213-740-2711
School of Theatre 213-821-2744

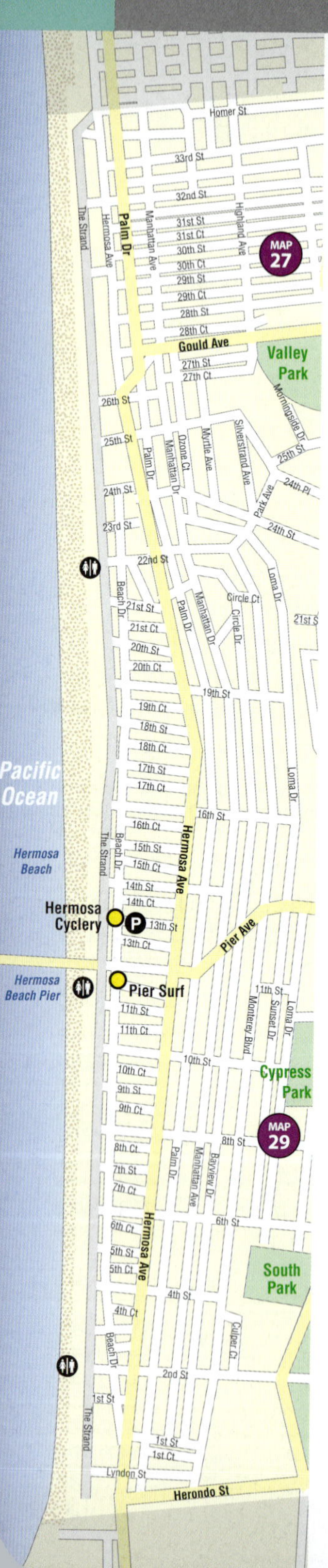

Overview

Hermosa means "beautiful" in Spanish, a descriptor not lost on the nearly 20,000 residents who call Hermosa Beach home. Hollywood certainly seems to take the place at name-value, filming hits like *The OC* and *Summerland* at the Pier on a regular basis. But glitz and glamour is the exception here—it's flip-flops, swim trunks, and tans that are the norm. The beach is teeming with surfers, volleyball players, and sunbathers, while joggers, bikers, skaters, and strollers line the Strand. Visit the City of Hermosa Beach website at www.hermosabch.org, or the Hermosa Beach Chamber of Commerce website at www.hbchamber.net, for listings of local events and activities. A summer favorite: movies on the beach at sunset.

As the official birthplace of surfing in California, Hermosa is home to the Surfers Walk of Fame, which honors big names like Bing Copeland, Hap Jacobs, and Greg Noll with bronze plaques embedded in the Pier. With its laid-back surfer mentality and compact town density, Hermosa Beach is a breezy alternative to the more ostentatious beach towns to the north.

Practicalities

Hermosa Beach is open daily from sunrise to sunset. During the summer, parking can be a pain, so come early and bring quarters. There is metered street parking for 25¢ per 15 minutes, or you can try the convenient new "cash key" (available for purchase at City Hall)—it works as a debit card, is accepted at all Hermosa meters, and is less likely to get lost in your seat cushions. A three-story lot on Hermosa Avenue is also available—rates vary depending on the time of year. Hint: If you don't mind walking, there's free 12-hour parking on Valley Drive (between 8th and 10th Streets). Restrooms are located on the new Pier Plaza and at 2nd Street, 11th Street, 14th Street, and 22nd Street.

Sports

It comes as little surprise that TV crews and volleyball players agree to use this beautiful location as a site for nationally televised AVP Volleyball Tournaments. Hermosa's other favorite pastime is honored every year when the International Surf Festival comes to neighboring Manhattan Beach (www.surffestival.org). The three-day event, held annually in August, features an amateur volleyball tournament complete with costumes and lots of libations as well as land activities like a two-mile beach run and a sand castle design contest, along with traditional surf and lifeguard competitions.

Surfing and volleyball lessons are always available right on the beach, as are rental boogie boards, surfboards, or skates. Pier Surf (21 Pier Ave, 310-372-2012), located just up from the Hermosa Beach Pier, rents surfboards for $12 an hour ($35 a day) and boogie boards for $6 an hour ($20 a day) with varying security deposits.

Hermosa Cyclery (20 13th St, 310-374-7816) provides a good selection of rental bikes, boogie boards, skates, umbrellas, and chairs at affordable prices; rates start at $7 an hour ($21 a day) for bikes and $6 an hour ($18 a day) for rollerblades. Check the Hermosa Cyclery website at www.hermosacyclery.com for a complete list of rental offers.

Hermosa Pier

The century-old Hermosa Pier just received a much-needed multi-stage renovation project. Among the improvements: fresh pylons, resurfacing, more lights, and a new three-story lifeguard station. The pier continues to serve as the epicenter and backdrop for most of the city's main events, including Fiesta Hermosa, a biannual arts and crafts festival.

Shopping

While Roxy and Quiksilver reign supreme in this surf-driven community, there are plenty of diverse shopping opportunities within walking distance of the beach along Pier Avenue, Hermosa Avenue, Artesia Boulevard, and the Pacific Coast Highway. The streets are lined with clothing and jewelry boutiques, sunglass huts, antiques showrooms, and quaint general stores featuring beach themed merchandise. If you're after fresh produce or flowers, the Farmers Market, located on Valley Drive (between 8th and 10th Streets), is open every Friday from noon until 4 pm, rain or shine.

Overview

Come to Manhattan Beach and it's almost like you've stepped onto the set of *The OC*, that show where the houses look good, the people look good, and the clothes look good. Multi-million dollar homes line the well-tended shorefront of the public beaches here. There's no shortage of trendy boutiques or places to eat in this beach community. Park your car and spend the afternoon walking down Manhattan Beach Boulevard and Manhattan Avenue for shops galore. Choose from on-the-run dining like a tasty beef pastrami sandwich from Papa Jake's or splurge on trendy Greek food at Petros Restaurant. But the beach here is really where its at—soak in the marvelous rays and miles of sand as you head out for volleyball, surfing, boogie boarding, body surfing, swimming, diving, and fishing.

For information about activities and events in the area, check out the City of Manhattan Beach website at www.ci.manhattan-beach.ca.us, or the Chamber of Commerce website at www.manhattanbeachchamber.net.

Practicalities

Manhattan Beach is open daily from sunrise until midnight. There are six metered parking lots and three free lots within walking distance of the beach. If you want good parking, though, you'd better get there early, as the conveniently located lots fill up fast. An underground parking facility, located at 1220 Morningside Drive, has 260 long-term meter spots and 200 short-term meter spots. If you're looking to park your Beamer convertible for beach time and you're short on cash, arrive early at Lot 8 off Valley Drive; the lot has 51 free spaces. Metered street parking is available, but one quarter buys you a measly 15 minutes. Note: during December, the city offers free three-hour parking at some meters as a little holiday gift to the diehard beach lovers.

Restrooms

Clean restrooms and showers are located at the end of the pier as well as at 8th Street, Manhattan Beach Boulevard, Marine Street, and 40th Street.

Sports

Surfers, boogie boarders, and body surfers all find decent breaks at Manhattan Beach, especially in El Porto (North Manhattan Beach). Everyone's happy to share the waves, but you gotta know your place: surfers go to the south of the pier, boogie boarders to the north, and everyone rides the waves in fear of infringing upon the posted swimming areas and enraging the lifeguards. For the land-loving folk, the bike path on the Strand separates the wheels from the pedestrians. There are plenty of volleyball nets (usually occupied by very tanned and toned athletes). The kiddies can enjoy the swing sets scattered along the beach.

Manhattan Pier

The pier at Manhattan Beach is a basic, no frills place, but it's worth a trip to see. Spend some contemplative time taking in the ocean and waves or fish off the pier. If you take a walk to the end, you'll reach the Roundhouse Marine Lab & Aquarium, an oceanographic teaching station. It's a small two-story building with a sampling of marine-life tanks and a touch pool. It is open to the public from 3 pm until sunset during the week and from 10 am until sunset on the weekends. Entry is free, although a $2 per person ($4 per family) donation is suggested (310-379-8117; www.roundhouseaquarium.org). Metered parking is available for $1 per hour. There are telescopes that offer terrific views of Palos Verdes and Catalina to the left and the northern beaches to the right. If you're lucky, you may even spot a dolphin or two.

Shopping

The streets within walking distance of downtown Manhattan Beach are treasure troves of eclectic shops and boutiques. Start at the intersection of Manhattan Beach Boulevard and Manhattan Avenue and walk a few blocks any direction and you'll find a great variety. The Manhattan Village Mall on Sepulveda Boulevard carries a mix of shops like Sephora, Macy's, and Pottery Barn and is just a short drive away.

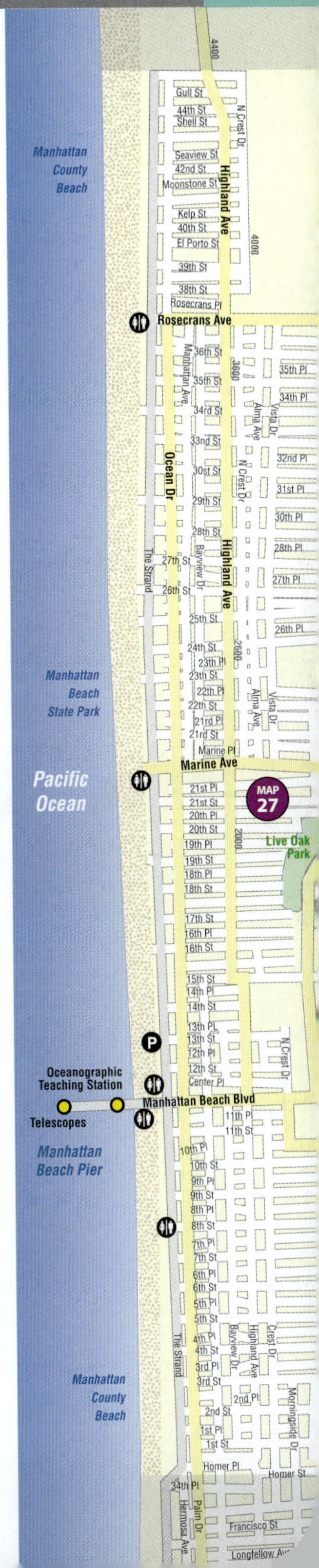

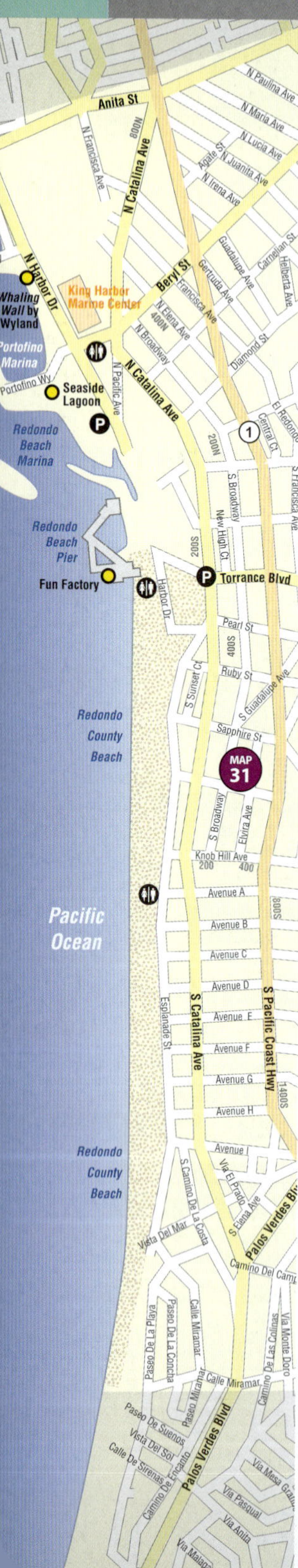

Overview

The Redondo Beach Harbor Enterprise occupies over 150 acres of land and water area, including the beach, parks, pier, boardwalk, and arcade. Redondo Beach may be a historic beach town, but it offers the most modern of amusements, from scuba diving to sport fishing. Because of the vast array of recreational activities it offers, Redondo Beach tends to be the most family-friendly of the South Bay beaches (which means the college kids head north to Hermosa, but you'll still find a share of shell-wearing surfer dudes). Famed environmental artist Wyland was so inspired by the natural beauty and sea life here that he created *"Whaling Wall 31"* in 1991—a spectacular mural that welcomes visitors on North Harbor Drive at Marina Way. From the beach, you get a beautiful view of the Palos Verdes Peninsula, and if you wait around until dusk, you'll be rewarded with a Southern Californian sunset that's so perfect, it might make you sick. For an up-to-date calendar of events, visit www.redondo.org.

Practicalities

Like most of the other South Bay beaches, Redondo is open daily during daylight hours. (You can still walk along the beach after sunset, but swimming is forbidden.) Between the pier parking structure (corner of Pacific Coast Hwy and Torrance Blvd) and the plaza parking structure (N Harbor Dr at Pacific Ave), you should have no trouble finding parking. Lots are open daily 11 am–7 pm, and charge $5 per day on weekdays and $7 per day on weekends during summer months. If you come during winter, you'll find that many things, including parking, are discounted. If you shop along the pier, be sure to validate your parking ticket. Metered street parking is also available, just make sure to keep it fed. Well-marked restrooms are located throughout the pier (and there's even one on the beach for bathers).

Sports

In addition to the usual beach activities of swimming, skating, and surfing, boating has gained quite a following in Redondo Beach. Whether you're launching your own or riding as a guest on an excursion boat, the Redondo Pier is a good departure point. The double-decked *Voyager* will take you on a 20- minute cruise of King's Harbor, the *Whaling Wall*, and the marinas. The *Voyager* is a good family activity, but the daredevils might prefer the *Ocean Racer* speedboat for a one-of-a-kind thrill ride. Avid anglers head out into the South Bay's waters for sport fishing opportunities, and cyclists speed to Redondo as a point of origin for LA County's 26-mile bike path that winds up the Pacific coast to Malibu.

Redondo Pier

The pier, boardwalk, and arcade together provide many dining options. The horseshoe-shaped pier holds a couple of upscale restaurants, but for less formal, fresh-from-the-ocean fare, head to any one of the great fish markets in the area (after all, Redondo Beach is known as the "seafood capital" of Southern California, and when in Rome…). Nestled next to the pier, the boardwalk is also stacked with restaurants, bars, and mostly tacky souvenir stores. Located under the pier, the Fun Factory is open seven days a week and features over 300 arcade and prize-redemption games, as well as a Tilt-A-Whirl and kiddie rides. Hours: Mon–Thurs 10am–10pm;Fri–Sat:10am–midnight; Sun: 10 am–10 pm. For more pier info, check out www.redondopier.com, or call 310-318-0631.

Seaside Lagoon

The Seaside Lagoon (200 Portofino Wy) is a saltwater lagoon, heated by a steam-generating plant, surrounded by man-made sunbathing beaches, beach volleyball courts, and a snack bar. The shallow lagoon is perfect for families—bring a picnic and spend the afternoon swimming under a lifeguard's watch. From 190th Street, go west toward the beach until the street ends, then turn left onto Harbor Drive, and proceed for about one mile. Parking is available at the Redondo Beach Marina and can be validated at the Lagoon. Admission costs $4.50 for adults and $3.25 for children ages 2–17. Hours: 10 am–5:45 pm, daily during the summer months. For more information, call 310-318-0681.

Shopping

When your interest in the shops along the pier and boardwalk begins to flag, check out Riviera Village. In South Redondo, between the Pacific Coast Highway and Catalina Avenue, south of Avenue 1, you'll find a bevy of unique boutiques, galleries, cafés, and restaurants.

Overview

Santa Monica Beach is the jewel in the crown of Los Angeles beaches. An offshore breakwater assures a gentle surf—good enough for neighborhood boogie boarders, novice surfers, and even the occasional pro in the everlasting search for that perfect wave. (For even better beginner waves, go to Manhattan Beach.) Aside from die-hard beach bums, Santa Monicans tend to stay away from the pier unless they're entertaining visitors. In 1909, the pier opened to an excited public and was a boom town of entertainment until the 1940s, when it experienced a bit of a mid-life crisis. The beloved structure was slated to be torn down after years of deterioration, but local residents rallied, and it was rebuilt in 1988. Film crews, photographers, and sun bunnies came flooding back, and today the place is buzzing with activity once again. Check out the Twilight Dance Series concerts on Thursday nights during the summer, featuring popular performers from a wide variety of musical genres. For more information, visit www.santamonicapier.org, www.santamonica.com, or call 310-319-6263.

Amusement Park

Located right on the Santa Monica Pier, Pacific Park Amusement Center is home to the nine-story Ferris Wheel, with a terrific view of the coastline and the city. Take a moonlit ride over the ocean on a summer night. The famous 1920s vintage carousel was featured in the Paul Newman/ Robert Redford movie *The Sting* and still costs just 25 cents for kids and 50 cents for adults. Other amusements include a fairly slow and uneventful rollercoaster, skeeball, air hockey, pinball, and video games. 310-260-8744; www.pacpark.com.

Camera Obscura

1450 Ocean Ave, 310-458-8644. Hours: Mon–Fri: 9 am–3 pm; Sat-Sun: 11am–3 pm;
Camera Obscura is another popular attraction. Entering the dark room on a sunny day, you can see images from the outside cast onto a table by a long-focus camera lens. The Camera Obscura—essentially a camera the size of a building—is in the Santa Monica Senior Recreation Center. Admission is free, just leave your driver's license at the Rec Center's office in exchange for the key. It may not be as exciting as the nearby ferris wheel, or as portable as your sleek, little digital camera, but it's definitely worth popping in.

Santa Monica Pier Aquarium

1600 Ocean Front Walk; 310-393-6149; www.healthebay.org/smpa.
Hours: Sat–Sun: 12:30pm-6 pm; Tues–Fri: 2 pm–6 pm
At the hands-on marine science aquarium, located underneath the carousel, exhibits focus on local sealife. Sea stars, crabs, snails, and sea urchins populate the touch tanks, but the shark tanks are strictly for eyes only. Suggested donation for admission is $5, but if you have no shame, you can pay as little as $2. Children under 12 enter free with an adult.

Practicalities

The parking lot on the north of the pier at 1550 PCH costs $5 weekdays and $7 weekends during the off-season, and $7 weekdays and $8 weekends during the summer months. There is metered parking along Ocean Avenue north and south of the pier. The visitor information stand is located on the corner of Ocean Avenue and Santa Monica Boulevard. You'll also find some rather grungy restrooms underneath and near the end of the pier.

Shopping

The best shopping in the area is two blocks east of Ocean Avenue along the Third Street Promenade. This three-block pedestrian mall is lined with restaurants, bars, movie theaters, and retail stores including everything from bookstores to swimwear shops. Venture a little south of the pier towards Main Street for more unique boutiques and restaurants. Le Sanctuaire is a fancy culinary boutique frequented by the professionals (2710 Main St, 310-581-8999); Splash Bath & Body sells scented soaps that you can smell a block away (2823 Main St, 310-581-4200); Blonde is the ultimate beach apparel boutique in a kitchy and fun setting (2430 Main St., 310-396-9113); and ZJ Boarding House supplies everything surf and snowboard-related (2619 Main St, 888-799-5646). Also check out Montana Avenue for more specialty shops and restaurants. Sample the best burger in LA at My Father's Office (1018 Montana Avenue, 310-393-2337); and don't miss the biannual Montana Avenue sidewalk sale held in early December and mid May every year.

Overview

Freaks, hippies, artists, and bohemians have been attracted to this stretch of oceanfront nuttiness since, well, the beginning. It was at Venice Beach that Jim Morrison and Ray Manzarek—old UCLA buddies—ran into each other in 1965 and decided to form The Doors. Venice Beach is also the famous backdrop of the 1970s roller-disco movie *Xanadu*, and the beach was home to legendary skateboarding crew the Z-Boys (as in, the guys in *Lords of Dogtown*). Nearby Venice High School, a Hollywood location favorite, substituted for Rydell High in *Grease* and was the set of Britney Spears's "Baby One More Time" video.

While some of the shops have acquired better paint jobs since Morrison's day, the funky attitude of the neighborhood still exists despite the influx of luxury lofts and the martini-and-Manolos crowd. The beach boardwalk is the place rock your bathing suit and flip flops, people-watch people watching you, and maybe pick up a steal (sometimes literally) from a wide-variety of non-commercial vendors. It's a chill, youth-friendly carnival melting pot replete with performance artists, psychics, bodybuilders, hand-in-hand couples, and people showing off their puppies. Step out to the beach to play volleyball, sunbathe, or perhaps brave the questionably clean LA bay for a surf or a swim. For hippies and people who don't mind them, the weekend sunset drum circles are a place to dance, play music, and celebrate the cosmic wonder of the end of another day in LA.

Practicalities

The beach area is closed nightly from 10 pm until 7 am. The main parking lot is located where North Venice intersects with Ocean Front Walk and is open 7 am to 8 pm weekdays ($5) and closes at 9 pm weekends ($6.50). Parking costs $3 before 9 am, but it goes up to $10 and up on summer weekends and holidays. If you're lucky and persistent, you might find free parking on the side streets. The area surrounding Venice Beach can get a bit seedy at night, so we don't recommend walking around alone after dark—unless that's your thing.

Sports

Considering its sunny seaside location, it comes as no surprise that Venice Beach is a hot spot for surfers, skaters, cyclists, and ballers. One of Venice Beach's main sporting attractions is world-famous Muscle Beach, which attracts an international set of weightlifters and spectators. For just five bucks, you can buy a day pass and pump iron with the best of them from 10 am to 6 pm, artificial enhancement not included (Venice Beach Recreation Center, 1800 Ocean Front Walk, 310-399-2775). The Recreation Center is also renowned for its high-level pick-up basketball and has popular paddle tennis and handball courts. Additionally, there is a roller rink, skate park, legal graffiti area, punching bag hookups, rings, parallel bars, and a climbing rope—in short, a monkey's paradise. Street vendors along the boardwalk rent out bikes and skates. The Redondo Beach bike path, which runs parallel to Venice Beach, is a perfect place to try out your rented wheels.

Venice Pier

The pier is open daily from 5 am to 10 pm, and the parking lot is located at Washington Boulevard & Ocean Front Walk. A popular spot for anglers, the pier is looking more sturdy than ever after recent renovations. Despite the abundance of locals fishing, be weary. In these parts the "catch of the day" may come with a mandatory tetanus shot. Parking costs $5 weekdays and $6.50 weekends. Restrooms are available on the pier, not off of it.

Shopping

From cheap t-shirts and sunglasses, 'tobacco' pipes and tattoos, to fancy surfboards and negotiable jewelry, Venice Beach offers quite a range of shopping opportunities in a unique bohemian environment. In addition to the shops and vendors along the boardwalk, one can also venture a few blocks inland to Abbot Kinney Boulevard (just east of Main St & Brooks Ave) for a beachtown stretch of art galleries and hipster shops. Every May over 60 area art galleries open up their studios to the public for the annual Venice Art Walk (www.venicefamilyclinic.org).

Overview

In 1978, idyllic Zuma Beach was the setting for an eponymous made-for-TV movie starring Suzanne Somers (also featuring Rosanna Arquette and Delta Burke). The premise involved an aging rocker who moved to the beach to try and "get away from it all," but who instead became wrapped up in the lives of beach-going teens. Though today old rockers opt to escape behind the high walls of their private beachfront compounds, the clean waters and mile-long stretch of broad, sandy beach still attract Malibu High students and a laid-back, local crowd of surfers, families, young beach bums, and sun-worshipers.

Getting to Zuma means taking a beautifully scenic drive along the Pacific Coast Highway—speaking of rock star compounds, you'll drive by Cher's on the way up. The beach is a 30-minute drive north from Santa Monica on a good day, so avoid the nightmarish weekend traffic on the PCH (especially in the summer) and get an early start.

Practicalities

The parking lot is open from 7 am to 7 pm daily and costs $4.75 to park in the winter, $6 in the summer. The lot has more than 2,000 spaces, but there's also plenty of free parking along the west side of the PCH. Be forewarned that a temperamental marine layer may not burn off until the early afternoon, if at all on some days, and the beach is often windy, so check the weather first and don't forget a cover-up. You may also want to pack some snacks before you head out, though there's a fast food stand near the volleyball courts and a small market across the highway. Get an early start if heading up to Malibu to avoid traffic and claim a good parking and beach spot.

Restrooms

Your typical beach-level of cleanliness should be expected in these restrooms, which also have showers and child-sized toilet stalls with walls so low you can peer over to your neighbor.

Sports

The wide, flat stretch of sand between lifeguard towers 6 and 7 features volleyball courts. The waves in this area can be strong enough for body surfing as well as board surfing. In other areas, visitors are allowed to fish and dive, though hopefully not in the same spot. For the kids, there's a swing set.

Surfing Beaches

Zuma's water is divided for surfers and swimmers, so one doesn't crash into the other. Malibu's coast is covered with more than 20 beaches and secret surfing spots. For experienced surfers, body surfers, and body boarders, a couple of good surfing beaches to the north of Zuma include Leo Carrillo and Nicholas Canyon Beach. The latter, known locally as Zero Beach, offers picnic tables, shore fishing, and plenty of parking. To the south, test the waters around Point Dume, or head straight for Surfrider, one of the most famous surfing beaches in the world. Located at the Malibu Pier, this surf spot's no secret, so if everyone's dropping in on your waves during summer months, you may have to hightail it or settle for volleyball. Check the LA County Coastal Monitoring Network for current weather and surf conditions (www.watchthewater.org/beach.cfm?bid=19).

Overview

Think of Marina Del Rey as Venice Beach's more conservative step-sibling. Just south of its flamboyant relative, Marina Del Rey is a cross between upscale condominium living at its finest and commercialized areas for tourists and locals alike. This man-made marina (one of the world's largest) is capable of sheltering over 5,000 sea-faring vessels and stands as a gateway to the Pacific for recreational and commercial vehicles. If you're looking to go out into the water in a boat, you can find it all here: charter a yacht, go for a brunch or dinner cruise, or spend the day whale watching. If you don't mind breaking out into a little sweat, get your own pedal boat or kayak to explore the waters. Amenities for boaters include beach-launching for small boats, a launch ramp for trailered boats, a sailing basin for boats and windsurfers, dry dock storage, a Sea Scout base, repair yards, fuel dock, pump-out stations, boat brokerages, and charter businesses. Visit www.beaches.co.la.ca.us or www.visitthemarina.com for more information on what the marina has to offer.

Most days throughout the year you'll find the weather warm enough to stop off at Burton Chace Park for a picnic. If you want to save a few coins, go during the week when you can park for free. It's usually quiet here, but during major holidays like the Fourth of July, you can find a pretty good crowd. You'll have to drop some extra bills, but it's worth it to grab dinner at Jer-ne (4375 Admiralty Wy, 310-823-1700) inside The Ritz-Carlton and take in the amazing view of the marina while you're there. Hit Baja Cantina for cheap and tasty grub and some great scoping and socializing on the patio (311 Washington Blvd. 310-821-2252). Fisherman's Village is a bit like hanging out at another spot tailor-made for tourists, but come see the live music and check out the breathtaking water view. You'll find kayaks, jet skis, ice cream, smoothies, free live concerts on the weekends, and, if you're here in early December, the annual Holiday Boat Parade.

Harbor Info

The entrance to the marina is situated between two jetties (north and south) that sit inside the breakwater that runs parallel to the shore. The north and south ends of the breakwater and the ends of both jetties are marked with lights that can be distinguished by their color and length between flashes: North Breakwater Light, 1 WHITE flash every six seconds; South Breakwater Light, 2 RED flashes every six seconds; North Jetty Light, 3 WHITE flashes every five seconds; South Jetty Light, 4 RED flashes every four seconds.

Practicalities

Located in the Santa Monica Bay 15 miles southwest of downtown LA, Marina Del Rey can be easily accessed from the 405 and the 90 freeways. Daily parking rates vary in the 15 lots surrounding the marina; however the lowest one can expect to pay is $5 for cars, and $7 for cars with boats in tow. Limited free parking is also available on Dock 52. If you plan on parking overnight, you will need to make arrangements with the harbormaster/sheriff's department beforehand (310-823-7762). There are also 18 metered boat washdown spaces, which cost 50 cents for three minutes (requires quarters). Restrooms are located at Fisherman's Village, near Mother's Beach, and next to the launch ramp.

Launch Ramp & Fuel Dock

Small, hand-carried vessels such as kayaks and tin boats are easily launched at the public beach in Basin D, also known as Mother's Beach because of the absence of surf, making it an ideal swimming beach for children. For larger vessels, there is a public launch ramp at the head of the first finger at Mindanao Way on the east side of the channel. The eight-lane ramp can get very busy, especially on the weekends and during summer months, so be prepared to wait. The fee is $7, and includes one launch, recovery, and 24-hour parking for your car. The fuel dock is located on the west side of the channel just inside the bend.

Guest Slips

The Los Angeles County Department of Beaches and Harbors offers boat slips to guests near Burton Chace Park. There is a free 4-hour tie-up dock between the H and G basins on the east side of the main channel, and overnight docking (for up to 7 days within a 30 day period) can be arranged at the Community Building in the park at a cost of 50 cents per foot per night. To obtain an overnight slip, you will need to produce your registration papers and identification. Overnight facilities include electricity, water, showers, and restrooms. If you are a yacht club member, try contacting the yacht clubs in the area to see if they offer reciprocal guest slips.

Harbor Patrol & Anchorage

The Harbor Patrol is run by the Los Angeles County Sheriff's Department and located on the east side of the main channel. They are on call 24 hours a day and can be reached on Channel 16, with 12 as the working channel (310-823-7762). During storms or other emergencies, anchoring is permitted in the north end of the entrance channel.

No Boat?

If you don't have your own water craft, several commercial boating companies leave from Dock 52 and provide all of the gear you will need for a great day of fishing, including rods, reels, and bait. If pier fishing is more your style, head down Fiji Way to Fisherman's Village and throw a line in from the docks.

Overview

The south-facing bay and nearby offshore breakwaters make Long Beach Marina one of the calmest and most popular boat mooring spots in Southern California. It ranks low on the snob-scale, too, making it a much better bet than its sister to the north, Marina Del Rey. The protected enclave and the idyllic boating conditions make sailing the number-one recreational activity in Long Beach, home of the Congressional Cup, Transpac, and the Olympic trial races. The 3,800-slip marina is run by the City of Long Beach and includes Alamitos Bay Marina (562-570-3215), Long Beach Shoreline Marina (562-570-4950), and Rainbow Harbor/Rainbow Marina (562-570-8636).

Practicalities

Daily parking is available near the marina. Boaters who wish to park in the launch parking lot for more than 24 hours need to visit the Alamitos Bay office and pay for a parking pass in advance.

Launch Ramps & Fuel Docks

Five separate launch ramps serve the Long Beach Marina population. The Granada Launch Ramp (Granada Ave and Ocean Blvd) and the Claremont Launch Ramp (Claremont and Ocean Blvds) are sand launches exclusively for small sailing vessels. Water skiers and larger vessels looking to get in the water need look no further than Marine Stadium (Appian Wy between 2nd and Colorado Aves). Boats in the stadium must be under 20 feet long, have a reverse gear, and travel counter-clockwise within the stadium. Davies Ramp, across from Marine Stadium, is the only launch open 24 hours a day. And last but not least, the South Shore Launch Ramp is a small boat launch ramp near the Queen Mary on Queensway Drive. All launch ramps cost $10 and are open year-round, usually from 8 am until dusk. For more information, call 562-570-8636.

Long Beach has two fuel docks—one in Downtown Shoreline Marina (562-436-4430) and one in Alamitos Bay (562-594-0888). The Alamitos fuel dock stocks propane, snacks, beer, ice, and frozen bait, along with gas and diesel fuels. The smaller Downtown Marine fuel dock features gas, CNG, and limited sundries. Both docks accept credit cards or cash. Fuel dock hours (May 31–Labor Day): Mon–Fri: 8 am–5 pm; Sat–Sun: 7 am–6 pm.

Guest Slips

Guest moorings can be rented year-round for 60¢ per foot per night. While it's always best to call ahead, it's only on holiday weekends that reservations are required (with 3,000 slips for rent, you can usually find a spot at short notice on weeknights).

Patrols

The Harbor Patrol looks after the water, while the Marine Patrol guards the land. All Lifeguard/Harbor Patrol boats are run by trained, professional lifeguards and are also equipped for emergencies such as fire, capsized boats, or pump-outs. If you need your boat towed, the Harbor Patrol/Rescue Boats will always oblige, but if it's not an emergency, they'll charge you for the towing.

No Boat?

If you're on a budget but you still want a piece of the action, check out the Belmont Pier at Ocean Boulevard and 39th Place, which offers free public fishing. No license is required as long as you stay on the pier (562-434-1542). If you decide to fish from the beach or the jetties, you'll need a salt-water fishing license. If you get tired of the salt and sand, you might opt for the Belmont Plaza Olympic Pool (4000 Olympic Plaza Dr, 562-570-1805), or grab a pint and a bite at the Belmont Brewing Company (25 39th Pl, 562-433-3891) on the pier. There are often events held along the shoreline that people enjoy from their boats, such as the Long Beach Jazz Festival. Unfortunately, there's no swimming allowed at the marina.

Overview

The wind known as "Hurricane Gulch" coming from Point Fermin into an area just outside the Cabrillo Marina provides first-rate sailing and windsurfing weather year-round. The 885 slips, friendly staff, and abundant amenities make this a pleasant marina to dock in for a few days. It's also the closest marina to Catalina (19.4 miles). For others, it's also a great place to run and bike, with waterfront restaurants for a quiet lunch or dinner and shopping available. Check out the marina's website at www.cymcabrillo.com or call the dockmaster at 310-732-2252. Keep your eyes open for Pedro's legendary Mike Watt; it is rumored he kayaks with pelicans every morning in the harbor.

Practicalities

Cabrillo Marina is easy to reach—just a shout from LA Airport. From the 405 or the I-5, take the 110 S and exit at Harbor Boulevard. There is plenty of free parking at the Cabrillo Marina and facilities include restrooms, laundry, water, electricity, showers, and lockers.

Launch Ramp & Fuel Dock

Run by the LA County Department of Recreation and Parks, the boat ramp is open 24 hours a day and has nearby space for trailer parking and boat washing, as well as restroom facilities. You will find fuel at the Cabrillo Marine Fuel Dock, which is located at Berth 31, 210 Whalers Walk.

Harbor Info

The breakwater entrance to the western end of San Pedro Bay is marked by the Los Angeles Harbor Lighthouse (33°42.5'N-118°15.0'W), also known as Angel's Gate. This marina has a lot of traffic, including huge ships and other commercial vehicles, so boat owners should study their charts in order to navigate the waters appropriately.

Guest Slips

Guest end-ties are available for overnight docking for boats up to 55 feet long for up to three days. Four mooring buoys are offered in the inner harbor for vessels up to 40 feet long, and in the outer harbor 14 mooring buoys are available for boats up to 50 feet long. However, overnight mooring is not permitted.

Harbor Patrol

The Port Warden and staff of the Los Angeles Harbor Department monitor the harbor. They are located at 425 S Palos Verdes Street, San Pedro.

No Boat?

Fishing is permitted from the Cabrillo Pier. During grunion season, the silvery fish emerge twice a month, like clockwork, to lay their eggs under a full or new moon. During part of the season, it is legal to catch these fish—but only by hand! If you want to participate you will need to take a flashlight. If you don't fancy getting wet, it's almost as much fun to watch—especially the people who try to lure them in by singing Barry White songs. The Cabrillo Marine Aquarium (3720 Stephen M. White Dr), a delightful way to spend a few hours with the kids, is nearby and free (with a suggested donation of $5 for adults and $1 for children and seniors). Visit www.cabrilloaq.org or call 310-548-7562 for more information. The 22nd Street Landing houses fishing and diving boats that can be taken out for half, 3/4, or full-day excursions of diving and deep-sea fishing. Whale-watching tours are also available. The beach and bathhouse are also enjoyable playgrounds.

Overview

Redondo Beach sits south of the communities of Manhattan Beach and Hermosa Beach, part of the South Bay beach communities. A home to families who make a comfortable living for themselves, Redondo Beach is a land by the sea with all the elements of fun in the sun, but less of the flash and pretense. It has four marinas—King Harbor, Port Royal, Portofino, and Redondo Beach—and over 1,400 boat slips. The marinas host seasonal activities, such as whale-watching in January, the annual Super Bowl Sunday 10K Run in February (with a beer garden at the finish line), and the Bayou Bash and Crawfish Boil, complete with music straight from New Orleans, in May. For those of you who just can't get enough seafood and fanfare, head out here in the fall for the Annual Redondo Beach Lobster Festival for live music, wacky seafood paraphernalia, carnival games, and, of course, more lobster than you'd care to eat. Between sailing, kayaking, and enjoying a seafood dinner by the water, let's just say there are worse things in life than having to spend a week at Redondo Beach.

Practicalities

The marina provides several double-spaced parking spots for vehicles with boat trailers. If you're hoping for a space during the summer months, you better head out early—the place gets mobbed. Expect to pay between $3 and $7 per day for parking, depending on the season and location.

Boat Hoist & Fuel Docks

Unlike most other marinas, the Redondo Beach Marina has a boat hoist instead of a launch ramp. Skilled hoist operators launch boats mechanically via slings using two five-ton hoists, which can lift boats up to 10,000 pounds and 30 feet long. Round-trip hoist fees are $8 for a hand-launch size boat, $18 for personal watercraft, $30 for boats 18-24 feet long, and $40 for boats over 25 feet long. Reservations are not needed. Locals with proof of boat registration can obtain boat hoist coupons from City Hall for $7.50. If you're launching a boat by hand, you'll want to go behind Seaside Lagoon, via the Redondo Beach Marina parking lot, or by Portofino Way.

Fuel docks are located at the commercial basin and across from the Harbor Patrol office.

Boat Hoist Regular Hours: Mon–Fri: 7 am–5 pm; Sat–Sun: 6 am–6 pm. Extended summer hours—6 am–6 pm on weekdays and 6 am–8 pm on weekends—begin Memorial Day weekend. For more information, visit www.rbmarina.com.

...Two If By Sea

If you're coming in from the water, use the lighted buoy to the SSW of the exterior jetty to guide you into the marina. The entrance is at the south end of the harbor, between two lighted jetties.

Guest Slips

King Harbor Marina (208 Yacht Club Wy, 310-376-6926) and the Redondo Beach Yacht Club both offer guest boat slips and docking accommodations. Boat slips come fully equipped with storage lockers, cable TV and phone hook-ups, laundry facilities, and plenty of parking.

Harbor Patrol

The Harbor Patrol office is located at the west end of Marina Way, adjacent to Moonstone Park. If you need them call 310-318-0632.

No Boat?

No worries! You can hire fishing rods, tackle, bait, and a salt water fishing license right on the Redondo Sport Fishing Pier. If you prefer being out on the water, fishing trips range from $32 ($27 kids) for a half-day to $650 for a ten-person charter boat for the day. For something a little racier, try sailing classes (310-937-3180) or a high-speed tour of the coast on the *Ocean Racer* (310-374-3481).

Restrooms

Restrooms are located in and around the harbor, on the Pier, and along the beach areas.

Redondo Beach Pier

The Redondo Beach Pier has a host of dining spots, a few bars, many touristy shops, and an arcade. If nothing else, you'll get a semi decent meal and find some places to pass the time. You can park at the Pier Parking Structure (100 W Torrance Blvd) south of the Boardwalk or the Plaza Parking Structure (180 N Harbor Dr) north of the Boardwalk. There's metered parking as well in the area. For seafood, try Oceanside Seafood (100-F Fishermans Wharf) and then make a stop at the Pier Bakery (100-M Fishermans Wharf) for fresh churros. Then you can browse through places like the Sunshine Kite Company and Shark Attack to round out your pier experience.

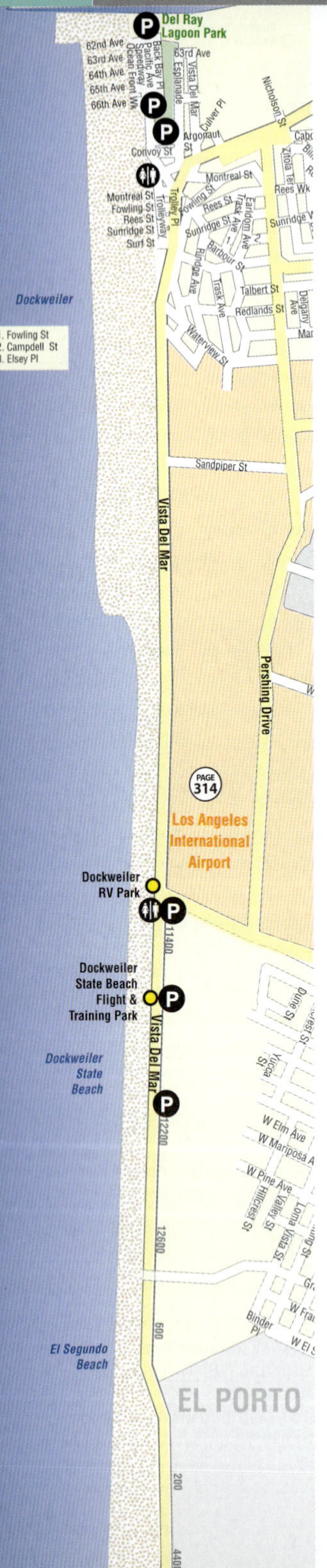

Overview

Dockweiler State Beach isn't the fanciest, most happening strip of sand in Los Angeles, but it's got a thing or two to give it some merit. This beach is part of the communities of Playa del Rey and El Segundo—two areas away from the freeways and hustle-n-bustle of the city that can almost make you forget you're in LA with their neighborhood-y vibe. Both mostly residential, Playa Del Rey and El Segundo are quiet seaside communities (well, except for the airplanes overhead) with a sprinkling of shops and a fair share of local restaurants. If you're hungry and want to bring a snack to the sand, try Beach Pizza in Playa Del Rey for a relatively inexpensive meal.

The beach starts by Ballona Creek, where you can set your sights on the yachts of Marina Del Rey across the way, and the beach ends three miles south at El Segundo. At this end of Dockweiler, if you catch a whiff of something awful, it's probably coming from the nearby Hyperion Wastewater Treatment Plant. The ocean breeze will help temper the smell a bit, but once in a while there's not much you can do about the stench. The Los Angeles Department of Beaches and Harbors has a website with some pretty basic information about Dockweiler. Visit http://beaches.co.la.ca.us/BandH/Beaches/Dockweiler.htm if you feel like taking a look.

Practicalities

Dockweiler is open daily from 7 am until 10 pm. On most days, especially when the weather is mediocre, you can find parking pretty easily in one of the lots along the beach or on the street. Playa Del Rey has one lot with a fee (a quarter for every fifteen minutes) at the end of Pacific Avenue and one free lot further south on Pacific Avenue. There's also a free lot by the playground off of Esplanade Street. El Segundo has two lots with fees on Vista Del Mar with entrances near the Imperial Highway. Lifeguard towers are manned on both sides of the beach, and this is also one of the few beaches in the LA area (Cabrillo Beach is the other one) where you can have a bonfire. Go to the area near El Segundo if you want to sit next to a fire pit. If you're hungry and can't bear to leave the seaside, stop off at the RC Grill, a concession stand located just north of Imperial Highway. On occasion, a hot dog vendor parks his cart in Playa Del Rey near the parking lot at the end of Pacific Avenue.

Restrooms

One set of public restrooms is located on the Playa Del Rey side of the beach and one set of restrooms is located at the El Segundo area. They are generally kept pretty clean, but as with all public restrooms, sometimes you have to lower your expectations juuust a bit.

Sports

You won't find a ton of amenities for sports out here, but you can expect to get a good game of volleyball going, and folks do occasionally surf or boogie board as well. The bike path tends to have light traffic passing through this part of the beach. When the sun's out, you'll find roller bladers and bikers making their way from Santa Monica to Manhattan Beach and back. There's also a hang gliding facility called the Dockweiler State Beach Flight Training Park that is perfect for beginners since the bluff isn't too steep and you have a nice patch of sand to cushion your landing. Windsports runs the program and offers a beginning lesson for $120. You can call 818-367-2430 for more information. The closest parking lot is located off Vista Del Mar just south of Imperial Highway. Expect to pay $2 from 6 am to 9 am, $5 from 9 am to 5 pm, and $2 from 5 pm to closing. The lot directly off of West Imperial Highway has a flat fee of $5 per day.

Dockweiler RV Park

One big draw to Dockweiler for out-of-towners is the RV Park. The unique thing about this place is that it's right on the beach. You'll find everything you need here, including hot showers, picnic tables, barbecue pits, RV spaces with hook-ups, dump stations, and a laundromat. Depending on the season and which space you get, expect to pay $24–32 per day to park your recreational vehicle. For an extra fee of two dollars per day, you can bring your pet, too. Make your reservations far in advance since this is a popular spot—you can reserve up to three months ahead of time by calling the office at 800-950-7275, Monday through Friday from 8 am–4 pm. Drive to 12001 Vista Del Mar and enter the park off of West Imperial Highway.

If you find yourself in the area for a summer swim at midnight, go to Main and Imperial in El Segundo for a late-night snack. There are a few 24 hour doughnut shops that cater to the late-night airport workers.

City of LA Tennis Courts

The city of Los Angeles runs two types of public tennis courts: Open Play courts, like the excellent ones at the **Mar Vista Recreation Center (Map 22)**, which are free and available on a first-come, first-served basis, and Reservation/Pay Tennis, like the **Cheviot Hills Recreation Center (Map 23)** courts, where hourly fees apply per court and reservations are required. Courts cost $5 per hour weekdays from 7 am until 4 pm, and $8 per hour all other times—$10 per hour/per court if you're booking tournaments. You must have a reservation card to reserve a court, and be aware they'll charge you $3 per "incident" if you don't show. Call (323) 644-3536 to purchase a reservation card, which runs $15 for residents and $30 for nonresidents and is good for one year. To reserve a court, call (213) 625-1010 and follow the verbal prompts or call (323) 644-3536. Hours vary depending on facility and date. Consult www.laparks.org/dos/sports/tennis/paytennis.htm or call Los Angeles Parks and Recreation at 323-586-6543 or 213-738-2965.

Tennis	*Address*	*Phone*	*Type of Court*	*No. of Courts*	*Map*
Griffith-Vermont Canyon	2715 Vermont Cyn	326-664-3521	Reservation / Pay	12, Unlit	4
Peck Park Community Center	560 N Western Ave	310-548-7580	Open Play / Free		4
Echo Park Rec	1632 Bellevue Ave	213-250-3578	Open Play / Free		5
Elysian Park Therapeutic	929 Academy Dr	323-226-1402	Open Play / Free		5
Riverside	3401 Riverside Dr	332-906-7953	Reservation / Pay	12	5
Queen Anne Rec Center	1240 West Blvd	323-857-1180	Open Play / Free		7
Lafayette Community Center	625 S Lafayette Pk Pl	213-387-9426	Open Play / Free		8
Shatto Rec Center	3191 W 4th St	213-386-8877	Open Play / Free		8
Daniels Field Sports Center	845 W 12th St	310-548-7728	Open Play / Free		9
Arthur Ashe Center	5001 Rodeo Rd	323-290-3141	Open Play / Free		10
Jim Gilliam Rec Center	4000 S La Brea Ave	323-291-5928	Open Play / Free		10
Loren Miller Rec Center	2717 Halldale Ave	323-734-1302	Open Play / Free		11
Van Ness Rec Center	5720 2nd Ave	323-296-1559	Open Play / Free		11
Ross Snyder Rec Center	1501 E 41st St	323-231-3964	Open Play / Free		12
South Park	345 E 51st St	213-847-6746	Open Play / Free		12
Ladera Park	6027 Ladera Park Ave	310-217-8361	LA County Tennis Courts		13
Algin Sutton Rec Center	8800 S Hoover St	323-753-5808	Open Play / Free		14
Harvard Rec Center	1535 W 62nd St	323-778-2579	Open Play / Free		14
Jesse Owens Park	9651 S Western Ave	323-241-6704	LA County Tennis Courts		14
St Andrews Rec Center	8701 S St Andrews Pl	213-485-1751	Open Play / Free		14
Pacific Palisades	851 Alma Real Dr	310-454-1412	Reservation / Pay	8	15
Rustic Canyon Rec Center	601 Latimer Rd	310-454-5734	Open Play / Free		15
Barrington Rec Center	333 S Barrington Ave	310-476-4866	Open Play / Free		16
Stoner Rec Center	1835 Stoner Ave	310-479-7200	Open Play / Free		19
Westwood	1350 Sepulveda Blvd	310-575-8299	Reservation / Pay	8	19
Oakwood Rec Center	767 California St	310-452-7479	Open Play / Free		21
Penmar Rec Center	1341 Lake St	310-396-8735	Open Play / Free		21
Glen Alla Park	4601 Alla Rd	310-396-1615	Open Play / Free		22
Mar Vista Rec Center	11430 Woodbine St	310-398-5982	Open Play / Free		22
Cheviot Hills	2551 Motor Ave	310-836-8879	Reservation / Pay	14	23
Westchester	7000 W Manchester Ave	310-649-4886	Reservation / Pay	8	26
Eagle Rock Rec Center	1100 Eagle Vista Dr	323-257-6948	Open Play / Free	Unlit	33
Yosemite Rec Center	1840 Yosemite Dr	323-257-1644	Open Play / Free		33
Glassell Park Rec Center	3650 Verdugo Rd	323-257-1863	Open Play / Free		36
Sycamore Grove Park	4702 N Figueroa St	323-225-0370	Open Play / Free		36
Montecito Heights Rec Center	4545 Homer St	213-485-5148	Open Play / Free		37
Arroyo Seco Park	5568 Via Marisol St	323-255-0370	Open Play / Free		38
El Sereno Rec Center	4721 Klamath Pl	323-225-3517	Open Play / Free		38
Aliso Pico Rec Center	370 S Clarence St	323-264-5261	Open Play / Free		40
Hazard Rec Center	2230 Norfolk St	213-485-6839	Open Play / Free		40
Hollenbeck Rec Center	415 S St Louis St	323-261-0113	Open Play / Free		40
Lincoln Park Rec Center	3501 Valley Blvd	213-847-1726	Open Play / Free		40
Belvedere Park	4914 E Cesar E Chavez Ave	323-260-2342	LA County Tennis Courts		41
City Terrace Park	1126 N Hazard Ave	323-260-2371	LA County Tennis Courts		41
Ruben F Salazar Park	3863 Whittier Blvd	323-260-2330	LA County Tennis Courts		41
Balboa	5651 Balboa Blvd	818-995-6570	Reservation / Pay	16	46
Reseda Rec Center	18411 Victory Blvd	818-881-3882	Open Play / Free		46
Van Nuys Rec Center	14301 Vanowen St	818-756-8131	Open Play / Free		47
Valley Plaza Rec Center	12240 Archwood St	818-765-5885	Open Play / Free		48
Victory-Vineland Rec Center	11112 Victory Blvd	818-985-9516	Open Play / Free		48
Studio City Rec Center	12621 Rye St	818-769-4415	Open Play / Free		51
Encino Park	16953 Ventura Blvd	818-995-1690	Open Play / Free		53
Van Nuys/Sherman Oaks	14201 Huston St	818-756-8223	Reservation / Pay	8	55
North Hollywood Rec Center	5301 Tujunga Ave	818-763-7651	Open Play / Free		56

Angeles National Forest
Switzer Falls
Eaton Canyon Falls
To Chantry Sturtevant
Van Nuys Airport
Sepulveda Dam Recreation Area
Burbank Airport
PAGE 316
MAP 56
Universal Studios
PAGE 262
Wilacre Park
Griffith Park
PAGE 246
Mt Lee
Ferndell/ Mt Hollywood
Dante's View
Runyon Canyon Park
MAP 2
Topanga State Park
PAGE 264
Mandeville Canyon
UCLA
PAGE 245
Elysian Park
Dodger Stadium
Will Rogers State Park
MAP 15
Temescal Canyon
To Malibu
Will Rogers State Beach
Santa Monica Municipal Airport
MAP 10
PAGE 273
Santa Monica Beach
Kenneth Hahn State Recreation Area
← To Point Dume State Beach
← To Malibu Creek State Park
PAGE 280
LAX
PAGE 314
Dockweiler State Beach
Manhattan Beach
PAGE 271
Redondo Beach
PAGE 272
PAGE 318
Long Beach Airport
Torrance Municipal Airport
Pacific Ocean

Overview

A week of bumper-to-bumper commuting will no doubt leave you desperate to escape the concrete jungle of LA. Angelenos enjoy a surprising number of great local hikes year-round, thanks to the city's average temperature of 70 degrees. And they do—if only to show off their designer sneaks or brag about an Orlando Bloom dog-walking sighting. Whether it's a casual jaunt through Runyon Canyon or an epic mountain trek in the Angeles National Forest, you're sure to find a hike that fits your ability and fitness level—just try to ignore the traffic on the drive to the trailhead.

Afoot and Afield in Los Angeles County by Jerry Schad (Wilderness Press) is an excellent resource, covering a total of 192 hikes accompanied by detailed maps. If you want to test out new terrain and make new friends, the Sierra Club organizes hikes throughout the city that range in difficulty and cater to a variety of special interests (www.angeles.sierraclub.org). Below you'll find a handful of hikes that come with our highest endorsement. Happy trails!

West Hollywood

Runyon Canyon Park

This is the perfect early-morning or after-work hike, as it's less than two miles and can be completed in an less than an hour. If the main path isn't enough of a workout for you, veer left just after the gates near the Vista entrance for a more challenging uphill climb. Runyon Canyon's no-leash western trail makes it a favorite for pooch owners, and the dog park at the base means an abundance of four-legged hikers. You might also see a downward dog or two at one of the free yoga classes that take place Monday through Thursday inside the park. Enter Runyon from either Fuller Street or Vista Street just north of Franklin Avenue, or try the northern trail options by entering from Mulholland Drive. Parking is available on neighboring streets, but check the signs for restrictions. www.runyon-canyon.com, 323-666-5046.

Griffith Park

Ferndell/Mt Hollywood

The relatively flat terrain of Ferndell makes it a popular choice for family hikes, and the rich plant life means that the area is almost always bathed in shade. Enter Griffith Park from Los Feliz Boulevard by turning left at Ferndell Drive. Enter at the beginning of the trail in Ferndell at the bottom entrance to Griffith Park, or cut your hike in half by entering at the north end of the Griffith Observatory parking lot at the Charlie Turner trailhead. The top of Mt. Hollywood is the reward, and—on a clear day—offers stunning views of the Pacific Ocean and the great urban sprawl.

Mount Lee (a.k.a. the Hollywood Sign)

While many a struggling actor toils for years to climb to the top in Hollywood, this trail is a sure thing. Drive up Beachwood Canyon to Hollyridge Drive. Hollyridge Trail will take you up to the summit of Mount Lee, where you can look down on the letters of the 450-foot-long Hollywood sign and enjoy 360-degree views of the LA basin and the San Fernando Valley. Enjoy it while it lasts—success in Hollywood is fleeting, and so are the smog-free views. The round trip is approximately three miles. Parking is free.

Dante's View

Unfortunately, this beautiful garden was destroyed in the May 2007 fire that swept through Griffin Park.

Baldwin Hills

Kenneth Hahn State Recreation Area

Located at 4100 South La Cienega Boulevard, Kenneth Hahn State Recreation Area features more than seven miles of trails for hiking from the Bowl Loop (just 0.8 miles) to the 2.6-mile Ridge Trail.

Pacific Palisades

Will Rogers State Park

The most popular walk in this park, located just north of Sunset Boulevard, is to the idyllic Inspiration Point. The hike is easy—almost too easy—and can be completed in one hour, round-trip. The view to Catalina on a clear day is lovely and makes for a nice change of pace. For a tougher challenge, go for the Backbone Trail, leading into the Santa Monica mountains up to Point Mugu. The trails at Will Rogers are open to hikers, mountain bikers, and horseback riders.

Temescal Canyon

Head north at the intersection of Sunset Boulevard and Temescal Canyon Road and park at Temescal Gateway Park. Once inside, you have two options—Canyon trail or Ridge trail. Be sure to follow the trail markers for the appropriately named Skull Rock, this hike's must-see. At approximately four miles round-trip, this hike is moderately difficult and takes about 2.5 hours.

Brentwood

Mandeville Canyon

The hike, which can be completed in less than two hours, begins with challenging, hilly terrain, but levels off after a bit. From Sunset Boulevard, go north on Mandeville Canyon Road until you reach Garden Land Road and find street parking. A fire road takes you to the Nike Missile Site, which has been turned into a park with restrooms and drink machines.

Pasadena/San Gabriel Valley

Chantry Flat/Sturtevant Falls

These waterfalls in Angeles National Forest are breathtaking, close to LA, and just a three-mile hike up a mountain—i.e. totally within reach. The hike to the falls passes private cabins nestled in the woods that look like something out of a fairy tale. Take the 210 to Santa Anita Avenue and head north. Follow the road up the mountain and use the parking lot at Chantry Flat. The whole trip can be completed in 90 minutes.

Eaton Canyon Falls

The Eaton Canyon Falls hike also leads to a waterfall, and it's especially friendly to dogs (on leashes) and kids because of its relatively flat terrain. The trail crosses over a creek several times during the 2-mile round trip, so you may get wet—dress accordingly and watch your footing. Exit the 210 at Altadena and travel north to the Eaton Canyon Natural Area (just past New York Drive).

Switzer Falls

This is not a difficult hike (roughly 4.5 miles round-trip, depending on how far afield you venture), but hopping over rock bridges and fallen logs while wading in the clear, cool waters takes some maneuvering. At the intersection with Bear Canyon, you can travel up the canyon for awesome views before doubling back. The sound of rushing waterfalls will stay with you long after you've returned to civilization. From the 210 Freeway in La Canada, follow 2 N (Angeles Crest Hwy) for ten miles into the Angeles National Forest. Stop at the Visitor Center at the intersection of Angeles Crest and Angeles Forest Highways to pick up your $5 day pass and map. Then continue on Angeles Crest for about a quarter mile to the Switzer Picnic Area, driving down to the parking lot near the stream. Stop for a sandwich or throw a burger on one of the grills before your trek toward Switzer Falls.

Studio City

Wilacre Park

This short and intense hike (2.7 hilly miles) can be finished in about an hour and is another great walk to save for the end of the day (especially in the hot summer months) or to do with a canine friend (only if leashed, unfortunately). Park ($1) in the gravel lot at the corner of Laurel Canyon Boulevard and Fryman Road and travel up the Dearing Mountain Trail. You'll emerge from the canyon in the midst of a residential neighborhood, on Iredell Lane. Follow this street back out to Fryman Road and turn left to return to the parking lot.

Malibu

Malibu Creek State Park

This 10,000-acre park offers horseback riding, camping, fishing, swimming, and, of course, hiking. The trail will take you on a moderately challenging 3.5-mile hike along gurgling creeks, past swimming holes, and to the spot where *M*A*S*H* was filmed. When you reach the fork in the road, hang a left toward the Visitor Center and follow signs to Rock Pool, a swimming hole popular with families and the site of the *Planet of the Apes* climbing rock. Retrace your steps back to the fork and turn left (away from the Visitor Center) to continue on the wild-flower-studded Crags Road trail. When you cross the creek, turn left to explore the marshy Century Lake, or turn right to hike to the *M*A*S*H* site—both make good turn-around points and, on the downhill trek back to the parking lot, you can enjoy the craggy mountain vistas, fragrant lavender fields, and chirping wildlife. Summers are hot and dusty, so visit the park after rainfall or in springtime to experience the scenery at its best. From the 101 Freeway, exit at Las Virgenes Road and follow the signs to Malibu Canyon. The entrance to the park is clearly marked just after Mulholland Highway. One bummer when you arrive—there's an $8 day-use fee. Our recommendation: park in the second lot and start at the Crags Road trail that runs past the bathrooms to avoid having to use the port-o-lets.

Point Dume State Beach

At 4 miles round trip, this trail is less of a hike and more of a sightseeing trip. While you may not break a sweat, the spectacular cliffside scenery and the semi-isolated beach at the end of the trail makes for a magical day in the great outdoors. From the 101 Freeway, exit at Kanan Road, follow it south for 12 miles, and then make a right on PCH. Turn left on Westward Beach Road and try to find parking before you hit the pay lot. If you can't score a free spot, at least you can drive to the trailhead, located at the far end of the parking lot. The viewing platform is a great place to take a break and to enjoy a marvelous view of the Santa Monica Bay, north Malibu coast, Santa Monica Mountains and, if you're lucky, Catalina Island. Dolphins almost always bob in the waves below, and watch for California gray whales between December and March. On the other side of the bluff, descend a stairway to Paradise Cove, a haven for tide-pool gazers and topless sunbathers. Follow the coast for about a mile to the pier, where you can enjoy a mid-hike meal at the Paradise Cove Beach Café. Check the tide tables before setting out or this hike may become a swim.

Los Angeles is famously dotted with blue swimming pools. Even for the unfortunate few without their own private pools, local municipal pools are abundant. The City of Los Angeles operates 59 pools: 47 seasonal (outdoor) pools and 12 year-round (8 indoor, 4 outdoor) pools. Individual cities and towns within Los Angeles County also run their own public pools, open to both residents and non-residents (with a discounted fee for residents). The best one by far is the **Santa Monica Swim Center (Map 18)**, located at Santa Monica College, featuring two nicely heated outdoor pools and diving area, with "Dive-in" movies on weekends.

The Aquatics Division of the City's Department of Recreation & Parks maintains all of the pool facilities, with the seasonal pools open during the summer from the third Saturday in June though Labor Day. Adults (ages 18 through 64) are required to pay a $1.50 admission charge; children and seniors swim for free.

The department also offers Learn to Swim classes for various ages and swimming abilities. The beginning toddler class for children aged 4 to 7 requires that parents participate with their child in the water. Students then progress to Level 1, which involves face-submerging and blowing bubbles, all the way up to Level 7, in which they will learn to complete 500 yards of continuous swimming using various strokes, conduct an in-water rescue, and perform a springboard dive in tuck and pike positions. Most pools also offer team sports, like inner-tube water polo, synchronized swimming, and lifeguard training. Visit your local pool for more information regarding classes and teams.

For public safety, there is an extensive published list of pool rules. Our favorite is "No snapping towels." For a complete list of pool rules and everything Aquatics Division–related, visit www.laparks.com/dos/aquatic/aquatic.htm. Check with the local Recreation & Parks department about municipalities in individual cities and towns.

Pools	*Address*	*Phone*	*Map*
Pan Pacific Pool	141 S Gardner St	323-975-4524	2
West Hollywood Pool	647 N San Vicente Blvd	323-848-6538	2
Hollywood Pool	1122 Cole Ave	323-957-4501	3
Echo Lake Pool	751 Echo Park Ave	213-847-8524	5
Echo Shallow Pool	1632 Bellevue Ave	213-580-3733	5
Griffith Park Pool	3401 Riverside Dr	323-644-6878	5
EG Roberts Indoor Pool	4526 W Pico Blvd	323-936-8483	7
MacArthur Park Lake	653 S Alvarado St	213-368-4160	8
Celes King III Indoor Pool	5001 Rodeo Dr	213-847-3406	10
John C Argue Swim Stadium	3980 S Menlo Ave	213-763-0129	11
Van Ness Pool	5720 2nd Ave	323-290-3134	11
Central Pool	1357 E 22nd St	213-765-0565	12
Ross Snyder Pool	1501 E 41st St	213-847-3430	12
South Park Pool	345 E 51st St	323-846-5366	12
Algin Sutton Pool	8800 S Hoover St	323-789-2826	14
Rustic Canyon Pool	601 Latimer Rd	310-230-0137	15
Santa Monica Swim Center	2225 16th St	310-458-8700	18
Stoner Park Pool	1835 Stoner Ave	310-575-8286	19
Mar Vista Pool	11655 Palms Blvd	310-390-2016	22
Venice High School Indoor Pool	2490 Walgrove Ave	310-575-8260	22
Cheviot Hills Pool	2693 Motor Ave	310-202-2844	23
Westchester Pool	9100 Lincoln Blvd	310-342-3164	25
Westwood Indoor Pool	1350 S Sepulveda Blvd	310-478-7019	32
Highland Park Pool	6150 Piedmont Ave	323-226-1669	33
Yosemite Pool	1840 Yosemite Dr	323-226-1668	33
Robinson Park	1081 N Fair Oaks Ave	626-585-2025	34
Glassell Park Pool	3704 Verdugo Rd	323-226-1670	36
Downey Pool	1775 N Spring St	323-226-1671	37
Richard Alatorre Indoor Pool	4721 Klamath St	323-276-3042	38
Costello Pool	3121 E Olympic Blvd	323-526-3073	40
Lincoln Park Pool	3501 Valley Blvd	213-847-3382	40
Pecan Pool	120 S Gless St	323-526-3042	40
Roosevelt Pool	456 S Mathews St	213-485-7391	40
Lanark Pool	21817 Strathern St	818-756-9364	42
Granada Hills Pool	16730 Chatsworth St	818-360-7107	44
Cleveland High Indoor Pool	8120 Vanalden Ave	818-756-9798	46
Lake Balboa	6300 Balboa Blvd	818-756-9743	46
Reseda Pool	18411 Victory Blvd	818-756-9361	46
Valley Plaza Swimming Pool	6715 Laurelgrove Ave	818-756-9362	48
Van Nuys Sherman Oaks Pool	14201 Huston St	818-783-6721	55
North Hollywood Pool	5301 Tujunga Ave	818-755-7654	56

Just like the city itself, Los Angeles's golf courses are diverse. They range in difficulty and lawn manicure, as well as in views (sweeping ocean vistas in Palos Verdes, power plants and overhead airplanes in El Segundo). This warm-weather city offers golf daily all year-round. On weekends, the best tee times are at the crack of dawn to avoid waiting. The city operates a total of 13 courses, including seven 18-hole championship courses, five 9-hole courses, and one 18-hole pony course. Call ahead for conditions, particularly after heavy rainfall. The County operates 16 courses as well (three 9-hole, 13 regulation 18-hole). In summer, bear in mind the weather, as temperatures can easily pass 100 degrees in the Valley. Book tee times early, as many novices forget their manners about letting others play through. Food, cocktail lounges, pro shops, lessons, and driving ranges accompany most golf clubs. In addition, individual cities and hotels have 3-par courses available to the public. Some public courses will require a city permit; check with the club when booking a tee time. We like the one at the **Marriott Hotel in Manhattan Beach (Map 27).** There's no real dress code (sneakers are permitted), but some people like to hide their handicap behind a smart pair of pants and polo shirt.

Golf Courses	*Address*	*Phone*	*Fee*	*Par*	*Map*
Roosevelt Golf Course	2650 N Vermont Ave	323-665-2011	$13.50 weekdays, $17 weekends	Par 33	4
Los Feliz Golf Course	3207 Los Feliz Blvd	323-663-7758	$4.50 weekdays, $6.50 weekends	Par 27	5
Maggie Hathaway Golf Course	9637 S Western Ave	323-755-6285	$5 weekdays, $7 weekends (18 hole)	Par 27	14
Arm and Hammer Pitch and Putt	601 Club View Dr	310-276-1604		Par 3	20
Penmar Golf Course	1233 Rose Ave	310-396-6228	$13.50 weekdays, $17 weekends	Par 33	21
Rancho Park	10460 W Pico Blvd	310-838-7373	$15 weekdays, $19 weekends (9-hole); $24 weekdays, weekends $31, (18-hole)	Par 71	23
Chester Washington Golf Course	1930 W 120th St	323-756-6975	$34 weekdays, $40 weekends	Par 70	25
Westchester Golf Course	6900 W Manchester Ave	310-649-9166	$19 weekdays, $22 weekends	Par 53	26
Marriott Manhattan Beach	1400 Park View Ave	310-546-7511	$12 weekdays, $14 weekends	Par 27	27
Alondra Park Golf Course	16400 S Prairie Ave	310-217-9919	$21.50 weekdays, $28 weekends	Par 72	28
Arroyo Seco Golf Course	1055 Lohman Ln	323-255-1506	$12 weekdays, $13 weekends	Par 3	34
Brookside Golf Course	1133 Rosemont Ave	626-796-0177	$52 weekdays, $64 weekends	Par 70	34
Alhambra Golf Course	630 S Almansor St	626-570-5059	$14.50 weekdays, $15.50 weekends	Par 70	39
Balboa/Encino Golf Course	16821 Burbank Blvd	818-995-1170	$15 weekdays, $19 weekends (9-hole); $24 weekdays, $31 weekends (18-hole)	Par 72	42
Van Nuys Golf Course	6550 Odessa Ave	818-785-8871	$11 weekdays, $13 weekends	Par 30; also an 18-hole Par 3	47
Woodley Lakes Golf Course	6331 Woodley Ave	818-756-9707	$11.50 weekdays, weekends $15 (9-hole); weekdays $22.50, weekends $28.50 (18-hole)	Par 72	47
De Bell Municipal Golf Course	1500 E Walnut Ave	818-845-0022	$38 weekdays, $43 weekends	Par 71	50
Altadena Golf Course	1456 E Mendocino St, Altadena	626-797-3821	$13.50 weekdays, $16.50 weekends	Par 36	n/a
Diamond Bar Golf Course	22751 Golden Springs Dr, Diamond Bar	909-861-8282	$21.50 weekdays, $28 weekends	Par 72	n/a
Eaton Canyon Golf Course	1150 Sierra Madre Villa Ave, Pasadena	626-794-6773	$13.50 weekdays, $16.50 weekends	Par 35	n/a
El Cariso Golf Course	13100 Eldridge Ave, Sylmar	818-367-8742	$29 weekdays, $34 weekends	Par 62	n/a
Knollwood Golf Course	12040 Balboa Blvd, Granada Hills	818-363-8161	$21.50 weekdays; $28.00 weekends	Par 72	n/a
La Mirada Golf Course	15501 Alicante Rd, La Mirada	562-943-7123	$21.50 weekdays, $33.50 weekends	Par 70	n/a
Lakewood Golf Course	3101 Carson St, Lakewood	562-429-9711	$34 weekdays, $40 weekends	Par 72	n/a
Los Amigos Golf Course	7295 Quill Dr, Downey	562-869-0302	$33 weekdays, $40 weekends	Par 70	n/a
Los Verdes Golf Course	7000 W Los Verdes Dr, Rancho Palos Verdes	310-377-7370	$21.50 weekdays, $28 weekends	Par 71	n/a
Marshall Canyon Golf Course	6100 Stephens Ranch Rd, La Verne	909-593-8211	$14.50 weekdays, $18 weekends	Par 71	n/a
Mountain Meadows	1875 Fairplex Dr, Pomona	909-629-1166	$22 weekdays, $29 weekends	Par 72	n/a
Santa Anita Golf Course	405 S Santa Anita Ave, Arcadia	626-447-2331	$33 weekdays, $40 weekends	Par 71	n/a
Victoria Golf Course	340 E 192nd St, Carson	310-323-6981	$21.50 weekdays,$28 weekends	Par 72	n/a
Wilson Golf Course	4730 Crystal Springs Dr, Los Angeles	323-663-2555	$15 weekdays,weekends $19 (9-hole), $24 weekdays, $31 weekends (18-hole)	Par 71	n/a

Driving Ranges	*Address*	*Phone*	*Fee*	*Map*
Chester Washington Golf Course	1930 W 120th St	323-756-6975	$6/bucket	25
Westchester Golf Course	6900 W Manchester Ave	310-649-9166	$3/5/$8 buckets	26
Alondra Park Golf Course	16400 S Prairie Ave	310-217-9919	$4.50/$9 buckets	28
Arroyo Seco Golf Course	1055 Lohman Ln	323-255-1506	$3/6/$8 buckets	34
Alhambra Golf Course	630 S Almansor St	626-570-5059	$3/$5/$7 buckets	39
Woodley Lakes Golf Course	6331 Woodley Ave	818-787-8163	$3/$5/$8 buckets	47
Altadena Golf Course	1456 E Mendocino St, Altadena	626-797-3821	$3 (33 balls)	n/a
Diamond Bar Golf Course	22751 Golden Springs Dr, Diamond Bar	909-861-8282	$6 bucket	n/a
Eaton Canyon Golf Course	1150 Sierra Madre Villa Ave, Pasadena	626-794-6773	$3 (33 balls)	n/a
El Cariso Golf Course	13100 Eldridge Ave, Sylmar	818-367-8742	$4/$7/$9 buckets	n/a
Knollwood Golf Course	12040 Balboa Blvd, Granada Hills	818-363-8161	$6/$10 buckets	n/a
La Mirada Golf Course	15501 Alicante Rd, La Mirada	562-943-7123	$10 buckets	n/a
Lakewood Golf Course	3101 Carson St, Lakewood	562-429-9711	$6/$10 buckets	n/a
Los Amigos Golf Course	7295 Quill Dr, Downey	562-869-0302	$4.50/7/9.50 buckets	n/a
Marshall Canyon Golf Course	6100 Stephens Ranch Rd, La Verne	909-593-8211	$6/$8/$10 buckets	n/a
Mountain Meadows	1875 Fairplex Dr, Pomona	909-629-1166	$6/10/20 reuseable cards	n/a
Santa Anita Golf Course	405 S Santa Anita Ave, Arcadia	626-447-2331	$5/$7/$8.50 buckets	n/a
Victoria Golf Course	340 E 192nd St, Carson	310-323-6981	$3/5/$8 buckets	n/a

Billiards

Billiards	Address	Phone	Fees	Map
Koray Billiard	401 S Vermont Ave	213-386-0402	$12/hr	8
Oriental Pool Room	2528 W Olympic Blvd	213-380-1310	$12/hr	8
Young Billiards	132 S Vermont Ave	213-387-9691	$12/hr	8
Young Dong Billiards	555 S Western Ave, Ste 202	213-368-0479	$12/hr	8
Sportsman's Family Billiards & Restaurant	3617 Crenshaw Blvd	323-733-9615	$9/hr	10
Raymond's Pool Room	5221 Avalon Blvd	323-234-1061	$8/hr	12
3rd Street Billiard Club	1410 3rd St Prom	310-394-4632	$12/hr	18
House of Billiards	1901 Wilshire Blvd	310-828-2120	$11/hr	18
Shark's Cove	1220 Hermosa Av	310-798-3932	$9/hr	29
Mr Lucky's Middleground	21020 Hawthorne Blvd	310-793-6948	$10/hr	31
Highland Park Billiards	5043 York Blvd	323-258-4427	$8/hr	33
Jake's Café and Billiards	38 W Colorado Blvd	626-568-1602	$12/hr	34
Jerry's Family Billards II	1312 N Lake Ave	626-791-5114	$12.50/hr	34
Bully's Billiards	21623 Devonshire St	818-341-3978	$10/hr	42
Plush Cue Recreation	20837 Roscoe Blvd	818-993-1450	$7.50/hr	42
Plush Pocket	16950 Parthenia St	818-893-1380	$10/hr	44
Canoga Billiard Parlor	22025 Sherman Wy	818-348-8798	$7.50/hr	45
Lucky 8 Ball Billiard	13325 Victory Blvd	818-786-9202	$8/hr	48
Fantasia Billiard	131 N San Fernando Blvd	818-848-6718	$12/hr	50
Charles Billiard	224 N Brand Blvd	818-547-4859	$12/hr	51
Green Room	4006 San Fernando Rd	818-548-0739	$10/hr	51
North Hollywood Billiards	11130 Magnolia Blvd	818-769-9144	$9.50/hr	56

Boxing

Train to be the next Oscar De La Hoya—onscreen or in the ring. If you like a bit of history with your blood, sweat, and tears, visit the Broadway Boxing Gym.

Gym	Address	Phone	Map
Hollywood Boxing Gym	1551 N La Brea Ave	323-845-1420	2
Wild Card Gym	1123 Vine St	323-461-4170	3
Broadway Boxing Gym	10730 S Broadway	323-755-9016	14

Just as Hollywood can take anything sincere and turn it into kitsch, Los Angeles has a way of taking true-blue Americana and making it seem forced and co-opted. So it is with the pastime of bowling. Luckily, for each too-hip alley in the city, there is another Suds and Rock place around the corner. **Lucky Strike Lanes (Map 3)** is as Hollywood as it gets. Located behind a velvet rope in the heart of tourist-driven Hollywood and Highland, you'll find more model/actor-types than league-nighters. After 7pm it becomes 21 and over and good luck getting a lane.

For a more true-to-its-roots experience, check out **AMF**'s **(Map 18)** lanes on Pico in Santa Monica. The rentals are fairly-priced, the attached diner is as down-home as you'll find on the Westside, and the bar serves bowling pin shaped long-necks. Just make sure to call ahead to avoid a league night. On the Eastside, **Shatto 39 Lanes (Map 8)** is not to be missed. The many lanes are populated by diehards, hipsters, teens, and families. There's a decent arcade, a full bar, and snackbar with the greasiest, cheapest tater tots in town.

To give yourself the pre-teen birthday party you never had, check out **Pickwick Bowling (Map 50)** in Burbank. A veritable wonderland of activity, this complex includes an arcade, ice-rink, and pro shop. Fridays and Saturdays at Pickwick bring on the fog, blacklights, and pop music, making for good group fun.

Bowling Alleys	*Address*	*Phone*	*Map*	
Lucky Strike Lanes	6801 Hollywood Blvd	323-467-7776	3	Weekdays $4.95–6.95 / game; Weekends $5.95–6.95; $3.95 for shoes
AMF Midtown Lanes	4645 Venice Blvd	323-933-7171	7	$4.50–$6 / game; $4.50 for shoes
Chateau 39 Lanes	3255 W 4th St	213-385-9475	8	$3–$3.75 / game; $2 for shoes
Shatto 39 Lanes	3255 W 4th St	213-385-9475	8	Weekdays $3–4.50 / game; Weekends $4.50 / game; $2.50 for shoes
AMF Bay Shore Lanes	234 Pico Blvd	310-399-7731	18	$4.50–$6 / game; $4.50 for shoes
AMF Mar Vista Lanes	12125 Venice Blvd	310-391-5288	22	$4.50–$6 / game; $4.50 for shoes
AMF El Dorado Lanes	8731 Lincoln Blvd	310-670-0688	25	$4.50–$6 / game; $4.50 for shoes
Gable House Bowl	22501 Hawthorne Blvd	310-378-2265	31	Weekdays $3.75-$5.00; Weekends $2-$5; $4.50 for shoes
AMF Bowl-O-Drome	21915 S Western Ave	310-328-3700	32	$4.50–$6 after 6pm; $4.50 for shoes
All Star Lanes	4459 Eagle Rock Blvd	323-254-2579	33	Weekdays $2.50–$3.50, Weekends $3.50, $2 for shoes
Palos Verdes Bowl	24600 Crenshaw Blvd	310-326-5120	36	Weekdays $3; Weekends $4.50, $3 for shoes
Alhambra Bowling Center	1400 E Valley Blvd	626-289-5168	39	Weekdays $2.25/game; Weekends $2.25–$4.50/game, $2-3.75 for shoes
AMF Rocket Lanes	9171 De Soto Ave	818-341-0070	42	$4.50–$6 / game; $4.50 for shoes
Brunswick Matador Bowl	9118 Balboa Blvd	818-892-8677	44	Weekdays $3.49–$5.49 / game; Weekends $5.49 per game; $3.99 for shoes
Canoga Park Bowl	20122 Vanowen St	818-340-5190	45	Weekdays $4–$5 / game, $15 / hour; Weekends $5 / game, $30 / hour; $3.25 for shoes
Corbin Bowl	19616 Ventura Blvd	818-996-2695	45	Weekdays $3.50–$4.50 / game, $16–$25 /hour; Weekends, $5.50 / game, $35/hour; $3.50 for shoes
Pickwick Center	1001 Riverside Dr	818-845-5300	50	Weekdays $3–$4 / game; Weekends $3.75–$5; $3 for shoes
Jewel City Bowl	135 S Glendale Ave	818-243-1188	51	Weekdays $3.50–$5.50 per game, $21–$34 per hour; Weekends $5.50 per game, $21–$34 per hour; $3 for shoes
Pinz Bowling Center	12655 Ventura Blvd	818-769-7600	56	Weekdays $4–$7 / game; Weekends $7 / game; $4 for shoes
Jillian's Hi-Life Lanes	1000 Universal Studios Blvd	818-985-8234	57	$4–$5.50 / game; $3.50 for shoes
AMF Bahama Lanes	3545 E Foothill Blvd, Pasadena	626-351-8858	n/a	$4.50–$6 / game; $4.50 for shoes
AMF Woodlake Lanes	23130 Ventura Blvd, Woodland Hills	818-225-7181	n/a	$4.50–$6 / game; $4.50 for shoes
Southwest Bowl	11633 S Western Ave, Los Angeles	323-757-2211	n/a	$2.50–$3.50 / game, $2 for shoes

Yoga	Address	Phone	Website	Map
BKS Lyengar Yoga	8233 W 3rd St	323-653-0357	www.iyila.org	2
City Yoga	7904 Santa Monica Blvd	323-654-2125	www.cityyoga.com	2
Dancing Shiva Yoga and Ayurveda	7466 Beverly Blvd	323-934-8332	www.dancingshiva.com	2
Earth's Power Yoga	7901 Melrose Ave	323-655-9642	www.earthspoweryoga.com	2
Liberation Yoga	124 S La Brea Ave	323-964-5222	www.liberationyoga.com	2
Tar Pit Yoga	636 S Burnside Ave	323-934-5171	www.tarpityoga.com	2
Yoga Ballet Studio	8250 W 3rd St	866-289-8939	www.swervestudio.com	2
Golden Bridge Yoga	6322 De Longpre Ave	323-936-1172	www.goldenbridgeyoga.com	3
Le Studio Yoga	1639 N Las Palmas Ave	323-559-6264	www.lestudioyoga.com	3
Karunga Yoga	1939 1/2 Hillhurst Ave	323-665-6242	www.karunayoga.net	4
Ashtanga Yoga	2815 Sunset Blvd, 2nd Fl	213-483-0400	www.ashtangayogala.org	5
Bikran Yoga Silverlake	3223 Glendale Blvd	323-668-2500	www.bikramyogasilverlake.com	5
Silverlake Yoga	2810 1/2 Glendale Blvd	323-953-0496	www.silverlakeyoga.com	5
Yoga East	2815 W Sunset Blvd	213-483-0400	www.yogaeast.us	5
Bikram Yoga	1862 S La Cienega Blvd	310-854-5800	www.bikramyoga.com	6
Bikran's Yoga College of India	1862 S La Cienega Blvd	310-854-5800	www.bikramyoga.com	6
The Blessings Center	1310 Carmona Ave	323-930-2803	www.gurutej.com/blessingscenter.html	6
Yoga West	1535 S Robertson Blvd	310-552-4647	www.yogawestla.com	6
Bala Yoga	142 N La Brea Ave	323-939-6424	www.yogainsideout.com	7
Center for Yoga	230 1/2 N Larchmont Blvd	323-464-1276	www.yogaworks.com	7
Yoga Circle Downtown	400 S Main St	213-620-1040	www.yogacircledowntown.com	9
Crenshaw Yoga and Dance	5426 Crenshaw Blvd	323-294-7148	www.crenshawyogaanddance.com	11
Center for Yoga	15327 W Sunset Blvd	310-454-7000	www.yogaworks.com	15
Maha Yoga	13050 San Vicente Blvd	310-889-0047	www.mahayoga.com	16
Center for Yoga	1426 Montana Ave	310-393-5150	www.yogaworks.com	18
Center for Yoga	2215 Main St	310-664-6470	www.yogaworks.com	18
Exhale Center for Sacred Movement	245 Main St	310-450-7676	www.sacredmovement.com	18
Exhale Mind and Body Spa	1422 2nd St	310-899-6222	www.exhalespa.com	18
Santa Monica Yoga	1640 Ocean Park Blvd	310-396-4040	www.santamonicayoga.com	18
Los Angeles Yoga	11740 San Vicente Blvd	310-826-9642	www.yogalosangeles.org/	19
Center for Yoga	1256 Westwood Blvd	310-234-1200	www.yogaworks.com	20
Para Yoga	1351 Westwood Blvd	310-745-1071	www.pureyoga.com	20
YAS Kimberely Fowler's	1101 Abbot Kinney Blvd	310-396-6993	www.go2yas.com	21
Sivananda Yoga Vendanta Center	13325 Beach Ave	310-822-9642	www.sivananda.org/la	22
Goda Yoga	9711 W Washington Blvd	310-287-1255	www.godayoga.com	24
Creative Chakra Downtown	3401 Pacific Ave	310-287-1255	www.creativechakra.com	25
The Awareness Center	2801 E Foothill Blvd	626-796-1567	www.insightyoga.com	34
Yoga House	11 W State St	626-403-3961	www.yogahouse.com	34
Progressive Power Yoga	21800 Burbank Blvd	800-545-9642	www.progressivepoweryoga.com	45
Yoga Blend	1921 W Magnolia Blvd	818-954-9642	www.yogablend.com	50
The Absolute Yoga and Pilates Studio	20855 Ventura Blvd	818-226-0695	www.theabsoluteyoga.com	52
The Yoga Loft	21228 Ventura Blvd	818-710-9057	www.yogaloftla.com	52
Sahaja Yoga Meditation Center	4565 Sherman Oaks Ave	866-972-4252	www.sahajayogala.org	54
Annie's Yoga Studio	4521-A Van Nuys Blvd	818-788-5960	www.anniesyoga.com	55
Angel City Yoga	12408 Ventura Blvd	818-788-9642	http://www.angelcityyoga.com	56
Yoga House	3808 W Riverside Dr	818-567-0471	www.yogahouse.com	57

Overview

From the old geezer skating on the Venice Boardwalk to the loose-limbed ingénue posing on her yoga mat, Angelenos love their exercise. All the fun options, not to mention the year-round sunshine, make it easy to join the city's tanned and toned without becoming a gym drone.

Play in the Park

The Los Angeles Department of Recreation and Parks oversees over 175 parks, including 59 swimming pools, 10 lakes, 13 golf courses, 69 tennis courts, 8 skateboarding parks, 9 dog parks, as well as numerous basketball, volleyball, and handball courts and baseball, softball, and soccer fields. Archery ranges are also available, as are beautiful, well maintained hiking trails. A variety of sports leagues and camps are offered for both children and adults and pick-up games of sports such as basketball and soccer are also popular. Visit www.laparks.org or call 888-LA-PARKS for more information.

Some of the cities within the Los Angeles metropolitan area maintain their own park and recreation departments including Santa Monica, Beverly Hills, West Hollywood, Burbank, Glendale, and Pasadena. Information about park and recreational opportunities in these cities can be found at: www.smgov.net or (310) 458-8411 for Santa Monica, www.beverlyhills.org or (310) 285-2536 for Beverly Hills, weho.org or (323) 848-6400 for West Hollywood, www.ci.burbank.ca.us or (818) 238-5330 for Burbank, www.ci.glendale.ca.us or (818) 548-2000 for Glendale, and www.ci.pasadena.ca.us or (626) 744-4000 for Pasadena.

Table Tennis

If you own your own paddle and watch the tournaments on ESPN, stop by the Westside Table Tennis Center (www.alphatabletennis.com) for tips from the pros.

Table Tennis Center	Address	Phone	Map
Westside Table Tennis Center	11755 Exposition Blvd	626-584-6377	19
Pasadena Table Tennis Club	85 E Holly St	626-584-6377	34

Horseback Riding

If you are more equine-inclined, check out one of the many companies offering guided trail rides and riding lessons. Looking for a novel way to spend a Friday night? Try one of the Sunset Ranch dinner rides through Griffith Park, which include a stop for margaritas at a restaurant with hitching posts.

Stable	Address	Phone	Map
Sunset Ranch Hollywood Stables	3400 N Beachwood Dr	323-469-5450	3
Griffith Park Horse Rental	480 Riverside Dr	818-840-8401	50
Traditional Equitation School	480 Riverside Dr	818-569-3666	50
Escape on Horseback	2623 Old Topanga Canyon Rd	818-591-2032	p264

Roller Skating

Here's your chance to dig those hot pants and leg warmers out of the far reaches of your closet. For the ultimate dance party on wheels, take to the streets of Santa Monica, Hollywood, or Downtown with the Friday Night Skate crew. Visit www.fridaynightskate.org for details.

Rinks & Lessons	Address	Phone	Map
Moonlight Rollerway Roller Skating Rink	5110 San Fernando Rd	818-241-3630	5
World on Wheels	4645 ½ Venice Blvd	323-933-3333	9
California Skate School	multiple locations, www.skateschool.com	888-880-ROLL	n/a

Paintball & Other Forms Combat Play

For information about local activities check out www.paintball-players.org or perhaps www.streetwars.net if this controversial urban stalking game is your thing.

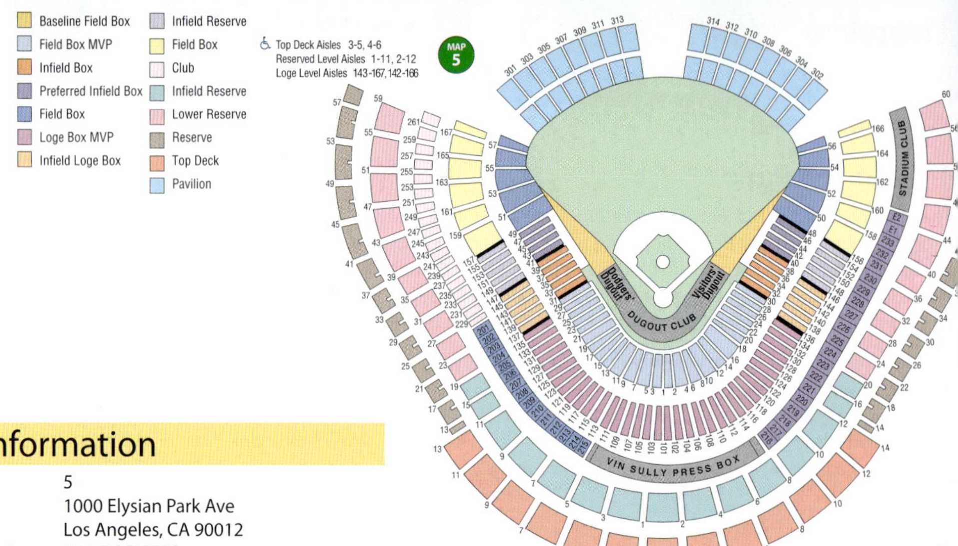

General Information

NFT Map:	5
Address:	1000 Elysian Park Ave Los Angeles, CA 90012
Information & Tickets:	866-DODGERS
Lost & Found:	866-DODGERS
Blue Crew Fan Club:	323-224-1315
Website:	www.dodgers.com

Overview

The Dodgers haven't brought a World Series win to Los Angeles in nearly two decades, but they'll always have one thing on their side: great California weather. There's nothing like catching a warm summer night or weekend afternoon game at the hilltop stadium. The view of nearby Chavez Ravine's rolling hills, the taste of an overpriced Dodger Dog (or why not a margarita and a Krispy Kreme doughnut?), and seeing the famous "Think Blue" sign in the distance can excite even the most cynical of Angelenos.

Even if the team isn't in tip-top shape, the stadium certainly is. A renovation unveiled for the 2006 season has restored the seating throughout the park, adding swanky baseline box seats and even a new adjacent park and picnic area. In a retro touch, the stadium has been restored to the original colors of its 1962 opening. Could a return to the glory days be on the horizon, too?

Win or lose, on game days just about the only sure bet is popping into the classic local dive bar, the Short Stop (1455 Sunset Blvd), for drink specials and plenty of folks in blue.

How to Get There—Driving

From the 101, exit at Alvarado, head north, then turn right on Sunset. Go approximately one mile and turn left on Elysian Park Avenue. You will run into Dodger Stadium. From the 110, take the Dodger Stadium exit and follow signs. From the 5 S, exit at Stadium Way, turn left, and follow the signs to Dodger Stadium. From the 5 N, exit at Stadium Way and turn left on Riverside Drive. Turn left onto Stadium Way and follow the signs.

Whenever possible, use surface roads. Sunset Boulevard will take you to Elysian Park Avenue. Beverly Boulevard is often less congested—and more direct—than Sunset Boulevard. Take Beverly to Alvarado, then follow directions above from the 101.

Parking

To make things more exciting for motorists, the Dodgers have instituted something called "Controlled Zone Parking", basically meaning that where you park will be determined by which parking gate you enter. This means that if you want to park near right field, you have to drive around until you find the corresponding gate. It's supposed to be easier…we'll see about that. Prices have gone up as well - general parking for cars and motorcycles is $15 and parking for large vehicles, including buses, motor homes, limousines, and other oversized vehicles costs $35.

How to Get There—Mass Transit

Getting to Dodger Stadium via mass transit once included a three-quarter-mile walk up an incredibly steep hill, but if you're a car-less fan, there is another option: the Roundtripper Station to Stadium Shuttle. Take the Metro to the Chinatown Gold Line Station or to Berth 6 of Union Station and hop on the shuttle. At Dodger Stadium you'll be dropped off in Lot 13, which is a short walk to Lot 5 and the entrance to all levels of the stadium. Buses leave Union Station every 15 minutes from 5:40 pm to 8 pm, and Chinatown every half-hour. Return service, leaving from Lot 13, begins at the top of the 8th inning and the last bus leaves 60 minutes after the last out or 11 pm, whichever comes first. A $2 round-trip ticket must be purchased at the station before boarding and Metro passes are not accepted. Unfortunately, the shuttle service is not available for all games, so call 866-DODGERS to check schedules.

If you take a cab to the game and you plan to depart from the stadium by cab, a taxi service is available in Lot 3 on the western side of the stadium or at the Union 76 Service Station near Lot 37 beyond the center field wall.

How to Get Tickets

You can order Dodgers tickets by phone, through the box office at Dodger Stadium (Monday through Saturday, 9 am to 5 pm and during all Dodger home games), and online through the Dodgers' website.

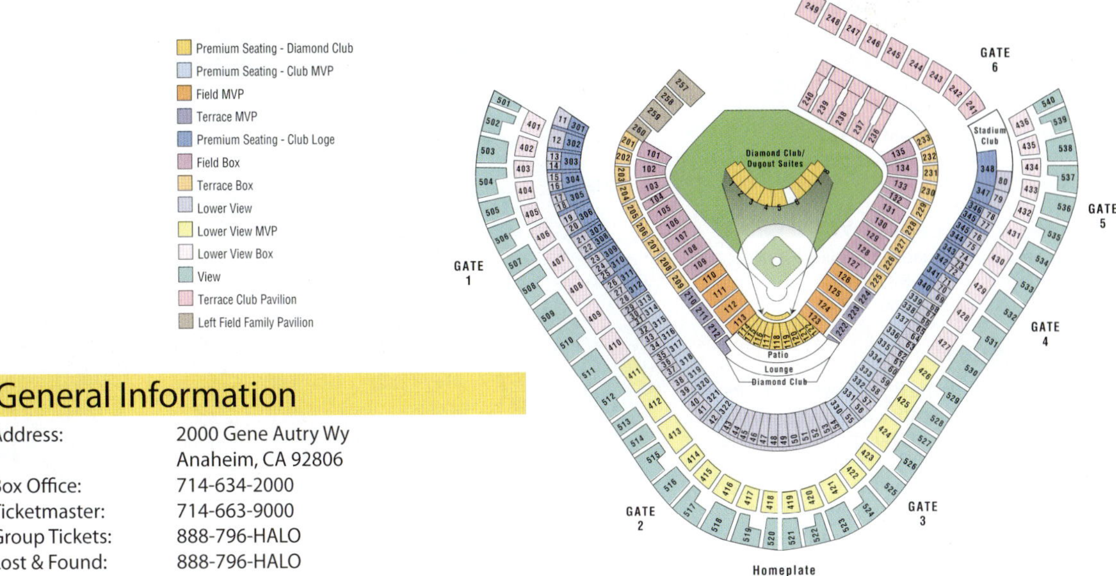

General Information

Address:	2000 Gene Autry Wy Anaheim, CA 92806
Box Office:	714-634-2000
Ticketmaster:	714-663-9000
Group Tickets:	888-796-HALO
Lost & Found:	888-796-HALO
Website:	http://losangeles.angels.mlb.com

Overview

No matter what they're calling the team this year (currently it's The Los Angeles Angels of Anaheim of the State of California in the country of the United States of America on the continent of North America), the Angels and their stadium are definitely a product of the OC. To a proper Angeleno, they just *feel* a little more put together, a little squarer, a little more hoity-toity than our precious Dodgers. Blame it on the filthy rich OC vibe, or on Anaheim's recent quest to separate itself into a thriving city independent of Disneyland.

That said, the stadium is sweet and comfortable and comes with all of the amenities that a modern-day baseball fan could want: three full-service restaurants, family-oriented seating, an interactive game area for the kids, and, of course, Vlad the Impaler. It's almost more amusement park than stadium. But if that's what it takes to get a new generation out to the old ball game, who can really complain?

How to Get There—Driving

From downtown, take 605 S to the CA-91/Artesia Freeway east. Take the I-5/Santa Ana Freeway exit on the right towards Santa Ana. Merge onto I-5 S and take the exit on the right towards Anaheim Boulevard/Haster Street/Katella Avenue. Turn left onto West Freedman Way, turn right onto South Anaheim Boulevard, and turn left onto East Katella Avenue.

Parking

The parking lot opens two-and-a-half hours prior to the start of the scheduled first pitch and, since there are only three entrances to the Angel Stadium parking lot (via Douglass Road, State College Boulevard, and Orangewood Avenue), we suggest you get there early. Parking staff will direct you towards vacancies. Day-of-game parking is $8 and oversized vehicles (greater than 20 feet in length) are $16.

The bus parking lot is located by the Orangewood Avenue entrance. Season ticket holders with parking coupons can use the Express Entry Lane on Orangewood Avenue.

How to Get There—Mass Transit

If you can get yourself to Union Station (Metro Red Line), you can catch the Amtrak Pacific Surfliner bound for San Diego, which stops not too far from the stadium at Anaheim Station. A one-way fare will set you back $10 and the Orange County Transportation Authority has a bus service to the ballpark. Call 800-636-RIDE for more information on bus schedules.

But unless you're watching a pitchers' duel or a complete blowout, the train may not be an option for most night games. The last train back to LA leaves Anaheim just after 10 pm, making an overnight stay in beautiful downtown Anaheim a definite possibility.

Patrons who require a taxi service from Angel Stadium can swing by the Guest Relations Center and ask a concierge to call them a cab.

How to Get Tickets

You can purchase tickets in person at the box office, which is open Monday through Saturday, as well as on Sunday game days, from 9 am to 5:30 pm, or by phoning the box office at 714-634-2000. Online tickets can be purchased through Ticketmaster at www.ticketmaster.com, or look for great seats for cheap on eBay where many locals put up their season tickets for sale.

General Information

NFT Map: 34
Address: 1001 Rose Bowl Dr
Pasadena, CA 91103
Phone: 626-577-3100
Ticketmaster: 213-480-3232
Website: www.rosebowlstadium.com
Rose Parade Grandstand Tickets: 626-795-4171
UCLA website: uclabruins.collegesports.com
UCLA tickets: 310-825-2101
Flea Market: 323-560-7469

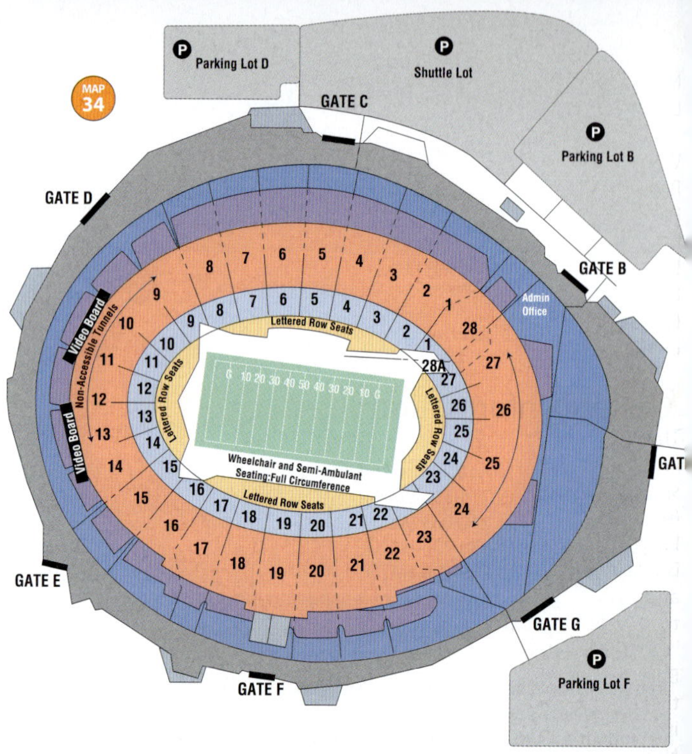

Overview

Everything about the Rose Bowl is big—its size, its reputation, its football games, its flea market, and the concerts it hosts. With seating for 90,000+ screaming fans, it's the largest stadium in Southern California. Every second Sunday of the month, the stadium hosts what it claims is the world's largest flea market. And once a year, it's the place to see the college kids lose their cool over the Big 10 and Pac 10 champs. The Rose Bowl is home to the UCLA Bruins football team and has hosted five NFL Super Bowl Games, the 1984 Olympic soccer matches, the 1994 Men's World Cup Soccer, and the 1999 Women's World Cup Soccer. It doesn't get much bigger than that.

While the stadium hosts world-class events, there's nothing particularly exceptional about the super-sized structure, except maybe its size. The stadium is moderately accessible by car, and the surrounding area of Pasadena offers good walking and shopping opportunities, with a choice of restaurants and sports bars where you can celebrate your team's victory—or drown out a nasty defeat.

Flea Market

On the second Sunday of each month, the flea market takes over the entire Rose Bowl complex. Inside the gates, you'll find a slapdash array of new merchandise, antique collectibles, vintage clothing, and goodness knows what else. All of which is just a precursor to what you'll find in the parking lots: the world's most overwhelming garage sale (come with patience, if not cash to burn). Entry into the flea market costs $7 after 9 am. If you want first dibs on the goods, you can gain early entry: admission costs $10 from 8 am to 9 am; $15 from 7 am to 8 am; and $20 from 5 am to 7 am. Serious shoppers arrive at dawn, and few go home empty-handed.

How to Get There—Driving

There is one major consideration you need to take into account when driving to the Rose Bowl—AVOID the 110 Pasadena Freeway at all costs! The best approach to the stadium is the Pasadena 210 Freeway. Take the Mountain/Seco/Arroyo Boulevard/Windsor exit and follow signs to the stadium. If you approach on the 134, exit at Linda Vista and follow signs. A less congested alternative if you're coming from the west is to take 134 to 2 North then take 210 East to Pasadena and exit at Mountain/Seco/Arroyo Boulevard/Windsor.

Parking

Parking for UCLA games costs $10 for cars, $20 for motor homes/ limousines, and is free of charge for buses. On Rose Bowl day, parking costs $25 for cars and $100 for motor homes. For the Rose Parade, paid parking is available on a first-come, first-served basis at various lots and parking structures near the parade route, including locations at Boston Court/Mentor, Union/El Molino, Euclid/Union, Raymond/Union, 40 North Mentor/Lake, 465 East Union near Los Robles, 44 South Madison near Green, 462 East Green near Los Robles, and Colorado/Los Robles.

How to Get There—Mass Transit

No city buses or trains stop near the stadium, but on Rose Bowl game day the MTA provides regular bus service from locations throughout the county. Call 800-266-6883 for departure locations. A shuttle is available on UCLA game days from Old Pasadena to the Stadium. The shuttle picks up fans at the Parsons Technology Building (100 W Walnut Ave). Parking costs $9, and the shuttle is free. Service begins four hours prior to the game and continues for one hour after the game.

How to Get Tickets

Tickets to the Rose Bowl, Rose Parade, and UCLA games can be purchased online through Ticketmaster.

General Information

NFT Map: 9
Location: 1111 S Figueroa St
Los Angeles, CA 90015
Website: www.staplescenter.com
Box Office: 213-742-7340
Parking: 213-742-7275
LA Sparks (WNBA): www.lasparks.com; 310-426-6033
LA Lakers (NBA): www.lakers.com; 310-426-6000
LA Clippers (NBA): www.clippers.com; 888-895-8662
LA Kings (NHL): www.lakings.com; 213-742-7100
LA Avengers (AFL): www.laavengers.com; 310-788-7744

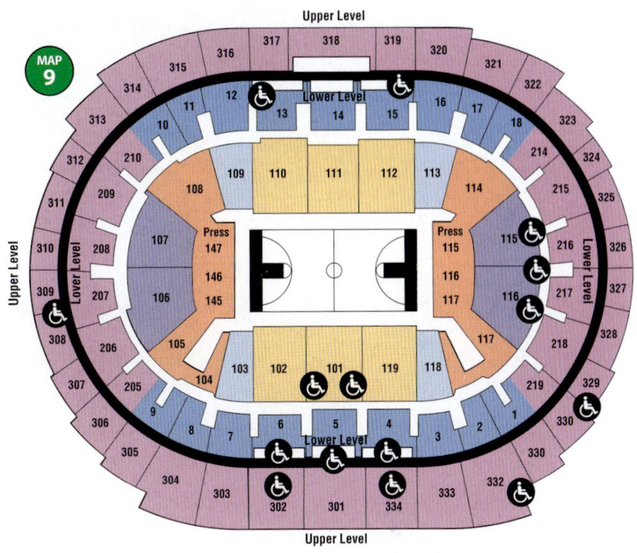

Overview

The STAPLES Center is hotter than ever for a few reasons. For starters, the Clippers, one of the many sports teams that call it home, are on a hot streak (some would say hotter than the city's precious Lakers). And, two, the revitalization of downtown LA is picking up steam, with more hip restaurants, bars, and clubs opening up every day. It's almost enough to make you ignore the downtown hobos.

Built in 1999, it's not only a sports mecca (hosting the Lakers, Clippers, Kings, Sparks, and Avengers) but it's also big enough to handle, say, the 2000 Democratic National Convention and Bruce Springsteen (just not on the same night). In stadium years, the STAPLES Center is no spring chicken, but the place still seems modern and is more than capable of handling the 19,000+ fans who flood its gates for the 230+ sports and entertainment events held annually. With concession stands at every turn, and the Fox Sports Sky Box's rowdy pub open before and after the games, food and booze will never be more than a couple of steps away (but, like all stadium concession stands, they jack up the prices just because they can and the food is mediocre at best). Even parking isn't all that bad, given downtown's cramped layout. And that's a major victory for any Angeleno right from the get-go.

How to Get There—Driving

The STAPLES Center is located in downtown Los Angeles, near the intersection of Routes 10 (Santa Monica) and 110 (Harbor). The best advice we can offer is to get off of the freeway as soon as possible and make your way to Olympic Boulevard. If you're coming from the north, take I-5 S (or 101 S) to 110 S (Harbor Freeway/Los Angeles). Exit at Olympic Boulevard and turn left onto 11th Street. Continue past Cherry Street and Georgian Street and the STAPLES Center is on the right. From the south, take the 110 N and exit at Adams Boulevard. Turn left onto Figueroa Street, then make another left at 11th Street.

Parking

Parking at the STAPLES Center is just about as easy as getting your hands on playoff tickets. Lot 7 opens at 8 am for guests visiting the box office, Fox Sports Sky Box, or Team LA store. Lots 1 and C open 2.5 hours before the start of an event. The remaining lots open 90 minutes before an event. The lots at STAPLES Center are overpriced (up to $30), and many are available only to VIPs and season ticket holders. If you're willing to arrive a little early for an event and walk a few blocks, there is a fair amount of cheaper parking available at various lots.

How to Get There—Mass Transit

The Metro Blue Line to Pico will land you just a block from the stadium. Buses 27, 28, 30, 31, 33, 81, 333, 434, 439, 442, 444, 445, 446, and 447 all stop in the vicinity.

How to Get Tickets

Tickets for Sparks, Lakers, Clippers, Kings, and Avengers games can all be purchased online through Ticketmaster at www.ticketmaster.com or through the individual websites and phone numbers listed above.

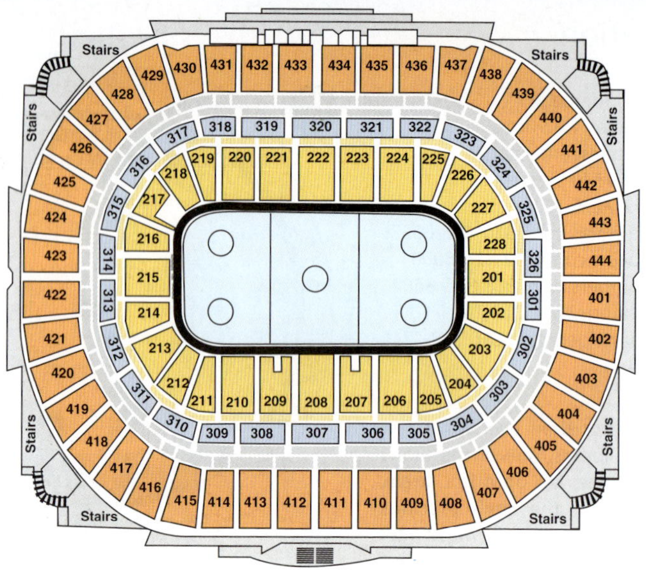

General Information

Location:	2695 East Katella Ave Anaheim, CA 92806
Admin Phone:	714-704-2400
Box Office Phone:	714-704-2500
Group Sales:	714-704-2420
Website:	www.arrowheadpond.com
Mighty Ducks Website (NHL):	www.mightyducks.com

Overview

Ever since the Ducks have proven themselves hockey contenders, the drive down to the OC to catch some action on the ice is almost worth it. Sure, it kind of blows getting there, especially if there's an event at Angels Stadium on that same night (they're right across the freeway from one another, guaranteeing road rage-inducing traffic congestion), but once inside, you'll discover that Anaheim's answer to the STAPLES Center is a snappy, efficient facility. (A facility that until recently had a much snappier name – Arrowhead Pond.) Whether you're one of the 17,000+ fans who flock to see the MOR-oriented line-up of music acts such as Rob Thomas or the latest WWE wrestling extravaganza, you'll appreciate the the friendly staff, the easy flow of people traffic, and the edible offerings that will find *you* before you find *them*. It's almost enough to clear up that road rage. Almost.

How to Get There—Driving

From Los Angeles, take 405 S to 22 E to 57 N. Exit on Katella Avenue and turn right, then turn left on Douglas Street. If you're approaching on I-5 S, exit on Katella Avenue and turn left, then go left on Douglas Street. From I-10, head east to 57 S and exit on Katella Avenue and turn left, then turn left on Douglas Street.

Parking

Parking for all events at the Honda Center is $12 for general parking, $20 preferred parking (if available), $25 limos, and $30 RVs and buses (unlimited drop-off and pick-up for an event).

How to Get There—Mass Transit

The Orange County Transit Authority provides transport to Honda Center. Check www.octa.net for schedules or phone 714-560-6272. In addition to OCTA, Amtrak's station is located within walking distance of the arena, in the parking lot at Angel Stadium. But Amtrak riders beware—the last train back to LA from Anaheim leaves shortly after 10 pm, so unless you're camping out or leaving early, you might want to make other arrangements for getting home after evening events.

How to Get Tickets

Tickets can be purchased in person at the box office or at Ticketmaster outlets, by calling your local Ticketmaster, or online at www.ticketmaster.com. The box office is open Monday through Friday, 10 am until 6 pm, and Saturday 10 am until 4 pm. Purchase same-day tickets on Sundays—the box office opens three hours before the scheduled event and sells tickets only to that day's event. A "wristband lottery" for any remaining tickets to popular events takes place the morning of the event, and line-ups begin at 7 am. But even if you're first in line and receive a wristband, obtaining a ticket is no guarantee. Fifteen minutes before tickets go on sale, one wristband number is drawn randomly and it becomes the starting number for ticket sales.

General Information

Address:	18400 Avalon Blvd Carson, CA 90746
General Information:	310-630-2000
Stadium Website:	www.homedepotcenter.com
LA Galaxy Website:	www.lagalaxy.com
LA Galaxy Tickets:	877-342-5299
Chivas USA Website:	http://chivas.usa.mlsnet.com
Chivas USA Tickets:	877-244-8271
Group Sales:	877-234-8425
Ticketmaster:	213-480-3232
Parking:	310-630-2060

Overview

The Home Depot Center is a jack of all trades: home of the LA Galaxy and Chivas USA soccer teams, the official training site of the US Track & Field team as well as USA cycling, the US Soccer Federation, and the US Tennis Association. Not to mention its one heck of a rockin' concert venue. Now that international soccer superstar David Beckham has announced his decision to join the LA Galaxy beginning summer 2007, the Home Depot will probably be henceforth known as 'Beckingham Palace.' We should have all known that something was in the plumbing when Beckham set up his youth soccer academy here in 2005. Hopefully "Goldenballs" will bring the sort of notoriety and attention to the sport that is so dearly needed in this country.

The Home Depot Center is definitely up to the task of becoming a world-renowned sporting venue with its 27,000 seat capacity soccer stadium, 8,000-seat tennis venue, a track-and-field stadium, a boxing ring, a 3,000-square-foot weight room, 30 tennis courts, nine soccer training fields, and a three-mile jogging trail. And speaking of attractions, The Home Depot Center has the best bathroom and food stand layouts around: they reside in a wide-open perimeter that is above not only the action on the field, but a majority of the seating, so the occasional trip to the bathroom or to go buy a margarita means that you'll miss none of the action. And let's not forget the parking: there's so much parking, you won't break a sweat getting into and out of the place. But with Beckham on board, let's see how long that lasts…

How to Get There—Driving

A lack of signs makes the Home Depot Center a little difficult to find. Leave time in your travel plans for getting lost.

Approaching on 110 S, exit on 190th Street and make a left. 190th Street becomes Victoria Street. Continue past Avalon Boulevard. For reserved parking, use Gates C or D on your right. For general unreserved parking, head further along and use Gates E or F on your right. From 110 N, take the Del Amo Boulevard exit and make a left on Figueroa Street. Make a right on Del Amo Boulevard and a left on Avalon Boulevard. For reserved parking, continue past University Drive and use Gate B on your right. For general unreserved parking, make a right on University Drive and use Gate I on your left.

From the 405 S, exit on Vermont. At the bottom of the ramp, make a left on 190th Street, which becomes Victoria Street. Follow directions for 110 S. From 405 N, exit on Avalon Boulevard, and make a right. Follow directions for 110 N.

Parking

Parking rates are different for each event. For a Galaxy or Chivas regular season game, parking costs between $10 and $15 per vehicle. For Galaxy playoffs or other special events, such as concerts, parking costs between $15 and $20 per vehicle. The lot generally opens two hours before game time, but tailgating is prohibited (whatever).

How to Get There—Mass Transit

Take the Metro Blue Line to the Artesia Station. Transfer to Metro Bus 130 and take it to Victoria Street and Avalon Boulevard.

How to Get Tickets

Tickets for all events can be purchased at the box office (Avalon and 184th St), through any Ticketmaster retail location, or online at www.ticketmaster.com. The box office is open Monday through Friday from 10 am-6 pm, as well as three hours before game time on event days.

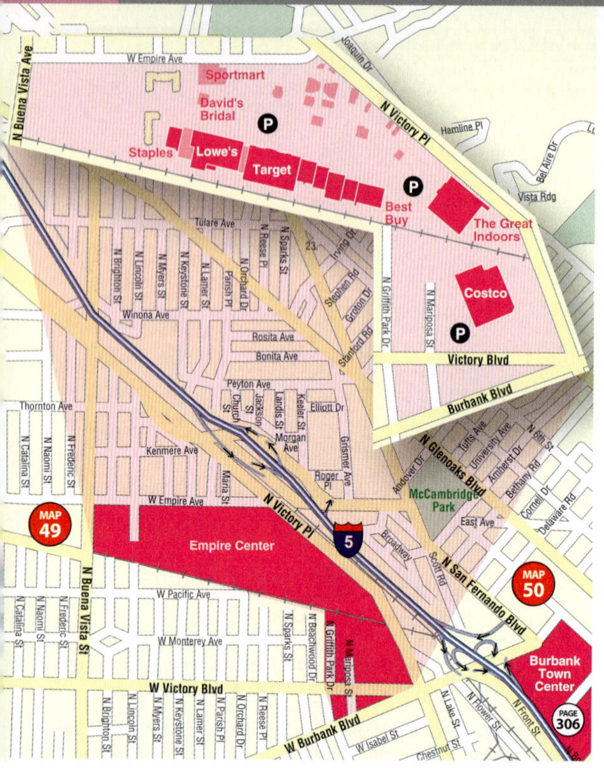

General Information

NFT Map:	49 & 50
Address:	1727 N Victory Pl Burbank, CA 91502

Shopping

The Burbank Empire Center is for serious shoppers. There is no leisurely window-shopping, no frivolous detours to mall staples like Claire's Accessories or Brookstone, no movie theater. The Empire Center is all about the essentials—life's most basic necessities, from super-sized televisions at Best Buy to supersized packs of legal pads at Staples to super-sized bags of Cheetos at Target. The center is home only to big-box retailers and national chains, and it expertly straddles the line between high end (The Great Indoors) and discount (Marshalls) with an emphasis on stores geared toward folks in the mood for nesting (Lowe's Home Improvement, Linens 'n Things, and the aforementioned Great Indoors). The absence of diversions makes the Burbank Empire Center an ideal place for holiday shopping—the roomy parking lot is easily navigated and there is a store that suits everyone on your list, from athlete (Sportmart) to crafter (Michaels) to toy-addicted kid (Target). And this utilitarian shopping center features an equally utilitarian hotel, the Marriott Courtyard, should your Empire experience prove to be too exhausting to make the drive home.

Food

As Homer would say, "Mmmm. Donuts." The arrival of Krispy Kreme was one of the biggest news stories to hit the area in years. (Matched only last spring, when Jet Blue announced direct service from Burbank to New York City.) You can also fuel up for a grueling day of paint-matching and window-treatment ordering at either Hometown Buffet or Outback Steakhouse. The Great Indoors has a Starbucks inside the store when shopping for shower curtains wears you down. A freestanding Starbuck's located in a cluster of restaurants bordering Empire Drive features extra room for the laptop-wagging set. Options for a mid-shopping respite run from the lighter fare of Jamba Juice, Subway, Sbarro, Wendy's and Panda Express, to the more substantial Outback Steakhouse, Olive Garden and Hometown Buffet (where the line begins forming about 10:30 a.m. and wraps around the building by noon, so plan accordingly).

Drawbacks

True to its name, the place is empire-sized. The Great Indoors and Lowe's are at opposite ends of the mall, which can be inconvenient for those on intensive home-improvement missions. The long walk can be especially rough on hot summer days when the heat is shimmering off the parking lot. The Burbank Empire Center is also adjacent to a very busy, very big Costco, which means the intersection of Burbank Boulevard, Victory Place, and Victory Boulevard can tie itself into quite a knot. The good news is that there are long left-turn arrows to ease you through.

How to Get There

From the 5 in either direction, exit at Burbank Boulevard. Head west on Burbank Boulevard to Victory Place and turn right. The Empire Center is about a mile down on your left. Just look for the signs shaped like airplanes and stores the size of airplane hangars. The Great Indoors is at the southern end of the mall; Target and Lowe's are at the northern end. In case you can't smell your way to them, the donuts are to be found on the east side of the mall where the stand-alone stores are located.

General Information

NFT Map: 2
Address: 8500 Beverly Blvd
Los Angeles, CA 90048
Phone: 310-854-0071
Website: www.beverlycenter.com

Shopping

Like a well-dressed phoenix rising from the ashes, the Beverly Center opened in 1982 to replace Kiddyland, a modest amusement park featuring a ferris wheel and pony rides. With its highly recognizable exterior escalators and plethora of bored housewives carrying pint-sized pets, this shopping stronghold is but an evolved version of Kiddyland. Despite the younger, scrappier Grove opening in 2002 and soaking up much of its limelight, the Beverly Center forges on and continues to be one of LA's premier shopping destinations. When it was announced that H&M was coming to town, shopping centers lobbied for the honors the way most cities lobby to host the Olympics. The Beverly Center is now home to one of the still-rare LA locations of the famous discount retailer. Who needs gold medals when you can buy babydoll dresses for $19.99?

Today's Beverly Center is something of a study in contrasts. Stores such as D&G, Louis Vuitton, Diesel, Dior, A/X Armani Exchange, Ben Sherman, and a brightly lit Bloomingdale's cater to 21st-century America's love affair with labels; but there's a distinct middle-of-the-road factor at the Beverly Center, embodied by the presence (persistence?) of GNC, Macy's, Brookstone, Sunglass Hut, and the rest of the chain gang. The scales may have been tipped on the luxe side with the closing of that staple of malls from coast to coast, the Gap. Shops like Forever 21, Claire's, and Steve Madden and eateries like the Grand Lux Café remind us all that the survival of the mall as a species depends on its ability to attract teenage girls and out-of-towners.

Food

The surprisingly sophisticated Wave Restaurant & Bar, smack-dab in the middle of the mall, is mainly frequented by mall employees and moviegoers who stop by to have a cocktail before their films begin. The eighth floor Food Court features all of the usual suspects (Auntie Anne's, Sbarro's, Panda Express, Starbucks, and the like). Patio seating is plentiful, non-smoking, and features an almost panoramic eastern view of the city. Street-level options include mall mainstays like CPK, PF Chang's and Chipotle Mexican Grill.

Drawbacks

This is a fairly popular mall in a busy part of town; it's bordered by another mall (the Beverly Connection, currently under renovation) and a huge medical center (Cedars-Sinai). That's why it's a good idea to enter from the San Vicente (westernmost and least-congested) side of the building. Although traffic flows well inside the mall, traffic in the parking lot does not. Stay cool—the good stuff's waiting upstairs. Don't be too intimidated by its size, because although it has eight levels, in classic LA style, five are parking. If it's women's clothes you're after, be advised that the Beverly Center best serves those under the age of 30 and smaller than a size 10. Beverly Cinemas 13 offers Dolby stereo and DTS sound, along with large auditoriums that feature balcony seating. Strangely there is no mall access to Bed, Bath and Beyond or the Macy's Men's Department—enter from the street or the valet parking area.

How to Get There—Driving

From the 10 in either direction, exit at La Cienega Boulevard. Head north on La Cienega for approximately 2.25 miles, and you'll see the behemoth just ahead on your left. Cross 3rd Street and turn left into the mall at the next signal. From the 101 in either direction, exit Highland Boulevard and head south on Highland for approximately two miles until you hit Beverly Boulevard. Turn right onto Beverly, and head west about two miles to La Cienega Boulevard. Make a left onto La Cienega Boulevard, and an immediate right into the mall.

General Information

NFT Map:	20
Address:	10250 Santa Monica Blvd Los Angeles, CA 90067
Phone:	310-277-3898
Website:	www.westfield.com/centurycity

Shopping

Though the mall may now be part of a large corporation, in our hearts and minds it will always be the Century City Shopping Center. Regardless of what it's called, Century City is a beacon on the Westside (but not too far west) that seems to say, "Bring me your tired, your hungry, your frazzled masses struggling to get away from fluorescent lighting and the overpowering scent of Cinnabon." In other words, this shopping center is an outdoor, upscale mall blessed with particularly temperate weather, a new state-of-the-art 15-screen movie theater, and a discerning selection of stores. On a good day, when the Bloomie's sale racks are stocked just-so and the nice fellow from Gelson's has unloaded the last of your grocery bags into the back of your station wagon, you'd swear that the happiest place on earth is not, in fact, in Orange County, but rather on Santa Monica Boulevard. Other times you will be wishing for a quick and painless death from the hordes of Beverly Hills teenagers/Paris Hilton wannabes who call this their home away from home.

Set around a gleaming Bloomingdale's, the mall is bright, cheerful, and glossy. Century City, like Sharon Stone, has undergone a massive make-over, renovation, and overall up-ending. Between Restoration Hardware, simplehuman, and the Bloomingdale's housewares department, bridal registries are covered. Another special treat is MaxMara (whose lovely coats you need only wear three or four days of the year in LA, but who's counting?).

Food

Lots of indoor and outdoor seating and a nice variety of cuisines await you in the new minimalist food court. (Think Spielberg's *The Terminal* meets the commissary on the Muir Space Station.) Gulen's Mediterranean and Tacone Wraps are both good. The coffee cart near the Discovery Channel Store has some tasty coffee and kind service. Houston's is great for a before- or after-movie dinner, but keep an eye on the time (see "Drawbacks" below) as there is often a long wait. Gulfstream is perfect for those that are looking for a high-end dining experience to go with their new Gap khakis.

Drawbacks

Construction or no, weekend parking is still a beast. Period. Generally, the farther you get from the mall entrance, the more likely you are to find a space. Or skip the tangled mess and consider valet parking at Gelson's or on the Santa Monica Boulevard side (free with your receipt if you spend at least $250). Another option is to have your car washed at Abluo Auto Spa while you shop: $16 for standard cars including tip (SUVs cost $18…suckers) and worth every penny (on parking Level A). Once the free parking limit is exceeded (three hours free; four with AMC Theater validation), the parking fees start racking up quickly and can result in considerable sticker-shock. Since all the ticket booths are not manned, make sure to pre-pay for parking before heading back to your car. Otherwise be prepared to become public enemy number one.

How to Get There

From the 405 in either direction, exit Santa Monica Boulevard and head east past Sepulveda. Make a slight jog right onto Little Santa Monica Boulevard, and follow it approximately one-and-a-half miles to the mall. The entrance is on your right just past Century Park. From Olympic Boulevard in either direction, head north on Avenue of the Stars to Constellation. Turn left on Constellation and look for the parking entrance 150 yards down on your right.

General Information

NFT Map: 32
Address: 21519-A Madrona Avenue
Torrance, CA 90503
Phone: 310-542-8525
Website: www.delamofashioncenter.com

Shopping

The shopping experience at the Del Amo Fashion Center can be much like gambling at a Las Vegas casino for three simple reasons. First, it's easy to lose track of time since you're surrounded by fluorescent lighting. Second, it's a maze that is hard to escape no matter how hard you try. Third, it's easy to spend your money on crap(s). Things are looking up a bit with the recent arrival of Anthropologie, Urban Outfitters and Lucky Strike Lanes. Better stores, including Crate and Barrel, are scheduled to arrive by fall of '07.

If you want everything under one roof, and you have a lot of time to kill, or you're a really focused shopper that can go straight to what you want, this is the place for you. You can't always find discount retailers such as T.J. Maxx, Marshalls, and Burlington Coat Factory alongside department stores like Macy's. Few malls have Old Navy and the Gap under one roof. This mall either offers a fantastic selection or suffers from chronic redundancy, depending on how you look at it. Let's count—ten jewelry stores, over a dozen shoe stores, and five optometric businesses. You simply need to decide if the sheer volume of stores is worth the physical effort and mental concentration required to tap it.

Food

The food court is centrally located and features Mexican, Mediterranean, and Pacific Rim cuisines in addition to fast-food offerings like Chick-fil-A and Hot Dog on a Stick. The area is clean, brightly lit, and well-attended. To break up a long expedition, consider going outside the mall. Black Angus (3405 W Carson St, 310-370-1523) and Lucille's Smokehouse BBQ (21420 Hawthorne Blvd, 310-370-7427), both adjacent to the mall, offer a chance to protein-load on pretty decent fare in relatively quiet surroundings.

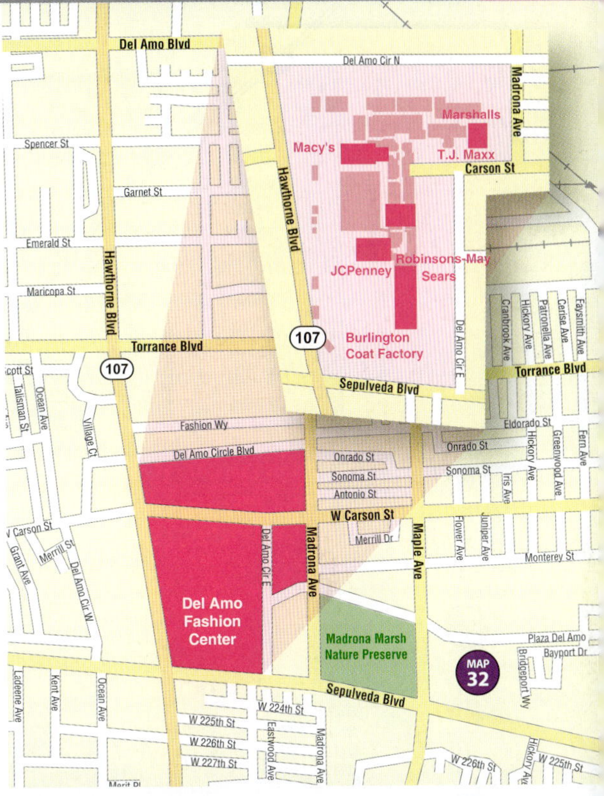

Drawbacks

The upside to the Del Amo Mall (lots of stores) is also its downfall (lots of stores). Besides the fact that you need your own GPS tracker to find where you're going, you need to hike on a mini expedition trek to get there. Del Amo is best approached with very comfortable shoes, an open mind, and an extra cup of coffee—from Kelley's, Starbucks, or Gloria Jean's Coffee. Shoppers seeking a smaller venue should consider the Galleria at South Bay as an alternate venue.

How to Get There

From the 405 S, exit Redondo Beach, head south on Prairie Avenue, and take Prairie approximately three miles. Turn right on Carson to enter the parking lot. From the 405 N, exit Artesia Boulevard and head west on Artesia to Prairie Avenue. Make a left at Prairie and continue on Prairie approximately three miles. Turn right on Carson to enter the parking lot. From the 110 in either direction, exit Carson and proceed west three miles on Carson to the Del Amo Fashion Center.

Malls • Galleria at South Bay

General Information

NFT Map: 30
Address: 1815 Hawthorne Blvd
Redondo Beach, CA 90278
Phone: 310-371-7546
Website: www.southbaygalleria.com

Shopping

All the malls bearing the name "Galleria" base their design (in theory at least) on the Galleria Vittorio Emmanuele in Milan, a four-story shopping center with a glass arcade roof that floods the space with natural light. Well, it's not Milan or even close, but you can see the glass structure effect at the South Bay Galleria. Your day might go like this—spend some time browsing such ubiquitous stores like Sharper Image and Things Remembered, go to the mundane food court, and see a movie with a noisy and rough teenage audience. You are much better off heading a few miles north to Century City for much more enjoyable shopping, dining, and movie-going experience.

Department stores include Mervyn's, Macy's and Nordstrom, all of which have rather poor selection when compared to their other Southern California locations. The mall has three stories of standard mall fare including Gap, Ann Taylor, and Bebe.

Food

The Galleria's food court, however, is excellent compared to much of the competition. Take the express escalator from the main floor and grab a table overlooking the fountain in center court. There's a nice range of food options from Great Khan Mongolian BBQ to the surprisingly good Red Rock Chili and Chick-fil-A (still not open on Sundays, though). The area is clean and well tended. If you're here to bring the little tikes around lunch time, between KB Toys and everyone else's kid running around, you'll blend right in. If you want to eat your meal in a quieter, less ricochet-prone setting, try California Pizza Kitchen (CPK) or Red Robin downstairs. For all you Internet surfers, bring your laptops—the food court has free WiFi.

Drawbacks

As with practically everywhere, weekend parking is a big hassle and not worth it. It's five dollars to valet. (Valets are near CPK on the east side and adjacent to Nordstrom on the west.) Hot tip: Check with the guest services booth just inside the Galleria, as they often have free valet passes stashed behind the counter.

How to Get There

From the 405 S, exit Hawthorne Boulevard and head south one mile. The mall entrance will be on your right.

From the 405 N, exit Redondo Boulevard and head west on Artesia approximately three-quarters of a mile to Hawthorne and make a left. The mall will be on your right.

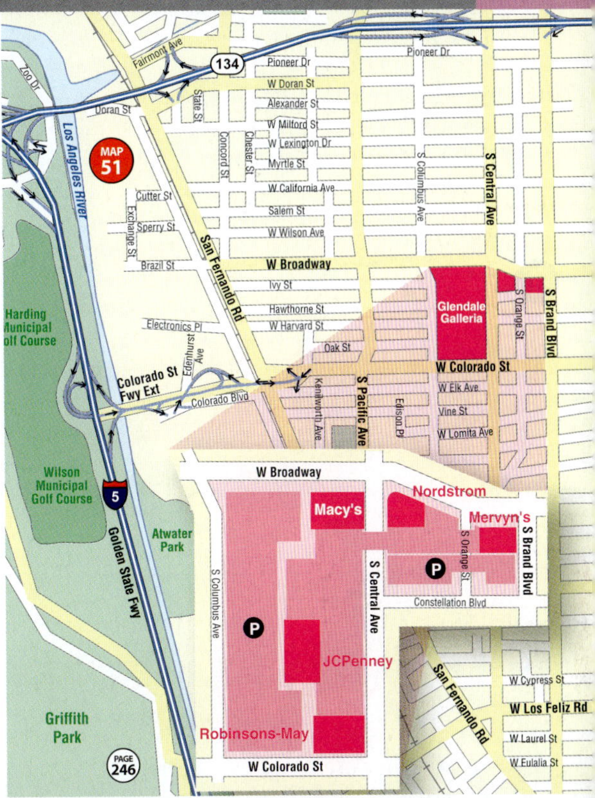

General Information

NFT Map:	51
Address:	2148 Glendale Galleria Glendale, CA 91210
Phone:	818-240-9481
Website:	www.glendalegalleria.com

Shopping

In the giant game of mall Tetris, Glendale Galleria is the "L": not only because of its shape, but also because it's simultaneously the most annoying and rewarding piece of the puzzle. It's the mall that locals love to hate—for all of its faults, you simply can't find a more comprehensive or utilitarian shopping experience. The mall is anchored by the usual stalwarts: Mervyn's, Macy's, JCPenney, Target, and Nordstrom. Coach, Swarovski, and the Apple store represent the high end at this otherwise middle-class temple of mass consumerism. You'll find typical mall fare like Hot Topic and Foot Locker mixed in with boutique-type stores. The Galleria has an impressive selection of dedicated children's stores including Janie & Jack, Naartjie, and the ubiquitous Gap Kids. Forever 21 and Charlotte Russe are the standard go-to for trendy Valley girls while their mothers can stock up on chi-chi cosmetics at Sephora, MAC, and Aveda. A motley crew of kiosks finishes off the retail landscape, peddling everything from "miracle" face creams to rhinestone-encrusted belt buckles.

Food

The Galleria's main food court is on the second level, but you can often smell it from the third. The smoke from The International Grill is mainly responsible—the popular kabob shop serves up steak, lamb chops, and Cornish game hen along with a selection of Armenian and American beers. You'll find everything you'd expect in a food court, including Panda Express, Cinnabon, La Salsa, and Hot Dog on a Stick. The third level has its own selection of fast-food restaurants, with Cleo & Cucci offering a more upscale selection of sandwiches, salads, and pastries.

Drawbacks

If malls aren't your thing, the Galleria probably won't change your mind: on a bad day, it can be a long, echoing chamber of crying babies and shrieking teenagers. The place is also short on elevators and escalators, meaning you may end up walking the length of a football field just to change floors. On the weekends, you run the risk of being swept up in the herds of stroller-pushers, young lovers, and junior high cliques that roam the mall's narrow corridors. Of course—to some hard-core shoppers—this is all just part of the fun.

How to Get There

From the 5 in either direction, exit Colorado and take Colorado east about a mile and a half. The entrance to the mall parking lot is at a light on the left a hundred or so yards before you get to the intersection at Central. From the 134 in either direction, exit Central/Brand Boulevard and head south on Brand about a mile and a half. Turn right on Broadway, and head west an eighth of a mile. The entrance to the mall parking lot is at a light on the left about a hundred or so yards after Central. Look for the "Galleria" sign. For Nordstrom's valet service, enter the smaller parking lot on the east side of Central, just south of Broadway.

General Information

NFT Map:	2
Address:	189 The Grove Dr Los Angeles, CA 90036
Phone:	323-900-8080
Website:	www.thegrovela.com

Shopping

Like Vegas, to which it has aptly been compared, the Grove polarizes Angelenos. There are those who hate it with a passion, resent the way it has commercialized the ancient, historic Farmers Market, and believe it has congested the streets of the Fairfax District beyond repair. Then there are the Grove supporters, open-minded, adaptable and happy consumers who can't help but smile when the dancing waters of the fountain break into yet another choreographed routine to the sound of Donna Summer's "Last Dance." Yes, the Grove is sterile. Yes, the Grove is pre-fab. But like the character of Melanie in *Gone With the Wind*, it's just so darned nice that we're able to table our cynicism for the length of a shopping trip and sing the mall's praises.

The Grove is fairly restrained, with just one anchor store—Nordstrom—and a small one at that. The emphasis here is on high end specialty stores. NikeWomen carries fitness wear for gym goddesses. This family-friendly mall houses the area's only Pottery Barn Kids and recently opened American Girl Place, home to a series of overpriced, over-accessorized dolls, a theater, and a cafe. The usual suspects—the Gap and its brethren—are well-represented, but the Grove also houses the unexpected: LA's first Barneys New York CO-OP, Amadeus Aveda Spa & Salon, and what might be the mall's most beautifully designed retail store, Anthropologie. If none of these stores fit your style, there's always Barnes & Noble. They've got something in everyone's size.

Food

We've got good news and bad news. The bad news is that there is no food court—only full-service restaurants, so lunch or dinner at the Grove is going to cost you. The Farm of Beverly Hills offers American comfort food, while the Wood Ranch BBQ & Grill is a carnivore's paradise. The good news is you can head for the adjacent Farmers Market and enjoy its less expensive, eclectic, and far-superior food stalls. The Gumbo Pot features the best muffuletta this side of N'awlins, ¡Loteria! Grill offers some of the finest Mexican specialties west of Alvarado, and there's no better place for breakfast than Kokomo. Also worth checking out are the handful of specialty kiosks, like Haägen-Dazs and Surf City Squeeze.

Drawbacks

The lack of cheap places to eat can be a drag, and traffic and parking are always a problem. Third Street gets congested, and the traffic light at Beverly Boulevard and The Grove Drive is so poorly timed that two cars are lucky to advance on a green light. Entering from Fairfax Avenue is your best bet.

How to Get There

From the 10 in either direction, exit at Fairfax and head north approximately three miles. Go through the intersection at Third and Fairfax and turn right at Farmers Market Way. Drive past the Farmers Market and enter The Grove's parking structure. From the 101 in either direction, exit at Highland and head south toward Franklin Avenue. Turn right onto Franklin, and continue until you hit La Brea Avenue. Make a left turn and continue south on La Brea to Third Street. Turn right onto Third Street, and continue until you reach The Grove Drive. Make a right turn into the mall. Parking at The Grove is free for the first hour, and $3 per hour for the 2nd and 3rd hours. Valet parking is also available near each of the main entrances of The Grove's parking structure and costs $8 for the first two hours and $2 for each block of 30 minutes thereafter.

General Information

NFT Map: 3
Address: 6801 Hollywood Blvd
Hollywood, CA 90028
Phone: 323-817-0220
Website: www.hollywoodandhighland.com

Shopping

Hollywood & Highland opened in late 2001 to much fanfare. Like the Strip in Las Vegas and the "new" Times Square, it's exceptionally clean, well-lit, and family-friendly. The center is most famous for its state-of-the-art Kodak Theater, which hosts the Academy Awards each year (right across from the Roosevelt Hotel, where the first Academy Awards was held in 1929). Yes, you heard correctly, the Oscars are held at a shopping mall! It's also home to Lucky Strike, a very glossy bowling alley serving a whole lotta top-shelf liquor. The complex provides a safe haven from panhandlers and impersonators of Spiderman and Charlie Chaplin on the Boulevard out front. It even boasts a variety of cozy dining options like Vert Brasserie—H&H wouldn't be Californian, after all, without a Wolfgang Puck outpost.

But let's be honest here: Hollywood & Highland is a gajillion-dollar complex built for the amusement of tourists who come to shop, take pictures of each other, and take pictures of each other shopping. Hollywood & Highland makes little effort to cater to the local set, which is why you won't find many locals here. At this point you have no doubt flipped to the front of this book to confirm that the title is "Not for Tourists." Understandable. We include it here, because eventually we all must entertain our paler friends from the eastern parts of the country who show up to visit in February for what seems to be the express purpose of telling us that California has neither weather nor seasons. But we digress.

Yeah, they've got a Build-A-Bear, a Hot Topic, even the Hollywood Pop Academy, which promises to turn you into tomorrow's Britney or Christina… at a price. But this mall tries to provide a little something else: a calendar of events like the wine & jazz summer series keeps the culture alive, while retail heavies like the flagship Virgin Megastore ensures relevance—even to locals. Besides, the convenience of the metro, along with shuttle services to the Pantages Theatre, Hollywood Bowl, and Griffith Observatory makes H&H an unavoidable convenience. Even Spiderman has to get home after a long day.

Food

Two high-profile local brands raise the meaning of mall food to an unprecedented level: CPK for pizza and the Wolfgang Puck brasserie, Vert. Koji's Sushi and Shabu Shabu is also a reliable choices for a lunch date. Green Earth Café serves up speciality coffees and iced blended drinks. The cream puffs at Beard Papa's will have you asking, "Krispy Kreme who? "The clever (and discreet) visitor might venture up to the Renaissance Marriott's rooftop pool for a spectacular view and a cool drink. On the elevator ride up be sure to practice your straight face when you tell the guards that you "totally didn't see the 'For Hotel Guests Only' sign."

Drawbacks

The drawbacks of Hollywood & Highland are pretty much the same as those of the Strip or the "new" Times Square: it's crowded, air-brushed, fabricated out of whole cloth, and devoid of organic materials—but that's why you moved here, right? Then there's the mind-boggling traffic in the area around the complex. The streets surrounding the place—Highland, Franklin, Orange, and Hollywood—get distressingly backed up on weekends. Also, the entrance to the never-crowded Mann Chinese 6 Theaters (not to be confused with the Grauman's legendary Chinese Theater next-door) is not well marked, so be sure to keep your eyes peeled. Parking at Hollywood & Highland costs $2 for up to four hours with validation. For an additional five bucks, you can splurge on valet.

How to Get There

If you're using mass transit, take the Red Line to the Hollywood & Highland station. Exit the station. Thumb your nose at the traffic all around you. From the 101 S, exit at Highland Avenue/Hollywood Bowl and merge onto Cahuenga Boulevard. Cahuenga becomes North Highland Avenue. Stay on Highland until Hollywood Boulevard. From the 101 N, exit at Highland Avenue/Hollywood Bowl and keep right at the fork in the ramp. Merge onto Odin Street, and turn left onto Highland Avenue. From 405 in either direction, exit onto Santa Monica Boulevard. Head east on Santa Monica Boulevard through Beverly Hills, West Hollywood, and into Hollywood. Turn left on Highland.

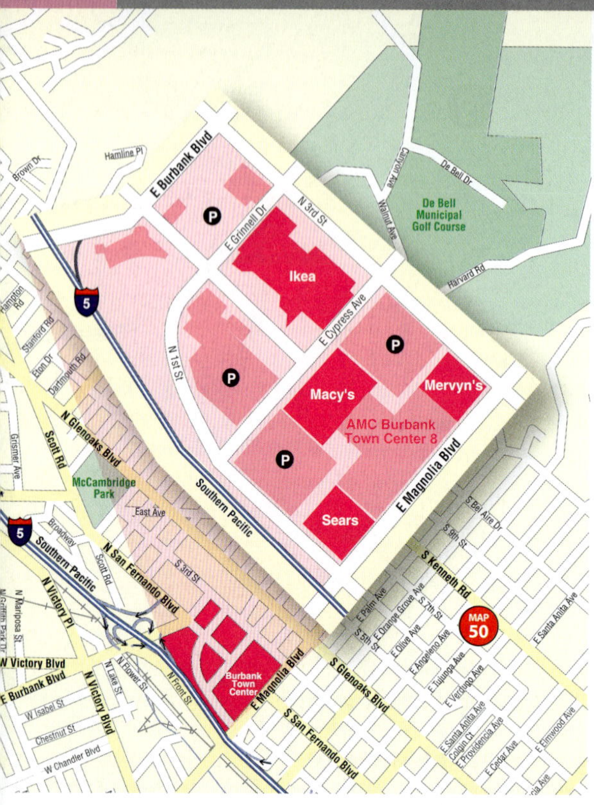

General Information

NFT Map:	50
Address:	201 E Magnolia Blvd Burbank, CA 91501
Phone:	818-566-8556
Website:	www.burbanktowncenter.com

Shopping

At some point in the early stages of their assimilation into LA, all new arrivals pass through the portals of IKEA, thus making Burbank Town Center the Ellis Island of Los Angeles. To see this area only for its prefab Swedish furnishings would be to miss the point entirely. It also has a full-service, mid-range mall (with an oversized chessboard on the first level centercourt), a boatload of movie theaters, and access to a rapidly developing stretch of San Fernando Boulevard where shoppers can browse movie scripts and used books, migrate toward the peculiar glow emanating from Urban Outfitters, and shoot a game of pool in between all the shopping, eating, and movie-going.

The Burbank Town Center mall itself provides the moderately-priced fare you'd expect from anchors such as Mervyn's, Macy's, and Sears. Sport Chalet is fun and well-stocked, while the newly-minted Bed, Bath & Beyond delivers its reliable supply of home furnishings and gadgetry. Women's clothing outlets (Georgiou, Lane Bryant, Express, and the like) outnumber men's (Corsine, Express Men, etc.) by nearly five to one, while kid magnets like KB Toys proliferate like bunnies at Easter. The chocolate-minded can get their fix at See's Candies. Outside the mall, Barnes & Noble is always good for pre- or post-movie browsing. The Virgin Megastore's closing has created a musical vacuum in the area, but audiophiles can still seek comfort at Circuit City.

Food

On the Magnolia Boulevard side of the mall's upper level, you'll find all of the standard Food Court fare, while Johnny Rockets, PF Chang's, and Pomodoro Cucina Italiana offer sit-down respites from mall madness. Just outside, along the strollable San Fernando Boulevard you'll find Market City Caffe (164 E Palm Ave, at San Fernando), specializing in Italian antipasti and inspired martinis; Romano's Macaroni Grill (102 E Magnolia Blvd), serving more Italian standards; Knight Restaurant (138 N San Fernando Blvd), offering savory Mediterranean treats; and Picanha Churrascaria (269 E Palm Ave), trotting out abundant quantities of Brazilian meat-on-a-stick fare. Hurried shoppers can also hit the drive-thru at In-N-Out Burger (761 N 1st St.) just outside the mall's 1st Street exit, or pause to admire the view over their meal at Hooters (600 N. 1st St).

Drawbacks

Three AMC Theaters with a total of 30 screens are clustered around Burbank Town Center, including one in the Burbank Town Center. Double-check your movie location before you go, or you'll surely miss the previews in a desperate dash between theaters. Parking gets complicated on weekends. Your best bet is to park in the East Garage on 3rd between San Jose and Magnolia.

How to Get There

From I-5 in either direction, exit at Burbank Boulevard and head east on Burbank to N 3rd Street. Turn right on 3rd and go four blocks. The East Parking Garage is on your right, the block after IKEA.

General Information

Address:	9301 Tampa Ave Northridge, CA 91324
Phone:	818-701-7051
Website:	www.northridgefashioncenter.com

Shopping

Although there's ample spending opportunity at Northridge Fashion Center, nothing did as much financial damage to it as 1994's earthquake. Since the quake, Northridge has been renovated twice to become the extravagant structure of retail magnificence you see today. With 200 stores, 10 restaurants, and a charming outdoor pedestrian area, there truly is something for everyone here. Cost Plus offers more exotic home décor ideas than you can shake a rain stick at, while conventionalists can rely on department store standards like Sears, JC Penney, and Macy's. With all that Northridge has to offer—including an Apple store, a Borders, and a ten-screen cinema—it's a shame that it's tucked just far enough out of the way that you'd never think to go there. However, if you're already headed to Sears for a fridge or new tires, or if you're fairly deep in the West San Fernando Valley, there's no reason not to go check it out.

Food

The NFC food court is clean, well-lit, and offers outdoor seating. You can choose between a variety of cuisines at restaurants like La Salsa, Sansei, and Surf City Squeeze. The line for Donatello's Pizza is always long, but it moves surprisingly fast. Sit-down restaurants in the complex include Red Robin (hamburgers) and On the Border Mexican Grill. For a break (weather permitting), sit outside on the patio at Wood Ranch BBQ for good food and better people watching.

Drawbacks

Whether you're coming from the 101 or the 118, the drive along Tampa can be slow. The parking lot fills up quickly, too, so in summer you may be in for a long, 100+ degree walk to and from the mall. There is a beautiful Gelson's supermarket nearby—far enough away from the main mall to require moving your car, but close enough to make you feel guilty for doing so.

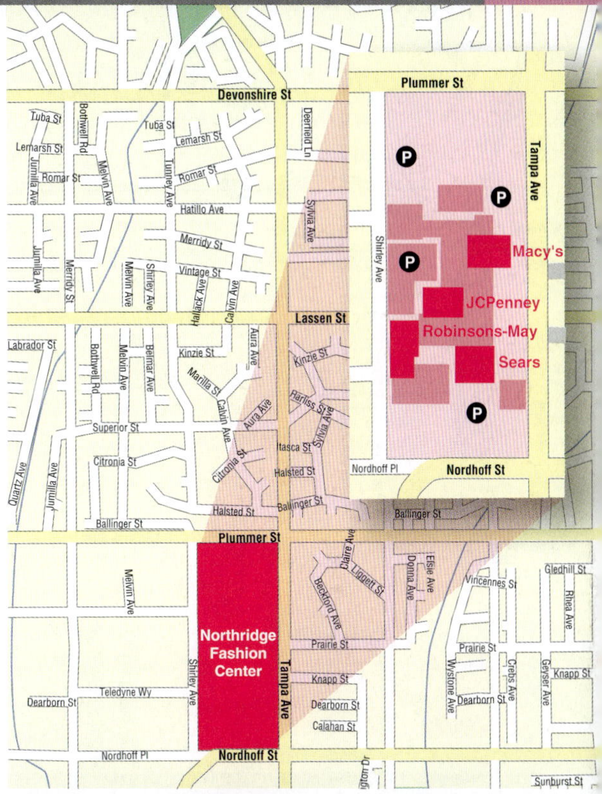

How to Get There

From the 101 in either direction, exit at Tampa Boulevard and head north on Tampa approximately four miles to Plummer. The mall entrance is on the left. From the 118 in either direction, exit at Tampa Boulevard and head south on Tampa approximately four miles to Plummer. The mall entrance is on the right.

General Information

NFT Map:	34
Address:	280 E Colorado Blvd Pasadena, CA 91101
Phone:	626-795-8891
Website:	www.paseocoloradopasadena.com

Shopping

If Carrie Bradshaw lived in LA (as if!) this is where she'd pick up her Manolo Blahniks. Paseo Colorado is a self-consciously upscale outdoor mall with the usual yadda yadda yadda stores. Fashionistas beat a path to DSW Shoe Warehouse for super-affordable designer shoes and drop by the venerable Loehmann's for discount chi-chi threads. Looking a little like Walt Disney's vision of a shopping mall (minus the life-size cartoon characters), Paseo Colorado boasts cutesy Mexican architecture and inviting open spaces that encourage strolling and exploration. Once inside the mall it's easy to forget you're just yards away from the busiest thoroughfare in Pasadena. Paseo Colorado proudly bills itself as an urban village; and it's true, you literally could live here—if you won the lottery—as light and airy apartment towers form the perimeter of the mall. Pick up your furnishings from the Bombay Company and Brookstone. Grocery shop at the world's most expensive supermarket—Gelson's—and meet your neighbors for a $5 happy hour martini or work your way through the "world's largest selection of draft beer" at the Yard House. If your jaw doesn't drop at the idea of single digit cocktail prices, you're not quite a local.

If you must move with the herd, know that Paseo Colorado is also home to Macy's, Tommy Bahama, and Ann Taylor Loft as well as a variety of smaller, more distinctive stores such as J. Jill. At the end of a hard day's consumerism, fold yourself into a seat in front of one of the Pacific Paseo Theater's fourteen screens.

Food

There isn't one centrally located food court, thank God, but there are a variety of places to eat on the second floor. Sit-down restaurants include Island's (huge burgers and frou-frou drinks with umbrellas in them) and PF Chang's China Bistro. Tokyo Wako has its fans if you're in the mood for sushi. During the day you can get takeout from Gelson's excellent deli and hot food sections...but aside from the aforementioned cheap drinks, Paseo Colorado isn't really a fine wining or dining location. Better to make the short hop to Old Town Pasadena for an eclectic array of really fine ethnic restaurants and street life.

Drawbacks

Avoid the permanently-full underground garage at all costs. Your endless gas-guzzling loops will easily take on the qualities of a Twilight Zone episode. There's plenty of street parking and it's safe. There isn't one contiguous second floor, so be sure and check the shopping directory before you head upstairs to your restaurant of choice.

How to Get There

From the 134 in either direction, exit at Marengo Avenue and head south on Marengo for a half-mile until you hit Colorado Boulevard. Parking is available in the structure on the right, just past Colorado.

From the 110 N, exit Fair Oaks Boulevard and head north on Fair Oaks to Colorado Boulevard. Turn right and head approximately a half-mile to Marengo Avenue. Turn right at Marengo Avenue to enter parking. There is also parking on the Green Street side of the Paseo. Don't forget to validate your parking ticket!

General Information

NFT Map: 18
Address: 395 Santa Monica Pl
Santa Monica, CA 90401
Phone: 310-394-1049
Website: www.santamonicaplace.com

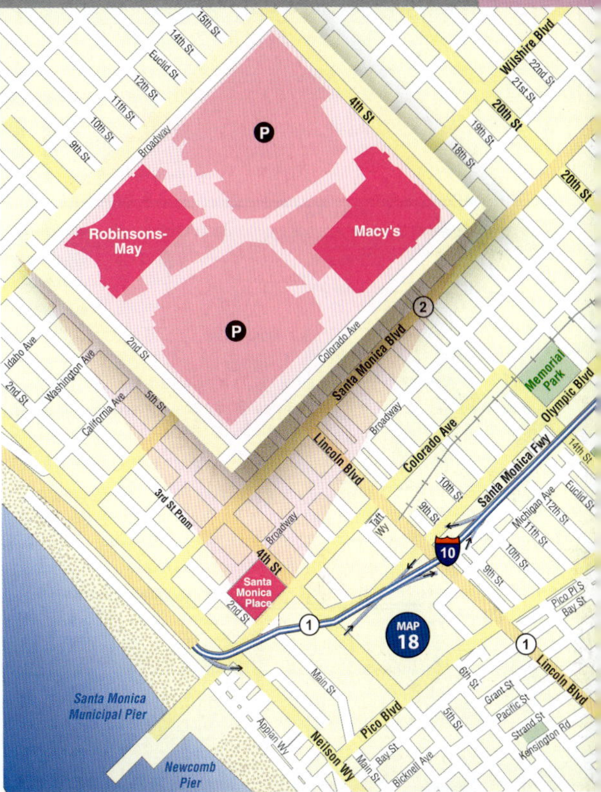

Shopping

Santa Monica Place is a perfectly average mall in a spectacular location. Adjacent to the 3rd Street Promenade, the mall, designed by Frank Gehry in 1980, is barely a quarter-mile from the beach. The location, combined with the usual line-up of unremarkable store offerings, make it hard to justify a visit. There are simply better places in the neighborhood to be. Better places, of course, unless it's raining. The typical mall shops serve the local Santa Monica community well for last-minute gifts and clothing necessities. Unless you know that what you're looking for is in one of the stores (Victoria's Secret, Brookstone, etc.), your best bet is to stroll around and take the mall on its own terms. Macy's is the only department store left, after acquisitions closed down Robinsons-May. Santa Monica Place caters to the young, so take your teenaged niece to Wet Seal and Forever 21. If you've arrived at the beach unprepared, you can buy bathing suits at one of the sporting goods stores and then find some new shades at Sun Shade or Sunglass Hut. (Both have good sales, making it worth at least a drive-by.)

Proposals were underway to renovate Santa Monica Place into a new development that includes office space, residential units, public parks, restaurants, and retail space, in conjunction with the Promenade, the Pier, and the Civic Center. However, the process is currently on hold indefinitely with no new updates. Until then, the mall will continue to operate as normal. More information about the project is available at www.santamonicaplace.com/redevelopment.

Food

The food court is bustling and cacophonous. Hot Dog on a Stick and Charlie Burgers will put you in a good-time mood if you're one of the lucky ones to snag a table, but more likely you'll have to place those orders "to go." Take them outside to eat on the Promenade, where the weather's better, anyway.

Drawbacks

This particular area of Santa Monica gets particularly congested on the weekends. Pedestrians, some on roller blades or skateboards, will wear out your patience. Once inside the mall, the clientele consists mostly of teens and tourists.

How to Get There

From 10 W, head north on Lincoln Boulevard for a quarter-mile until you hit Colorado Avenue. Head west on Colorado Avenue and enter the parking lot from that side.

From PCH heading east, exit at Ocean Avenue. Turn left on Ocean and then right on Colorado Avenue.

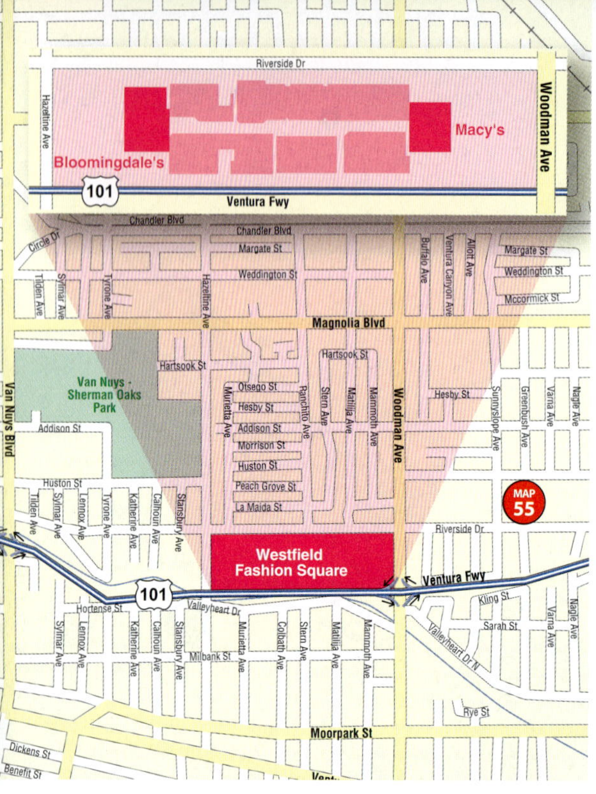

General Information

NFT Map:	55
Address:	14006 Riverside Dr Sherman Oaks, CA 91423
Phone:	818-783-0550
Website:	www.westfield.com/fashionsquare

Shopping

When fun-loving couples in their twenties evolve into responsible parents in their thirties, they move to the Valley. Indicative of this shift, while the Westfield Century City unveils a spanking new multiplex, the Westfield Fashion Square in Sherman Oaks is the recipient of a new kiddie playground and a passel of children's clothing stores (Naartjie, Janie & Jack, babystyle). The mood at the Fashion Square is cool, but not hip. Upscale, but not ostentatious. Entertaining, but not necessarily fun. The Fashion Square caters to the locals who have moved to Sherman Oaks because it is clean, tasteful and safe. Similar qualities may be found in the home furnishings dealers at the Fashion Square, a group which includes Pottery Barn, Williams Sonoma, and Z Gallerie.

Clothing choices are an equally predictable mix of Abercrombie & Fitch, the Gap, Banana Republic, and Victoria's Secret. The Square is not without its high-end perks—the Bloomingdale's shines and Teavana shows that there's a world of tea that goes way beyond Earl Grey. Expectant mothers are treated like queens with two apparel stores (babystyle, A Pea In the Pod) and a group of dedicated parking spots located close to the mall entrance reserved just for them. Those few Valley denizens without kids in tow can hold on to their freedom, shopping solo at the Apple store or pampering themselves at the Aspect Beauty health club and spa, which could only be further from the playground if it had been placed outside the mall on the other side of Riverside Drive.

Food

The choices in the Garden Café Food Court seem so limited that the most appealing lunch selection often seems to be an Ice Blended from the Coffee Bean & Tea Leaf and a Cinnabon, extra icing please. Chain restaurants rule, from healthy(-ish) chains like California Crisp or La Salsa to those that are decidedly not healthy at all (Carl's Jr., Sbarro). Downstairs options are more appealing. Barney's is a Westside institution that now offers burgers, sandwiches, and salads, and the California Pizza Kitchen ASAP offers a faster-food version of its usual dine-in menu. For your convienience and snacking pleasure, gumball machines are strewn throughout the mall, filled with assorted candy and chocolate treats.

Drawbacks

The long line of cars waiting to turn into the mall can frequently serve as a deterrent for shoppers, sending them off to stand-alone alternatives in nearby Studio City or Encino. Also, the absence of a supermarket, a movie theater, and a decent sit-down restaurant prevents the Fashion Square from being a destination in its own right.

How to Get There

From the 101 in either direction, exit Woodman. Head north on Woodman one block, and go left onto Riverside. The parking lot can be accessed on both the Riverside and the Hazeltine sides of the mall, though Bloomingdale's shoppers will want to enter on Hazeltine.

General Information

NFT Map: 45
Address: 6600 Topanga Canyon Blvd.
Canoga Park, CA 91303
Phone: 818-594-8732
Website: www.westfield.com/topanga/

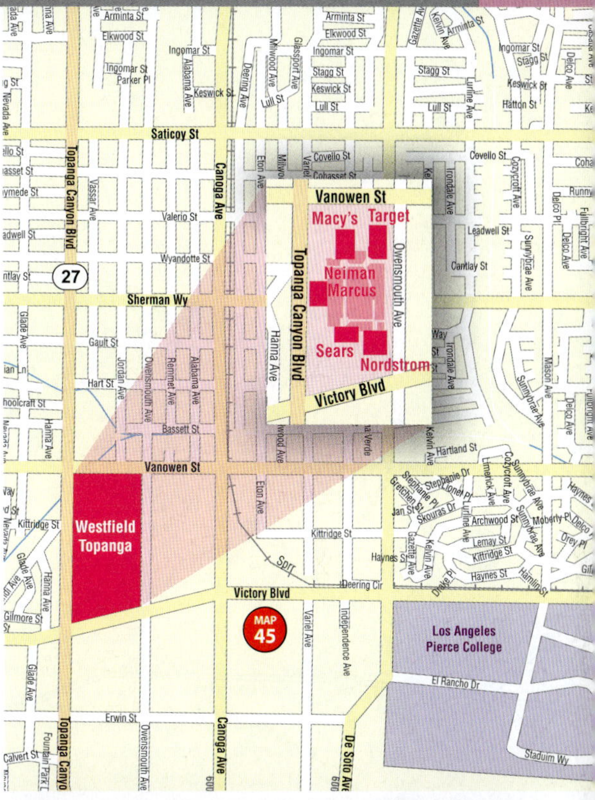

Shopping

For any Valley resident who has ever gone behind the Orange curtain to Costa Mesa and lamented, "Where is our South Coast Plaza?" we have an answer. It's in Canoga Park and it's called Westfield Topanga. Before the Northridge Quake did some serious damage, Topanga Plaza (as it was then known) was a run of the mill neighborhood mall. But out of the rubble has emerged a lesson in civic planning, a utopia, if you will, of how retail—and society—should be.

The brilliance of the Topanga mall is in how it manages to be the big tent that draws everyone in. Yes, Neiman Marcus is opening next year but Sears continues to anchor the mall from another end. The planner who thought to include a two-story Target along with a newly renovated Nordstrom deserves a Nobel Prize for malls. Low end, high end…it's all covered. The major apparel chains are all represented, along with an occasional higher-end surprise (Benetton and Hanna Andersson). Male shoppers have established a beachhead in the upper level "Canyon" with the one-two punch of the Apple Store and the spa-like Art of Shaving. For the home, there's a Crate & Barrel and a Pottery Barn, but what is Target for if not to knock off Crate & Barrel and Pottery Barn? Neiman Marcus is slated to open in 2008, bringing another batch of retail shops with it, including H&M. We cannot wait.

Food

The mall's egalitarian qualities extend to the food available to its guests. Westfield eschews the term "food court" for the far more posh "dining terrace." Choices there are a little more focused on Asian meals, from the sushi at Seiki-Shi Sushi to the Korean BBQ and kimchee at Sorabol, but it's all definitely fast food. If you've got the time (and the cash) spend a little more and have breakfast, lunch, or dinner at The Farm of Beverly Hills, an export from Beverly Hills and The Grove.

Drawbacks

In a bizarre attempt at world domination, the folks at Westfield now own both the former Topanga Plaza and a complex they call The Promenade just down the street (6100 Topanga Plaza). The good news is that together they are home to just about any retailer you might ever want to visit. The bad news is that there's no easy way to get to the Promenade from the Westfield Topanga and vice versa -- you can walk about five blocks, or drive and repark (an unbearable thought on a weekend evening). It's rumored that Westfield will one day connect the two malls by bridge or walkway or—we hope you're sitting down for this—build a new mall to unite the two squabbling ones that we have.

How To Get There:

Take the 101 to Topanga Canyon Blvd. and head north. Westfield Topanga will be the second mall on your right (the first being the Westfield Promenade), at Victory.

General Information

NFT Map:	23
Address:	10800 W Pico Blvd Los Angeles, CA 90064
Phone:	310-474-6255
Website:	www.westsidepavilion.com

Shopping

The Westside Pavilion is a rarity. A no-attitude shopping location with all the usual suspects in terms of stores and resources, but with solid ties to the local community. This may not sound exciting, but this mall has hotspots for everyone, including a dance studio, post office, and hairstylist. There are more kid's stores than you can hit in an afternoon: Gymboree, E.B. Games, Disney Store, and Three Cheeky Monkeys, to name a few. You can park the teens at Pop Star or Claire's Accessories. Dad will probably park himself at Sisley's Italian Kitchen wine bar while Mom is giving the plastic an airing at BCBG.

The mall is a long narrow space anchored by Nordstrom's and Macy's. Despite being home to over 160 stores it never feels crowded. The original space has an end-to-end skylight which gives a plein air feel even in winter. The newer annex is reached by way of a covered walkway across Westwood Boulevard. Periodically W.P. hosts wine and food samplings and honors local schools. There's even a monthly Kid's Club for the little brats that presents mimes, jugglers and puppet shows. On the upper level there's the ubiquitous food court and a couple of cozy movie theaters that actually show films you don't mind paying to see, including exclusive indie presentations not found anyplace else in the city. All in all a great, well-balanced mall.

Food

Not much to write home about. Basically, if you can fry it, put it on a stick, or smother it with cheese, you'll find a counter devoted to it in the food court. If you want real food, try Sisley's Italian Kitchen on the street level. Also surprisingly good is the Nordstrom Café, located inside the store on the top level. The best food, however, is just outside the mall: the Apple Pan (10801 W Pico Blvd) is a Los Angeles institution. The small shack serves affordable old-school hickory burgers in a lunch-counter setting. Be prepared to wait. Down the street on Pico is Louisa's Trattoria and the venerable (but pricey) Junior's Deli is just around the corner on Westwood Boulevard. It's been there for 50 years and some of the waitresses look as if they haven't missed a day. God bless 'em.

Drawbacks

Do not attempt to navigate the parking lot without medication and a pocketful of breadcrumbs. Hands down the worst, most confusing parking lot in the greater Los Angeles area. Take the express ramp directly to the top level. Or better yet, splurge on the best valet bargain in town—$3, no waiting. Enter next to Nordstrom. If you start thinking about trying your luck outside the structure, don't. There's minimal street parking and, since it's so close to both the 405 and 10 freeways, making your way around the surrounding streets (especially the biggies like Pico and Westwood) can be a slow-moving pain.

How to Get There

From the Valley, take 405 S and exit at the Pico/Olympic off ramp. Make a left to reach Pico Boulevard, and then another left. Continue east on Pico. Westside Pavilion extends from Westwood Boulevard to Overland Avenue. From the South Bay and Orange County, take 405 N, exit at National Boulevard and turn right. Make a left at Westwood Boulevard and travel north until you reach Pico Boulevard. From downtown LA, take 10 W and exit at Overland Avenue. Take a right on Overland Avenue heading north to Pico Boulevard. Westside Pavilion extends west from Overland Avenue to Westwood Boulevard. From Santa Monica, take 10 E and exit at National/Overland. Turn right on National and another right on Overland Avenue. Head north on Overland Avenue to Pico Boulevard.

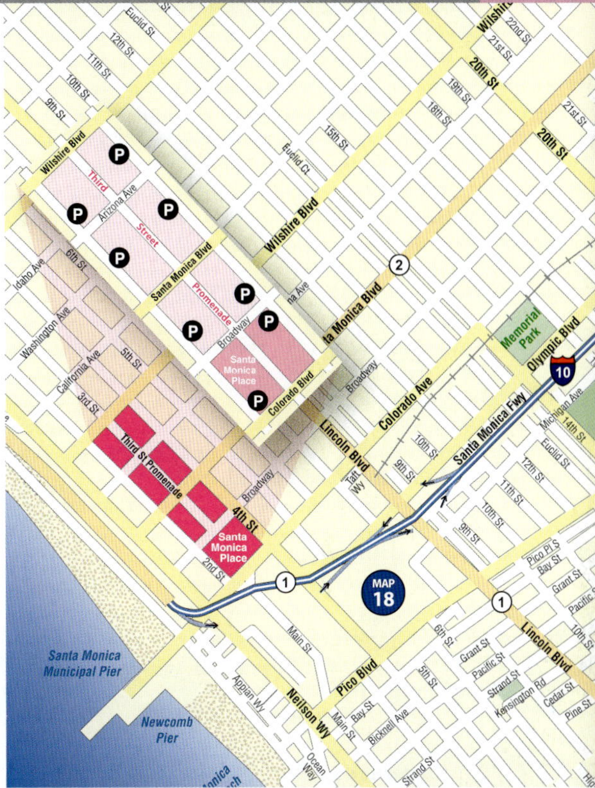

General information

NFT Map: 18
Website: www.thirdstreetpromenade.com

Shopping

Third Street Promenade is a tourist magnet with a force greater than gravity. The street is closed off to traffic from Wilshire to Colorado, providing wide-open walking space. Its outdoor shopping and alfresco dining options theoretically make it a pleasant place to spend an afternoon or evening, but its weekend crowds of high schoolers, out-of-towners, and visitors from the Inland Empire can make it a little less than charming to navigate. However, the Farmers Market on Wednesday and Saturday mornings lives up to its renowned reputation (Arizona & 3rd St). The usual mall suspects—Gap, J. Crew, Urban Outfitters, Pottery Barn, Victoria's Secret—flank the Promenade, intermixed with small boutiques selling cutesy, perhaps dubiously-priced clothes. The selection of stores clustered in one walkable area does make it easy for someone on a mission to quickly find exactly what he or she is looking to buy, and on the way one might even spot a celebrity browsing the magazines at the giant newsstand in the middle of the Promenade that features newspapers and magazines from all over the world. Additionally, three movie theaters span the Promenade and are a popular place to watch big premieres.

Food

Third Street Promenade offers up a range of eateries from McDonald's and Johnny Rocket's to more upscale Italian and Greek cuisines. Monsoon (1212 3rd Street Promenade) has a daily happy hour, along with sushi and potsticker deals, and a view of the tango entertainment on the street. Yankee Doodle's (1410 3rd Street Promenade) features 39 screens for sports watching over burgers and beer, and has several pool tables on two levels (also a good place to get quarters for parking meters). Gaucho Grill's Santa Monica location (1251 3rd Street Promenade) has a quiet, intimate dining room away from the outside hubbub. Though Broadway Deli (1457 3rd Street Promenade) is only an attempt to be a New York deli on the left coast, the food isn't so bad. Of course, dining weekday nights on the Promenade makes for a more soothing evening than on the weekends.

Drawbacks

Parking can be a challenge on the weekends, and if you park on the street, rest assured that the meter maids stand to watch the second your meter expires. Street performers often cause a clog up of pedestrian traffic as people stop to watch the man who juggles bowls or listen to the mini-Elvis crooning the King's songs a foot from the ground. But if you can snag an outdoor dining table, the people-watching is endless.

How to get there

From I-10 W, take the 5th Street exit going north. From PCH heading east, exit at Ocean Avenue. Turn left on Ocean and right on Colorado Avenue. Parking is available at a number of structures on 2nd and 4th Streets, and along Broadway and Colorado (free for the first two hours during the day).

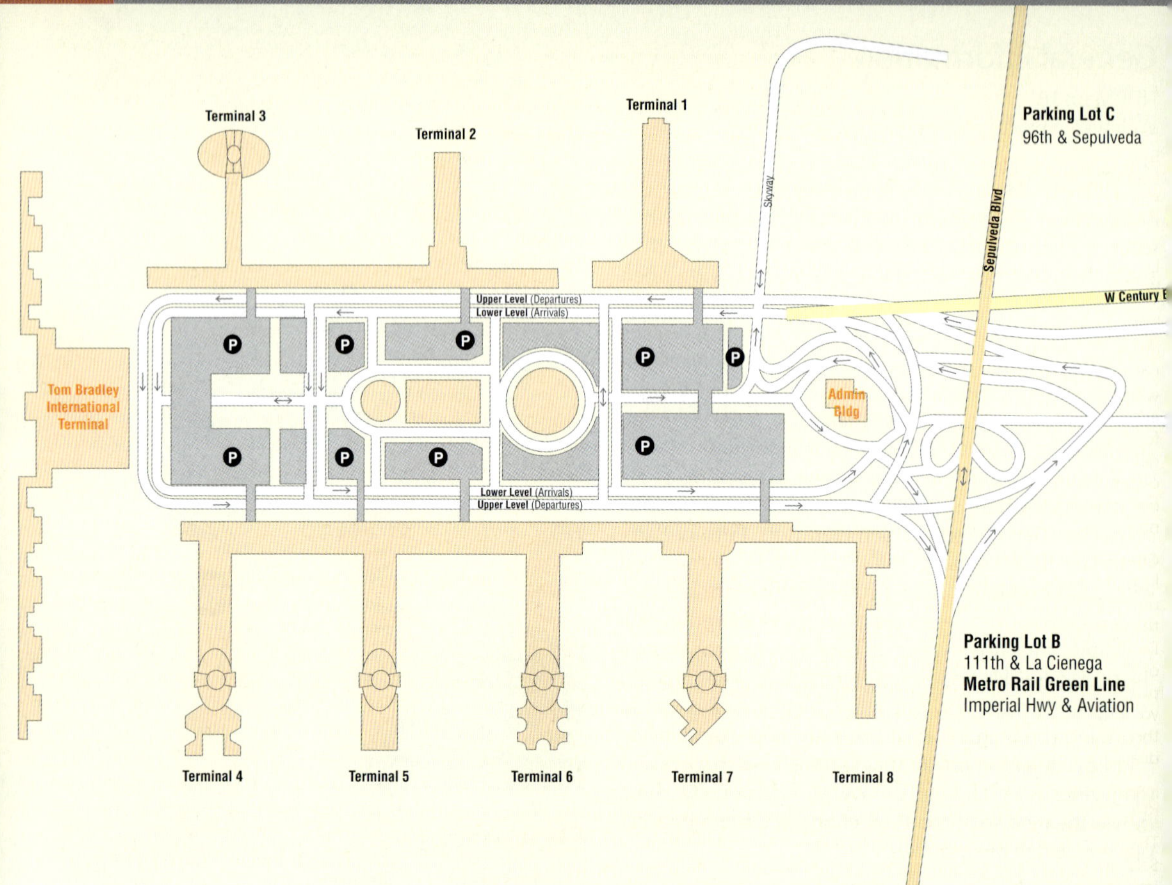

Airline	*Terminal*
Aer Lingus	TBIT
Aeroflot	TBIT
Aerolitoral	5
Aeromexico	5
Air Canada	2
Air Canada Jazz	
Air China	2
Air France	2
Air India	TBIT
Air Jamaica	5
Air New Zealand	2
Air Pacific	TBIT
Air Tahiti Nui	TBIT
AirTran Airways	3
Alaska Airlines	3, TBIT
All Nippon Airways (ANA)	TBIT
America West Airlines	1
American Airlines	4
American Eagle	4
American Trans Air (ATA)	3
Asiana Airlines	TBIT
Aviacsa Airlines	2

Airline	*Terminal*
Avianca Airlines	
British Airways	TBIT
Cathay Pacific Airways	TBIT
China Airlines	TBIT
China Eastern	TBIT
China Southern Airlines	5
Continental Airlines	6
Copa Airlines	6, TBIT
Delta Air Lines	5
El Al	TBIT
EVA Air	TBIT
Frontier Airlines	3
Hawaiian Airlines	2
Horizon Air	3
Japan Airlines	TBIT
KLM Royal Dutch Airlines	2
Korean Air	TBIT
LACSA Airlines	2
LAN Chile	TBIT
LAN Peru	TBIT
LTU International Airways	TBIT
Lufthansa	TBIT

Airline	*Terminal*
Malaysia Airlines	TBIT
Mexicana Airlines	TBIT
Midwest Express Airlines	3
Northwest Airlines	2
Philippine Airlines	TBIT
Qantas	4, TBIT
Singapore Airlines	TBIT
Southwest Airlines	1
Spirit Airlines	5
Sun Country Airlines	3
Swiss Int'l Air Lines	TBIT
TACA Int'l Airlines	2
Ted Airlines	7, 8
Thai Airways	TBIT
United Air Lines	6, 7, 8
United Express	7, 8
US Airways	1
Varig Brazilian Airlines	TBIT
Virgin Atlantic Airways	2
WestJet	3

** TBIT = Tom Bradley International Terminal*

General Information

Address:	1 World Way Los Angeles, CA 90045
Phone:	310-646-5252
Baggage Storage:	310-646-0222
Lost & Found:	310-417-0440
Police:	310-646-7911
First Aid:	310-215-6000
Customs Information:	310-215-2415
Los Angeles MTA:	800-266-6883
Website:	www.lawa.org

Overview

Los Angeles International Airport is one of the busiest airports in the world. Driving here is like braving a whirlpool with all its frustrating eddies, but as long as you start out correctly (take the upper ramp for departures, the lower one for arrivals) you'll be just fine. You can't get lost, because it's a big circle. Yes, a circle filled with honking traffic, overzealous parking cops, TV news trucks during the holidays, and a hustler or two looking to take advantage of lost tourists, but a circle nonetheless.

Give yourself plenty of time to get through the check in and security lines, especially during Thanksgiving and Christmas when the lines at terminal one will wrap around the check-in area, out the door and all the way to terminal two. Good thing it's warm in Los Angeles during December. Always check-in online if possible. Once you're through all of the hassle, each terminal offers a variety of places to grab a bite, pick up a magazine, or pep up with a coffee (Starbucks, of course). If you want to avoid eating airline food, try the Wolfgang Puck Café or the Gordon Biersch Brewery. Since security is so tight, you're forced to deal pretty much with whatever is in your airline's terminal.

How to Get There—Driving

The most direct route to LAX is unfortunately not the fastest. The San Diego Freeway (405) to the Century Freeway (105) leads right into the airport, but the 405 is almost always congested. The 105 has accommodating carpool lanes—which can be tantalizing when you're sitting in gridlock—but it's a mousetrap; the cops are primed to apprehend the fast and furiously late for their flights. The 110 to the 105 is another option, but if it's the 110 or the 405, you might as well flip a coin. As cab drivers know, surface roads are the preferable way to access LAX whenever possible. From the northern beach cities (Santa Monica, etc.), take Lincoln Boulevard south until it joins Sepulveda Boulevard. This will lead you right to LAX, but be prepared to make a sudden right turn into the airport. From the South Bay, Sepulveda is also the preferred route, but this time the airport will be on your left. The quickest route to LAX from Central LA is La Cienega Boulevard. South of Rodeo, La Cienega becomes a mini-freeway that rarely becomes congested except during rushhour. Take La Cienega to Century Boulevard, then turn right towards the airport.

How to Get There—Mass Transit

In a word: Don't. Though many buses will take you to LAX, the trip may last longer than your actual flight. Sure, you're getting a lot of bang out of your $1.25–$3 fare, but this is the way to go only if you have time for a "leisurely" ride to the airport, or if you're trying to log some field work for your anthro degree. City buses deposit passengers at the LAX Transit Center, where a free shuttle travels to each of the airport's terminals. Another free shuttle connects LAX to the Metro Green Line Aviation Station, where LA's Light Rail system ferries travelers to outlying areas like Redondo Beach (to the south) and Norwalk (to the east).

How to Get There—Really

If you're at all clever, convince a friend to drive you. If that's not an option, car services and taxis are truly the best way to go. The airport's FlyAway service from Van Nuys expanded in 2006 to shuttle passengers from downtown to LAX for $3 one-way ($2 for children). Park the car at Union Station for $6 a day or take MetroRail. Visit www.lawa.org for more information. Super Shuttle's rates start at under $20 and increase with distance from LAX (800-258-3826; www.supershuttle.com). Most local cab companies also offer a flat rate to LAX that can be economical for parties of two or more. Average cost for a one-way trip from Redondo Beach to LAX is $16; from Santa Monica it's $18; from downtown it's $27; from Van Nuys it's $40; and from Pasadena it's $50. Some taxi services are: Beverly Hills Cab Co. (310-273-6611), LA Yellow Cab (213-627-7000), and Valley Town Car Service (818-787-1900). Look for frequent coupons in the mail—they're worth it. Lastly, drive yourself to the airport and park at any number of long-term parking lots surrounding the airport. Free shuttles drop off and pick up at your terminal. The Parking Spot (5701 W Century Blvd) starts at $12.95 a day and offers valet and car washes. All Star Parking (6141 W Century Blvd) is located right next to the airport and has uncovered parking for $12.95 a day as well. Check the internet for frequent, advertised discounts, but be sure you know the location before arriving and give yourself plenty of time in case you have to wind around 12 floors to the roof. If you have a valet key, bring it in case that's the only option left, often the case on Fridays.

Parking

Two-hour metered parking is available on LAX's Lower/Arrival area opposite Terminals 1, 2A, 2B, 3, 4, 6, and 7. Fifteen minutes costs 25 cents. These spaces can be hard to spot, and you may find yourself in one of the pricier structures opposite each of the terminals. Parking in these lots costs $7 for up to two hours and $30 maximum. For long-term parking, it's best to use Lots B and C, but be sure to allow an extra half-hour in your schedule for dealing with the parking lot shuttle bus. Lot C is at Sepulveda Boulevard and 96th Street and rates are $10 for each 24 hours. Lot B is further away, at La Cienega and 111th Street, but less expensive at just $8 per day.

Car Rental

Advantage	310-671-0503
Alamo	888-826-6893
Avis	800-331-1212
Budget	310-642-4500
Dollar	800-800-4000
Enterprise	310-215-6856
Fox	800-225-4369
Hertz	800-654-3131
National	800-462-5266
Payless	310-342-5392
Thrifty	877-283-0898

Hotels

Best Western Airpark • 640 W Manchester Blvd • 800-233-8060
Comfort Inn • 850 N Sepulveda Blvd • 310-318-1020
Days Inn • 901 W Manchester Blvd • 310-649-0800
Hilton Garden Inn • 2100 E Mariposa Ave • 310-726-0100
Marriott Hotel • 5855 W Century Blvd • 310-641-5700
Motel 6 • 5101 W Century Blvd 310-419-1234
Sheraton Gateway • 6101 W Century Blvd • 310-642-1111
Travelodge • 5547 W Century Blvd • 310-649-4000

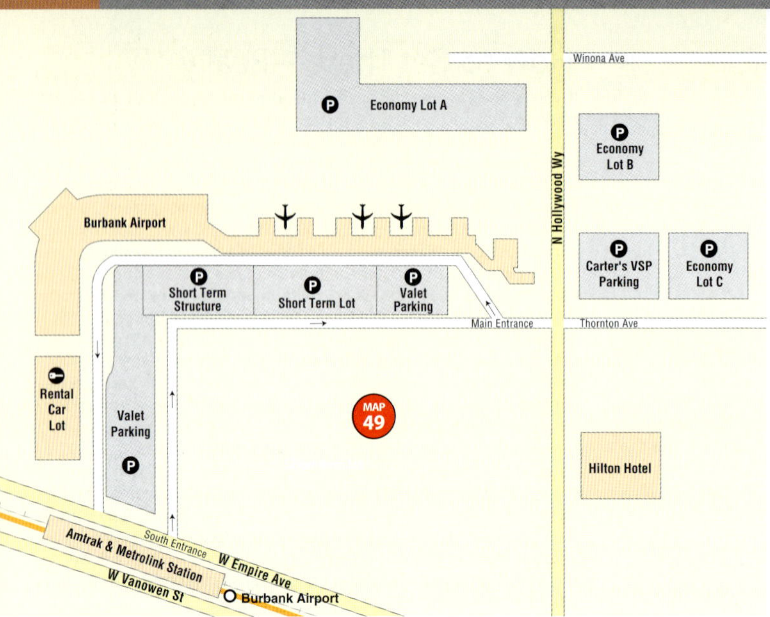

General Information

NFT Map:	49
Address:	2627 N Hollywood Wy Burbank, CA 91505
Phone:	818-840-8840
Parking Information:	818-565-1308
Website:	www.burbankairport.com

Overview

Burbank (BUR)—also known as the Bob Hope Airport (LA sure loves naming airports after old celebrities)—is a small, low-key, alternative to LAX, and a *must* if you live east of La Brea or in the San Fernando or San Gabriel Valleys. The parking is cheaper (especially in the nearby discount lots), the lines are shorter, and travelers coming through here are simply happier. From groups of partiers hopping a quick Southwest jaunt to Vegas to the smiling folks boarding the newly-added JetBlue service, Burbank is as stress-free as flying gets. Sure, the addition of JetBlue and Delta cross-country service has busied up the place and put some stress on the parking situation, but that's just a bit of turbulence during an otherwise smooth trip.

How to Get There—Driving

The airport is just off I-5, so if you're approaching from the north or south, take I-5 and exit atHollywood Way. Take Hollywood Way south and find the airport entrance on your right.

If you're coming from the west, take the 101 S to the 134 E and use the Hollywood Way exit. Travel north on Hollywood Way until you hit the airport on your left.

From the East, you can make your way to either the 134 W or I-5N and follow the above directions.

It's also possible, and often preferable, to drive to Burbank Airport from parts of the Valley by taking any number of surface roads. Burbank or Victory Boulevards provide a fairly direct route to the airport from the western end of the Valley. From all other directions, it's best to choose your favorite non-freeway route to Hollywood Way and take that straight into the airport.

How to Get There—Mass Transit

Similar to the rail systems in Europe and Japan, Metrolink and Amtrak trains both go right to the airport—well, almost. The terminals are just a short walk or free shuttle bus away.

The Burbank Airport station is on the Ventura County (yellow) Metrolink line and, depending on where you're coming from, during peak hours it will cost between $4.75 one-way (same zone) and $11.75 (if you're starting from the very end of the Orange County Line). Off-peak you can expect to pay between $3.50 and $8.75. Trains link up Monday–Friday only. 800-371-LINK; www.metrolinktrains.com.

Amtrak's Pacific Surfliner Train (which runs from San Diego to Paso Robles) makes a stop at the Burbank Airport Rail Station as does their Motor Coach Service to the San Joaquin trains in Bakersfield. 800-USA-RAIL; www.amtrak.com.

MTA buses are slower but cheaper. Numbers 94, 163, 165, and 394 all make stops at Burbank Airport. 800-COMMUTE; www.mta.net.

Parking

Short-term parking is located in the four-story garage across the entry road from the terminal. It can be pricey if you stick around for more than an hour or two: $2 for the first hour, $4 for the second, $6 for the third, $12 for the fourth, and up to a $30 daily maximum. There's economy (uncovered) parking in lots A, B, and C ($9 per day). A number of companies also offer covered long-term parking in locations adjacent to the airport. Got more money than time? Valet parking is $20 per day and located a scant 30 yards from the terminal.

Airlines

Alaska Airlines
American Airlines
Delta Air Lines
JetBlue Airways
Skybus Airlines
Southwest Airlines
United Air Lines
US Airways

Car Rental

On-Site:	
Alamo	800-327-9633
Avis	800-331-1212
Hertz	800-654-3131
National	800-227-7368
Off-Site:	
Advantage	800-777-5500
All-Rite	818-972-2490
Budget	800-527-0700
Discovery	800-641-4141
Enterprise	818-558-7336
Rent4Less	800-993-5377

Hotels

- **Anabelle Hotel** • 2011 W Olive Ave • 818-845-7800
- **Hilton** • 2500 N Hollywood Wy • 818-843-6000
- **Universal City Hilton & Towers** • 555 Universal Hollywood Dr • 818-506-2500
- **Ramada Inn** • 2900 N San Fernando Blvd • 818-843-5955
- **Safari Inn** • 1911 W Olive Ave • 818-845-8586
- **Sheraton** • 333 Universal Hollywood Dr • 818-980-1212
- **Travelodge** • 1112 N Hollywood Wy • 818-845-2408

General Information

Address:	18601 Airport Wy Santa Ana, CA 92707
Phone:	949-252-5200
Lost & Found:	949-252-5000
Website:	www.ocair.com

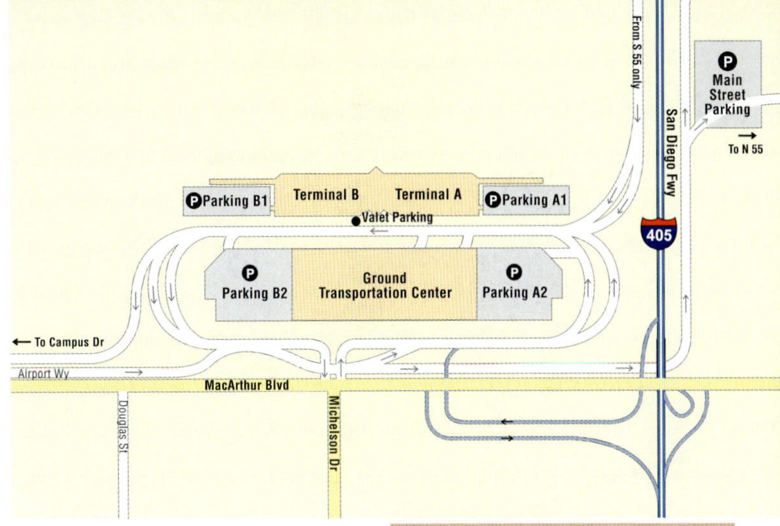

Overview

Though most of us typically associate John Wayne with dusty Hollywood westerns rather than aviation, Orange County has seen fit to name its only commercial airport after the leather-chapped actor, a longtime OC resident. They've even erected an impressive nine-foot bronze statue out front honoring the Duke in mid-swagger, complete with cowboy hat and spurs. Located well behind the "Orange Curtain," John Wayne Airport (SNA) is quite a trek from LA (approximately fifty miles), but airlines can sometimes make the commute worth your while with lower fares. Aesthetically, the airport makes a solid effort, featuring rotating art exhibits displayed on the departure level at each end of the terminal. Probably the best thing we can say about John Wayne Airport is that it isn't LAX.

How to Get There—Driving

Driving yourself or tapping that indebted buddy is definitely your best means of transportation to the airport. Sadly, most paths from LA County to John Wayne Airport at some point lead to the 405 Freeway—one of LA's more congested routes. The 405 will bring you closest to John Wayne, which lies just a short distance from the MacArthur Boulevard exit (CA-73). From downtown or the eastern part of Los Angeles, however, there is another option. Take the Santa Ana Freeway (5 S) to the Costa Mesa Freeway (55 S), exiting at the ramp marked "I-405 S to San Diego/John Wayne Airport," and follow the signs from there.

How to Get There—Mass Transit

From LA? You've got to be kidding. If you're dead-set on taking this course, you'd better have a LOT of free time. Several hours, in fact, as there are no direct bus routes that connect Los Angeles County with John Wayne Airport. However, for only $2.25 the MTA can get you as far as Disneyland on the 460. After the over-two-hour bus ride from downtown LA, get out and kill some time with a few rides on Space Mountain, then board Bus 43 heading south toward Costa Mesa, and take this to the corner of Harbor and MacArthur Boulevards. Are we there yet? Hardly. THEN transfer to Bus 76 heading east toward Newport Beach, which will take you right by the airport. All in all, you sure saved a bundle going the thrifty route for a grand total of $4.75, but not if you missed your flight.

How to Get There—Ground Transportation

A taxi ride from Los Angeles to John Wayne Airport starts at about $80. Some companies to consider are LA Yellow Cab, (213-627-7000) and the Beverly Hills Cab Company (310-273-6611). Leaving the airport, the John Wayne Airport Yellow Cab Service (800-535-2211) is the only company authorized to pick up fares. They'll charge around $90 from the airport to downtown. Compared to those prices, SuperShuttle (800-258-3826) is a veritable bargain at $65 from downtown LA to John Wayne.

Parking

Short-term lots (A1, A2, B1, and B2) charge $1 per hour with a $17 maximum per day. The Main Street long-term lot is also $1 per hour but only $12 per day with a courtesy shuttle to the terminal available every 15 minutes. Selected parking spaces are available in Lots A1 and B1 for a two-hour maximum, and are ideal for dropping people off and picking up, but you still have to fork over that $1. If you're really a high roller—or, say, on your way to Vegas—valet your car at $23 per day.

Airlines

Airlines	*Terminal*
Alaska Airlines	A
Aloha Airlines	B
America West Express	B
American Airlines	A
American Eagle	A
Continental Airlines	A
Delta Air Lines / Delta Connection	A
Frontier Airlines	B
Northwest Airlines	B
Southwest Airlines	B
United Air Lines / United Express	B
US Airways/American West Airlines	B

Car Rental

On-Site:	
Alamo	800-327-9633
Avis	800-230-4898
Budget	800-527-0700
Enterprise	800-736-8222
Hertz	800-654-3131
National	800-227-7368
Thrifty	800-847-4389
Off-Site:	
Advantage	800-777-5500
AM-PM	800-220-4310
Beverly Hills	800-479-5996
Fox/Payless	800-225-4369
Go Rent-A-Van	800-464-8267
OC Car & Truck	800-349-6061
Rent4Less	866-945-7368
Stop-Then-Go	888-704-7867
United Auto	866-878-6483

Hotels

Best Western • 2700 Hotel Terrace Dr • 714-432-8888

Embassy Suites • 1325 E Dyer Rd • 714-241-3800

Holiday Inn • 2726 S Grand Ave • 714-481-6300

Quality Suites • 2701 Hotel Terrace Dr • 714-957-9200

Travelodge • 1400 SE Bristol St • 714-557-8700

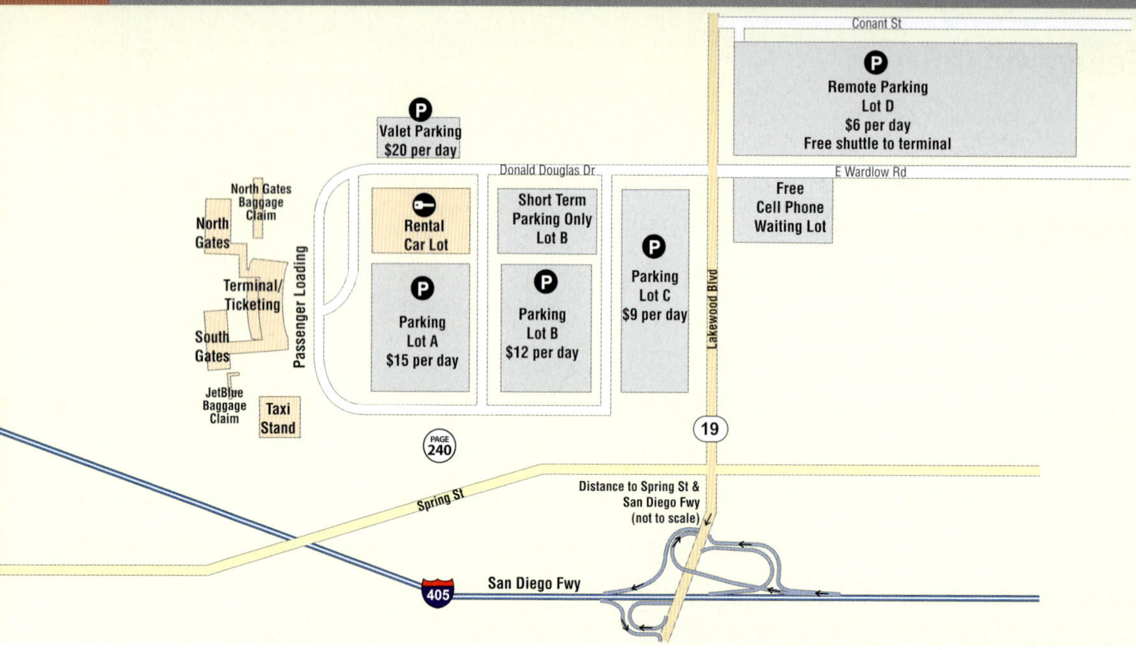

General Information

Address: 4100 Donald Douglas Dr,
Long Beach, CA 90808
Phone: 562-570-2619
Website: www.longbeach.gov/airport

Overview

What the Long Beach Airport (LGB) lacks in amenities, it makes up for with efficiency. The television show *Wings* comes to mind when popping into the quaint terminal (yes, that's *one* terminal) with its Art Deco style and historical aviation pictures. With a handful of carriers, some of which aren't represented at LAX, checking in is a snap. Retrieving your luggage is even easier. Flying into LGB sure beats the sensory overload of walking out into LAX's smog-ridden, traffic-choked arrivals area.

The best way to get there is by taking a shuttle service. Let someone else deal with the 405 while you read, nap, or crank up the iPod. Oh, and be sure to eat before you go, since your only options are a questionable-at-best snack bar, a stuffy upstairs restaurant, and maybe some of those Terra chips on JetBlue. A proposed expansion will undoubtedly change the dynamic to some degree, so enjoy it while you can.

How to Get There—Driving

Long Beach Airport can be reached easily from just about anywhere in the Los Angeles basin. From the 405, take the Lakewood Boulevard exit northbound. Proceed past Spring Street and turn left on the next stop light, which is Donald Douglas Drive. From the 91, take the Lakewood Boulevard exit and proceed southbound approximately four miles. Make a right at Donald Douglas Drive into the main airport entrance.

How to Get There—Mass Transit

For 90 cents the Long Beach Transit Bus Route 111 runs from Broadway to South Street via Lakewood Boulevard and makes a stop right at the airport (www.lbtransit.com; 562-591-2301). You can take the Blue Line train from downtown LA to the Transit Mall station in Long Beach to connect with the Route 111 bus (www.mta.net; 800-COMMUTE).

Taking a taxi, the best bet is a Long Beach Yellow Cab (562-435-6111). Alternatively, a number of van and limousine services are available including Advantage Ground Transportation (800-752-5211), SuperShuttle (800-BLUE-VAN), Airport Express Limousine (866-800-0700), and Diva Limousine (800-427-DIVA).

Parking

The first twenty minutes in all lots is free. Each hour after that will clock up $1. The maximum daily rate in the long-term parking lots is $15. Try the "Park & Walk" lot at the main airport entrance on the corner of Donald Douglas Drive and Lakewood Boulevard. The rate declines as you get farther from the airport, so decide how far you want to walk versus how much you want to spend ($12 versus $9 per day). If you've got a lot of time, try the $6 per day remote off-site lot at Lakewood Boulevard and Conant Street with a free shuttle to the airport. Valet parking is $22 per day. Short-term parking has a two-hour limit.

Hotels

Holiday Inn • 2640 N Lakewood Blvd • 562-597-4401
Marriott • 4700 Airport Plaza Dr • 562-425-5210
Residence Inn by Marriott • 4111 E Willow St • 562-595-0909

Airlines

Alaska Airlines (North Gates)
Delta Air Lines (North Gates)
America West/US Airways (North Gates)
JetBlue Airways (South Gates)

Car Rental

Avis	800-331-1212
Budget	800-221-1203
Enterprise	800-736-8222
Hertz	800-654-3131
National	800-227-7368

Airline	Phone	LAX	John Wayne	Burbank	Long Beach
Aer Lingus	800-474-7424	■			
Aeroflot	888-340-6400	■			
Aerolitoral	800-237-6639	■			
Aeromexico	800-237-6639	■			
Air Canada	888-247-2262	■			
Air Canada Jazz		■			
Air China	800-882-8122	■			
Air France	800-237-2747	■			
Air India	800-223-7776	■			
Air Jamaica	800-523-5585	■			
Air New Zealand	800-262-1234	■			
Air Pacific	800-227-4446	■			
Air Tahiti Nui	877-824-4846	■			
AirTran Airways	800-247-8726	■			
Alaska Airlines	800-426-0333	■	■	■	■
All Nippon Airways (ANA)	800-235-9262	■			
Aloha Airlines	800-367-5250		■		
America West Airlines	800-235-9292	■			■
American Airlines	800-433-7300	■	■	■	
American Eagle	800-433-7300	■	■		
American Trans Air	800-225-2995	■			
Asiana Airlines	800-227-4262	■			
Aviacsa Airlines	888-528-4227	■			
Avianca Airlines		■			
British Airways	800-247-9297	■			
Cathay Pacific Airways	800-233-2742	■			
China Airlines	800-227-5118	■			
China Eastern	626-583-1500	■			
China Southern Airlines	888-338-8988	■			
Continental Airlines	800-525-0280	■	■		
Copa Airlines (Panama)	800-359-2672	■			
Delta Air Lines	800-221-1212	■	■	■	■
Delta Connection			■		
El Al	800-352-5747	■			
EVA Air	800-695-1188	■			
Frontier Airlines	800-432-1359	■	■		

Airline	Phone	LAX	John Wayne	Burbank	Long Beach
Hawaiian Airlines	800-367-5320	■			
Horizon Air	800-547-9308	■			
Japan Airlines	800-525-3663	■			
JetBlue Airways	800-538-2583			■	■
KLM Royal Dutch Airlines	800-225-2525	■			
Korean Air	800-438-5000	■			
LACSA Airlines	800-225-2272	■			
LAN Chile	866-435-9526	■			
LAN Peru	866-435-9526	■			
LTU International Airways	866-266-5588	■			
Lufthansa	800-645-3880	■			
Malaysia Airlines	800-552-9264	■			
Mesa Airlines	800-637-2247		■		
Midwest Express Airlines	800-452-2022	■			
Northwest Airlines	800-225-2525	■	■		
Philippine Airlines	800-435-9725	■			
Qantas	800-227-4500	■			
Singapore Airlines	800-742-3333	■			
Skybus	n/a			■	
Southwest Airlines	800-435-9792	■	■	■	
Spirit Airlines	800-772-7117	■			
Sun Country Airlines	800-359-6786	■			
Swiss International Air Lines	877-359-7947	■			
TACA International Airlines	800-535-8780	■			
Ted Airlines	800-225-5833	■			
Thai Airways	800-426-5204	■			
United Air Lines	800-241-6522	■	■	■	
United Express	800-241-6522	■	■		
US Airways	800-428-4322	■	■	■	■
Varig Brazilian Airlines	800-468-2744	■			
Virgin Atlantic Airways	800-862-8621	■			
WestJet	888-937-8538	■			

Union Station

Union Station is located at 800 N Alameda Street between the Santa Ana Freeway (US 101) and Cesar E. Chavez Avenue. Built in 1939, it was considered the last great train station built in the United States. Its architecture alone renders it a stunning piece of Los Angeles history. With distinct Art Deco, Spanish Colonial, and Postmodern influences, it's impressive enough to merit a visit even if you're not looking to jump on a train. The scenic waiting room's ceiling stands 52 feet above its marble floors, and large, distinctive archways at each end give way to peaceful courtyards. Have you ever been in a train station that offered both the daily edition of the local paper *and* repose in a beautiful garden? Exactly. The station services three rail networks—the local Metro Rail Red Line, Amtrak (including the Pacific Sunliner and Coast Starlight Lines), and Southern California's Metrolink. Union Station is also home to the elegant Traxx Restaurant—a good spot to go if your boss is paying.

Amtrak

800-872-7245; www.amtrak.com

Amtrak, i.e. what passes for a reliable national rail network in this country, runs five major lines into LA's Union Station. The Pacific Surfliner (formerly the San Diegan) runs between San Diego, LA, and Santa Barbara, and on to San Luis Obispo and Paso Robles. You're not guaranteed to arrive on time, but at least you'll have beautiful ocean views to stare at if you're delayed. A one-way trip from San Diego to LA will set you back about $30 and will (hopefully) get you there in under three hours. Traveling the length of the line costs around $46. Since the Desert Wind line closed down, Amtrak no longer offers transportation to Las Vegas via train, but they do provide a bus service, which takes between five and six hours and costs $66 round trip.

Shuttle service to Bakersfield connects the Pacific Surfliner with the San Joaquin trains, which run from Bakersfield through Fresno to Oakland. The Coast Starlight runs the length of the coast from LA through Oakland, and up to Eugene-Springfield and Seattle. The LA-to-Oakland fare costs between $47 and $56 one-way (buying round-trip is no less expensive than buying two one-way tickets), and if you're traveling all the way to Seattle, you'll be paying about $139. If you're heading east, the Sunset Limited line will be your train of choice. It runs from LA through Tucson, Phoenix, San Antonio, Houston, New Orleans, Jacksonville, and Orlando. The Texas Eagle has a similar first leg and covers Los Angeles, Tucson, San Antonio, Dallas, Little Rock, St. Louis, and Chicago. The Southwest Chief goes from LA to Albuquerque to Kansas City to Chicago. Check the Amtrak website or call to check schedules on the days you wish to travel.

Metrolink

800-371-5465; www.metrolinktrains.com

Not to be confused with the MTA's Metro Rail, Metrolink is an above-ground rail network that serves Southern California, including Los Angeles County, Ventura County, San Bernardino County, Orange County, Riverside County, and San Diego County. The lines run as far south as Oceanside in San Diego County, and as far north as Montalvo in Ventura County and Lancaster in LA County. Fares are calculated according to the number of zones traversed. A one-way fare costs between $4.50 and $11.75 during peak times, and it is always cheaper to purchase a round-trip ticket ($7.25 peak, one zone) at the beginning of your journey rather than two one-way fares. At $30.50 for one zone and up to $105.25 for seven zones, the ten-trip pass is a good deal for frequent riders. Discounts are available at all times for senior and disabled riders and during off-peak hours for youth. Monthly passes are also available at varying rates.

Metro Rail

800-266-6883; www.mta.net

The Metro Rail network is really, at its best, a confusion of contradictions, debate, and public necessity. It's an expanding public transportation network in a city that is notorious for its lack of just that; it's a contentious subway system in a city with a Mediterranean climate and over 200 earthquake fault lines; but it's also one of the few things trying to shake things up in a city where the freeways have been allowed to run wild. Locked in a battle of ambivalence, a begged-for expansion has been delayed by NIMBYs and car-lovers who consider public transit irrelevant. Luckly, Mayor Villariagosa (a former president of the MTA) has been taking steps towards an extended Orange Line and the long-awaited "Subway to the Sea." And, as we come ever closer to paying four bucks for a gallon of gas, one has to wonder: Neglect your precious automobile...help save the environment in a potential death trap...well, it's a contentious debate thatseems like a real no-brainer.

The bus system is expanding in shaky bursts. With the new Orange Line in the Valley, one rarely wants to risk driving along Chandler. Granted, the street is all decked out with rather nice bus stops and the new eye-catching bus design is working hard to remind us that the bus isn't just for the blind and the homeless anymore. This new line even has its own transit lane, separate from the regular flow of traffic. But when the line opened, there was just accident upon accident between buses and confused Angelenos. The new traffic guidelines and signs at the intersections really are hard to miss, but apparently LA drivers are doing their best. So be careful—of the bus and your fellow autos.

With the Red, Blue, Gold, and Green Lines, the Rail system will carry you from the Valley to Hollywood to Downtown, over to Pasedena, and down to Redondo Beach. With stops at Union Station, Hollywood and Highland, the STAPLES Center, Universal City, and the Wiltern, one does feel the temptation to jump out of their car and onto the Metro Rail band wagon. The only real drawback is the limited hours, particularly obvious on weekend nights, when clubbing by rail would be possible, if only it didn't stop running at midnight.

As far as ticketing goes, the Metro Rail works off of the honor system. And by honor system, we mean the occasional threat of a ticket. While this may be hard to grasp for someone coming from a city with a reliable, untrusting transportation system, that's just how it's done here in the City of Angels. But you've been forewarned: Police check tickets onboard trains at random and unpredictable intervals, and if you fail to produce a valid ticket, you'll receive a fine a whole lot higher than the fare. Beware of eating or drinking on board as well—what seems like a minor infraction carries a major fine. Metro Rail sells a Monthly Metro Pass for $52 on their website.

Bicycles are happily allowed on the Metro Rail and buses. On the rail, they are not allowed on weekdays 6:30 am to 8:30 am and 4:30 pm to 6:30 pm. There are no restrictions during weekends and on holidays. Bicycle racks are available on a first-come, first-served basis, free of charge. Lockers may be rented for $75 for one year by calling 213-922-2660. Buses can accommodate two bikes per bus on their racks. The Orange Line provides a bikeway alongside its own transitway, as well as bike racks and bicycle parking at all of its stations.

North Hollywood
Universal City
Hollywood/Highland
Hollywood/Vine
Hollywood/Western
Vermont/Sunset
Vermont/Santa Monica
Vermont/Beverly
Wilshire/Western
Wilshire/Normandie
Wilshire/Vermont
Westlake/MacArthur Park
7th Street/Metro Center
Civic Center
Pershing Square
Union Station
Chinatown
Lincoln/Cypress
Heritage Square
Southwest Museum
Highland Park
Mission
Fillmore
Del Mar
Memorial Park
Lake
Allen
Sierra Madre Villa
Pico
Grand
San Pedro
Washington
Vernon
Slauson
Florence
Firestone
103rd St
Aviation/LAX
Hawthorne
Crenshaw
Vermont
Harbor Freeway
Avalon
Imperial/Wilmington
Long Beach
Lakewood
Norwalk
Mariposa
El Segundo
Douglas
Redondo
Compton
Artesia
Del Amo
Wardlow
Willow
Pacific Coast Highway
Anaheim
Pacific
5th Street
Transit Mall
1st Street
Pacific Ocean

Overview

An estimated 10 million people live in the 4,084 square miles of Los Angeles County, and while a railway system does exist, it is buses that make up the majority of LA's public transport network. Most, but not all, of the 300 bus routes through the city are run by the Metropolitan Transportation Authority (MTA). Fares and procedures vary between services. The websites for the services are excellent resources for route and schedule information, as well as trip planning. Fares for seniors, the disabled, and students can be as low as 25% of the full fare and differ for each service. Monthly passes offer regular riders a smaller discount. Up to two children (5 and under on MTA services, 4 and under on LADOT services) ride free with each fare-paying adult. Most buses don't give change, so be sure to carry exact change when boarding a bus. Fare machines take $1 bills, but they don't give change. If you're planning a multi-stage trip that involves bus, rail, and even Amtrak travel, the Metro Trip Planner website will tell you how to get from point A to point B, and it will conveniently detail times, fares, and directions (for details, see the Metro Trip Planner section on the next page).

Metropolitan Transportation Authority (MTA)

800-266-6883; www.mta.net

MTA buses are distinguished by their white color and distinctive orange stripes. Bus stops have a big black M on a white, rectangular sign. A single fare on an MTA bus costs $1.25 (45¢ for seniors/disabled). A transfer to a municipal bus costs 25¢ (10¢ for seniors/disabled)—ask your driver for one when you board. If you're changing buses again, buy another transfer from the driver when you hand in the first transfer. Transfers are good for an hour after you receive them. If you plan to switch to the Metro Rail, however, you'll have to pay $1.25 again; at this point, it might be cheaper to purchase a Day Pass, which allows you to board unlimited times for $3. Metro bus night fares (9 pm–5 am) cost 75¢ and 35¢ for seniors/disabled.

Frequent riders can save money by purchasing bags of ten tokens at local stores or supermarkets for $11 (which brings down your per-trip cost to $1.10). If you're a regular bus commuter, you might consider buying a weekly pass ($14), a semi-monthly pass ($27), or regular monthly pass ($52, and $12 for seniors/disabled). You can't just buy the semi-monthly and monthly passes anytime, though. They begin on the 25th or the 11th of each month and can be purchased in person from Metro Customer Centers and more than 600 sales outlet locations, or ordered through the mail and delivered to your home or office. MTA passes are valid on Commuter Express, DASH Downtown LA, Community Connection Routes 142, 147, 203, 208, and all Metro MTA rail and bus routes. LADOT passes are not valid on MTA services.

Los Angeles Department of Transportation (LADOT)

(213, 310, 323, or 818) 808-2273; www.ladottransit.com

DASH (Downtown Area Short Hop) shuttle system operates buses A, B, C, D, E, and F throughout downtown LA. The reliable service runs every five to twelve minutes, depending on the time of day and route, and costs only 25¢. The buses service downtown and also stop at the city's major landmark sites, including Union Station, the Convention Center, USC, Exposition Park, and the Garment District. DASH also runs services to many parts of west LA, including Venice, Hollywood, West Hollywood, Beverly Hills, Studio City and Watts, Wilmington, Northridge, Chatsworth, and Crenshaw.

The **Commuter Express** is mainly a commuter service for people living in suburbs such as Culver City, Westwood, Brentwood, Encino, Glendale, Burbank, Redondo Beach, and the San Fernando Valley, who work in downtown LA. The fare costs between 90¢ and $3.10. Seniors/disabled pay half the regular fare.

Community Connection serves the needs of city neighborhoods including San Pedro, Terminal Island, Long Beach Transit Mall, Griffith Park, and Beachwood Canyon. LADOT also operates a battery-powered trolley in San Pedro, which departs every 15 minutes. A one-way fare on the regular bus routes costs 90¢, and 45¢ for seniors/disabled, and the electric trolley costs 25¢ per ride.

The new **Holly Trolley** implements the Bunker Hill buses to carry club hoppers, diners, and other Hollywood explorers between Highland and Vine. For just a dollar, you can catch a ride until 4 am.

Municipal Buses

The Big Blue Bus serves Santa Monica, Malibu, and Venice, and it costs 75¢ to race between the beach towns. They also operate an express bus (Line 10) to downtown LA that costs $1.75 (25¢ seniors/disabled). If you buy a Little Blue Card, you'll save a couple of pennies per ride. The blue buses are instantly recognizable, and the stops are identified by a blue triangle on a light pole marked "Big Blue Bus." Even Paris Hilton and her little brown dog could figure this one out—that is, if she ever rode the bus. www.bigbluebus.com, 310-451-5444.

The **West Hollywood CityLine/DayLine** is a shuttle service that covers 18 locations in West Hollywood and costs 25¢ per ride. **West Hollywood Dollar Line** is a free shuttle service available only to seniors and the disabled, 800-447-2189.

Foothill Transit serves primarily the San Gabriel and Pomona Valleys, and fares cost between $1.00 for local trips and $3.65 for express service. Monthly passes cost between $55 for a local pass and up to $133 for a joint Foothills/MTA pass on the most expensive express route; www.foothilltransit.org, 626-967-3147.

Culver CityBus costs 75¢ (50¢ for students, 35¢ for seniors/disabled) and travels between Culver City, Venice, Mar Vista, LAX, and Westwood/UCLA. www.culvercity.org/bus

Orange County Transit Authority (OCTA)

www.octa.net, 714-636-7433

Regular fare on OCTA buses costs $1.25; senior and disability fares are a mere 50¢. A day pass entitles you to unlimited use of all local routes (excluding express routes 701 & 721) on the day it is purchased and costs $3 ($1 for seniors/disabled). A local monthly pass for OCTA services costs $45 ($15 for seniors/disabled). The express monthly pass (includes daily service to Los Angeles aboard routes 701 and 721) costs $128. Individual journeys on the 701 and 721 express routes to LA cost $3.75 and $2.50 if you have a day pass. (Metrolink monthly passes are now valid on local OCTA services.)

Ventura Intercity Service Transit Authority (VISTA)

www.goventura.org, 800-438-1112

Fixed bus routes will set you back $1 per ride (50¢ for seniors/disabled). Santa Paula and Fillmore dial-a-rides cost $1.50 (75¢ senior/disability), and the Conejo Connection/Coastal Express is $2 ($1 senior/disability). Monthly passes vary between $40 and $75, depending on the routes included in your package.

Metro Trip Planner

Search Engine: *www. socaltransport.org*

The search engine website is one of the best public transport facilities we've ever seen. It covers more than 45 of Southern California's transport networks including MTA buses and trains, OCTA and VISTA buses, Amtrak, Metrolink, MAX, and dozens of municipal services across Southern California.

The search facility prompts you to enter your start point, end point, the day you'd like to travel, the time you need to arrive at your destination, fare category, and special accommodations such as wheelchairs and bicycles. What you get in return is a detailed itinerary, including the type of transport, where it leaves from, the times it departs and arrives, the fare for each sector, and where you need to transfer. For example, if you were going from Universal Studios to Disneyland, leaving your departure point at noon, you would take the Red Metro Line at Universal City Station (12:05 pm—$1.25, get MTA transfer), get off at 7th Street Metro Center (12:25 pm) and take MTA Bus 460 Anaheim/Disneyland (12:32 pm, show driver transfer and pay $2.25). Get off at Disneyland at 2:22 pm and the entire journey will have cost you $3.50. The site even tells you that you should consider buying a Metro Day Pass for $3.00.

Start and end points can be addresses (including residential), intersections, or landmarks, and you can also decide whether you want the fastest itinerary, fewest transfers, or shortest walking distance. It's a good idea to try all three, as the travel times are often similar, and the cost difference is significant. If it doesn't recognize an intersection, reversing the street names sometimes helps. All in all, it's terrific resource for public transportation users—it's more clever and efficient, in fact, than the public transport system it tries to decode.

Overview

Driving in Los Angeles is not for the faint of heart, but in a city where geography is destiny, and viable mass transportation options are still thin on the ground (or under it, for that matter), we do what we must. Features peculiar to Los Angeles's motor landscape include "Sig-alerts"(legacy of the eponymous radio reporter Loyd C. "Sig" Sigmon, these reports denote unusual or hazardous freeway conditions that generally mean traffic has come to a stand-still) and a rush hour that goes from 7 am to 10 am, then picks up for a hydrocarbons happy hour again at 3 pm, lasting until after 8 pm. Even as gas prices soar to close to $4 a gallon, and commutes get longer and longer, no one seems to be driving any less, or any better, and people are still coming to the city in droves. So until the city succumbs to Ray Bradbury's dream of an LA monorail, here are a few NFT suggestions for surviving the LA roads.

The Ground Rules

1. The best offense is a good defense.

When the law says you have the right of way, don't be so presumptuous as to expect it will be yielded to you. Driving defensively in LA is like a modern basketball game: it's a full-on contact sport–but it's not supposed to be. LA drivers don't do the following: use turn signals, stay within the solid road lines, wait their turn, or concede that a few tons of steel in their way is any kind of a deterrent. Judging by the sense of urgency Los Angeles drivers often exhibit, you'd think they were all carrying transplant organs or plasma for the trauma ward in their back seats. No, they are just completely self-absorbed, and few of them have given up hand-held cells, especially while committing epic left turns.So keep your guard up. Accept that it's a mess, assume that the other driver is reckless and crazy, and make defensive driving your paranoid knee-jerk reaction of choice. Knowing that the other guy was in the wrong is not going to make the call to your insurance company any sweeter.

2. Plan a route. And then prepare to abandon it.

For any given drive, there is the logical route—the shortest distance between two points, the freeway, whatever. Much like the mythical beast that is "right of way," logic doesn't necessarily prevail. Accidents, roadwork, gawkers, Academy Award festivities, a refrigerator in the far right lane of the highway—these can all wreak havoc on your route of choice. Just as flight attendants instruct you to locate the emergency exit nearest you, we warn you to be aware of where you are at all times as you may need to bail out quite suddenly.

The road less traveled is often a glorious alternative, stop signs or not. However, beware the inherent gamble. These options are often two-lane roads. So all it takes is a Sunday driver, or enough people willing to gamble on the same alternative, and your plan is shot. LA traffic is the Las Vegas of American gridlock. Big money–be brave.

3. Traffic reports are your holy grail.

Gone are the days of watching the morning news. No one has the time. To help with the Sigalerts, we have www.sigalert.com. That's instant traffic updates the second before you're out the door. For on-the-go info, the radio is key. The young might lay claim to their indie rock stations and the post-graduates and middle-aged might have faith in NPR, but the truly erudite LA driver always switches over to the AM for traffic. 1070 AM has upwards of 6 traffic reports an hour. Yes, it may sound like the signal has traveled forward in time from the seventies, but their reports are comprehensive. They're not just aimed at those commuting from outside of LA and they're actually helpful. So get ready to multi-task and embrace the wonder of mixed media. You're not in Kansas anymore.

4. Keep your Thomas Guide within reach.

The Thomas Guide is undeniably an incredible resource, especially when driving in the hills. It's extremely detailed, and if it isn't in the guide, it's not in LA. However, this bulky book looks and feels like a city schematic, and it might as well be a life-size map of LA that has been cut into little rectangles and bound together in no particular order. While it's not difficult to use, it doesn't possess any definite logic. The old adage that you know you're an Angeleno when you can drive and use your Thomas Guide at the same time is truly the motto of the reckless, law-breaking, and accident-prone LA driver. So, if you want to keep your insurance rates down, plan ahead, keep the Thomas Guide at home, and find something more manageable for the car. Like, I don't know…your NFT guide? Or at least pull over before you break out that giant tome.

5. Make your left turns, do not let the left turns make you.

Nothing can mess up your progress across town—or, seemingly, in life--quite like waiting to make a left. You'd think you were on an organ transplant waiting list. Two problems here: not enough left turn arrows to go around (on some kind of endangered species list, apparently), and the major thoroughfares are functioning at 110% capacity (with no arrow, you ain't getting across). How many thousands of hours are lost collectively every day by drivers in Los Angeles waiting to go left onto Third Street from Normandie? From Fairfax onto Wilshire (and that's *with* an arrow)? From Cahuenga onto Sunset? We may never know.

Take control of the turns by taking advantage of other traffic lights. For example: say you're heading west on Sixth Street and need to make the left onto La Brea. This is a sad task, particularly in the morning. Knowing there are traffic lights to assist you, you could instead make a left on Sycamore (one block before La Brea), cross Wilshire at the light, turn right on Eighth Street, and then make your left onto La Brea with the aid of yet another light. By not trying to wait out La Brea and Sixth, you have also avoided having to pass through the dense mass of vehicles at La Brea and Wilshire. If you can turn left onto a side street without a light and return to your desired street for a left turn with less congestion, this will also help. Also, if you can pass your street and turn left into a side street or parking lot, you can turn around, make two easy rights and be on your street as the line builds at the left turn signal you left far far behind. Repeat these often enough and you will find yourself early to appointments and with more free time than you know what to do with.

6. Mind those yellow lights going red.
Simple, but true. First, there's the obvious risk of injury or death to you or your vehicle. But even worse, these days, your chances of getting caught by the law are increasing. More and more intersections are monitored by cameras, which take surprisingly clear photos of you smiling like the cat that caught the canary. The good thing is that they're required to post signs warning you of the cameras. The bad thing is that the ticket arrives in the mail a few days later;the fine varies depending upon which city's law you've violated. It's only a matter of time before they send an embossed sleeve for your pic, as if the light at Sunset & La Cienega might as well be the newest coaster at Magic Mountain.

7. You're never really lost in LA.
As long as you know where the hills are, you'll always be able to orient yourself and drive in the right direction. If you're in the Valley, the hills can always be found to the south. On the LA side of Mulholland, the hills are always to your north.

8. All bets are off when it rains.
Even with all the rain LA got in 2005, a mere sprinkle still sends LA drivers into a tailspin, leaving accidents in its wake and taking the lead story on the nightly news. You'd think they hadn't seen rain in 20 years, but apparently a dry LA summer does the trick. Santa Anas can make a light shower out of large-scale sprinkler systems, too. Proceed with extreme caution.

Shortcuts

Everybody has discovered at least one shortcut, of which they're extremely proud. Often, they keep these shortcuts even from their children and spouses. The discovery of a shared short cut can develop a bond that no frat or Masons lodge could ever hope to match. Like knowing where the traffic lights are, there is no way to function in LA without them. Here are a few recommendations.

Downtown

- Avoid the most congested part of the 110: Beaudry to the west and Figueroa to the east offer good alternatives.
- When heading east into downtown, try a more peripheral approach via Second Street or Olympic Boulevard.

Across Town

- Pico is better than Wilshire. Olympic is better than Pico. Venice is better than Olympic. Washington trumps all of them.
- Strangely, when going through Hollywood, Hollywood Boulevard itself is preferable to Sunset and can be preferable to Franklin, which backs up at Highland.
- Wilshire Boulevard through Beverly Hills into Westwood can coagulate badly. San Vicente-to-Sunset, and Burton-to-Little Santa Monica-to-Beverly Glen work well as alternates.
- Though Santa Monica Boulevard is actually a highway (the 2), it is not for cross-town trips, particularly through Hollywood/ West Hollywood. Years ago, when asked what advice she had for young actors in Hollywood, Bette Davis is said to have replied, "Take Fountain, dahhling." And what do you know? She's still right—even with the stop signs and the zig-zag around LeConte Junior High.

North-South

- Normandie moves pretty well between Koreatown and Los Feliz, as does Hillhurst/Virgil. When these are bad, a good short cut is Wilton/Arlington/Van Ness. Wilton hits Arlington at Olympic and then Van Ness at Slauson. This covers a lot of territory when you really need to cover some distance.
- Hauser and Cochran move way faster than La Brea, Fairfax, and Crescent Heights. Hauser can be used with Martel and then a short jog west to Gardner at Willoughby to get all the way to Franklin.
- Robertson is preferable to La Cienega. Just about everything is preferable to La Cienega.

Westside/Santa Monica

- 23rd Street morphs into Walgrove, getting you to Venice and points south in no time.
- Unfortunately, Santa Monica is something of a fox hole. Getting out is never easy. The 10 east is always bad, and Century City just makes things difficult with the larger buildings and shopping center drawing more traffic. Pico at times feels begrudgingly like your best bet. If you can jog south, try Palms. You'll be surprised.
- If you're trying to head north out of Santa Monica to the Valley, good luck. Head east on Montana, take that to Westgate just past San Vincente and head up to Sunset. Sunset takes you over the 405. This way you can check it out and see how bad it is. If necessary, turn around and head back to Sepulveda.
- Heading south from Beverly Hills, Beverwil to Castle Heights to Palms to Walgrove comes in handy.
- Carmelita in Beverly Hills is amazing. It picks up by Melrose and drops off at Wilshire. Even with the stop signs it will save you a lot of time, or at the bare minimum will get you away from Santa Monica. You can also jump on it heading south on Beverly to get to Wilshire and skip the Wilshire/Santa Monica intersection.
- National Boulevard is a strange and beautiful thing. Almost as strange as San Vicente. If you figure it out, drop us a note.

The Valley

- Moorpark and Riverside can pull through for you when the 101 and Ventura Boulevard fail you (and oh, they will).
- You'll save a lot of time by taking north-south roads that don't provide access to the 101. Whitsett and Colfax are underappreciated wonders–and usually allow easier left turns as well.
- When coming into the Valley on Beverly Glen and planning on heading back east, you can avoid the back up leading up to and on Ventura by taking Valley Vista. You can cut back to Ventura at several points or reconnect with it just before Coldwater Canyon.
- The Hollywood Freeway (the 170) can also help you, particularly if the 101/134 split is heavy.

Getting To and From the Valley

There are several options when traveling between the San Fernando Valley and points south, and none of them are especially attractive.

- The 405 too often turns into a parking lot. You might try Sepulveda Boulevard instead. Nice slalom effect on light days. When used in conjuction with the 405, this nice tag-team effort can sometimes save you some time.
- The 101 can be a terror in its own right. If you get on at Highland, as is the case when coming from Hollywood, Hancock Park, and the surrounding areas, you find yourself in the left-hand lane—with the rest of traffic moving at the speed of the Autobahn. If Burbank is your destination, you suddenly find yourself with only about 500 yards to cross no fewer than five lanes of traffic to exit at Barham Boulevard—a true test of one's driving mettle. Screenwriter/playwright Roger Kumble wrote in his play *Pay or Play* that there are two kinds of Angelenos, "101 People" and "Cahuenga People." Cahuenga people shy away from this act of bravado and prefer to drive the service road over the hill. Funny enough, he doesn't bother to categorize those smart enough to take whichever will get them to Point B faster.
- The Canyon roads all have their supporters and detractors. Those that opt for these routes over the highways are steadfast in their beliefs and stay true to their Canyon road of choice, but still, one must cop to the fact that the east/west positioning of the roads will often determine which one would be the best for you to use. That said: Laurel Canyon becomes less viable daily and recently has been partially rerouted due to mudslides. Coldwater Canyon backs up just about as easily. Benedict Canyon requires a little finessing. Beverly Glen is the user-friendliest of the four (Tyrone in Sherman Oaks runs into it at Ventura). Just like the highways, these roads improve greatly the earlier you can get to them. The increase in traffic from 7 am to 7:15 am is astounding.

The Freeways

When the freeway is moving and the weather is dry, Los Angeles is a beautiful place, and you never want to leave. The other 90% of the time, you fantasize about moving to San Francisco. Or about hurting someone. Where is the flashing highway marquee from *LA Story* when you need it? "LA wants to help you." If only…

Here's the thing: all freeways are not created equal and the 405 is the most unequal of all. Avoid it whenever possible, at least within a ten-mile radius of LAX. If it's at all convenient, La Cienega Boulevard is preferable as a north-south route. Heading south from Hollywood, La Cienega will actually lead you directly onto the 405, south of the airport, allowing you to overshoot the most common delays.

The 101 is also confusing. It's a north/south road, because its ultimate destination is Northern California, yet it crosses the San Fernando Valley in an east/west direction. The 101 is known as the Hollywood Freeway, at least while you're in Hollywood and Downtown. Once you reach the Valley, the 101 splits off toward Santa Barbara and becomes the Ventura Freeway. If you want to continue on the Hollywood Freeway, you must opt for the 170. Confused yet? Meanwhile, the 134 is known as the Ventura Freeway between I. 5 and I. 2, until it hooks up with the 101, which then becomes the Ventura Freeway. This is the best illustration we know for why the names of freeways are relatively meaningless here in LA.

Though not technically a freeway, the Pacific Coast Highway deserves special mention here. It's one of the most picturesque thoroughfares in LA, running—as its name implies—alongside the Pacific Coast. However, the PCH is plagued by mudslides, brushfires, and floods during the rainy season and often closed to traffic, stranding Malibu residents or forcing them to backtrack inland to pick up the 101. We guess that's the price you pay for beachfront property. (Speaking of beach: the shortest distance between Hollywood and Malibu is the 101 to Malibu Canyon. Period.)

Depending on where you are starting from and where you are going, the 2 and 210 Freeways may save you a lot of time by keeping you out of more congested parts of the city. Just beware of the 2 as it crawls through Echo Park on Alvarado Street.

A note on the freeway on-ramps: While most on-ramps are clearly mapped out, LA is rather fond of sketching out the path to a few of their ramps in a circuitous, unclear route that's less turn-left-for-north-and-right-for-south and more Where's Waldo? Just breathe. You'll figure it out, and make a mental note for next time.

DMV Locations

800-777-0133; www.dmv.ca.gov; Hours: Mon–Tues: 8 am–5 pm; Wed: 9 am–5 pm; Thurs–Fri: 8 am–5 pm. Many DMV offices are open the third Saturday each month from 8 am–12 pm. Check the website for details.

The Department of Motor Vehicles in California handles vehicle registrations,driving records,identification cards,and everything to do with driver's licenses--as well as aa cornucopia of other logistical, vehicle-related things almost equally as fascinating as the ones listed here. Thanks to our complete dependency on our vehicles, the department manages to dredge up a whopping $5.9 billion in revenue every year. (Maybe we're in the wrong business…) Much like the freeways they help populate, the DMV always involves long lines and much waiting. The DMV may be the LCD that LA needs; no amount of glam factor will ingratiate you with the broken-yet-still-somehow-not-wretched clerks.You can make an appointment via phone or their website and we highly recommend that you do. Some locations don't process registration issues, so make sure to check before you have to give up a great parking spot only to have to schlep to a sister location. We'd say that multiple trips to the DMV is like salt in the wounds, but, really, nothing is like multiple trips to the DMV.

Turn the world over on its side and everything loose will land in Los Angeles. —Frank Lloyd Wright

Useful Phone Numbers

Emergencies	911
Los Angeles City Hall	213-485-2121
CalTrans	213-897-3656
Department of Water & Power	800-342-5397
Southern California Edison	800-655-4555
The Gas Company	800-427-2200

Websites

www.notfortourists.com • The most comprehensive LA site there is. (And no, we weren't paid to say that.)

www.lacity.org • The city's official home on the web.

www.losangeles.com • From buying real estate to planning a night out on the town, this website has it all.

www.sigalert.com • Real-time traffic updates with an easy, snazzy interface.

http://losangeles.citysearch.com • Ultimate insider guide with reviews on shopping, dining and services

www.laalmanac.com • It's loaded with everything you could ever want to know about LA.

www.lapl.org • LA Public library's handy website—e.g., use the hold system to get a book sent to your library if you're not satisfied with your local branch.

www.lausd.k12.ca.us • Contact information and report cards for schools in your neighborhood.

www.blacknla.com • Online resource for LA-based African Americans featuring news articles, business listings, and local events.

www.la.com • Online resource for Angeleno luxuries, shopping, events, and nightlife.

Essential LA Songs

"Hooray for Hollywood" — Various, written by Johnny Mercer & Richard A. Whiting (1937)
"There's No Business Like Show Business" — Ethel Merman, written by Irving Berlin (1954)
"California Girls" — The Beach Boys (1965)
"California Dreamin' " — The Mamas & The Papas (1966)
"Ladies of the Canyon" — Joni Mitchell (1970)
"L.A. Woman" — The Doors (1971)
"I Am, I Said" — Neil Diamond (1971)
"You're So Vain" — Carly Simon (1972)
"Ventura Highway" - America (1972)
"Eggs and Sausage" — Tom Waits (1975)
"Hotel California" — The Eagles (1976)
"The Pretender" — Jackson Browne (1976)
"Los Angeles" — X (1980)
"Walkin' in LA" - Missing Persons (1982)
"Valley Girl" — Frank and Moon Unit Zappa (1982)
"I Love L.A." — Randy Newman (1983)
"My Life is Good" — Randy Newman (1983)
"Sunset Grill" — Don Henley (1984)
"Paradise City" — Guns N Roses (1987)
"Fallen Angel" — Poison (1988)
"F— Tha Police" — N.W.A. (1988)
"Free Fallin'" — Tom Petty (1989)
"Neighborhood" — Los Lobos (1990)
"All I Wanna Do" — Sheryl Crow (1993)
"California Love" — Tupac Shakur (1995)
"Malibu" — Hole (1998)
"Californication" — Red Hot Chili Peppers (1999)
"California" — Phantom Planet (2002)
"Beverly Hills" —Weezer (2005)
"Dani California" — Red Hot Chili Peppers (2006)

Less Practical Information

- Los Angeles averages 329 days of sunshine each year. Yet we still whine about the other 36.
- The longest street in Los Angeles is Sepulveda Boulevard, which runs 76 miles from the San Fernando Valley to Long Beach.
- With few exceptions, LA bars are legally prohibited from serving alcohol between the hours of 2 am and 6 am.
- The Library Tower (633 W Fifth St) is Los Angeles's tallest building (and was spectacularly taken out by aliens in the 1997 blockbuster *Independence Day*).
- The city boasts more stage theaters (80+) and museums (300) than any other city in the US. And New Yorkers say we have no culture.
- There are 527 miles of freeway and 382 miles of conventional highway in Los Angeles County. Bette Midler is determined to clean up all of them.
- Angelenos drive 92 million vehicle miles every day. This gives them ample time to admire the amber hues of our smog-riddled sunsets.
- Annually, LA residents consume over one billion pounds of red meat, over 300 billion pounds of ice cream, and absolutely no carbs whatsoever.

Essential LA Movies

The Big Sleep (1946)
Sunset Boulevard (1950)
Singin' in the Rain (1952)
Rebel Without a Cause (1955)
Chinatown (1974)
Shampoo (1975)
Big Wednesday (1978)
Grease (1978)
10 (1979)
Blade Runner (1982)
Fast Times at Ridgemont High (1982)
Valley Girl (1983)
To Live and Die in LA (1985)
Down and Out in Beverly Hills (1986)
Born in East LA (1987)
Less Than Zero (1987)
Pretty Woman (1990)
L.A. Story (1991)
Grand Canyon (1991)
The Player (1992)
Short Cuts (1993)
Pulp Fiction (1994)
Heat (1995)
Devil in a Blue Dress (1995)
Lords of Dogtown (2005)
Get Shorty (1995)
Swingers (1996)
Jackie Brown (1997)
L.A. Confidential (1997)
Volcano (1997)
Slums of Beverly Hills (1998)
The Muse (1999)
Mulholland Dr. (2001)
Laurel Canyon (2002)
Collateral (2004)
Crash (2005)

Los Angeles Timeline—a timeline of significant events in the history of Los Angeles (by no means complete)

1781: El Pueble de Nuestra Senora de la Reina de Los Angeles de Porciuncula—a.k.a. Los Angeles—is founded.
1822: Los Angeles becomes a Mexican City when Mexico wins its independence from Spain.
1842: Gold rush hits Southern California.
1850: LA County is established, City of LA is incorporated.
1880: USC is founded.
1881: Rail lines between LA and the East Coast are completed.
1881: *LA Times* begins printing.
1882: Electricity comes to downtown LA.
1887: The land is purchased for Hollywood: a church community planned to promote prohibition and clean living.
1890: First Tournament of Roses Parade.
1891: CalTech opens its doors.
1892: Abbott Kinney stakes his claim in Venice.
1894: Labor rioting breaks out in LA during national railroad strike.
1896: Griffith J. Griffith donates land that will become Griffith Park.
1899: LA Stock Exchange opens.
1902: City's first movie theater opens for business.
1909: Construction on LA aqueduct begins.
1910: Alice Stebbins Wells appointed to LA police force as the nation's first female policewoman.
1913: The Los Angeles Aqueduct brings water from the Owens Valley.
1915: Universal Studios opens.
1915: San Fernando Valley annexed by City of LA.
1919: UCLA is formed.
1922: Hollywood Bowl opens.
1923: The Hollywood Sign is erected.
1932: Tenth Olympic Games are held in LA.
1939: Union Station opens.
1940: Pasadena Freeway (later the 110) is LA's first freeway.
1946: KTLA is LA's first commercial television station.
1947: Black Dahlia murder. The case is never solved.
1953: The famed "four-level" opens, linking the 101 and 110 freeways.
1954: Completion of the Watts Towers.
1955: Disneyland opens.
1958: The Dodgers relocate from Brooklyn.
1960: The Lakers leave Minneapolis for LA.
1964: The Music Center opens Downtown.
1965: LACMA opens its doors.
1965: The Watts Riots.
1968: Robert Kennedy assassinated at Ambassador Hotel.
1969: Manson Murders.
1971: Sylmar Earthquake.
1974: J. Paul Getty Museum opens in Pacific Palisades.
1978: The Hollywood Sign is rebuilt with local celebs donating $27,700 per letter.
1980: Screen Actors Guild strike.
1984: The 23rd Olympics are held in LA.
1985: LA Lakers finally beat the Boston Celtics to take out NBA honors after losing nine finals to them previously.
1989: Mayor Tom Bradley elected to an unprecedented fifth term.
1991: Rodney King is beaten by four police officers.
1992: Verdict in King case leads to citywide rioting.
1992: Landers earthquake.
1993: Menendez murder trial #1.
1994: O.J. Simpson arrested after slow-speed chase down the 405.
1994: Northridge earthquake.
1995: Menendez murder trial #2.
1995: If it doesn't fit, you must acquit: O.J. found not guilty.
1995: Departure of Rams and Raiders leaves LA without a football team.
1997: The Getty Center opens in Brentwood.
2000: LA Lakers defeat Indiana Pacers for NBA title.
2001: Back-to-back NBA Championships for the LA Lakers.
2001: First championship for the WNBA's LA Sparks.
2002: Three-peat for the LA Lakers and Phil Jackson.
2002: Back-to-back WNBA Championships for the LA Sparks.
2002: Anaheim Angels win their first World Series.
2003: Famed Austrian-bodybuilder-turned-Hollywood-action-star adds another hyphenate. Arnold Schwarzenegger runs for the position of Governor of California during the recall election and wins.
2005: Actor and former child star Robert Blake found not guilty of his wife Bonnie Lee Bakley's murder.
2005: The city elects its first Latino mayor in 130 years.
2006: The WB and UPN merge to form the CW.
2006: LA serves as a focal point for the demonstrations and boycotts over the contentious proposed immigration legislation.
2007: USC beats Michigan in the Rose Bowl 32-18
2007: Fire in Griffith Park burns over 600 acres.

January

January	*Location*	*Description*
• Tournament of Roses Parade	Pasadena. Just follow the crowds.	A Southern California tradition. 117 years and counting. (Jan 1)
• Rose Bowl	The Rose Bowl, of course	"The Granddaddy of All Bowl Games." (Jan 1)
• Japanese New Year "Oshogatsu"	Little Tokyo	Soothe your New Year's hangover with the sound of Taiko drums. (Jan 1)
• Golden Globe Awards	Beverly Hilton Hotel	Unlike at the Oscars, the stars are allowed to drink, which leads to occasional embarrassing moments. (Jan 13)
• Kingdom Day Parade	Martin Luther King Blvd, at Crenshaw, at Grevillea Park	Parade commemorating the life of MLK, Jr. (Jan 21)

February

February	Location	Description
• Lunar New Year Parade & Festival	Pasadena	Parade along Colorado Blvd. (mid Feb)
• *LA Times* Travel Show	Long Beach Convention Center	Get outta town—at least in your head. (Feb 9–10)
• Firecracker Run 5K/10K	N Broadway & College St, Chinatown	Race celebrating Chinese New Year. (Feb 10)
• Pan African Film & Arts Festival	Magic Johnson Theaters, 3650 Martin Luther King Jr Blvd	One of America's largest festivals of black films and fine arts. (Feb 7–18)
• Chinese New Year	Chinatown & various locations	Features a parade, a street fair, and even a golf tournament. (mid Feb)
• Mardi Gras	El Pueblo Historical Monument, 125 Paseo de la Plaza	Celebrate Fat Tuesday on Olvera Street. (Feb 5).
• Brazilian Carnaval	Queen Mary, Long Beach	Samba your way down the Walk of Fame. (Feb)
• Nissan Open	Riviera Country Club, Pacific Palisades	The PGA championships come to the Westside. (Feb 11–17)
• Queen Mary Scottish Festival	Long Beach	Wear your tartan, eat your haggis!
• Ragga Muffins Festival	Long Beach Arena	Bob Marley's b-day celebration.
• Black History Parade & Festival	Jackie Robinson Center, Pasadena	Food, kids' play area, and the Black Inventions Museum. (mid Feb)
• Academy Awards	Kodak Theatre, Hollywood Blvd & Highland Ave	More revered as an LA holiday than Presidents' Day. (Feb 24)

March

March	Location	Description
• Los Angeles Marathon	Throughout LA	The one day a year we choose not to drive. (Mar 2)
• WestWeek	Pacific Design Center, WeHo	An interior design fest! (Mar).
• Big Bunny's Spring Fling	LA Zoo	Kiddie crafts and photo ops with "Big Bunny." (Mar. 21–23)
• Cesar E. Chavez Day	Olvera St	Honors the Mexican-American farm labor leader. (Mar 31)
• Wizard World Convention	LA Convention Center	Wizard's answer to ComiCon equals magical geeks! (Mar 14-16)

April

April	Location	Description
• Pasadena Cherry Blossom Festival	Rose Bowl	Japanese culture, great food, cool fighting. (first weekend in Apr)
• Blessing of the Animals	Olvera St	Check out the parade of house pets and wild animals. (Apr)
• Bunka Sai Japanese Cultural Festival	Ken Miller Rec Center, Torrance	Japanese culture, from judo to origami. (mid Apr)
• Garifuna Street Fest	Avalon Blvd, South Central LA	Celebrates largest Black ethnic group in Central America. (Apr)
• Jimmy Stewart Relay	Griffith Park	Like running a marathon, but with help. (Apr)
• Eco Maya Mother Earth Day Festival	Los Angeles City College	Ecology and the cooking of the Largest Tamal in the World (last week in Apr)
• 50+ Fitness Jamboree & Health Expo	Griffith Park	Includes 1K and 5K walks with celebrity seniors. (Last week in Apr)
• Toyota Grand Prix of Long Beach	Downtown Long Beach	Auto racing. (Apr 18–20)
• *Los Angeles Times* Festival of Books	UCLA campus	The city's biggest and coolest literary event (because we usually have a table). (Apr 26–27)
• Blooming of the Roses	Exposition Park Rose Garden	Stop and smell the roses. Literally. (Last week in Apr)
• Annual Arbor Day Festival	Cheviot Hills Park & Recreation Center	Trees aren't just for hugging. (Last week in Apr)
• Dolo Coker Scholarship Benefit Jazz Concert	Founder's Church, 3281 W 6th St	Supports young jazz hopefuls. (mid Apr)
• Santa Anita Derby	Santa Anita Racetrack, Arcadia	Big pre-Kentucky Derby race and festival. (Apr)
• Renaissance Pleasure Faire	Santa Fe Dam Recreation Area, Irwindale	Maidens, meade, and minstrels. (Apr–May)
• LA Zoo Earth Day Expo	LA Zoo	Meet Rascal the Recycling Raccoon. (Apr 20–21)
• Los Angeles Antiques Show	Santa Monica Air Center, Barker Hangar	Antiques galore. (late Apr)
• Indian Film Festival	ArcLight Cinemas, Hollywood	Go beyond Bollywood. (Apr)
• Feria de los Ninos Celebration	Hollenbeck Park, East LA	Ethnic food and entertainment with an emphasis on family-friendly activities. (late Apr)

May

May	*Location*	*Description*
• Fiesta Broadway	Downtown LA	The largest Cinco de Mayo celebration in the world. (First weekend of May)
• Cinco de Mayo Celebration	Olvera St	Celebrate Mexico's victory over the French. Que bueno! (May 5)
• LA Asian Pacific Film & Video Festival	Various locations	Showcases works by Pacific-American and international artists. (late April–early May)
• Revlon Run/Walk for Women Exposition Park	LA Memorial Coliseum,	5K race raises money for women's cancer causes. (May)
• Family FunFest and Kodomo-no-Hi	Japanese American Cultural & Community Center, Little Tokyo	Celebrate kids the Japanese way. (May)
• Silver Lake Film Festival	Silver Lake	Thinks it's the coolest film fest in town. (mid May)
• Affaire in the Gardens Art Show	Beverly Gardens Park, Beverly Hills	Art show. (mid May and mid Oct)
• Huntington Gardens Annual Plant Sale	San Marino	Let your garden grow. (mid May)
• Festival Dia de Las Madres	Vermont Ave & 8th St Downtown	Mother's Day street fair with food from Mexico, the Caribbean, and Latin America. (May 11)
• E3 Electronic Entertainment Expo	LA Convention Center	Boys and their toys (okay, some girls, too).
• Old Pasadena Summer Fest	Rose Bowl	Five fests in one range from eating to sports. (Memorial Day weekend)

June

June		
• Art & Design Walk	West Hollywood	Walk into 300+ showrooms, galleries, and boutiques. (early June)
• Life Cycle	San Francisco to Los Angeles	585-mile bicycle ride for AIDS-related charities. (early June)
Los Angeles Film Festival	Hollywood	A breath of cinematic fresh air. (June)
• Great American Irish Fair & Music Festival	Irvine	St. Patrick's Day in the summer. (mid June)
• Playboy Jazz Festival	Hollywood Bowl	Almost more jazz than you can handle. (mid June)
• Mariachi USA Festival	Hollywood Bowl	Traditional mariachi music, as well as Ballet Foklorico. (mid June)
• Christopher Street West	West Hollywood Park	Celebrates gay pride. (mid June)
• ArtWallah Festival of South Asian Arts	Barnsdall Art Park	Art festival of the South Asian Diaspora. (late June)
• Long Beach Chili Cook-off	Long Beach Marina Green	The competition really heats up (bad pun intended). (mid June)

July

July		
• At the Beach, LA Black Pride Festival	Westin Airport Hotel, Point Dume Beach in Malibu	Largest annual gathering of African-American lesbians and gay men in the world. (early Jul)
• Countrywide Classic	LA Tennis Center, UCLA	Tennis tournament. Used to be Mercedes Benz Cup. (last week in Jul)
• Outfest	DGA, 7920 Sunset Blvd	Gay and lesbian film festival. (early to mid Jul)
• Lotus Festival	Echo Park Lake	Celebrates Asian and Pacific cultures. (mid Jul)
• Central Avenue Jazz Festival	Central Ave b/w 42nd & 43rd Sts	Remembers Central Avenue as the hot spot it was in the 1920s–'50s. (late Jul)
• Twilight Dance Series	Santa Monica Pier	Dance away every Thursday from July to September.

August

August		
• Long Beach Jazz Festival	Long Beach	Jazz by the sea. (mid Aug)
• Nisei Week Japanese Festival	Little Tokyo	Celebrating Asian culture and community. (mid Aug)
• Marcus Garvey Day Parade & Festival	Elegant Manor, 3115 W Adams Blvd	Invites all to celebrate "Africa for the Africans at home or abroad." (mid Aug)
• Sunset Junction Street Fair	3600 to 4600 Sunset Blvd, LA	One of LA's funkiest neighborhoods puts on a fair. (late Aug)

September

September	*Location*	*Description*
• LA International Short Film Festival	ArcLight Cinemas, Hollywood	For movie lovers with short attention spans. (mid Sept)
• LA Greek Fest	St. Sophia Cathedral	Eat a gyro, break a plate. (early to mid Sept).
• Emmy Awards	Shrine Auditorium	TV's night to shine. (mid Sept)

• Lobster Festival	Location varies	Great food, good music, family fun, and cheap Maine Lobster. (mid Sept)
• Los Angeles City Birthday Celebration	El Pueblo Historical Monument, 125 Paseo de la Plaza	Happy Birthday, dear LA-ay, Happy Birthday to you! (Sept 4)
• Salvadoran Parade & Festival	LA City College	All things Salvadoran. (mid Sept)
• Mexican Independence Celebration	Olvera St	Traditional Mexican foods and entertainment. (mid Sept)
• LA County Fair	Fairplex in Pomona	Livestock, rides, and food on a stick. (Sept–Oct)
• Brazilian Street Carnival	Downtown Long Beach Promenade Theatre	Rio Brazilian fun.
• Thai Cultural Day	Location varies	Day-long celebration of Thailand. (mid Sept)
• Taste of Santa Monica	Santa Monica Pier	40 of the area's top restaurants participate. (mid Sept)
• Abbot Kinney Boulevard Festival	Abbot Kinney Blvd, Venice	Over 200 local arts & crafts vendors unite. (late Sept)
• Long Beach Blues Festival	Cal State Long Beach	Spend Labor Day weekend with blues heavyweights.

October

• West Hollywood Halloween & Costume Carnival	West Hollywood	Fabulous costumes make this the biggest bash in the nation. (Oct 31)
• AIDS Walk	West Hollywood Park	10K walkathon raises money for AIDS-related organizations.
• Affaire in the Gardens	Beverly Gardens Park, Beverly Hills	Twice-yearly art show. (mid Oct)
• Oktoberfest	Alpine Village, Torrance	German music, German beer, American hangover.
• Echo Park Arts Festival	Various	One of LA's artiest communities' time to shine.
• NOHO Theater & Arts Festival	Lankershim Blvd & Magnolia, North Hollywood	Performances scattered throughout the NOHO arts district. (early October)
• Harvest Festival of the ARTS	Pico Union Alvarado Terrace Park	Raising children's self-esteem through art. (late Oct)
• KTLA KIDS Day LA Celebration	Exposition Park and Recreation Center	Forget the kids. We want to hang out with Jennifer York. (mid Oct)
• Autumn in the Japanese Garden	Japanese Garden, 6100 Woodley Ave, Van Nuys	Learn origami or just stroll through the garden.
• Shipwreck Halloween Terrorfest	Queen Mary, Long Beach	Mazes and monsters on a real haunted boat! (weekends throughout Oct)
• Fall Festival at the Farmer's Market	Farmer's Market, Los Angeles	Carve a pumpkin, watch the leaves turn. (mid Oct)
• Long Beach Marathon	Long Beach	In case the LA Marathon didn't wear you out. (mid Oct)
• Day of the Dead	Hollywood Forever Cemetery	A true dead man's party. (late Oct)

November

• Dia de los Muertos Celebration	Olvera St	Traditional celebration of Mexico's Day of the Dead. (Nov 2)
• Arroyo Arts Collective Discovery Tour	Tour begins at Lummis Home, 200 E Ave 43	Local artists kindly open up their homes and studios. (mid Nov)
• Three Stooges Big Screen Event	Alex Theatre, 216 Brand Blvd, Glendale	Surely this will only interest silly cinephiles. (late Nov)
• Doo Dah Parade	Colorado Blvd, Pasadena	Irreverent spoof of the more stately Rose Parade. (Late Nov)
• Beverly Hills Flower & Garden Festival	Greystone Estate	Designer gardens, lectures, and tours. (mid Nov)
• Downtown on Ice, Winter Wonderland Skating Rink	Pershing Sq	Pretend you're at a tiny version of Rockefeller Center. (Nov–Dec)
• Griffith Park Holiday Light Festival	Crystal Springs Rd, Griffith Park	Drive-through tour of impressive lighting displays. (Nov–Dec)

December

• KROQ Acoustic Christmas	Universal Amphitheatre	Hot alternative bands feel the spirit of the season. (mid Dec)
• Marina del Rey Holiday Boat Parade	Main Channel, Marina del Rey	Imaginatively lit boats by crazy locals. (mid Dec)
• Navidad en la Calle Ocho	8th St at Normandie Ave	8th Street's answer to the Hollywood Christmas Parade. (late Dec)
• Las Posadas	Olvera St	Candlelit reenactment of Mary and Joseph's journey to Bethlehem. (Dec 16–24)
• Reindeer Romp	Los Angeles Zoo	Where Santa parks his reindeer (Dec)
• Long Beach Christmas Boat Parade of the Thousand Lights	Long Beach Downtown Marina	That's a lotta lights! (Dec 25)

Often, while trapped in LA traffic, it seems that your only options for coping are books-on-CD or trading in your car for a motorcycle. But never fear, the good news is that LA offers some of the most diverse radio programming anywhere, so there's always something to fit your mood—even if it involves a case of road rage. Of course, many of these stations now stream their music so you can listen at home, too—check out KPCC's and KCRW's podcasts, archives, and streams.

AM Stations

			Noteworthy Programs
570	KLAC	Talk	Lakers games and music so old it's cool.
600	KOGO	Talk	Talk with a conservative slant. Home of Dr. Laura, Art Bell, and, of course, Rush.
610	KAVL	Fox Sports	Lots of games, plus sports talk.
640	KFI	Talk	Talk radio that'll push your buttons, from Rush Limbaugh to Matt Drudge.
690	XTRA	Sports/Talk	UCLA basketball and football, as well as the Jim Rome show.
710	KSPN	ESPN Radio	Sports, sports, sports.
740	KBRT	Religious	The Word from Above broadcast from…Catalina Island!
790	KABC	News/Talk	Larry Elder, Bill O'Reilly, et al.
830	KMXE	Spanish	
870	KRLA	Talk	Lots of shows about health.
900	KALI	Spanish/Religious	
930	KHJ	Spanish/News	Regional Mexican music.
980	KFWB	News	News, Dodgers games, and traffic on all the ones (:01, :11, :21…)
1020	KTNQ	News/Talk (Spanish)	Galaxy soccer games.
1070	KNX	News	A poor man's NPR it might be, but they have fantastic traffic reports—and Food News is transfixing…
1110	KDIS	Radio Disney	Mickey Mouse, squeaky-clean pop tunes, and, of course, death metal.
1150	KXTA	Sports/Talk	Fox's radio affiliate. Dodger games are heard here.
1190	KXMX	Variety/Foreign Language	
1230	KYPA	Korean	Radio Korea.
1260	KKGO	Jazz	Everyone knows what this is.
1280	KFRN	Religious	"Family Radio."
1300	KAZN	Chinese	
1330	KWKW	Talk (Spanish)	News, talk, sports, and Laker games en español.
1390	KLTX	Spanish/Religious	
1430	KALI	Chinese	
1460	KTYM	Religious/Foreign language	
1510	KSPA	Oldies	Standards.
1540	KMPC	Sports	*The Phil Jackson Show, The Sporting News*.
1580	KBLA	Korean	Korean-language news, music, and lifestyle programming.
1650	KFOX	Korean	

FM Stations			*Noteworthy Programs*
88.1	KKJZ	Jazz & Blues	
88.5	KCSN	Classical/BBC	Their diverse line-up includes a Sunday morning commercial-free Beatles show.
88.7	KSPC	Alternative	College radio at its most bizarre.
88.9	KXLU	Eclectic	More college radio. Sample as you like.
89.3	KPCC	Eclectic/NPR	Straight up NPR, with *Morning Edition, All Things Considered, Car Talk,* and *This American Life.*
89.9	KCRW	Eclectic/NPR	*Morning Becomes Eclectic* breaks new bands; clever programming gives your brain a workout, too.
90.7	KPFK	Eclectic/Political	Talk radio with a very liberal slant.
91.5	KUSC	Classical	Relaxing classical, even in horrible traffic.
92.3	KHHT	R&B Oldies	Legendary Art Leboe knows how to get you in the mood.
92.7	KLIT	Adult Contemporary	
93.1	KCBS	Classic Rock/Pop	Some classic rock and a lotta hits make "Jack FM" a good deal.
93.5	KDAY	Hip-hop/R&B	Old and new hip-hop; features Dr. Dre—both of them!
93.9	KZLA	Country	
94.3	KBUA	Spanish	
94.7	KTWV	Smooth Jazz	"The Wave" is for fans of Kenny G and John Tesh.
95.1	KFRG	Country	"K-Frog" takes its amphibious theme very seriously.
95.5	KLOS	Classic Rock	Classic rock with Mark & Brian in the morning as a baby-boomer-funny alternative.
95.9	KFSH	Contemporary Christian	Ultra-clean-cut Christian pop and rock music.
96.3	KXOL	Spanish	Spanish pop and dance music.
96.7	KWIZ	Spanish	Spanish programming.
97.1	KLSX	Talk	Guy chatter galore, with Adam Corrolla in the morning and Tom Leykis in the afternoon.
97.5	KLYY	Spanish Pop/Rock	Modern Spanish hits.
97.9	KLAX	Mexican	Regional Mexican.
98.3	KRCV	Spanish	
98.7	KYSR	Adult Contemporary	First Bonaduce was out, then Jamie, Jack & Stench, looks like it's adult alternative 24-7, DJ-free
99.1	KGGI	Urban Contemporary	
99.5	KKLA	Religious	Religious talk radio.
99.9	KOLA	Rock Oldies	Plenty of '60s and '70s tunes, plus Beatles Brunch on Sundays.
100.3	KKBT	Urban Contemporary	Steve Harvey handles the morning shift; the mix shows are amazing.
101.1	KRTH	Oldies	It's always a kinder, gentler time on K-Earth.
101.9	KSCA	Spanish	Regional Mexican.
102.3	KJLH	R&B	Owner Stevie Wonder keeps this smooth station on track.
102.7	KIIS	Top 40	Find Ryan Seacrest here, plus more pop than you can handle.
103.1	KDLD	Indie	Totally alternative with the Sex Pistols' Steve Jones and other celeb DJs.
103.5	KOST	Adult Contemporary	Dedications all night with "Love Songs on the KOST."
103.9	KRCD	Spanish	Shares a signal with 98.3 KRCV.
104.3	KBIG	Adult Contemporary	Music from the '70s, '80s, and '90s. And occasionally the '00s.
105.1	KMZT	Classical	"K-Mozart" will have you "air-conducting" in you car.
105.9	KPWR	Dance/Urban	Big Boy's morning show cracks us up; the beats bounce the rest of the day.
106.3	KALI	Vietnamese	
106.7	KROQ	Modern Rock	Heavy on the hard stuff, this influential station breaks new bands all the time.
107.1	KSSE	Spanish	
107.5	KLVE	Spanish	Spanish adult contemporary.
107.9	KWVE	Religious	

Before children (BC), a day with nothing to do was just that. Or, as we liked to think of it, heaven. But when you have kids you have to have a plan—a series of them, actually. Plans for at-home, plans for being on-the-go. Rainy-day plans, too-hot-to-be-outside plans. Because this is LA, your plans have to be better than everybody else's plans or your kids will be doomed from the get-go. There are, of course, some bright spots to parenting in LA. Our endless summer means that you very rarely have to worry about lost jackets, mittens, or umbrellas. We also drive almost everywhere, making our choice of stroller far less important than our choice of black SUV, the preferred automobile of hip LA parents.

Essentials

Kids come into the world with nothing, yet by their first birthday their stuff fills up at least half the rooms in your house. Where does all of this accoutrement come from? Well, we can name a few of the culprits. Here are some of our favorite places for both the necessities and the more frivolous (but no less fun) purchases.

Map	*Store*	*Address*	*Phone*	*Description*
1	Auntie Barbara's	238 S Beverly Dr, Beverly Hills	310-285-0873	Vintage children's furnishings.
3	Flicka	204 N Larchmont Blvd	323-466-5822	Upscale kids' clothes.
15	Petite Ami	15301 Antioch St, Pacific Palisades	310-459-0011	Fancy children's apparel.
15	Ivy Greene for Kids	1020 Swarthmore Ave, Pacific Palisades	310-230-0301	Kids' formal wear.
15	Puzzle Zoo	1041 Swarthmore Ave, Pacific Palisades	310-454-8648	Toys galore.
16	Bellini Juvenile Designer Furniture	114 S Beverley Dr, Brentwood	310-859-7133	Nursery furniture.
18	The Acorn Store	1220 5th St, Santa Monica	310-451-5845	Wooden toys.
18	The Pump Station	2415 Wilshire Blvd, Santa Monica	310-998-1981	For nursing moms & tots.
18	Puzzle Zoo	1413 Third St Promenade, Santa Monica	310-393-9201	Awesome toy store.
18	This Little Piggy Wears Cotton	309 Wilshire Blvd, Santa Monica	310-260-2727	Comfy kids' clothes.
18	Every Picture Tells A Story	1311C Montana Ave, Santa Monica	310-451-2700	Art gallery & bookstore.
18	Moms The Word	910 Montana Ave, Santa Monica	310-451-9604	Maternity & nursing wear
19	Malina Children's Store	3304 Pico Blvd, Santa Monica	310-395-5965	High-end clothes.
20	Riginals	Century City Mall, 10250 Santa Monica Blvd, Century City	310-557-2532	High-end clothes.
20	Peanut Butter Playground	2042 Westwood Blvd, Westwood	310-475-5354	Upscale clothes & toys.
20	Traveling Tikes	10461 Santa Monica Blvd, Century City	310-234-9554	Strollers, bikes, & more.
23	Needles N' Tees	9223 W Pico Blvd	310-276-2531	Personalized items.
25	Sid & Me	8338 Lincoln Blvd, Westchester	310-670-5550	Everything for baby's room.
27	Baby A	1108 Manhattan Ave, Manhattan Beach	310-798-8086	Upscale gifts for tikes.
27	Babystyle	3200 Sepulveda Blvd, #C5, Manhattan Beach	310-802-0224	Website comes to life.
31	Little Moon	1813 S Catalina Ave, Redondo Beach	310-373-3766	Fancy frocks & the like.
34	Saturday's Child	2529 Mission St, San Marino	626-441-8888	High-end kids' stuff.
45	Babyland	7134 Topanga Canyon Blvd, Can Pk	818-704-7848	Affordable kids' furniture.
49	Gregory's Toys	16101 Ventura Blvd, Encino	818-906-2212	Toys, toys, toys.
49	A Mother's Haven	15928 Ventura Blvd, Encino	818-380-3111	Nursing products & support.
50	Juvenile Shop	13356 Ventura Blvd, Sherman Oaks	818-986-6214	One-stop baby shopping.
50	Burgundy Blue Outlet	4818 Fulton Ave, Sherman Oaks	818-981-7446	High-end, low-cost clothes.
50	Doll Shoppe	13300 Riverside Dr, Sherman Oaks	818-784-3655	Dolls & their accessories.
51	Safer Baby	13215 Ventura Blvd, Studio City	818-784-6628	One-stop baby-proofing.
51	Storyopolis	12348 Ventura Blvd, Studio City	818-509-5600	Children's literature & art.
51	M Fredric Kids	12128 Ventura Blvd, Studio City	818-985-9445	Cute & comfy clothes.
53	Harry Harris Children's Shoes	16744 Ventura Blvd, Encino	818-981-2641	First footwear.
53	Encino Kid	17157 Ventura Blvd, Encino	818-990-4510	Kids' clothing.
57	Wound & Wound Toy Co	1000 Universal Studios Blvd	818-509-8129	All things wind-up.

The Bestest of the Best

- **Most Kid-Friendly Mall:** The Grove, 189 The Grove Dr, 888-315-8883 (Map 2). They've got a trolley, a musical water fountain, and events for children such as puppet shows, arts, and crafts every Thursday morning. There's even a huge central lawn where you can catch a live band and eat ice cream. Oh, and there are shops and restaurants for parents, too.
- **Coolest Bookstore:** Storyopolis, 12348 Ventura Blvd, Studio City, 818-509-5600 (Map 51). Looking for *The Da Vinci Code*? Look somewhere else. This store sells only the most beautiful and beloved children's books, along with the artwork found within. Go for the story time, every day at 11 am.
- **Best Playground:** Shane's Inspiration, Griffith Park (Map 5). The playground was designed to allow handicapped children to play alongside their able-bodied peers on equipment that is colorful, innovative, and appealing to all. For a similar playground, check out Aidan's Place in Westwood Park, on Sepulveda Boulevard just south of Wilshire Boulevard.
- **Restaurant Most Welcoming to Kids:** Angeli Café, 7274 Melrose Ave, 323-936-9086 (Map 2). Sure, you could go to Shakey's or Chuck E. Cheese, but would you want to if you didn't have kids? Angeli Café is moderately priced, serves delicious pizzas and pastas, and provides young diners with their own ball of pizza dough to mold, shape, or fling at each other.
- **Most Surprising Place for Parents to Network:** Petting Zoo, Studio City Farmer's Market, Ventura Pl b/w Laurel Canyon & Ventura Blvd; Sundays, 8 am–1 pm (Map 56). Overall, the Studio City Farmer's Market is a kids' paradise on Sunday mornings. It features pony rides, a moon bounce, face painting, and a small train. Stand in the petting zoo long enough and you will encounter every person you have ever met in LA who has a child under the age of five. The animals are docile and the pen is kept as clean as is realistically possible. And the pig loves to have his belly rubbed.
- **Best Resource for New Mothers:** The Pump Station, 2415 Wilshire Blvd, Santa Monica, 310-998-1981 (Map 18). From breast pumps to nursing bras to high-end baby clothes, the Pump Station carries everything you need to get through the first few months of mommyhood. Even more useful, however, are the new-mother support groups, where lactation consultants/RNs can talk any nervous new mother down from the ledge.
- **Most Enjoyable Rainy Day Activity:** Tinker, 4337 Woodman Ave, Sherman Oaks, 818-784-7991, www.tinkertinker.com (Map 50). Only a parent could come up with a brilliant idea like Tinker. Here's how it works: "Art time" and basic materials are $5 per hour. Your child then selects a craft project from the wide variety they have at the store—dream catchers, t-shirts for painting, dolls and hats to sew and decorate, etc. (prices vary for each project)—and Tinker's friendly staff members guide them through the process. Classes featuring art, children's theater, knitting, and more are open to artists 5 and up. See www.tinkertinker.com for more info.

Parks for Playing

What makes for an excellent public park? In our opinion, any combination of the following: ample shade, well-maintained (and appealing or innovative) equipment, and an indefinable, overall good vibe. Most LA neighborhood parks feature at least a strip of grass and a slide or two, but these are some of the parks that are worth venturing out of your own neighborhood to explore:

- **Coldwater Canyon Park**, Coldwater Canyon Dr & N Beverly Dr, Beverly Hills (Map 1). The signs may say "No wading," but on any given day, dozens of kids splash through the man-made stream that runs through this park.
- **Roxbury Park**, Olympic Blvd & Roxbury Dr, Beverly Hills (Map 1). Not one, but two sizeable playgrounds with a wide variety of obstacles to climb on or slide down. Steam emanates from the dinosaur area every ten minutes or so.
- **West Hollywood Park**, San Vicente Blvd b/w Melrose Ave & Santa Monica Blvd, West Hollywood (Map 2). Run of the mill equipment, but a shady canopy covers the toddler play area. Great weekday "Tiny Tots" program.
- **Shane's Inspiration**, Griffith Park (Map 5). This colorful playground was designed to accommodate handicapped and able-bodied children alike.
- **Echo Park**, b/w Glendale Blvd & Echo Park Ave, just south of Sunset Blvd (Map 5). Lively crowds and a small lake, with paddleboats available for rent.
- **La Cienega Park**, La Cienega Blvd & Olympic Blvd (Map 6). Excellent music and dance classes for the smallest kids; colorful playground and chess players almost all day.
- **MacArthur Park**, 6th St & Alvarado St (Map 8). Small lake with paddleboats, as well as the chance to visit the park that inspired the epic '60s song.
- **Kenneth Hahn State Recreational Area**, La Cienega Blvd south of Rodeo Rd (Map 10). Hiking trails and a terrific play area for kids.
- **Douglas Park**, Wilshire Blvd & 25th St, Santa Monica (Map 19). Lots of grass and a water area that is home to several ducks.
- **Westwood Park**, Sepulveda Blvd b/w Wilshire Blvd & Santa Monica Blvd (Map 20). Features Aidan's Place, a playground designed to accommodate both handicapped and able-bodied children.
- **Penmar Playground**, Rose Ave & Penmar Ave, Venice (Map 21). Brand new playground and piñata pole, great for kids' birthday parties.
- **Culver City Park**, Jefferson Blvd & Duquesne Ave (Map 24). Features a 5000-square-foot skateboard park. Helmets required.

- **Polliwog Park**, N Redondo Ave & Manhattan Beach Blvd (Map 27). Park contains a pond as well as a playground area featuring a large, wooden, sunken galleon.
- **Seaside Lagoon**, 200 Portofino Wy, Redondo Beach (Map 31). Beach playground with a large, heated, saltwater swimming pool.
- **Garfield Park**, Stratford Ave & Mission Aly, South Pasadena (Map 34). Lots of shade and rolling green hills.
- **Lacey Park**, Monterey Rd & Virginia Rd, San Marino (Map 35). Includes a stroller/bicycle loop for fitness-minded moms and traveling tykes.
- **Lake Balboa Park**, Balboa Blvd & Victory Blvd (Map 46). Ducks to feed, a lake to walk around, and a great playground to boot.
- **Johnny Carson Park**, 400 S Bob Hope Dr & Riverside Dr (Map 50). Picturesque park home to numerous community events and festivals.
- **Encino Park**, Ventura Blvd & Genesta Ave (Map 53). Two shady playgrounds, at least one of which keeps the little ones fenced in.
- **Studio City Recreation Center (AKA Beeman Park)**, Beeman Ave & Rye St (Map 56). Lively, well-lit park serves as a community hub with large festivals for Halloween and Easter.

Rainy Day Activities—Indoor Playgrounds

Because wet weather is such an anomaly in Southern California, LA parents tend to lose it a little when forced to seek shelter indoors with the kids for a day or two. The kids, however, are perfectly happy, especially with a trip to some of LA's indoor playgrounds, where the temperature is always a pleasant 72 degrees and there's plenty of padding and cushions to break their fall.

- **Amy's Indoor Playground,** 1115 Mission Street, South Pasadena, (626)799-0304 (Map 34)
- **Bright Child**, 1415 4th St, Santa Monica, 310-393-4844 (Map 18)
- **Child's Play**, 2299 Westwood Blvd, Westwood, 310-470-4997 (Map 20)
- **Gymboree Play & Music**, Westside Pavilion, 10800 W Pico Blvd, West LA, 310-470-7780 (Map 23)
- **Gymboree Play & Music**, 14801 Ventura Blvd, Sherman Oaks, 818-905-6225 (Map 49)
- **Gymboree Play & Music**, 443 E Irving Dr, Suite F, Burbank, 818-955-8964 (Map 50)
- **Gymboree Play & Music**, 435 S Fair Oaks Ave, South Pasadena, 626-445-1122 (Map 34)
- **Under the Sea**, 2424 W Victory Blvd, Burbank, 818-567-9945 (Map 45)

Classes

Most of the play facilities listed above emphasize open play, allowing for parental spontaneity and the fickle nature of young children. However, with a little planning and structure (as counterintuitive as that might be), LA kids have a variety of classes available to them rivaling those of most Ivy League universities.

- **My Gym**, numerous locations around the LA area, visit www.my-gym.com for addresses. Gymnastics, circle time, and other traditionally kid-like activities.
- **Creative Space**, 6325 Santa Monica Blvd, Hollywood, 323-462-4600 (Map 2). An eclectic line-up of classes that includes Storybook Cooking for toddlers, knitting and breakdancing for the 'tweens, and yoga and scrapbooking for adults.
- **Creative Kids**, 11301 W Olympic Blvd, West LA, 310-473-6090 (Map 19). Their diverse schedule includes art classes for toddlers, dance and cooking for slightly older kids, and children's theater for ages 3–18.
- **Dance & Jingle**, 1900 W Mountain St, Glendale 818-845-3925 (Map 46). Highly sought-after music and movement class.
- **LA Zoo**, Zoo Dr, Griffith Park, 323-644-4200 (Map 51). The zoo's classes range from Toddler Totes, which involves singing, an animal guest, and a backpack filled with educational goodies, to Wild Planet, a more sophisticated program for adolescent zookeepers-in-training.
- **Music Together**, numerous locations around LA. Visit www.musictogether.com for more information. Teaches young children the fundamentals of rhythm and music through the modeling of parents and caregivers while exposing them to a wide array of music from diverse cultures and time periods.
- **Family Gallery Kits**, Skirball Cultural Center, 2701 N Sepulveda Blvd, 310-440-4500 (Map 49). Along with the center's ongoing arts and cultural exhibition, the organization provides an interactive kit packed with games, puzzles, and activities for 4–8 year olds.

Where to Go for More Information

Where to go for additional information:

- www.gocitykids.com
- www.at-la.com/@la-kid.htm
- local.thedaisychain.com/Los_Angeles_CA/
- *Fun and Educational Places to Go With Kids and Adults in Southern California* by Susan Peterson, Sunbelt Publications, 2001.

For the seriously ill or the terminally addicted to cosmetic surgery, Los Angeles boasts some of the most sought-after physicians and medical centers in the United States. The **UCLA Medical Center (Map 20)**, **Saint John's Medical Center (Map 18)**, and **Cedars-Sinai (Map 2)** are three of the best treatment facilities in the world. All have extensive networks of clinics and affiliated physicians around the city and county. Of the three Cedars has perhaps seen the longest list of celebrity births, deaths, and hospitalizations; Saint John's was the hospital that ushered adversaries Tom Cruise's and Brooke Shields's babies into the world. Of course, if you're experiencing a medical emergency, we advise you to go straight to the nearest hospital and/or shopping mall.

Emergency Rooms	*Address*	*Phone*	*Map*
Alhambra	100 S Raymond Ave	626-570-1606	39
Brotman	3828 Delmas Ter	310-836-7000	24
Cedars-Sinai Medical Center	8700 Beverly Blvd	310-423-8780	2
City of Angels	1711 W Temple St	213-989-6100	9
Daniel Freeman Memorial	333 N Prairie Ave	310-674-7050	13
Encino-Tarzana Regional Medical Center-Encino Campus	16237 Ventura Blvd	818-995-5000	54
Encino-Tarzana Regional Medical Center-Tarzana Campus	18321 Clark St	818-881-0800	46
Glendale Adventist	1509 Chevy Chase Dr	818-409-8000	51
Glendale Memorial	1420 S Central Ave	818-502-1900	51
Good Samaritan	1225 Wilshire Blvd	213-977-2121	9
Hollywood Presbyterian	1300 N Vermont Ave	213-413-3000	4
Huntington Memorial	100 W California Blvd	626-397-5000	34
LA County USC Medical Center	1200 N State St	323-226-2622	40
Little Company of Mary	4101 Torrance Blvd	310-540-7676	31
Los Angeles Community	4081 E Olympic Blvd	323-267-0477	41
Mission Community	14850 Roscoe Blvd	818-787-2222	47
Northridge - Roscoe Campus	18300 Roscoe Blvd	818-885-8500	46
Olympic Medical Center	5900 W Olympic Blvd	310-657-5900	6
Pacific Alliance	531 W College St	213-624-8411	9
Sherman Oaks	4929 Van Nuys Blvd	818-981-7111	55
Torrance Memorial	3330 Lomita Blvd	310-325-9110	32
UCLA Medical Center	10833 Le Conte Ave	310-825-7271	20

Other Hospitals	*Address*	*Phone*	*Map*
California Hospital Medical	1401 S Grand Ave	213-748-2411	9
Centinela	555 E Hardy St	310-673-4660	13
Children's	4650 W Sunset Blvd	323-660-2450	4
East LA Doctors	4060 Whittier Blvd	323-268-5514	41
Kaiser Foundation	4867 W Sunset Blvd	323-783-4011	4
Kaiser Foundation	6041 Cadillac Ave	323-857-2201	6
LA County Women's	1240 N Mission Rd	323-226-3054	40
Providence St Joseph Medical	501 S Buena Vista St	818-843-5111	50
St John's	1328 22nd St	310-829-5511	18
Valley Presbyterian	15107 Vanowen St	818-782-6600	47

Borrow a book from a friend and it sits on your nightstand for two years. Borrow that same book from the library and you have a deadline to meet—or a fine in your future. If it's instant gratification you seek, the Los Angeles Public Library stinks; but if you think of it as a kind of Amazon.com without shipping fees, it's a phenomenal service. The system works like Netflix: go online, find a book, select the branch to which you'd like your book sent, and—*voila*!—the library emails when said book is ready for pick-up. The drag is that you sometimes end up waiting months for the hottest bestsellers, but the price is right and the selection is vast.

The Library system offers more than just books—DVDs, CDs, and books-on-tape are all available to borrow. Computers are available, free of charge, for up to two hours a day at all branches. The Grandparents and Books program pairs senior citizens and kids for story time and games. This program is also available at most neighborhood branches. **The Los Angeles Central Library (Map 9)**, downtown, is worth a special trip. Its diverse collection of art includes the Children's Court, which features whimsical marble panels of kid-lit images like Alice in Wonderland and Mother Goose, and a breathtaking eight-story atrium.

Library	*Address*	*Phone*	*Map*
Alhambra Library	410 W Main St	626-570-5008	39
Allendale Branch	1130 S Marengo Ave	626-744-7260	34
Angeles Mesa	2700 W 52nd St	323-292-4328	11
Anthony Quinn Public Library	3965 E Cesar E Chavez Ave	323-264-7715	41
Arroyo Seco Regional	6145 N Figueroa St	323-255-0537	33
Atwater Branch	3379 Glendale Blvd	323-664-1353	5
Balch Art Research Library	5905 Wilshire Blvd	323-857-6116	6
Baldwin Hills Branch	2906 S La Brea Ave	323-733-1196	10
Benjamin Franklin Branch	2200 E 1st St	323-263-6901	40
Beverly Hills Public Library	444 N Rexford Dr	310-288-2220	1
Buena Vista Branch	300 N Buena Vista St	818-238-5620	50
Burbank Central Library	110 N Glenoaks Blvd	818-238-5600	50
Cahuenga Branch	4591 Santa Monica Blvd	323-664-6418	4
Canoga Park Branch	20939 Sherman Wy	818-887-0320	45
Chatsworth Branch	21052 Devonshire St	818-341-4276	42
Chinatown Branch	639 N Hill St	213-620-0925	9
City Terrace	4025 City Terrace Dr	323-261-0295	41
Crenshaw-Imperial Branch	11141 Crenshaw Blvd	310-412-5403	28
Culver City Julian Dixon	4975 Overland Ave	310-559-1676	24
Cypress Park Branch	1150 Cypress Ave	323-224-0039	36
Donald Bruce Kaufman	11820 San Vicente Blvd	310-575-8273	16
Eagle Rock	5027 Caspar Ave	323-258-8078	33
East Los Angeles	4837 E 3rd St	323-264-0155	41
Echo Park Library	1410 W Temple St	213-250-7808	9
Edendale Branch	2011 W Sunset Blvd	213-207-3000	5
El Camino Real	4264 Whittier Blvd	323-269-8102	41
El Retiro Branch	126 Vista Del Parque	310-375-0922	31
El Segundo Public Library	111 W Mariposa Ave	310-524-2722	27
El Sereno Branch	5226 Huntington Dr S	323-255-9201	38
Encino-Tarzana Branch	18231 Ventura Blvd	818-343-1983	53
Exposition Park Branch	3665 S Vermont Ave	323-732-0169	11
Fairfax Branch Library	161 S Gardner St	323-936-6191	2
Felipe De Neve Branch	2820 W 6th St	213-384-7676	8
Frances Howard Goldwyn	1623 Ivar Ave	323-856-8260	3
Franklin D Murphy Library (temporarily closed)	244 S San Pedro St	213-628-2725	9
Glendale Central Library	222 E Harvard St	818-548-2030	51
Goethe Institute-Los Angeles	5750 Wilshire Blvd	323-525-3388	6
Granada Hills Branch	10640 Petit Ave	818-368-5687	44
Grandview Library	1535 5th St	818-548-2049	50
Hawthorne	12700 Grevillea Ave	310-679-8193	28
Henderson Branch	4805 Emerald St	310-371-2075	31
Hermosa Beach Public Library	550 Pier Ave	310-379-8475	29
Hill Avenue Branch	55 S Hill Ave	626-744-7264	35
Hyde Park-Miriam Matthews Branch	2205 W Florence Ave	323-750-7241	14
Inglewood Public Library	101 W Manchester Blvd	310-412-5380	13
Jefferson Branch	2211 W Jefferson Blvd	323-734-8573	11
John C Fremont Branch	6121 Melrose Ave	323-962-3521	3
John Muir Branch	1005 W 64th St	323-789-4800	14
Junipero Serra Branch	4607 S Main St	323-234-1685	12
Katy Geissert Civic Center Library	3301 Torrance Blvd	310-618-5959	32
LA County Law Library	301 W 1st St	213-629-3531	9
LA County Law Library	6230 Sylmar Ave	818-374-2499	47
LA County Law Library	825 Maple Ave	310-222-8816	30
LA County Law Library-Pasadena	300 E Walnut St	626-356-5253	34
LA County Law Library-Santa Monica	1725 Main St	310-260-3644	18

La Pintoresca Branch	1355 N Raymond Ave	626-744-7268	34
Lamanda Park Branch	140 S Altadena Dr	626-744-7266	35
Lawndale Library	14615 Burin Ave	310-676-0177	28
Lennox	4359 Lennox Blvd	310-674-0385	13
Lincoln Heights Branch	2530 Workman St	323-226-1692	37
Little Tokyo Branch	203 S Los Angeles St	213-612-0525	9
Lloyd Taber	4533 Admiralty Wy	310-821-3415	25
Lomita	24200 Narbonne Ave	310-539-4515	32
Los Angeles Central Library	630 W 5th St	213-228-7000	9
Los Angeles Main Branch-Braille Institute Library	741 N Vermont Ave	800-808-2555	4
Los Feliz Branch	1874 Hillhurst Ave	323-913-4710	4
Malabar Branch	2801 Wabash Ave	323-263-1497	40
Malaga Cove Library	2400 Via Campesina	310-377-9584	31
Manhattan Beach	1320 Highland Ave	310-545-8595	27
Mar Vista Branch	12006 Venice Blvd	310-390-3454	22
Mark Twain Branch	9621 S Figueroa St	323-755-4088	14
Memorial Branch	4625 W Olympic Blvd	323-938-2732	7
Mid-Valley Regional Branch Library	16244 Nordhoff St	818-895-3650	44
Morningside Park Branch	3202 W 85th St	310-412-5400	14
MTA Library	1 Gateway Plz	213-922-4859	9
North Hollywood Regional	5211 Tujunga Ave	818-766-7185	56
North Torrance Branch	3604 Artesia Blvd	310-323-7200	30
Northridge Branch	9051 Darby Ave	818-886-3640	43
Northwest Branch	3323 W Victory Blvd	818-238-5640	49
Nursing Library	1237 N Mission Rd	323-226-6521	40
Pacific Palisades Branch	861 Alma Real Dr	310-459-2754	15
Pacific Park Branch	501 S Pacific Ave	818-548-3760	51
Palms-Rancho Park Branch	2920 Overland Ave	310-840-2142	23
Pasadena Central	285 E Walnut St	626-744-4066	34
Pico Union Branch	1030 S Alvarado St	213-368-7545	8
Pio Pico Koreatown Branch	694 S Oxford Ave	213-368-7647	8
Playa Vista Branch	6400 Playa Vista Dr	310-437-6680	25
Porter Ranch Branch	11371 Tampa Ave	818-360-5706	43
Redondo Beach North Branch	2000 Artesia Blvd	310-318-0677	29
Redondo Beach Public Library	303 N Pacific Coast Hwy	310-318-0675	31
Robert Louis Stevenson Branch	803 Spence St	323-268-4710	40
Robertson Branch	1719 S Robertson Blvd	310-840-2147	6
San Marino Public Library	1890 Huntington Dr	626-300-0777	39
San Rafael Branch	1240 Nithsdale Rd	626-744-7270	34
Santa Catalina Branch	999 E Washington Blvd	626-744-7272	35
Santa Monica Fairview Branch	2101 Ocean Park Blvd	310-450-0443	18
Santa Monica Montana Avenue Branch	1704 Montana Ave	310-829-7081	18
Santa Monica Ocean Park Branch	2601 Main St	310-392-3804	18
Santa Monica Public Library	601 Santa Monica Blvd	315-458-8600	18
Santa Monica Public Library (temporarily closed)	1343 6th St	310-458-8600	18
Sherman Oaks Library	14245 Moorpark St	818-205-9716	55
Sons of the Revolution Library	600 S Central Ave	818-240-1775	51
South Pasadena Library	1100 Oxley St	626-403-7340	34
Southeast Branch	23115 Arlington Ave	310-530-5044	32
Studio City Branch	12511 Moorpark St	818-755-7873	56
Sun Valley Branch	7935 Vineland Ave	818-764-1338	48
Valley Plaza Branch	12311 Vanowen St	818-765-9251	48
Van Nuys Branch	6250 Sylmar Ave	818-756-8453	47
Venice Branch	501 S Venice Blvd	310-821-1769	21
Vermont Square Branch	1201 W 48th St	323-290-7405	11
Vernon Branch	4504 S Central Ave	323-234-9106	12
View Park	3854 W 54th St	323-293-5371	10
Villa Parke Community Center Branch	363 E Villa St	626-744-6510	34
Walteria Branch	3815 W 242nd St	310-375-8418	31
Washington Irving Branch	4117 W Washington Blvd	323-734-6303	7
Water & Power Library	111 N Hope St	213-367-1995	9
West Hollywood	715 N San Vicente Blvd	310-652-5340	2
West Los Angeles Regional	11360 Santa Monica Blvd	310-575-8323	19
West Valley Regional	19036 Vanowen St	818-345-9806	46
Westchester Branch	7114 W Manchester Ave	310-348-1096	25
Westwood Branch	1246 Glendon Ave	310-474-1739	20
Will & Ariel Durant Branch	7140 W Sunset Blvd	323-876-2741	2
Wilshire Library	149 N St Andrews Pl	323-957-4550	7
Wiseburn	5335 W 135th St	310-643-8880	28
Woodcrest	1340 W 106th St	323-757-9373	14

Here's the deal in LA. West Hollywood's pretty-boy ground zero is located at **The Abbey**. Places further east down Santa Monica Boulevard, like **FuBar** and **Club7969**, trade in the gloss for raw power. FuBar is a little darker, wilder, and more intimate. 7969 is hot and packed on Saturdays with Hot Dog, Mario Diaz's sexy boy party. **O-Bar** is a swanky lounge that is cruising heaven. On Sunday afternoons, there's always Player/Size at **Here Lounge**, where, if you're lucky, the sun won't be the only thing to go down. Far from the reaches of WeHo, Silver Lake's gay scene is decidedly more mellow and friendly. **Akbar** is the place to go for cute, indie, normal-bodied boys, **Faultline** can give you that hot leather daddy moment we all need from time to time, and **The Eagle** is a mixed scene with retro porn playing and special nights catering to the ladies (Wednesday) and the bears (Thursday). To do it up gender-queer, check out Tiger Heat at **Circus Disco** on Thursdays, and Miss Kitty's at the **Dragonfly** on Fridays.

Hot girl action tends to be mixed in with the predominantly male scene in LA. So places like **The Abbey**, Beige at **The Falcon** (Tuesdays), Fuse (Thursdays) at **Here**, and Friday night GirlBar at **UltraSuede** or TruckStop at **Here** are also good places to meet the cute lipstick lesbian (*The L-Word* is set here for a reason) or sporty girl of your dreams. Like all of LA, the LGBT scene here is image-conscious, stylish, and physically fit. There is diversity to be had—you might just have to drive a bit further east and south of WeHo to find it. For hipster gals, check out Shotgun at **The Eagle** (Wednesdays) and for hip-hop hotties try Ladies Touch at **Little Temple** (1st Saturday). If you're further south, visit **Ripples** or **The Executive Suite** in Long Beach.

Websites

- **LA Gay & Lesbian Center • www.laglc.org**
  LA Gay and Lesbian Center is the largest and oldest in the country, and is an invaluable community resource offering legal, medical, outreach, and educational services, among many others.
- **Circuit Noize • www.circuitnoize.com**
  The premier source of circuit party information, parties, events, music, tickets, gay travel, and dancing.
- **Gay.com • www.gay.com**
  If you're looking for love online, this is the place to visit. Gay.com has hundreds of chat rooms for people around the country, with eight devoted to LA, two to Long Beach, and two to Orange County.
- **Gay and Lesbian Community Yellow Pages • www.glcyp.com** • Online version of Yellow Pages distributed through West Hollywood
- **Gay Los Angeles • www.gaylosangeles.com**
  Lesbian and gay directory for gay-owned and gay-friendly places in Los Angeles (bars, clubs, saunas, restaurants, and more).
- **West Hollywood • www.westhollywood.com**
  Comprehensive online guide to gay West Hollywood, featuring music, arts, videos, nightlife, circuits, classifieds, buzz, photos, and shopping.
- **QV Magazine • www.qvmagazine.com**
  Online edition of LA's gay Latino magazine.
- **Power Up • www.power-up.net**
  A group dedicated to promoting the visibility of gay women in film, entertainment, and media.
- **Los Angeles Tennis Association • www.lataweb.com**
  With more than 400 members, this is the largest gay and lesbian tennis club in the world. All skill levels welcome.
- **Greater Los Angeles Softball Association • www.lagaysoftball.com**
  This exclusively gay and lesbian league has more than 30 teams participating in their men's and women's divisions.
- **Gay Men's Chorus of Los Angeles • www.gmcla.com**
  Check out their site for performance dates and a rehearsal schedule.
- **Metropolitan Community Church • www.mccla.org**
  This popular church is gay- and lesbian-friendly and offers multi-denominational services.

Bookstores

- **A Different Light Bookstore** • 8853 Santa Monica Blvd (at San Vicente Blvd), West Hollywood • 310-854-6601 • www.adlbooks.com • Hours: 10 am–midnight, daily.
- **Circus of Books** (two locations) • 8230 Santa Monica Blvd (b/w Harper & LaJolla Aves), West Hollywood • 323-656-6533; and 4001 Sunset Blvd (at Sanborn Ave), Silver Lake • 323-666-1304 • www.circusofbooks.com • Hours: 6 am–2 am, daily.

Health Center & Support Organizations

LA Gay & Lesbian Center (LAGLC) McDonald Wright Building • 1625 N Schrader Blvd, Los Angeles, CA 90028 • 323-993-7400 • www.laglc.org

LAGLC offers the following services:

- Pedro Zamora Youth HIV Program • 323-993-7571
- Jeffrey Goodman Special Care Clinic • 323-993-7500
  12-Step Program Meetings including AA, Alanon, NA, Marijuana Anon, Crystal Meth Anon, Sexual Compulsives Anon, and Anorexics Anon.
- Counseling services including general, addiction recovery, domestic violence, and HIV/AIDS • 323-993-7500
- HIV Testing • 323-993-7500
- Audre Lorde Lesbian Health Clinic • 323-993-7500
- Sexual Health Program • 323-860-5855

AIDS Project Los Angeles • 213-201-1600 • www.apla.org • Assistance and information hotline for people living with AIDS.

HIV LA • www.hivla.org
An online resource in English and Spanish that helps people with HIV/AIDS find services available in Los Angeles County.

GLAAD Los Angeles • 5455 Wilshire Blvd #1500, Los Angeles, CA 90036 • 323-933-2240 • www.glaad.org

Gay & Lesbian Youth Talkline • 800-246-7743

The Trevor Project • www.trevorproject.org • Support line for LGBT youth.

Publications

From local news headlines to club listings, these LGBT publications bring you all the news that's gay. Most of these publications can be found in gay-friendly bookstores, cafes, bars, and various shops.

- **A & U** • 888.245.4333 • www.aumag.org
- **Blade** • 949-494-6945 • www.gayblade.com
- **Circuit Noize** • 818-769-9390 • www.circuitnoize.com
- **Cybersocket** • 323.650.9906 • www.cybersocket.com
- **Fab** • 323-655-5716 • www.gayfab.com
- **Frontiers** • 323-930-3220 • www.frontiersnewsmagazine.com
- **MetroSource LA** • 323-933-2300 • www.metrosource.com
- **POZ Magazine** • www.poz.com
- **QV Magazine** • 702-676-1427 • www.qvmagazine.com
- **The Lesbian News** • 800-458-9888 • www.lesbiannews.com
- **The Advocate** • 323-852-7200 • www.advocate.com
- **In Los Angeles Magazine** • 323.848.2200 • www.inlamagazine.com
- **Odyssey Magazine** • 323-874-8788 • www.odysseymagazine.net

Venues—Gay

- **Akbar** • 4356 W Sunset Blvd • Silver Lake • 323-665-6810
- **Arena** • 6655 Santa Monica Blvd • West Hollywood • 323-462-0714
- **Banana's Bar & Nightclub** • 7026 Reseda Blvd • Reseda • 818-996-2976
- **The Bullet** • 10522 Burbank Blvd & Cahuenga Blvd • North Hollywood • 818-762-8890
- **Club 7969** • 7969 Santa Monica Blvd (b/w Fairfax & Crescent Heights) • West Hollywood • 323-654-0280
- **Club Fuel** • 11608 Ventura Blvd & Laurel Canyon • Studio City • 818-506-0404
- **East West Lounge** • 8851 Santa Monica Blvd • West Hollywood • 310-360-6186
- **The Factory** • 652 N La Peer Dr (at Robertson) • West Hollywood • 310-659-4551
- **Faultline** • 4216 Melrose Ave • Silver Lake • 323-660-0889
- **Fiesta Cantina** • 8865 Santa Monica Blvd • West Hollywood • 310-652-8865
- **FuBar** • 7994 Santa Monica Blvd • West Hollywood • 323-654-0396
- **Gold Coast** • 8228 Santa Monica Blvd • West Hollywood • 323-656-4879
- **EAGLE LA** • 4219 Santa Monica Blvd • Silver Lake • 323-669-9472
- **Here** • 696 N Robertson Blvd • West Hollywood • 310-360-8455
- **Micky's** • 8857 Santa Monica Blvd • West Hollywood • 310-657-1176
- **MJ's** • 2810 Hyperion Ave • Silver Lake • 323-660-1503
- **Moonshadow** • 10437 Burbank Blvd • North Hollywood • 818-508-7008
- **Mother Lode** • 8944 Santa Monica Blvd (at San Vicente) • West Hollywood • 310-659-9700
- **Numbers** • 8741 Santa Monica Blvd • West Hollywood • 310-652-7700
- **O-bar** • 8279 Santa Monica Blvd • West Hollywood • 323-822-3300
- **Oil Can Harry's** • 11502 Ventura Blvd • Studio City • 818-760-9749
- **Rage** • 8911 Santa Monica Blvd (b/w Larrabee & San Vicente) • West Hollywood • 310-652-7055
- **Rawhide** • 10937 Burbank Blvd • North Hollywood • 818-760-9798
- **Roosterfish** • 1302 Abbot Kinney Blvd • Venice Beach • 310-392-2123
- **Trunks** • 8809 Santa Monica Blvd • West Hollywood • 310-652-1015
- **Ultra Suede** • 661 N Robertson Blvd (at Melrose Ave) • West Hollywood • 310-659-4551
- **Wonder Bar** • 2692 S La Cienega Ave • Los Angeles • 310-837-7443

Venues—Lesbian

- **Club 7969** (Michelle's XXX Review Tuesday) • 7969 Santa Monica Blvd (b/w Fairfax & Crescent Heights) • West Hollywood • 323-654-0280
- **The Eagle (Shotgun Wednesday)** • 4219 Santa Monica Blvd • Silver Lake • 323-669-9472
- **The Factory** (Girl Bar Friday) • 652 N La Peer Dr (at Robertson) • West Hollywood • 310-659-4551
- **Here** • (Fuse Thursday) • 696 N Robertson Blvd • 310-360-8455
- **Jewels Catch One** • 4067 W Pico Blvd (at Norton Ave) • Mid City • 323-734-8849
- **Little Temple (Ladies Touch)** • 4519 Santa Monica Blvd • Silver Lake • 323-660-4540
- **Normandie Room** • 8737 Santa Monica Blvd (at Hancock Ave) • West Hollywood • 310-659-6204
- **The Palms** • 8572 Santa Monica Blvd (at La Cienega) • West Hollywood • 310-652-1595

Venues—Both

- **The Abbey** • 692 N Robertson Blvd • 310-289-8410
- **Dream Discotheque** • 1717 Silver Lake Blvd • Los Angeles • 323-661-4380
- **The Echo** • 1822 W Sunset Blvd • Echo Park • 213-413-8200
- **The Falcon** (Beige, Tuesdays) • 7213 Sunset Blvd • Hollywood • 323-850-5350
- **Hamburger Marys** • 8288 Santa Monica Blvd • West Hollywood • 323-654-3800
- **Marix Tex-Mex Café** • 1108 N Flores St • West Hollywood • 323-848-2458
- **Red's Bar** • 2218 E First St • Los Angeles • 323-263-2995

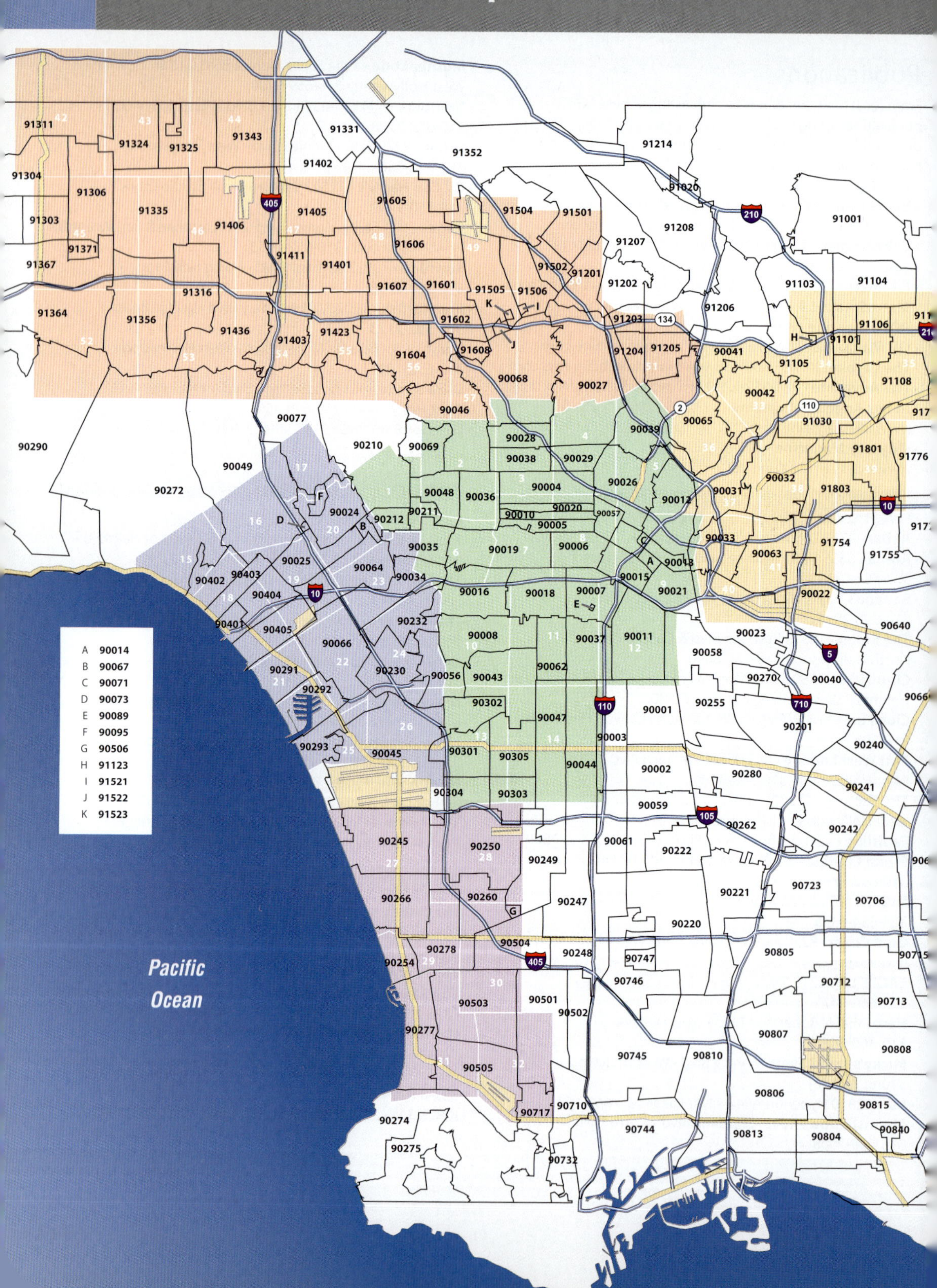
A 90014
B 90067
C 90071
D 90073
E 90089
F 90095
G 90506
H 91123
I 91521
J 91522
K 91523
Pacific Ocean
91311
91324
91325
91343
91331
91352
91214
91304
91402
91306
91335
91406
91405
91605
91504
91501
91020
91208
91001
91303
91371
91367
91411
91401
91606
91502
91201
91207
91202
91103
91104
91607
91601
91505
91506
91316
91364
91356
91436
91403
91423
91602
91604
91608
91203
91204
91205
91206
91041
91105
91106
91101
91108
90041
90042
90065
91030
90068
90027
90046
90077
90039
90210
90069
90028
90038
90029
90026
90290
90049
90272
90048
90036
90004
90020
90010
90005
90057
90012
90031
90032
91801
91776
91803
90024
90212
90211
90035
90019
90006
90033
90013
90063
91754
91755
90025
90064
90034
90402
90403
90404
90016
90018
90007
90015
90021
90022
90401
90405
90232
90008
90037
90011
90023
90058
90640
90066
90291
90230
90056
90043
90062
90270
90040
90292
90302
90047
90001
90255
90201
90293
90045
90301
90305
90044
90003
90002
90280
90240
90304
90303
90059
90241
90262
90242
90245
90250
90249
90061
90222
90266
90260
90247
90221
90723
90706
90220
90504
90278
90254
90248
90747
90746
90805
90712
90713
90503
90501
90502
90277
90807
90808
90505
90745
90810
90806
90815
90717
90710
90274
90744
90813
90804
90840
90275
90732
405
210
134
110
10
5
710
105
2

Map	Address	Zip
1	312 S Beverly Dr	90212
1	323 N Crescent Dr	90210
1	325 N Maple Dr	90210
2	1125 N Fairfax Ave	90046
2	7610 Beverly Blvd	90048
2	820 N San Vicente Blvd	90069
3	1425 N Cherokee Ave	90028
3	1615 Wilcox Ave	90028
3	6457 Santa Monica Blvd	90038
3	6801 Hollywood Blvd	90028
4	1825 N Vermont Ave	90027
5	1525 N Alvarado St	90026
5	3370 Glendale Blvd	90039
6	1270 S Alfred St	90035
6	4960 W Washington Blvd	90016
6	5350 Wilshire Blvd	90036
6	8383 Wilshire Blvd	90211
7	4040 W Washington Blvd	90018
8	2390 W Pico Blvd	90006
8	265 S Western Ave	90004
8	3751 W 6th St	90020
9	100 W Olympic Blvd	90015
9	1055 N Vignes St	90012
9	1122 E 7th St	90021
9	1660 Beverly Blvd	90015
9	1808 W 7th St	90057
9	2005 W 6th St	90057
9	300 N Los Angeles St	90012
9	350 S Grand Ave	90071
9	505 S Flower St	90071
9	750 W 7th St	90017
9	900 N Alameda St	90012
10	3650 W Martin Luther King Jr Blvd	90008
10	3894 Crenshaw Blvd	90008
11	1515 W Vernon Ave	90062
11	3585 S Vermont Ave	90007
11	5472 Crenshaw Blvd	90043
11	5832 S Vermont Ave	90044
12	4352 S Central Ave	90011
12	5115 S Figueroa St	90037
12	819 W Washington Blvd	90015
13	300 E Hillcrest Blvd	90301
13	4443 Lennox Blvd	90304
13	811 N La Brea Ave	90302
14	2200 W Century Blvd	90047
14	3212 W 85th St	90305
14	8200 S Vermont Ave	90044
15	15209 W Sunset Blvd	90272
15	15243 La Cruz Dr	90272
16	200 S Barrington Ave	90049
18	1025 Colorado Ave	90401
18	1217 Wilshire Blvd	90403
18	1248 5th St	90401
18	2720 Neilson Wy	90405
19	11270 Exposition Blvd	90064
19	11301 Wilshire Blvd	90073
19	11420 Santa Monica Blvd	90025
19	3010 WIlshire Blvd	90403
20	11000 Wilshire Blvd	90024
21	1601 Main St	90291
21	313 Grand Blvd	90291
22	3826 Grand View Blvd	90066
23	10850 W Pico Blvd	90064
23	3751 Motor Ave	90034
23	9911 W Pico Blvd	90035
24	11111 Jefferson Blvd	90230
24	9942 Culver Blvd	90232
25	13031 W Jefferson Blvd	90311
25	215 Culver Blvd	90293
25	4766 Admiralty Wy	90292
26	7381 La Tijera Blvd	90045
26	9029 Airport Blvd	90009
27	1007 N Sepulveda Blvd	90266
27	425 15th St	90266
28	12700 Inglewood Ave	90250
28	4320 Marine Ave	90260
29	2215 Artesia Blvd	90504
29	565 Pier Ave	90254
30	18080 Crenshaw Blvd	90504
30	1815 Hawthorne Blvd	90278
31	1201 N Catalina Ave	90277
32	1433 Marcelina Ave	90501
32	2510 Monterey St	90503
32	25131 Narbonne Ave	90717
32	291 Del Amo Fashion Sq	90503
33	5132 York Blvd	90042
33	5930 N Figueroa St	90042
33	7435 N Figueroa St	90041
34	1001 Fremont Ave	91030
34	1100 N Fair Oaks Ave	91103
34	1355 N Mentor Ave	91104
34	281 E Colorado Blvd	91101
34	600 Lincoln Ave	91109
34	870 S Raymond Ave	91105
34	99 W California Blvd	91105
35	2609 E Colorado Blvd	91107
35	2960 Huntington Dr	91108
35	967 E Colorado Blvd	91106
36	3950 Eagle Rock Blvd	90065
37	3001 N Broadway	90031
38	3316 N Eastern Ave	90032
38	4875 Huntington Dr	90032
39	1603 W Valley Blvd	91803
40	2016 E 1st St	90033
40	3641 E 8th St	90023
41	3729 E 1st St	90063
41	975 S Atlantic Blvd	90022
42	21606 Devonshire St	91311
43	18039 Chatsworth St	91344
43	19300 Rinaldi St	91326
43	9534 Reseda Blvd	91324
45	21801 Sherman Wy	91303
45	7655 Winnetka Ave	91306
45	8201 Canoga Ave	91304
46	5609 Yolanda Ave	91356
46	5805 White Oak Ave	91316
46	7320 Reseda Blvd	91335
47	15701 Sherman Wy	91406
47	6200 Van Nuys Blvd	91401
48	6242 Vantage Ave	91606
48	6535 Lankershim Blvd	91606
48	7035 Laurel Cyn Blvd	91605
49	2140 N Hollywood Wy	91505
49	3810 W Magnolia Blvd	91505
50	135 E Olive Ave	91502
50	1634 N San Fernando Blvd	91504
50	6444 San Fernando Rd	91201
51	1009 N Pacific Ave	91202
51	101 N Verdugo Rd	91206
51	120 E Chevy Chase Dr	91205
51	313 E Broadway	91205
52	22121 Clarendon St	91367
53	4930 Balboa Blvd	91316
54	14900 Magnolia Blvd	91403
56	11304 Chandler Blvd	91601
56	12450 Magnolia Blvd	91607
56	3950 Laurel Cyn Blvd	91604
57	10063 Riverside Dr	91602

** Last pick-up time, pm*

Map 1 • Beverly Hills

Beverly Hills Mail Box	9903 Santa Monica Blvd	4:30 pm
FedEx Kinko's	9680 Santa Monica Blvd	5:45 pm
FedEx Kinko's	9201 W Sunset Blvd	5:45 pm
FedEx Kinko's	9334 Wilshire Blvd	5:30 pm
Mail Boxes Etc	269 S Beverly Dr	5 pm
Mail Boxes Etc	9663 Santa Monica Blvd	5 pm
Mail Boxes Times	9461 Charleville Blvd	5:30 pm
Mailbox & Services	9190 W Olympic Blvd	5 pm
Self-Service	9440 Santa Monica Blvd	5:30 pm
Self-Service	312 S Beverly Dr	5 pm
Self-Service	325 N Maple Dr	5 pm
Self-Service	345 N Maple Dr	5 pm
Self-Service	421 N Rodeo Dr	5 pm
Self-Service	9171 Wilshire Blvd	5 pm
Self-Service	9220 W Sunset Blvd	5 pm
Self-Service	9300 Wilshire Blvd	5 pm
Self-Service	9301 Wilshire Blvd	5 pm
Self-Service	9401 Wilshire Blvd	5 pm
Self-Service	9454 Wilshire Blvd	5 pm
Self-Service	9460 Wilshire Blvd	5 pm
Self-Service	9465 Wilshire Blvd	5 pm
Self-Service	9595 Wilshire Blvd	5 pm
Self-Service	9665 Wilshire Blvd	5 pm
Self-Service	9701 Wilshire Blvd	5 pm
Self-Service	9720 Wilshire Blvd	5 pm
Self-Service	9777 Wilshire Blvd	5 pm
Self-Service	9601 Wilshire Blvd	5 pm
Self-Service	301 N Canon Dr	4:45 pm
Self-Service	9229 W Sunset Blvd	4:45 pm
Self-Service	9255 W Sunset Blvd	4:45 pm
Self-Service	9355 Wilshire Blvd	4:45 pm
Self-Service	9560 Wilshire Blvd	4:45 pm
Self-Service	433 N Camden Dr	4:30 pm
Self-Service	100 N Crescent Dr	4 pm
Self-Service	9292 Civic Center Dr	4 pm

Map 2 • West Hollywood

Banner Packaging	8231 W 3rd St	4 pm
Beverly Hills US Mailbox	311 N Robertson Blvd	4 pm
Box 2 Go	901 N Fairfax Ave	5 pm
Box and Mail	7162 Beverly Blvd	4 pm
Box and Ship	7304 Beverly Blvd	4 pm
Box Brothers	8533 Santa Monica Blvd	4:30 pm
The Box Depot	119 N Fairfax Ave	5 pm
Box & Ship Hollywood	8172 W Sunset Blvd	5 pm
Boxes & More	8491 W Sunset Blvd	5 pm
E and G Mail Boxes	357 S Fairfax Ave	5 pm
FedEx Kinko's	7630 W Sunset Blvd	5 pm
FedEx Kinko's	8471 Beverly Blvd	5 pm
Hybrid - Internet	8936 Santa Monica Blvd	5 pm
Mail Boxes Etc	8391 Beverly Blvd	4:15 pm
Mail Boxes PMB	7336 Santa Monica Blvd	5 pm
Mail Boxes & Things	8424 Santa Monica Blvd	5 pm
Mail & More On Hollywood	7095 Hollywood Blvd	5:30 pm
Mail Service Center	8721 Santa Monica Blvd	4:45 pm
Miracle Mail	5850 W 3rd St	4:30 pm
Mister Mail	7510 W Sunset Blvd	5:15 pm
Postal Center & More	8205 Santa Monica Blvd	5 pm
Rent Solution	8934 Santa Monica Blvd	5 pm
Russian Universal Service	1123 N Fairfax Ave	4:30 pm
Self-Service	7551 W Sunset Blvd	5:30 pm
Self-Service	7610 Beverly Blvd	5:15 pm
Self-Service	7753 Santa Monica Blvd	5:15 pm
Self-Service	8265 W Sunset Blvd	5:15 pm
Self-Service	116 N Robertson Blvd	5 pm
Self-Service	145 S Fairfax Ave	5 pm
Self-Service	7060 Hollywood Blvd	5 pm
Self-Service	7080 Hollywood Blvd	5 pm
Self-Service	7920 W Sunset Blvd	5 pm
Self-Service	8075 W 3rd St	5 pm
Self-Service	8222 Melrose Ave	5 pm
Self-Service	8500 Melrose Ave	5 pm
Self-Service	8635 W 3rd St	5 pm
Self-Service	8687 Melrose Ave	5 pm
Self-Service	8899 Beverly Blvd	5 pm
Self-Service	8981 W Sunset Blvd	5 pm
Self-Service	9000 W Sunset Blvd	5 pm
Self-Service	9060 Santa Monica Blvd	5 pm
Self-Service	1011 N Fuller Ave	4:45 pm
Self-Service	200 N Robertson Blvd	4:45 pm
Self-Service	250 N Robertson Blvd	4:45 pm
Self-Service	444 S San Vicente Blvd	4:45 pm
Self-Service	110 S Fairfax Ave	4:30 pm
Self-Service	189 The Grove Dr	4:30 pm
Self-Service	820 N San Vicente Blvd	4:30 pm
Self-Service	8730 W Sunset Blvd	4:30 pm
Self-Service	8436 W 3rd St	4 pm
Sunset Blvd Mailboxes	7119 W Sunset Blvd	4:30 pm
The UPS Store	8581 Santa Monica Blvd	4:45 pm
West Hollywood Mail & Msg	7985 Santa Monica Blvd	5 pm

Map 3 • Hollywood

FedEx Kinko's	6666 Lexington Ave	6 pm
FedEx Kinko's	6255 W Sunset Blvd	6 pm
FedEx Kinko's	1440 Vine St	5 pm
Highland Postal Center	1304 N Highland Ave	5 pm
Hollywood Mail Box	6767 W Sunset Blvd	5 pm
Mail Call	5870 Melrose Ave	5 pm
P S Postal Express	6217 Franklin Ave	5 pm
Rush Postal Center	6093 W Sunset Blvd	5 pm
Self-Service	1040 N Las Palmas Ave	5:45 pm
Self-Service	6464 W Sunset Blvd	5:30 pm
Self-Service	6922 Hollywood Blvd	5:30 pm
Self-Service	1680 Vine St	5:15 pm
Self-Service	6450 W Sunset Blvd	5:15 pm
Self-Service	6671 W Sunset Blvd	5:15 pm
Self-Service	846 N Cahuenga Blvd	5:15 pm
Self-Service	5300 Melrose Ave	5 pm
Self-Service	6430 W Sunset Blvd	5 pm
Self-Service	6525 W Sunset Blvd	5 pm
Self-Service	6565 W Sunset Blvd	5 pm
Self-Service	6801 Hollywood Blvd	5 pm
Self-Service	1440 Vine St	5 pm
Self-Service	1615 Wilcox Ave	4:30 pm
Self-Service	306 N Larchmont Blvd	4 pm
Village Mail Call	419 N Larchmont Blvd	5:15 pm

Map 4 • Los Feliz

Box Brothers	1954 Hillhurst Ave	5 pm
Copycat Pack-n-fly	2046 Hillhurst Ave	4:45 pm
Kingston Mail & Gift Mart	1555 N Vermont Ave	4 pm
Self-Service	1825 N Vermont Ave	5 pm
Self-Service	4021 Rosewood Ave	5 pm
Self-Service	1300 N Vermont Ave	4:30 pm
Self-Service	4546 W Sunset Blvd	4 pm
Self-Service	4661 W Sunset Blvd	4 pm

Map 5 • Silver Lake/ Echo Park/Atwater

Box and Ship	2590 Glendale Blvd	4:15 pm
Box Brothers	3108 Glendale Blvd	4 pm
Goinpostal Los Angeles	1166 Glendale Blvd	4:30 pm
Postalworks	2658 Griffith Park Blvd	5 pm
Self-Service	1525 N Alvarado St	5 pm
Self-Service	1910 W Sunset Blvd	5 pm
Self-Service	3370 Glendale Blvd	4:30 pm
Speedco Fax & Pack	3371 Glendale Blvd	4 pm

Map 6 • Miracle Mile/Mid-City

Adore Freight Shipping Etc	1494 S Robertson Blvd	4 pm
Beverly Hills Postal Center	8306 Wilshire Blvd	3:30 pm
Box Brothers	5353 Wilshire Blvd	4 pm
The Box Store	5657 Wilshire Blvd	5 pm
Business Partner	8901 Wilshire Blvd	4 pm
Digital Express	6404 Wilshire Blvd	5:15 pm
FedEx Kinko's	8950 W Olympic Blvd	5:45 pm
FedEx Kinko's	5500 Wilshire Blvd	5:30 pm
Mail Box Exchange	369 S Doheny Dr	4 pm
Mailbox Depot	6230-A Wilshire Blvd	5 pm
Postal Connection	287 S Robertson Blvd	4 pm
Self-Service	5670 Wilshire Blvd	5:30 pm
Self-Service	8484 Wilshire Blvd	5:30 pm
Self-Service	9033 Wilshire Blvd	5:30 pm
Self-Service	9100 Wilshire Blvd	5:30 pm
Self-Service	8383 Wilshire Blvd	5:30 pm
Self-Service	5900 Wilshire Blvd	5:15 pm
Self-Service	1833 S La Cienega Blvd	5 pm
Self-Service	195 S Robertson Blvd	5 pm
Self-Service	5350 Wilshire Blvd	5 pm
Self-Service	5455 Wilshire Blvd	5 pm
Self-Service	5700 Wilshire Blvd	5 pm
Self-Service	5750 Wilshire Blvd	5 pm
Self-Service	5757 Wilshire Blvd	5 pm
Self-Service	6100 Wilshire Blvd	5 pm
Self-Service	6300 Wilshire Blvd	5 pm
Self-Service	6500 Wilshire Blvd	5 pm
Self-Service	8500 Wilshire Blvd	5 pm
Self-Service	8730 Wilshire Blvd	5 pm
Self-Service	9107 Wilshire Blvd	5 pm
Self-Service	6404 Wilshire Blvd	5 pm
Self-Service	640 S San Vicente Blvd	4:45 pm
Self-Service	1270 S Alfred St	4:30 pm
Self-Service	6310 San Vicente Blvd	4:30 pm
Self-Service	8383 Wilshire Blvd	4 pm
Self-Service	50 N La Cienega Blvd	3:45 pm
United Mail Boxes	264 S La Cienega Blvd	4 pm

Map 7 • Hancock Park

Best Mailbox	5001 Wilshire Blvd	5 pm
Charlie Chan Printing	3974 Wilshire Blvd	4:20 pm
Color and Copy La Brea	5162 Wilshire Blvd	4 pm
Mail Box On Wilshire	3824 Wilshire Blvd	4:30 pm
The Mail Shoppe	137 N Larchmont Blvd	5 pm
Self-Service	4201 Wilshire Blvd	5:15 pm
Self-Service	3700 Wilshire Blvd	5 pm
Self-Service	4221 Wilshire Blvd	5 pm
Self-Service	4751 Wilshire Blvd	5 pm
Self-Service	4929 Wilshire Blvd	5 pm

** Last pick-up time, pm*

Self-Service	5055 Wilshire Blvd	5 pm
Self-Service	4601 Wilshire Blvd	4:30 pm
Wilshire Mail Boxes	5042 Wilshire Blvd	5 pm

Map 8 • Korea Town

Copy Express LA	3321 Wilshire Blvd	4 pm
FedEx Kinko's	3345 Wilshire Blvd	6 pm
Joy Express	139 N Western Ave	5 pm
Kebson Group	2500 Wilshire Blvd	5 pm
Mail Plus	269 S Western Ave	4:45 pm
Oneday Quick	450 S Western Ave	4 pm
Platinum Image	3550 Wilshire Blvd	5 pm
Self-Service	3600 Wilshire Blvd	5:30 pm
Self-Service	3055 Wilshire Blvd	5 pm
Self-Service	3250 Wilshire Blvd	5 pm
Self-Service	3255 Wilshire Blvd	5 pm
Self-Service	3435 Wilshire Blvd	5 pm
Self-Service	3450 Wilshire Blvd	5 pm
Self-Service	3530 Wilshire Blvd	5 pm
Self-Service	3660 Wilshire Blvd	5 pm
Self-Service	3699 Wilshire Blvd	5 pm
Self-Service	3731 Wilshire Blvd	5 pm
Self-Service	3751 W 6th St	5 pm
Self-Service	520 S La Fayette Park Pl	5 pm
Self-Service	3200 Wilshire Blvd	5 pm
Self-Service	3550 Wilshire Blvd	5 pm
Wizwa International	2975 Wilshire Blvd Ste 470	5 pm

Map 9 • Downtown

Chinatown Express Service	715 New High St	4 pm
City Business	603 S Los Angeles St	5:15 pm
FedEx Kinko's	735 S Figueroa St	6 pm
FedEx Kinko's	1149 S Hill St	5:50 pm
FedEx Kinko's	330 S Hope St	5:50 pm
FedEx Kinko's	554 S Grand Ave	5:50 pm
FedEx Kinko's	110 E 9th St	5:45 pm
FedEx Kinko's	835 Wilshire Blvd	5:45 pm
FedEx Kinko's	181 S Central Ave	5:30 pm
Joy Ship Center	2065 W 6th St	5 pm
Lecs USA	608 E 1st St	5 pm
Self-Service	333 S Hope St	5:45 pm
Self-Service	444 S Flower St	5:45 pm
Self-Service	1200 W 7th St	5:30 pm
Self-Service	550 S Hope St	5:30 pm
Self-Service	555 W 5th St	5:30 pm
Self-Service	601 S Figueroa St	5:30 pm
Self-Service	707 Wilshire Blvd	5:30 pm
Self-Service	1055 Wilshire Blvd	5:15 pm
Self-Service	1100 S San Pedro St	5:15 pm
Self-Service	112 W 9th St	5:15 pm
Self-Service	1150 S Olive St	5:15 pm
Self-Service	117 W 9th St	5:15 pm
Self-Service	1201 S Figueroa St	5:15 pm
Self-Service	2010 Wilshire Blvd	5:15 pm
Self-Service	207 S Broadway	5:15 pm
Self-Service	300 N Los Angeles St	5:15 pm
Self-Service	315 W 9th St	5:15 pm
Self-Service	350 S Figueroa St	5:15 pm
Self-Service	600 Wilshire Blvd	5:15 pm
Self-Service	624 S Grand Ave	5:15 pm
Self-Service	660 S Figueroa St	5:15 pm
Self-Service	750 W 7th St	5:15 pm
Self-Service	800 E 12th St	5:15 pm
Self-Service	800 W 6th St	5:15 pm
Self-Service	915 Wilshire Blvd	5:15 pm
Self-Service	312 N Spring St	5:10 pm
Self-Service	700 S Flower St	5:10 pm
Self-Service	900 Wilshire Blvd	5:10 pm
Self-Service	1545 Wilshire Blvd	5:05 pm
Self-Service	1000 W Temple St	5 pm
Self-Service	1000 Wilshire Blvd	5 pm
Self-Service	1055 W 7th St	5 pm
Self-Service	1127 Wilshire Blvd	5 pm
Self-Service	1200 Santee St	5 pm
Self-Service	1200 Wilshire Blvd	5 pm
Self-Service	1423 S Grand Ave	5 pm
Self-Service	1601 E Olympic Blvd	5 pm
Self-Service	1625 W Olympic Blvd	5 pm
Self-Service	201 N Figueroa St	5 pm
Self-Service	255 E Temple St	5 pm
Self-Service	261 S Figueroa St	5 pm
Self-Service	320 W 15th St	5 pm
Self-Service	333 S Beaudry Ave	5 pm
Self-Service	350 S Grand Ave	5 pm
Self-Service	420 E 3rd St	5 pm
Self-Service	445 S Figueroa St	5 pm
Self-Service	510 W 6th St	5 pm
Self-Service	515 S Figueroa St	5 pm
Self-Service	520 S Grand Ave	5 pm
Self-Service	601 W 5th St	5 pm
Self-Service	606 S Olive St	5 pm
Self-Service	627 S Central Ave	5 pm
Self-Service	650 S Hill St	5 pm
Self-Service	714 W Olympic Blvd	5 pm
Self-Service	777 S Figueroa St	5 pm
Self-Service	800 N Alameda St	5 pm
Self-Service	800 Wilshire Blvd	5 pm
Self-Service	801 S Figueroa St	5 pm
Self-Service	801 S Grand Ave	5 pm
Self-Service	810 N Alameda St	5 pm
Self-Service	818 W 7th St	5 pm
Self-Service	819 Santee St	5 pm
Self-Service	865 S Figueroa St	5 pm
Self-Service	888 S Figueroa St	5 pm
Self-Service	860 S Los Angeles St	5 pm
Self-Service	626 Wilshire Blvd	4:50 pm
Self-Service	420 Boyd St	4:45 pm
Self-Service	633 W 5th St	4:45 pm
Self-Service	800 S Figueroa St	4:45 pm
Self-Service	811 W 7th St	4:45 pm
Self-Service	1201 W 5th St	4:30 pm
Self-Service	634 S Spring St	4:30 pm
Self-Service	800 W 1st St	4:30 pm
Shipping Center	860 S Los Angeles	5:15 pm

Map 10 • Baldwin Hills

Copies Printscom	4076 S Crenshaw Blvd	4:30 pm
Mailboxex & More	5786 Rodeo Rd	5 pm
My Mailbox	3717 S La Brea Ave	4:30 pm
Self-Service	3650 W Martin Luther King Jr Blvd	5 pm
Self-Service	3870 Crenshaw Blvd	5 pm
Self-Service	5100 W Goldleaf Cir	5 pm
Self-Service	5120 W Goldleaf Cir	5 pm

Map 11 • South Central West

Self-Service	900 Exposition Blvd	5 pm
Self-Service	1150 W Jefferson Blvd	4:45 pm
Self-Service	3375 S Hoover St	4:45 pm
Self-Service	3667 McClintock Ave	4 pm
Self-Service	4401 Crenshaw Blvd	4 pm
Self-Service	840 Childs Way	4 pm

Map 12 • South Central East

Federal Express	3333 S Grand Ave	6 pm
FedEx Kinko's	2723 S Figueroa St	5 pm
Self-Service	1701 S Figueroa St	5:15 pm
Self-Service	155 W Washington Blvd	5 pm
Self-Service	1933 S Broadway	5 pm
Self-Service	3540 S Figueroa St	4:30 pm
Self-Service	639 W 34th St	4 pm

Map 13 • Inglewood

Mail Connexion	6709 La Tijera Blvd	5 pm
Marshall Enterprises	1336 Centinela Ave	3 pm
Postal Plus	309 E Hillcrest Blvd	4 pm
Self-Service	111 N La Brea Ave	5:30 pm
Self-Service	300 E Hillcrest Blvd	5 pm
Self-Service	401 S Prairie Ave	5 pm
Self-Service	1050 S Prairie Ave	4:30 pm
Self-Service	811 N La Brea Ave	4:30 pm

Map 14 • Inglewood East/ Morningside Park

Self-Service	2200 W Century Blvd	4:45 pm

Map 15 • Pacific Palisades

Channel Postal Center	130 W Channel Rd	3:15 pm
Palisadus Letter Shop	865 Via De La Paz	3:31 pm
Self-Service	15209 W Sunset Blvd	4:01 pm
Self-Service	860 Via De La Paz	4:01 pm
Self-Service	881 Alma Real Dr	4:01 pm

Map 16 • Brentwood

Brentwood Mail Box	11693 San Vicente Blvd	4:31 pm
Brentwood Shipping & Mail	212 26th St	4:01 pm
Mail Boxes Etc 1577	149 S Barrington Ave	5 pm
Self-Service	200 S Barrington Ave	5:16 pm
Self-Service	11611 San Vicente Blvd	5:01 pm
Self-Service	11661 San Vicente Blvd	5:01 pm
Self-Service	11726 San Vicente Blvd	5:01 pm
Self-Service	11777 San Vicente Blvd	5:01 pm
Self-Service	11812 San Vicente Blvd	5:01 pm
Self-Service	11911 San Vicente Blvd	5:01 pm
Self-Service	12011 San Vicente Blvd	4:46 pm
Self-Service	11999 San Vicente Blvd	4:06 pm

Map 17 • Bel Air/Holmby Hills

Self-Service	612 N Sepulveda Blvd	4:31 pm
Self-Service	308 Westwood Plz	4:01 pm

Map 18 • Santa Monica

Aim Mail Center #4	2461 Santa Monica Blvd	4:31 pm
Box Brothers	2113 Wilshire Blvd	4:31 pm
FedEx Kinko's	925 Wilshire Blvd	5:35 pm
FedEx Kinko's	601 Wilshire Blvd	5:01 pm
M&A World	1401 Ocean Ave	4:10 pm
The Mail House	1247 Lincoln Blvd	4:31 pm
Mail & Photo	1112 Montana Ave	3:46 pm
Ocean Park Mail & Bus	171 Pier Ave	5:31 pm
Post Tel Business Center	2118 Wilshire Blvd	4:30 pm
PostNet	410 Wilshire Blvd	4:45 pm
Self-Service	100 Wilshire Blvd	5:16 pm
Self-Service	1248 5th St	5:16 pm
Self-Service	1401 Ocean Ave	5:16 pm
Self-Service	501 Santa Monica Blvd	5:05 pm
Self-Service	120 Broadway	5:01 pm

** Last pick-up time, pm*

Map 18 • Santa Monica—*continued*

Location	Address	Time*
Self-Service	1245 16th St	5:01 pm
Self-Service	1250 6th St	5:01 pm
Self-Service	1299 Ocean Ave	5:01 pm
Self-Service	1601 Cloverfield Blvd	5:01 pm
Self-Service	1630 17th St	5:01 pm
Self-Service	1640 5th St	5:01 pm
Self-Service	1661 Lincoln Blvd	5:01 pm
Self-Service	1717 4th St	5:01 pm
Self-Service	1821 Wilshire Blvd	5:01 pm
Self-Service	1919 Santa Monica Blvd	5:01 pm
Self-Service	2001 Santa Monica Blvd	5:01 pm
Self-Service	2001 Wilshire Blvd	5:01 pm
Self-Service	2020 Santa Monica Blvd	5:01 pm
Self-Service	233 Wilshire Blvd	5:01 pm
Self-Service	2415 Main St	5:01 pm
Self-Service	2425 Colorado Ave	5:01 pm
Self-Service	2450 Colorado Ave	5:01 pm
Self-Service	2720 Neilson Way	5:01 pm
Self-Service	401 Wilshire Blvd	5:01 pm
Self-Service	429 Santa Monica Blvd	5:01 pm
Self-Service	501 Colorado Ave	5:01 pm
Self-Service	520 Broadway	5:01 pm
Self-Service	725 Arizona Ave	5:01 pm
Self-Service	902 Colorado Ave	5:01 pm
Self-Service	1437 7th St	5 pm
Self-Service	201 Wilshire Blvd	4:46 pm
Self-Service	2120 Colorado Ave	4:46 pm
Self-Service	530 Wilshire Blvd	4:46 pm
Self-Service	2444 Wilshire Blvd	4:32 pm
Self-Service	1422 2nd St	4:31 pm
Self-Service	1542 15th St	4:31 pm
Self-Service	1750 Ocean Park Blvd	4:31 pm
Self-Service	2040 Broadway	4:31 pm
Self-Service	2121 16th St	4:31 pm
Self-Service	217 Hampton Dr	4:31 pm

Map 19 • West LA/ Santa Monica East

Location	Address	Time*
American Livescan & Ship	11209 National Blvd	4:01 pm
Box Brothers	11701 Wilshire Blvd	4:50 pm
FedEx Kinko's	11819 Wilshire Blvd	5:31 pm
FedEx Kinko's	2139 S Bundy Dr	4:30 pm
Mail Boxes & More	11901 Santa Monica Blvd	4:31 pm
National Mailbox Center	2801 Ocean Park Blvd	5:01 pm
National Shipping Center	11664 National Blvd	5:05 pm
Postal & More	1158 26th St	5:01 pm
Save On Box	2215 S Sepulveda Blvd	4 pm
Self-Service	11420 Santa Monica Blvd	5:31 pm
Self-Service	11819 Wilshire Blvd	5:31 pm
Self-Service	11601 Wilshire Blvd	5:16 pm
Self-Service	11150 Santa Monica Blvd	5:15 pm
Self-Service	2730 Wilshire Blvd	5:03 pm
Self-Service	2811 Wilshire Blvd	5:02 pm
Self-Service	11111 Santa Monica Blvd	5:01 pm
Self-Service	11150 W Olympic Blvd	5:01 pm
Self-Service	11340 W Olympic Blvd	5:01 pm
Self-Service	11400 W Olympic Blvd	5:01 pm
Self-Service	11500 W Olympic Blvd	5:01 pm
Self-Service	11620 Wilshire Blvd	5:01 pm
Self-Service	11766 Wilshire Blvd	5:01 pm
Self-Service	11845 W Olympic Blvd	5:01 pm
Self-Service	11859 Wilshire Blvd	5:01 pm
Self-Service	11900 W Olympic Blvd	5:01 pm
Self-Service	12100 Wilshire Blvd	5:01 pm
Self-Service	12233 W Olympic Blvd	5:01 pm
Self-Service	12300 Wilshire Blvd	5:01 pm
Self-Service	12301 Wilshire Blvd	5:01 pm
Self-Service	12304 Santa Monica Blvd	5:01 pm
Self-Service	12400 Wilshire Blvd	5:01 pm
Self-Service	12424 Wilshire Blvd	5:01 pm
Self-Service	1640 S Sepulveda Blvd	5:01 pm
Self-Service	1815 Centinela Ave	5:01 pm
Self-Service	1849 Sawtelle Blvd	5:01 pm
Self-Service	1950 Sawtelle Blvd	5:01 pm
Self-Service	1990 S Bundy Dr	5:01 pm
Self-Service	2001 S Barrington Ave	5:01 pm
Self-Service	2052 S Bundy Dr	5:01 pm
Self-Service	2400 S Barrington Ave	5:01 pm
Self-Service	2425 Olympic Blvd	5:01 pm
Self-Service	2716 Ocean Park Blvd	5:01 pm
Self-Service	2800 28th St	5:01 pm
Self-Service	2850 Ocean Park Blvd	5:01 pm
Self-Service	3000 Olympic Blvd	5:01 pm
Self-Service	3130 Wilshire Blvd	5:01 pm
Self-Service	3223 Donald Douglas Loop S	5:01 pm
Self-Service	11377 W Olympic Blvd	5 pm
Self-Service	11755 Wilshire Blvd	4:46 pm
Self-Service	1620 26th St	4:46 pm
Self-Service	2525 Michigan Ave	4:46 pm
Self-Service	2530 Wilshire Blvd	4:46 pm
Self-Service	12121 Wilshire Blvd	4:45 pm
Self-Service	11628 Santa Monica Blvd	4:31 pm
Self-Service	12200 W Olympic Blvd	4:31 pm
Self-Service	2440 S Sepulveda Blvd	4:31 pm
Self-Service	3210 Ocean Park Blvd	4:31 pm
Self-Service	2100 Sawtelle Blvd	4:16 pm
Self-Service	2701 Ocean Park Blvd	4:01 pm
VIP Postal Services	12335 Santa Monica Blvd	4:46 pm

Map 20 • Westwood/ Century City

Location	Address	Time*
Box Brothers	1351 Westwood Blvd	5:01 pm
Box City 3	2056 Westwood Blvd	4:30 pm
Box & Ship	2180 Westwood Blvd	4:50 pm
FedEx Kinko's	1925 Century Park E	6 pm
FedEx Kinko's	10924 Weyburn Ave	5:31 pm
FedEx Kinko's	1520 Westwood Blvd	5:30 pm
Globex	1388 Westwood Blvd	3:40 pm
Mail and More In LA	2331 Westwood Blvd	4:45 pm
Mail Boxes Box & Ship	11041 Santa Monica Blvd	5:15 pm
Mail Boxes Etc - 4229	1875 Century Park E	5:01 pm
Pack and Ship	914 Westwood Blvd	5 pm
Plaza Printers	2025 Ave of The Stars	4:31 pm
Print Run	950 Gayley Ave	3:30 pm
Self-Service	1900 Ave of The Stars	5:35 pm
Self-Service	1801 Century Park E	5:31 pm
Self-Service	2080 Century Park E	5:31 pm
Self-Service	2121 Ave of The Stars	5:31 pm
Self-Service	10100 Santa Monica Blvd	5:16 pm
Self-Service	11000 Wilshire Blvd	5:15 pm
Self-Service	1901 Ave of The Stars	5:15 pm
Self-Service	10351 Santa Monica Blvd	5:01 pm
Self-Service	10390 Santa Monica Blvd	5:01 pm
Self-Service	10474 Santa Monica Blvd	5:01 pm
Self-Service	10585 Santa Monica Blvd	5:01 pm
Self-Service	10635 Santa Monica Blvd	5:01 pm
Self-Service	10850 Wilshire Blvd	5:01 pm
Self-Service	10877 Wilshire Blvd	5:01 pm
Self-Service	10880 Wilshire Blvd	5:01 pm
Self-Service	10920 Wilshire Blvd	5:01 pm
Self-Service	10960 Wilshire Blvd	5:01 pm
Self-Service	1800 Ave of The Stars	5:01 pm
Self-Service	1840 Century Park E	5:01 pm
Self-Service	1880 Century Park E	5:01 pm
Self-Service	1888 Century Park E	5:01 pm
Self-Service	1999 Ave of The Stars	5:01 pm
Self-Service	2029 Century Park E	5:01 pm
Self-Service	2049 Century Park E	5:01 pm
Self-Service	924 Westwood Blvd	5:01 pm
Self-Service	10940 Wilshire Blvd	5 pm
Self-Service	10990 Wilshire Blvd	5 pm
Self-Service	1100 Glendon Ave	5 pm
Self-Service	10250 Constellation Blvd	4:46 pm
Self-Service	10780 Santa Monica Blvd	4:46 pm
Self-Service	10866 Wilshire Blvd	4:46 pm
Self-Service	1000 Veteran Ave	4:31 pm
Self-Service	500 S Sepulveda Blvd	4:31 pm
Self-Service	2000 Ave of The Stars	4:30 pm

Map 21 • Venice

Location	Address	Time*
Aim Mail Center #120	13400 W Washington Blvd	4:05 pm
Postal Masters	333 Washington Blvd	4:15 pm
Self-Service	1501 Lincoln Blvd	5:01 pm
Self-Service	1601 Main St	5:01 pm
Self-Service	636b Venice Blvd	5:01 pm

Map 22 • Mar Vista

Location	Address	Time*
FedEx Kinko's	4325 Glencoe Ave	5:01 pm
Self-Service	12910 Culver Blvd	5:31 pm
Self-Service	3826 Grand View Blvd	5:31 pm
Self-Service	4501 Glencoe Ave	5:31 pm
Self-Service	4551 Glencoe Ave	5:16 pm
Self-Service	11965 Venice Blvd	5:01 pm
Self-Service	13323 W Washington Blvd	4:46 pm

Map 23 • Rancho Park/Palms

Location	Address	Time*
Mailboxes & More 24/7	3500 Overland Ave	4 pm
Self-Service	10801 National Blvd	5:01 pm
Self-Service	11270 Exposition Blvd	5:01 pm
Self-Service	2566 Overland Ave	5:01 pm
Self-Service	1180 S Beverly Dr	5 pm
Self-Service	3415 S Sepulveda Blvd	5 pm
Self-Service	3751 Motor Ave	5 pm
Self-Service	9911 W Pico Blvd	5 pm
Self-Service	10921 W Pico Blvd	4 pm
Us 24-7 Postal Center	9854 National Blvd	4 pm
Us 24/7 Postal Center	10008 National Blvd	4 pm
Westside Mailboxes N More	9162 W Pico Blvd	4:30 pm

Map 24 • Culver City

Location	Address	Time*
Culver Mail Box	10866 Washington Blvd	4:30 pm
FedEx Kinko's	5575 Sepulveda Blvd	5:45 pm
FedExStaffed	3700 S Robertson Blvd	6:15 pm
Self-Service	10202 Washington Blvd	5:30 pm
Self-Service	8985 Venice Blvd	5:30 pm
Self-Service	5701 W Slauson Ave	5:15 pm
Self-Service	100 Corporate Pointe	5 pm
Self-Service	11111 Jefferson Blvd	5 pm
Self-Service	11144 Washington Blvd	5 pm
Self-Service	301 Corporate Pointe	5 pm
Self-Service	400 Corporate Pointe	5 pm
Self-Service	9696 Culver Blvd	5 pm
Self-Service	9942 Culver Blvd	5 pm
Self-Service	3851 Overland Ave	4:30 pm
Self-Service	600 Corporate Pointe	4:15 pm

Map 25 • Marina Del Rey/ Westchester West

Location	Address	Time*
Box City 6	4220 Lincoln Blvd	4:30 pm
Federal Express	4170 Del Rey Ave	6:15 pm
Playa Postal Center	8117 W Manchester Ave	4 pm
Self-Service	4333 Admiralty Way	5:16 pm
Self-Service	4640 Admiralty Way	5:01 pm
Self-Service	4676 Admiralty Way	5:01 pm

** Last pick-up time, pm*

Self-Service	5419 McConnell Ave	5:01 pm
Self-Service	4720 Lincoln Blvd	4:30 pm
Self-Service	7001 World Way W	4:30 pm
Self-Service	7301 World Way W	4:30 pm
Self-Service	8055 W Manchester Ave	4:30 pm
Self-Service	322 1/2 Culver Blvd	4 pm

Map 26 • Westchester/ Fox Hills/Ladera Heights

Federal Express	11221 Hindry Ave	6:45 pm
FedEx Kinko's	5855 W Century Blvd	5 pm
Mail Call	8726 S Sepulveda Blvd	4:45 pm
Self-Service	11222 S La Cienega Blvd	5:30 pm
Self-Service	5757 W Century Blvd	5:30 pm
Self-Service	9800 S La Cienega Blvd	5:30 pm
Self-Service	9920 S La Cienega Blvd	5:30 pm
Self-Service	5777 W Century Blvd	5:15 pm
Self-Service	5933 W Century Blvd	5:15 pm
Self-Service	5959 W Century Blvd	5:15 pm
Self-Service	6080 Center Dr	5:15 pm
Self-Service	6167 Bristol Pkwy	5:15 pm
Self-Service	6701 Center Dr W	5:15 pm
Self-Service	9841 Airport Blvd	5:15 pm
Self-Service	419 Hindry Ave	5 pm
Self-Service	420 Hindry Ave	5 pm
Self-Service	5200 W Century Blvd	5 pm
Self-Service	5250 W Century Blvd	5 pm
Self-Service	6053 W Century Blvd	5 pm
Self-Service	6060 Center Dr	5 pm
Self-Service	6101 W Centinela Ave	5 pm
Self-Service	6133 Bristol Pkwy	5 pm
Self-Service	6151 W Century Blvd	5 pm
Self-Service	6225 W Century Blvd	5 pm
Self-Service	6601 Center Dr W	5 pm
Self-Service	7381 La Tijera Blvd	5 pm
Self-Service	8901 S La Cienega Blvd	5 pm
Self-Service	8939 S Sepulveda Blvd	5 pm
Self-Service	9029 Airport Blvd	5 pm
Self-Service	9133 S La Cienega Blvd	5 pm
Self-Service	6100 Center Dr	4:30 pm
Self-Service	8704 S Sepulveda Blvd	4:30 pm

Map 27 • El Segundo/ Manhattan Beach

Current Events	1140 Highland Ave	4 pm
FedEx Kinko's	630 N Sepulveda Blvd	5 pm
Manhattan Postal Center	2905 N Sepulveda Blvd	4 pm
Self-Service	1334 Park View Ave	5:45 pm
Self-Service	300 Continental Blvd	5:45 pm
Self-Service	300 N Sepulveda Blvd	5:45 pm
Self-Service	100 N Sepulveda Blvd	5:30 pm
Self-Service	1960 E Grand Ave	5:30 pm
Self-Service	2101 Rosecrans Ave	5:30 pm
Self-Service	2121 Park Pl	5:30 pm
Self-Service	2141 Rosecrans Ave	5:30 pm
Self-Service	222 N Sepulveda Blvd	5:30 pm
Self-Service	2221 Rosecrans Ave	5:30 pm
Self-Service	2250 E Imperial Hwy	5:30 pm
Self-Service	831 S Douglas St	5:30 pm
Self-Service	840 Apollo St	5:30 pm
Self-Service	880 Apollo St	5:30 pm
Self-Service	101 Continental Blvd	5:15 pm
Self-Service	1230 Rosecrans Ave	5:15 pm
Self-Service	130 E Grand Ave	5:15 pm
Self-Service	225 S Sepulveda Blvd	5:15 pm
Self-Service	3601 N Aviation Blvd	5:15 pm
Self-Service	1 Hornet Way	5 pm
Self-Service	1007 N Sepulveda Blvd	5 pm
Self-Service	2041 Rosecrans Ave	5 pm
Self-Service	2361 Rosecrans Ave	5 pm
Self-Service	2401 E El Segundo Blvd	5 pm
Self-Service	505 N Sepulveda Blvd	5 pm
Self-Service	601 N Nash St	5 pm
Self-Service	645 S Allied Way	5 pm
Self-Service	909 N Sepulveda Blvd	5 pm
Self-Service	898 N Sepulveda Blvd	5 pm
Self-Service	201 N Douglas St	4:45 pm
Self-Service	400 Continental Blvd	4:45 pm
Self-Service	14500 Aviation Blvd	4:30 pm
Self-Service	1600 Rosecrans Ave	4:30 pm
Self-Service	1700 E Imperial Ave	4:30 pm
Self-Service	425 15th St	4:30 pm
Self-Service	818 Manhattan Beach Blvd	4:15 pm
Self-Service	1700 E Walnut Ave	4 pm

Map 28 • Hawthorne

FedEx Kinko's	12600 Prairie Ave	6:30 pm
FedEx Kinko's	5201 W Rosecrans Ave	6 pm
Mailbox and Business Svcs	14402 Hawthorne Blvd	4:30 pm
Self-Service	3690 Redondo Beach Ave	5:30 pm
Self-Service	1 Northrop Ave	5 pm
Self-Service	5220 Pacific Concourse Dr	5 pm
Self-Service	5230 Pacific Concourse Dr	5 pm
Self-Service	5245 Pacific Concourse Dr	5 pm
Us 24/7 Postal Center	4001 Inglewood Ave	4 pm

Map 29 • Hermosa Beach

Aim Mail Center 118	1732 Aviation Blvd	4:45 pm
Beach Mail Box	2629 Manhattan Ave	4:30 pm
Box Brothers	2302 Artesia Blvd	4 pm
FedEx Kinko's	1139 Artesia Blvd	4:30 pm
Self-Service	2200 Pacific Coast Hwy	5 pm
Self-Service	2601 Manhattan Beach Blvd	5 pm
Self-Service	565 Pier Ave	5 pm
Self-Service	1426 Aviation Blvd	4:45 pm
Self-Service	1620 Aviation Blvd	4:45 pm
Self-Service	2215 Artesia Blvd	4:45 pm

Map 30 • Torrance North

Postal Boxes Etc	17252 Hawthorne Blvd	4:45 pm
Postal Planet Center	5120 W 190th St	4 pm
Postal Plus	17528 Hawthorne Blvd	4:30 pm
Self-Service	2908 Oregon Court	5:30 pm
Self-Service	3625 Del Amo Blvd	5:30 pm
Self-Service	3880 Del Amo Blvd	5:30 pm
Self-Service	18080 Crenshaw Blvd	5 pm
Self-Service	18411 Crenshaw Blvd	5 pm
Self-Service	3547 Voyager St	5 pm
Self-Service	Van Ness Ave & W 190th St	5 pm
Self-Service	17204 Hawthorne Blvd	4:45 pm

Map 31 • Redondo Beach

Beach N Boxes	817 Torrance Blvd	4:30 pm
Copy Bank	23215 Hawthorne Blvd	5 pm
FedEx Kinko's	21023 Hawthorne Blvd	6 pm
FedEx Kinko's	23325 Hawthorne Blvd	5:30 pm
FedEx Kinko's	1770 S Pacific Coast Hwy	4:30 pm
Packaging Store	1207 S Pacific Coast Hwy	4:15 pm
Post Net Riviera	217 Palos Verdes Blvd	4:15 pm
Postal Annex	553 N Pacific Coast Hwy	4 pm
Postal Place Plus	614 Torrance Blvd	4 pm
Postal Solutions	4733 Torrance Blvd	5 pm
Self-Service	21250 Hawthorne Blvd	5:30 pm
Self-Service	21535 Hawthorne Blvd	5:30 pm
Self-Service	23326 Hawthorne Blvd	5:30 pm
Self-Service	21311 Hawthorne Blvd	5:15 pm
Self-Service	3838 W Carson St	5:15 pm
Self-Service	200 S Pacific Coast Hwy	5 pm
Self-Service	205th & Beech	5 pm
Self-Service	22750 Hawthorne Blvd	5 pm
Self-Service	23430 Hawthorne Blvd	5 pm
Self-Service	4216 Pacific Coast Hwy	5 pm
Self-Service	1611 S Pacific Coast Hwy	4:45 pm
Self-Service	1201 N Catalina Ave	4:30 pm
Self-Service	1611 S Catalina Ave	4:30 pm
Self-Service	811 N Catalina Ave	4:15 pm
Self-Service	119 W Torrance Blvd	3:30 pm

Map 32 • Torrance South

Lomita Mail Car	2017 Lomita Blvd	4:30 pm
Mail Boxes Galore	1880 W Carson St	4:45 pm
Postal Annex	24325 Crenshaw Blvd	4:30 pm
The Postal Mart	2537 Pacific Coast Hwy	4:45 pm
Self-Service	23545 Crenshaw Blvd	5:30 pm
Self-Service	2501 W 237th St	5:30 pm
Self-Service	3305 Fujita St	5:30 pm
Self-Service	21171 S Western Ave	5:15 pm
Self-Service	Telo Ave & Fujita St	5:15 pm
Self-Service	1433 Marcelina Ave	5 pm
Self-Service	1815 W 213th St	5 pm
Self-Service	1820 W Carson St	5 pm
Self-Service	2377 Crenshaw Blvd	5 pm
Self-Service	2510 Monterey St	5 pm
Self-Service	25131 Narbonne Ave	5 pm
Self-Service	2601 Airport Dr	5 pm
Self-Service	2780 Skypark Dr	5 pm
Self-Service	3400 Torrance Blvd	5 pm
Self-Service	3424 W Carson St	5 pm
Self-Service	3440 Lomita Blvd	5 pm
Self-Service	3528 Torrance Blvd	5 pm
Self-Service	2720 Monterey St	4:45 pm
Self-Service	21081 S Western Ave	4:30 pm
Self-Service	3665 Pacific Coast Hwy	4:30 pm
Tri Postal Center	1658 W Carson St	5 pm

Map 33 • Highland Park

Eagle Express Services	4734 Eagle Rock Blvd	5 pm
Eaglerock Mail Center	2272 Colorado Blvd	4 pm
Self-Service	7435 N Figueroa St	4:30 pm
Self-Service	202 N Ave 64	4 pm

Map 34 • Pasadena

Aim Mail Center #144	700 Fair Oaks Ave	4:45 pm
Box & Ship	319 S Arroyo Pkwy	4 pm
Cal Oaks Box & Ship	422 S Pasadena Ave	4 pm
FedEx Kinko's	460 Fair Oaks Ave	4:45 pm
Post/pack & Ship	115 W California Blvd	4:30 pm
Self-Service	210 S De Lacey Ave	5:15 pm
Self-Service	46 Smith Aly	5:15 pm
Self-Service	1001 Fremont Ave	5 pm
Self-Service	1111 S Arroyo Pkwy	5 pm
Self-Service	145 Pasadena Ave	5 pm
Self-Service	150 E Colorado Blvd	5 pm
Self-Service	35 S Raymond Ave	5 pm
Self-Service	350 W Colorado Blvd	5 pm

** Last pick-up time, pm*

Map 34 • Pasadena—*continued*

Self-Service	600 S Lake Ave	5 pm
Self-Service	625 Fair Oaks Ave	5 pm
Self-Service	888 E Walnut St	5 pm
Self-Service	937 E Green St	5 pm
Self-Service	99 W California Blvd	5 pm
Self-Service	117 E Colorado Blvd	4:45 pm
Self-Service	200 E Del Mar Blvd	4:45 pm
Self-Service	460 N Fair Oaks Ave	4:45 pm
Self-Service	2600 Mission St	4:30 pm
Self-Service	600 Lincoln Ave	4:30 pm
Self-Service	85 E Holly St	4:30 pm
Self-Service	125 S Grand Ave	4 pm

Map 35 • Pasadena East/ San Marino

Box City 5	2650 E Colorado Blvd	4:30 pm
The Postmaster	2245 E Colorado Blvd	4:45 pm
Self-Service	1010 E Union St	5 pm
Self-Service	1224 E Green St	5 pm
Self-Service	2500 E Foothill Blvd	5 pm
Self-Service	2540 Huntington Dr	5 pm
Self-Service	2960 Huntington Dr	5 pm
Self-Service	967 E Colorado Blvd	5 pm
Self-Service	2060 Huntington Dr	4:45 pm
Self-Service	2609 E Colorado Blvd	4:30 pm
Self-Service	33 S Catalina Ave	4:30 pm
Self-Service	1055 E Colorado Blvd	4 pm
Self-Service	1623 E Washington Blvd	4 pm

Map 36 • Mt. Washington

FedExStaffed	2000 N San Fernando Rd	6 pm

Map 37 • Lincoln Heights

Self-Service	1900 N Main St	5 pm
Self-Service	1950 E Imperial Hwy	4:30 pm

Map 39 • Alhambra

Box-all Parcel Center	2107 W Commonwealth Ave	5 pm
Broad Solutions	630 E Main St	4 pm
Self-Service	1603 W Valley Blvd	5:15 pm
Self-Service	801 S Garfield Ave	5 pm
Self-Service	10 W Bay State St	4:45 pm
Self-Service	610 E Valley Blvd	4:30 pm

Map 40 • Boyle Heights

Self-Service	1200 N State St	5 pm
Self-Service	1240 N Mission Rd	4:45 pm
Self-Service	2010 Zonal Ave	4:45 pm
Self-Service	1969 Zonal Ave	4 pm

Map 41 • City Terrace/East LA

Self-Service	1000 Corporate Center Dr	5 pm
Self-Service	1255 Corporate Center Dr	5 pm
Self-Service	2540 Corporate Pl	5 pm

Map 42 • Chatsworth

Cell Plus	21534 Devonshire St	4 pm
Chatsworth Postal Center	21704 Devonshire St	4:30 pm
Mail & Box Depot	21911 Devonshire St	4:45 pm
Mail Boxes & Beyond	10200 Mason Ave	3:30 pm
Mailboxes & Lots More	21012 Devonshire St	4 pm
PostNet	9909 Topanga Canyon Blvd	4:45 pm
Self-Service	9430 Topanga Canyon Blvd	5 pm
Self-Service	9592 Topanga Canyon Blvd	5 pm
Self-Service	21606 Devonshire St	4:30 pm
Self-Service	21610 Lassen St	4:30 pm

Map 43 • Granada Hills / Northridge

B Brothers	8925 Reseda Blvd	4 pm
Cost Copy	18159 Parthenia St	4 pm
FedEx Kinko's	10725 Zelzah Ave	5 pm
FedEx Kinko's	9000 Tampa Ave	5 pm
Longs Drugs #533	19783 Rinaldi St	4 pm
Mail Box World	18543 Devonshire St	4:30 pm
Mail Depot	18533 Roscoe Blvd	5 pm
Pak & Ship All	9420 Reseda Blvd	5 pm
PostNet	9135 Reseda Blvd	5 pm
Self-Service	19215 Parthenia St	5 pm
Self-Service	19809 Prarie St	5 pm
Self-Service	19850 Plummer St	5 pm
Self-Service	9003 Reseda Blvd	5 pm
Self-Service	9200 Oakdale Ave	5 pm
Self-Service	9401 Oakdale Ave	5 pm
Self-Service	19500 Plummer St	4:30 pm
Self-Service	9301 Oakdale Ave	4:30 pm
Self-Service	9401 Corbin Ave	4:30 pm
Self-Service	11145 Tampa Ave	4 pm
Self-Service	18039 Chatsworth St	4 pm
Self-Service	18050 Chatsworth St	4 pm
US Mail Etc	9250 Reseda Blvd	4 pm
Xpress Mail and Packaging	19520 Nordhoff St	4 pm

Map 44 • Mission Hills / North Hills

Federal Express	16633 Schoenborn St	5:45 pm
Postal Plus	11024 Balboa Blvd	4 pm
Self-Service	8550 Balboa Blvd	4:45 pm

Map 45 • Canoga Park / Woodland Hills

Box Brothers	19714 Ventura Blvd	4 pm
Box City 7	7008 Topanga Canyon Blvd	3:30 pm
Express Pack & Ship	7657 Winnetka Ave	4:30 pm
FedEx Kinko's	21816 Victory Blvd	5 pm
FedExStaffed	21300 Vanowen St	6 pm
Mail Boxes Etc	19528 Ventura Blvd	4:30 pm
Postal Annex 5012	21781 Ventura Blvd	4 pm
PostNet Ca-217	20058 Ventura Blvd	4 pm
Self-Service	19303 Ventura Blvd	5 pm
Self-Service	20301 Ventura Blvd	5 pm
Self-Service	21271 Burbank Blvd	5 pm
Self-Service	21300 Victory Blvd	5 pm
Self-Service	21550 Oxnard St	5 pm
Self-Service	21600 Oxnard St	5 pm
Self-Service	21700 Oxnard St	5 pm
Self-Service	21800 Burbank Blvd	5 pm
Self-Service	21800 Oxnard St	5 pm
Self-Service	21820 Burbank Blvd	5 pm
Self-Service	21900 Burbank Blvd	5 pm
Self-Service	5500 Canoga Ave	5 pm
Self-Service	5550 Topanga Canyon Blvd	5 pm
Self-Service	5850 Canoga Ave	5 pm
Self-Service	5855 Topanga Canyon Blvd	5 pm
Self-Service	5959 Topanga Canyon Blvd	5 pm
Self-Service	6301 Owensmouth Ave	5 pm
Self-Service	6320 Canoga Ave	5 pm
Self-Service	6355 Topanga Canyon Blvd	5 pm
Self-Service	6400 Canoga Ave	5 pm
Self-Service	6351 Owensmouth Ave	4:45 pm
Self-Service	20501 Ventura Blvd	4:30 pm
Self-Service	21201 Victory Blvd	4:30 pm
Self-Service	21301 Burbank Blvd	4:30 pm
Self-Service	21650 Oxnard St	4:30 pm
Self-Service	5530 Corbin Ave	4:30 pm
Self-Service	5700 Canoga Ave	4:30 pm
Self-Service	22120 Clarendon St	4:15 pm
Self-Service	20201 Sherman Way	4 pm
Self-Service	21333 Oxnard St	4 pm
Self-Service	21801 Sherman Way	4 pm
Self-Service	22020 Clarendon St	4 pm
Self-Service	22121 Clarendon St	4 pm
Self-Service	6430 Independence Ave	4 pm
V-t Pharmacy	19300 Vanowen St	3:45 pm

Map 46 • Reseda

Postal Connections	19028 Ventura Blvd	4:15 pm
Reseda	18349 Sherman Way	4 pm
Self-Service	17750 Sherman Way	5 pm
Self-Service	18840 Ventura Blvd	4:45 pm
Self-Service	18425 Burbank Blvd	4:30 pm
Self-Service	18757 Burbank Blvd	4:30 pm
Self-Service	18801 Ventura Blvd	4:30 pm
Self-Service	5535 Balboa Blvd	4:30 pm
Self-Service	5805 White Oak Ave	4:30 pm
Self-Service	6914 Canby Ave	4:30 pm
Self-Service	6345 Balboa Blvd	4:30 pm
Self-Service	5609 Yolanda Ave	4 pm
Self-Service	7320 Reseda Blvd	4 pm
Wall Street Connection	18663 Ventura Blvd	4 pm

Map 47 • Van Nuys

B&E Postal Center	5632 Van Nuys Blvd	4 pm
Box City 1	16113 Sherman Way	4 pm
FedEx Kinko's	5810 Sepulveda Blvd	5:45 pm
Self-Service	16380 Roscoe Blvd	5:15 pm
Self-Service	15701 Sherman Way	5 pm
Self-Service	16461 Sherman Way	5 pm
Self-Service	16600 Sherman Way	5 pm
Self-Service	5990 Sepulveda Blvd	5 pm
Self-Service	7120 Hayvenhurst Ave	5 pm
Self-Service	14141 Covello St	4:45 pm
Self-Service	6200 Van Nuys Blvd	4:45 pm
Self-Service	7100 Hayvenhurst Ave	4:45 pm
Self-Service	5805 Sepulveda Blvd	4:30 pm
Self-Service	15107 Vanowen St	4:15 pm
Self-Service	6454 Van Nuys Blvd	4:15 pm
Van Nuys Print Center	14508 Erwin St	4 pm

Map 48 • North Hollywood

Armati Printing	12901 Sherman Way	4 pm
Box City 2	12800 Victory Blvd	4 pm
Mail Depot Etc	12450 Burbank Blvd	4 pm
Rockin Boxes	13636 Burbank Blvd	4 pm
Self-Service	6400 Laurel Canyon Blvd	5 pm
Self-Service	6180 Laurel Canyon Blvd	4:45 pm
Self-Service	12807 Sherman Way	4:30 pm
Self-Service	7254 Bellaire Ave	4:30 pm

Map 49 • Burbank

Self-Service	4605 Lankershim Blvd	5:30 pm
Self-Service	4640 Lankershim Blvd	5:30 pm
Self-Service	5503 Cahuenga Blvd	5:15 pm
Self-Service	2740 W Magnolia Blvd	4:45 pm
Self-Service	2924 W Magnolia Blvd	4:15 pm

** Last pick-up time, pm*

Map 50 • Burbank East/ Glendale West

Box Brothers	1806 W Olive Ave	5 pm
Boxes & Accessories	263 W Olive Ave	4:45 pm
Boxes and Ink	1812 W Burbank Blvd	4 pm
Central Pak & Mail	145 S Glenoaks Blvd	4:30 pm
FedEx Kinko's	250 E Olive Ave	5:30 pm
Pak & Ship All	1317 N San Fernando Blvd	4 pm
Self-Service	100 N 1st St	5:15 pm
Self-Service	1060 W Alameda Ave	5 pm
Self-Service	1700 Victory Blvd	5 pm
Self-Service	1918 W Magnolia Blvd	5 pm
Self-Service	2300 W Olive Ave	5 pm
Self-Service	303 N Glenoaks Blvd	5 pm
Self-Service	601 S Glenoaks Blvd	5 pm
Self-Service	101 S 1st St	4:45 pm
Self-Service	1213 Flower St	4:45 pm
Self-Service	221 W Alameda Ave	4:45 pm
Self-Service	333 N Glenoaks Blvd	4:45 pm
Smart Mailbox	101 N Victory Blvd	4 pm

Map 51 • Glendale South

ABC Mail Box	501 W Glenoaks Blvd	4 pm
FedEx Kinko's	225 N Brand Blvd	5 pm
Mail Boxes Etc	1125 E Broadway	4 pm
Mail Boxes Etc	249 N Brand Blvd	4 pm
Self-Service	100 W Broadway	5:15 pm
Self-Service	550 N Brand Blvd	5:15 pm
Self-Service	101 N Brand Blvd	5 pm
Self-Service	1400 S Central Ave	5 pm
Self-Service	144 N Glendale Ave	5 pm
Self-Service	230 N Maryland Ave	5 pm
Self-Service	315 Arden Ave	5 pm
Self-Service	330 N Brand Blvd	5 pm
Self-Service	425 E Colorado St	5 pm
Self-Service	425 W Broadway	5 pm
Self-Service	4820 San Fernando Rd	5 pm
Self-Service	500 N Brand Blvd	5 pm
Self-Service	500 N Central Ave	5 pm
Self-Service	505 N Brand Blvd	5 pm
Self-Service	700 N Brand Blvd	5 pm
Self-Service	700 N Central Ave	5 pm
Self-Service	517 E Wilson Ave	4:45 pm
Self-Service	101 N Verdugo Rd	4:30 pm
Self-Service	1010 N Central Ave	4:30 pm
Self-Service	130 N Brand Blvd	4:30 pm
Self-Service	300 W Glenoaks Blvd	4:30 pm
Self-Service	121 W Lexington Dr	4 pm
Self-Service	655 N Central Ave	4 pm
Self-Service	801 N Brand Blvd	4 pm

Map 52 • Tarzana / Woodland Hills

Function Junction	20841 Ventura Blvd	4 pm
Mailbox International	4872 Topanga Canyon Blvd	4 pm
Self-Service	20700 Ventura Blvd	5 pm
Self-Service	20750 Ventura Blvd	5 pm
Self-Service	20969 Ventura Blvd	5 pm
Self-Service	21031 Ventura Blvd	5 pm
Self-Service	21241 Ventura Blvd	5 pm

Map 53 • Encino

Encino Mail Boxes	4924 Balboa Blvd	5 pm
Encino Mail & More	18034 Ventura Blvd	4:45 pm
FedEx Kinko's	16652 Ventura Blvd	4 pm
Mail Boxes International	18375 Ventura Blvd	4 pm
PostNet	17328 Ventura Blvd	4:30 pm
Self-Service	16633 Ventura Blvd	5 pm
Self-Service	16830 Ventura Blvd	5 pm
Self-Service	17000 Ventura Blvd	5 pm
Self-Service	17337 Ventura Blvd	5 pm
Self-Service	17547 Ventura Blvd	5 pm
Self-Service	18321 Ventura Blvd	5 pm
Self-Service	4930 Balboa Blvd	4:45 pm
Self-Service	17301 Ventura Blvd	4:30 pm

Map 54 • Sherman Oaks West

All Boxed Inn	16161 Ventura Blvd	4:30 pm
Bizzy Box	16060 Ventura Blvd	4:30 pm
FedEx Kinko's	15720 Ventura Blvd	6 pm
Self-Service	15165 Ventura Blvd	5:15 pm
Self-Service	15233 Ventura Blvd	5:15 pm
Self-Service	15303 Ventura Blvd	5:15 pm
Self-Service	16530 Ventura Blvd	5:15 pm
Self-Service	14724 Ventura Blvd	5 pm
Self-Service	14900 Magnolia Blvd	5 pm
Self-Service	14900 Ventura Blvd	5 pm
Self-Service	15250 Ventura Blvd	5 pm
Self-Service	15760 Ventura Blvd	5 pm
Self-Service	15821 Ventura Blvd	5 pm
Self-Service	15910 Ventura Blvd	5 pm
Self-Service	15915 Ventura Blvd	5 pm
Self-Service	16000 Ventura Blvd	5 pm
Self-Service	16027 Ventura Blvd	5 pm
Self-Service	16030 Ventura Blvd	5 pm
Self-Service	16055 Ventura Blvd	5 pm
Self-Service	16130 Ventura Blvd	5 pm
Self-Service	16133 Ventura Blvd	5 pm
Self-Service	16200 Ventura Blvd	5 pm
Self-Service	16255 Ventura Blvd	5 pm
Self-Service	16311 Ventura Blvd	5 pm
Self-Service	16400 Ventura Blvd	5 pm
Self-Service	16501 Ventura Blvd	5 pm
Self-Service	15000 Ventura Blvd	4:45 pm
Self-Service	15060 Ventura Blvd	4:30 pm
Self-Service	15206 Ventura Blvd	4:30 pm
Self-Service	15300 Ventura Blvd	4:30 pm
Self-Service	15315 Magnolia Blvd	4:30 pm
Self-Service	15456 Ventura Blvd	4:30 pm
Self-Service	15928 Ventura Blvd	4:30 pm
Sherman Oaks Mail Service	14925 Magnolia Blvd	4 pm

Map 55 • Sherman Oaks East

Box Brothers	13824 Ventura Blvd	5 pm
Dickens Box	4335 Van Nuys Blvd	4:30 pm
Federal Mailbox Center	4570 Van Nuys Blvd	4:30 pm
FedEx Kinko's	4556 Van Nuys Blvd	5 pm
Mail Boxes & Things	12930 Ventura Blvd	4:30 pm
Mail Boxes-n-more	14320 Ventura Blvd	4 pm
Mailbox Services Plus	14431 Ventura Blvd	4 pm
Personally Yours Mail Box	13547 Ventura Blvd	4 pm
Post Masters	13351 Riverside Dr	4 pm
Self-Service	13400 Riverside Dr	5:15 pm
Self-Service	13701 Riverside Dr	5:15 pm
Self-Service	4400 Coldwater Canyon Ave	5:15 pm
Self-Service	5000 Van Nuys Blvd	5 pm
Self-Service	4730 Woodman Ave	4:45 pm
Self-Service	14011 Ventura Blvd	4:30 pm
Self-Service	14140 Ventura Blvd	4:30 pm

Map 56 • Studio City/ Valley Village

Aim Mail Center	5160 Vineland Ave	4 pm
American Post and Parcel	11333 Moorpark St	5:15 pm
Ez Pack & Ship	5424 Laurel Canyon Blvd	4:30 pm
FedEx Kinko's	12101 Ventura Blvd	5:30 pm
Laurelpark-mail&shipcenter	4346 Laurel Canyon Blvd	4 pm
Mailbox & Photo	4821 Lankershim Blvd	4 pm
Noho Mailboxes	5062 Lankershim Blvd	4 pm
Pack N Mail	11054 Ventura Blvd	4:45 pm
Self-Service	12101 Ventura Blvd	5:30 pm
Self-Service	5200 Lankershim Blvd	5:15 pm
Self-Service	12001 Ventura Pl	5 pm
Self-Service	12711 Ventura Blvd	5 pm
Self-Service	4370 Tujunga Ave	5 pm
Self-Service	11304 Chandler Blvd	4:45 pm
Self-Service	11846 Ventura Blvd	4:45 pm
Self-Service	12605 Ventura Blvd	4:45 pm
Self-Service	12450 Magnolia Blvd	4:30 pm
Self-Service	12650 Riverside Dr	4:30 pm
Self-Service	5161 Lankershim Blvd	4:30 pm
Studio City Postal Center	3940 Laurel Canyon Blvd	4 pm
Tlma Postal Stop	12115 Magnolia Blvd	4:30 pm
Universal Mail & Business	12400 Ventura Blvd	4:30 pm

Map 57 • Universal City/ Toluca Lake

Alico Global	10934 Ventura Blvd	4 pm
FedEx Kinko's	3575 Cahuenga Blvd W	6 pm
FedEx Kinko's	4100 W Riverside Dr	5:30 pm
FedEx Kinko's	3817 W Riverside Dr	3 pm
Mailbox Toluca Lake	10153 1/2 Riverside Dr	4:15 pm
Packaging Store	10218 Riverside Dr	4 pm
Self-Service	10 Universal City Plaza	5:30 pm
Self-Service	3500 W Olive Ave	5:30 pm
Self-Service	3151 Cahuenga Blvd W	5:15 pm
Self-Service	3365 Barham Blvd	5:15 pm
Self-Service	3900 W Alameda Ave	5:15 pm
Self-Service	3400 W Riverside Dr	5 pm
Self-Service	3800 Barham Blvd	5 pm
Self-Service	4100 W Alameda Ave	5 pm
Self-Service	4450 W Lakeside Dr	5 pm
Self-Service	6711 Forest Lawn Dr	5 pm
Self-Service	6735 Forest Lawn Dr	5 pm
Self-Service	6767 Forest Lawn Dr	5 pm
Self-Service	4144 Lankershim Blvd	4:30 pm

Important Phone Numbers

Life-Threatening Emergencies:	911
Citywide Services Directory:	311
Non-Emergency Information Line:	877-ASK-LAPD (275-5273)
Rape Victims Hotline:	626-793-3385
Suicide Hotline:	213-381-5111
Crime Victims Hotline:	213-485-6976
Domestic Violence Hotline:	800-978-3600
Missing Persons Unit:	213-485-5381
Sex Crimes Report Line:	213-485-2883
Legal Aid:	213-385-2202
Lights & Noise Complaints:	888-524-2845
California Highway Patrol:	323-906-3434
Terrorist Threats:	877-A-THREAT (284-7328)
Website:	www.lapdonline.org

Statistics

Statistics	2005	2004	2003	2002	2001
Homicides	487	518	517	647	605
Rapes	928	1,109	1,177	1,246	1,314
Robberies	13,453	14,024	16,486	17,072	17,065
Aggravated Assaults	15,502	25,851	30,341	18,940	18,965
Burglaries	21,543	22,811	24,871	24,893	25,442
Grand Thefts Auto	26,573	28,455	32,038	32,370	30,428

Police Stations

Alhambra Police Dept	211 S 1st St	626-570-5107	39
Beverly Hills Police	464 N Rexford Dr	310-550-4951	1
Burbank Police Dept	200 N 3rd St	818-238-3000	50
CSU Northridge Police Dept	18111 Nordhoff St	818-677-2111	43
Culver City Police Dept	4040 Duquesne Ave	310-837-1221	24
El Segundo City Police Dept	348 Main St	310-524-2200	27
Glendale Police Dept	131 N Isabel St	818-548-4840	51
Hawthorne Police Dept	12501 S Hawthorne Blvd	310-675-4443	28
Hermosa Beach Police Dept	540 Pier Ave	310-318-0360	29
Inglewood Police Dept	1 W Manchester Blvd	310-412-5111	13
Lawndale Sheriff Service Center	15331 Prairie Ave	310-219-2750	28
Los Angeles County Sheriff's Dept	5019 E 3rd St	323-264-4151	41
Los Angeles County Sheriff's Dept-Marina del Rey Station	13851 Fiji Wy	310-823-7762	25
Los Angeles County Sheriff's Dept-Universal Citywalk	1000 Universal Studios Blvd	818-622-9539	57
Los Angeles County Sheriff's Dept-West Hollywood Station	780 N San Vicente Blvd	310-855-8850	2
Los Angeles Police Dept	10250 Etiwanda Ave	818-832-0633	43
Los Angeles Police Dept	11640 Burbank Blvd	818-623-4016	48
Los Angeles Police Dept	12312 Culver Blvd	310-482-6334	22
Los Angeles Police Dept	1358 Wilcox Ave	213-972-2971	3
Los Angeles Police Dept	1546 W Martin Luther King Jr Blvd	213-485-2582	11
Los Angeles Police Dept	1663 Butler Ave	310-444-0701	19
Los Angeles Police Dept	19020 Vanowen St	818-374-7611	45
Los Angeles Police Dept	1936 E 1st St	323-266-5964	40
Los Angeles Police Dept	251 E 6th St	213-485-3294	9
Los Angeles Police Dept	2710 W Temple St	213-485-4061	8
Los Angeles Police Dept	3353 N San Fernando Rd	213-485-2563	51
Los Angeles Police Dept	3400 S Central Ave	310-846-6547	12
Los Angeles Police Dept	4861 W Venice Blvd	213-473-0476	7
Los Angeles Police Dept	6240 Sylmar Ave	818-756-8343	47
Los Angeles Police Dept - Administrative Office	150 N Los Angeles St	213-485-2121	9
Manhattan Beach Police Dept	420 15th St	310-802-5100	27
Pasadena Police Dept	207 N Garfield Ave	626-744-4501	34
Redondo Beach Police Dept Main Station	401 Diamond St	310-379-2477	31
San Marino Police Dept	2200 Huntington Dr	626-300-0720	35
Santa Monica Police Headquarters	333 Olympic Dr	310-458-8411	18
South Pasadena Police Dept	1422 Mission St	626-403-7270	34
Torrance Police Dept	3300 Civic Center Dr	310-320-2611	30

Many of Los Angeles' landmarks double as a tangible histories of the city. From elegant Art Deco and Spanish architecture to gooey bogs of tar, to the ubiquitous Angelyne and everything in between, a cruise around Los Angeles is more educational—and (gas prices permitting) much cheaper—than a day spent at Disneyland.

So go ahead and be a tourist in your own backyard! Go mural sighting in Echo Park and East LA; compare your shoe size with Marilyn Monroe's at **Grauman's Chinese Theate**r **(Map 3)** and have a drink at the historical **Pig 'n Whistle (Map 3)**; spend an afternoon of browsing in the downtown **LA Central Library (Map 9)** and stroll the surrounding Maguire Gardens before grabbing a bite at **Clifton's Cafeteria (Map 9)**; or take a train ride in **Griffith Park (Map 51)**, go for a round or two of golf (you've got four courses to choose from) and shuttle up to the Observatory to watch the sunset over a twinkling LA skyline.

Historical LA

Grand Central Market (Map 9) in downtown Los Angeles has been operating since 1917 and is still a great place to buy meat, produce, ice cream and your favorite Mexican delicacies. Just across the street is **Angel's Flight (Map 9)**, a relic from old LA's ancient trolley system. For you beachcombers out there, do what Angelino's have done for decades and ride the roller coaster at **Santa Monica Pier (Map 18)** after a day of surf and sand. Just south of Santa Monica, the remaining four **Venice Canals (Map 21)** (between Venice Boulevard and Sherman Canal Court) give you a sense of Abbot Kinney's original 1904 Italian vision for this beach community…give or take a million-dollar home or two.

Buildings

It's disgustingly easy to tear down buildings in LA and a good number of the city's legendary landmarks have long been razed (the Brown Derby, Coconut Grove). But those that do remain are quite extraordinary. Hollywood's cylindrical **Capitol Records Building (Map 3)** is evocative of a pile of vinyl on a spindle. Down the street is **Grauman's Chinese Theatre (Map 3)**, open since 1927, which can rightly claim to be the most famous movie theater in the world, thanks to its cement welcome mat. The Emerald City-like green **Wiltern Theater (Map 7)**, named for the intersection where it sits at Wilshire and Western, is a stunning example of Art Deco architecture. Downtown Los Angeles is home to a bevy of historical landmarks, among them the grand **Union Station (Map 9)**, built in 1939 in the Spanish-mission style, the **Bradbury Building (Map 9)** (of *Blade Runner* fame) is Victorian opulence and ingenuity at its finest, and the **Eastern Columbia Buildings (Map 9)** are dynamic by day and blaze the downtown skyline by night. The Persian-inspired **Shrine Auditorium (Map 12)**, former home of the Oscars, now hosts concerts and lesser award shows. And as a convergence of the holy and the post modern, there is the impressive strength and serenity of the **Cathedral of Our Lady of the Angels (Map 9)**, fascinating regardless of religious affiliation.

Outdoor Spaces

For all its freeways and urban sprawl, Los Angeles is no concrete jungle. There are some terrific places to have a picnic, go for a hike, hear music, cheer for your team, or just laze in the California sunshine. The athletic flock to **Pan Pacific Park (Map 2)** near the Miracle Mile for softball and basketball; families, hikers, golfers, and horseback riders recreate in rustic **Griffith Park (Map 51)**; golfers and sun worshippers head to the vast **Rancho Park (Map 23)** in Cheviot Hills; and those seeking a refreshing hike in the hills visit the **Hollywood Reservoir (Map 57)** or the ever-popular **Runyon Canyon (Map 2)**. And absolutely nothing can match an outdoor summertime concert at the **Hollywood Bowl (Map 3)** or the **Greek Theatre (Map 4)**—both boast awesome acoustics and make for a lovely evening of food, wine, and music. Much cherished by Angelinos and a fine example of mid century modern architecture, **Dodger Stadium (Map 5)** opened in 1962 and still remains free of an annoying corporate sponsor moniker. An enduring celebration of LA's Mexican heritage is **Olvera Street (Map 9)** off Cesar Chavez downtown, where traditional dances and Mariachis are the backdrop to some authentic Mexican dining.

Architecture

Always a forward-thinking city, Los Angeles has been attracting the funky and the innovative with its municipal reputation for starting trends. The results are evident in the colorful shapes of the **Pacific Design Center (Map 2)**, housing furniture, art galleries, and design offices. Two famous Frank Lloyd Wright–designed homes near Hollywood—the ailing **Ennis-Brown House (Map 4)** and the **Hollyhock House (Map 4)**—offer tours daily. LA's early 20th century explosion makes it an Art Deco heaven, boasting dozens of striking examples of the movement from the soaring **City Hall (Map 9)** to the opulent movie palaces that crowd Broadway, particularly the triumphant **Orpheum (Map 9).** The most recent architectural wonder in Los Angeles is, of course, Frank Gehry's **Walt Disney Concert Hall (Map 9)**. Resembling a carefully wadded crumple of metal, the building is quite impressive both inside and out. Running a close second to Gehry's LA opus is the new, expressively modern **Caltrans District 7 Headquarters (Map 9)** downtown.

Lowbrow Landmarks

Nobody did lowbrow better than the late great drunken saint of Los Angeles: Charles Bukowski. To relive the poetic debauchery, drop a few bucks and bet on the ponies at **Hollywood Park (Map 13)** near LAX; afterwards, take your winnings to tip the dancers at the seedy (yet historic) **Jumbo's Clown Room (Map 4)** in Hollywood, where the performers (like Courtney Love before them) gyrate to Tom Waits and The Clash. **Whisky A Go Go (Map 2)** is a distinct musical landmark surrounded by the garish cultural wasteland of the Sunset Strip. Once the home of legendary rock bands like The Doors, Love, Van Halen, and X, the Whisky has since lost its luster to a never ending line-up of wanna-be bands. However, it's still worth a look, for posterity's sake.

Lame, Bad, & Overrated Landmarks

If **Rock Walk (Map 2)** doesn't prove as rockin' as you had hoped, cross the street and head to **El Compadre (See Restaurants, Map 2)** for a kick-ass flaming margarita to tame those blues. Further down Sunset you'll find the **Sunset Strip (Map 2)**. Crowded with hordes of suburban drunk kids, gridlocked traffic, and cops at every corner, the Strip is best done once (before night falls) and left to the tourists thereafter. Many of the tourist traps on Hollywood Boulevard are a waste of traveler's checks; avoid the **Hollywood Wax Museum (Map 3)** at all costs, and the new **Hollywood & Highland Mall (Map 3)** is sterile and soulless. Also terribly overrated are the **La Brea Tar Pits (Map 6)**—smelly and boring, they've lost the arresting appeal they once possessed thousands of years ago. Skip eating at **Pink's (Map 2)**—a hot dog is, after all, only a hot dog and doesn't justify the wait in line. If you must, start your day (or end your night) with a Chicago Dog right as they open up at 9:30 am.

Underrated Landmarks

The **Silent Movie Theatre (Map 2)** on Fairfax was silenced for a number of years following the murder of its second owner, Lawrence Austin, in 1997, but now it's up and running again and definitely worth a visit. Continuing in the macabre vein of the dead and the silent, the oddly festive **Hollywood Forever Cemetery (Map 3)** is the final resting place of stars both famous (Douglas Fairbanks, Cecil B DeMille, Joey Ramone) and infamous (Bugsy Siegal!). Old films are frequently shown al fresco in the graveyard to a fun, hip crowd—check www.cinespia.org for details. For a little more Hollyweird, check out the **Magic Castle (Map 3)**—you can book a room here or go for dinner and a show put on by some of the world's premier smoke-and-mirror masters. Sticking with the weirdly metaphysical, head on over to the **Museum of Jurassic Technology (Map 24)** on Venice Boulevard for a peek into a cabinet of curiosities that will surely leave you dumbstruck.

Map 1 • Beverly Hills

Academy of Motion Pictures Arts & Sciences	8949 Wilshire Blvd • 310-247-3000	Brake for red carpets and klieg lights! Many premieres are held here.
Beverly Hills Civic Center	Rexford Dr & Santa Monica Blvd • 310-285-1000	Infrastructure for the rich and famous.
Beverly Hills Hotel	9641 Sunset Blvd • 310-276-2251	Legends have stayed at the Pink Palace.
Four Seasons Beverly Wilshire	9500 Wilshire Blvd • 310-275-5200	*Pretty Woman* stayed here.
Greystone Mansion	905 Loma Vista Dr • 310-550-4654	Amazing views of Beverly Hills at this public mansion estate. Luke and Laura got married here, and you can too.
Greystone Park	905 Loma Vista Dr • 310-550-4654	Formerly the Doheny Mansion, now a lovely public park.
Museum of Television & Radio	465 N Beverly Dr • 310-786-1000	Where reruns of old sitcoms are considered art.
Prada Store	469 N Rodeo Dr • 310-385-5959	Architect Rem Koolhaas gives BH something else to look at.
The Witch's House	516 Walden Dr	Fairytale haunt straight out of Hansel and Gretel.

Map 2 • West Hollywood

Case Study House #22 (Stahl House)	1636 Woods Dr	Pierre Koenig's architectural triumph that sums up the whole spirit of late twentieth-century architecture.
CBS Television City	Beverly Blvd & N Fairfax Ave • 323-575-2458	Wanna be on *The Price is Right*? Come on down!
The Chaplin Studios	1416 N La Brea Ave • 323-802-1500	Charlie Chaplin's charming English Tudor-esque studios, now the Jim Henson studio.
Chateau Marmont	8221 W Sunset Blvd • 323-656-1010	Chic hotel where John Belushi died.
Pacific Design Center	Melrose Ave & San Vicente Blvd • 310-657-0800	Nicknamed "The Blue Whale" for obvious reasons.
Pan Pacific Park	7600 Beverly Blvd • 323-939-8874	It's a storm drain! We mean, it's a park!
Pink's Famous Chili Dogs	709 N La Brea Ave • 323-931-4223	A line around the block; It's that famous.
Rock Walk	7435 Sunset Blvd • 323-874-1060	Mann's Chinese has John Wayne, the Rock Walk has Slash.
Runyon Canyon Park	Franklin Ave & Fuller Dr	Once Errol Flynn's estate, now a very popular off-leash hiking trail.
Santa Monica Blvd	Santa Monica Blvd b/w La Cienega Blvd & Robertson Blvd	The heart of gay West Hollywood.
Schindler House	833 N Kings Rd • 323-651-1510	A desert camp inspired this brilliant creation by architect Rudolph Schindler.
Silent Movie Theatre	611 N Fairfax Ave • 323-655-2520	Only the ticket prices will remind you that it's the 21st century.
Sunset Strip	Sunset Blvd b/w N Doheny Dr & N Fairfax Ave	Its clubs are still the center of LA's (bridge and tunnel) nightlife.
Whisky A Go Go	8901 Sunset Blvd • 310-652-4202	Music venue for legendary bands of yore.

Map 3 • Hollywood

Capitol Records Building	1750 N Vine St • 323-462-6252	Designed to look like a stack of records--remember those?
Crossroads of the World	6671 Sunset Blvd	Former 1930s shopping center with a nautical theme now deemed a cultural landmark.
El Capitan Theatre	6838 Hollywood Blvd • 800-347-6396	Live shows with movies in opulent historic theater.
Gower Gulch	W Sunset Blvd & N Gower St	Studio-adjacent intersection where cowboy extras used to congregate. Now a Western-themed strip-mall.
Grauman's Chinese Theatre	6925 Hollywood Blvd • 323-464-8111	See how your shoe size measures up against Sylvester Stallone's.
Grauman's Egyptian Theater	6712 Hollywood Blvd • 323-466-3456	Historic movie palace and home of American Cinematheque.
Hollywood Bowl	2301 N Highland Ave • 323-850-2000	Eclectic music and picnicking under the stars.
Hollywood Forever Cemetery	6000 Santa Monica Blvd • 323-469-1181	The only place in LA where you can still see Douglas Fairbanks and Tyrone Power.
Hollywood & Highland Mall	6801 Hollywood Blvd • 323-467-6412	Sterile, touristy mall that houses the Oscars.
Hollywood Roosevelt Hotel	7000 Hollywood Blvd • 323-466-7000	Recently renovated and rumored to be haunted by Marilyn Monroe.
Hollywood Walk of Fame	Hollywood Blvd from N Gower St to La Brea Ter • 323-469-8311	Tourists love this shrine to often-mediocre celebs.
Hollywood Wax Museum	6767 Hollywood Blvd • 323-462-8860	Celebrities in wax. Greeeat.
Lasky-DeMille Barn	2100 N Highland Ave • 323-874-2276	The birthplace of the Motion Picture Industry and now the Hollywood Heritage Museum.
Magic Castle of Hollywood	7025 Franklin Ave • 323-851-0800	Spend the night or catch a show--if you know a member.
Pantages Theater	6233 Hollywood Blvd • 323-468-1770	Go for the big Broadway shows.
Paramount Studios	5555 Melrose Ave • 323-956-5575	The last movie studio actually IN Hollywood.
Pig 'n Whistle	6714 Hollywood Blvd • 323-463-0000	Hollywood watering hole and restaurant dating back to the golden era.
Ripley's Believe It or Not	6780 Hollywood Blvd • 323-466-6335	More oddities, less exhausting than *Guinness Book*.

Map 4 • Los Feliz

American Film Institute	2021 N Western Ave • 323-856-7600	The next David Lynch might be honing his craft here right now. Or not.
Ennis-Brown House	2607 Glendower Ave • 323-660-0607	Frank Lloyd Wright's version of a Mayan temple.
The Figure 8 Mural	4334 W Sunset Blvd	Former cover art, this mural is now a tribute to departed indie fave Elliott Smith.
Greek Theatre	2700 N Vermont Ave • 323-468-1767	A more intimate alternative to the Hollywood Bowl.
Hollyhock House	4800 Hollywood Blvd • 323-644-6269	Another brilliant Frank Lloyd Wright design, open for public tours, love the fireplace.
Jumbo's Clown Room	5153 Hollywood Blvd • 323-666-1187	Seedy strip club where Courtney Love first exposed her "celebrity skin."
Silverlake Conservatory of Music	3920 Sunset Blvd • 323-665-3363	Neighborhood music school and hang-out courtesy of Chili Pepper Flea.

Map 5 • Silver Lake/Echo Park/Atwater

Angelus Temple	1100 Glendale Blvd • 213-816-1118	Founder claimed the Lord led her to the site.
Dodger Stadium	1000 Elysian Park Ave • 866-363-4377	With a view like this, who needs luxury boxes?
Echo Park	Glendale Blvd & Park Ave	The paddle boats alone are worth a trip.
Richard Neutra Houses	2200 Silver Lake Blvd	A can't-miss for architecture buffs.
Rowena Reservoir	Corner of Hyperion Ave & Rowena Ave	This strategically landscaped reservoir contains 10 million gallons of water and cost a few more million to build.
Silver Lake Reservoir	Silverlake Blvd & Duane St	Take a jog, a stroll, and a dog! There is an off-leash dog park at the reservoir's base.

Map 6 • Miracle Mile/Mid-City

A+D Museum	5900 Wilshire Blvd • 323-932-9393	All things architecture - check it out here.
Craft & Folk Art Museum	5800 Wilshire Blvd • 323-937-5544	If you like that sort of thing…
George C Page Museum of La Brea Discoveries	5801 Wilshire Blvd • 323-934-7243	Don't miss the La Brea Woman exhibit.
La Brea Tar Pits	Wilshire Blvd & S Curson Ave • 323-934-7243	It's just a big pool of tar, yet it continues to fascinate us.
LACMA West (former May Co Building)	6067 Wilshire Blvd • 323-933-4510	This Art Deco building used to be home to the May Co. Department Store.
Los Angeles County Museum of Art	5905 Wilshire Blvd • 323-857-6000	From King Tut to Jasper Johns, this museum covers it all.
Lula Washington Dance Theatre	5041 W Pico Blvd • 323-292-5852	Renowned African-American dance company with classes and residencies.
Petersen Automotive Museum	6060 Wilshire Blvd • 323-930-2277	Like you don't see enough cars in LA. Mediocre.
Zimmer Children's Museum	6505 Wilshire Blvd • 323-761-8989	Learning place for kids to explore.

Map 7 • Hancock Park

Getty House (Mayor's official residence)	605 S Irving Blvd • 323-930-6430	The home that LA's mayors use to par-tay.
Los Altos Apartments	4121 Wilshire Blvd • 323-464-0600	There is a waiting list for apartments in this historic Spanish-style building.
Wilshire Ebell Theatre & Club	4401 W 8th St • 323-939-1128	Renaissance-style buildings used mainly for private events.
Wiltern Theater	3780 Wilshire Blvd • 213-380-5005	Cool Art Deco building attracts equally cool, eclectic musical acts.

Map 8 • Korea Town

MacArthur Park	Wilshire Blvd & S Alvarado St	Avoid at night ,or you'll be melting in the dark!
Southwestern Law School	3050 Wilshire Blvd • 213-738-6700	Legendary Art Deco department store turned law school.

Map 9 • Downtown

Angel's Flight	W 4th St & Hill St • 213-626-1901	Due to a tragic accident, funicular is now simply a walkway.
Angeleno Heights	Carroll/Kellam/W Kensington Aves	Enclave of Victorian homes. Some lavished with astonishing TLC, some not.
Biltmore Hotel	506 S Grand Ave • 213-624-0052	Downtown's first lady of luxury hotels, the Biltmore is a testament to LA's lavish architectual heritage.
Bradbury Building	304 S Broadway	Eclectic and dramatic Victorian masterpiece that was featured in *Blade Runner*.
Caltrans District 7 Headquarters	100 S Main St	A solar behemoth that is as energy-efficient as it is commanding.
Cathedral of Our Lady of the Angels	555 W Temple St • 213-680-5200	Architectural Catholicism for the post-Y2K generation.
Chinatown	700-1000 N Broadway	It may not sound like much, but the slippery shrimp at Yang Chow can't be missed.
City Hall	200 N Spring St • 213-485-2121	Got a gripe? Here's the place to start.
Clifton's Cafeteria	648 S Broadway • 213-627-1673	Tri-level cafeteria with a woodsy theme and fake animals since 1931.
Coca-Cola Building	1334 S Central Ave	LA historic monument, looks like a luxury cruise ship.
Dorothy Chandler Pavilion	135 N Grand Ave • 213-972-0711	The Oscars are gone but the LA Opera is still here.
Eastern Columbia Buildings	849 S Broadway	Do not leave these off of your tour of LA's Art Deco gems.
El Pueblo de Los Angeles Historical Monument	Main St & Cesar E Chavez Ave • 213-628-1274	The real LA story, but with Mexican and Native American influence.
Garfield Building	403 W 8th St	Another Art Deco monument from LA's past. Check out the lobby.
The Geffen Contemporary at MOCA	152 N Central Ave • 213-626-6222	Formerly known as the "Temporary Contemporary," the museum is still going strong.
Grand Central Market	317 S Broadway • 213-625-5006	Mexican specialties and more.
Instituto Cultural Mexicano	125 Paseo de la Plz • 213-624-3660	Dedicated to the cultural exchange between American and Mexican cultures.
Japanese American National Museum	369 E 1st St • 213-625-0414	Chronicling the Japanese experience in the US.
LA Convention Center	1201 S Figueroa St • 213-741-1151	The building's green glass exterior is visible for miles.
Los Angeles Central Library	630 W 5th St • 213-228-7000	Grand downtown library.
Mayan Theater	1038 S Hill St • 213-746-4287	Spooky and cool. Check out the lobby if you can.
MOCA	250 S Grand Ave • 213-626-6222	Received much well-deserved attention for its wildly popular Andy Warhol retrospective.

Map 9 • Downtown—*continued*

Music Center	135 N Grand Ave • 213-972-7211	Four music venues in one.
Olvera Street	Olvera St	An authentic Mexican marketplace in the heart of downtown LA.
The Orpheum	842 S Broadway • 213-749-5171	Former Vaudeville house, now hosts and assortment of live events.
Oviatt Building	617 S Olive St	Art Deco treasure. Be sure to sneak a peek inside.
STAPLES Center	1111 S Figueroa St • 213-742-7333	If the Staples folk could find a way to play baseball inside the arena, they'd lure the Dodgers too.
Union Station	800 N Alameda St • 213-625-5865	Makes you wish people still traveled by train.
Walt Disney Concert Hall	141 S Grand Ave • 323-850-2000	Gehry's architectural masterpiece.
World Trade Center	350 S Figueroa St • 213-489-3337	Far less impressive than its former NY namesake, but a vital part of Downtown nonetheless.

Map 10 • Baldwin Hills

Kenneth Hahn State Recreation Area	4100 S La Cienega Blvd • 323-298-3660	Most people only think of this park as they're driving to LAX. That's a mistake.

Map 11 • South Central West

California Science Center	700 State Dr • 323-724-3623	Come for the exhibits and high-wire bicycle acts.
Exposition Park	Menlo Ave & S Park Dr • 213-765-5369	Forget the Coliseum and check out the Rose Garden. Or not.
LA County Museum of Natural History	900 Exposition Blvd • 213-763-3466	Kids just love the dinosaur fossils.

Map 12 • South Central East

LA Memorial Coliseum	3911 S Figueroa St • 213-747-7111	We're still waiting for that LA football team…
Shrine Auditorium	665 W Jefferson Blvd • 213-748-5116	The mosque design makes it one of the neighborhood's most visible buildings.

Map 13 • Inglewood

Great Western Forum	Manchester Ave & Prairie Ave • 310-330-7300	The Lakers' and Kings' former home is now the Faithful Central Bible Church. There's irony for you.
Hollywood Park	1050 S Prairie Ave • 310-419-1500	When you've just got to play the ponies…
Pann's Diner	6710 La Tijera Blvd • 323-776-3770	One of the best remaining examples in the country of '50s coffee shop design--and they serve a down-home tasty breakfast.
Randy's Donuts	805 W Manchester Blvd • 310-645-4707	Giant donut perched on top of this beloved donut stop.

Map 15 • Pacific Palisades

Eames House	203 Chautauqua Blvd • 310-459-9663	Iconic house that influenced modern architecture in the 'burbs.
Santa Monica Steps	4th St & Adelaide Dr	Climbing these is the most LA workout you can ever hope to have.
Self Realization Fellowship Lake Shrine Temple	17190 W Sunset Blvd • 310-454-4114	Stunning gardens.
Will Rogers State Historic Park	Sunset Blvd • 310-454-8212	Hiking, picnicking, and polo. Yes, polo.

Map 16 • Brentwood

Getty Center	1200 Getty Center Dr • 310-440-7300	Cool buildings (Meier), great garden (Irwin), fabulous views (God).

Map 17 • Bel Air/Holmby Hills

Beverly Hillbillies' House	700 Bel Air Rd	Former Clampett stomping ground.

Map 18 • Santa Monica

3rd Street Promenade	3rd St b/w Broadway & Wilshire	Day or night, there's always something going on.
Heritage Square	Main St & Ocean Park Blvd • 310-392-8537	A taste of 19th-century life amidst Starbucks and bagel shops.
Santa Monica Civic Auditorium/Civic Center	1855 Main St • 310-458-8551	Bizarre mix of cool rock concerts and antique sales.
Santa Monica Pier	Ocean Ave & Colorado Ave • 310-458-8900	Tiptoe through the tourists for a ride on the historic carousel.

Map 19 • West LA/Santa Monica East

Bergamot Station	2525 Michigan Ave • 310-828-6410	The best one-stop art experience you can have in LA.
Santa Monica Municipal Airport	3223 Donald Douglas Loop S • 310-458-8591	Home to lots of small planes and private jets. And an annual Barneys NY sale.

Map 20 • Westwood/Century City

Federal Building	Wilshire Blvd & Sepulveda Blvd	Picketers of any and all causes seem magnetically drawn to this building.
Fox Plaza (a.k.a. the *Die Hard* building)	2121 Ave of the Stars • 310-277-2121	Known to locals as "the *Die Hard* Building". Surely we don't have to explain.

Mormon Temple	10777 Santa Monica Blvd • 310-474-1549	Always one of the more festively-lit buildings at Christmastime.
Playboy Mansion	10236 Charing Cross Rd	We'd tell you all about it if only Hef would send us an invitation.
UCLA Hammer Museum	10889 Wilshire Blvd • 310-443-7000	Cutting-edge art museum with largely contemporary exhibits.
Wadsworth Theater	11000 Wilshire Blvd • 310-478-7578	They offer free jazz concerts on the first Sunday of every month.
Westwood Memorial Cemetery	1218 Glendon Ave • 310-272-2484	Marilyn Monroe and Natalie Wood are among the famous residents.

Map 21 • Venice

Chiat-Day Building	340 Main St • 310-305-5000	Frank Gehry's design features a large statue of binoculars marking its entrance.
Muscle Beach	1817 Ocean Front Wk • 310-578-6131	Don't forget to oil up first.
Venice Boardwalk	Ocean Front Wk	A freak show to some, while others thrive on the eclectic crowds. Marvel at the graffiti-bedecked palm trees.
Venice Canals	Venice Blvd & Pacific Ave	There used to be more than six, but they were deemed impractical and turned into roads.
Venice Pier	Far west end of Washington Blvd	It's been a casualty to weather conditions at least twice.
Windward Circle	Main St & Windward Ave	A great meeting place for those looking to spend the day at the beach.

Map 22 • Mar Vista

Mar Vista Tract	3500 Block of Beethoven St , Moore St, & Meier St, just south of Palms Blvd	Indulge your retro-modernist fetish.

Map 23 • Rancho Park/Palms

20th Century Fox Studios	10201 Pico Blvd • 310-277-2121	Check out the *Star Wars* mural. It's way cool.
Museum of Tolerance	9786 W Pico Blvd • 310-553-8403	A humbling experience that is worth a visit.
Rancho Park	10460 W Pico Blvd • 310-838-7373	Good, but crowded, municipal golf course.
Westside Pavilion Cinemas	10800 W Pico Blvd • 310-281-8223	We defy you to find your car at the end of any shopping expedition.

Map 24 • Culver City

Culver Hotel	9400 Culver Blvd • 310-838-7963	Home to many a munchkin during the shooting of The *Wizard of Oz*.
Helm's Bakery Building	3233 Helms Ave	They used to make bread, now they sell furniture.
Museum of Jurassic Technology	9341 Venice Blvd • 310-836-6131	The coolest. Check out Mary Davis's horn.
Sony Pictures Studios	10202 W Washington Blvd • 310-244-8687	Before Sony and Spider-Man, it was The Munchkins and MGM.

Map 25 • Marina Del Rey/Westchester West

Ballona Wetlands	Around Ballona Creek	Restored wetlands. View flora and fauna from walkway.
Fisherman's Village	13755 Fiji Wy • 310-823-5411	Quaint shopping and dining are geared to resemble a New England fishing town.
Marina City Towers	4333 Admiralty Wy • 310-822-0611	Massive condo complex that has even turned up on shows like *Melrose Place.*

Map 26 • Westchester/Fox Hills/Ladera Heights

Encounter Restaurant	209 World Wy N • 310-215-5151	Spaceship architecture from '60s with a 360-degree view.
Pann's Restaurant	6710 La Tijera Blvd • 323-776-3770Ê	Mid-century modern diner designed by Armet & Davis.

Map 27 • El Segundo/Manhattan Beach

Chevron Oil Refinery	East of Sepulveda Blvd, north of Rosecrans Ave	It ain't pretty, but it's definitely noticeable.
Manhattan Beach Pier	West of Manhattan Beach Blvd	Don't miss the Roundhouse Marine Studies Lab and Aquarium at the end of the pier!

Map 29 • Hermosa Beach

Hermosa Beach Fishing Pier	End of Pier Ave	Just bring your pole. There are bait and tackle shops right on the pier.

Map 33 • Highland Park

Eagle Rock Community Cultural Center	2225 Colorado Blvd • 323-226-1617	Classes, performances, and exhibitions for the local community.
Judson Studios	200 S Ave 66 • 323-255-0131	Stained glass like you've never seen before.
League of United Latin-American Citizens	4512 Eagle Rock Blvd • 202-833-6130	Helps to improve conditions for Latin-American Citizens nationwide.

Map 34 • Pasadena

Ambassador Auditorium	131 S St John Ave	Operated by the Worldwide Church of God.
Castle Green	99 S Raymond Ave • 626-793-0395	This Moorish Colonial marvel may be a has-been, but it's a beautiful one.

Map 34 • Pasadena—*continued*

Colorado Street Bridge	171 S Los Robles Ave • 626-795-9311	This stunning Beaux-Arts bridge is a romantic ode to Pasadena's majestic past.
Fenyes Mansion	470 W Walnut St • 626-577-1660	Beaux-Arts opulence at its best, the mansion's museum and gardens are open to the public for tours.
Gamble House	4 Westmoreland Pl • 626-449-4178	Pasadena's Craftsman style at its best.
Kidspace—An Interactive Museum	480 N Arroyo Blvd • 626-449-9144	Way cool kid-geared activities and exhibits.
Old Town	Fair Oaks Ave & Colorado Blvd	A fine example of urban regentrification at work.
Pasadena City Hall	100 N Garfield Ave • 626-744-4000	A lovely building with even lovelier gardens.
Pasadena Civic Auditorium	300 E Green St • 626-793-2122	Home to both the Pasadena Symphony and the People's Choice Awards.
Pasadena Playhouse State Theater	39 S El Molino Ave • 626-356-7529	Back in the day, the Playhouse's now-defunct acting school turned out many a movie star.
Rose Bowl	991 Rosemont Ave • 626-577-3100	UCLA football, Galaxy soccer games, and the infamous monthy swap meet.
Wrigley Mansion	391 S Orange Grove Blvd • 626-449-7673	Check out the Mission-style architecture.

Map 35 • Pasadena East/San Marino

El Molino Viejo	1120 Old Mill Rd • 626-449-5450	Southern California's first water-powered gristmill. Who needs Disney's California Adventure?
Huntington	1151 Oxford Rd • 626-405-2100	A perfect place to take relatives from out-of-town.
Lacy Park	1500 Virginia Rd • 626-300-0790	Second only to the Huntington, Lacy Park is 30 acres of gorgeous greenery

Map 36 • Mt. Washington

The Lummis Home	200 E Ave 43 • 323-222-0546	An original home conceived by an original man.
Mount Washington Hotel/ Self-Realization	3880 San Rafael Ave • 323-225-2471	Beautiful gardens, open to the public.

Map 37 • Lincoln Heights

Heritage Square Museum	3800 N Homer St • 626-449-0193	A cluster of buildings that have been saved from demolition through relocation to Heritage Square.

Map 39 • Alhambra

Ramona Convent School Museum	1701 W Ramona Rd • 626-282-4151	Some of the campus's buildings have been here since the 19th century.

Map 40 • Boyle Heights

The Brewery	620 Moulton Ave • 323-221-9204	Former Pabst Blue Ribbon brewery turned artists' studios.
El Corrido de Boyle Heights Mural	2336 E Cesar E Chavez Ave	Public art at its most colorful.
LA County USC Medical Center	1200 N State St • 323-226-2622	The facade may look familiar to viewers of *General Hospital.*
Mariachi Plaza	Boyle Ave & 1st St	Need a mariachi? Look no further!
San Antonio Winery	737 Lamar St • 323-223-1401	The last remaining winery along the LA river basin— check out the killer tasting room.

Map 41 • City Terrace/East LA

Mural: The Kennedy Saga II 1973 (City Terrace Park)	1126 N Hazard Ave	Located inside the City Terrace Park social hall.

Map 44 • Mission Hills / North Hills

Greer House	9200 Haskell Ave	Frank Lloyd Wright Jr. crawled out from under his father's shadow and built a house.
Sepulveda Unitarian Universalist Society Building	9550 Haskell Ave • 818-894-9251	A church shaped like an onion—only in LA.

Map 45 • Canoga Park / Woodland Hills

Antique Row	21500 block of Sherman Wy	It is what it is.

Map 47 • Van Nuys

Van Nuys Airport	16461 Sherman Wy • 818-785-8838	The world's busiest general aviation airport.

Map 49 • Burbank

NBC Television Studios	3000 W Alameda Ave • 818-840-4444	The line forms early for crowds hoping to view the daily *Tonight Show* taping.

Warner Ranch	Verdugo Ave & Pass Ave • 818-954-6000	That NY fountain where TV's "Friends" dance in the opening credits? Right here on the ranch.

Map 50 • Burbank East/Glendale West

Los Angeles Equestrian Center	480 Riverside Dr • 818-840-9066	Polo, dressage, and the Los Angeles Gay Rodeo.
Walt Disney Studios	500 S Buena Vista • 818-560-1000	The quirkiest architecture of all of the major motion picture studios.

Map 51 • Glendale South

Alex Theatre	216 N Brand Blvd • 818-243-2539	Former Vaudeville house opened in 1925.
Forest Lawn Memorial Park	1712 S Glendale Ave • 800-204-3131	The Disneyland of LA cemeteries.
Griffith Park	4730 Crystal Springs Dr • 323-913-4688	Ride the carousel.
Moonlight Rollerway	5110 San Fernando Rd • 818-241-3630	Time stands still at Glendale's premier roller-boogie spot.

Map 53 • Encino

Rancho de los Encinos State Historical Park	16756 Moorpark St • 818-784-4849	The rancho was damaged in the Northridge quake, but the park is still open.

Map 56 • Studio City/Valley Village

Brady Bunch House	11222 Dilling St	You too can pretend to be part of America's favorite blended family.
CBS Radford Studios	4024 Radford Ave • 818-655-5000	*Seinfeld's* NY sensibilities were actually found here, in the heart of the Valley.
El Portal Theatre	5269 Lankershim Blvd • 818-508-4234	Former Vaudeville/Silent Movie house now anchors the NoHo Arts District.

Map 57 • Universal City/Toluca Lake

Bob's Big Boy	4211 Riverside Dr • 818-843-9334	The original Bob's Big Boy, as if the giant "Big Boy" out front didn't tip you off.
Campo de Cahuenga	3912 Lankershim Blvd • 818-763-7651	This historic park is not regularly open to the public.
CityWalk	Universal Center Dr • 818-622-4455	Entering City Walk is like walking through the glitzy gates of mega-franchise hell.
Falcon Theatre	4252 W Riverside Dr • 818-955-8101	High-profile Valley theatre.
Hollywood Reservoir	East of Hwy 101 • 323-463-0830	Jog or stroll around lovely "Lake Hollywood."
Universal Studios	100 Universal Center Dr • 818-777-1000	New Yorkers scoff at the Studio's diminutive "tower."
Warner Brothers Studios	4000 Warner Blvd • 818-954-1744	The studio's water tower serves as a beacon for much of downtown Burbank.

Long Beach

Adelaide A Tichenor House	852 E Ocean Blvd	Historic Greene & Greene house.
Alexander House	5281 El Roble St	Red brick modernist house by famed architect John Lautner.
Aquarium of the Pacific	100 Aquarium Wy • 562-590-3100	See, learn, touch marine life! Interactive entertainment.
Art Theater	2025 E 4th St • 562-438-5435	One of the last Art Deco movie theaters standing in Long Beach.
California State University at Long Beach	1250 N Bellflower Blvd • 562-985-5761	One of the top state colleges, athletically and scholastically.
Catalina Landing	330 Golden Shore St • 562-435-2333	Go to, and come back from, Catalina Islandl
Edison Theater	213 E Broadway	This place has stories and ghosts in every wall panel.
Long Beach Convention & Visitor's Bureau	1 World Trade Ctr • 800-452-7829	It ain't just "lowa by the Sea" anymore.
Long Beach Museum of Art	2300 E Ocean Blvd • 562-439-2119	Fine collection inside, lovely grounds outside.
Matlock House	1560 Ramillo Ave	Beautiful pitched-roof house from Richard Neutra.
Museum of Latin-American Art	628 Alamitos Ave • 562-437-1689	Nationally reputable; bevy of time periods and artists featured.
The Pike at Rainbow Harbor	S Pine Ave & W Shoreline Dr • 563-432-8325	Former seaside playland reinterpreted as a concept mall.
Queen Mary Seaport	1126 Queens Hwy • 800-437-2934	This dame shuttled soldiers and ferried the uber-rich.
Seashell House	4325 E 6th St	A piece of 1920s folk art made from crushed sea shells.
Shoreline Village	419 Shoreline Village Dr • 562-435-2668	Buy a hat, grab a snack and fly a kite 100 yards away.
The Skinny House	798 Gladys Ave	Deemed the nation's narrowest home.
The Villa Riviera Hotel	800 E Ocean Blvd	Gothic wonder and former residence of Charlie Chaplin and Norma Talmadge.

San Pedro

Angel's Gate Cultural Center	3601 S Gaffey St • 310-519-0936	Don't miss this historical site.
Art Walk	W 4th St & S Pacific Ave	This is Who We Are, say San Pedro-ites.
Cabrillo Beach Bathhouse	3800 Stephen M White Dr • 310-548-7554	Renovated and worth a gander.
Catalina Express Terminal	Swinford St & N Harbor Blvd • 800-481-3470	Departs for and embarks from Catalina Island.
Point Fermin Lighthouse	807 W Paseo Del Mar	Charming Victorian lighthouse is one of the oldest on the west coast.
Ports O' Call	1100 Nagoy Wy	Ole touristy standby, still a pleasant afternoon.
San Pedro Farmer's Market	Mesa St, b/w 6th & 7th Sts	Avoid the traffic on Aviation to beach cities.

Los Angeles offers just a few too many hotel choices—so many, in fact, that it can easily induce a case of option paralysis. If you have money to spend, we offer this cheat-sheet to aid your decision-making. The **Chateau Marmont (Map 2)**: legendary, low-key, timeless. The **Four Seasons (Map 1)**: beautiful rooftop pool, excellent location, and with press junkets held year-round here, you never know who you might encounter on the elevator. Need a place to hide out while you recover from a "procedure?" The **Peninsula (Map 1)**, definitely. **Maison 140 (Map 1)** and the **Avalon Hotel (Map 1)** are stylish, sexy, and lighter-hearted than the more Baroque stuff you'd otherwise find in Beverly Hills. Similarly style-conscious and opening this year is their sibling property, the **Chamberlain (Map 2)** in West Hollywood. The **Sunset Marquis (Map 2)** has a famously fabulous scene at the Whiskey Bar on-premises—though you must be a hotel guest, or a bold-faced name, to belly-up.

Feeling architecturally significant? The **Sunset Tower Hotel (Map 2)**, an Art Deco gem, is back in business after extensive renovations and offers a substantially lower profile than Sunset Boulevard ball-hogs the **Standard (Map 9)** and the **Mondrian (Map 2)**. Out at the beach, within sight of the Santa Monica Pier but far from the maddening crowd, is the delicious **Hotel Casa Del Mar (Map 18)**. Next door is the famous **Shutters on the Beach (Map 18)**, a more rustic stay with five-star restaurants and service. If you are planning to spend a longish evening in Hollywood, book a room at the **Hollywood Roosevelt Hotel (Map 3)**—a landmark within stumbling distance of all of the star-studded clubs. And finally, when headed downtown, say, for an oversized night at the STAPLES Center or for your company's Christmas blow-out, book one of the Moroccan Suites at the **Figueroa Hotel (Map 9)**. It's a quirky, mysterious beauty, and once you've time-traveled through the well-decorated lobby, and sat down for a nightcap by the pool, you will wonder why it took you so long to find the place.

As with so many things, the best rates are always found online. Check out Tablet Hotels ("hotels for global nomads") for au courant, cool-design options; Luxury Link for the high-end stuff; Hotels.com, Hotwire, and Travelzoo to cast a wider net.

Map 1 • Beverly Hills

Avalon Hotel of Beverly Hills	9400 W Olympic Blvd	310-277-5221	$289
Beverly Crescent Hotel	403 N Crescent Dr	310-247-0505	$200
Beverly Hills Hotel	9641 Sunset Blvd	310-276-2251	$335
Beverly Hills Reeves Hotel	120 S Reeves Dr	310-271-3006	$89
Beverly Hilton	9876 Wilshire Blvd	310-274-7777	$252
Beverly Pavilion Hotel	9360 Wilshire Blvd	310-273-1400	$129
Four Seasons Beverly Wilshire	9500 Wilshire Blvd	310-275-5200	$375
Four Seasons Hotel	300 S Doheny Dr	310-273-2222	$425
Hotel Del Flores	409 N Crescent Dr	310-274-5115	$65 shared bath, $95 private bath
L'Ermitage Hotel	9291 Burton Wy	310-278-3344	$508
Maison 140	140 S Lasky Dr	310-281-4000	$191
Mosaic Hotel	125 S Spalding Dr	310-278-0303	$320
Peninsula Beverly Hills	9882 S Santa Monica Blvd	310-551-2888	$495
Summit Hotel Rodeo Drive	360 N Rodeo Dr	310-273-0300	$261

Map 2 • West Hollywood

Alta Cienega Motel	1005 N La Cienega Blvd	310-652-5797	$60
Bel Age	1020 N San Vicente Blvd	310-854-1111	$219
Best Western Sunset Plaza Htl	8400 W Sunset Blvd	323-654-0750	$179
Beverly Inn	7701 Beverly Blvd	323-931-8108	$60
Beverly Laurel Motor Hotel	8018 Beverly Blvd	323-651-2441	$79
Beverly Terrace Motor Hotel	469 N Doheny Dr	310-274-8141	$170
Bevonshire Lodge Motel	7575 Beverly Blvd	323-936-6154	$60
Chamberlain Hotel	1000 Westmount Dr	310-657-7400	$229
Chateau Marmont	8221 W Sunset Blvd	323-656-1010	$350
Days Inn	7023 W Sunset Blvd	323-464-8344	$94
Econo Lodge	7370 W Sunset Blvd	323-876-0330	$110
Elan Hotel Modern	8435 Beverly Blvd	323-658-6663	$189
Fairfax Motel	913 N Fairfax Ave	323-654-5570	$35
Farmer's Daughter Hotel	115 S Fairfax Ave	323-937-3930	$179
Grafton on Sunset	8462 Sunset Blvd	323-654-4600	$159
Guest House Inn	7721 Beverly Blvd	323-692-1777	$80
Highland Gardens Hotel	7047 Franklin Ave	323-850-0536	$109
Holiday Inn Express	1520 N La Brea Ave	323-464-3243	$126
Holloway Motel	8465 Santa Monica Blvd	323-654-2454	$60
Hollywood Seven Star Motel	1730 N La Brea Ave	323-876-2714	$65
Hollywood Seven Star Motel	7096 Yucca St	323-850-0831	$65
Hollywood Studio Inn	7160 W Sunset Blvd	323-874-6660	$68
Hollywood-La Brea Motel	7110 Hollywood Blvd	323-876-8000	$60
Hotel Sofitel	8555 Beverly Blvd	310-278-5444	$315
Hyatt on Sunset	8401 Sunset Blvd	323-656-1234	$255
Le Meridien At Beverly Hills	465 S La Cienega Blvd	310-247-0400	$289
Le Montrose	900 Hammond St	310-855-1115	$195
Le Parc	733 N W Knoll Dr	310-855-8888	$239
Mondrian	8440 W Sunset Blvd	323-650-8999	$395
Orbit Hotel	7950 Melrose Ave	323-655-1510	$22 shared, $69 private

The Orlando	8384 W 3rd St	323-658-6600	$259
Park Plaza Lodge	6001 W 3rd St	323-931-1501	$100
Ramada	8585 Santa Monica Blvd	310-652-6400	$129
Saharan Motel	7212 W Sunset Blvd	323-874-6700	$70
San Vicente Inn	845 N San Vicente Blvd	310-854-6915	$119
Standard	8300 W Sunset Blvd	323-650-9090	$225
Sunset Marquis Hotel	1200 N Alta Loma Rd	310-657-1333	$340
Sunset Tower Hotel	8358 Sunset Blvd	323-654-7100	$325
Travelodge	7051 W Sunset Blvd	323-462-0905	$99
Valadon Hotel	8822 Cynthia St	310-854-1114	$169

Map 3 • Hollywood

Best Inn	1822 N Cahuenga Blvd	323-467-2252	$45
Best Western Hollywood Hills Hotel	6141 Franklin Ave	323-464-5181	$136
Best Western Hollywood Plaza Inn	2011 N Highland Ave	323-851-1800	$110
Comfort Inn & Suites	2010 N Highland Ave	323-874-4300	$100
Dunes Sunset Motel & Coffee	5625 W Sunset Blvd	323-467-5171	$78
Econo Lodge Hollywood	777 Vine St	323-463-5671	$77
French Cottage	6757 W Sunset Blvd	323-464-9144	$50
Guest House international Inn	6700 W Sunset Blvd	323-467-6137	$60
Holiday Inn	2005 N Highland Ave	323-876-8600	$134
Hollywood Celebrity Hotel	1775 Orchid Ave	323-850-6464	$119
Hollywood Center Motel	6720 W Sunset Blvd	323-462-6051	$70
Hollywood Downtowner Motel	5601 Hollywood Blvd	323-464-7191	$60
Hollywood Guest Inn	6364 Yucca St	323-466-0524	$100
Hollywood Hills Hotel Apartments	1999 N Sycamore Ave	323-850-1909	$159
Hollywood International Youth Hostel	6820 Hollywood Blvd	323-463-0797	$17 dorm, $40 private
Hollywood Orchid Suites	1753 Orchid Ave	323-874-9678	$89
Hollywood Roosevelt Hotel	7000 Hollywood Blvd	323-466-7000	$259
Hotel Mark Twain	1622 Wilcox Ave	323-463-2111	$45
La Mirage Inn	1824 N Beachwood Dr	323-464-1824	$80
La Mirage Inn	6020 Franklin Ave	323-464-1824	$80
Las Palmas Hotel	1738 N Las Palmas Ave	323-464-9236	$40
Liberty Hotel	1770 Orchid Ave	323-962-1788	$79
Magic Castle of Hollywood	7025 Franklin Ave	323-851-0800	$160
Motel 6 Hollywood	1738 Whitley Ave	323-464-6006	$60
Orange Drive Manor Hollywood Hostel	1764 N Orange Dr	323-850-0350	$25 shared, $55 private
Renaissance Hollywood Hotel	1755 N Highland Ave	323-856-1200	$199
Rodeway Inn	6826 W Sunset Blvd	323-465-7186	$100
Sunset Inn	6830 W Sunset Blvd	323-466-9053	$50
Trylon Hotel	6515 Franklin Ave	323-851-7036	$55
Vagabond Inn	1133 Vine St	323-466-7501	$79
VIBE Hotel	5920 Hollywood Blvd	323-469-8600	$50
Villa Delle Stelle	6087 Harold Wy	323-876-8100	$285
Vine Lodge Hotel	1818 Vine St	323-464-9661	$50
Vista Hotel	1611 Vista Del Mar St	323-460-6000	$50
Western Plaza Motel	1066 N Wilton Pl	323-871-1126	$60

Map 4 • Los Feliz

Best Value Inn	5265 W Sunset Blvd	323-466-8521	$110
Bon-Air Motel	1727 N Western Ave	323-464-4154	$60
College Hotel	4620 Santa Monica Blvd	323-666-3785	$550/month
Comfort Inn	321 N Vermont Ave	323-665-0344	$110
Coral Sand Hotel	1730 N Western Ave	323-467-5141	$79
Days Inn	5410 Hollywood Blvd	323-463-7171	$81
Economy Inn	5308 W Sunset Blvd	323-466-9191	$55
Gershwin Hotel	5533 Hollywood Blvd	323-464-1131	$57
Harvard House Motel	5251 Hollywood Blvd	323-463-3238	$55
Holiday Inn Express	250 Silver Lake Blvd	213-387-5737	$131
Hollywood City Inn	1615 N Western Ave	323-469-2700	$60
Hollywood Inn Express	5131 Hollywood Blvd	323-663-1243	$105
Hollywood Premiere Motel	5333 Hollywood Blvd	323-466-1691	$65
Hollywood Stars Inn	5435 W Sunset Blvd	323-462-0062	$65
Hotel ROXY Hollywood	1655 N Western Ave	323-463-3106	$45
Ramada Hollywood	1160 N Vermont Ave	323-660-1788	$119
Sanborn GuestHouse	1005 1/2 Sanborn Ave	323-666-3947	$69
Super 8 Motel	1536 N Western Ave	323-467-3131	$69
Travelodge	1401 N Vermont Ave	323-665-5735	$75
Tropicana Inn Motel	5444 Fountain Ave	323-469-4999	$60
Value Inn	5200 W Sunset Blvd	323-666-0692	$45

Map 5 • Silver Lake/Echo Park/Atwater

Best Value Inn	811 N Alvarado St	213-413-0050	$79
Comfort Inn	2717 W Sunset Blvd	213-413-8222	$81
Los Feliz Motel	3101 Los Feliz Blvd	323-667-2567	$79
Olive Motel	2751 W Sunset Blvd	213-413-0300	$42
Super 8 Motel	1341 W Sunset Blvd	213-250-2233	$80

Map 6 • Miracle Mile/Mid-City

Annes Motel	1755 S La Cienega Blvd	310-837-5173	$60
Best Motel	5350 W Olympic Blvd	323-936-6966	$50
Best Western Carlyle Inn	1119 S Robertson Blvd	310-275-4445	$159
Cinema Motel	5274 W Washington Blvd	323-935-1526	$40
Gem Motel	4915 W Washington Blvd	323-934-3027	$55
Grand Motel	1479 S La Cienega Blvd	310-652-3644	$45
La Cienega Motel	1725 S La Cienega Blvd	310-559-1570	$50
Mansfield Motel	5000 W Washington Blvd	323-935-4060	$53
Olympic Motor Lodge	5850 W Olympic Blvd	323-936-1625	$70
Park Cienega Motor Hotel	1777 S La Cienega Blvd	310-837-5366	$50
Relax Inn Motel	1269 S La Brea Ave	323-939-3772	$60
Reno Motel	5136 W Washington Blvd	323-932-8251	$55
Royal Hawaiian Motel	1632 S La Brea Ave	323-937-2049	$55
Sea Way Motel	5961 Venice Blvd	323-933-2467	$55
Star Light Inn	1830 S La Brea Ave	323-932-8100	$60
Wilshire Crest Inn	6301 Orange St	323-936-5131	$82

Map 7 • Hancock Park

Dunes Wilshire Motor Hotel	4300 Wilshire Blvd	323-938-3616	$78
Friendship Motor Inn	1148 Crenshaw Blvd	323-937-1600	$50
Ramada Inn	3900 Wilshire Blvd	213-736-5222	$85
Rotex Hotel	3411 W Olympic Blvd	323-734-7373	$150

Map 8 • Korea Town

2 Normandie Tourist Hotel	605 S Normandie Ave	213-383-1351	$80
Alexandria Motel	300 S Alexandria Ave	213-385-6015	$60
Alvarado Inn Towner Motel	1212 S Alvarado St	213-383-4774	$50
Alvarado Palms Motel	931 S Alvarado St	213-480-8867	$50
Best Value Inn	906 S Alvarado St	213-388-3137	$49
Catalina 8 Inn	812 S Catalina St	213-739-8681	$65
Coronado Inn	682 S Coronado St	213-388-5277	$50
Days Inn	457 S Mariposa Ave	213-380-6910	$65
East West Hotel	3206 W 8th St	213-389-6711	$40
Eastern Hotel	1903 W Olympic Blvd	213-385-4002	$40
Garden Suites Hotel	681 S Western Ave	213-381-6000	$220
JJ Grand Hotel	620 S Harvard Blvd	213-383-3000	$149
LA Hamilton Tourist Hotel	3160 W 8th St	213-384-7768	$60
Lafayette Hotel	2731 Beverly Blvd	213-383-3182	$50
Mariposa Motel	518 S Mariposa Ave	213-388-1433	$60
Motel Inn	2787 W 8th St	213-487-0197	$55
New Seoul Hotel	2666 W Olympic Blvd	213-381-6262	$97
Oasis Motel	2200 W Olympic Blvd	213-385-4191	$55
Oxford Palace Hotel	745 S Oxford Ave	213-389-8000	$160
Park Plaza Hotel	607 S Park View St	213-384-5281	$60
Quality Inn	603 S New Hampshire Ave	213-385-4444	$69
Quality Inn & Suites Downtown	1901 W Olympic Blvd	213-385-7141	$79
Radisson Wilshire Plaza Hotel	3515 Wilshire Blvd	213-381-7411	$179
Rodeway Inn	1904 W Olympic Blvd	213-380-9393	$81
Vermont Motel	1717 S Vermont Ave	323-730-1578	$60
Western Inn	921 S Western Ave	323-733-2168	$75
Wilshire Inn	3400 W 3rd St	213-385-0061	$59

Map 9 • Downtown

Alvarado Inn	355 S Alvarado St	213-484-1883	$120
Barclay Hotel	103 W 4th St	213-626-5231	$40
Best Western Dragon Gate Inn	818 N Hill St	213-617-3077	$113
Best Western Mayfair Hotel	1256 W 7th St	213-484-9789	$89
Bixby Hotel	433 Wall St	213-620-1374	$30
Boyd Hotel	224 Boyd St	213-621-2693	$40
Cecil Hotel	640 S Main St	213-624-4545	$50
City Center Motel	1135 W 7th St	213-627-2581	$45
Comfort Inn Los Angeles	1710 W 7th St	213-616-3000	$85

Hotel	Address	Phone	Price
Courtland Hotel	520 Wall St	213-229-9697	$40
Daimaru Hotel	345 E 1st St	213-972-9208	$50
Days Inn	711 N Main St	213-680-0200	$89
Figueroa Hotel	939 S Figueroa St	213-627-8971	$90
Florence Hotel	310 E 5th St	213-229-9659	$40
Hilton Checkers Hotel	535 S Grand Ave	213-624-0000	$237
Holiday Inn	1020 S Figueroa St	213-748-1291	$159
Hollywood Inn Express	141 N Alvarado St	213-413-6699	$50
Jerry's Motel	285 Lucas Ave	213-481-8181	$65
Kawada Hotel	200 S Hill St	213-621-4455	$119
Knights Inn	1255 W Temple St	213-250-8925	$69
Little Tokyo Hotel	327 E 1st St	213-617-0128	$40
Madison Hotel	423 E 7th St	213-622-1508	$40
Marriott Hotels & Resorts	333 S Figueroa St	213-617-1133	$259
Millennium Biltmore Hotel	506 S Grand Ave	213-624-1011	$169
Milner Hotel	813 S Flower St	213-627-6981	$79
Miyako Inn & Spa	328 E 1st St	213-617-2000	$99
Motel de Ville	1123 W 7th St	213-624-8474	$48
New Otani Hotel & Garden	120 S Los Angeles St	213-629-1200	$189
Nutel Hotel	1906 W 3rd St	213-483-6681	$50
Olive Hotel	750 S Olive St	213-972-8931	$40
Omni Los Angeles Hotel	251 S Olive St	213-617-3300	$249
Paradise Motel	1116 W Sunset Blvd	213-250-9094	$65
Ramada Inn	611 S Westlake Ave	213-483-6363	$85
Royal Pagoda Motel	995 N Broadway	323-223-3381	$60
Royal Viking Motel	2025 W 3rd St	213-353-0619	$55
Sheraton	711 S Hope St	213-488-3500	$189
Standard Hotel	550 S Flower St	213-892-8080	$165
Stillwell Hotel	838 S Grand Ave	213-627-1151	$39
Travel Inn	401 S Westlake Ave	213-484-9306	$70
Westin Bonaventure Hotel	404 S Figueroa St	213-624-1000	$249
Wilshire Grand Hotel & Centre	930 Wilshire Blvd	213-688-7777	$169

Map 10 • Baldwin Hills

Hotel	Address	Phone	Price
Adams Motel	4905 W Adams Blvd	323-731-2165	$55
Baldwin Hills Motor Inn	3020 S La Brea Ave	323-732-0864	$75
Expo Inn	4523 Exposition Blvd	323-731-9293	$45
Jet Inn Motor Hotel	4542 W Slauson Ave	323-295-2544	$50
Universal Inn	3930 W Slauson Ave	323-299-7741	$50

Map 11 • South Central West

Hotel	Address	Phone	Price
Best Value Inn	4122 S Western Ave	323-294-5200	$73
Branco Motel	5501 S Western Ave	323-290-3563	$55
Harvard Motor Inn	1574 W Martin Luther King Jr Blvd	323-298-1018	$55
Mustang Motel	4121 S Western Ave	323-298-0351	$65
Raymona Motel	3211 W Jefferson Blvd	323-735-9077	$45
Sahara Inn	4501 S Vermont Ave	323-235-1904	$45
Santa Barbara Motel	1758 W Martin Luther King Jr Blvd	323-296-2576	$55
Snooty Fox Motor Inn	4120 S Western Ave	323-294-0083	$75

Map 12 • South Central East

Hotel	Address	Phone	Price
Broadway Motel	301 W 49th St	323-231-4303	$50
Casitas Motel	130 E 23rd St	213-747-8342	$40
City Motel	4731 S Figueroa St	323-232-4200	$45
Copacabana Inn	5304 S Figueroa St	323-234-1844	$45
Crown Inn	4760 S Broadway	323-232-2011	$55
Eastsider Motel	2133 S Central Ave	213-748-1048	$45
Radisson Hotel Midtown	3540 S Figueroa St	213-748-4141	$149
Sandpiper Motel	4112 S Central Ave	323-231-0249	$60
Vagabond Inn	3101 S Figueroa St	213-746-1531	$84

Map 13 • Inglewood

Hotel	Address	Phone	Price
Airport Motel	4054 W Century Blvd	310-671-0104	$50
Airport Park View Hotel	3900 W Century Blvd	310-677-8899	$40
American Inn	11025 S Prairie Ave	310-412-7100	$50
Best Western Air Park Hotel	640 W Manchester Blvd	310-677-7378	$90
Best Western Airport Plaza Inn	1730 Centinela Ave	310-568-0071	$90
Best Western Suites Hotel	5005 W Century Blvd	310-677-7733	$109
Cloud Nine Motel	537 W Manchester Blvd	310-674-1386	$55
Comfort Inn & Suites	4922 W Century Blvd	310-671-7213	$99
Crystal Inn	11163 S Prairie Ave	310-412-3888	

Map 13 • Inglewood—*continued*

Econo Lodge	4123 W Century Blvd	310-672-7285	$80
Economy Inn	439 W Manchester Blvd	310-674-8596	$56
Geneva Budget Motel	321 W Manchester Blvd	310-677-9171	$55
Holly Crest Hotel	4027 W Century Blvd	310-673-8612	$40
LA Adventurer All Suite Hotel	4200 W Century Blvd	310-419-0999	$70
La Brea Hotel	524 N La Brea Ave	310-672-1333	$30
Lotus Motel	437 W Manchester Blvd	310-672-5586	$65
Marletta's Motel	4849 W Century Blvd	310-677-7500	$45
Motel 6	5101 W Century Blvd	310-419-1234	$61
Ramada Limited	4300 W Century Blvd	310-419-1011	$79
Rodeway Inn	3940 W Century Blvd	310-672-4570	$65
Royal Century Hotel	4330 W Century Blvd	310-673-2400	$50
Sea Breeze Inn	4307 W Century Blvd	310-674-5444	$45
Super 8 Motel	4238 W Century Blvd	310-672-0740	$69
Tivoli Motor Hotel	4861 W Century Blvd	310-677-9181	$60
Topper Motel	4331 W Century Blvd	310-671-0424	$50
Westfield Inn	4652 W Century Blvd	310-671-6161	$60

Map 14 • Inglewood East/Morningside Park

Anand Motel	10210 S Western Ave	323-418-8488	$45
Atlas Motel	7322 S Western Ave	323-752-7542	$45
Boulevard Motel	6919 S Figueroa St	323-759-9302	$50
Cornett Motel	6345 Crenshaw Blvd	323-751-3227	$50
El Paso Inn	3220 W Florence Ave	323-751-4527	$55
Flight Motel	9501 S Figueroa St	323-777-9105	$45
Hoover Motel	9710 S Hoover St	323-755-9272	$65
Hyde Park Motel	6340 Crenshaw Blvd	323-752-0355	$55
Look Motor Inn	7827 Crenshaw Blvd	323-759-1623	$55
Orchid Motel	10720 S Figueroa St	323-242-9558	$45
Travel Inn Motel	7410 S Vermont Ave	323-778-7575	$50
Twenty-First Century Inn	10104 S Figueroa St	323-777-0477	$45
Western Motel	10411 S Vermont Ave	323-755-2596	$60

Map 15 • Pacific Palisades

Channel Road Inn	219 W Channel Rd	310-459-1920	$190

Map 16 • Brentwood

The Brentwood Inn	12200 W Sunset Blvd	310-476-9981	$219
Hotel Angelina	170 N Church Ln	310-476-6411	$195
Luxe Summit	11461 W Sunset Blvd	310-476-6571	$189

Map 17 • Bel Air/Holmby Hills

Hotel Bel Air	701 Stone Cyn Rd	310-472-1211	$375

Map 18 • Santa Monica

The Ambrose	1255 20th St	310-315-1555	$229
American Motel	1243 Lincoln Blvd	310-458-1411	$75
Bayside Hotel	2001 Ocean Ave	310-396-6000	$99
Best Western Ocean View	1447 Ocean Ave	310-458-4888	$197
Best Western Santa Monica Gateway Hotel	1920 Santa Monica Blvd	310-829-9100	$174
Cal Mar Hotel Suites	220 California Ave	310-395-5555	$159
Doubletree Guest Suites	1707 4th St	310-395-3332	$246
Fairmont Miramar	101 Wilshire Blvd	310-576-7777	$349
Georgian Hotel	1415 Ocean Ave	310-395-9945	$250
Holiday Inn	120 Colorado Ave	310-451-0676	$261
Holiday Motel	1102 Pico Blvd	310-450-9666	$70
Hotel California	1670 Ocean Ave	310-393-2363	$179
Hotel Carmel	201 Broadway	310-451-2469	$129
Hotel Casa Del Mar	1910 Ocean Wy	310-581-5533	$395
Hotel Ocenana	849 Ocean Ave	310-393-0486	$225
Le Merigot Santa Monica Beach	1740 Ocean Ave	310-395-9700	$359
Loews Santa Monica Beach Hotel	1700 Ocean Ave	310-458-6700	$349
Ocean Lodge	1667 Ocean Ave	310-451-4146	$130
Ocean Park Inn	2452 Lincoln Blvd	310-392-3966	$75
Pacific Sands Motel	1515 Ocean Ave	310-395-6133	$105
Palm Motel	2020 14th St	310-452-3861	$70
Radisson Hotel Huntley	1111 2nd St	310-394-5454	$419
Rest Haven Motel	815 Grant St	310-452-3977	$45
Santa Monica Motel	2102 Lincoln Blvd	310-392-6806	$55

Sea Shore Motel & Apartments	2637 Main St	310-392-2787	$95
Seaview Motel	1760 Ocean Ave	310-393-6711	$75
Sheraton Delfina Santa Monica	530 W Pico Blvd	310-399-9344	$249
Shutters on the Beach	1 Pico Blvd	310-458-0030	$445
Travelodge	1525 Ocean Ave	310-451-0761	$145
Viceroy	1819 Ocean Ave	310-260-7500	$391

Map 19 • West LA/Santa Monica East

Best Western Royal Palace & Suites	2528 S Sepulveda Blvd	310-477-9066	$96
Brooks Hotel	1541 Sawtelle Blvd	310-479-9404	$40
Comfort Inn	2815 Santa Monica Blvd	310-828-5517	$119
Days Inn	3007 Santa Monica Blvd	310-829-6333	$98
Holiday Inn Express,	11250 Santa Monica Blvd	310-478-1400	$136
Pavilions Motel	2338 Ocean Park Blvd	310-450-4044	$60
Travelodge	3102 Pico Blvd	310-450-5766	$119
Village Motel	2624 Santa Monica Blvd	310-828-0515	$70
West End Hotel	1538 Sawtelle Blvd	310-444-8990	175/week
Wilshire Motel	12023 Wilshire Blvd	310-478-3545	$90

Map 20 • Westwood/Century City

Beverly Hills Plaza Hotel	10300 Wilshire Blvd	310-275-5575	$155
Century Plaza Hotel	2025 Ave of the Stars	310-228-1234	$329
Courtyard By Marriott	10320 N Olympic Blvd	310-556-2777	$189
Hilgard House Hotel	927 Hilgard Ave	310-208-3945	$239
Holiday Inn Express Hotels	10330 W Olympic Blvd	310-553-1000	$152
Hotel Claremont	1044 Tiverton Ave	310-208-5957	$60
Intercontinantal	2151 Ave of the Stars	310-277-1234	$297
The Little Inn	10604 Santa Monica Blvd	310-475-4422	$60
Royal Palace Westwood	1052 Tiverton Ave	310-208-6677	$104
Royal Santa Monica Motel	10811 Santa Monica Blvd	310-475-3536	$60
Stars Inn	10269 Santa Monica Blvd	310-556-3076	$60
Travelodge	10740 Santa Monica Blvd	310-474-4576	$77
W Hotel	930 Hilgard Ave	310-208-8765	$335
The Westwood Hotel	10740 Wilshire Blvd	310-475-8711	$189

Map 21 • Venice

Best Western Marina Pacific Hotel & Suites	1697 Pacific Ave	310-452-1111	$149
Cadillac Hotel	8 Dudley Ave	310-399-8876	$95
Encore Motel	13432 Washington Blvd	310-823-5066	$60
Golden Star Motel	710 Rose Ave	310-399-1208	$70
Holiday Inn	737 Washington Blvd	310-821-4455	$109
Inn At Venice Beach	327 Washington Blvd	310-821-2557	$149
Jolly Roger Hotel	2904 Washington Blvd	310-822-2904	$85
Lincoln Inn	2447 Lincoln Blvd	310-822-0686	$75
Ramada Inn	3130 Washington Blvd	310-821-5086	$89
Rose Inn	2435 Lincoln Blvd	310-301-7073	$84
Venice Beach Cotel	25 Windward Ave	310-399-7649	$22 shared, $53 private
Venice Beach Hostel	1515 Pacific Ave	310-452-3052	$20 shared, $76 private
Venice Beach House	15 30th Ave	310-823-1966	$145
Venice Beach Suites	1305 Ocean Front Wk	310-396-4559	$107

Map 22 • Mar Vista

Culver Motel	11162 Culver Blvd	310-558-9769	$40
Econo Lodge	11933 W Washington Blvd	310-398-1651	$88
Paradise Motel	11750 W Washington Blvd	310-390-4044	$55
Sunbay Motels	12841 W Washington Blvd	310-306-7081	$69
Super 8 Motel	12664 W Washington Blvd	310-306-8243	$79
Villa Brasil Motel	11740 W Washington Blvd	310-636-0141	$70

Map 23 • Rancho Park/Palms

Crowne Plaza Hotel	1150 S Beverly Dr	310-553-6561	$208
Loews Beverly Hills	1224 S Beverwil Dr	310-277-2800	$249
Marriott Residence Inn	1177 S Beverly Dr	310-228-4100	$239
Royal Westwood Motel	2352 Westwood Blvd	310-475-4551	$67

Map 24 • Culver City

Astro Motel	3850 Sepulveda Blvd	310-398-3815	$60
Circle K Motel	5329 Sepulveda Blvd	310-391-9309	$40
Culver Hotel	9400 Culver Blvd	310-838-7963	$169
Deano's Motel	3868 Sepulveda Blvd	310-390-3511	$50

Map 24 • Culver City—*continued*

Half Moon Motel	3958 Sepulveda Blvd	310-391-5279	$55
Lindblade Hotel	8925 Lindblade St	310-839-1856	550/month
Metro Motel	8846 National Blvd	310-838-4554	$50
Ramada Inn	3930 Sepulveda Blvd	310-390-2189	$110
Sunburst Motel	3900 Sepulveda Blvd	310-398-7523	$79
Travelodge	11180 Washington Pl	310-839-1111	$99
Vista Motel	4900 Sepulveda Blvd	310-390-2014	$59
West End Hotel	3927 Van Buren Pl	310-838-1058	$220/week
Westchester Hotel	5630 Sawtelle Blvd	310-390-6534	$225/week

Map 25 • Marina Del Rey/Westchester West

Best Western Jamaica Bay Inn	4175 Admiralty Wy	310-823-5333	$189
Foghorn Harbor Inn	4140 Via Marina	310-823-4626	$168
Inn At Playa Del Rey	435 Culver Blvd	310-574-1920	$195
Marina Beach Marriott Resort	4100 Admiralty Wy	310-301-3000	$281
Marina Del Rey Courtyard	13480 Maxella Ave	310-822-8555	$219
Marina Del Rey Hotel	13534 Bali Wy	310-301-1000	$139
Marina International Hotel	4200 Admiralty Wy	310-301-2000	$109
Ritz Carlton Hotel	4375 Admiralty Wy	310-823-1700	$359

Map 26 • Westchester/Fox Hills/Ladera Heights

Courtyard by Marriott LAX	6161 W Century Blvd	310-649-1400	$189
Crowne Plaza Los Angeles Arprt	5985 W Century Blvd	310-642-7500	$109
Days Inn	901 W Manchester Blvd	310-649-0800	$67
Embassy Suites Hotel	9801 Airport Blvd	310-215-1000	$161
Extended Stayamerica	6531 S Sepulveda Blvd	310-568-9337	$110
Four Points Barcelo Hotel	5990 Green Valley Cir	310-641-7740	$135
Four Points Hotel By Sheraton	9750 Airport Blvd	310-645-4600	$145
Hampton Inn	10300 S La Cienega Blvd	310-846-3200	$99
Hilton Los Angeles Airport	5711 W Century Blvd	310-410-4000	$208
Holiday Inn	9901 S La Cienega Blvd	310-649-5151	$119
Howard Johnson Hotel LAX	8620 Airport Blvd	310-645-7700	$89
La Quinta Inn	5249 W Century Blvd	310-645-2200	$89
LAX Plaza Hotel	6333 Bristol Pkwy	310-670-3200	$145
Marriott Los Angeles Airport	5855 W Century Blvd	310-641-5700	$229
Radisson Hotel	6225 W Century Blvd	310-670-9000	$149
Radisson Hotel Los Angeles West	6161 W Centinela Ave	310-649-1776	$169
Renaissance Los Angeles Hotel	9620 Airport Blvd	310-337-2800	$199
Sandman Motel	850 W Manchester Blvd	310-649-6500	$49
Sheraton	6101 W Century Blvd	310-642-1111	$179
Super 8 Motel	9250 Airport Blvd	310-670-2900	$69
Travelodge	5547 W Century Blvd	310-649-4000	$80
Westin Los Angeles Airport	5400 W Century Blvd	310-216-5858	$162

Map 27 • El Segundo/Manhattan Beach

Belamar Hotel	3621 N Sepulveda Blvd	310-546-9162	$40
The Belmar	3501 N Sepulveda Blvd	310-750-0300	$182
Comfort Inn	850 N Sepulveda Blvd	310-318-1020	$110
Concord Hotel	221 Concord St	310-322-6116	$130/week
Courtyard By Marriott	2000 E Mariposa Ave	310-322-0700	$179
Doubletree Hotel	1985 E Grand Ave	310-322-0999	$185
El Camino Motel	3301 N Sepulveda Blvd	310-546-5464	$45
Embassy Suites Hotel	1440 E Imperial Ave	310-640-3600	$185
Hacienda Hotel—La Airport	525 N Sepulveda Blvd	310-615-0015	$99
Hi View Inn and Suites	100 S Sepulveda Blvd	310-374-4608	$89
Hilton Garden Inn LAX	2100 E Mariposa Ave	310-726-0100	$180
Holiday Inn Express Hotels	900 N Sepulveda Blvd	310-318-6132	$111
Homestead Studio Suites Hotel	1910 E Mariposa Ave	310-607-4000	$105
LAX Suites Motel	11838 Aviation Blvd	310-643-9905	$60
Marriott Manhattan Beach	1400 Park View Ave	310-546-7511	$249
Marriott Residence Inn	2135 E El Segundo Blvd	310-333-0888	$189
Residence Inn	1700 N Sepulveda Blvd	310-421-3100	$99
Sea View Inn	3400 Highland Ave	310-545-1504	$105
Seahorse Inn	233 N Sepulveda Blvd	310-376-7951	$65
Shade Hotel	1221 N Valley Dr	310-546-4995	$275
Spring Hill Suites Marriott	14620 Aviation Blvd	310-727-9595	$164
Summerfield Suites El Segundo	810 S Douglas St	310-725-0100	$184
Travelodge—LAX South	1804 E Sycamore Ave	310-615-1073	$84
Twin Towers Motel	11706 Aviation Blvd	310-643-5384	$40

Map 28 • Hawthorne

Acacia Inn	4307 W Imperial Hwy	310-674-3110	$50
Ayres Hotel Manhattan Beach	14400 Hindry Ave	310-536-0400	$179
Best Value Inn & Suites	4501 W Imperial Hwy	310-671-6017	$65
Best Western South Bay Hotel	15000 Hawthorne Blvd	310-973-0998	$90
Budget Inn Motel	14815 Hawthorne Blvd	310-675-8523	$50
Colonial Inn	4210 W El Segundo Blvd	310-355-1178	$45
Days Inn	15636 Hawthorne Blvd	310-676-7378	$68
Del Aire Inn	4610 W Imperial Hwy	310-673-4141	$55
Deluxe Motel	13640 Hawthorne Blvd	310-644-1154	$65
Diamond Inn	3735 W Imperial Hwy	310-674-1278	$45
Dream Inn	3201 W Imperial Hwy	310-412-0912	$50
El Rancho Inn	3900 W El Segundo Blvd	310-973-3522	$56
El Segundo Inn	4930 W El Segundo Blvd	310-644-4944	$70
Hawthorne Plaza Inn	12043 Hawthorne Blvd	310-973-3432	$60
Holiday Inn	14814 Hawthorne Blvd	310-676-1111	$189
Hollypark Motel	3928 W Imperial Hwy	310-674-3433	$45
Imperial Motel	4709 W Imperial Hwy	310-671-7700	$60
Kings Motel	3501 W Imperial Hwy	310-674-2196	$45
Manor Motel	4191 W El Segundo Blvd	310-675-9179	$45
Palm Hotel	4207 W El Segundo Blvd	310-644-2346	$175/week
Prairie Motel	15125 Prairie Ave	310-679-6850	$55
Ramada Inn	5250 W El Segundo Blvd	310-536-9800	$91
Tourist Lodge	3649 W Imperial Hwy	310-677-0112	$60
Town Place Suites By Marriott	14400 Aviation Blvd	310-725-9696	$159
Travelers Inn	14808 Hawthorne Blvd	310-675-5228	$70

Map 29 • Hermosa Beach

Beach House Inn at Hermosa	1300 The Strand	310-374-3001	$239
Best Western Galleria Inn	2740 Artesia Blvd	310-370-4353	$86
Grandview Inn	55 14th St	310-374-8981	$130
Hampton Inn & Suites	1530 Pacific Coast Hwy	310-318-7800	$129
Holiday Inn Express Hotel & Suites	125 Pacific Coast Hwy	310-798-9898	$126
Hotel Hermosa	2515 Pacific Coast Hwy	310-318-6000	$119
Quality Inn & Suites	901 Aviation Blvd	310-374-2666	$120
Sea Side Motel	1935 Artesia Blvd	310-376-0430	$75
Sea Sprite Ocean Front Motel	1016 The Strand	310-376-6933	$99

Map 30 • Torrance North

Del Amo Inn	20534 Hawthorne Blvd	310-542-9417	$50
Straybridge Suites	19901 Prairie Ave	310-371-8525	$200

Map 31 • Redondo Beach

Best Western Redondo Beach Inn	1850 S Pacific Coast Hwy	310-540-3700	$111
Best Western Sunrise	400 N Harbor Dr	310-376-0746	$139
Crowne Plaza	300 N Harbor Dr	310-318-8888	$189
Days Inn	4111 Pacific Coast Hwy	310-378-8511	$59
Driftwood Motel	3960 Pacific Coast Hwy	310-375-0511	$50
Homestead Studio Suites Hotel	3995 W Carson St	310-543-0048	$100
Moonlite Inn	625 S Pacific Coast Hwy	310-540-4058	$59
Palos Verdes Inn	1700 S Pacific Coast Hwy	310-316-4211	$51
The Portofino Hotel & Yacht Club	260 Portofino Wy	310-379-8481	$259
Ramada Unlimited	435 S Pacific Coast Hwy	310-540-5998	$84
Redondo Motel	711 S Pacific Coast Hwy	310-540-1888	$65
Redondo Pier Lodge	206 S Pacific Coast Hwy	310-318-1811	$93
Torrance Hilton at South Bay	21333 Hawthorne Blvd	310-540-0500	$161

Map 32 • Torrance South

Bartlett Motel	2364 Pacific Coast Hwy	310-325-0302	$55
Bestall Inn	2065 Pacific Coast Hwy	310-326-8288	$50
Cabrillo Hotel Of Torrance	1913 Cabrillo Ave	310-782-3531	$45
Courtyard By Marriott	2633 Sepulveda Blvd	310-533-8000	$169
Eldorado Coast Hotel	2037 Pacific Coast Hwy	310-534-0700	$55
Extended Stayamerica	3525 Torrance Blvd	310-540-5442	$95
Howard Johnson	3673 Torrance Blvd	310-316-5570	$85
Leo's Motel	1879 Lomita Blvd	310-326-0445	$40
Lomita Motel	2237 Pacific Coast Hwy	310-326-7530	$50
Plaza Hotel	1720 Cabrillo Ave	310-328-4671	$65
Pride Hotel	1806 Cabrillo Ave	310-533-9747	$130/week
Ramada Inn	2880 Pacific Coast Hwy	310-325-0660	$94

Map 32 • Torrance South—*continued*

Residence Inn	3701 Torrance Blvd	310-543-4566	$179
Super 8 Motel	2360 Sepulveda Blvd	310-534-4900	$70
Torrance Marriott	3635 Fashion Wy	310-316-3636	$199
Travelodge Torrance	2448 Sepulveda Blvd	310-539-9888	$82

Map 33 • Highland Park

Casa Lu-An Motel	1045 Colorado Blvd	323-257-6341	$55
Comfort Inn	2300 W Colorado Blvd	323-256-1199	$75
Eagle Rock Motel	7041 N Figueroa St	323-256-5106	$75
Highland Park Motel	4855 York Blvd	323-258-8444	$50
Islander Motel	1460 Colorado Blvd	323-257-8926	$55
Regency Inn	2378 Colorado Blvd	323-257-8168	$65
Rose Bowl Motel	1533 Colorado Blvd	323-258-8033	$50
Welcome Inn	1840 Colorado Blvd	323-256-1673	$65

Map 34 • Pasadena

Artists' Inn	1038 Magnolia St	626-799-5668	$135
Bissell House Bed & Breakfast	201 Orange Grove Ave	626-441-3535	$195
Hilton Pasadena	168 S Los Robles Ave	626-577-1000	$237
Livingstone Hotel & Apartments	139 S Los Robles Ave	626-795-3311	$65
Pasadena Courtyard By Marriot	180 N Fair Oaks Ave	626-403-7600	$219
Pasadena Inn	400 S Arroyo Pkwy	626-795-8401	$70
Ritz Carlton Huntington Hotel	1401 S Oak Knoll Ave	626-568-3900	$299
Sheraton Pasadena Hotel	303 Cordova St	626-449-4000	$199
Westin Pasadena Hotel	191 N Los Robles Ave	626-792-2727	$239

Map 35 • Pasadena East/San Marino

America's Best Value Inn	2860 E Colorado Blvd	626-792-3700	$54
Comfort Inn	2462 E Colorado Blvd	626-405-0811	$84
Kingston Inn	2156 E Colorado Blvd	626-793-9339	$70
Saga Motor Hotel	1633 E Colorado Blvd	626-795-0431	$77
Super 8 Motel	2863 E Colorado Blvd	626-449-3020	$69
Swiss Lodge	2800 E Colorado Blvd	626-449-1122	$45
Travelodge	2131 E Colorado Blvd	626-796-3121	$69
Vagabond Inn	1203 E Colorado Blvd	626-449-3170	$83
Westway Inn-Pasadena	1599 E Colorado Blvd	626-304-9678	$70

Map 36 • Mt. Washington

Triangle Motel	3951 Eagle Rock Blvd	323-255-2109	$60

Map 37 • Lincoln Heights

America Motel	2219 Pasadena Ave	323-227-9339	$45

Map 38 • El Sereno

Alhambra Motel	2800 W Valley Blvd	626-284-0410	$40
Ambassador Inn	2720 W Valley Blvd	626-308-1638	$55
Huntington Premiere Inn	5533 Huntington Dr N	323-221-8828	$50
Super 8 Motel	5350 Huntington Dr S	323-225-2310	$65
Valley Lodge Motel	4949 Valley Blvd	323-222-4949	$50

Map 39 • Alhambra

Alhambra Inn & Suites	2451 W Main St	626-284-5522	$74
Days Inn	15 N 1st St	626-308-0014	$61
Fremont Inn	2221 W Commonwealth Ave	626-300-0003	$93
Hilton Los Angeles-San Gabriel	225 W Valley Blvd	626-270-2700	$180
Lanai Motel	1749 W Valley Blvd	626-282-8421	$40

Map 40 • Boyle Heights

Hotel Antonio	229 N Soto St	323-264-5574	$40
Marengo Inn	2050 Marengo St	323-223-2080	$60
Soto Hotel	402 N Soto St	323-264-3388	$85/week

Map 41 • City Terrace/East LA

Com-On Inn	1560 Monterey Pass Rd	323-263-9888	$45
Vista Motel	4180 City Terrace Dr	323-260-7880	$55

Map 42 • Chatsworth

Comfort Inn	21603 Devonshire St	818-998-8888	$89
Paradise Lodge	20128 Roscoe Blvd	818-341-7200	$55
Radisson Hotel Chatsworth	9777 Topanga Cyn Blvd	818-709-7054	$135
Ramada Inn Chatsworth	21340 Devonshire St	818-998-5289	$89
Staybridge Suites by Intercontinental Hotel	21902 Lassen St	818-773-0707	$150

Map 43 • Granada Hills / Northridge

Extended Stayamerica	19325 Londelius St	818-734-1787	$100

Map 44 • Mission Hills / North Hills

Granada Motel	15543 Rinaldi St	818-366-5901	$50

Map 45 • Canoga Park / Woodland Hills

Best Western Canoga Park Motor	20122 Vanowen St	818-883-1200	$89
Canoga House Motor Hotel	7435 Winnetka Ave	818-341-9700	$65
Extended Stay America	20205 Ventura Blvd	818-710-1170	$90
Holiday Inn Hotels	21101 Ventura Blvd	818-883-6110	$87
Motel 6	7132 De Soto Ave	818-883-6666	$69
Movieland Motel	19335 Ventura Blvd	818-344-5886	$60
St George Motor Inn	19454 Ventura Blvd	818-345-6911	$77

Map 46 • Reseda

Howard Johnson Express Inn	7432 Reseda Blvd	818-344-5702	$69
Tarzana Inn	19170 Ventura Blvd	818-345-9410	$99

Map 47 • Van Nuys

Airtel Plaza Hotel	7277 Valjean Ave	818-997-7676	$139
Best Western Carriage Inn	5525 Sepulveda Blvd	818-787-2300	$125
Cabana Motel	5764 Sepulveda Blvd	818-780-8413	$65
Cinema Motel	6242 Sepulveda Blvd	818-786-3606	$55
El Cortez Motel	5746 Sepulveda Blvd	818-994-1900	$65
Holiday Inn	8244 Orion Ave	818-989-5010	$112
Hyland Motel	7041 Sepulveda Blvd	818-781-2780	$65
Le Rendezvous Motel	6501 Sepulveda Blvd	818-786-1564	$45
Motel 6	15711 Roscoe Blvd	818-894-9341	$50
Panorama Motel	8209 Sepulveda Blvd	818-786-4434	$55
Starlight Cottage	5450 Sepulveda Blvd	818-786-4722	$55
Town House Motel	6957 Sepulveda Blvd	818-782-8800	$65
Travelodge	6909 Sepulveda Blvd	818-787-5400	$80
Voyager Motor Inn	6500 Sepulveda Blvd	818-780-1142	$45

Map 48 • North Hollywood

Comfort Inn	6147 Lankershim Blvd	818-769-6600	$110
Pepper Tree Motel	5909 Lankershim Blvd	818-763-6959	$60
Ritz Motel	6021 Lankershim Blvd	818-769-7520	$55
Silver Saddle Motel	6235 Lankershim Blvd	818-766-5285	$65
Studio Lodge	11254 Vanowen St	818-760-1194	$40
Super 8 Motel	7541 Laurel Cyn Blvd	818-765-9800	$64
Village Inn Motel	7833 Lankershim Blvd	818-764-6007	$45

Map 49 • Burbank

Courtyard Los Angeles—Burbank/Airport	2100 W Empire Ave	818-843-5500	$209
Extended Stayamerica	2200 W Empire Ave	818-567-0952	$135
The Graciela	322 N Pass Ave	818-842-8887	$225
Hilton	2500 N Hollywood Wy	818-843-6000	$245
Quality Inn	2255 N Buena Vista St	818-848-1680	$83
Ramada Inn	2900 N San Fernando Blvd	818-843-5955	$91
Travelodge	1112 N Hollywood Wy	818-845-2408	$79

Map 50 • Burbank East/Glendale West

Anabelle Hotel	2011 W Olive Ave	818-845-7800	$149
Burbank Inn & Suites	180 W Alameda Ave	818-842-1114	$219
Glen Capri Motel	6700 San Fernando Rd	818-244-8434	$60
Griffith Park Motel	1634 Victory Blvd	818-244-5071	$45
Holiday Inn	150 E Angeleno Ave	818-841-4770	$143

Map 50 • Burbank East/Glendale West—*continued*

Homestead Studio Suites Hotel	1377 W Glenoaks Blvd	818-956-6665	$100
Olive Manor Motel	924 W Olive Ave	818-842-5215	$70
Providencia Motels	108 E Providencia Ave	818-842-6974	$50
Safari Inn	1911 W Olive Ave	818-845-8586	$110
Victory Motel Inn	1722 Victory Blvd	818-242-7052	$60

Map 51 • Glendale South

Best Western Inn	2911 Colorado Blvd	323-256-7711	$96
Brandwood Hotel	339 1/2 N Brand Blvd	818-244-3820	$75
Chariot Inn Motel	1118 E Colorado St	818-507-9600	$65
Days Inn	450 W Pioneer Dr	818-956-0202	$80
Econo Lodge	1437 E Colorado St	818-246-8367	$75
El Rio Motel	1515 E Colorado St	818-243-3157	$60
Glen Capri Inn & Suites	326 E Colorado St	818-246-7401	$70
Glendale Lodge	1510 E Colorado St	818-507-6688	$91
Glendale Motel	1523 E Colorado St	818-243-7126	$60
Golden Key	123 W Colorado St	818-247-0111	$104
Hilton	100 W Glenoaks Blvd	818-956-5466	$239
Motel Sakura-Glendale	1500 E Colorado St	818-243-8999	$75
Rodeway Inn	200 W Colorado St	818-246-7331	$70
Tropico Motel	401 W Chevy Chase Dr	818-242-5098	$46
Vagabond Inn	120 W Colorado St	818-240-1700	$84

Map 52 • Tarzana / Woodland Hills

AKU Inn	21830 Ventura Blvd	818-340-1000	$60
Comfort Inn Woodland Hills	20157 Ventura Blvd	818-347-8080	$87
Hilton & Towers Woodland Hills	6360 Canoga Ave	818-595-1000	$249
Marriott Hotels Resorts Suites	21850 Oxnard St	818-887-4800	$229
Super 8 Canoga Park	7631 Topanga Cyn Blvd	818-883-8888	$73
Warner Center Hilton & Tower	6320 Canoga Ave	818-596-4500	$160
Warner Gardens Motel	21706 Ventura Blvd	818-992-4426	$65

Map 53 • Encino

Tokyo Princess Inn	17448 Ventura Blvd	818-788-3820	$70

Map 54 • Sherman Oaks West

777 Motor Inn	4781 Sepulveda Blvd	818-788-3200	$53
Best West Inn	15485 Ventura Blvd	818-981-0500	$84
Courtyard by Marriott	15433 Ventura Blvd	818-981-5400	$209

Map 55 • Sherman Oaks East

Days Inn	12933 Ventura Blvd	818-789-6900	$76
Park Motel	12963 Ventura Blvd	818-501-9292	$65
Sportsmen's Lodge Hotel	12825 Ventura Blvd	818-769-4700	$152

Map 56 • Studio City/Valley Village

Best Western Inn	12600 Riverside Dr	818-763-9141	$149
Beverly Garland's Holiday Inn	4222 Vineland Ave	818-980-8000	$153
Carlton Motor Lodge	11811 Ventura Blvd	818-763-3515	$65
Colony Inn	4917 Vineland Ave	818-763-2787	$119
El Patio Inn	11466 Ventura Blvd	818-508-5828	$73
Studio City Inn	11733 Ventura Blvd	818-766-9599	$55

Map 57 • Universal City/Toluca Lake

Best Western	3910 W Riverside Dr	818-842-1900	$148
Holiday Inn Express Hotels	3241 Cahuenga Blvd W	323-845-1600	$128
Holiday Lodge Motel	3901 W Riverside Dr	818-843-1121	$80
Nite Inn	10612 Ventura Blvd	818-508-8022	$68
Sheraton Universal Hotel	333 Universal Hollywood Dr	818-980-1212	$199
Studio Place Inn	10740 Ventura Blvd	818-760-0555	$45
Universal City Hilton & Towers	555 Universal Hollywood Dr	818-506-2500	$179
Universal City Inn	10730 Ventura Blvd	818-760-8737	$79

As a local, you know of the many advantages to living in Los Angeles. Right up there with the ability to get a burger with avocado on every corner and the possibility of Christmas tree shopping in flip-flops is the abundance and proximity of neighborhood Farmers Markets. Sure, most places have Farmers Markets these days, but not like us Angelenos. Every day there is a market happening somewhere in the city, and each market has its own flavor and cultural or ethnic twist.

Vendors at the **Alhambra Farmers Market (Map 39)**, which caters to a predominantly Chinese population, carry vegetables and fruits you won't see on the Westside; the **Silver Lake (Map 4)** market is younger and funkier, offering Guatemalan crafts and leather goods. **Venice (Map 21)** is about food, but also features live music and pony rides for the kids (the latter occasionally picketed by local PETA activists). Both **South Pasadena (Map 34)** and **West Hollywood (Map 2)** are laid-back and small-town. The motherlode is to be found in **Hollywood (Map 3)**. On Sunday mornings, the intersection of Selma and Ivar explodes with orchids, the freshest veggies, and lively drum circles. Make sure to save time for the pupusas.

As the grandmama of them all, the **Santa Monica Wednesday Farmers Market (Map 18)**, is almost as impressive, where you can buy organic Heritage tomatoes a half a block from the Pacific Ocean. Chances are you'll also be rubbing shoulders with area chefs and celebrities. This market carries the largest selection of organic foods in the LA area and is worth the trip for the atmosphere and location alone. Check out what's in season before you go by tuning into KCRW's *Good Food*—they broadcast live reports from the market every weekend. Bon appetit.

Farmers Markets	*Address*	*Map*
Beverly Hills (Sun, 9 am–1 pm)	9300 Civic Center Dr	1
Melrose Place (Sun, 9 am–2 pm)	Melrose Pl & N Croft Ave	2
West Hollywood (Mon, 9 am–2 pm)	N Vista St & Fountain Ave	2
West Hollywood (Thurs, 2 pm–7 pm)	647 N San Vicente Blvd	2
Hollywood (Sun, 8 am–1 pm)	Ivar Ave & Selma Ave	3
Sears Parking Lot (Wed, 12:30-5:30)	5601 Santa Monica Blvd	3
Silver Lake Farmers Market (Sat, 8 am–1 pm)	3700 W Sunset Blvd	4
Atwater Village (Sun, 10 am–2 pm)	3250 Glendale Blvd	5
La Cienega Farmers Market (Thurs, 3 pm–7 pm)	1801 La Cienega Blvd	6
Larchmont Farmers Market (Sun, 10 am–2 pm)	N Larchmont Blvd & Beverly Blvd	7
Wilshire Center (Fri, 11:30 am–3 pm)	S Mariposa Ave & Wilshire Blvd	8
Little Tokyo (Tues, 10 am-2 pm)	E 2nd St & S San Pedro St	9
Los Angeles-7th & Figueroa (Thurs, Fri, Sat, 10 am–4 pm)	735 S Figueroa St	9
Los Angeles-Chinatown (Thurs, 4 pm–8 pm)	727 N Hill St	9
Leimert Park Village (Sat, 9 am–2 pm)	W 43rd St & Degnan Blvd	11
Los Angeles-Harambee (Sat, 10 am–4 pm)	Crenshaw Blvd & W Slauson Ave	11
St Agnes Catholic Church (Wed; Jun–Aug, 1 pm-6 pm; Sept–May, 2 pm–5 pm)	1432 W Adams Blvd	11
Los Angeles Central Ave (Sat, 9 am–1 pm)	43rd St & Central Ave	12
Pacific Palisades (Sun, 8 am–1:30 pm)	Swarthmore Ave & W Sunset Blvd	15
Brentwood (Sun, 9 am–1 pm)	S Gretna Green Wy & San Vicente Blvd	16
Farmers Market (Wed, 9 am–2 pm; Sat, 8:30 am–1 pm)	Arizona Ave & 2nd St	18
Santa Monica Saturday Organic (Sat, 8:30–1 pm)	Arizona Ave & 3rd St Prom	18
Santa Monica (Sun, 9:30 am–1 pm)	Ocean Park Blvd & Main St	18
Santa Monica Pico (Sat, 8 am–1 pm)	Pico Blvd & Cloverfield Blvd	19
West LA Civic (Sun, 9 am–2 pm)	1645 Corinth Ave	19
Farmers Market-Century City (Thurs, 11:30 am–3 pm)	Constellation Blvd & Ave of the Stars	20
Westwood Village (Thurs, 1 pm–7 pm)	Weyburn Ave & Westwood Blvd	20
Venice (Fri, 7 am–11 am)	Venice Blvd & Venice Wy	21
Culver City (Tues, 2 pm–7 pm)	Culver Blvd & Main St	24
Westchester (Wed, 8:30 am–1 pm)	W 87th St & Truxton Ave	26
Farmers Market-El Segundo (Thurs, 3pm–7pm)	Main St & E Pine Ave	27
Hermosa Beach (Fri, 12 pm–4 pm)	Valley Dr b/w 10th St & 8th St	29
Redondo Beach-Harbor Dr (Thurs, 8 am–1 pm)	N Harbor Dr & W Torrance Blvd	31
Torrance (Tues, 8 am–12 pm; Sat, 8 am–1 pm)	2200 Crenshaw Blvd	32
Eagle Rock Farmers Market (Fri 5 am–8:30 pm)	2100 Merton Ave	33
Pasadena Villa Park (Tues, 9 am–1 pm)	363 E Villa St	34
South Pasadena (Thurs 4 pm–8 pm)	Meridian Ave & Mission St	34
Pasadena Victory Park (Sat, 8:30 am–1 pm)	Paloma St & E Sierra Madre Blvd	35
Alhambra (Sun, 8:30 am–1 pm)	S Monterey St b/w E Main St & E Bay State St	39
Chatsworth (Sat, 8 am–1 pm)	Devonshire St & Canoga Ave	42
Northridge (Wed, 5 pm–9 pm)	9301 Tampa Ave	43
Encino (Sun, 8 am–1 pm)	17400 Victory Blvd	46
Tarzana (Sun, 8 am–12 pm)	19130 Ventura Blvd	46
Burbank (Sat, 8 am–12:30 pm)	E Olive Ave & S Glenoaks Blvd	50
Farmers Market-Glendale (Thurs, 9:30 am–1 pm)	100 N Brand Blvd	51
Woodland Hills (Sat, 8 am–4 pm)	6200 block of Topanga Cyn Blvd	52
Studio City Farmers Market (8 am–1 pm)	Ventura Pl b/w Laurel Cyn Blvd & Ventura Blvd	56

Overview

These days, Los Angeles has a good number of dog parks in which your beloved pooch can romp and play, and the list is growing--you can even find areas for the big bow-wows like German Shepherds and Mastiffs. For the little guys, like the feisty Yorkies or the ever-snorting pugs, there's the small dog park. If you and your canine buddy are making your way out to a fenced grassy area for a play date, consider a few rules to make everyone's life easier:

1. Make sure your four-legged child plays nice with the other kids.
2. If your dog drops the poop, you get to scoop. (Heck, most dog parks provide you with a poop bag and trashcan to make it even easier on you.)
3. If your dog is in heat, keep her at home.
4. If your dog generally snarls, snaps, and likes to sink his teeth into live meat, that means he shouldn't be socializing at a dog park.
5. If the sign says "for dogs up to 30 pounds" don't bring your Great Dane in—even if you swear she's well trained.
6. If your dog isn't spayed, neutered, or current with his vaccinations, it's best not to bring him.

We've compiled our own list of dog parks for you to scour. Each park has its own set of specific rules, so remember to read the signs when you enter.

For more information online, a great website to check is www.dogfriendly.com. It provides loads of information on dog-friendly parks, accommodations, attractions, restaurants, and retail stores. Try dogzone.org for all things canine in Southern California, including local dog parks and news. If you're into inflicting tutus upon your dog and parading her around on Halloween, they have information on that, too. Two other helpful websites can be found at www.laparks.org and www.dogpark.com.

The Boneyard, Culver City Dog Park

End of Duquesne in Culver City Park (South of Jefferson Blvd), Culver City

This place has been in the works since 2001, and as of April 2006, it has officially opened for public use. Just over an acre in size, this dog park has space designated for both big and little dogs. It's open every day of the week with no official hours except dawn to dusk. Bring your tennis balls and doggy bags, but leave the cigarettes at home. Water is provided at the doggie drinking fountains.

El Segundo Dog Park

600 E Imperial Ave, El Segundo

Located near LAX, you and Buster can fling Frisbees while watching the planes go by. Just be careful where you're walking while you're looking up. There are two areas: one for the little guys, 30 pounds and under, and one for the big boys, 31 pounds and up. Parking is a sure bet on the street adjacent to the park. Poop bags are provided for your convenience, along with trash receptacles. And don't worry all the bonding and frolicking will give you cotton mouth: they provide public drinking fountains for us two-legged folks and a lower model for the four-legged ones.

Long Beach Recreation Dog Park

5201 E 7th St (Cross Street is Park Ave), Long Beach

Ah, Long Beach: your dog finally has nearly two acres of fenced-in area in which to play. With separate areas for big dogs and little dogs, there's room for everyone's ego. The park is open from 6 am until 10 pm, and you and your canine can make a drink pit stop at the watering stations. Everyone's jonesing to get into this park, so if you're hard-up for play buddies for your dog (or, hey, for yourself) and you're in the area, do yourself a favor and stop here.. Want to strike up a convo with the hottie toting the Italian Greyhound? You can mention that this park was a set location for the 2005 Diane Lane and John Cusack film, *Must Love Dogs*.

Laurel Canyon Park

8260 Mulholland Dr (near Laurel Canyon Blvd), Studio City, 818-769-4415

Laurel Canyon Park boasts three acres of off-leash space in a fenced-in area. Dogs must be leashed between 10 am and 3 pm, but it's doggie anarchy between 6 am and 10 am and again from 3 pm until dusk. Other amenities include free parking, a small fenced-in children's play area, and a hot dog stand!

This is a spacious dog park, but it has drainage problems, so keep the towels handy, because your dog's going to come home fairly filthy; nonetheless, Laurel Canyon Park remains a popular place for dog lovers, and it attracts a healthy clot of celebrity pet owners. You're more likely to have a star sighting here than at the Chateau Marmont.

Silver Lake Recreation Center

1850 W Silver Lake Dr, Los Angeles, 323-644-3946

Open from 6 am until 10 pm, the Rec Center features 1.25 acres of off-leash running room. The only parking available is on the street. Silver Lake Recreation Center is a well-known meeting place for pooch owners, so if you're new to town and looking to make new friends with excellent fashion and intimidating scenester associations, take your dog down for a run. Just be mindful—the fastidious regulars here will be quick to bark at you if you don't securely shut the gates. Traffic tends to pick up around the curves, and it'd take only seconds for someone's beloved to leap from sanctuary to tragedy.

Runyon Canyon Park

2000 N Fuller Ave (north of Franklin Ave), Hollywood, 323-666-5046

Located in Hollywood, Runyon Canyon Park is almost completely undeveloped. While it doesn't have a fenced-in dog play area, dogs are permitted to roam the hiking trails unleashed, as long as they're with their owners. Within the 160-acre park, there are several hiking trails of varying difficulty with amazing views. You and your pooch can break a sweat together and enjoy the scenery next to a host of celebrities and their own canine buddies.

Westminster Dog Park

1234 Pacific Ave, Venice, 310-396-1615

This park features a fenced-in area with off-leash space for both large dogs and small dogs (under 25 lbs). Open from 6 am until 10 pm, you can usually find a spot in the lot adjacent to the dog park.

Barrington Dog Park

333 S Barrington Ave, Los Angeles, 310-476-4866

This 1.5-acre dog park located in Brentwood is open daily from 5 am to 10:30 pm and closes for maintenance on Tuesday mornings from 6 am to 10 am. The park is off-leash, fenced-in, and features separate sections for dogs big and small. The Friends of Barrington Dog Park maintain a website at www.fobdp.org that lists doggie resources, park news and events, as well as a photo gallery of the furry friends who frequent the park.

Sepulveda Basin Off-Leash Dog Park

17550 Victory Blvd, Encino, 818-756-7667

Featuring a five-acre off-leash area with half an acre for small pooches, Sepulveda Basin Dog Park is open daily from sunrise to sunset, except Friday mornings when it opens at 11 am. On-site parking can accommodate up to 100 cars. Whatever you do, avoid parking on White Oak Avenue or Victory Boulevard at all times, as ticketing agents here are eagle-eyed and vigilant. (Getting a ticket is a matter of "when," not "if.") Check out Randy's Sepulveda Basin Dog Park page at www.dog-park.com.

Griffith Park Dog Park

North end of John Ferraro Soccer Field on North Zoo Dr, Los Angeles, 323-913-4688

Griffith Park has its own dog park with compartmentalized areas for dogs big and little to roam off-leash. Open from 5 am to 10:30 pm every day of the week, the park has troughs to keep the dogs well-hydrated and a parking area for 40 cars. If you can't get enough outdoor space for your dog, explore the rest of Griffith Park. The trails across from the observatory are pro-dog, and you can even take your dog to the roof of the observatory via the outside stairs (though the dog's got to be on a leash). The one-mile train ride off Crystal Springs allows dogs onboard (accompanied by an adult, of course). We suggest that you pick up a map at the Ranger's Station (Crystal Spring and Griffith Park Drive) to check which trails allow dogs.

Beaches

While dogs, leashed or not, are prohibited from places like Venice Beach and the Ocean Front Walk, there are still some dog-friendly beaches and a core group of volunteer vigilantes fighting to keep it that way. Huntington Dog Beach (PCH and Golden West Street, www.dogbeach.org) is a beautiful one-mile stretch of beach that allows dogs on leashes, providing their owners pick up after them. The only place dogs are allowed off-leash is in the water, under supervision. Leo Carrillo State Beach (PCH 28 miles north of Santa Monica) also allows leashed dogs, but there are restrictions about where dogs can play—check the signs carefully before embarking on a beach adventure with your dog. Redondo Beach Dog Park is located away from the foreshore next to Dominguez Park (200 Flagler Lane and 190th Street, www.rbdogpark.com). A fenced-in area, Redondo Beach Dog Park has play spaces for large and small dogs. Long Beach has almost 3 acres of leash-free beach fun for dogs, located in the revitalized Belmont Shore area. Look for the signs marking the designated areas between Roycroft and Argonne Avenues.

Face it: pulling out a shiny new MacBook at your local Starbucks has a definite brag factor to it and, like it or not, automatically lumps you in with the hip crowd. So whether your laptop is just a fashion accessory to compliment your Jimmy Choos or whether you actually do use the infernal machine for work, LA is the place for you: WiFi connections abound around town and are mostly free. Chances are you'll find a friendly WiFi sign in most coffee shop windows, like at the **Sabor y Cultura (Map 3)** in Hollywood, **Groundwork** in Hollywood **(Map 3)** and Downtown **(Map 9),** and **Bourgeois Pig (Map 3)** in Hollywood. Or, for the defiantly autonomous, most of the Los Angeles Public Library branches (www.lapl.org) are wireless. Wi-Fi hotspots can be found in the most unlikely of places around the city: Santa Monica's **Krispy Kreme (Map 18)** and Hollywood's venerable dive bar **Boardner's (Map 3)** are all wireless**.** Even downtown's Pershing Square is wireless. A noble gesture, yes, but the services are lost on the homeless population who most often frequent the park.

T-Mobile allows you to "get more" at a price by offering high-speed wireless broadband Internet service in public locations such as Starbucks, Borders, FedEx Kinko's, Hyatt Hotels & Resorts, Red Roof Inn, and select airport and airport clubs. Access prices vary; consult www.hotspot.t-mobile.com for details. LAX offers Wi-Fi in certain terminals, as do several hotels including downtown's **Marriott (Map 9)**, the **Chateau Marmont (Map 2)** in West Hollywood, and LAX's **Courtyard (Map 26)**.

Check www.wififreespot.com/ca.html or www.wi-fihotspotlist.com for a complete list of local Wi-Fi opportunities—or if you don't find this morally objectionable, you could always try to tap into someone's network for free. Then again, if you're in LA, you most likely tossed your morals out the window somewhere south of Sunset.

WiFi	*Address*	*Phone*	*Map*
Aloha Island Coffee Company	153 S Beverly Dr	310-786-8257	1
Coffee Bean & Tea Leaf	233 S Beverly Dr	310-274-7801	1
Coffee Bean & Tea Leaf	445 N Beverly Dr	310-278-1865	1
It's Coffee Lovers Time	468 N Camden Dr	310-860-7451	1
Abbot's Habit Hollywood	7554 W Sunset Blvd	323-512-5278	2
At Coffee Shop	7200 Melrose Ave	323-938-9985	2
Buzz Coffee	7623 Beverly Blvd	323-634-7393	2
Café Marco	8200 Santa Monica Blvd	323-650-7742	2
Coffee Bean & Tea Leaf	300 S La Cienega Blvd	310-360-9777	2
Coffee Bean & Tea Leaf	5979 W 3rd St	323-934-7277	2
Coffee Bean & Tea Leaf	6333 W 3rd St	323-857-0461	2
Coffee Bean & Tea Leaf	7235 Beverly Blvd	323-934-1449	2
Coffee Bean & Tea Leaf	7502 Melrose Ave	323-782-0084	2
Coffee Bean & Tea Leaf	7915 W Sunset Blvd	323-851-8392	2
Coffee Bean & Tea Leaf	8500 Beverly Blvd	310-659-7330	2
Coffee Bean & Tea Leaf	8735 Santa Monica Blvd	310-659-8207	2
Coffee Bean & Tea Leaf	8789 W Sunset Blvd	310-659-1890	2
Coffee Bean & Tea Leaf	8793 Beverly Blvd	310-659-4592	2
Coffee Station	7801 Melrose Ave	323-653-2459	2
Creative City Café	7310 Santa Monica Blvd	323-851-1316	2
Cyber Java Internet Store	7080 Hollywood Blvd	323-466-5600	2
Dialog Coffee & Bakery	8766 Holloway Dr	310-289-1630	2
Insomnia	7286 Beverly Blvd	323-931-4943	2
Tully's Coffee	8631 W 3rd St	310-657-6466	2
101 Coffee Shop	6145 Franklin Ave	323-467-1175	3
Bourgeois Pig	5931 Franklin Ave	323-464-6008	3
Caffe Etc	6371 Selma Ave	323-464-8824	3
Coffee Bean & Tea Leaf	6255 W Sunset Blvd	323-962-7078	3
Coffee Bean & Tea Leaf	6922 Hollywood Blvd	323-467-7785	3
Sabor y Cultura	5625 Hollywood Blvd	323-466-0481	3
Stir Crazy Coffee Shop	6903 Melrose Ave	323-934-4656	3
Casbah Café	3900 W Sunset Blvd	323-664-7000	4
Coffee Bean & Tea Leaf	2081 Hillhurst Ave	323-913-3457	4
Lollicup	5259 Hollywood Blvd	323-216-7397	4
Mailbox Café	4845 Fountain Ave	323-953-7545	4
Night in Tunisia	710 N Heliotrope Dr	323-664-0600	4
Chango	1559 Echo Park Ave	213-977-9161	5
Kaldi Coffee & Tea	3147 Glendale Blvd	323-660-6005	5
Silverlake Coffee	2388 Glendale Blvd	323-913-0388	5
Backdoor Boba	5484 Wilshire Blvd	323-933-4020	6
Coffee Bean & Tea Leaf	1845 S La Cienega Blvd	310-815-1255	6
Coffee Bean & Tea Leaf	8328 Wilshire Blvd	323-852-9988	6

WiFi—*continued*	*Address*	*Phone*	*Map*
Café Americano	4001 Wilshire Blvd	213-427-3637	7
Coffee Bean & Tea Leaf	135 N Larchmont Blvd	323-469-4984	7
Coffeecana	3959 Wilshire Blvd	213-389-2838	7
Café de Flora	210 N Western Ave	323-960-0181	8
Coffee Break	363 S Western Ave	213-382-8802	8
Banquette Café	400 S Main St	213-626-2768	9
Café Take 5	328 E 1st St	213-621-3004	9
Coffee Bean & Tea Leaf	210 E Olympic Blvd	213-749-5746	9
Coffee Bean & Tea Leaf	601 W 5th St	213-689-8087	9
Coffee Bean & Tea Leaf	801 W 7th St	213-622-9748	9
Corner Bakery Café	801 S Figueroa St	213-239-0424	9
Gourmet Coffee Wherhouse Downtown	811 Traction Ave	213-626-8650	9
Groundwork Coffee	108 W 2nd St	213-620-9668	9
Lost Souls Café	124 W 4th St	213-617-7006	9
Tribal Café	1651 W Temple St	213-483-4458	9
Boba Loca	3617 S Vermont Ave	323-766-2622	11
Coffee Bean & Tea Leaf	3396 W Century Blvd	310-412-5083	14
Coffee Bean & Tea Leaf	15278 Antioch St	310-230-2587	15
Coffee Bean & Tea Leaf	11698 San Vicente Blvd	310-442-1019	16
The Coral Tree Café	11645 San Vicente Blvd	310-979-8733	16
Coffee Bean & Tea Leaf	1312 3rd St Prom	310-394-9737	18
Coffee Bean & Tea Leaf	1426 Montana Ave	310-453-2093	18
Coffee Bean & Tea Leaf	1804 Lincoln Blvd	310-581-7991	18
Coffee Bean & Tea Leaf	200 Santa Monica Blvd	310-260-0044	18
Coffee Bean & Tea Leaf	2901 Main St	310-392-1406	18
Coffee Bean & Tea Leaf	380 Santa Monica Pier	n/a	18
Coffee Bean & Tea Leaf	829 Wilshire Blvd	310-576-0560	18
Infuzion Café	1149 3rd St	310-393-9985	18
Starbucks Coffee and Hear Music	1429 3rd St Prom	310-319-9527	18
Talking Stick	1630 Ocean Park Blvd	310-450-6052	18
Velocity Café	2127 Lincoln Blvd	310-314-3368	18
Coffee Bean & Tea Leaf	3150 Ocean Park Blvd	310-396-6706	19
Lollicup	2012 Sawtelle Blvd	213-842-2898	19
The Office	256 26th St	310-917-4455	19
Tanner's Coffee Company	11901 Santa Monica Blvd	310-479-4533	19
Unurban	3301 Pico Blvd	310-315-0056	19
Boba Loca	10946 Weyburn Ave	310-443-8911	20
Coffee Bean & Tea Leaf	1001 Gayley Ave	310-208-1991	20
Coffee Bean & Tea Leaf	10401 Santa Monica Blvd	310-234-8411	20
Coffee Bean & Tea Leaf	11049 Santa Monica Blvd	310-473-6618	20
Coffee Bean & Tea Leaf	1500 Westwood Blvd	310-470-4226	20
Coffee Bean & Tea Leaf	1940 Century Park E	310-553-5254	20
Coffee Bean & Tea Leaf	950 Westwood Blvd	310-208-8018	20
Coffee Zinio	1731 Westwood Blvd	310-575-9999	20
Abbot's Habit	1401 Abbot Kinney Blvd	310-399-1171	21
The Cow's End	34 Washington Blvd	310-574-1080	21
Rumor Mill	11739 W Washington Blvd	310-397-5400	22
Coffee Bean & Tea Leaf	10800 W Pico Blvd	310-441-5918	23
Coffee Bean & Tea Leaf	10897 W Pico Blvd	310-441-1705	23
Coffee Bean & Tea Leaf	3470 S Sepulveda Blvd	310-313-0259	23
Synergy Café	4455 Overland Ave	310-559-8868	24
Tanner's Coffee	4342 Sepulveda Blvd	310-636-2727	24
Coffee Bean & Tea Leaf	13020 Pacific Prom	310-862-5725	25
Coffee Bean & Tea Leaf	13420 Maxella Ave	310-823-0858	25
Tanner's Coffee	200 Culver Blvd	310-574-2739	25
Eurotal	500 World Wy	310-645-2121	26
Coffee Bean & Tea Leaf	3008 N Sepulveda Blvd	310-546-3359	27
Coffee Bean & Tea Leaf	321 Manhattan Beach Blvd	310-545-2827	27
Coffee Attic	3901 Inglewood Ave	310-973-1900	28

WiFi—*continued*	*Address*	*Phone*	*Map*
Coffee Bean & Tea Leaf	1133 Artesia Blvd	310-374-9396	29
Coffee Bean & Tea Leaf	1227 Hermosa Ave	310-379-9249	29
Coffee Bean & Tea Leaf	1617 Pacific Coast Hwy	310-316-2416	29
Java Man	157 Pier Ave	310-379-7209	29
Planet Earth Eco Café	509 Pier Ave	310-318-1888	29
Coffee Bean & Tea Leaf	20301 Hawthorne Blvd	310-542-5401	30
Catalina Coffee Company	126 N Catalina Ave	310-318-2499	31
Catalina Coffee Company	126 N Catalina Ave	310-318-2499	31
Coffee Bean & Tea Leaf	21300 Hawthorne Blvd	310-792-8630	31
Coffee Cartel	1820 S Catalina Ave	310-316-6554	31
Coffee Bean & Tea Leaf	25345 Crenshaw Blvd	310-530-5443	32
The Coffee Table	1958 Colorado Blvd	323-255-2200	33
Bamboo Tea House	700 E Colorado Blvd	626-577-0707	34
Coffee Bean & Tea Leaf	18 S Fair Oaks Ave	626-449-5499	34
Coffee Bean & Tea Leaf	415 S Lake Ave	626-744-9370	34
Coffee Bean & Tea Leaf	700 S Fair Oaks Ave	626-403-2141	34
Coffee Tree	696 E Colorado Blvd	626-796-8256	34
Equator Coffee House	22 Mills Pl	626-564-8656	34
Jones Coffee Roasters	537 S Raymond Ave	626-564-9291	34
Kitty's Café	109 E Union St	626-795-2856	34
Coffee Club	12 Harkness Ave	626-683-8863	35
Coffee Bean & Tea Leaf	9 E Main St	626-570-1494	39
Lollicup	228 W Valley Blvd	626-308-1880	39
Coffee Bean & Tea Leaf	209 S Mednik Ave	323-263-9317	41
Barclays Coffee & Tea	8976 Tampa Ave	818-885-7744	43
Coffee Bean & Tea Leaf	18705 Devonshire St	818-360-8299	43
Muddhouse Coffee	9255 Reseda Blvd	818-886-5123	43
Perks	9028 Balboa Blvd	818-893-6507	44
Coffee Bean & Tea Leaf	19732 Ventura Blvd	818-346-4863	45
Coffee Bean & Tea Leaf	21801 Oxnard St	818-888-6321	45
Coffee Bean & Tea Leaf	5780 Canoga Ave	818-348-2609	45
Coffee Junction	19221 Ventura Blvd	818-342-3405	45
Coffee Bean & Tea Leaf	18505 Ventura Blvd	818-776-1178	46
Peet's	18973 Ventura Blvd	818-401-0263	46
Bobo Loca	12901 Sherman Wy	818-764-2622	48
Boba Loca	148 N San Fernando Blvd	818-842-0406	50
Coffee Bean & Tea Leaf	340 N San Fernando Blvd	818-842-2394	50
Krispy Kreme Doughnuts	1521 N Victory Pl	818-955-9015	50
Coffee Bean & Tea Leaf	300A N Glendale Ave	818-242-4074	51
Just Coffee	1010 N Glendale Ave	818-291-0240	51
Sidewalk Café	901 W Glenoaks Blvd	818-246-1000	51
Urartu Coffee	119 N Maryland Ave	818-242-9666	51
Coffee Bean & Tea Leaf	21851 Ventura Blvd	818-716-7981	52
Coffee Bean & Tea Leaf	17301 Ventura Blvd	818-906-9557	53
Coffee Bean & Tea Leaf	16101 Ventura Blvd	818-386-0935	54
Coffee Bean & Tea Leaf	12930 Ventura Blvd	818-783-8068	55
Espresso Grounded	14241 Ventura Blvd	818-501-0600	55
Lulu's Beehive	13203 Ventura Blvd	818-986-2233	55
Lulu's Beehive	13203 Ventura Blvd	818-986-2233	55
Amsterdam Café	10905 Magnolia Blvd	818-506-1938	56
Coffee Bean & Tea Leaf	12050 Ventura Blvd	818-506-4620	56
Coffee Bean & Tea Leaf	12501 Ventura Blvd	818-763-7271	56
Coffee Fix	12508 Moorpark St	818-762-0181	56
Jennifer's Coffee Connection	4397 Tujunga Ave	818-769-3622	56
Coffee Bean & Tea Leaf	1000 Universal Studios Blvd	818-763-1811	57
Coffee Bean & Tea Leaf	10121 Riverside Dr	818-763-4815	57

The fact that you would even look for an internet café in LA means you're definitely not a local. Unlike San Francisco, New York, or any European metropolis, shared computers and public internet access are slim pickings 'round these parts. Think of it as LA's way of saying 'Um, *hello*! Like, totally buy a BlackBerry!" So if you don't have a BlackBerry, if you can't borrow your friend's laptop, and if the boss won't let you use the internet (the jerk), then have fun: tracking down a shared computer with a halfway decent internet connection is about as much fun as the 405 freeway during rush hour.

Hollywood is about as close to European internet café culture as it gets with the excellent **Cyber Java** on Hollywood Boulevard **(Map 3)** and **Hybrid** in West Hollywood **(Map 2)**. You can try the LA Public Libraries as well: access is free, but you also get what you pay for. **Fedex Kinko's** is another sure bet (though charges are high) and some are even open 24 hours, including the popular Vine Street location in Hollywood **(Map 3)** and the Wilshire location in Beverly Hills **(Map 1)**. Granted, the going rate of $0.25 a minute is a scandal, but then again: beggars can't be choosers. And if you're that desperate to check your Hotmail, it just might be worth the investment.

Internet	*Address*	*Phone*	*Map*
FedEx Kinko's	8950 W Olympic Blvd	310-285-9591	1
FedEx Kinko's	9201 W Sunset Blvd	310-274-0714	1
FedEx Kinko's	9334 Wilshire Blvd	310-271-1258	1
FedEx Kinko's	9680 Santa Monica Blvd	310-859-2381	1
C&C Internet Café	7070 W Sunset Blvd	323-462-0013	2
Cyber Java Internet Store	7080 Hollywood Blvd	323-466-5600	2
Hybrid Internet Lounge	8936 Santa Monica Blvd	310-360-9248	2
FedEx Kinko's	7630 W Sunset Blvd	323-845-4501	2
FedEx Kinko's	8471 Beverly Blvd	323-782-6905	2
FedEx Kinko's	1440 Vine St	323-871-1300	3
FedEx Kinko's	6255 W Sunset Blvd	323-465-3305	3
Hollywood Internet Café	1770 N Highland Ave	323-978-0740	3
Mailbox Café	4845 Fountain Ave	323-953-7545	4
FedEx Kinko's	5500 Wilshire Blvd	323-937-0126	6
FedEx Kinko's	3345 Wilshire Blvd	213-381-4129	8
FedEx Kinko's	110 E 9th St	213-623-3614	9
FedEx Kinko's	330 S Hope St	213-620-8615	9
FedEx Kinko's	554 S Grand Ave	213-623-8129	9
FedEx Kinko's	735 S Figueroa St	213-624-9409	9
FedEx Kinko's	835 Wilshire Blvd	213-892-1700	9
FedEx Kinko's	2723 S Figueroa St	213-747-8341	12
FedEx Kinko's	601 Wilshire Blvd	310-576-7710	18
FedEx Kinko's	925 Wilshire Blvd	310-394-2914	18
FedEx Kinko's	11819 Wilshire Blvd	310-477-7756	19
FedEx Kinko's	2139 S Bundy Dr	310-826-8122	19
FedEx Kinko's	10924 Weyburn Ave	310-443-5501	20
FedEx Kinko's	1520 Westwood Blvd	310-475-0789	20
FedEx Kinko's	1925 Century Park E	310-203-9928	20
FedEx Kinko's	4325 Glencoe Ave	310-827-2297	22
FedEx Kinko's	5575 Sepulveda Blvd	310-313-2578	24
FedEx Kinko's	5855 W Century Blvd	310-665-5955	26
FedEx Kinko's	630 N Sepulveda Blvd	310-322-9141	27
FedEx Kinko's	5201 W Rosecrans Ave	310-297-6850	28
FedEx Kinko's	1139 Artesia Blvd	310-379-7433	29
FedEx Kinko's	1770 S Pacific Coast Hwy	310-792-8635	31
FedEx Kinko's	21023 Hawthorne Blvd	310-316-8455	31
FedEx Kinko's	23325 Hawthorne Blvd	310-373-2530	31
FedEx Kinko's	135 N Los Robles Ave	626-356-0483	34
FedEx Kinko's	460 Fair Oaks Ave	626-403-6690	34
FedEx Kinko's	855 E Colorado Blvd	626-793-6336	34
FedEx Kinko's	10725 Zelzah Ave	818-366-3761	43
FedEx Kinko's	9000 Tampa Ave	818-701-0362	43
FedEx Kinko's	21816 Victory Blvd	818-884-4465	45
FedEx Kinko's	5810 Sepulveda Blvd	818-780-2123	47
Hollywood Coffee	5734 Tujunga Ave	818-762-9189	48
FedEx Kinko's	250 E Olive Ave	818-558-3900	50
FedEx Kinko's	225 N Brand Blvd	818-500-1811	51
FedEx Kinko's	16652 Ventura Blvd	818-788-4243	53
FedEx Kinko's	15720 Ventura Blvd	818-783-2680	54
FedEx Kinko's	4556 Van Nuys Blvd	818-906-2679	55
FedEx Kinko's	12101 Ventura Blvd	818-980-2679	56
FedEx Kinko's	3575 Cahuenga Blvd W	323-876-3481	57
FedEx Kinko's	3817 W Riverside Dr	818-569-4914	57
FedEx Kinko's	4100 W Riverside Dr	818-567-1044	57

Self-Storage	*Address*	*Phone*	*Map*
Extra Space Storage	5825 Santa Monica Blvd	323-464-4780	3
Hollywood Bowl Self Storage	1847 Argyle Ave	323-460-6370	3
Hollywood & Bronson Self Storage	5900 Hollywood Blvd	323-464-6100	3
LA Security Storage	6372 Santa Monica Blvd	323-469-1402	3
Public Storage	6202 Willoughby Ave	323-467-0710	3
Public Storage	6801 Santa Monica Blvd	323-462-4836	3
Public Storage	6840 Santa Monica Blvd	323-871-2043	3
Storage USA	1860 Vine St	323-464-3020	3
USA Postal Center	6632 Lexington Ave	323-466-5763	3
BA Self Storage	620 N Heliotrope Dr	323-663-2299	4
Public Storage	3636 Beverly Blvd	213-380-2860	4
SAF Keep Self Storage	4996 Melrose Ave	818-840-8420	4
Storage USA	4728 Fountain Ave	323-663-8445	4
Storquest Self Storage	5138 W Sunset Blvd	323-660-9090	4
Extra Space Storage	2904 Casitas Ave	323-661-8100	5
Fort Self Storage	1651 S Central Ave	213-741-1666	5
Public Storage	1712 Glendale Blvd	323-663-4466	5
Store It All	2870 Los Feliz Pl	818-241-1200	5
Thriftee Storage	1717 Glendale Blvd	323-660-4600	5
U-haul	2671 Fletcher Dr	323-664-3516	5
Beverly Hills Self Storage	9014 Wilshire Blvd	310-274-6047	6
Public Storage	5570 Airdrome St	562-698-7214	6
Public Storage	5941 Venice Blvd	323-939-3573	6
Public Storage	6007 Venice Blvd	323-937-7296	6
Walter's Transfer & Moving	5850 Venice Blvd	323-933-8080	6
A-American Self Storage	4174 W Pico Blvd	323-731-5323	7
Central Self Storage	3611 W Washington Blvd	323-737-7137	7
Devon Self Storage	3611 W Washington Blvd	323-285-5745	7
A-American Self Storage	2500 W 6th St	213-385-0385	8
Safeway Self-Storage	116 S Western Ave	213-738-9048	8
Storage USA	2800 W Pico Blvd	323-733-4488	8
U-haul	1836 Arapahoe St	213-746-5910	8
U-Lock Storage	761 S Normandie Ave	213-388-2323	8
123 moving company	990 Main St	818-439-3474	9
A-American Self Storage	300 Avery St	213-626-1726	9
Devon Self Storage	801 E Commercial St	213-680-8900	9
Downtown Los Angeles Self Storage	1000 W 6th St	213-481-1010	9
Budget Self Storage	4411 W Slauson Ave	323-294-5230	10
Price Self Storage	3430 S La Brea Ave	323-299-2699	10
Public Storage	3401 S La Cienega Blvd	310-839-4018	10
Public Storage	3770 Crenshaw Blvd	323-292-7812	10
Public Storage	3821 W Jefferson Blvd	323-734-5490	10
Public Storage	5917 Burchard Ave	323-939-4531	10
Gibraltar Self Storage	1600 W Slauson Ave	323-759-0600	11
Public Storage	2703 W Martin Luther King Jr Blvd	323-291-3404	11
Storquest Self Storage	1701 W Slauson Ave	323-295-8500	11
A-American Self Storage	3625 S Grand Ave	213-749-3330	12
Devon Self Storage	700 E Slauson Ave	323-233-5160	12
Public Storage	1702 S San Pedro St	213-747-6366	12
A US Storage Centers	820 Industrial Ave	310-677-2544	13
A-American Self Storage	10101 Firmona Ave	310-674-6112	13
A-American Self Storage	10108 Condon Ave	310-680-7323	13
A-American Self Storage	10833 S Prairie Ave	310-672-6889	13
Extra Space Storage	3846 W Century Blvd	310-672-7900	13
U-haul	964 S La Brea Ave	310-671-9001	13
Crenshaw Self Storage	6725 Crenshaw Blvd	323-750-7867	14
Public Storage	365 W Manchester Ave	323-752-2807	14
U-Haul	11020 S Vermont Ave	323-756-8744	14
E-Z Storage	2105 Colorado Ave	877-351-6029	18
U-Haul	1747 Lincoln Blvd	310-450-6460	18
A-American Self Storage	2300 Federal Av	310-478-2211	19

Self-Storage—*continued*	*Address*	*Phone*	*Map*
E-Z Storage	11471 W Pico Blvd	877-351-6029	19
Olympic Self Storage	3250 Olympic Blvd	310-829-2525	19
Public Storage	11259 W Olympic Blvd	310-477-6025	19
Public Storage	11625 W Olympic Blvd	310-473-6223	19
Public Storage	1606 Cotner Ave	310-477-6777	19
Public Storage	2300 Purdue Ave	310-473-0800	19
Public Storage	3010 Wilshire Blvd	310-828-5473	19
Safe Store	2828 Donald Douglas Loop N	310-456-8157	19
Sawtelle Self Storage	2240 Sawtelle Blvd	310-235-1015	19
Storquest Self Storage	2531 Sawtelle Blvd	310-817-6710	19
Westside Self-Storage	2270 Centinela Ave	310-360-0456	19
Westwood Self Storage	1901 S Sepulveda Blvd	310-478-1901	19
Extra Space Storage	4095 Glencoe Ave	310-301-2527	21
Extra Space Storage	658 Venice Blvd	310-836-0084	21
A-American Self Storage	11802 W Washington Blvd	310-837-6630	22
E-Z Storage	12901 Culver Blvd	877-351-6029	22
Easy Storage	12901 Culver Blvd	310-577-3780	22
Lawndale Mini Storage	3701 Inglewood Blvd	310-536-6721	22
US Storage Centers	12700 Braddock Dr	310-827-5454	22
National Blvd Storage	10321 National Blvd	310-838-2300	23
Price Self Storage	10151 National Blvd	310-837-7700	23
Public Storage	11510 Jefferson Blvd	310-391-9929	24
Public Storage	3773 S Durango Ave	310-280-9000	24
Public Storage	5741 W Jefferson Blvd	310-842-3851	24
Public Storage	8512 National Blvd	310-839-1627	24
U-haul	8829 National Blvd	310-558-4561	24
Marina Del Rey Self Storage	4230 Del Rey Ave	310-577-1507	25
Public Storage	12681 W Jefferson Blvd	310-822-0821	25
Storquest Self Storage	12821 W Jefferson Blvd	310-301-7867	25
L.A. Airport/Westchester Self Storage	5221 W 102nd St	310-645-0900	26
Public Storage	10100 S La Cienega Blvd	310-641-3390	26
Public Storage	11102 S La Cienega Blvd	310-645-7450	26
Public Storage	5544 W Centinela Ave	310-645-4144	26
Public Storage	6701 S Sepulveda Blvd	310-215-3466	26
Springfield Storage & Parking	5431 W 104th St	310-670-7208	26
Storage EZ	6711 S Sepulveda Blvd	310-473-0069	26
Storage USA	5855 W Centinela Ave	310-412-0263	26
U-haul	940 W Florence Ave	310-674-1350	26
U-haul Co	5280 W Century Blvd	310-337-1137	26
A US Storage Centers	14680 Aviation Blvd	310-536-7100	27
California Storage Masters	1921 E Maple Ave	310-414-9294	27
Public Storage	1940 S Hughes Wy	310-322-0811	27
Storage USA	1017 E El Segundo Blvd	310-615-1042	27
405 Self Storage	12714 S La Cienega Blvd	310-725-0088	28
Gentle Giant Moving Company	13020 Yukon Ave	310-978-2939	28
Public Storage	14107 Crenshaw Blvd	310-973-5847	28
Redondo Torrance Mini Storage	3701 Inglewood Ave	310-536-6720	28
Redondo-Torrance Mini Storage	3401 W Rosecrans Ave	310-970-1800	28
Bay Self Storage & Moving	901 Hermosa Ave	310-379-2122	29
Everest Self Storage	871 S Aviation Blvd	310-643-7788	29
Hermosa Beach Mini Storage	490 Herondo St	310-372-0000	29
Hermosa Self-Storage	552 11th Pl	310-376-9401	29
A-1 Self Storage	20704 Earl St	310-371-9123	30
Magellan Storage	4320 W 190th St	310-370-7300	30
Public Storage	4460 Del Amo Blvd	310-370-6585	30
Self Storage America's Best	380 Crenshaw Blvd	310-212-7339	30
Spencer Street Self Storage	3925 Spencer St	310-370-4400	30
Stor-Mor	4300 Emerald St	310-542-7272	30
Store America	1415 Hawthorne Blvd	310-370-2383	30
Storquest Self Storage	20428 Earl St	310-256-3361	30
Torrance Self Storage	2515 Maricopa St	310-618-8900	30

Self-Storage—*continued*	*Address*	*Phone*	*Map*
US Storage Centers	1415 Hawthorne Blvd	310-370-2383	30
Redondo Van & Storage	325 Diamond St	310-376-7919	31
A US Storage Centers	23711 Crenshaw Blvd	310-517-0200	32
Public Storage	1724 Crenshaw Blvd	310-328-1378	32
Public Storage	3501 Lomita Blvd	310-539-3691	32
Torrance Western Self Storage	22011 S Western Ave	310-533-1146	32
U-haul	21707 S Western Ave	310-533-7037	32
Public Storage	2370 Colorado Blvd	323-256-8006	33
A-American Self Storage	511 S Fair Oaks Ave	626-744-3200	34
Arroyo Parkway Mini Storage	411 S Arroyo Pkwy	626-585-8800	34
Mini Storage	686 S Arroyo Blvd	626-440-1000	34
Public Storage	1240 Lincoln Ave	626-794-8934	34
Public Storage	171 S Arroyo Pkwy	626-287-6741	34
Public Storage	888 S Fair Oaks Ave	626-799-0470	34
Raymond Avenue Self Storage	421 S Raymond Ave	626-449-9215	34
Southmark Self Storage	919 Mission St	626-441-4444	34
U-haul	552 S Raymond Ave	626-795-6888	34
Colorado Blvd Self Storage	2581 E Colorado Blvd	626-711-2517	35
Public Storage	2773 E Colorado Blvd	626-792-8802	35
Public Storage	1776 Blake Ave	323-666-8835	36
Public Storage	3810 Eagle Rock Blvd	323-255-3048	36
Public Storage	4101 N Figueroa St	323-222-0024	36
SAF Keep Self Storage	2840 N San Fernando Rd	323-226-1900	36
Storquest Self Storage	2222 N Figueroa St	323-285-5812	36
Public Storage	4002 N Mission Rd	323-223-5520	37
Public Storage	4583 Huntington Dr S	323-223-2917	38
Public Storage	4889 Valley Blvd	323-223-1484	38
All Aboard Mini Storage	2000 W Mission Rd	626-284-5447	39
American Self Storage	2101 W Mission Rd	626-588-2700	39
PSA Private Storage Areas	600 S Garfield Ave	626-289-3232	39
U-Stor-It	2101 W Mission Rd	626-588-2700	39
Public Storage	649 S Boyle Ave	323-263-0656	40
Public Storage	4400 W Ramona Blvd	323-262-6005	41
Bekins Moving & Storage	20525 Nordhoff St	818-882-7220	42
E-Z Storage	9420 De Soto Ave	877-351-6029	42
Extra Space Storage	21536 Devonshire St	818-775-9700	42
Public Storage	9350 Topanga Cyn Blvd	818-882-2181	42
Storage Etc	20550 Lassen St	818-332-3986	42
Storage USA	20221 Prairie St	818-349-9211	42
Store & Lock	9111 Jordan Ave	818-727-0777	42
Trading Places Moving & Storage	20540 Superior St	818-701-9066	42
U-Store	20351 Prairie St	818-993-5070	42
All Aboard Mini Storage	18500 Eddy St	818-349-7882	43
Golden State Self Storage	18832 Rayen St	818-885-1611	43
Prodigy Moving & Storage	18659 Parthenia St	310-253-9808	43
Public Storage	19121 Parthenia St	818-349-3173	43
Public Storage	9341 Shirley Ave	818-349-1234	43
So Cal Self Storage	9000 Corbin Ave	818-882-2500	43
Air Ride Moving & Storage	17454 Chatsworth St	818-832-1270	44
Public Storage	9920 Balboa Blvd	818-700-0678	44
U-Haul	18160 Parthenia St	818-993-7470	44
A-American Self Storage	7900 Deering Ave	818-340-2929	45
A-American Self Storage	8050 Deering Ave	818-346-3514	45
Big Valley Self Storage	6061 De Soto Ave	818-703-7768	45
Canoga Self Storage	7700 Canoga Ave	818-999-6464	45
Public Storage	8111 Deering Ave	818-884-4642	45
Storage Etc	6030 Canoga Ave	818-347-7160	45
Warner Center Self Storage	21051 Oxnard St	818-703-0171	45
Warner Center Self Storage	6411 De Soto Ave	818-340-4949	45
Mid Valley Self Storage	6924 Canby Ave, Ste 110	818-705-4368	46

Self-Storage—*continued*	*Address*	*Phone*	*Map*
Public Storage	18440 Burbank Blvd	818-881-1717	46
Public Storage	7660 Balboa Blvd	818-994-4432	46
Storage Place	6836 Canby Ave	818-345-2696	46
VP Self Storage	18716 Oxnard St	818-705-1145	46
All Aboard Mini Storage	15101 Raymer St	818-785-3771	47
All Right Storage	6900 Van Nuys Blvd	818-786-4335	47
All Star Valley Moving And Storage	6639 Odessa Ave	818-787-8150	47
American Best Moving	15720 Stagg St	818-988-0816	47
Batee Investment	7400 Van Nuys Blvd	818-909-0012	47
Central Valley Self Storage	15025 Oxnard St	818-785-3259	47
City Self Storage of Van Nuys	7346 Sepulveda Blvd	818-780-6464	47
E-Z Storage	15330 Hatteras St	818-988-1112	47
Express Moving & Storage	7523 Woodman Pl	818-988-0041	47
Golden State Self Storage	15655 Roscoe Blvd	818-892-5669	47
Jackson's Moving & Storage	7523 Woodman Ave	818-363-5560	47
Oxnard Self Storage	14235 Oxnard St	818-786-8250	47
Panorama Self Storage	14647 Arminta St	818-786-0728	47
Public Storage	15350 Oxnard St	818-994-6163	47
Safe Storage	14601 Sherman Wy	818-442-9944	47
Vanowen Self Storage	16225 Vanowen St	818-376-1111	47
Wyandotte Self Storage	15319 Wyandotte St	818-781-1100	47
A Enterprise Self Storage	12540 Sherman Wy	818-765-1966	48
A Safe Place	7330 Varna Ave	818-764-9770	48
AA Universal Self Storage	6121 Lankershim Blvd	818-761-1600	48
All Aboard Mini Storage	7400 Coldwater Cyn Ave	818-765-4940	48
Coldwater Self Storage	7215 Coldwater Cyn Ave	818-780-8389	48
Dino's Storage	12641 Saticoy St S	818-503-3999	48
Extra Space Storage	11423 Vanowen St	818-503-3900	48
Extra Space Storage	13434 Saticoy St	818-779-2110	48
Pack Rat Self Storage	10920 Victory Blvd	818-487-6883	48
Personal Storage Garages	13005 Victory Blvd	818-508-9889	48
Public Storage	11620 Sherman Wy	818-765-6520	48
Public Storage	12510 Raymer St	818-764-7445	48
Public Storage	12940 Saticoy St	818-765-2944	48
Public Storage	7500 Whitsett Ave	818-982-6555	48
The Storage Company at Laurel Canyon	7361 Laurel Cyn Blvd	818-982-1927	48
Studio Self Storage	6200 Lankershim Blvd	818-505-6494	48
All Aboard Mini Storage	2801 Thornton Ave	818-845-4874	49
Burbank Self Storage	3203 N San Fernando Blvd	818-845-3040	49
Extra Storage	7670 N Hollywood Wy	818-767-7070	49
Personal Storage Garages	10847 Vanowen St	818-769-4491	49
Public Storage	10810 Vanowen St	818-760-2567	49
Public Storage	7521 N San Fernando Rd	818-767-2083	49
U-haul	7721 N Hollywood Wy	818-768-4100	49
A Enterprise Self Storage	6921 San Fernando Rd	818-845-8699	50
E-Z Storage	20 E Alameda Ave	877-351-6029	50
Extra Space Storage	175 W Verdugo Ave	818-895-5921	50
A-1 Self Storage	4427 San Fernando Rd	818-247-1444	51
Central Storage Distributors	403 S Central Ave	818-244-2721	51
Extra Space Storage	5120 San Fernando Rd	818-247-8235	51
Public Storage	3017 N San Fernando Rd	323-254-7532	51
Public Storage	4820 San Fernando Rd	818-507-1981	51
Encino Self-Storage	18019 Ventura Blvd	818-344-5668	53
Extra Space Storage	5225 Sepulveda Blvd	818-385-1755	54
Mcgee's Closet Self Storage	15111 Ventura Blvd	818-995-0972	54
A-1 Self Storage	5310 Vineland Ave	818-505-9800	56
Extra Space Storage	11570 Ventura Blvd	818-760-6549	56
Public Storage	12345 Ventura Ct	818-761-2345	56
Public Storage	5410 Vineland Ave	818-980-8791	56
Public Storage	10830 Ventura Blvd	818-762-5352	57

Van and Truck Rental	*Address*	*Phone*	*Map*
Budget Truck	9815 Wilshire Blvd	310-858-1635	1
U-Haul	1626 Wilcox Ave	323-464-8057	3
Penske	3636 Beverly Blvd	213-380-2672	4
U-Haul	1270 N Vermont Ave	323-913-9077	4
U-Haul	4550 Hollywood Blvd	323-666-7326	4
Budget	2870 Los Feliz Pl	323-665-7345	5
U-Haul	1717 Glendale Blvd	323-662-9973	5
U-Haul	2671 Fletcher Dr	323-664-3516	5
U-Haul	6108 W Pico Blvd	323-852-1810	6
U-Haul	116 S Western Ave	213-386-9758	8
U-Haul	1600 S Western Ave	323-731-3171	8
U-Haul	1836 Arapahoe St	213-746-5910	8
U-Haul	2451 Crenshaw Blvd	323-734-1125	10
U-Haul	2217 S Normandie Ave	323-734-8242	11
U-Haul	4167 S Western Ave	323-295-6122	11
Ryder	1508 S Alameda St	213-748-8606	12
U-Haul	1710 E Vernon Ave	323-232-1061	12
Penske	4900 W Century Blvd	310-532-3980	13
U-Haul	4858 W Century Blvd	310-330-0327	13
U-Haul	964 S La Brea Ave	310-671-9001	13
U-Haul	11020 S Vermont Ave	323-756-8744	14
U-Haul	8140 S Vermont Ave	323-541-0289	14
U-Haul	1453 Lincoln Blvd	310-394-0391	18
U-Haul	1747 Lincoln Blvd	310-450-6947	18
Budget	11700 Santa Monica Blvd	310-820-5262	19
Penske	2270 Centinela Ave	310-826-5900	19
U-Haul	11590 W Pico Blvd	310-479-1562	19
U-Haul	2240 Sawtelle Blvd	310-445-8614	19
U-Haul	2510 Wilshire Blvd	310-453-2762	19
U-Haul	3250 Olympic Blvd	310-829-4109	19
U-Haul	924 S Victory Blvd	818-845-7289	20
U-Haul	10321 National Blvd	310-202-1645	23
Budget	11510 Jefferson Blvd	310-390-9116	24
U-Haul	10610 Venice Blvd	310-839-1473	24
U-Haul	8829 National Blvd	310-558-4561	24
Penske	4500 Lincoln Blvd	310-306-2843	25
Budget	5560 W Manchester Blvd	310-670-1744	26
Ryder	5366 W 83rd St	310-670-6879	26
U-Haul	5600 Arbor Vitae St	310-568-0124	26
U-Haul	8911 Bellanca Ave	310-642-1130	26
U-Haul	9100 S Sepulveda Blvd	310-348-1951	26
U-Haul	940 W Florence Ave	310-410-1784	26
Penske	1910 S Hughes Wy	310-322-1992	27
U-Haul	1100 Manhattan Beach Blvd	310-545-7771	27
Penske	15312 Hawthorne Blvd	310-545-1241	28
U-Haul	4460 Imperial Hwy	310-671-0686	28
Budget	1081 Aviation Blvd	310-374-0247	29
Budget	20522 Hawthorne Blvd	310-370-3668	30
Budget	2515 Maricopa St	310-618-1828	30
Penske	20428 Earl St	310-214-0827	30
U-Haul	17528 Hawthorne Blvd	310-214-4668	30
U-Haul	24091 Hawthorne Blvd	310-378-4666	31
U-Haul	553 N Pacific Coast Hwy	310-318-2272	31
U-Haul	21707 S Western Ave	310-533-7037	32
U-Haul	4604 York Blvd	323-258-8865	33
Penske	888 S Fair Oaks Ave	626-799-1918	34
U-Haul	552 S Raymond Ave	626-795-6888	34

Van and Truck Rental	*Address*	*Phone*	*Map*
U-Haul	953 S Raymond Ave	626-403-2818	34
U-Haul	1816 E Villa St	626-795-0096	35
U-Haul	2106 E Colorado Blvd	626-564-8663	35
U-Haul	1206 Cypress Ave	323-227-4118	36
U-Haul	2524 W Main St	626-284-9473	38
U-Haul	5393 Alhambra Ave	323-225-9427	38
Budget	539 W Valley Blvd	626-284-2439	39
Penske	4400 W Ramona Blvd	323-262-1683	41
U-Haul	4237 E Cesar E Chavez Ave	323-268-1966	41
U-Haul	657 S Atlantic Blvd	323-266-4833	41
Penske	8921 De Soto Ave	818-886-7043	42
Penske	9350 Topanga Cyn Blvd	818-718-2482	42
U-Haul	20525 Nordhoff St	818-885-1091	42
U-Haul	21326 Devonshire St	818-709-4207	42
U-Haul	21500 Nordhoff St	818-709-7316	42
Budget	18505 Devonshire St	818-360-0137	43
Ryder	19133 Parthenia St	818-701-7000	43
U-Haul	18505 Devonshire St	818-831-0131	43
U-Haul	8659 Corbin Ave	818-717-8569	43
Budget	16930 Roscoe Blvd	818-709-0291	44
U-Haul	11062 Balboa Blvd	818-360-7825	44
U-Haul	18160 Parthenia St	818-993-7470	44
U-Haul	8658 Balboa Blvd	818-701-1493	44
Penske	20140 Sherman Wy	818-883-2864	45
U-Haul	20112 Sherman Wy	818-347-7686	45
U-Haul	21051 Oxnard St	818-884-8894	45
U-Haul	6411 De Soto Ave	818-704-8377	45
Budget	18312 Oxnard St	818-345-3571	46
Penske	7142 White Oak Ave	818-901-7042	46
U-Haul	18349 Sherman Wy	818-609-1213	46
U-Haul	6938 Reseda Blvd	818-708-1738	46
Budget	13717 Victory Blvd	818-997-7542	47
Budget	5651 Sepulveda Blvd	818-989-1401	47
Penske	15360 Oxnard St	818-902-5412	47
U-Haul	14106 Burbank Blvd	818-781-1760	47
U-Haul	15025 Oxnard St	818-989-7810	47
U-Haul	6900 Van Nuys Blvd	818-786-0117	47
U-Haul	7610 Van Nuys Blvd	818-786-6400	47
Budget	6200 Lankershim Blvd	818-508-9038	48
Penske	7500 Whitsett Ave	818-982-0654	48
U-Haul	11666 Victory Blvd	818-763-4381	48
U-Haul	5652 Vineland Ave	818-506-3675	48
U-Haul	6743 Fulton Ave	818-503-1070	48
U-Haul	7361 Laurel Cyn Blvd	818-764-7008	48
Penske	10560 Magnolia Blvd	818-762-0746	49
U-Haul	10631 Magnolia Blvd	818-766-6845	49
U-Haul	10907 Magnolia Blvd	818-763-1893	49
U-Haul	7721 N Hollywood Wy	818-768-4100	49
Penske	1633 Victory Blvd	818-848-8724	50
U-Haul	6820 San Fernando Rd	818-848-4587	50
U-Haul	726 S Flower St	818-972-9243	50
Budget	4103 Verdugo Rd	323-344-9107	51
Penske	4820 San Fernando Rd	818-507-1096	51
U-Haul	1313 S Brand Blvd	818-956-3740	51
U-Haul	5314 Topanga Cyn Blvd	818-932-1926	52
U-Haul	4388 Tujunga Ave	818-769-2947	56
U-Haul	4654 Laurel Cyn Blvd	818-752-4311	56

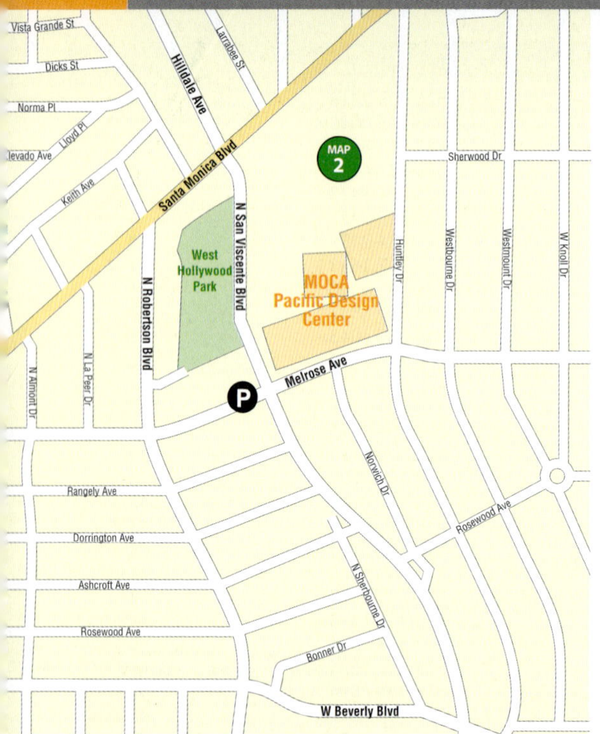

General Information

NFT Maps:	2 & 9
Main Address:	250 S Grand Ave Los Angeles, CA 90012
Phone:	213-626-6222
Website:	www.moca.org
Hours:	Mon & Fri: 11 am–5 pm; Thurs: 11 pm–8 pm; Sat & Sun: 11 am–6 pm; closed Tuesdays, Wednesdays, and major holidays
Admission:	adults: $8 (valid for all locations on the date of purchase); seniors & students: $5; children under 12: free; Thursdays after 5 pm: free

Overview

In a city where modern and contemporary generally refer to the latest plastic surgery or BMW, Los Angeles's Museum of Contemporary Art is a surprisingly refreshing destination. Located downtown in the shadow of the towering California Plaza, the museum sits catty-corner to Frank Gehry's Walt Disney Concert Hall. It is the only LA museum devoted exclusively to contemporary art (post-WWII)—if you're looking for Cézanne or Klimt, head to LACMA. This main building houses the impressive permanent collection, while the two satellite locations—in Little Tokyo and West Hollywood—display large installations and design-focused exhibits, respectively.

Between its three locations, MOCA offers an in-depth look at the art that shaped the latter half of the 20th century, as well as artists of the '00s that built reputations in places like the adjacent Chinatown art scene and those experimenting with interactive and digital media. And the museum enjoys no shortage of popularity. Perhaps due to a lack of non-cinematic art in LA, Angelenos love to brag about their cultural gem, even if all they do is shop the (fabulous) MOCA store. The museum is often lauded by critics and laymen alike for exhibitions like the successful Warhol (2001) and Basquiat (2005) retrospectives.

The entrance plaza of MOCA at Grand Avenue sports a massive sculpture by Nancy Rubins, composed mainly of stainless steel airplane parts. You can't miss it. Down below, MOCA's main location is a sprawling, subterranean maze that features exhibits culled from its more than 5,000 permanent works, courtesy of art world phenoms like Frank Stella, Roy Lichtenstein, Jackson Pollock, Lee Friedlander, Cindy Sherman, Tracy Emin and Steve McQueen.

It's also host to larger, traveling exhibitions, many of which include pieces loaned by the museum. MOCA has gained a reputation for mounting innovative retrospectives on contemporary artists and movements that have rarely been explored in such depth. Highlights include 2005's *Visual Music,* a look at the cross-stimulation of visual and aural senses through painting, film, music and projections, and 2006's *Robert Rauschenberg: Combines*, the first major exhibition dedicated to this pioneer of "combines." Summer nights bring Night Vision: MOCA After Dark, a ten-week program offering DJs, live performances, artmaking, screenings, spoken word, and more. Past guests include a performance by local indie darlings The Like and DJ sets by Steve Aoki.

MOCA at the Geffen Contemporary

152 Central Ave, 213-626-6222

Hours & Admission same as Grand Avenue location.

MOCA at the Geffen Contemporary—known as the "Temporary Contemporary" until a cool 5 mil from namesake David Geffen made it permanent—is a cavernous former police car garage in the heart of Little Tokyo. Past shows have included a 30-year retrospective on installation art in which many of the installations inhabited room-sized areas, and Gregor Schneider's *Dead House Ur* in which the artist reconstructed the entire interior of his childhood home. MOCA also uses this space in collaboration with other arts organizations to host gala events; in 2005 it co-hosted the GenArt independent designer runway shows that kicked off LA's Fashion Week.

Don't look for prototypical art exhibits here—the Geffen prides itself on wide-open industrial space and is decidedly anti-establishment. In 2007, *WACK! Art and the Feminist Revolution* explored the foundations of feminist art from 1965–80, while 2006's *Skin and Bones* examined parallel practices in fashion and architecture.

MOCA at the Pacific Design Center

8687 Melrose Ave, 310-289-5223

Hours: Tues, Wed, & Fri: 11 am–5 pm; Thurs: 11 am–8 pm, Sat & Sun: 11 am–6 pm; closed Mondays & major holidays

Admission: free

This smaller satellite location in West Hollywood opened in 2001 and is mainly used for exhibits that focus on one artist, architect, designer, or art collective. The museum's lot at the Pacific Design Center is a separate structure that's set away from the PDC's home-décor shops and across an expansive plaza where MOCA loves to throw its big fundraiser parties. This little, gallery-like space allows you to cruise through its two floors in about 20 minutes.

How to Get There—Driving

MOCA Grand Avenue: From the 110, exit at 4th Street. Turn left on Grand Avenue. The museum will be on your right.

MOCA at Geffen Contemporary: From the 101, exit at Los Angeles Street. Turn right on Los Angeles Street, then turn left on 1st Street. The museum will be on your left.

MOCA at the Pacific Design Center: From the 10, exit at Robertson Boulevard going north. Turn right on Melrose Avenue, then turn left on San Vicente Boulevard. The Design Center will be on your right. From the 101, exit west on Melrose Avenue. Turn right on San Vicente Boulevard. The Design Center will be on your right.

Parking

MOCA Grand Avenue: Parking is available for $8 in the Walt Disney Concert Hall parking garage on Grand Avenue. On the weekends, museum members can park for free in the California Plaza parking garage on Olive Street. Metered street parking is also available on Grand Avenue, 3rd Street, and Hope Street, but you'll only have two hours, max.

MOCA at Geffen Contemporary: Parking is available at the Advanced Parking Systems garage on Central Avenue for a daily flat rate of $4.25.

MOCA at the Pacific Design Center: Parking is available in the Pacific Design Center's lot on Melrose. The first 30 minutes are free, then it's $1 for each block of 30 minutes thereafter with an $8 maximum charge.

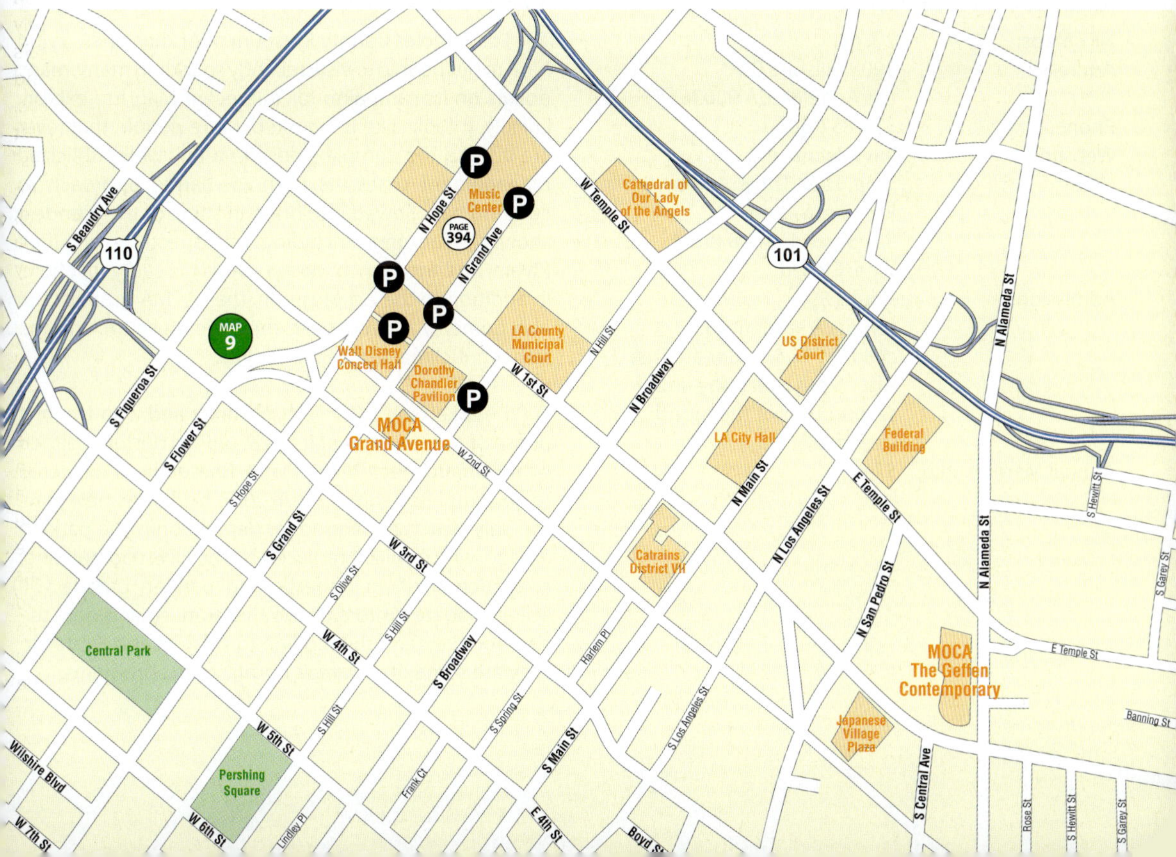

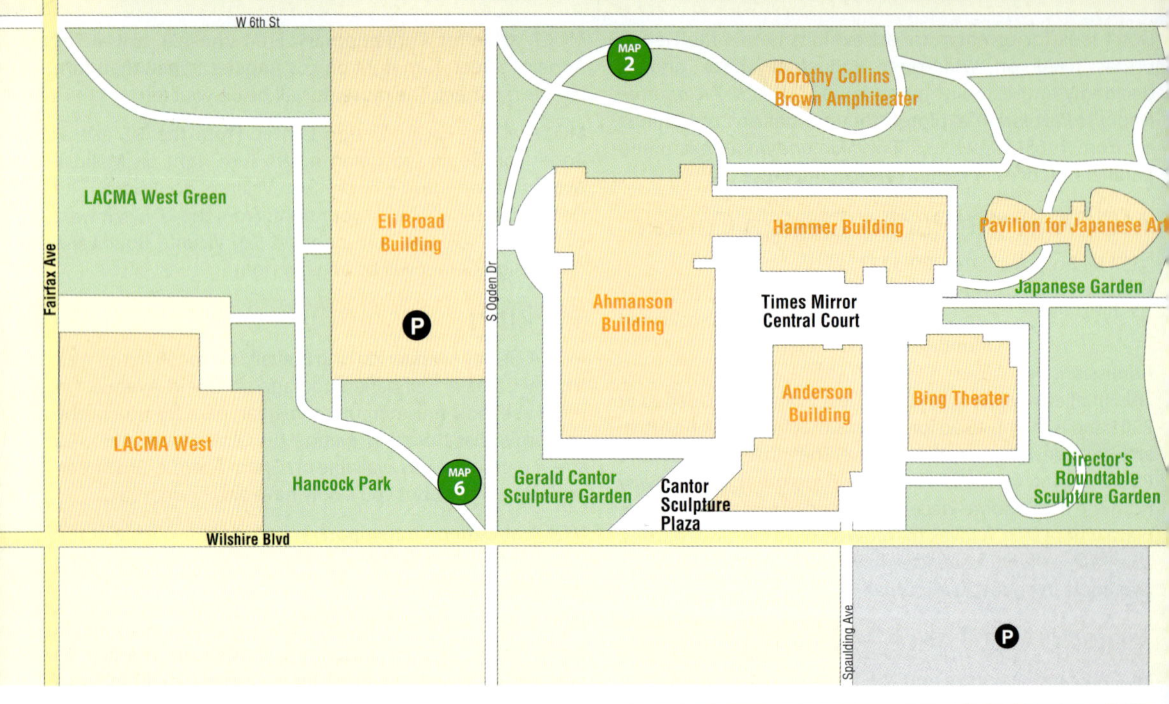

General Information

NFT Maps:	2 & 6
Address:	5905 Wilshire Blvd Los Angeles, CA 90036
Phone:	323-857-6000
Website:	www.lacma.org
Hours:	Mon, Tues, Thurs: 12 pm–8 pm Fri: 12 pm–9 pm Sat, Sun: 11 am–8 pm Wed: Closed
Admission:	Adults $9, seniors & students $5, children 17 & under are free After 5 pm every day and second Tues of the month, free for all
Annual Membership:	$75

Overview

The Los Angeles County Museum of Art has been trying hard to get people to visit, recently spending many, many dollars on its campaign for the recent Magritte exhibit. Luckily, it looks like it's worked. More people than ever are visiting the complex, despite a few well-publicized management crises. Its no-holds-barred approach to curating has allowed it to bring in some of the grandest shows in the area, including retrospectives of Klimt, Rivera, and the French Masters. A day is easily lost here; in addition to the Art Museum, the LACMA grounds are also home to a lovely park, the Page Museum, and the rather anticlimactic La Brea Tar Pits.

2006 marked LACMA's 40th birthday and also the first phase of construction of its new, unified design, helmed by Italian architect Renzo Piano. Phase one is expected to be completed sometime in 2007. Under the new plan, the only structure pegged for demolition is the parking garage, which will be replaced by the Eli Broad building; construction of an underground parking garage will accommodate visitors to the museum. Now if only the city would extend the red line to Wilshire and Fairfax to alleviate some of the area's horrific traffic problems.

LACMA East

The museum's collection is housed mainly in four buildings. The Anderson Building is home to LACMA's collection of modern and contemporary art. The permanent collection includes David Hockney's *Mulholland Drive; The Road to the Studio*, one of the most "LA" paintings that we know. Inside the Ahmanson Gallery, you'll find European paintings and sculpture from the 12th to 20th centuries as well as American art from the colonial period to World War II. The Hammer Building tends to hold temporary exhibitions, while the Pavilion for Japanese Art is a freestanding building that holds Japanese works from 3000 B.C. to the 20th century.

LACMA is also a great destination on weekend evenings. On Fridays, the museum is open late—until 9 pm—and there's live jazz in the Times Mirror Central Court from 5:30 pm until 8:30 pm. You can also hear live chamber music every Sunday at 6 pm in the Bing Theater. Both of these weekly concerts are free. The Bing Theater is also home to regular screenings of classic films, occasionally with a guest speaker. Movie tickets include admission to all of the galleries and cost $9 for the public and $6 for members, seniors, and students. Screenings are every Friday and Saturday at 7:30 pm.

LACMA West

In 1998, the Art Deco May Company department store reopened as LACMA West. The building has hosted special exhibits like 1999's Van Gogh show, but LACMA West is now the place in LA to view Latin American art. The building houses the Bernard and Edith Lewin Latin American Art Galleries, a collection dominated by Mexican modern masters. The collection rotates, but Diego Rivera and David Alfaro Siqueiros are among the artists whose work has been displayed here. Young art enthusiasts may enjoy the Boone Children's Gallery, which frequently incorporates works from the main museum's permanent collection. Admission is included along with your regular museum ticket.

The George C. Page Museum

Located just east of LACMA, the Page Museum is best known as the home of the La Brea Tar Pits. Almost everyone who moves to Los Angeles has heard of the Tar Pits in some context, and most make a pilgrimage at some point, hoping to see something dynamic, something bubbling, something interesting. What you end up seeing, however, is a large pool of tar. It's about as anticlimactic as it gets. The Tar Pits become exponentially more interesting during an eight-to-ten-week period, usually in July and August, when excavation takes place. It's during this time that museum-goers can watch paleontologists sift through the tar. The process is painstaking and oddly fascinating, even if it's hard to escape the feeling that everything cool has already been unearthed.

Inside the Page Museum, it's possible to view over one million specimens of fossils recovered from the Tar Pits. Among them are saber-toothed cats and mammoths. Sadly, there are no dinosaurs, but many a child has been riveted by the exhibit of the 9,000-year-old La Brea Woman, whose fossil is still the only human remains ever found in the Tar Pits.

Open Monday through Friday from 9:30 am until 5 pm, and from 10 am until 5 pm on Saturdays and Sundays. Adults $7, seniors and students $4.50, and children 5–12 $2. Admission is free on the first Tuesday of every month. 323-934-7243; www.tarpits.org.

How to Get There—Driving

From the 10, exit at Fairfax Avenue and drive north. Turn right at Wilshire Boulevard. The museum will be on your left. From the 101 S, exit at Highland and head south to Franklin. Turn right and take Franklin to La Brea. Make a left onto La Brea, and continue south to Wilshire Boulevard. Turn right on Wilshire, and the museum will be on your right.

Parking

There are parking lots on Wilshire, just across from the museum at Spaulding Avenue and at Ogden Drive. You have to pay for parking during the day, but the lots are free after 7 pm. If you're lucky, you'll nab one of the metered spots behind the museum (along 6th Street) that allow 4-hour parking from 8 am until 6 pm. Take lots of quarters with you. If you park in the parking structure, take a moment of silence for the previous parking structure, which featured historically significant murals by Margaret Kilgallen that were torn down. You can imagine what we think of that decision…

How to Get There—Mass Transit

MTA buses 20, 21, 217, and 720 all stop near the museum, on either Wilshire Boulevard or Fairfax Avenue.

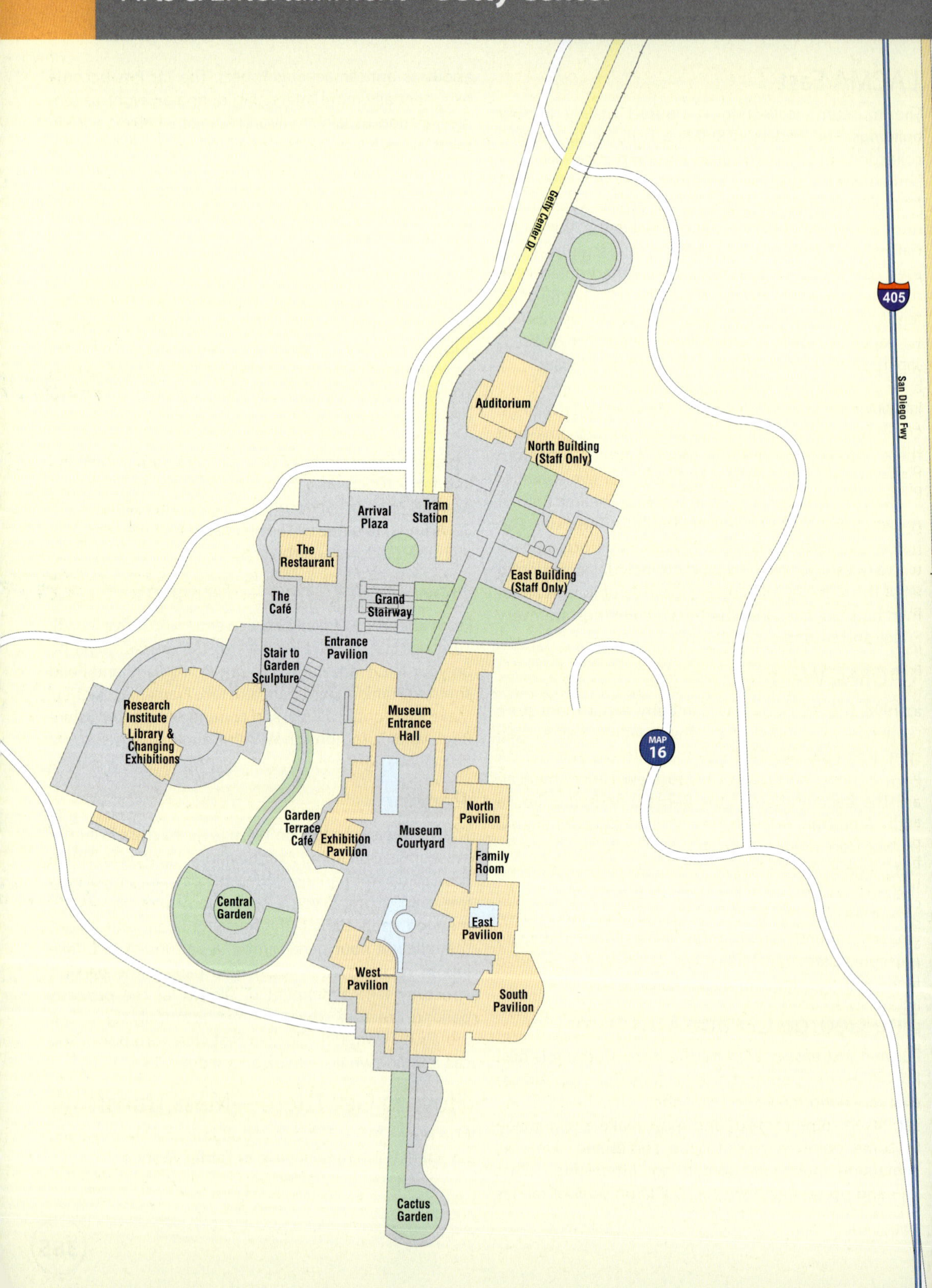
Getty Center Dr
405
San Diego Fwy
Auditorium
North Building
(Staff Only)
Arrival
Plaza
Tram
Station
The
Restaurant
The
Café
Grand
Stairway
East Building
(Staff Only)
Entrance
Pavilion
Stair to
Garden
Sculpture
Research
Institute
Library &
Changing
Exhibitions
Museum
Entrance
Hall
MAP
16
North
Pavilion
Garden
Terrace
Café
Exhibition
Pavilion
Museum
Courtyard
Family
Room
Central
Garden
East
Pavilion
West
Pavilion
South
Pavilion
Cactus
Garden

General Information

NFT Map: 16
Address: 1200 Getty Center Dr
Los Angeles, CA 90049
Phone: 310-440-7300
Website: www.getty.edu
Hours: Tues-Thurs & Sun: 10 am–6 pm
Fri & Sat: 10 am–9 pm
Closed Mondays and major holidays
Admission: free, but parking is $8

Overview

The Getty stands as one of most expensive museums in the world, and it's free for visitors. Even the $8 parking is a steal by LA standards (if you park in the residential areas you can just walk up to avoid the parking fee). So it's odd that so many Angelenos seem intimidated by it. Get in early, get a parking spot, and ride that tram up the hill to one of the most gorgeous places in Southern California. You don't even need to see one piece of official art to be blown away.

Designed by Richard Meier, the J. Paul Getty Center is a multi-sensory experience. From the building's amazing architecture to the Robert Irwin garden, which demands and afternoon stroll (or better yet, joining on one of the docent-led tours), the place is a work of art in itself.

If you think it's all stuffy, guess again. Hip programs such as the Friday Nights at the Getty fall series offer coolly eclectic music, readings, and screenings. Again, all of which are free. So what are you waiting for?

What to See

Oh, and there's art, too. The original Getty Museum began as a place for oilman J. Paul Getty to hang his large collection of art. Most art critics agree that although Getty's collecting habits proved prolific, his purchases were somewhat naïve. Though he never lived to see the museum, he left behind a staggering trust fund that has allowed the Getty to aggressively add to the collection over the years. The permanent collection includes several Van Goghs, among them the Getty's highest-profile acquisition, *Irises*. There are also Rembrandts, Cézannes, and a rare collaboration between Rubens and Brueghel. In addition to the mostly pre-20th-century paintings, the Getty boasts an impressive collection of photography from the late 1830s to the present. The ever-changing special exhibitions are a highlight of any visit to the Getty Center.

It may be impossible to see the entire collection in one visit—three hours is the absolute minimum you should plan on spending at the museum—and then there is the rest of the Getty Center. The Central Garden designed by Robert Irwin is intended to be (and most definitely is) a work of art on its own. The garden's benches and chairs invite visitors to relax and enjoy the view, which includes the entire Santa Monica Bay. Pay attention to the sound of the stream; Irwin placed rocks from different parts of the world to create different sounds as you descend into the garden. Meier's building design is also worth much more than a cursory look. The travertine marble used in the construction comes from the same source as that used to build the Coliseum in Rome and, if you look closely, you can sometimes spot fossils trapped inside the stone. Both highly trained aesthetes and novice admirers of beauty and design will notice and appreciate the sparseness and order of Meier's main buildings in contrast with Irwin's controlled chaos in the garden, which he re-landscapes seasonally.

If you can score yourself a library card to the research library (good luck!), you'll have access to one of the most amazing libraries in Los Angeles - from old optical toys like kaleidoscopes to Allan Kaprow's writings. There's an eclectic array of magical things here.

Where to Eat

The remote location means that you're basically limited to the Getty Center's dining facilities, but luckily the options here are many and all quite good. At the high end, The Restaurant is open for lunch every day and serves dinner from 5 pm until 9 pm on Fridays and Saturdays. Their menu is market-driven, so it changes frequently and serves healthy, California-style fare. Reservations are suggested and can be made by email or by calling 310-440-6810. Same-day reservations are sometimes available through the Visitor Information Desk.

The Café is run by the same management as The Restaurant, making the same high-quality food available in a more casual self-service setting. The Café is open Tuesday through Thursday from 11:30 am until 5:30 pm, on Friday and Saturday from 11:30 am until 8:30 pm, and Sunday from 11:30 am until 3 pm. Additionally, the Garden Terrace Café is a seasonal self-serve dining facility that overlooks the Central Garden.

There are also several coffee carts around the complex that carry lunch items and snacks. Should you opt to brown-bag it, a picnic area is located at the lower tram station and is open until 30 minutes before closing time.

How to Get There—Driving

Since local streets are often blocked, the best way to get to the Getty is to make your way to the 405 and exit at Getty Center Drive. Follow the signs into the parking garage. Parking is $8. Elevators for the parking garage are all color-coded, making it easy to remember where you've parked.

Once you park your car, you have two options for getting to the Getty Center. You can take the tram, which runs frequently, or you can walk to the top of the hill. Bear in mind that the walk is about a mile and at a very steep incline.

How to Get There—Mass Transit

MTA Bus 761 will drop you off right at the Getty's entrance on Sepulveda Boulevard.

Ranch House
Cafe & Museum Store
Conservation Training Laboratories
Antiquities and Conservation
Office Building
Barbara and Lawrence Fleischman Theatre
J. Paul Getty Museum
Inner Peristyle
East Garden
Herb Garden
Entry Pavillion
Outer Peristyle
Pacific Coast Hwy
1
Pacific Ocean

General Information

NFT Map: 15
Address: 17985 Pacific Coast Hwy
Pacific Palisades, CA 90272
Phone: 310-440-7300
Website: www.getty.edu
Hours: Thurs–Mon: 10 am–5 pm
Closed Tuesdays, Wednesdays, and major holidays.
Admission: Free (advanced, timed tickets required); Parking $8

Overview

Here's some rare truth in advertising. The Getty Villa actually feels like a real villa. Built in the '70s, it was the home of the J. Paul Getty Museum before it made its jump to the hilltop structure off the 405. After some remodeling, it's a vivid reproduction of the 1st century Villa del Papiri at Herculaneum in Italy. That means the main building surrounds a massive reflecting pool–filled peristyle (essentially a fancy courtyard with kick-ass columns; don't worry, we had to look it up too), with gorgeous gardens and plenty of places to take a nice stroll. Inside said column-lined buildings there's art from ancient Greece, Rome, and Etruria. An outdoor café and grassy areas that are just begging for a picnic or some lounging add to the whole leisurely Roman vibe. It's almost like you're part of the ruling empire all over again. Just don't get too comfy; we all know what happened to them.

What to See

Naked statues with broken arms, of course. Okay, and much more. The Villa is home to nearly 44,000 antiquities with about 1,200 on display at any time. Beyond the permanent collections, which are arranged by theme to better communicate their history, the Villa's exhibitions have included studies of glassmaking and architecture. Exhibitions are complemented by play readings, musical performances, demos, and other programs in a 250-seat auditorium or the old-school-like-a-Socratic-fool 450-seat outdoor classical theater. You don't have to be classically inclined to drop some cash in the gift shop, selling everything from 24k gold replicas of Roman jewelry to full gladiator getup for the 10-and-under set.

Where to Eat

Naturally, the Café at the Getty Villa specializes in Mediterranean fare: panini, pizzas, pastas, you know the drill. No reservations are required, they offer indoor and outdoor seating, and they do attempt to go the organic route when they can. It's open from 11 am to 4 pm.

If you just need a little nosh, the Espresso Cart near the Café entrance serves up coffee, cold drinks, and quicker food such as sandwiches and to-go salads. Why not get the most out of the great weather? With a little planning you can order a gourmet picnic lunch online and have it ready for you to enjoy at any of the Getty's public seating areas—all which come with a side of great views thanks to the coastal locale.

How to Get There—Driving

Sorry, you're going to have to fight your way down the Pacific Coast Highway for this one. Even trickier, you can only enter the Getty Villa by going northbound and being in the right-hand lane of PCH. Just hang on tight and make the turn into the Getty's parking lot (if you turn into the ocean, you went the wrong way). After that, the on-site parking structure is a snap.

How to Get There—Mass Transit

Los Angeles Metro Bus 534 stops near the Getty Villa entrance on Pacific Coast Highway.

General Information

NFT Map:	4
Address	2700 N Vermont Ave (in Griffith Park) Los Angeles, CA 90027
Hotline:	323-665-1927
Administration:	323-665-5857
Ticketmaster:	213-480-3232 or 714-740-2000
Website:	www.greektheatrela.com

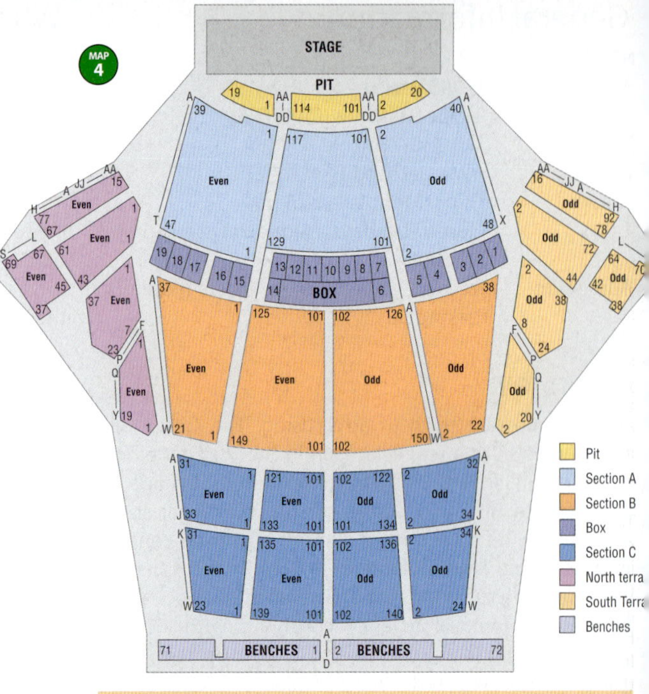

Overview

Sure, a majority of the acts that play the Greek are, shall we say, more *experienced* than most. But if you're feeling a bit nostalgic or ironic—and let's be honest, this is almost Silver Lake: you are—the Greek is *the* place to see WAR, a '70s-era soul fest, or Daryl Hall & John Oates… when the old folks' home lets them out so they can tour for the summer.

Next to the Hollywood Bowl, the Greek Theatre is LA's only other outdoor venue, and it's gorgeous. Nestled up in Griffith Park,—this sylvan amphitheater always feels cooler and less smoggy than the rest of the city. The Greek Theatre is about a third of the size of the Bowl, so you'll be hard pressed to find a bad seat. If the weather's right, the sky can be so clear that you might actually be able to impress your date by pointing out Orion and Polaris-- forgeting that you're in LA all together. No wonder the Coachella set is getting hip to the place. The Arcade Fire, Radiohead, Death Cab for Cutie, even Ashlee Simpson have all decided to go Greek during recent tours. None have trashed the place—yet.

How to Get There—Driving

From the 10, exit at Vermont and drive north to Griffith Park. From the 101 heading north, exit at Vermont Avenue. Turn right onto Vermont and follow it into Griffith Park. From the 101 heading south, exit at Vine Street. Go straight under the underpass, and you will be going east on Franklin Avenue. When you reach Western Avenue, turn left. Western will curve to the right and turn into Los Feliz Boulevard. Turn left at Vermont, and follow it into Griffith Park.

Parking

$15 at the Greek Theatre will buy you the stacked parking option (read: you can't leave until everyone around you does). For $45, you can get valet, allowing you to leave whenever the heck you want. Call 323-665-5857 to make advance reservations. (Yes, reservations for parking. We know, it sounds ridiculous.) The reservations office is open 10 am to 6 pm Monday through Friday, and 10 am until 12 pm the day of the show. All major credit cards are accepted. If you're really sly (or just lucky), you can score parallel parking along the many side roads around the Greek. You just have to hope the attendant directs you that way (it may be an option after stacked parking is full, we've never quite figured it out). This option costs $10 and you can leave whenever you want. Free shuttles will take you from your parking spot to the venue. If you're making a date of it and you're game for a stroll, parking on lively, venue-packed Hillhurst is also an option.

How to Get Tickets

The Greek Theatre's box office only sells tickets in person. They are open Monday through Friday 12 pm to 6 pm and Saturdays and Sundays 10 am to 4 pm. Tickets to all events are also available through Ticketmaster: www.ticketmaster.com, 213-480-3232.

General Information

NFT Map:	3
Address:	2301 N Highland Ave Hollywood, CA 90068
General Information:	323-850-2000
Website:	www.hollywoodbowl.org
Ticketmaster:	213-480-3232

Overview

You know the final scene in *Beaches*, where the divine Miss M sings *Wind Beneath My Wings* in that amazingly panoramic concert setting with impeccable acoustics? Yup, that's the Hollywood Bowl. This historic and beloved concert venue is another wonder of that sweet Hollywood magic. It's mere yards away from the 101 freeway, yet it feels like another world. Pack up your own food (and booze) take the hike up to the amphitheater seats, and soak up the sounds of Beethoven, something tasty from the Playboy Jazz Festival, or—if you prefer the hipper route—a mature mash-up such as Belle & Sebastian with the Los Angeles Philharmonic.

The bowl originally opened in 1922, although its signature "shell" recently endured a much-needed face-lift and debuted with improved acoustics in 2004. The official season runs from June through mid-September when fireworks light up the weekend and some twists on classical tunes (how about Bugs Bunny on Broadway?) make it a welcome event even for the uninitiated.
In other words, it's the place to bring your parents to show them that you appreciate the finer things in life–or bring that special date for a night under the stars. The program is varied and less expensive than you might think. So much so, it's almost amazing how many Angelenos *haven't* been to the Bowl. Don't let yourself be one of them.

How to Get There—Driving

The Hollywood Bowl is located on Highland Avenue, just north of Franklin Avenue. From the 10, exit at La Brea, and drive north. Turn right at Franklin Avenue, and head east until you reach Highland Avenue. Make a left turn, and the Bowl will be just ahead on your left. From the 101, exit at Highland Avenue and follow the signs to the Bowl.

Parking

There are a stingy 2,800 on-site parking spaces for an 18,000-seat amphitheater. If that doesn't stop you from wanting to park, you have to deal with pricey stacked parking lots operated by the Bowl. Pre-purchased parking is available through the box office in the Lower Terrace lot ($13), Upper Terrace lot ($12), and Odin Street lot ($12). Night-of parking, if available, costs $14 in the Terrace lots, $13 in Odin, and $13 in the Fairfield lots, located across Highland Avenue from the Bowl's main entrance. There are many privately run lots open for business when there's a concert, but skip those rip-offs. The way to do it is by parking at the Hollywood & Highland lot, validating your ticket at mall customer service (or picking up a quick snack), and walking up the hill with your picnic basket. You definitely won't be alone. It's cheaper, less difficult for the return trip home, and besides, a little exercise never killed anyone.

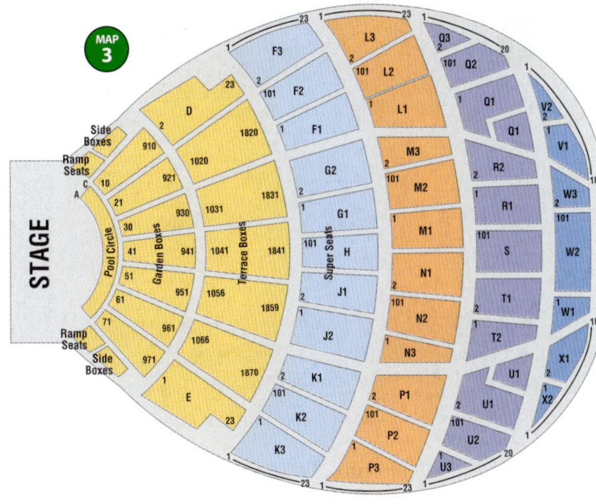

How to Get There—Mass Transit

The Park & Ride service, available for all "LA Phil Presents" concerts, lets you park at one of 15 lots around town and ride a shuttle to the Bowl for $5, round-trip. The BowlBus shuttle service offers free parking at three different locations and a $3 round-trip shuttle every 15 minutes or so starting 2.5 hours before show time. For Park & Ride and BowlBus information, visit the "Getting to the Bowl" section of www.hollywoodbowl.org.

The MTA Hollywood Bowl Shuttle (line 163) offers non-stop service to and from the Bowl when there's a concert. Catch the bus at Hollywood and Argyle, steps away from the Hollywood/Vine Metro Rail Red Line stop. The shuttle is free with a round-trip Metro Rail ticket. You can also take the 156 bus from the San Fernando Valley or LA. 800-266-6883; visit www.mta.net.

Where to Eat

Fill your basket with Trader Joe's Camembert, dry salami, and a bottle of two-buck-Chuck and join the thousands munching *en plein air* before the concert. Picnic areas open up to four hours before the concert, and tables are first come-first serve. If DIY is not your thing, the Hollywood Bowl offers a variety of overpriced dining choices, all owned and operated by Patina at the Bowl, part of chef Joachim Splichal's catering and restaurant empire. Whether it's lobster and Veuve Clicquot at the exclusive Pool Circle or popcorn from a concession stand, you will find something to simultaneously ease your hunger pains and the weight of your wallet. The Rooftop Grill offers sit-down service pre-concert, and the two Marketplace outlets sell sushi and other foodie nibbles to go.

Tickets

Subscription series go on sale earlier than individual seats for all "LA Phil Presents" concerts, and subscribers can add individual tickets to their orders before the general public. Individual tickets go on sale in May. Prices in those coveted box seats can approach $100 per person most nights, but the Bowl still offers their famous $1 seats for many concerts. Call the box office at 323-850-2000 or visit www.hollywoodbowl.com. Tickets are also available through Ticketmaster.

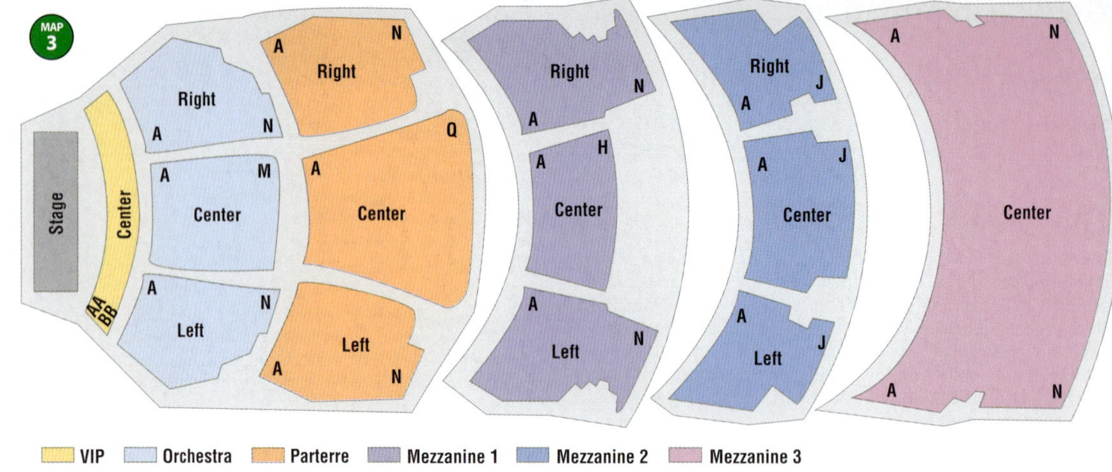

General Information

NFT Map:	3
Address:	6801 Hollywood Blvd Hollywood, CA 90028
Box Office:`	323-308-6363
Ticketmaster:	213-480-3232
Website:	www.kodaktheatre.com

Overview

The Kodak Theatre hosts two of Hollywood's most important events: the Academy Awards and the American Idol finale. Its location right in the heart of the Hollywood & Highland shopping complex means Nicole Kidman can pop over to the Gap for a new pair of skinny jeans after collecting her Best Actress award.

Not everything that takes place on its hallowed stage is Oscar-worthy. Val Kilmer bombed as Moses in a production of Jesus Christ Superstar, and Sesame Street Live is a more typical Kodak attraction. But that's Hollywood for ya—sometimes you get an Oscar, and sometimes you get Elmo.

Drawbacks that lessen the venue's cred include seats in the upper levels (the only ones that you can usually afford) raked at an alarmingly high angle and the fact that the red carpet for the Academy Awards actually rolls out through a mall. Maybe guided tours (adults $15, students & seniors $10) to see where recent nominees sat and gain access to the exclusive VIP room is money better spent if you're looking for some Hollywood magic.

The good news? The Hollywood & Highland entertainment complex, which houses the Kodak, is slowly improving with more shops and eateries like the ubiquitous California Pizza Kitchen. And if you want to balance a night of theater with a little trashiness, there's always Hooters across the street.

How to Get There—Driving

The Kodak Theatre is part of the Hollywood & Highland complex, found—*surprise!*—at the corner of Hollywood & Highland. From most parts of Los Angeles, the easiest way to reach this behemoth is via the 101 Freeway. Avoid the Highland Avenue exit if you can—it's always congested. Try the Cahuenga exit and head west on Hollywood Blvd, followed by a right onto Highland. Enter the parking garage via Highland next to the Renaissance Hollywood Hotel. From the south, you may want to avoid significant traffic downtown by taking the 10 to La Brea Avenue and heading north. Take La Brea all the way up to Franklin Avenue and turn right, then make another right onto Highland Avenue. Drive south until you reach the entrance for the parking garage.

Parking

The closest parking facility for the Kodak is the Hollywood & Highland parking garage. Escalators from said garage will deliver you virtually to the Kodak Theatre's doorstep and any merchant in the mall will validate your parking, making it a bargain at just $2 for four hours. (Valet parking is also available for an additional $5.) The parking garage is undoubtedly your best bet, as long as you don't forget to get validated and you don't mind the deep, cavernous, and impossibly-designed structure.

If you've got a little extra time, however, there are several lots that can be entered from Hollywood Boulevard that cater to the tourists who have come to see the Walk of Fame. Rates vary and tend to get more expensive as night falls and nightclubbers come out to play.

How to Get There—Mass Transit

The Metro Red Line stops at the Hollywood/Highland Station. This may actually be the easiest option for people coming from the Valley, especially when Highland Avenue backs up during Hollywood Bowl season. The 156, 212, 217, 312, and 717 buses also stop in the immediate vicinity of the Kodak. Once there, the convenient Holly Trolley can shuttle you around Hollywood between Highland and Vine for a mere dollar (free for LADOT Pass Holders).

How to Get Tickets

The box office at the Kodak Theatre, located on level one of the Hollywood & Highland center, is open Monday through Saturday from 10 am to 6 pm, and on Sundays from 10 am until 2:30 pm. Tickets are also available through Ticketmaster.

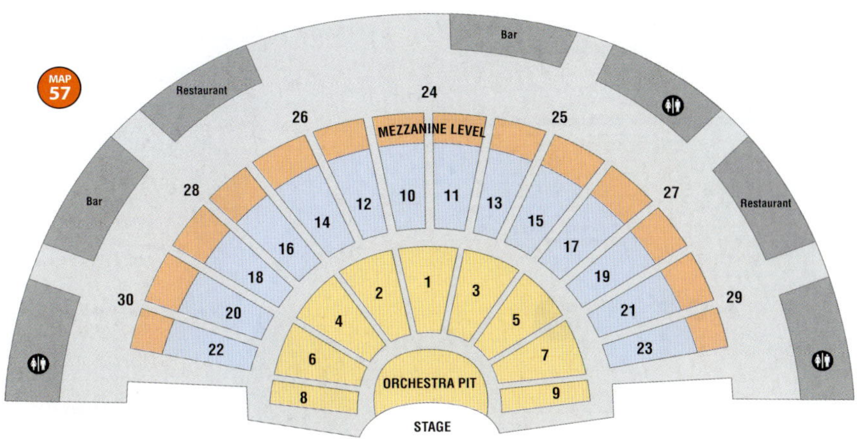

General Information

NFT Map:	57
Address:	100 Universal City Plz Universal City, CA 91608
Box Office:	818-622-4440
Ticketmaster:	213-252-8497
Website:	www.hob.com/venues/concerts/gibson

Overview

You may not see it at first blush, but the lengthily titled Gibson Amphitheatre at Universal CityWalk has a pretty rich history. It was originally an outdoor stunt stage for Universal Studios, then it was turned into an outdoor amphitheater hosting the likes of the Grateful Dead and Frank Sinatra before getting a roof in 1982, then a name change and new decor last year.

After all of that, the 6,000-seat Gibson stands as a medium-sized venue for medium-sized bands (either on their way to stardom or on their way, uh, down). In other words, this is the best place to catch everything from a packaged metal or reggaeton tour or any band that "VH1 Classic Presents" would get behind (think The O'Jays to Ringo Starr). The best thing about the place? Location, location, location. The adjoining Universal CityWalk is bigger than ever, offering plenty of places to eat and drink beforehand, making that whole dinner-and-a-show thing all the easier.

How to Get There—Driving

The Gibson Amphitheatre is located right outside the gates of the Universal Studios Hollywood theme park, just off the 101 Freeway. If you are coming from the north, take the 101 S and exit at Lankershim Boulevard. Turn left onto Cahuenga Boulevard and make a left onto Universal Center Drive. From there, head up the hill to the parking facilities. From the south, take the 101 N and exit at Universal Center Drive. Turn right at the first traffic light and drive up the hill to the parking facilities.

Parking

Parking at Universal Studios Hollywood costs $10 for the general parking lots and $20 for preferred parking. If you're happy to pay someone else to park your car, validated valet parking costs $5 for the first two hours and $2.50 per half hour thereafter. Without validation, valet parking is $7.50 for the first half hour and $2.50 for each half hour after that. Restaurants at Universal CityWalk provide validation for parking, but concession stands inside the Amphitheatre do not. Or, park for free at the Kiss & Ride lot adjacent to the Metro Red Line. Walk across the street from the subway station and get on the free shuttle up the hill to CityWalk, the theme park and Amphitheatre. Make sure to note what time the last shuttle leaves!

How to Get There—Mass Transit

The Universal City Metro Red Line stop is located just across Lankershim Boulevard from the Universal Studios entrance. If you cross the street from the subway station, the free shuttle mentioned above will take you up the hill to CityWalk, the theme park and Amphitheatre.

MTA buses 96, 150, 152, 156, 166, 240, and 750 also run to the Universal City Station.

How to Get Tickets

You can call the box office hotline at 818-622-4440 to hear what shows are playing. Tickets for most events are available through Ticketmaster, the Gibson Amphitheatre Main box office, or the CityWalk box office. The Main box office is open Thursday through Monday 1 pm–9 pm. The CityWalk Box Office is open daily 1 pm–9 pm (Fridays and Saturdays until 10:30 pm). Tickets may also be charged by phone at 213-252-TIXS (8497).

Sunset Blvd
Cesar E Chavez Ave
Pasadena Fwy
101
Hollywood Fwy
Cathedral of Our Lady of the Angels
Temple St
110
Harbor Fwy
Figueroa St
DWP Building
Hope St
Ahmanson Theatre
Mark Taper Forum
Dorothy Chandler Pavilion
Grand Ave
Kenneth Hahn Hall of Administration
MAP 9
Stanley Mosk Courthouse
Hill St
First St
Walt Disney Concert Hall
Hope St
Flower St
Second Pl
Second St
(Lower Grand below)
Olive St

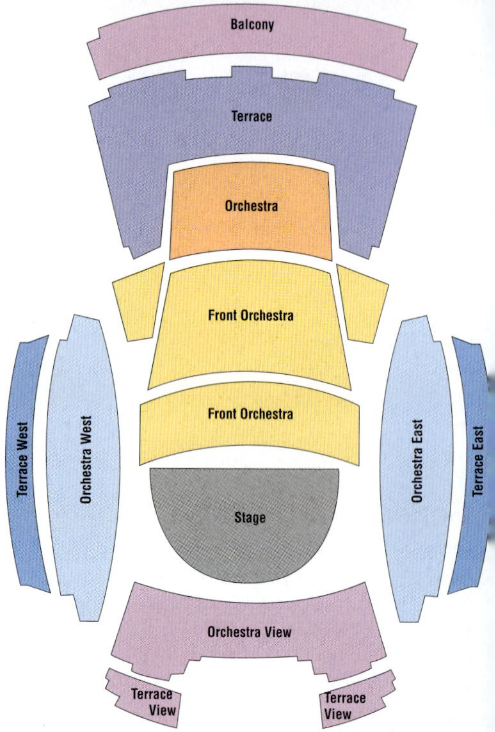

Balcony
Terrace
Orchestra
Front Orchestra
Front Orchestra
Terrace West
Orchestra West
Stage
Orchestra East
Terrace East
Orchestra View
Terrace View
Terrace View

Walt Disney Concert Hall

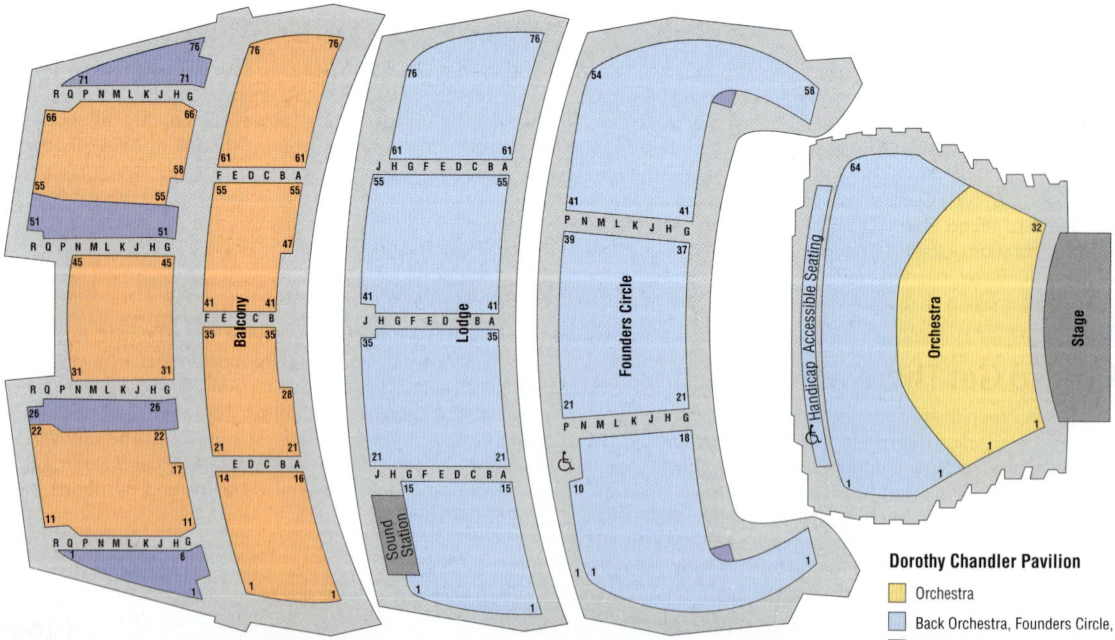

Balcony
Lodge
Sound Station
Founders Circle
Handicap Accessible Seating
Orchestra
Stage

Dorothy Chandler Pavilion

- Orchestra
- Back Orchestra, Founders Circle, Loc
- Balcony
- Obstructed View

General Information

NFT Map: 9
Address: 135 N Grand Ave
Los Angeles, CA 90012
Phone: 213-972-7211
Website: www.musiccenter.org

Overview

The Music Center brings world-renowned actors, dancers, and classical musicians to its four main venues in downtown LA. Whether it's a classic production of La Bohème or a new composition by John Adams, the Music Center's resident companies add much-lauded artistic gravitas to the city that is mocked for thinking frozen yogurt constitutes culture.

Walt Disney Concert Hall

The curving stainless-steel exterior of Frank Gehry's Walt Disney Concert Hall, erected October 2003, is now an iconic Southland image. The Los Angeles Philharmonic, led by music director Esa-Pekka Salonen, routinely sells out the house. Catching a concert in the state-of-the-art auditorium is something everyone in LA should experience at least once. Steep ticket prices are a paltry excuse: $15 can buy you a seat in the choral bench section, where you can look over the musicians' shoulders and follow along with their scores. These cheap seats are available by phone or at the Grand Avenue box office starting at noon on the Tuesday two weeks before the week of the concert. They sell-out within 30 minutes and are not available for all performances. For more information on the Los Angeles Philharmonic and Walt Disney Concert Hall, including schedules and tickets, visit www.laphil.org, or call 323-850-2000.

Under the baton of musical director Grant Gershon, the Grammy-nominated Los Angeles Master Chorale sings everything from avant-garde opera to Handel's Messiah (yes, you can sing along) in a hall that gives new meaning to "surround sound." $10 Public Rush seats (obstructed view) are available at the box office two hours before every performance on a cash-only, one-ticket-per-person basis. For Master Chorale schedules and tickets, visit www.lamc.org, or call 213-972-7282.

REDCAT

Short for the Roy and Edna Disney/CalArts Theater & Gallery, REDCAT is a slick black-box theater and art gallery operated by the California Institute of the Arts. REDCAT boasts an impressively diverse season of live performances and films highlighting innovative up-and-comers and cutting-edge performance artists from around the world. $10 Student Rush tickets are available at the box office 30 minutes before most performances on a cash-only, one-per-person (with ID) basis. For REDCAT schedules and tickets, visit www.redcat.org, or call 213-237-2800.

Dorothy Chandler Pavilion

The 3,197-seat Chandler, located on the southern end of the Music Center plaza, is home to the Los Angeles Opera and Music Center Dance programs. LA Opera, led by Plácido Domingo and music director Kent Nagano, presents greatest hits, new works, and intimate vocal recitals with stars like Renée Fleming. $20 Student and Senior Rush Tickets go on sale 90 minutes before selected performances on a cash-only, one-per-person basis (with valid ID only). Visit www.losangelesopera.com, or call 213-972-8001 for LA Opera tickets and schedules.

Dance at the Music Center is the organization responsible for bringing famed troupes such as the Merce Cunningham Dance Company and the American Ballet Theatre to the Chandler's stage. Student and Senior Rush Tickets priced $10–$15 are available at the Chandler box office two hours prior to curtain on a cash-only, one-per-person basis (with valid ID only). For more information, visit www.musiccenter.org, or call 213-972-0711.

Mark Taper Forum & Ahmanson Theatre

Center Theatre Group produces high-profile musicals, dramas, and comedies on the stages of the Mark Taper Forum and Ahmanson Theatre, most of which are on their way to or from Broadway Purchase tickets for either venue at the Ahmanson's box office, located on the north end of the Music Center plaza, or buy online. $12 rush tickets (balcony level) are available two hours before most performances on a cash-only, two-per-person basis. The Hot Tix! discount offers a certain percentage of tickets to each show for only $20. For more information on Center Theatre Group, including schedules and tickets, visit www.taperahmanson.com or call 213-628-2772. Non-affiliated, half-priced ticket consolidators abound, too. Check out Plays411.com or LAStageTix.com for discounts.

Where to Eat/Shop

The Patina Group operates all Music Center restaurants and concessions. Kendall's Brasserie & Bar, located on N Grand Avenue under the Chandler, has an impressive selection of imported beers and tasty French fare. Both the casual grab-and-go Spotlight Café and the sit-down burger spot Pinot Grill are centrally located between the Dorothy Chandler Pavilion and the Mark Taper Forum. Across First Street, the Walt Disney Concert Hall has a ho-hum sandwich shop in the lobby, so instead we recommend visitors try the wonderfully inventive and delicious meals prepared by super chef Joachim Splichal's fine-dining flagship, Patina. For more information on Patina's restaurants, visit www.patinagroup.com. REDCAT's minimal-yet-cozy Lounge is independently operated and serves snacks, coffee drinks, and cocktails.

The LA Phil Store is located in the Walt Disney Concert Hall lobby and sells gifts for music aficionados and architecture buffs, including T-shirts, jewelry, music recordings, and books. REDCAT, too, has a tiny giftshop specializing in art theory and biographies.

How To Get There—Driving

The Music Center is located in downtown Los Angeles near the intersection of the 110 and the 101 freeways.

Chandler/Ahmanson/Taper (135 N Grand Ave)
110 N and 110 S: Exit Temple, turn left on Temple, right on Grand, then turn right into the Music Center garage.

101 N: Exit at Grand, turn right on Grand, and turn right into the Music Center garage.

101 S: Exit on Temple, turn left on Temple, right on Grand, and turn right into the Music Center garage.

Walt Disney Concert Hall (111 S Grand Ave)
From 110 N: Exit on Fourth, continue straight, turn left on lower Grand, pass Kosciuszko, and turn left into the WDCH parking garage.

From 110 S: Exit at Hill, continue past Temple, turn right on First, left on Olive, right on Kosciuszko, right on lower Grand, and left into the WDCH parking garage.

From 101 N: Exit on Grand before the 110 interchange, turn right on Grand, right on Second, and right into the WDCH parking garage.

From 101 S: Exit at Temple, go straight onto Hope, turn left at Second Place, merge onto Kosciuszko from the middle lane, turn left on lower Grand, and turn left into the WDCH parking garage.

Parking

For self-parking at the Chandler, Ahmanson, or Taper, use the Music Center garage located on Grand Avenue between Temple and 1st Streets. Daytime parking costs $17 and the evening/event rate (after 4 pm for evening performances and 11 am for matinees) costs $8. Valet parking is available on Hope Street for $20.

The parking area located directly beneath WDCH has two entrances; one on 2nd Street and one on lower Grand Avenue. Valet parking is available on Hope Street for $20.

If you're buying or picking up tickets for any venue, the box office will validate for 30 minutes of free parking.

Additional parking options are within walking distance. County Lot 17 on Olive Street has parking for $8, DWP charges $5 (enter on Hope Street or 1st Street), or cruise through County Mall Parking VIP-style, with their underground tunnel to the Music Center Garage (enter on Grand Avenue) for $8.

How To Get There—Mass Transit

The MTA Metro Red Line stops at the Civic Center/Tom Bradley Station at First & Hill Streets, two blocks east of the Music Center. Metro Blue, Green, and Gold Lines connect with the Red Line.

Many bus lines stop near the center—consult the service providers listed below for routes and schedules.

MTA: 800-266-6883, www.mta.net
Foothill Transit: 800-743-3463, www.foothilltransit.org
Metrolink: 800-371-5465, www.metrolinktrains.com
Big Blue Bus: 310-451-5444, www.bigbluebus.com

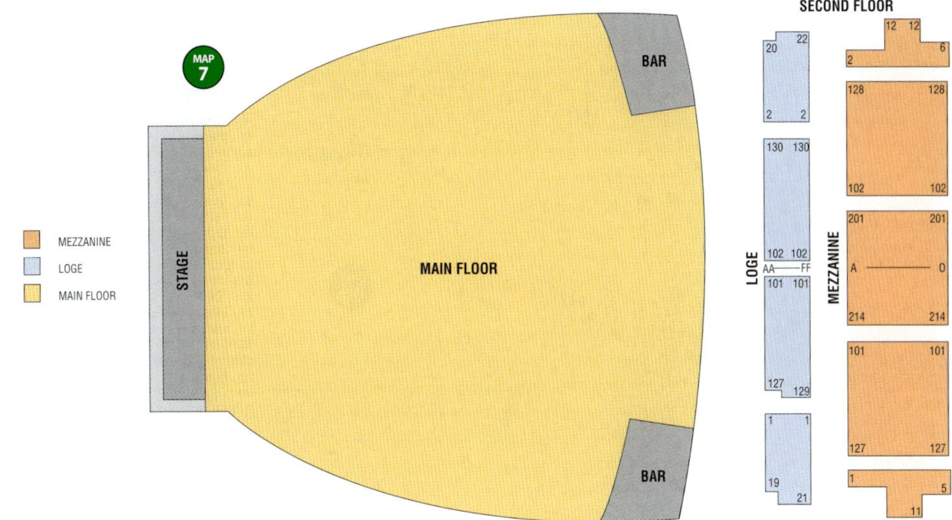

General Information

NFT Map:	7
Address:	3790 Wilshire Blvd Los Angeles, CA 90010
Phone:	213-388-1400
Box Office:	213-380-5005
Ticketmaster:	213-480-3232
Website:	www.wiltern.com

Overview

The Wiltern is undeniably one of LA's most beloved landmarks, with its trademark blue neon sign and imposing marquee watching over Wilshire Boulevard. With its omnipresent line snaked around the building, Wiltern looks like the hottest concert venue in town. A $1.5 million renovation in 2002 knocked out the lower level's 1,200 permanent seats located closest to the stage to make room for a first-come, first-served general admission area. So when Death Cab for Cutie or Belle & Sebastian come to town, you can guarantee every indie-loving teenager from LA to OC will be lined up for that prime pit spot. Don't worry, there is permanent seating available in the back for those who prefer to rock from their chairs.

The building's Art Deco architecture is so snazzy that the place was declared an official City of Los Angeles Historic-Cultural Monument, and its moderate size makes it a great place to catch a band before they hit arena status. Plus, there's a Denny's down the block, which means you can follow up that perfect Pixies concert with some Moons Over My Hammy and thank your lucky stars you're in LA.

How to Get There—Driving

Any number of east-west streets will take you to Western Avenue. The Wiltern is at the corner of Western and Wilshire. From the 10, exit at Western Avenue and drive north until you reach Wilshire Boulevard. The venue will be on your right. From the 101, use the Santa Monica Boulevard/Western Avenue exit and take Western south to Wilshire.

Parking

There are a number of parking lots in the area and limited street parking on and around Wilshire Boulevard. A large parking structure is available right behind the theater, which can be accessed from Oxford or Western. Lots generally charge between $5 and $20.

How to Get There—Mass Transit

The Metro Rail Red Line is a convenient and inexpensive way to reach the Wiltern and avoid paying for parking. The Wilshire/Western station is just across Wilshire from the theatre. A number of buses also access the Wiltern. Bus 720 runs along Wilshire Boulevard, while buses 207 and 357 run on Western Avenue. Routes 18 and 209 also stop near the theater.

How to Get Tickets

Buy tickets online or by phone through Ticketmaster. Or, skip the exorbitant fees and go straight to the box office—it's open three hours prior to showtimes.

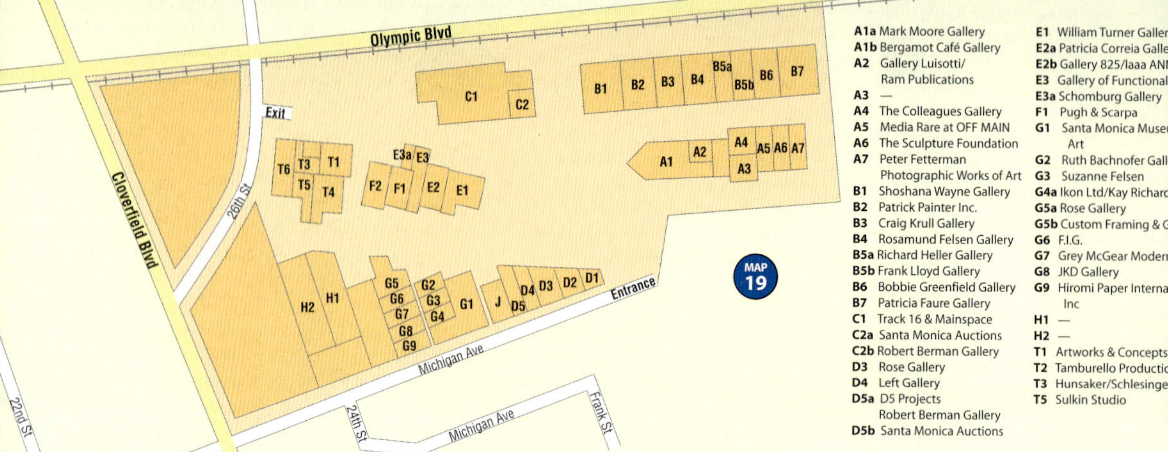

General Information

NFT Map:	19
Address:	2525 Michigan Ave Santa Monica, CA 90404
Bergamot Website:	www.bergamotstation.com
SMMOA Phone:	310-586-6488
SMMOA Website:	www.smmoa.org
Hours:	Tues–Sat: 11 am–6 pm, Closed Sun & Mon
Admission:	$3 suggested donation, $2 for artists, students, and seniors

Overview

Though looked upon as archaic by the current contemporary art scene in Los Angeles, Bergamot Station is still its own little "art walk" and there is an interesting one-stop art experience to be had. Originally a stop on the now-nonexistent Red Line trolley in the 1800s, Bergamot Station spent most of the last fifty years in a variety of incarnations from celery-packing facility to ice-making plant. After it was abandoned, the City of Santa Monica wisely saw the area's potential and asked developer Wayne Black to find an artistic use for the property. Boy, did he. By 1994, Bergamot Station was up and running as the largest art gallery complex and cultural center in Southern California. It now stands as eight acres of ideas, hopes, inspiration, and gratis wine and cheese (when you pop in for one of the many openings, that is).

What to See

Bergamot Station is home to almost forty galleries, each with its own personality. Rose Gallery deals in photographs and has shown a diverse line-up of artists from Manuel Alvarez Bravo to Wim Wenders. Patrick Painter, who shows Bas Jan Ader, is known for post-humously creating "new" works by deceased artists for profit's sake (undeniably unethical, but money does run the art-world). Track 16 focuses on modern and contemporary art and has featured artists like Karen Finley and Man Ray. The Gallery of Functional Art definitely shows art—but art that often doubles as furniture or lighting. Suzanne Felsen's unique jewelry is art by any definition of the word. One of the first Bergamot Galleries, the Shoshana Wayne Gallery, showcases artists such as Yoko Ono and Philip Argent. There is an eclectic variety to be seen at Bergamot Station and our advice is to use the complex as it was intended—park and stroll from one gallery to the next. If you keep a brisk pace, you can get through everything in an hour or two, but to get the most out of Bergamot Station, we would suggest spending an entire afternoon.

In addition to the galleries, Bergamot Station has several other tenants of note, including the Santa Monica Museum of Art. This non-collecting museum always features exhibits like no other museum in LA. Santa Monica Auctions features live art auctions of works by major artists. Hiromi Paper International is a retail shop that sells just one thing—paper. Hiromi's papers range from offbeat to exquisite, and most are so gorgeous that it would be a shame to write on them.

Where to Eat

Bergamot Café remains the complex's only option for breakfast or lunch. It's open Monday from 9 am until 4 pm, Tuesday through Friday from 9 am until 5 pm, and on Saturday from 10 am until 5 pm. They mainly serve sandwiches and salads. www.bergamotcafe.com. There are also some excellent restaurants in the area for a more leisurely lunch or a post-gallery dinner.

- **Il Moro**, 11400 W Olympic Blvd, 310-575-3530. Delicious pastas and Italian entrees.
- **LA Farm**, 3000 W Olympic Blvd, 310-449-4000. California-style cuisine in a beautiful patio setting.
- **JR Seafood**, 11901 Santa Monica Blvd, 310-268-2463. Your favorite Chinese dishes, with an emphasis on fish and seafood.

How to Get There—Driving

Located on Michigan Avenue in Santa Monica, just east of Cloverfield Boulevard, Bergamot Station is easily accessed from the 10 by exiting at Cloverfield/26th Street. Turn right at the first traffic light, Michigan Avenue, and stay on Michigan until it dead ends. The entrance to Bergamot Station will be on your left.

If you're taking surface streets, Olympic Boulevard is usually the best bet. Take Olympic to Cloverfield and turn left, then turn left again on Michigan Avenue. Bergamot Station is at the end of the street on the left-hand side.

LA is where art students go to art school to learn from famous artists. That being said, the art scene in LA is alive with many generations of artists coming out of these schools (check for MFA open studios for: UCLA, USC, Art Center, Cal Arts - you will be surprised to see what is happening amongst young artists; videos about boats and photographs of nothing, for instance). Currently the concentrated gallery areas are in Chinatown, Culver City, and at 6150 Wilshire. The Chinatown galleries - including **High Energy Constructs (Map 9), Trudi (Map 37),** and **Black Dragon Society (Map 9)** - can be found in walking vicinity of Hill Street and Chung King Court. Many are on the back alley of Chung King Road. There are small hidden galleries on side streets, so ask around. Also check out **Ooga Booga (See shopping, Map 9)**, a small store specializing in art-related goods, and have a lunch at **Via Cafe (See Restaurants, Map 9)**. The Culver City galleries are all on one block. Some highlights are **Blum & Poe (Map 10)** and **Anna Helwing Gallery (Map 10).** The **6150 Wilshire (Map 2)** galleries has **Marc Foxx, Roberts and Tilton** (who shows LA's famed photographer, Amir Zaki), and many others. **Bergamot Station (Map 19)** is becoming archaic but it is still worth a visit if you've got some free time. Usually when one gallery has an opening, all the other galleries in the vicinity have openings too, which makes one giant party of art and free beer. Check the LA Weekly for a listing of openings.

The Downtown Art Walk, held every second Thursday of the month, is a self-guided introduction to the local galleries. Visit **El Nopal Press (Map 9)**, a publisher of prints and lithographs by artists from Mexico and Los Angeles, or stop by **Bank (Map 9)** and the **Spring Arts Tower (Map 9)**, two of a growing list of galleries and artist spaces in Downtown's Historic Core on Main and Spring between Second and Ninth streets. In 2004, the area was designated "Gallery Row." Nearby **MOCA (Map 9)** offers free admission during Art Walk.

Just north of downtown in Boyle Heights, tour the resident artists' studios at the **Brewery Art Colony (Map 40)** during one of their twice-yearly art walks. Once a Pabst Blue Ribbon Brewery, the site is a warren of galleries and working studios.

Map 1 • Beverly Hills

Anderson Galleries	354 N Bedford Dr	310-858-1644
Andrew Weiss Gallery	179 S Beverly Dr	310-246-9333
Christie's Los Angeles	360 N Camden Dr	310-385-2600
Don O'Melveny Gallery	9009 Melrose Ave	310-273-6935
Gagosian Gallery	456 N Camden Dr	310-271-9400
Galerie Michael	430 N Rodeo Dr	310-273-3377
Galerie Yoram Gil	462 N Robertson Blvd	310-659-2641
Karen Lynne Gallery	216 N Canon Dr	310-858-8202
Latin American Masters	264 N Beverly Dr	310-271-4847
Martin Lawrence Gallery	460 N Rodeo Dr	310-777-0365
MB Fine Art	612 N Almont Dr	310-550-0050

Map 2 • West Hollywood

Acme	6150 Wilshire Blvd	323-857-5942
Adamson-Duvannes	484 S San Vicente Blvd	323-653-1015
Couturier Gallery	166 N La Brea Ave	323-933-5557
Curio 69	8764 Holloway Dr	310-659-1695
DiRT	7906 Santa Monica Blvd	323-822-9359
Earl McGrath Gallery	454 N Robertson Blvd	310-657-4257
Fahey/Klein Gallery	148 N La Brea Ave	323-934-2250
Forum Gallery Los Angeles	8069 Beverly Blvd	323-655-1550
Gallery 825, LAAA	825 N La Cienega Blvd	310-652-8272
Gallery Saint Germain	300 N Robertson Blvd	310-652-5511
Gemini GEL	8365 Melrose Ave	323-651-0513
George Stern Fine Arts	8920 Melrose Ave	310-276-2600
Glass Garage Fine Art Gallery	414 N Robertson Blvd	310-659-5228
Hamilton Selway Fine Art	8678 Melrose Ave	310-657-1711
Iturralde Gallery	116 S La Brea Ave	323-937-4267
Jack Rutberg Fine Arts	357 N La Brea Ave	323-938-5222
Jan Baum Gallery	170 S La Brea Ave	323-932-0170
Johnson Art Collection	8304B Melrose Ave	323-655-5738
Kantor/Feuer Gallery	7025 Melrose Ave	323-933-8976
Lacy Primitive & Fine Art	1240 Sierra Alta Wy	310-271-0807
Lev Moross Gallery	962 N La Brea Ave	323-512-0151
Louis Stern Fine Arts	9002 Melrose Ave	310-276-0147
Mak Center	835 N Kings Rd	323-651-1510
Manny Silverman Gallery	619 N Almont Dr	310-659-8256
Marc Foxx	6150 Wilshire Blvd	323-857-5571
Margo Leavin Gallery	812 N Robertson Blvd	310-273-0603
The Merry Karnowsky Gallery	170 S La Brea Ave	323-933-4408
Michael Hittleman Gallery	8797 Beverly Blvd	323-655-5364
Michael Kohn Gallery	8071 Beverly Blvd	323-658-8088
Morseburg Galleries	9089 Santa Monica Blvd	310-273-5207
Pacific Design Center	8687 Melrose Ave	213-621-1741
Papillon Gallery	462 N Robertson Blvd	310-289-1887
Regen Projects	633 N Almont Dr	310-276-5424
Riskpress Gallery	8533 Melrose Ave	310-659-4680
Roberts and Tilton	6150 Wilshire Blvd	323-549-0023
Silk Roads Design Gallery	145 N La Brea Ave	323-857-5588
Stephen Cohen Gallery	7358 Beverly Blvd	323-937-5525
Tasende Gallery	8808 Melrose Ave	310-276-8686
Tobey C Moss Gallery	7321 Beverly Blvd	323-933-5523
William A Karges Fine Art	427 N Canon Dr	310-276-8551

Map 3 • Hollywood

The Advocate Gallery, LA Gay and Lesbian Center	1625 Schrader Blvd	323-993-7400
Los Angeles Contemporary Exhibitions	6522 Hollywood Blvd	323-957-1777
Michael Dawson Gallery	535 N Larchmont Blvd	323-469-2186
Newspace Gallery	5241 Melrose Ave	323-469-9353

Map 4 • Los Feliz

Clair Obscur Gallery	4310 Melrose Ave	323-662-6693
La Luz de Jesus Gallery	4633 Hollywood Blvd	800-YRU-POOP

Map 5 • Silver Lake/Echo Park/Atwater

Black Maria Gallery	3137 Glendale Blvd	323-660-9393

Map 6 • Miracle Mile/Mid-City

Artbrokering.com	8621 Wilshire Blvd	323-939-3533
Don O'Melveny Gallery	5472 Wilshire Blvd	323-932-0076
Doublevision Gallery	5820 Wilshire Blvd	323-936-1553
Lawrence Asher Gallery	5820 Wilshire Blvd	323-935-9100
Paul Kopeikin Gallery	6150 Wilshire Blvd	323-937-0765

Map 9 • Downtown

626	626 S Spring St	213-614-8872
Acuna-Hansen Gallery	427 Bernard St	323-441-1624
Art Share-Warehhouse Gallery	801 E 4th Pl	213-687-4278
Bank	125 W 4th St	213-458-9921
Barnsdall Art Park	4800 Hollywood Blvd	323-644-6269
Bert Green Fine Art	102 W 5th St	213-624-6212
Black Dragon Society	961 Chung King Rd	310-620-0030
China Art Objects	933 Chung King Rd	213-613-0384
Cirrus Gallery	542 S Alameda St	213-680-3473
de Soto	108 W 2nd St	213-617-0434
Downtown Art Gallery	1611 S Hope St	213-255-2067
El Nopal Press at 5th St	109 W 5th St	323-581-7112
Fototeka	102 W 5th St	213-430-9044
Gallery Revisited	3204 Sunset Blvd	626-253-5266
The Geffen Contemporary at MOCA	152 N Central Ave	213-626-6222
Grand Avenue - MOCA	250 S Grand Ave	213-621-1745
The Happy Lion	963 Chung King Rd	213-625-1360
High Energy Constructs	990 N Hill St	323-227-7920
Infusion	719 South Spring St	213-683-8827
Japanese American Cultural and Community Center, George Doizaki Gallery	244 S San Pedro St	213-628-2725
Kristi Engle Gallery	453 S Spring St	213-629-2358
L2kontemporary Gallery	990 N Hill St, No 205	323-225-1288
LA Artcore	120 Judge John Aiso St	213-617-3274
MJ Higgins Gallery	244 S Main St	213-617-1700
NICHE.LA	453 S Spring St, #441	213-247-0002
Pharmaka	101 W 5th St	213-689-7799
Spring Arts Tower	453 S Spring St	213-623-4636
Transport Gallery	1308 Factory Pl	310-956-5344
Tropico de Nopal Gallery-Art Space	1665 Beverly Blvd	213-481-8112

Map 10 • Baldwin Hills

Anna Helwing Gallery	2766 S La Cienega Blvd	310-202-2213
Billy Shire Fine Art	5790 Washington Blvd	323-297-0600
Blum & Poe	2754 S La Cienega Blvd	310-836-2062
George Billis Gallery	2716 S La Cienega Blvd	310-838-3685
Q.E.D.	2622 S La Cienega Blvd	310-204-3334
Sandroni Rey	2762 S La Cienega Blvd	310-280-0111
sixspace	5803 Washington Blvd	323-932-6200
Susanne Vielmeter Los Angeles Projects	5795 Washington Blvd	323-933-2117
Taylor de Cordoba	2660 S La Cienega Blvd	310-559-9156

Map 11 • South Central West

USC -Fisher Gallery, University of Art Galleries	823 Exposition Blvd	213-740-4561

Map 12 • South Central East

Mixografia	1419 E Adams Blvd	323-232-1158

Map 13 • Inglewood

Jean Marc Gallery	906 N La Brea	323-659-2975

Map 15 • Pacific Palisades

Heritage Gallery	1300 Chautauqua Blvd	310-230-4340

Map 16 • Brentwood

Cambridge Art Gallery	200 26th St	310-451-2888
Del Mano Gallery	11981 San Vicente Blvd	310-476-8508
Leslie Sacks Fine Art	11640 San Vicente Blvd	310-820-9448
Mount St Mary's College—Jose Drudis-Biada Gallery	12001 Chalon Rd	310-954-4360

Map 18 • Santa Monica

18th Street Arts Complex	1639 18th St	310-453-3711
Angles Gallery	2230 Main St	310-396-5019
Christopher Grimes Gallery	916 Colorado Ave	310-587-3373
Crossroads School for Arts and Sciences-Sam Francis Gallery	1714 21st St	310-829-7391
Eames Office	850 Pico Blvd	310-396-5991
Enisen Gallery	2118 Wilshire Blvd	310-989-4069
Hamilton Galleries	1431 Ocean Ave	310-451-9983
LA Foto	806 Pico Blvd	310-664-1563
The Lowe Gallery	2034 Broadway	310-449-0184
M Hanks Gallery	3008 Main St	310-392-8820
Santa Monica College, Pete & Susan Barrett Art Gallery	11th St & Santa Monica Blvd	310-434-3434
Sylvia White Gallery	1013 Pico Blvd	310-452-4000
Terrence Rogers Fine Art	1231 5th St	310-394-4999

Map 19 • West LA/Santa Monica East

Art Source LA	2801 Ocean Park Blvd	310-452-4411
Berman Turner Projects	2525 Michigan Ave	310-315-9506
Bobbie Greenfield Gallery	2525 Michigan Ave	310-264-0640
Craig Krull Gallery	2525 Michigan Ave, Bldg B3	310-828-6410
Ernie Wolfe Gallery	1655 Sawtelle Blvd	310-473-1645
FIG Gallery	2525 Michigan Ave	310-829-0345
Frank Lloyd Gallery	2525 Michigan Ave	310-264-3866
Gail Harvey Gallery	2525 Michigan Ave	310-829-9125
Gallery 825 at Bergamot Station	2525 Michigan Ave	310-652-8272
Griffin Contemporary	2902 Nebraska Ave	310-586-6886
Hunsaker/Schlesinger Fine Art	2525 Michigan Ave	310-828-1133
JKD Gallery	2525 Michigan Ave	310-998-5888
Marylin Pink/Fine Arts	509 Avondale Ave	310-395-1465
Patricia Correia Gallery	2534 Michigan Ave	310-264-1760
Patricia Faure Gallery	2525 Michigan Ave	310-449-1479
Patrick Painter	2525 Michigan Ave	310-264-5988
Richard Heller Gallery	2525 Michigan Ave	310-453-9191
Robert Berman Gallery	2525 Michigan Ave	310-315-1937
Rosamund Felsen Gallery	2525 Michigan Ave	310-828-8488
Ruth Bachofner Gallery	2525 Michigan Ave	310-829-3300
Schomburg Gallery	2525 Michigan Ave	310-453-5757
Sherry Frumkin Gallery	3026 Airport Ave	310-397-7493
Shoshana Wayne Gallery	2525 Michigan Ave	310-453-7535
TAG, The Artists' Gallery	2903 Santa Monica Blvd	310-829-9556
Track 16 Gallery	2525 Michigan Ave	310-264-4678

Map 20 • Westwood/Century City

Italian Culture Institute - Spazio Italia	1023 Hilgard Ave	310-443-3250
Jonathan Novak Contemporary Art	1880 Century Park E	310-277-4997
White Room Gallery	10215 Santa Monica Blvd	310-859-2402

Map 21 • Venice

LA Louver Galleries	45 N Venice Blvd	310-822-4955
Light Space Gallery	1732 Abbot Kinney Blvd	310-301-6969
Off-Rose, The Secret Studio-Gallery of Venice	841 Flower Ave	310-664-8977
Sparc Art Gallery	685 Venice Blvd	310-822-9560

Map 22 • Mar Vista

The Venice Contemporary	12222 Venice Blvd	310-397-2244

Map 24 • Culver City

BLK/MRKT Gallery	6009 Washington Blvd	310-837-1989
Corey Helford Gallery	8522 Washington Blvd	310-287-2340
d.e.n. contemporary art	6023 Washington Blvd	310-559-3023
Duncan Miller Gallery	10959 Venice Blvd	310-838-2440
Fresh Paint Art Advisors	9355 Culver Blvd	310-558-9355
Koplin Del Rio Gallery	6031 Washington Blvd	310-836-9055
MC	6086 Comey Ave	323-939-3777
West Los Angeles College Art Gallery	4800 Freshman Dr	310-287-4200
Western Project	3830 Main St	310-838-0609

Map 25 • Marina Del Rey/Westchester West

Ben Maltz Gallery, Otis College of Art and Design	9045 Lincoln Blvd	310-665-6905
Loyola Marymount University - Laband Gallery	1 LMU Dr	310-338-2880

Map 28 • Hawthorne

Soicher Marin Gallery	12824 Cerise Ave	310-679-5000

Map 29 • Hermosa Beach

Cannery Row Studios	604 N Francisca Ave	888-366-1988
Gallery C	1225 Hermosa Ave	310-798-0102

Map 30 • Torrance North

El Camino College Art Gallery	16007 Crenshaw Blvd	310-660-3748
Joslyn Fine Arts Gallery	3320 Civic Center Dr	310-618-6340

Map 33 • Highland Park

Eagle Rock Community Cultural Center	2225 Colorado Blvd	323-226-1617
Judson Studios	200 S Ave 66	323-255-0131

Map 34 • Pasadena

Armory Northwest	965 N Fair Oaks Ave	626-792-5101
The Folk Tree	217 S Fair Oaks Ave	626-795-8733
The Folk Tree Collection	199 S Fair Oaks Ave	626-793-4828
Kelley Gallery	696 E Colorado Blvd	626-577-5657
Mendenhall Sobieski Gallery	40 Mills Pl	626-535-9757

Map 35 • Pasadena East/San Marino

Absolute Art Gallery	2326 Huntington Dr	626-285-8585
California Art Club Gallery at The Old Mill	1120 Old Mill Rd	626-449-5458
Huntington	1151 Oxford Rd	626-405-2100
Pasadena City College Art Gallery	1570 E Colorado Blvd	626-585-7721

Map 37 • Lincoln Heights

La Mano Press	1749 N Main St	323-227-0650
Plaza de la Raza, Boathouse Gallery	3540 N Mission Rd	323-223-2475

Map 38 • El Sereno

Luckman Gallery, Harriet & Charles Luckman Fine Arts Complex, California State University, Los Angeles	5151 State University Dr	323-343-6604
Trudi	510 Bernard St	323-404-8429

Map 40 • Boyle Heights

The Brewery Art Colony	676 S Ave 21	323-222-0222
East Los Angeles College, Vincent Price Gallery	1301 Cesar Chavez Ave	323-265-8650
Raid Projects Gallery	602 Moulton Ave	323-441-9593

Map 50 • Burbank East/Glendale West

Creative Arts Center Gallery	1100 W Clark Ave	818-238-5397

Map 51 • Glendale South

Harvest Gallery	938 N Brand Blvd	818-546-1000

Map 52 • Tarzana / Woodland Hills

Joseph Wahl Art Gallery	5305 Topanga Cyn Blvd	818-340-9245

Map 54 • Sherman Oaks West

Skirball Cultural Center	2701 N Sepulveda Blvd	310-440-4500
University of Judaism-Platt and Borstein Galleries	15600 Mulholland Dr	310-476-9777

Map 56 • Studio City/Valley Village

Soho Gallery	12202 Ventura Blvd	818-766-5569
Storyopolis	12348 Ventura Blvd	818-509-5600

Map 57 • Universal City/Toluca Lake

A Studio Gallery	4260 Lankershim Blvd	818-980-9100
Martin Lawrence Gallery	1000 University Center Dr	818-508-7867

Long Beach

Rio Hondo College Art Gallery	3600 Workman Mill Rd	562-692-0921

Los Angeles, the world's other film capital (we tip our hats to prolific Bollywood with awe and respect), is a moviegoer's paradise, offering a huge assortment of theaters playing old, new, revival, director's cuts, foreign, indie, gay, and silent films (and, of course, the rare gay-foreign-silent trifecta). The sprawling range of genres and theaters that cater to the movie-obsessed ensures that whatever your passion, you're bound to find something in this town to sate your cinematic tastes. With so many cinematic options it's no wonder no one reads in LA!

Palaces

Once you make it past the costumed Jack Sparrow and Spider-Man, **Grauman's Chinese Theatre (Map 3)** really is a sight to be seen (and not heard)—cavernous and elegantly lined with old velvet, but the acoustics could use an upgrade. The **ArcLight Hollywood (Map 3)** is civilized movie-going at its best with assigned seating, one of the best sound and picture systems in the world, and crying-baby-free 21-and-over screenings (but at a cost: $14 on Friday and Saturday nights; $11 otherwise). **The Bridge: Cinema de Lux (Map 26)** offers similar amenities to the Arclight but on the Westside. **Pacific's The Grove Stadium 14 (Map 2),** and **Paseo Stadium 14 (Map 34)** are big on swank and style and the new **AMC Century 15 (Map 20)** is satisfyingly super-sized, though the Saturday-night crowds tend to be, as well. The **Vista Theatre (Map 4)** in Silver Lake has leg-room galore and a beautiful Egyptian theme. The **AMC Magic Johnson Theatre 15 (Map 10)** in Baldwin Hills is also pleasingly palatial.

Jewel-Boxes

If you are of a certain age, it's possible that your love of film was born in a real theater—not at home in front of the VCR—watching something by Bergman, de Sica, or Renoir. If so, there are a handful of movie houses in LA where you can recapture some of that delicate, old-school thrill—regardless of what contemporary film might be playing. In this category we place **Landmark Regent (Map 20)**, **NuArt (Map 19)**, **NuWilshire (Map 18)**, and **Rialto (Map 34)** theatres. The **Fine Arts Theater (Map 6),** in particular, may be the quietest and most thoughtful film-going venue ever. The **Laemmle Music Hall 3 (Map 6)** and **Royal (Map 19)** theaters, as well as the intimate **Aero Theater (Map 18)** in Santa Monica, are also excellent in that capacity. Many of these old theaters do not have parking lots, so give yourself extra time.

Shoe Boxes

At $10 or more per ticket, we felt it irresponsible not to mention that some theaters are inherently disappointing in their size or layout. We cast no aspersions on their programming (most of which is beyond reproach), but want you to be prepared for smallish screens and/or unusual spatial configurations at **Westside Pavilion Cinemas (Map 23)**, the **Five Star Theaters Los Feliz 3 (Map 4)**, **Laemmle's Sunset 5 (Map 2)**, and the **Loews Beverly Center 13 (Map 2)**.

Independent

Laemmle and **Landmark** theaters are located throughout the city and can be counted on to play the low-budget, independent, foreign, or controversial film that you've been waiting to see. The **Five Star Theaters Los Feliz 3 (Map 4)** on Vermont screens a nice mix of indie and big-budget pictures, with a Wednesday "Mommy and Me" matinee at 10:30 am.

Bargains

The **Academy 6 (Map 35)** in Pasadena gives you a second chance to see first-run films you missed a month or so ago, as well as independent/foreign films that you might not have seen at all—tickets are as low as $4 if you go before six o'clock. Seven dollars will buy you admission to a double feature of second-run movies at the somewhat sketchy **Vine Theatre (Map 3)** (enter at your own risk); the two films are often oddly paired, though—an R-rated thriller and a G-rated animated feature, for instance. Also billing double features—although this movie match-up is strictly revival—is the enduringly popular **New Beverly Cinema (Map 2)**, where for $6 you can see two by Godard or a couple of spaghetti westerns.

Specialty

Every summer, the Los Angeles Conservancy presents classic films (*Roman Holiday*, anyone? *North by Northwest*?) in the historic theaters downtown on Broadway as part of their "Last Remaining Seats" program (on the web at www.laconservancy.org). For art films, with or without a narrative, check out the current listings at **REDCAT (Map 9)** in the Disney Hall. Frequently showing films that correspond with one of the current exhibits is the **Bing Theater (Map 6)** at LACMA—the museum also hosts the occasional film series as well as talks with legendary actors and directors.

Grauman's Egyptian Theater (Map 3) has been carefully restored to its 1922 grandeur by the folks of American Cinematheque, who also call this famous landmark their home; the theater features a veritable feast of film-geek favorites—director's cuts, anniversary specials, and films not on video. Summer Graveyard screenings at **Hollywood Forever Cemetery (Map 3)** allow film buffs to actually sit on the grave of the matinee idol projected on the screen while enjoying wine and cheese with hundreds of fellow Angelenos (check www.cinespia.org for details). While not technically a theater, **Cinespace (Map 3)**, a bar and restaurant in Hollywood, shows films nightly. **Pacific's El Capitan (Map 3)** theater across from Grauman's Chinese is a grand old palace owned by Disney and presents Disney films exclusively. Last, but certainly not least, is the historic **Silent Movie Theatre (Map 2)** on Fairfax. It is the only remaining silent theater in the world and has drawn in curious audiences for over sixty years with the bill of pre-talkie films and the murderous legend surrounding the theater.

Movie Theaters	*Address*	*Phone*	*Map*	
Academy 6	1003 E Colorado Blvd	626-229-9400	35	With $6 ticket prices and a great indie lineup, it's hard not to love the Academy.
Aero Theater	1328 Montana Ave	310-260-1528	18	This charming neighborhood favorite is owned by American Cinematheque--quality cinema guaranteed.
AMC Avco Center Cinemas	10840 Wilshire Blvd	310-475-0714	20	Decent and rather nondescript mainstream theatre.
AMC Broadway Cinemas 4	1441 3rd St Prom	310-458-1506	18	In the heart of the Promenade, the Broadway is a long time favorite.
AMC Burbank 16	125 E Palm Ave	818-953-9800	50	Burbank's premiere multiplex--and it's got the crowds to prove it.
AMC Century 15	10250 Santa Monica Blvd	310-289-4262	20	Great location makes this multiplex worth the trip.
AMC Del Amo 18	3525 W Carson St, Space 73	310-289-4262	32	Standard mall mega-plex.
AMC Galleria - South Bay Cinema 16	1815 Hawthorne Blvd	310-289-4262	30	It's in a mall, but manages to be decent despite the largely teenage demographic.
AMC Magic Johnson Theatre 15	4020 Marlton Ave	323-290-5900	10	Popular multiplex that is rather on the noisy side. Go early to avoid chatty crowds.
AMC Media Center 8	201 E Magnolia Blvd	818-953-9800	50	The fraternal twin of Media Center 6--this one is inside the mall.
AMC Media Center North 6	770 N 1st St	818-953-9800	50	The popular locale can make a Friday night movie quite an ordeal.
AMC Promenade 16	21801 Oxnard St	818-883-2262	45	The location is right, even if the prices aren't.
AMC Rolling Hills 20	2591 Airport Dr	310-289-4262	32	Go in with low expectations and…you won't be disappointed.
AMC Santa Monica 7 Plex	1310 3rd St Prom	310-289-4262	18	Convenient for promenade shoppers, but the theatre could do with an update or two.
AMC Theatres Marina Pacifica 12	6346 E Pacific Coast Hwy	562-435-4262	p. 241	First-run theatre with decent screens and sound.
AMC Theatres Pine Square 16	245 Pine Ave	562-435-4262	p. 241	Long-time Long Beach cinema is these days sadly neglected.
ArcLight Hollywood/Cinerama Dome	6360 W Sunset Blvd	323-464-1465	3	The crème de la crème of LA cinemas. No one does it better.
Art Theater	2025 E 4th St	562-438-5435	p. 241	Long Beach's oldest single-screen cinema features a variety of indie fare.
Billy Wilder Theater at the Hammer Museum	10899 Wilshire Blvd	310-206-3456	20	The UCLA Film & TV Archive's brand new home!
Bing Theater at LACMA	5905 Wilshire Blvd	323-857-6000	6	LACMA's huge variety of films varies monthly.
The Bridge: Cinema de Lux	6081 Center Dr	310-568-3375	26	There's something for everyone at the Bridge. IMAX, a restaurant, easy parking--what's not to love?
California Science Center IMAX	700 State Dr	213-744-7400	11	Impressive IMAX venue featuring family-friendly fare.
Century North Hollywood	12827 Victory Blvd	818-508-6004	48	Friendly valley theater.
Cinemark at the Pike	99 S Pine Ave	562-435-5754	p. 241	Fun and friendly stadium-style cinema.
Cineplex Marina Marketplace	13455 Maxella Ave	310-827-9588	25	This six-screen theater may be small, but it's big on the charm.
Cinespace	6356 Hollywood Blvd	323-817-3456	3	Have dinner and a movie in a clubby atmosphere.
Citywalk Stadium 19 with IMAX	100 Universal City Plz	818-508-0588	57	Recently underwent a massive (and dearly needed) refurbishment.
Echo Park Film Center	1200 N Alvarado St	213-484-8846	5	LA's DIY film hang out.
Edwards Atlantic Cinemas	700 W Main St	626-458-9748	39	In need of some TLC, but at least it's not crowded.
Edwards Renaissance Stadium 14	1 E Main St	626-300-8312	39	Excellent multiplex that's clean, comfortable and cute. (Yes, cute.)
The Fine Arts Theatre	8556 Wilshire Blvd	310-360-0455	6	It's no longer the Cecchi Gohri, but it's still all about independent film.

Movie Theaters—*continued*	*Address*	*Phone*	*Map*	
Five Star Theaters Los Feliz 3	1822 N Vermont Ave	323-664-2169	4	Single-screen venue bursting with personality and to-die-for popcorn. We kid you not.
Flagship University Village 3	3323 S Hoover St	213-748-6321	12	A totally fun triplex near USC that caters to the college crowd. Late night cult movies are a must.
Grauman's Chinese Theatre	6925 Hollywood Blvd	323-464-8111	3	The most famous movie theatre in the world, and rightly so.
Grauman's Egyptian Theater	6712 Hollywood Blvd	323-466-3456	3	The beautiful home of American Cinematheque features an eclectic variety of features, shorts, and documentaries.
Highland Theater	5604 N Figueroa St	323-256-6383	33	Good size, good sound, great prices: $3 on Tuesdays and Wednesdays!
Hollywood Forever Cemetery	6000 Santa Monica Blvd	323-469-1181	3	Watch a Jayne Mansfield film while sitting near her grave. Only in LA.
Laemmle Grande 4	345 S Figueroa St	213-617-0268	9	No fuss, no frills, and no fancy prices! Just plain good arthouse cinema.
Laemmle Monica 4	1332 2nd St	310-394-9744	18	Low-key and intimate indie arthouse theatre.
Laemmle Music Hall 3	9036 Wilshire Blvd	310-274-6860	6	A comfortable (and clean) arthouse theatre.
Laemmle One Colorado Cinemas	42 Miller Aly	626-744-1224	34	8-screen theater has slightly cheaper ticket prices than the norm.
Laemmle Playhouse 7	673 E Colorado Blvd	626-844-6444	34	State-of-the-art facilities in an old-world gem.
Laemmle Royal	11523 Santa Monica Blvd	310-477-5581	19	You gotta dig the Royal--as unpretentious as the films it showcases.
Laemmle Sunset 5	8000 W Sunset Blvd	323-848-3505	2	This LA favorite is an indie film lover's paradise…and then some.
Laemmle Town Center 5	17200 Ventura Blvd	818-981-9847	53	One of the Valley's few arthouse options, which means it should be a lot better than it is.
Landmark NuArt Theatre	11272 Santa Monica Blvd	310-281-8223	19	The eclectic Nuart is the consummate arthouse experience. Awesome flicks, atmosphere galore, and midnight movies!
Landmark NuWilshire Theatre	1314 Wilshire Blvd	310-281-8223	18	Legendary two-screen theater proudly offers the very best in independent film.
Landmark Regent Theatre	1045 Broxton Ave	310-281-8223	20	It's impossible not to love the Regent--everything that going to the movies is meant to be.
Landmark Rialto Theatre	1023 Fair Oaks Ave	626-388-2122	34	An exquisite single-screen palace since 1925.
Loews Beverly Center 13	8522 Beverly Blvd	310-652-7760	2	The Beverly Center's obligatory cinema. Convenient, if nothing else.
Majestic Crest Theatre	1262 Westwood Blvd	310-474-7866	20	Appropriately called majestic, the artwork is eye catching, the films fascinating, and the price is always right.
Mann Bruin	948 Broxton Ave	310-208-8998	20	Movie-premiere central. Fun destination for lesser mortals, too.
Mann Chinese 6	6801 Hollywood Blvd	323-464-8111	3	Just your average run-of-the-mill multiplex.
Mann Criterion 6	1313 3rd St Prom	310-395-1599	18	Decent and convenient, but with no discounts and overpriced food, there are better options in the area.
Mann Festival Westwood 1	10887 Lindbrook Dr	310-248-6266	20	There are better options in Westwood, but it gets the job done.
Mann Glendale Exchange 10	128 N Maryland Ave	818-549-0045	51	An older venue, but not nearly as crowded as its competitors.
Mann Glendale Marketplace 4	144 S Brand Blvd	818-547-3352	51	Comfortable, rarely crowded and close to the Galleria.

Movie Theaters—*continued*	*Address*	*Phone*	*Map*	
Mann Granada Hills 9	16830 Devonshire St	818-363-3679	44	Nothing fancy.(Not that you'd expect it anyway.)
Mann Plant 16	7876 Van Nuys Blvd	818-779-0323	47	Just your average run of the mill multiplex.
Mann Village Theatre Westwood	961 Broxton Ave	310-208-5576	20	Westwood's iconic theatre delivers the ultimate movie-going experience.
New Beverly Cinema	7165 Beverly Blvd	323-938-4038	2	Revival theater and a true LA original. The double features are legendary.
Old Town Music Hall	140 Richmond St	310-322-2592	27	Silent films + Wutlitzer pipe organ = truly awesome stuff.
Pacific Beach Cities 16	831 N Nash St	310-607-9630	27	16 screens, stadium seating and seriously long lines.
Pacific Culver Stadium 12	9500 Culver Blvd	310-360-9565	24	A great first-run theater that's totally convenient and big on comfort.
Pacific El Capitan	6838 Hollywood Blvd	323-467-7674	3	Elegant movie palace with an all-Disney bill. (At least it's cheaper than Disneyland.)
Pacific Fashion Center 10	9400 Shirley Ave	818-501-5121	43	It's hard to fault a theater with bathrooms cleaner than your Mom's.
Pacific Galleria Stadium	15301 Ventura Blvd	818-501-5121	54	Totally fab cinema: comfy seats, awesome screens and sound.
Pacific Manhattan Village	3560 N Sepulveda Blvd	310-640-1258	27	An initmate theatre with a fab selection of films, both mainstream and indie.
Pacific Paseo Stadium 14	336 E Colorado Blvd	626-568-9690	34	Big and pricey. Just like the movies it shows.
Pacific Sherman Oaks 5	14424 Millbank St	818-501-5121	55	Average and otherwise unimpressive if it weren't for the balconies--they're kinda cool.
Pacific Winnetka 21 Theaters	9201 Winnetka Ave	818-501-5121	42	An enormous 21 screen movie palace.
Pacific's The Grove Stadium 14	189 The Grove Dr	323-692-0164	2	Gorgeous cinema is big on swank and style, but its popularity is a problem come weekends.
REDCAT	631 W 2nd St	213-237-2800	9	Features film screenings, live performances, and a cracking good coffee lounge.
Redondo Beach Cinema 3	1509 Hawthorne Blvd	310-371-4567	30	There may be hipper alternatives, but it's as good a place as any if you just want to catch a movie.
Regency Fairfax	7907 Beverly Blvd	323-655-4010	2	$3 movie tickets? 'Nuff said.
Regency Fairfax 3	7907 Beverly Blvd	323-655-4012	2	Great cinema on the cheap. And we mean cheap.
Regent Showcase Theatre	614 N La Brea Ave	323-934-1770	2	Huge old-timey theatre that runs awesome foreign and indie flicks. Too bad the parking stinks.
Silent Movie Theatre	611 N Fairfax Ave	323-655-2520	2	A delightful one of a kind gem featuring pre-talkie films and live music accompaniment.
United Artists Long Beach Marketplace 6	6601 E Pacific Coast Hwy	562-430-2228	p. 241	So-so movie theatre with so-so movies.
United Artists Marina del Rey 6	4335 Glencoe Ave	310-823-3959	22	3 screens. Not much else.
Vine Theatre	6321 Hollywood Blvd	323-463-6819	3	Second-run movies at bargain prices.
Vista Theatre	4473 Sunset Blvd	323-660-6639	4	A wildly gaudy movie palace shows first runs and indie flicks.
Warner Grand Theatre	478 W 6th St	310-548-7672	p. 236	Lavish art deco movie palace hosts special screenings and live performances.
Westside Pavilion Cinemas	10800 W Pico Blvd	310-281-8223	23	Hey, the parking rocks. That alone validates the Pavillion's existence.

Who wants to be stuck in traffic on the 405 when you could instead be enjoying the wondrous museums LA has to offer? From dinosaur bones to ferry skeletons, Andy Warhol to Uta Barth, the Japanese Internment Camps to Japanese prints, this city has some amazing museums to check out.

Large/City

At the heart of the Miracle Mile is the **Los Angeles County Museum of Art (Map 6)**, or LACMA, with its comprehensive collection including Renaissance masterpieces, costumes and textiles, and African beadwork. The museum hosts weekly jazz and chamber music concerts and its Bing Theater shows documentaries and revival films. The **Page Museum (Map 6),** part of the LACMA campus, showcases fossils recovered from the La Brea Tar Pits that ooze nearby. In Brentwood, escape the hellish 405 and ascend by computer-operated tram to the **Getty Center (Map 16)**, a heavenly museum complex perched on a hilltop. The permanent collection includes works by Van Gogh, Cézanne, and Rembrandt, but the museum's spectacular views, gardens, and architecture steal the show. As it's one of the city's few free museums, all you'll pay for is parking. The Getty's sister museum, the **Getty Villa** in Malibu, re-opened its collection of antiquities in the winter of 2006. Downtown's **Museum of Contemporary Art (MOCA) (Map 9)** owns works by Lichtenstein, Rauschenberg, and Rothko and hosts hip opening-night parties. The **Museum of the American West** in Griffith Park mounts fascinating exhibits on subjects like the art of rawhide braiding and Jewish life along the Santa Fe Trail. Kids love to visit the creepy-crawly insect zoo at the **Natural History Museum of Los Angeles (Map 11)** in Exposition Park. In San Marino, bask in the glorious gardens at the **Huntington (Map 35)**, but don't miss the institution's world-renowned art and rare manuscript collections.

Small Collections

The **Norton Simon Museum (Map 34)** in Pasadena houses a fine private collection of European, American, and Asian art, including many of the bronze sculptures in Edgar Degas's *Dancer* series. Work by famed Harlem Renaissance artist Palmer C. Hayden is on display at the **Museum of African American Art (Map 10)** in Crenshaw. UCLA's **Hammer Museum (Map 20)** shows this year's cutting-edge artwork alongside last century's masterpieces. For a family field trip, try the **Craft & Folk Art Museum (Map 6)** or the **Zimmer Children's Museum (Map 6)** on Wilshire's Museum Row.

Specialty

Test your beliefs at the **Museum of Tolerance (Map 23)**, where interactive exhibits focus on the Holocaust and the American civil rights movement. The **Japanese American National Museum (Map 9)** in Little Tokyo hosts taiko drummers, sumi-e lessons, and special exhibitions such as the recent Isamu Noguchi retrospective. Indulge your favorite hot-rod historian at the **Petersen Automotive Museum (Map 6)** near LACMA, or nurse a beer on the real *Cheers* set at the **Hollywood Entertainment Museum (Map 8)**. The **Los Angeles Police Historical Society (Map 33)** displays bullets older than your grandfather, and the photos at the **African American Firefighter Museum (Map 51)** tell both the history of black firefighters and of Los Angeles. Complete with its very own exit off the 405, the **Skirball Cultural Center (Map 54)** is a premier Jewish cultural organization that offers socially relevant exhibitions along with regular musical and literary events.

Oddities

Culver City's **Museum of Jurassic Technology (Map 24)** is where you can find those aforementioned ferry skeletons (as well as some Russian tea in their tea room). Next door to the MJT is **CLUI (Center for Land Use Interpretation) (Map 24)**, a great exhibition space themed around land usage in the city. While not technically a museum, the LA County Coroner's Gift Shop, Skeletons in the Closet (See Shopping, Map 40), is a must-shop experience for the macabre or anyone looking for a chalk body outline beach towel. **The Museum of Television and Radio (Map 1)**, as implied by the name, is a must see for media fanatics.

Museums	*Address*	*Phone*	*Map*
A+D Museum	5900 Wilshire Blvd	323-932-9393	6
African American Firefighter Museum	1401 S Central Ave	213-744-1730	51
African American Museum	600 State Dr	213-744-7432	11
Alhambra Historical Society	1550 W Alhambra Rd	626-300-8845	39
Armory Center for the Arts	145 N Raymond Ave	626-792-5101	34
Blitzstein Museum of Art	428 N Fairfax Ave	323-852-4830	2
Cabrillo Marine Aquarium and State Beach	3720 Stephen M White Dr	310-548-7562	p. 236
California Heritage Museum	2612 Main St	310-392-8537	18

Museums	Address	Phone	Map
California Science Center	700 State Dr	323-724-3623	11
Chinese American Museum	425 N Los Angeles St	213-485-8567	9
CLUI (Center for Land Use Interpretation)	9331 Venice Blvd	310-839-5722	24
El Pueblo de Los Angeles Historical Monument	Main St & Cesar E Chavez Ave	213-628-1274	9
Geffen Contemporary	152 N Central Ave	213-626-6222	9
Getty Center	1200 Getty Center Dr	310-440-7300	16
Getty Villa	17895 Pacific Coast Hwy, Pacific Palisades	310-440-7300	n/a
Grier-Musser Museum	403 S Bonnie Brae St	213-413-1814	9
Hermosa Beach Historical Society Museum	710 Pier Ave	310-318-9421	29
Hollywood Entertainment Museum	3200 Wilshire Blvd	323-465-7900	8
Hollywood Guinness Museum	6764 Hollywood Blvd	323-463-6433	3
The Hollywood Heritage Museum	2100 N Highland Ave	323-874-4005	3
Hollywood Museum	1660 N Highland Ave	323-464-7776	3
Hollywood Wax Museum	6767 Hollywood Blvd	323-462-8860	3
Holyland Exhibition (by appointment only)	2215 Lake View Ave	323-664-3162	5
Huntington	1151 Oxford Rd	626-405-2100	35
Japanese American National Museum	369 E 1st St	213-625-0414	9
Kidspace—An Interactive Museum	480 N Arroyo Blvd	626-449-9144	34
L Ron Hubbard Life Exhibition	6331 Hollywood Blvd	323-960-3511	3
Los Angeles County Museum of Art	5905 Wilshire Blvd	323-857-6000	6
Los Angeles Craft & Folk Art Museum	5814 Wilshire Blvd	323-937-4230	6
Los Angeles Museum of the Holocaust	6435 Wilshire Blvd	323-651-3704	6
Los Angeles Police Historical Society	6045 York Blvd	323-344-9445	33
Mak Center	835 N Kings Rd	323-651-1510	2
Manhattan Beach Historical Society	1601 Manhattan Beach Blvd	310-374-7575	27
MOCA at the Pacific Design Center	8687 Melrose Ave	310-657-0800	2
Museum of African American Art	4005 Crenshaw Blvd	323-294-7071	10
Museum of Contemporary Art (MOCA)	250 S Grand Ave	213-621-1741	9
Museum of Jurassic Technology	9341 Venice Blvd	310-836-6131	24
Museum of Television & Radio	465 N Beverly Dr	310-786-1000	1
Museum of the American West	4700 Western Heritage Wy, Los Angeles	323-667-2000	n/a
Museum of Tolerance	9786 W Pico Blvd	310-553-8403	23
Natural History Museum of Los Angeles	900 Exposition Blvd	213-763-3466	11
Norton Simon Museum of Art	411 W Colorado Blvd	626-449-6840	34
Pacific Asia Museum	46 N Los Robles Ave	626-449-2742	34
Page Museum at the La Brea Pits	5801 Wilshire Blvd	323-934-7243	6
Pasadena Historical Museum	470 W Walnut St	626-577-1660	34
Pasadena Museum of California Art	490 E Union St	626-568-3665	34
Petersen Automotive Museum	6060 Wilshire Blvd	323-930-2277	6
Ripley's Believe It or Not	6780 Hollywood Blvd	323-466-6335	3
Santa Monica Historical Museum	1539 Euclid St	310-395-2290	18
Santa Monica Museum of Art	2525 Michigan Ave	310-586-6488	19
Skirball Cultural Center	2701 N Sepulveda Blvd	310-440-4500	54
Torrance Historical Society	1345 Post Ave	310-328-5392	32
Travel Town Museum	5200 Zoo Dr, Los Angeles	323-662-5874	n/a
UCLA Fowler Museum	Hilgard Ave & Sunset Blvd	310-825-4361	20
UCLA Hammer Museum	10889 Wilshire Blvd	310-443-7000	20
Western Museum of Flight	3315 Airport Dr	310-326-9544	32
Zimmer Children's Museum	6505 Wilshire Blvd	323-761-8989	6

General New/Used

LA's humongous selection of bookstores makes it easy to blow your grocery money on hard covers, even without a visit to the local **Barnes & Noble** or **Borders**.

Vroman's (Map 34) in Pasadena is over a century old, but its collection is as large and current as those at the big chains. **Dutton's**, another major independent, has locations in Brentwood **(Map 16)**, Beverly Hills **(Map 1)**, and Valley Village **(Map 56)**. (The Village store sells used books, too.) **Brand Bookshop (Map 51)** in Glendale lures customers with its eccentric window display (edible insect cookbook, anyone?), and keeps them turning the pages with over 100,000 used and out-of-print titles in every category imaginable.

The mothership of Southern California bookstores is **Acres of Books** in **Long Beach** (240 Long Beach Blvd). This airplane hangar–sized store carries over a million used, rare, and out-of-print books. Get lost in the stacks and channel your inner Ray Bradbury or Upton Sinclair, two of the institution's celebrated browsers.

Small New/Used

Skylight Books (Map 4) in Los Feliz has a well-edited collection of literary fiction, travel, local-interest, and film books, a resident kitty cat dozing in the window, and an impressive monthly lineup of literary events. **Small World Books (Map 21)** in Venice combines a fine selection of new titles with an ideal beachfront location. Downtown's **Caravan Bookstore (Map 9)**, the last of the old Bookseller's Row shops, carries rare and out-of-print works.

Specialty

If you're into something, odds are there's a bookshop that'll suit your interests. An intriguing selection of maps, travel guides, and photography books at **Distant Lands (Map 34)** in Pasadena inspires journeys by plane, train, or armchair. Likewise, West Hollywood's **Traveler's Bookcase (Map 2)** shelves over 14,000 books to stimulate your wanderlust. **Eso Won Books (Map 11)** in Baldwin Hills specializes in African-American literature and hosts frequent signings. **Dawson's Book Shop (Map 3)** in Hollywood is the source for antiquarian books on California history, Western Americana, and photography, and its gallery exhibits the likes of Ansel Adams, Edward Weston, and Eadweard Muybridge. The sleek **Equator Books (Map 21)** on Venice's trendy Abbot-Kinney strip specializes in rare and collectible coffee table tomes on surfing, call girls, and circus freaks.

West Hollywood is a microcosm of LA's literary scene, supporting a mind-boggling range of special interest bookstores. **Cook's Library (Map 2)** on 3rd Street stocks thousands of cookery books for Ferran Adria wannabes. **Mystery Pier (Map 2),** located on the Sunset Strip, is an antiquarian shop of the highest caliber, stocking first editions of American and British literature with an impressive collection of mystery and true crime titles. You can spend a day meditating in the stacks at the **Bodhi Tree Bookstore (Map 2)** on Melrose, purveyor of metaphysical titles both new and recycled. Check out the collection of dried herbs and crystal pendants along with the ethereal tomes. On Santa Monica, **A Different Light (Map 2)** caters to the area's gay, lesbian, bisexual, and transgender communities. **Circus of Books** in Silver Lake **(Map 4)** and West Hollywood **(Map 2)** has a large collection of gay erotica and pornography as well as zines and more mainstream gay and lesbian books. **Storyopolis (Map 56)** on Ventura specializes in children's literature, including rare and collectible titles from the turn of the 20th century. The store's readings, nifty lithograph collection, art classes, and sock hops (yes, sock hops!) keep kids and parents coming back for more.

Art/Film Books

LA is where art and entertainment collide, and the city's bookstores gather up the pieces. The eye-popping **Taschen (Map 1)** store in Beverly Hills stocks the iconoclast publisher's brand of luxe art tomes and naughty coffee table books. **Arcana (Map 18),** nuzzled in the ever-gentrifying 3rd Street Promenade, carries a staggering collection of art books dating from Abstract Impressionism to the present, organized by artist and theme. Where Arcana leaves off, **Hennessey + Ingalls (Map 18)** picks up. With an impressive collection of Renaissance monographs and architecture books, the store has as large a visual-arts collection as you'll find anywhere. **LACMA (Map 6)** and the **Getty (Map 16)** both carry exhibition catalogues and academic art books, and the **MOCA bookstore** has three locations in addition to its primary downtown residence **(Map 9)**: one at the Pacific Design Center **(Map 2)**, one at Main Street in Santa Monica **(Map 12)**, and another at the Geffen Contemporary **(Map 9)**. **Meltdown (Map 2)** in West Hollywood is famous for comics and collectibles, but its selection of graphic novels is equally strong. **Golden Apple** has two locations **(Map 2 & 43)** to delight your inner comic geek. **Book Soup (Map 2)** on the Sunset Strip boasts the best lineup of readings in the city and floor-to-ceiling shelves stocked with art, photography, film, and music-oriented titles.

Map 1 • Beverly Hills

Dutton's Beverly Hills	447 N Canon Dr	310-476-6947	Independent.
The Taschen Store	354 N Beverly Dr	310-274-4300	Art and photo books.

Map 2 • West Hollywood

A Different Light Bookstore	8853 Santa Monica Blvd	310-854-6601	Gay/lesbian.
Arundel Books	8380 Beverly Blvd	323-852-9852	Art and design books.
Audobon Society Bookstore	7377 Santa Monica Blvd	323-876-0202	Books on nature.
Automobile Books	8980 Santa Monica Blvd	310-657-5278	Books about cars.
Barnes & Noble	189 Grove Dr	323-525-0270	Chain.
The Bodhi Tree	8585 Melrose Ave	310-659-1733	New Age, spiritual.
Book Soup	8818 W Sunset Blvd	310-659-3110	Great independent bookstore.
Borders	330 S La Cienega Blvd	310-659-4045	Chain.

Circus of Books	8230 Santa Monica Blvd	323-656-6533	Gay/lesbian; general interest art/photo books.
The Cook's Library	8373 W 3rd St	323-655-3141	Cookbooks.
Golden Apple Comics	7018 Melrose Ave	323-658-6047	Comics.
Heaven Books	7740 Santa Monica Blvd	323-654-5486	Russian books.
Heritage Book Shop	8540 Melrose Ave	310-652-9486	Antiquarian books, rare finds.
Homework	139 S La Brea Ave	323-936-6139	Art, design, photography, architecture.
Houle Rare Books & Autographs	7260 Beverly Blvd	323-937-5858	Used and rare.
Illiterature	456 S La Brea Ave	323-937-3506	Art, photography, lifestyle, large print.
Interbook	7513 Santa Monica Blvd	323-882-6160	Russian books.
Kovcheg Russian Bookstore	7508 W Sunset Blvd	323-876-2749	Russian books.
Mega City One	7301 Melrose Ave	323-934-3373	Comics, etc.
Meltdown Comics & Collectibles	7522 Sunset Blvd	323-851-7223	Comics, graphic novels, and art books.
Michael R Thompson Booksellers	8242 W 3rd St	323-658-1901	Fine antiquarian and scholarly books.
MOCA at the Pacific Design Center	8687 Melrose Ave	310-289-5223	Contemporary art books and magazines.
Mystery Pier Books	8826 W Sunset Blvd	310-657-5557	First edition and rare books.
Samuel French Theatre & Film	7623 W Sunset Blvd	323-876-0570	Theater and film books.
St Petersberg Entertainment	7758 Santa Monica Blvd	323-654-0582	All things Russian.
Traveler's Bookcase	8375 W 3rd St	323-655-0575	Excellent shop for travelers.

Map 3 • Hollywood

A-Z Technical Book Store	1033 N Sycamore Ave	323-464-4322	Technical books.
Borders	1501 Vine St	323-463-8519	Chain.
Cosmopolitan Book Shop	7017 Melrose Ave	323-938-7119	General new and used.
Counterpoint Records and Books	5911 Franklin Ave	323-957-7965	Rare books and records
Daily Planet Book Store	5931 Franklin Ave	323-957-0061	New fiction.
Dawson's Book Shop	535 N Larchmont Blvd	323-469-2186	Rare books on the American West.
Edmund's Bookshop	6644 Hollywood Blvd	323-463-3273	Cinema and theatre books.
Hollywood Magic	6614 Hollywood Blvd	323-464-5610	Magic books.

Map 4 • Los Feliz

Aldine Books	4663 Hollywood Blvd	323-666-2690	Used.
Circus of Books	4001 W Sunset Blvd	323-666-1304	Gay books and magazines.
Comic Connection	1608 Hillhurst Ave	323-665-7715	Comic books.
Philosophical Bookstore	3910 Los Feliz Blvd	323-663-2167	Philosophy and spirituality.
Siam Books	5178 Hollywood Blvd	323-665-4236	Thai books.
Skylight Books	1818 N Vermont Ave	323-660-1175	Independent general interest.
Soap Plant	4633 Hollywood Blvd	323-663-0122	Eclectic selection.

Map 5 • Silver Lake/Echo Park/Atwater

Libreria Mexico de Echo Park	1632 W Sunset Blvd	213-250-4835	Hispanic general interest.
Mini-Melt	3151 Los Feliz Blvd	323-668-1212	Comic books, children's books.
Seven Crows Bookshop	2388 Glendale Blvd	323-913-9677	Used.

Map 6 • Miracle Mile/Mid-City

The Bookshelf at LACMA	5905 Wilshire Blvd	323-857-6146	Eclectic art books.
New Mastodon German Books	5820 Wilshire Blvd	323-525-1948	New and used German books.

Map 7 • Hancock Park

Chevalier's Books	126 N Larchmont Blvd	323-465-1334	General interest, new books.
Educational Bookstore	3005 W 6th St	213-387-3184	Educational books and school supplies.

Map 8 • Korea Town

Chong Books	2785 W Olympic Blvd	213-739-8107	Korean books.
Dong-A Book Plaza	3460 W 8th St	213-382-7100	Korean books.
Jeong Eum Sa	928 S Western Ave	213-738-9140	Korean books, some English.
Jump Q	4177 W 3rd St	213-365-6133	Educational books.
Kachi	401 S Vermont Ave	213-487-6921	Comics.
Korea One	170 S Western Ave	213-388-0914	Korean books.
Libreria Hispanoamerica	2502 W 6th St	213-384-6084	Spanish books.
Orange Comics	3500 W 8th St	213-383-5250	Comics.
Seojong Bookstore	3250 W Olympic Blvd	323-735-7374	Korean books.
Solomon Comics	2500 W 8th St	213-368-0076	Comics.
Student Books	244 S Oxford Ave	213-387-1582	K-7 textbooks.
Sung Ji Books	2837 W Olympic Blvd	213-388-2839	Korean books.
Western Comics	730 S Western Ave	213-385-7025	Korean comics.

Map 9 • Downtown

B Dalton	201 N Los Angeles St	213-687-3050	Chain.
Borders	700 W 7th St	213-624-5137	Chain.
Caravan Bookstore	550 S Grand Ave	213-626-9944	Out of print books.
China Bookstore	652 N Broadway	213-680-9230	Chinese books.
Great Wall Books & Art	970 N Broadway	213-617-2817	Chinese and medical books.
International Fashion Publications	110 E 9th St	213-622-5663	Fashion-related books.
Kinokuniya Bookstore	123 Astronaut Onizuka St E	213-687-4480	Japanese books, some English.
Libros Revolucion	312 W 8th St	213-488-1303	Spanish and English books.
MOCA at the Geffen Contemporary	152 N Central Ave	213-633-5323	Contemporary art books and magazines.
The MOCA Store	250 S Grand Ave	213-621-1710	Contemporary art books and magazines.
Niming Books	969 N Hill St	213-687-9817	Chinese books.
Thai Books & Music Dokya	1100 N Main St	323-342-9982	Thai books.

Map 11 • South Central West

Eso Won Books	4331 Degnan Blvd	323-290-1048	African-American books.
Libreria Azteca	1429 W Adams Blvd	323-733-4040	Spanish books.
University of Southern California Bookstore	840 Childs Wy	213-740-5214	Text and trade books.

Map 12 • South Central East

MOCA Santa Monica	2447 Main St	310-396-9833	Contemporary art books and magazines.
Pathfinder Bookstore	4229 S Central Ave	323-233-9372	Socialism.
Theosophy	245 W 33rd St	213-748-7244	Theosophy books.

Map 13 • Inglewood

Zarah's Books & Things	900 N La Brea Ave	310-330-1300	African-American books.

Map 14 • Inglewood East/Morningside Park

Bright Lights Children's Books	8461 S Van Ness Ave	323-971-1296	Multicultural children's books—Saturday only.
Express Yourself Books	1425 W Manchester Ave	323-750-4114	General interest books.

Map 15 • Pacific Palisades

Village Books	1049 Swarthmore Ave	310-454-4063	General.

Map 16 • Brentwood

Dutton's Brentwood	11975 San Vicente Blvd	310-476-6263	Great independent bookstore.
The Getty Museum Store	1200 Getty Center Dr	310-440-7300	Getty publications.

Map 17 • Bel Air/Holmby Hills

Dragon Books	2954 N Beverly Glen Cir	310-441-8545	Rare and antiquarian.
UCLA BookZone	308 Westwood Plz	310-206-4041	Very large college bookstore

Map 18 • Santa Monica

A&R Textbooks	1703 Pico Blvd	310-314-4361	Textbooks.
Angel City Bookstore & Gallery	218 Pier Ave	310-399-8767	Used art and literature.
Arcana Books on the Arts	1229 3rd St Prom	310-458-1499	Excellent art and architecture. Hard to find.
Barnes & Noble	1201 3rd St Prom	310-260-9110	Chain.
Barry R Levin Science Fiction	720 Santa Monica Blvd	310-458-6111	Science fiction, fantasy, and horror.
Borders	1415 3rd St Prom	310-393-9290	Chain.
Hennessey + Ingalls Art Books	214 Wilshire Blvd	310-458-9074	Superb art and architecture.
HI de Ho Comics & Books With Pictures	525 Santa Monica Blvd	310-394-2820	Comics
Kulturas Books	1700 Ocean Park Blvd	310-450-8707	General collection.
Novel Café	212 Pier Ave	310-396-8566	General interest, new, used and donated books.
Wilshire Books	3018 Wilshire Blvd	310-828-3115	Used books.

Map 19 • West LA/Santa Monica East

Alias Books	1650 Sawtelle Blvd	310-473-4442	Rare and out-of-print.
Asahiya Bookstore	2130 Sawtelle Blvd	310-575-3303	Japanese Books.
Collectors Exchange	3126 S Sepulveda Blvd	310-996-8811	Comic books
Gene de Chene Bookseller	11556 Santa Monica Blvd	310-477-8734	General.
RR News	11203 National Blvd	310-312-0405	News/periodicals.
Sawtelle Books & Music	11301 W Olympic Blvd	310-477-8686	Japanese books.

Map 20 • Westwood/Century City

Borders	10250 Santa Monica Blvd	310-552-1411	Chain.
Borders	1360 Westwood Blvd	310-475-3444	Chain.
Brentano's	10250 Santa Monica Blvd	877-449-2665	Chain in Century City Mall.

Dehkhoda Persian Bookstore	1387 Westwood Blvd	310-477-0044	Persian books.
Jay & Silent Bob's Secret Stash	1045 Westwood Blvd	310-824-1373	Comics.
Mystery Bookstore	1036 Broxton Ave	310-209-0415	Mystery.
Text Book Plus	927 Westwood Blvd	310-824-1155	College books.

Map 21 • Venice

Beyond Baroque Foundation	681 Venice Blvd	310-822-3006	Literary arts.
Equator Books	1103 Abbot Kinney Blvd	310-399-5544	Rare and collectibles.
Small World Books	1407 Ocean Front Wk	310-399-2360	General and mystery.

Map 22 • Mar Vista

Dreamworld Comics	12400 W Washington Blvd	310-390-7860	Contemporary art books and magazines
Sam Johnson's Bookshop	12310 Venice Blvd	310-391-5047	Rare and out-of-print.

Map 23 • Rancho Park/Palms

Barnes & Noble	10850 W Pico Blvd	310-475-4144	Chain.
Building News Bookstore	10801 National Blvd	310-474-7771	Construction books.
Children's Book World	10850 W Pico Blvd	310-559-2665	Children's books.

Map 24 • Culver City

Comic Ink	4267 Overland Ave	310-204-3240	Comic books.
Pepperdine Bookstore	6100 Center Dr	310-568-5741	College textbooks.

Map 25 • Marina Del Rey/Westchester West

Barnes & Noble	13400 Maxella Ave	310-306-3213	Chain.

Map 26 • Westchester/Fox Hills/Ladera Heights

Borders	6081 Center Dr	310-215-3720	Chain.
Borders Express	124 Fox Hills Mall	310-313-9352	Chain.
Crown Books	8655 S Sepulveda Blvd	310-568-9553	Bargain books, new.

Map 27 • El Segundo/Manhattan Beach

Barnes & Noble	1800 Rosecrans Ave	310-725-7025	Chain.
Borders	710 S Sepulveda Blvd	310-607-9196	Chain.
Comic Bug	1015 N Aviation Blvd	310-372-6704	Comic books.
Dave's Old Bookshop	350 N Sepulveda Blvd	310-376-0879	Used indie fiction.

Map 28 • Hawthorne

A Baseball Clubhouse and Comic Books	13308 Inglewood Ave	310-675-3333	Mostly baseball cards, some comic books.

Map 29 • Hermosa Beach

Book Value	2573 Pacific Coast Hwy	310-530-5343	Japanese books.
Eclectic Collector	1116 Hermosa Ave	310-374-4240	General used.

Map 30 • Torrance North

House Of Heroes Comics	18214 Prairie Ave	310-516-7800	Comics.
Kaede Shobo Japanese Bookstore	2147 W 182nd St	310-324-9892	Japanese books.

Map 31 • Redondo Beach

Book Again	5039 Torrance Blvd	310-542-1156	Used fiction.
Encore Books	1704 S Pacific Coast Hwy	310-540-1106	Used and rare.
Psychic Eye Bookshop	3902 Pacific Coast Hwy	310-378-7754	Metaphysical, self-help.
Sandpiper Books	4665 Torrance Blvd	310-371-2002	Used.

Map 32 • Torrance South

Asahiya Bookstore	3832 Sepulveda Blvd	310-787-0700	Japanese Books.
Barnes & Noble	21400 Hawthorne Blvd	310-370-5552	Chain.
Bookoff	2521 Pacific Coast Hwy	310-325-2388	Genereal used books.
Borders	3700 Torrance Blvd	310-540-7000	Chain.
Third Planet	3631 Pacific Coast Hwy	310-791-6227	Graphic novels and comics.
The WWII Store	1422 Marcelina Ave	310-533-4992	WWII…period.

Map 33 • Highland Park

Another World Comics & Books	1615 Colorado Blvd	323-257-7757	Comics, sci-fi.
Appleby Books	1007 N Ave 51	323-478-0655	Children's collectibles.
Imix Books	5052 Eagle Rock Blvd	323-257-2512	Spanish books.
Meltdown Comics & Collectibles	1613 Colorado Blvd	323-258-2300	Comics, graphic novels, and art books.

Map 34 • Pasadena

Alexandria Metaphysical Bookstore II	567 S Lake Ave	626-792-7885	Metaphysical books.
Apostrophe Books	289 E Green St	866-661-3031	Discount books.
Barnes & Noble	111 W Colorado Blvd	626-585-0362	Chain.
Book Alley	611 E Colorado Blvd	626-683-8083	Used art, literature, philosophy.
Book 'em Mysteries	1118 Mission St	626-799-9600	Mystery.
Bookhouse	1026 Fair Oaks Ave	626-799-0756	General used.
Borders	475 S Lake Ave	626-304-9773	Chain.
Bungalow News	746 E Colorado Blvd	626-795-9456	Magazines and paperbacks.
Cliff's Books	630 E Colorado Blvd	626-449-9541	Used.
Comic Odyssey	319 S Arroyo Pkwy	626-577-6696	Comic books.
Crown Books	900 Fair Oaks Ave	626-403-0010	Bargain books.
Distant Lands Travel Bookstore & Outfitter	56 S Raymond Ave	626-449-3220	Maps and travel books.
Gamble House	4 Westmoreland Pl	626-449-4178	Design, art, and architecture.
Norton Simon Museum of Art	411 W Colorado Blvd	626-449-6840	Museum shop.
Vroman's Bookstore	695 E Colorado Blvd	626-449-5320	Great independent bookstore.

Map 35 • Pasadena East/San Marino

Archives Bookshop	1396 E Washington Blvd	626-797-4756	Academics, philosophy, religious.
Cal-Gold Enterprises	2569 E Colorado Blvd	626-792-6161	Gold miners.
Comics Factory	1298 E Colorado Blvd	626-585-0618	Comics.
Cook Books	1388 E Washington Blvd	626-296-1638	Cook books.
Crossroads Books	1196 E Walnut St	626-795-8772	Rehab books.
Mitchell Books	1395 E Washington Blvd	626-798-4438	Mystery.
Oriental Book Store	1713 E Colorado Blvd	626-577-2413	Books on the Orient.
San Marino Toy & Book Shoppe	2424 Huntington Dr	626-309-0222	Children's books.

Map 38 • El Sereno

Legal Books Distributing	4247 Whiteside St	323-526-7110	Legal books warehouse.
Student Book Mart & Copy Center	1725 N Eastern Ave	323-262-5511	Textbooks for Cal-State.

Map 39 • Alhambra

Jilie	1283 E Valley Blvd	626-308-1466	Chinese books.
Kingston Culture Plaza	228 W Valley Blvd	626-570-1277	Chinese books.
Ng Hing Kee of Los Angeles	29 E Valley Blvd	626-943-9933	Chinese general interest.

Map 40 • Boyle Heights

Libreria & Discoteca Sonora	2403 E 1st St	323-263-0522	Spanish general, new and used.
Sears Book Center	2650 E Olympic Blvd	323-265-3153	Spanish books.

Map 43 • Granada Hills / Northridge

Anime Plus	8937 Reseda Blvd	818-773-7371	Anime.
Borders	9301 Tampa Ave	818-886-5443	Chain.
Crown Books	10821 Zelzah Ave	818-831-6000	Bargain books.
Golden Apple Comics	8967 Reseda Blvd	818-993-7804	Comics.

Map 44 • Mission Hills / North Hills

Bookhouse	17048 Devonshire St	818-832-0976	Children's, biography.
Continental Comics	17032 Devonshire St	818-368-8909	Comics.

Map 45 • Canoga Park / Woodland Hills

A&M Book Cellars	19801 Vanowen St	818-716-6259	Used books.
Builder's Bookstore	8001 Canoga Ave	818-887-7828	Construction books.
Collector's Paradise	7131 Winnetka Ave	818-999-9455	Comic books, graphic novels.
The Flip Side	19950 Ventura Blvd	818-883-9550	Comics and videos.
Libreria Soy Un Triufador	7223 Tampa Ave	818-993-7367	Hispanic general interest.
Massoglia Books	19801 Vanowen St	818-702-9529	Used books.
Pierce College - Bookstore	6201 Winnetka Ave	818-347-0313	Text and trade books.

Map 46 • Reseda

Imagine Center	18635 Ventura Blvd	818-345-1100	New age, spiritual.
Into The Mystic	18551 Ventura Blvd	818-345-0114	Metaphysical books and gifts.
Russian Gifts & Books	5424 Reseda Blvd	818-342-1668	Russian books.

Map 47 • Van Nuys

Bargain Books	14426 Friar St	818-782-2782	General used.
Comics & Fun	6411 Sepulveda Blvd	818-779-7643	Comic books, posters, magazines.
Epic Comics	7400 Van Nuys Blvd	818-781-3264	Comics.

Libreria El Quijote	14534 Victory Blvd	818-989-2411	Spanish books.
Recyclepedia	17216 Saticoy St	818-804-2772	Used and rare.
Russian Books	13757 Victory Blvd	818-781-7533	Russian books.
Theodore Front Musical Literature	16122 Cohasset St	818-994-1902	Books about music.

Map 48 • North Hollywood

Chamber of Comics	13545 Roscoe Blvd	818-780-4551	Comics

Map 49 • Burbank

American Opinion Books & Flags	5653 Cahuenga Blvd	818-769-4019	Right-wing books.
Autobooks/Aerobooks	3524 W Magnolia Blvd	818-845-0707	Auto and air.
Borders Express	201 E Magnolia Blvd	818-557-0828	Chain.
Dark Delicacies	4213 W Burbank Blvd	818-556-6660	Horror books.
Twice Told Tales	3427 W Magnolia Blvd	818-841-0652	Rare and out-of-print.
Woodbury University Book Store	7500 N Glenoaks Blvd	818-252-4828	College books.

Map 50 • Burbank East/Glendale West

A&S Bargain Books	301 N San Fernando Blvd	818-238-0371	Bargain books.
Astounding Fantasy Art Books & Comics	224 E Orange Grove Ave	818-953-7234	Art and comic books.
Automotive Book Stop	1508 W Magnolia Blvd	818-845-1202	The name says it all.
Barnes & Noble	731 N San Fernando Blvd	818-558-1383	Chain.
Best-Seller Bookshop	12 N San Fernando Blvd	818-845-1563	General used.
Book Castle's Movie World	212 N San Fernando Blvd	818-846-0459	Books on movies, theatre, dance, TV.
Kings Comic and Card Shop	420 N Glenoaks Blvd	818-562-1834	Comic books, graphic novels, sports.
Psychic Eye Bookshop	1011 W Olive Ave	818-845-8831	Metaphysical, self-help.

Map 51 • Glendale South

Abril Armenian Book Store	415 E Broadway	818-243-4112	Armenian books.
Barnes & Noble	245 N Glendale Ave	818-246-4677	Chain.
Berj Armenian Bookstore	422 S Central Ave	818-244-3830	Armenian books.
Bookfellows Fine & Rare Books	238 N Brand Blvd	818-545-0121	Rare books.
Borders	100 S Brand Blvd	818-241-8099	Chain.
Brand Bookshop	231 N Brand Blvd	818-507-5943	Used books.
Legacy Comic Books & Sportscards	123 W Wilson Ave	818-247-8803	Comics.
Mystery & Imagination Bookshop	238 N Brand Blvd	818-545-0206	Sci-Fi, fantasy, mystery.
Sardarabad Books	1111 S Glendale Ave	818-500-0790	Iranian books.
Young Scholar	233 N Central Ave	818-246-7063	Children's and teacher's books.

Map 52 • Tarzana / Woodland Hills

Barnes & Noble	6100 Topanga Cyn Blvd	818-704-3850	Chain.
Borders	6510 Canoga Ave	818-887-1999	Chain.

Map 54 • Sherman Oaks West

Barnes & Noble	16461 Ventura Blvd	818-380-1636	Chain.
Borders	14651 Ventura Blvd	818-728-6593	Chain.
Earth-2 Comics	15017 Ventura Blvd	818-386-9590	Comics.

Map 55 • Sherman Oaks East

Books on the Boulevard	13551 Ventura Blvd	818-905-0988	Hardcover non-fiction.
Borders Express	14006 Riverside Dr	818-788-8661	Chain owned by Borders.
Psychic Eye Bookshop	13435 Ventura Blvd	818-906-8263	Metaphysical, self-help.

Map 56 • Studio City/Valley Village

Alkimi: A Sacred Space for Transformation	12401 Ventura Blvd	818-985-4653	New Age, Mystical.
Bookstar	12136 Ventura Blvd	818-505-9528	Owned by B&N—chain.
Comicsmash	11824 Ventura Blvd	818-761-3753	Comic books.
DJ'S Universal Comics	11038 Ventura Blvd	818-761-3465	Comic books
Dutton's Books	5146 Laurel Cyn Blvd	818-769-3866	Great independent bookstore.
Laurel Park Newsstand	4346 Laurel Cyn Blvd	818-769-8583	Magazines.
Paris Bookstore	4820 Laurel Cyn Blvd	818-762-7557	Russian books.
Portrait of a Bookstore	4360 Tujunga Ave	818-769-3853	General interest indie bookstore.
Samuel French Theatre & Film	11963 Ventura Blvd	818-762-0535	Theater and film books.
Storyopolis	12348 Ventura Blvd	818-509-5600	Great children's bookstore.

Map 57 • Universal City/Toluca Lake

Geographia Map & Travel	4000 W Riverside Dr	818-848-1414	Maps and travel.
Iliad Bookshop	5400 Cahuenga Blvd	818-509-2665	Used literature, cinema, and arts.
Last Grenadier	820 N Hollywood Wy	818-848-9144	Military topics; role-play gaming books.
Upstart Crow	1000 Universal Center Dr	818-763-1811	General interest.

Overview

If you're trying to determine where you should be going in Los Angeles to find the best bars, scene, or music, you're probably in for more than you bargained for; or, if you're the Michiko Kakutani of inebriate decadence, maybe it's just enough. Where you go for your hedonistic splurges in LA is tantamount to declaring your political affiliation. Every city, god willing, is a raging pool of diversity. In LA, a city where the nightlife is an altar to transcendence, everyone casts themselves as the star of their own fever-dream fantasies. Battle lines are quickly drawn: the ropes and the ropes-not, those who favor the orchestral and those who seek the sweat straight from the lead singer's brow, the clubbers and loungers, beer chasers and oenophiles, the loyal neighborhood jointers and the hipsters drawn to the latest flame. Everyone here is dying for something to sneer at and something to which they can pledge their loyalty. For some, this is the supreme aesthetic mosh pit that they've been craving since the urge to split their hometown sprouted during puberty. For others, it's a cold, shallow battle of egos that leaves them nostalgic and dipping into yet another drink amid their own reverse snobbery. Either way, the good news is that there are choices galore, and they're breeding like rabbits.

Keeping track of it all can be like preparing for April 15th, and there are many ways/opinions on how this should be done. To begin with, there's *LA Weekly*, LA's premier free weekly, and the *LA Times* has its Calendar Live section—and each of these have online counterparts. There's also the omnipresent www.citysearch.com and an entire traffic jam of sites like www.la.com. One mention on Daily Candy means you can kiss your seat goodbye at your previously undiscovered neighborhood haunt—that's how hungry everyone in this town is for the "next big thing." And we're not going to even open the can of worms that is all the blogs, newsletters, and other web sites and publications dedicated to the LA nightlife. Is this sounding like finding a needle in a haystack yet? Well, it is and it isn't. Consider all of this a general arsenal. Soak it in and find your favorites. Anyway, remember, in LA, word of mouth is king. But here are some of our suggestions to get the ball rolling.

Best Dive Bars

You know you've entered a dive bar in Los Angeles when there's no velvet rope, no schmoozing the bouncer, and the inside smells of sweat and stale beer. Don't you dare order a schmancy Negroni or any rainbow-colored drink here—your request will be met with ironic laughter at best, a disgusted grunt at worst. A warning to oenophiles: these places stock the worst of the worst in wine, so don't even bother. Best stick to what dive bars do best: beer, shots, pool, and darts. Our favorite dive bar in LA is **White Horse (Map 3)** on the ground floor of Motel 8 on Western Avenue, just north of Sunset Boulevard; its red walls and black leatherette bar stools lend a sense of unpretentiousness, and the Romanian owner will feed you hot dogs and popcorn if you're nice...or tell you to "get lost" if you're not. If you like your dive bars dirty, **Power House (Map 3)** on Highland specializes in dingy booths and stiff drinks. While the Westside tends to shy away from cracked seats and beer nuts, the Eastside does dives well: a few great ones to checkout are the **Red Lion Tavern (Map 5)** in Silver Lake, **The Roost (Map 5)** in Atwater Village, or the slightly less ghetto **Short Stop (Map 5)**—conveniently just a block's stumble from one to the other in Echo Park. And nothing says "dive bar" like PBR, the drink of choice for many a patron at Highland Park's popular dive **Footsie's (Map 36)**. The morning after, head to **Ye Rustic Inn (Map 4)** for their weekend Bloody Mary Brunch—an interesting mix of locals and twenty-something hipsters love this amazing breakfast & drink affair for seven bucks.

Best Outdoor Spaces

Constant sun and an average temperature at a perfect 72 degrees mean that many LA bars drag their tables outside. For those of you who enjoy a smoke with your drink, outdoor seating is the only option. The *très rive gauche* **Figaro Café (Map 4)** on Vermont in Los Feliz lines up round marble tables to squeeze in thirsty hipsters. **Malo (Map 4)** on Sunset has an industrial-looking, yet surprisingly intimate, outdoor seating area with heating lamps. A happier Friday was never had than at **Ciudad's (Map 9)** happy hour at 5th and Fig downtown, where cheap mojitos, delicious tapas, and zesty Latin jazz spice up TGIF. **Blue on Blue (Map 1)** at the Avalon Hotel in Beverly Hills serves chilled martinis poolside (plan ahead and reserve a cabana). If you want to jump back in time into something off the beaten track, head into the back of the Figueroa Hotel for a drink by the pool on their nostalgic patio at the **Veranda Bar (Map 9)**. For stargazing through your beer goggles, the rooftop bar at **The Standard (Map 9)** can't be beat. Brit expats especially enjoy a pint in **The Cat & Fiddle's (Map 3)** leafy beer garden, ringing their mates in rainy ol' England to gloat about the balmy stateside summer nights.

Best Lounges

In a city where image is everything, the bigger-than-life style of LA's clubs tends to squash the urban reign of the almighty bar. Dives often seem a bit lost amid the velvet rope-gawking, and the current Cahuenga fascination distracts from simpler watering holes. What emerges is LA's answer to simplicity: the lounge. What passes for a stylish alternative in other cities is the modest choice in LA. But it doesn't matter, because a great lounge is a beautiful thing, and LA has some great ones. **Daddy's Lounge (Map 3)** is wonderfully classic bar: perched on plush couches and ottomans, groups of friends and couples get enveloped in dim lighting, the din of conversation, and tunes from a great jukebox. If it's too crowded, a lot of lounge-seeking Angelenos will head a block east on Sunset to **The Well (Map 3)**, another lounge by the same people who own Daddy's. Modish warmth is key to this lounge's hip brown and black design and tall leather banquettes, and their great jukebox mix and smooth transition from low-key hangout to loud and lively late night spot is a big draw. **The Brig (Map 21)** on Abbot Kinney in Venice is a chic, sleekly illuminated, mod dream. As swanky as it is (even down to its bathrooms), it's still a laid-back lounge where the cocktails and pool table pull rank. If you're looking for something a bit more dressed up, then the **East West Lounge (Map 2)** in WeHo is a good bet. This elegant bar is a martini safe-haven for the adult in you and those in WeHo looking for a break in their club schedule. Probably the most well-known local lounge, **The Dresden Room (Map 4)** solidified its fame with a cameo on the 1996 film Swingers, and comes with its very own lounge act. Say hi to Marty and Elayne when you go.

Best Beer Selection

There is oh so much more to beer than Bud and MGD, and places like **Father's Office (Map 18)**, with 30 microbrews on tap, and **The Library Alehouse (Map 18)**, with 29 on tap, are all the proof you'll need. Los Angeles's own brew, Angel City Brewing, is on draft in a number of locations including the vast and sporty **Hollywood Billiards (Map 3)** and the swanky **Loews Santa Monica Beach Hotel (Map 18)**. For a little adventure, try the Wednesday-night mystery brew at **Good Microbrew & Grill (Map 4)**. For three bucks you get a mystery beer from their eclectic collection of 150 bottled beers or their rotating selection of five draft beers (after you finish they'll let you know what you had). For a night in with your favorite rare ale, stock up at **Cost Plus World Market (Map2)**, where "Beers of the World" are sold by the 12-pack. Beer aficionados feel right at home at West Hollywood's **Red Rock(Map 2)**, where the extensive brew selection caters to the youngish crowds, and at **Backstage (Map 24)**, Culver City's reigning dive bar and karaoke headquarters. And last, but not at all least, there is the granddaddy of beer: **The Yard House (Map 34)**, with literally hundreds of beers on tap, and for some East Coast flavor, they offer the option of a half-yard glass. For those who like beer and love it on tap, welcome home.

Best Milieu

Décor varies greatly among all of the gin joints in this town. Drop by the **Bigfoot Lodge (Map 5)** in Atwater to swig down a few beers while you cozy up to Smokey the Bear. The owner of **Tiki Ti (Map 4)** in Los Feliz is so dedicated to the upkeep of his mini-Polynesian paradise that patrons will find the bar closed when he's in the islands "doing research." The **4100 Club (Map 4)** is like drinking in the belly of a Buddha with draped batiks, Persian lanterns, and intimate booths, yet it manages to keep the hippie vibe at bay. Try **Saints & Sinners (Map 24)** for a kitschy "naughty& nice" experience at a retro lounge space complete with a fire-happy bar staff. For upscale chic, **Casa del Mar (Map 18)** in Santa Monica delivers with a grand lobby/bar serving drinks with grand price tags, or try The Windows Lounge at the **Four Seasons Hotel (Map 2)**. **O-Bar (Map 2)** may seem like simply upscale WeHo food and cocktails, but take a step inside to experience how this oasis uses the elements to provide a unique hideaway. If you're looking for a great view, you're looking for **Yamashiro (Map 3)**. It's a famous Japanese restaurant in the Hollywood Hills, but skip the pricey meal and get a drink at the bar—and pick a table that takes advantage of one the best views of Los Angeles. **The Edison (Map 9)** downtown takes boiler room chic to a whole new level with its historically-accurate industrial vibe—just beware of the gate-keeping bouncers who hold a staunch no-tennis-shoe policy.

Best Dancing

So you think you can dance? Whether you shake your groove thing to Jay-Z, Ricky Martin, Bob Marley, or Cher, there is someplace for everyone to get down in Los Angeles. For hot and sweaty Havana nights, it doesn't get more authentic than Hollywood's **El Floridita (Map 3)** salsa club, located in a shady strip mall on Fountain and Vine. Downtown's legendary **Mayan (Map 9)** doubles as a concert venue and an exclusive salsa club with a strict dress code—be sure to call ahead for details. Over in the 90069, Boys Town boasts a plethora of gay dance clubs known for, um—stiff drinks, pulsating music, and buff bartenders. Some of the most popular include **The Factory/Ultra Suede (Map 2)**, **The Abbey (Map 2)**, **Micky's (Map 2)**, and **Rage (Map 2)**. For less hype, head to Los Feliz's **Akbar (Map 4)** to find a mixed crowd and a chill Eastside vibe. Central Hollywood has replaced the Strip as the hotspot for club-hopping twenty-somethings, celebrities, and indie hipsters. **Ivar (Map 3)**, **Cinespace (Map 3)**, **Avalon (Map 3)**, and **Spider Club (Map 3)** are all popular dance spots within a two-block radius. A couple of blocks west will land you smack in the middle of celebrity club-hopping central with clubs like **LAX (Map 3)**, **Parc (Map 3)**, and **Les Deux (Map 3)**. For more traditional Top 40 destinations, head to LA's own Times Square (Hollywood & Highland) for **The Highlands (Map 3)**. Even die-hard Hollywood fans flock to South Bay for Long Beach's ten-million-dollar club, **V20**. If hip-hop, dancehall, and reggae are more your style, hit up **Hollywood's Nacional (Map3)** on Fridays or **The Echo's (Map 5)** Dub Club on Wednesdays in Silver Lake. For a wild night out on the cheap check out **La Plaza (Map 2)** on La Brea, with DJs spinning ranchero music and fabulous Latino drag queen performances at 10 pm and midnight on the weekends.

Best Music

Out-of-work musicians are almost as plentiful in Los Angeles as out-of-work actors. Lucky for them, LA draws more than enough stadium-filling performances to help them keep the dream alive while offering plenty of smallish venues where they can showcase their talent. If you want your music grand, orchestral, and outdoors, then head to **The Hollywood Bowl (Map3)**. Pack a picnic, a blanket, and your significant other and head on up for a stunning view and some outstanding acoustics. The Bowl plays host to rock shows, classic bands, an impressive 4th of July fireworks show, and the occasional Garrison Keillor radio performance. The other great outdoor attraction is the **Greek Theatre (Map 4)**, a gorgeous venue in Griffith Park that catches both oldies & goodies and adventurous younger bands that are starting to warm up to this breath of fresh air. On the Sunset Strip, the dependable **House of Blues (Map 2)** draws in big names, while the **Key Club (Map 2)** mixes it up with top-billing performers and novelty events like Metal Skool on Monday nights. Local institutions like the **Whisky A Go-Go (Map 2)** and the **Viper Room (Map 2)** draw crowds for their reputations alone, while offering a mix of both established and undiscovered bands. Some adventurous performers and voyeurs take their chances at **Mr. T's Bowl (Map 33)**, a seedy former bowling alley in Highland Park. For the freshest indie bands and underground rock, try the **Henry Fonda Music Box (Map 3)** or **The Troubadour (Map2)**. **The Wiltern (Map 7)** and the **El Rey Theatre (Map 6)** in mid-Wilshire are local favorites for catching bigger bands at a smaller venue, while **Spaceland (Map 5)** in Silver Lake brings in locals and music insiders with more aggressive, alternative live music. **The Hotel Café (Map 3)** is undoubtedly LA's most- beloved acoustic venue, with a cozy New York vibe and some impressive names performing nightly. For live music that doesn't overpower the pub atmosphere, **Molly Malone's (Map 2)** is a deservedly popular spot. It's a great place to see a wide range of great bands (from alt rock to reggae) and then shoot some darts. For those looking for something more experimental (jazz, world music, fusion), the **Temple Bar (Map 18)** will satisfy with great music, a comfortable setting, and an eclectic menu to match. Those with more, ahem, evolved tastes can often be caught taking in a Friday night performance at the **Getty (Map 16)**, or a live music-silent film combo at the scandalous **Silent Movie Theater (Map2)**. Last but not least, the famous **Amoeba Music (Map 3)** packs in locals with (free!) live in-store performances—check their marquee for upcoming appearances.

Map 1 • Beverly Hills

Bar Noir	Maison 140, 140 S Lasky Dr	310-281-4000	Très petit hotel bar serves mondo martinis.
The Belvedere	Peninsula Hotel, 9882 S Santa Monica Blvd	310-551-2888	Classy hotel bar.
Blue on Blue	Avalon Hotel, 9400 W Olympic Blvd	310-407-7791	Mid-century modern poolside cocktails.
The Blvd	Regent Beverly Wilshire, 9500 Wilshire Blvd	310-275-5200	Hotel bar with clubby feel.
Trader Vic's	The Beverly Hilton, 9876 Wilshire Blvd	310-276-6345	Polynesian institution. Recently relocated.
Writer's Bar at L'Ermitage Hotel	9291 Burton Wy	310-278-3344	Sophisticated and elegant, the perfect spot for an intimate redezvous.

Map 2 • West Hollywood

The Abbey	692 N Robertson Blvd	310-289-8410	Mix, mingle, and make out in this West Hollywood gem.
Bar 1200	Sunset Marquis Hotel, 1200 N Alta Loma Rd	310-657-1333	So mellow, the star at your shoulder ain't no thing.
Bar at the Standard	8300 W Sunset Blvd	323-650-9090	This trendy spot is anything but standard.
Bar Lubitsch	7702 Santa Monica Blvd	323-654-1234	The vodka flows at this Russian bar.
Barney's Beanery	8447 Santa Monica Blvd	323-654-2287	A low-rent (but fun) LA institution.
Bel Age Hotel	1020 N San Vicente Blvd	866-282-4560	Hotel bar.
Club 7969	7969 Santa Monica Blvd	323-654-0280	Ravers rejoice! This place is all about the dance.
The Dime	442 N Fairfax Ave	323-651-4421	Unassuming yet hip watering hole.
Dominick's	8715 Beverly Blvd	310-652-2335	Entertainment industry hangout.
East West	8851 Santa Monica Blvd	310-360-6186	Sophisticated cocktail lounge that swings both ways.
El Carmen Tequila & Taco Bar	8138 W 3rd St	323-852-1552	Among the best margaritas in LA.
El Coyote	7312 Beverly Blvd	323-939-2255	Go for the drinks, not the food.
The Factory/Ultra Suede	652 N La Peer Dr	310-659-4551	Wildly popular gay dance club.
Falcon	7213 W Sunset Blvd	323-850-5350	Design-heavy restaurant with a smooth bar scene.
Formosa Café	7156 Santa Monica Blvd	323-850-9050	Train car drinks and rooftop bar. Avoid the food.
Fubar	7994 Santa Monica Blvd	323-654-0396	Cutest gay hipsters west of Avenue A.
Garden of Eden	7080 Hollywood Blvd	323-465-3336	And on the weekend G-d made debaucherous clubbers.
Genghis Cohen	740 N Fairfax Ave	323-653-0640	Acoustic music and Chinese food.
Guy's Bar	8713 Beverly Blvd	818-766-8311	Exclusive club where the bold and beautiful gather to schmooze.
Here	696 N Robertson Blvd	310-360-8455	Like an animated Hugo Boss ad, only gayer.
House of Blues	8430 Sunset Blvd	323-848-5100	Big(ger) acts on the Sunset Strip.
Jones	7205 Santa Monica Blvd	323-850-1727	Bathroom has nude pics of unruly patrons.
Key Club	9039 W Sunset Blvd	310-274-5800	Three different levels just in case the band on one level sucks.
La Plaza	739 N La Brea Ave	323-939-0703	Drag queens and ranchero music—ay yi yi!
Largo	432 N Fairfax Ave	323-852-1073	Jon Brion on Friday nights: a perfect LA experience.
Laugh Factory	8001 W Sunset Blvd	323-656-1336	Nightly comedy shows featuring local and mainstream talent.
Lola's	945 N Fairfax Ave	213-736-5652	Birthplace of the apple martini.
Micky's	8857 Santa Monica Blvd	310-657-1176	Drag queens and hot go-go boys every Monday.
Molly Malone's	575 S Fairfax Ave	323-935-1577	The ultimate neighborhood pub.
Monsieur Marcel	6333 W 3rd St	323-932-6855	Parisian wine bar in the Farmer's Market.
O-bar	8279 Santa Monica Blvd	323-822-3300	Civilized cocktails in boystown.
Pearl	665 N Robertson Blvd	310-358-9191	New WeHo hotspot tries for supper club scene. And succeeds.
Prey	643 N La Cienega Blvd	310-652-2012	Party promoters' dream club.
Privilege	8117 W Sunset Blvd	323-654-0030	Getting in the door is one.
Rage	8911 Santa Monica Blvd	310-652-7055	Hard-bodied boys cram the soft-rubber dance floor.
Rainbow Bar and Grill	9015 Sunset Blvd	310-278-4232	Those who rock will be saluted at this hairband hangout.
Red Rock	8782 Sunset Blvd	310-854-0710	Beers with a scene.
Roxy	9009 W Sunset Blvd	310-276-2222	A bastion of the Sunset Strip.
The Ruby	7070 Hollywood Blvd	323-467-7070	Popular dance club with a young crowd.
Saddle Ranch Chop House	8371 W Sunset Blvd	323-656-2007	Two words: mechanical bull.
Silent Movie Theatre	611 N Fairfax Ave	323-655-2520	If only the walls could talk at this scandelous film and performance venue.
The Skybar	8440 W Sunset Blvd	323-650-8999	Excuse me, you're standing on my Manolos…
Snake Pit Ale House	7529 Melrose Ave	323-653-2011	Fairfax District neighborhood bar.
St Nicks	8450 W Third St	323-655-6917	Great westside dive, complete with stocked jukebox.
Tower Bar	Sunset Tower Hotel, 8358 Sunset Blvd	323-654-7100	Restaubar in mobster Bugsy Siegel's old pad.
The Troubadour	9081 Santa Monica Blvd	310-276-6168	Legendary club where Tom Waits got his start.
The Village Idiot	7383 Melrose Ave	323-655-3331	Bustling British pub with surprisingly good food.
Viper Room	8852 Sunset Blvd	310-358-1880	After Johnny fled to France, scensters say it lost its bite.
Whisky A Go Go	8901 Sunset Blvd	310-652-4202	No sitting allowed, beer cups, five bands a night. Good times, bro.
Windows Lounge	Four Seasons Hotel, 300 S Doheny Dr	310-273-2222	Elegant hotel bar.
Winston's	7746 Santa Monica Blvd	323-654-0105	Über-lounge for Hollywood scenesters.

Map 3 • Hollywood

Amagi	6114 W Sunset Blvd	323-464-7497	Dive bar in the Gower Gulch. Home to the Karaoke Ninja.
ArcLight Café Bar & Balcony	6360 W Sunset Blvd	323-464-1478	Discuss the film over martinis and fried raviolis.
Arena Nightclub	6655 Santa Monica Blvd	323-462-0714	Mega-club hosting several popular weekly gay and lesbian events.
Avalon	1735 Vine St	323-462-8900	Old Palace, now Oakenfold and the Streets.
The Bar	5851 Sunset Blvd	323-468-9154	Formerly Raji's, now rocker bar/lounge.
Beauty Bar	1638 N Cahuenga Blvd	323-464-7676	Girlfriends gather for pre-party manicures and martinis.
Big Wang's	1562 N Cahuenga Blvd	323-469-2449	Texas brings good 'ol beer and wings to LA.
Birds	5925 Franklin Ave	323-465-0175	Unpretentious café/bar favored by the carefully disheveled.

Blu Monkey	5521 Hollywood Blvd	323-957-9000	Middle Eastern vibes in deep Hollywood.
Boardner's	1642 N Cherokee Ave	323-462-9621	Quiet watering hole becomes dance club.
Burgundy Room	1621 N Cahuenga Blvd	323-465-7530	If Johnny Rotten and Blondie had a kid. And the kid was a bar.
The Cat & Fiddle	6530 Sunset Blvd	323-468-3800	Pub plus patio draws Brits in search of better weather.
Catalina Bar & Grill	6725 W Sunset Blvd	323-466-2210	New location, same groovy jazz.
Cinespace	6356 Hollywood Blvd	323-817-3456	Movies, music, food, cocktails, and huge smoking room.
Circus Disco	6655 Santa Monica Blvd	323-462-1291	Eclectic Hollywood mega-(supper)club.
Dragonfly	6510 Santa Monica Blvd	323-466-6111	Alcoholics-in-training dance the night away in one of two rooms.
El Floridita	1253 N Vine St	323-871-8612	Salsa club (with lessons!).
Element	1642 N Las Palmas Ave	323-460-4632	Celebs and their publicists, rooftop VIPs.
Forty Deuce	5574 Melrose Ave	323-465-4242	Bourbon, burlesque, and beautiful people.
Frolic Room	6245 Hollywood Blvd	323-462-5890	Where Spacey searched his soul in *LA Confidential*.
Henry Fonda Music Box	6126 Hollywood Blvd	323-464-0808	Great place to see up-and-coming bands.
The Highlands	6801 Hollywood Blvd	323-461-9800	Club within the Hollywood & Highland complex.
Holly's	1651 Wilcox Ave	323-461-1400	Tougher door policy than a White House gala.
Hollywood Billiards	5750 Hollywood Blvd	323-465-0115	Huge sports bar.
Hollywood Canteen	1006 N Seward St	323-465-0961	Bette Davis's club got a makeover; still hot after all these years.
Hollywood Palladium (Temporarily Closed)	6215 W Sunset Blvd	323-962-7600	One of the premier music venues in LA. Closed for remodeling.
The Hotel Café	1623 1/2 N Cahuenga Blvd	323-461-2040	New York-style acoustic club draws a crowd.
Ivar	6356 Hollywood Blvd	323-465-4827	Ginormous club with industrial interior.
Joseph's	1775 Ivar Ave	323-462-8697	Where Britney met K-Fed.
King King	6555 Hollywood Blvd	323-960-5765	Live music, rotating DJs, very few jerks per capita.
Knitting Factory	7021 Hollywood Blvd	323-463-0204	LA outpost of top NYC eclectic music club. Love it.
La Velvet Margarita Cantina	1612 N Cahuenga Blvd	323-469-2000	Imagine a gothic circus in Tijuana…
The Larchmont	5657 Melrose Ave	323-467-4068	Deep house grooves and sushi.
LAX	1714 Las Palmas Ave	323-464-0171	Watch the B-list celebrities begging to be let in.
Les Deux	1638 N Las Palmas Ave	323-462-7674	The latest "it" club for stars and starlets.
M-Bar	1253 Vine St	323-856-0036	Liberace would have loved the interior.
Montmartre Lounge	6757 Hollywood Blvd	323-465-5369	Hollywood and rock scene playground.
Mood	6623 Hollywood Blvd	323-464-6663	Bali-inspired, go-go dancers in ripped t-shirts.
Musso & Frank Grill Bar	6667 Hollywood Blvd	323-467-5123	Hollywood's oldest bar.
Nacional	1645 Wilcox Ave	323-962-7712	Cuban-themed bar/lounge.
Parc	6683 Hollywood Blvd	323-465-6200	French-Asian restaurant turns velvet rope club.
Power House	1714 N Highland Ave	323-463-9438	Dive bar favorite.
Ritual Nightclub	1743 N Cahuenga Blvd	323-463-0060	Beware of the silicone bounce on the dance floor.
Rokbar	1710 N Las Palmas Blvd	323-461-5600	Tommy Lee's new joint. Same Hollywood crowd, better music.
The Room	1626 N Cahuenga Blvd	323-462-7196	More like a hallway; go through the alley to enter.
Spider Club at the Avalon	1735 Vine St	323-462-1307	The chic VIP hideaway away from packed partygoers.
Star Shoes	6364 Hollywood Blvd	323-462-7827	Vintage shoe salon and cocktails.
Three of Clubs	1123 N Vine St	323-462-6441	Low-key Hollywood hangout.
Tokio	1640 Cahuenga Blvd	323-464-2065	The always-packed dance floor makes for fun, if claustrophobic, times.
The Vanguard	6021 Hollywood Blvd	323-463-3331	Fashion and rock shows, electronica, drum 'n' bass.
The Well	6255 W Sunset Blvd	323-467-9355	Daddy's owners draw up a similar watering hole.
White Horse	1532 N Western Ave	323-462-8088	Serious drinking with Bukowski's ghost.
Xes	1716 N Cahuenga Blvd	323-461-8190	Don your bling and party with the Lakers.
Yamashiro	1999 N Sycamore Ave	323-466-5125	Romantic Japanese with a view.

Map 4 • Los Feliz

4100 Club	4100 W Sunset Blvd	323-666-4460	Red bohemian chic enclave where conversing is a reality.
Akbar	4356 W Sunset Blvd	323-665-6810	Your friendly neighborhood homo/hetero hangout.
The Derby	4500 Los Feliz Blvd	323-663-8979	Still swinging with cool cats and foxy felines.
Drawing Room	1800 Hillhurst Ave	323-665-0135	Tiny strip-mall dive, no pretense, TV 'n' locals.
The Dresden Room	1760 N Vermont Ave	323-665-4294	Home of Marty & Elayne's famed lounge act.
Figaro Café	1802 N Vermont Ave	323-662-1587	Great outdoor spot.
Gauntlet II	4219 Santa Monica Blvd	323-669-9472	Lez-be friends and leather pals.
Good Luck Bar	1514 Hillhurst Ave	323-666-3524	Confucius say: hook-ups likely.
Good Microbrew & Grill	3725 W Sunset Blvd	323-660-3645	Because beer is a comfort food.
il corral	662 N Heliotrope Dr	n/a	Kick-ass indie music venue.
Jumbo's Clown Room	5153 Hollywood Blvd	323-666-1187	The seediest little joint in Hollywood.
Little Temple	4519 Santa Monica Blvd	323-660-4540	The temple of boom for local and visiting DJs.
Malo	4326 W Sunset Blvd	323-664-1011	Fun, hip Mexican with intimate outdoor seating.
Smog Cutter	864 N Virgil Ave	23-660-4626	Hole-in-the-wall karaoke.
Tangier Lounge	2138 Hillhurst Ave	323-666-8666	Moroccan-themed Los Feliz spot with outdoor patio.
Tantra	3705 W Sunset Blvd	323-663-8268	Hollywood goes Bollywood in this erotically charged hotspot.
Tiki Ti	4427 W Sunset Blvd	323-669-9381	Fortify yourself with a famous Blood of the Bull.
Vermont	1714 N Vermont Ave	323-661-6163	Hot DJs and cool cocktails.
Ye Rustic Inn	1831 Hillhurst Ave	323-662-5757	If ye want pink drinks, get thee the hell out.

Map 5 • Silver Lake/Echo Park/Atwater

Bigfoot Lodge	3172 Los Feliz Blvd	323-662-9227	It's too bad boy scouts don't drink.
Club Tee Gee	3210 Glendale Blvd	323-669-9631	Dependable watering hole since 1946.
The Echo	1822 W Sunset Blvd	213-413-8200	Eastside hipster haven for DJ electronica and dancing.
Gold Room	1558 W Sunset Blvd	213-482-5259	Looks scarier from the outside than it is.
Johnny's Bar	2939 W Sunset Blvd	323-660-2276	Soju cocktails and pinup paintings.
Mixville Bar	2838 Rowena Ave	323-666-2000	Casual bar with outdoor seating adjacent to Edendale Grill.
MJ's	2810 Hyperion Ave	323-660-1503	Rage's hairier Eastside cousin.

Map 5 • Silver Lake/Echo Park/Atwater—*continued*

Red Lion Tavern	2366 Glendale Blvd	323-662-5337	Year-round Oktoberfest, plus schnitzel.
The Roost	3100 Los Feliz Blvd	323-664-7272	Cheap drinks, free popcorn, no frills.
Rudolpho's	2500 Riverside Dr	323-669-1226	Mexican by day; salsa dancing, cross-dressing by night.
Short Stop	1455 W Sunset Blvd	213-482-4942	Cool dive bar, seasonally packed with Dodger fans.
Silverlake Lounge	2906 Sunset Blvd	323-666-2407	Silver Lake's holy church of rock 'n' roll salvation.
Spaceland	1717 Silver Lake Blvd	323-661-4380	Smokin' alt. music venue.
Tam O'Shanter	2980 Los Feliz Blvd	323-664-0228	Me want prime rib and beer. Grrr.

Map 6 • Miracle Mile/Mid-City

El Rey	5515 Wilshire Blvd	323-936-6400	Diverse musical lineup.
The Joint	8771 W Pico Blvd	310-275-2619	Former jazz club, new renovation hosts wide array of music and scenesters.
The Mint	6010 Pico Blvd	323-954-9400	Casual acoustic venue with smokin' sound system.
Tom Bergin's	840 S Fairfax Ave	323-936-7151	Guinness and fifty years of paper shamrocks.

Map 7 • Hancock Park

Jewel's Catch One	4067 W Pico Blvd	323-737-1159	Think Madonna's "Material Girl" days.
Mixed Nuts Comedy Club	4000 W Washington Blvd	323-735-6622	Basic comedy club featuring unknowns and a 2-drink minimum.

Map 8 • Korea Town

Brass Monkey	659 Mariposa Ave	213-381-7047	One of the best of K-town karaokes, enter in back.
HMS Bounty	3357 Wilshire Blvd	213-385-7275	Nautical-themed old man bar patronized by the new kids.
La Fonda De Los Camperos	2501 Wilshire Blvd	213-380-5055	Traditional Latin music.
Orchid Karaoke Club	607 S Oxford Ave, 2nd Fl	213-251-8886	Sing and swill in your own private room.
The Prince	3198 7th St	213-389-1586	Smokin' waitresses, undercover celebs, cool.
R Bar	3331 W 8th St	213-387-7227	Koreatown bar that requires password for entry. (Hint: it's yo-ho-ho)

Map 9 • Downtown

Bar 107	107 W 4th St	213-625-7382	Kitschy hangout for jaded Hollywood outcasts and downtown dwellers.
Bonavista Lounge	Bonaventure Hotel, 404 Figueroa St	213-236-0802	Secret microbrewery, packed happy hour.
Broadway Bar	830 S Broadway	213-614-9909	Celebrating the glamorous side of cocktailing.
Ciudad	Union Bank Plaza, 445 S Figueroa St	213-486-5171	Best mojitos in LA, and a shockingly cheap feliz hour.
The Edison	108 W 2nd St	213-613-0000	Experience the roaring 20s with dancing flappers, hot jazz, and killer cocktails.
Gallery Bar	Millennium Biltmore Hotel, 506 S Grand Ave	213-624-1011	Specialty drink's the Black Dahlia: champagne + Guinness.
The Golden Gopher	417 W 8th St	213-614-8001	Outdoor smoking alley, chandeliers, gold gopher lamps.
Hop Louie	950 Mei Ling Wy	213-628-4244	Popular w/ the art crowd, cheap bevs.
La Cita	336 S Hill St	213-687-7111	Rock out to indie tunes under twinkle lights.
Mayan Theater	1038 S Hill St	213-746-4287	Salsa club with strict dress code, call for required attire.
Mountain Bar	473 Gin Ling Wy	213-625-7500	Art bar, Jorge Pardo did the bloody décor.
Oiwake	122 Japanese Village Plz Mall	213-628-2678	Karaoke restaubar with a serious songbook.
Pete's Café & Bar	400 S Main St	213-617-1000	The Downtown Martini has bleu cheese-stuffed olives.
Point Moorea Lounge	930 Wilshire Blvd	213-833-5100	Get Bali Hai on Polynesian libations.
Redwood Bar & Grill	316 W 2nd St	213-680-2600	Pirate-themed hangout - perfect for finding booty.
Roof Bar at the Standard Downtown	550 S Flower St	213-892-8080	Make an entrance upstairs, then stumble to your room.
The Smell	247 S Main St		All ages, no booze, but underground music.
Stock Exchange	618 S Spring St	213-489-3877	Upscale Art Deco dance club.
Veranda Bar	939 S Figueroa St	213-627-8971	Diverse crowd sits poolside, hidden within the Figueroa Hotel.

Map 10 • Baldwin Hills

Café Club Fais Do-Do	5253 W Adams Blvd	323-954-8080	Cajun food, eclectic music.
The Living Room	2636 Crenshaw Blvd	323-735-8748	Blues bar.
Mandrake	2692 S La Cienega Blvd	310-837-3297	Think art-students-talking-theory bar.

Map 11 • South Central West

Babe's Ricky Inn	4339 Leimert Blvd	323-295-9112	Blues music.

Map 13 • Inglewood

Hollywood Park	1050 S Prairie Ave	310-419-1500	Race track, nightclub, live music, games, etc.

Map 15 • Pacific Palisades

The Hideout	112 W Channel Rd	310-429-1851	Former speakeasy and gay dive turned hot Westside spot.
Pearl Dragon	15229 Sunset Blvd	310-459-9790	Cocktail lounge from Voda owners, full liquor license.

Map 17 • Bel Air/Holmby Hills

Hotel Bel Air Lounge	701 Stone Cyn Rd	310-472-1211	Where golddiggers and grandpas meet.

Map 18 • Santa Monica

14 Below	1348 14th St	310-451-5040	Pay-to-play rock 'n' roll bar.
Bar Copa	2810 Main St	310-452-2445	Low-lit, packed hip-hop beachside haven.
Big Dean's Café	1615 Ocean Front Wk	310-393-2666	Straight off the beach, fried locals.
Cameo Bar	Viceroy Hotel, 1819 Ocean Ave	310-260-7500	Chic hotel bar surrounding two swimming pools.
Casa del Mar	1910 Ocean Wy	310-581-5533	High-end hotel bar.
Circle Bar	2926 Main St	310-450-0508	Once divey, now trendy.
Cock N' Bull Pub	2947 Lincoln Blvd	310-399-9696	Irish pub.
Father's Office	1018 Montana Ave	310-393-2337	Bet your dad didn't have 30 beers on tap.
The Gaslite	2030 Wilshire Blvd	310-829-2382	Karaoke for the tone deaf.
Grill Restaurant	Fairmont Miramar Hotel, 101 Wilshire Blvd	310-319-3111	Hotel deluxe, waterfall included.
Harvelle's	1432 4th St	310-395-1676	You like your clubs dark and sexy.
Library Alehouse	2911 Main St	310-314-4855	No books, lots of beer.
Loews Santa Monica Beach Hotel	1700 Ocean Ave	310-458-6700	Swanky.
Lounge 217	217 Broadway	310-394-6336	Weekends packed with perfect 10s and tans.
Ma'Kai	101 Broadway Ave	310-434-1511	Award-winning bartenders use only the freshest ingredients for their cocktails.
O'Brien's	2941 Main St	310-396-4725	Neighborhood Irish pub.
Renee's Courtyard	522 Wilshire Blvd	310-451-9341	Spacious for an alleyway, hot staff.
The Room SM	1323 Santa Monica Blvd	310-458-0707	Westside station of Hollywood spot.
Rusty's Surf Ranch	256 Santa Monica Pier	310-393-7437	Surfboards, margs at sunset.
Shutters	1 Pico Blvd	310-458-0030	One of the "beachiest" Santa Monica hotel bars.
Temple Bar	1026 Wilshire Blvd	310-393-6611	Food, martinis, and good local music.
Voda	1449 2nd St	310-394-9774	In this NY-chic bar, vodka flows like, well, voda.
Ye Olde King's Head	116 Santa Monica Blvd	310-451-1402	Traditional English fare and beer.
Zanzibar	1301 5th St	310-451-2221	Grooves spun by KCRW's Garth Trinidad and Jason Bentley.

Map 19 • West LA/Santa Monica East

Air Conditioned	2819 Pico Blvd	310-829-3700	Sophisticated Westside lounge.
The Arsenal	12012 W Pico Blvd	310-575-5511	'60s era cool at this quite metro-for-the-Westside bar.
The Joker	2827 Pico Blvd	310-828-9235	Dive bar with chic clientele.
Liquid Kitty	11780 W Pico Blvd	310-473-3707	Westside lounge with martinis that will make you purr.
McCabe's Guitar Shop	3101 Pico Blvd	310-828-4497	Famed LA haunt for live acoustic music.
Plan B	11637 W Pico Blvd	310-312-3633	The Ladies Man would hang at this after 2 am cigar lounge.
Q's Billiards	11835 Wilshire Blvd	310-477-7550	Pool, pool, beer, and pool.
The Shack	2518 Wilshire Blvd	310-449-1171	Philly phans rejoice, get a cheesesteak, watch the Flyers.
Sonny McLean's Irish Pub & Restaurant	2615 Wilshire Blvd	310-449-1811	For homesick Red Sox fans.

Map 20 • Westwood/Century City

The Century Club	10131 Constellation Blvd	310-553-6000	Upscale rock club for the VH1 set.
Westwood Brewing Company	1097 Glendon Ave	310-209-2739	Microbrewery with comedy upstairs.
Whiskey Blue	W Hotel, 930 Hilgard Ave	310-443-8232	Modern, trendy hotel bar.

Map 21 • Venice

Baja Cantina	311 Washington Blvd	310-821-2252	Free chips 'n' salsa with your margs.
The Brig	1515 Abbot Kinney Blvd	310-399-7537	For trendy Westsiders too lazy to drive to Cahuenga.
Firehouse	213 Rose Ave	310-396-6810	Neighborhood bar.
James' Beach	60 N Venice Blvd	310-823-5396	Outdoor patio bar with ocean view.
The Other Room	1201 Abbot Kinney Blvd	312-226-6300	Plus/minus thirty bar. Fun ambition minus the Hollywood hustle.
Red Garter	2536 Lincoln Blvd	310-306-8300	Serving since the '60s. So, like, ancient history.
Roosterfish	1302 Abbot Kinney Blvd	310-392-2123	Friendly gay oasis in dude-ridden beach area.
The Town House	52 Windward Ave	310-392-4040	Oldest bar in Venice, trap door leads to bands.
Venice Whaler Bar & Grill	2 Washington Blvd	310-821-8737	Take out-of-town friends for buckets of beer, sunsets.

Map 22 • Mar Vista

Dear John's	11208 Culver Blvd	310-397-0276	Old-school piano bar.
Good Hurt	12249 Venice Blvd	310-390-1076	Medical-themed beer and wine remedies.

Map 23 • Rancho Park/Palms

Zabumba	10717 Venice Blvd	310-841-6225	Brazilian themed, Brazilian dancing, Brazilian live music.

Map 24 • Culver City

Backstage	10400 Culver Blvd	310-839-3892	Karaoke joint across from the Sony lot.
BottleRock	3847 Main St	310-836-9463	For oenophiles that like to rock.
Cinema Bar	3967 Sepulveda Blvd	310-390-1328	World's smallest honkytonk.
Jazz Bakery	3223 Helms Ave	310-271-9039	Live theatre-style jazz and yes, dessert.
Saints & Sinners	10899 Venice Blvd	310-842-8066	Churchy bordello décor for those who toe the line.

Map 25 • Marina Del Rey/Westchester West

Brennan's	4089 Lincoln Blvd	310-821-6622	Irish pub with turtle racing.

Map 26 • Westchester/Fox Hills/Ladera Heights

Sky Bar Lounge at Encounter Restaurant	209 World Wy	310-215-5151	Jetsons meets Star Trek with drinks.
Westchester Sports Grill	5630 W Manchester Ave	310-670-2366	All things sports.

Map 27 • El Segundo/Manhattan Beach

Baja Sharkeez	3801 Highland Ave	310-545-6563	Post-college hangout with good grub.
Beaches	117 Manhattan Beach Blvd	310-545-2523	Drink, dance, and sweat. Expect a line on weekends.
Ercole's	1101 Manhattan Ave	310-372-1997	Ultimate late-night meet-up spot; laid back meat market.
Hennessey's	313 Manhattan Beach Blvd	310-546-4813	Typical Irish pub; nuff said.
Mr. Pockets	516 N Sepulveda	310-372-4343	Über sports junkies bar with lots o' games.
OB's	3610 Highland Ave	310-546-1542	Taco Tuesdays and stiff jello shots = great venue for a blind date.
Panchos	3615 Highland Ave	310-545-6670	Great house band on weekends and killer margs.
Shark's Cove	309 Manhattan Beach Blvd	310-545-2683	Sports bar with nightly specials.
Shellback Tavern	116 Manhattan Beach Blvd	310-376-7857	Roll off the beach to this South Bay staple with good stiff drinks.
Side Door	900 Manhattan Ave	310-372-1684	South Bay's attempt at a Hollywood lounge.

Map 29 • Hermosa Beach

Aloha Sharkeez (temporarily closed)	52 Pier Ave	310-374-7823	Proving anytime is a good time for a beer.
Café Boogaloo	1238 Hermosa Ave	310-318-2324	New Orleans café with live music. Attracts 30+ crowd.
Comedy & Magic Club	1018 Hermosa Ave	310-372-1193	Off-Hollywood club with an all-star lineup.
Dragon	22 Pier Ave	310-372-4462	Hit the dance floor at this Hermosa hot spot.
Fat Face Fenner's Fishack	53 Pier Ave, 2nd Floor	310-379-5550	A local hangout: more bar, less nightclub.
Hennessey's	8 Pier Ave	310-372-5759	Only place in Hermosa with rooftop bar. Basic Irish pub.
Hermosa Beach Yacht Club	66 Hermosa Ave	310-376-6767	No ships are pulling in this port. Local dive with schooners of beer.
The Lighthouse Café	30 Pier Ave	310-376-9833	Jazz by the beach.
Mermaid	11 Pier Ave	310-374-9344	Enjoy cheap stiff drinks while ogling the babes on the Strand. Old timers meets local hipsters. Check out live piano music on Sundays.
Patrick Molloy's	50-A Pier Ave	310-798-9762	Good brews on tap inside and a shorter line outside.
The Pitcher House	142 Pacific Coast Hwy	310-374-0626	Rock 'n' roll bar with 50 years of history.
Sangria	68 Pier Ave	310-376-4412	Can be "Sangreasy" when the Hollywood kids invade the dance floor. Good tapas.
Shark's Cove	1220 Hermosa Ave	310-798-3932	Dark, divey, and kinda dank. Good venue for game watching.
The Underground	1334 Hermosa Ave	310-318-3818	English-themed sports pub with darts and pool. Attracts the ex-pats.

Map 31 • Redondo Beach

Mickie Finz Fish House and Bar	1710 S Catalina Ave	310-316-6658	It's trying really hard to make you like it. Lots of events and drink specials in a tiki atmosphere.
Naja's Place	154 Internatl Boardwalk	310-376-9951	Humongous selection of beer on tap; Go on weekends to see house hair band bang out tunes.
The Portofino Hotel & Yacht Club	260 Portofino Wy	310-379-8481	Jazz nights. On the water, great view, solid wine list.
Tony's on the Pier	210 Fishermans Wharf	310-374-1442	This place puts the "Old in Old School" - it's Vegas meets the Beach. Awesome ocean view and a campy live music.

Map 33 • Highland Park

All Star Lanes	4459 Eagle Rock Blvd	323-254-2579	Bowling? Ha! Locals flock for cheap drinks and wild karaoke.
The Chalet	1630 Colorado Blvd	323-258-8800	Alpine-themed bar high atop Eagle Rock.
Little Cave	5922 N Figueroa St	323-255-6871	Watch the stalagtites while sipping Bat-tinis.
Mr T's Bowl	5621 1/2 N Figueroa St	323-256-7561	Bowling alley turned rock club.

Map 34 • Pasadena

Bodega Wine Bar	260 E Colorado Blvd	626-793-4300	Ideal for chilled wines on warm nights.
Club 41	41 S De Lacey Ave	626-795-4141	Rat Pack steakhouse serves swank bevs.
Freddie's 35er Bar	12 E Colorado Blvd	626-356-9315	Neighborhood bar.
Ice House Comedy Club	24 N Mentor Ave	626-577-1894	Stand-up comedy, improv, booze.
Jake's Café and Billiards	38 W Colorado Blvd	626-568-1602	Pool hall and bar.
Lucky Baldwin's	17 S Raymond Ave	626-795-0652	Expat Brits, imported ales, high tea.
McMurphy's	72 Fair Oaks Ave	626-666-1445	Irish pub in Old Town.
The Muse	54 E Colorado Blvd	626-793-0608	Dance club with Salsa Thursdays.
Yard House	330 E Colorado Blvd	626-577-9273	More than 200 beers on tap.

Map 36 • Mt. Washington

Footsie's	2640 N Figueroa St	323-221-6900	Simply brilliant and hopefully the home of all future NFT release parties.

Map 39 • Alhambra

Azul Bar and Nightclub	129 W Main St	626-282-6320	Dance and drink your blues away.
California Brewing Co	100 W Main St	626-943-8430	Get some food with your beer.
The Granada	17 S 1st St	626-227-2572	Offers lessons and three dance floors to practice on.
Havana House	133 W Main St	626-576-0547	Dress-code-enforced cigar lounge.
Jay-dee Café	1843 W Main St	626-281-6887	Great dive bar.

Map 40 • Boyle Heights

Barbara's at the Brewery	Brewery Art Complex, 620 Moulton Ave	323-221-9204	Rub elbows with artists in old Pabst brewery.

Map 45 • Canoga Park / Woodland Hills

Corbin Bowl	19616 Ventura Blvd	818-996-2695	Ain't no Lucky Strike; serious bowlers abound.

Map 47 • Van Nuys

Robin Hood Pub	13640 Burbank Blvd	818-994-6045	Beer and bangers.

Map 48 • North Hollywood

Rawhide	10937 Burbank Blvd	818-760-9798	Gay bar features country music and line dancing.

Map 49 • Burbank

Champs Sports Pub	4103 W Burbank Blvd	818-840-9493	Old school sports pub, in both upkeep and M.O.
Dimples	3413 W Olive Ave	818-842-2336	Claims to be the "first karaoke club in America."
The Library Lounge	322 N Pass Ave	818-842-8887	Graciela's swanky-yet-cozy hotel bar with killer martinis.
Match	4657 Lankershim Blvd	818-766-0116	Formerly NoHo's Thunderbird Saloon; no signage.
NoBar	10622 Magnolia Blvd	818-753-0545	Plush, darkly fabulous interior belies the seedy exterior. First rate drinks and friendly folks.
Sardos	259 N Pass Ave	818-846-8126	Great karaoke.
Tinhorn Flats	2623 Magnolia Blvd	818-567-2470	Karaoke Thursday nights.

Map 50 • Burbank East/Glendale West

The Blue Room	916 S San Fernando Blvd	323-849-2779	Somewhat upscale neighborhood bar.

Map 51 • Glendale South

Far Niente	204 N Brand Blvd	818-242-3835	More polished than an actual dive.
Jax Bar and Grill	339 N Brand Blvd	818-500-1604	Jazz club.
Maurizio's	135 N Maryland Ave	818-247-5600	Sports bar and karaoke.
The Scene	806 E Colorado St	818-241-7029	Eastside hipsters and the DJs they love.

Map 55 • Sherman Oaks East

Coda	5248 Van Nuys Blvd	818-783-7518	NYC-style lounge w/ dress code, so not really.
Cozy's	14058 Ventura Blvd	818-986-6000	Ventura Blvd. blues club.
The Green Frog	13625 Moorpark St	818-788-4812	Straight up booze, booths, and billiards.
Lulu's Beehive	13203 Ventura Blvd	818-986-2233	A coffee bar with music, comedy, and open mic.
Muddy Moose Bar & Grill	12833 Ventura Blvd	818-755-5000	Sports bar with jazz music.

Map 56 • Studio City/Valley Village

Aura	12215 Ventura Blvd	818-487-1488	Supperclub brings glitz to the Valley.
Clear	11916 Ventura Blvd	818-980-4811	Transparent décor, trendy crowd.
Firefly	11720 Ventura Blvd	818-762-1833	Bookshelves paint the scene at this signless Valley draw.
Fox & Hounds	11100 Ventura Blvd	818-763-7976	English pub.
Foxfire Room	12516 Magnolia Blvd	818-766-1344	Unchanged since the '70s, a fun local dive bar.
La Ve Lee	12514 Ventura Blvd	818-980-8158	Brazilian, jazz, R&B, plus Middle Eastern food.
Maeve's Residuals	11042 Ventura Blvd	818-761-8301	Low-key entertainment industry hangout.
Oyster House Saloon	12446 Moorpark St	818-761-8686	Stellar bartenders sling drinks like pros.
Platinum Live	11345 Ventura Blvd	818-753-1771	Elegant hot night club with live music and TV events too.
The Sapphire	11938 Ventura Blvd	818-506-0777	Trendy club for the jr. studio exec.

Map 57 • Universal City/Toluca Lake

The Baked Potato	3787 Cahuenga Blvd	818-980-1615	Low-key jazz with your choice of fancy baked potatoes.
BB King's Blues Club	100 Universal Center Dr	818-622-5464	Nightly blues lineup and Sunday gospel brunch. Amen!
The Casting Office	3256 Cahuenga Blvd W	323-851-4300	Divey neighborhood strip-mall bar.
Minibar	3413 Cahuenga Blvd W	323-882-6965	Libations and white leather mod up Universal City.
Rumba Room	1000 Universal Studios Blvd	818-622-1226	City Walk salsa club.
The Smoke House	4420 W Lakeside Dr	818-845-3731	Keyboards Tues. -Thurs., Bands Fri. & Sat.
Timmy Nolan's	10111 Riverside Dr	818-985-3359	Irish pub.

Long Beach

49ers Tavern	5660 E Pacific Coast Hwy	562-494-7670	Nearly a landmark in itself; real tavern atmosphere.
The Belmont Brewing Company	25 39th Pl	562-433-3891	Try the Strawberry Blonde. Food's spectacular too.
Blue Café	210 The Promenade N	562-983-7111	Variety of bands, brews, pool tables upstairs, hipsters.
Joe Jost's	2803 E Anaheim St	562-439-5446	Opened in 1924 as a barbershop. Try the pickled eggs.
Mariposa	135 Pine Ave	562-437-2119	Decent food, trendy crowd, lotsa dancing.
Murphy's Pub	4918 E 2nd St	562-433-6338	Fun patio bar, great sandwiches. Don't spit on those walking below.
Portfolio Coffee House	2300 E 4th St	562-434-2486	TV shows film here; unbeatable atmosphere.
Rock Bottom Brewery	1 Pine Ave	562-308-2255	Chain microbrewery. Go figure.
The Sky Room	40 S Locust Ave	562-983-2703	Swanky Suppah Club, located atop The Breakers; 360-degree view.
V20	81 Aquarium Wy	866-402-5828	New joint in The Pike; upscale trendy revelers.

San Pedro

Godmother's	302 W 7th St	310-833-1589	Part of the ArtWalk scene.
June's Bar	1100 S Pacific Ave	310-833-4171	Warm, literally and figuratively.

Los Angeles is a city of strange juxtapositions when it comes to food. Hence, "fusion" was invented to please every palate and satisfy the giant melting pot that makes up this town. LA is where "Californian" cuisine was born, and you better believe it requires a lot more than just adding avocado. The city borrows many of its flavors from several different neighbors. With Mexico right next door, you can bet that authentic south-of-the-border dishes are served up in hundreds of restaurants citywide. The Pacific lapping at our sandy shores produces endless fresh seafood with an ocean view. In addition, California's abundant agriculture provides us with loads of fresh produce from local purveyors. Thanks to the strong Asian influence, tofu is prepared in ways no vegan could ever dream possible. For Atkins followers, LA's famous chophouses turn out some of the most succulent, buttery steaks imaginable. Let's just say, we Angelenos know how to eat it up.

Eating Old

Taix (Map 5) on Sunset in Echo Park has been serving up French country cuisine at peasant prices to Angelenos since 1927. Grab a tray and grin at all the stuffed woodsy creatures at **Clifton's Cafeteria (Map 9)** downtown, where Jell-O and brisket have been on the menu since 1931. **Philippe the Original (Map 9)** still serves their famous French dip sandwiches at long tables on the sawdust-covered dining room floor. During the exodus from a STAPLES Center event, don't pass up the **Original Pantry Café (Map 9)**, a 24-hour diner that claims to have never closed its doors since its opening more than 80 years ago, a feat that includes moving locations. **Musso & Frank Grill (Map 3)** has been operating since Hollywood was an infant in 1919, serving steaks, burgers, and other industry standards. **The Galley (Map 18)** is supposedly Santa Monica's oldest restaurant, serving steaks and seafood since 1934. Legend has it that Orson Welles once ate 18 hot dogs in one sitting at **Pink's (Map 2)** on La Brea—hundreds line up daily to challenge the portly actor's record.

Eating Cheap

Why make a run for the border when there are so many independent taquerias throughout LA? Many starving actors quell the hunger pangs at a number of hole-in-the-wall restaurants. Some of our favorite taco stands are the orange **Benito's (Maps 2, 3, 19)** throughout the city where $3 will buy you 5 "rolled tacos" or a burrito the size of a Chihuahua; also *delicioso* are the **¡Loteria! Grill (Map 2)** and **Poquito Mas (Maps 49, 50)**. If you are so stuffed that you think you're not seeing the bill correctly following a filling, yet inexpensive meal, you're most likely at one of the five **Versailles (Maps 6, 24, 27, 53, 57)** restaurants serving up authentic Cuban food. Still, our hands-down favorite for cheap eats is **Zankou Chicken (Maps 4, 35, 47)**, an Armenian, cash-only mini-chain with the most delectable poultry you will ever taste served with garlic sauce and pita.

Eating Hip

If any city does hip, it's Los Angeles, though unfortunately it occasionally does so to the detriment of the food. Recommended here are restaurants that are both hip *and* delicious. Head to **Café Stella (Map 4)** in Silver Lake to enjoy scrumptious and hearty French food with an extensive wine list. **AOC (Map 2)** on Third Street has so many tiny menu items to sample—along with at least 12 wines by the glass—that you may have to unbutton your Gucci slacks at the end of the meal. Often, "hip" is defined by scruffy-yet-sophisticated 20- and 30-somethings bobbling about a glass of wine while they tell you of their planned trajectory to fame and fortune. **Kate Mantilini**'s **(Map 1)** on Wilshire is where you'll find Westside hipsters eating steak sandwiches, while on the Eastside they tend to favor the outdoor patio at **Malo (Map 4)**, the petite quarters of **Blair's (Map 5)**, and the heat-lamp-aided **Edendale Grill (Map 5)** (a recent hotspot for low-key celebs who've escaped Hollywood). Also fashionably yummy is **Luna Park (Map 6)**—a San Francisco transplant that is as loud as the food is good.

Eating Late

For a city that needs it sleep to stay beautiful, a select few of LA's restaurants stay open for the late-night craves. **Fred 62 (Map 4)** on Vermont serves starving hipsters burgers, Asian noodles, gooey desserts, and great coffee 24 hours a day. For a late-night diner experience, head to the pop-art fabulous **Swingers (Map 2)** on Beverly Boulevard or the historic **Canter's Deli (Map 2)** on Fairfax, where you can also pick up bagels for the morning after. If you've just returned from Paris and are used to eating bistro-style at midnight, drive over the hill to Studio City's **Firefly (Map 56)** for *très magnifique*, if pricey, food and a lovely outdoor seating area. We'd be remiss to not mention the **Brite Spot Family Restaurant (Map 5)** in Echo Park; it's open until 4 am Thursday through Sunday and serves cheap diner favorites like grilled cheese and heaping plates of seasoned French fries, with featured DJ nights to boot.

Eating Ethnic

Often, but not always, the best ethnic restaurants are situated in the corresponding ethnic neighborhoods. A wealth of Ethiopian restaurants line Fairfax, just south of Olympic Boulevard; our favorite is **Nyala Ethiopian Cuisine (Map 6)**, where dishes like doro wat and injera can be sampled for less than $7 during the daily lunch buffet. The affordable four-course dinner at Armenian restaurant **Carousel (Map 51)** in East Hollywood is not to be missed. South Los Angeles is home to some of the city's best soul and Cajun food; for finger-licking gumbo try **Harold & Belle's (Map 11)** on Jefferson. Our tummies rumble just thinking about Koreatown. For an interactive and highly satisfying group dining experience, try one of the many Korean barbecue restaurants—we like **Soot Bull Jeep (Map 8)** on the cheap side and **Dong Il Jang (Map 8)** on the posh end. Don't worry if you can't read Korean, the menus have pictures that you can point to for ordering ease. In Little Tokyo, **Sushi Gen (Map 9)** can't be beat.

Eating Meat

From duck to filet mignon, from controversial foie gras to free-range chicken, we love to eat meat in the US of A. While California is supposed to be a national leader in the natural foods and vegetarian movement, you would never know from the assortment of restaurants serving every piece of the animal anatomy. For steaks, try **Arroyo Chop House (Map 34)** in Pasadena, **Mastro (Map 1)** in Beverly Hills, or the **Tam O'Shanter (Map 5)** in Silver Lake for prime rib. You can visit **Pink's (Map 2)** for several varieties of sausage, but for strictly German-style brats, give the **Red Lion Tavern (Map 5)** in Silver Lake a try. Let's not forget fish—downtown LA's **Water Grill**

(Map 9) is an upscale seafood destination, as is **Crustacean (Map 1)** in Beverly Hills. **Killer Shrimp (Maps 21, 56)** in Venice serves exactly what the restaurant's name states.

Eating Meatless

With an abundance of fresh vegetables and fruits in California, we like to go meatless once in a while. For this crunchy dining experience we'll head to **Real Food Daily (Maps 2)**, a chain of organic, vegan restaurants serving tempeh, tofu, and interesting noodle salads. **Mani's Bakery (Map 18)** serves a healthy breakfast all day, with enough non-meat options on its menu to satisfy the vegetarian in us. **A Votre Sante (Map 16)** in Brentwood has been dishing up vegetarian specialties since the 1980s, and they've managed to plump their menu without resorting to imitation meat products. To really own your veggie roots at **Home (Map 4)** in Los Feliz, order the yogurt, fruit, and granola concoction titled "My Sister the Tree Hugger."

Editor's Favorites

We have a penchant for oysters and sunsets at **Ocean Ave Seafood (Map 18)** in Santa Monica, and mouth-melting foie gras at **Joe's (Map 21)** on Abbott Kinney in Venice. **Max (Map 55)** is a pleasant and affordable surprise if ever stuck in the Valley. Waiting for a prosciutto sandwich at **Bay Cities (Map 21)** in Santa Monica is well worth it. **La Dijonaise Café (Map 24)** in Culver City takes out the expensive snobbiness in French dining but leaves all the decadent tastes. If you and your puka-shell necklace are still partying late in Hermosa Beach, a slice from **Paisano's (Map 29)** makes the best nightcap for a frat-boy night. A number of cupcake shops have sprouted across the area, but we prefer waiting on line at **Sprinkles Cupcakes (Map 1)** in Beverly Hills. And, as always, **In-N-Out Burger** (various locations) is a necessary staple.

Key: $: Under $10 / $$: $10–$20 / $$$: $20–$30 / $$$$: $30-40 / $$$$$: $40+;
** : Does not accept credit cards / † : Accepts only American Express / † † : Accepts only Visa and Mastercard.*
Times refer to kitchen closing time on weekend nights.

Map 1 • Beverly Hills

Baja Fresh	475 N Beverly Dr	310-858-6690	$	9 pm	Cheap, reliable Mexican.
Barney Greengrass	9570 Wilshire Blvd	310-777-5877	$$$	7 pm	An LA icon.
Basic Bites	443 N Beverly Blvd	310-247-9673	$	6 pm	Fresh sandwiches and salads.
The Belvedere	9882 Little Santa Monica Blvd	310-788-2306	$$$$	10:30 pm	Upscale hotel dining.
Blowfish Sushi	9229 Sunset Blvd	310-887-3848	$$$$	12 am	Sushi to die for.
Blue on Blue	9400 W Olympic Blvd	310-407-7791	$$$$	11 pm	Poolside cocktails—very LA.
The Blvd	9500 Wilshire Blvd	310-275-5200	$$$$	11 pm	For the *Pretty Woman* in us all.
Boe on the Crescent	403 N Crescent Dr	310-247-0505	$$	12 am	Small plates and casual atmosphere.
Brighton Coffee Shop	9600 Brighton Wy	310-276-7732	$$	5 pm	Comfort food.
Café Talesai	9198 W Olympic Blvd	310-271-9345	$	10 pm	Thai specialties with a twist.
Crustacean	9646 Little Santa Monica Blvd	310-205-8990	$$$$	11:30 pm	High-end Vietnamese.
Da Pasquale	9749 Little Santa Monica Blvd	310-859-3884	$$$	10:30 pm	Neighborhood Italian.
Dan Tana's	9071 Santa Monica Blvd	310-275-9444	$$$$	1 am	Old H'wood glamour—if you can get a table…
El Torito Grill	9595 Wilshire Blvd	310-550-1599	$$	11 pm	Okay food, better drinks.
Farm of Beverly Hills	439 N Beverly Dr	310-273-5578	$$$	10 pm	Yeehaw darlings! Farm-fresh salads and entrees.
Flavor of India	9045 Santa Monica Blvd	310-274-1715	$$$	11 pm	Dolly Parton likes the chicken tikka masala.
The Grill on the Alley	9560 Dayton Wy	310-276-0615	$$$$	11 pm	Hollywood power lunch spot.
Il Cono Gelateria	9461 Little Santa Monica Blvd	310-285-2045	$*	11 pm	Over 40 amazing flavors.
Kate Mantilini	9101 Wilshire Blvd	310-278-3699	$$$	2 am	Boxing-themed upscale bistro with knockout desserts.
La Conversation	638 N Doheny Dr	310-858-0950	$$	7 pm	Popular and *trés mignon* brunch and lunch bistro. A good place to eat and be seen.
La Scala	434 N Canon Dr	310-275-0579	$$$$	10:30 pm	Classic Italian.
Le Pain Quotidien	9630 Little Santa Monica Blvd	310-859-1100	$$	7 pm	Classy French sandwich shop.
Mastro's Steakhouse	246 N Canon Dr	310-888-8782	$$$$$	12 am	Great steaks; don't miss the upstairs piano bar.
Mulberry Street Pizzeria	240 S Beverly Dr	310-247-8100	$$	12 am	Thin-crust pizza.
Mulberry Street Pizzeria	347 N Canon Dr	310-247-8998	$$	12 am	Thin-crust pizza.
Nate 'n Al's	414 N Beverly Dr	310-274-0101	$$	9 pm	New York-style deli.
Nic's	453 N Canon Dr	310-550-5707	$$$$$	11 pm	Oysters and martinis--need we say more?
Polo Lounge	9641 Sunset Blvd	310-276-2251	$$$$$	2 am	The Grande Dame of hotel dining.
Sprinkles Cupcakes	9635 Little Santa Monica Blvd	310-274-8765	$	7 pm	LA's version of Magnolia Bakery.
Trader Vic's	9876 Wilshire Blvd	310-276-6345	$$$$	12 am	Old-school Polynesian-themed restaurant; fruity drinks and fried appetizers.
Xi'an	362 N Canon Dr	310-275-3345	$$$	11 pm	Healthy and delicious Chinese in a BH atmosphere.

Map 2 • West Hollywood

Ago	8478 Melrose Ave	323-655-6333	$$$$	11:30 pm	High-end Italian.
Albano's Brooklyn Pizza	7261 Melrose Ave	323-934-2494	$	12 am	Mulberry St. knockoff without the BH crowds.
Amalfi	143 N La Brea Ave	323-938-2504	$$$	12 am	Rustic, authentic Italian, good for groups.
Andre's Italian Restaurant	6332 W Third St	323-935-1246	$*	8.30 pm	Italian cafeteria complete with plastic flowers. Since 1963.
Angeli Caffe	7274 Melrose Ave	323-936-9086	$$$	11 pm	Starch-tastic bread and tasty pastas.

Map 2 • West Hollywood—*continued*

Angelini Osteria	7313 Beverly Blvd	323-297-0070	$$$	11 pm	Upscale Italian.
AOC	8022 W 3rd St	323-653-6359	$$$$	11 pm	Little plates, big wine selection, and savvy servers.
Azami Sushi Café	7160 Melrose Ave	323-939-3816	$$$$	10:30 pm	Fresh fish, fresh interior, fresh twist on sushi-fusion.
Balboa	8462 W Sunset Blvd	323-650-8383	$$$$	12 am	Steaks on the Sunset Strip.
Barefoot Bar & Grill	8722 W 3rd St	310-276-6223	$$$	11 pm	The California cuisine always draws crowds.
Basix Café	8333 Santa Monica Blvd	323-848-2460	$$	11 pm	Popular breakfast spot.
Benito's Taco Shop	7912 Beverly Blvd	323-938-7427	$	4 am	$3 burritos the size of your Chihuahua.
Beverly Hills Juice Club	8382 Beverly Blvd	323-655-8300	$*	6 pm	Drink this juice. Your intestines will thank you.
BLD	7450 Beverly Blvd	323-930-9744	$$$	11 pm	Stands for breakfast, lunch, and dinner—so good you'll want to try all three.
Bossa Nova	685 N Robertson Blvd	310-657-5070	$	1 am	Paradise for meat lovers.
Bossa Nova	7181 W Sunset Blvd	323-436-7999	$$	4 am	Savory Brazilian dishes. Open til 4 am.
Boule	420 N La Cienega Blvd	310-289-9977	$	7 pm	Don't miss the macaroons at this patisserie.
Buddha's Belly	7475 Beverly Blvd	323-931-8588	$$$	11 pm	Eat your way across Asia.
Bungalow Club	7174 Melrose Ave	323-936-5270	$$$$	1 am	Chic Moroccan-themed bar and outdoor dining.
Café Angelino	8735 W 3rd St	310-246-1177	$$	10 pm	Flaky thin crust pizzas.
Café Med	8615 Sunset Blvd	310-652-0445	$$	11:30 pm	Low-key Sunset Plaza Italian.
Café Vegan	7669 Beverley Blvd	323-937-3100	$	10 pm	Animal-friendly Thai food.
Campanile	624 S La Brea Ave	323-938-1447	$$$$	11 pm	Romantic Mediterranean.
Canter's Deli	419 N Fairfax Ave	323-651-2030	$$	24-hrs	Classic deli with swinging lounge attached.
Chameau	339 N Fairfax Ave	323-951-0039	$$$	11 pm	BYOB Moroccan.
Chateau Marmont	8221 W Sunset Blvd	323-656-1010	$$$$	24-hrs	Celeb-heavy scene, cuisine-light menu.
Chaya Brasserie	8741 Alden Dr	310-859-8833	$$$$	11 pm	Great food in a schmoozy setting.
Cheebo	7533 W Sunset Blvd	323-850-7070	$$	11 pm	Organic gourmet pizza and sandwiches.
Chipotle	121 N La Cienega Blvd	310-855-0371	$*	11 pm	Good 'n' fresh.
Cobras & Matadors	7615 Beverly Blvd	323-932-6178	$$	12 am	Hip, BYOB Tapas.
The Courtyard	8543 Santa Monica Blvd	310-358-0301	$$	1 am	The newest tapas place in town.
Cynthia's	8370 W 3rd St	323-658-7851	$$$	10:30 pm	American favorites. Order the cobbler—trust us...
Dolce Enoteca	8284 Melrose Ave	323-852-7174	$$$$	1 am	Ashton's Italian endeavor, still going strong.
Doughboys	8136 W 3rd St	323-651-4202	$	12 am	An anti-Atkins indulgence spot.
East India Grill	345 N La Brea Ave	323-936-8844	$	11 pm	Indian with a California twist.
Eat Well	8252 Santa Monica Blvd	323-656-1383	$††	3 pm	Hip chain for cheap comfort food.
Ed's Coffee Shop	460 N Robertson Blvd	310-659-8625	$††	3 pm	Home-cookin'.
El Compadre	7408 Sunset Blvd	323-874-7924	$$	2 am	Tasty Mexican with flaming, kick-ass margaritas.
Falcon	7213 W Sunset Blvd	323-850-5350	$$$	2 am	California chic cuisine best enjoyed with a posh cocktail
Farm of Beverly Hills	189 The Grove Dr	323-525-1699	$$$	11 pm	Yeehaw darlings! Farm-fresh salads and entrees.
Fish Grill	7226 Beverly Blvd	323-937-7162	$	2:30 pm	No-frills, super-fresh fish.
Fogo de Chao	133 N La Cienega Blvd	310-289-7755	$$$$	10:30 pm	An orgy of meat cooked Brazilian churrasco-style.
The French Crêpe Co	6333 W 3rd St	323-934-3113	$	10 pm	Even the crepe snobs love it.
French Quarter Market Place	7985 Santa Monica Blvd	323-654-0898	$$	3:30 am	Food for everyone, especially night owls.
Genghis Cohen	740 N Fairfax Ave	323-653-0640	$$$	11:30 pm	Chinese with live music.
Grace	7360 Beverly Blvd	323-934-4400	$$$$	11 pm	Chef Neil Fraser has been entertaining locals since 2002. Worth the splurge.
Greenblatts Delicatessen & Fine Wines	8017 W Sunset Blvd	323-656-0606	$	1:30 am	Kosher deli and wine shop.
Griddle Café	7916 W Sunset Blvd	323-874-0377	$$	4 pm	Brunch with the stars—of the WB.
Gumbo Pot	6333 W 3rd St	323-933-0358	$$	10 pm	Best Cajun in LA.
Hirozen	8385 Beverly Blvd	323-653-0470	$$$	10 pm	Great mini-mall sushi.
House of Blues	8430 Sunset Blvd	323-848-5100	$$$	11 pm	Saucy Cajun. Try Sunday's Gospel Brunch.
Hugo's	8401 Santa Monica Blvd	323-654-3993	$$	10 pm	Power brunches.
In-N-Out Burger	7009 W Sunset Blvd	800-786-1000	$	1:30 am	Top California burger joint.
The Ivy	113 N Robertson Blvd	310-274-8303	$$$$	11 pm	Broker a deal over traditional American fare.
JAR	8225 Beverly Blvd	323-655-6566	$$$$	11 pm	Upscale comfort food.
Joan's on Third	8350 W 3rd St	323-655-2285	$$	7:30 pm	Foodies can eat-in or carry out.
Jones	7205 Santa Monica Blvd	323-850-1727	$$	1:30 am	Cozy eatery with a nice menu.
King's Road Café	8361 Beverly Blvd	323-655-9044	$$	10 pm	Strongest coffee you'll ever drink.
Kokomo	6333 W 3rd St	323-933-0773	$$	9 pm	Standard American fare.
La Paella	476 S San Vicente Blvd	323-951-0745	$$$	10 pm	As authentic as you'll find this side of Barcelona.
Lala's	7229 Melrose Ave	323-934-6838	$$	11 pm	Casual Argentine. Great for lunch.
Le Pain Quotidien	8607 Melrose Ave	310-854-3700	$$	9 pm	Classy French sandwich shop.
The Little Door	8164 W 3rd St	323-951-1210	$$$$$	11 pm	Courtyard dining meets the farmers market.
Los Tacos	7954 Santa Monica Blvd	323-848-9141	$*	24-hrs	Cut your hangover off at the pass with the best Mexican in WeHo.

Loteria Grill	6333 W 3rd St	323-930-2211	$	10 pm	*Muy fresicita.*
Lucques	8474 Melrose Ave	323-655-6277	$$$$	12 am	Chez Panisse-style cooking in LA.
M Cafe de Chaya	7119 Melrose Ave	323-525-0588	$$	10 pm	Contemporary macrobiotic. Only in LA.
Mandarette	8386 Beverly Blvd	323-655-6115	$$	11:30 pm	Chinese fusion.
Miyagi's	8225 W Sunset Blvd	323-650-3524	$$$	2 am	Trendy sushi and cocktails.
Newsroom Café	120 N Robertson Blvd	310-652-4444	$$	10 pm	Star-laden vegetarian.
Numbers Restaurant	8741 Santa Monica Blvd	310-652-7700	$$$	11 pm	The food's not the only thing for sale.
Opaque	8401 W Sunset Blvd	800-710-1270	$$$$$	11 pm	Dinner in the dark. If you're into that sort of thing.
The Pig	612 N La Brea Ave	323-935-1116	$$	10 pm	Messy southern BBQ joint. Yum.
Pink's Famous Chili Dogs	709 N La Brea Ave	323-931-4223	$*	3 am	A line around the block; it's that famous.
Quality Food & Beverage	8030 W 3rd St	323-658-5959	$*	3:30 pm	Dog-friendly brunch hangout.
Real Food Daily	414 N La Cienega Blvd	310-289-9910	$$	11 pm	One of the healthiest-tasting restaurants in town.
Saddle Ranch Chop House	8371 W Sunset Blvd	323-656-2007	$$$	2 am	Chophouse with a mechanical bull.
Singapore's Banana Leaf	6333 W 3rd St	323-933-4627	$††	9 pm	Where the President of Singapore chows down when in LA.
The Standard	8300 W Sunset Blvd	323-650-9090	$$$	24-hrs	Late-night star watching.
Surya India	8048 W 3rd St	323-653-5151	$$$	9:45 pm	Tasty with a breezy interior.
Susina Bakery	7122 Beverly Blvd	323-934-7900	$	11 pm	French bakery and café.
Sweet Lady Jane	8360 Melrose Ave	323-653-7145	$$	11:30 pm	Decadent desserts to die for.
Swingers	8020 Beverly Blvd	323-653-5858	$	4 am	Classic late-night diner, both loved and hated.
Tagine	132 N Robertson Blvd	310-360-7535	$$$	10:30 pm	An eating experience with set menus of small plates.
TART	115 S Fairfax Ave	323-556-2608	$$$	10:30 pm	Farmer's Daughter restauraunt offers down-home food for WeHo types.
Taste	8454 Melrose Ave	323-852-6888	$$$	11 pm	Trendy Cali-fusion, Melrose-style.
The TEN20 Café	1020 N San Vicente Blvd	310-854-1111	$$$	11:30 pm	Swanky lounge atop the Bel Age hotel with views and live jazz shows.
Toast	8221 W Third St	323-655-5018	$$	11 pm	Great for celebrity spotting while you brunch.
Toi	7505 1/2 W Sunset Blvd	323-874-8062	$$$	4 am	Late night, hard rock Thai.
Tops	8593 Santa Monica Blvd	310-659-8843	$††	10 pm	Healthy burger and fries.
Trattoria Amici	469 N Doheny Dr	310-858-0271	$$$	10 pm	Pacific Italian chain.
Ulysses Voyage	6333 W Third St	323-939-9728	$$$	11:30 pm	Outdoor ouzo oasis.
Urth Caffé	8565 Melrose Ave	310-659-0628	$$	12 am	All organic lunch place, plus coffee and sweets.
Uzbekistan Restaurant	7077 W Sunset Blvd	323-464-3663	$$	11 pm	Your average strip-mall Uzbeki joint.
Vienna Café	7356 Melrose Ave	323-651-3822	$$	6 pm	People-watch while you brunch.
The Village Idiot	7383 Melrose Ave	323-655-3331	$$$	1 am	Bustling British pub with surprisingly good food.
Wokcano Café	8408 W 3rd St	323-653-1998	$$$	11:30 pm	Who cares about atmosphere when the Korean bbq is this good.
Wood Ranch BBQ & Grill	189 The Grove Dr	323-937-6800	$$	10:45	Get a heapin' pile of orangey goodness (a.k.a. sweet mashed potatoes).
Yabu	521 N La Cienega Blvd	310-854-0400	$$$	11:30 pm	Hip sushi and noodles.
Map 3 • Hollywood					
101 Coffee Shop	6145 Franklin Ave	323-467-1175	$$	3 am	Famous diner with yummy sweet-potato fries.
Ammo	1155 N Highland Ave	323-871-2666	$$$	11 pm	Trendy California comfort food.
Astro Burger	5601 Melrose Ave	323-469-1924	$*	1 am	Tasty meat-free burgers.
Benito's Taco Shop	6751 Santa Monica Blvd	323-466-9333	$	4 am	$3 burritos the size of your Chihuahua.
Big Wang's	1562 N Cahuenga Blvd	323-469-2449	$$	2 am	Unpretentious wing joint with celebrities. Karaoke Wednesdays.
Birds	5925 Franklin Ave	323-465-0175	$$	11 pm	Rotisserie chicken and beer.
California Chicken Café	6805 Melrose Ave	323-935-5877	$	10 pm	Popular cop hangout: the safest chicken in town.
California Vegan	7300 Sunset Blvd, Unit #A	323-874-9079	$††	10:30 pm	Good option for vegans, but only OK for the rest of us.
Chan Dara	310 N Larchmont Blvd	323-467-1052	$$$	11 pm	Huge Thai portions served by tiny Thai women.
Cinespace	6356 Hollywood Blvd	323-817-3456	$$$$	10 pm	Check that the kitchen is open before you go.
Citizen Smith	1602 N Cahuenga Blvd	323-461-5001	$$$	2 am	Down home meets uptown with this swanky spot specializing in comfort food.
Crispy Crust	1253 Vine St	323-467-2000	$$	12 am	Great delivery, a truly crispy crust.
Doughboys	1156 N Highland Ave	323-467-9117	$$	12 am	New York style bakery/café. Terrific soups and sandwiches
eat. on sunset	1448 N Gower St	323-461-8800	$$$$	10 pm	Former Pinot Hollywood got a face-lift.
Fabiolus Café	5255 Melrose Ave	323-464-5857	$$	10 pm	Dine in, deliver, or take-away Italian.
Fabiolus Café	6270 W Sunset Blvd	323-467-2882	$$	10 pm	Dine in, deliver, or take-away Italian.
Geisha House	6633 Hollywood Blvd	323-460-6300	$$$$	12 am	Sushi, sake and maybe get Punk'd.
Hola Fresh Mexican Grill	1807 N Cahuenga Blvd	323-466-0000	$	9:30 pm	Muy cheap Mexican eats with free delivery.
Hollywood and Vine	6263 Hollywood Blvd	323-464-2345	$$$	11:30 pm	Californian cuisine in a dressed-up 1940's Hollywood diner.

Map 3 • Hollywood—*continued*

Hungry Cat	1535 Vine St	323-462-2155	$$$	12 am	Seafood and hip cocktails. Killer bleu cheese burger.
Kung Pao Kitty	6445 Hollywood Blvd	323-465-0110	$$	12 am	Here fishy, fishy.
La Buca	5210 Melrose Ave	323-462-1900	$$	10:30 pm	Sophia Loren would eat at this tiny Italian ristorante.
La Poubelle	5907 Franklin Ave	323-465-0807	$$$	12 am	Gallic gourmet dining and '80s music.
Larchmont Deli	5210 Beverly Blvd	323-466-1193	$	5 pm	Try the pastrami.
Le Oriental Bistro	1710 N Highland Ave	323-462-3388	$	10:30 pm	Chinese for real.
Los Balcones del Peru	1360 Vine St	323-871-9600	$$	10 pm	Peruvian entrees & ceviches.
Magnolia	6266 W Sunset Blvd	323-467-0660	$$$	3 am	Familiar yet delicious bistro fare at new Hollywood hotspot. Try the mac-n-cheese.
Memphis	6541 Hollywood Blvd	323-465-8600	$$$$	1 am	Stick-to-your-ribs soul food in the heart of Hollywood.
Miceli's	1646 N Las Palmas Ave	323-466-3438	$$	12 am	Classic Hollywood Italian since 1949 (warning for the easily annoyed: singing waiters here).
Musso & Frank Grill	6667 Hollywood Blvd	323-467-7788	$$$$	11 pm	Old-fashioned American.
Off Vine	6263 Leland Wy	323-962-1900	$$$$	11:30 pm	Romantic Californian.
Palms Thai	5900 Hollywood Blvd	323-462-5073	$$	1:30 am	Thai Elvis impersonator!
Pig 'n Whistle	6714 Hollywood Blvd	323-463-0000	$$$	10 pm	Dine in "bed" or people-watch from a comfy booth.
Pizza Bella	1900 N Highland Ave	323-876-5961	$	11 pm	Good NY pizza (at least for LA).
Red Pearl Kitchen	6703 Melrose Ave	323-525-1415	$$	10 pm	Hidden gem boasting healthy Asian cuisine in ultra comfy digs.
Roscoe's House of Chicken 'n Waffles	1514 N Gower St	323-466-7453	$$	4 am	Southern-fried bonanza.
Skooby's Hot Dogs	6654 Hollywood Blvd	323-HOT-DOGS	$*	3 am	Tasty dogs with homemade chili.
Sushi Hiroba	776 Vine St	323-962-7237	$$$	11 pm	Sushi served on a conveyer belt.
Truly a Vegan Restaurant	5907 Hollywood Blvd	323-466-7533	$$††	10 pm	Thai without the meat on sticks.
Xiomara	6101 Melrose Ave	323-461-0601	$$$$	11 pm	Upscale Cuban with revolutionary mojitos.
Yamashiro	1999 N Sycamore Ave	323-466-5125	$$$$	11 pm	Romantic Japanese with a view.

Map 4 • Los Feliz

Alcove Bakery & Café	1929 Hillhurst Ave	323-644-0100	$	12 am	Brunch, lunch, gourmet food market, beautiful patio out front.
Alegria on Sunset	3510 W Sunset Blvd	323-913-1422	$$*	11 pm	Lively Mexican food made with home-style finesse.
Café Los Feliz	2081 N Hillhurst Ave	323-664-7111	$	6 pm	Neighborhoody gem. Exquisite tarts and cinnamon rolls.
Café Stella	3932 W Sunset Blvd	323-666-0265	$$$$	11 pm	Trendy French bistro and wine bar.
Casbah Café	3900 W Sunset Blvd	323-664-7000	$$	10 pm	Mint tea, pointy slippers, excellent local hang.
Casita Del Campo	1920 Hyperion Ave	323-662-4255	$$	10 pm	It's all about the margaritas.
Cha Cha Cha	656 N Virgil Ave	323-664-7723	$$$	11 pm	Caribbean food and sangria.
Cliff's Edge	3626 W Sunset Blvd	323-666-6116	$$	12 am	Cal-Euro tapas, upscale bohemian digs, and Silver Lake's swankiest patio.
Cobras and Matadors	4655 Hollywood Blvd	323-669-3922	$$$	12 am	Dark and delish. This tapas joint is great for indecisive diners.
Eat Well	3916 E Sunset Blvd	323-664-1624	$	3 pm	Hip chain for cheap comfort food.
El Conquistador	3701 W Sunset Blvd	323-666-5136	$$	11:30 pm	Mole olé!
Electric Lotus	4656 Franklin Ave	323-953-0040	$$	1 am	Hip Indian disco.
Farfalla Trattoria	1978 Hillhurst Ave	323-661-7365	$$$	11:30 pm	Inexpensive, reliable Italian.
Fred 62	1850 N Vermont Ave	323-667-0062	$$	24-hrs	Retro-styled diner with surprising menu.
Good Microbrew & Grill	3725 W Sunset Blvd	323-660-3645	$$$††	11 pm	Overpriced comfort food tempered by mucho bottled brews.
Hollywood Gelato Company	1936 Hillhurst Ave	323-644-3311	$	10:30 pm	Staid but flavorful rainbow of gelato, plus coffee and cupcakes.
Home	1760 Hillhurst Ave	323-669-0211	$$	11 pm	No place like this outdoor eatery. Try the waffle fries.
House of Pies	1869 N Vermont Ave	323-666-9961	$	3 am	Perfect pancakes and pecan pie—life's good.
The Kitchen	4348 Fountain Ave	323-664-3663	$$	1 am	Late-night comfort food.
Las Ranas Café Restaurant	654 N Hoover St	323-664-1588	$$††	9 pm	Cheap, tasty entrees and froggy décor.
Maco's Restaurant	1820 N Vermont Ave	323-660-1211	$$*	9 pm	Where the Japanese from Japan prefer to eat.
Madame Matisse	3536 W Sunset Blvd	323-662-4862	$$††	3:15 pm	Matchbox-sized and mellow French Café packed with regulars. BYOB.
Malo	4326 W Sunset Blvd	323-664-1011	$$$	12 am	Yummy Mexican for the hipster cheapskate.
Mexico City	2121 Hillhurst Ave	323-661-7227	$$$	11 pm	Arty Tex-Mex cantina.
Millie's	3524 Sunset Blvd	323-664-0404	$††	4 pm	The Devil's Mess is the best reason to be bad.
Mustard Seed Café	1948 Hillhurst Ave	323-660-0670	$$	5 pm	Tasty and laid-back; may take awhile to get the check!
Palermo	1858 N Vermont Ave	323-663-1178	$$	12:45 am	Uninspired, gooey, popular.
Paru's	5140 W Sunset Blvd	323-661-7600	$$	9:45 pm	Delicious South Indian food with lots of happy-smiley service.
Pinkberry	1726 N Vermont Ave	323-661-0411	$	12 am	Sample the "crackberry" with spunky diehards and suspicious newbies.

Scoops	712 N Heliotrope Dr	323-906-2649	$*	10 pm	Amazing vegan and non-vegan daily ice-cream. New flavors each day that are requested by the customers.
Shin	1972 Hillhurst Ave	323-664-1891	$$	11:30 pm	Japanese food, sushi, good salads.
Tantra	3705 W Sunset Blvd	323-663-8268	$$$$	12 am	Ultra-sexy Indian, with lounge.
Toad House	4503 Beverly Blvd	323-460-7037	$$$	1 am	Yummy pork. No toad.
Vermont	1714 N Vermont Ave	323-661-6163	$$$$	11:30 pm	Dine in style before heading to the punk show.
Yai on Vermont	1627 N Vermont	323-644-1076	$$*	10 pm	Kinda greasy but still divine. Comfy booths and great patio.
Yuca's	2056 Hillhurst Ave	323-662-1214	$*	6 pm	A busy shack serving luscious Yucatan-style burritos and tacos.
Zankou Chicken	5065 W Sunset Blvd	323-665-7845	$*	12 am	Palm-licking, Beck-serenaded chicken.

Map 5 • Silver Lake/Echo Park/Atwater

Astro Family Restaurant	2300 Fletcher Dr	323-663-9241	$	24-hrs	Relaxed '50s modern diner.
Baracoa Cuban Café	3175 Glendale Blvd	323-665-9590	$	9 pm	Home-style Cuban cooking.
Blair's	2903 Rowena Ave	323-660-1882	$$$$	11 pm	Silver Lake's premier eatery.
Brite Spot Family Restaurant	1918 W Sunset Blvd	213-484-9800	$	4 am	Classic Silver Lake late-night diner.
Café Tropical	2900 W Sunset Blvd	323-661-8391	$††	10 pm	Latin bakery and coffee house.
The Downbeat Café	1202 N Alvarado St	213-483-3955	$$	10 pm	Jazz café for neighborhood politicos.
Dusty's	3200 W Sunset Blvd	323-906-1018	$$$	1 am	Eclectic French bistro.
Edendale Grill	2838 Rowena Ave	323-666-2000	$$$$	11:30 pm	Former fire station serves American favorites—dine in or dine out.
Gingergrass	2396 Glendale Blvd	323-644-1600	$$	10:30 pm	Upscale Vietnamese food for a gringo palate.
Hard Times Pizza Co	2664 Griffith Park Blvd	323-661-5656	$$	11 pm	Sicilian- and Neopolitan-style pies to take out or eat in.
India Sweets and Spices	3126 Los Feliz Blvd	323-345-0360	$$	9 pm	Vegetarian delicacies, Indian groceries, and Bollywood hits under one roof.
La Parrilla	3129 W Sunset Blvd	323-661-8055	$$††	11 pm	Authentic Mexican, order the *molcajete azteca.*
Leela Thai	1737 Silver Lake Blvd	323-660-6100	$$*	11 pm	Inexpensive, delicious, friendly.
Mae Ploy	2606 W Sunset Blvd	213-353-9635	$$	10 pm	Home-style Thai food served with a smile.
Masa of Echo Park	1800 W Sunset Blvd	213-989-1558	$	11 pm	Neighborhood bakery and pizza house run by Patina vets.
Michelangelo Pizzeria	1637 Silver Lake Blvd	323-660-4843	$$††	10:30 pm	Italian fare with old-world flair.
Mimi's Café	2925 Los Feliz Blvd	323-668-1715	$$	11 pm	Average TGIF-style family restaurant.
Nicky D's Wood-Fired Pizza	2764 Rowena Ave	323-664-3333	$$	10 pm	Friendly local spot for NYC-style pies. Try the Garlic Clam pizza.
Pho' Café	2841 W Sunset Blvd	213-413-0888	$$*	12 am	Vietnamese noodle shop with hipster flavor.
Police Academy Café	1880 Academy Dr	323-221-5222	$	2 pm	Dine with the cadets.
Rambutan Thai	2835 W Sunset Blvd	213-273-8424	$$	11 pm	Trendy but good Thai favorites.
Red Lion Tavern	2366 Glendale Blvd	323-662-5337	$$	12 am	Go for the German brats.
Soycafe	1997 Hyperion Ave	323-663-7888	$*	n/a	Try a tofu/shitake sandwich.
Spain	1866 Glendale Blvd	323-667-9045	$$	10 pm	Sangria and paella without the airfare.
Taix	1911 W Sunset Blvd	213-484-1265	$$	11 pm	Say "Tex" and check out "Two-fer Tuesdays" for double the wine at this French standard.
Tam O'Shanter	2980 Los Feliz Blvd	323-664-0228	$$$$	11 pm	Scottish-English pub.

Map 6 • Miracle Mile/Mid-City

Baja Guadalajara Grill	1663 S La Cienega Blvd	310-860-1165	$$	8 pm	Hole-in-the-wall with incredible tamales.
Black Dog Coffee	5657 Wilshire Blvd	323-933-1976	$	5 pm	Friendly and tasty. Breakfast, lunch, coffee, dog biscuits.
Café Latte	6254 Wilshire Blvd	323-936-5213	$$	9 pm	California-style coffee and breakfast shop.
Crazy Fish	9105 W Olympic Blvd	310-550-8547	$$$	10:45 pm	Insanely popular sushi joint.
Fu's Palace	8751 W Pico Blvd	310-271-7887	$	11 pm	Crispy, spicy, sweet, and sour aromatic shrimp.
Lucy's	1373 S La Brea Ave	323-938-4337	$	24-hrs	A 24-hour drive-through taco stand that also sells chili dogs, burgers, and anything else bad for you.
Luna Park	672 S La Brea Ave	323-934-2110	$$$	11:30 pm	Cocktails, tasty food, lively scene. LA outpost of San Francisco original.
Merkato	1036 S Fairfax Ave	323-935-1775	$	11 pm	Eat with your hands at this Ethiopian joint.
Natalee Thai	998 S Robertson Blvd	310-855-9380	$$	10:30 pm	Popular Thai food.
Nyala Ethiopian Cuisine	1076 S Fairfax Ave	323-936-5918	$$	11 pm	Ethiopian serving unbeatable vegetarian $5.95 lunch buffet.
Rosalind's	1044 S Fairfax Ave	323-936-2486	$$	11 pm	Local favorite, Ethiopian.
Roscoe's House of Chicken 'n Waffles	5006 W Pico Blvd	323-934-4405	$$	2 am	Cheap Southern soul food chain.
Versailles	1415 S La Cienega Blvd	310-289-0392	$$	11 pm	The LA institution's garlicy Cuban grub will stay with you.
Wi Jammin	5103 Pico Blvd	323-965-9809	$	9 pm	A tiny hole-in-the-wall Carribbean restaurant where the local hairdressers hang out.

Map 7 • Hancock Park

Café du Village	139 N Larchmont Blvd	323-466-3996	$††	9:30 pm	French provincial meets modern American. Incroyable breakfasts.
Girasole	225 1/2 N Larchmont Blvd	323-464-6978	$$	10:30 pm	Tiny, cozy, delicious osso buco.
Kiku Sushi	246 N Larchmont Blvd	323-464-1200	$$	10:30 pm	All-you-can-eat sushi.
La Bottega Marino	203 N Larchmont Blvd	323-962-1325	$$	10 pm	Italian café/deli serving especially nice brunch.
La Luna	113 N Larchmont Blvd	323-962-2130	$$$	10 pm	Casual Italian trattoria.
Le Petit Greek	127 N Larchmont Blvd	323-464-5160	$$$	10 pm	Gyros, anyone?
Noah's New York Bagels	250 N Larchmont Blvd	323-466-2924	$	4 pm	Bagels and schmear with an NYC theme.
Prado	244 N Larchmont Blvd	323-467-3871	$$$	11 pm	Spicy Latin-Caribbean.
Village Pizzeria	131 N Larchmont Blvd	323-465-5566	$	10 pm	Might be LA's best NY-style pizza.
Z Pizza	123 N Larchmont Blvd	323-466-6969	$$	10 pm	Thin-crust deliciousness. A handful of sidewalk and indoor tables.

Map 8 • Korea Town

Cassell's Hamburgers	3266 W 6th St	213-480-5000	$*	4 pm	Legendary status lacking of late.
Dong Il Jang	3455 W 8th St	213-383-5757	$$	10 pm	Upscale Korean barbecue, also serving sushi.
El Cholo	1121 S Western Ave	323-734-2773	$$	11 pm	Long time favorite Mexican chain.
El Farolito	2737 W Pico Blvd	323-731-4329	$	10 pm	Chicken enchiladas.
Guelaguetza	3014 W Olympic Blvd	213-427-0608	$$	10 pm	Warm, informal, authentically Mexican dinning experience.
Hodori	1001 S Vermont Ave, Ste 102	213-383-3554	$††	24-hrs	24-hour Korean restaurant with killer barbecued beef.
Langers	704 S Alvarado St	213-483-8050	$$	4 pm	Great Jewish deli in MacArthur Park. Try the pastrami sandwiches.
Lowenbrau Keller	3211 Beverly Blvd	213-382-5723	$$††	10 pm	Décor looks like Germany threw up here.
M Grill	3832 Wilshire Blvd	213-389-2770	$$$	9:30 pm	Authentic Brazilian, sleek interior.
Mama's Hot Tamales	2122 W Seventh St	213-487-4300	$	3:30 pm	An amazing selection of tamales from all over Central and South America.
Papa Cristo's	2771 W Pico Blvd	323-737-2970	$	8 pm	Greek market and deli serving delicious gyros and souvlaki.
Parao	3680 Wilshire Blvd	213-383-8686	$$	n/a	Fusion fare with private karaoke rooms.
Pipers	222 N Western Ave	323-465-7701	$††	24 hrs	Dependable 24-hour diner.
Soot Bull Jeep	3136 W 8th St	213-387-3865	$$$	11 pm	Brilliant, smoky Korean BBQ—get the Spencer Steak.
Taylor's Steak House	3361 W 8th St	213-382-8449	$$$	10 pm	Old-fashioned steak house.
Tommy's	2575 Beverly Blvd	213-389-9060	$*	24-hrs	Their burgers are renowned.

Map 9 • Downtown

410 Boyd	410 Boyd St	213-617-2491	$$$	10 pm	Downtown secret for good food in a bar atmosphere.
626 Reserve	626B S Spring St	213-627-9800	$$	11 pm	Sophisti-cool afterwork hangout with a raging wine list.
Angelique Café	840 S Spring St	213-623-8698	$$	3:30 pm	Irresistably charming corner café that brings the best of France to LA... without the French.
Blossom Restaurant and Teas	426 S Main St	213-623-1973	$$	10 pm	Fresh authentic Vietnamese in "blossoming" downtown neighborhood.
Brooklyn Bagel	2217 Beverly Blvd	213-413-4114	$*	11 pm	Five-decade old authentic bagelry.
Café Pinot	700 W 5th St	213-239-6500	$$$$$	10 pm	Downtown's classy French bistro.
Casa La Golondrina	W 17 Olvera St	213-628-4349	$	9 pm	A historic setting for classic Mexican food complete with serenading Mariachis.
Checkers	535 S Grand Ave	213-624-0000	$$$$	9 pm	Upscale downtown pre-theater dining.
Cicada	617 S Olive St	213-488-9488	$$$$	9 pm	California Italian.
Ciudad	445 S Figueroa St	213-486-5171	$$$$	11 pm	Mod interior, killer mojitos, and eclectic pan-Latin menu.
Clifton's Cafeteria	648 S Broadway	213-627-1673	$††	7:30 pm	Tri-level cafeteria with a woodsy theme and fake animals since 1931.
Dakokuya	327 E 1st St	213-626-1680	$$	1 am	Not your college ramen.
Emerson's	862 S Los Angeles St	213-623-8807	$	5 pm	Specialty salads, sandwiches, and coffees.
Emerson's Café	606 S Olive St	213-623-3006	$	5 pm	Specialty salads, sandwiches, and coffees.
Empress Pavilion	988 N Hill St	213-617-9898	$$	10 pm	Specialty salads, sandwiches, and coffees.
Engine Co No 28	644 S Figueroa St	213-624-6996	$$$$	9 pm	Good firehouse-inspired eats.
Lamonica's NY Pizza	518 W 6th St	213-614-1100	$	6 pm	Best pizza in the neighborhood.
Mikado Sushi Roll & Teriyaki	1001 S Broadway	213-746-1481	$$††	8 pm	Scallops with avocado & grapefruit? Bring it on!
Mrs Beasley's	735 S Figueroa St	213-228-0227	$	5 pm	Baked goods, soups, sandwiches, coffee—also does gift baskets.
Nick & Stef's Steakhouse	330 S Hope St	213-680-0330	$$$$$	10:30 pm	Old-fashioned steaks in an ultra-modern downtown setting.
Noe	251 S Olive St	213-356-4100	$$$$	11 pm	Omni Hotel's upscale Japanese-American.
Oomasa	100 Japanese Village Plz Mall	213-623-9048	$$	12 am	Cozy, late-night, traditional Japanese fare.

Original Pantry Café	877 S Figueroa St	213-972-9279	$*	24-hrs	All-American diner open 24 hours since 1924.
Pacific Dining Car	1310 W 6th St	213-483-6000	$$$$	24-hrs	Steak all day, all night.
Patina	141 S Grand Ave	213-972-3331	$$$$	9:30 pm	French-Californian fusion.
Pete's Café & Bar	400 S Main St	213-617-1000	$$$	2 am	Great bar, big drinks, tasty American fare.
Philippe the Original	1001 N Alameda St	213-628-3781	$*	10 pm	The best French dips in town. Totally awesome.
Plum Tree Inn	913 N Broadway	213-613-1819	$$	10:30 pm	Delicious Chinese.
R-23	923 E 2nd St	213-687-7178	$$$$	10 pm	Stylish sushi in the LA arts district.
Rustic Canyon Wine Bar	1119 Wilshire Blvd	310-393-7050	$$$	11:30 pm	Hidden cave of wine.
Señor Fish	422 E 1st St	213-625-0566	$	9 pm	Tacos de fish.
Seoul Jung Korean	930 Wilshire Blvd	213-688-7880	$$$$	9:30 pm	Upscale Korean BBQ with fresh meat, fish, and veggies.
The Standard	550 S Flower St	213-892-8080	$$$	24-hrs	24-hour diner menu, post-party or in your room.
Suehiro Café	337 E 1st St	213-626-9132	$$	11 pm	Comfort food, Japanese-style, with comic books.
Sushi Gen	422 E 2nd St	213-617-0552	$$	9:40 pm	Excellent sushi favored by locals.
Tiara Café	127 E 9th St	213-623-3663	$$	3 pm	A good compromise if you're a carnivore dating a vegan.
TOT	345 E 2nd St	213-680-0344	$$	1 am	Good lunch spot for affordable Japanese. Try one of the tuna bowls.
Traxx at Union Station	800 N Alameda St	213-625-1999	$$	9 pm	As elegant and exquisite as Union Station itself.
Tribal Café	1651 W Temple St	213-483-4458	$	12 am	Filipino friendliness.
Via Café	451 Gin Ling Wy	213-617-1481	$*	11 pm	A small Vietnamese café in Chinatown near all the art galleries; mostly occupied by young artists and gallerists.
Water Grill	544 S Grand Ave	213-891-0900	$$$	9:30 pm	Expense-account dining to impress. And it's delicious.
Windows Steaks and Martinis	1150 S Olive St	213-746-1554	$$$$$	11 pm	Sky-top views, martinis, and steaks. Who could want anything more?
Yang Chow	819 N Broadway	213-625-0811	$$	10:30 pm	Popular Chinese chain.
Zip	744 E 3rd St	213-680-3770	$$	12 am	Fusion sushi in the heart of the Artists' District.

Map 10 • Baldwin Hills

Tasty Q	2959 Crenshaw Blvd	323-735-8325	$	11:30 pm	Fried birds—from whole turkeys to drumsticks.

Map 11 • South Central West

Aunt Rosa Lee's Mississippi Soul Food	2781 S Western Ave	323-733-8586	$$††	9 pm	Real soul food.
Harold & Belle's	2920 W Jefferson Blvd	323-735-3376	$$$	10 pm	Great Cajun food.
La Barca	2414 S Vermont Ave	323-735-6567	$$	11 pm	Mexican.
Phillip's Barbecue	4307 Leimert Blvd	323-292-7613	$$	11 pm	Southern-style ribs in southern LA.

Map 12 • South Central East

29th Street Café	2827 S Hoover St	213-746-2929	$$	11:30 pm	The spot in South Central for brunch.
Chano's Drive-In	3000 S Figueroa St	213-747-3944	$	3 am	Drive-in to dive into authentic Mexican food.
Pasta Roma	2827 S Figueroa St	213-742-0303	$	10 pm	University student hangout for cheap Italian.

Map 13 • Inglewood

Ibex Ethiopian Restaurant	630 N La Brea Ave	310-673-3392	$$	10 pm	Traditional Ethiopian cuisine, like we'd really know.
La Costa Mariscos Restaurant	597 S La Brea Ave	310-672-2083	$*	9 pm	Latin-styled fast food with the accent on seafood.
La Perla Restaurant	10623 S Prairie Ave	310-677-5277	$$	5 pm	Ernestina Murillo's kitchen serves up Latin American cuisine.
Little Belize Restaurant	217 E Nutwood St	323-574-4003	$$	9 pm	Get your Belizean fix on at this inexpensive spot.
Pann's Diner	6710 La Tijera Blvd	323-776-3770	$$††	11 pm	One of the best remaining examples in the country of '50s coffee shop design—and they serve a down-home tasty breakfast.
Thai Plate Restaurant	10311 Hawthorne Blvd	310-412-0111	$$	10 pm	This neighborhood-style restaurant's specialty is Northern Thai cuisine.

Map 14 • Inglewood East/Morningside Park

M&M Soul Food Restaurant	3300 W Manchester Blvd	310-673-5031	$$	10 pm	Consistently delicious.

Map 15 • Pacific Palisades

A La Tarte Bistrot	1037 Swarthmore Ave	310-459-6635	$$	4 pm	French.
Dante Palisades Restaurant	1032 Swarthmore Ave	310-459-7561	$$	10 pm	Italian food (closed from 3-5 pm).
Giorgio Baldi	114 W Channel Rd	310-573-1660	$$$$	10 pm	Memorable Tuscan cooking.
Kay 'n Dave's	15246 W Sunset Blvd	310-459-8118	$$	10 pm	Healthy Mexican with a family-friendly atmosphere.
Marix Tex Mex Café	118 Entrada Dr	310-459-8596	$$$	11 pm	Perfect for post-beach margaritas and tacos. Sandy patrons OK.
Modo Mio Cucina Rustica	15200 W Sunset Blvd	310-459-0979	$$$	10:30 pm	Oddly office-like outside; quiet, authentic, well-executed Italian inside.
Patrick's Roadhouse	106 Entrada Dr	310-459-4544	$$	6 pm	Quintessential place for breakfast at the beach.
Pure Energy Café	17383 W Sunset Blvd	310-573-4105	$	4 pm	Health-conscious Mexican food.
Robek's Juice	15280 Antioch St	310-230-3991	$	8 pm	Juice, salads, sandwiches.
Terry's	1028 Swarthmore Ave	310-454-6467	$$	9 pm	Breakfast, lunch, dinner, sandwiches, salads, omelettes.

Map 16 • Brentwood

A Votre Sante	13016 San Vicente Blvd	310-451-1813	$$	10 pm	Vegetarian health food.
The Brentwood	148 S Barrington Ave	310-476-3511	$$$$	11 pm	California-style comfort food.
Cheesecake Factory	11647 San Vicente Blvd	310-826-7111	$$	12:30 pm	American comfort food—and of course, cheesecake.
Chin Chin	11740 San Vicente Blvd	310-826-2525	$$	10 pm	Chinese chain run by non-Chinese.
City Bakery	225 26th St	310-656-3040	$	7 pm	NYC's iconic gourmet fare goes west.
The Coral Tree Café	11645 San Vicente Blvd	310-979-8733	$$	11 pm	Yummy lunch among the trophy wives and up-and-comers.
Daily Grill	11677 San Vicente Blvd	310-442-0044	$$$	10 pm	Home cooking.
Gaucho Grill	11754 San Vicente Blvd	310-447-7898	$$	11 pm	Argentine cuisine with lots of meat.
La Scala Presto	11740 San Vicente Blvd	310-826-6100	$$$	10 pm	Classic Italian.
Le Pain Quotidien	11702 Barrington Ct	310-476-0969	$$	7 pm	Classy French sandwich shop.
Pizzicotto	11758 San Vicente Blvd	310-442-7188	$$$	10 pm	Pizza and pasta.
Reddi Chick BBQ	225 26th St	310-393-5238	$*	7:30 pm	Chicken with a cult following.
Toscana	11633 San Vicente Blvd	310-820-2448	$$$$	11 pm	Tuscan with great pizzas.
Vincenti	11930 San Vicente Blvd	310-207-0127	$$$$	10 pm	Fine Italian food and wine with kitchen view.

Map 17 • Bel Air/Holmby Hills

Bel Air Bar & Grill	662 N Sepulveda Blvd	310-440-5544	$$$$	10 pm	Californian with quick Getty access.
Hotel Bel Air Dining Room	701 Stone Cyn Rd	310-472-1211	$$$$$	9 pm	Excellent nouvelle Cal-French for when you're feeling rich. Swanky bar.

Map 18 • Santa Monica

17th Street Café	1610 Montana Ave	310-453-2771	$$$	10 pm	California casual.
Akbar Cuisine of India	2627 Wilshire Blvd	310-586-7469	$$$	10 pm	Creative Indian cooking.
Angelato Café	301 Arizona Ave	310-656-9999	$*	12 am	Gelato in every flavor possible
Babalu	1002 Montana Ave	310-395-2500	$$$	11 pm	Caribbean, don't skip dessert.
Bagel Nosh	1629 Wilshire Blvd	310-451-8771	$	3 pm	No-frills bagel and coffee shop.
Bay Cities Italian Deli	1517 Lincoln Blvd	310-395-8279	$††	7 pm	Amazing Italian sandwich counter, Italian grocery, and long lines.
Border Grill	1445 4th St	310-451-1655	$$$	11 pm	Mexican restaurant run by popular TV chefs.
Broadway Deli	1457 3rd St Prom	310-451-0616	$$	1 am	Overpriced but popular deli food.
Buffalo Club	1520 Olympic Blvd	310-450-8600	$$$$$	12 am	Exclusive clubby dining.
Café Montana	1534 Montana Ave	310-829-3990	$$$	10 pm	A neighborhood staple.
California Chicken Café	2401 Wilshire Blvd	310-453-0477	$	10 pm	Good rotisserie chicken and sides. Cheap and fast.
Cha Cha Chicken	1906 Ocean Ave	310-581-1684	$$	10 pm	Caribbean chicken.
Chaya Venice	110 Navy St	310-396-1179	$$$$	12 am	Slightly upscale place to meet.
Chez Jay	1657 Ocean Ave	310-395-1741	$$$	11 pm	Californian seafood.
Chinois on Main	2709 Main St	310-392-9025	$$$$	10:30 pm	Wolfgang Puck does Chinese brilliantly.
Dhaba	2104 Main St	310-399-9452	$$	10 pm	Visit India with a Dhaba Dinner.
El Cholo	1025 Wilshire Blvd	310-899-1106	$$	11 pm	Popular Mexican chain.
Falafel King	1315 3rd St Prom	310-587-2551	$	10 pm	One of the cheapest, best meals on the Promenade.
Finn McCool's	2702 Main St	310-452-1734	$$	12 am	Neighborhood comfort food.
Fritto Misto	601 Colorado Ave	310-458-2829	$$	10:30 pm	Inexpensive California Italian.
Fromin's Delicatessen	1832 Wilshire Blvd	310-829-5443	$	10 pm	Old-school deli and diner.
The Galley	2442 Main St	310-452-1934	$$$$	11:30 pm	Steak and seafood in marine theme.
Houston's	202 Wilshire Blvd	310-576-7558	$$$	11 pm	Chain grill that caters to locals.
Jack 'n Jill's	510 Santa Monica Blvd	310-656-1501	$$	5 pm	Giant omelettes and long wait.
Library Alehouse	2911 Main St	310-314-4855	$$	11 pm	Beer and classy pub fare.
The Lobster	1602 Ocean Ave	310-458-9294	$$$$	11 pm	Definitely order the lobster.
Lula	2720 Main St	310-392-5711	$$	11 pm	Non-traditional Mexican cuisine with strong margaritas.
Ma'Kai	101 Broadway Ave	310-434-1511	$$$	12 am	Polynesian by the beach, award winning bartenders, and luaus on the last Sunday of every month.

Mani's	2507 Main St	310-396-7700	$	8 pm	Bakery, café, juices, sugarless cookies-oh my!
Michael D's Café & Catering	234 Pico Blvd	310-452-8737	$	10 pm	Next to bowling alley: scarf 'n' score!
Musha	424 Wilshire Blvd	310-576-6330	$$$	11:30 pm	Japanese-style tapas.
Newsroom Café	530 Wilshire Blvd	310-319-9100	$$	9:30 pm	Popular vegetarian lunch spot.
Ocean Ave Seafood	1401 Ocean Ave	310-394-5669	$$$$	11 pm	Upscale seafood by the beach with oyster happy hour.
Omelette Parlor	2732 Main St	310-399-7892	$	2:30 pm	Home of well-stuffed, three-egg omelettes.
On the Waterfront Café	205 Ocean Front Wk	310-392-0322	$$	9:30 pm	Sit outside, drink obscure German beer, and watch LA watch you as it strolls on by.
Sushi Roku	1401 Ocean Ave	310-458-4771	$$$	11:30 pm	Sushi by the beach.
Toi on Wilshire	1120 Wilshire Blvd	310-394-7804	$$	3 am	T-shirt, jeans, and big appetite required.
Trastevere	1360 3rd St Prom	310-319-1985	$$$	11:30 pm	Their gnocchi and olive dip rate a trip.
Tudor House	1403 2nd St	310-451-4107	$	6 pm	Lovely afternoon tea.
World Café	2820 Main St	310-392-1661	$$	1 am	Great mojitos and al fresco dining make up for disappointing food.
Ye Olde King's Head	116 Santa Monica Blvd	310-451-1402	$$	12 am	Traditional English fare and beer.

Map 19 • West LA/Santa Monica East

Asakuma	11701 Wilshire Blvd	310-826-0013	$$$	10 pm	More than just sushi.
Bandera	11700 Wilshire Blvd	310-477-3524	$$$	11 pm	Dimly-lit; yuppy-ish. Reliable New-American cuisine.
Benito's Taco Shop	11614 Santa Monica Blvd	310-442-9924	$	4 am	$3 burritos the size of your Chihuahua.
Bombay Café	12021 W Pico Blvd	310-473-3388	$$$	11 pm	Inspired Indian cuisine.
Chez Mimi	246 26th St	310-393-0558	$$$$	10 pm	Onion soup and other French staples.
Don Antonio's	11755 W Pico Blvd	310-312-2090	$$	11 pm	*Muy autentico.*
Hide Sushi	2040 Sawtelle Blvd	310-477-7242	$$$*	9 pm	Not for the sushi-phobic.
Il Forno	2901 Ocean Park Blvd	310-450-1241	$$$	10:30 pm	Northern Italian cuisine. Great pastas and NYC-style pizzas.
Il Grano	11359 Santa Monica Blvd	310-477-7886	$$$$	10:30 pm	This West LA authentic Italian has been drawing crowds for more than 10 years.
Il Moro	11400 W Olympic Blvd	310-575-3530	$$$$	10:30 pm	Creative Italian specialties.
Javan	11500 Santa Monica Blvd	310-207-5555	$$	12 am	Persian cuisine. Huge portions of tasty charbroiled meats.
Josie Restaurant	2424 Pico Blvd	310-581-9888	$$$$	11 pm	Reputable chef. Great interior. New-American cuisine.
Kay 'n Dave's	262 26th St	310-260-1355	$$	9:30 pm	Healthy Mexican with a family-friendly atmosphere.
La Bottega Marino	11363 Santa Monica Blvd	310-477-7777	$$	10 pm	Italian deli-restaurant. Affordable. Charming setting.
Lares	2909 Pico Blvd	310-829-4559	$$	1 am	Rich, authentic Mexican meals and potent margaritas.
Lazy Daisy	11913 Wilshire Blvd	310-477-8580	$$	3:30 pm	Great selection of salads and smoothies.
Le Saigon	11611 Santa Monica Blvd	310-312-2929	$$*	9:30 pm	Great Korean food.
Nook Neighborhood Bistro	11628 Santa Monica Blvd	310-207-5160	$$	3 pm	Traditional American with Euro flair.
Rae's Restaurant	2901 Pico Blvd	310-828-7937	$*	9 pm	Neighborhood hangout-they line up for breakfast!
Sushi Sasabune	12400 Wilshire Blvd	310-268-8380	$$	9:30 pm	No California Roll, no menu. Trust the chef.
Tlapazola Grill	11676 Gateway Blvd	310-477-1577	$$$	11 pm	Southern Mexican.
Typhoon	3221 Donald Douglas Loop S	310-390-6565	$$$	11 pm	Eclectic Pan-Asian. Aviation motif. Cool and chic.
Valentino	3115 Pico Blvd	310-829-4313	$$$$	11 pm	Classy Italian. Flawless. Dazzling wine list.
Violet	3221 Pico Blvd	310-453-9113	$$$	10 pm	Affordable small-plates restaurant serving gourmet Californian cuisine.
Vito	2807 Ocean Park Blvd	310-450-4999	$$$	10:30 pm	Reliable Italian.
Yabu	11820 W Pico Blvd	310-473-9757	$$$	10:30 pm	Hip sushi and noodles.
Yashima	11301 W Olympic Blvd, Ste 210	310-473-5297	$$$	10 pm	Japanese comfort food in udon form.
Zabie's	3003 Ocean Park Blvd	310-392-9036	$	4 pm	Neighborhood café. Friendly. Cheap. Good breakfast and lunch.

Map 20 • Westwood/Century City

Big Chill	10850 Olympic Blvd	310-441-0643	$*	11:30 pm	Best frozen yogurt in LA!
Carvel Ice Cream	11037 Santa Monica Blvd	310-444-0011	$	11 pm	East Coast ice cream institution.
Clementine	1751 Ensley Ave	310-552-1080	$$	7:30 pm	True American cuisine with a modern flair.
Diddy Riese Cookies	926 Broxton Ave	310-208-0448	$*	1 am	25¢ cookies and ice cream sandwiches.
Earth, Wind & Flour	1776 Westwood Blvd	310-470-2499	$$	11 pm	Boston-style pizzas and pastas, whatever that means.
Falafel King	1059 Broxton Ave	310-208-4444	$	12 am	Fast-food Middle Eastern.
Gardens on Glendon	1139 Glendon Ave	310-824-1818	$$$$	11 pm	Californian favorites.
Houston's	10250 Santa Monica Blvd	310-557-1285	$$$	11:30 pm	After-work favorite swanky grill.
In-N-Out Burger	922 Gayley Ave	800-786-1000	$	1:30 am	Top California burger joint.
Johnnie's NY Pizzeria	10251 Santa Monica Blvd	310-553-1188	$$	11 pm	New York-style pizza.
La Bruschetta	1621 Westwood Blvd	310-477-1052	$$$$	10:30 pm	Classic Italian. Their bruschetta is delicious.
La Cachette	10506 Santa Monica Blvd	310-470-4992	$$$$	10:30 pm	High-end French.
Matteo's Hoboken	2323 Westwood Blvd	310-474-1109	$$	9 pm	Southern Italian fare with a Jersey flair?
Napa Valley Grille	1100 Glendon Ave	310-824-3322	$$$$	11 pm	Upscale dining.

Map 20 • Westwood/Century City—*continued*

Stan's Donuts	10948 Weyburn Ave	310-208-8660	$*	11 pm	Try a Reese's Peanut Butter Cup donut.
Tengu	10853 Lindbrook Dr	310-209-0071	$$$$	11:30 pm	Hip Asian fare.

Map 21 • Venice

Abbot's Pizza	1407 Abbot Kinney Blvd	310-396-7334	$	11 pm	Bagel crust pizza.
Axe	1009 Abot Kinney Blvd	310-664-9787	$$$$	10:30 pm	Healthfood with a chef's touch, movie star approval, and a long wait.
Baja Cantina	311 Washington Blvd	310-821-2252	$$	11 pm	Mexican with seafood specialties and sizeable margaritas.
Beechwood	822 Washington Blvd	310-448-8884	$$$$	11 pm	Bright décor, Amuse Café entrees.
The Brick House	826 Hampton Dr	310-581-1639	$$	4 pm	Definitely a local hangout. Lunch and breakfast only. Great porch.
C&O Trattoria	31 Washington Blvd	310-823-9491	$$	11 pm	Cheap Italian.
Café 50's	838 Lincoln Blvd	310-399-1955	$$*	11 pm	All-American food without pretense.
Café Buna	3105 Washington Blvd	310-823-2430	$$	4 pm	Breakfast of champions with excellent coffee.
Canal Club	2025 Pacific Ave	310-823-3878	$$$	11 pm	Chinese-Cuban fusion.
Casablanca	220 Lincoln Blvd	310-392-5751	$$$	11 pm	Nice evening out, guaranteed.
Hal's Bar & Grill	1349 Abbot Kinney Blvd	310-396-3105	$$$	11 pm	Pub food.
Hama Sushi	213 Windward Ave	310-396-8783	$$$$	11 pm	Hip Japanese.
Jin Patisserie	1202 Abbot Kinney Blvd	310-399-8801	$	7 pm	Fabulous pastries and a soothing tea garden.
Joe's	1023 Abbot Kinney Blvd	310-399-5811	$$$$	11 pm	French-Californian unique cuisine, worth the prices.
Killer Shrimp	523 Washington Blvd	310-578-2293	$$	11 pm	An exotic option for seafood dining.
La Cabana Restaurant and Bar	738 Rose Ave	310-392-7973	$$	3 am	Very festive atmosphere and diverse meeting place.
Lilly's French Café	1031 Abbot Kinney Blvd	310-314-0004	$$	10.30 pm	Museum-like French dining.
Primitivo Wine Bistro	1025 Abbot Kinney Blvd	310-396-5353	$$$	12 am	Shabby chic Mediterranean tapas and wine bar.
Rose Café	220 Rose Ave	310-399-0711	$$	5 pm	Trendy eclectic Californian and pleasant brunch in art gallery.
The Terrace Café	7 Washington Blvd	310-578-1530	$$	1 am	Convenient lunch spot for rollerbladers.
Wabi-Sabi	1635 Abbot Kinney Blvd	310-314-2229	$$$	11 pm	Sushi.

Map 22 • Mar Vista

Asaya Restaurant	12740 Culver Blvd, #A	310-823-8944	$$*	9 pm	Local Japanese.
Aunt Kizzy's Back Porch	4325 Glencoe Ave	310-578-1005	$$	11 pm	Southern comfort food.
Centinela Café	4800 S Centinela Ave	310-391-2585	$	9 pm	Basic Mex/American, cheap.
Cora's Mexican Food	12565 W Washington Blvd	310-390-2007	$††	10 pm	Like its name. This place has heart.
Empanada's Place	3811 Sawtelle Blvd	310-391-0888	$*	8 pm	The name says it all.
Fioretto Trattoria	12740 Culver Blvd	310-448-8000	$$	9:30 pm	No-nonsense Italian.
Maxwell's Café	13329 W Washington Blvd	310-306-7829	$	2 pm	Hearty breakfasts and lunch.
Outdoor Grill	12630 Washington Pl	310-636-4745	$	9 pm	Quite literally. Big outdoor flesh grill!
Paco's Tacos	4141 S Centinela Ave	310-391-9616	$	11 pm	Cheap Tex-Mex.
Pepy's Galley	12125 Venice Blvd	310-390-0577	$*	11 pm	Unpretentious bowling alley diner.
Ronnie's Diner	12740 Culver Blvd, # J	310-578-9399	$††	2:30 pm	Mom-and-Pop in Marina Del Rey.
Sakura Japanese Restaurant	4345 S Centinela Ave	310-822-7790	$$	10 pm	Local sushi. Open for lunch.
Taqueria Sanchez	4341 S Centinela Ave	310-822-8880	$††	8 pm	Cheap n' plenty Mexican.

Map 23 • Rancho Park/Palms

Apple Pan	10801 W Pico Blvd	310-475-3585	$*	1 am	Famous hamburger joint.
Bourbon Street Shrimp	10928 W Pico Blvd	310-474-0007	$$	11 pm	Cajun and seafood.
Carvel Ice Cream	9618 W Pico Blvd	310-278-5411	$	11 pm	Cookie Puss, Fudgie the Whale, and more.
Delmonico's Seafood Grille	9320 W Pico Blvd	310-550-7737	$$$$	10:30 pm	Dependable old-school seafood.
Factor's Famous Deli	9420 W Pico Blvd	310-278-9175	$$	9:30 pm	New York diner/deli.
Guelaguetza	11127 Palms Blvd	310-837-1153	$$	10 pm	Authentic Oaxacan dishes.
Gyu-kaku	10925 W Pico Blvd	310-234-8641	$$$	12 am	Japanese-style Korean BBQ.
Hop Li	10974 W Pico Blvd	310-441-3708	$$	9:45 pm	Cantonese cuisine.
Jack Sprat's	10668 W Pico Blvd	310-837-6662	$$	10 pm	Healthy and boring.
John O'Groat's	10516 W Pico Blvd	310-204-0692	$$	3 pm	Breakfast hang-out.
Junior's	2379 Westwood Blvd	310-475-5771	$$	11:30 pm	A little bit of Brooklyn in West LA, including charmingly rude servers.
La Serenata Gourmet	10924 W Pico Blvd	310-441-9667	$$$	10:30 pm	Mexican with seafood specialties.
Lot 1224	1224 S Beverlywil Dr	310-277-2800	$$$	10:30 pm	Inventive hotel dining, locals swear by the Thai fried calamari.
Milky Way	9108 W Pico Blvd	310-859-0004	$$$	1:30 pm	Kosher dairy restaurant. Owned by Steven Spielberg's mom.
Overland Café	3601 Overland Ave	310-559-9999	$$	11 pm	Truly a casual California eatery.
Zen Bakery	10988 Pico Blvd	310-475-6727	$*	3 pm	Home of the muffin monk since 1975.

Map 24 • Culver City

Bamboo	10835 Venice Blvd	310-287-0668	$$$	11:30 pm	Caribbean.
Beacon	3280 Helms Ave	310-838-7500	$$$	9:30 pm	Fusion becomes a successful experiment.
Café Brasil	10831 Venice Blvd	310-837-8957	$$	10 pm	The fresh-squeezed juices are amazing!
Café Surfas	8777 Washington Blvd	310-558-1458	$	6 pm	Sandwiches made by food experts.
Conservatory for Coffee	10117 Washington Blvd	310-558-0436	$	6 pm	They roast their own and serve it up graciously.
Ford's Filling Station	9531 Culver Blvd	310-202-1470	$$$$	11 pm	Hip "gastropub" headed by Harrison Ford's chef son, Ben Ford.
Honey's Kettle Fried Chicken	9537 Culver Blvd	310-202-5453	$$	11 pm	Tasty fried chicken, mouth-watering biscuits.
In-N-Out Burger	9245 W Venice Blvd	800-786-1000	$	1:30 am	Top California burger joint.
Johnnie's Pastrami	4017 Sepulveda Blvd	310-397-6654	$*	3:30 am	The best dang dip in town. Great signage.
La Dijonaise Café et Boulangerie	8703 Washington Blvd	310-287-2770	$$	9 pm	Typical Parisian entrees without the stuffiness or high prices. Divine desserts.
Natalee Thai	10101 Venice Blvd	310-202-7003	$$	10:30 pm	Popular Pad Thai and curries.
Petrelli's Steakhouse	5615 S Sepulveda Blvd	310-397-1438	$$$	10 pm	Meat and potato lovers' paradise.
S&W Country Diner	9748 W Washington Blvd	310-204-5136	$*	3 pm	Yee-haw! Breakfast's on.
Santa Maria Barbecue Company	9552 Washington Blvd	310-842-8169	$$††	10 pm	Order BBQ indoors. Enjoy it outdoors.
Tito's Tacos	11222 Washington Pl	310-391-5780	$*	11:30 pm	Cheap taco stand.
Versailles	10319 Venice Blvd	310-558-3168	$	11 pm	The LA institution's garlicy Cuban grub will stay with you.

Map 25 • Marina Del Rey/Westchester West

Alejo's	4002 Lincoln Blvd	310-822-0095	$$	10 pm	Italian for bargain hunters.
Alejo's	8343 Lincoln Blvd	310-670-6677	$$	10 pm	Classic cheap Italian.
Antica Pizzeria	13455 Maxella Ave	310-577-8182	$$	10:30 pm	Classic Neapolitan pizzas and pastas.
Ballona	13455 Maxella Ave	310-822-8979	$$$	11 pm	Hans Rockenwagner does fish.
Café Del Rey	4451 Admiralty Wy	310-823-6395	$$$$	10 pm	Eclectic seafood.
Caffe Pinguini	6935 Pacific Ave	310-306-0117	$$$	10:30 pm	Italian on the beach.
Casa Escobar	14160 Palawan Wy	310-822-2199	$$	12 am	Great quesadillas and chimichangas!
Hacienda Del Rey	8347 Lincoln Blvd	310-670-8588	$$	12 am	No-frills cheap Mexican, in a good way.
Jer-ne	4375 Admiralty Wy	323-574-4333	$$$$$	10 pm	The Ritz Carlton's restaurant; amazing views.
Kanpai Japanese Sushi Bar and Grill	8325 Lincoln Blvd	310-338-7223	$$$	11 pm	Great sushi in a trendy, modern atmosphere.
The Shack	185 Culver Blvd	310-823-6222	$$	1:30 am	Cheap burgers and more.
Shanghai Red's	13813 Fiji Wy	310-823-4522	$$$	11 pm	Lovely Victorian-style restaurant with incredible brunch.
Tandoor-A-India	8406 Pershing Dr	310-822-1435	$$	11 pm	Cozy dining. Order the mango lassi.
Tony P's Dockside Grill	4445 Admiralty Wy	310-823-4534	$$	11 pm	Kick-back tavern with a nice breeze.
The Warehouse	4499 Admiralty Wy	310-823-5451	$$$	11 pm	Romantic enough to ask someone to marry you.

Map 26 • Westchester/Fox Hills/Ladera Heights

Buggy Whip	7420 La Tijera Blvd	310-645-7131	$$$$$	11 pm	Go for the piano bar more than the food.
Encounter Restaurant	209 World Wy N	310-215-5151	$$$	9:30 pm	Pre-flight futuristic meals.
In-N-Out Burger	9149 S Sepulveda Blvd	800-786-1000	$	1:30 am	Top California burger joint.
Paco's Tacos	6212 W Manchester Ave	310-645-8692	$	11 pm	Inexpensive Tex-Mex.
Panera Bread	8647 S Sepulveda Blvd	310-641-9200	$	9 pm	Excellent soup, coffee, sandwiches, and pastries.

Map 27 • El Segundo/Manhattan Beach

Avenue	1141 Manhattan Ave	310-802-1973	$$$$$	11 pm	Eclectic American with covered patio.
Back Home in Lahaina	916 N Sepulveda Blvd	310-374-0111	$	10 pm	Affordable Hawaiian barbecue with laid-back, beach-bum waiters.
Bora Bora	3505 Highland Ave	310-545-6464	$$$$	11 pm	American classics meets Polynesian. Big comfy booths. Mac 'n cheese is a must have.
Café Pierre	317 Manhattan Beach Blvd	310-545-5252	$$	11 pm	Fine dining with an eclectic menu.
Corkscrew Café	2201 Highland Ave	310-546-7160	$$	10:30 pm	Wine bar with small plates and patio with ocean view.
Cozymel's	2171 Rosecrans Ave	310-606-5464	$$	11 pm	Tex-Mex.
El Tarasco	316 Rosecrans Ave	310-545-4241	$	12 pm	Open late; good Mexican food a block from the beach.
Fonzs	1017 Manhattan Ave	310-376-1536	$$$	10 pm	Steak and seafood. Good for group dinners.
Houston's	1550 Rosecrans Ave	310-643-7211	$$$	10:30 pm	Casual, upscale American favorites.
Il Fornaio	1800 Rosecrans Ave	310-725-9555	$$$	11 pm	Tuscan chain.
The Kettle	1138 Highland Ave	310-545-8511	$$	24-hrs	24 hours, a block from the Manhattan Pier, good brunch.
Le Pain Quotidien	451 Manhattan Beach Blvd	310-546-6411	$$	7 pm	Tasty and healthy salads, sandwiches, and desserts.
Local Yolk	3414 Highland Ave	310-546-4407	$	2:30 pm	Get breakfast here after you drop Aunt Mira off at the airport.
Mama D's	1125 Manhattan Ave	310-546-1492	$$$	9:30 pm	Old school Italian with large portions. Complimentary garlic knots are delicious but lethal.

Map 27 • El Segundo/Manhattan Beach—*continued*

Mangiamos	128 Manhattan Beach Blvd	310-318-3434	$$$$	11 pm	Light Northern Italian with romantic wine grotto and big picture window for maximum people-watching.
Manhattan Beach Brewing Company	124 Manhattan Beach Blvd	310-798-2744	$$	12 pm	Burgers and home brewed beer.
North End Café	3421 Highland Ave	310-546-4782	$††	3 pm	Sandwiches, salads, and fries with four dipping sauces.
Petros	451 Manhattan Beach Blvd	310-545-4100	$$$$$	11 pm	Styling' Greek food in hip setting. Don't miss the limoncello shots.
Rock'n Fish	120 Manhattan Beach Blvd	310-379-9900	$$	11 pm	Always packed. Lunch and dinner from the sea.
Sloopy's	3416 Highland Ave	310-545-1373	$††	9 pm	Go for the burgers and patio seating.
Talias	1148 Manhattan Ave	310-545-6884	$$$$	11 pm	Upscale Italian in teeny tiny setting.
Towne	1142 Manhattan Ave	310-545-5405	$$$	11 pm	Upscale surf and turf.
Uncle Bill's Pancake House	1305 Highland Ave	310-545-5177	$$	3 pm	Breakfast by the beach.
Versailles	1000 N Sepulveda Blvd	310-937-6829	$$	11 pm	The LA institution's garlicy Cuban grub will stay with you.

Map 28 • Hawthorne

Daphne's Greek Café	2700 Marine Ave	310-676-9165	$	10 pm	Excellent baklava!
El Pollo Inka	15400 Hawthorne Blvd	310-676-6665	$$	10 pm	Chicken fit for Virococha.
Guru Palace	4850 W Rosecrans Ave	310-675-5533	$$	10 pm	Good vegetarian choices and great naan.
In-N-Out Burger	3801 Inglewood Ave	800-786-1000	$††	1:30 am	Top California burger joint.
Piggies	4601 W Rosecrans Ave	310-679-6326	$††	10 pm	Older style Greek coffee shop.

Map 29 • Hermosa Beach

Back on the Beach	445 Pacific Coast Hwy	310-393-8282	$$	9 pm	California food, California beach, California experience.
Big Mike's Philly Steaks & Subs	1314 Hermosa Ave	310-798-1499	$	9 pm	Best cheese steaks west of Philly.
Bobo's Chinese Deli	934 Hermosa Ave	310-372-8559	$$	10 pm	Suprisingly good designer Chinese.
Bottle Inn	26 22nd St	310-376-9595	$$$	9:30 pm	Campy old school Italian restaurant with phenemonal wine list.
Buona Vita	439 Pier Ave	310-379-7626	$$	11 pm	Best Italian in town. BYO vino.
Club Sushi	1200 Hermosa Ave	310-372-5939	$$$	10 pm	Overrated sushi in super fun clubby atmosphere.
Créme de la Crepe	424 Pier Ave	310-937-2822	$$	10 pm	Savory or sweet. How do you say "yum" in French?
El Burrito Jr	919 Pacific Coast Hwy	310-316-5058	$*	11 pm	Always a line outside this amazingly authentic Mexican food stand.
El Gringo	2620 Hermosa Ave	310-376-1381	$	11 pm	Cheap Mexican. Enjoy 2 for 1 tacos on Tuesday and sit on the open air roof.
Fritto Misto	316 Pier Ave	310-318-6098	$$	10:30 pm	Create your own pasta combo or choose a house special.
Good Stuff on the Strand	1286 The Strand	310-374-2334	$$	4 pm	Fabulous people watching on the Strand. Oh, and they have good healthy food too.
Havana Mania	3615 Inglewood Ave	310-725-9075	$$	11 pm	Cuban cuisine at its finest!
Hennessey's Tavern	8 Pier Ave	310-372-5759	$$	12 am	Californian favorites.
Il Boccaccio	39 Pier Ave	310-376-0211	$$$$	11 pm	Authentic Italian.
Jackson's Village Bistro	517 Pier Ave	310-376-6714	$$$	10:30 pm	Snug bistro with Euro-esque dishes. Minimal corkage fees.
La Sosta Enoteca	2700 Manhattan Ave	310-318-1556	$$$	11:30 pm	An Italian gem with charming waiters.
Le Petit Café	190 Hermosa Ave	310-379-1400	$$	9 pm	C'est Francais with good happy hour with 1/2 price apps and beer.
Martha's 22nd Street Grill	25 22nd St	301-376-7786	$$	3 pm	American fusion.
Mediterraneo	73 Pier Ave	310-318-2666	$$	11 pm	Try tapas on the patio.
Paisano's	1132 Hermosa Ave	310-376-9883	$	11 pm	Pizza straight from New York.
Pedone's Pizza	1332 Hermosa Ave	310-376-0949	$	3 pm	One of the few places at the beach where you can get NY-style pizza.
Phuket Thai	901 N Pacific Coast Hwy	310-374-9598	$$	11 pm	Try to say the name out loud without giggling! Tasty thai in pretty setting.
Ragin' Cajun Café	422 Pier Ave	310-376-7878	$$	10 pm	Blackened catfish is a favorite.
The Spot	110 2nd St	310-376-2355	$$*	10 pm	Vegetarian specialties.
Sushi Duke	201 Hermosa Ave	310-406-8986	$$$	10 pm	Hip sushi bar with funky drinks and outdoor patio.
Sushi Sei	1040 Hermosa Ave	310-379-6900	$$	10 pm	Pretty decent sushi for South Bay and OK atmosphere.
Union Cattle	1301 Manhattan Ave	310-798-8227	$$$	10 pm	Upscale urban cowboys dare to ride the bull. Funky library setting and open air dining upstairs. Good steaks.

Map 30 • Torrance North

Flossie's Restaurant	3566 Redondo Beach Blvd	310-352-4037	$*	8 pm	The fried chicken is legendary.

Map 31 • Redondo Beach

Bluewater Grill	665 N Harbor Dr	310-318-3474	$$$	11 pm	Fresh fish and seafood specialties.
The Bull Pen	314 Ave I	310-375-7797	$$	11 pm	Good old-school steak joint.
Captain Kidd's	209 N Harbor Dr	310-372-7703	$$	10 pm	Seafood dinners run from $7.99 to $22 for a whole lobster!
Catalina Coffee Company	126 N Catalina Ave	310-318-2499	$††	10 pm	Homier than Starbucks. Breakfast, sandwiches, and, of course, coffee.
Chez Melange	1716 S Pacific Coast Hwy	310-540-1222	$$$$	10 pm	Foodies from all over LA flock to the eclectic, Continental menu.
Christine	24530 Hawthorne Blvd	310-373-1952	$$$$	9:30 pm	Eclectic California-Mediterranean food.
Cialuzzis	601 N Pacific Coast Hwy	310-374-8581	$$*	10 pm	Neighborhood gem with real East Coast Italian food at low prices.
El Torito Grill	21321 Hawthorne Blvd	310-543-1896	$$	11 pm	Good food, great margaritas, free tortillas you can't stop eating.
Gina Lee's Bistro	211 Palos Verdes Blvd	310-375-4462	$$	11 pm	Neighborhoody Cal-Asian bistro food.
The Green Temple Vegetarian Restaurant	1700 S Catalina Ave	310-944-4525	$††	9 pm	Eat away the toxins at this organic, holistic garden spot. Worth it to see the groovy outdoor location.
Hennessey's Tavern	1712 S Catalina Ave	310-540-8443	$	1 am	Bar food at its finest, a great place to watch the game and drink hearty.
HT Grill	1701 S Catalina Ave	310-791-4849	$$	12 am	Innovative, eclectic bistro food at reasonable prices.
Japonica	1304 S Pacific Coast Hwy	310-316-9477	$$$*	12 am	Fresh designer sushi and private booths.
Kincaids	500 Fishermans Wharf	310-318-6080	$$$	11 pm	A room with an ocean view....and great seafood.
The Original Pancake House	1756 S Pacific Coast Hwy	310-543-9875	$	2 pm	Line up with the weekend breakfast crowd.
Pedone Pizza	1821 S Catalina Ave	310-373-6397	$	10 pm	Just follow the heavenly smell to NY style pizza.
Redondo Beach Brewing Company	1814 S Catalina Ave	310-316-8477	$$*		Basic brews and burgers.
Riviera Mexican Grill	1615 S Pacific Coast Hwy	310-540-2501	$$	10 pm	Casual; yummy quesadillas.
Splash	300 N Harbor Dr	310-798-5348	$$$	10:30 pm	Mediterrean bistro.
W's China Bistro	1410 S Pacific Coast Hwy	310-792-1600	$$	10 pm	Non-greasy, non-tacky Chinese. Really.
Zazou	1810 S Catalina Ave	310-540-4884	$$$$	11 pm	Mediterranian-Italian fusion.

Map 32 • Torrance South

Aioli	1261 Cabrillo Ave	310-320-9200	$$$	10 pm	Bistro features eclectic global dishes and tapas.
Depot	1250 Cabrillo Ave	310-787-7501	$$$$	10 pm	Broad range of chef Michael Shafer's culinary creations.
In-N-Out Burger	24445 Crenshaw Blvd	800-786-1000	$††	1:30 am	Top California burger joint.
Koji BBQ Buffet	1725 W Carson St	310-787-1820	$$††	10 pm	Cook your own Korean-style BBQ; over 100 menu items.
Mishima	21605 S Western Ave	310-320-2089	$$	10:30 pm	Noodle paradise.

Map 33 • Highland Park

Auntie Em's Kitchen	4616 Eagle Rock Blvd	323-255-0800	$	4 pm	Home-made, unique goodness.
Blue Hen Vietnamese Kitchen	1743 Colorado Blvd	323-982-9900	$$	10 pm	Family recipes with an organic update.
The Bucket	4541 Eagle Rock Blvd	323-257-5654	$††	8 pm	Servin' old-school burgers since 1935.
Café Beaujolais	1712 Colorado Blvd	323-255-5111	$$	9:30 pm	Delicious French romanticism, but for dinner only.
Capri Restaurant	4604 Eagle Rock Blvd	323-257-3225	$††	10 pm	Twin Italian bros serve up a warm neighborhood spot.
Casa Bianca	1650 Colorado Blvd	323-256-9617	$$*	1 am	Legendary pizza with atmosphere to spare.
Classic Thai Restaurant	1708 Colorado Blvd	323-478-0530	$††	9:30 pm	Bustling Thai with a home-y feel.
The Coffee Table	1958 Colorado Blvd	323-255-2200	$	9:30 pm	Spacious and satisfying bistro, bearable even on Sundays.
Colombo's	1833 Colorado Blvd	323-254-9138	$$	11 pm	Incredible Continental cuisine at reasonable prices.
Dave's Chillin-n-Grillin	2152 Colorado Blvd	323-490-0988	$*	9 pm	Dave serves fresh sandwiches, shakes, and more.
Eagle Rock Italian Bakery & Deli	1726 Colorado Blvd	323-255-8224	$	6 pm	Famous rum cake and amazing deli sandwiches.
El Arco Iris	5684 York Blvd	323-254-3401	$	10 pm	Mexican.
El Huarache Azteca	5225 York Blvd	323-478-9572	$*	8:30 pm	The best tacos, huaraches, tortas, and sopes in town.
Fatty's & Co	1627 Colorado Blvd	323-254-8804	$	10 pm	Eat a "Fat Elvis" for breakfast.

Map 33 • Highland Park—*continued*

Mia Sushi	4741 Eagle Rock Blvd	323-256-2562	$$$	11 pm	Cool sushi comes to the east side.
Original Tommy's	1717 Colorado Blvd	323-982-1746	$*	2 am	The chain's legendary chili burgers offer gassy goodness.
Pete's Blue Chip	1701 Colorado Blvd	323-478-9022	$*	12 am	Greasy burgers and everything else.
Señor Fish	4803 Eagle Rock Blvd	323-257-7167	$	9 pm	Amazing fish tacos and other hot stuff.
Sicha Siam	4403 Eagle Rock Blvd	323-344-8285	$$††	10 pm	Thai.
Spitz	2506 Colorado Blvd	323-257-5600	$††	10 pm	Do the "doner": a gyro in a toasted panini.
Villa Sombrero	6101 York Blvd	323-256-9784	$$	11 pm	Mexican.

Map 34 • Pasadena

750ml	966 Mission St	626-799-0711	$$$††	11 pm	Charming bistro with impressive wine list.
Akbar Cuisine of India	44 N Fair Oaks Ave	626-577-9916	$$$	11 pm	Creative Indian cooking.
Arroyo Chop House	536 S Arroyo Pkwy	626-577-7463	$$$$	11 pm	Take your father here for steaks.
Bar Celona	46 E Colorado Blvd	626-405-1000	$$	1 am	Tapas by the plate and hipsters by the glass.
Beckham Grill	77 W Walnut St	626-796-3399	$$	10 pm	Beer. Steak. Brilliant.
BrenArt Café and Gallery	53 E Union St	626-796-7460	$	4 pm	Bohemian gallery café serving fresh breakfasts all day!
Burger Continental	535 S Lake Ave	626-792-6634	$$	11:30 pm	Burgers and more.
Café Atlantic	69 N Raymond Ave	626-796-7350	$$	11 pm	Inexpensive and mouthwatering Cuban.
Café Bizou	91 N Raymond Ave	626-792-9923	$$$	11 pm	BYOB French bistro.
Café Santorini	64 W Union St	626-564-4200	$$$	12 am	Mediterranean magic on the rooftop terrace.
Celestino	141 S Lake Ave	626-795-4006	$$$$	10:30 pm	Italian.
Club 41	41 S De Lacey Ave	626-795-4141	$$$	10 pm	For carnivores and cocktail connoisseurs.
CrepeVine Bistro & Wine Bar	36 W Colorado Blvd, Ste 1	626-796-7250	$$	12 am	French comfort food and wine at un-French-like prices.
Firefly Bistro	1009 El Centro St	626-441-2443	$$	10 pm	Seasonal charm, tent style.
Five Sixty-One	561 E Green St	626-405-1561	$$$	8:30 pm	Culinary Arts students show off their stuff.
Gordon Biersch	41 Hugus Aly	626-449-0052	$$$	11 pm	Basic American brewpub.
Hop Li	526 Alpine St	213-680-3939	$$	10:30 pm	Inexpensive Chinese.
Houston's	320 S Arroyo Pkwy	626-577-6001	$$$	10 pm	Chain with a little something for everyone.
Julienne	2649 Mission St	626-441-2299	$$$	3:30 pm	Charming sidewalk bistro that is *très délicieux*.
Kansai	36 S Fair Oaks Ave	626-564-1560	$	10:30 pm	Cutesy Japanese vibe.
La Luna Negra	44 W Green St	626-844-4331	$$*	11 pm	Vibrant, colorful Spanish tapas bar.
La Maschera Ristorante	82 N Fair Oaks Ave	626-304-0004	$$$	10:30 pm	Italian restaurant with romantic wine and olive bar.
Magnolia Restaurant	492 S Lake Ave	626-584-1126	$$	11 pm	Chic and sexy with a tantalizingly creative menu.
Maison Akira	713 E Green St	626-796-9501	$$$$	10 pm	Light, French-Japanese cooking.
Marston's	151 E Walnut St	626-796-2459	$$	9:30 pm	Awesome breakfasts and traditional American dinners.
Mi Piace	25 E Colorado Blvd	626-795-3131	$$$	1:30 am	Italian chain with outdoor tables.
Parkway Grill	510 S Arroyo Pkwy	626-795-1001	$$$$	11 pm	Pasadena's perennial upscale favorite; live music in the bar.
Pie 'N Burger	913 E California Blvd	626-795-1123	$*	10 pm	Juicy burgers, homey pies.
Radhika's	140 Shoppers Ln	626-744-0994	$$$	9:45 pm	Tikka Masala and live jazz.
The Raymond	1250 S Fair Oaks Ave	626-441-3136	$$$$	10 pm	Romantic, special occasion dining.
Roscoe's House of Chicken n' Waffles	830 N Lake Ave	626-791-4890	$$	12 am	Cheap Southern chain.
The School Café	561 E Green St	626-683-7319	$	9 pm	Restaurant of the California School of Culinary Arts.
Shiro	1505 Mission St	626-799-4774	$$$$	9 pm	Low-key interior, sublime fusion cuisine.
Tonny's	843 E Orange Grove Blvd	626-797-0866	$$††	10 pm	24-hour Mexican grub.
Twin Palms	101 W Green St	626-577-2567	$$$$	10:30 pm	Hip, casual Californian.
Xiomara	69 N Raymond Ave	626-796-2520	$$$$	11 pm	Cuban continental, killer mojitos.
Yahaira's Café	698 E Colorado Blvd	626-844-3254	$$	9 pm	Mexicali fusion food.
Yujean Kang's	67 N Raymond Ave	626-585-0855	$$$$	10 pm	Chinese fusion.

Map 35 • Pasadena East/San Marino

Bistro 45	45 S Mentor Ave	626-795-2478	$$$$	10 pm	High-end gourmet food and wine.
Café Verde	961 E Green St	626-356-9811	$$	3 pm	Tiny and tasty BYOB spot.
Europane	950 E Colorado Blvd	626-577-1828	$††	5:30 pm	Sophisticated pastries for subtle palates.
In-N-Out Burger	2114 E Foothill Blvd	800-786-1000	$††	1:30 am	Top California burger joint.
Madeleine's Restaurant	1030 E Green St	626-440-7087	$$$	10 pm	Peerless French bistro with an impressive wine list.
Rose Garden Tea Room	1151 Oxford Rd	626-405-2100	$$	3:30 pm	The Huntington Library's famous tea room runs rather pricey, but is a definite don't miss.
Sushi Bar Yoshida	2026 Huntington Dr	626-281-9292	$$$	9:45 pm	San Marino's only place for raw fish and dim sum.
The Vault Bar & Grill	2675 E Colorado Blvd	626-683-3344	$$$	12 am	Popular for its steaks, sports bar and super sophisticated setting.
Zankou Chicken	1415 E Colorado Blvd	818-244-1937	$	11 pm	Cheap Armenian chain.

Map 36 • Mt. Washington

Chico's	100 N Ave 50	323-254-2445	$	9 pm	Mexican seafood.
La Abeja	3700 N Figueroa St	323-221-0474	$*	4 pm	Mexican.

Map 38 • El Sereno

Baguette du Jour	2436 W Valley Blvd	626-282-0109	$*	5 pm	Unusual French/Vietnamese sandwich shop
Bamboo House	2718 W Valley Blvd	626-458-8888	$	10 pm	Popular and authentic Chinese.
Brazusa	4880 Huntington Dr	323-342-9422	$	9:30 pm	A taste of Brazil. Music on weekends.
El Kora De Nayarit	4863 Huntington Dr N	323-223-3322	$*	9 pm	Seafood Nayarit style. Healthy.
Gaeta's Deli	3107 N Eastern Ave	323-227-5054	$*	5 pm	Smoothies, snacks for the after-school crowd.
Garfono's Pizza	5468 Valley Blvd	323-225-5464	$††	12 am	Tiny, local, cozy, thick crust.
Lee Kam Kee	2505 W Valley Blvd	626-282-7720	$$††	9:45 pm	Best Vietnamese place in the neighborhood.
Mi Casita Real Mexican Food	5189 Alhambra Ave	323-225-4800	$*	10 pm	Friendly little dive. Great salsa.
The Original Taco Room	5472 Valley Blvd	323-227-0284	$	9 pm	Also known as Ernie's Landmark under new management. Old self-serve salsa bar gone. Boo!
Tamale Man	3320 N Eastern Ave	323-221-5954	$††	7 pm	From sweet to savory, this man knows tamales. Hence the name.
Taqueria Guadalupana	3100 N Eastern Blvd	323-441-1036	$*	7 pm	East LA does carne asada right.

Map 39 • Alhambra

Angelo's Italian Restaurant	1540 W Valley Blvd	626-282-0153	$$	10 pm	Pizza worth the wait.
Charlie's Trio Café	47 W Main St	626-284-4943	$$	11 pm	Good, solid Italian.
Crane Sushi	17 W Main St	626-458-0388	$$	10:30 pm	Half-price sushi.
Crazy Sushi	201 E Bay State St	626-282-3557	$$	10 pm	Rock 'n' Roll sushi.
Crepe in the Grip	7 E Valley Blvd	626-284-1237	$*	11 pm	Truly bizarre food concept. Hand-held crepes, anyone?
Cuban Bistro	28 W Main St	626-308-3350	$$$	11 pm	Cuban comfort food and unorthodox cocktails that would make Fidel want to defect.
The Diner on Main	201 W Main St	626-281-3488	$	2 am	Great food. Nostalgic setting. The Real Deal.
El Ranchero Restaurant	511 S Garfield Ave	626-281-3452	$*	3 am	Mexican flavors in a friendly neighborhood setting.
Fosselman's Ice Cream Parlor	1824 W Main St	626-282-6533	$*	10 pm	Made on the premises since 1926.
Green Papaya Thai	1800 W Valley Blvd	626-282-1291	$	11 pm	Healthy and innovative Thai.
The Hat	1 W Valley Blvd	626-282-0140	$††	1 am	Best burgers for miles.
Hecho en Mexico	4976 S Huntington Dr	323-226-0010	$$	11 pm	Family restaurant. Authentic food.
Hop Woo	1 W Main St	626-289-7938	$$	11 pm	Good and authentic Chinese.
Indo Kitchen	5 N 4th St	626-282-1676	$$††	10 pm	Padang-style cooking.
La Parilla Mexicana	2938 W Valley Blvd	626-289-2412	$	9 pm	Family Mexican.
Little London Fish & Chips	19 S Garfield Ave	626-282-4477	$*	8 pm	Eat fish and chips like the Brits.
Mahan Indian Restaurant	2 S Garfield Ave	626-458-6299	$$	10 pm	Friendly family India.
Mission 261	261 S Mission Dr	626-588-1666	$	10 pm	Chinese fare from dim sum to dinner served in Mission-style former city hall.
MPV Seafood	1412 S Garfield Ave	626-289-3018	$$††	1 am	Seafood with an Asian twist.
Noodle Planet	700 W Valley Blvd	626-282-8855	$*	12 am	Every conceivable kind of noodle.
Perfectly Sweet	126 W Main St	626-282-9400	$††	10 pm	Decadent and deadly desserts.
Pho 79	29 S Garfield Ave	626-289-0239	$	10 pm	Go for the noodle soup and dessert drinks.
Phoenix Food Boutique	220 E Valley Blvd	626-299-1918	$$††	1 am	Limited menu for fast snacks and desserts.
Rick's Drive In & Out	132 W Main St	626-576-8519	$*	2 am	Fast food at its best.
Sam Woo Barbeque	514 W Valley Blvd	626-281-0038	$*	12 am	Chinese fast food.
Señor Fish	115 W Main St	626-299-7550	$$	9 pm	Eat Mexican seafood with Caltech students.
Thai Purple	27 N Garfield Ave	626-300-9083	$	11 pm	Small, unassuming, super-convenient for movie theaters.
Twohey's	1224 N Atlantic Blvd	626-284-7387	$	12 am	Old-style coffee shop.
Wahib's Middle East	910 E Main St	626-576-1048	$$	2 am	Very traditional Middle Eastern cooking.
Yazmin Malaysian Restaurant	27 E Main St	626-308-2036	$$††	10 pm	Go for the curry.

Map 40 • Boyle Heights

Barbara's at the Brewery	620 Moulton Ave	323-221-9204	$$	9 pm	Bar food and drinks for the art crowd.
Ciro's	705 N Evergreen St	323-267-8637	$	9 pm	Family fave for flautas.
El Tepeyac	812 N Evergreen Ave	323-267-8668	$$*	11 pm	Famous hole-in-the-wall Mexican.
King Taco	2400 E Cesar E Chavez Ave	323-264-3940	$*	3 am	The benevolent ruler of Mexican fast food.
La Parrilla	2126 E Cesar E Chavez Ave	323-262-3434	$$	10:30 pm	Better than average Mexican chain.
La Serenata de Garibaldi	1842 E 1st St	323-265-2887	$$$	11 pm	Creative Mexican seafood.

Map 41 • City Terrace/East LA

Granny's Donuts	1681 N Eastern Ave	323-266-6918	$*	10 pm	No granny. Just killer donuts.
Juanito's	4214 E Floral Dr	323-268-2365	$	4 pm	Tender tamales by the dozen.
Tamales Lilianas	4629 E Cesar E Chavez Ave	323-780-7265	$*	9 pm	The most famous tamales in LA.
Tamayo	5300 E Olympic Blvd	323-260-4700	$$	11 pm	Mexican.

Map 42 • Chatsworth

Los Chilenos	8408 Topanga Cyn Blvd	818-716-4169	$$††	10:30 pm	Chilean food.

Map 43 • Granada Hills / Northridge

Claim Jumper Restaurant	9429 Tampa Ave	818-718-2882	$$$	11 pm	A beef-eater's paradise; the night the giant potato ate the patrons; includes a full bar.
El Torrito Mexican Grill	8855 Tampa Ave	818-349-1607	$$	12 am	The Mexican-styled dishes are delicious and the atmosphere is fun.
Maria's Italian Kitchen Northridge	9161 Reseda Blvd	818-341-5114	$$	11 pm	This restaurant's motto, "Your Neighborhood Italian Restaurant," is a perfect fit.
On the Border Mexican Café	9301 Tampa Ave, # 210	818-885-2060	$$	11 pm	Mexican cuisine; features beef, chicken, or shrimp fajitas and a full bar.
University Club At Cal State	18111 Nordhoff St	818-677-2076	$$††	2 pm	California cuisine, sandwiches, Sunday brunch.

Map 44 • Mission Hills / North Hills

In-N-Out Burger	9858 Balboa Blvd	800-786-1000	$††	1:30 am	Top California burger joint.

Map 45 • Canoga Park / Woodland Hills

Follow Your Heart Café	21825 Sherman Wy	818-348-3240	$$	9 pm	Vegetarian cuisine.
In-N-Out Burger	19920 Ventura Blvd	800-786-1000	$	1:30 am	Top California burger joint.
Pasta Pomodoro	21600 Victory Blvd	818-340-2400	$$	10 pm	Inexpensive food from Milan.

Map 46 • Reseda

Amber's Chicken Kitchen	16900 Burbank Blvd	818-995-3200	$$††	8:30 pm	Chicken! Donuts and bagels for breakfast.
Madeleine Bistro	18621 Ventura Blvd	818-758-6971	$$$	10 pm	Upscale vegan dining. Remain hungry afterwards.
Melody's Mexican Kitchen	6747 Reseda Blvd	818-609-9062	$$*	10 pm	Great Mexican in a casual, artsy atmosphere.

Map 47 • Van Nuys

Dr Hogly Wogly's BBQ	8136 Sepulveda Blvd	818-780-6701	$$	10 pm	Texas BBQ.
In-N-Out Burger	7930 Van Nuys Blvd	800-786-1000	$	1:30 am	Top California burger joint.
Sam Woo Barbeque	6450 Sepulveda Blvd	818-988-6813	$*	10 pm	Peking duck to go or stay, Chinatown-style.
Zankou Chicken	5658 Sepulveda Blvd	818-781-0615	$*	10 pm	Palm-licking, Beck-serenaded chicken.

Map 48 • North Hollywood

In-N-Out Burger	5864 Lankershim Blvd	800-786-1000	$	1:30 am	Top California burger joint.
Miss Peaches Southern Cuisine	5643 Lankershim Blvd	818-760-4924	$$	9 pm	Southern specialties.

Map 49 • Burbank

Buchanan Arms	2013 W Burbank Blvd	818-845-0692	$$	10 pm	Sample British eats seated 'neath a portrait of the Queen.
Chili John's	2108 W Burbank Blvd	818-846-3611	$*	7 pm	Best chili this side of the Mississippi.
Coral Café	3321 W Burbank Blvd	818-566-9725	$	24-hrs	Burbank landmark serves breakfast 24/7, along with wholesome American favorites.
Full o' Life	2515 W Magnolia Blvd	818-845-8343	$	4 pm	Health food store/restaurant.
Le Petit Chateau	4615 Lankershim Blvd	818-769-1812	$$$	10 pm	Romantic little French bistro.
Mucho Mas	10405 Burbank Blvd	818-980-0300	$	10:30 pm	Mexican standards on the patio or in a cozy cavern.
Pinocchio's	3103 W Magnolia Blvd	818-845-3517	$	9 pm	Super cheap, great Italian deli.
Poquito Mas	10651 Magnolia Blvd	818-994-8226	$	10 pm	Cheap, fresh Mexican chain.
Porto's Bakery & Café	3614 W Magnolia Blvd	818-846-9100	$††	7:30 pm	Yummy Cuban sandwiches and an amazing array of baked goods.
Santa Fe Tacos	353 N Pass Ave	818-563-4324	$	9 pm	Great cheap Mexican.
Taste Chicago	603 N Hollywood Wy	818-563-2800	$	9 pm	Sweet Home Chicago comfort food.
Tony's Bella Vista	3116 W Magnolia Blvd	818-843-0164	$	9:45 pm	Italian standards in a friendly, straw-covered-Chianti-bottle setting.

Map 50 • Burbank East/Glendale West

Gordon Biersch	145 S San Fernando Blvd	818-569-5240	$$$	12 am	Basic American brewpub.
Gourmet 88	230 N San Fernando Blvd	818-848-8688	$$	11 pm	No fuss, no muss--just good Chinese.
Harry's Family Restaurant	920 N San Fernando Blvd	818-842-8755	$	24-hrs	American diner fare; open 24/7.
In-N-Out Burger	761 N 1st St	800-786-1000	$††	1:30 am	Top California burger joint.
Knight Restaurant	138 N San Fernando Blvd	818-845-4516	$$	10:45 pm	Savory Greek and Mediterranean dishes.
Mambo's Café	1701 Victory Blvd	818-545-8613	$$	9 pm	Little place packs powerful authentic Cuban punch.
Market City Caffé	164 E Palm Ave	818-840-7036	$$	11 pm	Inexpensive Italian chain.
Picanha Churrascaria	269 E Palm Ave	818-972-2100	$$	11 pm	Tasty Brazilian all-you-can-eat meat-on-a-stick.

Poquito Mas	2635 W Olive Ave	818-563-2252	$	11 pm	Cheap, fresh, Mexican chain.
Ribs USA	2711 W Olive Ave	818-841-8872	$$	11 pm	Cheap casual BBQ.
Riverside Café	1221 W Riverside Dr	818-563-3567	$$††	9 pm	Casual dining with a British flair.
Romano's Macaroni Grill	102 E Magnolia Blvd	818-729-9405	$$	11 pm	Standard Italian food and drink, and plenty of it.
Viva Fresh	900 W Riverside Dr	818-845-2425	$$	11 pm	Mexican restaurant/lounge.

Map 51 • Glendale South

Carousel	304 N Brand Blvd	818-246-7775	$$$	11 pm	Delicious Armenian food, BYO liquor.
Damon's Steakhouse	317 N Brand Blvd	818-507-1510	$$$	10 pm	Lots of red meat and cheesy tropical drinks.
Eat Well	1013 S Brand Blvd	818-243-5928	$††	3 pm	Comfort food, great breakfasts.
Ichiban	120 S Brand Blvd	818-242-9966	$$	11 pm	Affordable, fresh sushi.
Max's of Manila	313 W Broadway	818-637-7751	$	12 am	Famous Filipino fried chicken.
Porto's Bakery & Café	315 N Brand Blvd	818-956-5996	$††	7 pm	To-die-for Cuban pastries and cakes.

Map 52 • Tarzana / Woodland Hills

Toast	20969 Ventura Blvd	818-992-5500	$$$	11 pm	SoCal bistro food.

Map 53 • Encino

Bagel Nosh Deli & Restaurant	17271 Ventura Blvd	818-995-4545	$	9 pm	Bagels, sandwiches, salads, hamburgers.
Baklava Factory	17145 Ventura Blvd	818-728-1600	$	9 pm	European and Eastern pastries.
Buca di Beppo	17500 Ventura Blvd	818-995-3288	$$	11 pm	Lively, traditional Italian chain, dinner only.
California Wok	16656 Ventura Blvd	818-386-0561	$$	10:30 pm	Healthy Chinese food.
Catch 21	17316 Ventura Blvd	818-789-3474	$	9 pm	Seafood, chicken, ribs, salads.
Chili My Soul	4928 Balboa Blvd	818-981-7685	$	9 pm	Chili. Chili? Chili.
Jerry's Famous Deli	16650 Ventura Blvd	818-906-1800	$$	2 am	Everything from pizza to salads, Mexican to Jewish food.
Jerusalem Pizza	17942 Ventura Blvd	818-758-9595	$	1 am	Pizza!
Johnny Rockets	16901 Ventura Blvd	818-981-5900	$$	1 am	'50s-style family diner.
Kaiten Sushi	17302 Ventura Blvd	818-986-7003	$	10 pm	Sushi.
More Than Waffles	17200 Ventura Blvd	818-789-5937	$	4 pm	They don't lie: Belgian waffles and more.
Mulberry Street Pizzeria	17040 Ventura Blvd	818-906-8881	$$	12 am	Thin-crust NY-style pizza.
The Stand	17000 Ventura Blvd	818-788-2700	$	10 pm	Best hot dog in LA.
Versailles	17410 Ventura Blvd	818-906-0756	$$	11 pm	The LA institution's garlicy Cuban grub will stay with you.
Vittorio's Italian Cucina	17644 Ventura Blvd	818-986-9074	$$††	9 pm	Pasta, chicken, seafood.

Map 54 • Sherman Oaks West

California Chicken Café	15601 Ventura Blvd	818-789-8056	$	10 pm	Cheap and fresh chicken in every way on every day.
Delmonico's Lobster House	16358 Ventura Blvd	818-986-0777	$$$$$	11 pm	Upscale seafood.
Katsu-Ya Encino	16542 Ventura Blvd	818-788-2396	$$$	10 pm	Yummy raw fish.
Marmalade Café	14910 Ventura Blvd	818-905-8872	$$	11 pm	Salads and other CA cuisine.
Mel's Drive-In	14846 Ventura Blvd	818-990-6357	$	3 am	Upscale diner chain.
Panzanella	14928 Ventura Blvd	818-784-4400	$$$$$	11 pm	Higher-end Italian.
Wiener Factory	14917 Ventura Blvd	818-789-2676	$*	7 pm	Frank with loyal following.

Map 55 • Sherman Oaks East

Bistro Garden at Coldwater	12950 Ventura Blvd	818-501-0202	$$$$	11 pm	Longtime Studio City favorite. Take your parents!
Boneyard Bistro	13539 Ventura Blvd	818-906-7427	$$	11 pm	Fancy BBQ joint.
Café Bizou	14016 Ventura Blvd	818-788-3536	$$$	11 pm	Popular French bistro.
Carnival Restaurant	4356 Woodman Ave	818-784-3469	$$	10 pm	Lebanese food.
Casa Vega	13301 Ventura Blvd	818-788-4868	$$	1 am	Very popular restaurant and bar. Good food, even better margaritas.
The Dip	14333 Ventura Blvd	818-501-1850	$††	9 pm	Meat + Bread + Juice = Yum.
The Great Greek	13362 Ventura Blvd	818-905-5250	$$$	12 am	Lively, fun Greek.
Gyu Kaku	14457 Ventura Blvd	818-501-5400	$$	12 am	Korean BBQ via Japan.
Hugo's	12851 Riverside Dr	818-761-8985	$$	8 pm	Neighborhood restaurant and tea house, good food.
Hugo's Tacos	4749 Coldwater Cyn	818-762-7771	$*	10 pm	Yes, there is such a thing as gourmet tacos.
Il Tiramisu	13705 Ventura Blvd	818-986-2640	$$$	11 pm	Who says you need to leave LA for good Italian?
In-N-Out Burger	4444 Van Nuys Blvd	800-786-1000	$	1:30 am	Top California burger joint.
Iroha	12953 Ventura Blvd	818-990-9559	$$$$	12 am	Great sushi and ambience.
Jinky's	14120 Ventura Blvd	818-981-2250	$$	9:30 pm	Neighborhood diner known for breakfast.
Le Chine Wok	2958 Beverly Glen Cir	310-475-1146	$$	9:30 pm	Fancy Chinese.
Le Petit Restaurant	13360 Ventura Blvd	818-501-7999	$$$$	11 pm	Busy French bistro.
Maria's Italian Kitchen	13353 Ventura Blvd	818-906-0783	$$	11 pm	Casual family Italian.
Marrakesh	13003 Ventura Blvd	818-788-6354	$$	11 pm	Studio City Morroccan.
Max	13355 Ventura Blvd	818-784-2915	$$$$	11 pm	Eclectic California bistro menu.
Mazzarino's	12920 1/2 Riverside Dr	818-788-5050	$$	10 pm	Southern Italian pizza and more.

Map 55 • Sherman Oaks East—*continued*

Mistral Brasserie	13422 Ventura Blvd	818-981-6650	$$$$	11 pm	French bistro with cozy atmosphere.
Mulholland Grill	2932 Beverly Glen Cir	310-470-6223	$$$	10 pm	Neighborhood Northern Italian.
Pinot Bistro	12969 Ventura Blvd	818-990-0500	$$$$	10 pm	Creative California-French bistro.
Rive Gauche	14106 Ventura Blvd	818-990-3573	$$$$	11 pm	French bistro with courtyard setting.
Señor Fred	13730 Ventura Blvd	818-789-3200	$$$	11 pm	Upscale CA Mexican, NFT pick!
Stanley's	13817 Ventura Blvd	818-986-4623	$$	11:30 pm	Excellent salads, casual neighborhood restaurant and bar.

Map 56 • Studio City/Valley Village

Art's Deli	12224 Ventura Blvd	818-762-1221	$$	9 pm	New York-style deli.
Asanebo	11941 Ventura Blvd	818-760-3348	$$$	11:30 pm	Fantastic sashimi + retro setting = 1985 flashback.
Caioti Pizza Café	4346 Tujunga Ave	818-761-3588	$$	11 pm	Trendy, creative Italian.
Camille's Sidewalk Café	12265 Ventura Blvd	818-623-9009	$	9 pm	Sandwiches and wraps.
Carney's Express	12601 Ventura Blvd	818-761-8300	$	12 am	Fast-food institution.
Daichan	11288 Ventura Blvd	818-980-8450	$$††	9 pm	Japanese "soul food."
Dragon X	11400 Ventura Blvd	818-487-7000	$$	10 pm	Excellent Chinese takeout.
Du-par's	12036 Ventura Blvd	818-766-4437	$$	4 am	Cheap breakfast joint.
Eclectic Café	5156 Lankershim Blvd	818-760-2233	$$	11:30 pm	California cuisine and art—it's in the name.
Ernie's Taco House	4410 Lankershim Blvd	818-985-4654	$	10:45 pm	Legendary, old-school Mexican eats and drinks, for 50+ years.
Firefly	11720 Ventura Blvd	818-762-1833	$$$$	1 am	Gourmet French bistro with a cozy, clubby atmosphere.
Good Earth Restaurant & Bakery	12345 Ventura Blvd	818-506-7400	$	10 pm	Healthy meals served against a backdrop of soothing fountains.
Katsu-ya	11680 Ventura Blvd	818-985-6976	$$$$	10 pm	Great sushi; gets crowded on weekends. Try the baked crab roll in soy paper.
Killer Shrimp	4000 Colfax Ave	818-508-1570	$$	11 pm	Inexpensive shrimp only.
La Loggia	11814 Ventura Blvd	818-985-9222	$$$$	11 pm	Homestyle Italian.
Lala's Argentine Grill	11935 Ventura Blvd	818-623-4477	$$$	11 pm	Empanadas, chorizo, steak, and more. Trendy casual.
Matsuda	11837 Ventura Blvd	818-760-3917	$$$	10:30 pm	Yet another decent mini-mall sushi experience.
Maximilians	11330 Weddington St	818-980-6294	$$$$	10 pm	French food in an unlikely locale.
Mexicali	12161 Ventura Blvd	818-985-1744	$$	1 am	Lively California-Mexican.
My Little Cupcake	11925 Ventura Blvd	818-985-2253	$††	7 pm	There can never be too many cupcakes.
Next Door at La Loggia	11814 Ventura Blvd	818-985-9222	$$	12 am	Small but fancy plates.
Noosh Deli	5118 Lankershim Blvd	818-769-1844	$	8 pm	Satisfying, inexpensive Mediterranean fare.
Panera Bread	12131 Ventura Blvd	818-762-2226	$	9 pm	Freshly baked bread and tasty sandwiches; laptop-friendly.
Pit Fire Pizza	5211 Lankershim Blvd	818-980-2949	$$	10 pm	Trendy, crowded California-style pizza establishment. Great patio.
Salomi	5225 Lankershim Blvd	818-506-0130	$$	11 pm	Vegetarian-Indian cuisine with heat that's not for wimps.
Sitton's North Hollywood Diner	11329 Magnolia Blvd	818-761-3341	$	24-hrs	Basic American diner fare; open all night.
Sparks Woodfire Grill	11801 Ventura Blvd	818-623-8883	$$$	11 pm	Come for the meat, stay for the mojitos.
Sushi Dan Rockin' Sushi	11056 Ventura Blvd	818-985-2254	$$	11:30 pm	Excellent sushi on a budget. Fun atmosphere.
Sushi Nozawa	11288 Ventura Blvd	818-508-7017	$$$$	10 pm	Extreme sushi storefront.
Suzanne's Country Deli	11273 Ventura Blvd	818-762-9494	$	7 pm	Great salads and sandwiches. Bright and cheery.
Teru Sushi	11940 Ventura Blvd	818-763-6201	$$$$	11:30 pm	Basic—but delicious—sushi.
Todai	11239 Ventura Blvd #2	818-762-8311	$$$	10 pm	All-u-can-eat sushi. Japanese and Asian. Great value.
Tokyo Delve's Sushi Bar	5239 Lankershim Blvd	818-766-3868	$$$$	12 am	Sushi.
Vegan Plate	11943 Ventura Blvd	818-506-9015	$††	3 pm	Vegan food at mouthwatering prices. Spicy mint leaves a must!
Vitello's	4349 Tujunga Ave	818-769-0905	$$	11 pm	Robert Blake's favorite Italian.
Wine Bistro	11915 Ventura Blvd	818-766-6233	$$$	10:30 pm	Romantic, traditional menu.

Map 57 • Universal City/Toluca Lake

Bacco Trattoria	3821 W Riverside Dr	818-845-8036	$$	9 pm	Italian trattoria, wine bar, and marketplace.
Barsac Brasserie	4212 Lankershim Blvd	818-760-7081	$$$$	10:30 pm	French-Californian.
Buca di Beppo	1000 Universal Studios Blvd	818-509-9463	$$	11 pm	Lively traditional Italian chain, dinner only.
Ca' del Sole	4100 Cahuenga Blvd	818-985-4669	$$$$	11:30 pm	Italian with garden tables.
California Canteen	3311 Cahuenga Blvd	323-876-1702	$$	11 pm	French.
Chez Nous	10550 Riverside Dr	818-760-0288	$$$	10:30 pm	Big salads, pizza, eggs benedict, and nightly music, too.
Don Cuco	3911 W Riverside Dr	818-842-1123	$$	12 am	Cheap prices, strong margaritas, kitschy Mexican ambience.
Miceli's	3655 Cahuenga Blvd W	323-851-3345	$$	12 am	Lively, fun Italian known for its singing waiters.

Mo's	4301 Riverside Dr	818-845-3009	$$	11 pm	Hamburger haven.
Paty's	10001 Riverside Dr	818-761-0041	$$	10 pm	American classics.
Priscilla's Coffee	4150 W Riverside Dr	818-843-5707	$	12 am	All sorts of coffee.
Prosecco Restaurant	10144 Riverside Dr	818-505-0930	$$$	10 pm	Northern Italian.
The Smoke House	4420 W Lakeside Dr	818-845-3731	$$$	11 pm	Steakhouse.
Steak Joynt	4354 Lankershim Blvd	818-761-9899	$$$	11 pm	Steak and martinis the old fashioned way.
Versailles	1000 Universal Studios Blvd	818-505-0093	$$	12 am	The LA institution's garlicy Cuban grub will stay with you.
Wolfgang Puck Café	1000 Universal Studios Blvd	818-985-9653	$$	11 pm	Casual California chic.
Yamakawa	10118 Riverside Dr	818-763-8355	$$	10:30 am	Across the board Japanese.
Zach's Italian Café	10820 Ventura Blvd	818-762-4225	$$	10 pm	Satisfying Italian, with one of the city's best courtyards.

Long Beach

555 East	555 E Ocean Blvd	562-437-0626	$$$$	11 pm	High-end steakhouse, extensive wine list.
Alegria	115 Pine Ave	562-436-3388	$$$	12 am	Terrific tapas, flamenco music, sangria...ooh la la!
Bono's	4901 E 2nd St	562-434-9501	$$$	11 pm	That would be Chastity, the owner. Quality over quantity here.
Cha Cha	762 Pacific Ave	562-495-4242	$$*	12 am	What is "Caribbean fusion"? Pipe down and eatcher jerk chicken.
Christy's	3937 E Broadway	562-433-7133	$$$	10 pm	Owned by Sonny Bono's eldest daughter; superb Italian cuisine.
Chuck's Coffee Shop	4120 E Ocean Blvd	562-433-9317	$*	2:30 pm	Fun breakfast joint. Order the Weasel and greet Chuck himself.
Enrique's	6210 E Pacific Coast Hwy	562-498-3622	$$	10 pm	Unrivaled, authentic Mexican food. Prepare to fight over the appetizers.
Gladstone's	330 S Pine Ave	562-432-8588	$$$	11 pm	Scrumptious fish, lovely waterfront view.
King's Fish House	100 W Broadway	562-432-7463	$$$	11 pm	Point to your preferred lobster (in tank); extensive fish selection.
La Rizza's	1837 E 7th St	562-599-1080	$	11 pm	Cheerful gingham curtains, saucy Italian food.
La Traviata	301 Cedar Ave	562-432-8022	$$$$	10 pm	Diverse entrees, from French-Asian to Italian, each worth tasting.
Long Beach Café	615 E Ocean Blvd	562-436-6037	$$	12 am	Hidden amidst office buildings; it's a major find. Big portions.
L'Opera	101 Pine Ave	562-491-0066	$$$$	12 am	Even people born in Italy are impressed with the menu.
The Madison	102 Pine Ave	562-628-8866	$$$$	12 am	Lavish décor, varied menu, unremarkable food.
Open Sesame	5215 E 2nd St	562-621-1698	$	11 pm	This Lebanese food will blow your mind; it's that good.
Parker's Lighthouse	435 Shoreline Village Dr	562-432-6500	$$$	11 pm	Great for galas, receptions, and other celebrations.
Park Pantry	2104 E Broadway	562-434-0451	$	11 pm	The original. Meatloaf and octegonarians and honest American food.
Uncle Al's Seafood	400 E 1st St	562-436-2553	$$	9 pm	Fresh fish with Cajun and West African influences.
Utopia	445 E 1st St	562-432-6888	$$$	10 pm	A cosmopolitan menu; accompanied by jazz music on weekends.
Wasabi Japanese Restaurant	200 Pine Ave	562-901-0300	$$$	12 am	Dine or just people-watch; the place is always packed.
Yard House	401 Shoreline Village Dr	562-628-0455	$$$	1 am	World's largest selection of draft beer; decent food, too.

San Pedro

6th Street Bistro	354 W 6th St	310-521-8818	$$	9 pm	Flamenco dancing, first Thursday of every month!
Ante's Restaurant	729 Ante Perkov Wy	310-832-5375	$$	10 pm	Delicious Croatian food, homey atmosphere.
Beach City Grill	376 W 6th St	310-833-6345	$	8 pm	Funky and eclectic—the food and the surroundings.
Marcello Tuscany Room	470 W 7th St	310-519-7100	$$	10 pm	Choose this one when you're craving Italian.
Nam's Red Door	2253 S Pacific Ave	310-832-4120	$$	9 pm	Secret jewel of a Vietnamese restaurant.
Pacific Diner	3821 S Pacific Ave	310-831-5334	$$††	4 pm	The best place for a great breakfast.
Papadakis Taverna	301 W 6th St	310-548-1186	$$$	10 pm	Greek food, family owned, fun experience.
Ports O' Call Restaurant	Berth 76	310-833-3553	$$	10 pm	Eat outdoors and take in the view.
Rex's Café	2136 S Pacific Ave	310-519-7190	$††	2 pm	Breakfast and lunch only; you can't go wrong with either.
Think Bistro	1420 W 25th St	310-548-4797	$$	10 pm	Thought: If one Think is good, two are better.
Think Café	302 W 5th St	310-519-3662	$$	11 pm	Continental cuisine, cosy atmosphere.
The Whale and Ale	327 W 7th St	310-832-0363	$$$	10 pm	Delightful, hugely popular British pub.

It's been said there are four seasons in Los Angeles: spring, summer, fall, and awards season. With an intimidating index of outdoor malls and boutique-rich neighborhoods, Angelenos take full advantage of their city's balmy shopping weather. Although the fashion vanguard of New York, London, and Milan tend to condescend to LA designers, Los Angeles has long been the birthplace of trends thanks to the influence of film and television. The relationship is symbiotic, with celebrities moonlighting as designers and local stylists and designers achieving star status. People around the world can open a magazine on any given day and see what Nicole Richie is wearing as she schleps shopping bags and a triple non-fat mochaccino down Robertson Blvd. next to the caption: *They're just like us*! Shop on.

Shopping Districts

Los Angeles has wonderful shopping malls, but thankfully they're not a credit card–wielder's only option. In fact, LA has a surprising number of neighborhood shopping drags that feature lively, locally owned businesses should the whole "United States of Generica" thing get you down.

Downtown: Whether you're looking for flowers, textiles, toys, or jewelry, downtown has a district devoted to whatever your pleasure (i.e. poison) may be (even if the "district" turns out to be only one city block). The LA Fashion District (formerly called the "Garment District") is home to more than Santee Alley's knock-off handbags and shoes: it serves as the city's nucleus of showrooms, distributors, designers, and working fashion professionals. You'll also find an overwhelming assortment of fabrics for fashion or home design, flowers, produce, and housewares. This merchandise mecca is located between 6th Street to the north, the 10 Freeway to the south, Main Street to the west, and San Pedro Street to the east.

East on **Sunset Boulevard** from Los Feliz (especially once you've passed Maltman, and head on into Echo Park), a flotilla of furniture stores has begun to form. The options range from proper antiques to vintage to just plain old junk, but prices are still better than what you'd find in similarly themed venues to the west (for example, La Brea). You'll also find several indie boutiques like **Show Pony (Map 5)**, **The Kids are Alright (Map 5)**, and **Sirens and Sailors (Map 5)** that allow eastside hipsters access to their designer duds without losing cred by being seen at Fred Segal.

Los Feliz Village is the square mile-or-so delineated by Los Feliz Boulevard, Hillhurst Avenue, Vermont Avenue, and Hollywood Boulevard. In recent years, a rash of press excitement turned it from "America's hippest neighborhood" into its most-hyped. The din has died down a bit, though new cafés and boutiques open with stunning regularity. In the meantime, there are still enough family-owned restaurants and beloved local landmarks to keep it grounded.

Larchmont Boulevard, between Beverly and 1st Streets, is Hancock Park's friendly, low-key commercial area. A perfectly delightful place to shop for books, gifts, wine, and women's clothing, it is made all the more pleasant by the number of restaurants offering sidewalk seating for proper people watching. Not to be missed, the farmers market on Sundays always draws a crowd.

Fairfax High School is a decidedly appropriate divider between the two cliques that make up the shopping district known as **Melrose Avenue.** Stretching from La Brea to Fairfax, the eastern portion of Melrose is a nexus of tourists, tattoo shops, Harley riders, and vintage t-shirt outlets. West of Fairfax and until La Cienega, however, Melrose beckons the rich, popular kids with the siren call of posh boutiques like **Betsey Johnson (Map 2)**, **Tarina Tarantino (Map 2)**, **Miss Sixty (Map 2)**, and **Fred Segal (Maps 2 and 18)**.

Running parallel to Melrose to the south are two of LA's most up-and-coming shopping districts: **West 3rd Street** and **Beverly Ave**. 3rd Street has attracted fashion-forward boutiques like **Milk (Map 2), Aero & Co (Map 2)**, and **Satine (Map 2)**, who have made a home alongside LA pioneer **Trina Turk (Map 2)** and New York transplant **Hilary Rush (Map 2)**. On Beverly, cool furniture shops accompany the cutting-edge fashion offerings of boutiques like **Eduardo Lucero (Map 2)** and **Beige (Map 2)**. Both streets lead into the city's gargantuan shopping cartel that is the Grove and the Beverly Center, meaning you can shop the hippest undiscovered designers and still lunch at P.F. Chang's if you want.

Just past the Beverly Center is the played-out **Robertson Boulevard,** a shopping area killed by the hubris of one too many Hilton & co. sightings at Kitson. Home to an **American Apparel (Map 2)**, the popular **Lisa Kline (Map 2)**, and the still-trendy **Madison (Map 2)**, Robertson maintains its status in part due to its paparazzi mainstay, the Ivy restaurant.

No survey of Los Angeles shopping would be complete without at least a mention of the venerable **Rodeo Drive**. Known perhaps best for its cameo alongside Julia Roberts in *Pretty Woman*, Rodeo is home to the old guard: **Giorgio Armani (Map 1)**, **Gucci (Map 1)**, and **Chanel (Map 1)** all have boutiques here. You may not be able to buy anything, but you're guaranteed to see at least one celebrity, a handful of expensive sports cars, and a handful of gaping tourists.

On the west side, shopping becomes more of a birthright with areas like **Montana Avenue** accommodating Santa Monica's upper crust. The blocks between 7th and 17th Streets feature upscale boutiques selling sweaters, chic clothes for men and women, children's apparel, and jewelry. If you don't mind the myriad homeless or the dodgy street performers, the **3rd Street Promenade** in Santa Monica is a popular outdoor shopping area with pretty much anything you're looking to buy. For an artsy and laid back shopping day, head to **Abbot Kinney** in Venice where fancy furniture stores vie with surf shops and galleries for your attention and your dollar.

Over the hill in **Studio City**, Tujunga Avenue south of Moorpark keeps it real and local; it's another good spot for shoes, gifts, cards, and lazy weekend meals. Originally made famous by musicians Frank Zappa and Tom Petty, **Ventura Boulevard** isn't just for Valley Girls anymore. It's quickly become the Valley's answer to its popular West Hollywood and Beverly Hills counterparts with some of the hippest boutiques, cafés, and spas in Los Angeles.

Clothing

Fred Segal (Maps 2 and 18) (with stores on Melrose and on Broadway in Santa Monica) is, for many, the *arbiter dicta* of Los Angeles style. Even those who don't wear their high-end threads have to admit that their cosmetics and apothecary departments are exceptional. The store is actually a collection of boutiques, with the well-known **Ron Herman (Maps 1, 2, and 16)** carrying everything from Earnest Sewn jeans to C&C California tanks. Aside from the longstanding hegemony of Fred Segal, LA is home to countless intriguing boutiques and chain retail outlets in each pocket of town.

All of the standard department stores have an outpost in Los Angeles, including **Saks Fifth Avenue (Map 1)**, **Nordstrom (Map 2)**, **Bloomingdale's (Map 55)**, **Barney's (Map 1)**, and **Neiman Marcus (Map 1)**, among others. Many locals hit up the **Grove at Farmers Market (Map 2)** for a mix of department store looks and shabby chic trends from **Anthropologie (Map 1)** and **M Frederic (Map 2)**. The neighboring **Beverly Center (Map 2)** offers shoppers an eight level behemoth mall with retail favorites like **Diesel (Map 2)**, **Politix (Map 2)**, and **Ben Sherman (Map 2).**

Although not a shopping district in its own right, the stretch of La Brea is home to some of LA's most popular stores, including **Jet Rag (Map 2)**, a vintage landmark, and **American Rag (Map 2)**, featuring both vintage and new designer finds. Also on La Brea, **Buffalo Exchange (Map 54)** lets you buy and sell fashionable cast-offs and trendy accessories. Just remember to stay off La Brea after 4 p.m. They'll tow you, *stat*.

It can be said that Angelenos are just as preoccupied with their *under*clothing, and what better way for a girl to show off her Pilates-toned bod and year-round tan (or spray tan) than with sexy offerings from **Agent Provocateur (Map 2)** on Melrose or **Trashy Lingerie (Map 2)** on La Cienega. Or replicate the designer look with a Pussycat Dolls getup from the flagship **Frederick's of Hollywood (Map 3)** on Hollywood Blvd.

Housewares

Face-lifts are not relegated to bodily makeovers in Los Angeles—locals are constantly updating their pricey digs with furnishings from the city's many houseware and furniture shops. And there is no one dominant style in architecture—or interior design—so finding stuff that looks like "you" isn't too difficult a task. Finding it at a reasonable price is another matter entirely.

Those with big wallets will enjoy their visit to **HD Buttercup (Map 24)** at the Helms Bakery. They've got tens of thousands of square feet filled with beautiful furniture and other elegant household items from the spatial geniuses who brought you ABC Carpet in New York. **Berbere Imports (Map 10)**, also in the neighborhood, is a one-stop shop for teak furniture, Moroccan lamps, stone Buddhas, and terra cotta urns. On La Brea between Melrose and Wilshire are funky yet elegant furniture shops such as **Futurama (Map 2), Maison Midi (Map 2)**, and **Pom Pom (Map 3)**.

The folks at **Liz's Antique Hardware (Map 2)** can locate or recreate any doorknob or hinge you show them. **Koontz Hardware (Map 2)** in West Hollywood has everything from dishtowels to chainsaws packed into their Santa Monica Boulevard store. **Eames Office (Map 18)** in Santa Monica carries mid-century modern chairs and more.

Blueprint (Map 2) on Beverly offers a wide selection of affordable furniture; further down the street, **Sonrisa (Map 2)** is the go-to shop for lovers of steel furniture and clean lines. Yuppie professionals pass lazy Sundays shopping for furniture and housewares at local favorites **Crate & Barrel (Map 2)** at the Grove and **West Elm (Map 18)** in Santa Monica. Meanwhile, over the hill, Studio City's **Bedfellows (Map 56)** offers swanky furnishings for the boudoir.

Music

The enormous **Amoeba Music (Map 3)** on Sunset and Cahuenga has two floors of every type of music, DVD, and band-related geegaws you can imagine. Don't be intimidated by the long line—Ameoba is a well-oiled machine with 20 plus clerks and seasoned locals who know the drill. With several LA locations, **Penny Lane Records (Map 39)** offers used CDs and vinyl while Silver Lake's **Sea Level Records (Map 5)** is a local indie favorite. **Canterbury Record Shop (Map 34)** in Pasadena and Silver Lake's **Rockaway Records (Map 5)** also offer inspired browsing along the new-used continuum.

Food

Surfas (Map 24) in West LA has an impressive wholesale stock of imported gourmet food and restaurant supplies that is open to the public (but let's just keep that between us, got it?). Wildly popular and tasty is the French-style take-home deli and catering at **Joan's on Third (Map 2)**.

Despite the prevailing low-carb-mania, finding good cheese can be a tricky sojourn. Fortunately, **Say Cheese (Map 5)**, the **Cheese Store of Silver Lake (Map 4), Bristol Farms (Map 20),** and the **Cheese Store of Beverly Hills (Map 1)** carry everything from Abbaye to Humboldt Fog along with wine and other gourmet foods. For those exalted occasions when Two Buck Chuck simply will not do, **Silverlake Wine (Map 5)** and **Larchmont Village Wine & Cheese (Map 7)** are invaluable resources for good grape. **Victor's Liquor and Delicatessen (Map 3)** on Bronson is two-fold as a source for great meats, wines, and cheeses alongside an amazing sit-down restaurant that's been around for years.

Home to the aforementioned Two Buck Chuck, **Trader Joe's** is a Southern California institution with numerous locations where each and every item on the shelf is handpicked, sampled, and sold at reasonable prices. The **Hollywood/Ivar Farmers Market (Map 3)** is a Sunday tradition, where locals stock up on organic veggies and fresh hummus while enjoying live music from the reggae Rastafarian and other performers. Last, but certainly not least, is downtown's **Grand Central Market (Map 9)**, located on Broadway near 4th Street, which has been bustling with a diverse crowd ever since they opened in 1917.

Flea Markets & Sample Sales

Call it a flea market and you're likely to give away your East Coast roots. True Southern Californians refer to this Sunday afternoon activity by its regional name: swap meet. Call it what you will, there is no shortage of options to keep everyone from eBay fanatics to vintage furniture hounds happy. Perhaps the biggest and most well-known local swap meet, Pasadena's **Rose Bowl Flea Market (www.rosebowlstadium.com)** isn't for amateurs. Every second Sunday of the month (rain or shine), the flea market opens at 5 am for large crowds eager to stock up on antiques, vintage clothes, and plenty of beef jerky. If you want to start smaller, Fairfax High School hosts the **Melrose Trading Post (www.greenwayarts.org/tradingpost.htm)** every Sunday at the corner of Fairfax and Melrose. For just a $2 entrance fee, it's less pressure than the Rose Bowl, and you're more likely to find locals hocking new designer duds they can't fit in their closet anymore, or their burgeoning jewelry or t-shirt lines. And you can hit up **Jet Rag (Map 2)** on your way home—the vintage store holds a $1 parking lot sale every Sunday if you don't mind getting down on the cement and digging for bargains. The **Venice Beach Boardwalk** is a standard tourist trap of street performers, beggars, and souvenir shops, but it's worth the trip at least once.

Sample sales may seem a tad intimidating for the non-fashion-industry population, but can be well worth your time if you keep your ear to the ground and your cash at the ready. Some sample sales truly live up to the name and only offer sample sizes (usually a teeny size 2 or 4 and a size 6 shoe) but this isn't always the case. Some of the most popular local organizers are **Sassy City Chicks** (www.sassycitychicks.com), **Fashion Co-op** (www.fashioncoop.com), and **Billion Dollar Babes** (www.billiondollarbabes.com), each hosting a number of events locally. Consult their websites for more information about dates, times, and tickets. For chic home goods at a fraction of retail price, head to the **Dock Downtown** (www.thedockdowntown.com) sample sale, held monthly in (duh!) downtown LA. It's invitation-only, which simply means you have to sign up on their website.

As home to many designer showrooms, factories, and distributors, downtown Los Angeles is an excellent source for impromptu sample sales and designer co-ops. Check the **California Market Center (Map 9)** (www.californiamarketcenter.com) where some showrooms sell to the general public on the last Friday of the month.

FYI: Some sample sales have dressing rooms and accept credit cards, and some do not—so if you really want those half-price Chip & Pepper jeans, leave your modesty at home and pack the cashola.

Map 1 • Beverly Hills

Anthropologie	320 N Beverly Dr	310-385-7390	Unique, super-feminine clothes and accessories. Goldmine clearance.
Barney's New York	9570 Wilshire Blvd	310-276-4400	Upscale department store. It's not shopping—it's investing.
Chanel Boutique	400 N Rodeo Dr	310-278-5500	You can channel Coco here.
Cheese Store of Beverly Hills (Wine only)	419 N Beverly Dr	310-278-2855	High-quality cheese, even better olives. Also wine counseling.
Fritelli Donuts	350 N Canon Dr	310-276-1408	Fancy donuts in fancier digs.
Geary's of Beverly Hills	351 N Beverly Dr	310-273-4741	The place for wedding gifts and now wedding rings.
Giorgio Armani Boutique	436 N Rodeo Dr	310-271-5555	It's Rodeo Drive, baby.
Gucci	347 N Rodeo Dr	310-278-3451	Ignore the imitations; this is the original.
Mrs Beasley's/ Miss Grace Lemon Cake Co	255 1/2 S Beverly Dr	310-276-6516	How most Hollywood assistants' holiday weight is gained.
Neiman Marcus	9700 Wilshire Blvd	310-550-5900	High-end department store.
Prada Epicenter	343 N Rodeo Dr	310-278-8661	The conceptual Rem Koolhaas-designed store.
Ron Herman	325 N Beverly Dr	310-550-0910	Home of the "Citizens of Humanity" jeans.
Saks Fifth Avenue	9600 Wilshire Blvd	310-275-4211	Chi-chi department store.
Sprinkles Cupcakes	9635 Little Santa Monica Blvd	310-274-8765	Cupcakes with intimidating pedigree.
The Taschen Store	354 N Beverly Dr	310-274-4300	For all your art and fetish needs.

Map 2 • West Hollywood

Aardvark's Odd Ark	7579 Melrose Ave	323-655-6769	Score the piéce de résistance of your vintage Hawaiian shirt collection.
Aero & Co	8403 W 3rd St	323-653-4651	Part museum, part boutique, part toy store. Features local designers.
Agent Provocateur	7961 Melrose Ave	323-653-0229	Sexy undies annually contribute to Hollywood's baby boom.
American Apparel	104 N Robertson Blvd	310-274-6292	Simple clothing made sweatshop-free.
American Apparel	802 N San Vicente Blvd	310-659-0373	Simple clothing: sweatshop-free, but still scandalous.
American Rag	150 S La Brea Ave	323-935-3154	Trend-setting designer and vintage looks at a price.
Apple Store	189 The Grove Dr	323-965-8400	iParadise for Mac fanatics.
Beige	7274 Beverly Blvd	323-549-0064	Colorful boutique with an impressive designer palette.
Ben Sherman	8500 Beverly Blvd	310-657-3400	Tailored contemporary duds for those with a British persuasion.
Betsey Johnson	8050 Melrose Ave	323-852-1534	Clothes as funky as their namesake.
Blick Art Materials	7301 Beverly Blvd	323-933-9284	Corporate but comprehensive. Good selection of art magazines.
Blueprint	8366 Beverly Blvd	323-653-2439	Impressive showroom of modern, affordable furniture.
The Bodhi Tree	8585 Melrose Ave	310-659-1733	New-age bookshop and West Hollywood fixture.
Book Soup	8818 W Sunset Blvd	310-659-3110	The Roxy of LA bookstores.
Button Store	8344 W 3rd St	323-658-5473	Every button you could possibly need.
Centerfold Newsstand	716 N Fairfax Ave	323-651-4822	A satisfying panoply of printed media.
Chado Tea Room	8422 1/2 W 3rd St	323-655-2056	Where tea lovers go when they die.
Chateau Marmutt	8128 W 3rd St	323-653-2062	If you love your pet—and money is no object.
The Cook's Library	8373 W 3rd St	323-655-3141	Books on food for amateur chefs and professional eaters.
Cost Plus World Market	6333 W 3rd St	323-935-5530	An "everything" superstore.
Crate & Barrel	189 The Grove Dr	323-297-0370	Popular destination for chic home furnishings.
Decades	8214 1/2 Melrose Ave	323-655-0223	Discover the history—and future—of fashion.
Decades Two	8214 Melrose Ave	323-655-1960	Sometimes Chanel is better the second time around.
Denim Doctors	8044 W 3rd St	323-852-0171	They'll sell you vintage jeans or fix the ones you've already got.
Diesel	8500 Beverly Blvd	310-652-5504	High-grade fashion for the avant-garde.
Eduardo Lucero	7378 Beverly Blvd	323-933-2778	Local couture.
Ethel	8235 1/2 W 3rd St	323-658-8602	Great women's clothing, indie brands.
Flight 001	8235 3rd St	323-966-0001	Luxe luggage tags soothe pre-flight jitters, really.
Fornarina	8000 Melrose Ave	323-782-7901	Duds that are girly yet sexy—in a Euro kind of way.
Fred Segal	8100 Melrose Ave	323-651-4129	THE place to shop, first LA store to carry NFT, thanks Ron!
Futurama	446 N La Brea Ave	323-937-4522	Get your boomerang couch and chairs here.
Golden Apple Comics	7018 Melrose Ave	323-658-6047	Shangri-la for comic book lovers.
Guitar Center	7425 Sunset Blvd	323-874-1060	Their walk of fame alone is worth the trip.
Hilary Rush	8222 W Third St	323-852-0088	Eclectic, under-the-radar designers in a NY boutique setting.
I Martin	8330 Beverly Blvd	323-653-6900	They cater to both serious racers and the training wheels crowd.
Iconology	353 S La Brea Ave	323-965-9666	Classy (read: pricey) chic.
Jet Rag	825 N La Brea Ave	323-939-0528	Vintage; Sunday is $1 sale day in the parking lot.
Joan's on Third	8350 W 3rd St	323-655-2285	French-style take-home deli and catering.
Knit Café	8441 Melrose Ave	323-658-5648	The hippest knitting shop around.
Koontz Hardware	8914 Santa Monica Blvd	310-652-0123	If they don't carry it, it probably doesn't exist.
Kowboyz	8050 Beverly Blvd	323-653-6444	Vintage cowboy gear.
Lisa Kline	136 S Robertson Blvd	310-246-0907	Fashionable boutique with famous clientele.

Liz's Antique Hardware	453 S La Brea Ave	323-939-4403	Brave the crowds for doorknobs, hinges, nuts, and bolts.
M Frederic	189 The Grove Dr	323-939-9072	Retail haven for the young and trendy.
Madison	113 S Robertson Blvd	310-275-1930	Beautiful clothes for beautiful people.
Maison Midi	148 S La Brea Ave	323-935-3157	Homewares central for the Euro-trash set.
Mani's Bakery	519 S Fairfax Ave	323-938-8800	Desserts so delicious you'll never know they're sweetened with fruit juice.
Marc Jacobs	8400 Melrose Pl	323-653-5100	Marc Jacobs has arrived. Say "hi" to Winona if you see her.
Marc Jacobs Accessories	8401 Melrose Pl	323-653-0100	Marc by Marc Jacobs-—two Marcs are better than one!
Me & Ro	8405 Melrose Pl	323-782-1071	Über-trendy jewelry.
Milk	8209 W Third St	323-951-0330	Stylish fare, but prepare (yes) to be milked.
Miss Sixty	8070 Melrose Ave	323-655-7220	Jeans that'll take you from zero to sixty.
Mr Marcel's	6333 W 3rd St (Farmers Market)	323-935-9451	Gourmet French cheeses and wine bar.
Necromance	7220 Melrose Ave	323-934-8684	Morbid and eclectic, this boutique sells taxidermy and natural curios.
Nordstrom	189 The Grove Dr	323-930-2230	Awesome shoe department.
Paul Smith	8221 Melrose Ave	323-951-4800	The big fuschia store on Melrose.
Plastica	8405 W 3rd St	323-655-1051	All things trendy and plastic. So LA.
Pleasure Chest	7733 Santa Monica Blvd	323-650-1022	Popular sex shop with something for everyone, in a discreet setting.
Politix	8552 Beverly Blvd	310-659-1964	Best men's shoes in LA.
Pulp	452 S La Brea Ave	323-937-3505	For people who still write letters (or wish they did).
Restoration Hardware	131 N La Cienega Blvd	310-360-9651	Paint-by-number for impatient decorators. Staples and whimsies.
Ron Herman	8100 Melrose Ave	323-651-4129	There's something wrong about selling peasant skirts for $308 dollars.
Sam Ash Music	7360 Sunset Blvd	323-850-1050	Like the nearby Guitar Center, but far less intimidating.
Samy's Camera	431 S Fairfax Ave	323-938-4400	The only place to go to for cameras in LA.
Satine	8117 W 3rd St	323-655-2142	Sophisticated designer labels and shoes.
SEE Selective Eyewear Elements	131 N La Cienega Blvd	310-360-6998	Affordable Italian designer frames.
Solomon's	447 N Fairfax Ave	323-653-9045	Everything from seder plates to menorahs.
Sonrisa	7609 Beverly Blvd	323-935-8438	Industrial furniture for steel lovers.
Soolip	8646 Melrose Ave	310-360-0545	Cards, wrapping paper, and gifts you'd like to give to yourself.
Susina Bakery	7122 Beverly Blvd	323-934-7900	Not just a bakery—yummy chocolates, focaccia sandwiches, and beautiful cakes.
Sweet 9	7361 1/2 Melrose Ave	323-868-1658	Stylish cuts on the cheap.
Target	7100 Santa Monica Blvd	323-603-0004	Go for toothpaste, leave with a date.
Tarina Tarantino	7957 Melrose Ave	323-651-5155	Jewelry for pink ladies.
Trashy Lingerie	402 N La Cienega Blvd	310-652-4543	Trashy, yes, but they also sell high-quality custom-fitted lingerie.
Traveler's Bookcase	8375 W 3rd St	323-655-0575	A must-visit before any trip.
Trina Turk	8008 W 3rd St	323-651-1382	Resort wear from one of LA's most beloved designers.
Twentieth	8057 Beverly Blvd	323-904-1200	Modern furnishings and design.
Urban Outfitters	7650 Melrose Ave	323-653-3231	Trendy goods that might just go out of style before you leave the store.
Virgin Megastore	8000 W Sunset Blvd	323-650-8666	Hours of endless music-buying fun—if you can find parking!
Zipper	8316 W 3rd St	323-951-0620	Upscale gifts and funky home furnishings.

Map 3 • Hollywood

Amoeba Music	6400 Sunset Blvd	310-245-6400	Cavernous music store—used CDs, DVDs too. A dangerous place.
Conservatory Florist	1900 N Highland Ave	323-851-6290	Gorgeous, minimalist floral creations.
Cottage Antiques	5870 Melrose Ave	323-469-6444	Pricey, but lovely old things for home and garden.
Counterpoint Records and Books	5911 Franklin Ave	323-957-7965	Wide selection of gently used books and music.
Daily Planet Book Store	5931 Franklin Ave	323-957-0061	Books, magazines, and unusual gifts.
Edmund's Bookshop	6644 Hollywood Blvd	323-463-3273	Need to find a movie still from the '30s? It's here.
Frederick's of Hollywood	6751 Hollywood Blvd	323-957-5953	Lingerie that keeps nothing secret.
Half-Off Clothing	660 N Larchmont Blvd	323-463-6613	Discount designer duds.
Hollywood Hills Beauty Center and Spa	1915 N Highland Ave	323-874-5159	Deceptively large, unassuming spot offers cheap, good massages.
Hollywood Toy & Costume Shop	6600 Hollywood Blvd	323-464-4444	Quality medieval armor.
Native	5915 Franklin Ave	323-962-7710	Indie designers grace the famous Franklin strip.
Pom Pom	6819 Melrose Ave	323-938-6286	Rustic dining tables and vintage garden furniture.
Ray the Retoucher	1330 N Highland Ave	323-463-0555	Headshot help.
Victor's Liquor & Delicatessen	1915 N Bronson Ave	323-464-0275	Part sit-down restaurant, part wine, cheese, and deli offerings.
Vine American Party Store	5969 Melrose Ave	323-467-7124	Decorations and party favors for parties from New Year's to Hanukkah.

Map 4 • Los Feliz

American Apparel	4665 Hollywood Blvd	323-661-1407	Simple clothing: sweatshop-free, but still scandalous.
Atmosphere	1728 N Vermont Ave	323-666-8420	Co-ed hipster boutique for the fashion forward.
Bicycle Kitchen	706 N Heliotrope Dr	323-NO-CARRO	Non-profit community bicycle workshop.
Blue Rooster Art Supplies	1718 N Vermont Ave	323-661-9471	Everything for the starving artist, except food.
Camille Hudson	4685 Hollywood Blvd	323-953-0377	Lurvely shoes for the ladies.
Casbah Café	3900 W Sunset Blvd	323-664-7000	Café featuring gifts and home décor stuff a la Marocaine.
Cheese Store of Silver Lake	3926 W Sunset Blvd	323-644-7511	High-quality cheese and a great selection of cured meats, olives, and gourmet teas.
Glory	4659 Hollywood Blvd	323-644-5679	'50s Americana, cycles, and oddities.
Golden Needle Tailoring	2044 Hillhurst Ave	323-666-3365	Excellent spot for major alterations and custom tailoring when you got a few to spend.
Gypsy	3915 W Sunset Blvd	323-660-2556	Ponchos, Che tees, Mexican silver and assorted funkiness.
Half-Off Clothing	1748 N Vermont Ave	323-665-1526	Discount designer duds.
Lovecraft Bio-Fuels	4000 W Sunset Blvd	213-291-8587	Run your Benz on French fry grease.
LS	2120 Hillhurst Ave	323-913-1444	One-of-a-kind necklaces, bracelets, and earrings made of eclectic gemstones.
Naturemart & Bulk Bin	2080 Hillhurst Ave	323-667-1677	Neighborhood health-food store.
Oou	1764 N Vermont Ave	323-665-6263	Pretty things for pretty girls.
Ozzie Dots	4637 Hollywood Blvd	323-663-2867	Vintage clothes, costume rentals, loads o' fun.
Reform School	4014 Santa Monica Blvd	323-906-8660	Cool housewares for designophiles.
Rosetta Stone	1958 Hillhurst Ave	323-913-0369	Interior décor and design services.
Secret Headquarters	3817 W Sunset Blvd	323-666-2228	Embrace your secret comic book obsession here.
Serifos	3814 W Sunset Blvd	323-660-7467	Gifts for everyone, including yourself. Especially if "yourself" is a Volvo-driving Silver Lake mom.
Skylight Books	1818 N Vermont Ave	323-660-1175	Neighborhood fave, readings, mags, cat in the window.
Squaresville	1800 N Vermont Ave	323-669-8464	A staggering collection of vintage clothing, including high-end labels like Gucci and Pucci.
Steinberg & Sons	4712 Franklin Ave	323-660-0294	A slice of fashionista a la Nolita in old Los Angeles.
Una Mae's	4651 Kingswell Ave	323-662-6137	The going designer threads & killer discounted vintage rack.
Uncle Jer's	4459 W Sunset Blvd	323-662-6710	They sell everything from funky clothes to incense—and gift wrap it for free!
Village Gourmet	1927 Hillhurst Ave	323-660-3803	Cheese, spreads, cornichons, etc, adjacent to Alcove Café.
Wacko	4633 Hollywood Blvd	323-663-0122	Books, tchotchkes, party favors, and obscure tees.
White Trash Charms	1951 Hillhurst Ave	323-666-9585	More charming than trashy, indie clothes 'n' jewelry.
Y Que Trading Post	1770 Vermont Ave	323-664-0021	Gifts, trinkets, "Pluto: Never Forget" t-shirts.
Zoe & Sage	2134 Hillhurst Ave	323-906-1874	Cutie-pie clothes and jewelry and such for local hipsters.

Map 5 • Silver Lake/Echo Park/Atwater

American Apparel	2111 W Sunset Blvd	213-484-6464	Simple clothing made sweatshop-free.
Bittersweet Butterfly	1406 Micheltorena St	323-660-4303	Flowers and lingerie to really butter 'er up.
Edna Harte & Fay	2941 Rowena Ave	323-661-4070	Gifts, clothes, bags, cards, jewels from "the Queen of Silver Lake."
Grometville	2876 Rowena Ave	323-665-5524	For the baby punk rocker and her hipster mama.
Island LS	3038 Rowena Blvd	323-665-7454	Liza Shtromberg's jewelry, plus ethnic and unusual gifts and clothes.
The Kids Are Alright	2201 W Sunset Blvd	213-413-4014	Designer names for the Eastside set.
Le Pink	1545 Echo Park Ave	323-661-7465	Girly gifts, olde-time candy treats.
Mini-Melt	3151 Los Feliz Blvd	323-668-1212	Cutesy toys, comic books, and Japanese collectibles.
Panty Raid	2378 Glendale Blvd	323-668-1888	Tell your boyfriend/girlfriend about their frequent lingerie sales.
Pot-ted	3158 Los Feliz Blvd	323-665-3801	Tiles, fountains, wrought-iron furniture, enthusiastic advice from "exterior decorators."
Rockaway Records	2395 Glendale Blvd	323-664-3232	5000 square feet of used vinyl and CDs.
Say Cheese	2800 Hyperion Ave	323-665-0545	Great smelly cheese tastings.
Sea Level Records	1716 W Sunset Blvd	213-989-0146	Surprisingly well-stocked indie music shop.
Show Pony	1543 Echo Park Ave	213-482-7676	Hip, handmade clothing, unpretentious.
Silverlake Wine	2395 Glendale Blvd	323-662-9024	Snacks and hors d'oeuvres served with tastings at this convivial wine store.
Sirens and Sailors	1104 Mohawk St	213-483-5423	Local stylists' secret.
Video Journeys	2730 Griffith Park Blvd	323-663-5857	Rentals and sales for film lovers, not film snobs.

Map 6 • Miracle Mile/Mid-City

99 Cent Store	6121 Wilshire Blvd	323-939-9991	99-cent cell phone charger or a half gallon of soy milk.
Ace Gallery	5514 Wilshire Blvd	323-935-4411	Established in 1940, this up and down gallery showcases mostly local Los Angeles artists.
Albertson Wedding Chapel	5318 Wilshire Blvd	323-937-4919	Wanna get married NOW? Civil and Catholic services available.
Bang a Drum	1255 S La Brea Ave	800-495-1109	Hand drums, from Native American to Middle Eastern.
City Spa	5325 Pico Blvd	323-938-4800	Body wraps, massages, and steam rooms galore.
Feldmar Watch	9000 W Pico Blvd	310-274-8016	From Timex to Rolex, they've got it all.
Hansen's Cakes	1072 S Fairfax Ave	323-936-4332	Wedding cake central and imaginative birthday creations.
Kitson	115 S Robertson Blvd	310-859-2652	Overpriced wares inside and paparazzi outside.
Marinello Beauty School	6111 Wilshire Blvd	323-938-2005	A full-service beauty school with facials at half the going rate.
Miauhaus	1201 S La Brea Ave	323-933-6150	Art gallery spotlighting emerging and contemporary artists.
Oh My Nappy Hair!	805 S La Brea Ave	323-939-3999	Specializes in braids, locks, and extensions.
Pearl Art and Craft Supplies	1250 S La Cienega Blvd	310-854-4900	Art supplies for everyone from the career artist to the scrapbook hobbyist.
Tom Bergin's	840 S Fairfax Ave	323-936-7151	Guinness and fifty years of paper shamrocks.
Up Health Merchants	6051 San Vicente Blvd	323-935-3020	Vitamins, holistic remedies and other crunchy stuff.

Map 7 • Hancock Park

Absolute Tickets	144 N Larchmont Blvd	323-957-6699	Tickets to just about everything, if you've got a few bucks to spend.
Center for Yoga	230 1/2 N Larchmont Blvd	323-464-1276	Classes, clothing, books, incense, sticky mats, and deep breaths.
Chevalier Bookshop	126 N Larchmont Blvd	323-465-1334	Friendly staff and wonderfully diverse selection of titles.
Hans Custom Optik	212 N Larchmont Blvd	323-462-5195	Great selection of frames.
Kicks Sole Provider	143 N Larchmont Blvd	323-468-9794	Lots of stylin' sneaks.
Landis Department Store	140 N Larchmont Blvd	323-465-7998	A little bit of EVERTHING. The stationery department is especially good.
Larchmont Beauty Center	208 N Larchmont Blvd	323-461-0162	Arguably the best beauty supply store in the city.
Larchmont News Stand	230 N Larchmont Blvd	n/a	Good selection of newspapers and magazines.
Larchmont Village Wine, Spirits, & Cheese	223 N Larchmont Blvd	323-856-8699	When Two-Buck Chuck just won't do. Amateurs are just as welcome as oenophiles.
Leonidas Belgian Chocolates	201 N Larchmont Blvd	323-860-7966	Fine and finely wrapped cocoa lusciousness.
Picket Fences	214 N Larchmont	323-467-2140	Juicy Couture, Cosa Bella undies, Kaminski hats, cute gifts.

Map 8 • Korea Town

Seafood Market	110 N Vermont Ave	323-953-2689	These sea merchants don't mess around. Get there early.

Map 9 • Downtown

7 + Fig at Ernst & Young Plaza	735 S Figueroa St	213-955-7150	Downtown's only real shopping mall.
American Apparel	374 E 2nd St	213-687-0467	Simple clothing made sweatshop-free.
American Apparel Factory Store	747 Warehouse St	213-488-0226	Find irregular or overstock items at a fraction of retail price.
California Market Center	110 E 9th St	213-630-3600	Gift, home accent, and fashion showrooms, as well as a handful of restaurants.
Grand Central Market	317 S Broadway	213-625-5006	An LA legend since 1917 with produce, fish, meat, and ice cream all under one roof.
LA Flower Market	766 Wall St	213-622-1966	Say it with flowers, cheaply.
The MOCA Store	250 S Grand Ave	213-621-1710	Museum store's a haven for design.
Moskatel's	733 San Julian St	213-689-4590	They carry everything you need for a party. Except for the guests.
Munky King	441 Gin Ling Wy	213-620-8787	Chinatown art scene + designer action figures.
Ooga Booga	943 N Broadway, #203	213-617-1105	Cool store featuring LA artists.
Santee Alley	Maple Ave & E 12th St	213-488-1153	The perfect place to find convincing "Kate Spate" or "Prado" handbags.

Map 10 • Baldwin Hills

Berbere Imports	3049 S La Cienega Blvd	310-842-3842	Beautiful, old world furniture, textiles, accessories, statuary, lighting from all corners of the Mediterranean.
Graphaids	3030 La Cienega Blvd	310-204-1212	If you're not an artist, this store will make you wish you were.
Normandie Pate	3022 S Cochran Ave	323-939-5528	A Parisian oasis.

Map 11 • South Central West

Zambezi Bazaar	4334 Degnan Blvd	323-299-6383	African-American specialty store.

Map 14 • Inglewood East/Morningside Park

Costco	3560 W Century Blvd	310-242-2774	Buy it in bulk.

Map 15 • Pacific Palisades

Benton's Sporting Goods	1038 Swarthmore Ave	310-459-8451	Beach clothing and equipment.
Gelson's Market	15424 W Sunset Blvd	310-459-4483	When Trader Joe's won't cut it. Excellent foreign foods.
Gift Garden Antiques	15266 Antioch St	310-459-4114	Fine gifts from a smattering of decades.
Ivy Greene for Kids	1020 Swarthmore Ave	310-230-0301	Organic clothes for kids.
Palisades Playthings	1041 Swarthmore Ave	310-454-8648	Toys to educate or palliate.
The Prince's Table	1051 Swarthmore Ave	310-573-3667	Gifts and original paintings.
Village Books	1049 Swarthmore Ave	310-454-4063	Books. For the 5% of you that actually read.
Vivian's Boutique	970 Monument St	310-573-1326	Vivian hands out free earrings with purchase.
Whispers	1013 Swarthmore Ave	310-454-5582	De rigeur Malibu couture.

Map 16 • Brentwood

Dutton's Brentwood	11975 San Vicente Blvd	310-476-6263	Fantastic collection of books, outdoor reading area.
Falconhead	11911 San Vicente Blvd	310-471-7075	Cowboy's one-stop for boots, buckles, and belts.
PJ London	11661 San Vicente Blvd	310-826-4649	Women's fashions, mostly resale.
Porta Bella	11715 San Vicente Blvd	310-820-2550	Antique wood furniture—armchairs to armoires.
Ron Herman	11677 San Vicente Blvd	310-207-0927	$335 for a bikini? Does it do tricks?
Sugar Paper	225 26th St #27	310-451-7870	For all your pretty paper and stationary needs
SusieCakes	11708 San Vicente Blvd	310-442-2253	Let us eat cake.
Terra Cotta	11922 San Vicente Blvd	310-826-7878	Furniture in warm earthen colors.
Whole Foods Market	11737 San Vicente Blvd	310-826-4433	Fresh produce and groceries in Brentwood's hippie corner.

Map 18 • Santa Monica

Acorn Store	1220 5th St	310-451-5845	Unique toy store, handmade dolls and puppets.
Apple Store	1248 3rd St Prom	310-576-1011	iParadise for Mac fanatics.
Continental Shop	1619 Wilshire Blvd	310-453-8655	One stop shopping for everything from AbFab tapes to tea cozies.
Eames Office	850 Pico Blvd	310-396-5991	Who'd think that a desk chair could be fun?
Fred Segal	500 Broadway	310-394-9814	LA institution and celebrity-spotter's paradise. All the fun of the one on Melrose, minus the parking nightmares.
Helen's Cycles	2501 Broadway	310-829-1836	Bikes sold by people who know what they're talking about.
Herb King	2305 Main St	310-399-4470	One stop for herbs and homeopathic remedies.
Holy Guacamole, Neighborhood Taco Stand and Hot Sauce Emporium	2906 Main St	310-314-4850	Hot sauce heaven.
Horizons West	2011 Main St	310-392-1122	Everything for the surf and skate crowd.
Kiehl's	1516 Montana Ave	310-255-0055	No more mail-order. NY-fave beauty products.
Le Sanctuaire	2710 Main St	310-581-8999	Kitchen and dining boutique for Food Network fans.
London Sole	1331 Montana Ave	310-255-0937	Chic but comfortable flat-soled shoes.
Number One Beauty Supply	1426 Montana Ave	310-394-6968	A high-end Montana Ave selection at un-Montana Ave prices.
One Life Natural Foods	3001 Main St	310-392-4501	Produce, groceries, herbs, everything organic.
Palmetto	1034 Montana Ave	310-395-6687	Bath supplies, soap, natural beauty products.
Pump Station	2415 Wilshire Blvd	310-998-1981	Where new mothers turn for helpful advice and swell baby products.
Puzzle Zoo	1413 3rd St Prom	310-393-9201	Toy store caters to the sci-fi geek and child within us all.
REI	402 Santa Monica Blvd	310-458-4370	Everything you'll need for your camping trips.
Santa Monica Farms	2015 Main St	310-396-4069	Organic produce, groceries, juices, sandwiches to go.
Segway Los Angeles	1660 Ocean Ave	310-395-1395	If you can't afford the 5K price tag, rent one for $75 (2 hrs).
Starbucks Coffee and Hear Music	1429 3rd St Prom	310-319-9527	Knowledgable staff that lets you listen before you buy.
Step!	1004 Montana Ave	310-899-4409	Luxury and comfort in footware.
Tao Healing Arts Center	2309 Main St	310-396-4877	Learn to give a massage or just have one yourself.
This Little Piggy Wears Cotton	309 Wilshire Blvd	310-260-2727	Adorable, comfortable, irresistable and expensive baby and children's clothing
Tiffany & Jax	1244 3rd St Prom	310-260-8656	Here's to tasteful clothes for the ladies who lunch.
Tudor House	1403 2nd St	310-451-4107	British souvenirs and afternoon tea.
West Elm	1433 4th St	310-576-7270	It's where your metrosexual boyfriend got his coffee table.
Wildfiber	1453 14th St	310-458-2748	Bright knitting and yarn shop.
ZJ Boarding House	2619 Main St	310-392-5646	If it's flat and you can ride it, they've got it.

Map 19 • West LA/Santa Monica East

Any Occasion Balloons	12009 W Pico Blvd	310-473-9963	Every size balloon, in every shape and color imaginable.
Giant Robot Store	2015 Sawtelle Blvd	310-478-1819	Items from Asian pop culture.
Graphaids	12400 Santa Monica Blvd	310-820-0445	They appeal to both serious artists and doodlers.
Hiromi Paper International	2525 Michigan Ave	310-998-0098	Handcrafted paper so gorgeous you won't want to write on it.
McCabe's Guitar Shop	3101 Pico Blvd	310-828-4497	Geared more toward the fledgling Bob Dylan than Eddie Van Halen.
Musicians' Supply Shop	12010 Ohio Ave	310-478-7836	Huge selection of sheet music.
Record Surplus	11609 W Pico Blvd	310-478-4217	No glitz, no pizzazz. For serious music lovers only.
Utrecht Arts Supplies	11677 Santa Monica Blvd	310-478-5775	All manner of stuff for the artsy and the craftsy and helpful service.

Map 20 • Westwood/Century City

Bristol Farms	1515 Westwood Blvd	310-481-0100	Upscale grocery. Newest and biggest of its kind.
Cost Plus World Market	10860 Santa Monica Blvd	310-441-5115	An "everything" superstore.
Restoration Hardware	10250 Santa Monica Blvd	310-551-4995	All the beautiful unique furniture you can imagine!
Sugar Paper	1749 Ensley Ave	310-277-7804	For all your pretty paper and stationary needs
The Writer's Store	2040 Westwood Blvd	310-441-5151	Seminars, books, and computer software for writing.

Map 21 • Venice

Ananda	1354 Abbot Kinney Blvd	310-399-4186	Unique, affordable, beach Buddha fashion.
Brick Lane	1132 Abbot Kinney Blvd	310-392-2525	Pricey, imported UK duds.
Daisy Arts	1312 Abbot Kinney Blvd	310-396-8463	Luxurious Italian leather items. Open only occasionally and by appointment.
DNA	411 Rose Ave	310-399-0341	Shhh—this tiny designer outlet is a big secret.
Equator Books	1103 Abbot Kinney Blvd	310-399-5544	Amazing bookstore and artspace, with a focus on collectable and out-of-print.
Firefly	1413 Abbot Kinney Blvd	310-450-6288	Great for gifts. Better for yourself.
Green House Smoke Shop	1428 Abbot Kinney Blvd	310-450-6420	Tools for those high on life.
Heist	1104 Abot Kinney Blvd	310-450-6531	Decadent beachwear, sexy imperial classics, and well-edited denim.
Helen's Cycles	2472 Lincoln Blvd	310-306-7843	One of the best bike stores in the area.
Hydro Lab	1140 Abbot Kinney Blvd	310-450-7221	Skater/surfer duds.
Samy's Camera	585 Venice Blvd	310-450-4551	The only place to go to for cameras in LA.
The Starting Line	114 Washington Blvd	310-827-3035	If you are a serious walker or runner, this place is for you.
Venice Bike & Skate	21 Washington Blvd	310-301-4011	Rent yourself some boardwalk transport.
Waraku	1225 Abbot Kinney Blvd	310-452-5300	Specializing in custom sneakers and other cool clothes.

Map 22 • Mar Vista

A Mano Yarn Center	12808 Venice Blvd	310-397-7170	Yarn, classes, conversation, community.
The Los Angeles Wine Company	4935 McConnell Ave	310-306-9463	Stemware, gift bags, and wine accessories, too.
Mitsuwa Marketplace	3760 S Centinela Ave	310-398-2113	Everything Japanese. Fast food court.
Prebica Coffee	4325 Glencoe Ave	310-823-4446	They mainly supply fine restaurants, but here they can supply you.
Vanity Room	13217 W Washington Blvd	310-306-3336	Anthropologie-like boutique, but affordable.

Map 23 • Rancho Park/Palms

Adventure 16	11161 Pico Blvd	310-473-4574	Camping supplies that make city slickers want to commune with nature.

Map 24 • Culver City

Allied Model Trains	4411 Sepulveda Blvd	310-313-9353	It's so much more than just Lionel.
Civilization	8884 Venice Blvd	310-202-8883	Trendy and offbeat furniture that manages to look homey.
Culver City Home Brewing Supply	4358 1/2 Sepulveda Blvd	310-397-3453	Literally everything you need to brew beer.
Dovetail	8918 Venice Blvd	310-559-9431	Solid pine furniture for every room of your house.
HD Buttercup	3225 Helms Ave	310-558-8900	Interior-design mecca in Helms Bakery building.
Last Chance	8712 Washington Blvd	310-287-2333	Discount women's clothing from major brands.
Surfas	8777 W Washington Blvd	310-559-4770	They'll design your kitchen and stock it too.

Map 25 • Marina Del Rey/Westchester West

Jennifer Jeanne Boutique	8328 Lincoln Blvd	310-338-9300	Designer duds mixed with indie clothing.

Map 26 • Westchester/Fox Hills/Ladera Heights

D3 International	8705 Truxton Ave	310-568-9118	Hip tees, cool stuff from around the world.
Westfield Fox Hills Mall	294 Fox Hills Mall	310-390-5073	Middle-of-the-road fashion needs off I-40S.

Map 27 • El Segundo/Manhattan Beach

Bombshell	320 Manhattan Beach Blvd	310-372-0777	Trendy pricey clothes.
Diane's	125 Manhattan Beach Blvd	310-546-5868	Huge selection of bikinis and beachwear.
Dollyrocker	212 Manhattan Beach Blvd	310-374-3396	Rock star clothes and accessories.
Fry's Electronics	3600 Sepulveda Blvd	310-364-3797	Polynesian-themed electronic superstore.
GeoDecor	130 Penn St	310-322-4043	Fossils. This unusual store is open only by appointment.
Growing Wild	1201 Highland Ave	310-545-4432	Great floral creations.
Katwalk	312 Manhattan Beach Blvd	310-798-7399	Brilliant designer knockoffs at low prices
Lucky Brand Dungarees	1113 Manhattan Ave	310-798-8000	You can't help but get lucky here.
Magpie	1141 Highland Ave	310-546-5132	Classy, conversation-starting home décor.
Manhattan Surf & Sports	300 Manhattan Beach Blvd	310-318-7055	Become a professional volleyball player or at least dress like one.
Michael Stars	1114 Manhattan Ave	310-376-8700	A variety of one size fit all seasonless tanks and tops.
Sequins	912 Manhattan Ave	310-798-1788	Nifty home accessories and reasonably priced custom furniture.
Skechers USA	1121 Manhattan Ave	310-318-3116	Funky sneakers and sandals at corporate headquarters' shop.
Tabula Rasa Essentials	919 Manhattan Ave	310-318-3385	Greatest bath and body store ever. Ideal for girly-girl presents.

Map 29 • Hermosa Beach

Re:Style	138 Pier Ave	310-379-1706	For your more alternative attire.
Splash Bath & Body	132 Pier Ave	310-376-7270	Fizzy bath bombs, funky soaps, and rubber duckies.
Star's Antique Market	526 Pier Ave	310-318-2800	Grandma's barn in a beach town.
Yak & Yeti	116 Pier Ave	310-406-2890	Boho chic.

Map 31 • Redondo Beach

Cookin Stuff	22217 Palos Verdes Blvd	310-371-2220	Possibly the largest selection of cooking supplies for the layperson in all of LA County.
Cost Plus World Market	22929 Hawthorne Blvd	310-378-8331	An "everything" superstore.
Dive N Surf	504 N Broadway	310-372-8423	Surf shop catering to girlz.
Lindbergh Nutrition	3804 Sepulveda Blvd	310-378-9490	A mecca for bodybuilders and others wishing to "keep in the pink."

Map 33 • Highland Park

The Blissful Soul	4870 Eagle Rock Blvd	323-258-6900	Feel the shop's inner peace.
Blue Healer Imports	5058 Eagle Rock Blvd	323-982-9111	Hip Aussie imports, mate!
Cactus	4534 Eagle Rock Blvd	323-256-6117	South American art with a gallery space.
Colorado Wine Company	2114 Colorado Blvd	323-478-1985	Helpful owners and numerous tastings keep you *Sideways*.
Don's Music	4873 Eagle Rock Blvd	323-255-3551	Tiny, but packed with used vinyl and other treats.
Dr Music	1812 Colorado Blvd	323-258-9010	Everything a musician needs.
F*Art	2120 Colorado Blvd	323-254-3278	That means "functional art," silly.
Galco's Soda Pop Stop	5702 York Blvd	323-255-7115	Who knew there were so many different brands of root beer?
Imix Books	5052 Eagle Rock Blvd	323-257-2512	Alternative books, art, and ideas.
Lily Simone	5022 Eagle Rock Blvd	323-254-0530	Cute botique spot named after a dog.
Lucy Finch	5054 Eagle Rock Blvd	323-255-2565	Great vintage finds.
Mini-Melt Too	1613 Colorado Blvd	323-258-2300	Second sibling of cool comics 'n' more store, Meltdown.
Owl Talk	5060-B Eagle Rock Blvd	323-258-2465	Secondhand and new clothes.
Rockin' Baby Shop	5048 Eagle Rock Blvd	888-645-2227	Keep your kids looking cool.
Stained Glass Supplies	2104 Colorado Blvd	323-254-4361	Classes, supplies and other shiny things.
SW Hill Country	1412 Colorado Blvd	323-256-2500	Gear for urban (and real) cowboys.
Swanky Blanky	4807 Eagle Rock Blvd	323-478-9306	Hip duds for hipster babies.
That Yarn Store	1578 #4 W Colorado Blvd	323-256-9276	Knitting the community together with classes and special events.
Twerps	5060 Eagle Rock Blvd	323-256-7608	Not your regular kid stuff.

Map 34 • Pasadena

Angels School Supply	600 E Colorado Blvd	626-584-0855	Back to school isn't so bad after all.
The Art Store	44 S Raymond Ave	626-795-4985	Art supplies for everyone from the career artist to the scrapbook hobbyist.
Assistance League of Pasadena	820 E California Blvd	626-449-6590	Charity gift shop featuring all hand-crafted items. Great for baby gifts.
Bungalow News	746 E Colorado Blvd	626-795-9456	Monster newsstand.
Canterbury Record Shop	805 E Colorado Blvd	626-792-7184	New and used, plus DVD and video. Great jazz, blues, and classical.
Canyon Beachwear	34 Hugus Aly	626-564-0752	Bathing-suit-a-rama.
Carroll & Co	146 S Lake Ave	626-396-7060	Classic men's clothier.

Dreams of Tibet	20 E Holly St	626-585-8100	Folk arts, flags, and all manner of items to get you on the right side of the issue.
Elisa B	12 Douglas Aly	626-792-4746	Contemporary clothing for women.
Fine Kicks	88 E Colorado Blvd	626-744-0656	Great shoe selection.
Heritage Wine Co	155 N Raymond Ave	800-630-WINE	Tastings and sales of California wines.
Jacob Maarse Florists	655 E Green St	626-449-0246	Fabulous floral arrangements.
Lather	106 W Colorado Blvd	626-396-9636	Modern apothecary products that smell good and feel good.
Lush	24 E Colorado Blvd	626-792-0901	Super-fresh beauty and bath products.
Messarian Oriental Rugs	493 E Colorado Blvd	626-792-9858	Beautiful rugs from the Near and Middle East.
Nicole's Gourmet Imports	921 Meridian Ave	626-441-9600	French cheese rocks. And stinks.
Paperwhites	2491 Mission St	626-441-2196	Packaged cards, as well as custom invitations and announcements.
Pasadena Antique Mall	444 S Fair Oaks	626-449-7606	Dozens of dealers under one roof.
Penny Lane Records & Tapes	12 W Colorado Blvd	626-564-0161	Boasts the best selection of hard to find music in the city.
Rose Tree Cottage	828 E California Blvd	626-793-3337	English tea room and gift shop.
Run with Us	235 N Lake Ave	626-568-3331	For those who still have knees enough to run.
Stats	120 S Raymond Ave	626-795-9308	Every imaginable supply and bauble for your décor, floral, crafting projects.
Target	777 E Colorado Blvd	626-795-5472	Perfect-sized, not too big, two story, very manageable.
Three Dog Bakery	24 Smith Aly	626-440-0443	Fancy biscuits you'd be proud to offer man's best friend.
Vroman's Bookstore	695 E Colorado Blvd	626-449-5320	Indie, eclectic, and charming. Famous for its children's department, but stocks just about everything else too.
Z Gallerie	42 W Colorado Blvd	626-578-1538	Unique home items.

Map 35 • Pasadena East/San Marino

Aardvark's	1253 E Colorado Blvd	626-583-9109	Long established one stop destination for vintage clothing

Map 38 • El Sereno

Kohl's Department Store	1201 S Fremont Ave	626-289-7250	Latest addition to Alhambra shopping scene.

Map 39 • Alhambra

Lieberg's Hallmark Shop	101 E Main St	626-282-8454	Huge selection of cards and doodads.
Mervyn's	150 E Main St	626-300-0888	Old standby for women's clothing.
Mi Casita Rustica	135 W Main St	626-576-8143	Everything Mexican for your rustic home.
Penny Lane	110 W Main St	626-457-5787	Music, movies, games.
Ross Dress for Less	201 E Main St	626-281-8453	Popular discount stop for housewares, clothes, and shoes.

Map 40 • Boyle Heights

Skeletons in the Closet	1100 N Mission Rd	323-343-0760	County Coroner's gift shop stocks chalk outline beach towels and post-its.

Map 45 • Canoga Park / Woodland Hills

Babyland	7134 Topanga Cyn Blvd	818-704-7848	Bargain kids' stuff.
Green Thumb Nursery	21812 Sherman Wy	818-340-6400	Mega-nursery.
Kake Kreations	21851 Sherman Wy	818-346-7621	All your baking needs.
Promenade At Woodland Hills	6100 Topanga Cyn Blvd	818-594-8732	Dining, movies, and shops.
Westfield Shoppingtown Topanga	6600 Topanga Cyn Blvd	818-594-8732	Behemoth mall.

Map 46 • Reseda

Beauty Collection	18517 Ventura Blvd	818-881-8393	Well-stocked beauty supply.
Hobby Shack	5541 Balboa Blvd	818-995-1162	For crafters and hobbyists.

Map 47 • Van Nuys

Big Kid Collectable Toy Mall	14109 Burbank Blvd	818-785-9208	Maybe the coolest store in LA.
Educative Toys & Supplies	6416 Van Nuys Blvd	818-782-5580	School-supply heaven.
Star Restaurant Equipment & Supply	6178 Sepulveda Blvd	818-782-4460	Serious cookware.

Map 48 • North Hollywood

99 Cents Store	12711 Sherman Wy	818-764-9991	Plus tax!
Baklava Factory	12909 Sherman Wy	818-764-1011	Baklava and more.
Big Lots	13005 Sherman Wy	818-982-1687	Monster close-out store. Always something surprising and marked way, way down.
K-Mart	13007 Sherman Wy	818-764-0250	Welcome, shoppers…
Michael's	12809 Sherman Wy	818-901-8321	Arts, crafts, and classes.
Plummer's	12240 Sherman Way	818-765-0401	Cool furnishings for home and office.
Robin Hood	13638 Burbank Blvd	818-994-6045	Jolly 'ol goods from the UK.

Map 49 • Burbank

Arte de Mexico	5356 Riverton Ave	818-769-5090	Furniture and crafts with a Mexican flair.
Atomic Records	3812 W Magnolia Blvd	818-848-7090	Used records. An eclectic inventory at reasonable prices.
Dark Delicacies	4213 W Burbank Blvd	818-556-6660	Everything for your D&D/goth/horror/fantasy friend (we all have one).
Fry's Electronics	2311 N Hollywood Wy	818-526-8100	Huge electronics store with a B-movie, spaceship-themed exterior.
It's a Wrap	3315 W Magnolia Blvd	818-567-7366	Clothes previously worn by your favorite TV stars.
Jelly Bean Factory	927 N Hollywood Wy	818-848-4806	Governor Reagan would be in paradise.
Monte Carlo	3103 Magnolia Blvd	818-845-3517	Authentic Italian market.
Otto's Import Store & Delicatessen	2320 W Clark Ave	818-845-0433	All manner of Hungarian delicacies and deliciousness.
Swift	3212 W Magnolia Blvd	818-558-1289	Vintage goodies.
The Train Shack	1030 N Hollywood Wy	818-842-3330	Fun model train store.
Western Bagel	513 N Hollywood Wy	818-567-0413	Local favorite.

Map 50 • Burbank East/Glendale West

EQ3	308 N San Fernando Blvd	818-841-8110	Furniture for Ikea graduates.
Firing Line Indoor Shooting Ranges	1060 North Lake St	818-954-9810	Access your inner sniper at these 50-foot ranges.
Pickwick Center	1001 Riverside Dr	818-845-5300	Bowling alley, ice rink, often hosts antique or art fairs.
Skyblupink	314 N San Fernando Blvd	818-845-0226	Stylish accessories for the home.
Valley Dealer Exchange	6530 San Fernando Rd	818-845-4090	One of the most painless used car-buying experiences you will ever have.

Map 51 • Glendale South

Cost Plus World Market	223 N Glendale Ave	818-241-2112	An "everything" superstore.
Glendale Costume	746 W Doran St	818-244-1161	Amazing costume rental house.
Luigi's Pottery & Gardenware	5630 San Fernando Rd	818-246-7579	Fountains, tiles, heavy stuff to sit out in the garden.

Map 52 • Tarzana / Woodland Hills

Crazy Inkjets	4867 Topanga Cyn Blvd	818-346-5538	Discount toner, inkjets, etc.

Map 53 • Encino

Antik Shop	4909 Genesta Ave	818-990-5990	Funky antiques.
Hansen's Cakes	18432 Ventura Blvd	818-708-1208	Cakes for all occasions.
Herbalogics	17200 Ventura Blvd	818-990-9990	Get acupuncture and troll the herb store.
The Knot Garden	17200 Ventura Blvd	818-986-6642	A knitter's paradise.
Mitzvahland	16733 Ventura Blvd	818-788-5758	All things Judaica.
Nuts Landing	17028 Ventura Blvd	818-990-3211	Nutty gift baskets.
Rag Tattoo	17245 Ventura Blvd	818-990-7244	Funky clothing.
Sneaker Warehouse	16736 Ventura Blvd	818-995-8999	Shoes galore!

Map 54 • Sherman Oaks West

Buffalo Exchange	14621 Ventura Blvd	818-783-3420	Revolving door of used clothing. Buy, sell, trade.
Cost Plus World Market	15201 Ventura Blvd	818-205-9620	An "everything" superstore.
Drum Connection	4846 Libbit Ave	818-788-5550	Percussion!
Gregory's Toys	16101 Ventura Blvd	818-906-2212	Independent toy store.
Handmade Galleries	14556 Ventura Blvd	818-382-3444	Gifts and home stuff made by hand. From "huh?" to "wow."
The Laughter Store	15140 Ventura Blvd	866-LAUGH-42	Yuk yuk.
Party City	14735-A Ventura Blvd	818-981-0099	Discount party supplies.
Rubyjean	15000 Ventura Blvd, #101	818-990-2200	Helping turn Ventura Blvd into the new Robertson.
Sherman Oaks Galleria	Sepulveda Blvd & Ventura Blvd	818-382-4100	Take refuge from the Valley & shop like you're in LA.

Map 55 • Sherman Oaks East

Aunt Teek's Collectibles	14080 Ventura Blvd	818-784-3341	Antique furniture and collectables on consignment.
Baxter Northrup Music	14534 Ventura Blvd	818-788-7510	Great selection of sheet music. Also instrument sales.
Beauty Collection	13351 Riverside Dr	818-789-4999	Eclectic beauty supply.
Bel Air Spa	2980 N Beverly Glen Cir	310-470-6362	Well-known day spa frequented by ladies who lunch, as well as celebrities.
Belle Gray	13812 Ventura Blvd	818-789-4021	Celebrity couture.
Bloomingdale's	14060 Riverside Dr	818-325-2200	Quieter than the Century City location. Especially good shoes, kids, and women's departments.
Burgundy Blue Outlet	4818 Fulton Ave	818-981-7446	Discount upscale kids' clothes.
Café Unforgettable Cakes	14550 Ventura Blvd	818-783-5628	Excellent cakes and salad dressing, too.
Doll Shoppe	13300 Riverside Dr	818-784-3655	A leading source for dolls, miniatures, and doll houses, as well as a "doll hospital."
Juvenile Shop	13356 Ventura Blvd	818-986-6214	A civilized alternative to Babies 'R' Us.

Leda's Bakeshop	13722 Ventura Blvd	818-386-9644	Mini-cupcakes to die for.
Lightbulbs Unlimited	14446 Ventura Blvd	818-501-3492	Every bulb under the sun.
Mark's Garden	13838 Ventura Blvd	818-906-1718	Florist.
Pink Cheeks	14562 Ventura Blvd	818-906-8225	Spa. Claims to have invented the famous "playboy" bikini wax.
Runnergy	13541 Ventura Blvd	818-905-0020	Athletic shoes sold by athletic, knowledgeable staff.
Second Spin Records	14564 Ventura Blvd	818-986-6866	Reasonably priced used CDs.
Sportie LA	14510 Ventura Blvd	818-990-7575	Sneakers galore.
Tinker	4337 Woodman Ave	818-784-7991	Arts and crafts, sometimes with booze.

Map 56 • Studio City/Valley Village

The Artisan Cheese Gallery	12023 Ventura Blvd	818-505-0207	THE place for cheese.
Bedfellows	12250 Ventura Blvd	818-985-0500	Clocks, pillows, and bedside tables make wonderful bedfellows.
Crossroads Trading Co	12300 Ventura Blvd	818-761-6200	Upscale resale.
Dari	12184 Ventura Blvd	818-762-3274	One of the Valley's outposts for trendy women's clothes.
The Flask	12194 Ventura Blvd	818-761-5373	Newly renovated as a haven for fine wines.
Hoity Toity	4381 Tujunga Ave	818-766-2503	Upscale women's clothing boutique.
The Ivy	12318 Ventura Blvd	818-762-9844	Antique furniture and collectibles.
King's Western Wear	11450 Ventura Blvd	818-761-1162	Everything to "ride 'em cowboy" here.
Kit Kraft Hobby Shop	12109 Ventura Place	818-509-9739	Art supplies, model kits, and more.
La Knitterie Parisienne	12642 Ventura Blvd	818-766-1515	The best knitting store around.
Laura's Designer Resale Boutique	12426 Ventura Blvd	818-752-2835	Used celebrity clothes and more.
Marie et Cie	11704 Riverside Dr	818-508-5049	Coffee, home furnishings, and gifts all in one.
Maxwell Dog	12336 Ventura Blvd	818-505-8411	For the pampered pet.
Portrait of a Bookstore	4360 Tujunga Ave	818-769-3853	A very social bookstore, with great gifts, too.
Samuel French's Theatre & Film Bookshop	11963 Ventura Blvd	818-752-0535	Comprehensive resource for film and theatre books. No one elese does it better.
Storyopolis	12348 Ventura Blvd	818-509-5600	You can get lost in here for hours amidst the Dr. Seuss and Maurice Sendak books.
Tennis Ace	12544 Ventura Blvd	818-762-8751	Everything tennis! Clothes, shoes, balls, etc.
Tuesday Morning	11239 Ventura Blvd	818-508-5334	Home and housewares at a big discount.
Verona	4350 Tujunga Ave	818-508-6377	Shoe boutique. Handbags, too.
Village Gourmet	4357 Tujunga Ave	818-487-3807	Great gifts for the foodie in your life.
Village Market	11653 Moorpark St	818-761-4848	Old style, family-owned local market. Good deli.
Voila Boutique	12500 Magnolia Blvd	818-766-9449	Nice knock-offs to get you through each season.

Map 57 • Universal City/Toluca Lake

Cinema Secrets Beauty Supply	4400 W Riverside Dr	818-846-0579	Fabulous selection, including film makeup.
Geographia Map & Travel	4000 W Riverside Dr	818-848-1414	Amazing travel store--they've thought of everything.
Iliad Bookshop	5400 Cahuenga Blvd	818-509-2665	One of LA's best used bookstores. Zola, the one-eyed kitty, will greet you.
Pergolina	10139 Riverside Dr	818-508-7708	Gifts and items for home.
Simply Nature Day Spa	10067 Riverside Dr	818-506-8927	Unpretentious pampering spot.
Steel Casey	10624 Ventura Blvd	818-763-5667	Popular seller of retro office furniture.
Weekendz Only	10139 1/2 Riverside Dr	818-752-3695	Trendy boutique, great handbags and tees.

Long Beach

5001	5001 E 2nd St	562-438-3907	A smaller, kitschier, cleverer Z Gallerie.
Acres of Books	240 Long Beach Blvd	562-437-6980	Huge family-owned used bookstore; labyrinthine layout.
Buffalo Exchange	4608 E 2nd St	562-433-1991	Buy or sell gently worn designer labels here.
City Place	275 E 4th St	562-432-8325	Eight-block urban retail development, with some actual cool shops!
Kitchen Outfitters	5666 E 2nd St	562-434-2728	Classes, demonstrations, and cookware for the chef in you.
Mood Swings	455 E Ocean Blvd	562-437-6250	Unique designs and vintage jewelry; truly beautiful stuff.
Nordstrom Rack	300 The Promenade N	562-733-1223	Somehow this boosts Long Beach's cachet.
Olives Gourmet Grocer	3510 E Broadway	562-439-7758	This gourmet shop has no equal anywhere within 30 miles.
The Pike at Rainbow Harbor	Pine Ave & Shoreline Dr	562-432-8325	Entertainment available for every member of the family.
Z Gallerie	230 Pine Ave	562-491-0766	Unique home items.

San Pedro

Coyote Antiques	387 W 6th St	310-547-4222	A must, as you amble the ArtWalk.
Office Depot	810 N Western Ave	310-221-0162	Getcher office supplies here.
Ramona Bakery	1101 S Pacific Ave	310-832-0369	People travel for miles for the fresh strawberry cake.
Sav-On	950 N Western Ave	310-832-7258	Drugstore.

LA's theater scene struggles from being overshadowed by the film industry, but it makes up for this problem with the sheer number of theaters throughout the city. Though it's true that a struggling actor would sooner list his commercial credits than his Chekhov, the only real problem you'll have is deciding what to see on any given night. Theater Row on Santa Monica Boulevard is a good place to start. Running between Highland and Vine, there is a bevy of small theaters to choose from; check out the **Hudson Avenue Theater (Map 3), Elephant Asylum (Map 3),** and **The Unknown Theater (Map 2)**. The **2nd Stage (Map 3)** hosts a weekly play reading series, **The Complex (Map 3)** is almost never dark, and **The Lillian (Map 3)** puts on some of the best shows in the city.

The **Pantages Theater (Map 3)** in Hollywood hosts off-Broadway productions. The **Mark Taper Auditorium (Map 9)** and **The Geffen Playhouse (Map 20)** produce high-profile shows, often with big name talent. The **Ahmanson Theater (Map 9)**, downtown at the Music Center, mounts lavish shows fresh from, or on the way to, Broadway. Also downtown, **REDCAT (Map 9)** at the Disney Hall has an interesting and varied line-up of plays and performance art throughout the year. **The Kirk Douglas Theater (Map 24)** in Culver City is part of the Center Theater Group (along with the Ahmanson and The Mark Taper) and produces quirky and adventuresome plays in a beautiful space.

If you're looking for something more specific, check out The East/West Players presenting classics with a Pan-Asian bent at the **David Henry Hwang Theater (Map 9)**, the gay & lesbian-themed **Celebration Theater (Map 3)**, or Cornerstone Theater Company, which produces multi-ethnic, community-based works. The **Renberg Theater**, housed in the LA Gay & Lesbian Center's "Village" complex has an interesting line up of one-person shows and limited engagements.

The **Odyssey Theatre (Map 19)** in West LA is one of the oldest and most consistent companies in the city; **Theater of NOTE (Map 3)** in Hollywood takes interesting risks; and you'll always find something inspired playing at the **Black Dahlia (Map 6)**.

Theaters	*Address*	*Phone*	*Map*
2100 Square Feet	5615 San Vicente Blvd	323-936-6818	6
24th Street Theatre	1117 W 24th St	213-745-6516	11
2nd Stage Theater	6500 Santa Monica Blvd	323-661-9827	3
A Noise Within Theatre	234 S Brand Blvd	818-240-0910	51
ACME Comedy Theatre	135 N La Brea Ave	323-525-0202	2
Actor's Co-op	1760 N Gower St	323-462-8460	3
Actor's Gang	9070 Venice Blvd	310-838-4264	24
Actor's Playpen	1514 N Gardner St	323-874-1733	2
Actors Circle Theater School	7313 Santa Monica Blvd	323-882-8043	2
Actors Co-op at Crossley Terrace Theatre	1760 N Gower St	323-462-8460	3
Actors Forum Theater	10655 Magnolia Blvd	818-506-0600	49
Ahmanson Theater	135 N Grand Ave	213-628-2772	9
Alex Theatre	216 N Brand Blvd	818-243-2539	51
Ark Theater	1647 S La Cienega Blvd	323-969-1707	6
Attic Theater	5429 W Washington Blvd	323-525-0600	6
Avery Schreiber Theater	11050 Magnolia Blvd	866-811-4111	56
Bang Improv Studio	457 N Fairfax Ave	323-653-6886	2
Beverly Hills Playhouse	254 S Robertson Blvd	310-855-1556	6
Black Dahlia Theatre	5453 W Pico Blvd	323-525-0070	6
Boston Court Theater	70 N Mentor Ave	626-683-6883	35
Celebration Theater	7051 Santa Monica Blvd	323-957-1884	3
Celtic Arts Center	4843 Laurel Cyn Blvd	818-760-8322	56
Chandler Studio Theatre	12443 Chandler Blvd	818-786-1045	56
City Garage	1340 1/2 4th St	310-319-9939	18
Coast Playhouse	8325 Santa Monica Blvd	323-650-8507	2
Colony Theater	555 N 3rd St	818-558-7000	50
The Complex	6476 Santa Monica Blvd	323-465-0383	3
Coronet Theatre	366 N La Cienega Blvd	310-657-7377	2
David Henry Hwang Theater	120 Judge John Aiso St	213-625-7000	9
Deaf West Theatre	5112 Lankershim Blvd	818-762-2998	56
Dorothy Chandler Pavilion	135 N Grand Ave	213-972-0711	9
Ebell Theatre	4401 W 8th St	323-939-0126	7
El Portal Theatre	5269 Lankershim Blvd	818-508-0281	56
Electric Lodge	1416 Electric Ave	310-306-1854	21
Elephant Asylum Theater	6320 Santa Monica Blvd	323-962-0046	3
Elephant Stageworks	1076 Lillian Wy	323-962-0046	3
Empty Stage Theater	2372 Veteran Ave	310-470-3560	23
The Evidence Room Theater	2220 Beverly Blvd	213-381-7118	9
The Fake Gallery	4319 Melrose Ave	323-661-0786	4
Falcon Theatre	4252 W Riverside Dr	818-955-8101	57
Ford Amphitheater	2580 Cahuenga Blvd E	323-461-3673	3
Fountain Theater	5060 Fountain Ave	323-663-1525	4
Fremont Center Theater	1000 Fremont Ave	626-441-5977	34
Frida Kahlo Theater	2332 W 4th St	213-382-8133	8
Geffen Playhouse	10886 Le Conte Ave	310-208-5454	20
Gene Bua Acting for Life Theatre	3435 Magnolia Blvd	818-547-3810	49
Glendale Center Theatre	324 N Orange St	818-244-8481	51
Globe Playhouse	1107 N King's Rd	323-960-7863	2
Greenway Arts Alliance	544 N Fairfax Ave	323-655-7679	2
Groundling Theater	7307 Melrose Ave	323-934-9700	2
Harry Mastrogeorge Theater @ the Brewery Art Colony	600 Moulton Ave	323-227-5410	40
Hermosa Beach Playhouse	710 Pier Ave	310-372-4477	29
Highways	1651 18th St	310-315-1459	18

Theaters	Address	Phone	Map
Hollywood Bowl	2301 N Highland Ave	323-950-2000	3
Hollywood Fight Club Theater	6767 W Sunset Blvd	323-465-0800	3
The Hub	5245 Lankershim Blvd	818-508-0076	56
Hudson Avenue Theater	6539 Santa Monica Blvd	323-769-5858	3
Improv Olympic West	6366 Hollywood Blvd	323-962-7560	3
International City Theater	300 E Ocean Blvd	562-436-4610	p. 241
Ivar Theatre	1605 Ivar Ave	323-461-7300	3
Kirk Douglas Theatre	9820 Washington Blvd	213-628-2772	24
Knightsbridge Theatre	1944 Riverside Dr	323-667-0955	5
Lee Strasberg Creative Center	7936 Santa Monica Blvd	323-650-7777	2
Lex Theater	6760 Lexington Ave	323-957-5782	3
Lillian Theatre	1076 Lillian Wy	323-962-0046	3
Lonny Chapman Group Repertory Theatre	10900 Burbank Blvd	818-700-4878	49
Lost Studio	130 S La Brea Ave	323-933-6944	2
Lyric Hyperion Theatre	2106 Hyperion Ave	323-666-3259	5
Madrid Theatre	21622 Sherman Wy	818-347-9419	52
Magicopolis	1418 4th St	310-451-2241	18
Mark Taper Auditorium	630 W 5th St	213-228-7025	9
Masquer's Cabaret	8334 W 3rd St	323-653-4848	2
Matrix Theatre	7657 Melrose Ave	323-852-1445	2
McCadden Place Theater	1157 N McCadden Pl	323-463-2942	3
Met Theatre	1089 N Oxford Ave	323-957-1152	4
Meta Theater	7801 Melrose Ave	323-852-6963	2
Morgan-Wixson Theatre	2627 Pico Blvd	310-828-7519	19
National Comedy Theater	733 Seward St	323-871-1193	3
NoHo Actor's Studio	5215 Lankershim Blvd	818-763-5802	56
NoHo Arts Center	11136 Magnolia Blvd	818-508-7101	56
Odyssey Theatre	2055 S Sepulveda Blvd	310-477-2055	19
Pacific Resident Theater	705 Venice Blvd	301-822-8392	9
Pantages Theater	6233 Hollywood Blvd	323-468-1770	3
Pasadena Center	300 E Green St	626-793-2122	34
Pasadena Playhouse State Theater	39 S El Molino Ave	626-356-7529	34
Pico Playhouse	10508 W Pico Blvd	310-204-4440	23
Playhouse West School and Repertory Theater	4250 Lankershim Blvd	818-971-7191	57
Powerhouse Theater	3116 2nd St	310-396-3680	18
Raven Playhouse	5233 Lankershim Blvd	818-720-2009	56
REDCAT	631 W 2nd St	213-237-2800	9
Redondo Beach Performing Arts	1935 Manhattan Beach Blvd	310-937-6607	27
Riprap Studio Theater	5755 Lankershim Blvd	818-990-7498	48
Road Theatre Company at Lankershim Arts Center	5108 Lankershim Blvd	818-761-8838	56
Sacred Fools Theater	660 N Heliotrope Dr	310-281-8337	4
Sanford Meisner Theater	5124 Lankershim Blvd	818-509-9651	56
Santa Monica Playhouse & Group	1211 4th St	310-394-9779	18
Second City Training Center	6560 Hollywood Blvd	323-464-8542	3
Secret Rose Theater	11246 Magnolia Blvd	818-766-3691	56
Shakespeare Festival LA	1238 W 1st St	213-481-2273	9
Sierra Madre Playhouse	87 S Sierra Madre Blvd	626-256-3809	35
Skirball Cultural Center	2701 N Sepulveda Blvd	310-440-4500	54
Stage 52	5299 W Washington Blvd	323-549-9026	6
Stella Adler Academy of Acting	6773 Hollywood Blvd	323-465-4446	3
Studio/Stage	520 N Western Ave	323-463-3900	4
Tamarind Theater	5919 Franklin Ave	323-465-7980	3
Theater 68	5419 W Sunset Blvd	323-467-6688	4
The Theater District	804 N El Centro Ave	323-957-2343	3
Theater of NOTE	1517 N Cahuenga Blvd	323-856-8611	3
Theater West	3333 Cahuenga Blvd W	323-851-7977	57
Theatre Banchee	3435 W Magnolia Blvd	818-628-0688	49
Theatre Palisades	941 Temescal Cyn Rd	310-454-1970	15
Third Stage	2811 W Magnolia Blvd	818-842-4755	49
Torrance Cultural Arts Center	3330 Civic Center Dr N	310-781-7150	30
Tre Stage	1523 N La Brea Ave	323-850-7827	2
Two Roads Theater	4348 Tujunga Ave	866-811-4111	56
The Unknown Theater	1110 Seward St	323-466-7781	2
Victory Theatres	3326 W Victory Blvd	818-841-4404	49
Walt Disney Concert Hall	135 N Grand Ave	323-850-2000	9
West Valley Playhouse	7242 Owensmouth Ave	818-884-1907	52
Westchester Playhouse	8301 Hindry Ave	310-645-5156	26
Whitefire Theater	13500 Ventura Blvd	818-990-2324	55
Whitmore Lindley Theatre Center	11006 Magnolia Blvd	818-761-0704	56
Working Stage	1516 N Gardner St	323-851-2603	2
Works Theater	6569 Santa Monica Blvd	323-874-8205	3
Zephyr Theater	7456 Melrose Ave	323-852-9111	2
Zombie Joe's Underground Theatre	4850 Lankershim Blvd	818-202-4120	56

NEIGHBORHOODIES®
represent.
On-the-spot custom clothing
STORE L.A.
Hollywood & Highland
6801 Hollywood Blvd.
Hollywood, CA 90028
Tel: 323.960.0330
Present this ad for 20% in-store or use coupon code NFT online
THIRD 'N FAIRFAX
www.NEIGHBORHOODIES.com

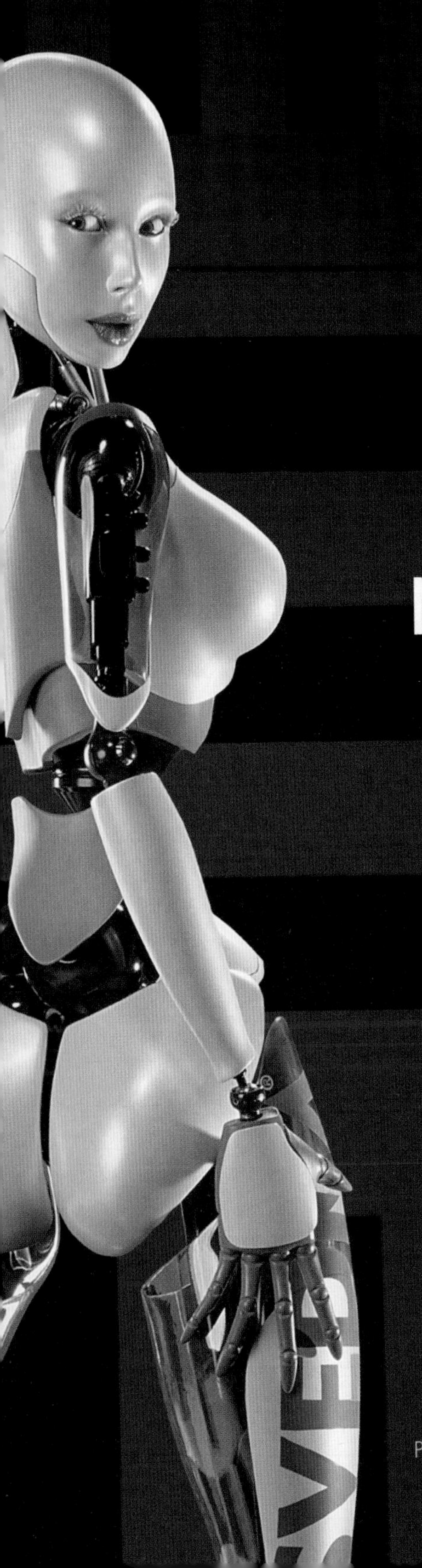

MAKE COCKTAILS
NOT WAR
- SVEDKA_GRL
SVEDKA
VOTED #1 VODKA OF 2033
PLAY RESPONSIBLY Svedka Vodka - 40% alc/vol. (80 proof), 100% grain neutral spirits,
product of Sweden, sole U.S. Importer: Spirits Marque One LLC, New York, NY.

GOLDEN APPLE
GA
TOYS, COMICS, T-SHIRTS,
DVDS, BOOKS, POSTERS,
& SO MUCH MORE!
Serving LA Since 1979
VISIT EITHER
SOUTHERN CALIFORNIA
LOCATION
LOS ANGELES
7711 MELROSE AVE.
(323) 658-6047
SAN FERNANDO VALLEY
8967 RESEDA BLVD.
(818) 993-7804
WWW.GOLDENAPPLECOMICS.COM
GRAPHIC NoVels
coMIX.

Key to City Abbreviations

AL Alhambra
BH Beverly Hills
BU Burbank
CH Chatsworth
CP Canoga Park
CU Culver City
EN Encino
ES El Segundo
GA **Gardena**
GH Granada Hills
GL Glendale
HA Hawthorne
HB Hermosa Beach
HC Harbor City
IN Inglewood
LA Los Angeles
LO Lomita
LW Lawndale
MA Marina Del Rey
MB Manhattan Beach
MH Mission Hills
MP Monterey Park
NH North Hollywood
NO North Hills
NR Northridge
PA Pasadena
PP Pacific Palisades
PV Palos Verdes Estates
RB Redondo Beach
RE Reseda
SC Studio City
SG San Gabriel
SM Santa Monica
SO Sherman Oaks
SP South Pasadena
SV Sun Valley
TO Torrance
TP Topanga
TZ Tarzana
VE Venice
VN Van Nuys
WH Woodland Hills

Street Index

Street Index

Street Index

Street Index

Street Index

Street Index